Oxford Mini School Dictionary & Thesaurus

Chief Editor: Robert Allen
Literacy Consultant: John Mannion

OXFORD
UNIVERSITY PRESS

OXFORD
UNIVERSITY PRESS

Great Clarendon Street, Oxford OX2 6DP

Oxford University Press is a department of the University of Oxford.
It furthers the University's objective of excellence in research,
scholarship, and education by publishing worldwide in

Oxford   New York

Auckland Cape Town Dar es Salaam Hong Kong Karachi
Kuala Lumpur Madrid Melbourne Mexico City Nairobi
New Delhi Shanghai Taipei Toronto

With offices in

Argentina Austria Brazil Chile Czech Republic France Greece
Guatemala Hungary Italy Japan Poland Portugal Singapore
South Korea Switzerland Thailand Turkey Ukraine Vietnam

Oxford is a registered trade mark of Oxford University Press
in the UK and in certain other countries

British Library Cataloguing in Publication Data
Data available

ISBN: 978 0 19 275697 8

13

Printed in India by Replika Press Pvt. Ltd.

Paper used in the production of this book is a natural, recyclable product
made from wood grown in sustainable forests. The manufacturing process
conforms to the environmental regulations of the country of origin.

Contents

Preface

The *Oxford Mini School Dictionary & Thesaurus* has been specially written for students aged 10 and above. It is particularly useful for students who are about to start secondary school and who need an up-to-date and student-friendly reference tool that they can use in the home and at school. This two-in-one reference book combines the features of a dictionary and a thesaurus in a convenient format with the two texts running in parallel one beneath the other. The dictionary aims at explaining the core vocabulary of English for school students, together with a selection of the curriculum vocabulary, and the thesaurus provides extra material for creative writing and vocabulary building.

The extensive Word Explorer section covers topics such as prefixes and suffixes, overused words, and writing tips.

The *Mini School Dictionary & Thesaurus* gives all the information students need for exam success in a simple, accessible, and portable format. It is an indispensable guide to a better understanding and more effective use of English.

The difference between a dictionary and a thesaurus

Dictionaries and thesauruses are tools to help you with using language. A dictionary tells you mostly about what words mean whilst a thesaurus helps you to put more words into use.

For instance, all of the following words have the same meaning in a dictionary; 'a place where people live': *house, home, dwelling, abode, residence.*

A thesaurus gives you a chance to choose which of these words you want to use.

Abode would be a good choice in a very formal piece of writing

House will be a suitable word for most uses

Home gives an idea of warmth and friendliness

When you are writing you might look up a word in a dictionary to check its exact meaning or spelling, but you use a thesaurus when you want to find more interesting or more exact way of expressing your ideas. Thesauruses organize words around key ideas and looking up a word can give you further ideas for writing.

Dictionary & Thesaurus features

headwords are in colour to find words easily

word classes (parts of speech) are given to build grammatical skills

heroic *ADJECTIVE* brave like a hero
▸ **heroically** *ADVERB*

hers *POSSESSIVE PRONOUN* belonging to her *The house is hers.*

⚠ **USAGE**
It is incorrect to write *her's*.

there are three types of panels: **usage notes** to support language use, **spelling tips** for tricky words, and **word histories** to increase language knowledge

herself *PRONOUN* she or her and nobody else *She cut herself.* *She herself has said it.* **by herself** alone; on her own

set **phrases** and idioms are defined

hertz *NOUN* a unit of frequency of electromagnetic waves

definitions are clear and accurate

▸ **WORD HISTORY**
named after H. R. *Hertz*, a German scientist

hesitant *ADJECTIVE* hesitating; undecided about what to do
▸ **hesitancy** *NOUN*

different **meanings** are clearly numbered

words that are **derived** from the headword are given at the end of entries

hide¹ *VERB* **1** to go where you cannot be seen **2** to keep from

---

hero *NOUN* • *a war hero*
▸ champion, brave man • *James had always been her hero.* ▸ idol, star • *The story had no real hero.*
▸ principal character, lead character

up-to-date example **sentences** and phrases show how words are used in context

headwords in the dictionary and thesaurus are on the same page

heroic *ADJECTIVE* • *heroic efforts*
▸ brave, courageous, noble, bold

hesitate *VERB* • *She hesitated at the front door.* ▸ pause, delay, falter, waver, wait

thousands of **synonyms** are included

vi

Aa

a *DETERMINER* (**an** before most vowel sounds) **1** one but not any special one *Find me a pen.* **2** each, every *once a day*

aardvark *NOUN* a nocturnal African animal with a long snout

aback *ADVERB* **taken aback** surprised

abacus *NOUN* **abacuses** a frame used for counting with beads sliding on wires

abandon *VERB* **1** to give up an idea **2** to leave someone or something without help ▸ **abandoned** *ADJECTIVE*, **abandonment** *NOUN*

abandon *NOUN* a careless and uncontrolled manner

abbey *NOUN* **abbeys** **1** a monastery or convent **2** a church that was once part of a monastery

abbot *NOUN* the head of an abbey

abbreviate *VERB* to shorten something

abbreviation *NOUN* a shortened form of a word or words, e.g. GCSE, St., USA

abdicate *VERB* **1** to resign from a throne **2** to give up an important responsibility ▸ **abdication** *NOUN*

abdomen *NOUN* **1** the lower front part of a person's or animal's body, containing the stomach and intestines **2** the rear section of an insect's body ▸ **abdominal** *ADJECTIVE*

abduct *VERB* to take a person away illegally ▸ **abduction** *NOUN*, **abductor** *NOUN*

abet *VERB* **abetting**, **abetted** to help or encourage someone to commit a crime

abide *VERB* to bear or tolerate something *I can't abide wasps.* **abide by** to keep to a law or a promise

abiding *ADJECTIVE* lasting or permanent

ability *NOUN* **abilities** **1** being able to do something **2** a talent

abject *ADJECTIVE* **1** wretched or miserable *abject poverty* **2** humble *an abject apology*

ablaze *ADJECTIVE* blazing; on fire

able *ADJECTIVE* **1** having the skill or opportunity to do something **2** skilful or clever ▸ **ably** *ADVERB*

abandon *VERB* • *to abandon a child* ▸ desert, leave behind, leave stranded • *to abandon a plan* ▸ cancel, drop, discontinue

ability *NOUN* • *the ability to travel the world* ▸ means, opportunity, power, resources, capability • *We admire her ability.* ▸ capability, competence, aptitude, expertise

• *many unusual abilities* ▸ talent, skill, accomplishment, gift • *the ability to do well* ▸ talent, skill, intelligence, aptitude

able *ADJECTIVE* • *an able student* ▸ talented, gifted, skilled, accomplished **able to** • *Are you able to come?* ▸ allowed to, free to

a
b
c
d
e
f
g
h
i
j
k
l
m
n
o
p
q
r
s
t
u
v
w
x
y
z

abnormal ADJECTIVE not normal; unusual ▸ **abnormally** ADVERB

abnormality NOUN **abnormalities** something that is not normal or usual

aboard ADVERB, PREPOSITION on or into a ship or aircraft or train

abode NOUN (formal) the place where someone lives

abolish VERB to put an end to a law or custom ▸ **abolition** NOUN

abominable ADJECTIVE very bad or unpleasant ▸ **abominably** ADVERB

abominate VERB to hate something very much ▸ **abomination** NOUN

aborigine NOUN one of the original inhabitants of a country ▸ **aboriginal** ADJECTIVE, NOUN **Aborigine** one of the original inhabitants of Australia who lived there before the Europeans arrived.

abort VERB to stop something before it has been completed

abortion NOUN an operation to remove an unborn child from the womb

abound VERB **1** to be plentiful or abundant **2** to have something in great quantities

about ADVERB, PREPOSITION **1** near in amount or time *about £5* **2** on the subject of *a book about animals* **3** in all directions *running about* **about to** going to do something

above ADVERB, PREPOSITION **1** higher than something **2** more than something

abrasive ADJECTIVE **1** rough and used for rubbing or scraping **2** rude and unpleasant

abreast ADVERB **1** side by side **2** keeping up with something

abridge VERB to shorten a book by using fewer words ▸ **abridgement** NOUN

abroad ADVERB in or to another country

abrupt ADJECTIVE **1** sudden or hasty *an abrupt departure* **2** rather rude and unfriendly; curt *an abrupt*

THESAURUS

abnormal ADJECTIVE • *abnormal results* ▸ unusual, uncommon, untypical, extraordinary, exceptional • *abnormal behaviour* ▸ strange, peculiar, odd, weird, curious

abolish VERB • *to abolish an unpopular tax* ▸ end, cancel, put an end to, revoke, eliminate

about PREPOSITION • *a book about bees* ▸ to do with, regarding,

concerning • *about thirty people* ▸ approximately, roughly, close to

above PREPOSITION • *above their heads* ▸ over, on top of, higher than • *above a hundred* ▸ over, more than, in excess of • *above me in rank* ▸ superior to, higher than

abrupt ADJECTIVE • *to come to an abrupt halt* ▸ sudden, quick, hasty, unexpected • *an abrupt manner* ▸ blunt, terse, gruff, rude, offhand

access VERB to find information stored in a computer

access NOUN **1** a way to enter or reach something **2** the right to use or look at something

accessible ADJECTIVE able to be reached or understood easily ▶ **accessibility** NOUN, **accessibly** ADVERB

accession NOUN **1** the act of becoming king or queen **2** something added

accessory NOUN accessories **1** an extra thing that goes with something **2** a person who helps another with a crime

accident NOUN something unexpected that causes injury or damage **by accident** by chance

accidental ADJECTIVE happening or done by chance ▶ **accidentally** ADVERB

accolade NOUN praise or a prize given for an achievement

accommodate VERB **1** to provide somebody with a place to live or work, or to sleep for the night **2** to help someone by providing something

accommodating ADJECTIVE willing to help or cooperate

accommodation NOUN somewhere to live, work, or sleep overnight

accompanist NOUN a musician who accompanies a singer or another musician

accompany VERB accompanies, accompanied **1** to go somewhere with somebody **2** to be present with something *Thunder accompanied the storm.* **3** to play music that supports a singer or another player ▶ **accompaniment** NOUN

accomplice NOUN a person who helps another to do wrong or commit a crime

THESAURUS

access NOUN • *The fans could not gain access to the stadium.* ▶ entry, admission, admittance, right of entry • *The building has no access at the front.* ▶ entrance, way in, approach

accident NOUN • *He was hurt in an accident.* ▶ misfortune, mishap, disaster, catastrophe • *She witnessed a traffic accident.* ▶ collision, smash, pile-up • *It was pure accident that we met.* ▶ chance, luck, coincidence, fate **by accident** • *They met by accident.*

▶ accidentally, by chance, coincidentally

accidental ADJECTIVE • *accidental damage* ▶ unintentional, chance, coincidental, unintended

accommodation NOUN • *three days' accommodation in Paris* ▶ board, lodging, housing, rooms

accompany VERB • *to accompany a friend* ▶ go with, escort, travel with, follow • *A note accompanied the flowers.* ▶ go with, be present with

accomplish VERB to do something successfully

accomplished ADJECTIVE skilled in something

accomplishment NOUN something you do well

accord NOUN agreement or consent **of your own accord** without being asked or compelled

accord VERB **1** to be consistent with something **2** (*formal*) to award something *They were accorded special privileges.*

accordance NOUN **in accordance with** in agreement with *in accordance with the rules*

according ADVERB **according to 1** as stated by **2** in relation to

accordingly ADVERB **1** in the way that is required **2** therefore

accordion NOUN a portable musical instrument like a large concertina with a keyboard, played by squeezing it and pressing the keys

account NOUN **1** a statement of money owed, spent, or received **2** an arrangement to keep money in a bank **3** a description or report **on account of** because of

account VERB **account for** to clarify why something happens

accountable ADJECTIVE having to explain why you have done something ▶ **accountability** NOUN

accountant NOUN a person who keeps or inspects financial accounts ▶ **accountancy** NOUN

accumulate VERB **1** to collect or pile up **2** to increase in quantity ▶ **accumulation** NOUN

accurate ADJECTIVE correct or exact ▶ **accurately** ADVERB, **accuracy** NOUN

accusation NOUN a statement accusing a person of a crime or wrong

accuse VERB to say that someone has committed a crime or wrong ▶ **accuser** NOUN

accomplish VERB • *to accomplish the task* ▶ achieve, fulfil, succeed in, complete, finish

account NOUN • *a full account of the incident* ▶ description, report, statement, explanation • *an account for the building work* ▶ invoice, statement, bill

account VERB **account for** • *It is difficult to account for the sudden change.* ▶ explain, justify, clarify, give reasons for

accumulate VERB • *to accumulate information* ▶ gather, collect, bring together, hoard, store up • *Leaves tend to accumulate.* ▶ build up, increase, grow

accurate ADJECTIVE • *an accurate account of what had happened* ▶ faithful, factual, true, truthful, exact • *She took accurate notes.* ▶ exact, precise, correct, careful, perfect

accuse VERB **accuse of** • *The men were accused of theft.* ▶ charge with, blame for, put on trial for, take to court for • *The banks are*

DICTIONARY

manner ▶ **abruptly** ADVERB, **abruptness** NOUN

abscess NOUN a painful swelling on the body where pus has formed

abscond VERB to go away secretly

abseil VERB to lower yourself down a steep cliff or rock by sliding down a rope

absent ADJECTIVE not here; not present ▶ **absence** NOUN

absent VERB **absent yourself** to stay away

absent-minded ADJECTIVE having your mind on other things; forgetful

absolute ADJECTIVE complete; not restricted *absolute power*

absolutely ADVERB completely; certainly

absolve VERB **1** to clear a person of blame or guilt **2** to release a person from a promise or obligation

absorb VERB **1** to soak up a liquid or gas **2** to deal with something and reduce its effect *The buffers*

absorbed the impact. **3** to take up a person's attention or time ▶ **absorption** NOUN

absorbent ADJECTIVE able to soak up liquids easily

abstain VERB **1** to keep yourself from doing something **2** to choose not to vote ▶ **abstention** NOUN

abstinence NOUN not doing something especially drinking alcohol

abstract ADJECTIVE **1** concerned with ideas and not solid objects **2** showing an artist's ideas or feelings and not a recognizable person or thing

abstract VERB to take out or remove ▶ **abstraction** NOUN

abstruse ADJECTIVE hard to understand

absurd ADJECTIVE ridiculous or foolish ▶ **absurdity** NOUN, **absurdly** ADVERB

abundance NOUN a large amount of something

THESAURUS

absent ADJECTIVE • *absent from work* ▶ away, off, missing • *an absent look* ▶ distracted, dreamy, faraway, preoccupied

absolute ADJECTIVE • *an absolute mess* ▶ complete, total, utter • *an absolute success* ▶ complete, total, outright, out-and-out • *the absolute truth* ▶ definite, positive, categorical, undoubted • *absolute rulers* ▶ autocratic, despotic, dictatorial, totalitarian, undemocratic

absorb VERB • *to absorb liquid* ▶ soak up, suck up, assimilate • *to absorb information* ▶ assimilate, take in, soak up, digest, comprehend • *The children were absorbed by their game.* ▶ preoccupy, engross, captivate, fascinate

absurd ADJECTIVE • *an absurd suggestion* ▶ ridiculous, preposterous, ludicrous, nonsensical, insane, mad

a
b
c
d
e
f
g
h
i
j
k
l
m
n
o
p
q
r
s
t
u
v
w
x
y
z

3

abundant ADJECTIVE plentiful
▸ **abundantly** ADVERB

abuse VERB 1 to use something badly or wrongly 2 to treat someone cruelly 3 to say unpleasant things about a person or thing

abuse NOUN 1 a wrong or bad use of something 2 physical harm or cruelty done to someone 3 offensive words or insults

abusive ADJECTIVE rude and insulting *abusive remarks*

abysmal ADJECTIVE extremely bad

abyss NOUN an extremely deep pit

academic ADJECTIVE 1 to do with education or studying 2 theoretical; having no practical use *an academic point*

academic NOUN a university or college teacher

academy NOUN **academies** 1 a school or college for specialized training 2 a society of scholars or artists

accelerate VERB to become or cause to become faster

acceleration NOUN 1 the rate at which the speed of something increases

accelerator NOUN the pedal that a driver presses to make a motor vehicle go faster

accent NOUN 1 the way a person pronounces the words of a language 2 emphasis or stress in a word 3 a mark placed over a letter to show how it is pronounced

accentuate VERB to emphasize something ▸ **accentuation** NOUN

accept VERB 1 to take a thing that is offered or presented 2 to say yes to an invitation or offer ▸ **acceptance** NOUN

acceptable ADJECTIVE pleasing or satisfactory ▸ **acceptably** ADVERB

abundant ADJECTIVE • *an abundant supply* ▸ plentiful, copious, ample, generous

abuse NOUN • *a serious abuse of authority* ▸ misuse, misapplication • *to yell abuse* ▸ insults, invective, obscenities, curses

abuse VERB • *Players were abusing the referee.* ▸ insult, be rude to, curse, swear at • *The judge had abused his authority.* ▸ misuse, misapply, exploit

abusive ADJECTIVE • *to yell abusive remarks* ▸ insulting, derogatory, rude, offensive

accept VERB • *to accept an offer* ▸ receive, take, get, welcome • *to accept responsibility* ▸ admit, acknowledge, bear, assume • *Reluctantly, he had to accept the decision.* ▸ agree to, go along with, accede to, comply with, abide by

acceptable ADJECTIVE • *an acceptable standard* ▸ adequate, satisfactory, reasonable, appropriate, suitable

activate VERB to start something working ▸ **activation** NOUN

active ADJECTIVE **1** taking part in many activities; energetic **2** functioning or working **3** (of a verb) in the form used when the subject of the verb is performing the action, e.g. *sells* in *The shop sells milk*. ▸ **actively** ADVERB, **activeness** NOUN

activist NOUN a person who is active in politics and social affairs

activity NOUN **activities 1** an action or occupation **2** an active or lively state

actor NOUN a person who acts in a play or film

actress NOUN a woman who acts in a play or film

actual ADJECTIVE really there or happening ▸ **actually** ADVERB

acumen NOUN a good ability to decide things

acupuncture NOUN treatment of the body by pricking parts with needles to relieve pain or cure disease ▸ **acupuncturist** NOUN

acute ADJECTIVE **1** sharp or strong *acute pain* **2** having a sharp mind ▸ **acutely** ADVERB, **acuteness** NOUN

acute accent NOUN A mark over a vowel, e.g. é in *résumé*

acute angle NOUN an angle of less than 90°

AD ABBREVIATION Anno Domini (Latin = in the year of Our Lord), used in dates counted from the birth of Christ

adamant ADJECTIVE firm and not giving way to persuasion

Adam's apple NOUN the lump at the front of a man's neck

adapt VERB **1** to change something for a new purpose **2** to become used to a new situation ▸ **adaptable** ADJECTIVE, **adaptation** NOUN

movement, energy • *the action of the play* ▸ story, plot, events

active ADJECTIVE • *an active time* ▸ busy, lively, eventful, energetic • *very active for her age* ▸ energetic, agile, sprightly, lively • *an active member of the group* ▸ hard-working, diligent, dedicated, enthusiastic • *Part of the old factory was still active.* ▸ working, functioning, in operation

activity NOUN • *a scene of great activity* ▸ liveliness, action, commotion, bustle, excitement

• *an activity involving everyone* ▸ job, task, project, scheme • *a leisure activity* ▸ interest, hobby, pastime

actual ADJECTIVE • *the actual damage* ▸ real, true, physical, genuine

acute ADJECTIVE • *an acute pain* ▸ sharp, severe, stabbing, burning, piercing • *an acute shortage* ▸ severe, drastic, serious, dire • *an acute illness* ▸ critical, sudden

adapt VERB • *to adapt to new surroundings* ▸ adjust, get used,

DICTIONARY

adaptor NOUN a device to connect pieces of equipment

add VERB 1 to put one thing with another 2 to make another remark **add up** 1 to make or find a total 2 (*informal*) to make sense

adder NOUN a small poisonous snake

addict NOUN a person with a habit they cannot give up ▸ **addicted** ADJECTIVE, **addiction** NOUN

addictive ADJECTIVE causing a habit that people cannot give up *an addictive drug*

addition NOUN 1 the process of adding 2 something added **in addition** also; as an extra thing ▸ **additional** ADJECTIVE, **additionally** ADVERB

additive NOUN a substance added to another in small amounts, e.g. as a flavouring in food

address NOUN 1 the details of the place where someone lives or can be contacted 2 a speech to an audience

address VERB 1 to write an address on a letter or parcel 2 to make a speech or remark to someone

adenoids PLURAL NOUN thick spongy flesh at the back of the nose and throat

adept ADJECTIVE very skilful

adequate ADJECTIVE enough or good enough ▸ **adequately** ADVERB, **adequacy** NOUN

adhere VERB to stick to something ▸ **adhesion** NOUN

adhesive ADJECTIVE sticky; making things stick

ad hoc ADJECTIVE, ADVERB done or arranged for a particular purpose *ad hoc decisions*

adjacent ADJECTIVE near or next *an adjacent room*

adjective NOUN a word that describes a noun or adds to its

THESAURUS

acclimatize yourself • *The vans are all adapted to carry dangerous substances.* ▸ modify, alter, convert, change, customize • *The story has been adapted for television.* ▸ edit, modify, alter

add VERB • *to add figures* ▸ add up, count up, calculate, find the sum of, work out • *A conservatory was added to the house.* ▸ build on, attach, add on, join **add to** • *Our shouts only added to the confusion.* ▸ increase, intensify, augment **add up** • *It was time to add up the*

scores. ▸ count up, calculate, find the sum of, work out

additional ADJECTIVE • *additional resources* ▸ extra, added, further, supplementary, increased

adequate ADJECTIVE • *an adequate standard of work* ▸ satisfactory, acceptable, sufficient, good enough • *adequate resources* ▸ sufficient, enough, suitable, appropriate

adjacent ADJECTIVE • *adjacent rooms* ▸ adjoining, neighbouring, next-door

meaning, e.g. *big, square*
► **adjectival** ADJECTIVE

adjoin VERB to be next to or joined to

adjourn VERB 1 to break off a meeting until a later time 2 to break off and go somewhere else *They adjourned to the library.*

adjournment NOUN a temporary pause in a meeting or activity

adjust VERB 1 to put a thing into its proper position or order 2 to alter something so that it is suitable
► **adjustable** ADJECTIVE

adjustment NOUN a slight alteration to something

administer VERB 1 to give or provide something 2 to manage business affairs

administrate VERB to manage public or business affairs
► **administrator** NOUN, **administrative** ADJECTIVE

administration NOUN 1 the management of a public or business affairs 2 the people who manage an organization etc. 3 the government

admirable ADJECTIVE worth admiring; excellent ► **admirably** ADVERB

admiral NOUN a naval officer of high rank

admire VERB 1 to look at something and enjoy it 2 to think that someone or something is very good ► **admiration** NOUN, **admirer** NOUN

admission NOUN 1 permission to go in 2 a charge for being allowed to go in 3 a statement admitting something

admit VERB **admitting, admitted** 1 to allow someone or something to come in 2 to state reluctantly that something is true

admittance NOUN permission to go into a private place

admittedly ADVERB as an agreed fact

ado NOUN **without more or further ado** without wasting any more time

adolescent NOUN a young person between being a child and being an adult ► **adolescence** NOUN

adjust VERB • *to adjust the tuning* ► modify, alter, regulate, balance, amend **adjust to** • *to adjust to new procedures* ► adapt to, get used to, acclimatize yourself to

admirable ADJECTIVE • *an admirable idea* ► praiseworthy, worthy, fine, commendable, excellent

admire VERB • *to be admired for efficiency* ► applaud, approve

of, respect, praise, look up to • *to admire a view* ► enjoy, appreciate, be delighted by

admit VERB • *They were not admitted to the house.* ► let in, allow in, grant access • *She admitted she had been there.* ► acknowledge, concede, confess, accept, own up

11

a
b
c
d
e
f
g
h
i
j
k
l
m
n
o
p
q
r
s
t
u
v
w
x
y
z

adopt VERB **1** to take a child into your family as your own **2** to accept something and use it ► **adoption** NOUN

adore VERB to love a person or thing very much ► **adorable** ADJECTIVE, **adoration** NOUN

adorn VERB to decorate ► **adornment** NOUN

adrenalin NOUN a hormone produced by the body when you are afraid or excited. It makes your heart beat faster and increases your energy.

adrift ADJECTIVE, ADVERB drifting or floating freely

adult NOUN a fully grown or mature person

adulterate VERB to make a thing impure or less good by adding

something to it ► **adulteration** NOUN

adultery NOUN the act of having sexual intercourse with someone other than your wife or husband ► **adulterer** NOUN, **adulterous** ADJECTIVE

advance NOUN **1** a forward movement **2** an increase **3** a loan or early payment **in advance** beforehand

advance VERB **1** to move forward or make progress **2** to lend or pay money ahead of the proper time ► **advancement** NOUN

advantage NOUN **1** something useful or helpful **2** (in tennis) the next point won after deuce **take advantage of** to use a person or thing profitably or unfairly

adopt VERB • *to adopt an official uniform* • *to adopt a more professional approach* ► take up, choose, accept, approve • *to adopt a child* ► foster, take in

adore VERB • *He still adores her.* ► love, dote on, idolize, worship • *We adore shopping.* ► love, like

adorn VERB • *The room was adorned with tapestries.* ► decorate, embellish, enhance, beautify

advance NOUN • *a major advance in cancer treatments* ► progress, development, improvement, step

advance VERB • *The soldiers began to advance.* ► move forward, proceed, press ahead, approach, gain ground • *Computer technology has advanced in the last*

few years. ► develop, evolve, improve • *Qualifications will advance your career.* ► benefit, boost, further, promote, assist

advanced ADJECTIVE • *advanced techniques* ► modern, sophisticated, up-to-date, progressive • *advanced ideas* ► forward-looking, innovative, pioneering, revolutionary, original • *advanced mathematics* ► higher, complex, complicated, difficult • *quite advanced for his age* ► mature, grown-up, sophisticated, well-developed

advantage NOUN • *Being tall is an advantage.* ► benefit, asset, help, convenience, boon **take advantage of** • *His friends all took*

advantageous ADJECTIVE giving an advantage; beneficial

Advent NOUN the four weeks before Christmas

adventure NOUN an exciting or challenging experience
▶ **adventurer** NOUN

adventurous ADJECTIVE willing to take risks and do new things

adverb NOUN a word that adds to the meaning of a verb or adjective or another adverb, e.g. *slowly*, *often*, and *downstairs*
▶ **adverbial** ADJECTIVE

adversary NOUN **adversaries** an opponent or enemy

adverse ADJECTIVE unfavourable or harmful *adverse effects*
▶ **adversely** ADVERB

⚠ **USAGE**
Do not confuse this word with *averse*.

adversity NOUN **adversities** trouble or misfortune

advert NOUN (*informal*) an advertisement

advertise VERB **1** to present and praise goods to the public to encourage them to buy or use them **2** to make something publicly known **3** to give information about a job vacancy
▶ **advertiser** NOUN

advertisement NOUN a public notice or announcement, especially one advertising goods or services in newspapers, on posters, or in broadcasts

advice NOUN **1** words that tell a person what they should do **2** a piece of information

advisable ADJECTIVE that is the wise thing to do

advise VERB **1** to give somebody advice **2** to inform someone
▶ **adviser** NOUN, **advisory** ADJECTIVE

advocate VERB to speak in favour of something *We advocate reform.*

advocate NOUN **1** a person who advocates a policy *an advocate of reform* **2** a lawyer presenting a person in a lawsuit

THESAURUS

advantage of him. ▶ exploit, make use of, profit by, manipulate

adventure NOUN • *a life full of adventures* ▶ exploit, escapade, deed, feat • *in search of adventure* ▶ excitement, danger, fun

adventurous ADJECTIVE • *an adventurous child* ▶ daring, bold, heroic, intrepid, valiant • *an adventurous time* ▶ eventful, exciting, challenging, dangerous

advertise VERB • *to advertise a new product* ▶ promote, publicize, market, announce, broadcast

advisable ADJECTIVE • *It is advisable to arrive early.* ▶ sensible, wise, prudent, a good idea

advise VERB • *He advised her to go the police.* ▶ recommend, encourage, counsel, instruct, warn • *The doctor advised a period*

aerate VERB **1** to add air to something **2** to add carbon dioxide to a liquid

aerial ADJECTIVE **1** in or from the air **2** to do with aircraft

aerial NOUN a wire or rod for receiving or transmitting radio or television signals

aerobatics PLURAL NOUN spectacular performances by flying aircraft ► **aerobatic** ADJECTIVE

aerobics PLURAL NOUN exercises to strengthen the heart and lungs ► **aerobic** ADJECTIVE

aerodrome NOUN a landing place for aircraft

aerodynamic ADJECTIVE designed to move through the air quickly and easily

aeronautics NOUN the study of aircraft and flying ► **aeronautic** ADJECTIVE, **aeronautical** ADJECTIVE

aeroplane NOUN a flying vehicle with engines and wings

aerosol NOUN a container that holds a liquid under pressure and can let it out in a fine spray

aerospace NOUN the earth's atmosphere and space beyond it

aesthetic ADJECTIVE to do with enjoying beautiful things

afar ADVERB far away

affable ADJECTIVE polite and friendly ► **affability** NOUN, **affably** ADVERB

affair NOUN **1** an event or matter *a grand affair* **2** a temporary sexual relationship outside marriage

affairs PLURAL NOUN the business and activities that are part of private or public life

affect VERB **1** to have an effect on **2** to pretend *We affected ignorance.*

affectation NOUN an unnatural manner that is intended to impress other people

affected ADJECTIVE pretended and unnatural

affection NOUN a strong liking for a person

affectionate ADJECTIVE showing affection; loving ► **affectionately** ADVERB

affidavit NOUN a legal statement written down and sworn to be true

affiliated ADJECTIVE officially connected with a larger organization

affinity NOUN affinities attraction or similarity between people or things

of rest. ► suggest, prescribe, urge, advocate

affair NOUN • *The meeting was an odd affair.* ► event, incident, episode, occurrence, occasion

affairs • *financial affairs* ► business, activities, concerns, matters

affect VERB • *Alcohol affects women and men differently.* ► have an

effect on, have an impact on, influence • *The sad news affected all of us.* ► upset, disturb, trouble, sadden, distress, touch • *to affect an accent* ► assume, feign, put on

affection NOUN • *to show affection for someone* ► fondness, friendship, attachment, devotion, warmth

affirm VERB to state something definitely ▶ **affirmation** NOUN

affix VERB to attach or add

affix NOUN a prefix or suffix

afflict VERB to cause someone to suffer

affliction NOUN something that causes pain or suffering

affluent ADJECTIVE having a lot of money ▶ **affluence** NOUN

afford VERB 1 to have enough money to pay for something 2 to have enough time or resources to do something 3 to be able to do something without a risk *You can't afford to wait.*

affront VERB to insult or offend someone

affront NOUN an insult

afield ADVERB at or to a distance *far afield*

afloat ADJECTIVE, ADVERB floating; on the sea

afraid ADJECTIVE frightened or alarmed *I'm afraid* I regret *I'm afraid I can't come.*

afresh ADVERB again; in a new way *start afresh*

African ADJECTIVE to do with Africa or its people

African NOUN an African person

aft ADVERB at or towards the back of a ship or aircraft

after PREPOSITION 1 later than *after tea* 2 behind in place or order *the letter after A* 3 trying to catch; pursuing *Run after him.* 4 in imitation or honour of *She is named after her aunt.* 5 about or concerning *He asked after you.*

after ADVERB 1 behind 2 at a later time

aftermath NOUN something that results from something bad or unpleasant *the aftermath of the earthquake*

afternoon NOUN the time from noon or lunchtime to evening

afterthought NOUN something you think of or add later

afterwards ADVERB at a later time

again ADVERB 1 another time; once more 2 besides; moreover

against PREPOSITION 1 touching or hitting *leaning against a wall* 2 in opposition to *They voted against the proposal.* 3 in preparation for protection against the cold

age NOUN 1 the length of time a person or thing has existed 2 a

afflict VERB • *to be afflicted by illness* ▶ trouble, bother, burden, distress

afford VERB • *We can't afford a holiday this year.* ▶ have enough money for, pay for, manage

afraid ADJECTIVE • *afraid of the dark* ▶ frightened, scared, terrified, intimidated (by), nervous • *I'm afraid all the food has gone.* ▶ sorry, regretful • *Don't be afraid to ask.* ▶ reluctant, hesitant, shy

age NOUN • *He was becoming affected by age.* ▶ old age, senility, decrepitude, decline • *the age of slavery* ▶ time, era, period, epoch, days

a
b
c
d
e
f
g
h
i
j
k
l
m
n
o
p
q
r
s
t
u
v
w
x
y
z

15

special period of history or geology *the ice age* **for ages** (*informal*) for a very long time

age VERB **ageing** to make or become old

aged ADJECTIVE **1** having the age of *a girl aged 12* **2** very old *an aged man*

agency NOUN **agencies 1** an office or business *a travel agency* **2** the means by which something is done

agenda NOUN a list of things to be done or discussed

agent NOUN **1** a person who organizes things for other people *a travel agent* **2** a spy *a secret agent*

aggravate VERB **1** to make something worse or more serious **2** (*informal*) to annoy ► **aggravation** NOUN

aggregate ADJECTIVE combined or total *the aggregate amount*

aggregate NOUN a total amount or score

aggression NOUN hostile or attacking action or behaviour

aggressive ADJECTIVE **1** hostile or violent **2** very determined and forceful ► **aggressively** ADVERB

aggressor NOUN a person or nation that starts an attack

aggrieved ADJECTIVE resentful because of being treated unfairly

aghast ADJECTIVE horrified

agile ADJECTIVE moving quickly and easily ► **agilely** ADVERB, **agility** NOUN

agitate VERB **1** to make someone feel upset or anxious **2** to stir up public interest **3** to shake something about ► **agitation** NOUN, **agitator** NOUN

ago ADVERB in the past *long ago*

agog ADJECTIVE eager and excited

agony NOUN **agonies** great pain or suffering ► **agonizing** ADJECTIVE

THESAURUS

age VERB • *Frank had aged in the last few years.* ► decline, degenerate, look older

aged ADJECTIVE • *an aged relative* ► elderly, old

aggravate • *The delays aggravated the situation.* ► worsen, exacerbate, intensify, make worse • *Their remarks aggravated us.* ► annoy, irritate, bother, anger

aggressive ADJECTIVE • *in an aggressive mood* ► hostile,

provocative, antagonistic, argumentative, violent

agile ADJECTIVE • *as agile as a monkey* ► nimble, lithe, graceful, supple, acrobatic

agitated ADJECTIVE • *She became agitated when they did not arrive.* ► upset, unsettled, anxious, confused, edgy, nervous

agony NOUN • *The victims died in agony.* ► pain, torment, suffering, anguish, distress

a
b
c
d
e
f
g
h
i
j
k
l
m
n
o
p
q
r
s
t
u
v
w
x
y
z

DICTIONARY

agree VERB **1** to think or say the same as another person **2** to say you will do something *I agreed to go.* **3** to suit a person's health or digestion

agreeable ADJECTIVE **1** willing **2** pleasant ▶ **agreeably** ADVERB

agreement NOUN **1** the act of agreeing **2** an arrangement that people have agreed on

agriculture NOUN the cultivating of land on a large scale and rearing livestock; farming ▶ **agricultural** ADJECTIVE

aground ADVERB, ADJECTIVE stranded on the bottom in shallow water

ah EXCLAMATION an exclamation of surprise, pity, or admiration

ahead ADVERB further forward; in front

ahoy EXCLAMATION a cry used at sea to call attention

aid NOUN **1** help **2** something that helps **3** money and supplies sent to help another country **in aid of** for the purpose of

aid VERB to help

aide NOUN an assistant

Aids NOUN a disease caused by the HIV virus, which weakens a person's ability to resist infections (from 'acquired immune deficiency syndrome')

ailing ADJECTIVE **1** ill; in poor health **2** in difficulties; not successful

ailment NOUN a slight illness

aim VERB **1** to point a weapon **2** to throw or kick in a particular direction **3** to try or intend to do something

THESAURUS

agree VERB • *Do you think they will agree?* ▶ approve, consent, be willing • *You must agree to take six books in the first year of membership.* ▶ promise, be willing, consent, undertake • *I think we all agree on the action needed.* ▶ concur, be unanimous, be united • *The accounts of all the witnesses agree.* ▶ match, correspond, tally, coincide

agree on • *to agree on a price* ▶ fix, settle, decide on, choose

agree to • *to agree to a request* ▶ accept, consent to, accede to, grant, allow **agree with** • *I don't agree with their decision.* ▶ support, defend, argue for, advocate

agreement NOUN • *a large measure of agreement* ▶ consensus, unanimity, accord, harmony, unity • *to reach an agreement* ▶ settlement, deal, pact, understanding, arrangement

aid NOUN • *foreign aid* ▶ help, support, assistance, relief

aid VERB • *an agreement to aid the poorest countries* ▶ help, assist, support, subsidize • *These measures will aid the process.* ▶ encourage, support, facilitate, expedite

aim VERB • *to aim a gun* ▶ point, direct, level, train • *We aim to finish this week.* ▶ intend, want, wish, plan

a
b
c
d
e
f
g
h
i
j
k
l
m
n
o
p
q
r
s
t
u
v
w
x
y
z

aim NOUN **1** the pointing of a weapon **2** a purpose or intention

aimless ADJECTIVE having no purpose ▸ **aimlessly** ADVERB

air NOUN **1** the mixture of gases that surrounds the earth **2** the open space above the earth **3** a tune or melody **4** an appearance or impression of something *an air of secrecy* **5** an impressive or haughty manner *put on airs*

air VERB **1** to put washing in a warm place to finish drying **2** to ventilate a room **3** to express an opinion

airborne ADJECTIVE **1** (of an aircraft) flying **2** carried by the air or by aircraft

air conditioning NOUN a system for controlling the temperature and quality of the air in a room or building ▸ **air conditioned** ADJECTIVE

aircraft NOUN **aircraft** an aeroplane, glider, or helicopter

aircraft carrier NOUN a large ship with a long deck where aircraft can take off and land

airfield NOUN an area with runways where aircraft can take off and land

air force NOUN the part of a country's armed forces that uses aircraft

airline NOUN a company that provides a regular service of transport by aircraft

airmail NOUN mail carried by air

airport NOUN a place where aircraft land and take off, with passenger terminals and other buildings

air raid NOUN an attack by aircraft dropping bombs

airship NOUN a large balloon with engines and a passenger compartment underneath

airtight ADJECTIVE sealed to prevent air escaping

airy ADJECTIVE **1** with plenty of fresh air **2** light as air **3** vague and insincere ▸ **airily** ADVERB

aisle NOUN a passage between rows of seats or between shelves in a large shop

ajar ADVERB, ADJECTIVE slightly open

akin ADJECTIVE related or similar

alabaster NOUN a kind of hard white stone

alacrity NOUN speed and willingness

alarm NOUN **1** a warning sound or signal **2** a feeling of fear or worry

alarm VERB to make someone frightened or anxious ▸ **alarming** ADJECTIVE

THESAURUS

aim NOUN • *Our aim is to win.* ▸ ambition, goal, objective, plan, intention, dream

alarm NOUN • *The woman looked round in alarm.* ▸ fear, fright, panic, terror, trepidation, dismay

• *Suddenly the alarm sounded.* ▸ signal, warning signal, distress signal, siren

alarm VERB • *The news alarmed us.* ▸ frighten, scare, shock, upset, panic

alarm clock NOUN a clock that can be set to sound at a fixed time to waken someone who is asleep

alas EXCLAMATION an exclamation of sorrow or regret

albatross NOUN a large seabird with long wings

albino NOUN **albinos** a person or animal with white skin and hair and pink eyes

album NOUN **1** a CD, record, or tape with a number of songs on it **2** a book with blank pages for keeping photographs or stamps

albumen NOUN the white of an egg

alchemy NOUN an early form of chemistry, concerned with turning ordinary metals into gold ▶ **alchemist** NOUN

alcohol NOUN **1** a colourless liquid made by fermenting sugar or starch **2** drinks containing this, e.g. wine, beer, and spirits

alcoholic ADJECTIVE containing alcohol

alcoholic NOUN a person who is addicted to alcohol ▶ **alcoholism** NOUN

alcove NOUN a section of a room that is set back from the main part

ale NOUN a kind of beer

alert ADJECTIVE watching and ready to act ▶ **alertness** NOUN

alert NOUN a warning or alarm **on the alert** keeping watch

alert VERB to warn someone of danger or make them aware of something

A level NOUN advanced level in GCSE

algae PLURAL NOUN plants that grow in water, with no true stems or leaves

algebra NOUN mathematics in which letters and symbols are used to represent quantities ▶ **algebraic** ADJECTIVE

alias NOUN a false or different name

alias ADVERB also called

alibi NOUN **alibis** evidence that a person accused of a crime was somewhere else when it took place

alien NOUN **1** a person from another country; a foreigner **2** (in science fiction) a being from another world

THESAURUS

alarming ADJECTIVE • *an alarming piece of news* ▶ frightening, upsetting, distressing, shocking, scary

alert ADJECTIVE • *to stay alert* ▶ attentive, vigilant, watchful, wide awake, on your guard • *mentally alert* ▶ sharp, quick-witted, alive, active, acute

alert VERB • *We alerted them to the problem.* ▶ warn (of), notify (of), inform (about)

alias NOUN • *Jack was not his real name, only an alias.* ▶ pseudonym, false name, assumed name, (said of a writer) pen name, (said of an actor) stage name

alien ADJECTIVE • *an alien landscape* ▶ strange, unfamiliar, foreign

19

alien ADJECTIVE **1** foreign **2** not part of a person's experience or character

alienate VERB to make a person unfriendly or unhelpful
▶ **alienation** NOUN

alight[1] ADJECTIVE **1** on fire **2** lit up

alight[2] VERB **1** to step out of a vehicle **2** (of a bird or insect) to fly down and settle

align VERB **1** to arrange things in a line **2** to join as an ally

alignment NOUN arrangement in a line or in a special way

alike ADJECTIVE, ADVERB **1** like one another **2** in the same way

alimony NOUN (American) money that someone is ordered to pay their wife or husband after they are separated or divorced

alive ADJECTIVE **1** living **2** alert or aware

alkali NOUN alkalis a chemical substance that neutralizes an acid to form a salt ▶ **alkaline** ADJECTIVE

all ADJECTIVE the whole number or amount of

all NOUN **1** everything or everyone **2** everybody

all ADVERB **1** completely *dressed all in white* **2** to each team or competitor *three goals all*

Allah NOUN the Muslim name of God

allay VERB to calm or relieve a fear or doubt

all-clear NOUN a signal that a danger has passed

allegation NOUN an accusation made without proof

allege VERB to say without being able to prove it
▶ **allegedly** ADVERB

allegiance NOUN loyalty to a person or country

allegory NOUN allegories a story in which the characters and events represent a deeper meaning, e.g. to teach a moral lesson
▶ **allegorical** ADJECTIVE

alleluia EXCLAMATION praise to God

allergy NOUN allergies intense sensitivity to something that can make you ill ▶ **allergic** ADJECTIVE

alleviate VERB to make something, e.g. pain or suffering, less severe ▶ **alleviation** NOUN

alley NOUN alleys **1** a narrow street or passage **2** a place for playing bowls or skittles

alliance NOUN an association formed by countries or groups who want to support each other

allied ADJECTIVE **1** joined as allies; on the same side **2** of the same kind

alligator NOUN a large reptile of the crocodile family

THESAURUS

• *alien beings* ▶ foreign, extra-terrestrial

alike ADJECTIVE • *to look alike* ▶ similar, identical, indistinguishable, the same

alive ADJECTIVE • *He was last seen alive a week ago.* ▶ living, live, breathing • *to keep old customs alive* ▶ active, in existence, current, flourishing, surviving

a
b
c
d
e
f
g
h
i
j
k
l
m
n
o
p
q
r
s
t
u
v
w
x
y
z

DICTIONARY

allocate VERB to set something aside for a particular purpose
▶ **allocation** NOUN

allot VERB allotting, allotted to give a share of something to different people

allotment NOUN **1** a small piece of rented land used for growing vegetables **2** an amount allotted

allow VERB **1** to permit **2** to provide someone with something *They are allowed £100 for books.* **allow for** to take into account
▶ **allowable** ADJECTIVE

allowance NOUN an amount of money given regularly for a particular purpose **make allowances** to be especially considerate

alloy NOUN a mixture of two or more metals

all right ADJECTIVE, ADVERB **1** satisfactory or adequate **2** in good condition

all-round ADJECTIVE general; not specialist *an all-round athlete*
▶ **all-rounder** NOUN

allude VERB to mention something briefly or indirectly

allure VERB to attract or fascinate someone ▶ **allure** NOUN, **alluring** ADJECTIVE

allusion NOUN a reference to something without actually naming it

alluvium NOUN sand and soil deposited by a river or flood
▶ **alluvial** ADJECTIVE

ally NOUN **1** a country in alliance with another **2** a person who cooperates with another

ally VERB allies, allied to form an alliance

almanac NOUN an annual publication containing a calendar and other information

almighty ADJECTIVE **1** having complete power **2** (informal) very great *an almighty din* **the Almighty** a name for God

almond NOUN an oval edible nut

almost ADVERB nearly but not quite

alms PLURAL NOUN (old use) money and gifts given to the poor

THESAURUS

allow VERB • *Smoking is not allowed.* ▶ permit, authorize, tolerate • *She allowed him to go home.* ▶ permit, let, authorize, give permission • *to allow more time* ▶ provide, set aside, grant, give

all right ADJECTIVE • *Everyone is all right now.* ▶ well, unhurt, unharmed, in good health, safe • *The food's all right, though not*

very exciting. ▶ satisfactory, acceptable, adequate, reasonable

ally NOUN • *a political ally* ▶ friend, supporter, helper, collaborator, partner

almost ADVERB • *We had almost reached home. almost a million people I was almost tempted to complain.* ▶ nearly, not quite, practically, virtually, just about

alone ADJECTIVE, ADVERB without any other people or things

along PREPOSITION following the length of *along the path*

along ADVERB **1** on or onwards *Push it along.* **2** accompanying somebody *Bring them along.*

alongside PREPOSITION, ADVERB next to something; beside

aloof ADJECTIVE unfriendly in manner

aloud ADVERB in a voice that can be heard

alpha NOUN the first letter of the Greek alphabet, equivalent to Roman *A, a*

alphabet NOUN the letters used in a language, arranged in a set order ▶ **alphabetical** ADJECTIVE, **alphabetically** ADVERB

alpine ADJECTIVE to do with high mountains *alpine plants*

already ADVERB by now; before now

Alsatian NOUN a German shepherd dog

also ADVERB in addition; besides

altar NOUN a table or similar structure used in religious ceremonies

alter VERB to make or become different; to change ▶ **alteration** NOUN

altercation NOUN a noisy argument or quarrel

alternate ADJECTIVE **1** happening or coming one after the other *alternate layers of sponge and cream* **2** one in every two *on alternate Fridays* ▶ **alternately** ADVERB

alternate VERB to use or come alternately ▶ **alternation** NOUN

alternating current NOUN electric current that reverses its direction at regular intervals

alternative ADJECTIVE available instead of something else ▶ **alternatively** ADVERB

alternative NOUN one of two or more possibilities

alternative medicine NOUN types of medical treatment that are not based on ordinary medicine, such as acupuncture and homeopathy

although CONJUNCTION despite the fact that

altimeter NOUN an instrument used in aircraft for showing the height above sea level

altitude NOUN the height of something above sea level

alone ADJECTIVE • *The children were alone in the house.* ▶ on your own, by yourself, solitary, single, unaccompanied, apart, separate, solo • *She often felt very*

alone. ▶ lonely, isolated, solitary, friendless, forlorn

alter VERB • *to alter the wording of the letter* ▶ change, adjust, modify, amend

DICTIONARY

altogether ADVERB **1** with all
included; in total **2** completely
3 on the whole

aluminium NOUN a lightweight
silver-coloured metal

always ADVERB **1** at all times
2 often *You are always
complaining.* **3** whatever happens
You can always sleep on the floor.

a.m. ABBREVIATION before noon

amalgam NOUN **1** an alloy of
mercury **2** a mixture or
combination

amalgamate VERB to mix or
combine ▶ **amalgamation** NOUN

amass VERB to heap up or collect

amateur NOUN a person who does
something out of interest and not
as a professional

amateurish ADJECTIVE not done or
made very well

amaze VERB to surprise somebody
greatly ▶ **amazement** NOUN

amazing ADJECTIVE very surprising
or remarkable

ambassador NOUN a person sent
to a foreign country to represent
their own government

amber NOUN a hard clear yellowish
substance used for making
jewellery

ambiguity NOUN **ambiguities**
uncertainty about the meaning of
something

ambiguous ADJECTIVE having
more than one possible meaning
▶ **ambiguously** ADVERB

ambition NOUN a strong desire to
be successful and achieve things

ambitious ADJECTIVE having a
strong desire to be successful

ambivalent ADJECTIVE having
conflicting feelings about a person
or situation ▶ **ambivalence** NOUN

THESAURUS

altogether ADVERB • *We are not
altogether satisfied.*
▶ completely, entirely, fully,
totally, perfectly

always ADVERB • *You are always
late.* ▶ every time, constantly,
repeatedly, habitually, invariably
• *He is always complaining.*
▶ forever, constantly, incessantly,
endlessly • *I will always remember
you.* ▶ for ever, permanently,
perpetually, evermore

amaze VERB • *It amazes me how big
the place is.* ▶ astonish, astound,
surprise, stagger, shock

amazing ADJECTIVE • *an amazing
sight* ▶ astonishing, astounding,
extraordinary, remarkable,
wonderful

ambition NOUN • *young people
with a lot of ambition* ▶ drive,
enthusiasm, enterprise, zeal • *Her
ambition is to become a model.*
▶ aim, dream, hope, goal,
objective, desire

ambitious ADJECTIVE • *an
ambitious politician* ▶ aspiring,
determined, enthusiastic
• *ambitious ideas* ▶ grand,
grandiose, large-scale, big

a
b
c
d
e
f
g
h
i
j
k
l
m
n
o
p
q
r
s
t
u
v
w
x
y
z

amble VERB to walk at a slow easy pace

ambulance NOUN a vehicle equipped to carry sick or injured people

ambush NOUN a surprise attack from a hidden position

ambush VERB to attack someone from a hidden position

amen EXCLAMATION a word used at the end of a prayer or hymn, meaning 'so be it'

amend VERB to alter something to improve it

amendment NOUN a change to improve something

amends PLURAL NOUN **make amends** to make up for having done something wrong

amenity NOUN **amenities** a pleasant or useful feature that a place has

American ADJECTIVE to do with the continent of America, or the USA
▶ **American** NOUN

amethyst NOUN a purple precious stone

amiable ADJECTIVE friendly and good-tempered ▶ **amiably** ADVERB

amicable ADJECTIVE friendly and likeable ▶ **amicably** ADVERB

amid or **amidst** PREPOSITION in the middle of; among

amino acid NOUN an acid found in proteins

amiss ADJECTIVE, ADVERB wrong or faulty **take something amiss** to be offended by what someone says

ammonia NOUN a colourless gas or liquid with a strong smell

ammunition NOUN a supply of bullets, shells, and grenades

amnesia NOUN a loss of memory

amnesty NOUN **amnesties** a general pardon for people who have committed a crime

amoeba NOUN **amoebas** a microscopic creature consisting of a single cell which constantly changes shape and can split itself in two

amok ADVERB **run amok** to rush about wildly or violently

among or **amongst** PREPOSITION **1** surrounded by *weeds among the flowers* **2** between *sweets divided among the children*

amoral ADJECTIVE having no moral standards

amorous ADJECTIVE showing or feeling sexual love

amorphous ADJECTIVE not having a definite shape

amount NOUN a quantity or total

THESAURUS

ambush NOUN • *to set up an ambush* ▶ surprise attack, trap

ambush VERB • *The gang ambushed passers-by.* ▶ waylay, attack, surprise, trap, intercept

amiable ADJECTIVES • *an amiable old fellow* ▶ friendly, agreeable, likeable, pleasant

amount NOUN • *the whole amount* ▶ quantity, sum, total, lot • *a*

amount VERB **amount to** to add up to or be equivalent to

amp NOUN **1** an ampere **2** (*informal*) an amplifier

ampere NOUN a unit for measuring electric current

amphetamine NOUN a drug used as a stimulant

amphibian NOUN **1** an animal able to live both on land and in water **2** a vehicle that can be used on land and in water

amphibious ADJECTIVE able to live or move on land and in water

amphitheatre NOUN a round open theatre with seats round a central arena

ample ADJECTIVE **1** quite enough **2** large ▶ **amply** ADVERB

amplifier NOUN a piece of equipment for making a sound or electrical signal louder or stronger

amplify VERB **amplifies, amplified 1** to make a sound or electrical signal louder or stronger **2** to explain in more detail ▶ **amplification** NOUN

amputate VERB to cut off an arm or leg by a surgical operation ▶ **amputation** NOUN

amuse VERB **1** to make a person laugh or smile **2** to make time pass pleasantly for someone ▶ **amusing** ADJECTIVE

amusement NOUN a way of passing time pleasantly

an DETERMINER SEE **a**

anaemia NOUN a poor condition of the blood that makes a person pale ▶ **anaemic** ADJECTIVE

anaesthetic NOUN a substance or gas that makes you unable to feel pain ▶ **anaesthesia** NOUN

anaesthetist NOUN a medical person qualified to give anaesthetics

anaesthetize VERB to give an anaesthetic to

⚠ **SPELLING**

This word can also be spelled *anaesthetise*.

anagram NOUN a word or phrase made by rearranging the letters of another word or phrase

anal ADJECTIVE to do with the anus

THESAURUS

large amount of computer memory ▶ quantity, volume, bulk, mass, supply

amount VERB **amount to** • *The cost amounted to several thousands.* ▶ add up to, come to, total, equal

ample ADJECTIVE • *an ample supply* ▶ plentiful, abundant, generous, liberal • *ample space* ▶ enough, adequate, sufficient, plenty of

amuse VERB • *The joke amused him.* ▶ entertain, delight, divert, cheer up, make laugh **amuse yourself** • *She amused herself by writing postcards.* ▶ occupy yourself, pass the time

amusing ADJECTIVE • *an amusing story* ▶ entertaining, enjoyable, witty, funny, humorous

analgesic NOUN a substance that reduces pain

analogy NOUN **analogies** a comparison between two things that are alike in some ways ► **analogous** ADJECTIVE

analyse VERB **1** to examine and interpret something **2** to separate something into its parts

analysis NOUN **analyses 1** a detailed examination of something **2** a separation of something into its parts ► **analytical** ADJECTIVE

anarchy NOUN **1** lack of government or control **2** lawlessness or complete disorder

anathema NOUN something you detest

anatomy NOUN the structure of a person's or animal's body, or the study of this ► **anatomical** ADJECTIVE, **anatomist** NOUN

ancestor NOUN someone from whom a person is descended ► **ancestral** ADJECTIVE, **ancestry** NOUN

anchor NOUN a heavy object attached to a ship by a chain or rope and dropped to the bottom of the sea to hold the ship still

anchor VERB **1** to fix or be fixed by an anchor **2** to fix firmly

anchovy NOUN **anchovies** a small fish with a strong flavour

ancient ADJECTIVE **1** very old **2** belonging to the distant past

ancillary ADJECTIVE helping or supporting *ancillary staff*

and CONJUNCTION a word used to link words and phrases *pens and pencils better and better*

anecdote NOUN an entertaining story about a real person or thing

anemone NOUN a plant with cup-shaped red, purple, or white flowers

anew ADVERB again; in a new or different way

angel NOUN **1** an attendant or messenger of God **2** a kind or beautiful person ► **angelic** ADJECTIVE

anger NOUN a strong feeling that you want to quarrel or fight with someone

anger VERB to make a person angry

angle NOUN **1** the space between two lines or surfaces that meet **2** the amount by which a line or

THESAURUS

ancestor NOUN • *We can trace our ancestors back to the Stuarts.* ► forebear, forefather, predecessor

ancient ADJECTIVE • *ancient buildings* ► old, historic, early, classical • *ancient civilizations* ► early, old, historic, prehistoric, bygone

anger NOUN • *Anger surged through him.* ► annoyance, irritation, exasperation, fury, rage

anger VERB • *Their rudeness angered us.* ► annoy, irritate, infuriate, incense, madden

angle NOUN • *the angle of the two walls* ► corner, intersection

surface must be turned to make it lie along another **3** a point of view

angle VERB **1** to put something in a slanting position **2** to present information from one point of view

angler NOUN a person who fishes with a fishing rod and line
▶ **angling** NOUN

angry ADJECTIVE **angrier**, **angriest** feeling or showing anger
▶ **angrily** ADVERB

anguish NOUN severe suffering or misery ▶ **anguished** ADJECTIVE

angular ADJECTIVE having angles or sharp corners

animal NOUN a living thing that can feel and move, usually other than a human

animate VERB **1** to make a thing lively **2** to produce something as an animated film

animated ADJECTIVE **1** lively and excited **2** (of a film) made by a process of animation

animation NOUN **1** a lively or excited state **2** the technique of making a film by photographing a series of still pictures and showing them rapidly one after another

animosity NOUN **animosities** a feeling of hostility

aniseed NOUN a sweet-smelling seed used for flavouring

ankle NOUN the part of the leg where it joins the foot

annex VERB **1** to take something and add it to what you have already **2** to add or join a thing to something else

annexe NOUN a building added to a larger or more important building

annihilate VERB to destroy something completely
▶ **annihilation** NOUN

anniversary NOUN **anniversaries** a day when you remember something special that happened on the same day in a previous year

announce VERB to make something known by saying it publicly or to an audience
▶ **announcement** NOUN

• *Let's look at the problem from another angle.* ▶ perspective, point of view, viewpoint, position

angry ADJECTIVE • *John looked angry. an angry look*
▶ annoyed, cross, irritated, enraged, furious **become angry**
• *The woman became angry.*
▶ lose your temper, fly into a rage, flare up, see red

anguish NOUN • *a cry of anguish*
▶ agony, pain, distress, suffering, grief

announce VERB • *to announce plans* ▶ make public, make known, declare, reveal • *The presenter announced the next act.*
▶ introduce, present

announcement NOUN • *an announcement from the Palace*
▶ statement, declaration,

a
b
c
d
e
f
g
h
i
j
k
l
m
n
o
p
q
r
s
t
u
v
w
x
y
z

DICTIONARY

announcer NOUN a person who announces items on radio or television

annoy VERB 1 to make a person slightly angry 2 to be troublesome to someone ▶ **annoyance** NOUN

annual ADJECTIVE 1 happening or done once a year 2 calculated over one year 3 living for one year or one season ▶ **annually** ADVERB

annual NOUN 1 a book that comes out once a year 2 an annual plant

annuity NOUN **annuities** a fixed annual allowance of money, especially from a kind of investment

annul VERB **annulling, annulled** to end a contract or arrangement legally ▶ **annulment** NOUN

anode NOUN the electrode by which electric current enters a device **COMPARE cathode**

anoint VERB to put oil or ointment on something in a religious ceremony

anomaly NOUN **anomalies** something that does not follow the general rule or that is unlike the usual or normal kind

anonymous ADJECTIVE without the name of the person responsible being known or made public *an anonymous donation* ▶ **anonymously** ADVERB, **anonymity** NOUN

anorak NOUN a waterproof jacket with a hood

anorexia NOUN an illness that makes a person so anxious to lose weight that they refuse to eat ▶ **anorexic** ADJECTIVE

another ADJECTIVE, PRONOUN a different or extra person or thing

answer NOUN 1 something said in return or reply 2 the solution to a problem

answer VERB 1 to give an answer to 2 to respond to a signal **answer**

THESAURUS

communiqué, proclamation, bulletin • *an announcement of the decision* ▶ declaration, notification, disclosure

annoy VERB • *The comments annoyed him.* ▶ irritate, anger, infuriate, enrage, madden

annoyed ADJECTIVE • *His mother looked annoyed.* ▶ irritated, angry, cross, displeased, infuriated

annoying ADJECTIVE • *an annoying grin* ▶ irritating, infuriating,

exasperating, maddening, tiresome

answer NOUN • *a quick answer* ▶ reply, response, reaction, riposte • *the answer to the question* ▶ solution, explanation • *Violence is no answer.* ▶ solution, remedy, way out • *his answer to the charge* ▶ defence, plea

answer VERB • *Answer the question. Will nobody answer me?* ▶ reply to, respond to, acknowledge, give an answer to,

back to reply cheekily or rudely
answer for to be responsible for

ant NOUN a small insect that lives as one of an organized group

antagonism NOUN a feeling of being unfriendly or hostile

antagonist NOUN an enemy or opponent

antagonistic ADJECTIVE unfriendly or hostile

antagonize VERB to make a person feel hostile or angry

⚠ SPELLING
This word can also be spelled
antagonise.

anteater NOUN an animal that feeds on ants and termites

antecedent NOUN a person or thing that lived or occurred at an earlier time

antelope NOUN a fast-running animal like a deer

antenna NOUN **1** (**antennae**) a feeler on the head of an insect or crustacean **2** (**antennas**) an aerial

anthem NOUN a religious or patriotic song, usually sung by a choir or group of people

anthology NOUN anthologies a collection of poems, stories, or songs

anthrax NOUN a disease of sheep and cattle that can also infect people

anthropoid ADJECTIVE like a human being

anthropology NOUN the study of human beings and their customs ▸ **anthropological** ADJECTIVE, **anthropologist** NOUN

antibiotic NOUN a substance (e.g. penicillin) that destroys bacteria or prevents them from growing

antibody NOUN antibodies a protein that forms in the blood as a defence against bacteria and other substances

anticipate VERB **1** to take action in advance about something you are aware of **2** to act before someone else does **3** to expect something ▸ **anticipation** NOUN, **anticipatory** ADJECTIVE

anticlimax NOUN a feeble or disappointing ending to something exciting

react to • *I'm not feeling well,' she answered.* ▸ reply, respond, retort, rejoin • *The encyclopedia will answer your problem.* ▸ solve, resolve, explain • *The accused answered all the charges.*
▸ refute, rebut, defend yourself against • *enough money to answer our needs* ▸ satisfy, serve, fulfil,

meet, fit • *a man answering the description* ▸ match, fit, correspond to, conform to

anticipate VERB • *It was impossible to anticipate all the problems.* ▸ prevent, pre-empt, forestall • *I anticipate that the result will be a draw.* ▸ expect, foresee, predict, forecast

a
b
c
d
e
f
g
h
i
j
k
l
m
n
o
p
q
r
s
t
u
v
w
x
y
z

anticlockwise ADVERB, ADJECTIVE moving in a direction opposite to the hands of a clock

antics PLURAL NOUN funny or foolish actions

anticyclone NOUN an area where air pressure is high, usually producing fine settled weather

antidote NOUN something that acts against the effects of a poison or disease

antifreeze NOUN a liquid added to water to make its freezing point lower

antipathy NOUN a strong dislike

antipodes PLURAL NOUN places on opposite sides of the earth **the Antipodes** Australia, New Zealand, and the areas near them, which are almost exactly opposite Europe ▶ **antipodean** ADJECTIVE

antiquated ADJECTIVE old-fashioned

antique ADJECTIVE **1** belonging to the distant past **2** very old

antique NOUN a valuable object from an older time

antiquities PLURAL NOUN objects that were made in ancient times

antiquity NOUN ancient times, especially of the Greeks and Romans

antiseptic ADJECTIVE **1** able to destroy bacteria **2** thoroughly clean and free from germs

antiseptic NOUN a substance that can destroy bacteria

antisocial ADJECTIVE unfriendly or inconsiderate towards other people

antithesis NOUN **antitheses** **1** the exact opposite of something **2** a contrast of ideas

antler NOUN the branching horn of a deer

antonym NOUN a word that is opposite in meaning to another, e.g. *good* and *bad*

anus NOUN the opening at the lower end of the alimentary canal, through which solid waste matter is passed out of the body

anvil NOUN a large block of iron on which a blacksmith hammers metal

anxious ADJECTIVE **1** worried **2** keen or eager *anxious to please us* ▶ **anxiously** ADVERB, **anxiety** NOUN

any ADJECTIVE, PRONOUN **1** one or some **2** no matter which *Come any time.*

THESAURUS

anxiety NOUN • *anxiety about money* ▶ concern, worry, unease, nervousness, dread • *a strong anxiety to please* ▶ eagerness, desire, enthusiasm, keenness

anxious • *Anxious relatives were waiting for news. Everyone is anxious about the next few weeks.* ▶ worried, concerned, nervous, troubled, tense • *anxious to please* ▶ eager, keen, enthusiastic

a
b
c
d
e
f
g
h
i
j
k
l
m
n
o
p
q
r
s
t
u
v
w
x
y
z

any ADVERB at all *Is this any good?*

anybody PRONOUN any person

anyhow ADVERB **1** in any case; whatever happens **2** in a careless way

anyone PRONOUN anybody

anything PRONOUN any thing

anyway ADVERB in any case; whatever happens

anywhere ADVERB in or to any place

aorta NOUN the main artery that carries blood away from the left side of the heart

apart ADVERB **1** away from each other **2** into pieces *It has come apart.* **apart from** excluding; other than

apartheid NOUN the political policy of keeping people of different races apart

apartment NOUN **1** a set of rooms **2** a flat

apathy NOUN lack of care or interest ▶ **apathetic** ADJECTIVE

ape NOUN an animal like a monkey but with no tail, e.g. a chimpanzee or gorilla

ape VERB to imitate or mimic

aperture NOUN an opening

apex NOUN the tip or highest point

aphid NOUN a tiny insect that sucks the juices from plants, e.g. a greenfly

aphorism NOUN a short witty saying

apiary NOUN **apiaries** a place where bees are kept

apiece ADVERB to, for, or by each *We got five pounds apiece.*

aplomb NOUN dignity and confidence

apologetic ADJECTIVE expressing regret ▶ **apologetically** ADVERB

apologize VERB to make an apology

⚠ **SPELLING**
This word can also be spelled *apologise.*

apology NOUN **apologies** a statement that you are sorry for something you have done

apostle NOUN a supporter of a person or belief, especially one of the twelve men sent out by Christ

apostrophe NOUN a punctuation mark (') used to show that letters have been missed out (as in *I can't* = I cannot) or to show possession (as in *the boy's book*)

appal VERB **appalling, appalled** to make a person shocked or horrified

apart ADVERB • *to be living apart* ▶ separately, independently, on your own **apart from** • *We are all here apart from him.* ▶ except (for), but for, aside from, besides, excepting, excluding

apologize VERB • *He apologized for his mistake.* ▶ say sorry, express regret, ask for forgiveness

appal VERB • *Violence appals most people.* ▶ horrify, shock, offend, disgust

DICTIONARY

appalling ADJECTIVE shocking; very unpleasant

apparatus NOUN the equipment for a particular experiment or task

apparent ADJECTIVE **1** clear or obvious **2** appearing to be true but not really so *their apparent indifference* ▸ **apparently** ADVERB

apparition NOUN **1** something strange or surprising that appears **2** a ghost

appeal VERB **1** to ask for something that you badly need *We'll appeal for more money.* **2** to ask for a decision to be changed **3** to seem attractive or interesting

appeal NOUN **1** an act of asking for something you need **2** an act of

asking for a decision to be changed **3** attraction or interest

appear VERB **1** to come into sight **2** to arrive **3** to seem

appearance NOUN what somebody or something looks like or seems to be

appease VERB to calm or pacify someone by agreeing to what they ask ▸ **appeasement** NOUN

append VERB to add at the end

appendage NOUN something added or attached at the end

appendicitis NOUN inflammation of the appendix

appendix NOUN **1** (**appendixes**) a small tube leading off from the intestine **2** (**appendices**) an extra section at the end of a book

THESAURUS

appalling ADJECTIVE • *appalling cruelty* ▸ horrifying, horrific, shocking, terrible, dreadful • *an appalling piece of work* ▸ dreadful, awful, terrible, atrocious, abysmal

apparent ADJECTIVE • *The crime had no apparent motive.* • *The sense of relief was apparent.* ▸ evident, obvious, discernible, clear

appeal NOUN • *an appeal for donations* ▸ call, request, cry • *The packaging improves the product's appeal.* ▸ attractiveness, charm, allure, charisma

appeal VERB appeal for • *to appeal for information* ▸ call for, beg for, ask for, request

appeal to • *The film role didn't appeal to him.* ▸ attract, interest, please, tempt

appear VERB • *A building appeared in the distance.* ▸ come into view, come into sight, be seen, arise • *These people still haven't appeared.* ▸ arrive, come, make an appearance • *A few problems have appeared.* ▸ arise, develop, emerge, come to light, occur • *The road appeared to lead nowhere.* ▸ seem, look • *Jake was appearing in the school play.* ▸ perform, take part, act

appearance NOUN • *a scruffy appearance* ▸ look, looks, demeanour • *an appearance of friendliness* ▸ semblance, air, pretence, facade, veneer

appetite NOUN **1** a desire for food **2** an enthusiasm for something

appetizer NOUN a small amount of food eaten before the main meal

⚠ **SPELLING**

This word can also be spelled *appetiser*.

appetizing ADJECTIVE looking and smelling good to eat

⚠ **SPELLING**

This word can also be spelled *appetising*.

applaud VERB **1** to show that you like something by clapping your hands **2** to express approval of

applause NOUN a show of approval by clapping

apple NOUN a round fruit with a red, yellow, or green skin

appliance NOUN a device or piece of equipment

applicable ADJECTIVE suitable or relevant

applicant NOUN a person who applies for a job or position

application NOUN **1** the action of applying for something **2** a formal request **3** the ability to concentrate on working **4** (*ICT*) a program designed for a particular purpose

apply VERB **applies, applied 1** to start using something **2** to make a formal request *I've applied for a job.* **3** to concern someone *This rule does not apply to you.* **4** to put one thing on another **apply yourself** to concentrate on working

appoint VERB **1** to choose a person for a job **2** to arrange or decide something officially *They will appoint a time for the meeting.*

appointment NOUN **1** an arrangement to meet or visit somebody at a particular time **2** a job or position

apposite ADJECTIVE (of a remark) suitable or relevant

THESAURUS

appetite NOUN • *A long walk will sharpen our appetite.* ► hunger, need for food • *an appetite for information* ► craving, longing, eagerness, desire, thirst

applaud VERB • *The audience applauded loudly.* ► clap, cheer, give an ovation, show your approval • *They applauded the youngsters' efforts.* ► commend, praise, acclaim, salute, congratulate

apply VERB • *Apply antiseptic cream to the cut.* ► put on, administer, spread • *to apply all skill and judgement* ► use, employ, exercise, utilize **apply for** • *to apply for a job* ► put in an application for, request **apply to** • *The rules only apply to England and Wales.* ► be relevant to, pertain to, refer to, relate to **apply yourself** • *It's hard work and you will need to apply yourself.* ► concentrate, be diligent, be industrious, work hard

appoint VERB • *They appointed her store manager.* ► name, nominate, choose (to be), engage (as)

a
b
c
d
e
f
g
h
i
j
k
l
m
n
o
p
q
r
s
t
u
v
w
x
y
z

apposition NOUN (*Grammar*) a construction in which two nouns referring to the same person or thing are placed together, e.g. *her dog Rufus*

appraise VERB to estimate the value or quality of a person or thing ► **appraisal** NOUN

appreciate VERB **1** to enjoy or value something **2** to understand something **3** to increase in value ► **appreciation** NOUN, **appreciative** ADJECTIVE

apprehend VERB **1** to seize or arrest someone **2** to understand something

apprehension NOUN **1** fear or worry **2** understanding **3** an arrest

apprehensive ADJECTIVE anxious or worried

apprentice NOUN a person who is learning a trade or craft from an

employer ► **apprenticed** ADJECTIVE, **apprenticeship** NOUN

approach VERB **1** to come near **2** to go to someone with a request or offer **3** to set about doing something

approach NOUN **1** a way or road to a place **2** a method of doing something

approachable ADJECTIVE friendly and easy to talk to

appropriate ADJECTIVE suitable or relevant ► **appropriately** ADVERB

appropriate VERB to take something for yourself ► **appropriation** NOUN

approval NOUN **1** a good opinion of somebody or something **2** formal agreement **on approval** taken by a customer for a trial period before being bought

THESAURUS

appreciate VERB • *I'd appreciate some help.* ► be grateful for, welcome, value, prize • *We appreciate good music.* ► enjoy, value, respect, like, think highly of • *I appreciate that you cannot stay long.* ► understand, recognize, realize, acknowledge, know

approach NOUN • *the approach of spring* ► arrival, coming, appearance, nearing • *an approach to the city* ► road, way in, entry, access • *The task needs a special approach.* ► method, procedure, technique, manner • *another approach to the problem* ► attitude, perspective, policy (for, regarding), point of view (on)

approach VERB • *A youth approached them.* ► move towards, come towards, go towards, come near • *The committee approached its task with determination.* ► set about, tackle, embark on, begin, undertake • *Should we approach the bank manager about a loan?* ► contact , speak to, sound out • *The cost was now approaching several millions.* ► border on, get close to, verge on

appropriate ADJECTIVE • *an appropriate time to ask questions* ► suitable, fitting, proper • *an appropriate comment* ► relevant, apposite, pertinent

DICTIONARY

approve *VERB* **1** to have a good opinion of a person or thing **2** to agree formally to something

approximate *ADJECTIVE* almost exact or correct but not completely so ▶ **approximately** *ADVERB*

approximate *VERB* to make or be almost the same as something ▶ **approximation** *NOUN*

apricot *NOUN* a juicy orange-coloured fruit with a stone in it

April *NOUN* the fourth month of the year

apron *NOUN* **1** a piece of clothing worn over the front of the body to protect other clothes **2** an area on an airfield where aircraft are loaded and unloaded

apse *NOUN* a domed semicircular part at the east end of a church

apt *ADJECTIVE* **1** likely; prone **2** suitable or relevant *an apt quotation* ▶ **aptly** *ADVERB*

aptitude *NOUN* a talent or ability

aquarium *NOUN* **aquariums** a tank or building for keeping live fish and other water animals

aquatic *ADJECTIVE* to do with water *aquatic sports*

aqueduct *NOUN* a bridge carrying a water channel across a valley

aquiline *ADJECTIVE* hooked like an eagle's beak

Arab *NOUN* a member of a Semitic people living in parts of the Middle East and North Africa ▶ **Arabian** *ADJECTIVE*

arabesque *NOUN* **1** (in dancing) a position with one leg stretched backwards in the air **2** an ornamental design of leaves and branches

Arabic *ADJECTIVE* to do with the Arabs or their language

Arabic *NOUN* the language of the Arabs

arabic numerals *PLURAL NOUN* the figures 1, 2, 3, 4, etc.

arable *ADJECTIVE* suitable for ploughing or growing crops on

arbiter *NOUN* **1** a person appointed to settle a disagreement **2** a person who is influential or sets standards

arbitrary *ADJECTIVE* chosen or done on an impulse, not according to a rule or law ▶ **arbitrarily** *ADVERB*

THESAURUS

approve *VERB* • *to approve a plan*
▶ support, accept, agree to, consent to, authorize **approve of**
• *They do not approve of these methods.* ▶ support, welcome, advocate, hold with, recommend

approximate *ADJECTIVE* • *All measurements are approximate.*
▶ rough, estimated, close, inexact

approximately *ADVERB*
• *approximately an hour*
▶ roughly, about, round about, more or less, in the region of

apt *ADJECTIVE* • *an apt reply*
▶ appropriate , suitable , fitting, proper • *He is apt to fall asleep.* ▶ inclined, liable, prone, likely

arbitrate VERB to settle a disagreement by arbitration

arbitration NOUN settlement of a disagreement by an impartial person who is not involved ▶ **arbitrator** NOUN

arboretum NOUN **arboretums** a place where trees are grown for study and display

arbour NOUN a shady place among trees

arc NOUN **1** part of the circumference of a circle **2** a luminous electric current passing between two electrodes

arcade NOUN a covered passage or area, usually with shops

arcane ADJECTIVE secret or mysterious

arch[1] NOUN **1** a curved structure that supports a bridge or roof **2** something shaped like this

arch VERB to form something into an arch

arch[2] ADJECTIVE pretending to be playful ▶ **archly** ADVERB

archaeology NOUN the study of ancient civilizations from the remains of their buildings and artefacts ▶ **archaeological** ADJECTIVE, **archaeologist** NOUN

archaic ADJECTIVE belonging to former or ancient times

archangel NOUN an angel of the highest rank

archbishop NOUN the chief bishop of a region

archer NOUN a person who shoots with a bow and arrows

archery NOUN the sport of shooting at a target with a bow and arrows

archipelago NOUN **archipelagos** a large group of islands

architect NOUN a person who designs buildings

architecture NOUN **1** the process of designing buildings **2** a particular style of building ▶ **architectural** ADJECTIVE

archive NOUN (ICT) a collection of computer files not in regular use

archives PLURAL NOUN the historical records of an organization or community

archivist NOUN a person trained to organize a set of archives

archway NOUN an arched passage or entrance

arctic ADJECTIVE very cold

ardent ADJECTIVE enthusiastic or passionate ▶ **ardently** ADVERB

ardour NOUN enthusiasm or passion

arduous ADJECTIVE needing much effort; laborious ▶ **arduously** ADVERB

area NOUN **1** the extent or measurement of a surface **2** a particular region or piece of land **3** a subject or special activity

THESAURUS

area NOUN • *an open area of land* ▶ expanse, stretch, patch, tract • *deprived urban areas* ▶ district, region, locality, neighbourhood, vicinity • *an area of study* ▶ field, domain, sphere, subject

arena NOUN the level area in the centre of an amphitheatre or sports stadium

aren't are not

arguable ADJECTIVE **1** able to be stated as a possibility **2** open to doubt; not certain ▸ **arguably** ADVERB

argue VERB **1** to disagree or exchange angry comments **2** to give reasons for a statement or opinion

argument NOUN **1** a disagreement or quarrel **2** a series of reasons for a statement or opinion

argumentative ADJECTIVE fond of arguing

aria NOUN a solo piece in an opera or oratorio

arid ADJECTIVE dry and barren

arise VERB **arose**, **arisen 1** to come into existence or to people's notice *A problem has arisen.* **2** to rise from a sitting or kneeling position

aristocracy NOUN people of the highest social rank; members of the nobility

aristocrat NOUN a member of the aristocracy ▸ **aristocratic** ADJECTIVE

arithmetic NOUN the science or study of numbers; calculation with numbers ▸ **arithmetical** ADJECTIVE

ark NOUN **1** (in the Bible) the ship in which Noah and his family escaped the Flood **2** a wooden box in which the writings of the Jewish Law were kept

arm¹ NOUN **1** each of the two limbs extending from the shoulder **2** something jutting out from a main part **3** the raised side part of a chair

arm² VERB **1** to supply with weapons **2** to prepare for war ▸ **armed** ADJECTIVE

armada NOUN a fleet of warships

armadillo NOUN **armadillos** a small burrowing animal covered with a shell of bony plates

armaments PLURAL NOUN the weapons of an army or country

argue VERB • *The children argue a lot.* ▸ quarrel, squabble, bicker, row • *The group argued late into the night.* ▸ discuss, debate, deliberate, dispute • *Some people argue that all ownership is theft.* ▸ contend, maintain, assert, claim, suggest

argument NOUN • *A fierce argument followed.* ▸ quarrel, disagreement, squabble, row,

altercation, dispute, fight • *a long argument about politics* ▸ discussion, debate, deliberation • *a convincing argument* ▸ case, line of reasoning, hypothesis, idea

arid ADJECTIVE • *an arid landscape* ▸ barren, parched, desert, dry

arise VERB • *Tell me if any problems arise.* ▸ occur, emerge, develop, appear, come to light

armature NOUN the current-carrying part of a dynamo or electric motor

armchair NOUN a comfortable chair with arms

armed forces or **armed services** PLURAL NOUN a country's army, navy, and air force

armful NOUN **armfuls** as much as you can carry in your arms

armistice NOUN an agreement to stop fighting in a war or battle

armour NOUN 1 a protective covering for the body, formerly worn in fighting 2 a metal protective covering on a warship or heavy military vehicle
▶ **armoured** ADJECTIVE

armoury NOUN **armouries** a place where weapons and ammunition are stored

armpit NOUN the hollow part below the top of the arm at the shoulder

arms PLURAL NOUN 1 weapons 2 a heraldic design on a shield

army NOUN **armies** 1 a large number of soldiers trained to fight on land 2 a large group of people

aroma NOUN a pleasant smell
▶ **aromatic** ADJECTIVE

around ADVERB, PREPOSITION all round; about

arouse VERB 1 to stir up a feeling in someone 2 to wake someone up

arrange VERB 1 to put things into a certain order 2 to form plans for something 3 to prepare music for particular instruments or voices

arrangement NOUN 1 a particular pattern or ordering of things 2 an agreement to do something

array NOUN 1 a display 2 an orderly arrangement

array VERB 1 to arrange in order 2 to dress or decorate

arrears PLURAL NOUN 1 money owed that should have been paid earlier 2 a backlog of work **in arrears** behind with payments

arrest VERB 1 to seize a person by the authority of the law 2 to stop or check a process or movement

arrest NOUN 1 the act of arresting somebody 2 the process of stopping something

THESAURUS

army NOUN • *an army of ten thousand soldiers* ▶ armed force, fighting force, force, militia • *an army of tourists* ▶ crowd, swarm, throng, horde

arouse VERB • *to arouse strong feelings* ▶ rouse, cause, kindle, provoke

arrange VERB • *to arrange the furniture* ▶ organize, set out, lay out, put in order, spread out • *to arrange an outing* ▶ organize, fix, plan, make arrangements for

arrest VERB • *They were arrested for shoplifting.* ▶ apprehend, detain, take into custody

arrive VERB **1** to reach the place you are going to **2** to reach a decision or agreement **3** to happen *The great day arrived.*
▶ **arrival** NOUN

arrogant ADJECTIVE unpleasantly proud and haughty ▶ **arrogantly** ADVERB, **arrogance** NOUN

arrow NOUN **1** a weapon with a pointed tip shot from a bow **2** a sign with a shape of an arrow, used for showing direction

arsenal NOUN a place where weapons and ammunition are stored or produced

arsenic NOUN a highly poisonous metallic substance

arson NOUN the crime of deliberately setting fire to a building ▶ **arsonist** NOUN

art NOUN **1** painting, drawing, or sculpture, or the things produced in this way **2** a skill *the art of debating*

artefact NOUN an object made by humans, especially in the past and of historical interest

artery NOUN **arteries 1** a tube that carries blood away from the heart **2** an important road or route
▶ **arterial** ADJECTIVE

artful ADJECTIVE clever and crafty
▶ **artfully** ADVERB

arthritis NOUN a disease that makes joints in the body stiff and painful ▶ **arthritic** ADJECTIVE

arthropod NOUN an animal of the group that includes insects, spiders, crabs, and centipedes

artichoke NOUN a kind of plant with a flower head used as a vegetable

article NOUN **1** a piece of writing published in a newspaper or magazine **2** an object **3** (*Grammar*) any of the words *a* or *an* (the indefinite article), or *the* (the definite article)

articulate ADJECTIVE able to speak and express ideas clearly

articulate VERB **1** to say or speak clearly **2** to connect by a joint
▶ **articulation** NOUN

articulated ADJECTIVE (of a vehicle) having two sections connected by a flexible joint

arrive VERB • *The guests started to arrive.* ▶ come, appear, enter, present yourself **arrive at** • *We arrived at the bus station.* ▶ reach, come to, get to

arrogant ADJECTIVE • *an arrogant manner* ▶ haughty, conceited, self-important, superior, pompous, snobbish

art NOUN • *a course in art* ▶ fine art, painting, sculpture, drawing, craftsmanship • *the art of writing* ▶ skill, talent, technique, gift, knack

article NOUN • *various household articles* ▶ object, item, thing, product • *a newspaper article* ▶ feature, report, review, account

a
b
c
d
e
f
g
h
i
j
k
l
m
n
o
p
q
r
s
t
u
v
w
x
y
z

artificial ADJECTIVE not natural; made by human beings in imitation of a natural thing
▶ **artificially** ADVERB, **artificiality** NOUN

artillery NOUN **1** large guns **2** the part of an army that uses these

artisan NOUN a skilled worker who makes things with their hands

artist NOUN **1** a person who paints pictures **2** an entertainer
▶ **artistry** NOUN

artistic ADJECTIVE **1** to do with art or artists **2** having a talent for art
▶ **artistically** ADVERB

arts PLURAL NOUN languages, literature, history, and other non-scientific subjects in which opinion and interpretation are very important **the arts** creative work such as painting, music, and writing

as ADVERB, CONJUNCTION **1** equally or similarly *This is just as easy.* **2** when or while *He fell as he got off the bus.* **3** because *As we were late, we missed the train.* **4** in a way that *Leave it as it is.*

as PREPOSITION in the function of *It acts as a handle.*

asbestos NOUN a fireproof material made up of fine soft fibres

ascend VERB **1** to go up **2** to rise or slope upwards **ascend the throne** to become king or queen

ascent NOUN **1** an upward climb or movement **2** a way up

ascertain VERB to find something out by asking

ascribe VERB to regard something as having a particular cause or reason *She ascribes her success to hard work.*

aseptic ADJECTIVE clean and free from bacteria that cause things to become septic

ash[1] NOUN the powder that is left after something has been burned **ashes** remains after something has been burned, especially of a human body after cremation

ash[2] NOUN a tree with silver-grey bark

ashamed ADJECTIVE feeling shame

ashen ADJECTIVE grey or pale

ashore ADVERB to or on the shore

artificial ADJECTIVE • artificial light • artificial trees ▶ synthetic, imitation, man-made, manufactured, fake • an artificial smile ▶ false, affected, fake, pretended

artistic ADJECTIVE • artistic skills ▶ creative, imaginative • an artistic design ▶ aesthetic, decorative, tasteful, elegant, beautiful

ascend VERB • He ascended the stairs. ▶ climb, climb up, go up, mount • The plane began to ascend. ▶ rise, soar, take off, lift off, fly up

ashamed ADJECTIVE • He was ashamed of his behaviour. ▶ sorry (for), apologetic (about), shamefaced (about), embarrassed (about), upset (about)

Asian ADJECTIVE to do with Asia or its people

Asian NOUN an Asian person

aside ADVERB 1 to or at one side 2 in reserve

aside NOUN words spoken so that only certain people will hear

asinine ADJECTIVE extremely stupid

ask VERB 1 to speak so as to find out or get something 2 to invite someone *Ask them to the party.*

askance ADVERB **look askance at** to regard a person or situation with distrust or disapproval

askew ADVERB, ADJECTIVE crooked; not straight or level

asleep ADVERB, ADJECTIVE sleeping

asparagus NOUN a plant whose young shoots are eaten as a vegetable

aspect NOUN 1 one part of a problem or situation 2 a person's or thing's appearance 3 the direction a room or building faces

asphalt NOUN a sticky black substance like tar, mixed with gravel to make road surfaces

asphyxia NOUN suffocation

asphyxiate VERB to suffocate ▸ **asphyxiation** NOUN

aspire VERB to have an ambition to achieve something *He aspires to be prime minister.*

aspirin NOUN a drug used to relieve pain or reduce fever

ass NOUN 1 a donkey 2 (*informal*) a stupid person

assail VERB to attack

assailant NOUN an attacker

assassin NOUN a person who kills an important person

assassinate VERB to kill an important person, especially for political reasons ▸ **assassination** NOUN

assault NOUN a violent attack

assault VERB to attack someone violently

assemble VERB 1 to bring or come together 2 to put the parts of something together

THESAURUS

ask VERB • *I'll ask him where it is.* ▸ enquire (of somebody), quiz (somebody about) • *to ask a question* ▸ put, pose, raise • *Ask them to get help.* ▸ request, beg, entreat, implore, urge • *Ask them round.* ▸ invite, summon **ask for** • *Ask for anything you need.* ▸ request, demand

asleep ADJECTIVE • *asleep in bed* ▸ sleeping, slumbering, dozing, napping

aspect NOUN • *looking at the problem from every aspect* ▸ side, angle, standpoint, respect

assault VERB • *he assaulted a police officer* ▸ attack, hit, strike, set upon, beat up

assault NOUN • *an assault on the enemy position* ▸ attack, onslaught, strike, offensive, raid

assemble VERB • *A crowd began to assemble.* ▸ gather, congregate, come together, collect • *The*

DICTIONARY

assembly NOUN **assemblies**
1 the process of coming together
2 a regular meeting, especially of all the members of a school **3** a parliament or other government body

assent VERB **1** to consent **2** to say you agree

assent NOUN consent or approval

assert VERB to state something firmly

assertion NOUN something said with force or confidence

assertive ADJECTIVE acting forcefully and with confidence

assess VERB to decide or estimate the value or quality of a person or thing ▸ **assessment** NOUN, **assessor** NOUN

asset NOUN something useful or valuable to someone

assets PLURAL NOUN a person's or company's property that could be sold to pay debts or raise money

assign VERB **1** to give a task or duty to someone **2** to appoint a person to perform a task

assignation NOUN an arrangement to meet someone, especially a lover

assignment NOUN a task or duty given to someone

assimilate VERB to take in and absorb something
▸ **assimilation** NOUN

THESAURUS

general assembled his forces.
▸ gather, collect together, bring together, convene, round up • *The cars are assembled abroad.*
▸ build, construct, manufacture, produce, put together

assert VERB • *She asserted that it was true.* ▸ declare, maintain, insist, argue, claim • *to assert your rights* ▸ insist on, claim, stand up for, uphold **assert yourself**
• *Some of the newer members are asserting themselves at meetings.*
▸ be assertive, be resolute, exert your influence

assertive ADJECTIVE • *assertive leadership* ▸ forceful, determined, resolute, confident, firm

assess VERB • *to assess the extent of the damage* ▸ evaluate, gauge,

judge, determine, estimate • *to assess students* ▸ judge, rate, appraise

asset NOUN • *A sense of humour is an asset.* ▸ benefit, advantage, blessing, help **assets** • *the company's assets* ▸ capital, resources, property, funds, goods

assign VERB • *to assign tasks* ▸ allocate, distribute, allot, give out, share out • *to assign an officer to the case* ▸ appoint, delegate, nominate, choose (for)

assignment NOUN • *a challenging assignment* ▸ task, piece of work, project, job, duty
• *the assignment of responsibilities* ▸ allocation, issuing, granting

assist VERB to help someone
► **assistance** NOUN

assistant NOUN **1** a person who assists another **2** a person who serves customers in a shop

associate VERB **1** to connect things in your mind **2** to have dealings with a group of people

associate NOUN a colleague or companion ► **associate** ADJECTIVE

association NOUN **1** an organization of people; a society **2** a connection or link in your mind

assorted ADJECTIVE of various sorts put together

assortment NOUN a mixed collection of things

assume VERB **1** to accept something without proof **2** to undertake **3** to put on an expression **assumed name** a false name ► **assumption** NOUN

assurance NOUN **1** a promise or guarantee **2** a kind of life insurance **3** confidence in yourself

assure VERB **1** to tell somebody confidently **2** to make certain

asterisk NOUN a star-shaped sign (*) used to draw attention to something

astern ADVERB at or to the back of a ship or aircraft

asteroid NOUN one of the small planets that orbit the sun between Mars and Jupiter

asthma NOUN a disease that makes breathing difficult
► **asthmatic** ADJECTIVE, NOUN

astigmatism NOUN a defect that prevents an eye or lens from focusing properly ► **astigmatic** ADJECTIVE

astonish VERB to surprise somebody very much
► **astonishment** NOUN

assist VERB • *Could you assist us for a while?* ► help, aid, support, give a hand to, lend a (helping) hand to

assistant NOUN • *The team leader has three assistants.* ► helper, subordinate, deputy, colleague, junior

assorted ADJECTIVE • *assorted objects* ► miscellaneous, mixed, different, various

assortment NOUN • *an assortment of paperbacks* ► mixture, selection, collection, variety, array

assume VERB • *I assumed the book was a gift.* ► presume, suppose, infer, deduce, surmise • *to assume responsibilities* ► take on, accept, undertake • *to assume a Scottish accent* ► adopt, put on, feign

assure VERB • *He assured me he would arrive in time.* ► promise, reassure, convince • *The win assured them a place in the finals.* ► ensure, secure, guarantee, make certain

astonish VERB • *We were astonished at the changes.* ► amaze, astound, surprise, stagger, shock

a
b
c
d
e
f
g
h
i
j
k
l
m
n
o
p
q
r
s
t
u
v
w
x
y
z

43

astound VERB to astonish or shock somebody very much

astray ADVERB, ADJECTIVE away from the right path or place or course of action **go astray** to be lost or mislaid

astride ADVERB, PREPOSITION with one leg on each side of something

astrology NOUN the study of the stars and planets and how they are supposed to influence people's lives ▶ **astrologer** NOUN, **astrological** ADJECTIVE

astronaut NOUN a person who travels in space

astronomical ADJECTIVE 1 to do with astronomy 2 (of a number or cost) extremely large

astronomy NOUN the study of the stars and planets and their movements ▶ **astronomer** NOUN

astute ADJECTIVE clever at understanding situations quickly ▶ **astutely** ADVERB

asylum NOUN 1 refuge and safety given to political refugees 2 (old use) a hospital for mentally ill people

at PREPOSITION used to show: 1 position or direction *at the top* Aim at the target. 2 time *at midnight* 3 level or price *They are sold at £10 each.* 4 cause *We were*

surprised at his mistake. **at all** in any way **at once** 1 immediately *Come at once.* 2 at the same time *It all happened at once.*

atheist NOUN a person who believes that there is no God ▶ **atheism** NOUN

athlete NOUN a person who is good at sport, especially athletics

athletic ADJECTIVE 1 physically strong and active 2 to do with athletes ▶ **athletically** ADVERB

athletics PLURAL NOUN physical exercises and sports, e.g. running, jumping, and throwing

atlas NOUN a book of maps

atmosphere NOUN 1 the air around the earth 2 a feeling or mood *a friendly atmosphere* ▶ **atmospheric** ADJECTIVE

atoll NOUN a ring-shaped coral reef

atom NOUN the smallest particle of a chemical element

atom bomb or **atomic bomb** NOUN a bomb exploded by atomic energy

atomic ADJECTIVE to do with an atom or atomic energy

atomic energy NOUN energy created by splitting the nuclei of certain atoms

THESAURUS

astonishing ADJECTIVE • *The results were astonishing.*
▶ amazing, astounding, staggering, extraordinary, incredible

astound VERB • *His arrogance astounded her.* ▶ astonish, amaze, surprise, stagger, shock

athletic ADJECTIVE • *an athletic physique* ▶ muscular, fit, well-built, strong, sporty

atmosphere NOUN • *gases escaping into the atmosphere*
▶ air, sky, ether • *the warm cosy atmosphere of the kitchen*

a
b
c
d
e
f
g
h
i
j
k
l
m
n
o
p
q
r
s
t
u
v
w
x
y
z

atomic number NOUN (Science) the number of protons in the nucleus of an atom

atomizer NOUN a device for making a liquid into a fine spray

⚠ **SPELLING**
This word can also be spelled **atomiser**.

atone VERB to make amends for having done wrong
▶ **atonement** NOUN

atrocious ADJECTIVE extremely bad
▶ **atrociously** ADVERB

atrocity NOUN atrocities something extremely bad or wicked; wickedness

attach VERB 1 to fix or join something to something else 2 to think of something as relevant to a situation or topic *We attach great*

importance to fitness. **attached to** fond of

attachment NOUN 1 the process of attaching 2 something attached 3 (ICT) a file sent with an email

attack NOUN 1 a violent attempt to hurt or overcome somebody 2 a piece of strong criticism 3 sudden illness or pain 4 the players in a team whose job is to score goals; an attempt to score a goal

attack VERB to make an attack on
▶ **attacker** NOUN

attain VERB to succeed in doing or getting something ▶ **attainable** ADJECTIVE, **attainment** NOUN

attainment NOUN an achievement

attempt VERB to make an effort to do something; to try

THESAURUS

▶ environment, surroundings, ambience, climate, mood

atrocious ADJECTIVE • *atrocious brutality* ▶ appalling, brutal, vicious, vile, horrifying

attach VERB • *Attach them to the wall with screws.* ▶ fix, fasten, secure, join, connect • *We attach great importance to punctuality.* ▶ assign, attribute, place (on)

attack NOUN • *an attack on the enemy position* ▶ assault, onslaught, strike, offensive, raid, charge, ambush, bombardment • *an attack on their honesty* ▶ criticism (of), tirade (against), outburst (against) • *an attack of coughing* ▶ fit, bout, convulsion, outbreak

attack VERB • *We attack the enemy position at dawn.* ▶ charge, bombard, assault, ambush, raid • *They attacked him on his way home.* ▶ assault, mug, jump on, ambush, set about • *to attack government policy* ▶ criticize, find fault with, denounce, condemn

attain VERB • *to attain high office* ▶ achieve, gain, win, get, reach

attempt NOUN • *a brave attempt* ▶ try, effort, endeavour

attempt VERB • *We attempted to persuade them.* ▶ try, endeavour, aim, strive, make an/every effort • *to attempt three questions* ▶ try, choose, answer

DICTIONARY

attempt NOUN an effort to do something; a try

attend VERB **1** to be present somewhere or go somewhere regularly **2** to look after someone **3** to spend time dealing with something

attendance NOUN **1** the act of attending or being present **2** the number of people present at an event

attendant NOUN a person who helps or accompanies someone

attention NOUN **1** concentration and careful thought **2** a position in which a soldier stands with feet together and arms straight downwards

attentive ADJECTIVE giving attention to something
▶ **attentively** ADVERB

attest VERB to declare or prove that something is true or genuine
▶ **attestation** NOUN

attic NOUN a room in the roof of a house

attire NOUN (formal) clothes

attired ADJECTIVE (formal) dressed

attitude NOUN **1** a way of thinking or behaving **2** the position of the body; posture

attorney NOUN **attorneys 1** a person appointed to act on behalf of another **2** (American) a lawyer

attract VERB **1** to seem pleasant or interesting to someone **2** to pull by a physical force *Magnets attract metal.*

attraction NOUN **1** the process of attracting, or the ability to attract **2** something that attracts visitors

attractive ADJECTIVE **1** pleasant or good-looking **2** interesting or appealing *an attractive idea*
▶ **attractively** ADVERB

attribute VERB to regard something as the cause or source *We attribute their success to hard work.* ▶ **attribution** NOUN

attribute NOUN a quality or characteristic

THESAURUS

attend VERB • *to attend an interview* ▶ go to/for, present yourself at, appear at, be present at • *The bride was attended by two bridesmaids.* ▶ escort, assist, accompany, guard, wait on
attend to • *to attend to the injured* ▶ look after, care for, tend, treat, help • *to attend to the details* ▶ deal with, take care of, look after, see to, organize

attentive ADJECTIVE • *an attentive audience* ▶ alert, vigilant, watchful, on the lookout • *an*

attentive helper ▶ thoughtful, considerate, kind, caring, understanding

attitude NOUN • *a positive attitude* ▶ outlook, approach, manner, frame of mind

attract VERB • *to attract a large audience* ▶ draw, bring, bring in, generate • *to be attracted by its beauty* ▶ enchant, entrance, captivate, lure, entice

attractive ADJECTIVE • *an attractive young woman* ▶ good-looking,

attuned ADJECTIVE adjusted to something

aubergine NOUN a deep purple fruit eaten as a vegetable

auction NOUN a public sale at which things are sold to the person who bids highest

auction VERB to sell something by auction ▸ **auctioneer** NOUN

audacious ADJECTIVE bold or daring ▸ **audaciously** ADVERB

audacity NOUN boldness or daring

audible ADJECTIVE loud enough to be heard ▸ **audibility** NOUN, **audibly** ADVERB

audience NOUN **1** people who have gathered to hear or watch something **2** a formal interview with an important person

audio NOUN the reproduction of recorded music or sounds

audio-visual ADJECTIVE using both sound and pictures to give information

audit NOUN an official examination of financial accounts to see that they are correct

audit VERB to make an audit of accounts

audition NOUN a test to see if an actor or musician is suitable for a job

audition VERB to give someone an audition

auditor NOUN a person qualified to audit accounts

auditorium NOUN **auditoriums** the part of a theatre or hall where the audience sits

augment VERB to increase or add to something ▸ **augmentation** NOUN

augur VERB to be a sign of what is to come *These successes augur well.*

August NOUN the eighth month of the year

august ADJECTIVE majestic or imposing

aunt NOUN **1** the sister of your father or mother **2** your uncle's wife

au pair NOUN a young person from abroad who works for a time in someone's home

aura NOUN a general feeling surrounding a person or thing *an aura of excitement*

aural ADJECTIVE to do with the ear or hearing ▸ **aurally** ADVERB

auspicious ADJECTIVE fortunate or favourable

austere ADJECTIVE very simple and plain ▸ **austerely** ADVERB, **austerity** NOUN

THESAURUS

nice-looking, pretty, striking, beautiful, gorgeous, lovely, charming, engaging, appealing, glamorous, stunning • *an attractive offer* ▸ appealing, agreeable, tempting, interesting

authentic ADJECTIVE • *an authentic painting* ▸ genuine, original, real, actual, legitimate • *an authentic story* ▸ accurate, factual, honest, reliable, truthful

a
b
c
d
e
f
g
h
i
j
k
l
m
n
o
p
q
r
s
t
u
v
w
x
y
z

authentic ADJECTIVE real; genuine
▶ **authentically** ADVERB,
authenticity NOUN

authenticate VERB to confirm
something as being authentic
▶ **authentication** NOUN

author NOUN the writer of a book,
play, poem, or article
▶ **authorship** NOUN

authoritarian ADJECTIVE strict in
enforcing obedience

authoritative ADJECTIVE having
proper authority or expert
knowledge

authority NOUN **authorities**
1 the right or power to give orders
2 a person or organization having
this power **3** an expert or a book
written by an expert

authorize VERB to give official
permission for something
▶ **authorization** NOUN

⚠ **SPELLING**

This word can also be spelled
authorise.

autism NOUN a disability that
means someone has difficulty
responding to their surroundings
or communicating with other
people ▶ **autistic** ADJECTIVE

autobiography NOUN
autobiographies the story of a
person's life written by himself or
herself ▶ **autobiographical**
ADJECTIVE

autocracy NOUN **autocracies**
rule by one person with unlimited
power

autocrat NOUN a person who
enforces rules harshly
▶ **autocratic** ADJECTIVE

autocue NOUN (*trademark*) a
device that displays the script for a
speaker or television presenter

autograph NOUN the signature of
a famous person

autograph VERB to write a
signature on

automated ADJECTIVE working by
automation

automatic ADJECTIVE **1** working
on its own without needing
control by people **2** done without
thinking ▶ **automatically** ADVERB

automation NOUN the use of
machines and automatic
processes

automaton NOUN **1** a robot **2** a
person who acts mechanically
without thinking

automobile NOUN (*American*) a
car

autonomy NOUN **1** the right of a
people to have their own
government **2** the right to act
independently ▶ **autonomous**
ADJECTIVE

autopsy NOUN **autopsies** an
examination of a body after death

autumn NOUN the season
between summer and winter
▶ **autumnal** ADJECTIVE

THESAURUS

automatic ADJECTIVE • *an
automatic reaction* ▶ instinctive,
spontaneous, involuntary,
unconscious, reflex, unthinking,
unintentional • *automatic doors*
▶ mechanical, automated,
computerized, programmed,
robotic

auxiliary ADJECTIVE giving help and support *auxiliary services*

auxiliary NOUN **auxiliaries** a helper

auxiliary verb NOUN a verb such as *do*, *have*, and *will*, used to form parts of other verbs, as in *I have finished*.

avail NOUN **to** or **of no avail** of no use *Their pleas for mercy were all to no avail.*

avail VERB **avail yourself of** to make use of

available ADJECTIVE ready or able to be used ▸ **availability** NOUN

avalanche NOUN a mass of snow or rock falling down the side of a mountain

avarice NOUN greed for money or possessions ▸ **avaricious** ADJECTIVE

avenge VERB to have revenge for something done to harm you ▸ **avenger** NOUN

avenue NOUN **1** a long wide street, often with trees down the sides **2** a means of doing something

average NOUN **1** the value obtained by adding several amounts together and dividing by the number of amounts **2** the usual or ordinary standard

average ADJECTIVE **1** worked out as an average *Their average age is 10.* **2** of the usual or ordinary standard

average VERB to work out or amount to as an average

averse ADJECTIVE opposed to something *I'm not averse to a bit of hard work.*

aversion NOUN a strong dislike

avert VERB **1** to turn something away *He averted his eyes.* **2** to prevent something

aviary NOUN a large cage or building for keeping birds

aviation NOUN the flying of aircraft ▸ **aviator** NOUN

avid ADJECTIVE keen or eager *an avid reader* ▸ **avidly** ADVERB

avocado NOUN **avocados** a pear-shaped fruit with a rough green skin and a creamy flesh

avoid VERB **1** to keep yourself away from someone or something **2** to keep yourself from doing or saying something ▸ **avoidable** ADJECTIVE, **avoidance** NOUN

avuncular ADJECTIVE kind and friendly towards someone younger

await VERB to wait for

THESAURUS

available ADJECTIVE • *All facilities will be available.* ▸ obtainable, accessible, ready, at/on/to hand, usable

average ADJECTIVE • *an average day* ▸ typical, normal, ordinary, usual, regular • *an average golfer* ▸ mediocre, undistinguished,

unremarkable, second-rate, passable

avid ADJECTIVE • *avid fans* ▸ keen, eager, enthusiastic, passionate, fervent

avoid VERB • *to avoid arguments* ▸ refrain from, stay clear of, steer

awake VERB **awoke, awoken** to wake up, or wake someone up

awake ADJECTIVE not asleep

awaken VERB **1** to wake up, or wake someone up **2** to stimulate a feeling or interest
▶ **awakening** NOUN

award VERB to give something officially as a prize, payment, or penalty

award NOUN something awarded, such as a prize or a sum of money

aware ADJECTIVE knowing or realizing something *Are you aware of the danger?*
▶ **awareness** NOUN

away ADVERB **1** to or at a distance **2** not at the usual place **3** out of existence *The water had boiled away.* **4** continuously or persistently *We worked away at it.*

away ADJECTIVE (of a game) played on an opponent's ground

awe NOUN fearful or deeply respectful wonder

awesome ADJECTIVE causing awe

awful ADJECTIVE **1** very bad *an awful accident* **2** (informal) very great *an awful lot of money*
▶ **awfully** ADVERB

awkward ADJECTIVE **1** difficult to use or deal with **2** not skilful; clumsy ▶ **awkwardly** ADVERB

awl NOUN a small pointed tool for making holes in leather or wood

awning NOUN a roof-like shelter made of canvas or plastic

awry ADVERB, ADJECTIVE **1** twisted to one side; crooked **2** not according to plan *go awry*

axe NOUN **1** a tool for chopping things **2** (informal) dismissal or redundancy **have an axe to grind** have a personal interest in something

THESAURUS

clear of • *to avoid responsibility*
▶ evade, escape, dodge, shirk, sidestep • *to avoid a collision*
▶ prevent, avert • *someone he was anxious to avoid* ▶ ignore, shun, keep away from, hide from, steer clear of • *to avoid alcohol*
▶ refrain from, desist from, abstain from

aware ADJECTIVE **aware of** • *to be aware of the dangers* ▶ conscious of, acquainted with, mindful of, informed about, familiar with

awe NOUN • *He regarded her with awe.* ▶ wonder, amazement, admiration, respect, reverence

awful ADJECTIVE • *awful weather*
▶ bad, terrible, dreadful, atrocious, appalling • *an awful smell* ▶ unpleasant, disgusting, nasty, horrible, foul • *awful news*
▶ grave, serious, bad, terrible, dreadful • *I felt awful for losing my temper.* ▶ guilty, remorseful, regretful, ashamed, sorry

awkward ADJECTIVE • *an awkward size* ▶ inconvenient, cumbersome, bulky, unwieldy • *awkward movements* ▶ clumsy, ungainly, inept, uncoordinated, gauche • *an awkward situation*
▶ difficult, troublesome, trying,

axe VERB **1** to cancel or abolish something **2** to reduce something by a large amount

axiom NOUN an established general truth or principle
► **axiomatic** ADJECTIVE

axis NOUN **axes 1** a line through the centre of a spinning object **2** a line dividing a thing in half **3** the horizontal or vertical line on a graph

axle NOUN the rod through the centre of a wheel, on which the wheel turns

aye ADVERB yes

annoying, perplexing • *an awkward silence* ► embarrassing, uncomfortable, uneasy • *an*

awkward person ► unreasonable, unhelpful, uncooperative, obstinate, exasperating

Bb

babble VERB **1** to talk very quickly without making sense **2** to make a murmuring sound ▶ **babble** NOUN

babe NOUN a baby

baboon NOUN a large monkey with a long muzzle and short tail

baby NOUN **babies** a very young child or animal

babyish ADJECTIVE childish or immature

babysit VERB **babysitting**, **babysat** to look after a child while its parents are out ▶ **babysitter** NOUN

bachelor NOUN **1** a man who has not married **2** someone who has a university degree *Bachelor of Arts*

back NOUN **1** the part furthest from the front **2** the back part of the body from the shoulders to the base of the spine **3** the part of a chair etc. that your back rests

against **4** a defending player near the goal in football etc.

back ADJECTIVE placed at or near the back

back ADVERB **1** to or towards the back **2** to the place you have come from *Go back home.* **3** to an earlier time or position *Give it back.*

back VERB **1** to move backwards **2** to give someone support or help **3** to bet on something **4** to cover the back of something **back out** to refuse to do what you agreed to do **back up 1** to give support or help to a person or thing **2** (ICT) to make a spare copy of a file or disk ▶ **backer** NOUN

backbone NOUN **1** the spine **2** the main support of an organization or undertaking

backfire VERB **1** (of a vehicle) to make a loud noise caused by an explosion in the exhaust pipe **2** (of a plan) to go wrong

background NOUN **1** the back part of a picture or scene **2** the

baby NOUN • *The woman was holding a baby.* ▶ babe, infant, toddler, child • *a baby car* ▶ miniature, mini, small-scale, diminutive

babyish ADJECTIVE • *babyish behaviour* ▶ childish, juvenile, puerile, immature, infantile

back NOUN • *a person's back* ▶ spine, backbone, spinal column • *the back of the vehicle* ▶ end, rear, tail-end • *the back of the building* ▶ rear, rear side • *the back of the ship* ▶ stern • *the back of an envelope* ▶ reverse • *the*

back of an animal ▶ rear, tail, hindquarters

back ADJECTIVE • *the back door* ▶ rear • *an animal's back legs* ▶ rear, hind • *the back row of the hall* ▶ end, rearmost

back VERB • *back into the parking space* ▶ reverse, go backwards, move back • *to back a plan* ▶ support, endorse, approve of, sponsor **back down** • *The government has had to back down.* ▶ give way, retreat, change your mind, yield

DICTIONARY

conditions influencing something **3** a person's family and upbringing **in the background** not noticeable or obvious

backhand NOUN a stroke made in tennis with the back of the hand turned outwards

backing NOUN **1** help or support **2** a musical accompaniment

backlash NOUN a violent reaction to an event

backlog NOUN an amount of work that still has to be done

backpack NOUN a pack carried on the back ▸ **backpacker** NOUN

backside NOUN (informal) the buttocks

backstroke NOUN a swimming stroke done lying on your back

back-up NOUN (ICT) a copy of a file or data kept for security

backward ADJECTIVE **1** going backwards **2** slow at learning or developing

backward ADVERB backwards

⚠ **USAGE**

The adverb *backward* is mainly used in American English.

backwards ADVERB **1** to or towards the back **2** with the back end going first **3** in reverse order **count backwards**

backwater NOUN a quiet place not affected by progress or new ideas

bacon NOUN smoked or salted meat from the back or sides of a pig

bacterium NOUN **bacteria** a microscopic organism that can cause disease ▸ **bacterial** ADJECTIVE

bad ADJECTIVE **worse, worst 1** not good **2** wicked or evil **3** serious or severe **a bad accident 4** ill or unhealthy **5** harmful **bad for your teeth 6** (of food) decayed or rotten

bade old past tense of **bid**²

THESAURUS

backing NOUN • **the backing of the unions** ▸ support, agreement, assistance, encouragement • **financial backing** ▸ support, funding, sponsorship • **a musical backing** ▸ accompaniment, orchestration

bad ADJECTIVE • **bad work** ▸ poor, substandard, unsatisfactory, awful, terrible, dreadful • **a bad driver** ▸ incompetent, poor, awful, terrible, dreadful • **a bad effect** ▸ harmful, damaging • **a bad child** ▸ naughty, badly behaved, disobedient,

mischievous • **leading a bad life** ▸ wicked, sinful, immoral • **bad language** ▸ vulgar, crude, foul, offensive • **bad news** ▸ unpleasant, unwelcome, upsetting • **a bad time to ask** ▸ unsuitable, inappropriate, difficult • **a bad accident** ▸ serious, severe, grave • **bad food** ▸ rotten, off, mouldy, sour (milk), rancid (butter) • **feeling bad** ▸ unwell, ill, sick • **a bad leg** ▸ injured, wounded, diseased • **to feel bad about something** ▸ guilty, remorseful, ashamed, conscience-stricken

badge NOUN a button or sign that you wear to show people who you are or what school or club etc. you belong to

badger NOUN a grey burrowing animal with a black and white head

badger VERB to pester or annoy someone

badly ADVERB **worse**, **worst** **1** in a bad way; not well **2** severely; causing much injury *badly wounded* **3** very much *We badly wanted to win.*

badminton NOUN a game in which players use rackets to hit a light object called a shuttlecock across a high net

baffle VERB to puzzle or confuse somebody ▸ **baffling** ADJECTIVE

bag NOUN a container made of a soft material **bags** (*informal*) plenty *bags of room*

bag VERB **bagging**, **bagged** **1** (*informal*) to catch or claim something **2** to put something into bags

bagatelle NOUN a game played on a board in which small balls are struck into holes

baggage NOUN luggage

baggy ADJECTIVE (of clothes) large and loose

bagpipes PLURAL NOUN a musical instrument in which air is squeezed out of a bag into pipes

bail[1] NOUN money paid as a guarantee that a person accused of a crime will return for trial if they are released in the meantime

bail VERB to provide bail for a person

bail[2] NOUN each of two small pieces of wood placed on top of the stumps in cricket

bail[3] VERB to scoop out water from a boat

bait NOUN **1** food that is put on a hook or in a trap to catch fish or animals **2** something that is meant to tempt someone

bait VERB **1** to put bait on a hook or in a trap **2** to try to make someone angry by teasing them

bake VERB **1** to cook in an oven **2** to make a thing hard by heating it **3** to make or become very hot

baker NOUN a person who bakes or sells bread or cakes ▸ **bakery** NOUN

balance NOUN **1** a steady position, with the weight or amount evenly distributed **2** the difference

THESAURUS

bad-tempered ADJECTIVE • thoroughly selfish and bad-tempered ▸ irritable, grumpy, testy, grouchy, cantankerous

baffle VERB • *The answer baffled him.* ▸ puzzle, perplex, bewilder, confuse

bag NOUN • *Put the shopping in a bag.* ▸ container, carrier bag, carrier • *We'll pack our bags.* ▸ case, suitcase • *She always carried a bag.* ▸ handbag, shoulder bag • *The walkers had bags on their backs.* ▸ backpack, rucksack

between money paid into an account and money paid out **3** an amount of money someone owes **4** a device for weighing

balance VERB to make or be steady or equal

balcony NOUN **balconies 1** a platform jutting out from the outside of a building **2** the upstairs part of a theatre or cinema

bald ADJECTIVE **1** having no hair on the top of the head **2** without details; blunt *a bald statement*
▶ **baldly** ADVERB

bale¹ NOUN a large bundle of hay, straw, or cotton tied up tightly

bale² VERB **bale out** to jump out of an aircraft with a parachute

ball¹ NOUN **1** a round object used in games **2** something with a round shape *a ball of string* **3** the rounded part of the foot at the base of the big toe

ball² NOUN a formal party where people dance

ballad NOUN a simple song or poem that tells a story

ballast NOUN heavy material carried in a ship to keep it steady

ball bearings PLURAL NOUN small steel balls rolling in a groove on which machine parts can move easily

ballerina NOUN a female ballet dancer

ballet (bal-ay) NOUN a stage entertainment that tells a story with dancing, mime, and music

ballistic ADJECTIVE to do with bullets and missiles

balloon NOUN **1** a thin rubber bag that can be inflated and used as a toy or decoration **2** a large round bag inflated with hot air or gas to make it rise in the air, often carrying a basket for passengers

ballot NOUN **1** a secret method of voting by making a mark on a piece of paper **2** a piece of paper on which a vote is made

ballroom NOUN a large room for formal dances

balm NOUN **1** a sweet-smelling ointment **2** something that soothes you

balmy ADJECTIVE **balmier,** **balmiest** soft and warm *a balmy breeze*

bamboo NOUN **1** a tall plant with hard hollow stems **2** a stem of the bamboo plant

ban VERB **banning, banned** to forbid something officially

ban NOUN an order that bans something

THESAURUS

bald ADJECTIVE • *a bald man*
▶ bald-headed, hairless, thin on top • *bald tyres* ▶ bare, smooth

ball NOUN • *The animal curled itself into a ball.* ▶ sphere, globe, orb • *a fancy-dress ball* ▶ dance, party

ban VERB • *to ban blood sports*
▶ prohibit, forbid, disallow, make illegal, stop

ban NOUN • *a ban on smoking*
▶ embargo, prohibition, bar, veto

banal (ba-**nahl**) ADJECTIVE ordinary and uninteresting ▶ **banality** NOUN

banana NOUN a long curved fruit with a yellow or green skin

band¹ NOUN **1** a strip or loop **2** a range of values or wavelengths

band² NOUN **1** an organized group of people **2** a group of people playing music together

band VERB to form an organized group

bandage NOUN a strip of material for binding up a wound ▶ **bandage** VERB

bandit NOUN a member of a gang of robbers who attack travellers

bandwagon NOUN **jump on the bandwagon** to join other people in something that is successful

bandy¹ ADJECTIVE having legs that curve outwards at the knees

bandy² VERB **bandies, bandied** to mention a story or rumour to a lot of people

bane NOUN a cause of trouble or worry *the bane of your life*

bang NOUN **1** a sudden loud noise like that of an explosion **2** a sharp blow or knock

bang VERB **1** to hit or shut something noisily **2** to make a sudden loud noise

bangle NOUN a stiff bracelet

banish VERB **1** to punish a person by ordering them to leave a place **2** to drive away doubts or fears ▶ **banishment** NOUN

banisters PLURAL NOUN a rail with upright supports beside a staircase

banjo NOUN **banjos** an instrument like a guitar with a round body

bank¹ NOUN **1** a slope **2** a long piled-up mass of sand, snow, or cloud **3** a row of lights or switches

bank¹ VERB **1** to build or form a bank **2** (of an aircraft) to tilt sideways while changing direction

bank² NOUN **1** a business that looks after people's money **2** a reserve supply *a blood bank*

bank VERB to put money in a bank **bank on** to rely on

band NOUN • *red with a blue band* ▶ strip, stripe, streak, line • *a band of followers* ▶ troop, group, gang, crew • *A band was playing.* ▶ orchestra, ensemble, group

bandit NOUN • *They were attacked by bandits.* ▶ robber, brigand, thief, outlaw, desperado

bang NOUN • *a bang on the head* ▶ bump, knock, blow, hit, thump, punch • *a loud bang* ▶ thud, crash, blast, explosion, boom

bang VERB • *to bang the table* ▶ hit, thump, strike, whack

banish VERB • *to banish their opponents* ▶ exile, expel, deport, send away • *to banish fears* ▶ remove, dispel, dismiss

bank NOUN • *a grassy bank* ▶ slope, rise, incline, embankment • *the bank of the lake* ▶ edge, border, shore, side • *a steep bank on the curve* ▶ camber, gradient, slope, tilt • *a*

b
c
d
e
f
g
h
i
j
k
l
m
n
o
p
q
r
s
t
u
v
w
x
y
z

banker NOUN a person who runs a bank

bankrupt ADJECTIVE unable to pay your debts ▸ **bankruptcy** NOUN

banner NOUN **1** a flag **2** a strip of cloth with a design or slogan on it, carried on two poles in processions

banns PLURAL NOUN an announcement in a church that a marriage is going to take place

banquet NOUN a large formal public meal

banter NOUN playful teasing or joking

bap NOUN a soft flat bread roll

baptism NOUN the ceremony of baptizing someone

baptize VERB to receive a person into the Christian Church in a ceremony in which they are given a name and sprinkled with water

⚠ SPELLING

This word can also be spelled *baptise*.

bar NOUN **1** a long piece of something hard **2** a counter or room where alcoholic drinks are served **3** a barrier or obstruction **4** each of the small equal sections into which music is divided *three beats to the bar* **5** the place in a lawcourt where the accused person stands **the Bar** barristers

bar VERB **barring**, **barred 1** to fasten something with a bar or bars **2** to block or obstruct something **3** to forbid or ban something

barb NOUN a backward-pointing spike on a spear, arrow, or fish hook, which makes the point stay in

barbarian NOUN an uncivilized or brutal person

barbaric or **barbarous** ADJECTIVE savage and cruel ▸ **barbarity** NOUN, **barbarism** NOUN

barbecue NOUN **1** a frame for grilling food over an open fire outdoors **2** a party with food cooked in this way

barbed wire NOUN wire with small spikes in it, used to make fences

barber NOUN a men's hairdresser

THESAURUS

bank of dials and switches ▸ row, panel, array, display • *a blood bank* ▸ store, reserve, stock, supply

banner NOUN • *banners flying from buildings* ▸ flag, pennant, standard, streamer

bar NOUN • *an iron bar* ▸ rod, pole, stick, stake, rail • *a bar of chocolate* • *a bar of soap* ▸ block, slab, tablet, chunk, piece • *a bar to progress* ▸ obstacle, barrier,

obstruction • *a drink at a bar* ▸ pub, public house, tavern

bar VERB • *The people were barred from entering the country.* ▸ ban, prohibit, forbid, exclude • *A crowd barred the way.* ▸ block, obstruct, hinder, impede

barbaric ADJECTIVE • *a barbaric attack* ▸ brutal, cruel, cold-blooded, inhuman, savage

a
b
c
d
e
f
g
h
i
j
k
l
m
n
o
p
q
r
s
t
u
v
w
x
y
z

bar code NOUN a set of black lines printed on goods and read by a computer to give information about them

bard NOUN (literary) a poet or minstrel

bare ADJECTIVE **1** without clothing or covering **2** empty *The cupboard was bare.* **3** plain; without details *the bare facts* **4** only just enough *the bare necessities*

bare VERB to uncover or reveal

barefaced ADJECTIVE bold or shameless *a barefaced lie*

barely ADVERB only just; with difficulty

bargain NOUN **1** an agreement about buying or selling something **2** something that you buy cheaply

bargain VERB to argue about a price **bargain for** to be prepared for or expect *more than you bargained for*

barge NOUN a long flat-bottomed boat used on canals

barge VERB to push or knock against someone roughly **barge in** to rush into a room rudely

baritone NOUN a male singer with a voice between a tenor and a bass

bark[1] NOUN the short harsh sound made by a dog or fox

bark VERB **1** (of a dog or fox) to make its cry **2** (of a person) to speak angrily

bark[2] NOUN the outer covering of a tree

barley NOUN a cereal plant from which malt is made

barley sugar NOUN a sweet made from boiled sugar

bar mitzvah NOUN a religious ceremony for Jewish boys aged 13

barmy ADJECTIVE (informal) crazy

barn NOUN a farm building for storing hay or grain etc.

barnacle NOUN a shellfish that attaches itself to rocks and the bottoms of ships

barometer NOUN an instrument that measures air pressure

baron NOUN **1** a member of the lowest rank of noblemen **2** a powerful owner of an industry or business *a newspaper baron*
▶ **baronial** ADJECTIVE

THESAURUS

bare ADJECTIVE • *bare flesh* ▶ naked, unclothed, uncovered, nude • *a bare landscape* ▶ barren, bleak, desolate, exposed, stark, empty, open, windswept • *bare trees* ▶ leafless, defoliated • *a bare room* ▶ empty, unfurnished, plain, simple, austere • *a bare wall* ▶ blank, clean, undecorated • *the bare facts* ▶ straightforward, plain, simple, basic, pure, essential, fundamental • *the bare*

necessities ▶ basic, essential, minimum

bare VERB • *to bare your arm* ▶ uncover, expose

bargain NOUN • *to make a bargain* ▶ agreement, deal, pact, pledge, promise • *a bargain at £12.99* ▶ good buy, good value

bargain VERB • *to bargain with the employers* ▶ negotiate, do a deal, barter, haggle

baroness NOUN a female baron or a baron's wife

baronet NOUN a nobleman ranking below a baron but above a knight

baroque NOUN a highly decorated style of architecture used in the 17th and 18th centuries

barracks NOUN a large building or group of buildings for soldiers to live in

barrage NOUN 1 heavy gunfire 2 a large amount of something *a barrage of questions* 3 a dam built across a river

barrel NOUN 1 a large rounded container with flat ends 2 the metal tube of a gun

barren ADJECTIVE 1 (of a woman) not able to have children 2 (of land) not fertile

barricade NOUN an improvised barrier across a street or door

barrier NOUN 1 a fence or wall that prevents people from getting past 2 something that stops you doing something

barrister NOUN a lawyer who represents people in a lawcourt

barrow NOUN 1 a wheelbarrow 2 a small cart that is pushed or pulled by hand

barter VERB to trade by exchanging goods for other goods

barter NOUN the system of bartering

base[1] NOUN 1 the part on which something stands or rests 2 a starting point or foundation; a basis 3 a headquarters for an expedition or military operation 4 (Chemistry) a substance that can combine with an acid to form a salt 5 each of the four corners that must be reached by a runner in baseball

base VERB to use something as a beginning or foundation *The story is based on facts.*

base[2] ADJECTIVE 1 dishonourable *base motives* 2 not of great value *base metals*

baseball NOUN an American game in which runs are scored by hitting a ball and running round a series of four bases

basement NOUN a room or storey below ground level

bash VERB to hit hard

bash NOUN 1 a hard hit 2 (informal) a try *have a bash at it*

bashful ADJECTIVE shy and self-conscious ► **bashfully** ADVERB

THESAURUS

barrel NOUN • *a barrel of beer* ► cask, keg, tub, drum

barrier NOUN • *barriers to keep out the crowd* ► barricade, fence, railing, wall • *a barrier to progress* ► obstacle, hindrance, impediment

base NOUN • *the base of the tower* ► foot, bottom, foundation • *a base for the expedition* ► headquarters, centre, camp

base VERB • *Base your story on events in the news.* ► build, construct, establish

basic *ADJECTIVE* forming the first or most important part *Bread is a basic food.*

basically *ADVERB* at the simplest or most fundamental level

basin *NOUN* **1** a deep bowl **2** a bowl with taps, for washing the hands and face **3** a sheltered area of water for mooring boats **4** the area from which water drains into a river

basis *NOUN* **bases** something to start from or add to; the main principle or ingredient

bask *VERB* to sit or lie comfortably in the sun

basket *NOUN* a container made of strips of flexible material or wire woven together

basketball *NOUN* a game in which goals are scored by putting a ball through a high net

bass [1] (bays) *NOUN* **1** the lowest part in music **2** a male singer with a deep voice

bass [2] (bas) *NOUN* **bass** a fish of the perch family

bassoon *NOUN* a bass woodwind instrument

baste *VERB* to moisten meat with fat while it is cooking

bastion *NOUN* **1** a projecting part of a fortified building **2** something that protects a belief or way of life

bat [1] *NOUN* a shaped piece of wood used to hit the ball in cricket or games **off your own bat** without help from other people

bat *VERB* **batting, batted** to use a bat in cricket or other games

bat [2] *NOUN* a flying animal that looks like a mouse with wings

batch *NOUN* a set of things or people dealt with together

bated *ADJECTIVE* **with bated breath** anxiously; hardly daring to speak

bath *NOUN* **1** a large container for water in which to wash the whole body **2** a washing of the body while sitting in water **3** a liquid in which something is placed *an acid bath*

bath *VERB* to wash in a bath

bathe *VERB* **1** to go swimming **2** to wash something gently ▶ **bather** *NOUN*

bathos *NOUN* a sudden change from a serious subject or tone to a ridiculous or trivial one

bathroom *NOUN* a room containing a bath

baths *PLURAL NOUN* a public swimming pool

THESAURUS

basic *ADJECTIVE* • *the basic principles of the subject* ▶ fundamental, main, key, principal, elementary • *basic washing facilities* ▶ plain, simple, crude, modest, unsophisticated

basin *NOUN* • *a basin full of water* ▶ bowl, dish, sink

basis *NOUN* • *a story with no factual basis* ▶ foundation, justification, support, base

baton NOUN **1** a thin stick used to conduct an orchestra **2** a short thick stick used in a relay race

battalion NOUN an army unit containing two or more companies

batten NOUN a strip of wood or metal that holds something in place

batter VERB to hit something hard and often

batter NOUN a beaten mixture of flour, eggs, and milk, used in cooking

battery NOUN **batteries 1** a device for storing and supplying electricity **2** a set of similar pieces of guns or other equipment **3** a series of cages in which poultry or animals are kept close together

battle NOUN **1** a fight between two armies **2** a struggle

battle VERB to fight or struggle

battlefield or **battleground** NOUN a place where a battle is fought

battlements PLURAL NOUN the top of a castle wall, with gaps for firing at the enemy

battleship NOUN a heavily armed warship

bauble NOUN a showy ornament of little value

baulk VERB **1** to stop and refuse to go on **2** to prevent someone from doing or getting something

bawl VERB to cry or shout noisily

bay¹ NOUN **1** a place where the shore curves inwards **2** an alcove in a room **3** a space or compartment for a special purpose *a parking bay*

bay² VERB (of a hunting dog) to make a long deep cry **at bay** cornered but defiant

bay³ NOUN a kind of laurel tree with leaves used in cooking

bayonet NOUN a blade fixed to the end of a rifle for stabbing

bay window NOUN a window that juts out from the main wall of a house

bazaar NOUN **1** a market place in an eastern country **2** a sale to raise money

bazooka NOUN a portable weapon for firing anti-tank rockets

batter VERB • *to batter on the door*
▶ pound, beat, knock • *Winds were battering the waterfront.*
▶ pound, buffet, lash, pummel

battle NOUN • *a battle between the two armies* ▶ fight, clash, encounter, engagement, action • *a legal battle* ▶ conflict, struggle, dispute • *a battle to save*

the library from closure
▶ campaign, crusade

battle VERB • *They battled to control the fire.* ▶ fight, struggle, strive

bay NOUN • *a bay on the coast*
▶ cove, inlet, gulf • *a loading bay*
▶ recess, alcove, booth, compartment

BC *ABBREVIATION* before Christ (used with dates)

> ⚠ **USAGE**
>
> Some people prefer to use BCE ('before the common era').

be *VERB* **am, are, is; was** or **were; being** or **been** **1** to exist or occupy a position *The shop is on the corner.* **2** to happen or take place *The wedding is tomorrow.* **3** used to form parts of other verbs *They are coming. He was attacked.*

beach *NOUN* the seashore by the water

beacon *NOUN* a light or fire used as a signal or warning

bead *NOUN* **1** a small piece of a hard substance with a hole for threading on a string or wire to make jewellery **2** a drop of liquid *beads of sweat*

beady *ADJECTIVE* (of the eyes) small and bright

beagle *NOUN* a small hound used for hunting hares

beak *NOUN* the hard horny part of a bird's mouth

beaker *NOUN* **1** a tall drinking mug **2** a glass container used in a laboratory

beam *NOUN* **1** a long thick bar of wood or metal **2** a ray or stream of light or other radiation **3** a happy smile

beam *VERB* **1** to smile happily **2** to send out a beam of light or other radiation

bean *NOUN* **1** a kind of plant with seeds growing in pods **2** its seed or pod eaten as food **3** the seed of coffee

bear[1] *NOUN* a large heavy animal with thick fur and large teeth and claws

bear[2] *VERB* **bore, borne** **1** to carry or support something **2** to have or show a mark or sign *He still bears the scar.* **3** to endure or stand something unpleasant *I can't bear the noise.* **4** to produce or give birth to *She bore him two sons.* **to bear in mind** to remember something and consider it **to bear out** to support or confirm an idea or argument ▶ **bearer** *NOUN*

be *VERB* • *There was someone in the room.* ▶ be present, exist, live d *He'd been there a long time.* ▶ remain, stay, wait, linger • *The next performance will be tomorrow.* ▶ take place, occur, happen

beach *NOUN* • *a picnic on the beach* ▶ shore, sand, seashore, coast

beam *NOUN* • *wooden beams* ▶ timber, joist, girder, rafter,

plank • *a beam of light* ▶ ray, shaft, gleam, stream

bear *VERB* • *The rope would not bear the weight.* ▶ support, carry, hold, take • *The document bore a signature.* ▶ show, display, possess • *The postman came, bearing a parcel.* ▶ carry, bring, convey, transport, deliver • *I cannot bear pain.* • *The noise is hard to bear.* ▶ put up with, endure, tolerate, stand, abide

bearable ADJECTIVE able to be endured; tolerable

beard NOUN hair on a man's chin
▶ **bearded** ADJECTIVE

beard VERB to challenge someone face to face

bearing NOUN 1 the way a person stands, walks, or behaves 2 relevance or connection *This has no bearing on the matter.* 3 the direction or position of one thing in relation to another 4 a part in a machine that connects moving parts so they run smoothly

beast NOUN 1 a wild four-footed animal 2 a cruel or vicious person

beastly ADJECTIVE **beastlier**, **beastliest** (*informal*) horrid or unpleasant

beat VERB **beat**, **beaten** 1 to hit a person or animal many times with a stick or weapon 2 to defeat someone or do better than them 3 to shape or flatten something by beating it 4 to stir a mixture vigorously in cooking 5 (of the

heart) to make regular movements **to beat up** to attack someone brutally

beat NOUN 1 a regular rhythm or stroke *the beat of your heart* 2 a strong rhythm in music 3 the regular route of a police officer

beautiful ADJECTIVE very attractive to see or hear or think about
▶ **beautifully** ADVERB

beauty NOUN **beauties** 1 the quality of being very attractive to see or hear or think about 2 a beautiful person or thing 3 a fine example of something

beaver NOUN 1 an animal with webbed feet and a large flat tail, that can gnaw through wood and dam streams 2 someone who works hard

beaver VERB to work hard *They are beavering away.*

because CONJUNCTION for the reason that **because of** for the reason of *He limped because of his bad leg.*

beast NOUN • *the roars of wild beasts* ▶ animal , creature, brute • *Her husband was a beast.* ▶ brute, monster, fiend, demon

beastly • *a beastly person* ▶ unkind, cruel, mean, nasty, spiteful

beat VERB • *to beat an animal* ▶ hit, strike, thrash, whip • *to beat eggs* ▶ whip, blend, mix, stir • *His heart was beating faster.* ▶ pound, race, thump, flutter • *to beat the enemy* • *to beat another team* ▶ defeat, overcome, conquer,

vanquish, crush **beat up** • *They got beaten up.* ▶ assault, attack

beat NOUN • *music with a strong beat* ▶ rhythm, pulse • *a policeman's beat* ▶ circuit, rounds, route

beautiful ADJECTIVE • *a beautiful young woman* ▶ attractive, pretty, lovely, glamorous, gorgeous, stunning

beauty NOUN • *the beauty of the scene* ▶ attractiveness, prettiness, loveliness, charm, splendour

a
b
c
d
e
f
g
h
i
j
k
l
m
n
o
p
q
r
s
t
u
v
w
x
y
z

beck NOUN **at someone's beck and call** always ready to do what they ask

beckon VERB to make a sign to a person to come

become VERB **became, become 1** to begin to be *It became dark.* **2** to suit or make attractive **become of** to happen to *What became of it?*

bed NOUN **1** a piece of furniture for lying on to sleep or rest **2** a piece of a garden where plants are grown **3** the bottom of the sea or of a river **4** a flat base or foundation **5** a layer of rock or soil

bedding NOUN mattresses and bedclothes

bedraggled ADJECTIVE very wet and untidy

bedridden ADJECTIVE too weak or ill to get out of bed

bedrock NOUN **1** solid rock beneath soil **2** the fundamental facts or principles on which an idea or belief is based

bedroom NOUN a room for sleeping in

bee NOUN a winged insect that lives in a hive and makes honey

beech NOUN a tree with smooth bark and glossy leaves

beef NOUN meat from a cow or bull

beefy ADJECTIVE having a solid muscular body ► **beefiness** NOUN

beehive NOUN a box or other container for bees to live in

beeline NOUN **make a beeline for** to go straight towards something

beer NOUN an alcoholic drink made with hops

beeswax NOUN a yellow substance produced by bees, used for polishing wood

beet NOUN a plant with a thick root used as a vegetable or for making sugar

beetle NOUN an insect with hard shiny wing covers

beetroot NOUN **beetroot** the dark red root of beet used as a vegetable

befall VERB **befell, befallen** (*formal*) to happen to someone

before ADVERB at an earlier time *Have you been here before?*

before PREPOSITION, CONJUNCTION **1** earlier than *I was here before you.* **2** in front of *He stood before the door.*

beforehand ADVERB earlier; in readiness

become VERB • *Caterpillars become butterflies.* ► grow into, turn into, change into, develop into • *to become rich* ► grow, come to be, turn • *to become*

prime minister ► be appointed, be elected, be chosen, be made

before ADVERB • *We have met before.* ► earlier, in advance, previously

beg VERB **begging, begged 1** to ask to be given money or food **2** to ask for something seriously or desperately

beggar NOUN **1** a person who lives by begging **2** (informal) a person described in some way *You lucky beggar!* ▸ **beggary** NOUN

begin VERB **began, begun 1** to do the earliest or first part of something **2** to come into existence *The problem began last year.* **3** to have something as the first part *The word begins with B.*

beginner NOUN a person who is just beginning to learn a subject

beginning NOUN the start of something

begot past tense of **beget**

behalf NOUN **on behalf of** for the benefit of someone else or as their representative *collecting money on behalf of cancer research*

behave VERB **1** to act in a particular way *They behaved badly.* **2** to show good manners

behaviour NOUN the way someone behaves ▸ **behavioural** ADJECTIVE

behead VERB to cut the head off a person or thing

behind ADVERB **1** at or to the back **2** at a place people have left *I'll leave it behind.* **3** late or not making good progress *behind with the rent*

behind PREPOSITION **1** at or to the back of **2** on the further side of **3** having made less progress than *behind the others at maths* **4** causing *What is behind all this trouble?*

behind NOUN (informal) a person's bottom

behold VERB **beheld** (old use) to see or look at ▸ **beholder** NOUN

THESAURUS

beg VERB • to beg for a favour ▸ plead, entreat, implore, beseech

begin VERB • to begin work ▸ start, set about, embark on, get down to • to begin with a question ▸ start, start off, open, get going • *Where did the rumour begin?* ▸ start, originate, spring up, emerge

beginner NOUN • a course for beginners ▸ novice, learner, starter, new recruit, trainee

beginning NOUN • the beginning of a new era ▸ start, birth, dawn, inception • from the beginning

▸ outset, start • *the beginning of the story* ▸ opening, start, prelude

behave VERB • to behave well ▸ conduct yourself, act, react, respond **behave yourself** • *Try to behave yourself.* ▸ be good, act correctly, be on your best behaviour

behaviour NOUN • disgusting behaviour ▸ conduct, manners, attitude

behind PREPOSITION • *Who is behind all this?* ▸ responsible for, the cause of, to blame for

a
b
c
d
e
f
g
h
i
j
k
l
m
n
o
p
q
r
s
t
u
v
w
x
y
z

beige NOUN, ADJECTIVE a pale brown colour

being NOUN 1 existence 2 a living person or animal

belated ADJECTIVE coming late; late ▶ **belatedly** ADVERB

belch VERB 1 to bring up wind from your stomach through your mouth 2 to send out a lot of fire or smoke ▶ **belch** NOUN

beleaguered ADJECTIVE experiencing a lot of difficulties or criticism

belfry NOUN **belfries** a tower or part of a tower in which bells hang

belief NOUN 1 the act of believing 2 something a person believes

believe VERB to think that something is true without having proof **believe in** to think that something exists or is good or can be relied on **make believe** to pretend in your imagination ▶ **believable** ADJECTIVE, **believer** NOUN

bell NOUN 1 a cup-shaped metal instrument that makes a ringing sound when struck by a hanging piece inside it 2 a device that makes a ringing or buzzing sound

bellow NOUN 1 the loud deep sound made by a bull or other large animal 2 a deep shout

bellow VERB to give a deep shout

bellows PLURAL NOUN a device for blowing out air, especially to stimulate a fire

belly NOUN **bellies** the abdomen or stomach

belong VERB to have a proper place *These things belong on the shelf.* **belong to** to be owned by

belongings PLURAL NOUN a person's possessions

beloved ADJECTIVE dearly loved

below ADVERB at or to a lower position; underneath

below PREPOSITION 1 lower than 2 less than

belief NOUN • *a strong belief in their innocence* ▶ conviction, confidence, opinion, certainty • *a belief in the value of a good diet* ▶ trust (in), reliance (on) • *religious belief* ▶ faith, ideology, creed

believe VERB • *That is hard to believe.* ▶ accept, be certain about, be convinced by • *I believe you are right.* ▶ think, suppose, consider, conclude, be of the opinion

belong VERB **belong to** • *It belongs to me.* ▶ be owned by, be

the property of **belong to** • *to belong to a club* ▶ be a member of, be affiliated with, be connected with • *They did not belong there.* ▶ feel welcome, have a place, be at home • *The book belongs on the top shelf.* ▶ be located, have a place, go

belongings NOUN • *Take all your belongings with you.* ▶ possessions, property, personal effects

below PREPOSITION • *below the surface* ▶ beneath, under, underneath, lower than • *below a*

belt NOUN **1** a strip of cloth, leather, or plastic worn round the waist **2** a band of flexible material used in machinery **3** a long narrow area *a belt of rain*

belt VERB **1** to put a belt round something **2** (*informal*) to hit

bench NOUN **1** a long seat **2** a long table for working at **the bench** the judges in a lawcourt

bend VERB **bent 1** to change from being straight **2** to stoop or turn downwards

bend NOUN a place where something bends; a curve or turn *a bend in the road*

beneath PREPOSITION **1** under; lower than **2** considered unworthy of *Cheating is beneath you.*

beneath ADVERB underneath

benefactor NOUN a person who gives money or other help

beneficial ADJECTIVE having a good or helpful effect

benefit NOUN **1** something that is helpful or profitable **2** a

government payment to someone in need **3** a payment from an insurance policy

benefit VERB **1** to do good to a person or thing **2** to receive a benefit

benevolent ADJECTIVE **1** kind and helpful **2** formed for charitable purposes *a benevolent fund*
▶ **benevolence** NOUN

benign ADJECTIVE **1** kindly **2** favourable **3** (of a tumour) not malignant

bent ADJECTIVE curved or crooked

bent on intending to do something

bent NOUN a talent for something

bequeath VERB to leave money or property to someone in a will

bequest NOUN something left to a person, especially in a will

bereaved ADJECTIVE suffering from the recent death of a close relative
▶ **bereavement** NOUN

bereft ADJECTIVE deprived of something *bereft of hope*

hundred ▶ under, less than
• *below me in rank* ▶ inferior to, subordinate to, lower than

bend VERB • *Bend the pipe round the tank.* ▶ curve, curl, angle, turn • *The road bends ahead.*
▶ turn, curve, veer, deviate, twist
bend down • *He bends down to pick up the paper.* ▶ stoop, bow, crouch, duck, kneel

bend NOUN • *a bend in the road*
▶ curve, turn, twist, corner

beneath PREPOSITION • *the ground beneath them* ▶ below, under, underneath, lower than

benefit NOUN • *the benefits of a healthy diet* ▶ advantage, reward, strength, convenience • *for your benefit* ▶ good, sake, welfare, advantage • *the unemployed on benefit* ▶ social security, welfare, assistance

bent ADJECTIVE • *a bent nail*
▶ crooked, twisted, misshapen, buckled

a
b
c
d
e
f
g
h
i
j
k
l
m
n
o
p
q
r
s
t
u
v
w
x
y
z

beret (bair-ay) NOUN a round flat cap

berry NOUN **berries** any small round round juicy fruit without a stone

berserk ADJECTIVE **go berserk** to become uncontrollably violent

berth NOUN **1** a sleeping place on a ship or train **2** a place where a ship can moor

berth VERB to moor in a berth

beseech VERB **beseeched** or **besought** to ask earnestly; to implore

beset VERB **besetting**, **beset** to trouble or harass from all sides *They are beset with problems.*

beside PREPOSITION **1** by the side of; near **2** compared with **be beside yourself** to be very excited or upset

besides PREPOSITION, ADVERB in addition to; also

besiege VERB **1** to surround a place to capture it **2** to crowd round someone famous

besought past tense of **beseech**

best ADJECTIVE of the most excellent kind; most able to do something

best ADVERB **1** in the best way; most **2** most or sensibly *We had best go.*

best man NOUN the bridegroom's chief attendant at a wedding

bestow VERB to present something to someone
► **bestowal** NOUN

bet NOUN **1** an agreement that you will receive money if you are correct in choosing the winner of a race or game or in predicting an event, and will lose your money if you are not correct **2** the money you risk losing in a bet

bet VERB **betting**, **bet** or **betted 1** to make a bet **2** (*informal*) to think most likely *I bet he forgot.*

betide VERB **woe betide you** you will be in trouble

betray VERB **1** to be disloyal to a person or country etc. **2** to reveal something by mistake
► **betrayal** NOUN

betrothed ADJECTIVE (*formal*) engaged to be married
► **betrothal** NOUN

better ADJECTIVE **1** more excellent; more satisfactory **2** recovered from illness **get the better of** to defeat or outwit

better ADVERB **1** in a better way; more **2** more usefully or sensibly *We had better go.* **be better off** to have more money or be more fortunate

best ADJECTIVE • *one of the best bookshops in London* ► leading, top, finest, foremost • *whatever you think best* ► most suitable, most appropriate, most sensible

betray VERB • *to betray a friend* ► let down, break your promise

to, double-cross, deceive • *to betray them to the authorities* ► inform on, denounce • *to betray a secret* ► reveal, give away, show, disclose, let slip

better ADJECTIVE • *a better place to live* ► superior, finer, preferable

better VERB **1** to improve something **2** to do better than ▸ **betterment** NOUN

between PREPOSITION, ADVERB **1** within two or more limits *between the walls* **2** from one place to another *the train line between London and Glasgow* **3** shared by *Divide the money between you.* **4** separating or comparing *I can't tell the difference between them.*

bevel VERB **bevelling, bevelled** to give a sloping edge to

bevy NOUN **bevies** a group of people

beware VERB to be careful *Beware of forgeries.*

bewilder VERB to puzzle someone completely ▸ **bewilderment** NOUN

bewitch VERB **1** to put a magic spell on someone **2** to delight someone

beyond PREPOSITION, ADVERB **1** further than; further on *beyond the fence* **2** too difficult for *The problem is beyond us.*

biannual ADJECTIVE happening twice a year ▸ **biannually** ADVERB

⚠ **USAGE**

Do not confuse this word with *biennial*.

bias NOUN **1** a tendency to favour one person or thing unfairly over another **2** a tendency to swerve **3** a slanting direction

biased ADJECTIVE unfairly favouring one over another; prejudiced

bib NOUN **1** a cloth or covering put under a baby's chin when eating **2** the part of an apron above the waist

Bible NOUN the sacred book of the Jews (the Old Testament) and of the Christians (the Old and New Testament)

biblical ADJECTIVE to do with or in the Bible

bibliography NOUN **bibliographies 1** a list of books about a subject **2** the study of books ▸ **bibliographical** ADJECTIVE

bicentenary NOUN **bicentenaries** a 200th anniversary

biceps NOUN the large muscle at the front of the arm above the elbow

bicker VERB to quarrel over unimportant things

bicycle NOUN a two-wheeled vehicle driven by pedals

bid NOUN **1** the offer of an amount you are willing to pay for something **2** an attempt

THESAURUS

• *feeling better* ▸ healthier, fitter, stronger, recovered

bewildered ADJECTIVE • *a bewildered look* ▸ puzzled, perplexed, baffled, mystified, confused

biased ADJECTIVE • *The judge was biased.* ▸ prejudiced, one-sided

bid NOUN • *a bid of £5,000* ▸ offer, tender, proposal, price • *a bid to discover the truth* ▸ attempt, effort, endeavour, try (at)

a
b
c
d
e
f
g
h
i
j
k
l
m
n
o
p
q
r
s
t
u
v
w
x
y
z

a
b
c
d
e
f
g
h
i
j
k
l
m
n
o
p
q
r
s
t
u
v
w
x
y
z

bid VERB **bidding, bid** or **bade 1** to make a bid **2** to say as a greeting or farewell *I bid you all good night.* **3** to command ▶ **bidder** NOUN

bidding NOUN **do someone's bidding** to do what they ask

bide VERB **bide your time** to wait for the right time to act

biennial ADJECTIVE **1** lasting for two years **2** happening once every two years ▶ **biennially** ADVERB

⚠ **USAGE**

Do not confuse this word with *biannual.*

bier NOUN a stand for a coffin

big ADJECTIVE **bigger, biggest 1** large **2** important *the big match* **3** more grown-up; elder *my big sister*

bigamy NOUN the crime of marrying a person when you are already married to someone else ▶ **bigamous** ADJECTIVE, **bigamist** NOUN

bigot NOUN a narrow-minded and intolerant person ▶ **bigoted** ADJECTIVE, **bigotry** NOUN

bike NOUN (*informal*) a bicycle or motorcycle

bikini NOUN **bikinis** a woman's two-piece swimsuit

bilateral ADJECTIVE **1** of or on two sides **2** between two people or groups *a bilateral agreement*

bile NOUN a bitter liquid produced by the liver, helping to digest fats

bilge NOUN **1** the bottom of a ship or the water that collects there **2** (*informal*) nonsense

bilingual ADJECTIVE **1** able to speak two languages well **2** written in two languages

bilious ADJECTIVE feeling sick; sickly

bill NOUN **1** a statement of charges for goods or services supplied **2** a poster **3** a programme of entertainment **4** the draft of a proposed law to be discussed by parliament **5** (*American*) a banknote **6** a bird's beak

billet NOUN a lodging for troops in a private house

billiards NOUN a game in which three balls are struck with cues on a cloth-covered table

billion NOUN **billions** or **billion** a thousand million (1,000,000,000) ▶ **billionth** ADJECTIVE and NOUN

billow NOUN a huge wave

billow VERB to rise or roll like waves

billy goat NOUN a male goat

bin NOUN a large container for rubbish or litter

binary ADJECTIVE **1** involving sets of two **2** consisting of two parts

binary system NOUN a system of expressing numbers by using

THESAURUS

big ADJECTIVE • *a big house* ▶ large, great, huge, enormous, colossal, immense • *a big difference* ▶ significant, important, substantial, considerable • *big*

ideas ▶ ambitious, grand, grandiose, far-reaching

bill NOUN • *a telephone bill* ▶ account, invoice, statement

the digits 0 and 1 only, used in computing

bind VERB **1** to fasten material round something **2** to fasten the pages of a book into a cover **3** to tie up or tie together **4** to make somebody agree to do something

bind NOUN (informal) a nuisance; a bore

binder NOUN a cover for loose sheets of paper

binding NOUN the covers and stitching of a book

binding ADJECTIVE (of an agreement or promise) that must be carried out or obeyed

bingo NOUN a game with cards on which numbers are crossed out as they are randomly called out

binoculars PLURAL NOUN an instrument with lenses for both eyes, for magnifying distant objects

biochemistry NOUN the study of the chemical composition and processes of living things
▶ **biochemist** NOUN

biodegradable ADJECTIVE able to be broken down by bacteria in the environment

biography NOUN **biographies** an account of a person's life
▶ **biographer** NOUN, **biographical** ADJECTIVE

biology NOUN the scientific study of the life and structure of living things ▶ **biological** ADJECTIVE, **biologist** NOUN

bionic ADJECTIVE (of a person or parts of the body) operated by electronic devices

biopsy NOUN **biopsies** examination of tissue from a living body

birch NOUN **1** a tree with slender branches and silver bark **2** a bundle of birch branches for flogging people

bird NOUN an animal with feathers, two wings, and two legs

Biro NOUN **Biros** (trademark) a kind of ballpoint pen

> **WORD HISTORY**
> named after its Hungarian inventor, L. *Bíró*

birth NOUN **1** the process of being born **2** a person's ancestry *of noble birth*

birth control NOUN ways of avoiding becoming pregnant

birthday NOUN the anniversary of the day a person was born

birthmark NOUN a coloured mark that is on a person's skin from birth

birth rate NOUN the number of children born in one year for every 1,000 people

biscuit NOUN a small flat kind of cake that has been baked until it is crisp

bisect VERB to divide something into two equal parts

bishop NOUN **1** an important member of the clergy in some

THESAURUS

bind VERB • *to bind things together*
▶ fasten, tie, secure, attach, join

• *A nurse bound their wounds.*
▶ bandage, dress, cover

churches **2** a chess piece shaped like a bishop's mitre

bison NOUN **bison** a large wild ox with shaggy hair on its head

bistro NOUN **bistros** a small restaurant

bit¹ NOUN **1** a small piece or amount **2** the part of a bridle that is put into a horse's mouth **3** the part of a tool that cuts or grips **a bit 1** a short distance or time **2** slightly *a bit nervous* **bit by bit** gradually

bit² past tense of **bite**

bit³ NOUN (ICT) the smallest unit of information in a computer, expressed as a choice between two possibilities

bitch NOUN **1** a female dog, fox, or wolf **2** (informal) a spiteful woman

bite VERB **bit, bitten 1** to cut or take something with your teeth **2** to penetrate or sting

bite NOUN **1** an act of biting *take a bite* **2** a wound or mark made by biting *an insect bite* **3** a snack

bitter ADJECTIVE **1** tasting sharp, not sweet **2** feeling or causing mental pain or resentment **3** very cold
▶ **bitterly** ADVERB

bizarre ADJECTIVE strange in appearance or effect

blab VERB **blabbing, blabbed** to let out a secret

black ADJECTIVE **1** of the darkest colour, like coal or soot **2** desperate or hopeless *The outlook is black.* **3** (of a person) having dark skin **4** (of coffee or tea) without milk

black NOUN the darkest colour

bit NOUN • *a bit of chocolate*
▶ piece, chunk, lump, hunk, fragment, slice *a bit* • *That was a bit hard.* ▶ rather, fairly, slightly, somewhat, a little
bit by bit • *Bit by bit I began to understand.* ▶ gradually, slowly, little by little

bite VERB • *He bit an apple.*
▶ munch, nibble, chew, crunch, gnaw • *She had been bitten by an insect.* ▶ sting **bite into** • *Acid starts to bite into the metal.* ▶ eat into, corrode, erode, wear away

bite NOUN • *a bite on the arm*
▶ nip, sting, pinch, wound • *a bite to eat* ▶ mouthful, snack, morsel, bit, nibble, piece, taste

bitter ADJECTIVE • *a bitter taste*
▶ sour, sharp, acid, tart • *a bitter disappointment* ▶ cruel, distressing, painful, unpleasant • *bitter remarks* ▶ harsh, cutting, caustic, hurtful, cruel • *to feel bitter* ▶ resentful, embittered, cynical, aggrieved • *a bitter quarrel* ▶ acrimonious, angry • *a bitter wind* ▶ biting, freezing, icy, raw, arctic

black ADJECTIVE • *black ink*
▶ jet-black, coal-black • *a black night* ▶ dark, unlit, moonless, starless, gloomy • *hands black from mending the mower* ▶ filthy, dirty, grimy, grubby, soiled • *in a black mood* ▶ miserable, glum, melancholy, despondent

black *VERB* to make a thing black
black out 1 to lose consciousness
2 to cover windows so that no light can penetrate

blackberry *NOUN* **blackberries** a sweet black berry

blackbird *NOUN* a songbird, the male of which is black

blackboard *NOUN* a dark board for writing on with chalk

blacken *VERB* to make or become black

blackguard (blag-ard) *NOUN* (old use) a wicked person

black hole *NOUN* a region in space with such strong gravity that no matter or radiation can escape from it

black ice *NOUN* thin transparent ice on roads

blacklist *NOUN* a list of people who are disapproved of or not trusted

black magic *NOUN* evil magic

blackmail *NOUN* the crime of demanding money from someone by threatening to reveal a secret about them

blackmail *VERB* to use blackmail on someone ► **blackmailer** *NOUN*

black market *NOUN* illegal buying and selling

blackout *NOUN* **1** darkness produced by covering windows **2** loss of consciousness

black sheep *NOUN* a member of a family or other group who is considered a failure or disgrace

blacksmith *NOUN* a person who makes and repairs iron things, especially horseshoes

bladder *NOUN* **1** the organ of the body in which urine collects **2** an inflatable bag inside a ball

blade *NOUN* **1** the flat cutting edge of a knife or tool **2** the flat wide part of an oar, spade, or propeller **3** a narrow leaf of grass or wheat

blame *VERB* to say that somebody or something has caused something wrong or bad

blame *NOUN* responsibility for what is wrong

blameless *ADJECTIVE* not responsible for a wrong; innocent

blanch *VERB* to make or become white or pale

blancmange (bla-monj) *NOUN* a jelly-like pudding made with milk

bland *ADJECTIVE* **1** having a mild flavour **2** gentle and casual *a bland manner*

blank *ADJECTIVE* **1** not written or printed on; unmarked **2** without expression *a blank look* **3** empty of thoughts *My mind's gone blank.*

blame *NOUN* • *He was cleared of all blame.* ► responsibility, guilt, liability, culpability • *Who got the blame for breaking the window?* ► criticism, censure, condemnation

blame *VERB* • *The report blamed the driver.* ► condemn, criticize, hold responsible, hold accountable

blank *ADJECTIVE* • *a blank page* ► empty, unused, clear, bare • *a*

a
b
c
d
e
f
g
h
i
j
k
l
m
n
o
p
q
r
s
t
u
v
w
x
y
z

DICTIONARY

blank NOUN **1** an empty space **2** a cartridge that does not fire a bullet

blanket NOUN **1** a warm cloth covering used on a bed etc **2** a thick soft covering *a blanket of snow*

blanket ADJECTIVE covering all cases *a blanket ban*

blank verse NOUN verse written without rhyme

blare VERB to make a loud harsh sound ▸ **blare** NOUN

blaspheme VERB to talk or write in a disrespectful way about sacred things

blasphemy NOUN **blasphemies** disrespectful talk about sacred things ▸ **blasphemous** ADJECTIVE

blast NOUN **1** a strong rush of wind or air **2** a loud noise, e.g. on a trumpet

blast VERB to blow up with explosives **blast off** to launch by the firing of rockets

blast-off NOUN the launching of a rocket

blatant ADJECTIVE very obvious *a blatant lie* ▸ **blatantly** ADVERB

blaze[1] NOUN a very bright fire or light

blaze VERB to burn or shine brightly

blaze[2] VERB **blaze a trail** to show the way for others to follow

blazer NOUN a jacket often worn as part of a uniform

bleach VERB to make or become white

bleach NOUN a substance used to make things white or for cleaning

bleak ADJECTIVE **1** bare and cold *a bleak hillside* **2** dreary or miserable *a bleak future*

bleary ADJECTIVE (of the eyes) watery and not seeing clearly ▸ **blearily** ADVERB

bleat NOUN the cry of a lamb, goat, or calf

bleat VERB to make a bleat

THESAURUS

blank look ▸ expressionless, impassive, vacant, deadpan, unresponsive

blare VERB • *Sirens were blaring.* ▸ blast, resound, screech, shriek

blast NOUN • *a blast of cold air* ▸ gust, rush, draught, squall • *injured in the blast* ▸ explosion

blast VERB • *Missiles blasted the building.* ▸ blow up, bomb, demolish, raze • *radios blasting out rock music* ▸ blare, boom

blatant ADJECTIVE • *a blatant lie* ▸ flagrant, brazen, barefaced, shameless

blaze NOUN • *It took hours to control the blaze.* ▸ fire, flames • *a blaze of light* ▸ burst, flash, gleam, streak

blaze VERB • *The fire began to blaze.* ▸ burn, flare up, be alight • *Lights blazed from the top floor.* ▸ shine, flash, gleam

bleak ADJECTIVE • *a bleak landscape* ▸ bare, barren, desolate, stark, empty

bleed VERB **bled 1** to lose blood **2** to draw blood or fluid from

bleep VERB to give out a short high sound as a signal ▶ **bleep** NOUN

blemish NOUN a flaw; a mark that spoils a thing's appearance

blemish VERB to spoil something

blench VERB to flinch

blend VERB to mix smoothly or easily

blend NOUN a smooth mixture

blender NOUN a machine for mixing food or turning it into liquid

bless VERB **1** to make sacred or holy **2** to bring God's favour on a person or thing

blessed (bless-id) ADJECTIVE sacred or holy

blessing NOUN **1** a prayer that blesses a person or thing **2** something to be glad of

blight NOUN **1** a disease that withers plants **2** something that spoils or damages something

blight VERB **1** to affect with blight **2** to spoil or damage something *Injuries blighted his career.*

blind ADJECTIVE **1** without the ability to see **2** without any thought *blind obedience* ▶ **blindness** NOUN

blind VERB **1** to make a person blind **2** to dazzle briefly

blind NOUN **1** a screen for a window **2** a deception *His journey was a blind.*

blindfold NOUN a strip of cloth tied round someone's eyes to prevent them from seeing

blindfold VERB to cover with a blindfold

blink VERB to shut and open your eyes rapidly ▶ **blink** NOUN

blinkers PLURAL NOUN pieces fixed on a bridle to prevent a horse from seeing sideways ▶ **blinkered** ADJECTIVE

bliss NOUN perfect happiness

blissful ADJECTIVE bringing great happiness ▶ **blissfully** ADVERB

blend VERB • *Blend the ingredients carefully.* ▶ mix, combine, stir together, merge • *The colours blend well.* ▶ harmonize, match, fit

blend NOUN • *a blend of several ingredients* ▶ mixture, mix, combination

blind ADJECTIVE • *blind from birth* ▶ sightless, unsighted, visually impaired, partially sighted • *blind to all dangers* ▶ oblivious, heedless (of), unaware (of), ignorant (of) • *a blind acceptance*

of criticism ▶ uncritical, indiscriminate, unreasoning, mindless • *a blind corner* ▶ concealed, hidden, obstructed

blind NOUN • *Pull down the blind.* ▶ screen, shade, cover, curtain, shutter

blind VERB • *The light blinded her for a few moments.* ▶ dazzle • *They are trying to blind us all with science.* ▶ confuse, deceive

bliss NOUN • *a life of bliss* ▶ joy, pleasure, happiness, heaven, paradise

a
b
c
d
e
f
g
h
i
j
k
l
m
n
o
p
q
r
s
t
u
v
w
x
y
z

blister NOUN a swelling like a bubble on skin

blister VERB (of the skin) to produce blisters

blitz NOUN **1** a sudden violent attack **2** an attack by air with bombs

blizzard NOUN a severe snowstorm

bloated ADJECTIVE swollen by fat, gas, or liquid

blob NOUN a small round mass of something *blobs of paint*

bloc NOUN a group of countries who have formed an alliance

block NOUN **1** a solid piece of something **2** an obstruction **3** a large building divided into flats or offices **4** a group of buildings

block VERB to obstruct a place or prevent something from moving or being used ▸ **blockage** NOUN

blockade NOUN the blocking of a place to prevent people and goods from going in or out

blockade VERB to set up a blockade of a place

block letters PLURAL NOUN plain capital letters

bloke NOUN (informal) a man

blond or **blonde** ADJECTIVE having fair hair or skin

blonde NOUN a girl or woman with fair hair

blood NOUN **1** the red liquid that flows through veins and arteries **2** ancestry *of royal blood* **in cold blood** deliberately and cruelly

blood group NOUN each of the classes or types of human blood

bloodhound NOUN a large dog able to track people by their scent

bloodshed NOUN the killing or wounding of people

bloodshot ADJECTIVE (of the eyes) sore and streaked with red

blood sport NOUN a sport that involves wounding or killing animals

bloodstream NOUN the blood circulating in the body

bloodthirsty ADJECTIVE eager for bloodshed

blob NOUN • *a blob of ice cream* ▸ drop, droplet, globule, lump

block NOUN • *a block of stone* ▸ chunk, hunk, slab, lump, piece • *a block in a pipe* ▸ blockage, obstruction, stoppage • *a block to progress* ▸ barrier, hindrance, impediment, obstacle

block VERB • *The drain was blocked with leaves.* ▸ choke, clog, bung up, jam, obstruct • *A van blocked access to the house.* ▸ obstruct,

bar, restrict • *The scheme was blocked.* ▸ stop, prevent, halt, thwart

bloodshed NOUN • *attempts to avoid further bloodshed* ▸ killing, slaughter, carnage, butchery, violence

bloodthirsty ADJECTIVE • *bloodthirsty attackers* ▸ brutal, murderous, cruel, barbaric, savage

DICTIONARY

blood vessel NOUN a tube carrying blood in the body, e.g. an artery or vein

bloody ADJECTIVE **bloodier**, **bloodiest 1** stained with blood **2** involving much bloodshed *a bloody battle*

bloom NOUN **1** a flower **2** the fine powder on fruit

bloom VERB (of a plant) to produce flowers

blossom NOUN a mass of flowers on a fruit tree

blossom VERB **1** to produce flowers **2** to develop into something fine

blot NOUN **1** a spot of ink **2** an ugly flaw or fault

blot VERB **blotting, blotted** to make a blot on something **blot out 1** to cross out thickly **2** to obscure

blotch NOUN an untidy patch of colour ▶ **blotchy** ADJECTIVE

blouse NOUN a loose piece of clothing for the upper body, worn by women

blow¹ VERB **blew, blown 1** to send out a current of air **2** to move in or with a current of air *Her hat blew off.* **3** to make or sound something by blowing *blow bubbles blow the whistle* **4** (of a fuse) to break **blow up 1** to inflate **2** to explode

blow NOUN the action of blowing

blow² NOUN **1** a hard knock or hit **2** a shock or disaster

blowpipe NOUN a tube for firing a dart or pellet by blowing

blubber NOUN the fat of whales or seals

THESAURUS

bloody ADJECTIVE • *a bloody wound* i bleeding, raw, gaping • *a bloody battle* ▶ fierce, gory, violent

bloom NOUN • *rose blooms* ▶ blossom, flower, bud

bloom VERB • *The roses have bloomed.* ▶ blossom, flower, open

blot NOUN • *a blot of ink* ▶ spot, blotch, mark, smudge, stain • *a blot on the landscape* ▶ eyesore, blemish, defect, flaw

blot VERB • *Ink blotted the page.* ▶ smudge, mark, spoil, spot, stain **blot out** • *A building blotted out the view.* ▶ hide, conceal, mask, obscure, cover

blow NOUN • *a blow on the head* ▶ knock, bang, hit, thump, smack • *The news was a terrible blow.* ▶ shock, setback, upset, disappointment, disaster

blow VERB • *The storm blew the ship on the rocks.* ▶ drive, sweep, fling • *Leaves were blowing across the drive.* ▶ drift, flutter, whirl, stream **blow out** • *to blow out hot air* ▶ puff out, blast out, breathe out, waft **blow up** • *to blow up tyres* ▶ inflate, pump up, fill, expand • *to blow up a photograph* ▶ enlarge, magnify • *to blow up a building* ▶ bomb, blast, detonate, dynamite, explode

DICTIONARY

blue ADJECTIVE **1** of the colour of a cloudless sky **2** unhappy or depressed

blue NOUN **1** the colour of a cloudless sky **out of the blue** unexpectedly

bluebell NOUN a plant with blue bell-shaped flowers

blue blood NOUN aristocratic or royal descent

bluebottle NOUN a large fly with a dark blue body

blueprint NOUN a detailed plan

blues NOUN slow sad jazz music **the blues** a sad feeling

bluff[1] VERB to deceive someone by pretending to be confident about something

bluff NOUN an act of bluffing; an unreal threat

bluff[2] ADJECTIVE frank and cheerful in manner

bluff NOUN a broad steep cliff

bluish ADJECTIVE rather blue

blunder NOUN a careless mistake

blunder VERB **1** to make a careless mistake **2** to move clumsily and uncertainly

blunderbuss NOUN an old type of gun with a wide mouth

blunt ADJECTIVE **1** having an edge that is not sharp **2** speaking in plain terms *a blunt refusal* ▶ **bluntly** ADVERB

blunt VERB to make something blunt

blur VERB **blurring**, **blurred** to make or become unclear or smeared

blur NOUN an unclear appearance

blurt VERB to say something suddenly or tactlessly

blush VERB to become red in the face from shame or embarrassment

blush NOUN a slight reddening

bluster VERB **1** to blow in windy gusts **2** to talk loudly and aggressively ▶ **blustery** ADJECTIVE

boa constrictor NOUN a large snake that curls round its prey and crushes it

boar NOUN **1** a wild pig **2** a male pig

THESAURUS

bluff VERB • *They must be bluffing us.* ▶ deceive, trick, mislead, hoodwink • *They are only bluffing.* ▶ pretend, sham, put on an act, lie

bluff NOUN • *The offer is probably a bluff.* ▶ deception, sham, trick, pretence, fake

blunder NOUN • *He admitted his blunder.* ▶ mistake, error, gaffe, slip

blunt ADJECTIVE • *a blunt knife* ▶ dull, unpointed, unsharpened

• *a blunt reply* ▶ abrupt, harsh, curt, gruff, rude

blur VERB • *The steam had blurred her glasses.* ▶ cloud, fog, obscure

blurred ADJECTIVE • *Everything looked blurred.* ▶ indistinct, blurry, fuzzy, hazy, misty

blush VERB • *She blushed as he kissed her hand.* ▶ go red, flush, glow

a
b
c
d
e
f
g
h
i
j
k
l
m
n
o
p
q
r
s
t
u
v
w
x
y
z

board NOUN **1** a flat piece of wood **2** a flat piece of stiff material, e.g. for playing a game **3** daily meals supplied in return for payment or work **4** a group of people running an organization **on board** on or in a ship, aircraft, or vehicle

board VERB **1** to go on board a ship, aircraft, or vehicle **2** to give or get meals and accommodation **board up** to block with fixed boards

boarder NOUN someone who receives board and lodging

boast VERB **1** to try to impress people about yourself or your achievements **2** to have something to be proud of *The town boasts a fine park.*

boast NOUN a boasting statement

boastful ADJECTIVE tending to boast ▸ **boastfully** ADVERB

boat NOUN a vehicle built to travel on water

boatswain (boh-sun) NOUN a ship's officer in charge of rigging, boats, and other equipment

bob VERB **bobbing, bobbed** to move quickly up and down

bobbin NOUN a small spool holding thread or wire in a machine

bobble NOUN a small round ornament, often made of wool

bobsleigh NOUN a sledge with two sets of runners

bode VERB to be a sign or omen of what is to come *It bodes well.*

bodice NOUN the upper part of a woman's dress

bodily ADJECTIVE to do with your body

bodily ADVERB by taking hold of the body *He was picked up bodily.*

bodkin NOUN a thick blunt needle

body NOUN **bodies 1** the structure of a person or animal, or the main part of this apart from the head and limbs **2** a corpse **3** the main part of something **4** a group of people acting together **5** a distinct object or piece of matter *heavenly bodies*

bodyguard NOUN a guard to protect a person from harm or attack

bog NOUN an area of wet spongy ground

THESAURUS

boast VERB • *He was still boasting about his win.* ▸ brag, crow, show off, gloat

boastful ADJECTIVE • *boastful of all her achievements* ▸ bragging, conceited, big-headed, vain

body NOUN • *the human body* ▸ frame, figure, form, physique, shape • *a blow to the body*

▸ trunk, torso • *a body floating in the river* ▸ corpse, cadaver, carcass

bog NOUN • *a bog on the moors* ▸ marsh, swamp, mire, morass, quagmire **bogged down** • *bogged down with all the work* ▸ slowed down, encumbered, hindered, stuck

boggle VERB to be amazed or puzzled *The mind boggles at the thought.*

bogus ADJECTIVE not real; sham

bogy NOUN **bogies 1** an evil spirit **2** something that frightens people

boil[1] VERB **1** to make or become hot enough to bubble and give off steam **2** to cook or wash something in boiling water **3** to be very hot

boil NOUN boiling point *Bring the milk to the boil.*

boil[2] NOUN an inflamed swelling under the skin

boiler NOUN a container in which water is heated

boiling point NOUN the temperature at which something boils

boisterous ADJECTIVE noisy and lively

bold ADJECTIVE **1** confident and courageous **2** cheeky or disrespectful **3** (of colours or designs) strong and vivid **4** (of type) extra dark and thick
► **boldly** ADVERB

bollard NOUN a short post on the street for controlling the movement of traffic

bolster NOUN a long pillow for placing across a bed

bolster VERB to add extra support

bolt NOUN **1** a sliding bar for fastening a door **2** a thick metal pin used with a nut for joining things **3** a shaft of lightning **4** an arrow shot from a crossbow **a bolt from the blue** an unwelcome surprise **bolt upright** with the back completely straight

bolt VERB **1** to fasten with a bolt **2** to run away or escape **3** to swallow food quickly

bomb NOUN a device that explodes causing great damage **the bomb** nuclear weapons

bomb VERB to attack a place with bombs

bogus ADJECTIVE • *a bogus address*
► fake, false, spurious, fraudulent

boil VERB • *Boil the potatoes in water.* ► cook, heat, simmer • *The water was beginning to boil.*
► bubble, steam

boil NOUN • *a boil on the skin*
► swelling, abscess, blister, spot

boisterous ADJECTIVE • *a boisterous game* ► lively, spirited, exuberant, rowdy

bold ADJECTIVE • *a bold traveller*
► brave, courageous, daring,

adventurous, fearless, heroic
• *bold remarks* ► brazen, cheeky, impertinent, impudent, insolent
• *bold colours* ► striking, strong, bright, clear, eye-catching

bolt NOUN • *the bolt on the door*
► catch, latch, lock • *Put a nut on the bolt.* ► pin, screw

bolt VERB • *to bolt the door*
► fasten, latch, lock, secure • *He bolted from the room.* ► dash, flee, fly, rush, sprint • *to bolt your food* ► gobble, gulp, wolf, guzzle

bombard VERB **1** to attack with gunfire or many missiles **2** to direct a large number of questions at somebody ► **bombardment** NOUN

bomber NOUN **1** someone who plants or sets off a bomb **2** an aeroplane from which bombs are dropped

bombshell NOUN a great shock

bond NOUN **1** a close friendship or connection between two or more people **2 bonds** ropes or chains used to tie somebody up **3** a spoken or written agreement

bond VERB to become closely linked or connected

bondage NOUN slavery or captivity

bone NOUN **1** one of the hard whitish parts that make up the skeleton of a person's or animal's body **2** the substance from which these parts are made

bone VERB to remove the bones from meat or fish

bone dry ADJECTIVE extremely dry

bonfire NOUN a large outdoor fire

bonnet NOUN **1** a hat with strings that tie under the chin **2** a Scottish beret **3** the cover over a car engine

bonny ADJECTIVE **bonnier**, **bonniest 1** healthy-looking **2** (Scottish) good-looking

bonus NOUN **1** an extra payment in addition to a person's normal wages **2** an extra benefit

bony ADJECTIVE **1** full of bones **2** thin without much flesh

boo VERB **boos**, **booing**, **booed** to shout in disapproval ► **boo** NOUN

booby NOUN **boobies** a babyish or stupid person

booby prize NOUN a prize given to someone who comes last in a contest

booby trap NOUN something designed to hit or injure someone unexpectedly

book NOUN a set of printed sheets of paper fastened together inside a cover

book VERB **1** to reserve a seat or room in a theatre, train, hotel, etc. **2** to make a note of a person's name when they have committed an offence

booklet NOUN a small thin book

bookcase NOUN a piece of furniture with shelves for books

bookmark NOUN **1** something to mark a place in a book **2** (ICT) a record of the address of a file or web page

THESAURUS

bond NOUN • a close bond between the brothers ► attachment, connection, tie, link, relationship **bonds** • The prisoner struggled to undo his bonds. ► chains, shackles, restraints

bonus NOUN • He worked extra hard to earn a bonus. ► extra payment, handout, reward • an unexpected bonus ► benefit, extra, addition, advantage, (informal) plus

boom VERB **1** to make a deep hollow sound **2** to be growing and prospering

boom NOUN **1** a deep hollow sound **2** prosperity or growth

boomerang NOUN a curved piece of wood that returns when it is thrown, originally used by Australian Aborigines

boon NOUN something helpful or pleasant

boor NOUN a person with bad manners ► **boorish** ADJECTIVE

boost VERB to increase the strength or value of a person or thing ► **booster** NOUN

boost NOUN **1** an increase **2** a piece of encouragement

boot NOUN **1** a shoe that covers the foot and ankle or leg **2** the compartment for luggage in a car

boot VERB **1** to kick hard **2** (ICT) to switch on a computer

booth NOUN an enclosed compartment for selling tickets, telephoning, etc.

booty NOUN valuable goods taken away by soldiers after a battle

booze NOUN (informal) alcoholic drink

border NOUN **1** the boundary of a country or the part near it **2** an edge **3** something placed round an edge **4** a strip of ground round a garden

border VERB to put or be a border to something

borderline NOUN a boundary

borderline ADJECTIVE only just belonging to a particular group or category *a borderline pass*

bore¹ VERB to drill a hole

bore NOUN **1** the width of the inside of a gun barrel **2** a hole made by boring

bore² VERB to seem dull and uninteresting to

bore NOUN a boring person or thing ► **boredom** NOUN

bore³ past tense of **bear**²

bored ADJECTIVE unhappy because something is uninteresting or you have nothing to do

boring ADJECTIVE dull and uninteresting

boom VERB • *The guns began to boom.* ► rumble, thunder, crash • *Business is booming.* ► thrive, prosper, flourish, do well

boom NOUN • *the boom of guns* ► bang, roar, sound, blast • *a boom in trade* ► upturn, upswing, boost, growth, improvement

boost VERB • *The award boosted our morale.* ► raise, lift, bolster, increase

boost NOUN • *a boost to morale* ► impetus, stimulus, lift • *a boost in sales* ► increase, expansion, growth, improvement

border NOUN • *the border of the lake* ► edge, margin, verge • *the border between two countries* ► frontier, boundary, borderline

boring ADJECTIVE • *a boring book* ► tedious, dull, dreary, monotonous, unexciting

a
b
c
d
e
f
g
h
i
j
k
l
m
n
o
p
q
r
s
t
u
v
w
x
y
z

DICTIONARY

born *ADJECTIVE* **1** having come into existence by birth **2** having a certain natural quality or ability *a born leader*

borne *past participle of* **bear**²

borough *NOUN* an important town or district

borrow *VERB* **1** to get something to use for a time **2** to obtain money as a loan ▶ **borrower** *NOUN*

bosom *NOUN* **1** a woman's breasts **2** the central part of something *the bosom of the family*

boss¹ *NOUN* (*informal*) a manager or chief person

boss *VERB* (*informal*) to order someone about

boss² *NOUN* a round raised knob or stud

bossy *ADJECTIVE* tending to order people about ▶ **bossiness** *NOUN*

botany *NOUN* the study of plants ▶ **botanical** *ADJECTIVE*, **botanist** *NOUN*

botch *VERB* to spoil something by poor or clumsy work

both *ADJECTIVE*, *PRONOUN* the two; all of two *both places I like both.*

both *ADVERB* **both ... and** not only ... but also *both large and ugly*

bother *VERB* **1** to cause somebody trouble or worry **2** to take trouble *Don't bother to reply.*

bother *NOUN* trouble or worry

bottle *NOUN* **1** a narrow-necked container for liquids **2** (*informal*) courage *They showed a lot of bottle.*

bottle *VERB* to put or store something in bottles **bottle up** to keep feelings to yourself

bottle bank *NOUN* a large container for putting glass bottles in for recycling

bottleneck *NOUN* **1** a narrow place where traffic cannot flow freely **2** a stage in an activity in which progress is slow

bottom *NOUN* **1** the lowest part; the base **2** the part furthest away *the bottom of the garden* **3** a person's buttocks

bottom *ADJECTIVE* lowest *the bottom shelf*

THESAURUS

boss *NOUN* • *The boss was away all week.* ▶ head, chief, manager, leader

boss *VERB* • *You have no right to boss me about.* ▶ order, push around, bully

bossy *ADJECTIVE* • *a bossy person* ▶ overbearing, high-handed, aggressive, bullying

bother *VERB* • *No one can bother us here.* ▶ disturb, trouble, pester,

annoy, upset • *nothing to bother about* ▶ concern yourself, be concerned, be worried, care, mind

bother *NOUN* • *There was some bother at the disco.* ▶ trouble, disturbance, difficulty, fuss • *It was a bother to keep the food hot.* ▶ nuisance, inconvenience, trouble, worry

bottom *NOUN* • *the bottom of the stairs* ▶ foot, base • *the bottom of the wall* ▶ foot, base, foundation

DICTIONARY

bough NOUN a large branch coming from the trunk of a tree

bought *past tense of* **buy**

boulder NOUN a large smooth stone

bounce VERB **1** to spring back when thrown against something **2** to make something bounce **3** (of a cheque) to be sent back by the bank because there is not enough money in the account **4** to jump or move suddenly

bounce NOUN **1** the action or power of bouncing **2** a lively confident manner *full of bounce*
▸ **bouncy** ADJECTIVE

bouncer NOUN a person who stops unwanted people coming in a place

bound¹ VERB **1** to jump or spring **2** to run with jumping movements

bound NOUN a bounding movement

bound² *past tense of* **bind**

bound ADJECTIVE obstructed or hindered by something *The*

airport is fog-bound. **bound to** certain to *He is bound to fail.*

bound³ ADJECTIVE going towards something *bound for India*

bound⁴ VERB to limit or be the boundary of *Their land is bounded by the river.*

boundary NOUN **boundaries** an edge or limit

bounds PLURAL NOUN limits *beyond the bounds of common sense* **out of bounds** where you are not allowed to go

bounty NOUN **bounties** **1** a generous gift **2** generosity in giving things **3** a reward for doing something

bouquet (boh-kay) NOUN a bunch of flowers

bout NOUN **1** a boxing or wrestling contest **2** a period of activity or illness

bovine ADJECTIVE to do with or like cattle

THESAURUS

• *the bottom of the car*
▸ underside, underneath • *the bottom of the sea* ▸ bed, depths, floor • *to get to the bottom of the problem* ▸ origin, root, source, heart

bounce VERB • *The ball hit the wall and bounced off.* ▸ rebound, spring up, ricochet

bound VERB • *A dog bounded up.*
▸ leap, jump, spring, bounce

bound ADJECTIVE • *Our friends are bound to help.* ▸ certain, sure, very likely **bound for** • *a train*

bound for the north ▸ going to, heading for, making for, off to, travelling towards

boundary NOUN • *a fence at the boundary* ▸ border, frontier, dividing line • *the boundary of the estate* ▸ bounds, confines, perimeter, outer edge, limit

bouquet NOUN • *a bouquet of flowers* ▸ bunch, spray, posy

bout NOUN • *a bout of coughing* ▸ attack, fit, outburst, burst • *a boxing bout* ▸ contest, match, fight, encounter, competition

bow¹ (rhymes with *go*) NOUN **1** a curved strip of wood with a tight string joining its ends, used for shooting arrows **2** a wooden rod with horsehair stretched between its ends, used for playing a stringed instrument **3** a knot made with loops

bow² (rhymes with *cow*) VERB **1** to bend the head or body forwards to show respect or as a greeting **2** to bend downwards *bowed by the weight*

bow NOUN the act of bowing the head or body

bow³ (rhymes with *cow*) NOUN the front part of a ship

bowels PLURAL NOUN the intestines

bowl¹ NOUN **1** a deep rounded container for food or liquid **2** the rounded part of something, e.g. a spoon

bowl² NOUN a heavy ball used in the game of **bowls** or in bowling, in which they are rolled towards a target

bowl VERB **1** to send a ball to be played by a batsman **2** to get a batsman out by bowling **3** to send a ball rolling

bow-legged ADJECTIVE having legs that curve outwards at the knees; bandy

bowler¹ NOUN a person who bowls

bowler² NOUN a man's stiff felt hat with a rounded top

> **WORD HISTORY**
>
> named after its designer, William *Bowler*

bowling NOUN **1** the game of bowls **2** the game of knocking down skittles with a heavy ball

bow tie NOUN a man's necktie tied into a bow

box¹ NOUN **1** a container with flat sides and usually a top or lid **2** a rectangular space to be filled in on a form, computer screen, etc. **3** a compartment in a public place such as a theatre **4** a hut or shelter **5** a small evergreen shrub

box VERB to put something in a box

box² VERB to fight with the fists as a sport ▸ **boxing** NOUN

boxer NOUN **1** a person who boxes **2** a smooth-haired dog that looks like a bulldog

Boxing Day NOUN the first weekday after Christmas Day

boy NOUN a male child ▸ **boyhood** NOUN

boycott VERB to refuse to have dealings with ▸ **boycott** NOUN

boyfriend NOUN a person's regular male friend or lover

boyish ADJECTIVE like a boy; youthful and lively

bra NOUN a piece of underwear worn by women to support their breasts

THESAURUS

bowl NOUN • *a bowl of soup*
▸ dish, basin

bowl VERB • *to bowl a ball*
▸ throw, toss, fling, hurl, pitch

box NOUN • *a box of pencils*
▸ carton, pack, packet, case

boy NOUN • *a young boy* ▸ lad, youngster

DICTIONARY

brace NOUN **1** a device for holding things in place **2** a pair *a brace of pheasants*

brace VERB to support something or make it firm against something

bracelet NOUN a piece of jewellery worn round the wrist

braces PLURAL NOUN straps over the shoulders, to hold up a pair of trousers

bracing ADJECTIVE making you feel refreshed and healthy

bracken NOUN a type of large fern that grows in open country

bracket NOUN **1** a mark used in pairs to enclose words or figures. There are round brackets ( ) and square brackets [ ]. **2** a support attached to a wall **3** a range between certain limits *a high income bracket*

brag VERB **bragging, bragged** to boast

braid NOUN **1** a plait of hair **2** a strip of cloth with a woven decorative pattern

braid VERB **1** to plait **2** to trim with braid

Braille (rhymes with *mail*) NOUN a system of representing letters by

raised dots which blind people can read by touch

brain NOUN **1** the organ inside the top of the head that controls the body **2** the mind; intelligence

brainwash VERB to force a person to accept new ideas or beliefs

brainwave NOUN a sudden bright idea

brainy ADJECTIVE **brainier, brainiest** clever or intelligent

braise VERB to cook slowly in a small amount of liquid

brake NOUN a device for slowing or stopping a vehicle

brake VERB to use a brake

bramble NOUN a blackberry bush or a prickly bush like it

bran NOUN ground-up husks of corn

branch NOUN **1** a woody arm-like part of a tree or shrub **2** a part of a railway, road, or river that leads off from the main part **3** a shop or office that belongs to a large organization

branch VERB to form a branch; to spread out **branch out** to start something new

THESAURUS

brain NOUN • *You need brains.*
▶ intelligence, intellect, common sense, understanding • *the brains of the family* ▶ intellectual, clever person, mastermind

brainy ADJECTIVE • *a brainy child*
▶ intelligent, clever, bright, gifted, intellectual

branch NOUN • *a branch of a tree*
▶ bough, limb, arm • *a branch of the government* ▶ department, section, division, part • *the company's overseas branches*
▶ office, bureau, agency

branch VERB • *The road branches ahead.* ▶ divide, fork **branch out**
• *to branch out into a new career*
▶ diversify, expand, extend

DICTIONARY

brand NOUN **1** a particular make of goods **2** a mark made by branding **3** a piece of burning wood

brand VERB **1** to mark cattle or sheep with a hot iron to identify them **2** to sell goods under a particular trademark

brandish VERB to wave something about

brand new ADJECTIVE completely new

brandy NOUN **brandies** a strong alcoholic drink, usually made from wine

brash ADJECTIVE loud and aggressive

brass NOUN **1** a metal alloy of copper and zinc **2** musical instruments made of brass, e.g. trumpets and trombones

brat NOUN an unpleasant or unruly child

bravado NOUN a display of boldness

brave ADJECTIVE having or showing courage ▶ **bravely** ADVERB

brave NOUN a Native American warrior

brave VERB to face and endure something bravely

bravery NOUN the quality of being brave; courage

bravo EXCLAMATION well done!

brawl NOUN a noisy quarrel or fight

brawl VERB to take part in a brawl

brawn NOUN muscular strength

brawny ADJECTIVE strong and muscular

bray VERB to make the loud harsh cry of a donkey ▶ **bray** NOUN

brazen ADJECTIVE openly disrespectful or shameless

brazier NOUN a metal framework for holding burning coals

breach NOUN **1** the breaking of an agreement or rule **2** a break or gap

⚠ **USAGE**
Do not confuse this word with **breech**.

breach VERB to break through or make a gap

bread NOUN a food made by baking flour, water, and yeast

breadth NOUN extent from side to side; width

THESAURUS

brand NOUN • *a new brand of margarine* ▶ make, kind, type, variety, sort

brand VERB • *The cattle are branded with hot irons.* ▶ mark, stamp, burn, label • *The men are all branded as troublemakers.* ▶ stigmatize, denounce, give (someone) the reputation of

brave ADJECTIVE • *a brave person* ▶ courageous, daring, intrepid, plucky, adventurous, fearless

bravery NOUN • *Everyone praised their bravery.* ▶ courage, boldness, daring, fearlessness, heroism

brawl NOUN • *a drunken brawl* ▶ fight, clash, scrap, scuffle, tussle

a
b
c
d
e
f
g
h
i
j
k
l
m
n
o
p
q
r
s
t
u
v
w
x
y
z

a
b
c
d
e
f
g
h
i
j
k
l
m
n
o
p
q
r
s
t
u
v
w
x
y
z

break VERB **broke, broken 1** to divide or fall into pieces by hitting or pressing **2** to damage or stop working properly **3** to fail to keep a promise or rule **4** to stop for a time *She broke her silence.* **5** to go suddenly or with force *They broke through.* **6** to appear suddenly *Day had broken.* **7** (of the weather) to change suddenly **8** (of a boy's voice) to deepen at puberty **9** (of waves) to fall in foam **break a record** to do better than anyone else has done **break down 1** to stop working properly **2** to collapse **break in** to train a wild animal **break into** to enter a place with force **break out 1** to begin suddenly **2** to escape **break the news** to make something known **break up 1** to break into small parts **2** to separate at the end of a school term **3** to end a relationship

break NOUN **1** a broken place; a gap **2** an escape or sudden dash **3** a short rest from work **4** (*informal*) a piece of luck; a fair chance **break of day** dawn

breakage NOUN **1** the act of breaking something **2** something broken

breakdown NOUN **1** a sudden failure to work **2** a period of mental illness **3** an analysis

breakfast NOUN the first meal of the day

break-in NOUN an illegal entry into a place to steal from it

breakneck ADJECTIVE dangerously fast *at breakneck speed*

break VERB • *The cup fell and broke.*
▶ shatter, smash, crack, split, splinter • *He broke the stick into three pieces.* ▶ split, cut, divide • *to break the law* ▶ contravene, disobey, flout, infringe • *Let's break for lunch.* ▶ pause, stop, take a break • *to break the power of the unions* ▶ defeat, crush, smash, subdue, suppress **break down** • *The car has broken down.*
▶ stop working, go wrong
• *Negotiations broke down.*
▶ fail, collapse, fall through, come to nothing **break in** • *Thieves had broken in during the night.*
▶ commit burglary, force your way in **break off** • *It was hard to*

break off before finishing the chapter. ▶ pause, stop, discontinue **break up** • *The meeting broke up after several hours.* ▶ finish, end, adjourn
• *The crowd began to break up.*
▶ disperse, scatter, disband, go their separate ways • *Jane and her boyfriend had recently broken up.* ▶ separate, split up, get divorced

break NOUN • *a break in a pipe*
▶ split, breach, fissure, crack, fracture • *a break in work*
▶ pause, rest, breathing space, interval, interlude • *without a break* ▶ interruption, disruption, halt, stop

breakthrough NOUN an important advance or achievement

bream NOUN **bream** a silvery fish with an arched back

breast NOUN **1** one of the two milk-producing fleshy parts on the upper front of a woman's body **2** a person's or animal's chest

breastbone NOUN the flat bone down the centre of the chest or breast

breastplate NOUN a piece of armour covering the chest

breaststroke NOUN a swimming stroke done on the front with the arms and legs pushed forwards and sideways

breath NOUN **1** air drawn into the lungs and sent out again *a breath of wind* **out of breath** panting **take your breath away** to surprise or delight you **under your breath** in a whisper

breathe VERB to take air into the lungs and send it out again

breather NOUN a pause for rest

breathless ADJECTIVE out of breath

breathtaking ADJECTIVE very surprising or beautiful

breech NOUN the back part of a gun barrel where the bullets are put in

⚠ **USAGE**

Do not confuse this word with *breach*.

breeches PLURAL NOUN trousers reaching to just below the knees

breed VERB **1** to produce children or young **2** to keep animals to produce young from them **3** to bring up or train **4** to create or produce *Poverty breeds disease*
▶ **breeder** NOUN

breed NOUN a variety of animals with qualities inherited from their parents

breeze NOUN a light wind
▶ **breezy** ADJECTIVE

breve NOUN a note in music, lasting eight times as long as a crotchet

brevity NOUN shortness; briefness

brew VERB **1** to make beer or tea **2** to develop *Trouble is brewing.*

brew NOUN a brewed drink

brewer NOUN a person who brews beer

brewery NOUN **breweries** a place where beer is brewed

briar NOUN a thorny bush, especially the wild rose

bribe NOUN money or a gift offered to influence a person

THESAURUS

breathe VERB • *to breathe fresh air*
▶ inhale, exhale, respire, puff, pant • *Don't breathe a word.*
▶ speak, whisper, let out

breed VERB • *Rabbits breed rapidly.*
▶ reproduce, produce young,

bear young, multiply • *Familiarity breeds contempt.* ▶ produce, cause, create

breed NOUN • *a rare breed of dog*
▶ variety, type, kind, sort

bribe VERB to give a bribe to
► **bribery** NOUN

brick NOUN **1** a small hard block of baked clay used in building **2** a rectangular block of something

brick VERB to close something with bricks *We bricked up the gap in the wall.*

bricklayer NOUN a builder who works with bricks

bride NOUN a woman on her wedding day ► **bridal** ADJECTIVE

bridegroom NOUN a man on his wedding day

bridesmaid NOUN a girl or woman who attends the bride at her wedding

bridge[1] NOUN **1** a structure built to take a path or road across a road, river, or railway **2** a high platform on a ship, for the officer in charge **3** the bony upper part of the nose **4** a piece of wood supporting the strings of a violin etc. **5** something that connects things

bridge VERB to make or form a bridge over something

bridge[2] NOUN a card game like whist, with bidding

bridle NOUN the part of a horse's harness that fits over its head

bridleway NOUN a road suitable only for horses

brief ADJECTIVE short or concise **in brief** in a few words ► **briefly** ADVERB

brief NOUN a set of instructions given to someone, especially to a barrister

brief VERB **1** to give a brief to a barrister **2** to instruct or inform someone concisely in advance

briefcase NOUN a flat case for carrying papers

briefs PLURAL NOUN short knickers or underpants

brier NOUN another spelling of briar

brigade NOUN **1** a large unit of an army **2** a group of people organized for a special purpose *the fire brigade*

brigadier NOUN an army officer who commands a brigade

brigand NOUN a member of a band of robbers

bright ADJECTIVE **1** giving a strong light; shining **2** intelligent **3** cheerful ► **brightly** ADVERB

brief ADJECTIVE • *a brief visit*
► short, quick, cursory, fleeting, short-lived • *a brief account of the incident* ► short, concise, succinct, pithy, incisive

brigand NOUN • *robbed by brigands* ► bandit, robber, thief, outlaw, desperado

bright ADJECTIVE • *bright colours*
► vivid, strong • *bright sunshine*
► shining, brilliant, glaring, blazing, dazzling • *a bright morning* ► sunny, fine, clear, cloudless • *a bright manner*
► cheerful, jaunty, lively • *a bright student* ► clever, intelligent, gifted, brilliant

DICTIONARY

brighten VERB to make or become brighter

brilliant ADJECTIVE **1** very bright; sparkling **2** very clever
▸ **brilliance** NOUN, **brilliantly** ADVERB

brim NOUN **1** the edge of a cup, bowl, etc. **2** the bottom part of a hat that sticks out

brimful ADJECTIVE full to the brim

brine NOUN salt water ▸ **briny** ADJECTIVE

bring VERB **brought** to cause a person or thing to come; to lead or carry **bring about** to cause to happen **bring off** to do successfully **bring up 1** to look after and train growing children **2** to mention a subject

brink NOUN **1** the edge of a steep place or of a stretch of water **2** the point beyond which something will happen *on the brink of war*

brisk ADJECTIVE quick and lively
▸ **briskly** ADVERB

bristle NOUN a short stiff hair on an animal, brush, etc. ▸ **bristly** ADJECTIVE

bristle VERB **1** (of an animal) to raise its bristles in anger or fear **2** to be indignant **bristle with** to be full of *bristling with problems*

brittle ADJECTIVE hard and easily broken

broach VERB to begin talking about something *to broach the subject*

THESAURUS

brighten VERB • *The weather brightened.* ▸ become sunny, become bright, clear up **brighten up** • *Pictures will brighten the place up.* ▸ cheer up, smarten up, enhance

brilliant ADJECTIVE • *brilliant light* ▸ bright, blazing, dazzling, glaring • *a brilliant student* ▸ clever, intelligent, outstanding, gifted • *a brilliant game* ▸ excellent, marvellous, wonderful, superb, exceptional

brim NOUN • *full to the brim* ▸ top, rim, edge, lip

bring VERB • *She brought me a mug of tea.* ▸ fetch, carry, deliver, take, transport • *Bring your friends into the garden.* ▸ escort, accompany, conduct, guide, lead

• *to bring attention* ▸ draw, attract, produce, cause **bring about** • *to bring about changes* ▸ cause, effect, achieve, create **bring out** • *to bring out a new edition* ▸ publish, release, issue, produce, print • *to bring out the funny side* ▸ emphasize, accentuate, underline, highlight, stress **bring up** • *to bring up children* ▸ raise, rear, educate, look after, teach • *to bring up a question* ▸ raise, mention, touch on

brisk ADJECTIVE • *a brisk pace* ▸ quick, rapid, fast, lively, energetic • *brisk exercise* ▸ vigorous, energetic • *a brisk trade* ▸ busy, lively, hectic

brittle ADJECTIVE • *brittle bones* ▸ breakable, fragile, frail, delicate

a
b
c
d
e
f
g
h
i
j
k
l
m
n
o
p
q
r
s
t
u
v
w
x
y
z

broad ADJECTIVE **1** large across; wide **2** full and complete *broad daylight* **3** in general terms; not detailed *in broad agreement* **4** strong and unmistakable *a broad hint* *a broad accent*
► **broadly** ADVERB

broadband NOUN (ICT) a continuous Internet connection using signals over a broad range of frequencies

broad bean NOUN a bean with large flat seeds

broadcast NOUN a programme transmitted on radio or television

broadcast VERB to transmit on radio or on television
► **broadcaster** NOUN

broaden VERB to make or become broader

broadside NOUN **1** the firing of all guns on one side of a ship **2** a piece of fierce criticism

brocade NOUN material woven with raised patterns

broccoli NOUN a kind of cauliflower with small green flower heads

brochure NOUN a booklet or pamphlet containing information

broil VERB **1** to cook on a fire or gridiron **2** to make or be very hot

broke ADJECTIVE (informal) having no money left

broken VERB SEE **break**

broker NOUN a person who buys and sells shares for other people

bronchitis NOUN a disease with inflammation of the tubes leading from the windpipe to the lungs

bronze NOUN **1** a metal alloy of copper and tin **2** something made of bronze **3** yellowish-brown
► **bronze** ADJECTIVE

Bronze Age NOUN the time when tools and weapons were made of bronze

bronze medal NOUN a medal awarded for third place in a competition

brooch (brohch) NOUN a piece of jewellery with a hinged pin for fastening it on to clothes

brood NOUN a group of young birds hatched together

broad ADJECTIVE • *a broad road*
► wide, big, great, large, vast • *a broad sweep of countryside*
► wide, extensive, vast, rolling
• *the broad outline of the story*
► general, rough, vague • *broad tastes* ► comprehensive, wide-ranging, universal • *a broad local accent* ► pronounced, strong, marked, noticeable • *a*

broad hint ► clear, direct, obvious, unmistakable

broken ADJECTIVE • *broken plates*
► smashed, shattered, cracked, split • *The television is broken.*
► faulty, defective, out of order, not working • *a broken man*
► defeated, crushed, beaten • *a broken marriage* ► failed, ended
• *broken sleep* ► interrupted, disturbed, disrupted

brood VERB **1** to sit on eggs to hatch them **2** to keep thinking and worrying about something

broody ADJECTIVE **1** (of a hen) wanting to sit on eggs **2** (of a woman) longing to have children **3** thoughtful or brooding

brook¹ NOUN a small stream

brook² VERB to tolerate *She will brook no argument.*

broom NOUN **1** a sweeping brush with a long handle **2** a shrub with yellow, white, or pink flowers

broomstick NOUN a long thick stick with twigs at one end, on which witches are said to fly

broth NOUN a kind of thin soup

brother NOUN **1** a son of the same parents as another person **2** a fellow member or worker
▸ **brotherly** ADJECTIVE

brotherhood NOUN
1 companionship between men **2** a society or association of men

brother-in-law NOUN
brothers-in-law 1 the brother of a married person's husband or wife **2** the husband of a person's sister

brow NOUN **1** an eyebrow **2** the forehead **3** the top of a hill or cliff

brown ADJECTIVE of a colour between orange and black, like the colour of dark wood

brown NOUN the colour of dark wood

browse VERB **1** to read or look at something casually **2** (of an animal) to feed on grass or leaves

bruise NOUN a dark mark made on the skin by hitting it

bruise VERB to give or get a bruise

brunette NOUN a woman with dark-brown hair

brunt NOUN **bear the brunt** to take the chief impact or strain

brush NOUN **1** an implement used for cleaning or painting or for smoothing the hair, with pieces of hair, wire, etc. set in a handle **2** the bushy tail of a fox **3** the act of brushing *Give it a good brush.* **4** a brief fight *a brush with the enemy*

brush VERB **1** to use a brush on something **2** to touch gently in passing **brush up** to revise a subject

brutal ADJECTIVE very cruel
▸ **brutality** NOUN, **brutally** ADVERB

brute NOUN **1** a brutal person **2** an animal ▸ **brutish** ADJECTIVE

bubble NOUN **1** a thin transparent ball of liquid filled with air or gas **2** a small ball of air in something
▸ **bubbly** ADJECTIVE

browse VERB • *browsing in a book*
▸ flick through, leaf through, look through, skim

brutal ADJECTIVE • *a brutal attack*
▸ savage, cruel, vicious, fierce, ferocious, barbaric

bubble NOUN **bubbles** • *soap bubbles* ▸ foam, froth, lather, suds

bubble VERB • *The water was bubbling.* ▸ boil, gurgle

bubbly ADJECTIVE • *a bubbly drink*
▸ fizzy, carbonated, sparkling • *a*

a
b
c
d
e
f
g
h
i
j
k
l
m
n
o
p
q
r
s
t
u
v
w
x
y
z

DICTIONARY

bubble VERB **1** to send up or rise in bubbles **2** to be very lively

buccaneer NOUN a pirate

buck[1] NOUN a male deer, rabbit, or hare

buck VERB (of a horse) to jump with its back arched **buck up** (informal) **1** to hurry **2** to cheer up

buck[2] NOUN **pass the buck** (informal) to pass the responsibility for something to another person

bucket NOUN a deep container with a handle, for carrying liquids etc. ► **bucketful** NOUN

buckle[1] NOUN a device for passing a belt or strap through to fasten it

buckle VERB to fasten with a buckle

buckle[2] VERB to bend or crumple **buckle down** to start working hard

bud NOUN a flower or leaf before it opens

Buddhism (buud-izm) NOUN a religion that follows the teachings of Gautama Buddha, who lived in the 5th century BC ► **Buddhist** NOUN

budding ADJECTIVE beginning to develop *a budding poet*

buddy NOUN **buddies** (informal) a friend

budge VERB to move slightly

budgerigar NOUN an Australian bird kept as a pet in a cage

budget NOUN **1** a plan for spending money **2** an amount of money set aside for a purpose ► **budgetary** ADJECTIVE

budget VERB to plan how much you are going to spend

budgie NOUN (informal) a budgerigar

buff ADJECTIVE of a dull yellow colour

buff VERB to polish with soft material

buffalo NOUN **buffalo** or **buffaloes** a large ox of Asia, Africa, and North America

buffer NOUN **1** something that softens the force of a blow or impact **2** (ICT) a temporary memory for text or data

buffet[1] (buu-fay) NOUN **1** a cafe at a station **2** a meal at which guests serve themselves

buffet[2] (buf-it) VERB to hit or knock strongly *Winds buffeted the coast.*

buffoon NOUN a person who plays the fool ► **buffoonery** NOUN

THESAURUS

bubbly personality ► vivacious, animated, vibrant, lively

buckle NOUN • *a belt buckle* ► clasp, clip, fastener, fastening

buckle VERB • *to buckle a coat* ► fasten, do up, secure • *The*

bridge began to buckle. ► bend, warp, twist, distort, contort

budge VERB • *The window wouldn't budge.* ► move, shift, give way, change position • *No one will budge.* ► change your mind, give way, yield, compromise

94

DICTIONARY

bug NOUN **1** an insect **2** an error in a computer program **3** a germ or virus **4** a hidden microphone for spying on people

bug VERB **bugging, bugged 1** to fit with a hidden microphone **2** (*informal*) to annoy

bugbear NOUN something you fear or dislike

buggy NOUN **buggies 1** a pushchair for young children **2** a light horse-drawn carriage

bugle NOUN a brass instrument like a small trumpet ▸ **bugler** NOUN

build VERB **built** to make something by putting the parts together **build in** to include **build up 1** to establish gradually **2** to accumulate **3** to cover an area with buildings

build NOUN the shape of someone's body *of slender build*

builder NOUN someone who puts up buildings

building NOUN **1** the process of constructing houses and other structures **2** a permanent built structure that people can go into

bulb NOUN **1** a thick rounded part of a plant from which a stem grows

up and roots grow down **2** a glass globe that produces electric light **3** a rounded part of something ▸ **bulbous** ADJECTIVE

bulge NOUN a rounded swelling; an outward curve

bulge VERB to swell out

bulk NOUN **1** the size of something, especially when it is large **2** the greater portion; the majority *The bulk of the population voted for it.* **in bulk** in large amounts

bulk VERB to increase the size or thickness of something

bulky ADJECTIVE **bulkier, bulkiest** taking up a lot of space

bull NOUN **1** the fully-grown male of cattle **2** a male seal, whale, or elephant

bulldog NOUN a dog of a powerful breed with a short thick neck

bulldoze VERB to clear with a bulldozer

bulldozer NOUN a vehicle with a wide metal blade or scoop in front, used for shifting soil or clearing ground

THESAURUS

build VERB • *to build an apartment block* ▸ construct, erect, put up, assemble **build up** • *to build up a business* ▸ establish, develop, create, expand • *Traffic is building up.* ▸ increase, intensify, grow, mount up

building NOUN • *a large grim building* ▸ structure, construction, premises, place

bulge NOUN • *a bulge in the curtains* ▸ bump, swelling, lump

bulk NOUN • *a large bulk* ▸ size, volume, dimensions, proportions, mass • *the bulk of the work* ▸ most, best part, majority

bulky ADJECTIVE • *a bulky parcel* ▸ sizeable, large, substantial, cumbersome

bullet NOUN a small piece of shaped metal shot from a rifle or revolver

bulletin NOUN **1** a short news announcement on radio or television **2** a regular newsletter or report

bulletproof ADJECTIVE able to keep out bullets

bullfight NOUN a public entertainment in which bulls are baited and killed in an arena
▶ **bullfighter** NOUN

bullion NOUN bars of gold or silver

bullock NOUN a young castrated bull

bull's-eye NOUN **1** the centre of a target **2** a hard shiny peppermint sweet

bully VERB **bullies, bullied** to use strength to hurt or frighten a weaker person

bully NOUN **bullies** someone who bullies people

bulwark NOUN **1** a wall of earth built as a defence **2** a defence or protection

bulwarks PLURAL NOUN a ship's side above the level of the deck

bum NOUN (informal) a person's bottom

bumble VERB to move or behave or speak clumsily

bumblebee NOUN a large bee with a loud hum

bump VERB **1** to knock against something **2** to move along with jolts **bump into** (informal) to meet by chance **bump off** (informal) to kill

bump NOUN **1** the action or sound of bumping **2** a swelling or lump
▶ **bumpy** ADJECTIVE

bumper¹ NOUN a protective bar along the front or back of a motor vehicle

bumper² ADJECTIVE unusually large or plentiful a bumper crop

bumpkin NOUN a country person with awkward manners

bumptious ADJECTIVE conceited and self-important

bun NOUN **1** a small round sweet cake **2** hair twisted into a round bunch at the back of the head

bully VERB • Some of them bullied him. ▶ persecute, torment, intimidate

bully NOUN • a school bully ▶ tormentor, persecutor, thug

bump VERB • to bump your head ▶ hit, strike, knock, bang • to bump up and down ▶ bounce, shake, jerk, jolt **bump into** • to bump into something ▶ collide

with, run into, crash into, bang into, hit

bump NOUN • to fall with a bump ▶ thud, thump, smack, crash, bang • a bump on the head ▶ swelling, lump, bulge

bumpy ADJECTIVE • a bumpy ride ▶ bouncy, rough, jerky, jolting • a bumpy surface ▶ uneven, rough, irregular, lumpy

bunch NOUN a number of things joined or fastened together

bundle NOUN a number of things tied or wrapped together

bundle VERB **1** to make a number of things into a bundle **2** to push hurriedly or carelessly *They bundled him into a taxi.*

bung NOUN a stopper for closing a hole in a barrel or jar

bung VERB (*informal*) throw *Bung it here.* **bunged up** completely blocked

bungalow NOUN a house on one floor

bungle VERB to do something very badly ▶ **bungler** NOUN

bunion NOUN a swelling on the joint of the big toe

bunk¹ NOUN a bed built like a shelf

bunk² NOUN **do a bunk** (*informal*) to run away

bunker NOUN **1** a store for fuel **2** a sandy hollow built as an obstacle on a golf course **3** an underground shelter

bunny NOUN **bunnies** (*informal*) a rabbit

Bunsen burner NOUN a small gas burner used in scientific work

bunting NOUN strips of small flags hung up to decorate streets and buildings

buoy (boi) NOUN a floating object anchored as a guide or warning

buoyant (boi-ant) ADJECTIVE **1** able to float **2** light-hearted or cheerful ▶ **buoyancy** NOUN

buoyed ADJECTIVE **buoyed up** cheerfully eager and excited

bur NOUN another spelling of **burr** (seed case)

burble VERB to make a gentle murmuring sound ▶ **burble** NOUN

burden NOUN **1** a heavy load **2** a worry or difficulty ▶ **burdensome** ADJECTIVE

burden VERB to put a burden on

bureau (bewr-oh) NOUN **bureaux 1** a writing desk **2** a business office *an information bureau*

bureaucracy (bewr-ok-ra-see) NOUN the use of too many rules and procedures, especially in government departments ▶ **bureaucratic** ADJECTIVE

bureaucrat (bewr-ok-rat) NOUN an official in a government department

burger NOUN a flat round cake of fried meat, eaten in a bread roll

THESAURUS

bunch NOUN • *A bunch of keys were hanging by the door.* ▶ bundle, cluster, collection, set, quantity • *I gave mum a bunch of flowers on her birthday.* ▶ bouquet, posy, spray • *a friendly bunch* ▶ group, set, band

bundle NOUN • *a bundle of papers* ▶ bunch, sheaf, collection, pack

burden NOUN • *heavy burdens* ▶ load, weight, bundle, cargo • *a large financial burden* ▶ responsibility, obligation, duty, worry, problem

burglar NOUN a person who breaks into a building in order to steal from it ► **burglary** NOUN

burgle VERB to steal from a place

burial NOUN the placing of a dead body in the ground

burly ADJECTIVE **burlier, burliest** strong and heavy

burn VERB **burned** or **burnt** 1 to glow with fire; to produce heat or light 2 to damage or destroy by fire, heat, or chemicals 3 to be damaged or destroyed by fire 4 to feel very hot

burn NOUN a mark or injury made by burning

burner NOUN the part of a lamp or cooker that gives out the flame

burning ADJECTIVE extreme; intense *a burning ambition*

burr NOUN 1 a prickly seed case of a plant or flower 2 a soft country accent

burrow NOUN a hole or tunnel dug by a small animal as a dwelling

burrow VERB 1 to dig a burrow 2 to search deeply

burst VERB **burst** 1 to break or force apart 2 to start suddenly *burst into flames burst out laughing* 3 to be very full *bursting with energy*

burst NOUN 1 a split caused by something bursting 2 something short and forceful *a burst of gunfire*

bury VERB **buries, buried** 1 to place a dead body in the ground 2 to put underground or cover up **bury the hatchet** to agree to stop quarrelling or fighting

bus NOUN a large public vehicle for carrying passengers

busby NOUN **busbies** a tall ceremonial fur hat worn by some regiments

burn VERB • *The fire burned all day.* ► be alight, be ablaze, blaze, glow, smoulder • *An incinerator will burn anything.* ► ignite, kindle, incinerate • *The heat began to burn our skin.* ► scorch, scald, blister, toast, singe

burning ADJECTIVE • *a burning building* ► blazing, flaming, ablaze, alight, on fire • *a burning pain* ► searing, acute, stinging • *a burning desire* ► intense, extreme, fervent, passionate • *a burning question* ► urgent, crucial, vital, important

burrow VERB • *to burrow under the fence* ► tunnel, excavate, dig, mine

burst VERB • *A tyre has burst.* ► rupture, split open • *Water burst through.* ► gush, surge, stream, pour, spurt • *A man burst into the room.* ► rush, run, charge

bury VERB • *to bury a bone* ► hide, conceal, cover • *to bury the dead* ► inter, lay to rest • *She buried herself in her work.* ► absorb, engross, occupy, immerse

DICTIONARY

bush NOUN **1** a shrub **2** wild uncultivated land in Africa or Australia ► **bushy** ADJECTIVE

bushel NOUN a measure for grain and fruit (8 gallons or or 36.4 litres)

business NOUN **1** a person's concern or responsibilities *That is my business.* **2** an affair or subject *tired of the whole business* **3** a shop or firm **4** the buying and selling of things

businesslike ADJECTIVE practical and well-organized

businessman or **businesswoman** NOUN **businessmen** or **businesswomen** a man or woman who works in business

busker NOUN a person who plays music in the street for money ► **busking** NOUN

bust¹ NOUN **1** a sculpture of a person's head and shoulders **2** the upper front part of a woman's body

bust² VERB **bust** (*informal*) to break something

bustle VERB to hurry in a busy or excited way

bustle NOUN hurried or excited activity

busy ADJECTIVE **busier, busiest 1** having a lot to do **2** full of activity **3** (of a telephone line) engaged ► **busily** ADVERB

busy VERB **busies, busied busy yourself** to occupy yourself; to keep busy

busybody NOUN **busybodies** a person who meddles or interferes

but CONJUNCTION however; nevertheless *I wanted to go, but I couldn't.*

but PREPOSITION except *no one but me*

but ADVERB only; no more than *We can but try.*

butcher NOUN **1** a person who cuts up meat and sells it **2** a person who kills cruelly or needlessly ► **butchery** NOUN

butcher VERB to kill cruelly or needlessly

butler NOUN the chief male servant in a large house

butt¹ NOUN **1** the thicker end of a weapon or tool **2** the stump of a used cigarette or cigar **3** a large cask or barrel **4** a target for ridicule or teasing

butt² VERB to push or hit with the head **butt in** to interrupt or meddle

THESAURUS

business NOUN • *a tricky business*
► matter, affair, issue, problem
• *to go about your business*
► work, job, occupation, employment • *a lot of new business* ► trade, trading, buying

and selling, commerce, dealings
• *to run a business* ► firm, company, establishment, enterprise, organization

busy ADJECTIVE • *busy at work*
► active, occupied, hard-pressed

butter NOUN a soft fatty food made by churning cream
▶ **buttery** ADJECTIVE

buttercup NOUN a wild plant with bright yellow cup-shaped flowers

butterfly NOUN **butterflies 1** an insect with large white or coloured wings **2** a swimming stroke in which both arms are lifted at the same time

butterscotch NOUN a kind of hard toffee

buttocks PLURAL NOUN the two fleshy rounded parts of your bottom

button NOUN **1** a knob or disc sewn on clothes as a fastening or ornament **2** a small knob pressed to work an electric device

button VERB to fasten something with a button or buttons

buttonhole NOUN **1** a slit through which a button passes to fasten clothes **2** a flower worn on a lapel

buttress NOUN a support built against a wall

buy VERB **bought** to become the owner of something by paying for it ▶ **buyer** NOUN

buy NOUN something that is bought

buzz NOUN a vibrating humming sound **get a buzz** (informal) to find something exciting

buzz VERB **1** to make a buzz **2** to be full of excitement

buzzard NOUN a large hawk

buzzer NOUN a device that makes a buzzing sound as a signal

by PREPOSITION **1** near; close to *Sit by me.* **2** using or through the agency of *We came by a short cut. cooking by gas a poem by Byron* **3** during *They travel by night.* **4** to the extent of *I missed it by inches.* **by the way** incidentally **by yourself** alone; without help

by ADVERB **1** near *He just stood by.* **2** past *People walked by.* **3** for future use *Put something by.* **by and by** soon; later on **by and large** on the whole

bye NOUN a run scored in cricket when the ball goes past the batsman without being touched

bye-bye EXCLAMATION goodbye

by-election NOUN an election to replace an MP who has died or resigned

THESAURUS

• *a busy person* ▶ active, energetic, diligent, industrious
• *a busy life* ▶ active, hectic, lively, strenuous, demanding
• *The manager is busy at the moment.* ▶ engaged, unavailable, occupied • *busy organizing a conference* ▶ occupied (with),

working (at), engaged (in), hard at work (on) • *The shops were busy all day.* ▶ crowded, teeming, bustling, swarming, full of people

buy VERB • *I will buy the drinks.*
▶ get, pay for, obtain

a b c d e f g h i j k l m n o p q r s t u v w x y z

bygone ADJECTIVE belonging to the past **let bygones be bygones** forgive and forget

bypass NOUN a road taking traffic round a city or congested area

bypass VERB to avoid something by going round it

bystander NOUN a person who sees an event in the street without being involved in it

byte NOUN (ICT) a unit for measuring computer data

byword NOUN a person or thing used as a famous example *a byword for quality*

Cc

cab NOUN **1** a taxi **2** a compartment for the driver of a lorry, train, bus, or crane

cabaret (kab-er-ay) NOUN an entertainment for customers in a restaurant or nightclub

cabbage NOUN a vegetable with green or purple leaves

cabin NOUN **1** a wooden hut or shelter **2** a room for sleeping on a ship **3** the part of an aircraft in which passengers sit

cabinet NOUN **1** a cupboard or container with drawers or shelves **2** the group of senior government ministers who meet regularly to decide policy

cable NOUN **1** a thick rope of fibre or wire **2** a covered group of wires laid underground for transmitting electrical signals **3** a telegram sent overseas

cable television NOUN a broadcasting service with signals transmitted by cable to subscribers

cacao (ka-kay-oh) NOUN a tree with a seed from which cocoa and chocolate are made

cache (kash) NOUN a hidden store of valuable things

cackle VERB **1** to make a loud silly laugh **2** to chatter noisily **3** to cluck loudly as a hen does
► **cackle** NOUN

cacophony NOUN cacophonies a loud unpleasant sound
► **cacophonous** ADJECTIVE

cactus NOUN cacti a type of prickly fleshy plant

cad NOUN (old use) a man who treats others badly

caddie NOUN a person who carries a golfer's clubs during a game

caddy NOUN caddies a small box for holding tea

cadet NOUN a young trainee in the armed forces or the police

cadge VERB to get something by asking for it without wanting to pay for it or work for it

cadmium NOUN a metal that looks like tin

Caesarean (siz-air-ee-an) NOUN a surgical operation for delivering a baby by cutting through the wall of the mother's womb

cafe (ka-fay) NOUN a small restaurant serving drinks and light meals

cafeteria NOUN a self-service cafe

THESAURUS

cabin NOUN • *We had a holiday in a cabin by the river.* ► hut, lodge, chalet, shack, shanty, shed, shelter • *a cabin on a ship* ► berth, compartment, sleeping quarters • *the driver's cabin* ► cab, compartment

cable NOUN • *The ship was moored with cables.* ► rope, cord, line, chain • *a power cable* ► wire, lead, line

cafe NOUN • *a snack at a local cafe* ► coffee shop, tea shop, snack bar, cafeteria, bistro

caffeine (kaf-een) NOUN a stimulant substance found in tea and coffee

caftan NOUN a long loose coat or dress

cage NOUN an enclosure with bars, in which birds or animals are kept

cage VERB to enclose in a cage

cagoule (kag-ool) NOUN a light waterproof jacket

cairn NOUN a pile of loose stones set up as a landmark or monument

cake NOUN **1** a baked food made from a mixture of flour, fat, eggs, and sugar **2** a shaped lump or mass *a cake of soap*

caked ADJECTIVE heavily covered with something thick such as mud

calamity NOUN **calamities** a disaster

calcium NOUN a chemical substance found in teeth, bones, and lime

calculate VERB **1** to work something out with mathematics **2** to plan or intend something ► **calculation** NOUN

calculating ADJECTIVE planning things carefully and selfishly

calculator NOUN a small electronic device for making calculations

calculus NOUN mathematics for working out problems about rates of change

calendar NOUN a chart or set of pages showing the dates of the month or year

calf[1] NOUN **calves** a young cow, bull, elephant, whale, or seal

calf[2] NOUN **calves** the fleshy back part of the leg below the knee

calibrate VERB to mark a gauge or instrument with a scale of measurements ► **calibration** NOUN

calibre (kal-ib-er) NOUN **1** the diameter of a tube or gun barrel **2** ability or importance *someone of your calibre*

call NOUN **1** a shout or cry **2** a visit **3** a telephone conversation **4** a summons

call VERB **1** to shout or speak loudly, especially to attract attention **2** to

calamity NOUN • *The decision was a calamity.* ► disaster, catastrophe, tragedy

calculate VERB • *Interest on the loan is calculated monthly.* ► work out, compute, count, add up

call NOUN • *a call for help* ► cry, shout, yell, scream • *a call for strike action* ► appeal, plea, demand, request

call VERB • '*Come here!*' *she called.* ► cry, shout, yell, exclaim • *I'll call you this evening.* ► phone, telephone, ring • *They called him Albert.* ► name, baptize, christen, dub • *Call me early tomorrow.* ► wake, wake up, get someone up, rouse • *The headteacher called them to her office.* ► summon, invite, order • *We'd better call the doctor.* ► send for, fetch,

telephone someone **3** to name a person or thing **4** to tell somebody to come to you **5** to make a short visit **call for 1** to come and collect **2** to need *The work calls for great care.* **call off** to cancel or postpone **call up** to summon to join the armed forces ▶ **caller** NOUN

call centre NOUN an office that deals with telephone enquiries from the public

calligraphy NOUN the art of fine handwriting

calling NOUN a profession or career

callipers PLURAL NOUN compasses for measuring the width of tubes or of round objects

callous ADJECTIVE hard-hearted or unsympathetic ▶ **callously** ADVERB

calm ADJECTIVE **1** quiet and still; not windy **2** not excited or agitated ▶ **calmly** ADVERB

calm VERB to make or become calm

calorie NOUN a unit for measuring an amount of heat or the energy produced by food ▶ **calorific** ADJECTIVE

calve VERB to give birth to a calf

calypso NOUN **calypsos** a West Indian song improvised by the singer on a topical theme

camber NOUN a slight upward curve on a road to allow drainage

camcorder NOUN a combined video camera and sound recorder

camel NOUN a large desert animal with a long neck and humped back, used for transport

cameo (kam-ee-oh) NOUN **cameos 1** a small hard piece of stone carved with a raised design **2** a short special part for a well-known actor in a play or film

camera NOUN a device for taking photographs, films, or television pictures

camouflage (kam-off-lahzh) NOUN a natural or artificial way of making things look like part of their surroundings, as a protection

camouflage VERB to disguise with camouflage

camp NOUN a place where people live in tents or huts for a short time

camp VERB **1** to put up a tent or tents **2** to have a holiday in a tent ▶ **camper** NOUN

summon, ask to come • *to call a meeting* ▶ convene, organize • *His mother called the next day.* ▶ visit, pay a visit **call for** • *The task calls for careful planning.* ▶ require, need, demand • *We'll call for you about six.* ▶ fetch, pick up, come for, collect **call off** • *The barbecue was called off.* ▶ cancel, abandon, postpone, adjourn

call on • *to call on friends* ▶ visit, go and see

callous ADJECTIVE • *a callous remark* ▶ heartless, hard-hearted, uncaring, insensitive, cruel

calm ADJECTIVE • *a calm sunny day* ▶ still, tranquil, quiet, peaceful • *a calm sea* ▶ smooth, still, flat, waveless • *He remained calm.* ▶ composed, collected, cool,

campaign NOUN **1** a series of battles in one area or with one purpose **2** a planned series of actions to arouse interest in something *an advertising campaign*

campaign VERB to take part in a campaign ► **campaigner** NOUN

campus NOUN the grounds of a university or college

can¹ AUXILIARY VERB **could 1** to be able to *He can speak three languages.* **2** to be allowed to *You can go if you like.*

can² NOUN **1** a sealed tin in which food or drink is preserved **2** a metal or plastic container for liquids

can VERB **canning, canned** to preserve food in a sealed can

canal NOUN **1** an artificial waterway for boats or drainage **2** a tube in a plant or animal body

canary NOUN **canaries** a small yellow songbird

cancan NOUN a lively dance in which the legs are kicked very high

cancel VERB **cancelling, cancelled 1** to stop something planned from happening **2** to stop an order or instruction **3** to mark a stamp or ticket as used **cancel out** to balance each other's effect *The good and harm cancel each other out.* ► **cancellation** NOUN

cancer NOUN **1** a disease in which harmful growths form in the body

2 a harmful growth or tumour ► **cancerous** ADJECTIVE

candid ADJECTIVE frank and honest ► **candidly** ADVERB

candidate NOUN **1** a person who wants to be elected or chosen for a particular job or position etc. **2** a person taking an examination ► **candidacy** NOUN, **candidature** NOUN

📖 **WORD HISTORY**

from Latin *candidus* 'white' (because Roman candidates for office wore a white toga)

---

candle NOUN a stick of wax with a wick through it, giving light when burning

candlestick NOUN a holder for a candle or candles

candour (kan-der) NOUN frankness; honesty

candy NOUN **candies** (American) sweets or a sweet

candyfloss NOUN a fluffy mass of thin strands of spun sugar

cane NOUN **1** the stem of a reed or tall grass **2** a thin stick

cane VERB to beat with a cane

canine ADJECTIVE to do with dogs

canister NOUN a metal container

canker NOUN a disease that rots the wood of trees and plants or causes ulcers and sores on animals

cannabis NOUN hemp smoked as a narcotic drug

THESAURUS

unruffled • *a calm temperament* ► serene, placid, phlegmatic, relaxed

cancel VERB • *to cancel a holiday* ► call off, abandon, drop, end • *to cancel a debt* ► revoke, annul

cannibal NOUN **1** a person who eats human flesh **2** an animal that eats animals of its own kind
▶ **cannibalism** NOUN

cannibalize VERB to take a machine or vehicle apart to provide spare parts for others
▶ **cannibalization** NOUN

⚠ SPELLING

This word can also be spelled *cannibalise*.

cannon NOUN a large heavy gun mounted on a carriage

cannonball NOUN a large solid ball fired from a cannon

cannot VERB can not

canny ADJECTIVE **cannier, canniest** shrewd and cautious ▶ **cannily** ADVERB

canoe NOUN a narrow lightweight boat, moved forwards with paddles ▶ **canoeing** NOUN, **canoeist** NOUN

canon NOUN **1** a general principle or rule **2** a clergyman at a cathedral

canonize VERB to declare officially that a dead person is a saint
▶ **canonization** NOUN

⚠ SPELLING

This word can also be spelled *canonise*.

canopy NOUN **canopies** a hanging cover above a throne or bed

cant NOUN **1** insincere or hypocritical talk **2** the slang or jargon of a particular group

can't cannot

cantankerous ADJECTIVE bad-tempered and quarrelsome

canteen NOUN **1** a restaurant for workers in a factory or office **2** a case or box containing a set of cutlery **3** a water flask

canter NOUN a gentle gallop

canter VERB to go or ride at a canter

canticle NOUN a song or chant with words taken from the Bible

cantilever NOUN a beam or girder fixed at one end and supporting a bridge

canton NOUN each of the districts into which Switzerland is divided

canvas NOUN **1** a kind of strong coarse cloth **2** a piece of canvas for painting on

canvass VERB to ask people for their support, e.g. in an election
▶ **canvasser** NOUN

canyon NOUN a deep river valley

cap NOUN **1** a soft hat with a peak **2** a cover or top **3** a small explosive strip used in a toy pistol **4** a cap awarded to players selected for a sports team

cap VERB **capping, capped 1** to put a cap or cover on something **2** to award a sports cap to someone chosen for a team **3** to do better than something **4** to put a limit on something

capability NOUN **capabilities** the ability or skill to do something

THESAURUS

cancel out • *One mistake could cancel out all our hard work.*
▶ counterbalance, wipe out, offset, make up for

capable ADJECTIVE able to do something ► **capably** ADVERB

capacity NOUN **capacities 1** the amount that something can hold **2** ability or capability **3** the position that someone occupies *in his capacity as commander-in-chief*

cape¹ NOUN a short cloak

cape² NOUN a piece of high land jutting into the sea

caper¹ VERB to jump about playfully

caper NOUN a playful prank or adventure

caper² NOUN a bud of a prickly shrub, pickled for use in cooking

capillary ADJECTIVE very narrow or fine

capital NOUN **1** the most important city in a country **2** a large letter used at the start of a name or sentence **3** the top part of a pillar **4** money or property that can be used to produce more wealth

capitalism NOUN an economic system in which trade and industry are controlled by private owners for profit, and not by the state

capitalist NOUN a person who supports capitalism

capitalize VERB **1** to write or print as a capital letter **2** to use something to your advantage *You should capitalize on your language skills.* ► **capitalization** NOUN

⚠ **SPELLING**

This word can also be spelled *capitalise*.

capital punishment NOUN punishment by being put to death

capitulate VERB to admit that you are defeated and surrender ► **capitulation** NOUN

cappuccino NOUN **cappuccinos** milky coffee made frothy with pressurized steam

capricious ADJECTIVE deciding or changing your mind impulsively ► **capriciously** ADVERB

capsize VERB (of a boat) to overturn

capstan NOUN a thick post used for winding a thick rope or cable

capsule NOUN **1** a gelatine case containing a dose of medicine, swallowed whole **2** a seed case on a plant, which splits open when ripe **3** a detachable compartment of a spacecraft

THESAURUS

capable ADJECTIVE • *a capable young woman* ► competent, able, accomplished, efficient, talented **be capable of** • *They are capable of all these tasks.* ► have the ability (to do), be competent (to do)

capacity NOUN • *a capacity of 30 litres* ► size, volume • *the*

capacity to motivate yourself ► ability, power, capability, skill, talent • *in his capacity as commander-in-chief* ► position, function, role

capsize VERB • *The boat capsized.* ► overturn, tip over, turn over, flip over

captain NOUN **1** a person in command of a ship or aircraft **2** the leader in a sports team **3** an army officer ranking next below a major **4** a naval officer ranking next below a commodore ► **captaincy** NOUN

caption NOUN **1** the words printed with a picture to describe it **2** a short title or heading in a newspaper or magazine

captivate VERB to charm or delight ► **captivation** NOUN

captive NOUN a person taken prisoner

captive ADJECTIVE **1** taken prisoner **2** unable to escape

captivity NOUN **1** the state of being captured **2** the confined state of an animal in a zoo

captor NOUN someone who has captured a person or animal

capture VERB **1** to take someone prisoner **2** to take or obtain by force, trickery, or charm **3** (ICT) to put data in a form that can be stored in a computer

capture NOUN the act of capturing someone or something

car NOUN **1** a motor car **2** a carriage of a train *dining car*

carafe (ka-raf) NOUN a glass bottle for serving wine or water

caramel NOUN **1** a kind of toffee tasting like burnt sugar **2** burnt sugar used for colouring and flavouring food

carat NOUN **1** a measure of weight for precious stones **2** a measure of the purity of gold

caravan NOUN **1** a vehicle towed by a car and used for living in **2** a group of people travelling together across desert country ► **caravanning** NOUN

carbohydrate NOUN a compound of carbon, oxygen, and hydrogen (e.g. sugar or starch)

carbolic NOUN a kind of disinfectant

carbon NOUN an element present in all living things and occurring in its pure form as diamond and graphite

carbonate NOUN a compound that gives off carbon dioxide when mixed with acid

carbonated ADJECTIVE (of a drink) having added carbon dioxide to make it fizzy

carbon dioxide NOUN a gas formed when things burn, or breathed out by humans and animals

carbuncle NOUN **1** an abscess in the skin **2** a bright-red gem

captive NOUN • *The captives wore handcuffs.* ► prisoner, convict, detainee, inmate, hostage

captive ADJECTIVE • *captive animals* ► caged, captured, confined, incarcerated • *The men* were held captive. ► locked up, imprisoned, jailed, under lock and key

capture VERB • *to capture prisoners* ► catch, arrest, apprehend, seize, take prisoner

carburettor NOUN a device for mixing fuel and air in an engine

carcass NOUN the dead body of an animal

card NOUN 1 thick stiff paper or thin cardboard 2 a small piece of stiff paper for writing or printing on to send messages or greetings or to record information 3 a small oblong piece of plastic with machine-readable information, issued to customers by banks and shops 4 a playing card **cards** PLURAL NOUN a game using playing cards **on the cards** likely; possible

cardboard NOUN a kind of thin board made of layers of paper or wood fibre

cardiac ADJECTIVE to do with the heart

cardigan NOUN a knitted jacket

cardinal NOUN a senior priest in the Roman Catholic Church

cardinal ADJECTIVE 1 chief or most important 2 deep scarlet, like a cardinal's cassock

cardinal number NOUN a number used for counting things, e.g. one, two, three, etc.

care NOUN 1 attention and thought *Proceed with care.* 2 protection or supervision *a child in her care* 3 worry or anxiety *free from care* **take care** to be especially careful **take care of** to look after

care VERB 1 to feel interested or concerned 2 to feel affection **care for 1** to have in your care 2 to be fond of

career NOUN the series of jobs that someone has as they make progress in their occupation

career VERB to rush along wildly

carefree ADJECTIVE without worries or responsibilities

THESAURUS

• *to capture a building* ► occupy, take, seize, secure

care NOUN • *Proceed with care.* ► caution, vigilance, watchfulness • *The job needs to be done with great care.* ► attention, thought, thoroughness, concentration • *free from care* ► worry, anxiety, trouble, problem, difficulty • *She left the baby in the care of a minder.* ► charge, safe keeping, supervision, protection

care VERB **care about** • *She cares about her staff.* ► interest yourself in, concern yourself about, mind about, bother about **care for**

• *The hospice cares for sick children.* ► look after, take care of, tend, provide for, nurse • *He cares for his grandchildren.* ► love, be fond of, adore, dote on • *I don't care for those biscuits.* ► like, fancy, feel like, be keen on

career NOUN • *a career in teaching* ► profession, occupation, job

carefree ADJECTIVE • *a carefree young girl* ► unworried, untroubled, cheerful, light-hearted, relaxed • *a carefree time* ► relaxing, restful, trouble-free, peaceful, quiet

DICTIONARY

careful ADJECTIVE **1** giving serious thought and attention to something; avoiding damage or danger; cautious ► **carefully** ADVERB

careless ADJECTIVE not taking proper care ► **carelessly** ADVERB

carer NOUN someone who looks after a person in need of care

caress NOUN a fond and gentle touch

caress VERB to touch fondly

caretaker NOUN a person employed to look after a school or other large building

cargo NOUN **cargoes** goods carried in a ship or aircraft

caricature NOUN an amusing or exaggerated picture of someone

caries NOUN **caries** decay in the teeth or bones

carnage NOUN the killing of many people

carnal ADJECTIVE to do with the body as opposed to the spirit

carnation NOUN a garden flower with a sweet smell

carnival NOUN a festival with a procession of people in fancy dress

carnivorous ADJECTIVE eating meat ► **carnivore** NOUN

carol NOUN a religious hymn sung at Christmas

carousel (ka-roo-sel) NOUN **1** a rotating conveyor belt for baggage at an airport **2** (American) a roundabout at a fair

carp¹ NOUN **carp** an edible freshwater fish

carp² VERB to complain constantly about trivial things

carpenter NOUN a person who makes things out of wood ► **carpentry** NOUN

carpet NOUN a thick soft covering for a floor ► **carpeted** ADJECTIVE, **carpeting** NOUN

carriage NOUN **1** each of the separate parts of a passenger train **2** a passenger vehicle pulled by horses **3** the process or cost of transporting goods **4** a moving part carrying or holding something in a machine

carriageway NOUN the part of a road on which vehicles travel

carrier NOUN **1** a person or thing that carries something **2** someone who transmits an illness without catching it

carrion NOUN dead and decaying flesh

THESAURUS

careful ADJECTIVE • Be careful. ► alert, vigilant, attentive, watchful • careful with your spending ► prudent, cautious, economical, thrifty • careful planning ► detailed, thorough, meticulous • a careful driver ► attentive, conscientious

careless ADJECTIVE • a careless driver   careless remarks ► inattentive, negligent, thoughtless, irresponsible, reckless • careless work ► slipshod, shoddy, slapdash, inaccurate • careless about money ► extravagant, reckless

a
b
c
d
e
f
g
h
i
j
k
l
m
n
o
p
q
r
s
t
u
v
w
x
y
z

carrot NOUN a plant with a thick orange-coloured root used as a vegetable

carry VERB **carries**, **carried** **1** to take something from one place to another **2** to support the weight of something **3** to take an amount into the next column when adding figures **4** (of sound) to reach a long way away **5** to approve a proposal at a meeting **be carried away** to be very excited **carry on** to continue **carry out** to put into practice

cart NOUN an open vehicle for carrying loads

cart VERB **1** to carry in a cart **2** (informal) to carry something heavy or tiring

cartilage NOUN tough white flexible tissue attached to a bone

cartography NOUN the process of drawing maps
▶ **cartographer** NOUN, **cartographic** ADJECTIVE

carton NOUN a cardboard or plastic container

cartoon NOUN **1** a funny or comic drawing **2** a series of drawings that tell a story **3** an animated film
▶ **cartoonist** NOUN

cartridge NOUN **1** a case containing the explosive for a bullet or shell **2** a container holding film, ink, etc.

cartwheel NOUN a handstand balancing on each hand in turn with arms and legs spread like spokes of a wheel

carve VERB **1** to make something by cutting wood or stone **2** to cut cooked meat into slices

cascade NOUN **1** a small waterfall **2** a lot of things falling or hanging down

cascade VERB **1** to fall like a cascade

case NOUN **1** a container or covering **2** a suitcase **3** an example of something existing or occurring *in all cases* **4** a police investigation *a murder case* **5** a set of facts or arguments *They put forward a good case.* **6** the form of a word that shows how it is used in a sentence, e.g. *him* is the objective case of *he* **in any case** whatever happens **in case** because something may happen

casement NOUN a window that opens on hinges at its side

cash NOUN **1** money in coin or notes **2** immediate payment for goods

carry VERB • to carry luggage
▶ convey, take, transfer, bring, lift, move • *The ships carry passengers and freight.*
▶ transport, convey, handle, ship • to carry the weight ▶ support, bear, hold up • *The job carries many responsibilities.* ▶ involve,

entail, require **carry on** • *We carried on as long as we could.*
▶ persevere, continue, go on, keep on **carry out** • to carry out orders ▶ obey, follow, execute, complete

case NOUN • *She put a few clothes in a case.* ▶ suitcase, bag, travel bag,

DICTIONARY

cash VERB to change a cheque etc. for cash

cashew NOUN a kind of small nut

cashier NOUN a person who deals with money in a bank or shop

cashmere NOUN very fine soft wool

cashpoint NOUN a cash dispenser

casing NOUN a protective covering

casino NOUN **casinos** a public building or room for gambling

cask NOUN a barrel for wine or other alcoholic drink

casket NOUN a small box for jewellery

casserole NOUN **1** a covered dish in which food is cooked and served **2** food cooked in a casserole

cassette NOUN a small sealed case containing recording tape, film, etc.

cast VERB **cast 1** to throw with force **2** to shed or throw off **3** to record a vote **4** to make something of metal or plaster in a mould **5** to choose performers for a play or film

cast NOUN **1** a shape made by pouring liquid metal or plaster into

a mould **2** the performers in a play or film

castanets PLURAL NOUN a pair of curved pieces of wood held in one hand by Spanish dancers and snapped together to make a clicking sound

castaway NOUN a shipwrecked person

cast iron NOUN a hard alloy of iron made by casting it in a mould

castle NOUN **1** a large old fortified building **2** a piece in chess, also called a *rook*

castor NOUN a small wheel on the leg of a piece of furniture

castor oil NOUN oil from the seeds of a tropical plant, used as a laxative

castor sugar NOUN finely-ground white sugar

castrate VERB to remove the testicles of a male animal
  ▶ **castration** NOUN

casual ADJECTIVE **1** happening by chance; not planned **2** not careful or methodical **3** informal; suitable for informal occasions *casual clothes* **4** not permanent *casual work* ▶ **casually** ADVERB

THESAURUS

trunk • *a packing case* ▶ box, chest, crate, container • *a handsome display case* ▶ cabinet, cupboard, showcase • *another case of mistaken identity* ▶ instance, example, occurrence • *Is that the case?* ▶ situation, position, state of affairs • *a police case* ▶ investigation, inquiry • *a*

legal case ▶ lawsuit, action, legal action

cast VERB • *He cast a coin into the fountain.* ▶ throw, toss, fling, sling • *The statue is cast in bronze.* ▶ mould, form, shape, model

casual ADJECTIVE • *a casual meeting* ▶ chance, unexpected, unforeseen, unplanned,

DICTIONARY

casualty NOUN **casualties**
someone who is killed or injured in
war or in an accident

cat NOUN **1** a small furry domestic
animal **2** a wild animal of the same
family as a domestic cat, e.g. a
lion, tiger, or leopard **let the cat
out of the bag** to reveal a secret

catacombs (kat-a-koomz) PLURAL
NOUN underground passages with
compartments for tombs

catalogue NOUN **1** a list of items
arranged in order **2** a book
containing a list of things for sale

catalogue VERB to enter
something in a catalogue

catamaran NOUN a boat with two
parallel hulls

catapult NOUN **1** a device with
elastic for shooting small stones
2 an ancient military weapon for
hurling stones etc.

catapult VERB to hurl or rush
violently

cataract NOUN **1** a large waterfall
or rush of water **2** a cloudy area
that forms in the eye and prevents
clear sight

catarrh (ka-tar) NOUN
inflammation in the nose that
makes it drip a watery fluid

catastrophe NOUN a sudden
great disaster ▶ **catastrophic**
ADJECTIVE

catch VERB **caught 1** to take and
hold something **2** to arrest or
capture **3** to overtake **4** to be in
time to get on a bus or train etc.
5 to be infected with an illness **6** to
hear *I didn't catch what you said.*
7 to discover someone doing
something wrong **8** to make or
become held or entangled on
something sharp **9** to hit or strike
The blow caught him on the nose.
catch fire to start burning **catch
on 1** to become popular **2** to
understand

catch NOUN **1** the act of catching
something **2** something caught or

THESAURUS

accidental • *a casual remark*
▶ offhand, spontaneous,
impromptu • *a casual
acquaintance* ▶ slight, vague • *a
casual approach to life* ▶ relaxed,
nonchalant, carefree, easy-going
• *a casual glance* ▶ cursory,
fleeting, passing, quick • *casual
clothes* ▶ informal

catastrophe NOUN • *The floods
were a catastrophe.* ▶ calamity,
tragedy, misfortune

catch VERB • *to catch a ball*
▶ seize, grab, take hold of, grip,

clutch • *to catch fish* ▶ hook, net,
land, trap • *to catch a thief*
▶ capture, arrest, apprehend • *to
catch a train* ▶ board, be in time
for, get to • *to catch an illness*
▶ contract, develop, get, go down
with • *She caught them in the act.*
▶ discover, find, surprise **catch up**
• *We can catch them up.* ▶ reach,
overtake, draw level with

catch NOUN • *the fishermen's catch*
▶ haul, net, booty, prize • *There
must be a catch.* ▶ snag,
disadvantage, difficulty,

a
b
c
d
e
f
g
h
i
j
k
l
m
n
o
p
q
r
s
t
u
v
w
x
y
z

worth catching **3** a hidden difficulty **4** a device for fastening something

catching ADJECTIVE (of an illness) infectious

catchment area NOUN **1** the area from which a hospital takes patients or a school takes pupils **2** the whole area from which water drains into a river or reservoir

catchphrase NOUN a familiar or popular phrase

catchy ADJECTIVE (of a tune) pleasant and easy to remember

categorical ADJECTIVE definite and absolute *a categorical refusal*
▸ **categorically** ADVERB

category NOUN **categories** a set of people or things classified as being similar to each other

cater VERB **1** to provide food **2** to provide what is needed ▸ **caterer** NOUN

caterpillar NOUN the wormlike larva of a butterfly or moth

cathedral NOUN the most important church of a district, usually the seat of a bishop

Catherine wheel NOUN a firework that spins round

✎ **WORD HISTORY**
named after St *Catherine*, who was martyred on a spiked wheel

cathode NOUN the electrode by which electric current leaves a device

cathode ray tube NOUN a tube used in televisions and monitors, in which a beam of electrons from a cathode produces an image on a fluorescent screen

Catholic ADJECTIVE belonging to the Roman Catholic Church
▸ **Catholicism** NOUN

Catholic NOUN a Roman Catholic

catholic ADJECTIVE including most things *catholic tastes*

catkin NOUN a spike of small soft flowers on trees such as hazel and willow

Catseye NOUN (trademark) one of a line of reflecting studs marking the centre or edge of a road

cattle PLURAL NOUN animals with horns and hoofs, kept by farmers for milk and beef

catty ADJECTIVE **cattier, cattiest** speaking or spoken spitefully

cauldron NOUN a large deep pot for boiling

cauliflower NOUN a cabbage with a large head of white flowers

cause NOUN **1** a person or thing that produces a result or effect **2** a reason *no cause for worry* **3** an aim or purpose for which people work

drawback, problem • *a window catch* ▸ latch, lock, fastening, bolt

category NOUN • *each category of writing* ▸ type, kind, sort, class

cater VERB **cater for** • *The hotel will cater for vegetarians.* ▸ provide

for, make arrangements for, feed, cook for

cause NOUN • *the cause of the explosion* ▸ source, origin, reason (for) • *no cause for alarm* ▸ reason, grounds, justification, need

DICTIONARY

cause *VERB* to be the cause of

causeway *NOUN* a raised road across low or marshy ground

caustic *ADJECTIVE* **1** able to burn or wear things away by chemical action **2** sarcastic

caution *NOUN* **1** care taken in order to avoid danger etc. **2** a warning

caution *VERB* to warn

cautionary *ADJECTIVE* giving a warning

cautious ► *ADJECTIVE* showing caution ► **cautiously** *ADVERB*

cavalcade *NOUN* a large procession

Cavalier *NOUN* a supporter of King Charles I in the English Civil War (1642–9)

cavalry *NOUN* soldiers who fight on horseback or in armoured vehicles

cave *NOUN* a large hollow place in a hill or cliff or underground

cave *VERB* **cave in 1** to fall inwards **2** to give way in an argument

caveman *NOUN* **cavemen** a person living in a cave in prehistoric times

cavern *NOUN* a large cave

cavernous *ADJECTIVE* (of a space) large and hollow

caviar or **caviare** (kav-ee-ar) *NOUN* the pickled roe of sturgeon or other large fish

cavil *VERB* **cavilling**, **cavilled** to raise petty objections

cavity *NOUN* **cavities** a hollow or hole

cavort *VERB* jump or run about excitedly

cc *ABBREVIATION* cubic centimetre(s)

CD *ABBREVIATION* compact disc

CD-ROM *ABBREVIATION* compact disc read-only memory; a compact disc on which large amounts of data can be stored and then displayed on a computer screen

CDT *ABBREVIATION* craft, design, and technology

cease *VERB* to stop or end

ceasefire *NOUN* a signal for armies to stop fighting or firing weapons

THESAURUS

cause *VERB* • *The weather caused delays.* ► bring about, result in, give rise to, lead to, produce • *Poor health caused him to give up work.* ► force, compel, lead, encourage, make

caution *NOUN* • *Extreme caution is needed.* ► care, attentiveness, carefulness, wariness, vigilance

• *let off with a caution* ► reprimand, warning

cautious *ADJECTIVE* • *a cautious man who avoided risks* ► careful, attentive, vigilant, prudent • *a cautious response* ► guarded, discreet, tactful

cease *VERB* • *Hostilities have ceased.* ► end, stop, finish, come or bring to an end, conclude

a
b
c
d
e
f
g
h
i
j
k
l
m
n
o
p
q
r
s
t
u
v
w
x
y
z

ceaseless ADJECTIVE not stopping

cedar NOUN an evergreen tree with hard fragrant wood

cede VERB to give up your rights to something

ceilidh (kay-lee) NOUN an informal gathering for music and dancing, especially in Scotland

ceiling NOUN **1** the flat surface under the top of a room **2** the highest limit of something

celebrate VERB **1** to do something enjoyable on a special day **2** to perform a religious ceremony ► **celebration** NOUN

celebrated ADJECTIVE famous

celebrity NOUN **celebrities 1** a famous person **2** fame

celery NOUN a vegetable with crisp white or green stems

celibate ADJECTIVE remaining unmarried or not having sex ► **celibacy** NOUN

cell NOUN **1** a small room in a prison, monastery, etc. **2** a microscopic unit of living matter **3** a device for producing electric current chemically **4** a small group or unit in an organization

cellar NOUN an underground room

cello (chel-oh) NOUN **cellos** a musical instrument like a large violin, placed between the knees of a player ► **cellist** NOUN

Cellophane NOUN (trademark) a thin transparent wrapping material

cellular ADJECTIVE to do with or containing cells

celluloid NOUN a kind of plastic

cellulose NOUN tissue that forms the main part of all plants and trees

Celsius (sel-see-us) ADJECTIVE measuring temperature on a scale using 100 degrees, in which water freezes at 0° and boils at 100°

Celtic (kel-tik) ADJECTIVE **1** to do with the peoples of ancient Britain and France before the Romans, or of their descendants in Ireland, Scotland, and Wales **2** of the languages of these peoples

cement NOUN **1** a mixture of lime and clay used in building **2** a strong glue

cement VERB **1** to put cement on **2** to join firmly

cemetery NOUN **cemeteries** a place where people are buried

cenotaph NOUN a monument to people who are buried elsewhere

censor NOUN an official who examines films, books, etc. and

THESAURUS

celebrate VERB • They celebrated with champagne. ► enjoy yourself, have fun, have a good time • to celebrate a golden wedding ► commemorate, mark, honour, remember

celebration NOUN • It was a fabulous birthday celebration. ► party, function, festivity • a cause for celebration ► festivities, merrymaking, enjoying yourself, partying

removes or bans anything that seems harmful ► **censorship** NOUN

censor VERB to ban or remove material from films, books, etc.

⚠ USAGE

Do not confuse this word with *censure*.

censure NOUN strong criticism or disapproval of something

censure VERB to criticize or disapprove of someone or something

⚠ USAGE

Do not confuse this word with *censor*.

census NOUN an official count of the population

cent NOUN a coin worth one-hundredth of a dollar

centaur NOUN (in Greek myths) a creature with the upper body, head, and arms of a man and the lower body of a horse

centenary NOUN **centenaries** a 100th anniversary

centigrade ADJECTIVE a temperature scale based on 100 degrees, especially Celsius

centilitre NOUN one hundredth of a litre

centimetre NOUN one hundredth of a metre

centipede NOUN a small crawling creature with many legs

central ADJECTIVE **1** to do with or at the centre **2** most important
► **centrally** ADVERB

central heating NOUN a system of heating a building by circulating hot water or hot air or steam from a central source

centralize VERB to bring under the control of a central authority
► **centralization** NOUN

⚠ SPELLING

This word can also be spelled *centralise*.

centre NOUN **1** the middle point or part **2** an important place **3** a building or place for a special purpose *a shopping centre*

centre VERB to place something at the centre **centre on 1** to be concentrated in **2** to have as the main subject or concern

centre of gravity NOUN the point in an object around which its mass is perfectly balanced

centrifugal ADJECTIVE moving away from the centre

century NOUN **centuries 1** a period of 100 years **2** 100 runs scored in cricket

ceramic ADJECTIVE to do with or made of pottery

ceramics PLURAL NOUN the art of making pottery

cereal NOUN **1** a grass producing seeds which are used as food,

central ADJECTIVE • *the central chamber* ► innermost, inner, interior, middle • *the central issues* ► chief, key, main, essential, principal, fundamental

centre NOUN • *the centre of a circle* ► middle, mid-point, heart, core, eye, bullseye • *The town hall is in the centre of the city.* ► middle, heart, nucleus

e.g. wheat, barley, rice **2** a breakfast food made from these seeds

⚠️ **USAGE**

Do not confuse this word with *serial*.

cerebral ADJECTIVE to do with the brain

cerebral palsy NOUN a condition caused by brain damage before birth, causing spasms of the muscles

ceremonial ADJECTIVE to do with a ceremony; formal
▶ **ceremonially** ADVERB

ceremonious ADJECTIVE full of ceremony; elaborately performed

ceremony NOUN **ceremonies** the formal actions carried out on an important occasion

certain ADJECTIVE **1** sure; without doubt **2** known but not named *a certain person*

certainly ADVERB **1** for certain **2** yes; of course

certainty NOUN **certainties 1** something that is sure to happen **2** the state of being sure

certificate NOUN an official written or printed statement giving information about a person etc. *a birth certificate*

certify VERB **certifies**, **certified** to declare formally that something is true ▶ **certification** NOUN

cessation NOUN (*formal*) the ending of something

CFC ABBREVIATION chlorofluorocarbon; a gas that is thought to be harmful to the environment

chafe VERB **1** to make or become sore by rubbing **2** to become impatient

chaff[1] NOUN husks of corn, separated from the seed

chaff[2] VERB to tease pleasantly

chaffinch NOUN a kind of finch

chain NOUN **1** a row of linked metal rings **2** a connected series of things *a mountain chain* **3** a number of shops or other businesses owned by the same company

chain VERB to fasten with a chain

chain reaction NOUN a series of happenings in which each causes the next

certain ADJECTIVE • *I was certain of it.* ▶ sure, confident, positive, convinced • *certain failure* ▶ inevitable, inescapable, unavoidable • *certain to win* ▶ sure, bound • *a certain person* ▶ particular, specific

certainly ADVERB • *This is certainly true.* ▶ undoubtedly, unquestionably, surely, undeniably, definitely

chain NOUN • *prisoners in chains* ▶ shackles, irons, manacles, handcuffs • *a chain of events* ▶ series, sequence, succession, string, course, train • *a chain of supermarkets* ▶ group, firm, series

chain VERB • *The bicycle was chained to a fence.* ▶ tie, fasten, secure, lock

chair NOUN **1** a seat with a back, for one person **2** the person in charge of a meeting

chair VERB to be in charge of a meeting

chairman or **chairperson** NOUN **chairmen** or **chairpersons** the person in charge of a meeting

chalet (shal-ay) NOUN **1** a Swiss hut or cottage **2** a small house in a holiday camp

chalice NOUN a large goblet for holding wine, especially in Christian services

chalk NOUN **1** soft white limestone **2** a white or coloured stick used on blackboards ► **chalky** ADJECTIVE

challenge NOUN **1** an exciting but difficult task or activity **2** a call to someone to take part in a contest

challenge VERB **1** to make a challenge to **2** to be a challenge to **3** to question whether something is true or correct ► **challenger** NOUN

challenging ADJECTIVE exciting but difficult

chamber NOUN **1** a room **2** a hall used for meetings of a parliament or a judicial body **3** a compartment in a weapon or piece of machinery

chambermaid NOUN a woman employed to clean bedrooms at a hotel

chameleon (ka-mee-lee-on) NOUN a small lizard that can change its colour to match its surroundings

chamois NOUN **1** (sham-wa) a small wild antelope living in the mountains **2** (sham-ee) a piece of soft yellow leather used for washing and polishing

champ VERB to munch or bite noisily

champagne (sham-payn) NOUN a sparkling white French wine

champion NOUN **1** a person, animal, or thing that has defeated all the others in a sport or competition **2** someone who actively supports a cause ► **championship** NOUN

champion VERB to support a cause by fighting or speaking for it

chance NOUN **1** an opportunity or possibility **2** the way things happen without being planned **take a chance** to take a risk

chance VERB **1** to happen by chance *I chanced to meet her.* **2** to risk something

THESAURUS

challenge VERB • to challenge an intruder ► confront, accost, take on • to challenge his abilities ► test, stretch • to challenge an enemy to a duel ► dare, invite, defy • to challenge the decision ► dispute, oppose, object to, question

chance NOUN • a slight chance of snow ► possibility, likelihood, risk, danger • Give them a chance. ► opportunity, turn • We were taking a chance. ► risk, gamble **by chance** • I found the earring by chance. ► by accident, accidentally

chancellor NOUN **1** an important government or legal official **2** the chief minister of the government in some European countries

Chancellor of the Exchequer NOUN the government minister in charge of a country's finances and taxes

chancy ADJECTIVE **chancier, chanciest** risky

chandelier NOUN a support for several lights or candles that hangs from the ceiling

change VERB **1** to make or become different **2** to exchange **3** to put on different clothes **4** to go from one train or bus etc. to another **5** to give smaller units of money, or money in another currency, for an amount of money

change NOUN **1** the process of changing **2** a difference in doing something **3** coins or notes of small values **4** money given back when the price is less than the amount handed over **5** a fresh set of clothes **6** a variation in routine

changeable ADJECTIVE likely to change; often changing

channel NOUN **1** a way for water to flow **2** a stretch of water connecting two seas **3** a broadcasting wavelength **4** the part of a river or sea deep enough for ships

channel VERB **channelling, channelled 1** to make a channel in something **2** to direct through a channel or in a particular direction

chant NOUN **1** a simple repeated tune in church music **2** a rhythmic call or shout

chant VERB **1** to sing a chant **2** to call out words in a rhythm

chaos (kay-oss) NOUN great confusion or disorder

chaotic ADJECTIVE in a state of great confusion ▶ **chaotically** ADVERB

chap NOUN (informal) a man

chapel NOUN **1** a small building or room used for Christian worship **2** a section of a large church with its own altar

chaplain NOUN a member of the clergy attached to a college, hospital, army regiment, etc.

change NOUN • *a change of plan* ▶ alteration, modification, variation • *A change will do you good.* ▶ novelty, variety • *I'm out of change.* ▶ coins, small change, loose change

change VERB • *to change life for ever* ▶ alter, transform, modify • *Things have changed.* ▶ alter, become different, develop • *to change a library book* ▶ exchange, swap, switch, replace

changeable ADJECTIVE • *changeable weather* ▶ variable, unsettled, unpredictable

chaos NOUN • *There was total chaos.* ▶ confusion, disorder, mayhem, pandemonium

chaotic ADJECTIVE • *a chaotic jumble of noise* ▶ disorderly, confused, disorganized, muddled

chapped ADJECTIVE with skin split or cracked from cold

chapter NOUN 1 a division of a book 2 the clergy of a cathedral or members of a monastery

char ¹ VERB **charring, charred** to make or become black by burning

char ² NOUN (informal) a woman employed as a cleaner

character NOUN 1 a person in a story, film, or play 2 all the qualities a person or thing has 3 a letter of the alphabet or other written symbol

characteristic NOUN a quality that forms part of a person's or thing's character

characteristic ADJECTIVE typical of a person or thing
▶ **characteristically** ADVERB

characterize VERB 1 to be a characteristic of 2 to describe the

character of ▶ **characterization** NOUN

⚠ **SPELLING**

This word can also be spelled *characterise*.

charade (sha-rahd) NOUN 1 a scene in the game (*charades*) in which people try to guess a word from other people's acting 2 a pretence

charcoal NOUN a black substance made from burnt wood, used for drawing

charge NOUN 1 the price asked for something 2 a rushing attack 3 the amount of explosive needed to fire a gun 4 an amount of stored electricity 5 an accusation that someone has committed a crime 6 a person or thing in someone's care **in charge** in control or authority

charge VERB 1 to ask a particular price 2 to rush forward in an attack 3 to give an electric charge to 4 to

character NOUN • *a forceful character* ▶ personality, temperament, nature • *The parks add a special character to the town.* ▶ distinctiveness, individuality • *without a stain on his character* ▶ reputation, name • *a charming character* ▶ person, individual, type • *a woman of character* ▶ integrity, honour • *a character in a play* ▶ part, role

charge NOUN • *The charges have increased.* ▶ fee, price, cost, tariff • *to face criminal charges* ▶ accusation, allegation • *a*

charge on enemy defences ▶ assault, attack, onslaught, offensive, raid **in charge of** • *in charge of the factory* ▶ responsible for, in control of, managing, running

charge VERB • *What do they charge for a coffee?* ▶ ask for, ask in payment, require • *The witness was charged with perjury.* ▶ accuse (of), prosecute (for), put on trial (for) • *The cavalry charged the enemy line.* ▶ attack, storm, rush, assault

accuse of committing a crime **5** to entrust with a responsibility or task

chariot NOUN a horse-drawn vehicle with two wheels, used in ancient times for fighting and racing ► **charioteer** NOUN

charity NOUN **charities 1** an organization helping people who are poor, ill, or disabled **2** the act of giving money or help to those in need **3** kindness and sympathy towards others ► **charitable** ADJECTIVE

charlatan (shar-la-tan) NOUN a person who falsely claims knowledge or ability

charm NOUN **1** the power to please or delight people **2** a magic spell **3** a small object believed to bring good luck **4** an ornament worn on a bracelet etc.

charm VERB **1** to give pleasure or delight to people **2** to put a spell on someone ► **charmer** NOUN, **charming** ADJECTIVE

chart NOUN **1** a map used in sailing ships or flying aircraft **2** an outline map showing special information

a weather chart **3** a diagram, list, or table of information **the charts** a list of the records that are most popular

chart VERB to make a chart of

charter NOUN **1** an official document granting rights **2** the act of chartering an aircraft, ship, or vehicle

chary (chair-ee) ADJECTIVE cautious about doing or giving something

chase VERB to go quickly after a person or thing to capture or catch them up ► **chase** NOUN

chasm (kazm) NOUN a deep opening in the ground

chassis (shass-ee) NOUN the framework on which a vehicle is built

chaste ADJECTIVE not having sex outside marriage or at all

chasten (chay-sen) VERB to make someone realize that they have done wrong

chastise VERB to punish or scold severely ► **chastisement** NOUN

chastity (chas-ti-ti) NOUN the state of being chaste or sexually pure

charity NOUN • *Show some charity.*
► goodwill, generosity, kindness, sympathy • *the charity of the public* ► financial assistance, generosity, donations, contributions

charm NOUN • *His charm and humour returned.*
► attractiveness, appeal, charisma, desirability • *magical charms* ► spell, incantation, • *a*

lucky charm ► trinket, talisman, amulet, mascot

charm VERB • *She charmed everyone with her stories.*
► delight, please, captivate, enchant

charming ADJECTIVE • *a charming baby* ► delightful, attractive, pleasant, endearing

chase VERB • *to chase intruders*
► pursue, run after, track, follow, hunt

DICTIONARY

chat NOUN a friendly conversation

chat VERB **chatting, chatted** to have a friendly conversation

chatter VERB **1** to talk about unimportant things **2** (of the teeth) to make a rattling sound from cold or fright

chatter NOUN chattering talk or sound

chatterbox NOUN a talkative person

chauffeur (shoh-fer) NOUN a person employed to drive a car

chauvinism NOUN **1** unthinking support for your own country **2** the belief that men are superior to women ▶ **chauvinist** NOUN, **chauvinistic** ADJECTIVE

cheap ADJECTIVE **1** low in price; not expensive **2** of poor quality ▶ **cheaply** ADVERB

cheapen VERB to make cheap

cheat VERB **1** to act dishonestly to gain an advantage **2** to trick or deceive somebody out of something

cheat NOUN a person who cheats

check[1] VERB **1** to make sure that something is correct or in good condition **2** to make something stop or go slower

check NOUN **1** the act of checking something **2** a pause or act of stopping **3** (American) a receipt; a bill in a restaurant **4** the situation in chess when the king is directly threatened

check[2] NOUN a pattern of squares ▶ **checked** ADJECTIVE

checkmate NOUN the winning situation in chess

checkout NOUN a place where goods are paid for in a supermarket

checkpoint NOUN a place on a road where traffic is stopped and checked

cheek NOUN **1** the side of the face below the eye **2** rude or disrespectful behaviour

cheeky ADJECTIVE rude or disrespectful ▶ **cheekily** ADVERB

THESAURUS

cheap ADJECTIVE • *a cheap edition of Shakespeare* ▶ inexpensive, low-priced, affordable, reasonable • *cheap digital watches* ▶ inferior, second-rate, shoddy • *cheap tabloid journalism* ▶ mean, despicable, low, contemptible

cheat VERB • *to cheat customers* ▶ swindle, defraud, deceive, exploit

cheat NOUN • *He called his brother a cheat.* ▶ swindler, deceiver, fraud

check VERB • *Police were checking vehicles.* ▶ examine, inspect, test, scrutinize • *to check an answer* ▶ verify, confirm, compare

check NOUN • *an official check of passports* ▶ inspection, examination

cheek NOUN • *What cheek I had!* ▶ audacity, effrontery, nerve, impertinence, insolence

cheeky ADJECTIVE • *a cheeky child* ▶ impudent, impertinent, insolent, disrespectful

a
b
c
d
e
f
g
h
i
j
k
l
m
n
o
p
q
r
s
t
u
v
w
x
y
z

cheer NOUN a shout of praise or encouragement

cheer VERB **1** to give a cheer **2** to gladden or encourage **cheer up** to make or become cheerful

cheerful ADJECTIVE **1** looking or sounding happy **2** pleasantly bright or colourful ▶ **cheerfully** ADVERB

cheerio EXCLAMATION (informal) goodbye

cheerless ADJECTIVE gloomy or dreary

cheers EXCLAMATION (informal) **1** good health **2** goodbye **3** thank you

cheery ADJECTIVE **cheerier**, **cheeriest** bright and cheerful

cheese NOUN a solid food made from milk

cheesecake NOUN a dessert made of a mixture of sweetened curds on a layer of biscuit

cheetah NOUN a large fast-running spotted animal of the cat family

chef NOUN the cook in a hotel or restaurant

chemical ADJECTIVE to do with or produced by chemistry

chemical NOUN a substance obtained by or used in chemistry

chemist NOUN **1** a person who makes or sells medicines **2** a shop selling medicines and toiletries **3** an expert in chemistry

chemistry NOUN the study of how substances combine and react with one another

cheque NOUN a printed form for writing instructions to a bank to pay money from an account

chequered ADJECTIVE marked with a pattern of squares

cherish VERB **1** to look after a person or thing lovingly **2** to be fond of

cherry NOUN **cherries** a small soft round fruit with a stone

cherub NOUN an angel shown as a chubby child with wings

chess NOUN a game for two players with sixteen pieces each (called **chessmen**) on a board of 64 squares (a **chessboard**)

chest NOUN **1** the front part of the body between the neck and the waist **2** a large strong box for storing things

chestnut NOUN **1** a tree that produces hard brown nuts **2** the nut of this tree **3** an old joke

THESAURUS

cheer VERB • to cheer the team ▶ applaud, clap, shout • The good news cheered them. ▶ comfort, console, gladden, encourage, make cheerful **cheer up** • I began to cheer up. ▶ take heart, perk up, brighten

cheer NOUN • The spectators gave her a cheer. ▶ hurrah, shout of approval, ovation, applause

cheerful ADJECTIVE • a cheerful person ▶ happy, jolly, joyful, buoyant, good-humoured, light-hearted

chevron (shev-ron) NOUN a V-shaped stripe on a sign or road marking

chew VERB to grind food between the teeth ► **chewy** ADJECTIVE

chic (sheek) ADJECTIVE stylish and elegant

chick NOUN a young bird

chicken NOUN **1** a young hen **2** a hen's flesh used as food

chicken ADJECTIVE (informal) lacking courage; cowardly

chicken VERB **chicken out** (informal) to fail to do something from fear

chickenpox NOUN a disease that produces red spots on the skin

chickpea NOUN the yellow seed of a plant of the pea family, eaten as a vegetable

chicory NOUN a plant with leaves that are used in salads

chide VERB to scold

chief NOUN **1** a leader or ruler of a people **2** a person with the highest rank or authority

chief ADJECTIVE most important; main ► **chiefly** ADVERB

chieftain NOUN the leader of a tribe or clan

chiffon (shif-on) NOUN a thin almost transparent fabric

chilblain NOUN a sore swollen place on a hand or foot, caused by cold

child NOUN **children 1** a young person; a boy or girl **2** a person's son or daughter

childhood NOUN the time when a person is a child

childish ADJECTIVE **1** like a child; unsuitable for a grown person **2** silly and immature ► **childishly** ADVERB

childless ADJECTIVE having no children

childlike ADJECTIVE like a child in appearance or behaviour

childminder NOUN a person who is paid to look after children while their parents are out

chill NOUN **1** unpleasant coldness **2** an illness that makes you shiver

chill VERB **1** to make a person or thing cold **2** (informal) to relax

chilli NOUN **chillies** the hot-tasting pod of a red pepper

THESAURUS

chief ADJECTIVE • the chief problem ► main, principal, fundamental, crucial, central • the chief cook ► head, senior, principal, leading

chiefly ADVERB • We were chiefly to blame for the damage. ► mainly, mostly, principally, predominantly

child NOUN • She was only a child. ► youngster, girl (or boy), baby, infant, kid • the child of Greek parents ► offspring, daughter (or son), descendant

childish ADJECTIVE • It was childish of him to say that. ► immature, babyish, puerile, juvenile, silly

chilly ADJECTIVE **chillier, chilliest**
1 rather cold **2** unfriendly
▶ **chilliness** NOUN

chime NOUN a series of notes sounded by a set of bells

chime VERB to make a chime

chimney pot NOUN a pipe fitted to the top of a chimney

chimney NOUN **chimneys** a tall pipe or structure that carries smoke away from a fire

chimpanzee NOUN a small African ape

chin NOUN the lower part of the face below the mouth

china NOUN thin delicate pottery

chink NOUN **1** a narrow opening **2** a chinking sound

chink VERB to make a sound like glasses or coins being struck together

chintz NOUN a shiny cotton cloth used for making curtains

chip NOUN **1** a thin piece cut or broken off something hard **2** a fried oblong strip of potato **3** a place where a small piece has been knocked off **4** a small counter used in games **5** a microchip **a chip on your shoulder** resentment about something

chip VERB **chipping, chipped** to knock small pieces off something

chipboard NOUN board made from chips of wood pressed and stuck together

chirp VERB to make short sharp sounds like a bird ▶ **chirp** NOUN

chirpy ADJECTIVE **chirpier, chirpiest** lively and cheerful

chisel NOUN a tool with a sharp end for shaping wood or stone

chisel VERB **chiselling, chiselled** to shape or cut with a chisel

chivalry NOUN kindness and consideration towards people less strong than yourself
▶ **chivalrous** ADJECTIVE

chive NOUN a small herb with leaves that taste like onions

chivvy VERB **chivvies, chivvied** to hurry someone along

chlorine NOUN a greenish-yellow gas used to disinfect water etc.

chloroform NOUN a liquid with a vapour that makes people unconscious

chlorophyll NOUN a substance in plants that traps sunlight and makes them green

chock-a-block ADJECTIVE crammed or crowded together

chock-full ADJECTIVE crammed full

chocolate NOUN **1** a solid brown food or powder made from roasted cacao seeds **2** a drink made with this powder **3** a sweet made of or covered with chocolate

choice NOUN **1** the act of choosing between things **2** the range of things from which someone can

THESAURUS

chilly ADJECTIVE • *a chilly evening*
▶ cold, crisp, fresh, cool, frosty
• *a chilly reception* ▶ unfriendly,
cool, lukewarm, unwelcoming,
hostile

choice NOUN • *We have no other choice now.* ▶ option, alternative,
possibility • *the viewers' choice of programmes* ▶ selection,
choosing, preference • *Write in*

choose *a wide choice of holidays*
3 a person or thing chosen

choice ADJECTIVE of the best quality

choir NOUN a group of people trained to sing together, especially in a church

choke VERB **1** to be unable to breathe, or to stop someone breathing **2** to clog or block up

choke NOUN a device controlling the flow of air into an engine

cholera (kol-er-a) NOUN a serious infectious disease causing vomiting and diarrhoea

cholesterol (kol-est-er-ol) NOUN a fatty substance that can clog the arteries

choose VERB chose, chosen **1** to decide from several possibilities **2** to decide to do something

choosy ADJECTIVE choosier, choosiest fussy and difficult to please

chop VERB chopping, chopped to cut or hit with a heavy blow

chop NOUN **1** a chopping blow **2** a small thick slice of meat

chopper NOUN **1** a small axe **2** (*informal*) a helicopter

choppy ADJECTIVE choppier, choppiest (of the sea) not smooth; full of small waves

chopsticks PLURAL NOUN a pair of thin sticks used for eating Chinese and Japanese food

choral ADJECTIVE to do with or sung by a choir or chorus

chord (kord) NOUN **1** a number of musical notes sounded together **2** a straight line joining two points on a curve

chore NOUN a regular or dull task

chortle VERB to give a loud chuckle
 ▶ **chortle** NOUN

chorus NOUN **1** the words repeated after each verse of a song or poem **2** music sung by a group of people **3** a group singing together

chorus VERB to sing or speak the same words at the same time

christen (kris-en) VERB **1** to baptize **2** to give a name to
 ▶ **christening** NOUN

Christian NOUN a person who believes in Jesus Christ and his teachings

Christian ADJECTIVE to do with Christians or their beliefs
 ▶ **Christianity** NOUN

THESAURUS

with your choice. ▶ selection, vote, nomination • *a wide choice* ▶ range, variety, selection, array, assortment

choose VERB • *We chose a quiet spot by the river.* ▶ pick, select, opt for, settle on, decide on • *Mark chose to go in first.*

 ▶ decide, elect, make up your mind, determine

chop VERB • *to chop wood* ▶ cut, hew • *to chop vegetables* ▶ cut up, slice, dice • *to chop down a tree* ▶ cut down, fell **chop off** • *to chop off a branch* ▶ sever, detach, lop off

a
b
c
d
e
f
g
h
i
j
k
l
m
n
o
p
q
r
s
t
u
v
w
x
y
z

Christmas NOUN the day (25 December) when Christians commemorate the birth of Jesus Christ

chromatic ADJECTIVE **1** to do with colours **2** (of a musical scale) going up or down in semitones

chrome NOUN chromium

chromium (kroh-mee-um) NOUN a shiny silvery metal

chromosome (kroh-mos-ohm) NOUN a tiny thread-like part of an animal cell or plant cell, carrying genes

chronic ADJECTIVE (of an illness) lasting for a long time
▶ **chronically** ADVERB

chronicle NOUN a record of events in the order in which they happened

chronological ADJECTIVE arranged in the order in which things happened
▶ **chronologically** ADVERB

chronology NOUN **chronologies** the arrangement of events according to their dates or the order in which they happened

chronometer (kron-om-it-er) NOUN a device for measuring time accurately

chrysalis NOUN the hard cover a caterpillar makes round itself before it changes into a butterfly or moth

chrysanthemum NOUN a garden flower that blooms in autumn

chubby ADJECTIVE **chubbier, chubbiest** plump

chuck[1] VERB (informal) to throw clumsily

chuck[2] NOUN **1** the gripping part of a lathe **2** the part of a drill that holds the bit

chuckle NOUN a quiet laugh

chuckle VERB to laugh quietly

chug VERB **chugging, chugged** to make the sound of an engine running slowly

chum NOUN (informal) a friend

chunk NOUN a thick piece of something ▶ **chunky** ADJECTIVE

church NOUN **1** a public building for Christian worship **2** a particular Christian religion

churlish ADJECTIVE bad-mannered and unfriendly

churn NOUN **1** a large can for transporting milk **2** a machine for beating milk to make butter

churn VERB **1** to make butter in a churn **2** to stir or swirl vigorously **churn out** to produce something in large quantities

chute NOUN a steep channel for people or things to slide down

chutney NOUN **chutneys** a strong-tasting sauce made with fruit, peppers, etc.

THESAURUS

chubby ADJECTIVE • *a chubby little baby* ▶ plump, tubby, podgy, round

chunk NOUN • *a chunk of cheese* ▶ lump, hunk, block, piece, slab

cider NOUN an alcoholic drink made from apples

cigar NOUN a roll of compressed tobacco leaves for smoking

cigarette NOUN a roll of shredded tobacco in thin paper for smoking

cinder NOUN a piece of partly burnt coal or wood

cine camera (sin-ee) NOUN a camera used for taking moving pictures

cinema NOUN 1 a place where films are shown 2 the business or art of making films

cinnamon NOUN a reddish-brown spice

cipher NOUN 1 a kind of code 2 the symbol 0, for nought or zero

circle NOUN 1 a perfectly round flat shape or thing 2 the balcony of a cinema or theatre 3 a number of people with similar interests

circle VERB 1 to move in a circle 2 to go round something

circuit (ser-kit) NOUN 1 a circular line or journey 2 a track for motor racing 3 the path of an electric current

circular ADJECTIVE 1 shaped like a circle; round 2 moving round a circle

circular NOUN a letter or advertisement sent to a number of people

circulate VERB 1 to go round continuously *Blood circulates in the body.* 2 to pass from place to

place 3 to send something to several people

circulation NOUN 1 the movement of blood around the body 2 the number of copies of a newspaper or magazine that are sold or distributed

circumcise VERB to cut off the fold of skin at the tip of the penis ▸ **circumcision** NOUN

circumference NOUN the line or distance round a circle

circumspect ADJECTIVE cautious and vigilant ▸ **circumspection** NOUN

circumstance NOUN a fact or condition connected with an event or person or action

circumstantial ADJECTIVE consisting of facts that suggest something but do not prove it *circumstantial evidence*

circus NOUN a travelling show performed in a tent, with clowns, acrobats, and sometimes performing animals

cistern NOUN a tank for storing water

citadel NOUN a fortress protecting a city

cite VERB to quote as an example ▸ **citation** NOUN

citizen NOUN a person belonging to a particular city or country

citizenry NOUN all the citizens of a place

THESAURUS

circle NOUN • *The children stood in a circle.* ▸ ring, round • *He has a*

new circle of friends. ▸ group, set, band, gang, party

a
b
c
d
e
f
g
h
i
j
k
l
m
n
o
p
q
r
s
t
u
v
w
x
y
z

citizenship NOUN the rights or duties of a citizen

citrus fruit NOUN a sharp-tasting fruit such as a lemon or orange

city NOUN **cities** a large important town, often having a cathedral

civic ADJECTIVE **1** to do with a city or town **2** to do with citizens

civics NOUN the study of the rights and duties of citizens

civil ADJECTIVE **1** polite and courteous **2** to do with citizens **3** to do with civilians; not military ▸ **civilly** ADVERB

civil engineering NOUN the work of designing roads, bridges, dams, etc. ▸ **civil engineer** NOUN

civilian NOUN a person who is not serving in the armed forces

civility NOUN politeness

civilization NOUN **1** a society or culture at a particular time in history *ancient civilizations* **2** a developed or organized way of life

⚠ **SPELLING**

This word can also be spelled *civilisation*.

civilize VERB **1** to bring culture and education to a primitive community **2** to improve a person's behaviour and manners

⚠ **SPELLING**

This word can also be spelled *civilise*.

civil service NOUN people employed by the government in various departments other than the armed forces

civil war NOUN war between groups of people of the same country

clad ADJECTIVE clothed or covered

claim VERB **1** to ask for something you believe you have a right to **2** to state something without being able to prove it ▸ **claimant** NOUN

claim NOUN **1** an act of claiming **2** something claimed

clairvoyant NOUN a person who can supposedly predict future events ▸ **clairvoyance** NOUN

clam NOUN a large shellfish

clamber VERB to climb with difficulty

clammy ADJECTIVE **clammier**, **clammiest** damp and slimy

clamour NOUN **1** a loud confused noise **2** a loud protest or demand

clamour VERB to make a loud protest or demand

THESAURUS

civil ADJECTIVE • *Try to be civil.*
▸ polite, respectful, well-mannered, courteous • *a civil wedding* ▸ secular, non-religious • *civil rights* ▸ social, public

claim VERB • *to claim a refund*
▸ ask for, request, demand

• *He claimed the witness had been lying.* ▸ allege, maintain, contend, assert

claim NOUN • *a claim for damages*
▸ application, demand, request
• *an incredible claim* ▸ assertion, allegation

clamp NOUN a device for holding things tightly

clamp VERB **1** to fix with a clamp **2** to fix firmly **clamp down on** to become stricter about something

clan NOUN a group of families having the same ancestor

clandestine ADJECTIVE done secretly; kept secret

clang VERB to make a loud ringing sound ▸ **clang** NOUN

clank VERB to make a sound like heavy pieces of metal banging together ▸ **clank** NOUN

clap VERB **clapping, clapped 1** to strike the palms of the hands together loudly, especially as applause **2** to slap in a friendly way *I clapped him on the shoulder.* **3** to put quickly *They clapped him into jail.*

clap NOUN **1** a sudden sharp noise, especially of thunder **2** a round of clapping **3** a friendly slap

clapper NOUN the hanging piece inside a bell that strikes it to make it sound

claptrap NOUN insincere or foolish talk

claret NOUN a kind of French red wine

clarify VERB **clarifies, clarified** to make something clear or easier to understand ▸ **clarification** NOUN

clarinet NOUN a woodwind instrument ▸ **clarinettist** NOUN

clarity NOUN the state of being clear or understandable

clash VERB **1** to make a loud sound like cymbals banging together **2** to happen inconveniently at the same time **3** to have a fight or argument **4** (of colours) to look unpleasant together ▸ **clash** NOUN

clasp NOUN **1** a device for fastening things **2** a tight grasp

clasp VERB **1** to grasp or hold tightly **2** to fasten with a clasp

class NOUN **1** a group of children or students who are taught together

clamp VERB • *Each shelf is clamped to three brackets.* ▸ fasten, fix, secure, attach, clip

clap VERB • *The audience clapped.* ▸ applaud, cheer

clarify VERB • *to clarify the problem* ▸ explain, throw light on, make clear

clash NOUN • *a metallic clash* ▸ crash, bang • *clashes between protesters and police* ▸ fight, conflict, hostilities

clash VERB • *The cymbals clashed.* ▸ crash, strike, bang • *Rival gangs*

clashed. ▸ disagree, quarrel, fight • *The interview clashes with my holiday.* ▸ coincide, come at the same time (as)

clasp NOUN • *The bracelet needs a strong clasp.* ▸ fastening, catch, hook, clip • *His clasp loosened a bit.* ▸ hold, grasp, grip, embrace

clasp VERB • *John clasped her in his arms.* ▸ hug, hold, embrace, squeeze • *She clasped his hand.* ▸ grasp, hold, grip, clutch

class NOUN • *the best class of hotel* ▸ category, grade • *a new class of*

a
b
c
d
e
f
g
h
i
j
k
l
m
n
o
p
q
r
s
t
u
v
w
x
y
z

131

DICTIONARY

2 a group of similar people, animals, or things **3** people of the same social or economic level **4** level of quality *first class*

class VERB to arrange things in classes or groups

classic ADJECTIVE generally regarded as excellent or important

classic NOUN a classic book, film, writer, etc.

classical ADJECTIVE **1** to do with ancient Greek or Roman literature, art, etc. **2** (of music) serious or conventional in style

classics NOUN the study of ancient Greek and Latin languages and literature

classified ADJECTIVE **1** put into classes or groups **2** (of information) officially secret and available only to certain people

classify VERB **classifies, classified** to arrange things in classes or groups ▶ **classification** NOUN

classroom NOUN a room in a school where lessons are held

clatter VERB to make a sound like hard objects rattling together

clatter NOUN a clattering noise

clause NOUN **1** a single part of a treaty, law, or contract **2** (*Grammar*) a part of a sentence, with its own verb

claustrophobia NOUN fear of being inside an enclosed space

claw NOUN **1** a sharp nail on a bird's or animal's foot **2** a claw-like part or device

claw VERB to grasp, pull, or scratch with a claw or hand

clay NOUN a stiff sticky earth that becomes hard when baked

clean ADJECTIVE **1** free of dirt or stains **2** fresh; not yet used **3** honourable; not unfair *a clean fight* **4** neat and effective *a clean catch*

THESAURUS

medicine ▶ type, kind, sort
• *social class* ▶ status, position • *a history class* ▶ form, set, group

class VERB • *Her performance was classed as a distinction.* ▶ classify, categorize, grade, rank

classic ADJECTIVE • *the classic book on the subject* ▶ definitive, established, best • *a classic example* ▶ typical, characteristic, perfect

classic NOUN • *The film is a classic.* ▶ masterpiece, model

classify VERB • *to classify plants by the shape of their leaves*

▶ categorize, class, group, organize, sort

clean ADJECTIVE • *clean clothes*
▶ washed, cleaned, laundered, pristine • *Keep the wound clean.*
▶ sterile, sterilized, healthy • *a clean sheet of paper* ▶ blank, unused, empty, plain • *clean air*
▶ pure, clear, fresh • *a clean life*
▶ honest, virtuous, moral, respectable • *a clean fight* ▶ fair, honest, sporting • *a clean cut*
▶ smooth, neat, straight, accurate
• *a clean break* ▶ complete, total, final

a
b
c
d
e
f
g
h
i
j
k
l
m
n
o
p
q
r
s
t
u
v
w
x
y
z

clean VERB to make clean

clean ADVERB completely *I clean forgot.*

cleaner NOUN 1 a person who cleans rooms 2 something used for cleaning

cleanliness (klen-li-nis) NOUN the quality of being clean

cleanly (kleen-lee) ADVERB in a clean way

cleanse (klenz) VERB 1 to clean 2 to make pure ▸ **cleanser** NOUN

clear ADJECTIVE 1 transparent; not muddy or cloudy 2 easy to see or hear or understand; distinct 3 free from obstacles or unwanted things 4 free from guilt *a clear conscience* ▸ **clearly** ADVERB, **clearness** NOUN

clear ADVERB 1 distinctly; clearly *We heard you loud and clear.* 2 completely *He got clear away.* 3 apart; not in contact *Stand clear of the doors.*

clear VERB 1 to make or become clear 2 to remove everything from *clear the table* 3 to show that someone is innocent or reliable 4 to jump over without touching 5 to get approval for **clear off** *or* **out** (*informal*) to leave **clear up** 1 to make things tidy 2 to become better or brighter

clearance NOUN 1 the process of getting rid of unwanted things 2 the space between two things

clearing NOUN an open space in a forest

clean VERB • *to clean the car* ▸ wash, hose down, shampoo, polish • *to clean the bathroom floor* ▸ wash, wipe, scrub, sweep, mop • *to clean clothes* ▸ launder, dry-clean • *to clean a room* ▸ dust, brush, spruce up • *to clean a wound* ▸ cleanse, wash, bathe, disinfect

clear ADJECTIVE • *clear instructions* ▸ plain, understandable, easy • *a clear case of discrimination* ▸ evident, obvious, plain, blatant • *a pool of clear water* ▸ transparent, translucent, crystalline • *a clear day* ▸ bright, cloudless, sunny, fine • *a clear complexion* ▸ fresh, unblemished • *a clear voice* ▸ pure, distinct • *The motorway was clear again.* ▸ open, unobstructed, unblocked

• *a clear conscience* ▸ untroubled, easy, guiltless

clear VERB • *The weather is clearing.* ▸ brighten, become brighter, turn fine • *Rain will slowly clear from the south.* ▸ disappear, fade out, dwindle, diminish, peter out • *to clear a backlog of work* ▸ complete, eliminate, deal with, get rid of • *to clear drains* ▸ unblock, unclog, free • *to clear the weeds* ▸ tidy, remove, get rid of, eliminate • *to clear the building* ▸ evacuate, empty, leave • *The ball cleared the bar.* ▸ go over, go above • *The appeal judges cleared him.* ▸ acquit, exonerate, free **clear up** • *to clear up the mess* ▸ tidy (up), clean (up) • *to clear up a misunderstanding* ▸ resolve, explain, straighten out

cleavage NOUN the hollow between a woman's breasts

cleave VERB **clove** or **cleft** or **cleaved**, **cloven** or **cleft** or **cleaved** to divide by chopping

cleaver NOUN a butcher's chopping tool

clef NOUN a symbol on a stave in music, showing the pitch of the notes as treble or bass

cleft NOUN a split in something

clemency NOUN gentle or merciful treatment

clench VERB to close the teeth or fingers tightly

clergy NOUN the priests and ministers of the Christian Church

clergyman or **clergywoman** NOUN **clergymen** or **clergywomen** a Christian minister

cleric NOUN a member of the clergy

clerical ADJECTIVE **1** to do with routine office work **2** to do with the clergy

clerk NOUN an office worker who writes letters and keeps records

clever ADJECTIVE **1** quick at learning and understanding **2** skilful ▶ **cleverly** ADVERB

cliché (klee-shay) NOUN a phrase or idea that is used so often that it has little meaning

click VERB to make a short sharp sound ▶ **click** NOUN

client NOUN a person who gets help or advice from a professional person such as a lawyer or accountant

clientele (klee-on-tel) NOUN customers or clients

cliff NOUN a steep rock face on a coast

climate NOUN the regular weather conditions of an area ▶ **climatic** ADJECTIVE

climax NOUN the most interesting or important point of a story or series of events

climb VERB **1** to go up or over or down something **2** to grow upwards **3** to go higher **climb down** to admit that you have been wrong ▶ **climb** NOUN, **climber** NOUN

clinch VERB **1** to settle something definitely **2** to clasp tightly ▶ **clinch** NOUN

cling VERB **clung** to hold on tightly

cling film NOUN a thin clinging transparent film, used to wrap food

clinic NOUN a place where patients see doctors for treatment or advice

THESAURUS

clever ADJECTIVE • a clever student ▶ intelligent, bright, gifted, brilliant, intellectual

climax NOUN • the climax of her career ▶ peak, summit, highlight, high point

climb VERB • to climb stairs ▶ ascend, go up, mount, move up • The plane climbed slowly. ▶ rise, ascend, fly up, soar • The road climbs steeply. ▶ rise, ascend, slope up

DICTIONARY

clinical ADJECTIVE **1** to do with the medical treatment of patients **2** cool and unemotional
▶ **clinically** ADVERB

clink VERB to make a thin sharp sound like glasses being struck together ▶ **clink** NOUN

clip [1] NOUN a fastener for keeping things together

clip VERB **clipping, clipped** to fasten with a clip

clip [2] VERB **clipping, clipped 1** to cut with shears or scissors **2** (*informal*) to hit someone

clip NOUN a short piece of film shown on its own

clipper NOUN an old type of fast sailing ship

clippers PLURAL NOUN an instrument for cutting hair

clique (kleek) NOUN a small group of people who stick together and keep others out

cloak NOUN a piece of outdoor clothing that hangs loosely from the shoulders

cloak VERB to cover or conceal

cloakroom NOUN **1** a place where coats and bags can be left by visitors **2** a toilet in a large building

clock NOUN **1** a device that shows the time **2** a measuring device with a dial or digital display

clock VERB **clock in** or **out** to register the time you arrive at or leave work

clockwise ADVERB, ADJECTIVE moving in the same direction as the hands of a clock

clockwork NOUN a mechanism with a spring that has to be wound up **like clockwork** very regularly

clod NOUN a lump of earth or clay

clog NOUN a shoe with a wooden sole

clog VERB **clogging, clogged** to block up

clone NOUN an animal or plant made from the cells of another and exactly like it

clone VERB to produce a clone of an animal or plant

close [1] ADJECTIVE **1** near **2** detailed or concentrated *close attention* **3** with little empty space *a close fit*

THESAURUS

clip VERB • *to clip a hedge* ▶ cut, trim, snip, prune

clog VERB • *to clog the drains* ▶ block, bung up, obstruct

close ADJECTIVE • *The house is fairly close.* ▶ near, nearby • *An agreement seemed close.* ▶ imminent, impending, at hand • *a close contest* ▶ even, level, evenly matched • *a close*

formation ▶ tight, dense, compact • *close friends* ▶ intimate, dear, devoted • *close attention* ▶ careful, thorough • *The weather was close.* ▶ humid, muggy, airless, sticky, clammy
close to • *a house close to the station* ▶ near, adjacent to, alongside, not far from • *close to tears* ▶ near to, on the verge of, on the brink of

a
b
c
d
e
f
g
h
i
j
k
l
m
n
o
p
q
r
s
t
u
v
w
x
y
z

DICTIONARY

4 in which competitors are nearly equal *a close contest* **5** (of the weather) humid and stuffy
▶ **closely** ADVERB

close ADVERB closely *close behind He held her close.*

close NOUN **1** a street that is closed at one end **2** an enclosed area in a town

close² VERB **1** to shut **2** to end
close in to get nearer

close NOUN the end of a performance or event

closet NOUN (American) a cupboard or storeroom

closet VERB to shut yourself away in private

close-up NOUN a photograph or piece of film taken at close range

closure NOUN the process of closing

clot NOUN **1** a small mass of blood, cream, etc. that has become solid **2** (informal) a silly person

clot VERB **clotting, clotted** to form clots

cloth NOUN **1** woven material or felt **2** a piece of this material **3** a tablecloth

clothe VERB to put clothes on someone

clothes PLURAL NOUN things worn to cover the body

clothing NOUN clothes

cloud NOUN **1** a mass of condensed water vapour floating in the sky **2** a mass of smoke or dust in the air

cloud VERB to become cloudy

cloudburst NOUN a sudden heavy rainstorm

cloudy ADJECTIVE **cloudier, cloudiest 1** full of clouds **2** not clear or transparent

clout VERB (informal) to hit

clout NOUN (informal) **1** a hit **2** power or influence

clove NOUN **1** the dried bud of a tropical tree, used as a spice **2** a section of a garlic bulb

clove² past tense of **cleave¹**

cloven past participle of **cleave¹**

clover NOUN a small plant usually with three leaves on each stalk **in clover** in ease and luxury

clown NOUN **1** a performer of amusing tricks and actions in a circus **2** a silly person

clown VERB to do silly things

THESAURUS

close VERB • *to close a door* ▶ shut, lock, secure, fasten, bolt • *to close a road* ▶ block off, cordon off, bar, barricade • *to close a meeting* ▶ conclude, end, stop • *to close the gap between rich and poor* ▶ narrow, reduce, lessen

clothes PLURAL NOUN • *a change of clothes* ▶ clothing, garments, attire, dress

cloud NOUN • *Visibility was affected by cloud.* ▶ haze, vapour, mist • *a cloud of steam* ▶ mass, billow, mist, puff

cloudy ADJECTIVE • *We looked out of the window at the cloudy sky.* ▶ overcast, dull, grey, gloomy • *The water went cloudy.* ▶ hazy, milky, murky, muddy

a b c d e f g h i j k l m n o p q r s t u v w x y z

cloying ADJECTIVE sickeningly sweet

club NOUN 1 a heavy stick used as a weapon 2 a stick with a shaped head used to hit the ball in golf 3 an organized group of people with a common interest 4 a playing card with black clover leaves on it

club VERB **clubbing, clubbed** to hit with a heavy stick **club together** to join with other people to pay for something

cluck VERB to make the cry of a hen ► **cluck** NOUN

clue NOUN something that helps to solve a puzzle or a mystery **not have a clue** (informal) to be ignorant or baffled

clump NOUN 1 a cluster or mass of things 2 a clumping sound

clump VERB 1 to form a cluster or mass 2 to walk with a heavy tread

clumsy ADJECTIVE **clumsier, clumsiest** 1 heavy and awkward

2 not skilful or tactful *a clumsy apology* ► **clumsily** ADVERB

cluster NOUN a small close group

cluster VERB to form a cluster

clutch[1] VERB to grasp tightly

clutch NOUN 1 a tight grasp 2 a device for connecting and disconnecting the engine of a motor vehicle to and from its gears

clutch[2] NOUN a set of eggs for hatching

clutter NOUN things lying about untidily

clutter VERB to fill with clutter

coach NOUN 1 a bus used for long journeys 2 a carriage of a railway train 3 a horse-drawn carriage with four wheels 4 an instructor in sports 5 a teacher giving private specialized tuition

coach VERB to instruct or train in sports

club NOUN • *the local book club* ► society, association, group, organization • *a heavy club* ► stick, cosh, cudgel, truncheon, baton

clue NOUN • *Give me a clue.* ► hint, indication, pointer, tip • *Police are looking for clues.* ► piece of evidence, lead

clump NOUN • *a clump of trees* ► group, cluster, collection • *a clump of grass* ► tuft, bundle, bunch • *a clump of earth* ► lump, clod, mass

clumsy ADJECTIVE • *a clumsy person* ► inept, bungling, bumbling, fumbling • *clumsy movements* ► awkward, ungainly, ungraceful, gawky

cluster NOUN • *a cluster of buildings* ► group, collection • *a cluster of people* ► crowd, group, gathering

clutch VERB • *They were clutching mugs of tea.* ► grip, grasp, clasp, hold

clutter NOUN • *a room full of clutter* ► mess, muddle, jumble, junk, rubbish

a
b
c
d
e
f
g
h
i
j
k
l
m
n
o
p
q
r
s
t
u
v
w
x
y
z

137

DICTIONARY

a b c d e f g h i j k l m n o p q r s t u v w x y z

coal NOUN a hard black mineral substance used for burning to supply heat

coalition NOUN a temporary alliance of political parties to form a government

coarse ADJECTIVE **1** not smooth or delicate; rough or harsh **2** composed of large particles; not fine **3** rude or vulgar

coarsen VERB to make or become coarse

coast NOUN the seashore or the land close to it ▸ **coastal** ADJECTIVE

coast VERB to ride downhill without using power

coat NOUN **1** a piece of outer clothing with sleeves **2** the hair or fur on an animal's body **3** a covering layer

coat VERB to cover something with a coating

coating NOUN a covering layer

coat of arms NOUN a crest on a shield

coax VERB to persuade gently or patiently

cob NOUN **1** the central part of an ear of maize, on which the corn grows **2** a sturdy horse for riding

cobalt NOUN a hard silvery-white metal

cobble¹ NOUN (also **cobblestone**) a rounded stone used for paving roads ▸ **cobbled** ADJECTIVE

cobble² VERB to make or mend roughly

cobbler NOUN someone who mends shoes

cobra NOUN a poisonous snake that can rear up

cobweb NOUN a thin sticky net made by a spider to trap insects

cocaine NOUN an addictive drug made from the leaves of a tropical plant

cock NOUN **1** a male chicken or other bird **2** a lever in a gun

cock VERB **1** to make a gun ready to fire by raising the cock **2** (of a dog) to turn the ears upwards when on the alert

cockatoo NOUN **cockatoos** a crested parrot

cockerel NOUN a young male chicken

cock-eyed ADJECTIVE (informal) crooked; not straight

cockle NOUN an edible shellfish

cockney NOUN **1** a person born in the East End of London **2** the speech of cockneys

cockpit NOUN the compartment for the pilot and crew of an aircraft

cockroach NOUN a dark brown beetle-like insect, often found in dirty houses

cocksure ADJECTIVE very sure; too confident

THESAURUS

coarse ADJECTIVE • *coarse sand* ▸ rough, unrefined, unprocessed, gritty • *coarse cloth* ▸ rough, harsh • *coarse language*

▸ crude, vulgar, offensive, foul, obscene

coax VERB • *to coax them back home* ▸ persuade, tempt, entice

cocktail NOUN a mixed alcoholic drink

cocky ADJECTIVE **cockier, cockiest** (*informal*) too self-confident

cocoa NOUN a hot drink made from a powder of crushed cacao seeds

coconut NOUN a large round nut from a palm tree, with a white flesh and milky juice

cocoon NOUN **1** the covering round a chrysalis **2** a protective wrapping

cocoon VERB to protect something by wrapping it up

cod NOUN cod a large edible sea fish

coddle VERB to cherish and protect carefully

code NOUN **1** a word or phrase used to represent a message to keep its meaning secret **2** a set of signs used in sending messages **3** a set of numbers or letters used to identify something **4** a set of laws or rules

code VERB to put a message into code

codify VERB **codifies, codified** to arrange laws or rules into a code or system ▶ **codification** NOUN

coeducation NOUN the education of boys and girls together ▶ **coeducational** ADJECTIVE

coefficient NOUN a number by which another number is multiplied

coerce (koh-erss) VERB to compel someone with threats or force ▶ **coercion** NOUN

coffee NOUN **1** a hot drink made from the roasted ground seeds of a tropical plant **2** these seeds

coffer NOUN a large strong box for holding money and valuables

coffin NOUN a long box in which a dead body is buried or cremated

cog NOUN a tooth-like part on the edge of a gear wheel

cogent (koh-jent) ADJECTIVE convincing *a cogent argument*

cognac (kon-yak) NOUN a kind of French brandy

cohere VERB to stick together ▶ **cohesion** NOUN, **cohesive** ADJECTIVE

coherent ADJECTIVE clear, reasonable, and making sense ▶ **coherently** ADVERB

coil NOUN something wound into a spiral

coil VERB to wind something into a coil

coin NOUN a round piece of metal used as money

coin VERB **1** to manufacture coins **2** to invent a word or phrase

coinage NOUN **1** a system of money **2** a new word or phrase

coincide VERB **1** to happen at the same time as something else **2** to be in the same place **3** to be the same *My opinion coincides with yours.*

THESAURUS

coil NOUN • *She put a coil of rope on the back of the boat.* ▶ loop, twist, ring

coil VERB • *He coiled her hair round his finger.* ▶ curl, wind, twine, loop

coincidence NOUN the happening of similar events at the same time by chance

coke NOUN solid fuel left when gas and tar have been extracted from coal

colander NOUN a bowl with holes in it, used for straining water from vegetables after cooking

cold ADJECTIVE 1 having a low temperature; not warm 2 unfriendly or unenthusiastic **get cold feet** to have doubts about doing something bold or ambitious ▸ **coldly** ADVERB, **coldness** NOUN

cold NOUN 1 a low temperature 2 an infectious illness that makes your nose run and your throat sore

cold-blooded ADJECTIVE 1 having a body temperature that changes according to the surroundings 2 callous; deliberately cruel

cold war NOUN a situation of hostility between nations without open fighting

colic NOUN pain in a baby's stomach

collaborate VERB 1 to work together on a task 2 to cooperate with an enemy of your country ▸ **collaboration** NOUN, **collaborator** NOUN

collage (kol-ahzh) NOUN a picture made by fixing small objects to a surface

collapse VERB 1 to break or fall to pieces 2 to become very weak or ill 3 to fold up

collapse NOUN 1 the act of collapsing 2 a breakdown

collapsible ADJECTIVE able to be folded up

collar NOUN 1 the part of a piece of clothing that goes round your neck 2 a band round the neck of an animal

collar VERB (informal) to seize or catch someone

colleague NOUN a person you work with

collect VERB 1 to bring people or things together 2 to find examples of things as a hobby 3 to come together 4 to ask for money or

---

THESAURUS

cold ADJECTIVE • a cold day ▸ chilly, cool, fresh, freezing, icy, bitter, wintry • to feel cold ▸ chilly, chilled, shivery, freezing, frozen • a cold reception ▸ unfriendly, unwelcoming, cool, frosty

collapse VERB • Part of the floor collapsed. ▸ fall in, cave in, give way, crumble • People were collapsing in the heat. ▸ faint, pass out, black out, keel over • The banking system was about

to collapse. ▸ fail, break down, founder

collapse NOUN • the collapse of part of the floor ▸ cave-in, disintegration, subsidence • the collapse of peace talks ▸ breakdown, failure

collect VERB • to collect data ▸ gather, accumulate, amass • to collect the children from school ▸ fetch, get, meet, call for • to

DICTIONARY

contributions from people **5** to go and fetch ▶ **collector** NOUN

collection NOUN **1** the process of collecting **2** things collected **3** money collected for a charity

collective ADJECTIVE to do with a group as a whole *our collective opinion*

collective noun NOUN a singular noun that refers to many individuals taken as a unit, e.g. *army* or *herd*

college NOUN a place where people can take courses after they have left school

collide VERB to crash into something ▶ **collision** NOUN

collie NOUN a dog with a long pointed face

colliery NOUN **collieries** a coal mine and its buildings

colloquial (col-oh-kwee-al) ADJECTIVE used in conversation but not in formal speech or writing ▶ **colloquially** ADVERB

collusion NOUN a secret agreement between two or more people who are trying to deceive or cheat someone

colon¹ NOUN a punctuation mark (:), often used to introduce a list

colon² NOUN the largest part of the intestine

colonel (ker-nel) NOUN an army officer in charge of a regiment

colonial ADJECTIVE to do with a colony or colonies abroad

colonize VERB to establish a colony in a country ▶ **colonist** NOUN, **colonization** NOUN

> ⚠ **SPELLING**
>
> This word can also be spelled *colonise.*

colonnade NOUN a row of columns

colony NOUN **colonies 1** an area of land that people of another country settle in and control **2** the people of a colony **3** a group of people or animals of the same kind living together

colossal ADJECTIVE very large; enormous

colour NOUN **1** the effect produced by waves of light of a particular wavelength **2** the use of various

THESAURUS

collect money ▶ raise, appeal for, ask for • *to collect stamps* ▶ keep, save, hoard, store • *People collected for the fireworks.* ▶ assemble, gather, come together

collection NOUN • *a collection of strange objects* ▶ assortment, accumulation, hoard, set, heap • *a collection of people* ▶ group, crowd, gathering • *a collection of poems* ▶ anthology, selection

collide VERB • *The vehicles collided.* ▶ crash, hit each other

collision NOUN • *a collision on the motorway* ▶ crash, accident, smash, pile-up

colossal ADJECTIVE • *a colossal building* ▶ huge, massive, enormous, gigantic, vast

colour NOUN • *over thirty beautiful colours* ▶ hue, shade, tint, tone

colours **3** the complexion of a
person's skin **4** a substance used
to colour things

colour VERB **1** to put colour on; to
paint or stain **2** to blush **3** to
influence what someone says or
believes

colour-blind ADJECTIVE unable to
see the difference between certain
colours

coloured ADJECTIVE having a
particular colour

colourful ADJECTIVE **1** full of colour
2 lively; having vivid details

colouring NOUN the colour of
something

colourless ADJECTIVE without
colour

colt NOUN a young male horse

column NOUN **1** a pillar
2 something long or tall and
narrow *a column of smoke* **3** a
vertical section of a page **4** a
regular article in a newspaper

columnist NOUN a journalist who
writes regularly for a newspaper

coma (koh-ma) NOUN a state of
deep unconsciousness caused by
illness or injury

comb NOUN **1** a toothed strip of
wood or plastic used to tidy the
hair **2** the red crest on the head of
a hen or turkey

comb VERB **1** to tidy the hair with a
comb **2** to search thoroughly

combat NOUN a fight

combat VERB to fight or resist

combatant NOUN someone who
takes part in a fight

combination NOUN **1** the
process of joining together **2** a
number of people or things
combined **3** a series of numbers or
letters needed to open a lock

combine VERB to join or mix
together

combustible ADJECTIVE able to be
set on fire

combustion NOUN the process of
burning

come VERB **came**, **come 1** to move
towards this place **2** to reach a
condition or result *to come to a
decision* **3** to happen *How did you
come to lose it?* **4** to occur or be

• *colour in your cheeks* ► bloom,
glow, redness, rosiness

colour VERB • *to colour it blue*
► paint, tint, dye, stain • *His face
began to colour.* ► blush, flush, go
red • *to colour your judgement*
► influence, affect

colourful ADJECTIVE • *colourful
flowers* ► bright, brilliant, vibrant,
multicoloured • *a colourful*

account ► graphic, vivid,
dramatic, exciting

combine VERB • *to combine visits*
► merge, amalgamate, join (to)
• *to combine to defeat the enemy*
► cooperate, collaborate, join
forces, unite

come VERB • *Our friends have come.*
► arrive, appear, visit • *Spring
came early.* ► occur, happen

DICTIONARY

present *It comes on the next page.*
5 to result *This comes of being
careless.* **come across** to find or
meet by chance **come by** to
obtain **come in for** to receive a
share of **come to 1** to amount to
2 to become conscious again

comedian NOUN a performer who
entertains by making the audience
laugh

comedy NOUN **comedies 1** a play
or film that makes people laugh
2 humour

comet NOUN an object moving
across the sky with a bright tail of
light

comfort NOUN **1** a comfortable
feeling or condition **2** a person or
thing that gives comfort

comfort VERB to make a person
less unhappy; to soothe

comfortable ADJECTIVE **1** free
from worry or pain **2** pleasant to
use or wear *comfortable shoes*
▶ **comfortably** ADVERB

comic ADJECTIVE making people
laugh ▶ **comical** ADJECTIVE,
comically ADVERB

comic NOUN **1** a children's
magazine containing comic strips
2 a comedian

comic strip NOUN a series of
drawings telling a story, especially
a funny one

comma NOUN a punctuation mark
(,) used to mark a pause in a
sentence or to separate items in a
list

command NOUN **1** a statement
telling somebody to do something
2 authority or control **3** the ability
to use or do something *a good
command of Japanese*

THESAURUS

come about ▶ happen, occur
come across • *I came across an old
friend.* ▶ find, encounter,
discover, meet **come round** • *It
took nearly an hour for her to come
round after the operation.*
▶ recover, wake **come to** • *They
came to a river.* ▶ reach, arrive at,
get to • *The shirt came to his
knees.* ▶ reach, extend to

comfort NOUN • *to live in comfort*
▶ ease, luxury • *some words of
comfort* ▶ consolation,
sympathy, commiseration,
encouragement, reassurance

comfort VERB • *to comfort
someone* ▶ console, soothe,
encourage, reassure

comfortable ADJECTIVE • *a
comfortable chair* ▶ snug, cosy,
relaxing, pleasant, soft, warm
• *comfortable shoes*
▶ well-fitting, well-made • *a
comfortable lifestyle*
▶ prosperous, pleasant, well-off,
luxurious

comic ADJECTIVE • *a comic effect*
▶ comical, humorous, funny,
amusing, entertaining

command NOUN • *to shout a
command* ▶ order, instruction
• *twenty men under his command*
▶ authority, control, direction,
leadership • *a good command of
French* ▶ knowledge, mastery,
grasp, understanding

a
b
c
d
e
f
g
h
i
j
k
l
m
n
o
p
q
r
s
t
u
v
w
x
y
z

command VERB **1** to give a command to **2** to have authority over **3** to deserve and get *They command our respect.*

commandant NOUN a military officer in charge of a place or group of people

commandeer VERB to take or seize something for use in a war

commander NOUN **1** a person who has command **2** a naval officer

commandment NOUN a sacred command, especially one of the Ten Commandments in the Old Testament of the Bible

commando NOUN **commandos** a soldier trained to carry out dangerous raids

commemorate VERB to be a celebration or reminder of some past event or person
► **commemoration** NOUN, **commemorative** ADJECTIVE

commence VERB (*formal*) to begin ► **commencement** NOUN

commend VERB **1** to praise *He was commended for bravery.* **2** to entrust *We commend him to your care.* ► **commendation** NOUN

commendable ADJECTIVE deserving praise

comment NOUN a brief opinion or explanation

comment VERB to make a comment

commentary VERB **1** a description of an event by someone who is watching it **2** a set of explanatory notes
► **commentator** NOUN

commerce NOUN trade and the services that assist it, e.g. banking and insurance

commercial ADJECTIVE **1** to do with commerce **2** paid for by advertising *commercial television* **3** profitable ► **commercially** ADVERB

commercial NOUN an advertisement on radio or television

commercialized ADJECTIVE changed in order to make more money

⚠ **SPELLING**

This word can also be spelled *commercialised.*

commiserate VERB to sympathize ► **commiseration** NOUN

commission NOUN **1** a task formally given to someone **2** an appointment to be an officer in the armed forces **3** a group of people given authority to do or

THESAURUS

command VERB • to command the troops to advance ► order, instruct, direct, call on, require, bid • to command a squadron ► be in charge of, be in command of, have command of, lead, head, manage, supervise, rule, control

comment NOUN • some interesting comments ► remark, opinion, observation

comment VERB **comment on** • The article commented on the problem. ► mention, discuss, refer to, touch on

investigate something **4** a payment to someone for providing a service on your behalf

commission VERB to give a commission to

commissionaire NOUN an attendant in uniform at the entrance to a large building

commissioner NOUN **1** an official appointed by commission **2** a member of a commission

commit VERB **committing, committed 1** to do or perform *to commit a crime* **2** to place in someone's care or custody **3** to promise to give time or money available for a particular purpose

commitment NOUN **1** the work, belief, and loyalty that a person gives to a system or organization **2** something that you have to do regularly *work commitments*

committal NOUN **1** the act of committing a person to prison **2** the act of giving a body for burial or cremation

committee NOUN a group of people appointed to deal with a particular matter

commodity NOUN **commodities** a product for buying and selling

commodore NOUN **1** a naval officer ranking next below a rear admiral **2** the commander of part of a fleet

common ADJECTIVE **1** ordinary or usual **2** occurring often *a common mistake* **3** for all or most people *the common good* **4** shared *a common interest* **5** vulgar **in common** shared by two or more people or things ▶ **commonly** ADVERB

common NOUN a piece of land for public use

commoner NOUN a member of the ordinary people

commonplace ADJECTIVE ordinary or usual

common room NOUN an informal room for students or teachers at a school or college

common sense NOUN normal good sense in thinking or behaviour

commonwealth NOUN **1** a group of independent countries **2** a country made up of several states **the Commonwealth** an association of Britain and countries that used to be part of the British Empire

commotion NOUN a noisy uproar

THESAURUS

common ADJECTIVE • *Accidents are quite common.* ▶ frequent, regular, usual, normal, standard, everyday • *a common belief* ▶ widespread, general, popular, universal • *the common good* ▶ collective, communal, public

• *Her friends were too common for her.* ▶ inferior, low-class, vulgar, coarse

commotion NOUN • *a commotion across the street* ▶ disturbance, uproar, racket, hullabaloo, rumpus

communal ADJECTIVE shared by several people ▶ **communally** ADVERB

commune¹ NOUN a group of people living together and sharing everything

commune² VERB to talk together

communicate VERB **1** to pass news or information to other people **2** (of rooms) to have a connecting door

communication NOUN **1** the process of communicating **2** something communicated; a message **communications** PLURAL NOUN links between places (e.g. roads, railways, telephones, radio)

communicative ADJECTIVE willing to talk or give information

communion NOUN religious fellowship **Communion** the Christian ceremony in which consecrated bread and wine are given to worshippers

Communism NOUN a political system in which the state controls property and the means of production ▶ **Communist** NOUN

communism NOUN a system in which property is shared by the community

community NOUN **communities 1** the people living in an area **2** a group with similar interests or origins

commute VERB to travel daily to and from work ▶ **commuter** NOUN

compact ADJECTIVE closely or neatly packed together

compact NOUN a small flat container for face powder

compact VERB to join or press firmly together or into a small space

compact disc NOUN a small plastic disc on which music or data is stored as digital signals and is read by a laser beam

companion NOUN **1** a person you spend time with or travel with **2** one of a matching pair of things ▶ **companionship** NOUN

company NOUN **companies 1** a number of people together **2** a business firm **3** having people with you **4** visitors **5** a section of a battalion

compact ADJECTIVE • *a compact version of the machine* ▶ small, little, petite, portable • *a compact encyclopedia* ▶ concise, condensed, brief

companion NOUN • *He spoke to his companions.* ▶ friend, associate, comrade, colleague, partner

company NOUN • *I miss her company.* ▶ companionship, fellowship, friendship • *We are expecting company.* ▶ visitors, guests, callers • *an insurance company* ▶ firm, business, corporation, establishment • *a local theatre company* ▶ group, troupe, society, association

comparable ADJECTIVE able to be compared, similar ▸ **comparably** ADVERB

comparative ADJECTIVE compared with others *They live in comparative comfort.* ▸ **comparatively** ADVERB

compare VERB to put things together to see how they are similar or different **compare with** to be similar to or as good as

comparison NOUN the act of comparing

compartment NOUN one of the spaces into which something is divided

compass NOUN a device that shows direction, with a magnetized needle pointing to the north **compasses** or **pair of compasses** a device for drawing circles

compassion NOUN pity or mercy ▸ **compassionate** ADJECTIVE

compatible ADJECTIVE 1 able to live or exist together 2 able to be

used together ▸ **compatibility** NOUN

compatriot NOUN a person from the same country as another

compel VERB **compelling**, **compelled** to force somebody to do something

compelling ADJECTIVE 1 convincing *a compelling argument* 2 interesting or attractive

compensate VERB 1 to give a person money etc. to make up for a loss or injury 2 to have a balancing effect ▸ **compensation** NOUN

compère (kom-pair) NOUN a person who introduces the performers in a show or broadcast

compete VERB to take part in a competition

competent ADJECTIVE able to do a particular thing ▸ **competence** NOUN, **competently** ADVERB

competition NOUN 1 a game or race or other contest in which

compare VERB • *to compare our results* ▸ check (against), contrast, juxtapose, match **compare with** • *Our achievements hardly compare with yours.* ▸ match, equal, compete with, rival

compel VERB • *to compel him to give evidence* ▸ force, oblige, order, pressurize **be compelled to** • *She was compelled to admit the truth.* ▸ have to, be obliged to, have no choice but to

compete VERB • *to compete in a tournament* ▸ take part, participate, enter, go in for

competent ADJECTIVE • *a competent builder* ▸ capable, accomplished, qualified, skilful, efficient • *a competent performance* ▸ adequate, satisfactory, acceptable, reasonable

competition NOUN • *fierce competition* ▸ opposition, rivalry • *She came first in the competition.*

people try to win **2** the people competing with you
► **competitive** ADJECTIVE

competitor NOUN someone who competes; a rival

compile VERB to put things together into a list or collection
► **compiler** NOUN, **compilation** NOUN

complacent ADJECTIVE smugly satisfied ► **complacency** NOUN, **complacently** ADVERB

complain VERB to say that you are annoyed or unhappy about something

complaint NOUN **1** a statement complaining about something **2** an illness

complement NOUN **1** the quantity needed to fill or complete something **2** (*Grammar*) the word or words used after verbs such as

be and become to complete the sense

complement VERB to go well together with something else or make it complete

complementary ADJECTIVE completing or adding to something else

complementary angle NOUN either of two angles that add up to 90°

complete ADJECTIVE **1** having all its parts **2** finished **3** thorough; in every way *a complete surprise*
► **completely** ADVERB

complete VERB **1** to make a thing complete **2** to add what is needed
► **completion** NOUN

complex ADJECTIVE **1** difficult to understand or do **2** made up of parts ► **complexity** NOUN

THESAURUS

► contest, match, tournament, game, championship, race

competitor ADJECTIVE • *We must not be complacent.* ► smug, self-satisfied, overconfident

complain VERB • *always complaining about things*
► protest, grumble, whinge, find fault (with), make a complaint

complaint NOUN • *a series of complaints about their behaviour*
► objection (to), criticism (of), protest (about), grumble • *little cause for complaint* ► grievance, dissatisfaction • *a heart complaint*
► disorder, disease, illness, infection

complete ADJECTIVE • *the complete story* ► whole, full, entire, total • *The exercise is now complete.*
► completed, finished, ended • *a complete fool* ► absolute, utter, out-and-out, thorough • *complete rubbish* ► utter, absolute, sheer, pure, total

complete VERB • *to complete your training* ► finish, end, conclude
• *to complete an application form*
► fill in, fill out, answer

completely ADVERB • *completely honest* ► totally, absolutely, utterly, entirely, perfectly

complex ADJECTIVE • *a complex subject* ► complicated, intricate, involved

complex NOUN **1** a set of related buildings or facilities on the same site **2** a group of feelings or ideas that influence a person's behaviour

complexion NOUN the natural colour and appearance of the skin of the face

complicate VERB to make a thing more complicated or difficult

complicated ADJECTIVE **1** difficult to understand or do **2** made up of many parts

complication NOUN something that complicates things or adds difficulties

complicity NOUN the state of being involved in a crime or bad action

compliment NOUN something good you say about a person or thing **compliments** PLURAL NOUN good wishes given in a message

compliment VERB to pay someone a compliment; to congratulate

complimentary ADJECTIVE **1** expressing a compliment **2** given free of charge *complimentary tickets*

comply VERB **complies, complied** to obey laws or rules

component NOUN one of the parts from which a thing is made

compose VERB **1** to form or make up *The class is composed of 20 students.* **2** to write music or poetry **3** to arrange in good order

composed ADJECTIVE calm or quiet

composer NOUN a person who writes music

composite ADJECTIVE made up of different parts or styles

composition NOUN **1** the process of composing **2** a piece of music or writing **3** the parts that make something

compost NOUN decayed leaves and grass used as a fertilizer

composure NOUN a calm manner

compound[1] ADJECTIVE made of two or more parts or ingredients

compound NOUN a compound substance

compound VERB to put together; to combine

compound[2] NOUN a fenced area containing buildings

comprehend VERB **1** to understand **2** to include

comprehensible ADJECTIVE understandable

comprehensive ADJECTIVE including all or many kinds of people or things

compress (kom-press) VERB to press together or into a smaller

complicated ADJECTIVE • *a complicated story* ► complex, intricate, involved, elaborate

compose VERB • *to compose music   to compose a letter*

► write, create, arrange, devise, make up, produce **be composed of** • *The team is composed of six players.* ► consist of, comprise, contain, include

DICTIONARY

space ► **compression** NOUN,
compressor NOUN

compress (kom-press) NOUN a soft
pad or cloth pressed on the body
to stop bleeding or reduce
inflammation

comprise VERB to include or
consist of *The pentathlon
comprises five events.*

compromise NOUN the settling
of a dispute by each side accepting
less than it wanted

compromise VERB **1** to settle by
a compromise **2** to expose
someone to danger or suspicion

compulsion NOUN a strong and
uncontrollable desire to do
something

compulsive ADJECTIVE having a
strong and uncontrollable desire

compulsory ADJECTIVE required to
be done; not optional

compunction NOUN a guilty
feeling about doing something
*had no compunction about leaving
them*

compute VERB to calculate
► **computation** NOUN

computer NOUN an electronic
machine that stores and analyses
information

comrade NOUN a companion who
shares in your activities
► **comradeship** NOUN

con VERB conning, conned
(*informal*) to swindle

concave ADJECTIVE curved like the
inside of a ball or circle

conceal VERB to hide something or
keep something secret
► **concealment** NOUN

concede VERB **1** to admit that
something is true **2** to grant or
allow a right

conceit NOUN too much pride in
yourself

conceited ADJECTIVE having too
high an opinion of yourself

conceivable ADJECTIVE able to be
imagined or believed
► **conceivably** ADVERB

conceive VERB **1** to become
pregnant **2** to form an idea or plan;
to imagine

THESAURUS

compromise VERB • *We had to
compromise.* ► make
concessions, meet halfway, strike
a balance, negotiate • *to
compromise a reputation*
► undermine, discredit,
jeopardize, risk

compulsory ADJECTIVE • *a
compulsory question*
► obligatory, mandatory,
required

conceal VERB • *to conceal
something under your clothes*
► hide, cover up, disguise • *He
could barely conceal his frustration.*
► hide, suppress, keep secret

conceited ADJECTIVE • *a conceited
person* ► vain, boastful, arrogant,
haughty

conceive VERB • *hard to conceive
what it was like* ► imagine,

concentrate VERB **1** to give your full attention or effort to something **2** to bring or come together in one place

concentration NOUN **1** the process of concentrating **2** the amount dissolved in each part of a liquid

concentric ADJECTIVE having the same centre

concept NOUN an idea
▶ **conceptual** ADJECTIVE

conception NOUN **1** the process of conceiving **2** an idea

concern VERB **1** to affect or be important to somebody **2** to worry somebody **3** to have as its subject

concern NOUN **1** something that concerns you **2** a worry **3** a business

concerned ADJECTIVE **1** worried **2** involved in or affected by something

concerning PREPOSITION on the subject of; about

concert NOUN a musical entertainment

concerted ADJECTIVE done in cooperation with others *a concerted effort*

concertina NOUN a musical instrument with bellows, played by squeezing

concerto (kon-chert-oh) NOUN **concertos** or **concerti** a piece of music for a solo instrument and an orchestra

concession NOUN **1** the process of conceding **2** something conceded **3** a reduction in price for certain types of people
▶ **concessionary** ADJECTIVE

conciliate VERB **1** to win over by friendliness **2** to help people to agree ▶ **conciliation** NOUN

THESAURUS

envisage, visualize, understand, comprehend

concentrate VERB • *Troops concentrated on the border.*
▶ gather, mass, collect
concentrate on - *to concentrate on your work* ▶ pay attention to, keep your mind on, focus on, think about

concept NOUN • *a hard concept to grasp* ▶ idea, notion, principle, theory

concern VERB • *This concerns everyone.* ▶ affect, involve, apply to, be relevant to • *The news*

concerned us deeply. ▶ worry, disturb, upset, trouble

concern NOUN • *concern for others* ▶ consideration, thought • *no concern of ours* ▶ affair, business, responsibility, problem • *a cause for concern* ▶ anxiety, worry, unease • *a publishing concern* ▶ company, firm, business, organization

concerned ADJECTIVE • *to look concerned* ▶ worried, anxious, troubled, upset • *the people concerned* ▶ involved, connected

a
b
c
d
e
f
g
h
i
j
k
l
m
n
o
p
q
r
s
t
u
v
w
x
y
z

a
b
c
d
e
f
g
h
i
j
k
l
m
n
o
p
q
r
s
t
u
v
w
x
y
z

concise ADJECTIVE giving much information in a few words
▶ **concisely** ADVERB

conclude VERB 1 to bring or come to an end 2 to form an opinion by reasoning

conclusion NOUN 1 an ending 2 an opinion formed by reasoning

conclusive ADJECTIVE putting an end to all doubt ▶ **conclusively** ADVERB

concoct VERB 1 to make something by putting ingredients together 2 to invent *to concoct an excuse* ▶ **concoction** NOUN

concord NOUN friendly agreement or harmony

concordance NOUN an index of the words used in a book or an author's works

concourse NOUN an open area through which people pass, e.g. at an airport

concrete NOUN cement mixed with sand and gravel, used in building

concrete ADJECTIVE 1 able to be touched and felt; not abstract 2 definite *concrete evidence*

concur VERB concurring, concurred to agree ▶ **concurrence** NOUN

concussion NOUN a temporary injury to the brain caused by a blow to the head ▶ **concussed** ADJECTIVE

condemn VERB 1 to say that you strongly disapprove of something 2 to sentence to a particular punishment 3 to declare a building unfit for use
▶ **condemnation** NOUN

condensation NOUN 1 the process of condensing 2 drops of liquid formed by vapour condensing

condense VERB 1 to make a liquid denser or more compact 2 to put something into fewer words 3 to change from gas or vapour to liquid

condescend VERB to act in a superior way towards someone
▶ **condescension** NOUN

THESAURUS

concise ADJECTIVE • *a concise summary* ▶ brief, succinct, short

conclude VERB • *Hostilities concluded at midnight.* ▶ finish, end, stop, cease • *The jury concluded that he was guilty.* ▶ decide, infer, deduce, judge

conclusion NOUN • *the conclusion of the speech* ▶ end, finish, close • *Our conclusion proved to be*

correct. ▶ deduction, decision, judgement, opinion

condemn VERB • *to condemn violence* ▶ deplore, denounce • *They condemned us for our behaviour.* ▶ criticize, denounce • *The court condemned them.* ▶ convict, find guilty, sentence

condense VERB • *to condense ten episodes into one* ▶ shorten, reduce, abridge, cut

condition NOUN **1** the state or fitness of a person or thing *in good condition* **2** the situation or surroundings that affect something *working conditions* **3** something required as part of an agreement *on condition that* only if

condition VERB **1** to put something into a healthy or proper condition **2** to train someone to behave or react in a particular way

conditional ADJECTIVE depending on certain actions or events
▸ **conditionally** ADVERB

conditioner NOUN a substance put on the hair to keep it in good condition

condolence NOUN an expression of sympathy for someone

condone VERB to forgive or ignore a wrong or bad action

conducive ADJECTIVE helping to cause or produce something *Noisy surroundings are not conducive to work.*

conduct VERB **1** to lead or guide **2** to be the conductor of an orchestra or choir **3** to manage or direct something **4** to allow heat, light, sound, or electricity to pass along or through **5** to behave *They conducted themselves with dignity.*

conduct NOUN behaviour

conduction NOUN the process of conducting heat or electricity

conductor NOUN **1** a person who directs the performance of an orchestra or choir **2** a person who collects the fares on a bus **3** something that conducts heat or electricity

cone NOUN **1** a circular object that narrows to a point at one end **2** an ice cream cornet **3** the dry fruit of a pine or other tree **4** a plastic cone-shaped marker on a road

confectionery NOUN sweets and chocolates

confer VERB **conferring, conferred 1** to grant a right or title on someone **2** to hold a discussion

conference NOUN a meeting for discussion

THESAURUS

condition NOUN • *in good condition* ▸ order, state, shape • *a medical condition* ▸ disorder, illness, disease, complaint • *conditions attached to membership* ▸ requirement, proviso, terms, restriction, limitation

conduct VERB • *to conduct visitors round the building* ▸ escort,

guide, accompany, take, lead • *to conduct a survey* ▸ organize, coordinate, carry out

conduct NOUN • *good conduct* ▸ behaviour, demeanour, attitude • *the conduct of the nation's affairs* ▸ management, direction, handling, running

153

DICTIONARY

confess VERB to state that you have done something wrong

confession NOUN an admission of having done wrong

confetti NOUN small pieces of coloured paper thrown by guests at a wedding

confide VERB to tell someone a secret *I will confide in you.*

confidence NOUN **1** a feeling of belief in yourself and your ability to do things well **2** firm trust **3** something told confidentially **in confidence** as a secret

confidence trick NOUN a trick to swindle someone after persuading them to trust you

confident ADJECTIVE showing or feeling confidence ▶ **confidently** ADVERB

confidential ADJECTIVE meant to be kept secret ▶ **confidentially** ADVERB

confine VERB **1** to keep something within limits *Confine your remarks to the subject.* **2** to keep someone in a place

confined ADJECTIVE narrow or restricted

confinement NOUN **1** imprisonment **2** the time when a woman gives birth to a baby

confines PLURAL NOUN the limits or boundaries of an area

confirm VERB **1** to show that something is true or correct **2** to make a thing definite *to confirm a booking* **3** to make a person a full member of a Christian Church ▶ **confirmation** NOUN

THESAURUS

confess VERB • *to confess to a crime* ▶ admit guilt, plead guilty, own up

confidence NOUN • *to face the future with confidence* ▶ optimism, positiveness, certainty, hope, trust **have confidence in** *They have confidence in their abilities.* ▶ trust, believe (in)

confident ADJECTIVE • *confident that the money will be found* ▶ optimistic, hopeful, sure, certain, convinced • *a confident gesture* ▶ self-assured, self-confident, assertive, positive

confidential ADJECTIVE • *a confidential report* ▶ secret, top secret, private, personal, classified • *a confidential secretary* ▶ personal, private

confine VERB • *She confined her writing to short stories.* ▶ restrict, limit, keep • *He was confined in the Tower.* ▶ enclose, imprison, keep, shut, cage

confirm VERB • *to confirm suspicions* ▶ support, corroborate, back up • *to confirm a booking* ▶ verify, guarantee, formalize, make official • *to confirm that you are coming* ▶ affirm, assert, give an assurance

confiscate VERB to take something away as a punishment ► **confiscation** NOUN

conflict NOUN a fight or disagreement

conflict VERB to differ or disagree

conform VERB to keep to accepted rules or customs ► **conformist** NOUN, **conformity** NOUN

confound VERB to puzzle or confuse

confront VERB **1** to come or bring face to face in a hostile way **2** to face up to and deal with ► **confrontation** NOUN

confuse VERB **1** to make a person puzzled or muddled **2** to mistake one thing for another ► **confusion** NOUN

congeal VERB to become jelly-like in cooling

congenial ADJECTIVE pleasant or agreeable *a congenial companion* ► **congenially** ADVERB

congenital ADJECTIVE existing from birth ► **congenitally** ADVERB

congested ADJECTIVE crowded or blocked up ► **congestion** NOUN

congratulate VERB to tell a person that you are pleased about their success or good fortune ► **congratulation** NOUN

congregate VERB to assemble or come together

congregation NOUN a group of people who have come together for religious worship

Congress NOUN the parliament of the USA

congress NOUN a meeting for discussion

conical ADJECTIVE shaped like a cone ► **conically** ADVERB

conifer NOUN an evergreen tree with cones ► **coniferous** ADJECTIVE

conjecture NOUN a guess ► **conjectural** ADJECTIVE

conjugal ADJECTIVE to do with marriage

THESAURUS

conflict NOUN • *an industrial conflict* ► dispute, disagreement, confrontation • *a military conflict* ► war, struggle, clash, battle, fight

conform VERB • *It's best to conform.* ► comply, acquiesce, fit in, obey the rules

confront VERB • *to confront an intruder* ► challenge, accost, stand up to, take on • *to confront the problem* ► tackle, face up to, deal with

confuse VERB • *to confuse the issue* ► complicate, muddle, cloud

• *Too much detail will confuse us.* ► puzzle, bewilder, perplex, baffle

confused ADJECTIVE • *confused about what was happening* ► puzzled, bewildered, perplexed, baffled • *a confused pile* ► untidy, disorderly, disorganized, muddled • *confused accounts of the incident* ► vague, muddled, unclear

congratulate VERB • *to congratulate her on her success* ► praise, compliment, commend, applaud

a
b
c
d
e
f
g
h
i
j
k
l
m
n
o
p
q
r
s
t
u
v
w
x
y
z

conjunction NOUN a word that joins words or groups of words, e.g. *and* or *but*

conjure VERB to perform tricks that look like magic ► **conjuror** NOUN

conker NOUN the hard shiny brown nut of the horse chestnut tree

connect VERB to join together or link

connection NOUN **1** a point where two things are connected; a link **2** a train, bus, etc. that leaves a station soon after another arrives

connive (kon-yv) VERB **connive at** to take no notice of a wrong or bad action ► **connivance** NOUN

connoisseur (kon-a-ser) NOUN a person with great experience and knowledge of something

conquer VERB to defeat or overcome ► **conqueror** NOUN

conquest NOUN **1** a victory **2** conquered territory

conscience NOUN a feeling of what is right and wrong in what you do

conscientious ADJECTIVE careful and honest about doing your work properly ► **conscientiously** ADVERB

conscious ADJECTIVE **1** awake and knowing what is happening **2** aware of something *I was not conscious of the time.* **3** done deliberately *a conscious decision* ► **consciously** ADVERB, **consciousness** NOUN

consecutive ADJECTIVE following one after another ► **consecutively** ADVERB

consensus NOUN the opinion of most people

consent VERB to say that you are willing to do or allow what someone wants

THESAURUS

connect VERB • *to connect speakers to an amplifier* ► link, attach, join, fasten • *The two crimes could be connected.* ► link, relate, associate

connection NOUN • *a connection between money and power* ► relationship, link, association, correlation

conquer VERB • *to conquer a country* ► seize, capture, overrun, occupy, invade • *to conquer the enemy* ► defeat, beat, overcome, crush • *to conquer fears* ► overcome, suppress, master, control

conquest NOUN • *the conquest of the territory* ► capture, invasion, occupation, defeat

conscientious ADJECTIVE • *a conscientious worker* ► hard-working, diligent, industrious, careful, meticulous

conscious ADJECTIVE • *to remain conscious* ► awake, aware, alert • *a conscious attempt to deceive* ► deliberate, intentional, calculated, planned, premeditated

consent VERB • *to consent to do something* ► agree, be willing

DICTIONARY

consent NOUN agreement to what someone wants

consequence NOUN 1 something that happens as the result of an event or action 2 importance *of no consequence*

consequent ADJECTIVE happening as a result ▸ **consequently** ADVERB

conservation NOUN preservation of the natural environment or old buildings ▸ **conservationist** NOUN

Conservative NOUN a person who supports the Conservative Party, a British political party that favours private business and industry ▸ **Conservative** ADJECTIVE

conservative ADJECTIVE 1 liking traditional ways and disliking changes 2 moderate or cautious; not extreme *a conservative estimate* ▸ **conservatism** NOUN

conservatory NOUN **conservatories** a room with a glass roof and large windows, built against an outside wall of a house

conserve VERB to prevent something valuable from being changed or wasted

consider VERB 1 to think carefully about something, especially to make a decision 2 to think *Consider yourself lucky.*

considerable ADJECTIVE fairly large *a considerable amount* ▸ **considerably** ADVERB

considerate ADJECTIVE taking care not to inconvenience or hurt others ▸ **considerately** ADVERB

consideration NOUN 1 careful thought 2 a fact that must be kept in mind

considering PREPOSITION taking something into consideration *The car runs well, considering its age.*

consign VERB to hand something over formally

consignment NOUN a batch of goods sent to someone

THESAURUS

consent to • *to consent to a request* ▸ agree to, allow, grant, permit

consequence NOUN • *a consequence of global warming* ▸ result, effect, outcome, repercussion, side-effect • *of little consequence* ▸ importance, significance

consider VERB • *to consider the possibilities* ▸ think about, contemplate, ponder, weigh up, study • *I consider it a privilege.*

▸ regard (as), think, judge, believe (to be)

considerable ADJECTIVE • *a considerable amount* ▸ substantial, sizeable, significant, reasonable, large

considerate ADJECTIVE • *to be considerate to others* ▸ kind, thoughtful, helpful, caring, sensitive

consideration NOUN • *careful consideration* ▸ thought, attention, deliberation

DICTIONARY

consist VERB to be made up or composed of *The flat consists of three rooms.*

consistency NOUN **consistencies 1** thickness or stiffness, especially of a liquid **2** the quality of being regular

consistent ADJECTIVE **1** keeping to a regular pattern or style **2** not contradictory ▶ **consistently** ADVERB

consolation NOUN something that makes you feel less unhappy or disappointed

console[1] (kon-sohl) VERB to comfort someone who is unhappy or disappointed

console[2] (kon-sohl) NOUN a panel of controls or switches

consolidate VERB to make or become secure and strong ▶ **consolidation** NOUN

consonant NOUN a letter that is not a vowel, e.g. b, c, d, and f

consort (kon-sort) NOUN the husband or wife of a monarch

consort (kon-sort) VERB to be in someone's company

consortium NOUN **consortiums** a group of business companies acting together

conspicuous ADJECTIVE easily seen; noticeable ▶ **conspicuously** ADVERB

conspiracy NOUN **conspiracies** a plot to do something illegal

conspire VERB to take part in a conspiracy ▶ **conspirator** NOUN

constable NOUN a police officer of the lowest rank

constant ADJECTIVE **1** not changing; happening all the time **2** faithful or loyal ▶ **constancy** NOUN, **constantly** ADVERB

constant NOUN something that does not change, especially a number

constellation NOUN a group of stars

constipated ADJECTIVE unable to empty the bowels easily or regularly ▶ **constipation** NOUN

THESAURUS

consist VERB **consist of •** *to consist of different things* ▶ be composed of, comprise, be made of, include, contain

consistent ADJECTIVE • *a consistent pattern of behaviour* ▶ steady, stable, regular, unchanging

console VERB • *His friends tried to console him.* ▶ comfort, encourage, soothe, sympathize with, cheer

conspicuous ADJECTIVE • *conspicuous in bright clothes* ▶ noticeable, distinct, prominent, clearly visible, easily seen • *conspicuous bravery* ▶ obvious, evident, outstanding, exceptional

constant ADJECTIVE • *the constant hum of traffic* ▶ continuous, continual, ceaseless, incessant, endless • *a constant speed* ▶ steady, regular, stable, even, fixed • *a constant friend* ▶ faithful, loyal, devoted, true, reliable

constituency NOUN
constituencies a district represented by a Member of Parliament elected by the people who live there

constituent NOUN 1 one of the parts that form a whole thing 2 someone who lives in a constituency ▸ **constituent** ADJECTIVE

constitute VERB to make up or form something *Twelve months constitute a year.*

constitution NOUN 1 a set of laws or principles about how a country is organized and governed 2 the condition of the body in regard to health *a strong constitution* 3 the composition of something ▸ **constitutional** ADJECTIVE

constraint NOUN 1 force or compulsion 2 a restriction

constrict VERB to squeeze or tighten something by making it narrower ▸ **constriction** NOUN

construct VERB to make something by putting the parts together ▸ **constructor** NOUN

construction NOUN 1 the process of constructing 2 a

building or other thing put together 3 words put together to form a phrase or sentence 4 an interpretation of what someone says

constructive ADJECTIVE helpful and positive

construe VERB to interpret or explain

consul NOUN a government official who represents their country in another country ▸ **consular** ADJECTIVE

consulate NOUN the office of a consul

consult VERB to go to a person or book for information or advice ▸ **consultation** NOUN

consultant NOUN 1 a person who gives expert advice 2 a senior hospital doctor

consume VERB 1 to eat or drink something 2 to use up 3 to destroy

consumer NOUN a person who buys goods or services

consumption NOUN 1 the act of consuming 2 an amount consumed

THESAURUS

construct VERB • *to construct a new bridge* ▸ build, erect, put up, assemble • *to construct a new form of society* ▸ create, devise, develop, design

consult VERB • *He wanted to consult the workforce.* ▸ speak to, confer with, seek advice from

• *Consult your doctor.* ▸ see, ask, get advice from

consume VERB • *to consume food and drink* ▸ eat, drink, devour, swallow • *to consume fuel* ▸ use, expend, swallow up • *Fire consumed the buildings.* ▸ destroy, devastate, wipe out, ravage

a
b
c
d
e
f
g
h
i
j
k
l
m
n
o
p
q
r
s
t
u
v
w
x
y
z

contact NOUN **1** the act of touching **2** communication between people **3** a person you can communicate with

contact VERB to get in touch with a person

contagious ADJECTIVE spreading by contact with an infected person

contain VERB **1** to have inside **2** to consist of **3** to hold back *Try to contain your laughter.*

container NOUN **1** a box or bottle etc. designed to contain something **2** a large box-like object for transporting goods

contaminate VERB to make dirty or impure or diseased
► **contamination** NOUN

contemplate VERB **1** to look at something thoughtfully **2** to

consider or think about doing something ► **contemplation** NOUN, **contemplative** ADJECTIVE

contemporary ADJECTIVE **1** belonging to the same period **2** modern or up-to-date *contemporary furniture*

contemporary NOUN **contemporaries** a person of roughly the same age as someone else

contempt NOUN a feeling of despising a person or thing

contemptible ADJECTIVE deserving contempt

contemptuous ADJECTIVE feeling or showing contempt
► **contemptuously** ADVERB

contend VERB **1** to struggle in a fight or against difficulties **2** to

contact NOUN • *physical contact* ► touch, touching, proximity • *contact between Europe and Africa* ► communication, connection, association • *an electrical contact* ► connection, join • *my contact in Italy* ► associate, acquaintance

contact VERB • *I'll contact them next week.* ► notify, communicate with, get in touch with, call, speak to

contain VERB • *a box containing wine* ► hold, accommodate • *The book contains photographs.* ► include, incorporate, consist of, be composed of • *to contain your impatience* ► restrain, curb, suppress, control, stifle, limit

contemplate VERB • *to contemplate the scene* ► look at, view, observe, survey, watch • *She contemplated what might happen.* ► think about, consider, deliberate, mull over, plan • *He contemplated leaving.* ► consider, think about, intend (to) • *She sat quietly and contemplated.* ► reflect, ponder, think, meditate

contemporary ADJECTIVE • *information from contemporary accounts* ► contemporaneous, of the time • *contemporary music* ► modern, current, present-day, fashionable

contempt NOUN • *She had nothing but contempt for them.* ► disgust, scorn, disdain, loathing

compete **3** to state or declare *We contend that he is innocent.*
► **contender** NOUN

content[1] (kon-**tent**) ADJECTIVE pleased or satisfied

content NOUN happiness or satisfaction

content VERB to make a person pleased or satisfied

content[2] (**kon**-tent) NOUN or **contents** PLURAL NOUN what something contains

contented ADJECTIVE pleased with what you have; satisfied
► **contentedly** ADVERB

contest (**kon**-test) NOUN a competition or struggle

contest (kon-**test**) VERB **1** to dispute or argue about something **2** to compete in

contestant NOUN a person taking part in a contest

context NOUN **1** the words that come before and after a particular

word or phrase and help to fix its meaning **2** the background to an event that helps to explain it

continent NOUN one of the main masses of land in the world (Europe, Asia, Africa, North America, South America, Australia, and Antarctica) **the Continent** the mainland of Europe ► **continental** ADJECTIVE

contingency NOUN **contingencies** something that may happen but cannot be known for certain

contingent NOUN a section of a larger group

continual ADJECTIVE happening all the time at intervals *continual interruptions* ► **continually** ADVERB

continue VERB **1** to do something without stopping **2** to begin again after stopping ► **continuation** NOUN

THESAURUS

content ADJECTIVE • *content with the situation* ► happy, contented, satisfied, pleased, glad

content NOUN • *the content of the book* ► subject matter, subject, theme, message • *a high fat content* ► element, ingredient, substance • *to smile with content* ► happiness, contentment, satisfaction, pleasure

contented ADJECTIVE • *a contented feeling* ► happy, content, satisfied, pleased, glad

contest NOUN • *a song contest* ► competition, tournament,

match • *a contest for the leadership* ► struggle, challenge, battle, duel

contest VERB • *to contest an election* ► enter, compete in, take part in, participate in • *to contest the decision* ► oppose, challenge, dispute, object to

continual ADJECTIVE • *continual breakdowns* ► constant, repeated, frequent, regular, ceaseless

continue VERB • *to continue the search* ► carry on, maintain, keep up, keep going, persevere with,

a b c d e f g h i j k l m n o p q r s t u v w x y z

continuous ADJECTIVE going on without a break *continuous rain* ▶ **continuously** ADVERB, **continuity** NOUN

contort VERB to twist or force out of the usual shape ▶ **contortion** NOUN

contortionist NOUN a person who can twist their body into unusual positions

contour NOUN **1** a line on a map joining the points that are the same height above sea level **2** an outline

contraband NOUN smuggled goods

contraception NOUN prevention of pregnancy

contraceptive NOUN a substance or device that prevents pregnancy

contract (kon-trakt) NOUN a legal agreement to do something

contract (kon-trakt) VERB **1** to make or become smaller **2** to make a contract **3** to catch an illness

contraction NOUN **1** the process of contracting **2** a shortened form of a word or words, e.g. *can't* for *cannot*

contractor NOUN a person who makes a contract to do work or supply goods

contradict VERB **1** to say that something said is not true or that someone is wrong **2** to say the opposite of ▶ **contradiction** NOUN

contradictory ADJECTIVE saying or meaning the opposite of something else

contraption NOUN a strange-looking device or machine

THESAURUS

proceed with, prolong, pursue, (*more informal*) stick at • *We'll continue later.* ▶ resume, restart, begin again, recommence • *Talks continued all week.* ▶ last, carry on, go on, endure, persist, keep on, linger, live on, remain, stay, survive

continuous ADJECTIVE • *three days of continuous rain* ▶ uninterrupted, constant, steady, endless, incessant, non-stop

contract NOUN • *a legal contract* ▶ agreement, settlement, deal, treaty

contract VERB • *The glass contracts as it cools.* ▶ shrink, reduce, become smaller, decrease • *to contract an illness* ▶ develop, catch, get, become infected by, be taken ill with

contradict VERB • *I didn't like to contradict him.* ▶ disagree with, challenge, oppose, speak against • *The evidence contradicts earlier conclusions.* ▶ conflict with, be at odds with, be inconsistent with • *The statement was contradicted by the Prime Minister.* ▶ deny, repudiate, rebut, dispute

DICTIONARY

contrary ADJECTIVE 1 (kon-tra-ree) of the opposite kind or direction 2 (kon-trair-ee) awkward and obstinate

contrary (kon-tra-ree) NOUN the opposite **on the contrary** the opposite is true

contrast (kon-trahst) NOUN 1 a clear difference between things 2 something showing a clear difference

contrast (kon-trahst) VERB 1 to compare or oppose two things to show they are different 2 to be clearly different

contribute VERB 1 to give money or help jointly with others 2 to write something for a newspaper or magazine 3 to help to cause

something ▸ **contributor** NOUN, **contributory** ADJECTIVE

contribution NOUN something given or offered jointly with others

contrite ADJECTIVE sorry for having done wrong

contrivance NOUN an ingenious device

contrive VERB 1 to plan cleverly 2 to find a way of doing or making something

control NOUN power or authority to make someone or something do what you want

control VERB controlling, controlled 1 to have control over 2 to hold a feeling in check ▸ **controller** NOUN

THESAURUS

contrary ADJECTIVE (with the stress on con-) • the contrary view ▸ opposite, opposing, contrasting, different (with the stress on -trary, pronounced like Mary) • a contrary child ▸ perverse, awkward, difficult, obstinate, disobedient **contrary to** • contrary to all expectations ▸ in conflict with, at odds with

contrast NOUN • a contrast between words and actions ▸ difference, dissimilarity, disparity, contradiction

contrast VERB • People contrast the two brothers. ▸ compare, differentiate, distinguish, make distinctions between **contrast with** • Her fair hair contrasted with her dark dress. ▸ set off, complement, clash with

contribute VERB • to contribute money ▸ give, donate, provide, supply **contribute to** • The weather contributed to the success. ▸ play a part in, add to, be a factor in, have a hand in

control NOUN • control over the business ▸ authority, power, management, jurisdiction, command • to exercise control ▸ restraint, self-control, composure • the aircraft's controls ▸ switch, knob, button, lever, dial **gain control of** • to gain control of the country ▸ take over, dominate, win, seize

control VERB • to control the resources ▸ be in charge of, manage, have authority over, administer, run • Please try to

a
b
c
d
e
f
g
h
i
j
k
l
m
n
o
p
q
r
s
t
u
v
w
x
y
z

controls PLURAL NOUN the switches and instruments used to control a machine

controversial ADJECTIVE causing argument or disagreement

controversy NOUN **controversies** a long argument or disagreement

conundrum NOUN **conundrums** a riddle or difficult question

convalesce VERB to be recovering from an illness ▶ **convalescence** NOUN

convalescent NOUN someone who is recovering from an illness

convection NOUN the passing through of heat within liquid, air, or gas

convector NOUN a heater that circulates warm air by convection

convene VERB to summon or assemble for a meeting ▶ **convener** NOUN

convenience NOUN **1** the quality of being convenient **2** something that is convenient **3** a public lavatory

convenient ADJECTIVE easy to use or deal with or reach ▶ **conveniently** ADVERB

convent NOUN a place where nuns live and work

convention NOUN **1** an accepted way of doing things **2** a formal assembly

conventional ADJECTIVE **1** done or doing things in the accepted way **2** (of weapons) not nuclear ▶ **conventionally** ADVERB

converge VERB to come towards the same point ▶ **convergence** NOUN, **convergent** ADJECTIVE

conversant ADJECTIVE (formal) familiar with something *conversant with the rules*

conversation NOUN talk between people ▶ **conversational** ADJECTIVE

converse[1] (kon-verss) VERB to have a conversation

converse[2] (kon-verss) ADJECTIVE opposite; contrary ▶ **conversely** ADVERB

converse NOUN the opposite of something *the converse is true*

conversion NOUN the process of converting

THESAURUS

control your temper. ▶ restrain, check, curb, repress

convenient ADJECTIVE • *a convenient time to come* ▶ suitable, appropriate, fitting, agreeable • *the most convenient option* ▶ practical, handy, useful, helpful • *a convenient shopping*

centre ▶ nearby, accessible, handy, at hand

conventional ADJECTIVE • *conventional ideas* ▶ traditional, orthodox, established, customary, mainstream • *a conventional person* ▶ conservative, traditional, conformist

convert (kon-vert) VERB **1** to change something **2** to cause a person to change their beliefs **3** to kick a goal after scoring a try in rugby football ▶ **converter** NOUN

convert (kon-vert) NOUN a person who has changed their beliefs

convertible ADJECTIVE able to be converted

convertible NOUN a car with a folding roof

convex ADJECTIVE curved like the outside of a ball or circle

convey VERB **1** to transport **2** to communicate a message or idea ▶ **conveyor** NOUN

conveyance NOUN **1** the process of conveying **2** a vehicle for transporting people

conveyancing NOUN the process of transferring ownership of land or buildings from one person to another

conveyor belt NOUN a continuous moving belt for moving objects from one place to another

convict (kon-vikt) VERB to declare that a person is guilty of a crime

convict (kon-vikt) NOUN a convicted person in prison

conviction NOUN **1** the process of being convicted of a crime **2** a firm opinion or belief

convince VERB to make a person feel certain that something is true

convoy NOUN a group of ships or lorries travelling together

convulse VERB to make violent movements of the body ▶ **convulsive** ADJECTIVE

convulsion NOUN **1** a violent movement of the body **2** a violent upheaval

coo VERB **coos**, **cooing**, **cooed** to make a soft murmuring sound ▶ **coo** NOUN

cook VERB to prepare food by heating it

cook NOUN a person who cooks

cooker NOUN a piece of kitchen equipment for cooking

cookery NOUN the cooking of food

cool ADJECTIVE **1** fairly cold **2** calm; not enthusiastic **3** (informal) good or fashionable ▶ **coolly** ADVERB

THESAURUS

convert VERB • to convert the loft into a workroom ▶ adapt, change, turn, modify, reorganize • to convert digital data into audio signals ▶ turn, change, transform, translate

convey VERB • to convey passengers to the city centre ▶ transport, carry, take, transfer, move • to convey a meaning ▶ communicate, get across

convince VERB • It will be difficult to convince them. ▶ persuade, prove to, reassure, win over

cool ADJECTIVE • the cool air of early morning ▶ fresh, crisp, chilly, bracing, chilled • a cool response. ▶ unfriendly, chilly, lukewarm, hostile • to keep cool in a crisis ▶ calm, composed, clear-headed, self-controlled, unflustered

DICTIONARY

cool VERB to make or become cool
► **cooler** NOUN

coop NOUN a cage for poultry

cooped up ADJECTIVE having to
stay in a small uncomfortable
place

cooperate VERB to work helpfully
with other people ► **cooperation**
NOUN, **cooperative** ADJECTIVE

coordinate VERB to organize
people or things to work together
► **coordination** NOUN,
coordinator NOUN

coordinate NOUN one of a set of
numbers or letters used to fix the
position of a point on a graph or
map

coot NOUN a waterbird with a white
patch on its forehead

cop VERB **copping**, **copped**
cop it (informal) to get into
trouble

cop NOUN (informal) a police officer

cope VERB to manage or deal with
something successfully

copier NOUN a device for copying
documents

copious ADJECTIVE plentiful; in large
amounts ► **copiously** ADVERB

copper NOUN 1 a reddish-brown
metal 2 a reddish-brown colour
3 a coin made of copper

copse NOUN a small group of trees

copy NOUN **copies** 1 a thing made
to look like another 2 something
written or printed out again from
its original form 3 one of a number
of specimens of the same book
etc.

copy VERB **copies**, **copied** 1 to
make a copy of something 2 to do
the same as someone else

copyright NOUN the legal right to
print a book, reproduce a picture,
record a piece of music, etc.

THESAURUS

(informal) • She thinks she's cool.
► fashionable, trendy, stylish

cool VERB • to cool the room
► chill, make cooler, lower the
temperature of • to cool the drinks
► chill, refrigerate, make cold
• Their enthusiasm began to cool.
► lessen, reduce, diminish

cooperate VERB • to cooperate in
an operation ► collaborate, unite,
work together, join forces, team
up **cooperate with** • He refused
to cooperate with them. ► assist,
help, support, work with

co-operative ADJECTIVE • pleasant
and cooperative ► helpful,
obliging, accommodating,

supportive, willing • a cooperative
effort ► joint, combined,
collective, concerted

cope VERB • too old to cope alone
► manage, survive, carry on, get
by, fend for yourself **cope with**
• so many problems to cope with
► deal with, handle, manage

copy NOUN • a copy of the letter
► duplicate, photocopy, facsimile
• The painting is a copy.
► reproduction, model, imitation,
fake, forgery, clone

copy VERB • to copy a passage from
a book ► write out, make a copy
of, duplicate • to copy paintings
► reproduce, forge, fake • to copy

coral NOUN **1** a hard substance formed by the skeletons of tiny sea creatures massed together **2** a pink colour

cord NOUN **1** a long thin flexible strip of twisted threads or strands **2** a piece of flex **3** a cord-like structure in the body *the spinal cord* **4** corduroy

cordial NOUN a fruit-flavoured drink

cordial ADJECTIVE warm and friendly
▶ **cordially** ADVERB

cordon NOUN a line of people, ships, fortifications, etc. placed round an area to guard or enclose it

corduroy NOUN cotton cloth with velvety ridges

core NOUN the part in the middle of something, especially of fruit

corgi NOUN corgis a small dog with short legs and upright ears

cork NOUN **1** the lightweight bark of a kind of oak tree **2** a stopper for a bottle

cork VERB to close with a cork

corkscrew NOUN **1** a device for removing corks from bottles **2** a spiral

corn NOUN **1** the seed of wheat and similar plants **2** a plant, such as

wheat, grown for its grain **3** a small hard lump on the foot

cornea NOUN the transparent covering over the pupil of the eye

corner NOUN **1** the angle or area where two lines or walls or roads meet **2** a free hit or kick from the corner of a hockey or football field

corner VERB **1** to drive someone into a position from which it is difficult to escape **2** to travel round a corner **3** to get hold of all or most of something

cornerstone NOUN **1** a stone built into the corner at the base of a building **2** something that is a vital foundation

cornet NOUN **1** a cone-shaped wafer holding ice cream **2** a musical instrument like a trumpet

cornflakes PLURAL NOUN toasted maize flakes eaten as a breakfast cereal

cornflour NOUN flour made from maize or rice

cornflower NOUN a wild plant with blue flowers

cornice NOUN an ornamental moulding on walls below the ceiling

corny ADJECTIVE **cornier**, **corniest** (*informal*) (of a joke) repeated so often that it is no longer funny

THESAURUS

someone else ▶ imitate, mimic, impersonate

core NOUN • *the earth's core*
▶ centre, heart, middle, nucleus

corner NOUN • *Turn left at the corner.* ▶ bend, curve, turning

• *The women sat in the corner of the cafe.* ▶ nook, niche, recess, alcove

corner VERB • *The animal had cornered its prey.* ▶ trap, shut in, capture, catch

a
b
c
d
e
f
g
h
i
j
k
l
m
n
o
p
q
r
s
t
u
v
w
x
y
z

coronation NOUN a ceremony to crown a king or queen

coroner NOUN an official who holds an inquiry into the cause of a death

coronet NOUN a small crown

corporal[1] NOUN a soldier ranking next below a sergeant

corporal[2] ADJECTIVE to do with the body

corporal punishment NOUN physical punishment such as spanking or caning

corporation NOUN 1 a group of people elected to govern a town 2 a group of people legally authorized to act as an individual in business

corps (kor) NOUN 1 a unit in an army 2 a group of people in a job

corpse NOUN a dead body

corpuscle NOUN a red or white cell in the blood

correct ADJECTIVE 1 true or accurate 2 done or said in the right way ▶ **correctly** ADVERB

correct VERB 1 to make a thing correct 2 to mark the mistakes in

something ▶ **correction** NOUN, **corrective** ADJECTIVE

correspond VERB 1 to write letters 2 to agree or match 3 to be similar or equivalent

correspondence NOUN 1 letters or the writing of letters 2 similarity or agreement

correspondent NOUN 1 a person who writes letters 2 a person who writes news reports for a newspaper or broadcasting station

corridor NOUN a passage in a building

corroborate VERB to help to confirm a statement ▶ **corroboration** NOUN

corrode VERB to destroy metal gradually by chemical action ▶ **corrosion** NOUN

corrosive ADJECTIVE able to corrode something

corrugated ADJECTIVE shaped into alternate ridges and grooves

corrupt ADJECTIVE 1 dishonest; accepting bribes 2 bad; wicked 3 decaying

THESAURUS

correct ADJECTIVE • *correct information* ▶ right, accurate, true, precise, reliable, factual • *the correct course of action* ▶ right, proper, appropriate, suitable, acceptable • *correct behaviour* ▶ proper, decent, well-mannered

correct VERB • *to correct a mistake* ▶ rectify, put right, make good, amend • *to correct work* ▶ mark, assess, evaluate, appraise

correspond VERB • *The friends corresponded for years.* ▶ communicate, exchange letters, write to each other **correspond to** • *words that correspond to the thought* ▶ match, fit, conform to, agree with, be consistent with

corrupt ADJECTIVE • *corrupt politicians* ▶ dishonest, unscrupulous, untrustworthy, crooked, disreputable • *a corrupt*

DICTIONARY

corrupt VERB **1** to make dishonest or wicked **2** to spoil or cause to decay ▸ **corruptible** ADJECTIVE

corruption NOUN dishonesty; the practice of bribery

corset NOUN a close-fitting piece of underwear worn to support the body

cosh NOUN a heavy weapon

cosmetic NOUN a substance (e.g. powder or lipstick) put on the skin to make it look more attractive

cosmetic ADJECTIVE done only for appearance

cosmic ADJECTIVE to do with the universe or outer space

cosmopolitan ADJECTIVE including people from many countries

cosset VERB to treat someone very kindly and lovingly

cost NOUN **1** the amount of money needed to buy or do **2** the effort or loss needed to achieve something

cost VERB cost **1** to have a certain amount as its price or charge **2** to cause the loss of *The war cost us many lives.* **3** (past tense is **cost** or

costed) to estimate the cost of something

costly ADJECTIVE **costlier, costliest** having a high price

costume NOUN clothes for a particular purpose or of a particular date

cosy ADJECTIVE **cosier, cosiest** warm and comfortable ▸ **cosily** ADVERB

cosy NOUN **cosies** a cover placed over a teapot or boiled egg to keep it hot

cot NOUN a baby's bed with high sides

cottage NOUN a small simple house

cottage cheese NOUN soft white cheese made from skimmed milk

cotton NOUN **1** a soft white substance covering the seeds of a tropical plant **2** a thread made from this substance **3** cloth made from cotton thread

cotton wool NOUN soft fluffy wadding originally made from cotton

couch NOUN a long soft seat with one end raised

THESAURUS

society ▸ sinful, immoral, decadent, wicked, evil

cost NOUN • *the cost of a ticket* ▸ price, charge (for), expense, rate (for), value • *the cost in human lives* ▸ loss, suffering, sacrifice, price

cost VERB • *Each item costs a pound.* ▸ be priced at, sell for, go for, come to, fetch

costly ADJECTIVE • *costly designer clothes* ▸ expensive, overpriced, exorbitant, pricey

costume NOUN • *a prize for the best costume* ▸ outfit, dress, ensemble, clothing, suit

cosy ADJECTIVE • *a cosy little house* ▸ snug, comfortable, warm, homely, secure, relaxing

a
b
c
d
e
f
g
h
i
j
k
l
m
n
o
p
q
r
s
t
u
v
w
x
y
z

169

cough VERB to send out air from the lungs with a sudden sharp sound ▸ **cough** NOUN

could past tense of **can**²

couldn't could not

council NOUN a group of people elected to organize or discuss something, especially to organize the affairs of a town or county

councillor NOUN a member of a town or county council

counsel NOUN 1 expert advice 2 a barrister representing someone in a lawsuit

counsel VERB **counselling, counselled** to give expert advice to

counsellor NOUN an adviser

count¹ VERB 1 to say numbers in their correct order 2 to find the total of 3 to include in a total *six of us, counting the dog* 4 to be important 5 to regard or consider *to count it an honour* **count on** to rely on

count NOUN 1 an instance of counting 2 a number reached by counting 3 a charge or accusation

count² NOUN a foreign nobleman

countdown NOUN a count backwards to zero before an event

countenance NOUN a person's face or expression

countenance VERB to tolerate or approve of

counter¹ NOUN 1 a flat surface over which customers are served in a shop 2 a small round playing piece used in board games 3 a device for counting things

counter² VERB 1 to counteract 2 to return an opponent's blow

counteract VERB to act against something and reduce or prevent its effects ▸ **counteraction** NOUN

counter-attack VERB to attack to oppose an enemy's attack ▸ **counter-attack** NOUN

counterfeit (kownt-er-feet) ADJECTIVE fake; not genuine

counterfeit NOUN a forgery or imitation

counterfeit VERB to forge or make an imitation of

counterpart NOUN a person or thing that corresponds to another

counterpoint NOUN a method of combining melodies in harmony

countess NOUN 1 a woman with the rank of count 2 the wife or widow of a count or earl

countless ADJECTIVE too many to count

THESAURUS

count VERB • *counting the number of people present* ▸ add up, calculate, work out, check
• *People should feel that they count.* ▸ matter, be important, have significance **count on** • *You can*

count on my support. ▸ rely on, depend on, bank on, be sure of, trust

countless ADJECTIVE • *countless reasons* ▸ innumerable, untold, numerous, endless, infinite

a
b
c
d
e
f
g
h
i
j
k
l
m
n
o
p
q
r
s
t
u
v
w
x
y
z

country *NOUN* **countries 1** the land a nation occupies **2** all the people of a country **3** areas away from towns and cities

countryside *NOUN* areas away from towns and cities, with fields, trees, and villages

county *NOUN* **counties** a major division of a country

coup (koo) *NOUN* a sudden action taken to win power

couple *NOUN* two people or things considered together; a pair

couple *VERB* to fasten or link two things

couplet *NOUN* a pair of lines in rhyming verse

coupon *NOUN* a piece of paper that gives you the right to receive or do something

courage *NOUN* the ability to face danger or difficulty or pain when you are afraid ► **courageous** *ADJECTIVE*

courgette *NOUN* a kind of small vegetable marrow

courier *NOUN* **1** a messenger **2** a person employed to guide tourists

course *NOUN* **1** the direction which something takes **2** a series of events or actions **3** a series of lessons or exercises **4** a part of a meal **5** a racecourse or golf course **of course** without a doubt; as we expected

course *VERB* to move or flow freely

court *NOUN* **1** the royal household **2** a lawcourt or the judges and lawyers in it **3** an enclosed area for games such as tennis or netball **4** a courtyard

THESAURUS

country *NOUN* • *a country of warlike people* ► nation, land, state, territory, realm • *to return to your country* ► homeland, home, native land, mother country • *to appeal to the country in an election* ► people, nation, public, population, community • *lovely open country* ► landscape, countryside, terrain, scenery, environment

couple *NOUN* • *a couple dancing on the balcony* ► pair, twosome, duo, husband and wife • *in the next couple of days* ► few, two or three

courage *NOUN* • *It takes courage to argue with them.* ► bravery,

daring, nerve, audacity, pluck, heroism

courageous *ADJECTIVE* • *a courageous attempt* ► brave, daring, audacious, plucky, adventurous

course *NOUN* • *a beginner's course* ► programme of study, course of study, classes, lessons • *to change course* ► direction, route, way, itinerary • *to change the course of history* ► progress, development, advance, evolution • *the best course to adopt* ► plan, plan of action, procedure, method • *six laps of the course* ► track, circuit, ground, stadium

court VERB to try to win somebody's love or support

courteous (ker-tee-us) ADJECTIVE polite and helpful ► **courteously** ADVERB, **courtesy** NOUN

courtier NOUN (old use) a companion of a king or queen at court

courtly ADJECTIVE dignified and polite

court martial NOUN **courts martial** 1 a court for trying people who have broken military law 2 a trial in this court

court-martial VERB **court-martialling, court-martialled** to try a person by a court martial

courtship NOUN 1 the process of courting someone 2 the mating ritual of some birds and animals

courtyard NOUN a space surrounded by walls or buildings

cousin NOUN a child of your uncle or aunt

cove NOUN a small bay

coven (kuv-en) NOUN a group of witches

cover VERB 1 to place one thing over or round another 2 to travel a certain distance 3 to aim a gun at or near somebody 4 to protect by insurance or a guarantee 5 to be enough money to pay for something 6 to deal with or include **cover up** to hide an awkward fact or piece of information

cover NOUN 1 a thing used for covering something else 2 the binding of a book 3 something that hides or shelters

coverage NOUN the amount of time or space given to reporting an event in a newspaper or broadcast

covert ADJECTIVE done secretly

covet (kuv-it) VERB to want very much to have something belonging to someone else ► **covetous** ADJECTIVE

courteous ADJECTIVE • helpful and courteous ► polite, civil, considerate, respectful, well-mannered

cover NOUN • a plastic cover ► covering, envelope, wrapper, case • Lift the cover. ► lid, top, cap • The book has a blue cover. ► jacket, dust jacket • a thick cover of snow ► covering, layer, coating, blanket, carpet • The trees provide cover. ► shelter, protection, refuge, defence • a

cover for spying activities ► front, facade, pretext, disguise

cover VERB • She covered her knees with a blanket. ► enclose, protect, hide • The car was covered in mud. ► coat, cake, plaster, smother • The book covers all these topics. ► deal with, consider, include, contain • The money should cover most of our needs. ► cater for, be enough for, meet

cow¹ NOUN **1** the female of cattle **2** the female of an elephant, whale, or seal

cow² VERB to subdue by bullying

coward NOUN a person who has no courage and shows fear in a shameful way ► **cowardly** ADJECTIVE

cowardice NOUN lack of courage

cowboy NOUN a man in charge of grazing cattle on a ranch in the USA

cower VERB to crouch or shrink back in fear

cowl NOUN **1** a monk's hood **2** a hood-shaped covering on a chimney

cowslip NOUN a wild plant with small yellow flowers

cox NOUN a person who steers a rowing boat

coy ADJECTIVE pretending to be shy or modest ► **coyly** ADVERB

coyote (koi-oh-ti) NOUN a North American wolf

crab NOUN a shellfish with ten legs, the first pair being a set of pincers

crab apple NOUN a small sour apple

crack NOUN **1** a line on the surface of something that has broken but not come apart **2** a narrow gap **3** a sudden sharp noise **4** a knock **5** (informal) a joke **6** a drug made from cocaine

crack ADJECTIVE (informal) first-class *a crack shot*

crack VERB **1** to make or get a crack **2** to make a sudden sharp noise **3** to break down **4** to tell a joke **crack down on** (informal) to stop something illegal or against the rules **get cracking** (informal) to get busy

cracker NOUN **1** a paper tube that bangs when pulled apart **2** a thin biscuit

crackle VERB to make small cracking sounds ► **crackle** NOUN

crackling NOUN crisp skin on roast pork

cradle NOUN **1** a small cot for a baby **2** a supporting framework

cradle VERB to hold gently

craft NOUN **1** a job needing skilful use of the hands **2** skill **3** cunning or trickery **4** a boat or small ship

craftsman NOUN craftsmen a person who is good at a craft ► **craftsmanship** NOUN

THESAURUS

cowardly ADJECTIVE • *a cowardly person* ► weak, timid, faint-hearted, spineless

crack NOUN • *a plate with a crack in it* ► break, chip, chink, split • *a crack on the head* ► blow, bang, knock, smack, hit • *a crack of thunder* ► bang, crash, explosion, burst

crack VERB • *She dropped a cup and cracked it.* ► break, split, shatter, splinter, chip • *a problem that's hard to crack* ► solve, work out, puzzle out **crack down on** • *a drive to crack down on street crime* ► reduce, end, stop, eradicate, clamp down on

crafty ADJECTIVE **craftier, craftiest** cunning ► **craftily** ADVERB

crag NOUN a steep piece of rough rock ► **craggy** ADJECTIVE

cram VERB **cramming, crammed** 1 to push many things into a space so that it is too full 2 to learn facts quickly for an exam

cramp NOUN pain caused by a muscle tightening suddenly

cramp VERB to hinder someone's freedom or growth

cramped ADJECTIVE in a space that is too small or tight

cranberry NOUN **cranberries** a small sour red berry

crane NOUN 1 a machine for lifting and moving heavy objects 2 a large wading bird with long legs and neck

crane VERB to stretch your neck to try to see something

crane fly NOUN **crane flies** a flying insect with long thin legs

cranium NOUN the skull

crank NOUN 1 an L-shaped part used for changing the direction of movement in machinery 2 an eccentric person ► **cranky** ADJECTIVE

crank VERB to move by means of a crank

cranny NOUN **crannies** a small crack or opening

crash NOUN 1 the loud noise of something breaking or colliding 2 a violent collision or fall 3 a sudden drop or failure

crash VERB 1 to make or have a crash 2 to cause to crash 3 to move with a crash 4 (of a computer) to stop working suddenly

crash ADJECTIVE short and intensive *a crash course*

crass ADJECTIVE 1 very obvious or shocking *crass ignorance* 2 very stupid

crafty ADJECTIVE • *a crafty way of avoiding the problem* ► cunning, clever, shrewd, ingenious, wily

cram VERB • *They were cramming burgers into their mouths.* ► stuff, force, press, squeeze, jam • *How did we manage to cram into such a tiny car?* ► crowd, crush, squeeze

cramped ADJECTIVE • *the cramped quarters of the submarine* ► restricted, confined, poky, narrow, tight

crash NOUN • *a loud crash in the kitchen* ► bang, smash, clash, clatter, clang, thump, thud, boom • *a car crash* ► accident, collision, smash, bump, pile-up • *a stock-market crash* ► collapse, failure, fall, ruin

crash VERB • *The company crashed.* ► fail, collapse, fold, go under • *Parts of the roof crashed.* ► collapse, fall, topple **crash into** • *to crash into a tree* ► hit, strike, smash into, collide with, bump into

DICTIONARY

crate NOUN **1** a packing case made of wooden strips **2** an open container for carrying bottles

crater NOUN **1** the mouth of a volcano **2** a hollow caused by an explosion or impact

cravat NOUN a short wide scarf worn by men round the neck instead of a tie

crave VERB to want very much

craving NOUN a strong desire or longing

crawl VERB **1** to move with the body close to the ground **2** to move slowly **3** to be covered with crawling things ► **crawler** NOUN

crawl NOUN **1** a crawling movement **2** a very slow pace **3** an overarm swimming stroke

crayon NOUN a coloured stick or pencil for drawing

craze NOUN a temporary enthusiasm

crazed ADJECTIVE driven insane

crazy ADJECTIVE **crazier, craziest** insane or foolish ► **crazily** ADVERB

creak NOUN a harsh squeak like a stiff door hinge ► **creaky** ADJECTIVE

creak VERB to make a creak

cream NOUN **1** the fatty part of milk **2** a yellowish-white colour **3** a food containing or looking like cream **4** a soft substance **5** the best part of something ► **creamy** ADJECTIVE

cream VERB to take the cream off **cream off** to remove the best part of something

crease NOUN **1** a line made in something by folding **2** a line on a cricket pitch marking a batsman's or bowler's position

crease VERB to make creases in

create VERB **1** to bring into existence; to make or produce **2** (*informal*) to make a fuss

THESAURUS

crate NOUN • *three crates of books* ► case, packing case, box, tea chest

crawl VERB • *to crawl out of the cave* ► creep, edge, inch, slither, clamber **be crawling with** • *be crawling with tourists* ► be full of, be overrun by, be teeming with, be packed with

craze NOUN • *the latest craze* ► fad, trend, fashion, rage, obsession

crazy ADJECTIVE • *It was crazy to think they would agree.* ► absurd, ridiculous, ludicrous, foolish, idiotic, stupid • *She was going*

crazy with all the work. ► mad, insane, out of your mind, demented • *crazy about golf* ► made, passionate, keen (on), devoted (to)

crease NOUN • *The cloth was full of creases.* ► wrinkle, crinkle, line

crease VERB • *to crease your clothes* ► crumple, crinkle, crush, rumple

create VERB • *to create a new work* ► produce, make, generate, develop, compose, design • *to create a business* ► set up, start, found, establish • *The decision created resentment.* ► cause,

DICTIONARY

creation NOUN **1** the act of creating something **2** something created

creative ADJECTIVE showing imagination and thought as well as skill ▸ **creativity** NOUN

creator NOUN a person who creates something

creature NOUN a living being

crèche (kresh) NOUN a place where babies and young children are looked after while their parents are at work

credentials PLURAL NOUN documents showing a person's identity, qualifications, etc.

credible ADJECTIVE able to be believed; convincing ▸ **credibility** NOUN, **credibly** ADVERB

credit NOUN **1** a source of pride or honour **2** praise or acknowledgement for an achievement or good quality **3** an arrangement by which a person pays for something at a later time **4** an amount of money in an account at a bank **5** belief or trust

I put no credit in this rumour.

credits a list of people involved in a film or television programme

credit VERB **1** to believe **2** to say that a person has done or achieved something *Columbus is credited with the discovery of America.* **3** to enter something as a credit in a financial account

credit card NOUN a card authorizing a person to buy on credit

creditor NOUN a person to whom money is owed

credulous ADJECTIVE too ready to believe things; gullible

creed NOUN a set or formal statement of beliefs

creek NOUN **1** a narrow inlet **2** a small stream

creep VERB **crept 1** to move along close to the ground **2** to move quietly **3** to come gradually **4** (of the flesh) to prickle with fear

creep NOUN **1** a creeping movement **2** (*informal*) an unpleasant person

THESAURUS

bring about, lead to, produce, result in

creative ADJECTIVE • *to be creative in your writing* ▸ imaginative, inventive, original, artistic, inspired

creature NOUN • *the largest living creatures* ▸ animal, living thing, beast • *the poor creature* ▸ wretch, fellow, chap, person

credible ADJECTIVE • *a credible explanation* ▸ believable,

plausible, reasonable, possible, convincing

credit NOUN • *to deserve credit* ▸ praise, acclaim, approval, recognition

credit VERB • *It is difficult to credit such an unlikely story.* ▸ accept, believe, trust, have confidence in

creep VERB • *to creep along the floor* ▸ crawl, slither, slink, wriggle, edge, inch • *They crept down the stairs.* ▸ slip, sneak, steal, tiptoe

a
b
c
d
e
f
g
h
i
j
k
l
m
n
o
p
q
r
s
t
u
v
w
x
y
z

the creeps (*informal*) a nervous feeling caused by fear or dislike

creeper NOUN a plant that grows along the ground or up a wall etc.

creepy ADJECTIVE **creepier**, **creepiest** frightening and sinister

cremate VERB to burn a dead body to ashes ▸ **cremation** NOUN

crematorium NOUN **crematoriums** a place where corpses are cremated

creosote NOUN an oily brown liquid painted on wood to preserve it

crêpe paper NOUN paper with a wrinkled surface

crescendo (krish-en-doh) NOUN **crescendos** a gradual increase in loudness

crescent NOUN 1 a narrow curved shape coming to a point at each end 2 a curved street

cress NOUN a plant with hot-tasting leaves, used in salads

crest NOUN 1 a tuft of hair, skin, or feathers on a bird's head 2 the top of a hill or wave 3 a badge or design ▸ **crested** ADJECTIVE

crestfallen ADJECTIVE disappointed or dejected

crevasse (kri-vass) NOUN a deep open crack in a glacier

crevice NOUN a narrow opening in a rock or wall

crew[1] NOUN 1 the people working in a ship or aircraft 2 a group working together *a camera crew*

crew[2] *past tense of* **crow**[2]

crib NOUN 1 a baby's cot 2 a manger 3 a translation used by students

crib VERB **cribbing**, **cribbed** to copy someone else's work

cribbage NOUN a card game

crick NOUN painful stiffness in the neck or back

cricket[1] NOUN a game played outdoors between teams of 11 with a ball, bats, and two wickets ▸ **cricketer** NOUN

cricket[2] NOUN a brown insect like a grasshopper

crime NOUN 1 an action that breaks the law 2 unlawful activity

criminal NOUN a person who has committed a crime ▸ **criminal** ADJECTIVE

crimson ADJECTIVE of a deep red colour ▸ **crimson** NOUN

THESAURUS

creepy ADJECTIVE • *The place gave her creepy feelings.* ▸ frightening, eerie, spooky, scary, weird, sinister

crime NOUN • *a decrease in street crime* ▸ lawbreaking, lawlessness, wrongdoing, dishonesty • *Blackmail is a serious*

crime. ▸ offence, misdemeanour, illegal act

criminal NOUN • *a gang of criminals* ▸ lawbreaker, villain, offender, wrongdoer, convict, culprit

criminal ADJECTIVE • *criminal behaviour* ▸ illegal, unlawful, dishonest, corrupt

cringe VERB to shrink back in fear

crinkle VERB to make or become wrinkled ► **crinkly** ADJECTIVE

cripple VERB 1 to make a person lame 2 to weaken or damage seriously

crisis NOUN **crises** a time of great danger or difficulty

crisp ADJECTIVE 1 very dry and breaking with a snap 2 fresh and stiff 3 cold and dry *a crisp morning* 4 brisk and sharp *a crisp manner*
► **crisply** ADVERB

crisp NOUN a thin fried slice of potato, sold in packets

criss-cross ADJECTIVE, ADVERB with crossing lines

criss-cross VERB to move backwards and forwards across

criterion NOUN **criteria** a standard for judging or deciding something

critic NOUN 1 a person who gives opinions on books, plays, films, music, etc. 2 a person who finds fault

critical ADJECTIVE 1 criticizing 2 to do with critics or criticism 3 at a crisis; very serious ► **critically** ADVERB

criticism NOUN 1 the process of criticizing 2 the work of a critic

criticize VERB to say that a person or thing has faults

⚠ **SPELLING**

This word can also be spelled *criticise*.

croak VERB to make a deep hoarse sound like a frog ► **croak** NOUN

crochet (kroh-shay) NOUN a kind of needlework done with a hooked needle

crochet VERB to make with crochet

crock NOUN 1 a piece of crockery 2 (*informal*) a decrepit person or thing

crockery NOUN household china

cringe VERB • to cringe with fear ► cower, shrink back, recoil, flinch, shy away

crisp ADJECTIVE • *The biscuits in the tin were new and crisp.* ► crunchy, crispy, brittle, crumbly • *a crisp morning in November* ► fresh, brisk, bracing, refreshing

critical ADJECTIVE • *highly critical of the foreign policy* ► disapproving, disparaging (about), scathing (about), uncomplimentary (about) • *a critical assessment of*

his work ► analytical, objective, evaluative • *the critical moment* ► crucial, vital, decisive, all-important • *in a critical condition* ► serious, grave, dangerous

criticism NOUN • to come in for criticism ► disapproval, blame, censure, reproach

criticize VERB • *Police criticized motorists for excessive speed.* ► condemn, find fault with, denounce, blame

crocodile NOUN **1** a large tropical reptile with a thick skin, long tail, and huge jaws **2** a line of schoolchildren walking in pairs

crocus NOUN a small plant with yellow, purple, or white flowers

croft NOUN a small rented farm in Scotland ► **crofter** NOUN

croissant (krwah-son) NOUN a flaky crescent-shaped bread roll

crone NOUN an old woman

crony NOUN **cronies** a close friend or companion

crook NOUN **1** a shepherd's stick with a curved end **2** something bent or curved **3** (informal) a person who makes a living dishonestly

crook VERB to bend or make into a hook

crooked ADJECTIVE **1** bent or twisted; not straight **2** dishonest

croon VERB to sing softly and gently

crop NOUN **1** something grown for food **2** a whip with a loop instead of a lash **3** part of a bird's throat **4** a short haircut

crop VERB **cropping, cropped 1** to cut or bite off **2** to produce a crop **crop up** to happen unexpectedly

cropper NOUN **come a cropper** (informal) **1** to have a bad fall **2** to fail badly

croquet (kroh-kay) NOUN a game in which players use mallets to drive wooden balls through hoops in the ground

cross NOUN **1** a mark or shape made like + or X **2** an upright post with another piece of wood across it, used in ancient times for crucifixion; this as a symbol of Christianity **3** a mixture of two different things

cross VERB **1** to go across something **2** to draw a line or lines across something **3** to make the

THESAURUS

crooked ADJECTIVE • *The picture looks crooked.* ► askew, lopsided, offcentre, slanting • *a maze of crooked paths* ► winding, twisting, tortuous, zigzag • *a crooked finger* ► bent, misshapen, deformed • *crooked officials* ► criminal, dishonest, corrupt

crop NOUN • *a crop of apples* ► harvest, yield

crop VERB • *Sheep were cropping grass.* ► graze on, browse on, eat, nibble • *to crop hair* ► cut short, clip, trim, snip **crop up** • *The same*

problems keep cropping up. ► occur, arise, appear, come up, happen

cross NOUN • *a cross between a yak and a cow* ► hybrid, cross-breed, combination (of), mixture (of)

cross VERB • *The two roads cross.* ► intersect, meet • *to cross the river* ► go across, pass over, ford • *to cross the field* ► go across, walk across, traverse • *A bridge crosses the stream.* ► span, bridge, go across, extend across • *Try not to cross him.* ► oppose, annoy, defy, thwart **cross out** • *to*

a
b
c
d
e
f
g
h
i
j
k
l
m
n
o
p
q
r
s
t
u
v
w
x
y
z

DICTIONARY

sign or shape of a cross **4** to produce something from two different kinds **cross out** to draw a line across unwanted writing

cross ADJECTIVE **1** annoyed or bad-tempered **2** going from one side to another **cross winds**
▶ **crossly** ADVERB

crossbar NOUN a horizontal bar, especially between two uprights

crossbow NOUN a powerful bow with a mechanism for pulling and releasing the string

cross-examine VERB to question someone carefully to test answers given to previous questions, especially in a lawcourt
▶ **cross-examination** NOUN

cross-eyed ADJECTIVE with eyes that look or seem to look towards the nose

crossfire NOUN lines of gunfire that cross each other

crossing NOUN a place where people can cross a road or railway

cross-legged ADJECTIVE, ADVERB with ankles crossed and knees spread apart

crossroads NOUN a place where two or more roads cross one another

cross-section NOUN **1** a drawing of something as if it had been cut through **2** a typical sample

crosswise ADVERB, ADJECTIVE with one thing crossing another

crossword NOUN a puzzle in which words have to be found from clues and written into blank squares in a grid

crotch NOUN the part between the legs where they join the body

crotchet NOUN a note in music, usually representing one beat (♩)

crotchety ADJECTIVE bad-tempered

crouch VERB to lower your body, with your arms and legs bent

croup (kroop) NOUN a disease causing a hard cough and difficulty in breathing

crow[1] NOUN a large black bird **as the crow flies** in a straight line

crow[2] VERB **crowed** or **crew 1** to make a shrill cry as a cock does **2** to boast ▶ **crow** NOUN

crowbar NOUN an iron bar used as a lever

crowd NOUN a large number of people in one place

THESAURUS

cross out part of the sentence
▶ delete, strike out, erase

cross ADJECTIVE • *They were getting cross about the wait.* ▶ angry, annoyed, upset, irate, bad-tempered, cantankerous, crotchety, irritable, grumpy

crouch VERB • *to crouch behind a tree* ▶ squat, kneel, stoop, bend, bob down, hunch

crowd NOUN • *The crowd dispersed quickly.* ▶ throng, gathering, multitude, mob, horde, rabble • *a large crowd at the ground* ▶ audience, spectators, attendance

DICTIONARY

crowd VERB **1** to come together in a crowd **2** to cram

crown NOUN **1** an ornamental headdress worn by a king or queen **2** (often **Crown**) the sovereign **3** the highest part of a road or hill **4** a former coin worth 5 shillings (25p) **Crown Prince** or **Crown Princess** the heir to the throne

crown VERB **1** to place a crown on someone as a symbol of royal power or victory **2** to form or cover or decorate the top of **3** to be a successful end to something **4** (informal) to hit on the head

crow's nest NOUN a lookout platform high up on a ship's mast

crucial (kroo-shal) ADJECTIVE most important ▶ **crucially** ADVERB

crucible NOUN a melting pot for metals

crucifix NOUN a model of Christ on the cross

crucify VERB **crucifies, crucified** to put a person to death by nailing or binding the hands and feet to a cross ▶ **crucifixion** NOUN

crude ADJECTIVE **1** in a natural state; not yet refined **2** not well finished; rough **3** vulgar ▶ **crudely** ADVERB, **crudity** NOUN

cruel ADJECTIVE **crueller, cruellest** causing pain or suffering ▶ **cruelly** ADVERB, **cruelty** NOUN

cruet NOUN a set of small containers for salt, pepper, oil, etc. for use at the table

cruise NOUN a pleasure trip in a ship

cruise VERB **1** to sail or travel at a moderate speed **2** to go on a cruise

cruiser NOUN **1** a fast warship **2** a large motor boat

crumb NOUN a tiny piece of bread, cake, or biscuit

THESAURUS

crowd VERB • to crowd round
▶ gather, collect, cluster, congregate, huddle, swarm • The team had to crowd into the tiny room. ▶ stream, push, pile, pack, squeeze, flock

crowded ADJECTIVE • a crowded beach ▶ packed, congested, overcrowded, swarming, teeming, overflowing

crucial ADJECTIVE • a crucial role to play ▶ major, central, decisive, important • Secrecy is crucial. ▶ paramount, essential, vital

crude ADJECTIVE • crude oil
▶ unrefined, unpurified,

unprocessed, natural, raw • a crude method ▶ primitive, simple, basic, rudimentary, amateurish • crude humour ▶ coarse, indecent, vulgar, offensive, obscene

cruel ADJECTIVE • cruel men
▶ brutal, savage, vicious, barbaric, callous, cold-blooded, pitiless, ruthless • a cruel blow ▶ severe, harsh, bitter

crumb NOUN • crumbs of bread
▶ fragment, grain, morsel, scrap, bit

DICTIONARY

crumble VERB to break or fall into small pieces

crumble NOUN a pudding made with fruit cooked with a crumbly topping

crumbly ADJECTIVE easily breaking into small pieces

crumpet NOUN a soft flat cake made with yeast, eaten toasted with butter

crumple VERB 1 to crush or become crushed into creases 2 to collapse loosely

crunch VERB to crush noisily, e.g. between your teeth

crunch NOUN a crunching sound **the crunch** (*informal*) a crucial event or turning point ▶ **crunchy** ADJECTIVE

Crusade NOUN a military expedition made by Christians in the Middle Ages to recover Palestine from the Muslims who had conquered it ▶ **Crusader** NOUN

crusade NOUN a campaign in a good cause

crush VERB 1 to press something so that it breaks or is damaged 2 to squeeze tightly 3 to defeat completely

crush NOUN 1 a crowd of people pressed together 2 a drink made with crushed fruit

crust NOUN 1 the hard outer layer of something, e.g. bread 2 the rocky outer layer of the earth

crustacean NOUN an animal with a shell, e.g. a crab, lobster, or shrimp

crusty ADJECTIVE **crustier**, **crustiest** 1 having a crisp crust 2 irritable or bad-tempered ▶ **crustily** ADVERB

crutch NOUN a support like a long walking stick for helping a lame person

cry NOUN **cries** 1 a loud wordless sound expressing pain, grief, joy, etc. 2 a shout 3 a spell of crying

THESAURUS

crumble VERB • *The damaged buildings began to crumble.* ▶ disintegrate, break up, collapse, fall apart • *to crumble the soil* ▶ crush, grind, pound, break into pieces

crumple VERB • *to crumple your clothes* ▶ crease, crush, crinkle, squash

crunch VERB • *to crunch biscuits* ▶ munch, chomp, devour

crush VERB • *to crush your arm* ▶ squash, squeeze, mangle, mash,

break, bruise • *to crush the dress* ▶ crease, crumple, crinkle, squash • *to crush a rebellion* ▶ suppress, quell, quash, put down, defeat

crush NOUN • *a crush by the doors* ▶ crowd, throng, congestion, jam

crust NOUN • *The paint formed a hard crust.* ▶ covering, skin, surface, shell

cry NOUN • *a cry of pain* ▶ call, shout, yell, shriek, scream, screech, roar, bellow • *a cry for help* ▶ appeal, plea

cry VERB **cries**, **cried 1** to shed tears **2** to call out loudly

crypt NOUN a room under a church

cryptic ADJECTIVE having a secret meaning that is hard to find
► **cryptically** ADVERB

crystal NOUN **1** a clear transparent mineral like glass **2** very clear high-quality glass **3** a small solid piece of a substance with a symmetrical shape *ice crystals*

crystalline ADJECTIVE made of crystals

crystallize VERB **1** to form into crystals **2** to become definite in form ► **crystallization** NOUN

⚠ **SPELLING**

This word can also be spelled *crystalise.*

cub NOUN a young lion, tiger, fox, or bear

Cub or **Cub Scout** NOUN a member of the junior branch of the Scout Association

cubby hole NOUN a small compartment

cube NOUN **1** an object that has six equal square sides, like a box or dice **2** the number produced by multiplying something by itself twice *The cube of 3 is 3 x 3 x 3 = 27.*

cube VERB **1** to multiply a number by itself twice *4 cubed is 4 x 4 x 4 = 64.* **2** to cut into cubes

cube root NOUN the number that gives a particular number if it is multiplied by itself twice *The cube root of 27 is 3.*

cubic ADJECTIVE **1** three-dimensional **2** denoting volume *cubic metre*

cubicle NOUN a compartment within a room

cuboid (kew-boid) NOUN an object with six rectangular sides

cuckoo NOUN **cuckoos** a bird with a two-note cry that lays its eggs in the nests of other birds

cucumber NOUN a long vegetable with a green skin

cud NOUN half-digested food that a sheep or cow brings back from its first stomach to chew again

cuddle VERB to put your arms closely round; to hug ► **cuddly** ADJECTIVE

cudgel NOUN a short thick stick used as a weapon

cudgel VERB **cudgelling**, **cudgelled** to beat with a cudgel

cue[1] NOUN a signal for an actor to speak or come on stage

cue[2] NOUN a long stick for striking the ball in billiards or snooker

cuff NOUN **1** the end of a sleeve round the wrist **2** a sharp slap with the hand **off the cuff** without rehearsal or preparation

cuff VERB to hit with the hand

cufflink NOUN each of a pair of fasteners for shirt cuffs

THESAURUS

cry VERB • *Debbie was about to cry.*
► weep, shed tears, sob, howl, whimper, snivel, blubber, bawl, wail • *'Come on!' cried Sam.*

► call, yell, exclaim, shout, shriek, scream, bawl

cuddle VERB • *to kiss and cuddle*
► hug, embrace, hold, clasp

cuisine (kwiz-een) NOUN a style of cooking

cul-de-sac NOUN a street that is closed at one end

culinary ADJECTIVE to do with cooking

cull VERB 1 to pick out and kill a number of animals from a larger number 2 to select and use ► **cull** NOUN

culminate VERB to reach the highest or last point ► **culmination** NOUN

culpable ADJECTIVE deserving blame

culprit NOUN the person who is to blame for something

cult NOUN 1 a religious sect 2 a film, rock group, etc. that is popular with a particular group of people

cultivate VERB 1 to use land to grow crops 2 to grow or develop things by looking after them ► **cultivation** NOUN, **cultivator** NOUN

cultivated ADJECTIVE having good manners and education

culture NOUN 1 appreciation and understanding of literature and the arts 2 the customs and traditions of a people 3 (Science) a quantity of bacteria or cells grown

for study 4 the cultivation of plants ► **cultural** ADJECTIVE

cultured ADJECTIVE educated to appreciate literature, art, music, etc.

cumbersome ADJECTIVE clumsy to carry or manage

cumulative ADJECTIVE increasing by continuous additions

cunning ADJECTIVE 1 clever at deceiving people 2 cleverly designed or planned

cunning NOUN 1 skill in deceiving people 2 skill or ingenuity

cup NOUN 1 a small container for drinking from 2 anything shaped like a cup 3 a goblet-shaped ornament given as a prize

cup VERB **cupping, cupped** to form your hands into the shape of a cup

cupboard NOUN a piece of furniture with a door, for storage

cupful NOUN **cupfuls** the amount a cup will hold

curable ADJECTIVE able to be cured

curate NOUN a member of the clergy who helps a vicar

curator (kewr-ay-ter) NOUN a person in charge of a museum or gallery or a part of one

THESAURUS

culprit NOUN • *He was not the culprit after all.* ► guilty party, person responsible, offender, criminal, wrongdoer

cunning ADJECTIVE • *a cunning plan* ► crafty, wily, sly, devious

• *cunning detective work* ► skilful, clever, shrewd, ingenious

cunning NOUN • *You will need all your cunning.* ► craftiness, shrewdness, astuteness, deviousness

curb VERB to restrain *curb your impatience*

curb NOUN a restraint *a curb on spending*

> ⚠ **USAGE**
>
> Do not confuse this word with *kerb*.

curd NOUN or **curds** PLURAL NOUN a thick substance formed when milk turns sour

curdle VERB to form into curds

cure VERB 1 to free someone from an illness 2 to stop something bad 3 to preserve food by drying or smoking it

cure NOUN 1 the process of freeing from an illness 2 something that cures a person or thing

curfew NOUN 1 an order for people to remain indoors after a certain time until the next day 2 the time fixed for this

curiosity NOUN **curiosities** 1 the state of being curious 2 something unusual and interesting

curious ADJECTIVE 1 wanting to find out about things; inquisitive 2 strange or unusual ► **curiously** ADVERB

curl NOUN a curve or coil, e.g. of hair

curl VERB to form into curls **curl up** to sit or lie with your knees drawn up

curling NOUN a game played on ice with large flat stones

curly ADJECTIVE **curlier, curliest** having many curls

currant NOUN 1 a small black dried grape used in cookery 2 a small round red, black, or white berry

currency NOUN **currencies** 1 the money in use in a country 2 the general use of something

THESAURUS

curb VERB • *to curb your temper*
► restrain, suppress, control

cure VERB • *to cure an illness*
► heal, treat, alleviate, ease, relieve • *The fault is difficult to cure.* ► correct, rectify, repair, put right

cure NOUN • *a cure for cancer*
► treatment, remedy, medicine, antidote, therapy • *her unexpected cure* ► recovery, healing

curious ADJECTIVE • *curious about the reasons* ► inquisitive, intrigued, interested, puzzled • *a curious jerking motion* ► strange, odd, peculiar, queer, bizarre

curl NOUN • *a mass of curls* ► wave, ringlet, coil, loop • *a pattern with repeated curls* ► loop, spiral, swirl, twist, curve • *a curl of smoke* ► spiral, coil, swirl

curl VERB • *Smoke curled from the chimney.* ► coil, spiral, swirl • *The path curls round old tree trunks.* ► wind, twist, snake, zigzag • *to curl an arm round* ► wind, twine, wrap • *to curl your hair* ► crimp, wave, frizz, perm

curly ADJECTIVE • *thick curly hair*
► wavy, curled, crinkly, frizzy, permed

DICTIONARY

current ADJECTIVE happening now; used now ▸ **currently** ADVERB

current NOUN **1** water or air etc. moving in one direction **2** the flow of electricity along a wire etc. or through something

current affairs PLURAL NOUN political events in the news

curriculum NOUN **curricula** a course of study in a school or university

curry[1] NOUN **curries** food cooked with spices that taste hot ▸ **curried** ADJECTIVE

curry[2] VERB **curries**, **curried** **curry favour** to seek favour by flattery

curse NOUN **1** a call for a person or thing to be harmed **2** something very unpleasant **3** an angry word or words

curse VERB **1** to make a curse **2** to use a curse against

cursor NOUN a flashing symbol on a computer screen, that moves to show where new data will be put

cursory ADJECTIVE hasty and not thorough ▸ **cursorily** ADVERB

curt ADJECTIVE brief and hasty or rude *a curt reply* ▸ **curtly** ADVERB

curtail VERB **1** to cut short **2** to reduce or limit ▸ **curtailment** NOUN

curtain NOUN a piece of material hung at a window or door or at the front of a stage

curtsy NOUN **curtsies** a bow made by putting one foot behind the other and bending the knees

curtsy VERB **curtsies**, **curtsied** to make a curtsy

curve VERB to bend smoothly

curve NOUN a curved line or shape ▸ **curvy** ADJECTIVE

cushion NOUN **1** a cloth cover filled with soft material for resting on **2** anything soft or springy that acts as a support

cushion VERB to protect from the effects of a knock or shock

cushy ADJECTIVE (*informal*) pleasant and easy

cusp NOUN a pointed end where two curves meet

custard NOUN a sweet yellow sauce made with milk and eggs

THESAURUS

curse NOUN • *to put a curse on them* ▸ malediction, jinx • *the curse of unemployment* ▸ affliction, scourge, misfortune • *to let out a curse* ▸ swear word, oath

curse VERB • *He was cursing and shouting.* ▸ swear, blaspheme **be cursed with** • *to be cursed with sickness* ▸ be afflicted with, be plagued with, be burdened with

curve NOUN • *a series of curves in the road* ▸ bend, turn, twist • *a window with a curve at the top* ▸ arch, arc, bow, crescent

curve VERB • *The river curved to the west.* ▸ bend, twist, wind, snake

curved ADJECTIVE • *a curved roof* ▸ arched, rounded, convex • *The road was narrow and curved.* ▸ twisty, meandering

a
b
c
d
e
f
g
h
i
j
k
l
m
n
o
p
q
r
s
t
u
v
w
x
y
z

custody NOUN **1** care and supervision **2** imprisonment

custom NOUN **1** the usual way of behaving or acting **2** regular business from customers

customary ADJECTIVE according to custom; usual ► **customarily** ADVERB

customer NOUN a person who uses a shop, bank, or other business

customs PLURAL NOUN **1** taxes charged on goods brought into a country **2** the officials who collect these

cut VERB **cutting, cut 1** to divide or separate by using a sharp implement **2** to wound **3** to reduce in amount or size **4** to divide a pack of playing cards **5** to

hit a ball with a chopping movement **6** to go through or across something **7** to switch off electrical power or an engine etc. **8** (in a film) to move to another shot or scene **9** to make a sound recording **cut a corner** to pass round it very closely **cut and dried** already decided **cut in** to interrupt **cut off 1** to remove by cutting **2** to stop a supply of

cut NOUN **1** an act of cutting; the result of cutting **2** a small wound **3** (informal) a share

cute ADJECTIVE (informal) **1** attractive in a pretty way **2** smart; clever

cuticle NOUN the skin round a nail

cutlass NOUN a short sword with a broad curved blade

cutlery NOUN knives, forks, and spoons

THESAURUS

custom NOUN • old local customs ► tradition, practice, convention, habit • our usual custom ► practice, habit, routine • to attract custom ► business, trade, customers

customer NOUN • to attract younger customers ► shopper, buyer, client, consumer

cut NOUN • a cut on his hand ► gash, wound, injury, nick, scratch, graze • a cut in pay ► reduction, decrease

cut VERB • to cut a finger ► gash, wound, injure, slash, nick, scratch, graze • to cut vegetables ► slice, chop, dice, cube • to cut the grass ► trim, clip, crop, mow • to cut prices ► reduce, lower • to cut

parts of the story ► omit, remove, delete, take out • to cut your essay ► shorten, abridge, reduce • The remarks cut her deeply. ► hurt, offend, upset, wound **cut down** • to cut down trees ► fell, lop **cut off** • to cut off a finger ► sever, chop off, amputate, hack off, remove • to cut off a supply ► disconnect, discontinue, interrupt • Storms cut off the village. ► isolate, separate **cut out** • to cut out inefficiencies ► remove, eliminate, get rid of **cut up** • Cut the meat up into small cubes. ► chop, slice, dice, carve

cute ADJECTIVE • a cute little puppy ► appealing, lovely, delightful, attractive, pretty, adorable

cutlet NOUN a thick slice of meat for cooking

cut-out NOUN a shape cut out of paper, cardboard, etc.

cut-price ADJECTIVE sold at a reduced price

cutting NOUN 1 a steep-sided passage cut through high ground for a road or railway 2 a piece cut out of a newspaper or magazine 3 a piece cut from a plant to form a new plant

cuttlefish NOUN a sea creature with ten arms

cyanide NOUN a highly poisonous chemical

cycle NOUN 1 a bicycle or motorcycle 2 a series of events regularly repeated ▶ **cyclic** ADJECTIVE, **cyclical** ADJECTIVE

cycle VERB to ride a bicycle ▶ **cyclist** NOUN

cyclone NOUN a wind that rotates round a calm central area ▶ **cyclonic** ADJECTIVE

cygnet (sig-nit) NOUN a young swan

cylinder NOUN an object with straight sides and circular ends ▶ **cylindrical** ADJECTIVE

cymbal NOUN a percussion instrument consisting of a metal plate that is struck to make a ringing sound

⚠ **USAGE**

Do not confuse this word with *symbol*.

cynic (sin-ik) NOUN a person who believes that people act for selfish or bad reasons ▶ **cynical** ADJECTIVE, **cynicism** NOUN

cypress NOUN an evergreen tree with dark leaves

cyst (sist) NOUN a swelling containing fluid or soft matter

czar (zar) NOUN another spelling of **tsar**

Dd

dab NOUN **1** a quick gentle touch with something damp **2** a small lump *a dab of butter*

dab VERB **dabbing, dabbed** to touch quickly and gently

dabble VERB **1** to splash something about in water **2** to do something as a hobby

dachshund (daks-huund) NOUN a small dog with a long body and short legs

dad or **daddy** NOUN (*informal*) father

daddy-long-legs NOUN a crane fly

daffodil NOUN a yellow flower that grows from a bulb

daft ADJECTIVE (*informal*) silly or stupid

dagger NOUN a stabbing weapon like a short sword

dahlia (day-lee-a) NOUN a garden plant with brightly-coloured flowers

daily ADVERB, ADJECTIVE every day

dainty ADJECTIVE **daintier, daintiest** small and pretty
▶ **daintily** ADVERB

dairy NOUN **dairies** a place where milk, butter, and cheese are produced or sold

daisy NOUN **daisies** a small flower with white petals and a yellow centre

dale NOUN a valley

dally VERB **dallies, dallied** to dawdle or waste time

dam NOUN a wall built to hold back water

dam VERB **damming, dammed** to hold back water with a dam

damage NOUN harm or injury done to something

damage VERB to harm or spoil something

damages PLURAL NOUN money paid as compensation for an injury or loss

Dame NOUN the title of a lady who has been given the equivalent of a knighthood

dame NOUN a comic middle-aged woman in a pantomime, played by a man

damn VERB to curse or condemn
▶ **damnation** NOUN

damp ADJECTIVE slightly wet; not quite dry

THESAURUS

daft ADJECTIVE • *a daft idea* ▶ silly, stupid, absurd, foolish, crazy

dainty ADJECTIVE • *a dainty lace handkerchief* ▶ delicate, elegant, pretty

damage NOUN • *The burglars caused some damage.* ▶ destruction, devastation, havoc, harm, injury

damage VERB • *to damage properties* ▶ spoil, wreck, harm, injure

damp ADJECTIVE • *a damp cloth* ▶ moist, wet, soggy • *The air was damp and cold.* ▶ wet, drizzly, rainy

a
b
c
d
e
f
g
h
i
j
k
l
m
n
o
p
q
r
s
t
u
v
w
x
y
z

DICTIONARY

damp NOUN moisture in the air or on a surface

damp VERB **1** to make slightly wet **2** to reduce the strength of

dampen VERB **1** to make damp **2** to reduce the strength of

damper NOUN a metal plate that can be moved to increase or decrease the amount of air flowing into a fire or furnace etc. **put a damper on** to make less enjoyable

damsel NOUN (old use) a young woman

damson NOUN a small dark-purple plum

dance VERB to move in time to music

dance NOUN **1** a set of movements used in dancing **2** a piece of music for dancing **3** a party with dancing ▸ **dancer** NOUN

dandelion NOUN a yellow wild flower with jagged leaves

dandruff NOUN tiny white flakes of dead skin in a person's hair

D and T ABBREVIATION design and technology

dandy NOUN **dandies** a man who likes to look well-dressed

danger NOUN **1** something unsafe or harmful **2** the possibility of suffering harm or death

dangerous ADJECTIVE likely to cause harm or difficulty ▸ **dangerously** ADVERB

dangle VERB to hang or swing loosely

dank ADJECTIVE damp and chilly

dappled ADJECTIVE marked with patches of a different colour

dare VERB **1** to be brave or bold enough to do something **2** to challenge someone to do something risky

dare NOUN a challenge to someone to do something risky

daredevil NOUN a person who is very bold and reckless

dark ADJECTIVE **1** with little or no light **2** not light in colour *a dark*

THESAURUS

dampen VERB • *to dampen a cloth* ▸ moisten, wet, damp • *to dampen enthusiasm* ▸ lessen, diminish, discourage

dance VERB • *to dance around playfully* ▸ caper, cavort, jig, jump, leap, prance, skip

dance NOUN • *to go to a dance* ▸ ball, disco

danger NOUN • *a danger of flooding* ▸ risk, threat, chance, possibility, likelihood • *a danger to public health* ▸ threat, hazard,

risk • *a sense of danger* ▸ insecurity, vulnerability, uncertainty • *in danger* ▸ peril, jeopardy, (at) risk

dangerous ADJECTIVE • *dangerous work* ▸ risky, unsafe, hazardous, perilous • *dangerous driving* ▸ reckless, careless • *a dangerous criminal* ▸ ruthless, violent, vicious, desperate

dare VERB • *No one dared to say anything.* ▸ have the courage, be

DICTIONARY

suit **3** having dark hair **4** sinister or evil ► **darkness** NOUN

dark NOUN **1** the absence of light *to see in the dark* **2** the time when the sun has set *after dark*

darken VERB to make or become dark

darling NOUN someone who is loved very much

darn VERB to mend a hole in material by weaving threads across it

darn NOUN a place that has been darned

dart NOUN **1** an object with a sharp point, thrown at a target **2** a quick movement

dart VERB to run suddenly and quickly

darts NOUN a game in which darts are thrown at a circular target (a *dartboard*)

dash VERB **1** to run quickly **2** to throw a thing violently against something

dash NOUN **1** a short quick run; a rush **2** energy or liveliness **3** a small amount *a dash of lemon*

juice **4** a short line (-) used in writing or printing

dashboard NOUN a panel with dials and controls in front of the driver of a vehicle

dashing ADJECTIVE lively and showy

data (day-ta) NOUN pieces of information

database NOUN (ICT) a store of information held in a computer

date¹ NOUN **1** the time when something happens or happened or was done **2** an appointment to meet someone at an agreed time

date VERB **1** to give a date to **2** to have existed from a particular time *The building dates from 1684.* **3** to seem old-fashioned

date² NOUN a small sweet brown fruit from a palm tree

daub VERB to paint or smear clumsily ► **daub** NOUN

daughter NOUN a female child

THESAURUS

brave enough • *She dared him to jump.* ► challenge, defy

dark ADJECTIVE • *a dark room* ► dim, dingy, gloomy, unlit, shadowy • *a dark night* ► black, pitch-black, starless, moonless • *a dark colour* ► deep, strong • *a dark secret* ► mysterious, hidden, obscure • *dark thoughts* ► pessimistic, gloomy, sombre, grim

darling ADJECTIVE • *his darling wife* ► dear, dearest, beloved

dash VERB • *to dash home* ► rush, race, tear, hasten, hurry, speed, sprint, dart, fly • *to dash a plate against the wall* ► smash, crash, hurl, throw

data NOUN • *to collect data* ► information, details, facts and figures, statistics

DICTIONARY

a
b
c
d
e
f
g
h
i
j
k
l
m
n
o
p
q
r
s
t
u
v
w
x
y
z

daughter-in-law NOUN
 daughters-in-law a son's wife

daunting ADJECTIVE difficult or alarming

dawdle VERB to go slowly and lazily ► **dawdler** NOUN

dawn NOUN the time when the sun rises

dawn VERB 1 to grow light in the morning 2 to begin to be realized *The truth dawned on them.*

day NOUN 1 the 24 hours between midnight and the next midnight 2 the light part of this time 3 a particular day *sports day* 4 a period of time *in my day*

daybreak NOUN dawn

daydream NOUN pleasant thoughts of something you would like to happen

daydream VERB to have daydreams

daylight NOUN 1 the light of day 2 dawn

day-to-day ADJECTIVE ordinary; happening every day

dazed ADJECTIVE unable to think or see clearly ► **daze** NOUN

dazzle VERB 1 to make you unable to see clearly because of too much bright light 2 to amaze or impress

DC ABBREVIATION direct current

dead ADJECTIVE 1 no longer alive 2 not lively 3 not functioning; no longer in use 4 exact or complete *a dead loss*

deaden VERB to make pain or noise weaker

dead end NOUN 1 a road or passage with one end closed 2 a situation where no progress can be made

THESAURUS

dawdle VERB • *Ruth dawdled back.*
 ► stroll, amble, wander

dawn NOUN • *at dawn*
 ► daybreak, sunrise, first light
 • *the dawn of civilization*
 ► beginning, start, birth, origin

day NOUN • *during the day*
 ► daytime, daylight • *the leading musician of the day* ► age, period, time, era

dazed ADJECTIVE • *She was dazed by the news.* ► stunned, shocked, bewildered, confused

dazzle VERB • *The sunlight dazzled him.* ► blind • *The beauty of the place dazzled her.* ► overwhelm, impress, amaze

dead ADJECTIVE • *Both her parents were dead.* ► deceased, departed, passed on, gone • *a dead animal* ► lifeless, killed • *a dead language* ► extinct, obsolete, died out • *feet dead with cold* ► numb, deadened, insensitive • *The battery was dead.* ► flat, defunct, not working, burnt out, useless • *The place is dead on a Monday night.* ► lifeless, dreary, boring, dull

dead ADVERB • *dead straight*
 ► completely, absolutely, perfectly, utterly

deaden VERB • *to deaden the noise*
 ► muffle, soften, reduce, stifle, weaken • *to deaden the pain*
 ► numb, dull, alleviate, soothe

dead heat NOUN a race in which two or more winners finish exactly together

deadline NOUN a time limit

deadlock NOUN a situation in which no progress can be made

deadly ADJECTIVE **deadlier, deadliest** likely to kill

deaf ADJECTIVE **1** unable to hear **2** unwilling to listen ► **deafness** NOUN

deafen VERB to be so loud that it is difficult to hear anything else ► **deafening** ADJECTIVE

deal VERB **dealt 1** to hand out **2** to give out cards for a card game **3** to do business *to deal in antiques* **deal with 1** to be concerned with *The book deals with whales and dolphins.* **2** to take action about

I'll deal with the washing-up. ► **dealer** NOUN

deal NOUN **1** an agreement or bargain **2** someone's turn to deal at cards *a good deal* or *a great deal* a large amount

dean NOUN **1** a member of the clergy **2** the head of a university or department

dear ADJECTIVE **1** loved very much **2** a polite greeting in letters **3** expensive ► **dearly** ADVERB

dearth (derth) NOUN a shortage or lack of something

death NOUN the end of life

deathly ADJECTIVE like death

debar VERB **debarring, debarred** to forbid or ban

debatable ADJECTIVE questionable; that can be argued against

deadly ADJECTIVE • *a deadly poison* ► lethal, noxious, harmful, dangerous • *a deadly disease* ► fatal, life-threatening, terminal

deafening ADJECTIVE • *a deafening roar* ► loud, piercing, ear-splitting, booming, thunderous

deal VERB • *to deal the cards* ► give out, distribute, share out, divide • *to deal a blow* ► deliver, inflict, give • *to deal in stocks and shares* ► trade, do business, buy and sell, traffic **deal with** • *a difficult issue to deal with* ► handle, manage, cope with, sort out • *The book deals with several important topics.* ► cover, tackle, explain

deal NOUN • *business deals* ► agreement, arrangement, contract, understanding • *to look for the best deal* ► buy, bargain **a good deal** or **a great deal** • *We have achieved a great deal.* ► a lot, much, plenty, a large amount

dear ADJECTIVE • *dear friends* ► beloved, close, valued • *Fruit is dear at this time of year.* ► expensive, costly, overpriced, exorbitant

death NOUN • *his uncle's death* ► dying, passing, passing away, end • *many deaths* ► casualty, fatality • *the death of all their dreams* ► end, finish, collapse, ruin **put to death** • *The rebels were put to death.* ► execute, kill

DICTIONARY

debate NOUN a formal discussion

debate VERB to hold a debate

debilitating ADJECTIVE causing weakness

debit NOUN an entry in an account showing how much money is owed

debit VERB to remove money from an account

debonair (deb-on-air) ADJECTIVE carefree and confident

debris (deb-ree) NOUN scattered fragments or wreckage

debt (det) NOUN something that you owe someone **in debt** owing money

debtor (det-or) NOUN a person who owes money

debut (day-bew) NOUN the first public appearance, e.g. of an actor

decade NOUN a period of ten years

decadent ADJECTIVE abandoning normal moral standards
  ▸ **decadence** NOUN

decaffeinated ADJECTIVE (of coffee or tea) with the caffeine removed

decanter NOUN a decorative glass bottle for serving wine

decathlon NOUN an athletic contest in which each competitor takes part in ten events

decay VERB **1** to rot or go bad **2** to become less good or less strong
  ▸ **decay** NOUN

deceased ADJECTIVE dead

deceit (dis-eet) NOUN the act of making a person believe something that is not true

deceitful ADJECTIVE using deceit
  ▸ **deceitfully** ADVERB

deceive VERB to make a person believe something that is not true
  ▸ **deceiver** NOUN

December NOUN the twelfth month of the year

decent ADJECTIVE **1** respectable and honest **2** reasonable or adequate

THESAURUS

debate NOUN • *a debate about personal freedom* ▸ discussion, argument, exchange of views, dispute

debate VERB • *to debate an idea* ▸ discuss, consider, exchange views on, argue • *I am debating whether to go.* ▸ consider, think over, ponder, contemplate

decay VERB • *The body had decayed.* ▸ decompose, rot, putrefy • *The old palace had decayed.* ▸ deteriorate, decline, crumble, disintegrate, fall apart

deceit NOUN • *lies and deceit* ▸ deception, duplicity, trickery, cheating, fraud

deceitful ADJECTIVE • *deceitful and irresponsible* ▸ dishonest, untruthful, untrustworthy, underhand

deceive VERB • *not easy to deceive them* ▸ trick, fool, mislead, dupe, cheat

decent ADJECTIVE • *not decent* ▸ proper, respectable, appropriate, suitable • *a decent person* ▸ honest, trustworthy, reliable, courteous, polite • *a*

DICTIONARY

a decent income **3** (informal) kind or helpful ▸ **decency** NOUN, **decently** ADVERB

deception NOUN the act of deceiving someone

deceptive ADJECTIVE misleading ▸ **deceptively** ADVERB

decibel (dess-ib-el) NOUN a unit for measuring the loudness of sound

decide VERB **1** to make a choice about what to do or have **2** to settle a contest or argument ▸ **decider** NOUN

decided ADJECTIVE **1** having clear and definite opinions **2** noticeable a decided difference ▸ **decidedly** ADVERB

deciduous ADJECTIVE (of a tree) losing its leaves in autumn

decimal ADJECTIVE using tens or tenths

decimal NOUN a fraction with tenths shown as numbers after a point (e.g. 0.3,1.5)

decimal point NOUN the dot in a decimal fraction

decimate VERB to kill or destroy a large part of

decipher VERB **1** to work out the meaning of a coded message **2** to work out the meaning of untidy writing ▸ **decipherment** NOUN

decision NOUN **1** the act of deciding **2** what you have decided **3** determination

decisive ADJECTIVE **1** settling or ending something a decisive victory **2** able to make decisions quickly and firmly ▸ **decisively** ADVERB

deck NOUN **1** a floor on a ship or bus **2** a pack of playing cards **3** a turntable on a record player

deck VERB to decorate

deckchair NOUN a folding chair with a canvas or plastic seat

declare VERB **1** to say something clearly or firmly **2** to admit to income or goods on which a tax has to be paid **3** to end a cricket innings before all the batsmen are out **declare war** to announce that you are starting a war ▸ **declaration** NOUN

decline VERB **1** to refuse **2** to become weaker or smaller **3** to slope downwards **4** to give the

THESAURUS

decent meal ▸ good, nice, pleasant, agreeable

decide VERB • decided to become a journalist ▸ resolve, determine, make up your mind, choose, plan, aim • to decide the issue ▸ determine, judge, adjudicate on

decision NOUN • the jury's decision ▸ verdict, ruling, conclusion, judgement, recommendation

decisive ADJECTIVE • a decisive win ▸ definite, significant, convincing, crucial • a decisive leader ▸ firm, forceful, resolute, strong-minded, unhesitating

declare VERB • to declare your intentions ▸ announce, proclaim, affirm, reveal, divulge • He declared that he was ready. ▸ announce, assert, state, insist, claim, vow

a
b
c
d
e
f
g
h
i
j
k
l
m
n
o
p
q
r
s
t
u
v
w
x
y
z

196

DICTIONARY

various forms of a noun, pronoun, or adjective

decline NOUN a gradual decrease or loss of strength

decode VERB to work out the meaning of something written in code ▶ **decoder** NOUN

decompose VERB to decay or rot ▶ **decomposition** NOUN

decompression NOUN reducing air pressure

decor (day-kor) NOUN the style of furnishings and decorations

decorate VERB **1** to make something look more beautiful or colourful **2** to put fresh paint or paper on walls **3** to give someone a medal ▶ **decoration** NOUN, **decorator** NOUN

decorative ADJECTIVE pretty or ornamental

decorum (dik-or-um) NOUN polite and dignified behaviour

decoy (dee-koi) NOUN something used to tempt a person or animal into a trap or into danger

decoy (dik-oi) VERB to tempt a person or animal into a trap etc.

decrease VERB to make or become smaller or fewer

decrease NOUN the amount by which something decreases

decree NOUN an official order or decision

decree VERB to make a decree

decrepit ADJECTIVE old and weak

dedicate VERB **1** to devote all your time or energy to something **2** to name a person at the beginning of a book, as a tribute ▶ **dedication** NOUN

deduce VERB to work something out from known facts ▶ **deducible** ADJECTIVE

deduct VERB to subtract part of something

deduction NOUN **1** the process of deducting; something deducted **2** the process of deducing; a conclusion reached

THESAURUS

decorate VERB • *to decorate a tree* ▶ adorn, embellish, beautify • *to decorate a house* ▶ paint, renovate, refurbish • *to be decorated for bravery* ▶ honour, reward

decoration • *elaborate decoration* ▶ ornamentation, trimmings • *a decoration for bravery* ▶ award, medal

decrease NOUN • *a decrease in crime levels* ▶ reduction, decline, lessening (of), drop

decrepit ADJECTIVE • *a decrepit old cottage* ▶ dilapidated, ramshackle, tumbledown, derelict

dedicated ADJECTIVE • *a dedicated musician* ▶ devoted, committed, keen, loyal, enthusiastic

deduce VERB • *He deduced that she must be a good cook.* ▶ conclude, reason, work out, infer, surmise

deduct VERB • *The cost was deducted from his allowance.* ▶ subtract, knock off, take away

DICTIONARY

deed NOUN 1 something that someone has done 2 a legal document

deem VERB (formal) to consider I deem it an honour.

deep ADJECTIVE 1 going a long way down or back or in a deep well deep cupboards 2 measured from top to bottom or front to back six feet deep 3 intense or strong deep colours deep feelings 4 low-pitched, not shrill ▸ **deeply** ADVERB

deepen VERB to make or become deeper

deep-freeze NOUN a freezer

deer NOUN deer a fast-running animal, the male of which has antlers

deface VERB to spoil the surface of something ▸ **defacement** NOUN

defamatory ADJECTIVE attacking a person's good reputation ▸ **defamation** NOUN

default VERB to fail to do what you have agreed to do ▸ **defaulter** NOUN

default NOUN 1 failure to do something 2 (ICT) the action a computer performs unless given another command

defeat VERB 1 to win a victory over someone 2 to baffle or be too difficult for

defeat NOUN 1 the process of defeating someone 2 a lost game or battle

defect (dif-ekt or dee-fekt) NOUN a flaw or imperfection

defect (dif-ekt) VERB to desert your own country and join the enemy ▸ **defection** NOUN, **defector** NOUN

THESAURUS

deed NOUN • a heroic deed ▸ act, action, feat, exploit

deep ADJECTIVE • a deep well ▸ bottomless, fathomless • a deep disappointment ▸ intense, profound, extreme, serious • a deep mystery ▸ obscure, secret, mysterious, unfathomable • deep affection ▸ intense, heartfelt, fervent, ardent • deep in conversation ▸ absorbed, engrossed, immersed • a deep sound ▸ low, low-pitched, booming • deep colours ▸ dark, rich, vivid, strong, intense

deepen VERB • The mystery deepened. ▸ increase, intensify, grow

defeat VERB • to defeat the enemy ▸ beat, overcome, conquer, vanquish • The task defeated them. ▸ frustrate, confound, baffle

defeat NOUN • the defeat of Napoleon ▸ conquest, overthrow, victory (over) • to face defeat ▸ failure, loss, setback, humiliation

defect NOUN • defects in the machinery ▸ fault, flaw, imperfection, weakness, error

defective ADJECTIVE having defects; not working properly ► **defectiveness** NOUN

defence NOUN 1 the act of defending something 2 the soldiers, weapons, etc. that a country uses to protect itself 3 something that defends or protects 4 the case put forward on behalf of a defendant in a lawsuit 5 the players in a defending position in a game

defenceless ADJECTIVE having no defences

defend VERB 1 to protect against an attack or accusation 2 to try to prove that an accused person is not guilty ► **defender** NOUN

defendant NOUN a person accused in a lawcourt

defensive ADJECTIVE 1 used or done for defence 2 anxious about being criticized ► **defensively** ADVERB

defer¹ VERB deferring, deferred to postpone ► **deferment** NOUN, **deferral** NOUN

defer² VERB deferring, deferred to give way to a person's wishes or authority

defiance NOUN open opposition or disobedience

defiant ADJECTIVE defying; openly disobedient ► **defiantly** ADVERB

deficiency NOUN deficiencies 1 a lack or shortage 2 a defect ► **deficient** ADJECTIVE

deficit (def-iss-it) NOUN 1 the amount by which a total is too small 2 the amount by which spending is greater than income

define VERB 1 to explain what a word or phrase means 2 to show clearly what something is 3 to show a thing's outline ► **definable** ADJECTIVE

definite ADJECTIVE 1 clearly stated; exact *a definite promise* 2 certain or settled

definite article NOUN the word 'the'

definitely ADVERB certainly; without any doubt

definition NOUN 1 an explanation of what a word or phrase means

defective ADJECTIVE • *defective brakes* ► faulty, broken, malfunctioning

defence NOUN • *to speak in defence of their actions* ► support, justification • *a defence against attack* ► protection, shield, barricade

defend VERB • *to defend the country* ► protect, guard, safeguard, secure • *to defend his actions* ► justify, vindicate

defiant ADJECTIVE • *He remained defiant.* ► obstinate, stubborn, disobedient, confrontational

definite ADJECTIVE • *a definite opinion* ► clear, explicit, certain, precise • *definite signs of improvement* ► distinct, clear, obvious, noticeable, unmistakable

definitely ADVERB • *She definitely hadn't been there.* ► certainly, positively, surely, without doubt, unquestionably

2 clearness of outline in a photograph or picture

definitive ADJECTIVE **1** finally settling something *a definitive victory* **2** not able to be bettered *the definitive history of the war*

deflate VERB **1** to let out air from a tyre or balloon **2** to make someone feel less proud or less confident

deflation NOUN **1** the process of deflating **2** a feeling of disappointment

deflect VERB to make something turn aside ► **deflection** NOUN, **deflector** NOUN

deforestation NOUN the process of clearing away trees from an area

deformed ADJECTIVE badly or abnormally shaped ► **deformity** NOUN

defraud VERB to take something from a person by fraud; to cheat or swindle

defrost VERB **1** to thaw out something frozen **2** to remove the ice and frost from a refrigerator or windscreen

deft ADJECTIVE skilful and quick ► **deftly** ADVERB, **deftness** NOUN

defunct ADJECTIVE no longer in use or existing

defuse VERB **1** to remove the fuse from a bomb **2** to make a situation less dangerous or tense

defy VERB **defies**, **defied 1** to resist openly; to refuse to obey **2** to challenge a person to do something you think impossible *I defy you to prove this.*

degenerate VERB to become worse or lower in standard ► **degeneration** NOUN

degenerate ADJECTIVE having become immoral or bad ► **degeneracy** NOUN

degrading ADJECTIVE humiliating

degree NOUN **1** a unit for measuring temperature **2** a unit for measuring angles **3** amount or extent *to some degree* **4** an award to someone at a university or college who has successfully finished a course

dehydrated ADJECTIVE dried up; with all moisture removed ► **dehydration** NOUN

deign (dayn) VERB to be gracious enough to do something

deity (dee-it-ee) NOUN **deities** a god or goddess

THESAURUS

definitive ADJECTIVE • *the definitive film guide* ► authoritative, official, ultimate, complete • *a definitive reply* ► decisive, conclusive, categorical, final

deflect VERB • *to deflect a blow* ► divert, turn aside, parry, fend off

deformed ADJECTIVE • *a deformed body* ► misshapen, contorted, crippled, twisted, malformed

defy VERB • *to defy an order* ► disobey, flout, disregard, contravene, resist • *She defied him to admit it.* ► challenge, dare

dejected ADJECTIVE sad or depressed ► **dejection** NOUN

delay VERB 1 to make someone or something late 2 to postpone

delay NOUN the process of delaying, or the time this lasts *an hour's delay*

delegate NOUN a person who represents others and acts on their instructions

delegate VERB to give someone a task or duty to do

delegation NOUN 1 the act of delegating 2 a group of delegates

delete VERB to cross out or remove something written or printed or stored on a computer ► **deletion** NOUN

deliberate ADJECTIVE 1 done on purpose; intentional 2 slow and careful ► **deliberately** ADVERB

deliberate VERB to discuss or think carefully ► **deliberation** NOUN

delicacy NOUN **delicacies** 1 a delicate state 2 a piece of delicious food

delicate ADJECTIVE 1 fine and graceful 2 fragile and easily damaged 3 pleasant and not strong or intense 4 becoming ill easily 5 needing great care or tact *a delicate situation* ► **delicately** ADVERB

delicatessen NOUN a shop that sells cooked meats, cheeses, salads, etc.

delicious ADJECTIVE tasting or smelling very pleasant ► **deliciously** ADVERB

delight VERB 1 to please someone very much 2 to take great pleasure in something

delight NOUN great pleasure

THESAURUS

dejected ADJECTIVE • *to look dejected* ► sad, miserable, despondent, disheartened, depressed

delay VERB • *The traffic delayed them.* ► detain, hold up, make late • *to delay the start* ► postpone, put off, defer, adjourn • *no time to delay* ► linger, dally, take your time

delay NOUN • *long traffic delays* ► hold-up, wait, stoppage

deliberate ADJECTIVE • *deliberate sabotage* ► intentional, calculated, conscious, planned, premeditated • *slow deliberate footsteps* ► careful, steady, measured, methodical

delicate ADJECTIVE • *delicate fabrics* ► fine, exquisite, flimsy, fragile • *a delicate child* ► weak, frail, sickly • *a delicate matter* ► difficult, tricky, sensitive, embarrassing

delicious ADJECTIVE • *a delicious meal* ► tasty, appetizing, mouth-watering, scrumptious, succulent

delight VERB • *to delight someone with a song* ► please, thrill, captivate, entrance, amuse

delight NOUN • *She laughed with delight.* ► pleasure, happiness, joy, enjoyment

a
b
c
d
e
f
g
h
i
j
k
l
m
n
o
p
q
r
s
t
u
v
w
x
y
z

DICTIONARY

delightful ADJECTIVE very pleasing
▶ **delightfully** ADVERB

delinquent NOUN a young person who breaks the law ▶ **delinquent** ADJECTIVE, **delinquency** NOUN

delirious ADJECTIVE 1 in a state of mental confusion 2 extremely excited or enthusiastic
▶ **deliriously** ADVERB

delirium NOUN a state of mental confusion caused by fever 2 wild excitement

deliver VERB 1 to take letters or goods to a place 2 to give a speech or lecture 3 to help with the birth of a baby 4 to aim or strike a blow or attack 5 to rescue or set free

delivery NOUN **deliveries** 1 the process of delivering 2 something delivered

dell NOUN a small valley with trees

delta NOUN a triangular area at the mouth of a river

delude VERB to deceive or mislead

deluge NOUN 1 a large flood 2 a heavy fall of rain 3 something coming in great numbers

deluge VERB to overwhelm

delusion NOUN a false belief

de luxe ADJECTIVE of very high quality

delve VERB to search deeply

demand VERB 1 to ask for something firmly or forcefully 2 to need *The work demands great skill.*

demand NOUN 1 a firm or forceful request 2 a desire to have something *a great demand for computers* **in demand** wanted or needed

demanding ADJECTIVE 1 needing skill or effort 2 needing a lot of attention

demeaning ADJECTIVE lowering a person's dignity; humiliating

demeanour (dim-een-er) NOUN a person's behaviour or manner

demented ADJECTIVE driven mad; crazy

demise (dim-yz) NOUN (formal) death

demo NOUN **demos** (informal) a demonstration

THESAURUS

delighted VERB • *He was delighted to see her.* ▶ thrilled, overjoyed, excited, ecstatic, pleased, happy

delightful ADJECTIVE • *a delightful occasion* ▶ pleasant, lovely, enjoyable, marvellous, wonderful

deliver VERB • *to deliver a package* ▶ take, bring, send, convey, transport • *to deliver a verdict* ▶ give, announce, declare • *to deliver a blow* ▶ deal, aim, strike, administer

demand NOUN • *to agree to demands* ▶ request, requirement, claim, ultimatum • *no demand for their products* ▶ call, market, need

demand VERB • *to demand a pay rise* ▶ request, ask for, call for, claim, insist on

demanding ADJECTIVE • *a demanding child* ▶ insistent, nagging, trying, tiresome • *a demanding task* ▶ difficult, challenging, testing, hard, tough

a
b
c
d
e
f
g
h
i
j
k
l
m
n
o
p
q
r
s
t
u
v
w
x
y
z

democracy NOUN **democracies**
1 government of a country by representatives elected by the people **2** a country governed in this way

Democrat NOUN a member of the Democratic Party in the USA

democrat NOUN a supporter of democracy ▶ **democratic** ADJECTIVE, **democratically** ADVERB

demography (dim-og-ra-fee) NOUN the study of statistics to do with populations
▶ **demographic** ADJECTIVE

demolish VERB **1** to knock a building down and break it up **2** to destroy completely
▶ **demolition** NOUN

demon NOUN **1** a devil; an evil spirit **2** a fierce or forceful person ▶ **demonic** ADJECTIVE

demonstrate VERB **1** to show or prove something **2** to take part in a demonstration
▶ **demonstrator** NOUN

demonstration NOUN **1** the process of demonstrating **2** a march or meeting to promote an opinion or cause

demonstrative ADJECTIVE
1 showing or proving something **2** showing feelings or affection openly

demoralize VERB to dishearten someone or weaken their confidence ▶ **demoralization** NOUN

⚠️ **SPELLING**

This word can also be spelled demoralise.

demote VERB to reduce to a lower position or rank ▶ **demotion** NOUN

den NOUN **1** an animal's lair **2** a private room

denial NOUN the act of denying or refusing

denigrate VERB to blacken the reputation of ▶ **denigration** NOUN

denim NOUN a kind of strong blue cotton cloth used to make jeans or other clothes

denomination NOUN **1** a name or title **2** a religious group with a special name **3** a unit of weight or of money

denominator NOUN the number below the line in a fraction, showing how many parts the whole is divided into, e.g. 4 in $\frac{3}{4}$

THESAURUS

demolish VERB • to demolish a row of houses ▶ destroy, wreck, flatten, knock down, obliterate

demonstrate VERB • The evidence demonstrates a major change. ▶ show, indicate, prove, illustrate • to demonstrate in the streets ▶ protest, march, parade, rally

demonstration NOUN • a demonstration of skill and creativity ▶ display, exhibition, presentation • a public demonstration ▶ protest, rally, march, sit-in, vigil

den NOUN • He worked in his den upstairs. ▶ retreat, hideaway, sanctuary

denote VERB to mean or indicate P *denotes parking.* ▸ **denotation** NOUN

denounce VERB to speak strongly against; to accuse ▸ **denunciation** NOUN

dense ADJECTIVE **1** thick or packed closely *dense fog dense crowds* **2** (*informal*) stupid ▸ **densely** ADVERB

density NOUN **1** thickness **2** (*Science*) the proportion of mass to volume

dent NOUN a hollow left in a surface where something has pressed or hit it

dent VERB to make a dent in

dental ADJECTIVE to do with the teeth

dentist NOUN a person who is trained to take care of teeth ▸ **dentistry** NOUN

dentures NOUN a set of false teeth

denude VERB to make bare or naked ▸ **denudation** NOUN

denunciation NOUN the act of denouncing

deny VERB **denies**, **denied 1** to say that something is not true **2** to refuse to give or allow something **deny yourself** to go without something you want

deodorant NOUN a substance that removes unpleasant smells

depart VERB to go away; to leave

department NOUN one section of a large organization or shop

departure NOUN the act of departing

depend VERB **depend on** to rely on or be controlled by

dependable ADJECTIVE reliable

dependant NOUN a person who depends on another, especially financially

⚠ **USAGE**

Do not confuse this word with *dependent*, which is an adjective.

dependency NOUN **dependencies 1** dependence **2** a country that is controlled by another

dependent ADJECTIVE relying or depending *two dependent*

THESAURUS

dense ADJECTIVE • *a dense forest* ▸ thick, tightly packed, compact, impenetrable • *dense smoke* ▸ thick, heavy, concentrated • *too dense to understand* ▸ stupid, foolish, slow, unintelligent

deny VERB • *to deny all charges* ▸ reject, dismiss, contradict, refute • *to deny people their rights* ▸ refuse, forbid

depart VERB • *The officials departed.* ▸ leave, go, go away, withdraw

department NOUN • *a government department* ▸ section, division, unit, branch, office, bureau

depend VERB **depend on 1** *to depend on someone* ▸ rely on, count on, need, trust **2** *Choice depends on money.* ▸ be dependent on, hinge on, revolve around

dependable ADJECTIVE • *strong and dependable* ▸ reliable, trustworthy, faithful, loyal

children They are dependent on us.
► **dependence** NOUN

⚠️ **USAGE**

Do not confuse this word with *dependant*, which is a noun.

depict VERB 1 to show something in a painting or drawing 2 to describe ► **depiction** NOUN

deplete (dip-leet) VERB to reduce the amount of ► **depletion** NOUN

deplore VERB to think something very bad or unwelcome
► **deplorable** ADJECTIVE

deploy VERB 1 to place troops or weapons in positions for use 2 to use something effectively
► **deployment** NOUN

deport VERB to send an unwanted foreign person out of a country
► **deportation** NOUN

depose VERB to remove a person from power

deposit NOUN 1 an amount of money paid into a bank 2 money paid as a first instalment 3 a layer of solid matter in or on the earth

deposit VERB 1 to put something down 2 to pay money as a deposit
► **depositor** NOUN

depot (dep-oh) NOUN 1 a place where things are stored 2 a place where buses or trains are kept and repaired 3 a headquarters

depraved ADJECTIVE behaving wickedly ► **depravity** NOUN

deprecate (dep-rik-ayt) VERB to say that you disapprove of something

⚠️ **USAGE**

Do not confuse this word with *depreciate*.

depreciate (dip-ree-shee-ayt) VERB to make or become lower in value
► **depreciation** NOUN

⚠️ **USAGE**

Do not confuse this word with *deprecate*.

depress VERB to make you sad or unhappy

THESAURUS

depict VERB • *The painting depicts a village.* ► show, portray, illustrate, represent • *The author depicts his own childhood.*
► describe, recount, portray

deplorable ADJECTIVE • *deplorable behaviour* ► disgraceful, shameful, inexcusable, shocking, reprehensible • *deplorable conditions* ► awful, terrible, atrocious, lamentable, miserable

deplore VERB • *to deplore violence*
► condemn, disapprove of, denounce, abhor

depot NOUN • *a military depot*
► store, storehouse, base • *a bus depot* ► garage, station, terminus, headquarters

depress VERB • *The news depressed us.* ► sadden, upset, discourage, dishearten

depressed ADJECTIVE • *was tired and depressed* ► unhappy, sad, dejected, despondent, miserable, downcast

depressing ADJECTIVE • *a cold, depressing day* ► gloomy, bleak, dreary, dismal, drab, sombre

DICTIONARY

depression NOUN **1** a feeling of great sadness or hopelessness **2** a long period when trade is slack

deprive VERB to take or keep something away from somebody ▶ **deprivation** NOUN

depth NOUN **1** deepness; how deep something is **2** the deepest or lowest part

deputation NOUN a group of people sent as representatives

deputize VERB to act as someone's deputy

⚠ SPELLING

This word can also be spelled deputise.

deputy NOUN **deputies** a person appointed to act as a substitute for another

derail VERB to cause a train to leave the rails ▶ **derailment** NOUN

deranged ADJECTIVE insane ▶ **derangement** NOUN

derby (dar-bi) NOUN **derbies** a sports match between two teams from the same area

derelict ADJECTIVE abandoned and left to fall into ruin ▶ **dereliction** NOUN

deride VERB to laugh at with contempt or scorn

derision NOUN scorn or ridicule

derisive ADJECTIVE mocking; scornful ▶ **derisively** ADVERB

derisory ADJECTIVE absurdly inadequate *a derisory offer*

derivation NOUN the origin of a word

derivative ADJECTIVE derived from something; not original ▶ **derivative** NOUN

derive VERB **1** to obtain something from a source **2** to form or originate from something *words that are derived from Latin*

dermatology NOUN the study of the skin and its diseases ▶ **dermatologist** NOUN

derogatory ADJECTIVE scornful or severely critical

descant NOUN a tune sung or played above the main tune

descend VERB to go down **be descended from** to have as an ancestor

descendant NOUN a person who is descended from someone

descent NOUN the act of descending

THESAURUS

• *depressing thoughts* ▶ sad, upsetting, disheartening, melancholy

deprive VERB **deprive of** • *The war deprived her of her income.* ▶ deny, dispossess of, rob of

derelict ADJECTIVE • *derelict buildings* ▶ dilapidated, ramshackle, run-down, tumbledown, ruined

descend VERB • *The plane descended.* ▶ come down, go down, drop, fall, sink, dive • *The road descends to a village.* ▶ slope, dip, drop, fall **be descended from** • *to be descended from an Italian family* ▶ come from, spring from

descent NOUN • *the descent into the valley* ▶ way down, drop, dip, slope • *a person of British descent*

describe VERB **1** to say what someone or something is like **2** to draw in outline

description NOUN **1** a statement that describes someone or something **2** sort or kind *houses of every description* ▶ **descriptive** ADJECTIVE

desert (dez-ert) NOUN a large area of dry sandy land

⚠ USAGE

Do not confuse this word with *dessert*.

desert (diz-ert) VERB **1** to leave a person or place without intending to return **2** to run away from the army ▶ **deserter** NOUN, **desertion** NOUN

desert island NOUN an uninhabited tropical island

deserts (diz-erts) PLURAL NOUN what a person deserves

deserve VERB to have a right to; to be worthy of ▶ **deservedly** ADVERB

desiccated ADJECTIVE dried *desiccated coconut*

design NOUN **1** a drawing or pattern **2** the way something is made or arranged

design VERB **1** to draw a design for **2** to plan or intend for a special purpose ▶ **designer** NOUN

designate VERB to mark or describe as something particular ▶ **designation** NOUN

desirable ADJECTIVE **1** pleasing; worth having **2** worth doing; advisable

desire NOUN a feeling of wanting something ▶ **desirous** ADJECTIVE

desire VERB to wish for

▶ ancestry, parentage, origin, family

describe VERB • *to describe an incident* ▶ report, relate, narrate, recount, explain • *to describe a circle* ▶ draw, mark out, trace **describe as** • *I would never describe him as 'charming'.* ▶ call, refer to, classify, portray, present

description NOUN • *a detailed description* ▶ account, explanation, report, narration, commentary (on) • *furniture of every description* ▶ sort, kind, variety, type

desert VERB • *Her husband had deserted her.* ▶ abandon, leave, forsake, walk out on • *Soldiers were deserting.* ▶ abscond, defect, turn tail, run away

deserve VERB • *to deserve a holiday* ▶ be entitled to, have a right to, be worthy of, have earned • *to deserve praise* ▶ merit, justify, warrant

design VERB • *to design a building* ▶ plan, draw plans of • *to design a new kind of engine* ▶ create, invent, develop, devise, think up

design NOUN • *a design for the new building* ▶ plan, blueprint, drawing, prototype, model • *a fresh bright design* ▶ pattern, style

desire NOUN • *a desire to travel* ▶ wish, longing, yearning, inclination, impulse

desire VERB • *to desire peace* ▶ want, wish for, long for, yearn for, need

desist (diz-ist) VERB to stop doing something

desk NOUN a piece of furniture with a flat top, used for writing or working

desktop ADJECTIVE small enough to use on a desk

desolate ADJECTIVE 1 lonely and sad 2 uninhabited ▸ **desolation** NOUN

despair NOUN a feeling of hopelessness

despair VERB to feel despair

despatch VERB another spelling of **dispatch** ▸ **despatch** NOUN

desperate ADJECTIVE 1 extremely serious or hopeless 2 having a great need for something 3 reckless and ready to do anything ▸ **desperation** NOUN

despicable ADJECTIVE hateful; contemptible

despise VERB to feel contempt for a person or thing

despite PREPOSITION in spite of

despondent ADJECTIVE sad or gloomy ▸ **despondency** NOUN

despot NOUN a tyrant

dessert (diz-ert) NOUN a sweet course served as the last part of a meal

⚠ **USAGE**

Do not confuse this word with *desert*.

destination NOUN the place to which a person or thing is travelling

destined ADJECTIVE having a certain destiny; intended

destiny NOUN **destinies** what will happen or has happened to somebody or something

destitute ADJECTIVE having no home or food or money ▸ **destitution** NOUN

destroy VERB to ruin or put an end to ▸ **destruction** NOUN, **destructive** ADJECTIVE

destroyer NOUN a fast warship

THESAURUS

despair NOUN • *in a state of despair* ▸ hopelessness, despondency, gloom, misery, depression

despair VERB • *Do not despair.* ▸ lose hope, give up hope, lose heart, be demoralized

desperate ADJECTIVE • *a desperate cry* ▸ despairing, hopeless, inconsolable, distressed, miserable • *a desperate shortage of food* ▸ acute, critical, severe, serious, grave • *desperate criminals* ▸ violent, wild, dangerous

despise VERB • *to despise their way of life* ▸ scorn, disdain, look down on, detest, loathe

destiny NOUN • *Destiny had helped them.* ▸ fate, chance, luck, providence • *in control of his destiny* ▸ future, fortune, fate

destitute ADJECTIVE • *destitute with two children to care for* ▸ penniless, poverty-stricken, homeless, down and out

destroy VERB • *to destroy a building* ▸ demolish, ruin, wreck, obliterate, blow up • *to destroy their hopes* ▸ wreck, ruin, spoil

DICTIONARY

detach VERB to unfasten or separate

detachment NOUN **1** the state of being impartial **2** a small group of soldiers sent on a special duty

detail NOUN **1** a small part of a design or plan or decoration **2** a small piece of information
▶ **detailed** ADJECTIVE

detain VERB **1** to keep someone waiting **2** to keep someone confined to a place ▶ **detention** NOUN

detect VERB to notice or discover
▶ **detection** NOUN

detective NOUN a person who investigates crimes

detention NOUN **1** the act of detaining someone **2** a punishment in which a pupil is made to stay late at school

deter VERB **deterring, deterred** to discourage or prevent from doing something

detergent NOUN a substance used for cleaning or washing things

deteriorate VERB to become worse ▶ **deterioration** NOUN

determination NOUN **1** a firm intention to achieve something **2** the act of deciding something

determine VERB **1** to decide *The time of the meeting is yet to be*

THESAURUS

• *to destroy the enemy* ▶ kill, slaughter, annihilate

destruction NOUN • *destruction of the forests* ▶ devastation, damage, demolition

detach VERB • *to detach the cover* ▶ remove, unfasten, disconnect, take off, separate

detail NOUN • *accurate in every detail* ▶ feature, aspect, characteristic, point • *an eye for detail* ▶ precision, exactness, accuracy • *in detail* • *to comment in detail* ▶ in depth, thoroughly, methodically

detailed ADJECTIVE • *a detailed description* ▶ precise, exact, comprehensive, complete, elaborate

detain VERB • *to detain suspects* ▶ arrest, apprehend, hold in custody, imprison • *Something*

must have detained them.
▶ delay, hold up, hinder

detect VERB • *to detect smoke in the building* ▶ notice, become aware of, perceive, identify, spot • *to detect a crime* ▶ discover, uncover, expose, reveal, find out

deteriorate VERB • *His health deteriorated.* ▶ worsen, weaken, decline, fail, get worse • *These materials deteriorate.* ▶ decay, degenerate, disintegrate, decompose

determination NOUN • *a determination to win* ▶ resolution, resolve, will • *You will need a lot of determination.* ▶ dedication, tenacity, persistence, drive

determine VERB • *to determine the size of the problem* ▶ find out, discover, establish, identify • *This*

a
b
c
d
e
f
g
h
i
j
k
l
m
n
o
p
q
r
s
t
u
v
w
x
y
z

determined. **2** to cause or influence **3** to find out or calculate

determined ADJECTIVE fully decided; having a firm intention

determiner NOUN (Grammar) a word (such as *a*, *the*, *some*) that modifies a noun

deterrent NOUN something that may deter people from a particular action ► **deterrence** NOUN

detest VERB to dislike something very much

detonate VERB to explode or cause to explode ► **detonation** NOUN, **detonator** NOUN

detour NOUN a roundabout route instead of the normal one

detract VERB to lessen the amount or value ► **detraction** NOUN

detriment NOUN harm or disadvantage

detrimental ADJECTIVE harmful or disadvantageous ► **detrimentally** ADVERB

deuce NOUN a score of 40 points on each side in tennis

devalue VERB **1** to reduce the value of **2** to reduce the value of a country's currency ► **devaluation** NOUN

devastate VERB **1** to destroy completely **2** to make someone extremely upset ► **devastation** NOUN

develop VERB **1** to make or become bigger or better **2** to come gradually into existence *Storms developed.* **3** to begin to have or use *to develop bad habits* **4** to use an area of land for building **5** to produce pictures on photographic film

development NOUN **1** the process of growing or becoming better **2** use of land for building **3** a new or unexpected occurrence

will determine what happens next.
► control, decide, dictate, influence

determined ADJECTIVE
• *determined he will have his way*
► adamant, insistent, convinced, resolute, intent (on having) • *a determined young woman*
► strong-willed, single-minded, strong-minded, resolute, tenacious

detest VERB • *I detest that kind of talk.* ► hate, loathe, dislike, despise, deplore

develop VERB • *Our plans have developed.* ► advance, evolve,

progress, grow, get better, improve • *An argument developed.*
► arise, ensue, emerge, start, begin, come about • *to develop the business* ► expand, extend, diversify, build up • *to develop your reading skills* ► improve, expand, advance, evolve

development NOUN • *the development of a road network*
► evolution, growth, expansion, spread, improvement • *recent developments in the Middle East*
► event, occurrence, change, incident

DICTIONARY

deviate VERB to turn aside from a course or from what is usual ► **deviation** NOUN

device NOUN 1 something made for a particular purpose 2 a design used as a decoration or emblem

devil NOUN 1 an evil spirit 2 a wicked or cruel person ► **devilish** ADJECTIVE, **devilry** NOUN

devious ADJECTIVE 1 roundabout; not direct *a devious route* 2 not straightforward; underhand

devise VERB to invent or plan

devoid ADJECTIVE lacking or without something *work devoid of merit*

devolution NOUN the process of giving power to local or regional government

devote VERB to give completely *He devoted his time to sport.*

devoted ADJECTIVE loving or loyal

devotee NOUN an enthusiast

devotion NOUN great love or loyalty

devour VERB 1 to eat hungrily or greedily 2 to destroy

devout ADJECTIVE earnestly religious or sincere ► **devoutly** ADVERB

dew NOUN tiny drops of water that form at night on surfaces in the open air

dexterity (deks-terri-tee) NOUN skill in handling things

diabetes NOUN a disease in which there is too much sugar in the blood ► **diabetic** ADJECTIVE, NOUN

diabolical ADJECTIVE very bad or wicked

diagnose VERB to find out what disease a person has ► **diagnosis** NOUN

diagonal NOUN a straight line joining opposite corners ► **diagonal** ADJECTIVE, **diagonally** ADVERB

diagram NOUN a drawing or picture that shows the parts or working of something

THESAURUS

device NOUN • *a device for converting data into audio signals* ► tool, implement, contraption, gadget, invention, machine

devil NOUN • *tempted by the Devil* ► Satan, Lucifer, the Evil One, the Prince of Darkness • *green-skinned devils holding tridents* ► demon, fiend

devious ADJECTIVE • *a devious route* ► indirect, winding, rambling, circuitous, roundabout • *a devious person* ► underhand, deceitful, scheming, cunning, sneaky

devise VERB • *to devise a history project* ► conceive, think up, make up, plan, design

devote VERB • *to devote more time to the work* ► dedicate, set aside, commit

devoted ADJECTIVE • *a devoted husband* ► loyal, faithful, dedicated, loving, caring, committed

diagram NOUN • *a diagram of the digestive system* ► plan, drawing, chart, outline, sketch, illustration, picture

a
b
c
d
e
f
g
h
i
j
k
l
m
n
o
p
q
r
s
t
u
v
w
x
y
z

dial NOUN a circular object with numbers or letters round it

dial VERB **dialling, dialled** to call a telephone number by using a dial or buttons

dialect NOUN the words and pronunciations used by people in one district but not in the rest of a country

dialogue NOUN **1** the words spoken by characters in a play, film, or story **2** a conversation

diameter NOUN **1** a line drawn straight across a circle or sphere and passing through its centre **2** the length of this line

diamond NOUN **1** a hard precious stone **2** a shape with four equal sides and four angles that are not right angles **3** a playing card with red diamond shapes on it

diaper NOUN (American) a baby's nappy

diaphragm (dy-a-fram) NOUN a layer of muscle separating the chest from the abdomen and used in breathing

diarrhoea (dy-a-ree-a) NOUN frequent watery emptying of the bowels

diary NOUN **diaries** a book in which the events of each day are written

dice NOUN **dice** a small cube marked with dots on its sides, used in games

dice VERB **1** to cut food into small cubes

dictate VERB **1** to speak or read something aloud for someone else to write down **2** to give firm orders ▸ **dictation** NOUN

dictator NOUN a ruler with unlimited power

dictatorial ADJECTIVE like a dictator; domineering

diction NOUN **1** a way of speaking words **2** a writer's choice of words

dictionary NOUN **dictionaries** a book that contains words in alphabetical order with their meanings

didn't did not

die¹ VERB **dying 1** to stop living or existing **2** to stop burning or functioning *The fire died down.* **be dying for** or **to** (informal) to want to have or do something very much

die² NOUN a device that stamps a design on coins or medals

diesel NOUN **1** an engine that works by burning oil in compressed air **2** fuel for this kind of engine

THESAURUS

dictator NOUN • *a cruel dictator* ▸ tyrant, despot

dictatorial ADJECTIVE • *a dictatorial regime* ▸ autocratic, authoritarian, totalitarian, undemocratic

die VERB • *He died young.* ▸ pass away, pass on, lose your life, meet your end, decease • *Hopes are dying.* ▸ fade, dwindle, sink, disappear, vanish, wither, melt away

a
b
c
d
e
f
g
h
i
j
k
l
m
n
o
p
q
r
s
t
u
v
w
x
y
z

diet NOUN **1** a course of special meals followed for health or to lose weight **2** the sort of foods someone eats

diet VERB to follow a diet

differ VERB **1** to be different **2** to disagree

difference NOUN **1** the state of being different; the way in which things differ **2** the remainder left after one number is subtracted from another **3** a disagreement

different ADJECTIVE **1** unlike; not the same **2** separate or distinct *three different occasions* ▸ **differently** ADVERB

differentiate VERB to make or recognize differences

difficult ADJECTIVE needing a lot of effort or skill; not easy

difficulty NOUN **difficulties 1** the state of being difficult **2** something that causes a problem

diffident ADJECTIVE shy and not self-confident ▸ **diffidence** NOUN

diffuse (dif-yooz) VERB to spread widely or thinly *diffused lighting* ▸ **diffusion** NOUN

diffuse (dif-yooss) ADJECTIVE **1** spread widely **2** using many words

dig VERB **digging**, **dug 1** to take up soil with a spade or fork **2** to poke something in **3** to seek or discover by investigating

differ VERB • *Opinions differ.*
▸ vary, diverge, be different • *to differ about what to do*
▸ disagree, argue, fall out, quarrel

difference NOUN • *There was a big difference in their ages*
▸ contrast, distinction, dissimilarity **difference of opinion** • *to have a difference of opinion* ▸ disagreement, misunderstanding, argument, quarrel

different ADJECTIVE • *many different answers to the question*
▸ dissimilar, varying, opposed, contradictory • *The house looked different.* ▸ changed, altered, transformed, unfamiliar • *to try something different* ▸ unusual, new, fresh, original • *Every person's fingerprint is different.*

▸ unique, distinctive, individual, special

difficult ADJECTIVE • *a difficult problem* ▸ complicated, complex, hard, tricky, problematical, baffling • *a difficult task* ▸ hard, arduous, demanding, strenuous, tough, challenging • *difficult neighbours* ▸ troublesome, tiresome, uncooperative, unhelpful

difficulty NOUN • *to be in difficulty* ▸ trouble, distress, hardship, adversity • *The cost might be a difficulty.* ▸ problem, complication, snag, hitch, obstacle

dig VERB • *to dig a hole in the garden* ▸ burrow, excavate, tunnel, gouge out, hollow out • *to dig someone in the ribs* ▸ poke, prod, jab, nudge, shove

DICTIONARY

dig NOUN **1** an archaeological excavation **2** a poke **3** an unpleasant remark

digest (dy-jest) VERB **1** to soften and change food in the stomach for the body to absorb **2** to take information into your mind ► **digestion** NOUN

digest (dy-jest) NOUN a summary of news or information

digestive ADJECTIVE to do with digestion

digger NOUN a machine for digging

digit (dij-it) NOUN **1** any of the numbers from 0 to 9 **2** a finger or toe

digital ADJECTIVE **1** to do with or using digits **2** (of a watch or clock) showing the time with a row of figures **3** (of a computer, recording, etc.) storing data or sound as a series of binary digits

dignified ADJECTIVE having dignity

dignitary NOUN **dignitaries** an important official

dignity NOUN a calm and serious manner

digress VERB to stray from the main subject ► **digression** NOUN

dike NOUN another spelling of **dyke**

dilapidated ADJECTIVE falling to pieces

dilate VERB to make or become wider or larger ► **dilation** NOUN

dilemma NOUN a situation in which it is difficult to choose between two possibilities, both unwelcome

diligent ADJECTIVE hard-working ► **diligence** NOUN

dilute VERB to make a liquid weaker by adding water or other liquid ► **dilution** NOUN

dim ADJECTIVE **dimmer, dimmest 1** not bright or clear; only faintly lit **2** (informal) stupid ► **dimly** ADVERB

dim VERB **dimming, dimmed** to make or become dim

dime NOUN (American) a ten-cent coin

dimension NOUN **1** a measurement such as length,

THESAURUS

dignified ADJECTIVE • *a calm and dignified manner* ► noble, stately, solemn, majestic, grand

dignity NOUN • *to accept misfortune with dignity* ► calmness, self-control, decorum • *the dignity of the occasion* ► grandeur, formality, solemnity

dilemma NOUN • *to be in a dilemma about what to do*

► quandary, predicament, difficulty

dim ADJECTIVE • *dim shapes in the distance* ► vague, indistinct, unclear, fuzzy, blurred • *a dim room* ► dark, dingy, gloomy, dismal

dim VERB • *The sky dimmed.* ► grow dark, darken, blacken, cloud over • *to dim the lights* ► turn down, fade, lower

DICTIONARY

width, area, or volume **2** size or extent ▸ **dimensional** ADJECTIVE

diminish VERB to make or become smaller ▸ **diminution** NOUN

diminutive ADJECTIVE very small

dimple NOUN a small hollow or dent in the skin ▸ **dimpled** ADJECTIVE

din NOUN a loud annoying noise

dine VERB to have dinner

diner NOUN **1** someone eating dinner **2** (*American*) a small inexpensive restaurant

dinghy (ding-ee) NOUN **dinghies** a kind of small boat

dingo NOUN **dingoes** an Australian wild dog

dingy (din-jee) ADJECTIVE **dingier, dingiest** dirty-looking

dinner NOUN the main meal of the day, at midday or in the evening

dinosaur (dy-noss-or) NOUN a prehistoric reptile, often of enormous size

dip VERB **dipping, dipped** to put down or go down, especially into a liquid

dip NOUN **1** the act of dipping **2** a downward slope **3** a quick swim **4** a substance into which things are dipped

diphtheria (dif-theer-ee-a) NOUN a serious disease that causes inflammation in the throat

diphthong (dif-thong) NOUN a vowel sound made up of two sounds, e.g. *oi* in point or *ou* in loud

diploma NOUN a certificate awarded by a college for completing a course

diplomacy NOUN **1** the work of making agreements with other countries **2** skill in dealing with people

diplomat NOUN **1** a person employed in diplomacy **2** a tactful person

diplomatic ADJECTIVE **1** to do with diplomats or diplomacy **2** tactful ▸ **diplomatically** ADVERB

dire ADJECTIVE dreadful or serious *in dire need*

THESAURUS

diminish VERB • *His angry feelings diminished.* ▸ decrease, reduce, lessen, subside

din NOUN • *hard to hear above the din* ▸ racket, uproar, rumpus, noise, commotion

dingy ADJECTIVE • *a dingy hallway* ▸ gloomy, dismal, dim, dreary, dark

dip VERB • *to dip your hand in the water* ▸ immerse, lower, plunge, submerge, dunk • *The path dips towards the village.* ▸ descend, slope down, go down

dip NOUN • *a dip in the ground* ▸ slope, depression, hole, hollow • *a dip in sales* ▸ decrease, fall, decline • *a quick dip in the river* ▸ bathe, swim, splash, paddle

diplomatic ADJECTIVE • *a diplomatic response* ▸ tactful, sensitive, considerate, polite

dire ADJECTIVE • *in a dire state* ▸ terrible, dreadful, awful, appalling • *a dire warning* ▸ ominous, gloomy, grim • *in dire need of help* ▸ urgent, desperate, serious, grave

DICTIONARY

direct ADJECTIVE **1** as straight as possible **2** going straight to the point; frank **3** exact *the direct opposite*

direct VERB **1** to tell someone the way **2** to guide or aim in a certain direction **3** to control or manage **4** to order

direct current NOUN electric current flowing only in one direction

direction NOUN **1** the line along which something moves or faces **2** the process of directing
▶ **directional** ADJECTIVE

directions PLURAL NOUN information on how to use or do something or how to get somewhere

directive NOUN a command

directly ADVERB **1** by a direct route *Go directly home.* **2** immediately *Please come directly.*

director NOUN **1** a person in charge of a business **2** a person who directs the making of a film, programme, or play

directory NOUN **directories 1** a book containing a list of people with their addresses and telephone numbers **2** (*ICT*) a group of files

direct speech NOUN a person's words expressed in the form in which they were said

dirge NOUN a slow sad song

dirt NOUN earth or soil; anything that is not clean

dirty ADJECTIVE **dirtier, dirtiest 1** not clean; soiled **2** unfair; dishonourable *a dirty trick*

THESAURUS

direct ADJECTIVE • *the direct route*
▶ straight, shortest, quickest, non-stop • *a direct answer*
▶ honest, straightforward, frank, candid, sincere • *direct opposites*
▶ absolute, exact, complete

direct VERB • *to direct a project*
▶ manage, run, administer, be in charge of, control • *An official directed them to the exit.* ▶ show the way, give directions to, guide, point • *The books are directed at teenagers.* ▶ target, aim, design (for) • *The judge directed the jury.*
▶ instruct, order, command, advise

direction NOUN • *in another direction* ▶ way, route, course

directions • *regular directions on new medicines* ▶ instructions, guidelines, orders

dirt NOUN • *a room covered in dirt*
▶ grime, filth, muck, dust, slime, mess, pollution • *to scratch about in the dirt* ▶ earth, soil, mud, clay

dirty ADJECTIVE • *dirty clothes*
▶ filthy, grimy, grubby, soiled, stained, mucky, unwashed • *a dirty room* ▶ dusty, filthy, messy, squalid • *dirty water* ▶ muddy, murky, polluted, impure • *dirty tricks* ▶ corrupt, dishonest, illegal, unfair, unsporting • *a dirty joke* ▶ rude, indecent, obscene, offensive • *a dirty look* ▶ angry, hostile, resentful, black

DICTIONARY

3 indecent; obscene ▶ **dirtily**
ADVERB

disable VERB to make something
unable to work or act

disabled ADJECTIVE unable to use
part of the body properly because
of illness or injury ▶ **disability**
NOUN

disadvantage NOUN something
that hinders or is unhelpful
▶ **disadvantageous** ADJECTIVE

disadvantaged ADJECTIVE
suffering from a disadvantage,
especially having less money or
fewer opportunities than most
people

disagree VERB **1** to have or
express a different opinion **2** to

have a bad effect *Rich food
disagrees with me.*
▶ **disagreement** NOUN

disagreeable ADJECTIVE
unpleasant

disappear VERB to stop being
visible; to vanish
▶ **disappearance** NOUN

disappoint VERB to fail to do
what someone hopes for
▶ **disappointment** NOUN

disappointed ADJECTIVE unhappy
because a hope has not been
achieved

disapprove VERB to have an
unfavourable opinion of
▶ **disapproval** NOUN

THESAURUS

disabled ADJECTIVE • *disabled
visitors* ▶ handicapped,
incapacitated, lame, paralysed

disadvantage NOUN • *a major
disadvantage* ▶ drawback, snag,
problem, inconvenience, nuisance

disagree VERB • *We often
disagree.* ▶ argue, fall out,
quarrel, squabble, bicker, clash
disagree with • *She disagrees
with everything he says.*
▶ contradict, argue with, object to

disagreement NOUN • *to have
a disagreement* ▶ argument,
quarrel, squabble, dispute • *some
disagreement between the two
stories* ▶ difference, dissimilarity,
discrepancy

disappear VERB • *The crowd
disappeared.* ▶ vanish, disperse,
evaporate, melt away • *a way of

life that has disappeared* ▶ die
out, become extinct, vanish

disappoint VERB • *We will try not
to disappoint you.* ▶ let down, fail,
dissatisfy • *Their hopes were
disappointed.* ▶ thwart, frustrate,
dash

disappointed ADJECTIVE • *I was
disappointed when they left.*
▶ unhappy, upset, let down,
dissatisfied, dejected, crestfallen

disappointment NOUN • *a
feeling of disappointment*
▶ regret, sadness, sorrow,
dissatisfaction • *The result was a
disappointment.* ▶ let-down,
setback, blow

disapproval NOUN • *She showed
her disapproval.* ▶ dislike,
displeasure, criticism

disapprove VERB **disapprove of**
• *to disapprove of gambling*

a b c **d** e f g h i j k l m n o p q r s t u v w x y z

DICTIONARY

disarm VERB **1** to give up using weapons **2** to take away someone's weapons

disarmament NOUN reduction of a country's armed forces or weapons

disarray NOUN a state of disorder

disaster NOUN **1** a bad accident or misfortune **2** a complete failure ▶ **disastrous** ADJECTIVE

disband VERB to stop working as a group

disbelieve VERB to be unwilling to believe something ▶ **disbelief** NOUN

disc NOUN **1** a round flat object **2** a layer of cartilage between vertebrae in the spine **3** a CD or record

discard VERB to throw away or put aside

discern VERB to see or recognize clearly ▶ **discernible** ADJECTIVE

discerning ADJECTIVE showing good judgement

discharge VERB **1** to release a person **2** to dismiss from a job **3** to send out a liquid or substance **4** to pay a debt

discharge NOUN **1** the process of discharging **2** something that is discharged

disciple NOUN **1** a person who follows the teachings of a leader **2** any of the original followers of Christ

disciplinarian NOUN a person who believes in strict discipline

discipline NOUN **1** orderly and obedient behaviour **2** a subject for study ▶ **disciplinary** ADJECTIVE

discipline VERB **1** to train to be orderly and obedient **2** to punish

disc jockey NOUN a person who introduces and plays records

disclose VERB to reveal or make known ▶ **disclosure** NOUN

disco NOUN a place where CDs or records are played for dancing

discolour VERB to spoil the colour of; to stain ▶ **discoloration** NOUN

THESAURUS

▶ dislike, object to, frown on, condemn, criticize

disaster NOUN • *an air disaster* ▶ tragedy, catastrophe, calamity • *a complete disaster for them* ▶ failure, fiasco, catastrophe

disastrous ADJECTIVE • *a disastrous fire* ▶ terrible, dreadful, catastrophic, calamitous, devastating

discard VERB • *to discard old clothes* ▶ get rid of, dispose of, throw away, cast off, reject

discharge VERB • *to discharge fumes* ▶ emit, give out, pour out, give off, exude, belch, release, secrete, produce, send out, eject, expel • *to discharge an employee* ▶ dismiss, fire, sack, throw out • *to discharge someone from hospital* ▶ dismiss, fire, make redundant, remove, sack, throw out

discipline NOUN • *more discipline in the classroom* ▶ control, order, self-control, strictness, obedience

discomfort NOUN a lack of comfort

disconcert VERB to make a person feel uneasy

disconnect VERB to break the connection between; to detach ▶ **disconnection** NOUN

disconnected ADJECTIVE not having a connection between its parts

discontent NOUN lack of contentment; dissatisfaction ▶ **discontented** ADJECTIVE, **discontentment** NOUN

discontinue VERB to stop doing something; to end

discord NOUN 1 disagreement; quarrelling 2 musical sounds producing a harsh or unpleasant sound ▶ **discordant** ADJECTIVE

discount NOUN a sum taken off a price

discount VERB to ignore or disregard something

discourage VERB 1 to take away someone's enthusiasm or confidence 2 to try to persuade someone not to do something ▶ **discouragement** NOUN

discourteous ADJECTIVE not courteous; rude ▶ **discourtesy** NOUN

discover VERB 1 to find or find out 2 to be the first person to find something

discovery NOUN **discoveries** 1 the process of discovering 2 something discovered

discredit VERB 1 to cause to be doubted 2 to damage the reputation of

discreet ADJECTIVE 1 cautious about what you say 2 not showy ▶ **discreetly** ADVERB

⚠ USAGE

Do not confuse this word with *discrete*.

discrepancy NOUN **discrepancies** a difference

discount NOUN • *a £5 discount* ▶ reduction, deduction, cut, rebate

discount VERB • *to discount rumours* ▶ disregard, reject, disbelieve, ignore

discourage VERB • *The audience was discouraged from asking questions.* ▶ deter, dissuade, prevent, put off • *Her cool response discouraged them.* ▶ demoralize, dishearten

discover VERB • *The children discovered a secret door.* ▶ find, locate, come across, uncover,

stumble on • *We discovered that he had been lying.* ▶ find out, learn, realize • *Faraday discovered electricity.* ▶ invent, develop, pioneer

discovery NOUN • *a major new discovery* ▶ invention, innovation, breakthrough • *the discovery of the body* ▶ finding, detection, uncovering, unearthing

discreet ADJECTIVE • *discreet enquiries* ▶ careful, cautious, tactful, considerate, sensitive

discrepancy NOUN • *a discrepancy between the two*

between things which should be the same

discrete ADJECTIVE separate or distinct

> ⚠ USAGE
>
> Do not confuse this word with *discreet*.

discretion (dis-kresh-on) NOUN
1 caution in what you say or do
2 freedom to decide for yourself about something

discriminate VERB 1 to notice the differences between things
2 to treat people unfairly because of their race, sex, or religion

discrimination NOUN 1 unfair treatment because of race, sex, or religion 2 sensitive taste or judgement

discus NOUN a thick heavy disc thrown in athletic contests

discuss VERB to talk with other people about a subject
> **discussion** NOUN

disease NOUN an unhealthy condition; an illness ▶ **diseased** ADJECTIVE

disentangle VERB to free from tangles or confusion

disfigure VERB to spoil the appearance of ▶ **disfigurement** NOUN

disgorge VERB to pour or send out

disgrace NOUN 1 shame; loss of approval or respect 2 something that causes shame

disgrace VERB to bring disgrace on

disgraceful ADJECTIVE shameful; very bad ▶ **disgracefully** ADVERB

disgruntled ADJECTIVE discontented or resentful

disguise NOUN something used to disguise

versions of the story
▶ inconsistency, difference, dissimilarity, incompatibility

discriminate VERB • to discriminate between the two theories ▶ distinguish, differentiate, tell the difference
• to discriminate against women ▶ be biased, be prejudiced, be intolerant (towards)

discuss VERB • to discuss problems ▶ debate, talk about, consider, confer about

discussion NOUN • a lively discussion ▶ debate, dialogue, conversation, talk, argument, exchange of views

disease NOUN • a country afflicted by disease ▶ illness, sickness, bad health, ailment, malady

disgrace NOUN • a public disgrace ▶ dishonour, shame, humiliation, embarrassment

disgrace VERB • to disgrace his family ▶ shame, bring shame on, humiliate, embarrass

disgraceful ADJECTIVE • disgraceful behaviour ▶ shameful, shocking, dreadful, dishonourable

disguise NOUN • a convincing disguise ▶ costume, outfit, fancy dress, camouflage, impersonation, cover

a
b
c
d
e
f
g
h
i
j
k
l
m
n
o
p
q
r
s
t
u
v
w
x
y
z

disguise VERB **1** to make a person or thing look different **2** to conceal your feelings

disgust NOUN a feeling that something is very unpleasant or disgraceful

disgust VERB to cause disgust in

dish NOUN **1** a plate or bowl for food **2** something having this shape **3** food prepared for eating

dish VERB (informal)

dish out to give out; to distribute

dishcloth NOUN a cloth for washing dishes

dishearten VERB to cause to lose hope or confidence

dishevelled ADJECTIVE ruffled and untidy

dishonest ADJECTIVE not honest ▶ **dishonesty** NOUN

dishonour NOUN, VERB to bring disgrace to ▶ **dishonourable** ADJECTIVE

disillusion VERB to correct a wrong belief that someone has

disinclined ADJECTIVE unwilling to do something

disinfect VERB to destroy the germs in ▶ **disinfection** NOUN

disinfectant NOUN a substance used for disinfecting

disintegrate VERB to break up into small parts or pieces ▶ **disintegration** NOUN

disinterested ADJECTIVE not influenced by personal interest; impartial *disinterested advice*

⚠ **USAGE**

This word does not mean the same as *uninterested*.

disjointed ADJECTIVE (of talk or writing) not fitting well together well and so difficult to understand

disk NOUN (ICT) a circular storage device for data

THESAURUS

disguise VERB • *to disguise your appearance* ▶ hide, conceal, camouflage • *to disguise your anger* ▶ hide, conceal, cover up **disguise yourself as** • *I disguised myself as a postman.* ▶ dress up as, impersonate, pretend to be, pose as

disgust NOUN • *to feel disgust* ▶ revulsion, dislike, loathing, horror, repugnance, repulsion

disgust VERB • *The food disgusted me.* ▶ revolt, sicken, nauseate, offend, outrage, horrify, shock

disgusting ADJECTIVE • *a disgusting smell* ▶ revolting, sickening,

nauseating, offensive, repulsive, loathsome

dishevelled ADJECTIVE • *dishevelled hair* ▶ untidy, bedraggled, unkempt, scruffy, messy

dishonest ADJECTIVE • *a dishonest official* ▶ deceitful, untruthful, cheating, double-dealing, corrupt, untrustworthy

dishonesty NOUN • *a charge of dishonesty* ▶ corruption, fraud, cheating, deceit, lying

disinterested ADJECTIVE • *a disinterested attitude* ▶ impartial, neutral, unbiased, unprejudiced

DICTIONARY

dislike NOUN a feeling of not liking someone or something

dislike VERB to feel that you do not like someone or something

dislocate VERB to move or force a bone from its proper position ▶ **dislocation** NOUN

dislodge VERB to move or force something from its place

disloyal ADJECTIVE not loyal ▶ **disloyally** ADVERB, **disloyalty** NOUN

dismal ADJECTIVE 1 gloomy 2 of poor quality ▶ **dismally** ADVERB

dismantle VERB to take to pieces

dismay NOUN a feeling of surprise and disappointment ▶ **dismayed** ADJECTIVE

dismiss VERB 1 to send away 2 to remove from a job 3 to stop

thinking about ▶ **dismissal** NOUN, **dismissive** ADJECTIVE

dismount VERB to get off a horse or bicycle

disobedient ADJECTIVE not obedient ▶ **disobediently** ADVERB, **disobedience** NOUN

disobey VERB to refuse to do what you are told

disorder NOUN 1 untidiness 2 public fighting or rioting 3 an illness

disorderly ADJECTIVE disorganized; untidy

disorganized ADJECTIVE muddled and badly organized ▶ **disorganization** NOUN

⚠ **SPELLING**

This word can also be spelled *disorganised*.

THESAURUS

dislike NOUN • *a dislike of big cities* ▶ aversion (to), hatred, loathing, disgust (for)

dislike VERB • *to dislike long journeys* ▶ hate, detest, object to, disapprove of, despise

dismal ADJECTIVE • *a dismal little room* ▶ gloomy, dingy, dim, dreary, dark • *dismal faces* ▶ sad, glum, gloomy, miserable

dismay NOUN • *her dismay at the loss* ▶ alarm, shock, surprise, distress

dismiss VERB • *to dismiss an attendant* ▶ send away, discharge, free, let go, release • *to dismiss employees* ▶ sack, fire, give someone notice, lay

off • *to dismiss the allegations* ▶ reject, discount, disregard, drop • *to dismiss thoughts from the mind* ▶ remove, banish, dispel

disobedient ADJECTIVE • *a disobedient child* ▶ naughty, badly behaved, disruptive, rebellious, unruly

disobey VERB • *to disobey the rules* ▶ break, defy, flout, rebel against, ignore

disorganized ADJECTIVE • *The room looked disorganized.* ▶ untidy, disorderly, messy, confused, chaotic • *I was careless and disorganized.* ▶ unmethodical, slapdash, slovenly, scatterbrained

a
b
c
d
e
f
g
h
i
j
k
l
m
n
o
p
q
r
s
t
u
v
w
x
y
z

disown VERB to refuse to acknowledge as yours

disparage VERB to speak of in a belittling way

dispatch VERB 1 to send off to a destination 2 to kill

dispatch NOUN 1 the act of dispatching 2 a report or message sent

dispel VERB **dispelling, dispelled** to scatter or drive away

dispense VERB 1 to distribute or deal out 2 to prepare medicine according to prescriptions **dispense with** to do without something

dispenser NOUN a device or machine that supplies a quantity of something *a cash dispenser*

disperse VERB to scatter ▶ **dispersal** NOUN

displace VERB 1 to shift from its place 2 to take a person's or thing's place ▶ **displacement** NOUN

display VERB to show clearly

display NOUN 1 an exhibition 2 something displayed

displease VERB to annoy or not please someone ▶ **displeasure** NOUN

disposable ADJECTIVE made to be thrown away after use

disposal NOUN the process of getting rid of something **at your disposal** ready for you to use

dispose VERB to place in position; to arrange **dispose of** to get rid of

disposed ADJECTIVE ready and willing **be well disposed** to be friendly

disposition NOUN 1 a person's nature or qualities 2 an arrangement

dispense VERB • *to dispense drinks* ▶ distribute, give out, pass round, provide • *to dispense medicines* ▶ supply, prepare, make up **dispense with** • *to dispense with the formalities* ▶ dispose of, disregard, ignore, get rid of, do without

disperse VERB • *Troops dispersed the demonstrators.* ▶ break up, split up, scatter, drive away • *The crowd dispersed quickly.* ▶ break up, split up, separate, scatter, disappear • *Birds disperse the seed.* ▶ scatter, spread, distribute

display NOUN • *a display of horsemanship* ▶ exhibition, demonstration, show, spectacle, presentation

display VERB • *a room to display the exhibits* ▶ show, exhibit, present • *to display knowledge* ▶ show, reveal, demonstrate

displease VERB • *The decision displeased him.* ▶ annoy, anger, irritate, infuriate, enrage, madden

dispose VERB **dispose of** • *to dispose of soiled nappies* ▶ get rid of, throw away, destroy, discard, jettison

disproportionate ADJECTIVE out of proportion; too large or too small

disprove VERB to show that something is not true

dispute VERB 1 to argue or debate 2 to quarrel 3 to raise an objection to

dispute NOUN 1 an argument or debate 2 a quarrel **in dispute** being argued about

disqualify VERB **disqualifies, disqualified** to bar someone from a competition for breaking the rules ▶ **disqualification** NOUN

disquiet NOUN anxiety or worry ▶ **disquieting** ADJECTIVE

disregard VERB to ignore

disregard NOUN the act of ignoring something

disrepair NOUN bad condition from being neglected

disreputable ADJECTIVE not respectable

disrepute NOUN bad reputation

disrespect NOUN lack of respect; rudeness ▶ **disrespectful** ADJECTIVE

disrupt VERB to put into disorder ▶ **disruption** NOUN, **disruptive** ADJECTIVE

dissatisfied ADJECTIVE not satisfied ▶ **dissatisfaction** NOUN

dissect VERB to cut something up in order to examine it ▶ **dissection** NOUN

dissent NOUN strong disagreement

dissent VERB to disagree strongly

dissident NOUN a person who disagrees with those in authority

dissipate VERB 1 to disappear or scatter 2 to waste or squander ▶ **dissipation** NOUN

dissolute ADJECTIVE having an immoral way of life

dissolution NOUN the formal ending of an arrangement, especially a marriage

dissolve VERB 1 to make or become liquid; to melt 2 to end a

dispute VERB • *We disputed with them.* ▶ debate, argue, quarrel • *to dispute a claim* ▶ challenge, contest, question, oppose, deny

dispute NOUN • *a matter of dispute* ▶ debate, discussion, controversy, argument, disagreement

disqualify VERB • *to be disqualified from driving* ▶ ban, bar, exclude, prohibit

disregard VERB • *to disregard the interruptions* ▶ ignore, take no notice of, pay no attention to

disrespectful ADJECTIVE • *disrespectful towards his elders* ▶ rude, discourteous, impertinent, impolite, cheeky

disrupt VERB • *to disrupt plans* ▶ interrupt, break up, disturb, upset, interfere with

dissatisfied ADJECTIVE • *dissatisfied with the answer* ▶ discontented, disappointed, unhappy, disgruntled, upset

dissolve VERB • *The powder dissolves in water.* ▶ disintegrate, disperse, melt

marriage or partnership **3** to end a parliament or assembly

dissuade VERB to persuade somebody not to do something ► **dissuasion** NOUN

distance NOUN the amount of space between two places **in the distance** far away but visible

distant ADJECTIVE **1** far away **2** not friendly or sociable **3** not closely related ► **distantly** ADVERB

distaste NOUN dislike

distasteful ADJECTIVE unpleasant

distil VERB distilling, distilled to purify a liquid by boiling it and condensing the vapour ► **distillation** NOUN

distiller NOUN a person or firm that makes alcoholic drinks by distilling ► **distillery** NOUN

distinct ADJECTIVE **1** easily heard or seen; noticeable **2** clearly separate or different ► **distinctly** ADVERB

⚠ **USAGE**

Do not confuse this word with *distinctive*.

distinction NOUN **1** a difference **2** excellence or honour **3** an award or high mark

distinctive ADJECTIVE easy to recognize or identify *a distinctive uniform* ► **distinctively** ADVERB

⚠ **USAGE**

Do not confuse this word with *distinct*.

distinguish VERB **1** to make or notice differences between things **2** to see or hear something clearly **3** to bring honour to ► **distinguishable** ADJECTIVE

distance NOUN • *the distance between the two vehicles* ► space, gap, interval, length • *in the distance* • *a church spire in the distance* ► far away, far off, in the background, on the horizon

distant ADJECTIVE • *distant countries* ► far-off, faraway, remote, outlying • *a distant memory* ► vague, dim, faint, indistinct • *a distant manner* ► cool, aloof, detached, reserved, unfriendly

distinct ADJECTIVE • *four distinct categories* ► separate, discrete, individual • *a distinct improvement* ► clear, definite, marked, obvious

distinction NOUN • *a clear distinction between their views and ours* ► difference, contrast, dissimilarity • *a writer of distinction* ► importance, significance, note, renown, fame • *to serve with distinction* ► honour, credit, merit, courage

distinctive ADJECTIVE • *distinctive markings* ► special, characteristic, typical, individual, unique

distinguish VERB • *to distinguish between good and bad* ► differentiate, discriminate, tell the difference • *We could distinguish a line of trees.* ► see, make out, identify, perceive

a
b
c
d
e
f
g
h
i
j
k
l
m
n
o
p
q
r
s
t
u
v
w
x
y
z

distinguished ADJECTIVE
1 excellent and famous 2 dignified in appearance

distort VERB 1 to pull or twist out of its normal shape 2 to give a false account of ▶ **distortion** NOUN

distract VERB to take a person's attention away from something

distraction NOUN 1 something that distracts your attention 2 an amusement 3 great worry or distress

distraught (dis-trawt) ADJECTIVE very worried or upset

distress NOUN great sorrow or trouble

distress VERB to cause distress to

distribute VERB 1 to deal or share out 2 to spread or scatter

▶ **distribution** NOUN, **distributor** NOUN

district NOUN part of a town or country

distrust NOUN lack of trust; suspicion ▶ **distrustful** ADJECTIVE

distrust VERB not to trust

disturb VERB 1 to spoil the peace or rest of 2 to cause to worry 3 to move something from its position

disturbance NOUN 1 an argument or an outbreak of violence 2 the act of disturbing or interrupting

disuse NOUN the state of not being used any more

disused ADJECTIVE no longer used

THESAURUS

distinguished ADJECTIVE • *a distinguished statesman*
▶ famous, well known, eminent, celebrated, renowned

distort VERB • *His face was distorted with pain.* ▶ twist, contort, deform • *to distort the truth* ▶ twist, misrepresent

distract VERB • *A noise distracted him.* ▶ disturb, divert, sidetrack

distraught ADJECTIVE • *The poor woman looked distraught.*
▶ upset, distressed, frantic

distress NOUN • *She could hardly hide her distress.* ▶ suffering, misery, anguish, unhappiness, despair, grief • *the distress of extreme poverty* ▶ hardship, adversity

distress VERB • *The news distressed him.* ▶ upset, sadden, trouble, bother, worry

distribute VERB • *to distribute leaflets* ▶ give out, hand out, circulate, issue • *The money was distributed among his heirs.*
▶ share out, divide up, apportion • *The seed should be distributed evenly.* ▶ scatter, spread, disperse

district NOUN • *a shopping district*
▶ area, region, quarter, locality, neighbourhood

distrust VERB • *The public distrusts politicians.* ▶ mistrust, be suspicious of, disbelieve, doubt, question

disturb VERB • *He did not want to disturb the neighbours.* ▶ bother, interrupt, annoy, intrude on • *Try not to disturb the books and papers.* ▶ move, muddle, mix up

a
b
c
d
e
f
g
h
i
j
k
l
m
n
o
p
q
r
s
t
u
v
w
x
y
z

225

ditch NOUN a trench dug to hold water or carry it away

ditch VERB **1** (*informal*) to bring an aircraft down in a forced landing on the sea **2** (*informal*) to abandon or discard something

dither VERB to hesitate nervously

ditto NOUN (used in lists) the same again

ditty NOUN **ditties** a short song

divan NOUN a bed or couch without a raised back or sides

dive VERB **1** to go underwater, especially head first **2** to move down quickly ► **dive** NOUN

diver NOUN a person who works underwater in a special suit with an air supply

diverge VERB to separate and go in different directions ► **divergent** ADJECTIVE, **divergence** NOUN

diverse ADJECTIVE of several different kinds ► **diversity** NOUN

diversify VERB **diversifies**, **diversified 1** to make or become

varied **2** to involve yourself in different things
► **diversification** NOUN

diversion NOUN **1** an alternative route for traffic **2** a recreation or entertainment

divert VERB **1** to turn something aside from its course **2** to entertain or amuse ► **diverting** ADJECTIVE

divide VERB **1** to separate into smaller parts **2** to share among several people **3** to find how many times one number is contained in another ► **divider** NOUN

dividend NOUN **1** a share of business profits **2** a number that is to be divided by another

dividers PLURAL NOUN a pair of compasses for measuring distances

divine ADJECTIVE **1** belonging to or coming from God **2** like a god **3** (*informal*) excellent; extremely beautiful ► **divinely** ADVERB

THESAURUS

dither VERB • *He dithered over which suit to wear.* ► hesitate, waver

dive VERB • *a dive into the water* ► leap, jump, drop, plunge • *The hawk dived towards its prey.* ► descend, drop, swoop, plunge, plummet

diverge VERB • *The roads diverged.* ► separate, divide, part • *Our opinions diverge.* ► differ, disagree, be different

divert VERB • *The plane was diverted to another airport.*

► redirect, reroute, switch • *We tried to divert them with funny stories.* ► amuse, entertain, distract, keep happy

divide VERB • *to divide into groups* ► separate, split • *We divided the food between us.* ► share out, allocate, distribute • *to divide the eggs according to size* ► sort, classify, grade, organize, group

divine ADJECTIVE • *divine worship* ► holy, sacred, religious • *a divine being* ► supernatural, godlike, heavenly, immortal

divinity NOUN **divinities** 1 a divine state 2 a god or goddess 3 the study of religion

division NOUN 1 the process of dividing 2 a dividing line or thing 3 a section

divisive ADJECTIVE causing disagreement within a group

divisor NOUN a number by which another is to be divided

divorce NOUN the legal ending of a marriage

divorce VERB 1 to separate from a husband or wife by divorce 2 to separate

divulge VERB to reveal secret or sensitive information

Diwali (di-wah-lee) NOUN a Hindu religious festival of lamps, held in October or November

DIY ABBREVIATION do-it-yourself

dizzy ADJECTIVE **dizzier, dizziest** confused or giddy, or causing this

state ► **dizzily** ADVERB, **dizziness** NOUN

DJ ABBREVIATION disc jockey

DNA ABBREVIATION deoxyribonucleic acid, a substance in chromosomes that stores genetic information

do VERB **does, did, done** 1 to perform or carry out *Do your work.* 2 to deal with *I'll do the dinner.* 3 to act or behave *They do as they please.* 4 to succeed or manage *You are doing very well.* 5 used to form negative statements and questions *I do not like this. Do you want it?* 6 used for emphasis *I do hope you can come.* 7 used to avoid repeating a verb that has just been used *We work as hard as they do.* **do away with** to get rid of **do up** 1 to fasten 2 to repair or redecorate

do NOUN (*informal*) a party or other social event

THESAURUS

division NOUN • *divisions in modern society* ► split, disagreement, conflict • *the division of Germany* ► dividing, splitting, partitioning, separation • *the overseas division of the company* ► department, branch, office • *the division of the spoils* ► distribution, dividing up, sharing out

dizzy ADJECTIVE • *Leaping about made her dizzy.* ► giddy, faint, shaky, light-headed

do VERB • *a lot of work to do* ► carry out, attend to, deal with, cope with, complete, finish • *Do as you please.* ► behave, act, conduct yourself • *A glass of water will do.*

► suffice, be enough, be adequate, be acceptable • *Shall I do the lunch now?* ► prepare, make, get ready • *She went to do her hair.* ► arrange, style, brush, comb • *He is doing languages.* ► study, learn, take a course in • *to do very well* ► get on, progress, succeed **do away with** • *to do away with outdated practices* ► abolish, get rid of, put an end to, dispense with **do up** • *to do up your laces* ► tie, fasten, secure • *to do up an old house* ► renovate, restore, refurbish, decorate **do without** • *to do without sleep* ► dispense with, give up, manage without

docile ADJECTIVE willing to obey

dock[1] NOUN **1** a part of a harbour where ships are loaded and repaired **2** an enclosure for the accused or witnesses in a lawcourt

dock VERB **1** to bring or come into a dock **2** (of a spacecraft) to join with another in space

dock[2] NOUN a weed with broad leaves

dock[3] VERB **1** to cut short an animal's tail **2** to reduce someone's wages or supplies

docker NOUN a labourer who loads and unloads ships

docket NOUN a document or label listing the contents of a package

dockyard NOUN an open area with docks and equipment for ships

doctor NOUN **1** a person who is trained to treat sick or injured people **2** a person who holds an advanced degree at a university *Doctor of Music*

doctrine NOUN a belief held by a religious or political group

document NOUN a written or printed paper giving information or evidence about something
  ▶ **documentation** NOUN

documentary ADJECTIVE **1** consisting of documents *documentary evidence* **2** showing real events or situations

documentary NOUN **documentaries** a film giving information about real events

doddery ADJECTIVE unsteady from old age

dodge VERB to move quickly to avoid someone or something

dodge NOUN **1** a dodging movement **2** (*informal*) a clever way of doing something

dodgem NOUN a small electric car at a funfair, driven to bump or avoid others

dodgy ADJECTIVE **dodgier**, **dodgiest** (*informal*) **1** awkward or tricky **2** not working properly **3** dishonest

dodo NOUN **dodos** a large extinct bird that was unable to fly

doe NOUN a female deer, rabbit, or hare

doesn't does not

dog NOUN a four-legged animal that barks, often kept as a pet

dog VERB **dogging**, **dogged** to follow closely

dog-eared ADJECTIVE (of a book) with the corners worn from use

docile ADJECTIVE • *a docile nature*
  ▶ gentle, compliant, meek, mild, obedient

dodge VERB • *to dodge a blow*
  ▶ avoid, duck, evade • *to dodge the issue* ▶ avoid, evade, fudge, sidestep • *to dodge between*

parked cars ▶ dart, dive, duck, swerve, jump

dodge NOUN • *a clever dodge*
  ▶ ruse, ploy, trick, scheme

dodgy ADJECTIVE • *dodgy travel agents* ▶ dishonest, deceitful, unreliable

a b c **d** e f g h i j k l m n o p q r s t u v w x y z

dogged (dog-id) ADJECTIVE
persistent or obstinate
► **doggedly** ADVERB

dogma NOUN a belief or principle
that must be accepted by
members of a religion

dogmatic ADJECTIVE expressing
ideas in a firm way and not willing
to accept other ideas
► **dogmatically** ADVERB

doh NOUN a name for the keynote
of a scale in music, or the note C

do-it-yourself ADJECTIVE suitable
for an amateur to do or make at
home

doldrums PLURAL NOUN an
uninteresting or depressing time

> **WORD HISTORY**
> originally ocean regions near the
> equator where there is little or no
> wind

dole VERB **dole out** to distribute

dole NOUN (informal) money paid by
the state to unemployed people

doleful ADJECTIVE sad or sorrowful
► **dolefully** ADVERB

doll NOUN a toy model of a person

dollar NOUN a unit of money in the
USA and some other countries

dollop NOUN (informal) a lump of
something soft

dolphin NOUN a sea animal like a
small whale with a beak-like snout

domain (dom-ayn) NOUN **1** a
kingdom **2** an area of knowledge
or interest

dome NOUN a roof shaped like the
top half of a ball ► **domed** ADJECTIVE

domestic ADJECTIVE **1** to do with
the home or household **2** (of
animals) kept by people; not wild
► **domestically** ADVERB

domesticated ADJECTIVE (of
animals) trained to live with
humans

dominate VERB **1** to control by
being stronger or more powerful
2 to be conspicuous or prominent
► **dominant** ADJECTIVE, **domination**
NOUN

domineering ADJECTIVE behaving
in a dominating way

dominion NOUN **1** authority or
control over others **2** an area over
which someone rules

dogged ADJECTIVE • *dogged efforts*
► determined, persistent,
tenacious, single-minded

dogmatic ADJECTIVE • *a dogmatic
point of view* ► stubborn,
arrogant, opinionated

dole VERB **dole out** • *to dole out the
food* ► give out, share out,
distribute

dominant ADJECTIVE • *the
dominant member of the*

partnership ► leading, main,
principal, prominent • *to play a
dominant role* ► controlling,
leading, powerful, influential

dominate VERB • *to dominate the
meeting* ► control, monopolize,
rule

domineering ADJECTIVE • *a
domineering mother*
► authoritarian, overbearing,
tyrannical

domino NOUN **dominoes** a small flat oblong piece of wood or plastic marked with dots or a blank space at each end, used in the game called dominoes

don VERB **donning, donned** to put on a coat etc.

donate VERB to present money or a gift to a fund or institution ▶ **donation** NOUN

donkey NOUN **donkeys** an animal that looks like a small horse with long ears

donor NOUN someone who gives something *a blood donor*

don't do not

doodle VERB to scribble or draw absent-mindedly ▶ **doodle** NOUN

doom NOUN a grim fate that you cannot avoid

doomed ADJECTIVE **1** destined to a grim fate **2** bound to fail or be destroyed

doomsday NOUN the end of the world

door NOUN a hinged or movable barrier used to open or close an entrance

doorstep NOUN the step or piece of ground just outside a door

doorway NOUN the opening into which a door fits

dope NOUN **1** (informal) an illegal drug **2** (informal) a stupid person ▶ **dopey** ADJECTIVE

dope VERB (informal) to give a drug to

dormant ADJECTIVE **1** sleeping **2** living or existing but not active

dormitory NOUN **dormitories** a room for several people to sleep in

dormouse NOUN **dormice** an animal like a large mouse that hibernates in winter

dosage NOUN the size of a dose of medicine

dose NOUN an amount of medicine taken at one time

dose VERB to give a dose of medicine to

dossier (doss-ee-ay) a set of documents containing information about a person or event

dot NOUN a tiny spot

dot VERB **dotting, dotted** to mark with dots

dotage (doh-tij) NOUN a condition of weakness of mind caused by old age

dote VERB **dote on** to be very fond of

double ADJECTIVE **1** twice as much or as many **2** having two things or

donation NOUN • *voluntary donations* ▶ gift, contribution

donor NOUN • *an anonymous donor* ▶ provider, contributor, benefactor, sponsor

doom NOUN • *a feeling of doom* ▶ ruin, destruction, disaster, catastrophe

doomed ADJECTIVE • *The project was doomed.* ▶ ill-fated, cursed, jinxed

dot NOUN • *a picture of tiny dots* ▶ spot, speck, point, mark

double NOUN • *It was either you or your double.* ▶ lookalike, clone, twin, spitting image

parts that form a pair *a double-barrelled gun* **3** suitable for two people *a double bed* ▶ **doubly** ADVERB

double NOUN **1** a double quantity or thing **2** a person or thing that looks exactly like another

double VERB **1** to make or become twice as much or as many **2** to bend or fold in two **3** to turn back sharply

double bass NOUN a musical instrument with strings, like a large cello

double-cross VERB to deceive or cheat

double-decker NOUN a bus with two floors, one above the other

double glazing NOUN a window of two sheets of glass with a space between, to retain heat or keep out noise

doubt NOUN a feeling of not being sure about something

doubt VERB to feel doubt

doubtful ADJECTIVE **1** feeling doubt **2** making you feel doubt ▶ **doubtfully** ADVERB

doubtless ADVERB probably

dough NOUN **1** a thick mixture of flour and water used for making bread or pastry **2** (*informal*) money ▶ **doughy** ADJECTIVE

doughnut NOUN a round bun that has been fried and covered in sugar

dour (doo-er) ADJECTIVE stern and gloomy-looking

douse VERB **1** to put into water or pour water over **2** to put out a light

dove NOUN a kind of pigeon

dowager NOUN a woman who holds a title or property after her husband has died

dowdy ADJECTIVE **dowdier**, **dowdiest** shabby or unfashionable ▶ **dowdily** ADVERB

double VERB • *to double your efforts* ▶ increase, multiply
double back • *He doubled back and crossed the bridge.* ▶ turn back, return, backtrack, retrace your steps

double-cross VERB • *to double-cross your friends* ▶ cheat, betray, deceive

doubt NOUN • *some doubt about their identity* ▶ uncertainty, confusion • *plagued by doubt* ▶ indecision, uncertainty, lack of confidence, mistrust, suspicion

doubt VERB • *I doubt whether they will be there.* ▶ question, think it

unlikely • *I do not doubt their motives.* ▶ disbelieve, distrust, question, suspect

doubtful ADJECTIVE • *I was doubtful about leaving.* ▶ hesitant, uncertain, unsure, undecided, sceptical • *It was doubtful whether the witness would back him up.* ▶ uncertain, questionable, dubious, debatable, in doubt • *doubtful of their conclusions* ▶ unsure, suspicious, distrustful, wary, sceptical • *The chances of success are doubtful.* ▶ unlikely, improbable, uncertain

down[1] ADVERB **1** to or in a lower place or position or level *to fall down* **2** to a source or place etc. *to track down* **3** in writing *Take down these instructions.* **4** as an immediate payment *£50 down*

down PREPOSITION downwards through or along or into *down the stairs*

down ADJECTIVE unhappy or depressed *feeling down*

down[2] NOUN fine soft feathers or hair ▶ **downy** ADJECTIVE

downcast ADJECTIVE **1** (of the eyes) looking down **2** dejected

downfall NOUN **1** a fall from power or prosperity **2** a heavy fall of rain or snow

downgrade VERB to make less important or valuable

downhill ADVERB, ADJECTIVE down a slope

download VERB to transfer data from a large computer system to a smaller one

downpour NOUN a heavy fall of rain

downright ADVERB, ADJECTIVE complete or completely *a downright lie*

downs PLURAL NOUN grass-covered hills

downstairs ADVERB, ADJECTIVE to or on a lower floor

downstream ADJECTIVE, ADVERB in the direction in which a stream flows

down-to-earth ADJECTIVE sensible and practical

downward ADJECTIVE, ADVERB going towards what is lower ▶ **downwards** ADVERB

dowry NOUN **dowries** property or money brought by a bride to her husband when she marries him

doze VERB to sleep lightly ▶ **doze** NOUN, **dozy** ADJECTIVE

dozen NOUN a set of twelve

drab ADJECTIVE **drabber**, **drabbest** **1** not colourful **2** dull or uninteresting

draft NOUN **1** a rough sketch or plan **2** a written order for a bank to pay out money

draft VERB **1** to prepare a draft **2** to select for a special duty

drag VERB **dragging**, **dragged** **1** to pull something heavy along **2** to search a river or lake

drag NOUN **1** something tedious or unpleasant **2** (*informal*) women's clothes worn by men

down ADJECTIVE • *He felt down all day.* ▶ depressed, dejected, sad, unhappy, miserable

downright ADJECTIVE • *downright lies* ▶ utter, absolute, total, complete

drab ADJECTIVE • *drab furnishings* ▶ dowdy, shabby, dreary, dingy, dull

draft NOUN • *a draft of a speech* ▶ outline, sketch, abstract, first version, rough version, plan

drag VERB • *She dragged a chair over to the table.* ▶ pull, draw, haul, heave • *Time began to drag.* ▶ become tedious, crawl, go slowly, move slowly, pass slowly

dragon NOUN 1 (in stories) a fire-breathing monster with wings 2 a fierce person

dragonfly NOUN **dragonflies** an insect with a long thin body and two pairs of transparent wings

drain NOUN 1 a pipe or ditch for taking away water or other liquid 2 something that uses up strength or resources

drain VERB 1 to take away water through a drain 2 to flow or trickle away 3 to empty liquid out of a container 4 to use up strength or resources ► **drainage** NOUN

drake NOUN a male duck

drama NOUN 1 a play 2 the writing or performing of plays 3 a series of exciting events

dramatic ADJECTIVE 1 to do with drama 2 exciting and impressive *a dramatic change* ► **dramatically** ADVERB

dramatist NOUN a person who writes plays

dramatize VERB 1 to make a story into a play 2 to make something seem exciting ► **dramatization** NOUN

⚠ **SPELLING**

This word can also be spelled *dramatise*.

drape VERB to hang loosely over something

drapery NOUN cloth arranged in loose folds

drastic ADJECTIVE having a strong or violent effect ► **drastically** ADVERB

draught (drahft) NOUN 1 a current of cold air indoors 2 the depth of water needed to float a ship 3 a swallow of liquid ► **draughty** ADJECTIVE

draughts NOUN a game played with 24 round pieces on a chessboard

draughtsman NOUN **draughtsmen** 1 a person who makes drawings 2 a piece used in the game of draughts

THESAURUS

drain NOUN • *The drain was blocked.* ► channel, ditch, pipe, drainpipe, gutter

drain VERB • *to drain water from the tank* ► draw off, empty, remove, bleed • *to drain the glass* ► empty, drink up, finish off, polish off • *The water drains into the river.* ► seep, leak out, ooze, trickle • *The colour had drained from her face.* ► fade, vanish, disappear

drama NOUN • *to study drama* ► acting, dramatics, the theatre,

the stage • *a family drama* ► scene, incident, crisis, commotion

dramatic ADJECTIVE • *a dramatic production* ► theatrical, stage • *a dramatic rescue* ► exciting, thrilling • *a dramatic change* ► big, substantial, significant, marked

drastic ADJECTIVE • *drastic measures to reduce pollution* ► extreme, harsh, severe, radical

DICTIONARY

draw VERB drew, drawn **1** to make a picture or outline by making marks on a surface **2** to pull **3** to take out *draw water* **4** to attract *The fair drew large crowds.* **5** to have the same score on both sides **6** to move or come *to draw near* **7** to write out a cheque to be cashed **8** to form a conclusion

draw NOUN **1** the drawing of lots **2** the drawing out of a gun *He was quick on the draw.* **3** an attraction **4** a drawn game

drawback NOUN a disadvantage

drawbridge NOUN a bridge over a moat, hinged to be raised or lowered

drawer NOUN **1** a sliding compartment in a piece of furniture **2** a person who draws

drawing NOUN a picture or outline

drawl VERB to speak slowly or lazily
► **drawl** NOUN

dread NOUN great fear

dread VERB to fear very much
► **dreaded** ADJECTIVE

dreadful ADJECTIVE **1** terrible **2** (*informal*) very bad *had a dreadful time* ► **dreadfully** ADVERB

dreadlocks PLURAL NOUN hair worn in ringlets or plaits

dream NOUN **1** a series of pictures or events in the mind during sleep **2** an ambition or idea

dream VERB dreamt *or* dreamed **1** to have a dream or dreams **2** to have an ambition **3** to think something might happen *I never dreamt she would leave.* **dream**

THESAURUS

draw VERB • *to draw a shape*
► sketch, trace, outline, doodle
• *to draw a chair close to the fire*
► pull, drag, haul • *to draw the curtains* ► close, shut, open • *The show drew large audiences.*
► attract, bring in • *That is the conclusion I drew.* ► reach, arrive at • *The teams drew.* ► tie, be even, be equal

drawback NOUN • *The climate is a drawback.* ► disadvantage, problem, nuisance, snag, hitch

drawing NOUN • *drawings of the children* ► sketch, picture , illustration

dread VERB • *He dreaded the winter.* ► fear, be afraid of, worry about

dread NOUN • *a feeling of dread*
► fear, anxiety, trepidation, foreboding

dreadful ADJECTIVE • *a dreadful accident* ► terrible, awful, horrible, ghastly, shocking • *a dreadful person* ► unpleasant, nasty, awful

dream NOUN • *a dream about lizards* ► nightmare, fantasy, vision, hallucination • *to walk around in a dream* ► daydream, reverie, trance, daze • *His dream is to run a pub.* ► ambition, wish, desire

dream VERB • *She dreamed she was on a journey.* ► imagine, fantasize • *I dream of playing for England.*
► long (to play), yearn (to play), fantasize (about) **dream up** • *to*

up to invent or imagine ► **dreamer** NOUN

dreamy ADJECTIVE **dreamier**, **dreamiest** 1 half-asleep 2 vague or unclear ► **dreamily** ADVERB

dreary ADJECTIVE **drearier**, **dreariest** 1 dull or tedious 2 gloomy ► **drearily** ADVERB

dredge VERB to drag up by scooping at the bottom of a river or the sea ► **dredger** NOUN

dregs PLURAL NOUN the last drops and sediment at the bottom of a glass or bottle

drench VERB to make wet all through; soak

dress NOUN 1 a woman's or girl's piece of clothing with a bodice and skirt 2 clothes or costume *fancy dress*

dress VERB 1 to put clothes on 2 to prepare food for cooking or eating 3 to put a dressing on a wound

dresser NOUN a sideboard with shelves for dishes

dressing NOUN 1 a bandage or plaster for a wound 2 a mixture of oil, vinegar, etc. for a salad

dressing gown NOUN a loose garment for wearing over pyjamas or a nightdress

dribble VERB 1 to let saliva trickle out of your mouth 2 (of a liquid) to flow in drops 3 to move the ball forward with short movements in football or hockey ► **dribble** NOUN

drier NOUN a device for drying things

drift VERB 1 to be carried gently along by water or air 2 to move along slowly and casually 3 to live aimlessly ► **drifter** NOUN

drift NOUN 1 a drifting movement 2 a mass of snow or sand piled up by the wind 3 the general meaning of what someone says

drill NOUN 1 a tool or machine for making holes 2 repeated exercises in training

drill VERB 1 to make a hole with a drill 2 to teach with repeated exercises

drily ADVERB in a dry way

drink VERB **drank**, **drunk** 1 to swallow liquid 2 to drink alcoholic drinks, especially in large amounts ► **drinker** NOUN

drink NOUN 1 an amount of liquid for drinking 2 an alcoholic drink

dream up an excuse ► invent, devise, think up, concoct

dreary ADJECTIVE • *a dreary story* ► dull, boring, uninteresting, tedious • *dreary countryside* ► dull, gloomy, dismal, bleak

dress NOUN • *formal dress* ► clothes, clothing, garments,

attire • *a beautiful red dress* ► frock, gown, robe

dress VERB • *He dressed quickly.* ► put on clothes, get dressed • *A nurse dressed the wound.* ► bandage, put a dressing on, tend

drink VERB • *She drank her tea.* ► sip, swallow, gulp down, swill

a
b
c
d
e
f
g
h
i
j
k
l
m
n
o
p
q
r
s
t
u
v
w
x
y
z

drip VERB **dripping, dripped** to fall or let something fall in drops

drip NOUN **1** a drop of falling liquid **2** apparatus for dripping liquid into the veins

dripping NOUN fat from roasted meat

drive VERB **drove, driven 1** to make something or someone move **2** to operate a motor vehicle or a train etc. **3** to force someone to do something *Hunger drove them to steal.* **4** to force someone into a state *You are driving me crazy.* **5** to move with force *Rain drove against the window.* ▸ **driver** NOUN

drive NOUN **1** a journey in a vehicle **2** a track for vehicles through the grounds of a house **3** the transmitting of power to machinery **4** energy or enthusiasm **5** a hard stroke in cricket or golf

etc. **6** an organized effort *a sales drive*

drivel NOUN silly talk; nonsense

drizzle NOUN fine light rain

droll ADJECTIVE amusing in an odd way

drone VERB **1** to make a deep humming sound **2** to talk in a deep dull voice

drone NOUN **1** a droning sound **2** a male bee

drool VERB to dribble **drool over** to be very emotional about liking something

droop VERB to hang down weakly

drop NOUN **1** a tiny amount of liquid **2** a fall or decrease **3** a descent **4** a small round sweet

drop VERB **dropping, dropped 1** to fall **2** to let something fall **3** to become lower or less **4** to abandon or stop dealing with **5** to set down a passenger from a

drip VERB • *Water dripped on the floor.* ▸ drop, plop, splash, dribble, leak, trickle

drive VERB • *I'll drive them to the station.* ▸ take, transport, carry • *Can you drive a tractor?* ▸ operate, control, handle • *She drives everywhere.* ▸ go by car, travel by car • *The teachers drove their students very hard.* ▸ work, push • *Poverty drove them to crime.* ▸ force, push, compel, urge • *He drove a nail into the wall.* ▸ hammer, bang, ram

drive NOUN • *a short drive into town* ▸ trip, ride, journey, excursion,

outing • *You need plenty of drive.* ▸ motivation, ambition, initiative, determination, enthusiasm • *a drive to recruit blood donors* ▸ campaign, effort, appeal

droop VERB • *The flowers began to droop.* ▸ wither, wilt, flop, hang

drop NOUN • *a drop of water* ▸ droplet, drip, blob, bead, spot • *a drop of milk* ▸ dash, spot, small amount • *a drop of 100 metres* ▸ descent, fall, plunge • *a drop in prices* ▸ reduction, decrease, cut

drop VERB • *to drop the tray* ▸ let fall, let go of, release • *to drop to*

DICTIONARY

vehicle **drop in** to visit someone casually **drop out** to stop taking part in something

droppings PLURAL NOUN the dung of animals or birds

drought (drout) NOUN a long period of dry weather

drove NOUN a moving herd or flock **droves** a large number of people

drown VERB **1** to die or kill by suffocation underwater **2** to flood or drench **3** to suppress a sound with a louder one

drowsy ADJECTIVE **drowsier, drowsiest** slightly sleepy
► **drowsily** ADVERB

drubbing NOUN a severe defeat

drudge NOUN a person who does hard or tedious work ► **drudgery** NOUN

drug NOUN **1** a substance used in medicine **2** a substance taken because it affects the senses or the mind, e.g. a narcotic or stimulant, especially one causing addiction such as heroin or cocaine

drug VERB **drugging, drugged** to give a drug to

Druid (droo-id) NOUN a priest of an ancient Celtic religion in Britain and France

drum NOUN **1** a musical instrument made of a skin or parchment stretched over a round frame, beaten with sticks **2** a cylindrical object or container

drum VERB **drumming, drummed 1** to beat a drum **2** to tap repeatedly with the fingers
► **drummer** NOUN

drunk ADJECTIVE not able to control your behaviour through drinking too much alcohol

drunk NOUN a person who is drunk

drunkard NOUN a person who is often drunk

drunken ADJECTIVE **1** drunk **2** caused by drinking alcohol *a drunken brawl*

dry ADJECTIVE **drier, driest 1** without water or moisture **2** thirsty **3** tedious or dull **4** (of remarks or humour) said in a

THESAURUS

your knees ► sink, fall, go down
• *to drop a claim* ► abandon, give up, discontinue • *to drop your friends* ► desert, abandon, disown, reject • *to drop prices* ► reduce, lower, cut • *He was dropped from the team.*
► exclude, leave out (of) • *The plane dropped a thousand feet.*
► nosedive, sink

drowsy ADJECTIVE • *drowsy in the heat* ► sleepy, dozy, lethargic, somnolent, (*more informal*) snoozy

drum NOUN • *a drum of oil*
► barrel, canister, cask, butt, keg

drunk ADJECTIVE • *The men got drunk.* ► intoxicated, inebriated, tipsy

dry ADJECTIVE • *miles of dry desert*
► arid, parched, barren, scorched
• *a dry story* ► dull, boring, tedious, dreary, monotonous
• *dry humour* ► droll, ironic, wry, subtle

matter-of-fact or ironical way
► **drily** ADVERB, **dryness** NOUN

dry VERB **dries**, **dried** to make or become dry

dual ADJECTIVE composed of two parts; double

⚠ **USAGE**

Do not confuse this word with *duel*.

dub[1] VERB **dubbing**, **dubbed** 1 to make someone a knight by touching them on the shoulder with a sword 2 to give a nickname to

dub[2] VERB **dubbing**, **dubbed** to change or add new sound to the soundtrack of a film or to a recording

dubious (dew-bee-us) ADJECTIVE doubtful or uncertain
► **dubiously** ADVERB

duchess NOUN 1 a woman with the same rank as a duke 2 the wife or widow of a duke

duchy NOUN **duchies** the territory of a duke

duck NOUN 1 a swimming bird with a flat beak 2 a batsman's score of no runs at cricket 3 a ducking movement

duck VERB 1 to bend down quickly to avoid something 2 to go or

push quickly underwater 3 to dodge or avoid doing something

duckling NOUN a young duck

duct NOUN a tube or channel through which liquid, gas, air, or cables can pass

ductile ADJECTIVE (of metal) able to be drawn out into fine strands

dud NOUN (*informal*) something useless or broken

due ADJECTIVE 1 expected or scheduled *due in ten minutes* 2 owing; needing to be paid 3 that ought to be given; rightful *due respect due to* as a result of

due ADVERB exactly *due east*

due NOUN 1 something you deserve or have a right to 2 a fee *harbour dues*

duel NOUN a fight between two people, especially with pistols or swords ► **duelling** NOUN, **duellist** NOUN

⚠ **USAGE**

Do not confuse this word with *dual*.

duet NOUN a piece of music for two players or singers

duffel coat NOUN a thick overcoat with a hood, fastened with toggles

THESAURUS

dubious ADJECTIVE • *I was dubious about the idea.* ► doubtful, hesitant, uncertain, unsure • *a dubious excuse* ► suspect, suspicious, untrustworthy, unreliable

due ADJECTIVE • *Your subscription is due.* ► owing, owed, payable, outstanding • *She drove with due

care.* ► proper, appropriate, necessary, suitable • *the respect due to an eminent statesman* ► deserved (by), merited (by), appropriate (for), suitable (for)
due to • *Death was due to a heart attack.* ► caused by, the result of • *The game was cancelled due to bad weather.* ► owing to, because of, on account of, as a result of

DICTIONARY

dugout NOUN **1** an underground shelter **2** a bench for coaches and substitutes beside a sports pitch **3** a canoe made by hollowing out a tree trunk

duke NOUN a member of the highest rank of nobility
▶ **dukedom** NOUN

dull ADJECTIVE **1** not bright or clear *dull weather* **2** stupid **3** uninteresting *a dull concert* **4** not sharp *a dull pain a dull thud*
▶ **dully** ADVERB

duly ADVERB **1** in the due or proper way **2** at the expected time

dumb ADJECTIVE **1** without the ability to speak **2** silent **3** (*informal*) stupid

dumbfounded ADJECTIVE too astonished to speak

dummy NOUN **dummies** **1** something made to look like a person or thing **2** an imitation teat given to a baby to suck

dump NOUN **1** a place where rubbish is left or stored **2** (*informal*) a dull or unattractive place **in the dumps** depressed or unhappy

dump VERB **1** to get rid of something unwanted **2** to put down carelessly

dumpling NOUN a piece of dough cooked in a stew

dumpy ADJECTIVE **dumpier**, **dumpiest** short and fat

dunce NOUN a person who is slow at learning

dune NOUN a mound of loose sand shaped by the wind

dung NOUN solid waste matter excreted by an animal

dungarees PLURAL NOUN trousers with a piece in front covering the chest and held up by straps

dungeon (dun-jon) NOUN an underground prison cell

dunk VERB to dip something into liquid

duo (dew-oh) NOUN **duos** a pair of people, especially musicians

dupe VERB to deceive

THESAURUS

dull ADJECTIVE • *dull colours* ▶ dark, drab, dreary, sombre • *a dull winter morning* ▶ gloomy, overcast, dark, dim, dismal • *dull reading* ▶ boring, tedious, uninteresting, unexciting, monotonous • *a dull pupil* ▶ stupid, slow, unintelligent, dim, slow-witted

dumb ADJECTIVE • *She kept dumb while the others argued.* ▶ silent, mute, speechless • *He's not as dumb as he makes out.* ▶ stupid, unintelligent, foolish

dummy NOUN • *The gun was a dummy.* ▶ imitation, fake, sham, toy, model • *a ventriloquist's dummy* ▶ doll, puppet, manikin, figure

dump NOUN • *We've a lot to take to the dump.* ▶ tip, rubbish heap, junk yard

dump VERB • *Old cars had been dumped.* ▶ discard, dispose of, get rid of, scrap, throw away • *She dumped her shopping on the floor.* ▶ drop, put down, throw down, deposit

DICTIONARY

duplicate NOUN an exact copy or imitation

duplicate VERB to make or be a duplicate ▶ **duplication** NOUN

durable ADJECTIVE strong and likely to last ▶ **durability** NOUN

duration NOUN the length of time something lasts

duress (dewr-ess) NOUN the use of force or threats to get your way

during PREPOSITION **1** through the course of *It rained during the night.* **2** at a point in the course of *They arrived during our meal.*

dusk NOUN twilight in the evening

dusky ADJECTIVE dark or shadowy

dust NOUN tiny particles of earth or other solid material

dust VERB **1** to wipe away dust **2** to sprinkle with dust or powder

dustbin NOUN a bin for household rubbish

duster NOUN a cloth for dusting things

dustman NOUN a person employed to take away household rubbish

dusty ADJECTIVE **dustier**, **dustiest** **1** covered with dust **2** like dust

dutiful ADJECTIVE doing your duty; obedient ▶ **dutifully** ADVERB

duty NOUN **1** what you ought to do or must do **2** a task that must be done **3** a tax charged on some goods **on** or **off duty** actually doing (or not doing) your regular work

duvet (doo-vay) NOUN a thick quilt used on a bed instead of blankets

DVD ABBREVIATION digital video (or versatile) disc, a disc used for storing audio or video information, especially films

dwarf NOUN **dwarfs** or **dwarves** a very small person or thing

dwarf VERB to make something seem small by contrast

dwell VERB **dwelt** to live in a place **dwell on** to think or talk about constantly ▶ **dweller** NOUN

dwelling NOUN a building for living in

dwindle VERB to get smaller gradually

dye NOUN a substance used to colour fabrics etc.

dye VERB **dyeing** to colour something with dye

THESAURUS

dust NOUN • *covered in dust* ▶ dirt, grime, filth

dusty ADJECTIVE • *The tables were dusty.* ▶ dirty, filthy, grubby • *a light dusty substance* ▶ powdery, chalky

duty NOUN • *a strong sense of duty* ▶ responsibility, loyalty, obligation • *one of his duties*

▶ job, role, task, assignment • *the duty on tobacco* ▶ tax, levy, charge

dwindle VERB • *The population dwindled.* ▶ decrease, decline, diminish, shrink

dye NOUN • *a yellow dye* ▶ colouring, pigment, stain, tint

a
b
c
d
e
f
g
h
i
j
k
l
m
n
o
p
q
r
s
t
u
v
w
x
y
z

dyke NOUN **1** a long wall or embankment holding back water **2** a ditch for draining water from land

dynamic ADJECTIVE **1** energetic or forceful **2** (of a force) producing motion ▶ **dynamically** ADVERB

dynamics NOUN **1** the study of force and motion **2** (*Music*) different levels of loudness and softness

dynamite NOUN a powerful explosive

dynamo NOUN **dynamos** a machine that generates electricity

dynasty NOUN **dynasties** a line of rulers or leaders from the same family ▶ **dynastic** ADJECTIVE

dysentery (dis-en-tree) NOUN a disease causing fever and diarrhoea

dyslexia NOUN special difficulty in being able to read and spell ▶ **dyslexic** ADJECTIVE

Ee

each ADJECTIVE, PRONOUN every; every one *each child each of you*

eager ADJECTIVE strongly wanting to do something ▶ **eagerly** ADVERB, **eagerness** NOUN

eagle NOUN a large bird of prey with keen sight

ear¹ NOUN **1** the organ of the body used for hearing **2** hearing ability *a good ear*

ear² NOUN the spike of seeds at the top of a stalk of corn

eardrum NOUN a membrane in the ear that vibrates when sounds reach it

earl NOUN a member of the British nobility below a marquess ▶ **earldom** NOUN

early ADJECTIVE, ADVERB **earlier**, **earliest 1** before the usual or expected time **2** near the beginning *early in the book*

earn VERB **1** to receive money for doing work **2** to deserve

earnest ADJECTIVE showing serious feelings or intentions ▶ **earnestly** ADVERB

earnings PLURAL NOUN money paid for work

earphones PLURAL NOUN a listening device that fits over the ears

earring NOUN a piece of jewellery worn on the ear

earshot NOUN the distance within which a sound can be heard

earth NOUN **1** the planet that we live on **2** the ground; soil **3** the hole where a fox or badger lives **4** connection to the ground to complete an electrical circuit

earth VERB to connect an electrical circuit to the ground

earthenware NOUN pottery made of coarse baked clay

earthly ADJECTIVE concerned with life on earth rather than with life after death

earthquake NOUN a violent movement of part of the earth's surface

earthworm NOUN a worm that lives in the soil

THESAURUS

eager ADJECTIVE • *eager faces* ▶ keen, enthusiastic • *eager to see us* ▶ keen, anxious, determined • *eager for more adventure* ▶ longing, yearning, intent (on)

early ADJECTIVE • *early symptoms of the disease* ▶ first, initial, preliminary • *early civilizations* ▶ ancient, primitive, prehistoric

earn VERB • *to earn a salary* ▶ receive, be paid, make • *to earn*

gratitude ▶ deserve, merit, warrant, be worthy of

earnest ADJECTIVE • *an earnest attempt to help* ▶ committed, determined • *an earnest person* ▶ serious, thoughtful, solemn

earth NOUN • *life on earth* ▶ this world, the planet, the globe • *the soft earth* ▶ soil, loam, clay, ground

earthy ADJECTIVE **earthier, earthiest 1** like earth or soil **2** coarse and vulgar

earwig NOUN a crawling insect with pincers at the end of its body

> **WORD HISTORY**
> called this because it was once thought to crawl into people's ears

ease NOUN freedom from trouble or effort or pain

ease VERB **1** to make less painful or less tight or troublesome **2** to move gently into position **3** to become less severe *The pain has eased.*

easel NOUN a stand for supporting a blackboard or painting

easily ADVERB **1** without difficulty; with ease **2** by far *easily the best* **3** very likely *They could easily be wrong.*

east NOUN **1** the direction where the sun rises **2** the eastern part of a country, city, etc.

east ADJECTIVE, ADVERB towards or in the east; coming from the east

Easter NOUN the Sunday (in March or April) when Christians commemorate the resurrection of Christ

easterly ADJECTIVE **1** coming from the east **2** facing the east

eastern ADJECTIVE of or in the east

eastward ADJECTIVE, ADVERB towards the east ► **eastwards** ADVERB

easy ADJECTIVE **easier, easiest** able to be done or used or understood without trouble **take it easy** to relax

eat VERB **ate, eaten 1** to chew and swallow as food **2** to have a meal **3** to use up or destroy gradually

eaves PLURAL NOUN the overhanging edges of a roof

eavesdrop VERB **eavesdropping, eavesdropped** to listen secretly to a private

THESAURUS

ease NOUN • *the ease with which he completed the task* ► skill, dexterity, facility, naturalness • *a life of ease* ► comfort, luxury, wealth, relaxation, leisure

ease VERB • *to ease the pain* ► relieve, alleviate, lessen • *to ease the tension* ► reduce, relax, decrease • *eased the stopper out of the bottle* ► guide, slide, slip, edge

easily ADVERB • *easily the brightest student* ► by far, without doubt, undoubtedly, definitely, undeniably • *managed the work*

easily ► comfortably, effortlessly, with ease, with no difficulty

easy ADJECTIVE • *an easy task* ► simple, straightforward, undemanding, effortless • *easy instructions* ► simple, straightforward, clear, uncomplicated, user-friendly • *an easy life* ► comfortable, carefree, untroubled, leisurely, relaxed

eat VERB • *to eat a biscuit* ► consume, devour, to nibble, to chew, to munch, to crunch, swallow, guzzle, bolt, wolf down

conversation ▶ **eavesdropper**
NOUN

ebb NOUN **1** the movement of the
tide when it is going out **2** a low
point *Our courage was at a low
ebb.*

ebb VERB **1** to flow away from the
land **2** to weaken or become less

ebony NOUN a hard black wood

eccentric (ik-sen-trik) ADJECTIVE
behaving strangely
▶ **eccentrically** ADVERB,
eccentricity NOUN

echo NOUN echoes a sound that is
heard again as it is reflected off a
surface

echo VERB **echoes, echoing,
echoed 1** to make an echo **2** to
repeat a sound or saying

éclair (ay-klair) NOUN a finger-
shaped cake of pastry with a
creamy filling

eclipse NOUN the blocking of the
sun's or moon's light when the
moon or the earth is in the way

eclipse VERB **1** to block the light
and cause an eclipse **2** to be much
better or more important than

ecology (ee-kol-o-jee) NOUN the
study of living things in relation to

their environment ▶ **ecological**
ADJECTIVE, **ecologist** NOUN

economic (ee-kon-om-ik) ADJECTIVE
1 to do with economy or
economics **2** profitable

economical ADJECTIVE careful
with resources ▶ **economically**
ADVERB

economics NOUN the study of
how money is earned and used
▶ **economist** NOUN

economize VERB to be
economical; to use or spend less

⚠ **SPELLING**

This word can also be spelled
economise.

economy NOUN **economies 1** the
management of a country's or
household's income and spending
2 the careful use of resources **3** a
saving

ecosystem NOUN all the plants
and animals in a particular area
considered in terms of their
relationship with their
environment

ecstasy NOUN **1** a feeling of great
delight **2** an illegal drug that
causes hallucinations ▶ **ecstatic**
(ik-stat-ik) ADJECTIVE

• *Where shall we eat tonight?*
▶ have a meal, have dinner, dine

eccentric ADJECTIVE • *eccentric
behaviour* ▶ unconventional,
odd, strange, weird, bizarre

echo VERB • *The sound echoed
across the hall.* ▶ reverberate,
resound, ring, resonate

economical ADJECTIVE • *Travelling
by train is more economical.*
▶ inexpensive, cost-effective,
reasonable • *economical with their
money* ▶ thrifty, careful, prudent,
sensible

economize VERB • *to economize
by growing your own vegetables*
▶ save money, cut costs, spend
less

eczema (eks-im-a) NOUN a skin disease causing rough itching patches

eddy NOUN **eddies** a swirling patch of water or air or smoke etc.

eddy VERB **eddies, eddied** to swirl

edge NOUN **1** the part along the side or end of something **2** the sharp part of a knife or other cutting instrument **3** special interest or excitement

edge VERB **1** to be the edge or border of **2** to put a border on **3** to move gradually *He edged away.*

edgeways ADVERB with the edge forwards or outwards

edgy ADJECTIVE **edgier, edgiest** tense and irritable ► **edginess** NOUN

edible ADJECTIVE suitable for eating; not poisonous

edict NOUN an official command

edit VERB **1** to be the editor of a newspaper or other publication **2** to make written material ready for publishing **3** to choose and put the parts of a film or tape recording etc. into order

edition NOUN **1** the form in which something is published **2** all the copies of a book

editor NOUN a person who edits something

editorial ADJECTIVE to do with editing or editors

editorial NOUN a newspaper article giving the editor's opinions

educate VERB to provide with education ► **educated** ADJECTIVE

education NOUN the training of people's minds and abilities to acquire knowledge and develop skills ► **educational** ADJECTIVE

eel NOUN a long snake-like fish

eerie ADJECTIVE **eerier, eeriest** strange in a frightening or mysterious way ► **eerily** ADVERB

efface VERB to wipe or rub out ► **effacement** NOUN

effect NOUN **1** a change or result **2** an impression that is produced by something *a cheerful effect*

effect VERB to make something happen *to effect changes*

⚠ USAGE

Do not confuse this word with *affect*.

edge NOUN • *the edge of the lake* ► border, bank, fringe, verge, perimeter

edge VERB • *She edged closer to the table.* ► creep, inch, sidle

educated ADJECTIVE • *an educated person* ► learned, knowledgeable, cultured, well-read, informed

education NOUN • *a first-class education* ► schooling, training,

teaching, instruction, tuition, coaching, curriculum

eerie ADJECTIVE • *an eerie silence* ► weird, strange, uncanny, sinister, spooky

effect NOUN • *The effect of the changes was to confuse everyone.* ► result, consequence, upshot, outcome, conclusion • *to have a profound effect* ► impact, impression

DICTIONARY

effective ADJECTIVE **1** producing the effect that is wanted **2** impressive and striking

effeminate ADJECTIVE (of a man) having feminine qualities
► **effeminacy** NOUN

effervesce (ef-er-vess) VERB to give off bubbles of gas
► **effervescence** NOUN, **effervescent** ADJECTIVE

efficient ADJECTIVE doing work well; effective ► **efficiency** NOUN, **efficiently** ADVERB

effigy NOUN **effigies** a model or sculptured figure

effort NOUN **1** the use of energy; the energy used **2** something difficult or tiring **3** an attempt *a good effort*

effusive ADJECTIVE making a great show of affection or enthusiasm
► **effusively** ADVERB

e.g. ABBREVIATION for example

egg[1] NOUN **1** a round object containing an embryo, produced by a bird, fish, reptile, or insect **2** a hen's or duck's egg used as food **3** an ovum

egg[2] VERB to urge or encourage

eggplant NOUN (American) an aubergine

ego (eeg-oh) NOUN a person's self or self-respect

egotist (eg-oh-tist) NOUN a conceited person who is always talking about himself or herself
► **egotism** NOUN, **egotistic** ADJECTIVE

Eid (eed) NOUN a Muslim festival marking the end of Ramadan

eiderdown NOUN a quilt stuffed with feathers or other soft material

eight NOUN, ADJECTIVE the number 8
► **eighth** ADJECTIVE, NOUN

eighteen NOUN, ADJECTIVE the number 18 ► **eighteenth** ADJECTIVE, NOUN

eighty NOUN, ADJECTIVE **eighties** the number 80 ► **eightieth** ADJECTIVE, NOUN

either ADJECTIVE, PRONOUN **1** one or the other of two *Either team can win. either of them* **2** both of two *on either side of the road*

either ADVERB also; similarly *If you won't go, I won't either.*

either CONJUNCTION (used with **or**) the first of two possibilities *He is either ill or drunk. Either come in or go away.*

THESAURUS

effective ADJECTIVE • *no effective alternative* ► good, useful, successful, worthwhile • *an effective opposition* ► able, capable, competent • *effective arguments* ► convincing, persuasive

efficient ADJECTIVE • *efficient housekeeping* ► well-organized,

methodical, systematic • *an efficient assistant* ► capable, competent, able, well-organized

effort NOUN • *to make an effort* ► attempt, try, endeavour • *It took considerable effort.* ► energy, exertion, trouble • *a team effort* ► achievement, accomplishment, feat, success

ejaculate VERB **1** (of a man) to produce semen from the penis **2** (formal) to suddenly say something ▶ **ejaculation** NOUN

eject VERB **1** to send out forcefully **2** to force someone to leave ▶ **ejection** NOUN

eke (eek) VERB **eke out** to make something last by using small amounts

elaborate (il-ab-er-at) ADJECTIVE having many parts or details; complicated ▶ **elaborately** ADVERB

elaborate (il-ab-er-ayt) VERB to explain or work out in detail ▶ **elaboration** NOUN

elapse VERB (of time) to pass

elastic NOUN cord or material woven with strands of rubber so that it can stretch

elastic ADJECTIVE able to be stretched and return to its original length

elated ADJECTIVE feeling very pleased ▶ **elation** NOUN

elbow NOUN the joint in the middle of the arm

elbow VERB to push with the elbow

elder¹ ADJECTIVE older *my elder brother*

elder NOUN **1** an older person **2** an official in certain Churches

elder² NOUN a tree with white flowers and black berries

elderberry NOUN **elderberries** a berry from an elder tree

elderly ADJECTIVE rather old

eldest ADJECTIVE oldest

elect VERB **1** to choose by voting **2** to choose to do something

elect ADJECTIVE chosen by a vote but not yet in office *the president elect*

election NOUN the process of electing people, especially Members of Parliament

electorate NOUN all the people who can vote

electric ADJECTIVE **1** to do with or worked by electricity **2** causing sudden excitement *an electric effect* ▶ **electrical** ADJECTIVE

electrician NOUN a person skilled in working with electrical equipment

electricity NOUN a form of energy carried by certain particles of matter (electrons and protons), used for lighting, heating, and power

electrify VERB **electrifies**, **electrified 1** to give an electric

THESAURUS

elaborate ADJECTIVE • *elaborate schemes to raise money* ▶ complicated, intricate, detailed, involved • *elaborate wood carvings* ▶ ornate, decorative, intricate, fancy

elderly ADJECTIVE • *elderly people* ▶ aged, ageing, old

elect VERB • *to elect a leader* ▶ choose, select, vote for, pick, appoint

election NOUN • *the election of a president* ▶ selection, choosing • *next year's election* ▶ poll, vote, ballot

a
b
c
d
e
f
g
h
i
j
k
l
m
n
o
p
q
r
s
t
u
v
w
x
y
z

charge to **2** to supply with electric power **3** to thrill with excitement ▶ **electrification** NOUN

electrocute VERB to kill by electricity ▶ **electrocution** NOUN

electrode NOUN a solid conductor through which electricity enters or leaves a vacuum tube

electromagnet NOUN a magnet worked by electricity
▶ **electromagnetic** ADJECTIVE

electron NOUN a particle of matter with a negative electric charge

electronic ADJECTIVE produced or worked by a flow of electrons
▶ **electronically** ADVERB

electronics NOUN the use or study of electronic devices

elegant ADJECTIVE graceful and dignified ▶ **elegance** NOUN

elegy NOUN **elegies** a sorrowful or serious poem

element NOUN **1** (Science) a substance that cannot be split up into simpler substances, composed of atoms that have the same number of protons **2** each of the parts that make up a thing **3** a basic or elementary principle *the*

elements of algebra **4** a wire or coil that gives out heat in an electric fire or cooker **the elements** weather conditions, such as rain, wind, and cold

elementary ADJECTIVE dealing with the simplest stages of something; easy

elephant NOUN a large animal with a trunk, large ears, and tusks

elevate VERB to lift or raise to a higher position ▶ **elevation** NOUN

elevator NOUN (*American*) a lift in a building

eleven ADJECTIVE, NOUN the number 11 ▶ **eleventh** ADJECTIVE, NOUN

elf NOUN (in fairy tales) a small being with magic powers

eligible ADJECTIVE qualified or suitable for something
▶ **eligibility** NOUN

eliminate VERB to get rid of
▶ **elimination** NOUN

élite (ay-leet) NOUN a group of people with privileges which are not given to others

elk NOUN a large kind of deer

ellipse NOUN an oval shape

THESAURUS

elegant ADJECTIVE • *an elegant building* ▶ attractive, stylish, graceful, tasteful • *a tall elegant woman* ▶ beautiful, graceful, fashionable, chic

element NOUN • *only one element of the situation* ▶ component, factor, part, aspect • *an element of truth* ▶ amount, trace, hint, touch

elementary ADJECTIVE • *an elementary course* ▶ basic, rudimentary, fundamental, introductory • *The answer to the question is elementary.* ▶ simple, easy, straightforward, uncomplicated

eligible ADJECTIVE **be eligible for**
• *You are eligible for a grant.* ▶ be entitled to, qualify for, be allowed

elm NOUN a tall tree with rough leaves

elocution NOUN the art of speaking clearly and correctly

elongated ADJECTIVE made longer; lengthened ► **elongation** NOUN

elope VERB to run away secretly to get married ► **elopement** NOUN

eloquent ADJECTIVE speaking fluently and expressing ideas vividly ► **eloquence** NOUN

else ADVERB 1 besides; other *Someone else did it.* 2 otherwise; if not *Run or else you'll be late.*

elsewhere ADVERB somewhere else

elude VERB 1 to avoid being caught by 2 to be too difficult to remember or understand *The name eludes me.* ► **elusive** ADJECTIVE

email NOUN 1 a system of sending messages and data from one computer to another by means of a network 2 a message sent in this way

email VERB to send by email

emancipation NOUN the process of setting people free from slavery or other restraints

embalm VERB to preserve a dead body from decay by using spices or chemicals

embankment NOUN a bank of earth or stone holding back water or supporting a road or railway

embargo NOUN **embargoes** an official ban on trade with a country

embark VERB to put or go on board a ship or aircraft **embark on** to begin something new or challenging ► **embarkation** NOUN

embarrass VERB to make someone feel awkward or ashamed ► **embarrassment** NOUN

embassy NOUN **embassies** the office and staff of an ambassador in a foreign country

embed VERB **embedding, embedded** to fix firmly in something solid

embellish VERB to decorate or add details to ► **embellishment** NOUN

embers PLURAL NOUN small pieces of glowing coal or wood in a dying fire

embezzle VERB to take dishonestly money that was left in your care ► **embezzlement** NOUN

emblem NOUN a symbol that represents something *an emblem of friendship*

embody VERB **embodies, embodied** 1 to include or contain 2 to express in a visible form

---

THESAURUS

eloquent ADJECTIVE • *an eloquent speech* ► expressive, articulate, moving, stirring, powerful

embarrassed ADJECTIVE • *was feeling embarrassed*

► uncomfortable, awkward, ashamed, shy, self-conscious

embarrassing ADJECTIVE
• *an embarrassing mistake*
► awkward, humiliating, mortifying

DICTIONARY

art that embodies a view of life
► **embodiment** NOUN

embossed ADJECTIVE decorated with a raised design

embrace VERB **1** to hold closely in your arms **2** to include **3** to accept or adopt a cause or belief

embrace NOUN a hug

embroider VERB **1** to decorate cloth with needlework **2** to add details to a story to make it more interesting ► **embroidery** NOUN

embryo (em-bree-oh) NOUN **embryos** a baby or young animal in its earliest stages

emend VERB to remove errors from a piece of writing

emerald NOUN a bright-green precious stone

emerge VERB **1** to come out or appear **2** to become known
► **emergence** NOUN

emergency NOUN **emergencies** a sudden serious event that needs immediate action

emigrant NOUN a person who goes to live in another country

emigrate VERB to leave your own country to live in another
► **emigration** NOUN

eminent ADJECTIVE famous and respected ► **eminently** ADVERB

emission NOUN fumes or radiation

emit VERB **emitting**, **emitted** to send out light, heat, fumes, etc.

emotion NOUN a strong feeling in the mind, such as love, anger, or hate

emotional ADJECTIVE having or causing strong feelings

emotive ADJECTIVE likely to cause strong feelings

empathize VERB to share the feelings of another person

> ⚠ **SPELLING**
>
> This word can also be spelled *empathise*.

empathy NOUN the ability to understand and share in someone else's feelings

emperor NOUN a man who rules an empire

emphasis NOUN **emphases** **1** special importance given to

THESAURUS

embrace VERB • *The old man embraced his son.* ► hug, clasp, hold, cuddle • *to embrace a new idea* ► accept, welcome, take on

emerge VERB • *A cyclist emerged from the entrance.* ► come out, appear, come into view • *Another version of the story later emerged.* ► become known, become evident, be revealed, come to light

eminent ADJECTIVE • *an eminent scientist* ► distinguished, famous, prominent, well known, renowned

emit VERB • *Vehicle exhausts emit hydrocarbons.* ► discharge, release, give off

emotional ADJECTIVE • *an emotional tribute* ► moving, touching, poignant • *an emotional person* ► passionate, demonstrative, sensitive

something **2** stress put on a word or part of a word

emphasize VERB to put emphasis on

⚠ **SPELLING**

This word can also be spelled *emphasise*.

emphatic ADJECTIVE using emphasis; spoken strongly ► **emphatically** ADVERB

empire NOUN **1** a group of countries ruled by one country **2** a large business organization controlled by one person or group

employ VERB **1** to pay a person to do work **2** to make use of *to employ modern methods*

employee NOUN a person who works for a person or organization

employer NOUN a person or organization that employs people

employment NOUN paid work

empower VERB to give someone the power to do something

empress NOUN **1** a woman who rules an empire **2** the wife of an emperor

empty ADJECTIVE **emptier, emptiest 1** containing nothing or nobody **2** not likely to have any effect *empty promises* ► **emptiness** NOUN

empty VERB **empties, emptied** to make or become empty

emu NOUN **emus** a large Australian bird like an ostrich

emulate VERB to try to do as well as someone ► **emulation** NOUN

emulsion NOUN **1** a creamy or slightly oily liquid **2** a kind of water-based paint

enable VERB to give the means or ability to do something

enact VERB **1** to make a law **2** to perform ► **enactment** NOUN

enamel NOUN **1** a shiny substance for coating metal **2** paint that dries hard and shiny **3** the hard shiny surface of teeth

THESAURUS

emphasize VERB • *emphasized the need to stay calm* ► stress, underline, focus on, highlight, draw attention to

emphatic ADJECTIVE • *an emphatic refusal* ► firm, forceful, vehement, definite

employ VERB • *to employ over a hundred people* ► pay, hire, take on, engage

employment NOUN
• *employment as a shop assistant* ► work, a job, a post, a position, a livelihood

empty ADJECTIVE • *an empty house* ► vacant, unoccupied,

uninhabited, abandoned, deserted • *His life felt empty.* ► aimless, futile, worthless, hollow • *empty threats* ► vain, idle, meaningless

empty VERB • *to empty the washing machine* ► unload, unpack, remove • *to empty a glass* ► drain

enable VERB • *a law to enable individuals to own shares* ► allow, permit, authorize • *The free time will enable him to take up a hobby.* ► allow, permit, let, help, make it possible for

a
b
c
d
e
f
g
h
i
j
k
l
m
n
o
p
q
r
s
t
u
v
w
x
y
z

enamel VERB **enamelling, enamelled** to coat or decorate with enamel

enamoured ADJECTIVE fond of

encapsulate VERB to express an idea clearly and concisely

enchant VERB **1** to put under a magic spell **2** to fill with delight and wonder

encircle VERB to surround

enclave NOUN a country's territory lying entirely within another country

enclose VERB **1** to put a wall or fence round **2** to include in a letter or package

enclosure NOUN **1** the act of enclosing **2** an enclosed area **3** something included with a letter or parcel

encompass VERB **1** to surround **2** to contain or include

encore (on-kor) NOUN an extra item performed at a concert after applause for the main items

encounter VERB **1** to meet unexpectedly **2** to experience *We encountered some difficulties.*

encounter NOUN **1** an unexpected meeting **2** a battle

encourage VERB **1** to give confidence or hope to **2** to try to persuade **3** to help something happen or develop *to encourage healthy eating*
  ▸ **encouragement** NOUN

encroach VERB **1** to intrude on someone's rights **2** to go further than the proper limits
  ▸ **encroachment** NOUN

encrypt VERB to put information into a special code for security
  ▸ **encryption** NOUN

encumber VERB to be a burden to
  ▸ **encumbrance** NOUN

encyclopedia NOUN a book or set of books containing information on many subjects

encyclopedic ADJECTIVE giving information about many different things

end NOUN **1** the last part of something **2** each half of a sports pitch **3** destruction or death **4** a purpose *for your own ends*

THESAURUS

enclose VERB • *A fence enclosed the garden.* ▸ surround, circle, border, contain • *Enclose payment with your order.* ▸ include, insert

encourage VERB • *to encourage the players* ▸ cheer, inspire, reassure, hearten, spur on • *keen to encourage small businesses* ▸ support, promote, help • *Clever marketing encourages sales.*
  ▸ increase, boost, help, promote

• *Her mother encouraged her to take up medicine.* ▸ persuade, urge

encouragement NOUN • *a little encouragement* ▸ support, reassurance, inspiration, cheering up

end NOUN • *at the end of the garden* ▸ edge, boundary, limit, extremity • *the end of the story* ▸ conclusion, ending, climax • *a*

DICTIONARY

end VERB to bring or come to an end

endanger VERB to cause danger to

endear VERB to make someone fond of you ► **endearing** ADJECTIVE

endearment NOUN a word or phrase expressing love or affection

endeavour (en-dev-er) VERB to try hard

endeavour NOUN a strong attempt

endemic (en-dem-ik) ADJECTIVE (of a disease) often found in a certain area or group of people

ending NOUN the last part

endless ADJECTIVE never stopping ► **endlessly** ADVERB

endorse VERB 1 to confirm or give your approval to something 2 to sign your name on the back of a document ► **endorsement** NOUN

endow VERB 1 to provide a source of income to establish something *to endow a scholarship* 2 to provide with an ability or quality *They were endowed with great talent.* ► **endowment** NOUN

endurance NOUN the ability to put up with difficulty or pain for a long period

endure 1 to suffer or put up with difficulty or pain 2 to continue to exist ► **endurable** ADJECTIVE

enemy NOUN **enemies** 1 someone who opposes or seeks to harm another 2 a nation or army at war with another

energetic ADJECTIVE full of energy ► **energetically** ADVERB

energy NOUN **energies** 1 strength to do things; liveliness 2 (*Science*) the ability of matter or radiation to do work 3 power obtained from fuel and other resources

THESAURUS

means to achieve an end ► aim, goal, purpose, objective

end VERB • *The programme ends at midnight.* ► finish, conclude, come to an end, close • *to end a relationship* ► break off, stop, halt, discontinue • *plans to end the scheme* ► abolish, terminate, finish, put an end to

ending NOUN • *a story with an exciting ending* ► end, conclusion, finish, close, climax

endurance NOUN • *a test of endurance* ► stamina, strength,

staying power, determination, perseverance

endure VERB • *pain greater than anyone can endure* ► tolerate, bear, withstand, suffer • *love that will endure* ► last, survive, persist, prevail

energetic ADJECTIVE • *an energetic person* ► active, lively, dynamic, enthusiastic, tireless • *energetic exercises* ► strenuous, vigorous, rigorous, arduous

energy NOUN • *full of energy* ► vitality, vigour, strength, drive, zeal, exuberance • *new sources of energy* ► power, fuel

a
b
c
d
e
f
g
h
i
j
k
l
m
n
o
p
q
r
s
t
u
v
w
x
y
z

a
b
c
d
e
f
g
h
i
j
k
l
m
n
o
p
q
r
s
t
u
v
w
x
y
z

enfold VERB to surround or be wrapped round something

enforce VERB to make people obey a law or rule ▶ **enforcement** NOUN

engage VERB 1 to arrange to employ or use 2 to occupy the attention of *to engage someone in conversation* 3 to begin a battle with

engaged ADJECTIVE 1 having promised to marry somebody 2 in use; occupied

engagement NOUN 1 a promise to marry 2 an arrangement to meet 3 a battle

engaging ADJECTIVE attractive or charming

engine NOUN 1 a machine that provides power 2 a vehicle that pulls a railway train

engineer NOUN an expert in engineering

engineer VERB 1 to plan and build machines and large structures 2 to cause to happen by clever planning

engineering NOUN the design and building of machines and

large structures such as roads and bridges

engrave VERB to carve something on a surface

engross VERB to occupy the whole attention of

engulf VERB to flow over and cover completely

enhance VERB to make a thing more attractive or increase its value ▶ **enhancement** NOUN

enigma NOUN something difficult to understand; a mystery

enigmatic (en-ig-mat-ik) ADJECTIVE mysterious and puzzling ▶ **enigmatically** ADVERB

enjoy VERB to get pleasure from something ▶ **enjoyment** NOUN

enjoyable ADJECTIVE pleasant and satisfying

enlarge VERB to make bigger ▶ **enlargement** NOUN

enlighten VERB to give more knowledge or information to ▶ **enlightenment** NOUN

enlist VERB 1 to join the armed forces 2 to obtain the support or help of

enliven VERB to make more lively

engage VERB • *to engage a nanny* ▶ hire, employ, recruit, take on, appoint • *to engage the enemy* ▶ fight, do battle with, clash with

engrossed ADJECTIVE • *engrossed in a book* ▶ absorbed, immersed, preoccupied (by), gripped (by)

enjoy VERB • *to enjoy a holiday* ▶ like, love, take pleasure from or in, appreciate, delight in, relish

• *to enjoy privileges* ▶ have, benefit from, experience **enjoy yourself** ▶ have fun, have a good time

enjoyable ADJECTIVE • *an enjoyable occasion* ▶ pleasant, agreeable, delightful, satisfying, rewarding, entertaining, amusing

enlarge VERB • *to enlarge a photograph* ▶ increase, expand

enmity NOUN a state of being an enemy; hostility

enormity NOUN 1 great wickedness *the enormity of the crime* 2 great size; hugeness *the enormity of the task*

> ⚠ **USAGE**
> Many people regard the use of sense 2 as incorrect, and it is usually better to use *magnitude* instead.

enormous ADJECTIVE very large; huge ▶ **enormously** ADVERB

enough ADJECTIVE, NOUN, ADVERB as much or as many as necessary *enough food* *I have had enough. Are you warm enough?*

enquire VERB 1 to ask for information *He enquired if I was well.* 2 to investigate carefully

> ⚠ **USAGE**
> See the note at **inquire**.

enquiry NOUN 1 a question 2 an investigation

enrage VERB to make very angry

enrich VERB make richer or more satisfying ▶ **enrichment** NOUN

enrol VERB enrolling, enrolled 1 to become a member of a society 2 to make someone a member ▶ **enrolment** NOUN

ensemble (on-sombl) NOUN 1 a group of things that go together 2 a group of musicians 3 a matching set of clothes

ensign NOUN a military or naval flag

enslave VERB to make a slave of ▶ **enslavement** NOUN

ensue VERB to happen afterwards or as a result

ensure VERB to make certain of *The right diet can ensure good health.*

> ⚠ **USAGE**
> Do not confuse this word with *insure*.

entail VERB to involve as a result *This plan entails danger.*

entangle VERB 1 to tangle 2 to make complicated ▶ **entanglement** NOUN

enter VERB 1 to come in or go in 2 to put into a list or book 3 to key into a computer 4 to register as a competitor

enterprise NOUN 1 the ability to act independently and set up new projects 2 business activity *private enterprise*

enterprising ADJECTIVE willing to try new or adventurous projects

enormous ADJECTIVE • *an enormous insect* ▶ huge, gigantic, immense, massive, colossal

ensure VERB • *to ensure a good night's sleep* ▶ guarantee, make sure, secure, confirm

enter VERB • *to enter a building* ▶ go in or into, come in or into,

gain access to, set foot in • *A bullet entered his chest.* ▶ penetrate, pierce, puncture • *The Americans entered the war.* ▶ join, take part in, participate in • *to enter a competition* ▶ go in for, take part in • *to enter your details* ▶ record, register, note, write down

a
b
c
d
e
f
g
h
i
j
k
l
m
n
o
p
q
r
s
t
u
v
w
x
y
z

a
b
c
d
e
f
g
h
i
j
k
l
m
n
o
p
q
r
s
t
u
v
w
x
y
z

DICTIONARY

entertain VERB **1** to amuse **2** to have as guests **3** to consider ► **entertainer** NOUN

entertainment NOUN something performed before an audience

enthral VERB **enthralling, enthralled** to give great pleasure or interest to

enthusiasm NOUN a strong liking, interest, or excitement ► **enthusiast** NOUN

enthusiastic ADJECTIVE full of enthusiasm ► **enthusiastically** ADVERB

entice VERB to attract or persuade by offering something pleasant ► **enticement** NOUN

entire ADJECTIVE whole or complete ► **entirely** ADVERB

entirety (int-I-rit-ee) NOUN the whole of something

entitle VERB to give the right to have or do something ► **entitlement** NOUN

entitled ADJECTIVE having as a title

entity NOUN **entities** something that exists separately from other things

entrails PLURAL NOUN the intestines

entrance[1] (en-trans) NOUN **1** the way into a place **2** the act of entering

entrance[2] (in-trahns) VERB to fill with intense delight

entrant NOUN someone who enters for an examination or competition

entreat VERB to ask earnestly

entreaty NOUN **entreaties** an earnest request

entrenched ADJECTIVE (of an idea) firmly established

entrust VERB to place in someone's care

entry NOUN **entries 1** an entrance **2** an item entered in a list, diary, or reference book **3** something entered in a competition

THESAURUS

entertain VERB • *stories to entertain the children* ► amuse, divert, delight, cheer up, make laugh • *to entertain friends* ► receive, play host to, welcome

enthusiasm NOUN • *acted with enthusiasm* ► eagerness, excitement, energy, keenness, zeal • *the latest enthusiasm* ► interest, passion, craze

enthusiastic ADJECTIVE • *enthusiastic supporters* ► eager, keen, passionate, ardent, fervent

entrance NOUN • *the entrance to the building* ► entry, way in,

door, gate • *the entrance of the guests* ► entry, appearance, arrival, approach • *People were refused entrance.* ► admission, admittance, entry, access

entry NOUN • *the entry to the grounds* ► entrance, way in, door, gate • *They were allowed entry.* ► admission, admittance, entrance, access • *the entry in the diary* ► record, note • *an entry in a competition* ► candidate, competitor, contender, contestant, participant, player

envelop (en-vel-op) *VERB* to cover or wrap round completely

envelope (en-ve-lohp) *NOUN* a wrapper or covering, especially for a letter

enviable *ADJECTIVE* likely to be envied

envious *ADJECTIVE* feeling envy

environment *NOUN*
1 surroundings, especially as they affect people's lives 2 the natural world of the land, sea, and air
▶ **environmental** *ADJECTIVE*

environmentalist *NOUN* a person who wishes to protect or improve the environment

envisage *VERB* 1 to picture in the mind 2 to imagine as being possible

envoy *NOUN* an official representative sent by one government to another

envy *NOUN* **envies** 1 a feeling of discontent when someone else is more fortunate than you 2 something that causes this feeling

envy *VERB* **envies, envied** to feel envy towards

enzyme *NOUN* a kind of substance that assists chemical processes

ephemeral *ADJECTIVE* lasting only a short time

epic *NOUN* 1 a long poem or story about heroic deeds 2 a spectacular film

epicentre *NOUN* the point where an earthquake reaches the earth's surface

epidemic *NOUN* an outbreak of a disease among the people of an area

epigram *NOUN* a short witty saying

epilepsy *NOUN* a disease of the nervous system, causing convulsions ▶ **epileptic** *ADJECTIVE* & *NOUN*

epilogue *NOUN* a short section at the end of a book or play

episode *NOUN* 1 one event in a series of happenings 2 one programme in a radio or television serial

epistle *NOUN* a letter, especially one in the New Testament of the Bible

epitaph *NOUN* words written on a gravestone or describing a person who has died

THESAURUS

envious *ADJECTIVE* • *envious of their success* ▶ jealous, resentful, grudging

environment *NOUN* • *a natural environment* ▶ habitat, location, setting, surroundings, conditions **the environment** • *threatening the environment* ▶ the natural world, the earth, the planet

envy *NOUN* • *envy at her good luck* ▶ jealousy, bitterness, resentment

envy *VERB* • *He envied her success.* ▶ be jealous of, be envious of, resent, begrudge

episode *NOUN* • *a happy episode* ▶ incident, event, occurrence
• *the final episode of the series* ▶ instalment, part, section, programme

epithet NOUN an adjective or special name

epitome (ip-it-um-ee) NOUN a perfect example of something *the epitome of kindness*

epoch NOUN a long period of time

equal ADJECTIVE **1** the same in amount, size, or value **2** having the necessary strength or ability *equal to the task* ▸ **equally** ADVERB

equal NOUN a person or thing that is equal to another

equal VERB **equalling, equalled 1** to be the same in amount, size, or value **2** to match or be as good as

equality NOUN the state of being equal

equalize VERB to make equal

⚠ SPELLING

This word can also be spelled *equalise*.

equate VERB to regard as equal or equivalent

equation NOUN (Maths) a statement that two things are equal, e.g. $3 + 4 = 2 + 5$

equator NOUN an imaginary line round the earth at an equal distance from the North and South Poles ▸ **equatorial** ADJECTIVE

equestrian ADJECTIVE to do with horse riding

equilateral (ee-kwi-lat-er-al) ADJECTIVE (of a triangle) having all sides equal

equilibrium NOUN **1** a balance between different forces, influences, etc. **2** a balanced state of mind

equine ADJECTIVE of or like a horse

equinox NOUN the time of year when day and night are equal in length (about 20 March in spring, about 22 September in autumn)

equip VERB **equipping, equipped** to supply with what is needed

equipment NOUN the things needed for a particular purpose

equitable ADJECTIVE fair and sensible

equity (ek-wit-ee) NOUN fairness

equivalent ADJECTIVE equal in importance, meaning, value, etc.

THESAURUS

equal ADJECTIVE • *houses of equal size* ▸ identical, similar, the same, comparable, uniform • *an equal contest* ▸ even, balanced, level, evenly matched **equal to** • *equal to the task* ▸ capable of, adequate for, good enough for, suitable for

equal VERB • *Her performance equalled the world record.* ▸ match, reach, be as good as • *Three and ten equals thirteen.* ▸ add up to, amount to

equip VERB • *Each seat is equipped with headphones.* ▸ provide, supply, furnish, fit

equipment NOUN • *recording equipment* ▸ apparatus, appliances, tools, gear

equivalent ADJECTIVE • *a degree or an equivalent qualification* ▸ comparable, similar, corresponding

DICTIONARY

equivalent NOUN something that is equivalent

era (eer-u) NOUN a major period of history

eradicate VERB to get rid of
► **eradication** NOUN

erase VERB 1 to rub out 2 to remove or wipe out ► **eraser** NOUN

erect ADJECTIVE standing straight up

erect VERB to set up or build

erection NOUN 1 the process of erecting 2 something erected

ermine NOUN 1 a kind of weasel 2 its white fur

erode VERB to wear away

erosion NOUN the wearing away of the earth's surface by the action of water, wind, etc.

erotic ADJECTIVE arousing sexual feelings ► **erotically** ADVERB

err (er) VERB 1 to make a mistake 2 to do wrong

errand NOUN a short journey to take a message, fetch goods, etc.

erratic (ir-at-ik) ADJECTIVE 1 not regular 2 not reliable
► **erratically** ADVERB

erroneous ADJECTIVE incorrect; mistaken ► **erroneously** ADVERB

error NOUN a mistake

erupt VERB 1 to burst out 2 (of a volcano) to shoot out lava
► **eruption** NOUN

escalate VERB to make or become greater or more extreme
► **escalation** NOUN

escalator NOUN a staircase with steps moving up or down

escapade NOUN an adventure

escape VERB 1 to get free or away 2 to avoid something unpleasant *to escape punishment* 3 to be forgotten by *Her name escapes me for the moment.*

escape NOUN 1 an act of escaping 2 a way to escape

escarpment NOUN a steep slope at the edge of high level ground

escort (ess-kort) NOUN someone accompanying a person or thing for company or protection

THESAURUS

errand NOUN • *a few errands to do* ► job, task, duty, assignment

erratic ADJECTIVE • *erratic behaviour* ► changeable, unpredictable, variable

error NOUN • *many factual errors* ► mistake, inaccuracy, slip, blunder, fault

escape VERB • *They must have had help to escape.* ► get away, break free, break loose, run away, abscond • *Oil was escaping.*

► leak, seep, ooze, discharge • *to escape serious injury* ► avoid, evade

escape NOUN • *an escape from prison* ► breakout, getaway, flight • *an escape of gas* ► leak, emission, discharge

escort NOUN • *The police provided an escort.* ► guard, bodyguard, convoy • *a royal escort* ► attendant, entourage, train, retinue

escort (iss-kort) *VERB* to act as an escort to

Eskimo *NOUN* a name formerly used for Inuit

⚠ **USAGE**

The name *Inuit* is preferred.

especially *ADVERB* specially; more than anything else

espionage *NOUN* spying

essay *NOUN* a short piece of writing in prose

essence *NOUN* **1** the most important quality or element of something **2** a concentrated liquid

essential *ADJECTIVE* completely necessary ► **essentially** *ADVERB*

essential *NOUN* an essential thing

establish *VERB* **1** to set up an organization or relationship **2** to show to be true *He established his innocence.*

establishment *NOUN* a business firm or other institution

estate *NOUN* **1** an area of land with houses or factories on it **2** a large area of land owned by one person **3** the property of someone who has died

estate agent *NOUN* a person whose business is selling or letting houses and land

estate car *NOUN* a car with a door at the back giving access to an inside luggage compartment

esteem *VERB* to think very highly of

esteem *NOUN* respect and admiration

esteemed *ADJECTIVE* highly respected and admired

ester *NOUN* a kind of chemical compound

estimate (ess-tim-at) *NOUN* a rough calculation or guess about an amount or value

escort *VERB* • *We will escort you to your seat.* ► take, lead, guide, accompany, conduct

especially *ADVERB* • *Property is especially expensive.* ► particularly, exceptionally, extremely, remarkably • *Patients, especially those with head injuries, become disoriented.* ► particularly, mainly, principally, chiefly

essential *ADJECTIVE* • *essential information* ► necessary, vital, important, crucial, key

establish *VERB* • *to establish a business* ► set up, found, create

establishment *NOUN* • *the establishment of a new republic* ► creation, formation, foundation • *a publishing establishment* ► business, concern, enterprise, venture, undertaking, company

estate *NOUN* • *a housing estate* ► development • *an estate worth millions* ► assets, possessions, wealth, property, belongings, holdings

estimate *NOUN* • *The painter will provide an estimate.* ► price, quotation, reckoning, specification, valuation, calculation

estimate (ess-tim-ayt) *VERB* to make an estimate ► **estimation** *NOUN*

estranged *ADJECTIVE* unfriendly after having been friendly or loving ► **estrangement** *NOUN*

estuary *NOUN* **estuaries** the mouth of a river where it reaches the sea

etc. *ABBREVIATION* (short for **et cetera**) and other similar things; and so on

etch *VERB* to engrave a picture with acid on a metal plate, especially for printing

etching *NOUN* a picture printed from an etched metal plate

eternal *ADJECTIVE* lasting for ever ► **eternally** *ADVERB*

eternity *NOUN* **eternities** **1** a time that has no end **2** (*informal*) a very long time

ether (ee-ther) *NOUN* **1** a colourless liquid with fumes that are used as an anaesthetic **2** the upper air

ethereal *ADJECTIVE* light and delicate ► **ethereally** *ADVERB*

ethical *ADJECTIVE* **1** to do with ethics **2** morally right; honourable ► **ethically** *ADVERB*

ethics (eth-iks) *PLURAL NOUN* standards of right behaviour

ethnic *ADJECTIVE* belonging to a particular race or group of people

etiquette (et-ik-et) *NOUN* the rules of correct behaviour

etymology *NOUN* **etymologies** **1** the origin of a word and its meaning **2** the study of the origins of words

EU *ABBREVIATION* European Union

eucalyptus (yoo-kal-**ip**-tus) *NOUN* **1** a kind of evergreen tree **2** a strong-smelling oil obtained from its leaves

Eucharist (yoo-ker-ist) *NOUN* the Christian ceremony commemorating the Last Supper of Christ and his disciples

eulogy (yoo-loj-ee) *NOUN* **eulogies** a speech or piece of writing praising a person or thing

eunuch (yoo-nuk) *NOUN* a man who has been castrated

euphemism (yoo-fim-izm) *NOUN* a mild word or phrase used instead of an offensive or frank one, e.g. *pass away* instead of *die* ► **euphemistic** *ADJECTIVE*

euphoria (yoo-for-ee-a) *NOUN* a feeling of general happiness

euro *NOUN* **euros** the basic unit of currency used by some members of the EU since 1999

European *ADJECTIVE* to do with Europe or its people ► **European** *NOUN*

euthanasia (yooth-an-**ay**-zee-a) *NOUN* the act of causing a person with a terminal illness to die gently and without pain

THESAURUS

estimate *VERB* • to estimate the cost ► assess, calculate, evaluate, guess, work out

eternal *ADJECTIVE* • eternal happiness ► everlasting, never-ending, unending, undying

a
b
c
d
e
f
g
h
i
j
k
l
m
n
o
p
q
r
s
t
u
v
w
x
y
z

evacuate VERB **1** to move people away from a dangerous place **2** to make empty ▶ **evacuation** NOUN

evacuee NOUN a person who has been evacuated

evade VERB to avoid by cleverness or trickery

evaluate VERB estimate the value of something; assess
▶ **evaluation** NOUN

evaporate VERB **1** to change from liquid into steam or vapour **2** to cease to exist *Their enthusiasm evaporated.* ▶ **evaporation** NOUN

evasion NOUN **1** the act of evading **2** an evasive answer or excuse

evasive ADJECTIVE trying to avoid giving an answer; not frank or straightforward

eve NOUN the day or evening before an important day or event *New Year's Eve*

even[1] ADJECTIVE **1** level and smooth **2** not varying **3** calm; not easily upset *an even temper* **4** equal *The scores were even.* **5** (of a number) able to be divided exactly by two
get even to take revenge
▶ **evenly** ADVERB, **evenness** NOUN

even VERB to make or become even

even ADVERB used to emphasize a word or statement *They ran even faster.*

even-handed ADJECTIVE fair and impartial

evening NOUN the time at the end of the day before the night

event NOUN **1** something important that happens **2** an item forming part of a sports contest

eventful ADJECTIVE full of happenings

eventual ADJECTIVE happening at last *our eventual success*
▶ **eventually** ADVERB

THESAURUS

evade VERB • *to evade responsibilities* ▶ avoid, shirk, shun, dodge, sidestep • *to evade capture* ▶ avoid, elude, escape

even ADJECTIVE • *an even surface* ▶ flat, smooth, level • *an even temperament* ▶ calm, stable, placid, even-tempered • *the even ticking of the clock* ▶ steady, regular, constant, unvarying • *The scores were even.* ▶ level, equal, identical, the same

even VERB **even out** • *to even out the wrinkles* ▶ smooth, straighten, flatten, level
even up • *to even up the scores* ▶ level, balance, equalize

evening NOUN • *It was evening when we reached home.* ▶ dusk, sunset, sundown, nightfall, twilight

event NOUN • *an annual event* ▶ occurrence, occasion, activity, affair, function • *a sporting event* ▶ game, match, competition, tournament

eventful ADJECTIVE • *an eventful week* ▶ busy, lively, exciting, interesting, action-packed

eventual ADJECTIVE • *the eventual outcome* ▶ final, ultimate, ensuing, resulting, overall

eventuality NOUN **eventualities** something that may happen

ever ADVERB **1** at any time *the best thing I ever did* **2** always *ever hopeful* **3** (*informal*) used for emphasis *Why ever not?*

evergreen ADJECTIVE having green leaves all the year ► **evergreen** NOUN

everlasting ADJECTIVE lasting for ever or for a long time

every ADJECTIVE each without any exceptions *We enjoyed every minute.* **every one** each one **every other** every second one

⚠️ **USAGE**

Every should be used with a singular verb and singular pronouns: Every house has its own garden.

everybody or **everyone** PRONOUN every person

everyday ADJECTIVE ordinary; usual *everyday clothes*

everything PRONOUN all things; all

everywhere ADVERB in every place

evict VERB to force someone to leave the house they are living in ► **eviction** NOUN

evidence NOUN **1** anything that gives people reason to believe something **2** information given in a lawcourt to prove something

evident ADJECTIVE obvious; clearly seen ► **evidently** ADVERB

evil ADJECTIVE morally bad; wicked ► **evilly** ADVERB

evil NOUN **1** wickedness **2** something unpleasant or harmful

evocative ADJECTIVE inspiring memories or feelings

evoke VERB to produce or inspire memories or feelings

evolution NOUN **1** gradual change into something different **2** the development of animals and plants from earlier or simpler forms of life ► **evolutionary** ADJECTIVE

evolve VERB to develop gradually

ewe (yoo) NOUN a female sheep

everlasting ADJECTIVE • *everlasting joy* ► eternal, never-ending, undying, enduring, infinite

everyday ADJECTIVE • *an everyday occurrence* ► commonplace, common, frequent, ordinary, familiar

evidence NOUN • *evidence of human life* ► proof, confirmation • *The evidence helped convict them.* ► testimony, statement, information

evident ADJECTIVE • *It was evident that he didn't like her.* ► clear, obvious, apparent, plain

evil ADJECTIVE • *an evil king* ► wicked, bad, immoral, vile • *an evil smell* ► nasty, foul, noxious, unpleasant, offensive • *an evil influence* ► bad, harmful, destructive, pernicious

evil NOUN • *a crime of the utmost evil* ► wickedness, sinfulness, immorality, depravity, vileness

DICTIONARY

ewer (yoo-er) NOUN a large water jug

exacerbate (eks-ass-er-bayt) VERB to make worse

exact ADJECTIVE 1 correct; precise 2 giving all details *exact instructions*

exact VERB to insist on and obtain

exacting ADJECTIVE making great demands *an exacting task*

exactly ADVERB 1 precisely; with all details 2 used in reply as a strong form of agreement

exaggerate VERB to make something seem bigger, better, or worse than it really is
► **exaggeration** NOUN

exalt VERB 1 to raise in rank or status 2 to praise highly
► **exaltation** NOUN

exam NOUN an examination

examination NOUN 1 a test of a person's knowledge or skill 2 an act of examining or inspecting *a medical examination*

examine VERB 1 to test a person's knowledge or skill 2 to look at closely or in detail ► **examiner** NOUN

> **WORD HISTORY**
> from a Latin word meaning 'to weigh accurately'

example NOUN 1 anything that represents something of the same kind 2 a person or thing worth imitating

exasperate VERB to annoy very much ► **exasperation** NOUN

excavate VERB to dig out or uncover by digging ► **excavation** NOUN, **excavator** NOUN

THESAURUS

exact ADJECTIVE • *exact in their work*
► careful, precise, accurate, painstaking • *exact measurements*
► precise, accurate, correct • *an exact copy* ► identical, faithful

exactly • *She looks exactly like her mother.* ► precisely, entirely, absolutely, completely, totally
• *Describe the scene exactly.*
► accurately, precisely, faithfully, in detail

exaggerate VERB • *to exaggerate the scale of the problem*
► overstate, over-emphasize, overestimate, overstress

examination NOUN • *an examination of the accounts*
► inspection, scrutiny, study, analysis • *a written examination in*

history ► exam, test, paper • *a medical examination* ► check-up, check

examine VERB • *to examine the company accounts* ► inspect, scrutinize, study, investigate, check, analyse, probe • *Students are examined at the end of each year.* ► test, assess • *The defence counsel will examine the witness.*
► question, cross-examine, interrogate

example NOUN • *a fine example of a Tudor building* ► specimen, instance, illustration, sample • *to follow their example* ► model, pattern, standard, ideal • *punished as an example to others*
► warning, lesson, deterrent

a b c d e f g h i j k l m n o p q r s t u v w x y z

DICTIONARY

exceed VERB **1** to be greater than **2** to go beyond the limit of

exceedingly ADVERB very; extremely

excel VERB **excelling, excelled 1** to be better than **2** to do very well

Excellency NOUN the title of high officials such as ambassadors and governors

excellent ADJECTIVE of high quality; extremely good ▶ **excellence** NOUN

except PREPOSITION not including *They all left except me.*

except VERB to exclude or leave out

⚠ **USAGE**

Do not confuse this word with *accept*.

excepting PREPOSITION except

exception NOUN a person or thing that is left out or does not follow

the general rule **take exception to** to object to or resent

exceptional ADJECTIVE **1** very unusual **2** outstandingly good ▶ **exceptionally** ADVERB

excerpt (ek-serpt) NOUN a passage taken from a book or speech or film etc.

excess NOUN too much of something

excessive ADJECTIVE too much or too great ▶ **excessively** ADVERB

exchange VERB to give something and get something else in return

exchange NOUN **1** the act of exchanging **2** a place where stocks and shares are bought and sold **3** a place where telephone connections are made

exchequer NOUN a national treasury into which taxes and other public funds are paid

THESAURUS

exceed VERB • *to exceed expectations* ▶ surpass, outdo, beat, better

excel VERB • *to excel all the others* ▶ do better than, beat, surpass, outdo • *to excel at music* ▶ shine, do well, stand out, be outstanding

excellent ADJECTIVE • *an excellent idea* ▶ very good, first-class, outstanding, superb, remarkable, exceptional, wonderful, marvellous, brilliant

exception NOUN • *with a few exceptions* ▶ oddity, abnormality, peculiarity, special case, freak

exceptional ADJECTIVE • *exceptional ability* ▶ excellent, very good, first-class, outstanding, superb, remarkable • *exceptional weather* ▶ unusual, abnormal, untypical, extraordinary, freakish

excessive ADJECTIVE • *excessive drinking* ▶ extreme, immoderate, extravagant, *The cost proved excessive.* ▶ unreasonable, exorbitant

exchange VERB • *The players exchanged shirts.* ▶ swap, switch, change • *I exchanged my old bike for a smart new one.* ▶ swap, trade, barter, substitute

DICTIONARY

excise[1] (eks-I'z) NOUN a tax charged on certain goods

excise[2] (iks-I'z) VERB to remove by cutting

excitable ADJECTIVE easily excited

excite VERB 1 to make eager and enthusiastic about something 2 to cause a feeling or reaction to *excite great interest*

excitement NOUN a strong feeling of eagerness or pleasure

exclaim VERB to shout or cry out in eagerness or surprise

exclamation NOUN 1 the act of exclaiming 2 a word or words cried out

exclamation mark NOUN the punctuation mark (!) placed after an exclamation

exclude VERB 1 to shut somebody or something out 2 to leave out of consideration ▶ **exclusion** NOUN

exclusive ADJECTIVE 1 including only certain people *an exclusive club* 2 not existing elsewhere *an exclusive offer* **exclusive of** not

including *the cost exclusive of tax* ▶ **exclusively** ADVERB

excrement NOUN waste matter excreted from the bowels

excrete VERB to get rid of waste matter from the body ▶ **excretion** NOUN

excruciating ADJECTIVE 1 extremely painful 2 hard to put up with

excursion NOUN a short journey made for pleasure

excuse (iks-kewz) VERB 1 to forgive 2 to release from a duty or commitment

excuse (iks-kewss) NOUN a reason given to explain a wrongdoing or mistake

execute VERB 1 to put to death as a punishment 2 to perform or produce ▶ **execution** NOUN

executioner NOUN an official who executes a condemned person

executive NOUN 1 a senior person in a business organization 2 the

THESAURUS

excite VERB • *The prospect excited them.* ▶ thrill, interest, exhilarate

excited ADJECTIVE • *The children became excited.* ▶ happy, animated, lively, thrilled, exuberant, enthusiastic, worked up, elated

exciting ADJECTIVE • *an exciting story* ▶ thrilling, exhilarating, gripping, dramatic, eventful, action-packed

exclude VERB • *anxious to exclude troublemakers* ▶ keep out,

prevent, deter, ban, disallow • *He excluded his own name from the list.* ▶ omit, leave out, miss out • *The figures exclude taxes.* ▶ omit, not include

excuse VERB • *We cannot excuse bad behaviour.* ▶ justify, defend, condone, tolerate • *She found it hard to excuse them.* ▶ forgive, pardon

excuse NOUN • *the usual feeble excuses* ▶ explanation, defence, reason • *no excuse for what they did* ▶ justification, vindication

part of a government that puts decisions into effect

executive ADJECTIVE having the authority to carry out plans or laws

executor (ig-zek-yoo-ter) NOUN an official appointed to carry out the instructions in a will

exemplary (ig-zem-pler-ee) ADJECTIVE good as an example to others *exemplary conduct*

exemplify VERB **exemplifies, exemplified** to be an example of

exempt ADJECTIVE not having to do something that others have to do

exempt VERB to make exempt
▶ **exemption** NOUN

exercise NOUN **1** the practice of using your body to keep it strong and healthy **2** a piece of work done for practice

exercise VERB **1** to do exercises **2** to give exercise to an animal **3** to use *Exercise more care.*

exert VERB to bring into use *to exert authority* ▶ **exertion** NOUN

exhale VERB to breathe out
▶ **exhalation** NOUN

exhaust VERB **1** to make very tired **2** to use up completely
▶ **exhaustion** NOUN

exhaust NOUN **1** the waste gases or steam from an engine **2** the system they pass through

exhaustive ADJECTIVE thorough *an exhaustive search*
▶ **exhaustively** ADVERB

exhibit VERB to show or display in public ▶ **exhibitor** NOUN

exhibit NOUN an item on display in a gallery or museum

exhibition NOUN a collection of things put on display for people to look at

exhibitionist NOUN a person who behaves in a way that is meant to attract attention
▶ **exhibitionism** NOUN

exhilarate VERB to make someone happy and excited
▶ **exhilarating** ADJECTIVE, **exhilaration** NOUN

exhort VERB to try hard to persuade someone
▶ **exhortation** NOUN

exercise NOUN • *regular exercise*
▶ physical activity, working out, exertion, training

exhaust VERB • *Her day out had exhausted her.* ▶ tire out, wear out, fatigue, weary, tax, strain • *to exhaust the supply* ▶ use up, consume, drain, deplete, empty, finish off, go through, spend, sap

exhausted ADJECTIVE • *I felt exhausted.* ▶ tired, worn out, shattered, weary

exhausting ADJECTIVE • *an exhausting journey* ▶ tiring, difficult, strenuous, gruelling, demanding

exhibition NOUN • *an exhibition of sculpture* ▶ display, presentation, show

a
b
c
d
e
f
g
h
i
j
k
l
m
n
o
p
q
r
s
t
u
v
w
x
y
z

exhume VERB to dig up a body that has been buried ► **exhumation** NOUN

exile VERB to banish

exile NOUN **1** a period of having to live away from your own country **2** a person sent away from their own country

exist VERB **1** to be present as part of what is real **2** to stay alive

existence NOUN **1** the state of being **2** life or a particular type of life *a miserable existence*

exit NOUN **1** the way out of a building **2** the act of leaving

exit VERB to leave; to go out

exodus NOUN the departure of many people, especially from their country

exonerate VERB to free from blame or guilt

exorbitant ADJECTIVE (of an amount charged) much too great

exorcize VERB to drive out an evil spirit ► **exorcism** NOUN, **exorcist** NOUN

⚠ USAGE

This word can also be spelled *exorcise.*

exotic ADJECTIVE **1** strange or unusual *exotic clothes* **2** from another part of the world *exotic plants*

expand VERB to make or become larger or fuller ► **expansion** NOUN, **expansive** ADJECTIVE

expanse NOUN a wide area

expansive ADJECTIVE **1** wide and large **2** talkative

expect VERB **1** to think or believe that something is likely to happen **2** to want or demand *to expect courtesy*

exile VERB • *to exile your enemies*
► expel, banish, deport, drive out

exile NOUN • *punished with exile*
► banishment, expulsion, deportation • *a group of political exiles* ► émigré, deportee, outcast, refugee

exist VERB • *animals that no longer exist* ► live, occur, be alive • *to exist on a modest income*
► survive, live, subsist, keep going

existence NOUN • *the very existence of these organizations*
► survival, continuation • *a dreary existence* ► way of life, lifestyle

existing ADJECTIVE • *the existing arrangements* ► current, present, prevailing

exit NOUN • *the building's main exit*
► way out, door, gate • *a quick exit*
► departure, retreat, leaving

exotic ADJECTIVE • *exotic places*
► faraway, distant, remote, exciting, romantic • *exotic birds*
► foreign, tropical • *exotic dress*
► colourful, unusual, unconventional

expand VERB • *to expand the business* ► develop, enlarge, extend • *The metal expands.*
► increase in size, become larger, swell, grow, stretch

expect VERB • *to expect better results* ► hope for, predict, anticipate • *to expect obedience*
► want, demand, insist on, require

expectant ADJECTIVE **1** expecting something to happen **2** (of a woman) pregnant

expectation NOUN **1** belief that something will happen **2** something you expect to happen

expedient ADJECTIVE practical and convenient rather than fair

expedient NOUN a means of doing something difficult

expedite VERB to make something happen more quickly

expedition NOUN **1** a journey made for a special purpose **2** speed or promptness

expel VERB **expelling, expelled** **1** to send or force out *a fan to expel stale air* **2** to make a person leave a school or country

expend VERB to spend or use up

expenditure NOUN the spending or using up of money or effort

expense NOUN **1** a cost **2** something that causes a cost

expensive ADJECTIVE costing a lot

experience NOUN **1** knowledge gained from doing or seeing things **2** an event you have taken part in

experience VERB to take part in an event

experienced ADJECTIVE having skill or knowledge from experience

experiment NOUN a test to get information or try to prove something

experiment VERB to carry out an experiment ▶ **experimentation** NOUN

• *I expect they missed the train.* ▶ think, suppose, assume, imagine, guess

expel VERB • *He was expelled from the country.* ▶ banish, exile, deport, drive out

expensive ADJECTIVE • *an expensive holiday* ▶ costly, dear, high-priced, exorbitant

experience NOUN • *to learn by experience* ▶ practice, participation, involvement, taking part • *to gain experience* ▶ skill, knowledge, understanding • *a terrifying experience* ▶ incident, event, episode, ordeal, adventure

experience VERB • *to experience difficulties* ▶ meet, encounter, face, suffer

experienced ADJECTIVE • *an experienced actor* ▶ expert, skilled, qualified, trained, professional • *an experienced woman of the world* ▶ mature, sophisticated, worldly wise, knowing

experiment NOUN • *experiments with laser technology* ▶ test, investigation, trial, piece of research • *The new library hours are an experiment.* ▶ trial, trial run, try-out

experiment VERB **experiment with** • *You need to experiment with the camera's different settings.* ▶ test, try out, investigate, explore, do tests on

DICTIONARY

experimental ADJECTIVE done as a trial or experiment
➤ **experimentally** ADVERB

expert NOUN a person with great knowledge or skill in a subject

expert ADJECTIVE having great knowledge or skill ➤ **expertly** ADVERB

expertise (eks-per-**teez**) NOUN expert ability

expire VERB **1** to come to an end **2** to die **3** to breathe out air

expiry NOUN the time when something ends

explain VERB **1** to make clear to someone; to show the meaning of **2** to account for

explanation NOUN a statement explaining something

explanatory (iks-**plan**-at-er-ee) ADJECTIVE giving an explanation

explicit ADJECTIVE stated or stating something openly and exactly
➤ **explicitly** ADVERB

explode VERB **1** to burst or suddenly release energy with a loud noise **2** to cause a bomb to go off **3** to increase suddenly or quickly

exploit (eks-**ploit**) NOUN a brave or exciting deed

exploit (iks-**ploit**) VERB **1** to use or develop to good effect **2** to make use of a person selfishly
➤ **exploitation** NOUN

exploratory ADJECTIVE for the purpose of exploring

explore VERB **1** to travel to make discoveries **2** to examine a subject or idea carefully ➤ **exploration** NOUN, **explorer** NOUN

THESAURUS

expert NOUN • *advice from an expert* ➤ specialist, professional, authority • *an expert at board games* ➤ master, genius, virtuoso

expert ADJECTIVE • *expert advice* ➤ skilled, professional, qualified, specialist • *an expert swimmer* ➤ skilful, talented, accomplished, proficient, competent

explain VERB • *to explain the problem* ➤ describe, clarify, make clear, spell out, elucidate • *hard to explain such stupidity* ➤ account for, justify, excuse, defend, give reasons for

explanation NOUN • *an explanation for what happened* ➤ justification, reason, account, excuse, defence • *What can the explanation be?* ➤ cause, reason,

motive • *a brief explanation of the ideas* ➤ description, account, clarification, elucidation

explicit ADJECTIVE • *explicit instructions* ➤ clear, plain, direct, precise • *an explicit criticism* ➤ open, direct, frank, candid

exploit NOUN • *brave exploits* ➤ feat, deed, adventure

exploit VERB • *to exploit mineral resources* ➤ make use of, utilize, use, take advantage of • *exploiting the workers* ➤ take advantage of, use, mistreat, oppress

explore VERB • *to explore the neighbourhood* ➤ look around, inspect, take a look at, tour • *to explore the possibility* ➤ investigate, examine, look into, consider

explosion NOUN 1 the exploding of a bomb etc.; the noise made by exploding 2 a sudden great increase

explosive ADJECTIVE able to explode

explosive NOUN a substance that can explode

export (ek-spawt) VERB to send goods abroad to be sold
► **exportation** NOUN, **exporter** NOUN

export (ek-spawt) NOUN 1 the exporting of goods 2 something exported

expose VERB 1 to reveal or uncover 2 to allow light to reach a photographic film

exposure NOUN 1 the harmful effects of being exposed to cold weather without protection 2 the exposing of photographic film to the light 3 a piece of film exposed in this way

express ADJECTIVE 1 going or sent quickly 2 clearly stated *express orders*

express NOUN a fast train or bus

express VERB 1 to put into words 2 to press or squeeze out

expression NOUN 1 the look on a person's face 2 a word or phrase 3 a way of speaking or of playing music to show your feelings 4 the act of expressing

expressive ADJECTIVE expressing meaning clearly or vividly

expressly ADVERB 1 clearly and plainly *expressly forbidden* 2 specially *designed expressly for you*

expulsion NOUN the act of expelling or being expelled, especially from a school

exquisite (eks-kwiz-it) ADJECTIVE very beautiful and delicate
► **exquisitely** ADVERB

extend VERB 1 to stretch out 2 to make or become longer or larger

explosion NOUN • *a loud explosion* ► blast, bang, boom, burst, crash

explosive ADJECTIVE • *explosive substances* ► volatile, combustible • *an explosive situation* ► tense, highly charged, dangerous

expose VERB • *to expose faults* ► reveal, uncover, bring to light

express ADJECTIVE • *an express train* ► fast, high-speed, non-stop • *his express wish* ► clear, definite, explicit

express VERB • *to express your wishes* ► communicate,

convey, voice, articulate, put into words

expression NOUN • *a puzzled expression* ► look, appearance, face, countenance • *old-fashioned expressions* ► phrase, idiom, saying • *She read the letter with expression.* ► emotion, feeling, passion, poignancy

extend VERB • *to extend power* ► expand, enlarge, increase, develop • *to extend a meeting* ► lengthen, prolong, continue • *to extend thanks* ► offer, proffer, present • *The fields extend to the river.* ► reach, go, continue

3 to offer or give ▸ **extendible** ADJECTIVE

extension NOUN **1** a part added on, especially to a building **2** an extra telephone linked to the main one

extensive ADJECTIVE covering a large area or range ▸ **extensively** ADVERB

extent NOUN **1** the area or length of something **2** level or scope *the full extent of his power*

extenuating ADJECTIVE making something bad seem less so *extenuating circumstances* ▸ **extenuation** NOUN

exterior ADJECTIVE outer; outside

exterior NOUN the outside of a building

exterminate VERB to destroy or kill all of ▸ **extermination** NOUN

external ADJECTIVE outside ▸ **externally** ADVERB

extinct ADJECTIVE not existing or active any more *an extinct bird an extinct vocano*

extinction NOUN the process of making or becoming extinct

extinguish VERB **1** to put out a fire or light **2** to put an end to

extol VERB **extolling, extolled** to praise highly

extort VERB to obtain by force or threats ▸ **extortion** NOUN

extortionate ADJECTIVE charging far too much

extra ADJECTIVE more than is needed or usual

extra ADVERB more than usually *extra strong*

extra NOUN **1** an extra person or thing **2** a person acting as part of a crowd in a film or play

extract (iks-trakt) VERB to take out or remove ▸ **extractor** NOUN

extract (eks-trakt) NOUN **1** a passage taken from a book, speech, film, etc. **2** a substance separated or obtained from another

extraction NOUN **1** the process of extracting **2** a person's descent *of Russian extraction*

THESAURUS

extension NOUN • *an extension to the house* ▸ addition, annexe, wing

extent NOUN • *thirty square metres in extent* ▸ area, size, expanse, dimensions • *the extent of the damage* ▸ amount, degree, scale, scope, size, quantity, range

external ADJECTIVE • *an external surface* ▸ outer, outside, exterior

extinct ADJECTIVE • *an extinct species* ▸ lost, vanished, died out, dead • *an extinct volcano* ▸ inactive, extinguished

extra ADJECTIVE • *extra money* ▸ additional, more, further, supplementary • *a lot of extra food* ▸ spare, excess, surplus, superfluous, leftover

extra ADVERB • *He worked extra hard.* ▸ especially, exceptionally, particularly, extremely

extra NOUN • *The holiday was a welcome extra.* ▸ addition, bonus

a
b
c
d
e
f
g
h
i
j
k
l
m
n
o
p
q
r
s
t
u
v
w
x
y
z

extradite VERB to hand over a person accused of a crime to the country where the crime was committed ► **extradition** NOUN

extraneous (iks-tray-nee-us) ADJECTIVE added from outside *extraneous noises*

extraordinary ADJECTIVE very unusual or strange
► **extraordinarily** ADVERB

extraterrestrial ADJECTIVE from beyond the earth's atmosphere

extraterrestrial NOUN a being from outer space

extravagant ADJECTIVE spending or using too much
► **extravagance** NOUN

extravaganza NOUN a spectacular show or display

extreme ADJECTIVE **1** very great or intense *extreme cold* **2** furthest away *the extreme north* **3** going to great lengths in actions or opinions ► **extremely** ADVERB

extreme NOUN **1** something extreme **2** either end of something

extremity (iks-trem-it-ee) NOUN **extremities 1** an extreme point; the very end **2** extreme danger

extricate VERB to free from a difficult position or situation
► **extrication** NOUN

extrovert NOUN a person who is sociable and communicative

exuberant (ig-zew-ber-ant) ADJECTIVE lively and cheerful
► **exuberance** NOUN

exude VERB **1** to give off moisture, a smell, etc. **2** to display openly *to exude confidence*

exult VERB to rejoice greatly
► **exultant** ADJECTIVE, **exultation** NOUN

eye NOUN **1** the organ of the body used for seeing **2** the ability to see *keen eyes* **3** the small hole in a needle **4** the centre of a storm

THESAURUS

extraordinary ADJECTIVE • *an extraordinary story*
► remarkable, amazing, astonishing, unusual, strange, wonderful, fantastic, unbelievable, incredible

extravagant ADJECTIVE • *an extravagant lifestyle* ► lavish, luxurious, indulgent, wasteful

extreme ADJECTIVE • *extreme tiredness* ► great, intense, exceptional, extraordinary,

acute • *extreme measures*
► drastic, serious, radical, desperate, severe • *in the extreme north* ► far, farthest, distant, remote • *extreme political opinions* ► radical, extremist, fanatical

extreme NOUN • *from one extreme to the other* ► limit, extremity, end

eye NOUN • *a sharp eye* ► eyesight, vision

a
b
c
d
e
f
g
h
i
j
k
l
m
n
o
p
q
r
s
t
u
v
w
x
y
z

DICTIONARY

eye *VERB* **eyeing** to look at closely

eyeball *NOUN* the ball-shaped part of the eye inside the eyelids

eyebrow *NOUN* the fringe of hair growing above each eye

eyelash *NOUN* each of the short hairs that grow on an eyelid

eyelid *NOUN* each of the two folds of skin that close over the eyeball

eyesight *NOUN* the ability to see

eyesore *NOUN* something large and ugly

eyewitness *NOUN* a person who saw an accident or crime take place

eyrie (eer-ee) *NOUN* the nest of an eagle or other bird of prey

THESAURUS

eye *VERB* • *He eyed the visitors carefully.* ▶ look at, watch, observe, view, gaze at, glance at, scrutinize, examine

Ff

fable NOUN a short story, often about animals, with a moral or lesson

fabric NOUN **1** cloth **2** the basic framework of a building

fabricate VERB **1** to construct or manufacture something **2** to invent a story or excuse ► **fabrication** NOUN

fabulous ADJECTIVE **1** great or wonderful **2** told of in fables and myths ► **fabulously** ADVERB

facade (fas-ahd) NOUN **1** the front of a building **2** a deceptive outward appearance

face NOUN **1** the front part of the head **2** the expression on a person's face **3** the front or upper side of something **4** a surface of a block or cube ► **facial** ADJECTIVE

face VERB **1** to look or have the front towards something *The house faces the sea.* **2** to have to deal with *Explorers face many dangers.* **3** to

cover with a layer of different material

facelift NOUN **1** surgery to remove wrinkles, done to make someone look younger **2** a renovation or improvement to the appearance of something

facet (fas-it) NOUN **1** each side of a cut stone or jewel **2** one aspect of a situation or problem

facetious (fas-ee-shus) ADJECTIVE trying to be funny at an unsuitable time *facetious remarks* ► **facetiously** ADVERB

facile (fas-yl) ADJECTIVE done or produced easily or with little thought

facilitate VERB to make easier to do ► **facilitation** NOUN

facility (fas-il-it-ee) NOUN **facilities 1** buildings and equipment for doing things *sports facilities* **2** ease or skill

facsimile (fak-sim-il-ee) NOUN an exact copy

THESAURUS

fable NOUN • *the fable of the fox and the crow* ► story, tale, parable

fabric NOUN • *a cotton fabric* ► cloth, material • *the fabric of the building* ► structure, framework, frame

fabricate VERB • *to fabricate evidence* ► invent, make up, concoct

fabulous ADJECTIVE • *a fabulous time* ► wonderful, marvellous,

fantastic, splendid, magnificent • *fabulous places in stories* ► legendary, mythical, imaginary

face NOUN • *a lovely face* ► features, countenance, visage • *an angry face* ► expression, look, appearance, countenance • *a cube of six faces* ► side, surface, plane

face VERB • *The hotel faces the lake.* ► overlook • *to face criticism* ► meet, encounter, experience

a
b
c
d
e
f
g
h
i
j
k
l
m
n
o
p
q
r
s
t
u
v
w
x
y
z

fact NOUN something that is certainly true

faction NOUN a small united group within a larger one

factor NOUN **1** something that affects a situation or result *Hard work is an important factor.* **2** a number by which a larger number can be divided exactly

factory NOUN **factories** a large building where machines are used to make goods

factual ADJECTIVE based on facts; containing facts ► **factually** ADVERB

faculty NOUN **faculties 1** any of the powers of the body or mind (e.g. sight, speech, understanding) **2** a department teaching a particular subject in a university or college

fad NOUN **1** an unusual like or dislike **2** a temporary fashion or craze ► **faddy** ADJECTIVE

fade VERB **1** to lose colour or strength **2** to disappear gradually **3** to make something become gradually weaker or stronger

faeces (fee-seez) PLURAL NOUN solid waste matter passed out of the body

fag NOUN **1** something tiring or tedious **2** (*informal*) a cigarette

fagged out tired out; exhausted

Fahrenheit ADJECTIVE measuring temperature on a scale on which water freezes at 32° and boils at 212°

fail VERB **1** to be unable to do something **2** to become weak or useless; to break down **3** not to do something you should have done *They failed to warn me.* **4** to be unsuccessful in an exam or test **without fail** for certain; whatever happens

failing NOUN a weakness or fault

fact NOUN • *a proven fact* ► reality, truth, certainty **facts** • *to take all the facts into account* ► evidence, information, details, data

factor NOUN • *Cost is a key factor.* ► element, component, feature, aspect

factory NOUN • *a factory that made parts for tractors* ► manufacturing plant, workshop, works

factual ADJECTIVE • *a factual description of the events* ► truthful, accurate, realistic, objective

fad NOUN • *a passing fad* ► craze, fashion, trend, vogue, obsession

fade VERB • *The light has faded the colours.* ► bleach, lighten, whiten • *The music began to fade.* ► decrease, diminish, weaken, decline, dwindle, disappear • *The flowers had faded by now.* ► wither, wilt, droop

fail VERB • *All attempts failed.* ► be unsuccessful, go wrong, miscarry, fall through • *The business had failed.* ► collapse, founder, go bankrupt • *Her daughter had failed to contact her.* ► neglect, forget, omit • *His health was failing.* ► deteriorate, decline, weaken • *They say we have failed them.* ► let down, disappoint, desert • *to*

DICTIONARY

failure NOUN 1 the act of failing 2 a person or thing that has failed

faint ADJECTIVE 1 pale or dim; not distinct 2 weak or giddy; nearly unconscious 3 slight *a faint hope* ► **faintly** ADVERB

faint VERB to become unconscious for a short time

⚠ **USAGE**

Do not confuse this word with *feint*.

fair[1] ADJECTIVE 1 right or just; according to the rules *a fair fight* 2 (of hair or skin) light in colour 3 (of weather) fine or favourable 4 moderate; quite good *a fair number* ► **fairness** NOUN

fair[2] NOUN 1 a group of outdoor entertainments including

sideshows and stalls 2 an exhibition or market

fairground NOUN an open space for holding a fair

fairly ADVERB 1 justly; according to the rules 2 moderately *fairly good*

fairy NOUN **fairies** an imaginary small creature with magic powers

fairy story or **fairy tale** NOUN a traditional story about fairies, giants, etc.

faith NOUN 1 strong belief or trust 2 a religion

faithful ADJECTIVE 1 loyal and trustworthy 2 true to the facts *a faithful account* ► **faithfully** ADVERB

fake NOUN something that looks genuine but is not; a forgery

THESAURUS

fail an exam ► be unsuccessful in, not pass

failure NOUN • *The negotiations ended in failure.*
► disappointment, defeat, disaster • *The plan proved to be a failure.* ► disaster, catastrophe, fiasco, mistake, flop • *a failure in the power supply* ► breakdown, fault, malfunction

faint ADJECTIVE • *a faint smell of gas*
► slight, vague, weak • *a faint pink colour* ► pale, light, hazy • *a faint cry* ► quiet, muffled, muted, feeble, weak • *a faint possibility*
► slight, slim, small, vague, remote • *to feel faint* ► dizzy, giddy, light-headed, weak

fair ADJECTIVE • *It isn't fair to blame them.* ► just, reasonable, honourable • *a fair assessment of*

the situation ► honest, reasonable, objective, dispassionate • *a fair chance of success* ► moderate, reasonable, average, decent, satisfactory • *a fair amount of traffic*
► considerable, moderate, average • *fair hair* ► blond(e), light • *fair weather* ► fine, dry, bright, clear, sunny

fairly ADVERB • *fairly good*
► reasonably, moderately, quite

faithful ADJECTIVE • *a faithful friend*
► loyal, devoted, reliable, trustworthy, close • *a faithful record* ► accurate, true

fake NOUN • *One of the paintings was a fake.* ► forgery, copy, imitation, reproduction, replica • *The man is a fake.* ► fraud, impostor, cheat

fake

DICTIONARY

fake VERB **1** to make a copy or forgery of **2** to pretend *to fake illness*

falcon NOUN a bird of prey used to hunt other birds or game

fall VERB **fell, fallen 1** to come or go down under its own weight **2** to decrease or become lower **3** (of a place) to be captured in war **4** to die in battle **5** to happen *A silence fell.* **6** to become *She fell asleep.*

fall NOUN **1** the action of falling **2** (*American*) autumn, when leaves fall

fallacy (fal-a-see) NOUN **fallacies** a false or mistaken idea or belief

fallible (fal-ib-ul) ADJECTIVE liable to make mistakes ► **fallibility** NOUN

fallout NOUN radioactive material carried in the air after a nuclear explosion

fallow ADJECTIVE (of land) ploughed and left without crops for a time

falls PLURAL NOUN a waterfall

false ADJECTIVE **1** untrue or incorrect **2** not genuine; artificial **3** treacherous or deceitful

falsehood NOUN a lie

falsetto NOUN **falsettos** a man's voice forced into speaking or singing higher than is natural

falsify VERB **falsifies, falsified** to alter dishonestly; to make false ► **falsification** NOUN

falter VERB **1** to hesitate when you move or speak **2** to become weaker *His courage faltered.*

fame NOUN the state of being very well-known ► **famed** ADJECTIVE

familiar ADJECTIVE **1** well-known; often seen or experienced

THESAURUS

fake VERB • *to fake a death certificate* ► forge, fabricate, counterfeit, falsify

fake ADJECTIVE • *The diamonds were fake.* ► imitation, artificial, synthetic, false, bogus, radioactive • *a wad of fake banknotes* ► counterfeit, forged

fall VERB • *He stumbled and fell.* ► tumble, topple, trip over, keel over, collapse • *Flood levels began to fall at last.* ► drop, go down, subside, recede • *Bombs continued to fall.* ► drop, descend, plummet • *Prices are expected to fall.* ► go down, decrease, drop

fall NOUN • *He was hurt in a fall.* ► tumble, trip, topple, stumble, collapse • *a fall in house prices*

► drop, decline, decrease, reduction • *the fall of Troy* ► surrender, capitulation, defeat • *the fall of the Roman Empire* ► downfall, collapse, ruin, failure, destruction

false ADJECTIVE • *a false alibi* ► untrue, invented, concocted • *a false friend* ► unfaithful, disloyal, unreliable, untrustworthy • *false hair* ► artificial, unreal, imitation, synthetic, fake • *a false belief* ► incorrect, erroneous, mistaken, wrong

fame NOUN • *Their fame spread.* ► renown, reputation, popularity, celebrity, stardom

2 knowing something well **3** very friendly ▸ **familiarity** NOUN

familiarize VERB to make yourself familiar with something

⚠ **SPELLING**

This word can also be spelled *familiarise*.

family NOUN **families 1** parents and their children **2** a group of related plants or things

famine NOUN a serious shortage of food in an area

famished ADJECTIVE very hungry

famous ADJECTIVE known to many people

fan¹ NOUN a device or machine for making air move about

fan VERB **fanning, fanned** to send a current of air on

fan² NOUN an enthusiastic admirer or supporter

fanatic NOUN a person who is extremely or wildly enthusiastic about something

fanatical ADJECTIVE extremely or wildly enthusiastic

fanciful ADJECTIVE **1** imagining things **2** imaginary

fancy NOUN **fancies 1** a liking **2** imagination

fancy ADJECTIVE decorated or elaborate; not plain

fancy VERB **fancies, fancied 1** to have a liking or desire for **2** to imagine or believe

fancy dress NOUN unusual costume worn for a party, e.g. to look like a famous person

fanfare NOUN a short piece of loud music played on trumpets

fang NOUN a long sharp tooth

fantasize VERB to imagine something pleasant or strange

⚠ **SPELLING**

This word can also be spelled *fantasise*.

fantastic ADJECTIVE **1** (*informal*) excellent **2** strange or unusual **3** designed in a fanciful way

THESAURUS

familiar ADJECTIVE • *familiar faces* ▸ well-known, recognizable • *a familiar friend* ▸ close, intimate, dear • *a friendly and familiar atmosphere* ▸ informal, casual, relaxed

famous ADJECTIVE • *a famous singer* ▸ well-known, renowned, great, celebrated, acclaimed, admired

fan NOUN • *a fan of rock music* ▸ admirer, lover, fanatic, devotee, enthusiast

fancy ADJECTIVE • *fancy patterns* ▸ elaborate, decorative, ornate

• *fancy clothes* ▸ showy, ostentatious, gaudy

fancy VERB • *I fancied I could see a light.* ▸ imagine, think, believe • *I fancy a doughnut.* ▸ feel like, want, desire • *the boy she had fancied* ▸ like, have a crush on

fantastic ADJECTIVE • *a fantastic time* ▸ wonderful, marvellous, fabulous, splendid, magnificent • *a fantastic story* ▸ extraordinary, incredible, unbelievable

fantasy NOUN **fantasies**
something imaginary or fantastic

far ADVERB **1** at or to a great distance **2** much; by a great amount *far worse*

far ADJECTIVE distant or remote *on the far side*

farce NOUN **1** a comedy based on ridiculous situations **2** an absurd or false situation or series of events ► **farcical** ADJECTIVE

fare NOUN **1** the price charged to make a journey **2** food and drink

fare VERB to make progress

farewell EXCLAMATION, NOUN goodbye

far-fetched ADJECTIVE unlikely, difficult to believe

farm NOUN **1** an area of land for growing crops or keeping animals for food **2** a farmer's house

farm VERB **1** to grow crops or keep animals for food **2** to use land for growing crops

farmer NOUN a person who owns or manages a farm

farrow NOUN a litter of young pigs

farther ADVERB, ADJECTIVE at or to a greater distance; more distant

farthest ADVERB, ADJECTIVE at or to the greatest distance; most distant

farthing NOUN a former British coin worth one-quarter of an old penny

fascinate VERB to be very attractive or interesting to ► **fascination** NOUN

fascism (fash-izm) NOUN an extreme dictatorial form of government ► **fascist** NOUN

fashion NOUN **1** the popular style of clothes or other things **2** a way of doing something

fashion VERB to make in a particular shape or style

fashionable ADJECTIVE following the fashion of the time; popular ► **fashionably** ADVERB

fast¹ ADJECTIVE **1** moving or done quickly; rapid **2** allowing fast movement *a fast road* **3** showing a time later than the correct time *Your watch is fast.* **4** firmly fixed or attached **5** (of colour) not likely to fade

fast ADVERB **1** quickly **2** firmly *stuck fast* **fast asleep** in a deep sleep

THESAURUS

far ADJECTIVE • *far places* ► distant, faraway, remote, foreign

fascinate VERB • *The story fascinated them.* ► interest, intrigue, captivate, enthrall

fascinating ADJECTIVE • *a fascinating book* ► interesting, intriguing, engrossing, captivating, enthralling

fashion NOUN • *the fashion for long dresses* ► trend, vogue, craze

• *behaving in an odd fashion* ► way, manner

fashionable ADJECTIVE • *a fashionable hotel* ► stylish, popular, chic, elegant

fast ADJECTIVE • *a fast car* ► quick, rapid, speedy, swift, high-speed

fast ADVERB • *The train was travelling fast.* ► quickly, rapidly, swiftly, speedily, at full speed

• *stuck fast in the mud* ► tightly,

a
b
c
d
e
f
g
h
i
j
k
l
m
n
o
p
q
r
s
t
u
v
w
x
y
z

fast[2] VERB to go without food
► **fast** NOUN

fasten VERB to fix one thing firmly
to another ► **fastener** NOUN,
fastening NOUN

fast food NOUN hot food that is
quickly prepared and served

fastidious ADJECTIVE **1** fussy and
hard to please **2** very careful about
small details

fat NOUN **1** the white greasy part of
meat **2** oil or grease used in
cooking

fat ADJECTIVE **fatter, fattest**
1 having a thick round body
2 thick *a fat book* **3** full of fat

fatal ADJECTIVE causing death or
disaster ► **fatally** ADVERB

fatality (fa-tal-it-ee) NOUN
fatalities a death caused by an
accident or war

fate NOUN **1** a power that is thought
to make things happen **2** what will
happen or has happened to a
person

fated ADJECTIVE certain to do or
suffer something bad or
unpleasant

fateful ADJECTIVE bringing events
that are important and usually
unpleasant *that fateful day*
► **fatefully** ADVERB

father NOUN **1** a male parent **2** a
priest ► **fatherhood** NOUN

father VERB to be the father of

father-in-law NOUN
fathers-in-law the father of a
married person's husband or wife

fathom NOUN a unit used to
measure the depth of water, equal
to 1.83 metres or 6 feet

fathom VERB **1** to measure the
depth of **2** to work out a problem

fatigue NOUN **1** tiredness
2 weakness in metals

fatten VERB to make or become fat

fatty ADJECTIVE **fattier, fattiest** like
fat; containing fat

fatuous ADJECTIVE silly or foolish
► **fatuously** ADVERB

fault NOUN **1** anything that makes a
person or thing imperfect **2** the

THESAURUS

securely • *fast asleep* ► deeply,
sound, completely

fasten VERB • *a jacket that you*
fasten at the back ► do up, tie,
close, button up • *Brackets are*
fastened to the wall. ► fix, attach,
secure, bolt

fat ADJECTIVE • *a fat person* ► plump,
tubby, large, stout, rotund, portly,
overweight, obese • *a fat book*
► thick, bulky, chunky

fatal ADJECTIVE • *a fatal blow*
► deadly, mortal, lethal • *a fatal*
illness ► deadly, incurable,
terminal • *a fatal mistake*
► disastrous, catastrophic

fate NOUN • *whatever fate has to*
offer ► destiny, luck, chance,
providence • *a terrible fate*
► death, demise, end

fault NOUN • *a fault in the*
manufacturing process ► defect,
problem, weakness, flaw,

a
b
c
d
e
f
g
h
i
j
k
l
m
n
o
p
q
r
s
t
u
v
w
x
y
z

responsibility for something wrong **3** a break in a layer of rock
▶ **faultless** ADJECTIVE

fault VERB to find faults in; to criticize

faulty ADJECTIVE **faultier, faultiest** having a fault or faults

faun NOUN an ancient country god with a goat's legs, horns, and tail

fauna NOUN the animals of a certain area or period of time

favour NOUN **1** a kind or helpful act **2** approval or goodwill **3** friendly support shown to one person or group

favour VERB to like or support

favourable ADJECTIVE **1** helpful or advantageous **2** showing approval
▶ **favourably** ADVERB

favourite ADJECTIVE liked more than others

favourite NOUN a person or thing that is favoured

favouritism NOUN a tendency to be kinder to one person than to others

fawn¹ NOUN **1** a young deer **2** a light-brown colour

fawn² VERB to get someone to like you by flattering them

fax NOUN **1** a machine that sends an exact copy of a document electronically **2** a copy produced by this

fax VERB to send a copy of a document using a fax machine

> ✎ **WORD HISTORY**
>
> a shortening of *facsimile* 'an exact copy'

faze VERB (informal) to make someone feel confused or shocked

fear NOUN a feeling that something unpleasant may happen
▶ **fearless** ADJECTIVE

fear VERB to feel fear; to be afraid

THESAURUS

malfunction, snag • *a fault in their argument* ▶ flaw, error, inaccuracy, mistake • *He has his faults.* ▶ failing, weakness, flaw, defect • *The error was my fault.*
▶ responsibility, mistake, error

faulty ADJECTIVE • *a faulty machine*
▶ broken, defective, malfunctioning, out of order

favour NOUN • *She regards us with great favour.* ▶ approval, goodwill, kindness, friendliness • *Could you do me a favour?*
▶ good turn, kindness, good deed

favour VERB • *I favour casual clothes.* ▶ prefer, like • *The*

government favours a policy of peace. ▶ support, recommend, back, promote

favourite ADJECTIVE • *her favourite nephew* ▶ best-loved, most-liked, preferred, special

fear NOUN • *a feeling of fear*
▶ terror, fright, horror, alarm, panic, dread • *hard to overcome your fears* ▶ anxiety, concern, unease, misgiving

fear VERB • *They all feared him.*
▶ be afraid of, be scared of, be terrified of, dread • *I fear you may be right.* ▶ think, suspect

a b c d e f g h i j k l m n o p q r s t u v w x y z

DICTIONARY

fearful ADJECTIVE **1** feeling fear; afraid **2** causing fear or horror ► **fearfully** ADVERB

fearsome ADJECTIVE frightening

feasible ADJECTIVE able to be done ► **feasibility** NOUN, **feasibly** ADVERB

feast NOUN **1** a large splendid meal **2** a religious festival

feast VERB to have a feast

feat NOUN a brave or clever deed

feather NOUN one of the light coverings that grow from a bird's skin ► **feathery** ADJECTIVE

feather VERB to cover or line with feathers

feature NOUN **1** any part of the face (e.g. the mouth, nose, or eyes) **2** an important or noticeable part **3** a special newspaper article or programme **4** the main film in a cinema programme

feature VERB to make or be a noticeable part of something

February NOUN the second month of the year

fed past tense of **feed**.
fed up (*informal*) unhappy or bored

federal ADJECTIVE of a system in which several states are ruled by a central government but are responsible for their own internal affairs

federation NOUN a group of federal states

fee NOUN a charge for work or a service

feeble ADJECTIVE weak; without strength ► **feebly** ADVERB

feed VERB **fed 1** to give food to a person or animal **2** to eat ► **feeder** NOUN

feed NOUN food for animals or babies

feedback NOUN comments from users of something

feel VERB **felt 1** to touch something to find out what it is like **2** to be aware of **3** to experience **4** to give a certain

THESAURUS

feasible ADJECTIVE • *a feasible plan* ► possible, practical, workable, achievable, viable

feast NOUN • *a feast fit for a king* ► meal, banquet

feat NOUN • *a feat of great daring* ► act, deed, exploit

feature NOUN • *some notable features* ► characteristic, detail, quality, aspect, trait • *a magazine feature* ► article, report, story, item, piece **features** • *her fine features* ► face, countenance, expression

fed up ADJECTIVE • *feeling tired and fed up* ► depressed, dejected,

despondent, miserable, down **be fed up with** • *I was fed up with all the whinging.* ► be sick of, be tired of, be bored with

feeble ADJECTIVE • *feeble attempts to protest* ► weak, ineffective • *too feeble to stand up* ► weak, frail, delicate, sickly • *a feeble character* ► weak, spineless, timid

feed VERB • *a large family to feed* ► nourish, give food to, provide for, cater for • *They spend all their time consuming and sleeping.* ► eat, consume, take food

feel VERB • *He felt the back of his head.* ► touch, stroke, handle

DICTIONARY

sensation *feels warm* **feel like** to want

feel NOUN the sensation caused by feeling something

feeler NOUN 1 a long thin projection on an insect's or crustacean's body; an antenna 2 a cautious question or suggestion

feeling NOUN 1 the ability to feel things; the sense of touch 2 an emotion 3 a thought or opinion

feign (fayn) VERB to pretend

feint (faynt) NOUN a pretended attack or punch

feint VERB to make a feint

> ⚠ **USAGE**
>
> Do not confuse this word with *faint*.

feisty ADJECTIVE **feistier**, **feistiest** lively and rather aggressive

> 🔖 **WORD HISTORY**
>
> from an old word *feist* 'an old dog'

feline ADJECTIVE to do with cats

fell [1] *past tense of* **fall**

fell [2] VERB to cut or knock down

fell [3] NOUN a piece of wild hilly country

fellow NOUN 1 a friend or companion 2 a man or boy 3 a member of a learned society

fellow ADJECTIVE of the same group or kind *fellow teachers*

fellowship NOUN 1 friendship 2 a group of friends

felony (fel-on-ee) NOUN **felonies** a serious crime

felt [1] *past tense of* **feel**

felt [2] NOUN a thick fabric made of fibres of wool or fur

female ADJECTIVE of the sex that can bear offspring or produce eggs or fruit

female NOUN a female person, animal, or plant

feminine ADJECTIVE 1 to do with or like women 2 (in some languages) belonging to the class of words which includes words referring to women ▸ **femininity** NOUN

feminist NOUN a person who believes that women should have

THESAURUS

• *She felt a gun in her side.*
▸ sense, notice, perceive, be aware of • *to feel pain*
▸ experience, suffer, go through • *We feel you should apologize.*
▸ believe, think, consider **feel like**
• *I feel like a drink.* ▸ want, fancy

feel NOUN • *a warm feel* ▸ texture, touch • *a good feel for the music*
▸ aptitude, flair, talent

feeling NOUN • *the feeling of power* ▸ sensation, sense,

awareness • *I had a feeling she wouldn't be coming.* ▸ idea, suspicion, inkling, notion • *a friendly feeling* ▸ atmosphere, ambience, climate • *to speak with feeling* ▸ emotion, passion, tenderness, warmth • *to lose feeling in your arm* ▸ sensation, sense of touch

fell VERB • *Dead trees have to be felled quickly.* ▸ chop down, cut down

DICTIONARY

the same rights and status as men ► **feminism** NOUN

fen NOUN an area of low-lying wet ground

fence NOUN 1 a flat upright barrier round an area 2 a structure for a horse to jump over

fence VERB 1 to put a fence round 2 to fight with swords as a sport ► **fencer** NOUN

fend VERB **fend for yourself** to take care of yourself **fend off** to keep a person or thing away

fender NOUN a low barrier round a fireplace

fennel NOUN a herb with yellow flowers

ferment (fer-ment) VERB to bubble and change chemically, e.g. by the action of yeast ► **fermentation** NOUN

⚠️ **USAGE**

Do not confuse this word with *foment*.

ferment (fer-ment) NOUN an excited or agitated condition

fern NOUN a plant with feathery leaves and no flowers

ferocious ADJECTIVE fierce or savage ► **ferociously** ADVERB, **ferocity** NOUN

ferret NOUN a small weasel-like animal

ferret VERB to search for something in small spaces

ferry NOUN **ferries** a ship used for transporting people or things across water

ferry VERB **ferries**, **ferried** to transport across water

fertile ADJECTIVE 1 (of soil) producing good crops 2 able to produce offspring 3 able to produce ideas *a fertile imagination* ► **fertility** NOUN

fertilize VERB 1 to add substances to the soil to make it more fertile 2 to put pollen into a plant or sperm into an egg or female animal so that it develops seed or young ► **fertilization** NOUN

⚠️ **SPELLING**

This word can also be spelled *fertilise*.

fertilizer NOUN chemicals or manure added to the soil to make it more fertile

fervent ADJECTIVE showing warm or strong feeling

fester VERB 1 to become septic and filled with pus 2 to cause resentment

festival NOUN 1 a time of religious celebration 2 an organized series of concerts, films, performances, etc.

festive ADJECTIVE 1 to do with a festival 2 joyful

festivity NOUN **festivities** a festive occasion or celebration

THESAURUS

ferocious ADJECTIVE • *a ferocious attack* ► fierce, savage, brutal, violent, vicious

fertile ADJECTIVE • *fertile soil* ► fruitful, productive, rich • *a*

fertile mind ► imaginative, inventive, creative

festival NOUN • *a music festival* ► celebration, carnival, pageant

DICTIONARY

fetch VERB **1** to go for and bring back **2** to be sold for a particular price

fete (fayt) NOUN an outdoor entertainment with stalls and sideshows

fete VERB to honour with celebrations

fetus (fee-tuhs) NOUN a developing embryo; an unborn baby ► **fetal** ADJECTIVE

feud (fewd) NOUN a long-lasting quarrel

feudal (few-duhl) ADJECTIVE to do with the system used in the Middle Ages in which people could farm land in exchange for work done for the owner ► **feudalism** NOUN

fever NOUN **1** a high body temperature, with an illness **2** excitement or agitation ► **feverish** ADJECTIVE

few ADJECTIVE not many

few NOUN a small number of people or things

fiancé or **fiancée** (fee-ahn-say) NOUN a man or woman who is engaged to be married

fiasco (fee-as-koh) NOUN **fiascos** a complete failure

fib NOUN a lie about something unimportant

fib VERB **fibbing, fibbed** to lie about something trivial

fibre NOUN **1** a fine thread **2** a substance made of thin threads **3** material in food that stimulates the action of the intestines

fibreglass NOUN **1** fabric made from glass fibres **2** plastic containing glass fibres

fickle ADJECTIVE constantly changing; not loyal

fiction NOUN stories about made-up events ► **fictional** ADJECTIVE

fictitious ADJECTIVE imagined or untrue

fiddle VERB **1** to play the violin **2** to tinker with something **3** (informal) to alter accounts dishonestly ► **fiddler** NOUN

fiddle NOUN **1** a violin **2** (informal) a swindle or deception

fiddly ADJECTIVE **fiddlier, fiddliest** small and awkward to use or do

THESAURUS

fetch VERB • *She went to fetch a bucket.* ► get, fetch, collect, pick up, obtain • *Will you fetch me from the station?* ► collect, pick up, transport, bring, get • *to fetch a doctor* ► send for, call for, summon • *The house might fetch a million.* ► sell for, be sold for, raise, make

feud NOUN • *a family feud* ► dispute, conflict, vendetta

few ADJECTIVE • *Few details are available.* ► not many, hardly any,

a small number of • *Buses are few at this time of night.* ► scarce, scant, in short supply

few PRONOUN • *I only have a few left.* ► small number, handful, couple

fickle ADJECTIVE • *fickle friends* ► changeable, unfaithful, unreliable

fiddle VERB • *to fiddle the accounts* ► alter, falsify, tamper with

fiddle with • *fiddling with the controls* ► play about with, tinker with, tamper with

a b c d e f g h i j k l m n o p q r s t u v w x y z

DICTIONARY

fidelity NOUN **1** faithfulness or loyalty **2** accuracy, especially of sound reproduction

fidget VERB to make small restless movements ▶ **fidgety** ADJECTIVE

fidget NOUN a person who fidgets

field NOUN **1** a piece of land with grass or crops **2** an area of interest or study

field VERB **1** to stop or catch the ball in cricket or other ball games **2** to deal with a difficult question effectively

field marshal NOUN an army officer of the highest rank

fieldwork NOUN practical work or research

fiend (feend) NOUN **1** an evil spirit; a devil **2** a wicked or cruel person **3** an enthusiast *a fresh-air fiend*

fiendish ADJECTIVE **1** very wicked or cruel **2** extremely difficult

fierce ADJECTIVE **fiercer**, **fiercest** **1** angry and violent or cruel **2** intense *fierce heat*

fiery ADJECTIVE **1** full of flames or heat **2** full of emotion **3** easily made angry

fife NOUN a small shrill flute

fifteen NOUN, ADJECTIVE **1** the number 15 **2** a team in rugby union football ▶ **fifteenth** ADJECTIVE, NOUN

fifth ADJECTIVE, NOUN next after the fourth ▶ **fifthly** ADVERB

fifty NOUN, ADJECTIVE **fifties** the number 50 ▶ **fiftieth** ADJECTIVE & NOUN

fifty-fifty ADJECTIVE, ADVERB **1** shared equally between two **2** evenly balanced *a fifty-fifty chance*

fig NOUN a soft fruit full of small seeds

fight NOUN **1** a struggle against somebody using hands or weapons **2** an attempt to achieve or overcome something *the fight against poverty*

fight VERB **fought** **1** to have a fight **2** to attempt to overcome a difficulty ▶ **fighter** NOUN

figment NOUN something imagined *a figment of the imagination*

THESAURUS

fidget VERB • *The heat made me fidget.* ▶ wriggle, twitch, jiggle, shuffle about

fierce ADJECTIVE • *a fierce dog* ▶ ferocious, vicious, savage, wild • *fierce competition* ▶ strong, intense, keen • *fierce resentment* ▶ passionate, intense, strong, powerful • *a fierce pain* ▶ acute, severe, intense

fight NOUN • *to get into a fight* ▶ brawl, fracas, tussle, struggle • *fights with her boyfriend*

▶ argument, quarrel, row, squabble, difference of opinion • *the fight for women's rights* ▶ struggle, battle, campaign • *a championship fight* ▶ contest, match

fight VERB • *Some men were fighting in the street.* ▶ brawl, tussle, struggle, grapple, wrestle • *Her sons all fought in the war.* ▶ serve, be a soldier, take up arms • *We are always fighting.* ▶ argue, quarrel, row, squabble • *to fight proposals to cut jobs* ▶ oppose,

a
b
c
d
e
f
g
h
i
j
k
l
m
n
o
p
q
r
s
t
u
v
w
x
y
z

figurative ADJECTIVE using a figure of speech; metaphorical, not literal

figure NOUN **1** the symbol of a number **2** an amount or value **3** a diagram or illustration **4** a shape **5** the shape of a person's body **6** a person **7** a representation of a person or animal in painting etc.

figure VERB to appear or take part in something **figure out** to work something out

figurehead NOUN an important person with no real power

figure of speech NOUN **figures of speech** a word or phrase used for special effect, e.g. *a flood of letters*

filament NOUN a thin wire in a light bulb, which gives out light

filch VERB (*informal*) to steal in a sly way

file¹ NOUN a metal tool with a rough surface, rubbed on wood or metal to shape or smooth it

file VERB to shape or smooth with a file

file² NOUN **1** a folder or box for keeping papers in order **2** a collection of data stored under

one name in a computer **3** a line of people one behind the other

file VERB **1** to put into a file **2** to walk in a file

fill VERB **1** to make or become full **2** to block up a hole or cavity **3** to do the work involved in a job

fillet NOUN a piece of fish or meat without bones

fillet VERB to remove the bones from fish or meat

filling NOUN **1** something used to fill a hole or gap **2** something put in a pie or sandwich

filling station NOUN a place where petrol is sold from pumps

filly NOUN **fillies** a young female horse

film NOUN **1** a motion picture shown in cinemas or on television **2** a strip of thin plastic coated with material that is sensitive to light, used for taking photographs **3** a thin layer of grease

film VERB to record on film

filter NOUN a device for holding back dirt or other unwanted material from a liquid or gas etc. that passes through it

resist, combat • *to fight for basic rights* ► campaign, battle

figure NOUN • *The figure was higher than last year.* ► number, total, sum, amount • *The third figure is an eight.* ► digit, numeral, number • *an exact figure* ► amount, price, sum • *a lovely figure* ► shape, physique, build, body • *a public figure* ► personality, character, celebrity

fill VERB • *to fill a suitcase* ► pack, load • *Fill the holes and gaps.* ► plug, stop, block up, seal • *to fill the room* ► crowd, pack • *to fill new posts* ► take up, occupy, be appointed to **fill in** • *to fill in a form* ► complete

film NOUN • *going to see a film* ► movie, picture, feature • *a film of dust* ► layer, covering, coating

filter VERB to pass through a filter

filth NOUN disgusting dirt

filthy ADJECTIVE **filthier, filthiest**
1 disgustingly dirty **2** obscene or offensive

fin NOUN **1** a thin flat part on the body of a fish **2** a flat piece on an aircraft or rocket

final ADJECTIVE **1** last **2** not allowing disagreement ▶ **finally** ADVERB

final NOUN the last in a series of contests

finale (fin-ah-lee) NOUN the last section of a piece of music

finalist NOUN a competitor in a final

finalize VERB to put into a final form

⚠ **SPELLING**

This word can also be spelled *finalise*.

finance NOUN **1** the use of money **2** money paying for something

finances PLURAL NOUN money resources; funds

finance VERB to provide the money for ▶ **financier** NOUN

financial ADJECTIVE to do with finance ▶ **financially** ADVERB

finch NOUN a small bird with a short bill

find VERB **found 1** to get or see by looking or by chance **2** to learn by experience *He found that it was hard work.* **3** to decide and give a verdict *The jury found him guilty.*
find out to get or discover information

find NOUN something useful that has been found

findings PLURAL NOUN conclusions from an investigation

fine¹ ADJECTIVE **1** of high quality; excellent **2** (of weather) dry and sunny **3** very thin; consisting of small particles **4** in good health
▶ **finely** ADVERB

THESAURUS

filth NOUN • *the filth on the floor*
▶ dirt, muck, grime, mud

filthy ADJECTIVE • *The house was filthy.* ▶ dirty, grubby, mucky, uncleaned, unwashed • *a filthy trick* ▶ nasty, mean, vile, despicable • *in a filthy mood*
▶ bad, foul, bad-tempered

final ADJECTIVE • *the final month of their course* ▶ last, closing, concluding • *the final minutes of the match* ▶ last, closing, dying
• *The judges' decision is final.*
▶ definite, absolute, indisputable, irrevocable

finally ADVERB • *He finally agreed.*
▶ eventually, ultimately, at last

financial ADJECTIVE • *financial affairs* ▶ monetary, economic

find VERB • *I have found my watch.*
▶ discover, come across, chance on, locate, retrieve, track down
• *You may find this strange.*
▶ think, consider, believe • *You will find that it's better to be honest.* ▶ discover, learn, realize
• *to find success* ▶ achieve, attain, win, get **find out** • *to find out what happened* ▶ learn, discover

fine ADJECTIVE • *a fine achievement*
▶ good, great, excellent,

a
b
c
d
e
f
g
h
i
j
k
l
m
n
o
p
q
r
s
t
u
v
w
x
y
z

DICTIONARY

fine² NOUN money which has to be paid as a punishment

fine VERB to impose a fine on

fine arts PLURAL NOUN painting, sculpture, and music

finery NOUN fine clothes or decorations

finesse (fin-ess) NOUN skill and elegance in doing something

finger NOUN 1 each of the separate parts of the hand 2 a narrow piece of something

finger VERB to touch or feel with your fingers

fingerprint NOUN a mark made by the tiny ridges on the fingertip, used as a means of identification

finicky ADJECTIVE fussy about details

finish VERB to bring or come to an end

finish NOUN 1 the last stage of something 2 the surface or coating on a surface

finite (fy-nyt) ADJECTIVE limited in amount or size

fir NOUN an evergreen tree that produces cones

fire NOUN 1 the process of burning that produces light and heat 2 material burning to give heat 3 a

device using electricity or gas to heat a room 4 the shooting of guns *Hold your fire!*

fire VERB 1 to set fire to 2 to bake pottery or bricks in a kiln 3 to shoot a gun or missile 4 to dismiss from a job 5 to excite

firearm NOUN a small gun or pistol

fire brigade NOUN a team of firefighters

fire drill NOUN a rehearsal of the procedure that needs to be followed in case of a fire

fire engine NOUN a large vehicle that carries firefighters and equipment to put out large fires

firefighter NOUN a person trained to put out fires

firefly NOUN **fireflies** a kind of beetle that gives off a glowing light

fireman NOUN **firemen** a male firefighter

fireplace NOUN an open structure for holding a fire in a room

firework NOUN a device containing chemicals that shoot out coloured patterns when lit

firing squad NOUN a group of soldiers ordered to shoot a condemned person

THESAURUS

outstanding, remarkable • *a fine day* ▶ bright, fair, dry, clear, sunny • *a pen with a fine tip* ▶ thin, narrow • *fine clothes* ▶ elegant, stylish, smart, chic, fashionable • *a fine adjustment* ▶ small, minor • *It's fine to write to me here.* ▶ all right, acceptable

finish NOUN • *an exciting finish* ▶ ending, close, completiion

finish VERB • *to finish the work* ▶ complete, end, finalize • *The film finishes at ten.* ▶ end, stop, conclude • *We've finished the biscuits.* ▶ use up, eat, consume, exhaust

firm NOUN a business organization

firm ADJECTIVE **1** not giving way when pressed **2** steady; not shaking or moving **3** definite and not changing *a firm belief*
► **firmly** ADVERB

first ADJECTIVE coming before all others in time or order ► **firstly** ADVERB

first ADVERB before everything else *Finish this first.*

first NOUN a person or thing that is first

first aid NOUN treatment given to an injured person

first-class ADJECTIVE **1** using the best class of a service **2** excellent

first-hand ADJECTIVE, ADVERB obtained directly *first-hand experience*

fish NOUN **fish** or **fishes** an animal that lives in water and breathes through gills

fish VERB to try to catch fish

fisherman NOUN **fishermen** a person who tries to catch fish

fishmonger NOUN a shopkeeper who sells fish

fishy ADJECTIVE **fishier**, **fishiest**
1 smelling or tasting of fish
2 (*informal*) doubtful or suspicious

fission NOUN the splitting of the nucleus of an atom to release energy

fissure (fish-er) NOUN a narrow opening or crack

fist NOUN a tightly closed hand

fit¹ ADJECTIVE **fitter**, **fittest**
1 suitable or good enough *a meal fit for a king* **2** in good physical condition **3** ready or likely *fit to collapse* ► **fitness** NOUN

fit VERB **1** to be the right size and shape **2** to put into place *to fit a lock* **3** to alter or make suitable

fit NOUN the way something fits *a good fit*

fit² NOUN an attack of an illness, laughter, etc.

fitful ADJECTIVE happening in short periods, not steadily ► **fitfully** ADVERB

firm ADJECTIVE • *firm ground* ► hard, solid, unyielding, compact • *firm foundations* ► secure, steady, strong, stable • *firm action* ► strong, determined, resolute • *a firm commitment* ► definite, agreed, settled • *a firm friend* ► loyal, faithful, devoted

first ADJECTIVE • *the first attempt* ► initial, opening, preliminary • *the first inhabitants* ► original, earliest, oldest • *the first consideration* ► main, principal, prime, key, foremost

fit ADJECTIVE • *She looked remarkably fit.* ► healthy, well, able-bodied, in good form • *vehicles fit for commercial use* ► suitable, appropriate, equipped, ready • *fit to be a parent* ► able, competent, qualified, worthy

fit VERB • *to fit all the pieces together* ► join, match, arrange, assemble • *Make the punishment fit the crime.* ► match, suit, be appropriate to

a
b
c
d
e
f
g
h
i
j
k
l
m
n
o
p
q
r
s
t
u
v
w
x
y
z

DICTIONARY

fitting ADJECTIVE proper or suitable

fitting NOUN something fixed or fitted

five NOUN, ADJECTIVE the number 5

fix VERB 1 to fasten or place firmly 2 to make permanent 3 to decide or arrange *fix a date for the party* 4 to repair

fix NOUN (informal) an awkward situation

fixation NOUN a strong interest or a concentration on one idea

fixture NOUN 1 something fixed in its place 2 a sports event arranged for a particular day

fizz VERB to make a hissing sound

fizzle VERB to make a slight fizzing sound

fizzy ADJECTIVE **fizzier, fizziest** (of a drink) having a lot of small bubbles

flabbergasted ADJECTIVE very surprised

flabby ADJECTIVE **flabbier, flabbiest** fat and soft, not firm ▸ **flabbiness** NOUN

flag NOUN 1 a piece of cloth with a distinctive pattern on it, used as

the symbol of a country or organization 2 a slab of stone

flag VERB **flagging, flagged** 1 to become tired or weak 2 to signal with a flag or by waving

flagon NOUN a large bottle or container for wine or cider

flagrant (flay-gruhnt) ADJECTIVE very bad and noticeable *flagrant rudeness*

flagship NOUN a ship that carries an admiral

flair NOUN a natural ability or talent *a flair for languages*

⚠ USAGE

Do not confuse this word with **flare**.

flak NOUN 1 shells fired by anti-aircraft guns 2 strong criticism

flake NOUN 1 a very light thin piece of something 2 a small flat piece of falling snow ▸ **flaky** ADJECTIVE

flake VERB come off in flakes

flamboyant ADJECTIVE very showy in appearance or manner

flame NOUN a tongue-shaped portion of fire or burning gas

THESAURUS

fix VERB • *to fix a notice* ▸ fasten, tie, pin, attach • *to fix posts into the ground* ▸ place, position, set, embed • *I can fix it for you.* ▸ arrange, organize • *to fix a date* ▸ set, decide on, agree on, arrange • *The television needs to be fixed.* ▸ mend, repair, put right

fizz VERB • *The water fizzed.* ▸ bubble, foam, froth, effervesce

fizzy ADJECTIVE • *fizzy drinks* ▸ sparkling, bubbly, carbonated, effervescent

flabby ADJECTIVE • *soft and flabby* ▸ loose, floppy, slack, limp

flair NOUN • *a flair for languages* ▸ talent, aptitude, gift • *She dresses with great flair.* ▸ style, elegance, taste

flamboyant ADJECTIVE • *his flamboyant appearance* ▸ colourful, showy, ostentatious

flame

DICTIONARY

flame *VERB* to produce flames

flamenco *NOUN* a lively Spanish style of guitar playing and dance

flamingo *NOUN* **flamingos** a wading bird with long legs and pale pink feathers

flammable *ADJECTIVE* able to be set on fire

flan *NOUN* a tart open on top

flank *NOUN* the side of an animal's body or an army

flannel *NOUN* **1** a soft cloth for washing **2** a soft woollen material

flap *VERB* **flapping, flapped 1** to wave about **2** (*informal*) to fuss or panic

flap *NOUN* **1** a covering part that is fixed at one edge **2** the action or sound of flapping **3** (*informal*) a fuss or panic

flare 1 to blaze with a sudden bright flame **2** to become angry suddenly **3** to become gradually wider

flare *NOUN* **1** a sudden bright flame or light, especially one used as a signal **2** a gradual widening

⚠ USAGE
Do not confuse this word with **flair**.

flash *NOUN* **1** a sudden bright flame or light **2** a device for making a sudden bright light for taking photographs **3** a sudden display of anger, wit, etc.

flash *VERB* **1** to make a flash **2** to appear or move quickly

flashback *NOUN* a scene in a film or story that goes back to earlier events

flashy *ADJECTIVE* **flashier, flashiest** gaudy or showy

flask *NOUN* **1** a bottle with a narrow neck **2** a container for keeping drinks hot

flat *ADJECTIVE* **flatter, flattest**
1 having no curves or bumps; smooth and level **2** lying at full length *flat on the ground* **3** (of a tyre) having no air inside **4** (of the feet) without the normal arch underneath **5** complete *a flat refusal* **6** dull; not changing **7** (of a drink) no longer fizzy **8** (of a battery) unable to produce any more electric current **9** (*Music*) one semitone lower than the natural note **flat out** as fast as possible

THESAURUS

flap *VERB* • *to flap in the wind*
▸ flutter, sway, swing, wave • *to flap its wings* ▸ beat, flutter

flash *VERB* • *Lights flashed.*
▸ shine, blaze, gleam, glint, sparkle

flash *NOUN* • *a flash of light*
▸ blaze, burst, gleam, glint, flicker
• *a flash of inspiration* ▸ burst, rush

flat *ADJECTIVE* • *a flat surface* ▸ level, smooth, even, horizontal • *She lay flat on the bed.* ▸ outstretched, prostrate, spread out • *a flat sea* ▸ calm, still, smooth, waveless
• *His voice was flat and lifeless.*
▸ dull, boring, monotonous, tedious, unexpressive • *a flat refusal* ▸ direct, outright

DICTIONARY

flat NOUN **1** a set of rooms on one floor for living in **2** a punctured tyre

flatten VERB to make or become flat

flatter VERB **1** to praise someone insincerely **2** to make a person or thing seem more attractive than they really are ► **flattery** NOUN

flaunt VERB to display in a showy way

⚠️ **USAGE**

Do not confuse this word with *flout*.

flavour NOUN **1** the taste of something **2** a characteristic quality

flavour VERB to give a flavour to ► **flavouring** NOUN

flaw NOUN a fault or imperfection ► **flawed** ADJECTIVE

flawless ADJECTIVE without a flaw; perfect

flax NOUN a plant producing fibres from which linen is made

flay VERB to strip the skin from a dead animal

flea NOUN a small jumping insect that sucks blood

fleck NOUN **1** a small patch of colour **2** a particle or speck ► **flecked** ADJECTIVE

fledgling NOUN a young bird when its feathers have grown

flee VERB **fled** to run or hurry away

fleece NOUN **1** the woolly hair of a sheep or similar animal **2** a soft warm article of clothing ► **fleecy** ADJECTIVE

fleet NOUN a number of ships, aircraft, or vehicles

fleeting ADJECTIVE passing quickly

flesh NOUN **1** the soft substance of the bodies of people and animals **2** the body as opposed to the mind or soul **3** the soft part of fruit ► **fleshy** ADJECTIVE

flex VERB to bend or stretch

flex NOUN flexible insulated wire for carrying electric current

flexible ADJECTIVE **1** easy to bend or stretch **2** able to be changed ► **flexibility** NOUN

THESAURUS

flat NOUN • *They live in a small flat.* ► apartment, maisonette

flatter VERB • *He enjoyed flattering her.* ► praise, compliment

flavour NOUN • *a spicy flavour* ► taste, tang, savour • *a story with an oriental flavour* ► character, feel, mood

flavour VERB • *to flavour food* ► season, spice

flaw NOUN • *a flaw in their reasoning* ► defect, fault, imperfection, weakness

flee VERB • *She had to flee to her room.* ► run away, bolt, fly, escape

fleet NOUN • *a fleet of ships* ► flotilla, armada, convoy, navy

flexible ADJECTIVE • *a flexible rod* ► bendable, pliable • *flexible working hours* ► adaptable, adjustable, variable

flick NOUN a quick light hit or movement

flick VERB to hit or move with a flick

flicker VERB 1 to burn or shine unsteadily 2 to move quickly to and fro

flicker NOUN a flickering light or movement

flight NOUN 1 the act of flying 2 a journey in an aircraft 3 an escape 4 a series of stairs or steps 5 a group of flying birds or aircraft

flighty ADJECTIVE **flightier**, **flightiest** silly and frivolous

flimsy ADJECTIVE **flimsier**, **flimsiest** thin and weak

flinch VERB to move or shrink back from fear or pain

fling VERB **flung** to throw hard or carelessly

fling NOUN 1 a brief time of enjoyment 2 a brief romantic affair 3 a vigorous dance

flint NOUN a hard kind of stone

flip VERB **flipping**, **flipped** 1 to flick 2 (*informal*) to lose your temper

flip NOUN a flipping movement

flippant ADJECTIVE not showing proper seriousness ▶ **flippancy** NOUN

flipper NOUN 1 a limb that some water-living animals use for swimming 2 a flat rubber shoe worn for swimming

flirt VERB to behave as though sexually attracted to someone to amuse yourself ▶ **flirtation** NOUN

flirt NOUN a person who flirts ▶ **flirtatious** ADJECTIVE

flit VERB **flitting**, **flitted** to fly or move lightly and quickly ▶ **flit** NOUN

flitter VERB to flit about

float VERB 1 to stay on the surface of a liquid or in air 2 to make something float

float NOUN 1 a device that floats 2 a display vehicle in a procession

flock[1] NOUN a group of sheep, goats, or birds

flock VERB to gather or move in a crowd

flock[2] NOUN a tuft of wool or cotton

floe NOUN a sheet of floating ice

flick NOUN • *a flick of the head* ▶ jerk, toss, flip • *a few flicks with a duster* ▶ touch, brush, stroke

flight NOUN • *a short history of flight* ▶ flying, aviation, air travel • *the flight of a missile* ▶ path, trajectory • *the king's flight to safety* ▶ escape, retreat, fleeing

flimsy ADJECTIVE • *a flimsy barrier* ▶ fragile, rickety, shaky, weak • *a flimsy excuse* ▶ feeble, weak, poor, unconvincing

flinch VERB • *to flinch in fear* ▶ wince, recoil, shrink back

fling VERB • *He flung the gun into the river.* ▶ throw, hurl, toss, sling

float VERB • *boats floating on the water* ▶ sail, bob, drift • *A cloud floated across the sky.* ▶ drift, glide, hover, slide

flock VERB • *People flocked from all quarters.* ▶ gather, assemble, crowd, jostle

a
b
c
d
e
f
g
h
i
j
k
l
m
n
o
p
q
r
s
t
u
v
w
x
y
z

flog VERB **flogging, flogged 1** to beat or whip **2** (*informal*) to sell

flood NOUN **1** a large amount of water spreading over a place **2** a huge amount

flood VERB **1** to cover with a flood **2** to come in great amounts

floodlight NOUN a lamp with a broad bright beam to light up a building or public place ▶ **floodlit** ADJECTIVE

floor NOUN **1** the part of a room that people walk on **2** a storey of a building; all the rooms at the same level

floor VERB **1** to put a floor into a building **2** (*informal*) to knock someone down **3** (*informal*) to baffle someone

floorboard NOUN one of the boards forming the floor of a room

flop VERB **flopping, flopped 1** to fall or sit down clumsily **2** to hang or sway heavily and loosely **3** (*informal*) to fail

flop NOUN **1** a flopping movement or sound **2** (*informal*) a failure

floppy ADJECTIVE **floppier, floppiest** hanging loosely; not firm or rigid ▶ **floppiness** NOUN

floppy disk NOUN (*ICT*) a flexible disc holding data for use in a computer

flora NOUN the plants of a particular area or period

floral ADJECTIVE made with flowers

florid (flo-rid) ADJECTIVE **1** red and flushed **2** elaborate and ornate

florist NOUN a seller of flowers

floss NOUN **1** silky thread or fibres **2** a soft medicated thread pulled between the teeth to clean them

flotilla NOUN a fleet of boats or small ships

flotsam NOUN objects found floating after a shipwreck

flounce¹ VERB to move in an impatient or annoyed manner ▶ **flounce** NOUN

flounce² NOUN a wide frill

flounder VERB **1** to move clumsily **2** to make mistakes

flour NOUN a fine powder of wheat or other grain, used in cooking ▶ **floury** ADJECTIVE

flourish VERB **1** to grow or develop strongly **2** to be successful **3** to wave about dramatically

THESAURUS

flood NOUN • *The flood cut off the village.* ▶ inundation, deluge • *a flood of protests* ▶ succession, torrent, barrage, storm

flood VERB • *The dam burst, flooding the town.* ▶ inundate, swamp, submerge, engulf • *Light flooded the room.* ▶ fill, swamp • *People flooded into the building.* ▶ pour, stream, swarm, crowd, flock

flop NOUN • *The show was a flop.* ▶ failure, disaster, fiasco

floppy ADJECTIVE • *a large floppy hat* ▶ limp, droopy, dangling, sagging

flounder VERB • *to flounder in swampy ground* ▶ struggle, falter, wallow, stumble

flourish VERB • *Plants flourish in this soil.* ▶ thrive, prosper, bloom,

flourish NOUN a showy or dramatic sweeping movement or stroke

flout VERB to disobey a rule or instruction openly

⚠ USAGE
Do not confuse this word with *flaunt*.

flow VERB 1 to move along smoothly or continuously 2 to gush out 3 to hang loosely *flowing hair* 4 (of the tide) to come in towards the land

flow NOUN 1 a flowing movement or mass 2 a steady continuous stream *a flow of ideas* 3 the movement of the tide when it is coming in

flower NOUN 1 the part of a plant from which seed and fruit develop 2 a blossom and its stem ▶ **flowery** ADJECTIVE

flower VERB to produce flowers

flu NOUN influenza

fluctuate VERB to rise and fall ▶ **fluctuation** NOUN

flue NOUN a pipe or tube through which smoke or hot gases are drawn off

fluent (floo-ent) ADJECTIVE 1 skilful at speaking clearly 2 able to speak a foreign language well ▶ **fluency** NOUN

fluff NOUN a fluffy substance

fluff VERB (*informal*) to make a small mistake

fluffy ADJECTIVE **fluffier, fluffiest** having a mass of soft fur or fibres

fluid NOUN a substance able to flow freely as liquids and gases do

fluid ADJECTIVE 1 able to flow freely 2 not fixed or definite ▶ **fluidity** NOUN

fluke NOUN a success achieved by luck

flummox VERB (*informal*) to baffle

fluorescent ADJECTIVE creating light from radiation ▶ **fluorescence** NOUN

fluoridation NOUN the process of adding fluoride to drinking water

fluoride NOUN a chemical substance that is thought to prevent tooth decay

flurry NOUN **flurries** 1 a sudden whirling gust of wind, rain, or snow 2 a short period of activity or excitement

THESAURUS

succeed • *She flourished an umbrella.* ▶ wave, brandish, wield

flout VERB • *to flout the law* ▶ disobey, defy, break

flow VERB • *to flow through pipes* ▶ run, stream, trickle, ooze, spurt, gush

flow NOUN • *the flow of blood to the brain* ▶ movement, circulation, stream, motion, current

fluffy ADJECTIVE • *a big fluffy towel* ▶ furry, woolly, fleecy, velvety, soft

fluke NOUN • *a lucky fluke* ▶ chance, piece of luck

flush¹ VERB **1** to blush **2** to clean or remove with a fast flow of water

flush NOUN **1** a blush **2** a fast flow of water **3** (in card games) a hand of cards of the same suit

flush² ADJECTIVE **1** level with the surrounding surface **2** having plenty of money

fluster VERB to make nervous and confused ► **fluster** NOUN

flute NOUN a musical instrument consisting of a long pipe held across the mouth, with holes stopped by fingers or keys

flutter VERB **1** to flap the wings quickly **2** to move or flap quickly and irregularly

flutter NOUN a fluttering state or movement

flux NOUN constant change or flow

fly¹ NOUN **flies 1** a small flying insect **2** an artificial fly used as bait in fishing **3** the front opening of a pair of trousers

fly² VERB **flies, flew, flown 1** to move through the air with wings or in an aircraft **2** (of a flag) to wave in the air **3** to move or pass quickly **4** to flee from a place ► **flyer** NOUN

flyover NOUN a bridge carrying one road or railway over another

flywheel NOUN a heavy wheel used to regulate machinery

foal NOUN a young horse

foam NOUN **1** a white mass of tiny bubbles on liquid **2** a spongy kind of rubber or plastic ► **foamy** ADJECTIVE

foam VERB to form bubbles

fob¹ NOUN **1** a chain for a pocket watch **2** a tab on a key ring

fob² VERB **fobbing, fobbed
fob off** to get rid of someone with an excuse

focal ADJECTIVE to do with or at a focus

focus NOUN **1** the distance from an eye or lens at which an object appears clearest **2** the point at which rays seem to meet **3** something that is a centre of interest or attention

focus VERB **1** to adjust the focus of **2** to concentrate

fodder NOUN food for horses and farm animals

foe NOUN (literary) an enemy

fog NOUN thick mist ► **foggy** ADJECTIVE

fogy NOUN **fogies** a person with old-fashioned ideas

foible NOUN a slight peculiarity in someone's character

flush VERB • to flush with embarrassment ► blush, go red, redden, colour, glow • to flush impurities from the body ► cleanse, rinse out, wash out, swill

fly VERB • A flock of birds flew past. ► glide, flit, flutter, hover, soar • A gull flew into the air. ► rise, soar, ascend • to fly aircraft ► pilot, operate • A flag was flying. ► flutter, flap, wave

DICTIONARY

foil¹ NOUN **1** a thin sheet of metal **2** a person or thing that makes another look better in contrast

foil² NOUN a long narrow sword used in fencing

foil³ VERB to prevent from being successful

foist VERB to make a person accept something inferior or unwelcome

fold¹ VERB to bend or turn so that one part lies on another part

fold¹ NOUN a line where something is folded

fold² NOUN an enclosure for sheep

folder NOUN a folding cover for loose papers

foliage NOUN the leaves of a tree or plant

folk PLURAL NOUN people

folklore NOUN old beliefs and legends

follow VERB **1** to go or come after **2** to do a thing after something else **3** to take as a guide or

example **4** to take an interest in the progress of **5** to understand **6** to result from

follower NOUN a supporter or disciple

folly NOUN **follies 1** foolishness **2** a foolish action

foment (fo-ment) VERB to arouse or stimulate deliberately

⚠ **USAGE**

Do not confuse this word with *ferment*.

fond ADJECTIVE **1** loving or liking a person or thing **2** (of hopes) foolishly optimistic

fondle VERB to touch or stroke lovingly

font NOUN **1** a basin in a church, for holding water for baptism **2** a set of characters used in printing

food NOUN a substance that an animal or plant can take into its body to help it to grow

THESAURUS

foil VERB • *to foil their efforts*
▶ thwart, frustrate, hamper, hinder, stop

fold VERB • *to fold the sheets*
▶ double over, bend, crease, tuck

fold NOUN • *folds in the curtains*
▶ pleat, crease, tuck

follow VERB • *He followed them as far as the corner.* ▶ go after, walk behind, trace the footsteps of • *A police officer followed them.*
▶ pursue, stalk, track, shadow, tail
• *to follow the instructions* ▶ carry out, obey, observe, heed, conform

to • *to follow his meaning*
▶ understand, comprehend, grasp

folly NOUN • *an act of folly*
▶ foolishness, stupidity, silliness, madness

fond ADJECTIVE • *her fond father*
▶ loving, adoring, devoted **be fond of** • *We are fond of dancing.*
▶ be keen on, like, love

food NOUN • *had gone a week without food* ▶ nourishment, sustenance • *I'll bring some food.*
▶ refreshments, provisions, something to eat

fool NOUN **1** a silly person **2** a jester or clown **3** a creamy pudding with crushed fruit in it

fool VERB **1** to behave in a joking way **2** to trick or deceive

foolhardy ADJECTIVE bold but foolish; reckless

foolish ADJECTIVE not having good sense or judgement; unwise

foolproof ADJECTIVE easy to use or do correctly

foot NOUN **1** the lower part of the leg below the ankle **2** the lowest part *the foot of the hill* **3** a measure of length, 12 inches or about 30 centimetres **4** a unit of rhythm in a line of poetry

footage NOUN a length of film

football NOUN **1** a game played by two teams which try to kick a ball into their opponents' goal **2** the ball used in this game
► **footballer** NOUN

foothold NOUN a place to put your foot when climbing

footing NOUN **1** balance with the foot *to lose your footing* **2** the nature of a relationship *on a friendly footing*

footnote NOUN a note printed at the bottom of the page

footpath NOUN a path for pedestrians

footprint NOUN a mark made by a foot or shoe

footstep NOUN **1** a step taken in walking or running **2** the sound of this

for PREPOSITION **1** sent to or intended for *a letter for you* **2** in the direction of *set out for home* **3** during or over *walk for three hours* **4** at the price of *We bought it for £50.* **5** because of *fined for speeding* **6** in support of *to play for your country* **7** in order to *doing it for the money* **for ever** for all time; always

for CONJUNCTION because *They hesitated, for they were afraid.*

forage VERB to go searching for food or fuel

foray NOUN a sudden attack or raid

forbear VERB forbears, forbearing, forbore, forborne to refrain from something *We forbore to mention it.*

forbearance NOUN patience with someone or something difficult or tiresome

forbid VERB forbade, forbidden **1** to order someone not to do something **2** to refuse to allow

THESAURUS

fool NOUN • *to act like a fool*
► idiot, imbecile, clown, dope, moron

fool VERB • *We easily fooled him.*
► deceive, trick, dupe • *I thought you were just fooling.* ► pretend, joke, tease

foolish ADJECTIVE • *a foolish remark*
► stupid, silly, daft, crazy, mad

foolproof ADJECTIVE • *a foolproof method* ► infallible

forbid VERB • *to forbid the use of calculators* ► ban, prohibit, disallow, exclude, veto, outlaw

forbidding ADJECTIVE unfriendly in appearance

force NOUN 1 strength or power 2 (Science) an influence, which can be measured, that causes something to move 3 an organized group of police, soldiers, etc.

force VERB 1 to use force to get or do something; to make or compel 2 to break open by force

forceful ADJECTIVE strong and vigorous

forceps NOUN pincers or tongs used by surgeons and dentists

forcible ADJECTIVE done by force; forceful ▶ **forcibly** ADVERB

ford NOUN a shallow place for crossing a river on foot

fore ADJECTIVE, ADVERB at or towards the front *fore and aft*

fore NOUN the front part

forearm NOUN the arm from the elbow to the wrist or fingertips

forebears PLURAL NOUN ancestors

foreboding NOUN a feeling that trouble is coming

forecast NOUN a statement about the future

forecast VERB **forecast** to make a forecast

forecourt NOUN an enclosed area in front of a building

forefathers PLURAL NOUN ancestors

forefinger NOUN the finger next to the thumb

forefront NOUN the very front

foregoing ADJECTIVE preceding; previously mentioned

foregone conclusion NOUN a result that is inevitable

foreground NOUN the part of a scene, picture, or view that is nearest to you

forehand NOUN a stroke made in tennis with the palm of the hand turned forwards

forehead NOUN the part of the face above the eyes

foreign ADJECTIVE 1 belonging to another country 2 not belonging naturally *a foreign body*

forbidding ADJECTIVE • *a forbidding appearance* ▶ grim, ominous, menacing, unfriendly

force NOUN • *It took some force to open the door.* ▶ strength, might, effort, energy, muscle, power, weight • *the force of the explosion* ▶ intensity, strength, impact • *to use force* ▶ violence, aggression • *a peace-keeping force* ▶ army, group, corps, unit, team

force VERB • *We will force them to do it.* ▶ make, compel, oblige,

pressurize, order • *to force a door* ▶ break open, smash

forceful ADJECTIVE • *a forceful personality* ▶ strong, dynamic, powerful, assertive • *forceful arguments* ▶ strong, compelling, convincing

foreign ADJECTIVE • *foreign countries* ▶ overseas, distant, remote, exotic, faraway • *foreign branches of the company* ▶ overseas, international

foreigner NOUN a person from another country

foreleg NOUN an animal's front leg

foreman NOUN **foremen 1** a worker in charge of a group of workers **2** the leader of a jury

foremost ADJECTIVE, ADVERB first in position or rank

forensic (fer-en-sik) ADJECTIVE to do with or used in lawcourts

forerunner NOUN a person or thing that comes before another

foresee VERB **foresaw, foreseen** to realize what is going to happen

foreshadow VERB to be a sign of something to come

foresight NOUN the ability to foresee and prepare for future needs

foreskin NOUN the fold of skin covering the tip of the penis

forest NOUN trees and undergrowth covering a large area ► **forested** ADJECTIVE

forestall VERB to prevent somebody or something by taking action first

forestry NOUN the planting and care of forests

foretell VERB **foretold** to tell in advance; to prophesy

forethought NOUN careful thought and planning for the future

forewarn VERB to warn beforehand

foreword NOUN a preface

forfeit (for-fit) VERB to pay or give up something as a penalty ► **forfeiture** NOUN

forfeit NOUN something forfeited

forge[1] NOUN a place where metal is heated and shaped; a blacksmith's workshop

forge VERB **1** to shape metal by heating and hammering **2** to copy something in order to deceive people ► **forgery** NOUN

forge[2] VERB **forge ahead** to move forward steadily

forget VERB **forgetting, forgot, forgotten 1** to fail to remember **2** to stop thinking about

forgetful ADJECTIVE tending to forget ► **forgetfully** ADVERB

forget-me-not NOUN a plant with small blue flowers

forgive VERB **forgave, forgiven** to stop feeling angry with

forge VERB • *to forge swords* ► make, work, cast, mould, shape • *to forge a signature* ► fake, falsify, copy

forgery NOUN • *The painting is a forgery.* ► fake, copy, imitation, reproduction

forget VERB • *I forgot my passport.* ► leave behind, miss out, omit, overlook • *She forgot to lock the door.* ► omit, neglect, fail • *This is not something we can easily forget.* ► ignore, disregard, dismiss, think no more of

forgetful ADJECTIVE • *a forgetful person* ► absent-minded, inattentive, vague, dreamy

forgive VERB • *It is hard to forgive them.* ► excuse, pardon, exonerate, let off • *to forgive such*

somebody about something
► **forgiveness** NOUN

forgo VERB **forgoes, forwent, forgone** to give up or go without

fork NOUN **1** a small tool with prongs for lifting food to your mouth **2** a large tool with prongs used for digging or lifting **3** a place where something divides into two or more parts

fork VERB **1** to lift or dig with a fork **2** to divide into branches **3** to follow one of these branches *Fork left after a mile.* **fork out** (*informal*) to pay out money

forlorn ADJECTIVE alone and unhappy **forlorn hope** the only faint hope left

form NOUN **1** the shape, appearance, or condition of something **2** the way something exists *Ice is a form of water.* **3** a class in school **4** a bench **5** a piece of paper with spaces to be filled in

form VERB **1** to shape or construct something **2** to come into existence.

formal ADJECTIVE **1** strictly following the accepted rules or customs **2** serious and stiff in manner ► **formally** ADVERB

formality NOUN **formalities 1** formal behaviour **2** something done to obey a rule or custom

format NOUN **1** the shape and size of something **2** the way something is arranged or organized **3** (ICT) the way data is organized for processing or storage by a computer

format VERB **formatting, formatted** (ICT) to organize data in the correct format

formation NOUN a special arrangement or pattern

formative ADJECTIVE forming or developing something

former ADJECTIVE of an earlier time **the former** the first of two people or things mentioned

THESAURUS

rudeness ► excuse, condone, overlook, ignore

form NOUN • *a form of blackmail* ► kind, type, sort • *the human form* ► body, frame, shape, figure • *a form to fill in* ► document, questionnaire, sheet • *a new form at school* ► class, set, group, stream • *in good form* ► condition, shape, health

form VERB • *to form a plan* ► devise, formulate, develop, put together, work out • *The pots were formed from clay.* ► make, fashion, shape • *to form a club*

► set up, establish, found, begin • *Ice was forming.* ► appear, develop, materialize • *Six players form a team.* ► make up, constitute, compose

formal ADJECTIVE • *a formal manner* ► aloof, prim, staid, stiff • *a formal occasion* ► solemn, official, dignified • *a formal education* ► conventional, institutional

former ADJECTIVE • *her former husband* ► ex-, past, previous • *in former times* ► earlier, past, ancient

DICTIONARY

formerly ADVERB at an earlier time; previously

formidable (for-mid-a-bul) ADJECTIVE **1** difficult to deal with or do *a formidable task* **2** frightening

formula NOUN **formulae** or **formulas** **1** (Science) a set of chemical symbols **2** a list of substances **3** a fixed wording

formulate VERB to express an idea or plan clearly and exactly
▶ **formulation** NOUN

forsake VERB **forsook, forsaken** to desert or abandon

fort NOUN a fortified building

forth ADVERB onwards or forwards **and so forth** and so on

forthcoming ADJECTIVE **1** happening soon **2** willing to give information

forthright ADJECTIVE frank and outspoken

forthwith ADVERB immediately

fortification NOUN a wall or building built to make a place strong against attack

fortify VERB **fortifies, fortified** **1** to make a place strong against attack **2** to strengthen

fortitude NOUN courage in bearing pain or trouble

fortnight NOUN a period of two weeks ▶ **fortnightly** ADVERB & ADJECTIVE

fortress NOUN a fortified building or town

fortuitous ADJECTIVE happening by chance; accidental
▶ **fortuitously** ADVERB

⚠ USAGE

Note that this word does not mean the same as *fortunate*.

fortunate ADJECTIVE lucky
▶ **fortunately** ADVERB

fortune NOUN **1** good luck **2** a large amount of money

forty NOUN, ADJECTIVE **forties** the number 40 **forty winks** a short light sleep ▶ **fortieth** ADJECTIVE & NOUN

forum NOUN a meeting for public discussion

forward ADJECTIVE **1** placed or going forwards **2** having made more than the normal progress **3** too bold

forward ADVERB forwards

forward NOUN a player in the front line of a team

THESAURUS

formerly ADVERB • *work formerly done by volunteers* ▶ previously, in the past, at one time, once

fortunate ADJECTIVE • *fortunate not to be sent off* ▶ lucky, in luck

fortune NOUN • *a major change of fortune* ▶ fate, destiny, luck • *good fortune* ▶ chance, luck,

providence • *to leave her fortune to charity* ▶ money, wealth, riches

forward ADJECTIVE • *a forward movement* ▶ onward, advancing • *forward planning* ▶ advance, future • *a forward manner* ▶ bold, brazen, precocious, assertive, cheeky

forward VERB **1** to send on a letter to a new address **2** to help to make progress

forwards ADVERB **1** to or towards the front **2** in the direction you are facing

fossil NOUN the remains or traces of a prehistoric animal hardened in rock ▶ **fossilized** ADJECTIVE

fossil fuel NOUN a natural fuel such as coal or gas that is formed from the remains of plants and animals

fossilize VERB to turn into a fossil ▶ **fossilization** NOUN

⚠ **SPELLING**

This word can also be spelled *fossilise*.

foster VERB **1** to bring up someone else's child as your own **2** to help to grow or develop

foster child NOUN a child who is fostered

foster parent NOUN a parent who fosters a child

foul ADJECTIVE **1** tasting or smelling unpleasant **2** (of weather) rough or stormy **3** breaking the rules of a game ▶ **foully** ADVERB

foul NOUN an action that breaks the rules of a game

foul VERB **1** to make or become foul **2** to commit a foul against

foul play NOUN a violent crime, especially murder

found [1] *past tense of* **find**

found [2] VERB to establish or provide money for

foundation NOUN **1** the solid base on which a building stands **2** the founding of something **3** a charitable institution

founder [1] NOUN a person who founds an institution

founder [2] VERB **1** (of a ship) to fill with water and sink **2** to stumble or fall **3** to fail completely

foundling NOUN a child found abandoned

foundry NOUN **foundries** a factory or workshop where metal or glass is made

fount NOUN a fountain

fountain NOUN a structure in which a jet of water shoots up into the air

four NOUN, ADJECTIVE the number 4 ▶ **fourth** ADJECTIVE, NOUN

fourteen NOUN, ADJECTIVE the number 14 ▶ **fourteenth** ADJECTIVE, NOUN

fowl NOUN a bird, especially one kept for its eggs or meat

fox NOUN a wild animal that looks like a dog with a long furry tail

fox VERB to deceive or puzzle

foxglove NOUN a tall plant with flowers like the fingers of gloves

✎ **WORD HISTORY**

called this because the flowers look like the fingers of a glove

THESAURUS

foul ADJECTIVE • *a foul smell* ▶ nasty, horrible, disgusting, revolting, vile • *a foul mess on the floor* ▶ dirty, filthy, nasty, mucky

• *a foul crime* ▶ wicked, evil, vile, despicable • *foul language* ▶ obscene, indecent, offensive

foyer (foy-ay) NOUN the entrance hall of a theatre or large building

fraction NOUN **1** a number that is not a whole number, e.g. $\frac{1}{2}$, 0.5 **2** a tiny part

fractious (frak-shus) ADJECTIVE irritable ► **fractiously** ADVERB, **fractiousness** NOUN

fracture NOUN the breaking of a bone in the body

fracture VERB to break

fragile ADJECTIVE easy to break or damage ► **fragility** NOUN

fragment NOUN **1** a small piece broken off **2** a small part ► **fragmentary** ADJECTIVE

fragrant ADJECTIVE having a pleasant smell ► **fragrance** NOUN

frail ADJECTIVE **1** not strong or healthy **2** fragile ► **frailty** NOUN

frame NOUN **1** a holder that fits round the outside of a picture **2** a rigid structure that supports something **3** a human or animal body *He has a small frame.* **4** a single exposure on a cinema film **frame of mind** the way you think or feel for a while

frame VERB **1** to put a frame on or round **2** to incriminate

framework NOUN **1** a frame supporting something **2** a basic plan or system

franchise NOUN **1** the right to vote in elections **2** a licence to sell a firm's goods or services in a certain area

frank ADJECTIVE making your thoughts and feelings clear ► **frankly** ADVERB

frantic ADJECTIVE wildly agitated or excited ► **frantically** ADVERB

fraternal (fra-tern-al) ADJECTIVE to do with brothers; brotherly ► **fraternally** ADVERB

fraternity NOUN **fraternities 1** a brotherly feeling **2** a group of people with the same interest

fraternize VERB to associate with other people in a friendly way ► **fraternization** NOUN

⚠ **SPELLING**

This word can also be spelled *fraternise.*

fraud NOUN **1** the crime of swindling people **2** an fake

fragile ADJECTIVE • *fragile china* ► delicate, weak, breakable, easily damaged • *a fragile ceasefire* ► flimsy, precarious

fragment NOUN • *fragments of pottery* ► piece, bit, particle, chip, scrap

frame NOUN • *a strong lightweight frame* ► framework, structure, construction • *a portrait in a gilt*

frame ► surround, mount, border, setting

frank ADJECTIVE • *frank opinions* ► honest, open, candid, truthful

frantic ADJECTIVE • *frantic about their safety* ► anxious, worried, distraught • *frantic attempts to locate the luggage* ► hectic, frenzied

fraud NOUN • *accused of fraud* ► fraudulence, swindling,

DICTIONARY

fraudulent (fraw-dew-lent) *ADJECTIVE* involving fraud; deceitful or dishonest

fraught *ADJECTIVE* **1** tense or upset **2** filled with *fraught with danger*

fray [1] *NOUN* a fight or conflict *ready for the fray*

fray [2] *VERB* **1** to become ragged with loose threads **2** (of tempers or nerves) to become strained

freak *NOUN* a strange or abnormal person or thing ► **freakish** *ADJECTIVE*

freckle *NOUN* a small brown spot on the skin ► **freckled** *ADJECTIVE*

free *ADJECTIVE* **freer, freest 1** able to do what you want **2** not costing any money **3** not fixed **4** not having or being affected by something **5** not being used or

occupied **6** generous *very free with their money* ► **freely** *ADVERB*

free *VERB* to set free

freedom *NOUN* the state of being free; independence

freehand *ADJECTIVE, ADVERB* (of a drawing) done without the aid of instruments

freehold *NOUN* the possession of land or a house as its absolute owner

free-range *ADJECTIVE* (of poultry) not caged but allowed to move about freely

freeway *NOUN* (American) a motorway

freewheel *VERB* to ride a bicycle without pedalling

THESAURUS

cheating, deception • *The offer was a fraud.* ► trick, hoax, swindle, deception • *They exposed him as a fraud.* ► impostor, cheat

fraudulent *ADJECTIVE* • *fraudulent dealings* ► dishonest, illegal, unlawful, criminal

fraught *ADJECTIVE* • *looked tired and fraught* ► anxious, tense, worried, distressed

freak *NOUN* • *a genetically engineered freak* ► oddity, mutant • *a weight-training freak* ► fanatic, enthusiast, addict

free *ADJECTIVE* • *free tickets* ► complimentary, gratis, free of charge, on the house • *The people longed to be free.* ► independent, self-governing, emancipated • *The wanted man is still free.* ► at liberty, on the loose, at large • *free*

time ► spare, available • *The bathroom is free now.* ► vacant, empty, available, not in use • *free with her money* ► generous, lavish • *Are you free on Friday?* ► available, unoccupied • *free to choose* ► able, allowed, permitted

free *VERB* • *to free prisoners* ► release, liberate, set free • *to free the trapped victims* ► rescue, release, extricate

freedom *NOUN* • *to value your freedom* ► liberty, liberation, release • *The country fought for its freedom.* ► independence, self-government • *the freedom to choose* ► ability, opportunity, chance

freely *ADVERB* • *to talk freely* ► openly, frankly, honestly

freeze VERB **froze, frozen 1** to turn into ice **2** to make or be very cold **3** to keep at a fixed level **4** to become still

freeze NOUN **1** a period of freezing weather **2** the freezing of wages or prices

freezer NOUN a refrigerator in which food can be frozen quickly and stored

freight (frayt) NOUN goods transported as cargo

freighter NOUN a ship or aircraft carrying cargo

frenzy NOUN **frenzies** a state of wild excitement ▸ **frenzied** ADJECTIVE

frequency NOUN **frequencies 1** the rate at which something happens **2** the number of vibrations made each second by a wave of sound, radio, or light

frequent (freek-went) ADJECTIVE happening often ▸ **frequently** ADVERB

frequent (frik-wuhnt) VERB to visit a place often

fresco NOUN **frescoes** a picture painted on a wall or ceiling when the plaster is still wet

fresh ADJECTIVE **1** newly made or arrived; not stale **2** not tinned or preserved *fresh fruit* **3** cool and clean *fresh air* **4** (of water) not salty **5** cheeky

freshen VERB to make or become fresh

freshwater ADJECTIVE living in rivers or lakes, not the sea

fret¹ VERB to worry or be upset ▸ **fretful** ADJECTIVE

fret² NOUN a bar or ridge on the neck of a guitar

friar NOUN a male member of a Roman Catholic religious order who has vowed to live a life of poverty ▸ **friary** NOUN

friction NOUN **1** the rubbing of one thing against another **2** bad feeling between people ▸ **frictional** ADJECTIVE

freeze VERB • *In winter the river freezes.* ▸ ice over, solidify • *to freeze prices* ▸ fix, hold, limit

freight NOUN • *passenger and freight services* ▸ cargo, goods, merchandise • *air freight* ▸ transportation, shipment

frenzy NOUN • *in a state of frenzy* ▸ hysteria, turmoil, agitation • *a frenzy of anger* ▸ fit, outburst, paroxysm

frequent ADJECTIVE • *frequent warnings* ▸ regular, repeated,

constant, countless • *a frequent visitor* ▸ habitual, regular, common

fresh ADJECTIVE • *fresh fruit and vegetables* ▸ natural, raw • *fresh ideas* ▸ new, original, innovative, up-to-date • *a batch of fresh recruits* ▸ young, youthful, inexperienced • *feeling fresh after a shower* ▸ refreshed, rested, revived, invigorated • *a fresh wind* ▸ cold, cool, brisk, bracing

a
b
c
d
e
f
g
h
i
j
k
l
m
n
o
p
q
r
s
t
u
v
w
x
y
z

Friday NOUN the day of the week following Thursday

fridge NOUN a refrigerator

friend NOUN a person you like who likes you

friendly ADJECTIVE **friendlier friendliest** behaving like a friend ► **friendliness** NOUN

friendship NOUN being friends

frieze (freez) NOUN a strip of designs round a wall

fright NOUN **1** a sudden great fear **2** a person or thing that looks ugly or ridiculous

frighten VERB to make or become afraid ► **frightened** ADJECTIVE

frightful ADJECTIVE awful; very great or bad ► **frightfully** ADVERB

frigid ADJECTIVE **1** extremely cold **2** unfriendly

frill NOUN **1** a gathered or pleated trimming on a dress or curtain

2 an unnecessary extra benefit ► **frilly** ADJECTIVE

fringe NOUN **1** a decorative edging with threads hanging down loosely **2** a straight line of hair over the forehead **3** the edge of something

frisk VERB **1** to jump or run about playfully **2** to search somebody by running the hands over their clothes

frisky ADJECTIVE **friskier, friskiest** playful or lively ► **friskily** ADVERB

fritter¹ NOUN a slice of meat, potato, or fruit coated in batter and fried

fritter² VERB to waste time or money gradually

frivolous ADJECTIVE seeking pleasure in a light-hearted way ► **frivolity** NOUN

frizzy ADJECTIVE **frizzier, frizziest** (of hair) in tight curls

THESAURUS

friend NOUN • *stay with a friend*
► acquaintance, companion, mate, pal

friendly ADJECTIVE • *friendly staff*
► pleasant, kind, agreeable, amiable, likeable, approachable, sociable • *a friendly atmosphere*
► pleasant, warm, welcoming
• *friendly since childhood* ► close, affectionate, intimate, familiar

friendship NOUN • *Their friendship grew.* ► relationship, friendliness, comradeship, affection, closeness, love

fright NOUN • *to get a fright*
► scare, shock, surprise
• *overcome by fright* ► fear, alarm, terror, horror, dread, panic

frighten VERB • *The noises frightened them.* ► scare, startle, alarm, shock, terrify, petrify, panic

frightened ADJECTIVE • *The children were tired and frightened.*
► scared, afraid, alarmed, terrified, petrified, shocked, panicky

frightful ADJECTIVE • *a frightful time*
► awful, terrible, dreadful, appalling

a
b
c
d
e
f
g
h
i
j
k
l
m
n
o
p
q
r
s
t
u
v
w
x
y
z

fro ADVERB **to and fro** backwards and forwards

frock NOUN a girl's or woman's dress

frog NOUN a small jumping animal that can live both in water and on land

frogman NOUN **frogmen** a swimmer equipped to swim underwater

frolic NOUN a lively cheerful game or entertainment

frolic VERB **frolicking, frolicked** to play about in a lively cheerful way

from PREPOSITION **1** used to show a starting point in space or time or order *from London to Paris from 9 a.m. to 5 p.m.* **2** used to show separation *Take the gun from him.* **3** used to show origin or cause *I suffer from headaches.*

front NOUN **1** the part or side that comes first or is the most important or furthest forward **2** the place where fighting is happening in a war **3** an approaching mass of air ► **frontal** ADJECTIVE

front ADJECTIVE of the front; in front

frontier NOUN the boundary between two countries or regions

frost NOUN **1** powdery ice that forms on surfaces in freezing weather **2** weather with a temperature below freezing point

frost VERB to cover with frost

frostbite NOUN harm done to the body by very cold weather ► **frostbitten** ADJECTIVE

frosty ADJECTIVE **frostier frostiest 1** cold with frost **2** unfriendly and unwelcoming ► **frostily** ADVERB

froth NOUN a white mass of tiny bubbles on liquid ► **frothy** ADJECTIVE

frown VERB to wrinkle your forehead when angry or worried

frown NOUN a frowning movement or look

frugal (froo-gal) ADJECTIVE **1** spending little money **2** costing very little *a frugal meal* ► **frugally** ADVERB

fruit NOUN **1** the seed container that grows on a tree or plant **2** a good result of doing something ► **fruity** ADJECTIVE

fruitful ADJECTIVE having good results

fruitless ADJECTIVE producing no results

THESAURUS

front NOUN • *the front of the house* ► facade, exterior • *the front of a boat* ► prow, bow • *the front of a car* ► nose • *the front of the queue* ► head, start, beginning • *a brave front* ► appearance, manner

frosty ADJECTIVE • *a frosty autumn morning* ► cold, crisp, bitter,

freezing • *a frosty reception* ► unfriendly, unwelcoming, cool

frown VERB • *The woman frowned at them.* ► scowl, glower, glare

fruitful ADJECTIVE • *a fruitful crop* ► productive, rich, abundant • *fruitful discussions* ► successful, useful, productive

DICTIONARY

frustrate VERB to prevent from doing something or from happening ▸ **frustration** NOUN

fry [1] VERB **fries, fried** to cook in hot fat ▸ **fryer** NOUN

fry [2] PLURAL NOUN very young fish

fudge [1] NOUN a soft sugary sweet

fudge [2] VERB to avoid giving clear information

fuel NOUN something that is burned to produce heat or power

fuel VERB **fuelling, fuelled** to supply with fuel

fug NOUN (informal) a stuffy atmosphere in a room

fugitive (few-jit-iv) NOUN a person who is running away from the authorities

fulcrum NOUN the point on which a lever is placed

fulfil VERB **fulfilling, fulfilled** to perform or complete ▸ **fulfilment** NOUN

full ADJECTIVE **1** containing as much or as many as possible **2** having many people or things *full of ideas* **3** complete *the full story* **4** the greatest possible *at full speed* **5** fitting loosely; with many folds *a full skirt* **in full** with nothing left out

full ADVERB completely and directly *It hit him full in the face.*

full moon NOUN the moon when it is visible as a complete disc

full stop NOUN the dot used as a punctuation mark at the end of a sentence

fully ADVERB completely

fumble VERB to hold or handle clumsily

fume VERB **1** to give off fumes **2** to be very angry

fumes PLURAL NOUN strong-smelling smoke or gas

fun NOUN amusement or enjoyment **make fun of** to make people laugh at

THESAURUS

frustrate VERB • *The lack of progress was frustrating them.* ▸ exasperate, discourage, irritate • *Bad weather frustrated attempts at a rescue.* ▸ thwart, foil, defeat, prevent

fulfil VERB • *to fulfil an ambition* ▸ achieve, realize, carry out • *to fulfil obligations* ▸ meet, complete, comply with

full ADJECTIVE • *His glass was still full.* ▸ filled, brimming, overflowing, topped up • *The trains would be full.* ▸ crowded, packed,

crammed, congested • *too full to do anything* ▸ well fed, satisfied, replete • *a full list* ▸ complete, comprehensive • *the full story* ▸ entire, complete, total, unabridged • *a full life* ▸ exciting, eventful, interesting, busy

fumble VERB • *He fumbled for his wallet.* ▸ grope, feel about • *She fumbled about in the dark.* ▸ stumble, blunder, stagger

fun NOUN • *to have some fun* ▸ enjoyment, pleasure, entertainment, amusement

a
b
c
d
e
f
g
h
i
j
k
l
m
n
o
p
q
r
s
t
u
v
w
x
y
z

DICTIONARY

a b c d e f g h i j k l m n o p q r s t u v w x y z

function NOUN 1 a role or purpose 2 an important event 3 a basic computer peration 4 (*Maths*) a variable quantity whose value depends on the value of other variable quantities

function VERB 1 to perform a function 2 to work properly

functional ADJECTIVE 1 working properly 2 useful

fund NOUN 1 money collected 2 a stock or supply

fund VERB to supply with money

fundamental ADJECTIVE basic; essential ▸ **fundamentally** ADVERB

funeral NOUN the ceremony of burying or cremating a dead person

funereal (few-neer-ee-al) ADJECTIVE gloomy or depressing

funfair NOUN a fair consisting of amusements and sideshows

fungus NOUN fungi a plant that grows on decayed material, such as a mushroom or a toadstool

funk NOUN a style of popular music with a strong beat, based on jazz and blues

funky ADJECTIVE funkier, funkiest 1 (of music) having a strong beat 2 fashionable; trendy

funnel NOUN 1 a metal chimney on a ship or steam engine 2 a narrowing tube for pouring things into a narrow opening

funny ADJECTIVE funnier, funniest 1 that makes you laugh or smile 2 strange or odd *a funny smell* ▸ **funnily** ADVERB

fur NOUN 1 the soft hair on some animals 2 animal skin with the fur on it, used for clothing

furious ADJECTIVE 1 very angry 2 violent or intense *furious heat* ▸ **furiously** ADVERB

furlong NOUN one-eighth of a mile, 220 yards

furniture NOUN tables, chairs, and other movable things in a building

furrow NOUN 1 a long cut in the ground made by a plough 2 a deep groove 3 a wrinkle

THESAURUS

function NOUN • *the function of the organization* ▸ role, job, responsibility • *an official function* ▸ event, occasion, party, gathering

fund NOUN • *an emergency fund* ▸ pool, kitty, store, supply **funds** • *Funds are running low.* ▸ money, cash, savings

fund VERB • *to fund the railways* ▸ pay for, finance

fundamental ADJECTIVE • *fundamental principles* ▸ basic, main, elementary, key, principal

funny ADJECTIVE • *a funny story* ▸ amusing, humorous, comical, witty, hilarious, entertaining • *a funny coincidence* ▸ strange, odd, peculiar, curious, queer, weird

furious ADJECTIVE • *She was furious when she found out.* ▸ angry, enraged, infuriated, incensed, irate

DICTIONARY

furrow VERB to make furrows in

furry ADJECTIVE **furrier, furriest** like fur; covered with fur

further ADVERB, ADJECTIVE **1** at or to a greater distance **2** more; additional *further enquiries*

further VERB to help or develop *to further your career*

furthermore ADVERB also; moreover

furthest ADVERB, ADJECTIVE at or to the greatest distance; most distant

furtive ADJECTIVE stealthy; trying not to be seen

fury NOUN **furies** wild anger or rage

furze NOUN gorse

fuse NOUN **1** a safety device that breaks an electric circuit **2** a length of material used for setting off an explosive

fuse VERB **1** to stop working because a fuse has melted **2** to blend together

fuselage (few-zel-ahzh) NOUN the main body of an aircraft

fusion NOUN **1** the action of blending or merging **2** the uniting of atomic nuclei, releasing energy

fuss NOUN **1** unnecessary excitement or bustle **2** an agitated protest

fuss VERB to make a fuss

fussy ADJECTIVE **fussier, fussiest** **1** inclined to make a fuss **2** choosing very carefully **3** full of unnecessary details ▶ **fussily** ADVERB, **fussiness** NOUN

fusty ADJECTIVE **fustier, fustiest** smelling stale or stuffy

futile ADJECTIVE useless; having no result ▶ **futility** NOUN

futon (foo-ton) NOUN a padded mattress that rolls out to form a bed

future NOUN **1** the time that will come; what is going to happen **2** (*Grammar*) the tense of a verb that indicates something

THESAURUS

further ADJECTIVE • *further information* ▶ more, additional, extra

furtive ADJECTIVE • *furtive glances* ▶ secretive, surreptitious, sly, stealthy

fury NOUN • *She could not hide her fury.* ▶ anger, rage, wrath • *The storm struck with immense fury.* ▶ force, ferocity, fierceness, violence

fuss NOUN • *a lot of fuss about the missing money* ▶ commotion, excitement, confusion, upset • *to*

get the job done with no fuss ▶ bother, trouble, difficulty

fuss VERB • *He begged her not to fuss.* ▶ fret, worry, get worked up

fussy ADJECTIVE • *fussy about their food* ▶ finicky, fastidious, particular, choosy

futile ADJECTIVE • *a futile struggle* ▶ pointless, useless, fruitless, vain, unsuccessful

future NOUN • *a bright future for them* ▶ outlook, prospects, expectations, destiny • *our plans*

a
b
c
d
e
f
g
h
i
j
k
l
m
n
o
p
q
r
s
t
u
v
w
x
y
z

happening in the future,
expressed by using 'shall', 'will', or
'be going to'

future _ADJECTIVE_ belonging or
referring to the future

futuristic _ADJECTIVE_ very modern,
as if belonging to the future

fuzz _NOUN_ something light or fluffy

fuzzy _ADJECTIVE_ **fuzzier, fuzziest**
1 like fuzz; covered with fuzz
2 blurred; not clear

for the future ► time to come,
time ahead

future _ADJECTIVE_ • _the future king_
► next, coming, approaching,
forthcoming

fuzzy _ADJECTIVE_ • _a large fuzzy head_
► fluffy, woolly, fleecy, downy,
velvety • _a fuzzy picture_
► blurred, unfocused, vague,
hazy, unclear

a
b
c
d
e
f
g
h
i
j
k
l
m
n
o
p
q
r
s
t
u
v
w
x
y
z

Gg

gabble VERB to talk too quickly to be understood

gable NOUN the pointed part at the top of an outside wall

gadget NOUN a small useful tool

Gaelic (gay-lik) NOUN the Celtic languages of Scotland and Ireland

gaffe NOUN an embarrassing blunder

gag NOUN 1 something put into a person's mouth to prevent them speaking 2 a joke

gag VERB **gagging, gagged 1** to put a gag on **2** to prevent from making comments **3** to retch

gaggle NOUN a flock of geese

gaiety NOUN cheerfulness

gaily ADVERB in a cheerful way

gain VERB 1 to get something you did not have before 2 (of a clock or watch) to become ahead of the correct time **gain on** to come closer to someone else moving

gain NOUN something gained; a profit or improvement

gait NOUN a way of walking or running *a shuffling gait*

gala (gah-la) NOUN **1** a festival or celebration **2** a set of sports contests

galaxy NOUN **galaxies** a large group of stars ▸ **galactic** ADJECTIVE

gale NOUN a strong wind

gall NOUN boldness or impudence

gallant ADJECTIVE brave or heroic ▸ **gallantry** NOUN

galleon NOUN in former times, a large Spanish sailing ship

gallery NOUN **galleries 1** a room or building for showing works of art **2** the highest balcony in a cinema or theatre **3** a long room or passage

galley NOUN **galleys 1** an old type of ship driven by oars **2** the kitchen in a ship or aircraft

galling ADJECTIVE annoying or humiliating

gallivant VERB to wander about for fun

gallon NOUN a unit used to measure liquids, 8 pints or 4.546 litres

gallop NOUN a fast pace by a horse

gallop VERB to go or ride at a gallop

gallows NOUN a framework with a noose for hanging criminals

gadget NOUN • *a kitchen full of gadgets* ▸ tool, utensil, appliance, contraption, device

gain VERB • *to gain a large profit* ▸ earn, bring in, obtain, acquire • *to gain a reputation* ▸ earn, get, achieve, acquire

• *to gain speed* ▸ increase, gather, pick up

gain NOUN • *financial gain* ▸ profit, income, advantage, benefit, reward

gallant ADJECTIVE • *a gallant band of soldiers* ▸ brave, courageous, heroic

galore
DICTIONARY
garbage

galore ADVERB in large numbers
bargains galore
galvanize VERB 1 to stimulate into activity 2 to coat iron with zinc to protect it from rust

⚠ **SPELLING**

This word can also be spelled *galvanise*.

gamble VERB 1 to bet on the result of a game, race, or other event 2 to take risks ► **gambler** NOUN
gamble NOUN 1 a bet or chance 2 a risky attempt
gambol VERB **gambolling**, **gambolled** to jump or skip about in play
game NOUN 1 a form of play or sport, especially one with rules 2 a scheme or trick 3 wild animals or birds hunted for sport or food
game ADJECTIVE brave and enterprising
gamma NOUN the third letter of the Greek alphabet, equivalent to Roman *G, g*
gamma rays PLURAL NOUN very short X-rays emitted by radioactive substances
gammon NOUN ham that has been cured like bacon

gander NOUN a male goose
gang NOUN 1 a group of people who do things together 2 a group of criminals
gang VERB **gang up on** to join together to fight or bully someone
gangling ADJECTIVE tall, thin, and awkward-looking
gangrene (gang-green) NOUN decay of body tissue in a living person
gangster NOUN a member of a gang of violent criminals
gangway NOUN 1 a gap for passing between rows of seats 2 a bridge for walking on and off a ship
gannet NOUN a large seabird which catches fish by diving
gaol (jayl) NOUN a different spelling of *jail* ► **gaol** VERB, **gaoler** NOUN
gap NOUN 1 a break or opening 2 an interval
gape VERB to stare with your mouth open
garage NOUN 1 a building for a vehicle 2 a place that services and repairs vehicles
garbage NOUN household rubbish

THESAURUS

game NOUN • *playing a new game* ► pastime, diversion, amusement, sport, activity • *the big game on Saturday* ► match, contest, tournament, competition • *I know how to deal with his little game.* ► scheme, trick, plot, plan • *to play a game on someone* ► joke, trick, prank

gang NOUN • *a gang of youths* ► band, group, crowd, pack, mob
gap NOUN • *a gap in a wall* ► opening, space, hole, break, crack, chink • *a gap in the fighting* ► pause, break, interruption • *the gap between rich and poor* ► divide, gulf, rift
gape VERB • *He gaped at her in surprise.* ► stare, gaze, gawp

garble VERB to give a confused account of

garden NOUN a piece of ground where flowers, fruit, or vegetables are grown

gardener NOUN someone who looks after a garden ▸ **gardening** NOUN

gargle VERB to wash the throat by pushing air through a liquid at the back of the mouth

gargoyle NOUN an ugly or comical face carved on a building

garish (gair-ish) ADJECTIVE very bright or highly coloured

garland NOUN a wreath of flowers worn or hung as a decoration

garlic NOUN a plant with a bulb divided into cloves, used for flavouring food

garment NOUN a piece of clothing

garnish VERB to decorate food

garnish NOUN a decoration on food

garrison NOUN troops guarding a fortified building

garter NOUN a band of elastic to hold up a sock or stocking

gas¹ NOUN **gases** **1** a substance, such as oxygen, that can move freely and is not liquid or solid at ordinary temperatures **2** a gas that can be burned, used as a fuel

gas VERB **gasses, gassing, gassed** to kill or injure with gas

gas² NOUN (informal) (American) short for **gasoline**

gaseous (gas-ee-us) ADJECTIVE in the form of a gas

gash NOUN a long deep cut or wound

gash VERB to make a gash in

gasket NOUN a layer of soft material sealing a joint between metal surfaces

gasoline NOUN (American) petrol

gasp VERB **1** to breathe in suddenly from shock or surprise **2** to struggle to breathe ▸ **gasp** NOUN

gassy ADJECTIVE **gassier, gassiest** fizzy

gastric ADJECTIVE to do with the stomach

gate NOUN **1** a movable barrier on hinges, used as a door in a wall or fence **2** a place for waiting to board an aircraft **3** the number of people attending a sports event

gateau (gat-oh) NOUN **gateaus** or **gateaux** a large rich cream cake

gatecrash VERB to go to a private party without being invited

gateway NOUN an opening containing a gate

gather VERB **1** to come or bring together **2** to collect gradually

THESAURUS

gash NOUN • *a gash on the head*
▸ cut, slash, wound, injury

gash VERB • *to gash your hand*
▸ cut, slash, wound, injury

gather VERB • *A crowd gathered.*
▸ assemble, collect, come

together, congregate • *to gather your things* ▸ collect, assemble • *to gather flowers* ▸ pick, pluck, harvest • *I gather you have been unwell.* ▸ understand, believe

3 to collect as harvest **4** to understand or learn *I gather you've been ill.* **5** to pull cloth into folds

gathering NOUN a meeting of people

gaudy ADJECTIVE **gaudier, gaudiest** showy and bright
▸ **gaudily** ADVERB

gauge (gayj) NOUN **1** a standard measurement **2** the distance the rails of a railway **3** a measuring instrument

gauge VERB **1** to measure **2** to estimate

gaunt ADJECTIVE looking thin and unwell

gauntlet NOUN a glove with a wide cuff over the wrist

gauze NOUN **1** thin transparent woven material **2** fine wire mesh

gave past tense of **give**

gay ADJECTIVE **1** homosexual **2** cheerful **3** brightly coloured

gaze VERB to look at something steadily

gaze NOUN a long steady look

gazelle NOUN a small antelope

gazette NOUN **1** a newspaper **2** an official journal

gazetteer NOUN a list of place names

GCSE ABBREVIATION General Certificate of Secondary Education

gear NOUN **1** a set of wheels with cogs that transmit power **2** (*informal*) equipment or clothing

gear VERB **gear to** to make something match or be suitable

gearbox NOUN a case enclosing gears

gel NOUN a jelly-like substance

gelatin NOUN a clear jelly-like substance used to make jellies

gem NOUN **1** a precious stone **2** an excellent person or thing

gender NOUN **1** (*Grammar*) the group in which a noun is classed in some languages, e.g. masculine, feminine, or neuter **2** a person's sex

gene (jeen) NOUN the part of a living cell that controls which characteristics are inherited from parents

genealogy (jee-nee-al-o-jee) NOUN **genealogies** the study of family history and ancestors

genera (jen-e-ra) PLURAL NOUN plural of **genus**

general ADJECTIVE **1** to do with most people or things **2** not detailed; broad *the general idea*

THESAURUS

gaudy ADJECTIVE • *nothing too gaudy* ▸ garish, lurid, flashy, loud

gauge VERB • *to gauge public opinion* ▸ assess, evaluate • *to gauge the distance* ▸ measure, calculate

gaunt ADJECTIVE • *a gaunt figure* ▸ thin, haggard, drawn, emaciated, scrawny

general ADJECTIVE • *in general terms* ▸ broad, rough, vague, loose • *suitable for general use* ▸ regular, typical, normal,

general NOUN a senior army officer

general election NOUN an election of Members of Parliament for the whole country

generalize VERB to make a statement that is true in most cases ▶ **generalization** NOUN

> ⚠ **SPELLING**
>
> This word can also be spelled *generalise*.

generally ADVERB **1** usually **2** in a general sense

general practitioner NOUN a doctor who treats all kinds of diseases

generate VERB to produce or create

generation NOUN **1** the process of producing **2** a single stage in a family **3** all the people born at about the same time

generator NOUN a machine for producing electricity

generic (jin-*e*-rik) ADJECTIVE belonging to a whole class or group

generous ADJECTIVE **1** willing to give or share **2** plentiful
▶ **generosity** NOUN

genetic (jin-et-ik) ADJECTIVE **1** to do with genes **2** to do with inherited characteristics ▶ **genetically** ADVERB

genetics NOUN the study of genes and genetic behaviour

genial (jee-nee-al) ADJECTIVE kindly and cheerful

genie (jee-nee) NOUN (in stories) a spirit who can grant wishes

genitals PLURAL NOUN the external sexual organs

genius NOUN **1** an unusually able person **2** a great ability *a genius for music*

genocide (jen-o-syd) NOUN deliberate extermination of a race of people

genome (jen-ohm) NOUN (*Science*) all the genes in one cell of a living thing

genteel (jen-teel) ADJECTIVE trying to seem polite and refined

gentle ADJECTIVE **1** mild or kind; not rough **2** not harsh or severe *a gentle breeze* ▶ **gently** ADVERB

ordinary, universal, everyday • *a general pay increase*
▶ comprehensive, universal

generally ADVERB • *It is generally a mistake to ignore them.*
▶ normally, as a rule, on the whole, usually

generate VERB • *to generate business* ▶ create, produce, make, cause

generous ADJECTIVE • *a generous nature* ▶ kind, kind-hearted,

benevolent, unselfish, charitable • *a generous helping* ▶ large, lavish, ample

genius NOUN • *It doesn't take a genius to work it out.*
▶ mastermind, great thinker, prodigy, expert • *a genius for music* ▶ talent, gift, flair, aptitude

gentle ADJECTIVE • *a gentle person*
▶ kind, calm, placid, tender, sympathetic, compassionate • *a gentle breeze* ▶ light, faint, soft

a
b
c
d
e
f
g
h
i
j
k
l
m
n
o
p
q
r
s
t
u
v
w
x
y
z

gentleman NOUN **gentlemen 1** a well-mannered man **2** a man of good social position

gentry PLURAL NOUN upper-class people

genuine ADJECTIVE real; not faked or pretending

genus (jee-nus) NOUN **genera** a group of similar animals or plants

geography NOUN the study of the earth's surface and of its climate and products ► **geographer** NOUN, **geographical** ADJECTIVE

> **WORD HISTORY**
>
> from Greek *ge* 'earth' and *graphein* 'to write'

geology NOUN the study of the structure of the earth's crust and its layers ► **geological** ADJECTIVE, **geologist** NOUN

geometric ADJECTIVE **1** to do with geometry **2** made up of straight lines and angles ► **geometrical** ADJECTIVE

geometry NOUN the study of lines, angles, surfaces, and solids in mathematics

geranium NOUN a garden plant with red, pink, or white flowers

gerbil (jer-bil) NOUN a small brown rodent kept as a pet

geriatric (je-ree-at-rik) ADJECTIVE to do with the care of old people

germ NOUN **1** a small organism causing disease **2** a tiny living structure from which a plant or animal may develop

German measles NOUN rubella

German shepherd NOUN a large strong dog, often used by the police

germicide NOUN a substance that kills germs

germinate VERB (of a seed) to produce roots and shoots ► **germination** NOUN

gestation (jes-tay-shun) NOUN the process of carrying a fetus in the womb

gesticulate VERB to make expressive movements ► **gesticulation** NOUN

gesture (jes-cher) NOUN **1** a movement that expresses what a person feels **2** an action that shows goodwill

gesture VERB to say something by making a gesture

get VERB **getting, got 1** to obtain or receive *to get first prize* **2** to become *Don't get angry!* **3** to reach a place *We'll get there soon.*

THESAURUS

• *a gentle slope* ► gradual, slight, easy

genuine ADJECTIVE • *a genuine Picasso* ► authentic, original, real, true

get VERB • *Will you get my book?* ► fetch, bring, collect, pick up • *to get an award* ► receive,

acquire, achieve, obtain • *It's getting cold.* ► become, turn, grow • *We'll get there soon.* ► arrive, reach, come to • *I got a cold.* ► catch, come down with, develop • *I'll get her to come tomorrow.* ► ask, instruct, order, request

4 to put or move *I can't get my shoe on.* **5** to prepare *Will you get the tea?* **6** to persuade or order *Get him to come here.* **7** to catch an illness **8** (*informal*) to understand *I don't get that.* **get over** to recover from an illness **get up 1** to stand up **2** to get out of bed in the morning

getaway NOUN an escape after committing a crime

geyser (gee-zer or gy-zer) NOUN a natural hot spring

ghastly ADJECTIVE **1** very unpleasant or bad **2** looking pale and ill ▶ **ghastliness** NOUN

gherkin (ger-kin) NOUN a small pickled cucumber

ghetto (get-oh) NOUN **ghettos** a deprived area of a city where immigrants or other minorities live

ghost NOUN the spirit of a dead person that appears to the living ▶ **ghostly** ADJECTIVE

ghoulish (gool-ish) ADJECTIVE enjoying things that are grisly or unpleasant

giant NOUN (in stories) a creature like a huge person

giant ADJECTIVE very large

gibberish (jib-er-ish) NOUN nonsense

gibbon NOUN an ape with long arms

gibe (jyb) NOUN another spelling of **jibe**

giddy ADJECTIVE **giddier**, **giddiest** feeling unsteady and dizzy ▶ **giddiness** NOUN

gift NOUN **1** something you give someone **2** a natural talent *a gift for music*

gifted ADJECTIVE having a special talent

gigabyte (gi-ga-byt) NOUN (ICT) a unit of information equal to one thousand million bytes, or (more precisely) 2^{30} bytes

THESAURUS

ghastly ADJECTIVE • *a ghastly murder* ▶ terrible, horrible, horrific, gruesome • *a ghastly time* ▶ unpleasant, awful, terrible, nasty, revolting

ghost NOUN • *a ghost in the house* ▶ phantom, spectre, spirit

ghostly ADJECTIVE • *a ghostly figure* ▶ unearthly, eerie, phantom, weird, supernatural

giant NOUN • *a giant of a man* ▶ monster, ogre, colossus

giant ADJECTIVE • *four giant chimneys* ▶ huge, enormous, gigantic, colossal, massive

giddy ADJECTIVE • *The heat made her giddy.* ▶ dizzy, faint, weak, light-headed

gift NOUN • *a generous gift* ▶ present, donation, contribution, handout, offering • *a gift for languages* ▶ talent, flair, aptitude

gifted ADJECTIVE • *a gifted musician* ▶ talented, able, accomplished, capable, skilful

gigantic (jy-gan-tik) ADJECTIVE extremely large

giggle VERB to laugh in a silly way ▶ **giggle** NOUN

gild VERB to cover with a thin layer of gold

gills PLURAL NOUN the part of the body through which a fish breathes

gilt NOUN a thin covering of gold or gold paint

gilt ADJECTIVE gilded; gold-coloured

gimmick NOUN something unusual done to attract attention

gin NOUN an alcoholic drink flavoured with juniper berries

ginger NOUN the hot-tasting root of a tropical plant, used for flavouring ▶ **ginger** ADJECTIVE

ginger VERB to make more lively

gingerbread NOUN a ginger-flavoured cake or biscuit

gingerly ADVERB cautiously

Gipsy NOUN **Gipsies** another spelling of **Gypsy**

giraffe NOUN an African animal with long legs and a long neck

girder NOUN a metal beam supporting part of a building or bridge

girdle NOUN **1** a belt or cord worn round the waist **2** a tight corset

girl NOUN a female child or young woman ▶ **girlhood** NOUN

girlfriend NOUN a person's regular female friend or lover

girlish ADJECTIVE like a girl; young and attractive

giro (jy-roh) NOUN a system of sending money directly from one bank account to another

girth NOUN the distance round something

gist (jist) NOUN the essential points or general sense of a story or argument

give VERB **gave**, **given 1** to let someone have something **2** to make or do **give a laugh 3** to bend or collapse when pressed **give in** to admit defeat **give up** to stop ▶ **giver** NOUN

glacial ADJECTIVE made of or produced by ice

gigantic ADJECTIVE • *a gigantic building* ▶ huge, enormous, colossal, immense, massive

give VERB • *to give them money* ▶ provide with, present with, supply with, award, donate • *to give a message* ▶ pass on, convey, communicate, transmit, send, deliver • *to give your life*
▶ sacrifice, lose, devote • *to give trouble* ▶ cause, make, create, start • *to give a party* ▶ hold, organize, arrange • *to give a shout* ▶ utter, emit, let out • *to give a warning* ▶ issue, deliver **give in** • *They had to give in after a while.* ▶ surrender, submit, capitulate, yield **give up** • *Don't give up now.* ▶ quit, stop, concede defeat

glacier NOUN a mass of ice that moves slowly down a mountain valley

glad ADJECTIVE **1** pleased; expressing joy **2** giving pleasure *the glad news*

gladden VERB to make glad

glade NOUN an open space in a forest

gladiator (glad-ee-ay-ter) NOUN a man trained to fight for public entertainment in ancient Rome

glamorize VERB to make something seem glamorous or romantic

⚠ **SPELLING**

This word can also be spelled *glamorise.*

glamorous ADJECTIVE excitingly attractive

glamour NOUN attractiveness; romantic charm

glance VERB **1** to look briefly **2** to strike at an angle and slide off *The ball glanced off his bat.* ▶ **glance** NOUN

gland NOUN an organ of the body that separates substances from the blood so that they can be used or passed out of the body
▶ **glandular** ADJECTIVE

glare VERB **1** to shine with a bright or dazzling light **2** to stare angrily
▶ **glare** NOUN

glaring ADJECTIVE very obvious *a glaring error*

glass NOUN **1** a hard brittle substance that allows light to pass through **2** a drinking container made of glass **3** a mirror or lens
▶ **glassy** ADJECTIVE

glasses PLURAL NOUN a pair of lenses in a frame, worn over the eyes to improve eyesight

glaze VERB **1** to fit a window or building with glass **2** to give a shiny surface to

glaze NOUN a shiny surface or coating

glazier (glay-zee-er) NOUN a person who fits glass

gleam VERB to shine brightly

glad ADJECTIVE • *I am glad you came.*
▶ pleased, happy, delighted, thrilled, overjoyed • *They were glad to help* ▶ pleased, willing, keen

glamorous ADJECTIVE • *a glamorous woman* ▶ beautiful, elegant, gorgeous, stylish • *a glamorous lifestyle* ▶ exciting, colourful, dazzling, glittering

glare VERB • *She glared at him.*
▶ stare angrily, glower, scowl, frown

glare NOUN • *an angry glare*
▶ stare, scowl, glower, frown • *the glare of the lights* ▶ dazzle, shine, blaze, brilliance

glaring ADJECTIVE • *a glaring error*
▶ obvious, conspicuous, blatant

gleam VERB • *The brass gleamed in the moonlight.* ▶ glimmer, glint, glow, shine, glisten

a
b
c
d
e
f
g
h
i
j
k
l
m
n
o
p
q
r
s
t
u
v
w
x
y
z

324

gleam NOUN **1** a beam of soft light **2** a small amount of hope

glean VERB to gather information bit by bit

glee NOUN mischievous delight
▶ **gleeful** ADJECTIVE, **gleefully** ADVERB

glen NOUN a narrow valley in Scotland

glib ADJECTIVE speaking or writing readily but not sincerely or thoughtfully

glide VERB **1** to move along smoothly **2** to fly without using an engine ▶ **glide** NOUN

glider NOUN an aircraft without an engine that flies by floating on warm air currents

glimmer NOUN **1** a faint light **2** a small sign or trace

glimmer VERB to shine with a faint, flickering light

glimpse VERB to see briefly
▶ **glimpse** NOUN

glint NOUN a brief flash of light

glint VERB to shine with a flash of light

glisten (glis-en) VERB to shine like something wet or oily

glitter VERB to shine or sparkle

glitter NOUN tiny sparkling pieces used for decoration

gloat VERB to be pleased in an unkind way about someone's misfortune

global ADJECTIVE **1** to do with the whole world **2** to do with the whole of a system ▶ **globally** ADVERB

globalization NOUN the process by which a business or organization becomes international

⚠ **SPELLING**

This word can also be spelled *globalisation.*

global warming NOUN the increase in the temperature of the earth's atmosphere

globe NOUN **1** a map of the whole world on a ball **2** something shaped like a ball

globule (glob-yool) NOUN a small rounded drop

gloom NOUN **1** darkness **2** sadness or despair

gleam NOUN • *the gleam of lights*
▶ glimmer, glint, glow, shimmer

glide VERB • *A boat glided past.*
▶ slide, slip, sail, skim • *The gulls were gliding overhead.* ▶ drift, soar, sail, float, fly

glimpse NOUN • *a quick glimpse of the house* ▶ glance, peep, look, sight, view

global ADJECTIVE • *global communications* ▶ worldwide, international • *a global solution to the problem* ▶ total, comprehensive, general

gloom NOUN • *They peered out into the gloom.* ▶ darkness, dimness, shade, shadow, twilight, obscurity • *a feeling of gloom* ▶ depression, dejection, despondency

gloomy ADJECTIVE **gloomier**, **gloomiest 1** almost dark **2** depressed or depressing
▶ **gloomily** ADVERB

glorify VERB **glorifies**, **glorified 1** to give great praise or honour to **2** to make a thing seem more splendid or attractive than it really is *a film that glorifies war*
▶ **glorification** NOUN

glorious ADJECTIVE splendid or magnificent

glory NOUN **glories 1** fame and honour **2** praise **3** beauty or magnificence

glory VERB **glories**, **gloried** to rejoice or take great pleasure

gloss¹ NOUN the shine on a smooth surface

gloss VERB to make a thing glossy

gloss² VERB **gloss over** to mention a fault or mistake only briefly

glossary NOUN **glossaries** a list of difficult words with their meanings explained

glossy ADJECTIVE **glossier**, **glossiest** smooth and shiny

glove NOUN a covering for the hand with divisions for each finger and the thumb

glow NOUN **1** brightness and warmth without flames **2** a warm or cheerful feeling *a glow of pride*

glow VERB to shine with a soft warm light

glower (rhymes with *flower*) VERB to stare angrily

glucose NOUN a form of sugar found in fruit juice and honey

glue NOUN a sticky substance used for sticking things together
▶ **gluey** ADJECTIVE

glue VERB to stick with glue

glum ADJECTIVE miserable or depressed

THESAURUS

gloomy ADJECTIVE • *a gloomy hall*
▶ dark, dingy, dim, dismal • *a gloomy expression* ▶ miserable, glum, dejected, unhappy • *a gloomy outlook* ▶ pessimistic, depressing, bleak

glorious ADJECTIVE • *a glorious victory* ▶ magnificent, splendid, celebrated, great • *a glorious view* ▶ wonderful, spectacular, magnificent, beautiful, stunning

glory NOUN • *the glory of competing for your country* ▶ distinction, honour, prestige, fame • *glory to God* ▶ praise, adoration, thanksgiving, worship

gloss NOUN • *a fine gloss on the surface* ▶ shine, sheen, brightness, lustre

glossy ADJECTIVE • *a glossy finish* ▶ bright, lustrous, polished, burnished, glassy

glow VERB • *Lights glowed.* ▶ shine, gleam, glimmer, flicker • *to glow with pleasure* ▶ shine, blush

glow NOUN • *the glow of the street lights* ▶ shine, gleam, glimmer • *a glow in her cheeks* ▶ flush, blush, rosiness

glum ADJECTIVE • *to feel glum* ▶ miserable, gloomy, dejected, unhappy

glut NOUN an excessive supply

glutinous ADJECTIVE glue-like or sticky

glutton NOUN a person who eats too much ▶ **gluttonous** ADJECTIVE, **gluttony** NOUN

glycerine (glis-er-een) NOUN a thick sweet colourless liquid

gnash (nash) VERB to grind the teeth together

gnat (nat) NOUN a tiny fly that bites

gnaw (naw) VERB to keep on biting something hard

gnome (nohm) NOUN (in stories) a dwarf that lives underground

gnu (noo) NOUN **gnu** or **gnus** a large ox-like antelope

go VERB **goes**, **going**, **went**, **gone** **1** to move from one place to another **2** to leave **3** to lead from one place to another *The road goes to Bristol.* **4** to become **He went pale.** **5** to make a sound *The*

gun went bang. **6** to belong *Plates go on that shelf.* **go off 1** to explode **2** to become stale **3** to stop liking something **go on** to continue **go out** to stop burning or shining **go through** to experience something unpleasant or difficult

go NOUN **goes 1** a turn or try **2** (informal) energy or liveliness *full of go*

goad VERB to stir into action by annoying

goal NOUN **1** the place where a ball must go to score a point in football, hockey, etc. **2** a point scored in this way **3** something you are trying to achieve

goalkeeper NOUN a player who defends the goal

goat NOUN an animal related to the sheep, with horns and a beard and long hair

THESAURUS

go VERB • *to go towards the door*
▶ move, advance, proceed, walk, make your way, progress • *We are going to London.* ▶ travel, journey, make a trip • *Several guests had already gone.* ▶ leave, depart, withdraw • *My purse had gone.* ▶ disappear, vanish • *The path goes to the village.* ▶ lead, continue, extend, stretch • *All the money goes to charity.* ▶ be given, be donated • *His hair had gone grey.* ▶ turn, become, grow • *I hope things go well for them.*
▶ work out, turn out, develop • *The coat and hat don't go.*

▶ match, blend, suit one another • *The car won't go.* ▶ start, work, function, run • *Where do these books go?* ▶ belong, be placed, be kept • *The time will go quickly.*
▶ pass, elapse **go away** • *She wanted them all to go away.*
▶ leave, depart **go through** • *to go through a difficult time*
▶ suffer, experience, endure **go with** • *Will you go with them?*
▶ accompany, escort • *I'm not sure this tie goes with my shirt.*
▶ match, suit

goal NOUN • *to achieve your goal*
▶ aim, objective, ambition, target

gobble VERB to eat quickly and greedily

gobbledegook NOUN (informal) technical language or jargon that is difficult to understand

goblet NOUN a drinking glass with a long stem and a base

goblin NOUN (in stories) a mischievous ugly elf

God NOUN the creator of the universe in Christian, Jewish, and Muslim belief

god NOUN a divine male being who is worshipped

godchild NOUN **godchildren** a child who has a godparent
▶ **god-daughter** NOUN, **godson** NOUN

goddess NOUN a divine female being who is worshipped

godparent NOUN a person at a child's christening who agrees to take responsibility for the child's religious upbringing
▶ **godfather** NOUN, **godmother** NOUN

godsend NOUN a piece of unexpected good luck

goggles PLURAL NOUN large glasses for protecting the eyes from wind, water, dust, etc.

going NOUN **good going** quick progress

gold NOUN **1** a precious yellow metal **2** a deep yellow colour
▶ **gold** ADJECTIVE

golden ADJECTIVE **1** made of gold **2** coloured like gold **3** precious or excellent *a golden opportunity*

goldfinch NOUN a bird with yellow feathers in its wings

goldfish NOUN a small red or orange fish

gold medal NOUN a medal awarded for first place in a competition

goldsmith NOUN a person who makes articles in gold

golf NOUN an outdoor game played by hitting a small white ball with a club into a series of holes on a prepared ground ▶ **golfer** NOUN

gondola (gond-uhl-uh) NOUN a boat with high pointed ends used on the canals in Venice

gondolier NOUN the person who moves a gondola along with a pole

gong NOUN a large metal disc that makes an echoing sound when it is hit

good ADJECTIVE **better**, **best**
1 having the right qualities *a good book* **2** kind *good of you to help* **3** well-behaved *a good boy* **4** skilled or talented *a good pianist* **5** healthy; giving benefit *Exercise*

THESAURUS

good ADJECTIVE • *a good person*
▶ kind, honest, virtuous, moral, upright, trustworthy • *a good hotel* ▶ fine, high-quality, excellent, outstanding • *The children were being good.*
▶ well-behaved, obedient, well-mannered • *a good thing to do* ▶ proper, right, correct, appropriate • *a good swimmer*
▶ capable, able, proficient, accomplished, talented • *a good*

is good for you. **6** thorough *a good clean* **7** large; considerable *a good distance away*

good NOUN **1** something good *to do good* **2** benefit *for your own good* **for good** for ever **no good** useless

goodbye EXCLAMATION a word used when you leave somebody

goodness NOUN **1** the quality of being good **2** the good part of something

goods PLURAL NOUN **1** things that are bought and sold **2** things that are transported by train or road

goodwill NOUN a kindly feeling towards others

goody NOUN **goodies** (*informal*) **1** something good to eat **2** a hero or good person in a story

gooey ADJECTIVE sticky or slimy

goose NOUN **geese** a large water bird with webbed feet and a long neck

gooseberry NOUN **gooseberries** a small green fruit that grows on a prickly bush

goose pimples or **goosebumps** PLURAL NOUN small bumps on the skin caused by cold or fear

gore[1] VERB to wound by piercing with a horn or tusk

gore[2] NOUN thickened blood from a cut or wound

gorge NOUN a narrow valley with steep sides

gorge VERB to eat greedily

gorgeous ADJECTIVE magnificent or beautiful

gorilla NOUN a large powerful ape

⚠ **USAGE**

Do not confuse this word with *guerrilla*.

gorse NOUN a prickly bush with small yellow flowers

gory ADJECTIVE **gorier, goriest** **1** covered with blood **2** with much bloodshed *a gory battle*

friend ► true, loyal, close, dear, trustworthy, dependable • *a good party* ► enjoyable, pleasant, agreeable • *a good clean* ► thorough, complete • *a good number of people* ► considerable, substantial, fair • *good of you to come* ► kind, generous, considerate • *a good time to call* ► convenient, suitable, appropriate • *food that is good for you* ► healthy, wholesome, nutritious, nourishing • *good reasons for going* ► valid, genuine, convincing

goodness NOUN • *a lot of goodness in these people* ► virtue, good, generosity, honesty

goods PLURAL NOUN • *the supply of goods and services* ► merchandise, products

goodwill NOUN • *full of goodwill* ► kindness, generosity, friendliness

gorgeous ADJECTIVE • *a gorgeous woman* ► beautiful, lovely, glamorous, stunning • *a gorgeous view* ► magnificent, spectacular, splendid, wonderful

gosh EXCLAMATION an exclamation of surprise

gosling NOUN a young goose

gospel NOUN 1 the teachings of Christ 2 something you can safely believe to be true

> **WORD HISTORY**
> from Old English *god spel* 'good news'

gossip VERB to talk trivially about other people

gossip NOUN 1 trivial talk or rumours about other people 2 a person who enjoys gossip
 ▶ **gossipy** ADJECTIVE

got past tense of **get**
have got to possess *Have you got a car?* **have got to** must *I have got to go now.*

gouge (gowj) VERB to scoop or force out by pressing

goulash (goo-lash) NOUN a meat stew seasoned with paprika

gourd (goord) NOUN the rounded hard-skinned fruit of a climbing plant

gourmet (goor-may) NOUN a person who appreciates good food and drink

gout NOUN a disease that causes painful swelling of the toes, knees, and fingers

govern VERB 1 to be in charge of the affairs of a country or region 2 to control or determine

governess NOUN a woman who teaches children at their home

government NOUN 1 the group of people who are in charge of the affairs of a country 2 the process of governing

governor NOUN 1 a person who governs a state or colony 2 a person who runs or helps to run an institution

gown NOUN 1 a woman's long dress 2 a loose robe worn by lawyers, members of a university, etc.

GP ABBREVIATION general practitioner

grab VERB **grabbing**, **grabbed** to take hold of firmly or suddenly

grace NOUN 1 beauty of movement 2 goodwill or favour 3 dignity or good manners *He had the grace to apologize.* 4 a short prayer of thanks at a meal 5 the title of a duke, duchess, or archbishop *Your Grace*

grace VERB to bring honour or dignity to someone or something *The mayor graced us with his presence.*

graceful ADJECTIVE beautiful and elegant ▶ **gracefully** ADVERB

govern VERB • *to govern the country* ▶ run, rule, be in charge of

grab VERB • *She grabbed him by the arm.* ▶ seize, grasp, grip, clutch • *Someone grabbed her credit card.* ▶ snatch, steal, take

grace NOUN • *to move with grace* ▶ elegance, poise, gracefulness

graceful ADJECTIVE • *clothes that are light and graceful* ▶ elegant, flowing, stylish, beautiful

gracious ADJECTIVE kind and honourable

grade NOUN **1** a step in a scale of quality or rank **2** a mark showing the quality of work

grade VERB to sort or divide into grades

gradient (gray-dee-uhnt) NOUN a slope or the steepness of a slope

gradual ADJECTIVE happening slowly but steadily ► **gradually** ADVERB

graduate (grad-yoo-ayt) VERB **1** to be awarded a university or college degree **2** to divide into graded sections ► **graduation** NOUN

graduate (grad-yoo-at) NOUN a person who has a university or college degree

graffiti NOUN words or drawings scribbled or sprayed on a wall

graft NOUN **1** a shoot from a plant or tree fitted into another to form a new growth **2** a piece of transplanted body tissue

graft VERB to insert or transplant as a graft

grain NOUN **1** a small hard seed or similar particle **2** cereal plants **3** a

small amount *a grain of truth*
4 the pattern of lines made by the fibres in a piece of wood or paper

gram NOUN a unit of mass or weight in the metric system

grammar NOUN **1** the rules for using words correctly **2** a book about these rules

grammar school NOUN a secondary school for children with academic ability

grammatical ADJECTIVE following the rules of grammar ► **grammatically** ADVERB

granary NOUN **granaries** a storehouse for grain

grand ADJECTIVE **1** splendid and impressive **2** most important or highest-ranking **3** including everything *a grand total*

grandad NOUN (informal) grandfather

grandchild NOUN **grandchildren** the child of a person's son or daughter ► **granddaughter** NOUN, **grandson** NOUN

grandeur (grand-yer) NOUN impressive beauty

grade NOUN • *a higher grade*
► mark, score, level • *the top grade* ► class, category • *officers in the lower grades* ► rank, level

grade VERB • *to be graded by size*
► sort, classify, categorize, group
• *to grade course work* ► mark, assess, evaluate, rate

gradual ADJECTIVE • *a gradual change* ► steady, slow, continuous, step-by-step • *a*

gradual slope ► gentle, slight, easy

gradually ADVERB • *to fade gradually* ► slowly, little by little, steadily, gently

grand ADJECTIVE • *a grand palace*
► magnificent, splendid, majestic
• *a grand old lady*
► distinguished, illustrious, eminent

a b c d e f **g** h i j k l m n o p q r s t u v w x y z

DICTIONARY

grandfather NOUN the father of a person's father or mother

grandiose (grand-ee-ohss) ADJECTIVE large and impressive

grandma NOUN (informal) grandmother

grandmother NOUN the mother of a person's father or mother

grandpa NOUN (informal) grandfather

grandparent NOUN a grandfather or grandmother

grandstand NOUN a building open at the front with seats for spectators at a racecourse or sports ground

granite NOUN a very hard kind of rock used for building

granny NOUN **grannies** (informal) grandmother

grant VERB **1** to give or allow to grant a request **2** to admit that something is true

grant NOUN a sum of money awarded for a special purpose

Granth (grunt) NOUN the sacred scriptures of the Sikhs

granular ADJECTIVE like grains

granule NOUN a small grain

grape NOUN a small green or purple berry that grows in bunches on a vine, used to make wine

grapefruit NOUN a large round yellow citrus fruit

grapevine NOUN **1** a vine with grapes growing on it **2** a means of spreading news

graph NOUN a diagram showing how two quantities or variables are related

graphic ADJECTIVE **1** to do with drawing or painting a graphic artist **2** (of a description) lively and vivid ▸ **graphically** ADVERB

graphics PLURAL NOUN diagrams, lettering, and drawings, especially pictures that are produced by a computer

graphite NOUN a soft black form of carbon used for the lead in pencils

grapple VERB **1** to struggle with **2** to seize **3** to try to deal with a problem

grasp VERB **1** to seize and hold firmly **2** to understand

grasp NOUN **1** a person's understanding of a subject **2** a firm hold

THESAURUS

grant VERB • to grant you a scholarship ▸ give, award • to grant a request ▸ allow, consent to, permit

grant NOUN • a grant to repair the roof ▸ award, allowance, subsidy, contribution, donation, endowment • a student grant ▸ bursary, scholarship, sponsorship, grant

graphic ADJECTIVE • a graphic description ▸ vivid, explicit, striking, dramatic, colourful

grasp VERB • He grasped her hand. ▸ grip, clasp, clutch, grab, seize, hang on to • to grasp the point ▸ understand, comprehend

grasp NOUN • to escape his grasp ▸ grip, hold, clutch, control • within his grasp ▸ reach, power

a
b
c
d
e
f
g
h
i
j
k
l
m
n
o
p
q
r
s
t
u
v
w
x
y
z

grasping ADJECTIVE greedy

grass NOUN **1** a plant with green blades and stalks that are eaten by animals **2** ground covered with grass; lawn ► **grassy** ADJECTIVE

grasshopper NOUN a jumping insect that makes a shrill noise

grate¹ NOUN **1** a metal framework that keeps fuel in a fireplace **2** a fireplace

grate² VERB **1** to shred into small pieces by rubbing on a rough surface **2** to make a harsh unpleasant sound **3** to sound harshly

grateful ADJECTIVE thankful for something that has been done for you ► **gratefully** ADVERB

grater NOUN a device for grating food

gratify VERB **gratifies, gratified** to please or satisfy ► **gratification** NOUN

grating NOUN a framework of metal bars across an opening

gratitude NOUN a feeling of being grateful

gratuitous (gra-tew-it-us) ADJECTIVE done without good reason; uncalled for

grave¹ NOUN the place where a dead body is buried

grave² ADJECTIVE serious or solemn ► **gravely** ADVERB

grave accent (rhymes with *starve*) NOUN a backward-sloping mark over a vowel, as in *à*

gravel NOUN small stones mixed with coarse sand ► **gravelled** ADJECTIVE

gravestone NOUN a stone monument over a grave

graveyard NOUN a burial ground

gravitate VERB to move or be attracted towards something

gravitation NOUN **1** the process of gravitating **2** the force of gravity

gravity NOUN **1** the force that pulls everything towards the earth **2** seriousness

gravy NOUN a hot brown sauce made from meat juices

graze VERB **1** to feed on growing grass **2** to scrape the skin slightly **3** to touch lightly in passing

THESAURUS

• *a good grasp of the subject*
► understanding, comprehension

grateful ADJECTIVE • *grateful for all the support* ► thankful, appreciative (of), indebted, obliged

grave ADJECTIVE • *a grave error* ► serious, important, significant, crucial, momentous • *a grave expression* ► serious, solemn, sombre, earnest

gravity NOUN • *the gravity of the situation* ► seriousness, importance, magnitude • *the gravity of his manner* ► solemnity, dignity

graze VERB • *to graze a knee* ► scrape, cut, scratch • *Cattle grazed in the fields.* ► feed, browse, crop

DICTIONARY

graze NOUN a raw place where skin has been scraped

grease NOUN 1 any thick oily substance 2 melted fat

grease VERB to put grease on

greasy ADJECTIVE **greasier**, **greasiest** containing or covered in grease

great ADJECTIVE 1 very large; much more than normal 2 very important or talented *a great writer* 3 (*informal*) very good or enjoyable *great to see you* 4 older or younger by one generation *great-grandmother* ▸ **greatly** ADVERB

greed NOUN a constant desire for more than you need

greedy ADJECTIVE **greedier** **greediest** wanting more food, money, or other things than you need ▸ **greedily** ADVERB

green ADJECTIVE 1 of the colour of grass, leaves, etc. 2 concerned with protecting the environment 3 inexperienced

green NOUN 1 the colour of grass, leaves, etc. 2 an area of land with grass

greenery NOUN green leaves or plants

greenfly NOUN **greenfly** a small green insect that sucks the juice from plants

greengrocer NOUN someone who sells fruit and vegetables

greenhouse NOUN a glass building in which plants are protected from the cold

greens PLURAL NOUN green vegetables, such as cabbage and spinach

greet VERB 1 to meet and welcome 2 to receive *They greeted the song*

THESAURUS

greasy ADJECTIVE • *greasy hair*
▸ oily, shiny, waxy • *greasy marks*
▸ oily, fatty, slimy

great ADJECTIVE • *a great mountain*
▸ large, huge, enormous, gigantic, massive, colossal • *a great advantage* ▸ considerable, special, extreme • *great statesmen* ▸ famous, eminent, celebrated, distinguished • *great advances in medicine* ▸ big, important, significant, crucial, vital • *a great party* ▸ excellent, enjoyable, marvellous, wonderful, fantastic

greed NOUN • *to eat with greed*
▸ hunger, gluttony, ravenousness • *greed for money* ▸ avarice,

acquisitiveness, desire, selfishness • *a greed for power* ▸ appetite, desire, need, longing

greedy ADJECTIVE • *a greedy eater*
▸ gluttonous, ravenous, voracious, insatiable • *greedy for money* ▸ avaricious, acquisitive, mercenary, grasping • *greedy for power* ▸ eager, avid, longing

green ADJECTIVE • *a green garden*
▸ leafy, grassy, verdant • *green issues* ▸ environmental, ecological, conservationist

greet VERB • *to greet visitors*
▸ welcome, say hello to, receive, hail

a
b
c
d
e
f
g
h
i
j
k
l
m
n
o
p
q
r
s
t
u
v
w
x
y
z

with applause. **3** to present itself to *A strange sight greeted our eyes.*

greeting NOUN words or actions used to greet someone

greetings PLURAL NOUN good wishes

gregarious (grig-**air**-ee-us) ADJECTIVE fond of company

grenade (grin-**ayd**) NOUN a small bomb thrown by hand

grey ADJECTIVE of a colour between black and white ▶ **grey** NOUN

greyhound NOUN a slender racing dog with smooth hair

grid NOUN **1** a pattern of bars or lines crossing each other **2** a network of cables carrying electricity over a large area

grief NOUN deep sorrow, especially at a person's death

grievance NOUN a cause for complaining

grieve VERB **1** to feel deep sorrow at a person's death **2** to make a person feel very sad

grievous (gree-vus) ADJECTIVE **1** causing grief **2** serious

grill NOUN **1** a heated element on a cooker, sending heat downwards **2** food cooked under this

grill VERB **1** to cook under a grill **2** to question closely

grille NOUN a metal grating over a window or opening

grim ADJECTIVE **grimmer**, **grimmest 1** stern or severe **2** unpleasant or unattractive ▶ **grimly** ADVERB

grimace NOUN a twisted expression on the face

grimace VERB to make a grimace

grime NOUN dirt in a layer on a surface

grimy ADJECTIVE **grimier**, **grimiest** covered in a layer of dirt

grin NOUN a broad smile

grin VERB **grinning**, **grinned** to smile broadly

grind VERB **1** to crush into powder **2** to sharpen on a rough surface **3** to rub harshly together

grip VERB **gripping**, **gripped** to hold firmly

greeting NOUN • *to call out a greeting* ▶ hello, welcome

greetings • *birthday greetings* ▶ good wishes, best wishes, congratulations

grey ADJECTIVE • *a grey beard* ▶ silver, silvery, whitish, grizzled • *a grey day* ▶ cloudy, overcast, gloomy, dreary

grief NOUN • *overcome by grief* ▶ sadness, sorrow, mourning, bereavement

grieve VERB • *She grieved for her mother.* ▶ mourn, lament, weep, cry

grim ADJECTIVE • *a grim expression* ▶ stern, severe, harsh • *the grim prospect of death* ▶ unpleasant, dreadful, terrible

grip VERB • *He gripped her hand.* ▶ grasp, clasp, clutch, grab, seize • *The film gripped everyone.* ▶ engross, absorb, fascinate, captivate

DICTIONARY

grip NOUN **1** a firm hold **2** a handle **3** a travelling bag **get to grips with** to begin to deal with

gripe VERB (informal) to grumble or complain

gripe NOUN a complaint

gripping ADJECTIVE (of a story etc.) exciting

grisly ADJECTIVE **grislier, grisliest** causing horror or disgust

⚠ **USAGE**

Do not confuse this word with *grizzly*.

gristle NOUN tough rubbery tissue in meat ▶ **gristly** ADJECTIVE

grit NOUN **1** tiny pieces of stone or sand **2** courage and endurance

grit VERB **gritting, gritted 1** to spread grit over **2** to clench your teeth

gritty ADJECTIVE **grittier, grittiest 1** like grit or covered in grit **2** showing courage

grizzle VERB to whimper or whine

grizzled ADJECTIVE streaked with grey hairs

grizzly ADJECTIVE **grizzlier, grizzliest** grey or grey-haired

⚠ **USAGE**

Do not confuse this word with *grisly*.

grizzly bear NOUN a large fierce bear of North America

groan VERB to make a long deep sound in pain or disapproval ▶ **groan** NOUN

grocer NOUN a person who sells food and household goods

groceries PLURAL NOUN goods sold by a grocer

groggy ADJECTIVE **groggier, groggiest** dizzy and unsteady after illness or injury

groin NOUN the hollow between the thigh and the trunk of the body

groom NOUN **1** a person who looks after horses **2** a bridegroom

groom VERB **1** to clean and brush a horse **2** to train for a job or position

groove NOUN a long narrow channel cut in a surface ▶ **grooved** ADJECTIVE

grope VERB to feel about for something you cannot see

gross (grohss) ADJECTIVE **1** fat and ugly **2** obvious or shocking *gross stupidity* **3** bad-mannered **4** total *gross income* ▶ **grossly** ADVERB

gross NOUN twelve dozen (144)

grotesque (groh-**tesk**) ADJECTIVE strange and ugly in appearance

grotto NOUN **grottoes** an artificial cave

ground[1] past tense of **grind**

THESAURUS

grip NOUN • *a firm grip* ▶ hold, grasp, clasp, clutch

groove NOUN • *a groove in the rock* ▶ channel, furrow, hollow, rut

gross ADJECTIVE • *a gross exaggeration* ▶ extreme, blatant, flagrant, obvious • *gross income* ▶ total, inclusive, overall

a b c d e f **g** h i j k l m n o p q r s t u v w x y z

DICTIONARY

ground[2] NOUN **1** the solid surface of the earth **2** a sports field **3** land of a certain kind *marshy ground*

ground VERB **1** to keep an aircraft from flying **2** to stop a child from going out

grounding NOUN basic training or instruction

groundless ADJECTIVE without reason

grounds PLURAL NOUN **1** the gardens of a large house **2** solid particles that sink to the bottom of liquid **3** reasons *grounds for suspicion*

groundwork NOUN the first work done for a task

group NOUN a number of people or things that come or belong together

group VERB to put together in a group or groups

grouse[1] NOUN grouse a bird with feathered feet, hunted as game

grouse[2] VERB (informal) to grumble or complain ▸ **grouse** NOUN

grove NOUN a small group of trees

grovel VERB **grovelling**, **grovelled 1** to crawl on the ground **2** to act in an excessively humble way

grow VERB **grew**, **grown 1** to become bigger or greater **2** to develop **3** to plant and look after **4** to become *grew tired* **grow up** to become an adult

growl VERB to make a deep angry sound in the throat ▸ **growl** NOUN

grown-up NOUN An adult person ▸ **grown-up** ADJECTIVE

growth NOUN **1** the process of growing **2** something that has

THESAURUS

ground NOUN • *The ground was wet.* ▸ earth, soil, turf • *The plane rose from the ground.* ▸ land, surface **grounds** • *a large house in its own grounds* ▸ land, estate, gardens

group NOUN • *divided into groups* ▸ set, section • *a reading group* ▸ club, circle, society, association • *a group of islands* ▸ cluster, collection, formation, bunch, clump • *a group of fans* ▸ crowd, band, body, gang, bunch • *They sorted the books into groups.* ▸ category, type, sort, kind

group VERB • *Chairs are grouped around coffee tables.* ▸ arrange, organize • *We group the books*

according to size. ▸ classify, categorize, sort **group together** • *Farmers grouped together to cooperate.* ▸ unite, join together, join forces, team up

grow VERB • *The baby grew fast.* ▸ get bigger, get larger, increase in size • *Their debts are growing.* ▸ increase, mount up, multiply • *to grow roses* ▸ cultivate, produce, propagate, farm • *It was growing dark.* ▸ become, turn • *The business is growing.* ▸ expand, develop, flourish, thrive

growth NOUN • *a growth in population* ▸ increase, expansion • *hormones that aid growth* ▸ growing, development,

grown **3** a lump or tumour on or
inside a person's body

grub NOUN **1** a tiny worm-like
creature that will become an
insect; a larva **2** (informal) food

grubby ADJECTIVE **grubbier,
grubbiest** rather dirty
► **grubbiness** NOUN

grudge NOUN a feeling of
resentment or ill will to bear a
grudge

grudge VERB to resent having to
give or allow

gruelling ADJECTIVE exhausting

gruesome ADJECTIVE horrible or
disgusting

gruff ADJECTIVE having a rough voice
or manner

grumble VERB to complain in a
bad-tempered way ► **grumble**
NOUN

grumpy ADJECTIVE **grumpier,
grumpiest** bad-tempered
► **grumpily** ADVERB

grunt VERB to make the gruff snort
of a pig ► **grunt** NOUN

guarantee NOUN **1** a formal
promise **2** a statement by the
maker of a product that it will be
put right if faulty

guarantee VERB **1** to give a
guarantee **2** to make something
certain ► **guarantor** NOUN

guard VERB **1** to protect or keep
safe **2** to watch over and prevent
from escaping

maturing • economic growth
► expansion, development,
progress, advance • to have a
growth removed ► tumour, lump,
swelling

grudge NOUN • to have a grudge
► grievance, resentment

gruelling ADJECTIVE • a gruelling
journey ► exhausting, arduous,
strenuous

gruesome ADJECTIVE • the
gruesome remains ► horrible,
horrific, grisly, gory

gruff ADJECTIVE • a gruff voice
► harsh, rough, hoarse, husky • a
gruff manner ► abrupt, brusque,
curt, blunt

grumble VERB • to grumble about
the noise ► complain, protest,
whine, moan, whinge

grumble NOUN • grumbles about
the weather ► complaint, moan,
groan, protest

grumpy ADJECTIVE • grumpy in the
morning ► bad-tempered,
irritable, crotchety, cantankerous,
stroppy

guarantee NOUN • a six-month
guarantee ► warranty • a
guarantee of success ► promise,
commitment, assurance

guarantee VERB • cannot
guarantee that this will work
► promise, swear, assure, give
your word • a reservation will
guarantee a seat ► secure,
ensure, make sure of

guard VERB • Troops guarded the
house. ► protect, watch over,
safeguard, defend • An escort
guarded the prisoners.
► supervise, watch over, control

a
b
c
d
e
f
g
h
i
j
k
l
m
n
o
p
q
r
s
t
u
v
w
x
y
z

a
b
c
d
e
f

g

h
i
j
k
l
m
n
o
p
q
r
s
t
u
v
w
x
y
z

guard NOUN **1** the act of guarding *under close guard* **2** someone guarding a person or place **3** a group of soldiers or police acting as a guard **4** a railway official in charge of a train **5** a protecting device

guardian NOUN **1** someone who guards **2** a person who is legally in charge of a child in place of the child's parents ▸ **guardianship** NOUN

guerrilla (ger-il-a) NOUN a member of a small unofficial army who fights by making surprise attacks

> ⚠ **USAGE**
>
> Do not confuse this word with *gorilla*.

guess NOUN an opinion or answer given without certain knowledge

guess VERB to make a guess

guesswork NOUN something you do by guessing

guest NOUN a person who is staying at another person's house or hotel etc.

guffaw VERB to laugh noisily ▸ **guffaw** NOUN

guidance NOUN **1** the act of guiding **2** advice on problems

Guide NOUN a member of the Girl Guides Association, an organization for girls

guide NOUN **1** a person who shows others the way or points out interesting sights **2** a book giving information about a place

guide VERB to show someone the way or how to do something

guide dog NOUN a dog trained to lead a blind person

guidelines PLURAL NOUN rules or information about how something should be done

guild (gild) NOUN a society of people with similar skills or interests

THESAURUS

guard NOUN • *guards at the border* ▸ sentry, sentinel, lookout, patrol, watchman • *a prison guard* ▸ jailer, prison officer, warder, warden

guess NOUN • *That's my guess.* ▸ estimate, feeling, prediction, hunch

guess VERB • *to guess the weight of the cake* ▸ estimate, reckon, judge, predict, gauge • *I guess I should say sorry.* ▸ suppose, believe, think

guest NOUN • *guests for dinner* ▸ visitor, company, caller • *a hotel*

guest ▸ resident, patron, client, customer

guidance NOUN • *to offer guidance* ▸ advice, help, direction, instruction, guidelines

guide NOUN • *a guide to show you the way* ▸ escort, leader, navigator • *a guide to follow* ▸ model, example, guideline, pointer

guide VERB • *I asked her to guide me back.* ▸ lead, direct, show, take, accompany, escort • *to guide students in their work* ▸ advise, direct, supervise, teach

guile (rhymes with *mile*) NOUN craftiness; cunning

guillotine (gil-ot-een) NOUN **1** a machine with a heavy blade for beheading criminals **2** a machine for cutting paper

guillotine VERB to behead or cut with a guillotine

guilt NOUN **1** the fact of having committed an offence **2** a feeling that you are to blame

guilty ADJECTIVE **guiltier, guiltiest 1** having done wrong **2** feeling or showing guilt *a guilty conscience*
▶ **guiltily** ADVERB

guinea (gin-ee) NOUN **1** a former British gold coin worth 21 shillings (£1.05) **2** this amount of money

guinea pig NOUN **1** a small furry animal without a tail **2** someone used as the subject of an experiment

guise (guys) NOUN an outward disguise or pretence

guitar NOUN a musical instrument played by plucking the strings
▶ **guitarist** NOUN

gulf NOUN **1** a large area of the sea partly surrounded by land **2** a large difference

gull NOUN a seagull

gullet NOUN the passage from the throat to the stomach

gullible ADJECTIVE easily deceived

gully NOUN **gullies** a narrow channel carrying water

gulp VERB **1** to swallow hastily or greedily **2** to make a loud swallowing noise from fear

gulp NOUN **1** the act of gulping **2** a large mouthful of liquid

gum NOUN **1** the firm flesh in which the teeth are rooted **2** a sticky substance produced by some trees and shrubs, used as glue **3** a sweet made with gum or gelatin **4** chewing gum ▶ **gummy** ADJECTIVE

gum VERB **gumming, gummed** to cover or stick with gum

gumption NOUN (*informal*) common sense

gun NOUN a weapon that fires shells or bullets

gun VERB **gunning, gunned gun down** to shoot and kill with a gun

gunfire NOUN the firing of guns

gunpowder NOUN an explosive powder

gunshot NOUN a shot fired from a gun

gurdwara NOUN a Sikh temple

THESAURUS

guilt NOUN • *The jury was sure of his guilt.* ▶ guiltiness, culpability, blame • *to feel guilt* ▶ shame, remorse, self-reproach, regret

guilty ADJECTIVE • *guilty of assault* ▶ culpable, blameworthy, at fault, responsible, in the wrong • *to feel guilty* ▶ ashamed, remorseful, sorry, repentant, regretful

gulf NOUN • *the gulf between rich and poor* ▶ gap, contrast, chasm, divide, rift

gun NOUN • *He threatened her with a gun.* ▶ firearm, weapon, pistol, revolver, rifle, shotgun

gurgle VERB to make a low bubbling sound ▸ **gurgle** NOUN

guru NOUN **1** a Hindu religious leader **2** an influential teacher

gush VERB **1** to flow suddenly or quickly **2** to talk too enthusiastically or emotionally ▸ **gush** NOUN

gust NOUN a sudden rush of wind, rain, or smoke ▸ **gusty** ADJECTIVE

gust VERB to blow in gusts

gusto NOUN great enjoyment or enthusiasm

gut NOUN the lower part of the digestive system; the intestine

gut VERB **gutting, gutted 1** to remove the guts from **2** to remove or destroy the inside of *Fire gutted the building.*

guts PLURAL NOUN **1** the digestive system; the insides of a person or thing **2** (*informal*) courage

gutted ADJECTIVE (*informal*) extremely disappointed or upset

gutter NOUN a long narrow water channel at the side of a street or along the edge of a roof

guttural ADJECTIVE throaty and harsh-sounding

guy[1] NOUN **1** a figure representing Guy Fawkes, burned on 5 November in memory of a plot to blow up Parliament on that day in 1605 **2** (*informal*) a man

guy[2] NOUN a rope used to secure a tent

guzzle VERB to eat or drink greedily ▸ **guzzler** NOUN

gym (jim) NOUN **1** a gymnasium **2** gymnastics

gymkhana (jim-kah-na) NOUN a series of horse-riding contests and other sports events

gymnasium NOUN a place equipped for gymnastics

gymnast NOUN an expert in gymnastics

gymnastics PLURAL NOUN exercises to develop the muscles ▸ **gymnastic** ADJECTIVE

Gypsy NOUN **Gypsies** a member of a community of people, also called travellers, who travel from place to place

gyrate (jy-rayt) VERB to move in circles or spirals ▸ **gyration** NOUN

gyroscope (jy-ro-skohp) NOUN a navigation device that keeps steady in a rolling ship

THESAURUS

gush VERB • *Blood gushed from the wound.* ▸ pour, spurt, squirt, stream

Hh

habit NOUN **1** something that you do often and are used to **2** something that is hard to give up **3** the dress worn by a monk or nun

habitat NOUN the place in which an animal or plant lives naturally

habitation NOUN a place to live in

habitual ADJECTIVE done by habit; usual ► **habitually** ADVERB

hack VERB **1** to chop or cut roughly **2** (*informal*) to break into a computer system

hacker NOUN a person who breaks into a computer system, especially that of a company or government

hackles PLURAL NOUN **make someone's hackles rise** to make them angry

hackneyed ADJECTIVE (of a word or phrase) used often and no longer interesting

hacksaw NOUN a saw for cutting metal

haddock NOUN **haddock** a small sea fish used as food

hadn't had not

haemoglobin (heem-a-gloh-bin) NOUN the red substance that carries oxygen in the blood

haemophilia (heem-o-fil-ee-a) NOUN a disease that causes dangerous bleeding from even a slight cut ► **haemophiliac** NOUN, ADJECTIVE

haemorrhage (hem-er-ij) NOUN bleeding, especially inside a person's body

hag NOUN an ugly old woman

haggard ADJECTIVE looking ill or very tired

haggis NOUN a Scottish food made from sheep's offal

haggle VERB to argue about a price or agreement

haiku (hy-koo) NOUN a Japanese form of poem, written in three lines of five, seven, and five syllables

hail[1] NOUN frozen drops of rain

hail VERB to fall as hail

hail[2] VERB to call out to **hail from** to come from *He hails from Ireland.*

hailstone NOUN a piece of hail

hair NOUN **1** a soft covering growing on the heads and bodies of people and animals **2** one of the threads forming part of this

hairbrush NOUN a brush for grooming the hair

haircut NOUN **1** the act of cutting a person's hair **2** a hairstyle

hairdresser NOUN a person who cuts and arranges people's hair

hair-raising ADJECTIVE terrifying

hairstyle NOUN a way of cutting and arranging the hair

THESAURUS

habit NOUN • *healthy eating habits* ► practice, custom, pattern, routine • *her habit*

of twirling her hair ► mannerism, quirk, trick, gesture, custom, practice

a
b
c
d
e
f
g
h
i
j
k
l
m
n
o
p
q
r
s
t
u
v
w
x
y
z

hairy ADJECTIVE **hairier, hairiest** covered with hair

hajj NOUN the Muslim pilgrimage to Mecca

hake NOUN **hake** a sea fish used as food

halal ADJECTIVE keeping to Muslim law about the preparation of meat

hale ADJECTIVE strong and healthy *hale and hearty*

half NOUN **halves** each of two equal parts into which something can be divided

half ADVERB partly; not completely *only half cooked*

half-brother or **half-sister** NOUN a brother or sister by one parent only

half-hearted ADJECTIVE not enthusiastic

half mast NOUN the position of a flag halfway up the flagpole as a mark of respect for a person who has died

half-term NOUN a short holiday in the middle of a term

half-time NOUN the point or interval halfway through a game

halfway ADJECTIVE, ADVERB at a point half the distance or amount between two places or times

halibut NOUN a large flat fish used as food

> ### WORD HISTORY
>
> from *holy butt* (the name of a fish), because it was eaten on holy days, when meat was not allowed

hall NOUN **1** a space or passage inside the front entrance of a house **2** a large room or building used for public events

hallmark NOUN **1** an official mark on gold and silver showing its quality **2** a characteristic by which something is recognized

hallo EXCLAMATION a word of greeting

hallowed ADJECTIVE honoured as being holy

Hallowe'en NOUN 31 October, traditionally a time when ghosts and spirits are believed to be present

hallucinate VERB to see something that is not really there ▶ **hallucination** NOUN

halo NOUN **haloes** a circle of light round the head of a holy person in paintings

halt VERB to stop

halt NOUN **1** a stop or standstill *come to a halt* **2** a small stopping place on a railway

---

THESAURUS

hairy ADJECTIVE • *a hairy chest*
▶ furry, shaggy, woolly, bristly, downy

hall NOUN • *the village hall*
▶ assembly hall, meeting room, auditorium, concert hall • *Leave your coat in the hall.* ▶ hallway, entrance hall, lobby, foyer

halt VERB • *Strikes halted production.* ▶ stop, terminate, block • *Traffic halted on the bridge.* ▶ stop, wait, come to a halt, pull up • *Work has halted.* ▶ cease, stop, break off

halt NOUN • *to come to a halt*
▶ stop, standstill, pause

halter NOUN a rope or strap put round a horse's head for guiding it

halve VERB 1 to divide into halves 2 to reduce to half

ham NOUN meat from a pig's leg

hamburger NOUN a fried cake of minced beef

hamlet NOUN a small village

hammer NOUN a tool with a heavy metal head for driving in nails

hammer VERB 1 to hit with a hammer 2 to knock loudly

hammock NOUN a bed made of a length of cloth or netting hung up by the ends

hamper[1] NOUN a large box-shaped basket with a lid

hamper[2] VERB to hinder or prevent from working freely

hamster NOUN a small furry animal with cheek pouches for carrying grain

hamstring NOUN a tendon at the back of the knee

hand NOUN 1 the end part of the arm below the wrist 2 a pointer on a clock or dial 3 a worker; a member of a ship's crew 4 the cards held by a player in a card game 5 side or direction *the right-hand side* 6 help or aid *Give me a hand.* 7 applause *a big hand* **at hand** near; available **by hand** using your hand or hands **hands down** winning easily **in hand** being dealt with **on hand** available **out of hand** out of control

hand VERB to give or pass to someone

handbag NOUN a small bag for holding a purse and personal articles

handcuffs PLURAL NOUN a pair of metal rings linked by a chain, for fastening the wrists of a prisoner

handcuff VERB to fasten with handcuffs

handful NOUN **handfuls** 1 as much as can be carried in one hand 2 a few people or things 3 a troublesome person or task

THESAURUS

hammer VERB • *to hammer on the door* ▶ beat, batter, knock, pummel, pound

hamper VERB • *Bad weather hampered the rescue.* ▶ hinder, obstruct, hold up, restrict • *Her bandaged hand hampered her.* ▶ hinder, encumber, impede, restrain, hold back

hand NOUN • *a person's hand* ▶ fist, palm • *the hand of a gauge* ▶ pointer, indicator • *The factory*

took on more hands. ▶ worker, employee, labourer **at hand** ▶ close by, handy, accessible, available

hand VERB • *He handed her a letter.* ▶ give, offer, pass, deliver **hand out** or **round** • *to hand out forms* ▶ distribute, give out **hand over** • *to hand over a large sum* ▶ give, pay, donate • *to hand over prisoners* ▶ deliver up, surrender

handicap NOUN a disability or disadvantage ► **handicapped** ADJECTIVE

handicraft NOUN artistic work done with the hands

handiwork NOUN **1** something made by hand **2** something someone has done

handkerchief NOUN **handkerchieves** a small square of cloth for wiping the nose or face

handle NOUN the part of a thing by which it is held or controlled

handle VERB **1** to touch or feel with your hands **2** to deal with ► **handler** NOUN

handlebars PLURAL NOUN a bar with handles for steering at the front of a bicycle or motorcycle

handout NOUN **1** money given to a needy person **2** a sheet of information given out in a lesson or talk

handsome ADJECTIVE **1** good-looking **2** generous *a handsome gift*

hands-on ADJECTIVE involving actual experience

handstand NOUN an act of balancing on your hands with your feet in the air

handwriting NOUN writing done by hand ► **handwritten** ADJECTIVE

handy ADJECTIVE **handier**, **handiest 1** convenient or useful **2** good at using the hands

handyman NOUN **handymen** a person who does odd jobs

hang VERB **hung 1** to fix or be fixed at the top or side so it is off the ground **2** to stick wallpaper to a wall **3** to decorate with ornaments **4** to remain in the air or as something unpleasant *Smoke hung over the city.* **5** (with *past tense* & *past participle* **hanged**) to

---

THESAURUS

handicap NOUN • *Their poor French was a handicap.*
► disadvantage, difficulty, problem, drawback, hindrance • *a physical handicap* ► disability, impairment

handle VERB • *Do not handle the exhibits.* ► touch, feel, hold, finger, pick up • *He handled the situation well.* ► control, cope with, deal with, manage • *a smaller car that he could handle more easily* ► control, drive, manoeuvre, steer

handsome ADJECTIVE • *a handsome man* ► good-looking, attractive • *a handsome building*

► elegant, attractive, striking, imposing • *a handsome profit* ► large, big, sizeable, generous

handy ADJECTIVE • *a handy tool* ► useful, convenient, practical, helpful • *handy with a screwdriver* ► skilful, adept, able • *Keep your timer handy.* ► accessible, available, ready

hang VERB • *Baskets of flowers hung from the lampposts.* ► dangle, swing, be suspended • *Curtains hang from every window.*
► drape, drop, cascade • *to hang pictures* ► fix, attach, fasten, display

execute a condemned person by hanging them from a rope round the neck

hangar NOUN a large shed for aircraft

hanger NOUN a device for hanging clothes

hang-glider NOUN a framework in which a person can glide through the air ▸ **hang-gliding** NOUN

hangover NOUN an unpleasant feeling after drinking too much alcohol

hank NOUN a coil or piece of wool, thread, etc.

hanker VERB to feel a longing for something

hanky NOUN **hankies** (*informal*) a handkerchief

Hanukkah (hah-noo-ka) NOUN the eight-day Jewish festival of lights beginning in December

haphazard ADJECTIVE done or chosen at random, without planning

hapless ADJECTIVE having no luck

happen VERB **1** to take place; to occur **2** to do something by chance *I happened to see him.*

happening NOUN something that happens; an event

happy ADJECTIVE **happier**, **happiest 1** pleased or contented **2** fortunate *a happy coincidence* **3** willing *happy to help* ▸ **happily** ADVERB, **happiness** NOUN

harangue (ha-rang) VERB to make a long aggressive speech to ▸ **harangue** NOUN

harass (ha-ras) VERB to trouble or annoy persistently ▸ **harassment** NOUN

harbour NOUN a place where ships can shelter or unload

harbour VERB **1** to keep in your mind *to harbour a grudge* **2** to give shelter to

haphazard ADJECTIVE • *things strewn about in a haphazard fashion* ▸ random, arbitrary, chaotic, disorganized

happen VERB • *Something strange happened.* ▸ occur, take place, arise, transpire

happening NOUN • *all the happenings of that week* ▸ event, incident, occurrence

happiness NOUN • *a feeling of great happiness* ▸ contentment, joy, gladness, pleasure, bliss, elation

happy ADJECTIVE • *happy faces* ▸ cheerful, contented, smiling, joyful, delighted, thrilled, overjoyed • *happy to help* ▸ pleased, glad, willing, delighted

harass VERB • *They have been harassing us.* ▸ pester, torment, persecute, hassle

harbour NOUN • *boats down in the harbour* ▸ port, dock, marina, quay, waterfront

harbour VERB • *to harbour a criminal* ▸ hide, protect, shelter

a
b
c
d
e
f
g
h
i
j
k
l
m
n
o
p
q
r
s
t
u
v
w
x
y
z

DICTIONARY

hard ADJECTIVE **1** firm or solid; not soft **2** difficult to do or understand **3** severe or stern **4** causing suffering *hard luck* **5** using great effort *a hard worker* **6** (of drugs) strong and addictive **7** (of water) containing minerals that reduce lathering

hard ADVERB with great effort *to work hard*

hardboard NOUN stiff board made of compressed wood pulp

hard disk NOUN (ICT) a computer disk able to store large amounts of data

harden VERB to make or become hard

hard-hearted ADJECTIVE unkind or unsympathetic

hardly ADVERB only just; only with difficulty *can hardly speak*

hardship NOUN difficult conditions or suffering

hardware NOUN **1** metal implements and tools **2** (ICT) the machinery of a computer as opposed to the software

hardy ADJECTIVE **hardier**, **hardiest** able to endure cold or difficult conditions ▶ **hardiness** NOUN

hare NOUN an animal like a rabbit but larger

harem (har-eem) NOUN the part of a Muslim palace or house where the women live

hark VERB to listen

harlequin NOUN a pantomime character who wears a costume of mixed colours

harm VERB to damage or injure

harm NOUN damage or injury

harmful ADJECTIVE causing harm or injury

THESAURUS

hard ADJECTIVE • *The ground is too hard to play on.* ▶ solid, firm, compact • *hard work* ▶ strenuous, arduous, exhausting, demanding • *a hard problem* ▶ difficult, complicated, involved, baffling, puzzling • *a hard taskmaster* ▶ strict, harsh, firm, stern • *a hard blow* ▶ heavy, forceful, strong, powerful, violent

hard ADVERB • *to work hard* ▶ diligently, industriously, steadily • *raining hard* ▶ heavily, steadily • *She looked hard at them.* ▶ intently, intensely, closely

hardly ADVERB • *hardly surprising* ▶ not at all, by no means • *He*

hardly knew her. ▶ scarcely, barely, only slightly

hardship NOUN • *to cause hardship* ▶ suffering, misery, unhappiness

hardy ADJECTIVE • *hardy walkers* ▶ tough, fit, robust, strong

harm NOUN • *to cause harm to the public* ▶ injury, damage, suffering, hurt

harm VERB • *to harm the hostages* ▶ hurt, injure • *to harm the environment* ▶ damage, spoil, ruin

harmful ADJECTIVE • *the harmful effects of smoking* ▶ damaging, detrimental, unhealthy, destructive

harmless ADJECTIVE not causing any harm; safe

harmonic ADJECTIVE to do with harmony in music

harmonica NOUN a mouth organ

harmonious ADJECTIVE
1 combining together in a pleasant or effective way
2 sounding pleasant 3 peaceful and friendly

harmonize VERB to combine together in a pleasant way
► **harmonization** NOUN

⚠ **SPELLING**

This word can also be spelled *harmonise.*

harmony NOUN **harmonies** 1 a pleasant combination of musical notes 2 a state of being friendly

harness NOUN the straps put round a horse's head and neck for controlling it

harness VERB 1 to put a harness on a horse 2 to control and use

harp NOUN a musical instrument with strings stretched down a triangular frame and plucked with the fingers ► **harpist** NOUN

harpoon NOUN a spear attached to a rope, used for killing whales

harpsichord NOUN an instrument like a piano but with strings that are plucked

harrow NOUN a heavy device pulled over the ground to break up the soil

harrowing ADJECTIVE upsetting or distressing

harry VERB **harries, harried** to harass or worry

harsh ADJECTIVE 1 rough and unpleasant 2 severe or cruel
► **harshly** ADVERB

hart NOUN a male deer

harvest NOUN 1 the time when ripened corn, fruit, or vegetables are gathered in 2 the crop that is gathered in

harvest VERB to gather in a crop

hash NOUN 1 a dish of small pieces of fried meat and vegetables 2 the symbol #

hashish NOUN a drug made from hemp

hasn't has not

hassle NOUN (*informal*) something difficult or annoying

hassle VERB (*informal*) to annoy or pester someone

haste NOUN a hurry **make haste** to act promptly

harmless ADJECTIVE • *a harmless substance* ► safe, innocuous, non-toxic, non-poisonous • *harmless fun* ► safe, inoffensive

harmony NOUN • *living in harmony* ► friendship, agreement, peace, unity • *musical harmony* ► tunefulness, melody

harsh ADJECTIVE • *a harsh voice* ► shrill, grating, grasping • *harsh measures* ► severe, strict, draconian, punitive • *harsh words* ► sharp, bitter, unfriendly, unkind • *the harsh rule of a tyrant* ► cruel, savage, brutal, strict, intolerant

a
b
c
d
e
f
g
h
i
j
k
l
m
n
o
p
q
r
s
t
u
v
w
x
y
z

hasten VERB to hurry

hasty ADJECTIVE **hastier, hastiest** hurried; done too quickly
▸ **hastily** ADVERB

hat NOUN a covering for the head

hatch¹ NOUN a covered opening in a floor, wall, etc.

hatch² VERB **1** to break out of an egg **2** to keep an egg warm until a young bird comes out **3** to form a plot

hatchback NOUN a car with a sloping back hinged to open at the top

hatchet NOUN a small axe

hate VERB to dislike very strongly

hate NOUN extreme dislike

hateful ADJECTIVE arousing hatred

hatred NOUN extreme dislike

hat-trick NOUN three successes in a row

haughty ADJECTIVE **haughtier, haughtiest** proud and arrogant
▸ **haughtily** ADVERB

haul VERB to pull or drag with great effort

haul NOUN an amount of booty

haulage NOUN **1** the transporting of goods **2** a charge for this

haunch NOUN the buttock and top part of the thigh

haunt VERB **1** (of ghosts) to appear often in a place **2** to visit a place often **3** (of a memory) to linger in the mind ▸ **haunted** ADJECTIVE

haunt NOUN a place that you often visit

have VERB **has, had 1** to possess or own *We have two dogs.* **2** to contain *The tin has tea in it.* **3** to experience *He had a shock.* **4** to be obliged to do something *We have to go now.* **5** to allow *I won't have him disturbed.* **6** receive or accept

THESAURUS

hasty ADJECTIVE • *a hasty retreat*
▸ quick, hurried, swift, rapid • *a hasty decision* ▸ rash, impulsive, imprudent

hate VERB • *to hate one another*
▸ loathe, detest, dislike • *I hate to bother them.* ▸ be sorry, regret, be reluctant

hate NOUN • *feelings of hate*
▸ hatred, loathing, detestation, dislike • *a list of their pet hates*
▸ dislike, bugbear, bane

hatred NOUN • *a legacy of fear and hatred* ▸ hate, loathing, detestation, hostility, bad feeling

haughty ADJECTIVE • *a haughty toss of the head* ▸ proud, arrogant, self-important, disdainful

haul VERB • *She hauled the heavy box across the floor.* ▸ pull, drag, heave, tug

have VERB • *They have a house in France.* ▸ own, possess, be the owner of • *She had a letter from her boyfriend.* ▸ receive, get, be sent • *They are having a party next door.* ▸ hold, give, organize, arrange • *The apartment has five rooms.* ▸ contain, comprise, consist of, include • *We had trouble parking.* ▸ experience, encounter • *I have a bad cold.*

DICTIONARY

Will you have a sweet? **7** to get something done *I'm having my watch mended.* **8** used to form the past tense of verbs *He has gone.*

haven NOUN a safe place or refuge

haven't have not

havoc NOUN great destruction or disorder

hawk¹ NOUN a bird of prey with very good eyesight

hawk² VERB to carry goods about to sell ▸ **hawker** NOUN

hawthorn NOUN a thorny tree with small red berries

hay NOUN dried grass for feeding to animals

hay fever NOUN irritation of the nose, throat, and eyes, caused by pollen or dust

haystack or **hayrick** NOUN a large neat pile of hay packed for storing

haywire ADJECTIVE out of control

hazard NOUN **1** a danger or risk **2** an obstacle on a golf course

hazard VERB to chance or risk

hazardous ADJECTIVE risky or dangerous

haze NOUN thin mist

hazel NOUN **1** a bush with small nuts **2** a light brown colour

hazelnut NOUN a nut of a hazel tree

hazy ADJECTIVE **hazier**, **haziest** **1** misty **2** vague or uncertain ▸ **hazily** ADVERB

H-bomb NOUN a hydrogen bomb

he PRONOUN the male person or animal being talked about

head NOUN **1** the part of the body containing the brains, eyes, and mouth **2** the brains or mind **3** a talent or ability *a good head for figures* **4** the side of a coin on which someone's head is shown **5** a person *It costs £5 a head.* **6** the top or front of something **7** the person in charge **8** a headteacher

head VERB **1** to be at the top or front of something **2** to hit a ball

THESAURUS

▸ be suffering from, be afflicted by

haven NOUN • *a safe haven* ▸ refuge, shelter, sanctuary

hazard NOUN • *a health hazard* ▸ danger, risk, threat

hazardous ADJECTIVE • *hazardous road conditions* ▸ dangerous, risky, perilous, unsafe

hazy ADJECTIVE • *hazy weather* ▸ misty, cloudy, foggy • *hazy memories* ▸ vague, indistinct, unclear

head NOUN • *He hit his head on a beam.* ▸ skull, crown • *the head of the company* ▸ chief, chairman, president, principal • *a good head for figures* ▸ brain, intellect, intelligence • *a head for figures* ▸ aptitude, gift, talent

head ADJECTIVE • *the head chef* ▸ chief, senior, principal

head VERB • *to head a team of researchers* ▸ lead, be in charge of, oversee **head for** • *heading for the station* ▸ go or move towards, make for, aim for

349

DICTIONARY

with the head **3** to move in a particular direction **head off** to force someone to turn aside by getting in front of them

headache NOUN **1** a pain in the head **2** (informal) a worrying problem

headdress NOUN a covering or decoration for the head

header NOUN the act of heading the ball in football

heading NOUN a word or words put at the top of a piece of printing or writing

headland NOUN a large piece of high land jutting out into the sea

headlight NOUN a powerful light at the front of a vehicle

headline NOUN a heading in large print in a newspaper

headlong ADVERB, ADJECTIVE **1** falling head first **2** hastily

headmaster NOUN a male headteacher

headmistress NOUN a female headteacher

head-on ADVERB, ADJECTIVE (of a collision) with the front parts meeting

headphones PLURAL NOUN a pair of earphones on a band that fits over the head

headquarters NOUN the place from which an organization is controlled

headstone NOUN a stone set up on a grave; a gravestone

headstrong ADJECTIVE determined to do what you want

headteacher NOUN the person in charge of a school

headway NOUN progress

heal VERB to make or become healthy

health NOUN **1** the condition of a person's body or mind **2** a good state of health *in sickness and in health*

healthy ADJECTIVE **healthier, healthiest 1** being well and free from illness **2** producing good health *a healthy diet* ▶ **healthily** ADVERB

heap NOUN an untidy pile **heaps** PLURAL NOUN (informal) plenty *heaps of time*

heap VERB **1** to put into a heap **2** to put on large amounts

hear VERB **heard 1** to take in sounds through the ears **2** to receive news or information **3** to

THESAURUS

healthy ADJECTIVE • *healthy food* ▶ nutritious, nourishing, wholesome • *feeling fit and healthy* ▶ fit, well, in good health, in good shape

heap NOUN • *a heap of old newspapers* ▶ pile, stack, mass,

mound **heaps** • *heaps of time* ▶ plenty, a lot

heap VERB • *to heap cakes on their plates* ▶ pile, stack

hear VERB • *You can hear the traffic.* ▶ make out, catch, listen to, discern • *I heard that you were*

try a case in a lawcourt ► **hearer**
NOUN

hearing NOUN **1** the ability to hear **2** a legal trial or investigation

hearsay NOUN rumour or gossip

hearse NOUN a vehicle for taking a coffin to a funeral

heart NOUN **1** the organ of the body that pumps the blood **2** a person's feelings or emotions; sympathy **3** courage *take heart* **4** the middle or most important part **5** a curved shape representing a heart **6** a playing card with red heart shapes on it **break a person's heart** to make them very unhappy **by heart** memorized

heart attack NOUN a sudden and painful failure of the heart to work properly

heartbroken ADJECTIVE very upset or unhappy

hearten VERB to make a person feel encouraged

heartfelt ADJECTIVE felt deeply

hearth NOUN the floor of a fireplace

heartless ADJECTIVE without pity or sympathy

hearty ADJECTIVE **heartier**, **heartiest 1** strong and vigorous **2** enthusiastic and sincere *hearty thanks* **3** (of a meal) large
► **heartily** ADVERB

heat NOUN **1** a hot condition, or the form of energy causing this **2** hot weather **3** anger or other strong feeling **4** a first round in a contest

heat VERB to make or become hot

heater NOUN a device for heating

heath NOUN open land with low shrubs

heathen NOUN a person who does not believe in any of the world's chief religions

heather NOUN an evergreen plant with small purple, pink, or white flowers

heatwave NOUN a long period of hot weather

leaving. ► be told, learn, gather, find out

heart NOUN • *the heart of the city* ► centre, middle • *the heart of the problem* ► essence, nub, crux, root • *His heart rules his head.* ► feelings, emotion • *to lose heart* ► enthusiasm, eagerness, courage, determination • *She has a lot of heart.* ► compassion, feeling, sympathy, tenderness

hearty ADJECTIVE • *a hearty laugh* ► enthusiastic, sincere, warm • *a*

hearty appetite ► big, healthy, strong • *a hearty meal*
► substantial, generous, large

heat NOUN • *The fire gave out a lot of heat.* ► warmth, hotness, glow • *the summer heat* ► hot weather, warmth, high temperatures, humidity

heat VERB • *to heat food* ► cook, heat up, reheat • *a room difficult to heat* ► keep warm, warm up

DICTIONARY

heave VERB **heaved** (when used of ships **hove**) **1** to lift or move something heavy **2** (*informal*) to throw **3** to rise and fall ▶ **heave** NOUN

heaven NOUN **1** the place believed in some religions to be the dwelling of God **2** a very pleasant state **the heavens** the sky

heavenly ADJECTIVE **1** to do with heaven **2** in the sky *heavenly bodies* **3** (*informal*) very pleasing

heavy ADJECTIVE **heavier**, **heaviest** **1** weighing a lot **2** great in amount or force *heavy rain* **3** large or massive *a heavy door* **4** needing much effort *heavy work* ▶ **heavily** ADVERB

heavyweight NOUN **1** a heavy person **2** a boxer of the heaviest weight ▶ **heavyweight** ADJECTIVE

Hebrew NOUN the language of the Jews in ancient Palestine and modern Israel

heckle VERB to interrupt a public speaker with awkward questions ▶ **heckler** NOUN

hectare (hek-tar) NOUN a unit of area equal to 10,000 square metres or just over 2 acres

hectic ADJECTIVE full of activity

hector VERB to talk to someone in a bullying way

hedge NOUN a row of bushes forming a barrier or boundary

hedge VERB **1** to surround with a hedge **2** to avoid giving an answer

hedgehog NOUN a small animal covered with long prickles

hedgerow NOUN a hedge of bushes bordering a field

heed VERB to pay attention to

heed NOUN **take** or **pay heed** to give attention to something

heedless ADJECTIVE taking no notice

heel¹ NOUN the back part of the foot

heel VERB **1** to repair the heel of a shoe **2** to kick with your heel

heel² VERB (of a ship) to lean over to one side

hefty ADJECTIVE **heftier**, **heftiest** large and strong

THESAURUS

heave VERB • *to heave back the gates* ▶ haul, drag, pull, lift

heavenly ADJECTIVE • *heavenly music* ▶ celestial, divine, angelic • *a heavenly time* ▶ beautiful, delightful, marvellous, wonderful

heavy ADJECTIVE • *too heavy to lift* ▶ weighty, massive, bulky • *a heavy man* ▶ large, fat, corpulent, overweight • *a heavy meal* ▶ substantial, hearty, filling, large, solid • *a heavy blow* ▶ hard,

forceful, violent, powerful • *heavy losses* ▶ large, substantial, considerable • *heavy work* ▶ strenuous, arduous, demanding • *heavy rain* ▶ strong, intense, torrential

hectic ADJECTIVE • *three hectic days* ▶ busy, frantic, manic, chaotic

hefty ADJECTIVE • *a hefty young man* ▶ stocky, burly, well-built, strapping, muscular, big, heavy

heifer (hef-er) NOUN a young cow

height NOUN **1** extent from top to bottom or foot **2** a high place **3** the most intense part *the height of the season*

heighten VERB to make or become higher or more intense

heinous (hay-nus or hee-nus) ADJECTIVE very wicked *a heinous crime*

heir (say as air) NOUN a person who inherits property

heiress (air-ess) NOUN a female heir to a fortune

heirloom (air-loom) NOUN a valued possession handed down in a family for several generations

helicopter NOUN a kind of aircraft with a large horizontal propeller or rotor

helium (hee-lee-um) NOUN a light colourless gas that does not burn

helix (hee-liks) NOUN **helices** a spiral

hell NOUN **1** a place where, in some religions, wicked people are thought to be punished after they die **2** a very unpleasant place

hellish ADJECTIVE (informal) very difficult or unpleasant

hello EXCLAMATION a word of greeting

helm NOUN the handle or wheel used to steer a ship

helmet NOUN a strong covering worn to protect the head

help VERB **1** to do something useful for someone **2** to make better or easier *will help you to sleep* **3** to prevent yourself *can't help coughing* **4** to serve food to ► **helper** NOUN

help NOUN **1** the act of helping **2** a person or thing that helps

helpful ADJECTIVE giving help; useful ► **helpfully** ADVERB

helping NOUN a portion of food

height NOUN • *the height of the tower* ► tallness, highness, altitude • *at the height of their fame* ► peak, high point, climax, zenith **heights** • *the mountain heights* ► summit, top, peak, crest

help VERB • *Will you help me?* ► assist, aid, lend a hand • *Foreign visits will help your languages.* ► improve, enhance, bolster • *She took aspirin to help her headache.* ► relieve, reduce, ease, soothe

help NOUN • *We could do with some help.* ► assistance, support, aid, cooperation, advice • *Would a screwdriver be of help?* ► use, service, benefit

helpful ADJECTIVE • *a helpful assistant* ► obliging, willing, cooperative, thoughtful, considerate • *A hammer might be helpful.* ► useful, of use, beneficial, valuable

helping NOUN • *a good helping of pudding* ► portion, serving, plateful, bowlful, ration

a
b
c
d
e
f
g
h
i
j
k
l
m
n
o
p
q
r
s
t
u
v
w
x
y
z

353

helpless ADJECTIVE unable to act without help

helpline NOUN a telephone service giving advice to callers

helter-skelter ADVERB in great haste

helter-skelter NOUN a spiral slide at a fair

hem NOUN the edge of a piece of cloth, folded over and sewn down

hem VERB **hemming, hemmed** put a hem on **hem in** to surround and restrict

hemisphere NOUN **1** half a sphere **2** half the earth *the southern hemisphere*

hemp NOUN **1** a plant that produces fibres for making cloth and ropes **2** the drug cannabis, made from this plant

hen NOUN **1** a female bird **2** a female fowl

hence ADVERB **1** from this time or place **2** therefore

henceforth ADVERB from now on

henna NOUN a reddish-brown dye used for colouring hair

hepatitis NOUN inflammation of the liver

heptagon NOUN a flat shape with seven sides ► **heptagonal** ADJECTIVE

her PRONOUN the form of **she** used as the object of a verb or after a preposition

her ADJECTIVE belonging to her *her house*

herald NOUN **1** in former times, an official who made announcements and carried important messages **2** a person or thing that is a sign of something to come

herald VERB to show that something is coming

heraldry NOUN the study of coats of arms ► **heraldic** (hir-al-dik) ADJECTIVE

herb NOUN a plant used for flavouring or for making medicine ► **herbal** ADJECTIVE

herbivorous (her-biv-er-us) ADJECTIVE eating plants ► **herbivore** NOUN

herd NOUN **1** a group of animals that feed together **2** a mass of people

herd VERB to gather or move together

here ADVERB in or to this place

hereafter ADVERB from now on

hereby ADVERB by this act

hereditary ADJECTIVE passed from one generation to the next

heredity NOUN the inheriting of physical or mental characteristics from parents or ancestors

heresy (herri-see) NOUN **heresies** a religious opinion that disagrees with the main beliefs

helpless ADJECTIVE • *She felt helpless and frustrated.*
► powerless, impotent, weak, vulnerable, defenceless

herd NOUN • *a herd of animals*
► pack, flock • *a herd of tourists* ► crowd, mass, throng, horde

heretic (herri-tik) NOUN a person who supports a heresy

heritage NOUN the property that someone has inherited

hermit NOUN a person who lives alone, usually for religious reasons

hernia NOUN a condition in which an internal part of the body pushes through a weak point in another part

hero NOUN **heroes 1** a person who is admired for bravery **2** the chief male character in a story

heroic ADJECTIVE brave like a hero
► **heroically** ADVERB

heroin NOUN a strong addictive drug made from morphine

heroine NOUN **1** a woman who is admired for bravery **2** the chief female character in a story

heroism NOUN bravery

heron NOUN a wading bird with long legs and a long neck

herring NOUN **herring** or **herrings** a sea fish used as food

hers POSSESSIVE PRONOUN belonging to her *The house is hers.*

⚠ **USAGE**

It is incorrect to write *her's*.

herself PRONOUN she or her and nobody else *She cut herself. She herself has said it.* **by herself** alone; on her own

hertz NOUN a unit of frequency of electromagnetic waves

📖 **WORD HISTORY**

named after H. R. *Hertz*, a German scientist

hesitant ADJECTIVE hesitating; undecided about what to do
► **hesitancy** NOUN

hesitate VERB to be slow or uncertain in speaking, moving, etc. ► **hesitation** NOUN

heterosexual ADJECTIVE attracted to people of the opposite sex; not homosexual ► **heterosexual** NOUN

hew VERB **hewn** to chop or cut with an axe etc.

hexagon NOUN a flat shape with six sides ► **hexagonal** ADJECTIVE

hey EXCLAMATION an exclamation used to attract attention or to express surprise or interest

heyday NOUN the time of a thing's greatest success or prosperity

hi EXCLAMATION an exclamation used as a friendly greeting

hiatus (hy-ay-tuhs) NOUN a gap in something that is otherwise continuous

hibernate VERB (of an animal) to spend the winter in a state like deep sleep ► **hibernation** NOUN

hiccup NOUN **1** a high gulping sound made when the breath is

THESAURUS

hero NOUN • *a war hero*
► champion, brave man • *James had always been her hero.* ► idol, star • *The story had no real hero.*
► principal character, lead character

heroic ADJECTIVE • *heroic efforts*
► brave, courageous, noble, bold, daring

hesitate VERB • *She hesitated at the front door.* ► pause, delay, falter, waver, wait

briefly interrupted **2** a hitch or setback

hiccup VERB **hiccuping, hiccuped** to make the sound of a hiccup

hide¹ VERB **1** to go where you cannot be seen **2** to keep from being seen **3** to keep secret

hide² NOUN an animal's skin

hide-and-seek NOUN a game of looking for people who are hiding

hideous ADJECTIVE very ugly or unpleasant

hideout NOUN a place to hide from other people

hiding¹ NOUN a state of being hidden *go into hiding*

hiding² NOUN a beating

hierarchy (hyr-ar-kee) NOUN **hierarchies** an organization that puts people one above another in rank

hieroglyphics (hyr-o-glif-iks) PLURAL NOUN pictures or symbols used in ancient Egypt to represent words

hi-fi NOUN equipment for reproducing recorded sound with high quality

higgledy-piggledy ADVERB, ADJECTIVE mixed up; in great disorder

high ADJECTIVE **1** reaching a long way upwards *high hills* **2** far above the ground or sea *high clouds* **3** measuring from top to bottom *two metres high* **4** above average level in importance, quality, amount, etc. *high rank high prices* **5** (of meat) beginning to go bad **6** (informal) affected by a drug

high ADVERB at or to a high level or position etc. *high above them*

highbrow ADJECTIVE intellectual

hidden ADJECTIVE • *a hidden entrance* ▶ concealed, secret, invisible, disguised, camouflaged • *a hidden meaning* ▶ abstruse, ulterior

hide VERB • *to hide in a cupboard* ▶ conceal yourself, take cover, lie low, keep out of sight • *to hide the jewels* ▶ conceal, secrete, store away, bury • *to hide your disapproval* ▶ disguise, conceal, suppress, mask • *Clouds hid the moon.* ▶ obscure, block out, conceal

hideous ADJECTIVE • *a hideous grin* ▶ ugly, repulsive, repellent • *a hideous experience* ▶ awful,

horrible, ghastly, terrible, appalling

high ADJECTIVE • *a high mountain* ▶ tall, lofty, towering • *a high position in the government* ▶ senior, prominent, top-ranking, important, powerful • *high moral principles* ▶ noble, lofty, honourable • *high prices* ▶ inflated, excessive, exorbitant • *a high voice* ▶ high-pitched, shrill, sharp, piercing • *high standards* ▶ excellent, outstanding • *high winds* ▶ strong, powerful, violent • *a high opinion* ▶ favourable, positive, good

higher education NOUN education at a university or college

high jump NOUN an athletic contest in which competitors jump over a high bar

highlands PLURAL NOUN mountainous country
► **highland** ADJECTIVE, **highlander** NOUN

highlight NOUN 1 the most interesting part of something 2 a light-coloured area or streak

highlight VERB to draw special attention to

highly ADVERB 1 extremely *highly amusing* 2 very favourably *thought highly of them*

highly-strung ADJECTIVE nervous and easily upset

Highness NOUN the title of a prince or princess

high-rise ADJECTIVE (of a building) having many storeys

high road NOUN a main road

high school NOUN a secondary school

high spirits PLURAL NOUN cheerful and lively behaviour
► **high-spirited** ADJECTIVE

high street NOUN the main street of a town

highway NOUN a main road or route

highwayman NOUN **highwaymen** a man who robbed travellers on highways

hijack VERB to seize control of an aircraft or vehicle during a journey
► **hijack** NOUN, **hijacker** NOUN

hike VERB to walk a long distance in the countryside ► **hike** NOUN, **hiker** NOUN

hilarious ADJECTIVE very funny
► **hilariously** ADVERB, **hilarity** NOUN

hill NOUN a piece of land that is higher than the ground around it
► **hilly** ADJECTIVE

hillock NOUN a small hill

hilt NOUN the handle of a sword or dagger

him PRONOUN the form of **he** used as the object of a verb or after a preposition

himself PRONOUN he or him and nobody else *He cut himself. He himself has said it.* **by himself** alone; on his own

hind[1] ADJECTIVE at the back *hind legs*

hind[2] NOUN a female deer

hinder VERB to get in the way of or make things difficult for
► **hindrance** NOUN

Hindi NOUN one of the languages of India

hindmost ADJECTIVE furthest behind

hindquarters PLURAL NOUN an animal's hind legs and rear parts

hill NOUN • *the top of the hill* ► high ground, hillock, ridge, peak • *a steep hill* ► slope, rise, gradient, incline, ascent

hinder VERB • *Power failures have hindered production.*
► hamper, hold up, interfere with, prevent

hindsight NOUN knowledge or understanding about something after it has happened

Hinduism NOUN one of the religions of India

hinge NOUN a joining device on which a lid or door turns when it opens

hinge VERB 1 to fix with a hinge 2 to depend

hint NOUN 1 a useful idea or piece of advice 2 a slight indication or suggestion

hint VERB to make a hint

hinterland NOUN the district lying inland from the coast

hip ¹ NOUN the bony side of the body between the waist and the thigh

hip ² NOUN the fruit of the wild rose

hippie NOUN a young person who joins with others to live in an unconventional way, often based on ideas of peace and love

hippo NOUN hippos (informal) a hippopotamus

hippopotamus NOUN a large African animal that lives near water

hire VERB 1 to pay to have use of something 2 to lend for payment
▶ **hirer** NOUN

hire NOUN the act of hiring

his ADJECTIVE, POSSESSIVE PRONOUN belonging to him his house The house is his.

hiss VERB to make a sound like an s
▶ **hiss** NOUN

historian NOUN a person who writes or studies history

historic ADJECTIVE famous or important in history

historical ADJECTIVE 1 to do with history 2 that actually existed or took place historical events
▶ **historically** ADVERB

history NOUN histories the study or description of what happened in the past

hit VERB hitting, hit 1 to come forcefully against a person or thing 2 to have a bad effect on Famine hit the country.

hit NOUN 1 an act of hitting; a blow or stroke 2 a shot that hits the target 3 something very successful

hint NOUN • a few casual hints
▶ clue, sign, tip, pointer, signal, indication • a hint of sadness in her voice ▶ trace, tinge, touch, suggestion

hint VERB • He hinted we might get an award. ▶ suggest, imply, indicate **hint at** I'm not sure what she was hinting at. ▶ allude to, refer to, imply, suggest

historic ADJECTIVE • a historic meeting ▶ famous, important, momentous, significant

historical ADJECTIVE • historical events ▶ real, true, actual, authentic, documented

hit VERB • He hit his leg. ▶ strike, smack, slap, thump, whack • A lorry hit the barrier. ▶ crash into, run into, collide with, smash into • Famine hit the country. ▶ strike, afflict

hit NOUN • a hit on the head ▶ blow, punch, thump, knock, smack, slap • The party had been a huge hit. ▶ success, triumph

hitch VERB **1** to raise or pull with a slight jerk **2** to fasten with a loop or hook **3** to hitch-hike

hitch NOUN **1** a slight difficulty causing delay **2** a hitching movement **3** a knot

hitch-hike VERB to travel by getting lifts from passing vehicles ▸ **hitch-hiker** NOUN

hither ADVERB to or towards this place

hitherto ADVERB until this time

HIV ABBREVIATION human immunodeficiency virus; the virus that causes Aids

hive NOUN **1** a box or other container for bees to live in **2** the bees living in a beehive

hoard NOUN a carefully saved store of money, treasure, food, etc.

hoard VERB to store away ▸ **hoarder** NOUN

⚠ **USAGE**

Do not confuse this word with *horde*.

hoarding NOUN a tall fence covered with advertisements

hoar frost NOUN a white frost

hoarse ADJECTIVE having a rough or croaking voice

hoary ADJECTIVE white or grey from age

hoax VERB to deceive somebody as a joke ▸ **hoax** NOUN

hob NOUN a flat surface on a cooker, for cooking food

hobble VERB to limp or walk with difficulty

hobby NOUN **hobbies** an activity done for pleasure

hobgoblin NOUN a mischievous or evil spirit

hobnob VERB **hobnobbing, hobnobbed** to spend time together

hockey NOUN a game played by two teams with curved sticks and a hard ball

hoe NOUN a tool for scraping up weeds

hoe VERB **hoes, hoeing, hoed** to scrape or dig with a hoe

hog NOUN **1** a male pig **2** (*informal*) a greedy person

hog VERB **hogging, hogged** (*informal*) to take more than your share of

Hogmanay NOUN New Year's Eve in Scotland

hoist VERB to lift up with ropes or pulleys

THESAURUS

hoard NOUN • *a huge hoard of jewellery* ▸ cache, store, stock, pile, supply

hoard VERB • *to hoard supplies* ▸ store, save, amass, accumulate

hoarse ADJECTIVE • *a voice that was hoarse from shouting* ▸ rough, harsh, gruff, husky

hoax NOUN • *The virus warning was a hoax.* ▸ joke, practical joke, prank, trick, spoof

hobby NOUN • *fishing as a hobby* ▸ pastime, leisure activity, interest

hoist VERB • *to hoist cargo on deck* ▸ raise, lift, heave, winch up

hold VERB **held 1** to have and keep in your hands **2** to have room for *The jug holds two pints.* **3** to support *won't hold my weight* **4** to believe or consider *to hold us responsible* **5** to cause something to take place *to hold a meeting* **6** to keep in custody **hold up 1** to hinder **2** to stop and rob

hold NOUN **1** the act of holding; a grasp **2** something to hold on to **3** the part of a ship where cargo is stored

holdall NOUN a large portable bag or case

holder NOUN a person or thing that holds something

hold-up NOUN **1** a delay **2** a robbery with force

hole NOUN **1** a hollow place; a gap or opening **2** a burrow **3** (*informal*) an unpleasant place

hole VERB to make a hole or holes in

holiday NOUN **1** a day or time when people do not go to work or school **2** a time to enjoy yourself away from home

holiness NOUN the state of being holy or sacred **His Holiness** the title of the Pope

hollow ADJECTIVE with an empty space inside; not solid

hollow ADVERB completely *beat them hollow*

hollow NOUN a hollow or sunken place

hollow VERB to make hollow

holly NOUN an evergreen bush with shiny prickly leaves and red berries

hollyhock NOUN a plant with large flowers on a very tall stem

holocaust NOUN a huge destruction by fire **the Holocaust** the mass killing of Jews by the Nazis from 1939 to 1945

hold VERB • *holding a briefcase* ► clasp, clutch, grip, cling on to • *to hold her in my arms* ► hug, embrace, clasp • *must hold a valid passport* ► possess, have, own • *to hold a meeting* ► call, convene, conduct • *Police are holding him.* ► detain, keep in custody, imprison • *to hold a senior position* ► have, occupy, fill • *to hold six to eight people* ► take, accommodate, have room for • *to hold someone responsible* ► believe, consider, think • *I hope the good weather will hold.* ► continue, last, carry on

hold up • *The bridge is held up by*

columns. ► support, shore up, carry • *Work on the roof was held up.* ► delay, hinder

hold NOUN • *to release your hold* ► grip, grasp, clutch • *to have a hold over someone* ► influence, power, control

hole NOUN • *a large hole in the road* ► opening, hollow, trench, ditch • *holes in the plaster* ► gap, split, crack, puncture, tear • *an animal's hole* ► burrow, den, lair

hollow ADJECTIVE • *a hollow space* ► empty, concave, sunken • *a hollow laugh* ► dull, low, muffled • *a hollow promise* ► insincere, false, empty • *a hollow victory*

DICTIONARY

hologram NOUN a laser photograph with a three-dimensional image

holster NOUN a leather case in which a pistol or revolver is carried

holy ADJECTIVE **holier**, **holiest**
1 belonging or devoted to God
2 consecrated *holy water*
► **holiness** NOUN

homage NOUN an act or expression of respect or honour

home NOUN 1 the place where a person lives or was born 2 a place where those who need help are looked after 3 the place to be reached in a race or game

home ADJECTIVE 1 to do with your own home or country *home industries* 2 played on a team's own ground *a home match*

home ADVERB 1 to or at home *Is she home yet?* 2 to the point aimed at *Push the bolt home.*

home VERB **home in on** to move towards a target

homeless ADJECTIVE having no home

homely ADJECTIVE simple and ordinary

home-made ADJECTIVE made at home, not bought

homeopathy NOUN the treatment of disease by tiny doses of drugs that produce symptoms similar to the disease
► **homeopathic** ADJECTIVE

homesick ADJECTIVE sad when away from home

homework NOUN school work that is done at home

homicide NOUN the killing of one person by another ► **homicidal** ADJECTIVE

homing ADJECTIVE (of a pigeon) trained to fly home

homogeneous (hom-o-**jeen**-ee-us) ADJECTIVE formed of people or things of the same kind

homograph NOUN a word that is spelt like another but has a different meaning or origin, e.g. *bat* (a flying animal) and *bat* (for hitting a ball)

THESAURUS

► worthless, futile, vain, meaningless, pointless

holy ADJECTIVE • *holy men and women* ► saintly, godly, pious, devout, religious, spiritual, virtuous, pure • *a holy place* ► sacred, consecrated, sanctified

home NOUN • *forced to leave their homes* ► house, dwelling, place of residence, accommodation • *miles from home* ► native land, homeland, birthplace,

motherland, fatherland • *to go into a home* ► institution, nursing home, shelter

homeless ADJECTIVE • *homeless people* ► destitute, vagrant, down-and-out

homely ADJECTIVE • *a homely atmosphere* ► friendly, informal, relaxed, easygoing, familiar, intimate, congenial, comfortable, cosy

a b c d e f g h i j k l m n o p q r s t u v w x y z

homophone NOUN a word with the same sound as another, e.g. *son* and *sun*

homosexual ADJECTIVE attracted to people of the same sex
► **homosexual** NOUN, **homosexuality** NOUN

honest ADJECTIVE being truthful and not cheating ► **honestly** ADVERB, **honesty** NOUN

honey NOUN a sweet sticky food made by bees

honeycomb NOUN a wax structure made by bees to hold their honey and eggs

honeymoon NOUN a holiday spent together by a newly-married couple

honeysuckle NOUN a climbing plant with fragrant yellow or pink flowers

honk NOUN a loud sound like that made by a goose or an old car horn

honk VERB to make a honk

honorary ADJECTIVE **1** given as an honour *an honorary degree* **2** unpaid *the honorary treasurer*

honour NOUN **1** great respect or reputation **2** a person or thing that brings honour **3** something a person is proud to do *an honour to meet you* **4** honesty and loyalty *a person of honour* **5** an award given as a mark of respect

honour VERB **1** to feel or show honour for **2** to keep to the terms of an agreement or promise **3** to acknowledge and pay a cheque etc.

honourable ADJECTIVE deserving honour; honest and loyal
► **honourably** ADVERB

hood NOUN **1** a covering of soft material for the head and neck **2** a folding roof or cover **3** (*American*) the bonnet of a car ► **hooded** ADJECTIVE

THESAURUS

honest ADJECTIVE • *an honest person*
► upright, honourable, virtuous, law-abiding • *honest practices*
► legal, lawful, legitimate, above-board • *an honest mistake*
► genuine, real, authentic • *an honest opinion* ► sincere, open, frank, truthful

honesty NOUN • *to demand complete honesty* ► truthfulness, trustworthiness, integrity, fairness • *to speak with complete honesty* ► sincerity, candour, frankness, bluntness

honour NOUN • *a man of honour*
► honesty, integrity, principle, decency • *to receive honours*

► award, accolade, tribute, distinction, commendation • *the honour of an invitation*
► privilege, distinction • *to be received with honour* ► praise, acclaim, admiration

honour VERB • *to honour the visitors* ► praise, applaud, commend • *to honour a commitment* ► fulfil, respect, keep

honourable ADJECTIVE
• *honourable motives* ► honest, sincere, reputable, trustworthy
• *honourable achievements*
► distinguished, illustrious, great

DICTIONARY

hoodwink VERB to deceive

hoof NOUN **hoofs** or **hooves** the horny part of the foot of a horse etc.

hook NOUN a bent or curved piece of metal etc. for hanging things on or for catching hold of something

hook VERB **1** to fasten with or on a hook **2** to catch a fish with a hook **3** to hit a ball in a curving path
► **hooked** ADJECTIVE

hooligan NOUN a rough and violent young person
► **hooliganism** NOUN

hoop NOUN a ring made of metal or wood

hooray EXCLAMATION another spelling of **hurray**

hoot VERB **1** to make a sound like that made by an owl **2** to laugh loudly ► **hoot** NOUN

hooter NOUN a horn or siren that makes a hooting sound

hop[1] VERB **hopping, hopped 1** to jump on one foot **2** (of an animal) to spring from all feet at once

hop NOUN a hopping movement

hop[2] NOUN a climbing plant used to give beer its flavour

hope NOUN **1** the feeling of wanting and expecting something to happen **2** a person or thing that gives hope

hope VERB to want and expect something

hopeful ADJECTIVE **1** feeling hope **2** likely to be good or successful
► **hopefully** ADVERB

hopeless ADJECTIVE **1** without hope **2** very bad at something
► **hopelessly** ADVERB

hopscotch NOUN a game of hopping into squares drawn on the ground

horde NOUN a large group or crowd

⚠ **USAGE**
Do not confuse this word with *hoard*.

horizon NOUN the line where the earth and the sky appear to meet

THESAURUS

hop VERB • *He hopped up onto the bench.* ► jump, leap, spring

hope NOUN • *the hope of being in the team* ► ambition, dream, desire, wish • *some hope of a better future* ► prospect, expectation, likelihood

hope VERB • *I hope to answer all your questions.* ► aim, intend, plan **hope for** • *to hope for a quick response* ► expect, want, wish for

hopeful ADJECTIVE • *hopeful about winning a conflict* ► optimistic,

confident • *hopeful signs*
► promising, encouraging, favourable, reassuring

hopeless ADJECTIVE • *in hopeless bewilderment* ► despairing, desperate, wretched • *a hopeless situation* ► desperate, serious, critical, impossible, beyond hope
• *hopeless at board games*
► incompetent, poor, inept, useless

horde NOUN • *a horde of journalists*
► crowd, throng, pack, mob

a
b
c
d
e
f
g
h
i
j
k
l
m
n
o
p
q
r
s
t
u
v
w
x
y
z

a
b
c
d
e
f
g
h
i
j
k
l
m
n
o
p
q
r
s
t
u
v
w
x
y
z

horizontal ADJECTIVE level; parallel to the horizon ▶ **horizontally** ADVERB

hormone NOUN a substance produced in the body and carried by the blood to stimulate other organs in the body ▶ **hormonal** ADJECTIVE

horn NOUN **1** a hard growth on the head of a bull, cow, ram, etc. **2** a brass instrument played by blowing **3** a device for making a warning sound ▶ **horned** ADJECTIVE, **horny** ADJECTIVE

hornet NOUN a large kind of wasp

hornpipe NOUN a sailors' dance

horoscope NOUN a prediction of future events based on the positions of stars

horrendous ADJECTIVE extremely unpleasant

horrible ADJECTIVE **1** horrifying **2** very unpleasant or nasty ▶ **horribly** ADVERB

horrid ADJECTIVE horrible

horrific ADJECTIVE horrifying ▶ **horrifically** ADVERB

horrify VERB **horrifies, horrified 1** to make someone feel afraid or disgusted **2** to shock

horror NOUN **1** great fear or disgust **2** a person or thing causing horror

horse NOUN **1** a large four-legged animal used for riding on and for pulling carts etc. **2** a piece of gymnastic equipment for vaulting over

horsepower NOUN a unit for measuring the power of an engine, equal to 746 watts

horseshoe NOUN a curved piece of metal nailed to a horse's hoof

horticulture NOUN the art of gardening ▶ **horticultural** ADJECTIVE

hose NOUN a flexible tube for directing a flow of water

hose VERB to water or spray with a hose

hospice (hosp-iss) NOUN a nursing home for people who are very ill or dying

horrible ADJECTIVE • *a horrible accident* ▶ dreadful, horrific, terrible, awful • *a horrible smell* ▶ unpleasant, disagreeable, nasty, awful, revolting • *He was being horrible.* ▶ nasty, unkind, unpleasant, disagreeable, objectionable

horrific • *horrific injuries* ▶ dreadful, appalling, frightful, terrible

horrify VERB • *stories that horrified readers* ▶ terrify, frighten, scare, petrify • *The news horrified them.* ▶ shock, appal, outrage

horror NOUN • *to scream in horror* ▶ terror, fear, fright • *to react with horror* ▶ shock, outrage, disgust, revulsion • *the full horror of the attack* ▶ awfulness, ghastliness, savagery

DICTIONARY

hospitable ADJECTIVE welcoming; liking to give hospitality
► **hospitably** ADVERB

hospital NOUN a place providing medical treatment for people who are ill or injured

hospitality NOUN the welcoming of guests or strangers with food and entertainment

host¹ NOUN **1** a person who has guests and looks after them **2** the presenter of a television or radio programme

host VERB to organize and take charge of a party or other event

host² NOUN a large number of people or things

host³ NOUN (in Christianity) the bread consecrated at Holy Communion

hostage NOUN a person who is held prisoner until demands are met

hostel NOUN a building where travellers, students, or other groups can stay or live

hostess NOUN a woman who has guests and looks after them

hostile ADJECTIVE **1** unfriendly *a hostile glance* **2** opposed to something **3** to do with an enemy *hostile aircraft* ► **hostility** NOUN

hot ADJECTIVE **hotter**, **hottest**
1 having great heat or a high temperature **2** (of food) highly spiced **3** passionate or excitable *a hot temper*

hot VERB **hotting**, **hotted**
hot up (*informal*) to become more exciting

hot dog NOUN a hot sausage in a bread roll

hotel NOUN a building where people pay to stay for a night or several nights

hothead NOUN an impetuous person ► **hotheaded** ADJECTIVE

hothouse NOUN a heated greenhouse

hotly ADVERB intensely *a hotly disputed point*

hotplate NOUN a heated surface for cooking food

hotpot NOUN a kind of stew

hound NOUN a dog used in hunting or racing

hound VERB to pursue or harass

THESAURUS

hospitable ADJECTIVE • *a hospitable family* ► friendly, sociable, welcoming

hostile ADJECTIVE • *a hostile crowd* ► aggressive, confrontational, angry, unfriendly, warlike • *a hostile climate* ► harsh, unfavourable, inhospitable

hostility NOUN • *to react with hostility* ► antagonism, enmity, animosity, opposition, hatred

hot ADJECTIVE • *hot weather* ► warm, balmy, boiling, blazing, roasting, scorching, sweltering • *a hot meal* ► cooked, piping, sizzling • *a hot curry* ► spicy, peppery, piquant • *a hot temper* ► fierce, angry, violent

hour NOUN one twenty-fourth part of a day and night; sixty minutes

hourly ADVERB, ADJECTIVE every hour

house (howss) NOUN 1 a building for people to live in 2 a building for a special purpose *opera house* 3 a government assembly *House of Commons* 4 one of the divisions in some schools 5 a family or dynasty *the House of Tudor*

house (howz) VERB to provide accommodation for

houseboat NOUN a boat for living in

household NOUN all the people living in the same house

housekeeper NOUN a person employed to look after a household

housekeeping NOUN the business of looking after a household

housewife NOUN **housewives** a woman who does the housekeeping for her family

housework NOUN cleaning and cooking and other work done in a house

housing NOUN accommodation; houses

hovel NOUN a small shabby house

hover VERB 1 to stay in one place in the air 2 to wait about nearby

hovercraft NOUN a vehicle that travels on a cushion of air produced by its engines

how ADVERB 1 in what way; by what means *How do you do it?* 2 to what extent or amount *How high can you jump?* 3 in what condition *How are you?*

however ADVERB 1 regardless of how *You can never win, however hard you try.* 2 all the same *Later, however, he left.*

howl NOUN a long loud cry or sound, like that made by a dog or wolf

howl VERB 1 to make a howl 2 to weep loudly

howler NOUN (*informal*) a foolish mistake

HQ ABBREVIATION headquarters

hub NOUN 1 the central part of a wheel 2 the central point of interest or activity

hubbub NOUN a loud confused noise of voices

huddle VERB 1 to crowd closely together 2 to curl your body closely ▸ **huddle** NOUN

house NOUN • *a row of terraced houses* ▸ home, dwelling, abode, residence • *the house of Stuart* ▸ dynasty, clan, family

house VERB • *The cabins housed twenty people.* ▸ accommodate, lodge, shelter, take in

hover VERB • *A bird hovered above us.* ▸ float, hang, flutter, drift, fly • *He hovered outside.* ▸ linger, wait about, loiter

huddle VERB • *to huddle together* ▸ crowd, gather, squeeze, snuggle

DICTIONARY

hue NOUN a colour or tint

huff NOUN a period of sulking

huff VERB to blow hard

hug VERB hugging, hugged 1 to clasp tightly in your arms 2 to keep close to

hug NOUN a tight embrace

huge ADJECTIVE extremely large; enormous ▶ **hugely** ADVERB

hulk NOUN 1 the body or wreck of an old ship 2 a large clumsy person or thing ▶ **hulking** ADJECTIVE

hull NOUN the framework of a ship

hullabaloo NOUN an uproar

hullo EXCLAMATION a word of greeting

hum VERB humming, hummed 1 to sing a tune with your lips closed 2 to make a low continuous sound like that of a bee

hum NOUN a humming sound

human ADJECTIVE to do with human beings

human NOUN a human being

human being NOUN a man, woman, or child

humane ADJECTIVE kind-hearted and merciful ▶ **humanely** ADVERB

humanist NOUN a person who is concerned with people's needs and with finding rational ways to solve human problems rather than relying on religious belief ▶ **humanism** NOUN

humanitarian ADJECTIVE concerned with people's welfare ▶ **humanitarian** NOUN

humanity NOUN 1 people in general 2 the state of being human 3 being humane **humanities** PLURAL NOUN arts subjects such as history, literature, and music, not sciences

humble ADJECTIVE 1 modest; not proud or showy 2 of low rank or importance ▶ **humbly** ADVERB

humble VERB to make a person feel humble

humbug NOUN 1 insincere or dishonest talk 2 a hard peppermint sweet

humdrum ADJECTIVE dull and not exciting

humid (hew-mid) ADJECTIVE (of air) warm and damp ▶ **humidity** NOUN

THESAURUS

hue NOUN • *a range of bright hues*
▶ colour, shade, tone

hug VERB • *to hug closely*
▶ embrace, clasp, cuddle, squeeze

huge ADJECTIVE • *a huge building*
▶ enormous, gigantic, immense, massive, colossal, vast

humane ADJECTIVE • *humane methods* ▶ kind, compassionate, considerate, sympathetic, merciful

humble ADJECTIVE • *in a humble and contrite manner* ▶ meek, self-effacing, respectful, submissive • *a humble house in the suburbs* ▶ modest, simple, plain, lowly, unpretentious

humid ADJECTIVE • *a humid day*
▶ muggy, clammy, sultry, sticky

a
b
c
d
e
f
g
h
i
j
k
l
m
n
o
p
q
r
s
t
u
v
w
x
y
z

humiliate VERB to make a person feel disgraced or ashamed
► **humiliation** NOUN

humility NOUN a humble state

hummingbird NOUN a small tropical bird that makes a humming sound by beating its wings rapidly

humorous ADJECTIVE full of humour; amusing

humour NOUN **1** an amusing aspect of something; what makes people laugh **2** the ability to enjoy comical things *a sense of humour* **3** a person's mood *a good humour*

humour VERB to keep a person happy by agreeing to what they want

hump NOUN **1** a rounded lump or mound **2** a growth at the top of a person's back

hump VERB to carry with difficulty

humus (hew-mus) NOUN rich earth made by decayed plants

hunch[1] NOUN a feeling about what is true or is going to happen

hunch[2] VERB to bend your shoulders with your back rounded

hunchback NOUN someone with a hump on their back
► **hunchbacked** ADJECTIVE

hundred NOUN, ADJECTIVE the number 100 ► **hundredth** ADJECTIVE, NOUN

hundredweight NOUN a unit of weight equal to 112 pounds (about 50.8 kilograms)

hunger NOUN **1** a feeling of needing food **2** a strong desire

hunger VERB to have a strong desire

hungry ADJECTIVE **hungrier, hungriest** feeling hunger
► **hungrily** ADVERB

humiliate VERB • *to humiliate them with reminders of their mistakes* ► embarrass, mortify, demean, shame

humiliating ADJECTIVE • *a humiliating defeat* ► embarrassing, mortifying, ignominious, degrading, demeaning

humorous ADJECTIVE • *humorous episodes* ► amusing, funny, comical, hilarious, entertaining

humour NOUN • *a conversation spiced with humour* ► wit, jokes, jesting, hilarity, comedy • *in a bad humour* ► mood, temper

hump NOUN • *a hump in the road* ► bump, protuberance, bulge, mound, lump

hunch NOUN • *no more than a hunch* ► feeling, intuition, inkling, suspicion

hunch VERB • *to hunch the shoulders* ► arch, curve, bend

hunger NOUN • *faint with hunger* ► lack of food, malnutrition, starvation, famine • *a hunger for knowledge* ► desire, yearning, longing, thirst

hungry ADJECTIVE • *hungry again by 3 o'clock* ► in need of food, ravenous, famished, starving

DICTIONARY

hunk NOUN a large piece of something

hunt VERB **1** to chase and kill animals for food or as a sport **2** to search for ▸ **hunter** NOUN

hunt NOUN **1** an act of hunting **2** a group of hunters

hurdle NOUN **1** an upright frame to be jumped over in hurdling **2** an obstacle or difficulty

hurl VERB to throw with great force

hurly-burly NOUN busy noisy activity

hurray or **hurrah** EXCLAMATION a shout of joy or approval

hurricane NOUN a storm with a strong wind

hurried ADJECTIVE done in a hurry ▸ **hurriedly** ADVERB

hurry VERB **hurries, hurried 1** to move or act quickly **2** to try to make someone be quick

hurry NOUN **1** the act of hurrying **2** a need to hurry

hurt VERB **hurt 1** to cause pain or injury to **2** to suffer pain *My leg hurts.* **3** to upset or offend

hurt NOUN physical or mental pain or injury

hurtful ADJECTIVE causing pain or offence

hurtle VERB to move very rapidly

husband NOUN the man to whom a woman is married

husbandry NOUN **1** farming **2** management of resources

THESAURUS

hunt VERB • *to hunt foxes* ▸ chase, track, trail, pursue • *still hunting for the keys* ▸ search, look, rummage

hunt NOUN • *the hunt for clues* ▸ search, quest, pursuit (of)

hurdle NOUN • *He fell at the last hurdle.* ▸ fence, jump, barrier • *one more hurdle to overcome* ▸ obstacle, difficulty, problem

hurl VERB • *to hurl a ball* ▸ throw, fling, toss

hurry VERB • *We must hurry.* ▸ be quick, hasten, make speed • *to hurry home* ▸ rush, hasten, dash, speed

hurry NOUN • *no need for hurry* ▸ haste, urgency

hurt VERB • *My arm hurts.* ▸ be sore, be painful, ache, throb, sting • *Derek hurt his leg.* ▸ injure, wound, maim, bruise • *The criticism hurt her.* ▸ upset, distress

hurt NOUN • *the hurt on her leg* ▸ injury, wound, pain • *the hurt he had caused her* ▸ distress, suffering, sadness

hurt ADJECTIVE • *a hurt animal* ▸ injured, wounded, maimed • *to feel hurt* ▸ upset, distressed, wounded

hurtful ADJECTIVE • *hurtful remarks* ▸ upsetting, distressing, unkind, spiteful, mean, painful

hurtle VERB • *A train was hurtling towards them.* ▸ speed, rush, career, charge, shoot

DICTIONARY

hush VERB to make or become quiet

hush NOUN silence

hush-hush ADJECTIVE (informal) highly secret

husk NOUN the dry outer covering of some seeds and fruits

husky¹ ADJECTIVE **huskier, huskiest 1** hoarse **2** big and strong; burly

husky² NOUN **huskies** a large dog used in the Arctic for pulling sledges

hustle VERB **1** to hurry **2** to push or shove rudely

hut NOUN a small roughly-made house or shelter

hutch NOUN a box-like cage for a pet animal

hyacinth NOUN a sweet-smelling flower that grows from a bulb

hybrid NOUN **1** a plant or animal produced by combining two different species or varieties **2** something that combines parts of two different things

hydrangea (hy-drayn-ja) NOUN a shrub with clusters of pink, blue, or white flowers

hydrant NOUN a special tap in the street for attaching a large hose to draw off water

hydraulic ADJECTIVE worked by the force of water or other fluid

hydroelectric ADJECTIVE using water power to produce electricity
▸ **hydroelectricity** NOUN

hydrofoil NOUN a boat designed to skim over the surface of water

hydrogen NOUN a lightweight gas that combines with oxygen to form water

hydrogen bomb NOUN a powerful bomb using energy created by the fusion of hydrogen nuclei

hydrolysis NOUN (Science) the chemical reaction of a substance with water

hyena NOUN a wild animal that makes a shrieking howl

hygiene (hy-jeen) NOUN the practice of keeping things clean to remain healthy and prevent disease ▸ **hygienic** ADJECTIVE

hymn NOUN a religious song of praise

hype NOUN (informal) extravagant publicity or advertising

hyperactive ADJECTIVE always active and unable to relax

hyperbole (hy-per-bol-ee) NOUN dramatic exaggeration for special effect, e.g. 'I've had thousands of letters'

hyperlink NOUN (ICT) a place in a computer document that provides a link to another document

THESAURUS

hush NOUN • *A hush fell on the room.* ▸ silence, quiet, calm, stillness

hush VERB • *He told us to hush.* ▸ be quiet, be silent

hut NOUN • *a hut in the woods* ▸ cabin, shack, shed, shelter

hygienic ADJECTIVE • *hygienic conditions* ▸ clean, sanitary, germ-free, sterile

a b c d e f g h i j k l m n o p q r s t u v w x y z

hypertext NOUN (ICT) a computer document that contains links to other documents

hyphen NOUN a short dash used to join words or parts of words together (e.g. in *hit-and-miss*)

hyphenate VERB to join or spell with a hyphen ► **hyphenation** NOUN

hypnosis NOUN a condition like a deep sleep in which a person's actions may be controlled by another person ► **hypnotic** ADJECTIVE

hypnotism NOUN the process of producing hypnosis in a person ► **hypnotist** NOUN

hypnotize VERB to produce hypnosis in

⚠ **SPELLING**

This word can also be spelled *hypnotise*.

hypochondriac (hy-po-**kon**-dree-ak) NOUN a person who constantly worries that they are ill ► **hypochondria** NOUN

hypocrite (**hip**-o-krit) NOUN a person who pretends to be more

virtuous than they really are ► **hypocrisy** (hip-ok-riss-ee) NOUN, **hypocritical** ADJECTIVE

hypodermic ADJECTIVE injecting drugs under the skin

hypotenuse (hy-**pot**-i-newz) NOUN the longest side in a right-angled triangle

hypothermia NOUN the condition of having a body temperature well below normal

hypothesis (hy-**poth**-i-sis) NOUN **hypotheses** a suggestion or argument that has not yet been proved true or correct ► **hypothetical** ADJECTIVE

hysterectomy (hist-er-**ek**-tom-ee) NOUN **hysterectomies** the surgical removal of the womb

hysteria NOUN wild uncontrollable excitement or panic

hysterical ADJECTIVE **1** in a state of hysteria **2** (*informal*) extremely funny ► **hysterically** ADVERB

hysterics (hiss-**te**-riks) PLURAL NOUN a fit of hysteria

hysterical ADJECTIVE • *hysterical fans* ► overwrought, frenzied, uncontrollable, frantic, wild,

delirious • *a hysterical film* ► hilarious, funny, amusing, comical

a
b
c
d
e
f
g
h
i
j
k
l
m
n
o
p
q
r
s
t
u
v
w
x
y
z

Ii

I *PRONOUN* a word used to refer to the person speaking or writing

ice *NOUN* **1** frozen water **2** an ice cream ▶ **icy** *ADJECTIVE*

ice *VERB* **1** to make or become icy **2** to put icing on a cake

iceberg *NOUN* a large mass of ice floating in the sea

ice cream *NOUN* a sweet creamy frozen food

ice hockey *NOUN* a form of hockey played on ice

ice rink *NOUN* a place made for skating

icicle *NOUN* a pointed hanging piece of ice formed when dripping water freezes

icing *NOUN* a sugary substance for decorating cakes

icon *NOUN* **1** a sacred painting or mosaic of a holy person **2** (*ICT*) a small symbol or picture on a computer screen

ICT *ABBREVIATION* information and communication technology

idea *NOUN* **1** a plan or thought formed in the mind **2** an opinion or belief **3** a feeling that something is likely

ideal *ADJECTIVE* perfect; completely suitable ▶ **ideally** *ADVERB*

ideal *NOUN* **1** a standard that people try to achieve **2** a person or thing regarded as perfect

idealist *NOUN* a person with high ideals ▶ **idealism** *NOUN*, **idealistic** *ADJECTIVE*

identical *ADJECTIVE* exactly the same ▶ **identically** *ADVERB*

identification *NOUN* **1** a document that proves who you are **2** the process of identifying someone or something

identify *VERB* **identifies**, **identified** **1** to recognize as being a certain person or thing **2** to treat as identical to something else **3** to share someone's feelings ▶ **identifiable** *ADJECTIVE*

identity *NOUN* **identities** **1** who or what a person or thing is **2** the

THESAURUS

icy *ADJECTIVE* • *an icy blast of air* ▶ freezing, biting, bitter, arctic • *icy roads* ▶ frozen, ice-covered, slippery

idea *NOUN* • *This is our idea.* ▶ plan, suggestion, intention, scheme, proposal • *other ideas on the subject* ▶ view, opinion, thought • *the idea of an afterlife* ▶ concept, notion, theory • *no idea this might happen* ▶ suspicion, feeling, inkling

• *some idea of the cost* ▶ estimate, approximation, guess

ideal *ADJECTIVE* • *ideal conditions* ▶ perfect, excellent, optimum

identify *VERB* • *to identify a suspect* ▶ recognize, pick out, name • *to identify areas for action* ▶ establish, recognize, discover, spot **identify with** • *to identify with the story's hero* ▶ sympathize with, empathize with, relate to

state of being the same **3** distinctive character

ideology NOUN **ideologies** a set of political beliefs and aims ▶ **ideological** ADJECTIVE

idiocy NOUN foolishness

idiom NOUN a phrase with a meaning that cannot be guessed from the words in it, e.g. *in hot water* (= in trouble) ▶ **idiomatic** ADJECTIVE

idiosyncrasy NOUN **idiosyncrasies** a person's own way of behaving or doing something

idiot NOUN a stupid or foolish person

idiotic ADJECTIVE stupid or foolish ▶ **idiotically** ADVERB

idle ADJECTIVE **1** doing no work; lazy **2** not in use or working **3** useless or pointless *idle gossip* ▶ **idly** ADVERB

idle VERB **1** to be idle **2** (of an engine) to be working slowly ▶ **idler** NOUN

idol NOUN **1** an image that is worshipped as a god **2** a famous person who is widely admired

idolize VERB to admire someone very much ▶ **idolization** NOUN

⚠ **SPELLING**

This word can also be spelled *idolise*.

idyll NOUN **1** a beautiful scene or situation **2** a poem describing a peaceful or romantic scene

idyllic ADJECTIVE very happy or beautiful

i.e. ABBREVIATION that is

if CONJUNCTION **1** on condition that; supposing that **2** whether

igloo NOUN an Inuit round house built of snow

ignite VERB **1** to set fire to **2** to catch fire

ignition NOUN **1** the process of igniting **2** the part of a motor engine that starts the fuel burning

ignoble ADJECTIVE not noble; shameful

ignominious ADJECTIVE humiliating; bringing disgrace ▶ **ignominy** NOUN

ignorant ADJECTIVE not knowing much or anything ▶ **ignorance** NOUN

ignore VERB to take no notice of

THESAURUS

idiotic ADJECTIVE • *an idiotic suggestion* ▶ stupid, silly, foolish

idle ADJECTIVE • *an idle person* ▶ lazy, indolent, slothful, work-shy • *idle machinery* ▶ unused, out of service • *idle speculation* ▶ pointless, aimless, meaningless

ignorant ADJECTIVE • *ignorant of events* ▶ unaware, uninformed (about), oblivious (to) • *an ignorant person* ▶ uneducated, illiterate

ignore VERB • *too serious to ignore* ▶ disregard, overlook, take no notice of • *Helen had ignored him.* ▶ snub, spurn, shun, give the cold shoulder to

a
b
c
d
e
f
g
h
i
j
k
l
m
n
o
p
q
r
s
t
u
v
w
x
y
z

iguana (ig-wah-na) NOUN a large tree-climbing tropical lizard

ilk NOUN **of that ilk** (*informal*) of that kind

ill ADJECTIVE **1** unwell; in bad health **2** bad or harmful *no ill effects*

ill ADVERB badly **ill at ease** uncomfortable

ill NOUN harm

illegal ADJECTIVE not legal; against the law ▸ **illegality** NOUN, **illegally** ADVERB

illegible ADJECTIVE impossible to read ▸ **illegibility** NOUN, **illegibly** ADVERB

illegitimate ADJECTIVE born of parents who are not married to each other

illicit ADJECTIVE against the law; not allowed ▸ **illicitly** ADVERB

illiterate ADJECTIVE unable to read or write ▸ **illiteracy** NOUN

illness NOUN a form of bad health

illogical ADJECTIVE not logical; not reasoning correctly ▸ **illogicality** NOUN, **illogically** ADVERB

illuminate VERB **1** to light up **2** to decorate with lights **3** to help to explain ▸ **illumination** NOUN

illusion NOUN **1** something that appears to be real but is not **2** a false idea or belief ▸ **illusory** ADJECTIVE

illusionist NOUN a conjuror

illustrate VERB **1** to show something by pictures, examples, etc. **2** to put illustrations in a book ▸ **illustrator** NOUN

illustration NOUN a picture in a book or magazine

illustrious ADJECTIVE famous and distinguished

image NOUN **1** a picture or statue of a person or thing **2** a mental picture of something **3** a strong likeness to someone else **4** the public reputation of a person or organization

imagery NOUN a writer's or speaker's use of words to produce pictures in the mind

imaginable ADJECTIVE able to be imagined

imaginary ADJECTIVE existing in the imagination; not real

ill ADJECTIVE ▸ **to feel ill** ▸ sick, unwell, poorly, off colour, nauseous ▸ *no ill effects* ▸ harmful, damaging, adverse

illegal ADJECTIVE ▸ *illegal activity* ▸ unlawful, criminal, wrong

illness NOUN ▸ *the exact nature of the illness* ▸ disease, disorder, sickness, infirmity, affliction

illusion NOUN ▸ *an illusion created by mirrors* ▸ deception, trick,

hallucination ▸ *no illusions about the difficulty of the task* ▸ delusion, misapprehension

image NOUN ▸ *images of the saints* ▸ picture, portrait, depiction, representation ▸ *the image on the screen* ▸ picture, reproduction ▸ *the image he had of university* ▸ impression, perception, idea

imaginary ADJECTIVE ▸ *an imaginary country* ▸ imagined,

a
b
c
d
e
f
g
h
i
j
k
l
m
n
o
p
q
r
s
t
u
v
w
x
y
z

imagination NOUN the ability to imagine things in a creative way

imaginative ADJECTIVE having or showing imagination

imagine VERB **1** to form pictures or ideas in the mind **2** to suppose

imam NOUN a Muslim religious leader

imbalance NOUN a lack of balance

imbecile NOUN an idiot ► **imbecile** ADJECTIVE, **imbecility** NOUN

imitate VERB to copy or mimic ► **imitator** NOUN

imitation NOUN **1** the process of imitating **2** a copy that imitates

immaculate ADJECTIVE **1** perfectly clean; spotless **2** without any fault or blemish

immaterial ADJECTIVE unimportant; not mattering

immature ADJECTIVE not mature ► **immaturity** NOUN

immediate ADJECTIVE **1** happening or done without any delay

2 nearest *our immediate neighbours* ► **immediacy** NOUN

immediately ADVERB without delay; straight away

immense ADJECTIVE exceedingly great; huge ► **immensity** NOUN

immerse VERB **1** to put completely into a liquid **2** to absorb in thought ► **immersion** NOUN

immigrant NOUN a person who comes to live in a country

immigrate VERB to come into a country to live there ► **immigration** NOUN

imminent ADJECTIVE likely to happen at any moment

immobile ADJECTIVE not moving; not able to move ► **immobility** NOUN

immobilize VERB to stop from moving or working ► **immobilization** NOUN

⚠ **SPELLING**

This word can also be spelled *immobilise*.

THESAURUS

fictional, invented, made-up, unreal, mythical

imaginative ADJECTIVE • *an imaginative description* ► creative, inventive, original, inspired, clever

imagine VERB • *to imagine life on a desert island* ► visualize, envisage, picture • *I imagine you'd like us to pay you now.* ► suppose, assume, presume

immediate ADJECTIVE • *to take immediate action* ► instant,

prompt, urgent, swift, quick • *immediate neighbours* ► nearest, closest

immediately ADVERB • *to return immediately* ► straight away, at once, directly, right away

immense ADJECTIVE • *two immense towers* ► huge, great, enormous, gigantic, massive

imminent ADJECTIVE • *An invasion seemed imminent.* ► close, near, impending, about to happen

immoral ADJECTIVE morally wrong; improper ► **immorality** NOUN

⚠️ **USAGE**

Do not confuse this word with *amoral*, which means 'having no moral standards'.

immortal ADJECTIVE 1 living for ever; not mortal 2 famous for all time ► **immortal** NOUN, **immortality** NOUN

immune ADJECTIVE 1 safe from catching a disease 2 not affected by *immune to his charms* ► **immunity** NOUN

immunize VERB to make a person immune from a disease, e.g. by vaccination ► **immunization** NOUN

⚠️ **SPELLING**

This word can also be spelled *immunise*.

imp NOUN 1 a small devil 2 a mischievous child ► **impish** ADJECTIVE

impact NOUN 1 a collision; the force of a collision 2 an influence or effect

impair VERB to damage or weaken

impala NOUN an African antelope

impale VERB to pierce or fix on a pointed object

impart VERB to tell information or news

impartial ADJECTIVE not favouring one side more than the other; not biased ► **impartiality** NOUN, **impartially** ADVERB

impassable ADJECTIVE (of a road) not able to be travelled along

impasse (am-pass) NOUN a situation in which no progress can be made

impassive ADJECTIVE not showing any emotion ► **impassively** ADVERB

impatient ADJECTIVE 1 not patient; in a hurry 2 eager to do something without waiting ► **impatience** NOUN, **impatiently** ADVERB

impeach VERB to bring a person to trial for a serious crime against their country ► **impeachment** NOUN

impeccable ADJECTIVE faultless; perfect ► **impeccably** ADVERB

impede VERB to hinder or get in the way of

impediment NOUN 1 a hindrance 2 a defect

impel VERB impelling, impelled 1 to urge or drive someone to do something 2 to drive forward

impending ADJECTIVE soon to happen; imminent

impenetrable ADJECTIVE 1 impossible to get through 2 incomprehensible

THESAURUS

immoral ADJECTIVE • *immoral behaviour* ► wrong, unethical, sinful, wicked, evil

impartial ADJECTIVE • *impartial advice* ► objective, unbiased, balanced, detached, neutral

impatient ADJECTIVE • *to grow impatient* ► restless, agitated, fretful, anxious, tetchy, jumpy • *impatient to start* ► anxious, eager, keen, avid

a
b
c
d
e
f
g
h
i
j
k
l
m
n
o
p
q
r
s
t
u
v
w
x
y
z

imperative ADJECTIVE **1** essential **2** (*Grammar*) expressing a command

imperceptible ADJECTIVE too small or gradual to be noticed

imperfect ADJECTIVE not perfect ▸ **imperfectly** ADVERB

imperfection NOUN a fault or weakness

imperial ADJECTIVE to do with an empire or its rulers

imperialism NOUN the policy of extending a country's empire or its influence ▸ **imperialist** NOUN

impersonal ADJECTIVE not affected by personal feelings ▸ **impersonally** ADVERB

impersonate VERB to pretend to be another person ▸ **impersonation** NOUN

impertinent ADJECTIVE insolent; not showing proper respect ▸ **impertinence** NOUN

impervious ADJECTIVE not affected by something *impervious to criticism*

impetuous ADJECTIVE acting hastily without thinking

impetus NOUN **1** the force that makes an object start moving **2** an influence causing something to happen or develop

impinge VERB **impinge on** to have an effect on

implacable ADJECTIVE determined to remain hostile or opposed ▸ **implacably** ADVERB

implant (im-plahnt) VERB to insert or fix in ▸ **implantation** NOUN

implant (im-plahnt) NOUN an organ or piece of tissue inserted in the body

implement NOUN a tool

implement VERB to put into action ▸ **implementation** NOUN

implicate VERB to involve in a crime or wrongdoing

implication NOUN something implied without being said

implicit ADJECTIVE **1** implied without being said **2** unquestioning *implicit obedience* ▸ **implicitly** ADVERB

implode VERB to burst or explode inwards ▸ **implosion** NOUN

implore VERB to beg somebody to do something

imply VERB **implies**, **implied** to suggest something without actually saying it ▸ **implication** NOUN

import (im-pawt) VERB to bring in goods from abroad to be sold

import (im-pawt) NOUN **1** the importing of goods **2** something imported

important ADJECTIVE **1** having or able to have a great effect **2** having

THESAURUS

impertinent ADJECTIVE • *an impertinent remark* ▸ rude, impolite, insolent, cheeky

implore VERB • *They implored him to come home.* ▸ beg, urge

imply VERB • *to imply that we are wrong* ▸ suggest, hint, insinuate

important ADJECTIVE • *an important decision* ▸ significant, momentous, crucial, vital • *an*

a b c d e f g h i j k l m n o p q r s t u v w x y z

great authority or influence
► **importance** NOUN

impose VERB to put or inflict *It imposes a strain upon us.* **impose on** to put an unfair burden on someone

imposition NOUN an unfair burden or inconvenience

impossible ADJECTIVE **1** not possible **2** (*informal*) annoying; unbearable ► **impossibility** NOUN, **impossibly** ADVERB

impostor NOUN a person who dishonestly pretends to be someone else

impotent ADJECTIVE powerless; unable to take action
► **impotence** NOUN, **impotently** ADVERB

impound VERB to confiscate or take possession of

impoverished ADJECTIVE made poor or weak

impractical ADJECTIVE not practical

impregnable ADJECTIVE strong enough to be safe against attack

impregnate VERB to fertilize or make pregnant

impress VERB **1** to make a person admire something **2** to fix firmly in the mind

impression NOUN **1** an effect produced on the mind *can make a big impression* **2** a vague idea **3** an imitation of a person or a sound

impressive ADJECTIVE making a strong impression; important or good

imprint NOUN a mark pressed into or on something

imprison VERB to put or keep in prison ► **imprisonment** NOUN

improbable ADJECTIVE unlikely
► **improbability** NOUN, **improbably** ADVERB

impromptu ADJECTIVE, ADVERB without any rehearsal or preparation

improper ADJECTIVE **1** unsuitable or wrong **2** indecent

important person ► powerful, influential, prominent, distinguished

impossible ADJECTIVE • *an impossible task* ► impractical, unrealistic, hopeless, out of the question, unachievable

impress VERB • *The evidence did not impress the jury.* ► move, stir, excite, have an impact on

impression NOUN • *the impression they were hiding something* ► feeling, sense,

suspicion, idea, hunch • *make a good impression* ► effect, impact, influence • *a favourable impression of them* ► opinion, view, assessment • *a good impression of the Prime Minister* ► imitation, impersonation, parody

impressive ADJECTIVE • *an impressive start* ► good, great, striking, first-class • *an impressive building* ► magnificent, imposing, splendid

improve VERB to make or become better ► **improvement** NOUN

improvise VERB to make or perform without preparation ► **improvisation** NOUN

impudent ADJECTIVE cheeky or disrespectful ► **impudence** NOUN

impulse NOUN a sudden strong desire to do something

impulsive ADJECTIVE done or acting on impulse

impunity (im-pewn-it-ee) NOUN freedom from punishment

impure ADJECTIVE not pure or clean ► **impurity** NOUN

in PREPOSITION 1 at or inside *in a box* 2 within the limits of *in two hours* 3 into *fall in a puddle* 4 consisting of *a serial in four parts* 5 occupied with; a member of *He is in the army.* 6 by means of *to pay in cash* **in all** in total number; altogether

in ADVERB 1 so as to be inside *Do come in.* 2 at home 3 in action or power **be in for** to be likely to get *be in for a shock*

inability NOUN lack of ability or power

inaccurate ADJECTIVE not accurate

inactive ADJECTIVE not active ► **inaction** NOUN, **inactivity** NOUN

inadequate ADJECTIVE 1 not enough 2 not able to cope or deal with something ► **inadequacy** NOUN

inane ADJECTIVE silly; without sense ► **inanely** ADVERB, **inanity** NOUN

inappropriate ADJECTIVE not appropriate

inaudible ADJECTIVE not loud enough to be heard ► **inaudibly** ADVERB

inaugurate VERB 1 to start or introduce something new and important 2 to formally establish in office ► **inauguration** NOUN

inborn ADJECTIVE existing from birth

inbred ADJECTIVE 1 inborn 2 produced by inbreeding

incapable ADJECTIVE not able to do something

incapacitate VERB to make a person or thing unable to do something

incense (in-sens) NOUN a substance making a spicy smell when it is burnt

incense (in-sens) VERB to make angry

THESAURUS

improve VERB • *ways to improve the service* ► make better, enhance, upgrade • *Relations have improved.* ► get better, progress, advance, develop • *The patient began to improve.* ► recover, get better, recuperate • *to improve their offer* ► increase, raise

impulsive ADJECTIVE • *impulsive behaviour* ► impetuous, spontaneous, rash, reckless

inaccurate ADJECTIVE • *inaccurate copies* ► inexact, imprecise, incorrect, wrong

incapable ADJECTIVE • *incapable of answering* ► incompetent, unable, useless

incentive NOUN something that encourages a person to do something

inception NOUN the beginning of something

incessant ADJECTIVE continuing without a pause; unceasing

inch NOUN a measure of length, one twelfth of a foot (about 2.5 centimetres)

inch VERB to move gradually

incidence NOUN the extent or frequency of something

incident NOUN an event

incidental ADJECTIVE happening as a minor part of something else
▶ **incidentally** ADVERB

incinerator NOUN a device for burning rubbish

incise VERB to cut or engrave into a surface

incision NOUN a cut made in a surgical operation

incisive ADJECTIVE clear and sharp

incite VERB to urge a person to act
▶ **incitement** NOUN

inclination NOUN **1** a tendency **2** a liking or preference

incline (in-klyn) VERB **1** to lean or slope **2** to bend forward in a nod or bow **3** to cause or influence **be inclined to** to tend to

incline (in-klyn) NOUN a slope

include VERB to make or consider as part of a group of things
▶ **inclusion** NOUN

inclusive ADJECTIVE including everything

incoherent ADJECTIVE not speaking or reasoning in an orderly way

income NOUN money received regularly from work or investments

incomparable (in-komp-er-abul) ADJECTIVE without an equal

incompatible ADJECTIVE not able to exist or be used together

incompetent ADJECTIVE unable to do something well

incomplete ADJECTIVE not complete

incomprehensible ADJECTIVE not able to be understood
▶ **incomprehension** NOUN

incident NOUN • *an incident from his childhood* ▶ event, episode, occurrence, experience • *an incident in the town centre* ▶ disturbance, commotion, fracas, scene

include VERB • *Activities include swimming and aerobics.* ▶ incorporate, consist of, involve, comprise, contain • *a package that includes flights and hotels*

▶ cover, allow for, take into account

incompetent ADJECTIVE • *too incompetent to do the job properly* ▶ inept, incapable, unqualified, inefficient, clumsy, bungling

incomplete ADJECTIVE • *work that is still incomplete* ▶ unfinished, not finished

incomprehensible ADJECTIVE • *an incomprehensible remark*

a
b
c
d
e
f
g
h
i
j
k
l
m
n
o
p
q
r
s
t
u
v
w
x
y
z

DICTIONARY

inconceivable ADJECTIVE not able
to be imagined; most unlikely

inconclusive ADJECTIVE not
conclusive

incongruous ADJECTIVE out of
place or unsuitable

inconsiderate ADJECTIVE not
considerate towards other people

inconsistent ADJECTIVE not
consistent ▸ **inconsistency** NOUN

inconspicuous ADJECTIVE not
attracting attention

incontinent ADJECTIVE not able to
control the bladder or bowels
▸ **incontinence** NOUN

inconvenience NOUN
something inconvenient

inconvenience VERB to cause
inconvenience to

inconvenient ADJECTIVE not
convenient

incorporate VERB to include as a
part of something larger
▸ **incorporation** NOUN

incorrect ADJECTIVE not correct
▸ **incorrectly** ADVERB

incorrigible ADJECTIVE not able to
be reformed

increase (in-krees) VERB to make or
become larger or more

increase (in-krees) NOUN **1** the
process of increasing **2** the
amount by which a thing increases

incredible ADJECTIVE impossible to
believe ▸ **incredibly** ADVERB

incredulous ADJECTIVE unwilling
to believe something
▸ **incredulity** NOUN

incriminate VERB to show a
person to have been involved in a
crime ▸ **incrimination** NOUN

THESAURUS

▸ confusing, baffling,
unintelligible, incoherent
• *incomprehensible writing*
▸ illegible, indecipherable

inconsiderate ADJECTIVE
• *inconsiderate behaviour*
▸ thoughtless, insensitive, selfish

inconsistent ADJECTIVE
• *inconsistent attitudes*
▸ changeable, unreliable, erratic,
variable • *several inconsistent
versions of the legend*
▸ conflicting, contradictory,
incompatible

inconvenient ADJECTIVE • *an
inconvenient moment*
▸ awkward, difficult, unsuitable,
inappropriate

incorrect ADJECTIVE • *incorrect
answers* ▸ wrong, false,
erroneous, inaccurate, mistaken

increase VERB • *Applications have
increased.* ▸ rise, grow, swell,
multiply, expand, spread • *to
increase demand* ▸ raise, boost,
strengthen, develop, expand

increase NOUN • *an increase in size*
▸ growth, enlargement,
expansion • *an increase in pay*
▸ rise

incredible ADJECTIVE • *an
incredible feat* ▸ magnificent,
marvellous, spectacular,
remarkable, wonderful • *an
incredible story* ▸ unbelievable,
implausible, far-fetched, unlikely

incubate VERB to hatch eggs by keeping them warm
▶ **incubation** NOUN

incubator NOUN **1** a device for keeping a premature baby warm and supplied with oxygen **2** a device for incubating eggs

incur VERB incurring, incurred to bring something on yourself *to incur expenses*

incurable ADJECTIVE not able to be cured ▶ **incurably** ADVERB

indebted ADJECTIVE owing money or gratitude

indecent ADJECTIVE not decent; improper ▶ **indecency** NOUN

indeed ADVERB **1** used to strengthen a meaning *very hot indeed* **2** really; truly *I am indeed surprised.*

indefinite ADJECTIVE not definite; vague ▶ **indefinitely** ADVERB

indefinite article NOUN the word 'a' or 'an'

indelible ADJECTIVE impossible to rub out or remove

indent VERB to start a line of writing or printing further in from the margin than other lines
▶ **indentation** NOUN

independent ADJECTIVE **1** not dependent on any other person or thing **2** (of a country) free of foreign rule **3** not connected with something ▶ **independence** NOUN

indescribable ADJECTIVE too extraordinary to be described

indeterminate ADJECTIVE not fixed or decided exactly

index NOUN **1** (**indexes**) an alphabetical list of subjects in a book **2** (**indices**) (*Maths*) the raised number written to the right of another (e.g. 3 in 2³) showing how many times the first one is to be multiplied by itself

index VERB to put into an index

index finger NOUN the forefinger

indicate VERB **1** to point out or make known **2** to be a sign of
▶ **indication** NOUN, **indicator** NOUN

indicative ADJECTIVE giving an indication

indict (ind-yt) VERB to charge a person with a crime
▶ **indictment** NOUN

indifferent ADJECTIVE **1** not caring or interested **2** not good
▶ **indifference** NOUN

indefinite ADJECTIVE • *for an indefinite period* ▶ unspecified, unknown, unlimited

independent ADJECTIVE • *an independent country* ▶ autonomous, sovereign, self-governing • *an independent person* ▶ free, self-reliant, self-sufficient, liberated • *an independent opinion* ▶ impartial, unbiased, objective

indicate VERB • *a signal to indicate success* ▶ show, signify, denote d *Good sales indicate the book's popularity.* ▶ show, demonstrate, be a sign of, suggest • *to indicate your choice* ▶ specify, point out

indifferent ADJECTIVE • *His voice showed how indifferent he was.* ▶ unconcerned, uncaring, nonchalant • *an indifferent meal* ▶ mediocre, ordinary, average

indigenous ADJECTIVE growing or originating in a particular country

indigestible ADJECTIVE difficult to digest

indigestion NOUN pain or discomfort while digesting food

indignant ADJECTIVE angry at something unfair ▸ **indignation** NOUN

indignity NOUN **indignities** treatment that makes a person feel humiliated

indigo NOUN a deep-blue colour

indirect ADJECTIVE not direct ▸ **indirectly** ADVERB

indiscreet ADJECTIVE not discreet; revealing secrets ▸ **indiscretion** NOUN

indiscriminate ADJECTIVE not choosing carefully; haphazard ▸ **indiscriminately** ADVERB

indispensable ADJECTIVE essential

indisposed ADJECTIVE slightly unwell

indistinct ADJECTIVE not clear

indistinguishable ADJECTIVE not able to be told apart

individual ADJECTIVE **1** of or for one person **2** single or separate *each individual word* ▸ **individually** ADVERB

individual NOUN one person, animal, or plant

indivisible ADJECTIVE not able to be divided or separated

indoctrinate VERB to fill someone's mind with ideas or beliefs which they accept unthinkingly ▸ **indoctrination** NOUN

indolent ADJECTIVE lazy ▸ **indolence** NOUN

indoor ADJECTIVE used or done inside a building *indoor games*

indoors ADVERB inside a building

indubitable ADJECTIVE not able to be doubted ▸ **indubitably** ADVERB

induce VERB **1** to persuade **2** to produce or cause ▸ **induction** NOUN

inducement NOUN an incentive

indulge VERB to allow someone what they want

indulgent ADJECTIVE kind and lenient ▸ **indulgence** NOUN

industrial ADJECTIVE to do with industry

industrialized ADJECTIVE (of a country or district) having many industries ▸ **industrialization** NOUN

⚠ SPELLING

This word can also be spelled *industrialised*.

THESAURUS

indignant ADJECTIVE • *indignant letters from readers* ▸ angry, irate, affronted, incensed, offended, furious, fuming

indirect ADJECTIVE • *a quieter indirect route* ▸ roundabout, circuitous, meandering • *an*

indirect insult ▸ disguised, ambiguous, implied

individual ADJECTIVE • *an individual style* ▸ characteristic, distinctive, special, unique, personal

industrious ADJECTIVE working hard

industry NOUN **industries 1** the making of goods in factories **2** a branch of this **3** hard work

inedible ADJECTIVE not edible

ineffective ADJECTIVE not effective; inefficient
▸ **ineffectively** ADVERB

inefficient ADJECTIVE not efficient
▸ **inefficiency** NOUN

ineligible ADJECTIVE not eligible or qualified

inept ADJECTIVE lacking skill
▸ **ineptitude** NOUN

inequality NOUN **inequalities** an unequal or unfair state

inert ADJECTIVE **1** not moving or reacting **2** (*Science*) (of a gas) not combining with other substances

inertia (in-er-sha) NOUN **1** the state of being inert or slow to take action **2** (*Science*) the tendency for a moving thing to keep moving

inescapable ADJECTIVE unavoidable

inevitable ADJECTIVE unavoidable; sure to happen ▸ **inevitably** ADVERB

inexorable ADJECTIVE relentless
▸ **inexorably** ADVERB

inexpensive ADJECTIVE not expensive; cheap
▸ **inexpensively** ADVERB

inexperience NOUN lack of experience ▸ **inexperienced** ADJECTIVE

inexplicable ADJECTIVE impossible to explain ▸ **inexplicably** ADVERB

infallible ADJECTIVE never wrong or failing ▸ **infallibility** NOUN, **infallibly** ADVERB

infamous (in-fam-us) ADJECTIVE having a bad reputation; wicked ▸ **infamy** NOUN

infancy NOUN early childhood

infant NOUN a baby or young child

infantile ADJECTIVE **1** to do with infants **2** childish

infantry NOUN soldiers fighting on foot

infatuated ADJECTIVE filled with foolish love ▸ **infatuation** NOUN

infect VERB to pass on a disease to

infection NOUN an infectious disease or condition

infectious ADJECTIVE **1** (of a disease) able to be spread by air or water **2** quickly spreading *infectious laughter*

infer VERB **inferring, inferred** to draw a conclusion from what

industrious ADJECTIVE • *an industrious student*
▸ hard-working, conscientious, diligent

ineffective ADJECTIVE • *ineffective protests* ▸ unsuccessful, unproductive, useless, futile • *an ineffective leader* ▸ inadequate, ineffectual, weak, inept

inevitable ADJECTIVE • *inevitable delays* ▸ unavoidable, inescapable

infallible ADJECTIVE • *an infallible solution* ▸ foolproof, unfailing, guaranteed, certain

infer VERB • *to infer from the results* ▸ conclude, deduce, assume, guess

someone says or does
► **inference** NOUN

⚠ USAGE

Do not use this word to mean *imply* or *suggest*.

inferior ADJECTIVE less good or important ► **inferiority** NOUN

inferior NOUN a person who is lower in position or rank

infernal ADJECTIVE to do with or like hell *infernal regions* ► **infernally** ADVERB

inferno NOUN **infernos** a huge fire that is out of control

infertile ADJECTIVE not fertile
► **infertility** NOUN

infest VERB (of pests) to be present in large numbers in a place
► **infestation** NOUN

infidelity NOUN unfaithfulness

infiltrate VERB to get into an organization gradually in order to control it ► **infiltration** NOUN, **infiltrator** NOUN

infinite ADJECTIVE endless; without a limit ► **infinitely** ADVERB

infinitesimal ADJECTIVE extremely small

infinitive NOUN (*Grammar*) the basic form of a verb (e.g. *come* and *kill*, sometimes preceded by *to* (e.g. *I want to come*)

infinity NOUN an infinite number or distance or time

infirm ADJECTIVE weak from old age or illness ► **infirmity** NOUN

infirmary NOUN **infirmaries** a hospital

inflamed ADJECTIVE **1** red and swollen **2** angry

inflammable ADJECTIVE able to be set on fire

inflammation NOUN painful redness or swelling in a part of the body

inflammatory ADJECTIVE likely to make people angry

inflate VERB **1** to fill with air or gas **2** to increase too much
► **inflatable** ADJECTIVE

inflation NOUN **1** a general rise in prices

inflection NOUN (*Grammar*) an ending or form of a word used to change its role in a sentence, e.g. *take, takes, taking, took*

inflexible ADJECTIVE **1** not able to be bent **2** unable to be persuaded

inflict VERB to make a person suffer something

influence NOUN **1** the power to affect other people or things **2** a person or thing with this power

inferior ADJECTIVE • *inferior rank* ► lesser, lower, subordinate, junior • *inferior quality* ► poor, mediocre, substandard, shoddy

infinite ADJECTIVE • *to need infinite patience* ► endless, limitless, boundless, unlimited • *infinite*

numbers of chimneys ► countless, innumerable, numberless

influence NOUN • *ideas that have a large influence* ► effect, impact, control, power (over), authority (over)

a
b
c
d
e
f
g
h
i
j
k
l
m
n
o
p
q
r
s
t
u
v
w
x
y
z

DICTIONARY

influence *VERB* to have an influence on

influential *ADJECTIVE* having great influence

influenza *NOUN* an infectious disease causing fever

influx *NOUN* the arrival of people or things

inform *VERB* to give information to

informal *ADJECTIVE* not formal ► **informality** *NOUN*, **informally** *ADVERB*

informant *NOUN* someone who gives information

information *NOUN* knowledge or facts

informative *ADJECTIVE* giving a lot of information

informed *ADJECTIVE* knowing about something

informer *NOUN* a person who gives information to the police

infra-red *ADJECTIVE* below or beyond red in the spectrum

infrastructure *NOUN* the basic services and systems of a country

infringe *VERB* **1** to break a rule or law **2** to encroach on a person's rights ► **infringement** *NOUN*

infuriate *VERB* to make angry

ingenious *ADJECTIVE* **1** clever at inventing things **2** cleverly made ► **ingenuity** *NOUN*

ingot *NOUN* a lump of gold or silver in the form of a brick

ingrained *ADJECTIVE* (of feelings or habits) deeply fixed

ingratitude *NOUN* lack of gratitude

ingredient *NOUN* one of the parts of a mixture

inhabit *VERB* to live in a place ► **inhabitant** *NOUN*

inhale *VERB* to breathe in ► **inhaler** *NOUN*

inherent *ADJECTIVE* existing naturally in someone or something

inherit *VERB* **1** to receive property when someone dies **2** to receive from parents ► **inheritance** *NOUN*

inhibit *VERB* to hinder or restrain ► **inhibited** *ADJECTIVE*

THESAURUS

influence *VERB* • *Parents influence their children.* ► affect, have an effect on, guide, direct, control • *attempts to influence the jury* ► sway, coerce, pressurize, bias, prejudice

influential *ADJECTIVE* • *an influential politician* ► important, powerful, authoritative, leading

informal *ADJECTIVE* • *an informal conversation* ► casual, relaxed, natural, easy-going • *an informal*

style of writing ► colloquial, idiomatic, popular • *informal clothes* ► casual, everyday, comfortable, leisure

infuriate *VERB* • *a stubborn refusal that infuriated her* ► anger, enrage, exasperate, annoy, irritate

ingenious *ADJECTIVE* • *an ingenious solution* ► clever, inventive, imaginative, creative, cunning

inhabit *VERB* • *to inhabit a house* ► live in, occupy, dwell in

inhibition NOUN a feeling of embarrassment or worry that prevents a person from acting in a natural way

inhuman ADJECTIVE cruel; without pity or kindness ► **inhumanity** NOUN

inhumane ADJECTIVE not humane

initial NOUN the first letter of a word or name

initial VERB **initialling, initialled** to mark or sign with the initials of your name

initial ADJECTIVE at the beginning *the initial stages* ► **initially** ADVERB

initiate VERB **1** to start **2** to admit to a group ► **initiation** NOUN

initiative NOUN the right or ability to take action

inject VERB to put a medicine or drug into the body ► **injection** NOUN

injunction NOUN a legal order not to do something

injure VERB to harm or hurt someone

injury NOUN **injuries** an instance of harm or damage

injustice NOUN an unjust action or treatment

ink NOUN a black or coloured liquid used in writing and printing

inkling NOUN a slight idea or suspicion

inland ADJECTIVE, ADVERB in or towards the interior of a country

inlet NOUN a strip of water reaching into the land from a sea or lake

inmost ADJECTIVE most inward; furthest in

inn NOUN a country hotel or pub

innards PLURAL NOUN (informal) the internal organs of a person or animal

innate ADJECTIVE inborn or natural

inner ADJECTIVE inside; nearer to the centre ► **innermost** ADJECTIVE

innings NOUN the turn of a cricket team or player to bat

innocent ADJECTIVE **1** not guilty or bad **2** harmless ► **innocence** NOUN

THESAURUS

inhuman ADJECTIVE • *inhuman treatment of prisoners* ► brutal, cruel, barbaric, inhumane

initial ADJECTIVE • *an initial reaction* ► first, original, earliest • *an initial payment* ► opening, preliminary, starting, introductory

initiative NOUN • *applicants with initiative* ► resourcefulness, inventiveness, enterprise, drive, energy, dynamism • *to lose the initiative* ► advantage, upper hand, lead • *a peace initiative*

► proposal, plan, scheme, strategy

injure VERB • *He was injured in a fight.* ► hurt, harm, wound, maim • *She injured her arm.* ► hurt, damage, break, crush

innocent ADJECTIVE • *He swore that he was innocent.* ► not guilty, guiltless, blameless • *They looked so innocent.* ► pure, virtuous, childlike, trusting • *innocent fun* ► harmless, innocuous, inoffensive

innocuous ADJECTIVE harmless

innovation NOUN something completely new ▸ **innovative** ADJECTIVE

innuendo NOUN **innuendoes** an indirect reference to something insulting or rude

innumerable ADJECTIVE too many to be counted

inoculate VERB to inject with a vaccine or serum as a protection against a disease ▸ **inoculation** NOUN

inoffensive ADJECTIVE not giving offence

inordinate ADJECTIVE excessive ▸ **inordinately** ADVERB

inorganic ADJECTIVE not of living organisms; of mineral origin

input NOUN data put into a computer

inquest NOUN an official inquiry into a sudden death

inquire VERB **1** to investigate carefully **2** to ask for information

inquiry NOUN **inquiries 1** an official investigation **2** a question

inquisition NOUN a detailed investigation

inquisitive ADJECTIVE fond of asking questions

insane ADJECTIVE mad ▸ **insanity** NOUN

insatiable ADJECTIVE impossible to satisfy

inscribe VERB to write or carve

inscription NOUN words written or carved

inscrutable ADJECTIVE mysterious

insect NOUN a small animal with six legs and no backbone

insecure ADJECTIVE not secure or safe ▸ **insecurity** NOUN

insensible ADJECTIVE unconscious or unaware

insensitive ADJECTIVE not sensitive

inseparable ADJECTIVE not able or wanting to be separated ▸ **inseparably** ADVERB

insert VERB to put a thing into something else ▸ **insertion** NOUN

inshore ADVERB, ADJECTIVE near or nearer to the shore

inside NOUN the inner side, surface, or part

inside ADJECTIVE, ADVERB on or to the inside

inside PREPOSITION on or to the inside of *inside the box*

inquiry NOUNS • *a formal inquiry into the incident* ▸ investigation, inquest

inquisitive ADJECTIVE • *an inquisitive mind* ▸ curious, questioning, enquiring, interested

insane ADJECTIVE • *to be declared insane* ▸ mad, deranged, crazy, demented, mentally ill • *would be insane to try it* ▸ mad, crazy, foolish, stupid

insecure ADJECTIVE • *The house was insecure.* ▸ unsafe, unprotected, vulnerable • *to feel insecure* ▸ anxious, worried, unconfident

insidious ADJECTIVE causing harm gradually

insight NOUN the ability to understand things

insignificant ADJECTIVE not important or influential
▸ **insignificance** NOUN

insincere ADJECTIVE not sincere
▸ **insincerity** NOUN

insinuate VERB 1 to hint something unpleasant 2 to become gradually involved
▸ **insinuation** NOUN

insipid ADJECTIVE lacking flavour or interest

insist VERB to be firm in saying or asking ▸ **insistent** ADJECTIVE

insolent ADJECTIVE rude and insulting ▸ **insolence** NOUN

insoluble ADJECTIVE impossible to solve or dissolve

insomnia NOUN an inability to sleep ▸ **insomniac** NOUN

inspect VERB to examine carefully
▸ **inspection** NOUN, **inspector** NOUN

inspiration NOUN 1 a sudden good idea 2 an inspiring influence

inspire VERB to fill a person with ideas or enthusiasm

install VERB to put in position
▸ **installation** NOUN

instalment NOUN 1 each of several payments 2 each part of a story

instance NOUN an example

instant ADJECTIVE happening or ready immediately

instant NOUN a moment

instantaneous ADJECTIVE happening immediately

instead ADVERB in place of something else

instep NOUN the top of the foot between the toes and the ankle

instigate VERB to cause to happen
▸ **instigation** NOUN

instil VERB instilling, instilled to put ideas into a person's mind gradually

insignificant ADJECTIVE • *insignificant differences*
▸ unimportant, trivial, small, meaningless

insincere ADJECTIVE • *an insincere smile* ▸ false, deceitful, dishonest, pretended

insist VERB • *He insisted he had done everything they had asked.*
▸ maintain, assert, claim, declare, stress

insolent ADJECTIVE • *an insolent attitude* ▸ rude, impolite, impertinent, disrespectful, cheeky

inspect VERB • *to be inspected by a surveyor* ▸ check, examine, investigate, scrutinize

inspire VERB • *a simple tune that inspired him to write a musical*
▸ stimulate, motivate, prompt, encourage

instant ADJECTIVE • *instant access to the information* ▸ immediate, instantaneous, prompt, fast, direct

instant NOUN • *finished in an instant* ▸ moment, second, minute, flash

a
b
c
d
e
f
g
h
i
j
k
l
m
n
o
p
q
r
s
t
u
v
w
x
y
z

instinct NOUN a natural tendency or ability ▶ **instinctive** ADJECTIVE

institute NOUN a society or organization

institute VERB to establish or found

institution NOUN 1 a public organization 2 a habit or custom

instruct VERB 1 to teach a person a subject or skill 2 to tell a person what they must do ▶ **instruction** NOUN, **instructor** NOUN

instructive ADJECTIVE giving knowledge or information

instrument NOUN 1 a device for producing musical sounds 2 a tool or device

instrumental ADJECTIVE 1 performed on musical instruments 2 helping to make something happen

insubordinate ADJECTIVE disobedient or rebellious ▶ **insubordination** NOUN

insufferable ADJECTIVE unbearable

insufficient ADJECTIVE not enough

insular ADJECTIVE like an island

insulate VERB to cover or protect to prevent heat, cold, or electricity, etc. from passing in or out ▶ **insulation** NOUN

insulin NOUN a substance that controls the amount of sugar in the blood

insult (in-sult) VERB to hurt a person's feelings or pride

insult (in-sult) NOUN an insulting remark

insuperable ADJECTIVE unable to be overcome *an insuperable difficulty*

insurance NOUN an agreement to compensate someone for a loss, damage, or injury, etc., in return for a payment made in advance

insure VERB to protect with insurance

⚠ **USAGE**

Do not confuse this word with ensure.

intact ADJECTIVE not damaged; complete

intake NOUN the number of people or things accepted

intangible ADJECTIVE not able to be touched; not solid

THESAURUS

instinct NOUN • *an instinct to follow them* ▶ impulse, inclination, hunch, feeling, sixth-sense

instruct VERB • *a tutor to instruct the children* ▶ coach, educate, train, teach • *The officials instructed us to wait behind the barrier.* ▶ order, direct, command, advise

instrument NOUN • *a sharp instrument* ▶ tool, implement, device, appliance, gadget, machine

insult VERB • *did not want to insult us* ▶ offend, mock, affront, snub, sneer at

insult NOUN • *The remark was an insult.* ▶ affront, slight, criticism, snub

integer NOUN a whole number (e.g. 0, 3, 19), not a fraction

integral (in-tig-ral) ADJECTIVE **1** being an essential part of something **2** whole or complete

integrate VERB **1** to make into a whole **2** to bring people together ► **integration** NOUN

integrity NOUN honesty

intellect NOUN the ability to reason

intellectual ADJECTIVE **1** to do with or using the intellect **2** having a good intellect

intellectual NOUN a person with a good intellect

intelligence NOUN **1** the state of being intelligent **2** information of military value

intelligent ADJECTIVE able to learn and understand well

intelligible ADJECTIVE able to be understood ► **intelligibility** NOUN

intend VERB to have something in mind as what you want to do

intense ADJECTIVE **1** very strong or great **2** feeling things strongly ► **intensity** NOUN

intensify VERB **intensifies**, **intensified** to make or become more intense

intensive ADJECTIVE concentrated; using a lot of effort over a short time

intent NOUN intention

intent ADJECTIVE **intent on** determined to do something

intention NOUN a purpose or plan

intentional ADJECTIVE deliberate ► **intentionally** ADVERB

integrity NOUN • *No one doubts their integrity.* ► honesty, sincerity, reliability

intelligence NOUN • *a person of great intelligence* ► intellect, brainpower, wisdom, understanding • *intelligence regarding terrorist attacks* ► information, report, warning, news, knowledge

intelligent ADJECTIVE • *a highly intelligent writer* ► clever, bright, acute, sharp, perceptive

intelligible ADJECTIVE • *The message was barely intelligible.* ► understandable, comprehensible, legible, clear

intend VERB • *I intend to apply for a grant.* ► propose, mean, plan, aim • *The book is intended for learners of English.* ► design, destine, mean

intense ADJECTIVE • *intense pain* ► extreme, severe, fierce, strong, powerful

intent ADJECTIVE • *intent on visiting her friends* ► keen (to), resolved (to), determined (to) • *an intent look* ► attentive, engrossed, absorbed, preoccupied

intention NOUN • *our intention to accept the offer* ► aim, objective, plan, ambition, goal

intentional ADJECTIVE • *The action was intentional.* ► deliberate,

a
b
c
d
e
f
g
h
i
j
k
l
m
n
o
p
q
r
s
t
u
v
w
x
y
z

DICTIONARY

inter VERB **interring, interred** to bury

interactive ADJECTIVE (ICT) allowing information to be sent immediately between a computer system and its user

intercede VERB to intervene on behalf of another person ▸ **intercession** NOUN

intercept VERB to stop or catch a person or thing that is going from one place to another ▸ **interception** NOUN

interchange VERB to exchange or alternate ▸ **interchangeable** ADJECTIVE

interchange NOUN a major road junction

intercom NOUN a system of telephone communication between parts of a building

intercourse NOUN communication between people

interest NOUN **1** a feeling of wanting to know about something **2** something that interests

someone **3** an advantage **4** money paid in return for money lent

interest VERB to attract the interest of

interface NOUN (ICT) a connection between parts of a computer system

interfere VERB **1** to take part in something that is not your concern **2** to get in the way

interference NOUN **1** the act of interfering **2** distortion of a radio or television signal

interim ADJECTIVE temporary *an interim arrangement*

interior ADJECTIVE inner

interior NOUN the inside of something

interject VERB to interrupt someone ▸ **interjection** NOUN

interlude NOUN **1** an interval **2** something happening between other events

intermediary NOUN **intermediaries** someone who tries to settle a dispute

THESAURUS

premeditated, intended, planned, conscious

interest NOUN • *a matter of great interest* ▸ importance, significance, consequence • *interests including rock-climbing* ▸ hobby, pastime, activity

interest VERB • *an idea that interests me* ▸ appeal to, excite, fascinate, intrigue

interested ADJECTIVE • *No one seemed interested.* ▸ curious, enthusiastic, excited, keen,

fascinated, absorbed • *the interested parties* ▸ affected, involved, concerned

interesting ADJECTIVE • *an interesting idea* ▸ fascinating, exciting, intriguing, attractive, appealing

interfere VERB **interfere in** • *to interfere in her friends' lives* ▸ intervene, meddle in, pry into

interfere with • *A headache interfered with his thoughts.* ▸ inhibit, hinder, hamper

intermediate ADJECTIVE coming between two things

interminable ADJECTIVE long and tedious ► **interminably** ADVERB

intermission NOUN an interval or pause

intermittent ADJECTIVE happening at intervals; not continuous ► **intermittently** ADVERB

internal ADJECTIVE happening or situated inside ► **internally** ADVERB

international ADJECTIVE 1 to do with or belonging to more than one country 2 agreed between nations ► **internationally** ADVERB

international NOUN a sports contest between different countries

Internet NOUN an international computer network that allows users to communicate and exchange information

interpret VERB 1 to explain or translate 2 to perform music ► **interpretation** NOUN, **interpreter** NOUN

interrogate VERB to question someone closely or formally

► **interrogation** NOUN, **interrogator** NOUN

interrogative ADJECTIVE expressing a question

interrupt VERB 1 to break in on what someone is saying 2 to prevent from continuing ► **interruption** NOUN

intersect VERB 1 to divide a thing by passing or lying across it 2 (of lines or roads) to cross each other ► **intersection** NOUN

interval NOUN 1 a time between two events or parts 2 a space between two things

intervene VERB 1 to come between two events 2 to try to stop something ► **intervention** NOUN

interview NOUN a formal meeting with someone to obtain information

interview VERB to hold an interview with someone

intestine NOUN the tube along which food passes after the stomach

intimate (in-tim-at) ADJECTIVE 1 friendly 2 private and personal ► **intimacy** NOUN

THESAURUS

internal ADJECTIVE • *an internal courtyard* ► inner, interior, central • *the country's internal affairs* ► domestic, home, interior

interrupt VERB • *She opened her mouth to interrupt.* ► butt in, break in, cut in, intervene • *People began to interrupt him.* ► heckle, disrupt, butt in on • *to interrupt their holiday* ► suspend, break off, discontinue

interval NOUN • *an interval of 20 minutes* ► intermission, interlude, break, pause

intimate ADJECTIVE • *an intimate friendship* ► close, loving, affectionate • *an intimate*

DICTIONARY

intimate (in-tim-ayt) *VERB* to hint at something ► **intimation** *NOUN*

intimidate *VERB* to frighten with threats ► **intimidation** *NOUN*

into *PREPOSITION* **1** to the inside of *went into the house* **2** to a different condition *It broke into pieces.*

intolerable *ADJECTIVE* unbearable ► **intolerably** *ADVERB*

intonation *NOUN* the tone or pitch of the voice in speaking

intone *VERB* to recite in a chanting voice

intoxicate *VERB* **1** to make drunk **2** to excite ► **intoxication** *NOUN*

intransitive *ADJECTIVE* (of a verb) not having a direct object, e.g. *walk* in *We walked to the station.*

intrepid *ADJECTIVE* fearless and brave

intricate *ADJECTIVE* very complicated ► **intricacy** *NOUN*, **intricately** *ADVERB*

intrigue (in-treeg) *VERB* **1** to interest very much **2** to plot or scheme

intrigue *NOUN* secret plotting

intrinsic *ADJECTIVE* being part of the essential nature of something *intrinsic value* ► **intrinsically** *ADVERB*

introduce *VERB* **1** to bring into use **2** to make a person known to other people

introduction *NOUN* **1** the act of introducing **2** a piece at the beginning of a book explaining its contents ► **introductory** *ADJECTIVE*

introspective *ADJECTIVE* examining your own thoughts and feelings ► **introspection** *NOUN*

introvert *NOUN* someone who does not like to talk about their own thoughts and feelings with other people

intrude *VERB* to join in without being wanted ► **intrusion** *NOUN*, **intrusive** *ADJECTIVE*

intruder *NOUN* **1** someone who intrudes **2** a burglar

THESAURUS

atmosphere ► friendly, welcoming, warm, relaxed, cosy • *intimate thoughts* ► personal, private, secret, confidential • *an intimate knowledge of the area* ► detailed, deep, in-depth

intrepid *ADJECTIVE* • *intrepid climbers* ► brave, bold, courageous, daring

intricate *ADJECTIVE* • *intricate designs* ► complex, elaborate, complicated, involved, sophisticated

introduce *VERB* • *She introduced us to her husband.* ► present, make known, acquaint • *to introduce some new features* ► bring in, institute, start, begin • *to introduce the show* ► present, host, announce

intrude *VERB* **intrude on** • *no right to intrude on a person's privacy* ► break in on, interrupt, butt in on

intruder *NOUN* • *Intruders left the house in a mess.* ► trespasser, burglar, housebreaker, thief

intuition NOUN the power to know or understand things naturally ► **intuitive** ADJECTIVE

Inuit (in-yoo-it) NOUN **1** a member of a people living in northern Canada and Greenland; an Eskimo **2** the language of the Inuit

⚠ USAGE

Inuit is preferred to *Eskimo*.

inundate VERB to flood or overwhelm ► **inundation** NOUN

inured (in-yoord) ADJECTIVE used to something unpleasant

invade VERB to attack and enter a country ► **invader** NOUN

invalid (in-va-leed) NOUN a person who is ill or weakened by illness

invalid (in-val-id) ADJECTIVE not valid ► **invalidity** NOUN

invalidate VERB to make invalid ► **invalidation** NOUN

invaluable ADJECTIVE extremely valuable

⚠ USAGE

This is not the opposite of *valuable*, which is *valueless*.

invasion NOUN the act of invading a country

invent VERB to make or think of something new ► **invention** NOUN, **inventive** ADJECTIVE, **inventor** NOUN

inventory (in-ven-ter-ee) NOUN **inventories** a detailed list of things

inverse ADJECTIVE opposite or reverse

invert VERB to turn something upside down ► **inversion** NOUN

invertebrate NOUN an animal without a backbone ► **invertebrate** ADJECTIVE

inverted commas PLURAL NOUN a pair of punctuation marks (' ' or " ") put round quotations and spoken words

invest VERB **1** to use money to make a profit **2** to give someone an honour ► **investor** NOUN

investigate VERB to find out as much as you can about ► **investigation** NOUN, **investigator** NOUN

investment NOUN **1** an amount of money invested **2** something in which money is invested

invade VERB • *to invade the country from the south* ► march into, occupy, enter, raid, attack

invalid ADJECTIVE • *His licence was invalid.* ► void, unacceptable, worthless • *to prove the idea invalid* ► false, incorrect, untrue

invaluable ADJECTIVE • *an invaluable member of the team* ► important, crucial,

indispensable, irreplaceable, precious

invent VERB • *to invent a new board game* ► create, devise • *to invent an excuse* ► make up, concoct, fabricate

investigate VERB • *The police were investigating the discovery of a body.* ► inquire into, look into, examine, explore, study, gather evidence about

a
b
c
d
e
f
g
i
j
k
l
m
n
o
p
q
r
s
t
u
v
w
x
y
z

inveterate ADJECTIVE firmly established *an inveterate liar*

invidious ADJECTIVE causing resentment because of unfairness

invigorate VERB to give a person strength or courage

invincible ADJECTIVE not able to be defeated ▶ **invincibility** NOUN

invisible ADJECTIVE not able to be seen

invite VERB 1 to ask a person to come or do something 2 to be likely to cause *to invite disaster* ▶ **invitation** NOUN

inviting ADJECTIVE attractive or tempting

invoice NOUN a written request for payment

invoke VERB 1 to appeal or pray to ▶ **invocation** NOUN

involuntary ADJECTIVE not deliberate ▶ **involuntarily** ADVERB

involve VERB 1 to have as a part or make necessary 2 to make someone take part in something ▶ **involvement** NOUN

involved ADJECTIVE 1 complicated 2 taking part

inward ADJECTIVE 1 on the inside 2 going or facing inwards

inward ADVERB inwards

inwards ADVERB towards the inside

iodine NOUN a chemical substance used as an antiseptic

ion NOUN an electrically charged particle

iota NOUN a tiny amount of something *not an iota of truth in the story*

IQ ABBREVIATION intelligence quotient; a number indicating a person's intelligence

irascible ADJECTIVE easily becoming angry

irate ADJECTIVE angry

iridescent ADJECTIVE coloured like a rainbow ▶ **iridescence** NOUN

iris NOUN 1 the coloured part of the eyeball 2 a plant with long pointed leaves and large flowers

irk VERB to bother or annoy

THESAURUS

invincible ADJECTIVE • *invincible power* ▶ mighty, unbeatable, indestructible, unconquerable

invisible ADJECTIVE • *invisible in the dark* ▶ hidden, concealed, undetectable, unseen

invite VERB • *invited us to dinner* ▶ ask, welcome, summon • *to invite trouble* ▶ provoke, cause, generate

involve VERB • *a job that involves travel* ▶ necessitate, entail, require • *decisions that involve everybody* ▶ affect, concern, interest, include, touch • *to involve people in community work* ▶ engage, occupy, absorb

involved ADJECTIVE • *a long and involved story* ▶ complicated, complex, elaborate, confusing • *is totally involved in the work* ▶ occupied, engrossed, absorbed, preoccupied

DICTIONARY

irksome ADJECTIVE annoying or tiresome

iron NOUN 1 a hard grey metal 2 a device for pressing clothes or cloth 3 a tool made of iron ► **iron** ADJECTIVE

iron VERB to smooth clothes or cloth with an iron

Iron Age NOUN the time when tools and weapons were made of iron

ironic ADJECTIVE using irony; full of irony ► **ironical** ADJECTIVE, **ironically** ADVERB

ironmonger NOUN a shopkeeper who sells tools and household equipment ► **ironmongery** NOUN

irons PLURAL NOUN shackles or fetters

irony NOUN **ironies** 1 saying the opposite of what you mean in order to emphasize it 2 an oddly contradictory situation

irrational ADJECTIVE not rational; illogical ► **irrationally** ADVERB

irregular ADJECTIVE 1 not regular; uneven 2 against the rules or custom ► **irregularity** NOUN

irrelevant ADJECTIVE not relevant ► **irrelevance** NOUN

irreparable ADJECTIVE unable to be repaired ► **irreparably** ADVERB

irreplaceable ADJECTIVE unable to be replaced

irrepressible ADJECTIVE always lively and cheerful

irresistible ADJECTIVE too strong or attractive to be resisted ► **irresistibly** ADVERB

irrespective ADJECTIVE not taking something into account *irrespective of cost*

irresponsible ADJECTIVE not showing a proper sense of responsibility ► **irresponsibly** ADVERB

irreverent ADJECTIVE not reverent or respectful ► **irreverence** NOUN

irrevocable (ir-rev-ok-a-bul) ADJECTIVE unable to be altered ► **irrevocably** ADVERB

irrigate VERB to supply land with water for crops ► **irrigation** NOUN

irritable ADJECTIVE easily annoyed; bad-tempered

irritant NOUN something that annoys or causes itching

THESAURUS

irrational ADJECTIVE • *an irrational fear of flying* ► illogical, unreasonable, senseless, unjustifiable

irregular ADJECTIVE • *an irregular surface* ► uneven, rough, bumpy • *an irregular heartbeat* ► variable, erratic, haphazard, intermittent

irrelevant ADJECTIVE • *irrelevant details* ► inappropriate, unnecessary, inessential, extraneous

irresponsible ADJECTIVE • *an irresponsible attitude* ► reckless, rash, inconsiderate, thoughtless, careless • *irresponsible people* ► immature, unreliable, untrustworthy

DICTIONARY

irritate VERB **1** to annoy **2** to cause itching ▸ **irritation** NOUN

Islam NOUN the religion of Muslims ▸ **Islamic** ADJECTIVE

island NOUN a piece of land surrounded by water ▸ **islander** NOUN

isle (say as i'll) NOUN an island

isn't is not

isobar (I-so-bar) NOUN a line on a map connecting places that have the same atmospheric pressure

isolate VERB to place apart or alone ▸ **isolation** NOUN

isosceles (I-soss-il-eez) ADJECTIVE (of a triangle) having two sides of equal length

isotope NOUN (Science) a form of an element that differs from other forms in the structure of its nucleus but has the same chemical properties as the other forms

issue VERB **1** to supply or give out **2** to send out information or a warning **3** to publish **4** to come or go out

issue NOUN **1** a subject for discussion or concern **2** a particular edition of a newspaper or magazine **3** the process of issuing **4** (formal) children He died without issue.

isthmus NOUN a narrow strip of land connecting two larger pieces of land

IT ABBREVIATION information technology

it PRONOUN the thing being talked about

italic ADJECTIVE printed with sloping letters (called italics, like this)

itch VERB **1** to feel a tickling sensation in the skin **2** to long to do something

itch NOUN an itching feeling ▸ **itchy** ADJECTIVE

item NOUN one thing in a list or group of things

itinerant ADJECTIVE travelling from place to place

itinerary NOUN itineraries a list of places to be visited on a journey

THESAURUS

irritable ADJECTIVE • an irritable look on his face ▸ bad-tempered, grumpy, tetchy, crotchety, cantankerous

irritate VERB • letting silly things irritate me ▸ annoy, anger, infuriate, exasperate, madden

isolate VERB • political views that isolated them from their contemporaries ▸ separate, set apart, segregate, detach, alienate

issue NOUN • political issues ▸ matter, concern, subject, topic,

affair • a special issue of the magazine ▸ edition, publication, instalment

issue VERB • to issue a statement ▸ give out, publish, release, circulate, distribute, deliver, announce

item NOUN • an item of equipment ▸ article, piece, bit, object • a news item ▸ report, article, account, feature • several items on the agenda ▸ topic, subject, matter, point

its *POSSESSIVE PRONOUN* belonging to it
The cat hurt its paw.

 USAGE

Do not use an apostrophe unless you mean 'it is' or 'it has' (see the next entry).

it's it is *or* it has

⚠ **USAGE**

Do not confuse *its* and *it's*.

itself *PRONOUN* it and nothing else
by itself on its own; alone

ivory *NOUN* **ivories** the hard white substance forming elephants' tusks

ivy *NOUN* **ivies** a climbing plant with shiny leaves

a
b
c
d
e
f
g
h
i
j
k
l
m
n
o
p
q
r
s
t
u
v
w
x
y
z

Jj

jab VERB **jabbing, jabbed** to push or poke roughly

jab NOUN **1** a jabbing movement **2** (informal) an injection

jabber VERB to speak quickly and indistinctly ► **jabber** NOUN

jack NOUN **1** a device for lifting a heavy weight **2** a playing card with a picture of a young man

jack VERB to lift with a jack

jackal NOUN a wild animal like a dog

jackass NOUN **1** a male donkey **2** a stupid person

jackdaw NOUN a kind of small crow

jacket NOUN **1** a short coat reaching to the hips **2** a paper wrapper for a book

jack-in-the-box NOUN a toy figure on a spring that leaps from a box when the lid is lifted

jackknife VERB (of an articulated lorry) to skid and swing against itself

jackpot NOUN an amount of prize money that increases until someone wins it

Jacobite NOUN a supporter of the exiled Stuarts after the abdication of James II (1688)

Jacuzzi (ja-koo-zi) NOUN (trademark) a large bath with underwater jets of water

jade NOUN a green stone that is carved to make ornaments

jaded ADJECTIVE tired and bored

jagged (jag-id) ADJECTIVE having a rough uneven edge

jaguar NOUN a South American animal like a leopard

jail NOUN a prison

jail VERB to put into prison ► **jailer** NOUN

Jain (say as Jane) NOUN a believer in an Indian religion similar to Buddhism

jam NOUN **1** a thick sweet food made of fruit boiled with sugar **2** a crush of people or vehicles **in a jam** in a difficult situation

jam VERB **jamming, jammed 1** to make or become unable to move **2** to crowd or squeeze into a space

jamb (jam) NOUN a side post of a doorway or window frame

jamboree NOUN a large party or celebration

jam-packed ADJECTIVE tightly packed; congested

jab VERB • *jabbed him in the ribs*
► poke, prod, dig

jagged ADJECTIVE • *a jagged edge*
► spiky, uneven, rough

jam NOUN • *a jam on the motorway*
► tailback, hold-up, blockage • *in a bit of a jam* ► predicament,

quandary, dilemma • *home-made jam* ► preserve, jelly, marmalade

jam VERB • *to jam people in*
► cram, pack, squeeze, stuff, squash • *to jam the door open*
► prop, wedge • *The window has jammed.* ► stick, seize

a
b
c
d
e
f
g
h
i
j
k
l
m
n
o
p
q
r
s
t
u
v
w
x
y
z

jangle VERB to make a harsh ringing sound ► **jangle** NOUN

janitor NOUN a caretaker

January NOUN the first month of the year

jar¹ NOUN a container made of glass or pottery

jar² VERB **jarring**, **jarred** 1 to cause an unpleasant jolt 2 to sound unpleasantly harsh

jargon NOUN special words used by a profession or group

jasmine NOUN a shrub with yellow or white flowers

jaundice NOUN a disease in which the skin becomes yellow ► **jaundiced** ADJECTIVE

jaunt NOUN a short trip for pleasure

jaunty ADJECTIVE **jauntier**, **jauntiest** lively and cheerful ► **jauntily** ADVERB

javelin NOUN a light spear for throwing

jaw NOUN the lower part of the face round the mouth

jay NOUN a brightly coloured bird

jazz NOUN a kind of music with strong rhythm, often improvised

jazzy ADJECTIVE **jazzier**, **jazziest** bright and colourful

jealous ADJECTIVE 1 unhappy because someone is better or luckier than you 2 careful in keeping something ► **jealousy** NOUN

jeans PLURAL NOUN trousers made of strong cotton fabric

Jeep NOUN (trademark) a small sturdy army vehicle

jeer VERB to scoff at ► **jeer** NOUN

jelly NOUN **jellies** 1 a soft transparent food 2 a soft slippery substance ► **jellied** ADJECTIVE

jellyfish NOUN a sea animal with a body like jelly

jemmy NOUN **jemmies** a burglar's crowbar

jeopardize (jep-er-dyz) VERB to put in danger or at risk

⚠ **SPELLING**

This word can also be spelled *jeopardise*.

jeopardy (jep-er-dee) NOUN danger of harm or failure

jerk VERB 1 to make a sudden sharp movement 2 to pull suddenly

jerk NOUN a sudden sharp movement

THESAURUS

jar NOUN • *a jar of honey* ► pot, glass, container

jar VERB • *The fall jarred her whole body.* ► jolt, jerk, shake

jealous ADJECTIVE • *jealous of her ability* ► envious, resentful, grudging

jeer VERB • *to jeer the speakers* ► mock, taunt, scoff, sneer

jeer NOUN • *jeers from his mates* ► taunt, sneer, jibe, insult

jerk VERB • *She jerked her hand away.* ► pull, tug, wrench, yank • *The car jerked forward.* ► jolt, lurch, bump

jerk NOUN • *He pulled the handle with a jerk.* ► tug, pull, wrench, yank • *to stop with a jerk* ► jolt, lurch, bump

jerkin NOUN a sleeveless jacket

jerky ADJECTIVE **jerkier, jerkiest** moving in jerks ► **jerkily** ADVERB

jersey NOUN **jerseys 1** a pullover with sleeves **2** a plain machine-knitted material

jest NOUN a joke

jest VERB to make jokes

jester NOUN a professional entertainer at a royal court in the Middle Ages

jet¹ NOUN **1** a stream of water, gas, flame, etc. **2** an aircraft driven by engines that send out a jet of hot gases

jet² NOUN **1** a hard black mineral substance **2** a deep glossy black colour

jetsam NOUN goods thrown overboard and washed ashore

jettison VERB **1** to throw overboard **2** to get rid of

jetty NOUN **jetties** a small landing stage

Jew NOUN a member of a people descended from the ancient tribes of Israel ► **Jewish** ADJECTIVE

jewel NOUN a precious stone ► **jewelled** ADJECTIVE

jeweller NOUN a person who sells or makes jewellery

jewellery NOUN jewels and similar ornaments for wearing

jib¹ NOUN **1** a triangular sail stretching forward from a ship's front mast **2** the arm of a crane

jib² VERB **jibbing, jibbed** to be reluctant or unwilling to do something

jiffy NOUN **jiffies** (informal) a moment

jig NOUN a lively jumping dance

jig VERB **jigging, jigged** to move up and down quickly

jigsaw NOUN a puzzle in which pieces have to be put together to make a picture

jihad NOUN a war or struggle undertaken by Muslims

jilt VERB to abandon a boyfriend or girlfriend

jingle VERB to make or cause to make a tinkling sound

jingle NOUN **1** a jingling sound **2** a simple verse or tune

jingoism NOUN an unreasonable belief that your country is superior to others ► **jingoistic** ADJECTIVE

jinx NOUN a person or thing that brings bad luck

jitters PLURAL NOUN (informal) a nervous feeling

jittery ADJECTIVE nervous

job NOUN **1** work that someone does regularly to earn a living **2** a piece of work to be done

THESAURUS

jet NOUN • *a jet of water* ► stream, spurt, squirt, spout, fountain

jingle NOUN • *the jingle of her bracelet* ► jangle, clink, tinkle • *an advertising jingle* ► slogan, song, catchline

jingle VERB • *coins jingling in their pockets* ► jangle, clink

job NOUN • *a job involving weekend work* ► occupation, employment, post, work, career • *a long job* ► task, piece of work,

DICTIONARY

jockey NOUN **jockeys** a person who rides horses in races

jocular ADJECTIVE joking
► **jocularity** NOUN

jodhpurs (jod-perz) PLURAL NOUN trousers for horse riding, fitting closely from the knee to the ankle

jog VERB **jogging, jogged 1** to run or trot slowly **2** to give a slight push ► **jogger** NOUN

jog NOUN **1** a slow run or trot **2** a slight knock or push

join VERB **1** to put or come together **2** to take part with others in an activity *I joined the search party.* **3** to become a member of

join NOUN a place where things join

joiner NOUN a person who makes wooden furniture ► **joinery** NOUN

joint NOUN **1** a place where two things are joined **2** a large piece of meat cut ready for cooking

joint ADJECTIVE shared or done by two or more people or groups
► **jointly** ADVERB

joist NOUN a beam supporting a floor or ceiling

joke NOUN something said or done to make people laugh

joke VERB **1** to make jokes **2** to tease or not be serious

joker NOUN **1** someone who jokes **2** an extra playing card with a jester on it

jolly ADJECTIVE **jollier, jolliest** cheerful and good-humoured

jolly ADVERB (*informal*) very *jolly good*

jolly VERB **jollies, jollied** (*informal*) **jolly along** to keep someone cheerful

jolt VERB **1** to shake with a sudden movement **2** to move along jerkily **3** to give someone a shock

jolt NOUN **1** a jolting movement **2** a shock

THESAURUS

undertaking, project, chore • *my job to lock up* ► responsibility, duty, task

jog VERB • *He jogged her elbow.* ► nudge, prod, jolt, jar • *a clue to jog my memory* ► prompt, stir • *jogging through the park* ► trot, run

join VERB • *Join the two pieces together.* ► connect, fasten, attach, stick, tie, glue • *to join the army* ► enlist in, enrol in, volunteer for, become a member of • *to join the peace march* ► follow, go along with, accompany • *The two roads join*

here. ► meet, come together, converge

join NOUN • *to see the join* ► joint, connection, seam

joint ADJECTIVE • *a joint exhibition* ► combined, shared, collaborative, cooperative, collective

joke NOUN • *to tell jokes* ► funny story, witticism, wisecrack

joke VERB • *to joke with friends* ► tell jokes, crack jokes, have a laugh • *I was only joking.* ► fool, tease, hoax, kid

jolt VERB • *The car jolted along.* ► bump, bounce, jerk, shake • *His*

403

DICTIONARY

jostle VERB to push roughly in a crowd

jot VERB **jotting**, **jotted** to write quickly

jotter NOUN a notepad or notebook

joule (jool) NOUN (*Science*) a unit of work or energy

journal NOUN **1** a newspaper or magazine **2** a diary

journalist NOUN a person who writes for a newspaper or magazine ► **journalism** NOUN

journey NOUN **journeys** the process of going from one place to another

journey VERB to make a journey

joust (jowst) VERB (in medieval times) to fight on horseback with lances ► **joust** NOUN

jovial ADJECTIVE cheerful and good-humoured ► **joviality** NOUN

jowl NOUN the jaw or cheek

joy NOUN **1** a feeling of pleasure or happiness **2** a thing that causes this

joyful ADJECTIVE very happy ► **joyfully** ADVERB

joyous ADJECTIVE full of joy

joyride NOUN a drive in a stolen car ► **joyrider** NOUN

joystick NOUN **1** the control lever of an aircraft **2** a control device in computer games

jubilant ADJECTIVE rejoicing or triumphant ► **jubilation** NOUN

jubilee (joo-bil-ee) NOUN a special anniversary

Judaism (joo-day-izm) NOUN the religion of the Jewish people

judder VERB to shake noisily or violently

judge NOUN **1** a person who hears cases in a lawcourt **2** a person who applies the rules in a competition **3** someone who is good at forming opinions

judge VERB **1** to act as a judge **2** to form and give an opinion **3** to estimate

judgement NOUN **1** the process of judging **2** the decision made by

THESAURUS

anger jolted her. ► startle, surprise, shock

journalist NOUN • *local journalists* ► reporter, correspondent, columnist, feature-writer

journey NOUN • *a journey through three countries* ► trip, itinerary, travels, voyage

joy NOUN • *a look of joy* ► delight, pleasure, happiness, gladness, bliss

joyful ADJECTIVE • *joyful enthusiasm* ► cheerful, happy, delighted, elated

judge NOUN • *The judges could not agree.* ► adjudicator, arbitrator, assessor • *a good judge of art* ► connoisseur, authority (on), expert (on), critic

judge VERB • *A magistrate will judge the case.* ► try, hear, decide • *to judge the best entries* ► assess, appraise, decide, evaluate

judgement NOUN • *the judgement of the court* ► verdict, decision, ruling, pronouncement, sentence • *a lack of judgement*

a lawcourt **3** an opinion **4** the ability to judge wisely

judicial ADJECTIVE to do with lawcourts or judges ► **judicially** ADVERB

judiciary NOUN the judges of a country

judicious ADJECTIVE showing good sense or judgement ► **judiciously** ADVERB

judo NOUN a Japanese method of self-defence

jug NOUN a container for liquids, with a handle and a lip

juggernaut NOUN a large articulated lorry

juggle VERB **1** to toss and catch objects skilfully **2** to rearrange things ► **juggler** NOUN

jugular ADJECTIVE to do with the throat or neck

juice NOUN **1** the liquid from fruit or vegetables **2** a liquid produced by the stomach

juicy ADJECTIVE **juicier**, **juiciest** containing a lot of juice

jukebox NOUN a machine that automatically plays a record you have selected when you put a coin in

July NOUN the seventh month of the year

jumble VERB to mix up into a confused mass

jumble NOUN a confused mixture or muddle

jumble sale NOUN a sale of second-hand goods

jumbo NOUN jumbos
1 something very large **2** an elephant

jump VERB **1** to move up suddenly from the ground into the air **2** to go over something by jumping **3** to pass over or miss out **4** to move suddenly in surprise

jump NOUN **1** a jumping movement **2** a sudden rise or change

jumper NOUN a jersey

► understanding, wisdom, sense, common sense

juicy ADJECTIVE • *a juicy pear*
► succulent, tender, moist, soft, ripe

jumble VERB • *to jumble the papers*
► muddle, disorganize, mix up, confuse

jumble NOUN • *in a jumble on the floor* ► muddle, mess, clutter, chaos

jump VERB • *A dog jumped off the chair.* ► leap, spring, bound,

bounce, hop • *to jump a fence*
► vault, clear • *jumping about in the garden* ► skip, leap, prance, cavort • *A noise made him jump.*
► start, jerk, jolt, flinch

jump NOUN • *With a jump he reached the other side.* ► leap, bound, spring, vault, hop • *The horse cleared the last jump.*
► fence, hurdle, ditch, gate • *a huge jump in house prices* ► rise, increase • *She woke up with a jump.* ► start, jerk, jolt, shock

a b c d e f g h i **j** k l m n o p q r s t u v w x y z

jumpy ADJECTIVE **jumpier, jumpiest** nervous and edgy

junction NOUN **1** a join **2** a place where roads or railway lines meet

juncture NOUN a point of time

June NOUN the sixth month of the year

jungle NOUN a thick tangled forest in a tropical country ► **jungly** ADJECTIVE

junior ADJECTIVE **1** younger **2** for young children *a junior school* **3** lower in rank *junior officers*

junior NOUN a junior person

juniper NOUN an evergreen shrub

junk[1] NOUN things of no value

junk[2] NOUN a Chinese sailing boat

junk food NOUN food that is not nourishing

junk mail NOUN unwanted advertising sent by post

jurisdiction NOUN authority or official power

juror NOUN a member of a jury

jury NOUN **juries** a group of people appointed to give a verdict in a lawcourt

just ADJECTIVE **1** giving proper consideration to everyone's claims **2** deserved *a just reward* ► **justly** ADVERB

just ADVERB **1** exactly *just what I wanted* **2** only; simply *I just wanted to see him.* **3** by a small amount *just below the knee* **4** only a little while ago *She has just gone.*

justice NOUN **1** fair treatment **2** a judge or magistrate

justification NOUN good reason

justify VERB **justifies, justified 1** to show that something is fair or just **2** to arrange lines of text with an even margin ► **justifiable** ADJECTIVE

jut VERB **jutting, jutted** to stick out

jute NOUN fibre from tropical plants

juvenile ADJECTIVE **1** of or for young people **2** childish

juvenile NOUN a young person

juxtapose VERB to put things side by side ► **juxtaposition** NOUN

THESAURUS

jumpy ADJECTIVE • *tired and jumpy* ► nervous, edgy, jittery, tense

junior ADJECTIVE • *a junior official* ► low-ranking, subordinate, young

junk NOUN • *a cupboard full of old junk* ► rubbish, clutter, oddments, garbage, scrap

just ADJECTIVE • *a just ruler* ► fair, equitable, even-handed, unbiased • *a just punishment* ► fair, deserved, appropriate, suitable

justice NOUN • *their sense of justice* ► fairness, fair play, integrity, right • *the administration of justice* ► the law, legal proceedings

justify VERB • *cannot justify this behaviour* ► excuse, defend, account for, explain

jut VERB **jut out** • *Shelves jutting out on one wall.* ► stick out, project, protrude, extend

Kk

kaleidoscope (kal-y-dos-kohp) NOUN a tube to look through to see changing patterns

kangaroo NOUN an Australian animal that jumps on its hind legs

karaoke (ka-ri-oh-ki) NOUN an entertainment of singing against a pre-recorded backing

karate (ka-rah-tee) NOUN a Japanese method of self-defence using the hands and feet

kayak NOUN a small canoe

KB or **Kb** ABBREVIATION kilobytes

kebab NOUN small pieces of meat or vegetables cooked on a skewer

keel NOUN the long piece of wood or metal along the bottom of a boat

keel VERB **keel over** to fall down or overturn

keen[1] ADJECTIVE **1** enthusiastic or interested **2** sharp *a keen edge* *keen eyesight* **3** (of the wind) very cold ► **keenness** NOUN

keen[2] VERB to wail in mourning

keep VERB **kept 1** to have and look after **2** to stay or cause to stay in the same condition **3** to do something continually *He keeps laughing.* **4** (of food) to last without going bad **5** to respect and not break *keep your word*

keep NOUN **1** the food etc. that needed to live **2** a strong tower in a castle

keeper NOUN **1** a person who looks after an animal, building, etc. **2** a goalkeeper or wicketkeeper

keeping NOUN care and attention *in safe keeping*

keepsake NOUN a gift in memory of the person who gave it

keg NOUN a small barrel

kelvin NOUN (Science) the SI unit of thermodynamic temperature

kennel NOUN a shelter for a dog

kerb NOUN the edge of a pavement

kernel NOUN the part inside the shell of a nut or fruit

kerosene NOUN paraffin

kestrel NOUN a small falcon

ketchup NOUN a thick sauce made from tomatoes

a
b
c
d
e
f
g
h
i
j
k
l
m
n
o
p
q
r
s
t
u
v
w
x
y
z

THESAURUS

keen ADJECTIVE • *keen to play football* ► eager, enthusiastic, anxious, determined, impatient • *keen competition* ► intense, fierce, strong • *keen eyesight* ► sharp, clear, powerful

keep VERB • *something for you to keep* ► retain, hold on to, possess • *to keep quiet* ► remain, stay,

continue to be • *keeps twitching his ears* ► persist in, go on, continue, carry on • *We'll try not to keep you long.* ► detain, delay, hold up, keep waiting • *to keep you from continuing* ► deter, hinder • *to keep a promise* ► observe, fulfil, carry out, comply with • *Where do you keep the coats?* ► store, put, stow

a
b
c
d
e
f
g
h
i
j
k
l
m
n
o
p
q
r
s
t
u
v
w
x
y
z

kettle NOUN a container with a spout for boiling water

kettledrum NOUN a drum made of a large metal bowl with a skin stretched over the top

key NOUN 1 a piece of metal shaped to open a lock 2 a device for winding up a clock or clockwork mechanism 3 a small lever to be pressed by a finger on a piano or computer 4 a system of notes in music 5 an explanation 6 a list of symbols used in a map or table

key VERB to type information into a computer

keyboard NOUN the set of keys on a piano, typewriter, or computer

keyhole NOUN the hole through which a key is put into a lock

keypad NOUN a small keyboard or set of buttons used to operate a telephone, television, etc.

kg ABBREVIATION kilogram

khaki NOUN a dull yellowish-brown colour used for military uniforms

kibbutz NOUN a farming commune in Israel

kick VERB to hit or move with your foot

kick NOUN 1 a kicking movement 2 (informal) a thrill

kick-off NOUN the start of a football match

kid NOUN 1 (informal) a child 2 a young goat 3 the skin of a young goat

kid VERB kidding, kidded (informal) to deceive playfully

kidnap VERB kidnapping, kidnapped to take someone away by force ▸ **kidnapper** NOUN

kidney NOUN kidneys an organ in the body that removes waste products from the blood

kill VERB 1 to end the life of 2 to destroy or put an end to ▸ **killer** NOUN

kill NOUN the act of killing an animal

killing NOUN an act causing death

kiln NOUN an oven for hardening pottery or bricks

kilo NOUN a kilogram

kilobyte NOUN a unit of computer data equal to 1,024 bytes

kilogram NOUN a unit of mass or weight equal to 1,000 grams

kilometre NOUN a unit of length equal to 1,000 metres

kilowatt NOUN a unit of electrical power equal to 1,000 watts

kilt NOUN a kind of pleated skirt worn by men

THESAURUS

key NOUN • the key to a problem ▸ clue, pointer, lead, answer • a key to a map ▸ guide, index, explanation, glossary

kick VERB • to kick a ball ▸ boot, hit, drive, send • to kick a habit (informal) ▸ give up, quit, break

kidnap VERB • preparing to kidnap a businessman ▸ abduct, capture, seize, snatch

kill VERB • to kill the prisoners ▸ murder, put to death, slay, slaughter, exterminate, assassinate • to kill all hopes

kimono NOUN **kimonos** a long loose Japanese robe

kin NOUN a person's relatives **next of kin** a person's closest relative

kind[1] NOUN a sort or type

kind[2] ADJECTIVE friendly and helpful ► **kindly** ADVERB, **kindness** NOUN

kindergarten NOUN a school or class for young children

kind-hearted ADJECTIVE kind and considerate

kindle VERB **1** to start a flame **2** to begin burning

kindly ADJECTIVE **kindlier**, **kindliest** kind

kinetic ADJECTIVE to do with or produced by movement *kinetic energy*

king NOUN **1** a country's male ruler who reigns because of his birth **2** the most important piece in chess **3** a playing card with a picture of a king

kingdom NOUN **1** a country ruled by a king or queen **2** a major division of the natural world

kingfisher NOUN a bird with blue feathers that dives to catch fish

king-size or **king-sized** ADJECTIVE extra large

kink NOUN a short twist in a rope, wire, etc.

kinsman or **kinswoman** NOUN **kinsmen** or **kinswomen** a male or female relation

kiosk NOUN **1** a telephone box **2** a stall for selling newspapers etc.

kip NOUN (*informal*) a short sleep

kipper NOUN a smoked herring

kiss NOUN the act of touching lips as a sign of affection

kiss VERB to give someone a kiss

kit NOUN **1** equipment or clothes **2** a set of parts for fitting together

kitchen NOUN a room in which meals are prepared and cooked

kite NOUN **1** a light covered framework flown in the wind on a string **2** a large hawk

kith and kin friends and relatives

kitten NOUN a young cat

kitty NOUN **kitties** a fund of money for a special purpose

kiwi (kee-wee) NOUN **kiwis** a New Zealand bird that cannot fly

► end, destroy, dash, extinguish, put an end to, finish

kind NOUN • *a new kind of rock music* ► sort, type, style, form, variety

kind ADJECTIVE • *a kind friend* ► caring, good, kind-hearted, kindly, considerate, sympathetic, thoughtful, obliging, tender-hearted, benevolent

kindness NOUN • *to show kindness* ► consideration, thoughtfulness, generosity, goodwill, understanding

kit NOUN • *a tool kit* ► equipment, gear, implements, appliances • *furniture made from kits* ► set of parts, self-assembly set, flatpack • *a football kit* ► strip, colours, outfit, clothes

a b c d e f g h i j k l m n o p q r s t u v w x y z

kiwi fruit NOUN a fruit with thin hairy skin and green flesh

kleptomania NOUN an uncontrollable urge to steal
▶ **kleptomaniac** NOUN

km ABBREVIATION kilometre

knack NOUN a special skill

knapsack NOUN a bag carried on the back by soldiers and hikers

knave NOUN 1 a rogue 2 a jack in playing cards

knead VERB to press and stretch dough with the hands

knee NOUN the joint in the middle of the leg

kneecap NOUN the bone covering the front of the knee joint

kneel VERB knelt to be or get yourself in a position on your knees

knell NOUN the sound of a bell rung solemnly after a death

knickers PLURAL NOUN underpants worn by women and girls

knick-knack NOUN a small ornament

knife NOUN knives a tool with a blade for cutting

knife VERB to stab with a knife

knight NOUN 1 a man who can put Sir before his name 2 (in the Middle Ages) a warrior of high social rank 3 a piece in chess, with a horse's head ▶ **knighthood** NOUN

knit VERB knitting, knitted or knit to make clothing by looping wool with needles or a machine
▶ **knitting** NOUN

knob NOUN 1 the round handle of a door, drawer, etc. 2 a round lump 3 a round button or switch 4 a small round piece *a knob of butter*
▶ **knobbly** ADJECTIVE, **knobby** ADJECTIVE

knock VERB 1 to hit hard to make a noise 2 to produce by hitting *to knock a hole in the wall* 3 (*informal*) to criticize unfavourably **knock out** to make unconscious

knock NOUN the act or sound of knocking

knocker NOUN a hinged device on a door, for knocking

knockout NOUN 1 the act of knocking someone out 2 a contest in which the loser in each round has to drop out

knoll NOUN a small round hill

knack NOUN • *a knack of asking the right question* ▶ gift, flair (for), talent (for)

knife VERB • *The victim had been knifed repeatedly.* ▶ stab, slash, pierce, cut, wound

knob NOUN • *the knobs on the old tree trunk* ▶ bump, lump, projection, protuberance

knock VERB • *to knock on the door* ▶ bang, rap, tap, thump, pound • *to knock your knee* ▶ bump, hit, strike, bang **knock down** • *to knock down houses* ▶ demolish, level, destroy

knock NOUN • *The car has taken a few knocks.* ▶ blow, bump, bang, shock, collision, smash

knot NOUN **1** a place where a piece of string, rope, etc. is twisted round itself or another piece **2** a tangle or lump **3** a round spot on a piece of wood where a branch joined it **4** a cluster of people or things **5** a unit of speed for ships and aircraft, equal to 1.85 kilometres per hour

knot VERB **1** to tie or fasten with a knot **2** to entangle

knotty ADJECTIVE **knottier, knottiest 1** full of knots **2** difficult or puzzling

know VERB **knew, known 1** to have something in your mind that you have learned or discovered **2** to recognize or be familiar with

knowing ADJECTIVE showing that you know something

knowledge NOUN **1** the fact of knowing **2** all that is known

knowledgeable ADJECTIVE having a lot of knowledge
▶ **knowledgeably** ADVERB

knuckle NOUN a joint in the finger

knuckle VERB **knuckle down** to begin to work hard

koala (koh-ah-la) NOUN an Australian animal like a small bear

Koran NOUN the sacred book of Islam

kosher ADJECTIVE keeping to Jewish laws about the preparation of food

krypton NOUN an inert gas present in the earth's atmosphere and used in fluorescent lights

kudos (kew-doss) NOUN honour and glory

kung fu NOUN a Chinese method of self-defence

THESAURUS

knot NOUN • *a knot in a rope* ▶ tie, twist, join

know VERB • *Does she know we are here?* ▶ realize, be aware, understand, appreciate • *I don't know any German.* ▶ understand, speak, have knowledge of, be familiar with • *He knows me from our student days.* ▶ be acquainted with, have met, be friends with • *He had known much better times.* ▶ experience, live through, go through

knowing ADJECTIVE • *a knowing look* ▶ meaningful, expressive, suggestive

knowledge NOUN • *She had an extensive knowledge of the subject.* ▶ understanding, comprehension, mastery, grasp • *technical knowledge* ▶ expertise, skill, understanding, know-how, proficiency • *no knowledge of these people* ▶ acquaintance (with), familiarity (with) • *a wide range of knowledge* ▶ learning, education, erudition, scholarship

knowledgeable ADJECTIVE • *a knowledgeable man* ▶ educated, learned, well informed

LI

lab NOUN (informal) a laboratory

label NOUN a small piece of paper, cloth, etc. attached to something to give information about it

label VERB **labelling, labelled 1** to put a label on **2** to identify with a name

laboratory NOUN **laboratories** a place equipped for scientific experiments

laborious ADJECTIVE **1** needing a lot of hard work **2** lengthy and tedious

labour NOUN **1** hard work **2** a task **3** workers **4** the contractions of the womb during childbirth

labour VERB **1** to work hard **2** to explain or discuss at tedious length

labourer NOUN a person who does heavy manual work

Labrador NOUN a large black or light-brown dog

laburnum NOUN a tree with hanging yellow flowers

labyrinth NOUN a complicated set of passages or paths

lace NOUN **1** net-like material with decorative patterns of holes in it **2** a piece of thin cord for fastening shoes etc.

lace VERB **1** to fasten with a lace **2** to thread a cord through

lack NOUN the state of being without something

lack VERB to be without

lackadaisical ADJECTIVE lacking energy; feeble

lackey NOUN **lackeys 1** a male servant **2** a person who behaves or is treated like a servant

lacking ADJECTIVE not having something, or not having enough

laconic ADJECTIVE using few words ▸ **laconically** ADVERB

lacquer NOUN a hard glossy varnish ▸ **lacquered** ADJECTIVE

lacrosse NOUN a game using a stick with a net on it to catch and throw a ball

lad NOUN a boy or youth

ladder NOUN **1** a set of rungs between two upright pieces of

label NOUN • the label on the packet ▸ tag, sticker, ticket • a record label ▸ brand, company

label VERB • to label people as troublemakers ▸ identify, brand, categorize, define

laborious ADJECTIVE • a laborious process ▸ hard, arduous, difficult, slow

labour NOUN • needs a lot of labour ▸ work, effort, exertion, toil • to

take on extra labour ▸ staff, workers, employees

labour VERB • to labour day and night ▸ work, toil, slave

lack NOUN • a lack of money ▸ shortage, deficiency, scarcity, absence

lack VERB • The film lacks drama. ▸ be without, be short of, be deficient in

wood or metal, used for climbing up or down **2** a row of undone stitches in a pair of tights or stockings

laden ADJECTIVE carrying a load

ladle NOUN a large deep spoon for lifting and pouring liquids

ladle VERB to lift and pour a liquid with a ladle

lady NOUN **ladies 1** a well-mannered woman **2** a woman of good social position ▸ **ladyship** NOUN

ladybird NOUN a small flying beetle, usually red with black spots

ladylike ADJECTIVE (of a woman) well-mannered

lag[1] VERB **lagging**, **lagged** to fail to keep up with others

lag NOUN a delay

lag[2] VERB **lagging**, **lagged** to wrap pipes or boilers etc. in insulating material

lager (lah-ger) NOUN a light beer

lagoon NOUN a salt-water lake separated from the sea by sandbanks or reefs

laid past tense of **lay**.

laid-back ADJECTIVE (informal) relaxed and easy-going

lain past participle of **lie**[2].

lair NOUN a sheltered place where a wild animal lives

lake NOUN a large area of water surrounded by land

lama NOUN a Buddhist priest or monk in Tibet and Mongolia

lamb NOUN **1** a young sheep **2** meat from a lamb

lame ADJECTIVE **1** unable to walk normally **2** weak; not convincing *a lame excuse* ▸ **lamely** ADVERB, **lameness** NOUN

lament NOUN a statement, song, or poem expressing grief or regret

lament VERB to express grief or regret about ▸ **lamentation** NOUN

lamentable (lam-in-ta-bul) ADJECTIVE regrettable or deplorable

laminated ADJECTIVE made of thin layers or sheets pressed together *laminated plastic*

lamp NOUN a device for producing light from electricity, gas, or oil

lamppost NOUN a tall post with a lamp at the top

lamprey NOUN **lampreys** a small eel-like water animal

lance NOUN a long spear

lance VERB to cut open a boil etc. with a knife

lance corporal NOUN a soldier ranking between a private and a corporal

lancet NOUN a pointed two-edged knife used in surgery

land NOUN **1** the part of the earth's surface not covered by sea **2** the ground or soil **3** a country

land VERB **1** to arrive on land or the shore **2** to bring an aircraft to the

lag VERB • *to be lagging behind* ▸ straggle, trail, dawdle

land NOUN • *several acres of land* ▸ ground, farmland, open space • *a land steeped in history*

▸ country, nation, state • *to reach land* ▸ dry land, terra firma, shore

land VERB • *The troops landed.* ▸ disembark, go ashore, alight, arrive • *The ship will land at Calais.*

a
b
c
d
e
f
g
h
i
j
k
l
m
n
o
p
q
r
s
t
u
v
w
x
y
z

a
b
c
d
e
f
g
h
i
j
k
l
m
n
o
p
q
r
s
t
u
v
w
x
y
z

ground **3** (*informal*) to obtain *to land a job* **4** (*informal*) to present with a problem

landed ADJECTIVE **1** owning land **2** consisting of land

landing NOUN **1** the level area at the top of a staircase **2** the act of bringing or coming to land **3** a place where people can get on and off a boat

landlady NOUN **landladies 1** a woman who lets rooms to lodgers **2** a woman who runs a pub

landlocked ADJECTIVE almost or entirely surrounded by land

landlord NOUN **1** a person who lets a house, room, or land to a tenant **2** a person who runs a pub

landlubber NOUN (*informal*) a person who is not used to the sea

landmark NOUN **1** an object that is easily seen in the distance **2** an important event

landmine NOUN an explosive mine laid near the surface of the ground

landowner NOUN a person who owns a large amount of land

landscape NOUN **1** a view of a particular area of countryside or

town **2** a picture of the countryside

landslide NOUN **1** a mass of soil and rocks sliding down a slope **2** an overwhelming victory in an election

lane NOUN **1** a narrow country road **2** a strip of road for a single line of traffic

language NOUN **1** words and their use **2** the words used by a particular people

> **WORD HISTORY**
> from Latin *lingua* 'tongue'

languid ADJECTIVE slow and lacking energy ► **languor** NOUN

languish VERB **1** to live in miserable conditions **2** to become weak or listless

lank ADJECTIVE (of hair) long and limp

lanky ADJECTIVE **lankier, lankiest** awkwardly thin and tall

lantern NOUN a transparent case for holding a light

lap [1] NOUN **1** the level place between the knees and the waist of someone sitting **2** one circuit round a racetrack

THESAURUS

► dock, berth, moor, anchor • *The plane has landed.* ► touch down, come in to land

landmark NOUN • *a landmark visible for miles* ► feature, sight, marker • *a landmark in history* ► turning point, milestone

landscape NOUN • *the landscape of the Highlands* ► scenery, countryside, environment • *a*

painting of a landscape ► scene, panorama, view

language NOUN • *the language of the media* ► vocabulary, style, speech • *written in plain language* ► wording, phrasing • *the grammar of language* ► speech, writing, communication

lap NOUN • *three laps of the track* ► circuit, round, circle, loop

lap VERB **lapping, lapped** to overtake another competitor in a race to become one or more laps ahead

lap ² VERB **lapping, lapped 1** to take up liquid by moving the tongue **2** to make a gentle splash against

lapel (la-pel) NOUN a flap folded back at the front edge of a coat or jacket

lapse NOUN **1** a slight mistake or failure **2** an amount of time between two events *a lapse of two months*

lapse VERB **1** to pass or slip gradually *to lapse into unconsciousness* **2** to be no longer valid

laptop NOUN a portable computer for use while travelling

lapwing NOUN a black and white bird with a crested head and a shrill cry

larceny NOUN the crime of stealing possessions

larch NOUN a tall deciduous tree that bears small cones

lard NOUN melted pig fat used in cooking

larder NOUN a cupboard or small room for storing food

large ADJECTIVE of more than the ordinary size **at large** free; not captured

largely ADVERB to a great extent *is largely responsible*

lark ¹ NOUN a light brown songbird

lark ² NOUN (informal) a bit of fun

lark VERB (informal)
lark about to have fun

larva NOUN **larvae** an insect in the first stage of its life

laryngitis NOUN inflammation of the larynx, causing hoarseness

larynx (la-rinks) NOUN **larynxes** or **larynges** the part of the throat that contains the vocal cords

lasagne (laz-an-ya) NOUN a dish made from sheets of pasta with minced meat and cheese

laser NOUN a device that makes a strong narrow beam of light or other electromagnetic radiation

lap VERB • *Waves lapped against the rocks.* ▶ wash, splash, strike • *The dog lapped a bowl of water.* ▶ drink, sip, lick, gulp

lapse NOUN • *a lapse of attention* ▶ failure, slip, mistake • *a lapse of two months* ▶ interval, gap, pause, break

lapse VERB • *to lapse into unconsciousness* ▶ slide, slip,

drop, fall • *Membership will lapse soon.* ▶ expire, run out, stop

large ADJECTIVE • *a large house* ▶ big, great, sizeable, substantial, huge, enormous, massive, vast • *a large man* ▶ big, burly, hefty, stocky, strapping • *a large supply of food* ▶ plentiful, abundant, copious, generous, ample • *large areas of forest* ▶ widespread, extensive, large-scale

DICTIONARY

lash NOUN **1** a stroke with a whip or stick **2** the cord or cord-like part of a whip **3** an eyelash

lash VERB **1** to beat with a whip or stick **2** to tie with cord **lash out** to speak or hit out angrily

lashings PLURAL NOUN plenty

lass NOUN a girl or young woman

lasso NOUN **lassos** a rope with a sliding noose at the end, used for catching cattle or wild horses

lasso VERB **lassoes**, **lassoing**, **lassoed** to catch an animal with a lasso

last¹ ADJECTIVE, ADVERB **1** coming after all others; final **2** latest; most recent *last night* **3** least likely *the last person I'd have thought of* **the last straw** a final thing that makes a problem unbearable

last NOUN **1** a person or thing that is last **2** the end *fighting to the last*

last² VERB **1** to continue or go on existing **2** to be enough for

last³ NOUN a block used for repairing shoes and making them by hand

lastly ADVERB in the last place; finally

latch NOUN a small bar fastening a door or gate

latch VERB to fasten with a latch

late ADJECTIVE, ADVERB **1** after the usual or expected time **2** near the end *late in the afternoon* **3** recent *the latest news* **4** recently dead *the late king*

lately ADVERB recently

latent (lay-tent) ADJECTIVE existing but not active or visible

lateral ADJECTIVE **1** to do with the side or sides **2** sideways *lateral movement* ▶ **laterally** ADVERB

latex NOUN the milky juice of the rubber tree

lath NOUN a narrow thin strip of wood

lathe (layth) NOUN a machine for holding and turning pieces of wood while they are being shaped

lather NOUN a mass of froth

lather VERB to form a lather

Latin NOUN the language of the ancient Romans

latitude NOUN **1** the distance of a place from the equator, measured in degrees **2** freedom of action

latrine (la-treen) NOUN a toilet in a camp or barracks

latter ADJECTIVE later *the latter part of the year* **the latter** the second of two people or things mentioned

THESAURUS

last ADJECTIVE • *better than last time* ▶ previous, preceding, recent, former • *the last person in the queue* ▶ final, endmost • *one last look* ▶ final, concluding, ultimate

last VERB • *The storm lasted all night.* ▶ continue, carry on, keep on, persist

late ADJECTIVE • *over an hour late* ▶ overdue, delayed, slow, belated, tardy, unpunctual • *the late king* ▶ deceased, dead, former

latter ADJECTIVE • *the latter part of the month* ▶ later, closing, concluding, second

latterly ADVERB recently

lattice NOUN a framework of crossed strips or bars

laud VERB (formal) to praise

laudable ADJECTIVE deserving praise ▶ **laudably** ADVERB

laudatory ADJECTIVE expressing praise

laugh VERB to make the sounds that show you are happy or think something is funny ▶ **laughable** ADJECTIVE

laugh NOUN the sound of laughing

laughter NOUN the act, sound, or manner of laughing

launch¹ VERB 1 to send a ship from the land into the water 2 to send a rocket into space 3 to set a thing moving 4 to make available 5 to start *to launch an attack*

launch NOUN the launching of a ship, spacecraft, or new product

launch² NOUN a large motor boat

launder VERB to wash and iron clothes etc.

launderette NOUN a place fitted with washing machines that people pay to use

laundry NOUN **laundries** 1 a place where clothes etc. are washed 2 clothes etc. for washing

laurel NOUN an evergreen shrub with smooth shiny leaves

lava NOUN molten rock that flows from a volcano and becomes solid when it cools

lavatory NOUN **lavatories** a toilet

lavender NOUN 1 a shrub with sweet-smelling purple flowers 2 a light-purple colour

lavish ADJECTIVE 1 generous 2 plentiful

lavish VERB to give generously

law NOUN 1 a rule or set of rules 2 the profession of lawyers 3 (informal) the police 4 a scientific principle *the law of gravity*

lawcourt NOUN a room or building in which a judge or magistrate hears evidence and decides whether someone has broken the law

lawful ADJECTIVE allowed by the law ▶ **lawfully** ADVERB

laugh VERB • began to make them laugh ▶ giggle, chuckle, chortle, snigger, titter, guffaw **laugh at** • *They may laugh at me.* ▶ mock, ridicule, make fun of, scoff at, jeer at

laugh NOUN • a loud laugh ▶ chuckle, chortle, snigger, titter, guffaw • *It would be a laugh.* ▶ joke, piece of fun, adventure

launch VERB • to launch a ship ▶ float, set afloat • to launch the

shuttle ▶ fire, propel, send off, blast off • to launch an attack ▶ begin, start, open, set up

lavish ADJECTIVE • a lavish meal ▶ sumptuous, elaborate, extravagant, luxurious

law NOUN • a new law on gambling ▶ regulation, ruling, rule, act, bill • the laws of logic ▶ rule, principle

lawful ADJECTIVE • a lawful arrest ▶ legal, legitimate, allowed, proper

a
b
c
d
e
f
g
h
i
j
k
l
m
n
o
p
q
r
s
t
u
v
w
x
y
z

a
b
c
d
e
f
g
h
i
j
k
l
m
n
o
p
q
r
s
t
u
v
w
x
y
z

lawless ADJECTIVE not having or obeying laws

lawn NOUN an area of closely cut grass in a garden or park

lawyer NOUN a person qualified to give advice about the law

lax ADJECTIVE slack; not strict
► **laxity** NOUN

laxative NOUN a medicine that stimulates the bowels to empty

lay ¹ VERB **laid 1** to put something down in a particular place or way **2** to arrange things **3** to place *laid the blame on his sister* **4** to form or prepare *We laid our plans.* **5** to produce an egg **lay off** to stop employing someone for a while **lay on** to supply or provide

lay ² past tense of **lie** ²

lay ³ ADJECTIVE **1** not belonging to the clergy **2** not professional

layabout NOUN an idle person who avoids work

lay-by NOUN a place where vehicles can stop beside a main road

layer NOUN a single thickness or coating

layman NOUN **laymen** a person who does not have special knowledge of a subject

layout NOUN an arrangement of parts according to a plan

laze VERB to spend time in a lazy way

lazy ADJECTIVE **lazier, laziest** not wanting to work ► **lazily** ADVERB, **laziness** NOUN

lead ¹ (leed) VERB **led 1** to take or guide by going in front **2** to be winning in a race or contest **3** to be in charge of **4** to be a way or route *a path leading to the beach* **5** to live or experience *to lead a dull life*

lead ² (leed) NOUN **1** a leading place or part or position *She took the lead on the final bend.* **2** guidance

lax ADJECTIVE • *lax discipline* ► slack, casual, lenient

lay VERB • *He laid the map on the table.* ► put, place, set, spread • *to lay plans* ► form, make, devise, prepare • *to lay the blame* ► assign, attach, attribute • *to lay a table* ► arrange, set out, organize

layer NOUN • *a layer of paint* ► coating, coat, covering, film, sheet • *a layer of rock* ► seam, stratum

lazy ADJECTIVE • *a lazy person* ► idle, indolent, slothful, work-shy, lethargic • *a lazy time* ► quiet, relaxing, peaceful

lead VERB • *She led her guests out.* ► conduct, guide, show, escort, steer • *to lead the delegation* ► head, be in charge of, be the leader of, manage, command • *leading for most of the race* ► be in front, be in the lead • *to lead a happy life* ► spend, have, pass

lead NOUN • *to provide a lead* ► example, guidance, leadership, direction • *an important new lead* ► clue, hint, tip • *to take the lead* ► first place, front position • *to play the lead* ► principal role, chief part, starring role • *let the dog off the lead* ► leash, tether, chain

or example *We should be taking a lead on this issue.* **3** a clue to be followed **4** a strap or cord for leading a dog or other animal **5** an electrical wire attached to something

lead [2] (led) NOUN **1** a soft heavy grey metal **2** the substance in a pencil, made of graphite that marks the paper

leaden ADJECTIVE **1** made of lead **2** heavy and slow **3** dark grey *leaden skies*

leader NOUN **1** the person in charge of a group **2** the person who is winning **3** a leading article in a newspaper ► **leadership** NOUN

leaf NOUN **leaves 1** a flat green part growing from a branch or stem **2** the paper forming one page of a book **3** a thin sheet or flap ► **leafy** ADJECTIVE

leaflet NOUN a piece of paper printed with information

league NOUN **1** a group of competing teams **2** a group of people or nations working together

leak NOUN **1** an escape of liquid or gas **2** the revealing of secret information ► **leaky** ADJECTIVE

leak VERB **1** to escape or let out through a leak **2** to reveal secret information ► **leakage** NOUN

lean [1] ADJECTIVE thin or lacking fat

lean [2] VERB **leaned** or **leant 1** to bend your body **2** to put or be in a sloping position **3** to rest against something **4** to rely or depend on for help

leaning NOUN a tendency or preference

leap VERB **leaped** or **leapt** to jump vigorously ► **leap** NOUN

leapfrog NOUN a game in which players jump with legs apart over others bending down

leap year NOUN a year with an extra day in it (29 February)

leader NOUN • *the leader of the team* ► head, chief, director, manager, principal, boss • *one of the country's leaders* ► ruler, chief

leak NOUN • *several leaks in the roof* ► hole, opening, crack, puncture • *a gas leak* ► escape, discharge • *a leak of information* ► disclosure, revelation

leak VERB • *Oil was leaking from the tank.* ► seep, escape, ooze, spill, trickle, drip • *to leak information* ► reveal, disclose, divulge, give away

lean ADJECTIVE • *a tall lean figure* ► thin, skinny, slender, slim • *a lean harvest* ► meagre, scanty, sparse, poor

lean VERB • *The trees were leaning in the wind.* ► slant, incline, bend, tilt, tip, slope • *to lean against the fence* ► rest, support yourself, prop yourself up, recline

leap VERB • *to leap over the gate* ► jump, spring, vault, bound • *to leap to your feet* ► spring, jump • *Prices have leapt.* ► soar, rise, rocket, increase

DICTIONARY

learn VERB **learned** or **learnt** 1 to get knowledge or skill 2 to find out about something

learned (ler-nid) ADJECTIVE having or showing much knowledge

learner NOUN a person who is learning something

learning NOUN knowledge got by study

lease NOUN an agreement to allow someone to use a building or land etc. for a fixed period in return for payment

lease VERB to allow or obtain the use of by lease

leash NOUN a dog's lead

least ADJECTIVE, ADVERB very small in amount etc.

least NOUN the smallest amount or degree

leather NOUN material made from animal skins ▶ **leathery** ADJECTIVE

leave VERB **left** 1 to go away from a person or place 2 to cause

something to stay as it is 3 to go away without taking 4 to give responsibility for something *left the decision to you* 5 to put something to be collected or passed on **leave out** to omit or exclude

leave NOUN official permission to be away

lecherous ADJECTIVE showing strong sexual desire

lectern NOUN a stand for a large book

lecture NOUN 1 a formal talk 2 a serious warning

lecture VERB to give a lecture to ▶ **lecturer** NOUN

led past tense of **lead**[1]

ledge NOUN a narrow shelf

ledger NOUN an account book

lee NOUN the sheltered side away from the wind

leech NOUN a blood-sucking worm

THESAURUS

learn VERB • *to learn a language* ▶ master, acquire a knowledge of, understand, pick up • *to learn a poem* ▶ memorize, learn by heart, know

learned ADJECTIVE • *a learned piece of writing* ▶ scholarly, intellectual, educated, erudite

learner NOUN • *still a learner* ▶ beginner, novice, apprentice, pupil, trainee

leave VERB • *time to leave* ▶ depart, set off, go, take your leave, say goodbye • *She left the*

house. ▶ depart from, quit, vacate • *His wife has left him.* ▶ desert, abandon • *to leave your job* ▶ quit, give up, resign from • *I left my case on the train.* ▶ lose, mislay, leave behind • *Leave it to me to sort out.* ▶ entrust, hand over

leave NOUN • *leave from the army* ▶ free time, time off, holiday, vacation

lecture NOUN • *a lecture on modern art* ▶ talk, discourse, speech • *a stern lecture* ▶ reprimand, scolding, rebuke

leek NOUN a long green and white vegetable of the onion family

leer VERB to look at someone in a lustful or unpleasant way ▶ **leer** NOUN

leeway NOUN extra space or time available

left¹ ADJECTIVE, ADVERB **1** on or towards the west if you are facing north **2** (of politics) in favour of socialist or radical views ▶ **left-hand** ADJECTIVE

left NOUN the left-hand side or part etc.

left² past tense of **leave**

left-handed ADJECTIVE using the left hand in preference

leg NOUN **1** one of the limbs on which a person or animal stands or moves **2** each of the supports of a chair or table **3** one stage of a journey **4** each of a pair of sports matches

legacy NOUN **legacies** property left to a person in a will

legal ADJECTIVE **1** lawful **2** to do with the law ▶ **legally** ADVERB

legality NOUN the state of being legal

legalize VERB to make legal

⚠ **SPELLING**

This word can also be spelled *legalise*.

legate NOUN an official representative

legend NOUN a traditional story

legendary ADJECTIVE **1** existing in legend **2** famous for a long time

leggings PLURAL NOUN tight-fitting trousers worn by women

legible ADJECTIVE clear enough to read ▶ **legibility** NOUN, **legibly** ADVERB

legion NOUN **1** a division of an army **2** a large number of people

legionnaire NOUN a member of an association of former soldiers

legionnaires' disease NOUN a serious form of pneumonia caused by bacteria

legislate VERB to make laws ▶ **legislation** NOUN, **legislative** ADJECTIVE

legislature NOUN a country's parliament or law-making assembly

legitimate ADJECTIVE **1** born of married parents **2** acceptable or reasonable ▶ **legitimacy** NOUN

THESAURUS

legal ADJECTIVE • *activity that is not legal* ▶ lawful, legitimate, permitted, proper, aboveboard, allowed

legend NOUN • *legends from the past* ▶ myth, story, folk tale, fable

legible ADJECTIVE • *writing that was barely legible* ▶ readable, clear, intelligible, distinct

legitimate ADJECTIVE • *legitimate reasons for what they did* ▶ valid, sound, acceptable, justifiable • *a legitimate heir* ▶ lawful, legal, rightful, genuine, authentic, real

leisure NOUN • *a life of leisure* ▶ ease, relaxation, enjoyment, pleasure, luxury • *never has*

a
b
c
d
e
f
g
h
i
j
k
l
m
n
o
p
q
r
s
t
u
v
w
x
y
z

a
b
c
d
e
f
g
h
i
j
k
l
m
n
o
p
q
r
s
t
u
v
w
x
y
z

leisure NOUN time that is free from work ► **leisured** ADJECTIVE

leisurely ADJECTIVE done without hurrying *a leisurely stroll*

lemming NOUN a small mouse-like animal of Arctic regions that is said to run headlong into the sea and drown during its mass migration

lemon NOUN **1** an yellow fruit with a sour taste **2** a pale yellow colour

lemonade NOUN a lemon-flavoured drink

lemur (lee-mer) NOUN a monkey-like animal

lend VERB lent **1** to give someone something they have to give back **2** to give or add a quality *lent dignity to the occasion* **lend a hand** to help in a task

length NOUN **1** extent from one end to the other **2** a strip cut from a larger piece

lengthen VERB to make or become longer

lengthways or **lengthwise** ADVERB from end to end; along the longest part

lengthy ADJECTIVE going on for a long time

lenient ADJECTIVE not strict ► **leniency** NOUN

lens NOUN **1** a curved piece of glass or plastic used to focus in glasses, cameras, etc. **2** the transparent part of the eye

Lent NOUN a time of fasting observed by Christians before Easter

lent past tense of **lend**

lentil NOUN a kind of small bean

leopard (lep-erd) NOUN a large spotted animal of the cat family

leotard (lee-o-tard) NOUN a close-fitting piece of clothing worn for dancing, gymnastics, etc.

leper NOUN a person who has leprosy

leprechaun (lep-rek-awn) NOUN an elf that looks like a little old man

leprosy NOUN an infectious disease that makes parts of the body waste away ► **leprous** ADJECTIVE

THESAURUS

enough leisure ► free time, spare time, time off

leisurely ADJECTIVE • *a leisurely stroll* ► slow, gentle, unhurried, relaxed

lend VERB • *to lend money* ► loan, advance

length NOUN • *a length of twenty metres* ► extent, measurement, stretch, distance • *the length of the wait* ► duration, extent, period, time

lengthen VERB • *The days began to lengthen.* ► grow longer, draw out, stretch, elongate, extend • *to lengthen the time* ► extend, increase, prolong

lengthy ADJECTIVE • *a lengthy journey* ► long, protracted, drawn out, extended

lenient ADJECTIVE • *too lenient with him* ► soft, easygoing, tolerant

DICTIONARY

lesbian NOUN a homosexual woman

less ADJECTIVE, ADVERB smaller in amount; not so much

less NOUN a smaller amount

less PREPOSITION minus; deducting *£100 less tax*

lessen VERB to make or become less

lesser ADJECTIVE not so great as the other *the lesser evil*

lesson NOUN **1** a period of teaching **2** something to be learned **3** an example or experience

lest CONJUNCTION (old use) to prevent *Remind us, lest we forget.*

let VERB **letting, let 1** to allow **2** to leave *Let it alone.* **3** to give someone use of a house or building in return for payment **let down** to disappoint or fail **let off 1** to excuse from a duty or punishment **2** to cause to explode **let up** (informal) **1** to relax **2** to become less intense

lethal (lee-thal) ADJECTIVE causing death ► **lethally** ADVERB

lethargy NOUN lack of energy ► **lethargic** ADJECTIVE

letter NOUN **1** a symbol representing a sound **2** a written message

lettering NOUN letters drawn or painted

lettuce NOUN a garden plant with broad crisp leaves used in salads

leukaemia (lew-kee-mee-a) NOUN a disease of the white corpuscles in the blood

level ADJECTIVE **1** flat or horizontal **2** at the same height or position

level NOUN **1** height, depth, position, or value in relation to other things *a level surface* **3** a tool that shows whether something is level

level VERB **levelling, levelled 1** to make or become level **2** to aim or direct

level crossing NOUN a place where a road crosses a railway at the same level

THESAURUS

lessen VERB • *to lessen the pain*
► reduce, decrease, alleviate, minimize • *Her love would never lessen.* ► diminish, decrease, fade, weaken, shrink

lesson NOUN • *a French lesson*
► class, period, lecture, seminar • *a lesson to all of them*
► example, warning, deterrent

let VERB • *Let them go on the trip.*
► allow, permit, give permission, authorize, agree to • *to let rooms*
► rent out, hire out

level ADJECTIVE • *a level surface*
► flat, even, smooth, horizontal • *The scores were level.* ► equal, even, balanced

level NOUN • *promoted to a senior level* ► rank, standing, position • *a high level of absences* ► amount, quantity, extent, degree • *The water rose to a dangerous level.*
► height, altitude • *on this level of the building* ► floor, storey

level VERB • *to level the surface*
► smooth, even out, flatten

lever NOUN **1** a bar for lifting or forcing something **2** a handle for operating machinery

lever VERB to lift or move with a lever

leverage NOUN **1** the force of a lever **2** power or influence

levitate VERB to rise in the air ► **levitation** NOUN

levity NOUN unsuitable humour

levy VERB **levies**, **levied** to impose a tax or other payment

levy NOUN **levies** an amount of money paid in tax

lewd ADJECTIVE indecent or crude

liability NOUN **liabilities 1** legal responsibility **2** a debt or obligation **3** a disadvantage

liable ADJECTIVE **1** likely to do or suffer something **2** legally responsible

liaise (lee-ayz) VERB (*informal*) to act in cooperation with someone

liaison (lee-ay-zon) NOUN communication and cooperation

liar NOUN a person who tells lies

libel NOUN an untrue statement that damages a person's reputation ► **libellous** ADJECTIVE

libel VERB **libelling**, **libelled** to make a libel about someone

liberal ADJECTIVE **1** giving or given generously **2** not strict; tolerant ► **liberally** ADVERB

liberate VERB to set free ► **liberation** NOUN, **liberator** NOUN

liberty NOUN **liberties** freedom to speak and act **take liberties** to behave impolitely

librarian NOUN a person in charge of or of a library

library NOUN **libraries 1** a place where books are kept for use or loan **2** a collection of books, records, films, etc.

libretto NOUN **libretti** or **librettos** the words of an opera

lice *plural of* **louse**

licence NOUN **1** an official permit to do or use or own something **2** special freedom to avoid the usual rules or customs

license VERB to authorize by law

lichen (ly-ken) NOUN a dry-looking plant growing on rocks, walls, etc.

lick VERB **1** to pass the tongue over **2** to touch lightly **3** (*informal*) to defeat

lick NOUN **1** an act of licking **2** a slight application of paint etc.

lid NOUN a cover for a box or pot etc.

lie¹ NOUN a deliberate untrue statement

liable ADJECTIVE • *not liable for any damage* ► responsible, answerable, to blame • *liable to break* ► likely, apt, prone, inclined

liberal ADJECTIVE • *a liberal supply* ► generous, plentiful, copious, abundant • *liberal attitudes*

► broad-minded, tolerant, progressive

liberate VERB • *to liberate people from slavery* ► free, set free, release, rescue, save

lie NOUN • *telling lies* ► untruth, falsehood, deception, invention

DICTIONARY

lie VERB **lies**, **lied** to tell a lie

lie² VERB **lies**, **lay**, **lain** **1** to be or get in a flat or resting position **2** to be or remain

lieutenant (lef-ten-ant) NOUN **1** an officer in the army or navy **2** a deputy

life NOUN **lives 1** the period between birth and death **2** the state of being alive **3** living things **4** liveliness *full of life*

lifebelt NOUN a ring of buoyant material to support a person in water

lifeboat NOUN a boat for rescuing people at sea

lifebuoy NOUN a device to support a person needing rescue in water

lifeguard NOUN a person qualified to rescue swimmers in difficulty

life jacket NOUN a jacket of buoyant material to support a person in water

lifeless ADJECTIVE unconscious or without life

lifelike ADJECTIVE looking like a real person or thing

lifelong ADJECTIVE lasting for a whole life

lifetime NOUN the time someone is alive

lift VERB **1** to raise or pick up **2** to rise up **3** to remove a restriction

lift NOUN **1** a device for taking people or goods from one floor or level to another in a building **2** a ride in someone else's car

lift-off NOUN the launch of a rocket or spacecraft

ligament NOUN a tough flexible tissue that holds the bones of the body together

light¹ NOUN **1** radiation that makes things visible **2** a lamp or other source of light **3** a flame

light ADJECTIVE **1** full of light; not dark **2** pale

light VERB **lit** or **lighted 1** to start a thing burning **2** to provide light for

light² ADJECTIVE **1** having little weight; not heavy **2** small in

THESAURUS

life NOUN • *full of life* ► vitality, energy, liveliness, vigour

lift VERB • *She lifted the chair.* ► raise, pick up, hoist, heave • *to lift off the ground* ► rise, ascend, go up • *to lift your spirits* ► raise, boost, revive, perk up • *The ban has been lifted.* ► cancel, revoke, remove • *The mist had lifted.* ► clear, disperse, disappear

light NOUN • *not enough light* ► brightness, illumination, luminescence, glow • *a light on in the bedroom* ► lamp, lantern, torch, bulb • *to work in the light*

► daylight, light of day, daytime, sunlight

light ADJECTIVE • *a light load* ► slight, lightweight, flimsy, insubstantial, portable • *a light blue* ► pale, faint, pastel • *a light meal* ► modest, simple, insubstantial • *a little light reading* ► entertaining, easy • *light on her feet* ► nimble, agile, graceful

light VERB • *to light a fire* ► kindle, ignite, set alight, set fire to, switch on • *Searchlights lit the sky.* ► illuminate, light up, brighten, shine on

a
b
c
d
e
f
g
h
i
j
k
l
m
n
o
p
q
r
s
t
u
v
w
x
y
z

amount or force *light rain*
3 needing little effort *light work*
4 cheerful, not sad *with a light
heart* **5** not serious or profound
light music ▶ **lightly** ADVERB

lighten VERB to make or become
brighter or less heavy

light-hearted ADJECTIVE cheerful

lighthouse NOUN a tower with a
bright light to guide or warn ships

lighting NOUN lamps, or the light
they provide

lightning NOUN a flash of bright
light produced during a
thunderstorm

lightweight NOUN unimportant

light year NOUN the distance light
travels in one year (about 6 million
million miles)

like¹ VERB **1** to think a person or
thing is pleasant or satisfactory
2 to wish *I'd like to come.*

like² PREPOSITION **1** in the manner of
swims like a fish **2** in a suitable
state for *looks like rain. I feel like a
cup of tea.* **3** such as *things like art
and music*

like ADJECTIVE similar

likeable ADJECTIVE easy to like;
pleasant

likelihood NOUN being likely;
probability

likely ADJECTIVE **likelier, likeliest**
1 expected to happen or be true
2 expected to do something

liken VERB to compare

likeness NOUN **1** a similarity in
appearance **2** a portrait

likewise ADVERB similarly; in the
same way

liking NOUN a feeling that you like
something

lilac NOUN a bush with purple or
white flowers

lilt NOUN a light pleasant rhythm
▶ **lilting** ADJECTIVE

lily NOUN **lilies** a garden plant with
trumpet-shaped flowers

limb NOUN **1** a leg, arm, or wing **2** a
large branch of a tree

limber VERB **limber up** to exercise
in preparation for a sport

limbo¹ NOUN **in limbo** in an
uncertain situation

limbo² NOUN a West Indian dance
in which the dancer bends
backwards to pass under a low bar

lime¹ NOUN a white chalky
substance used in making cement

like VERB • *to like someone* ▶ be
fond of, be attached to, care for,
adore, admire, respect • *Do you
like dancing?* ▶ enjoy, appreciate,
be keen on, love

like ADJECTIVE • *very like each other*
▶ similar to, the same as, identical

likeable ADJECTIVE • *a likeable
person* ▶ pleasant, personable,
nice, friendly

likely ADJECTIVE • *An inquiry was
likely.* ▶ probable, possible,
expected • *a likely explanation*
▶ believable, plausible, credible,
convincing, reasonable,
acceptable

liking NOUN • *a liking for rock
music* ▶ affection, fondness, love,
weakness

lime [2] NOUN a green fruit like a small round lemon

lime [3] NOUN a tree with yellow flowers

limelight NOUN **in the limelight** getting publicity

limerick NOUN an amusing poem with five lines

limestone NOUN a kind of rock from which lime is obtained

limit NOUN 1 a line or point where something ends 2 the greatest amount allowed

limit VERB 1 to keep within certain limits 2 to be a limit to

limitation NOUN a limit or restriction

limited ADJECTIVE kept within limits *a limited choice*

limousine (lim-oo-zeen) NOUN a large luxurious car

limp [1] VERB to walk lamely

limp NOUN a limping walk

limp [2] ADJECTIVE not stiff or firm

limpet NOUN a small shellfish that clings to rocks

limpid ADJECTIVE (of liquids) clear or transparent

linchpin NOUN a pin through the end of an axle keeping a wheel in position

line [1] NOUN 1 a long thin mark 2 a row or series of people or things 3 a length of rope, string, wire, etc. 4 a railway 5 a company operating a transport service 6 a way of doing things or behaving 7 a telephone connection

line VERB 1 to mark with lines 2 to form into a line

line [2] VERB to cover the inside of

lineage (lin-ee-ij) NOUN a line of descendants from an ancestor

linear (lin-ee-er) ADJECTIVE 1 arranged in a line 2 to do with a line or length

linen NOUN 1 cloth made from flax 2 shirts, sheets, and other items originally made of linen

liner NOUN a large passenger ship

linesman NOUN **linesmen** an official in football or tennis etc. who decides whether the ball has crossed a line

linger VERB to be slow to leave

lingerie (lan-zher-ee) NOUN women's underwear

THESAURUS

limit NOUN • *a limit of ten thousand tickets* ▶ restriction, maximum, cut-off point, restraint, ceiling • *as far as the city limits* ▶ boundary, border, edge, perimeter, periphery

limit VERB • *to limit numbers* ▶ restrict, curb, restrain, control, fix

limp ADJECTIVE • *a limp hand* ▶ soft, loose, slack, weak, floppy

line NOUN • *a line of cars* ▶ queue, row, file, column, procession • *to draw a line* ▶ stroke, underline, strip, band, bar • *to take a tough line* ▶ approach, policy, stance • *to attach a line to the post* ▶ cord, rope, string, cable, wire

a
b
c
d
e
f
g
h
i
j
k
l
m
n
o
p
q
r
s
t
u
v
w
x
y
z

a
b
c
d
e
f
g
h
i
j
k
l
m
n
o
p
q
r
s
t
u
v
w
x
y
z

linguist NOUN an expert in languages

linguistics NOUN the study of languages and of language
▶ **linguistic** ADJECTIVE

liniment NOUN a soothing body lotion

lining NOUN a layer that covers the inside of something

link NOUN **1** a ring or loop in a chain **2** a connection or relationship

link VERB to join together
▶ **linkage** NOUN

links NOUN a golf course near the sea

linnet NOUN a kind of finch

lino NOUN linoleum

linoleum NOUN a stiff shiny floor covering

linseed oil NOUN oil obtained from the seeds of flax plants

lint NOUN a soft material for covering wounds

lintel NOUN a horizontal piece of wood or stone etc. above a door or other opening

lion NOUN a large strong flesh-eating animal of the cat family found in Africa and India

lioness NOUN a female lion

lip NOUN **1** either of the two fleshy edges of the mouth **2** the edge of a

cup or crater **3** the pointed part at the top of a jug for pouring

lip-read VERB **lip-read** to understand what a person says by watching the lips

lipstick NOUN a stick of a waxy substance for colouring the lips

liquefy VERB **liquefies, liquefied** to make or become liquid

liqueur (lik-yoor) NOUN a strong sweet alcoholic drink

liquid NOUN a substance that flows freely but has a constant volume

liquid ADJECTIVE **1** in the form of a liquid **2** easily converted into cash
▶ **liquidity** NOUN

liquidate VERB **1** to pay off or settle a debt **2** to close down a bankrupt business ▶ **liquidation** NOUN, **liquidator** NOUN

liquidize VERB to make into a liquid or pulp ▶ **liquidizer** NOUN

⚠ **SPELLING**

This word can also be spelled *liquidise.*

liquor NOUN an alcoholic drink

liquorice NOUN a black substance from a plant, used as a sweet

lisp NOUN a fault in speech in which *s* and *z* are pronounced like *th*

lisp VERB to speak with a lisp

list[1] NOUN a number of items written one after another

link NOUN • *links between families*
▶ bond, tie, relationship, attachment • *a rail link*
▶ connection, line

link VERB • *to link the crimes*
▶ connect, associate, draw a

connection between • *to link together* ▶ join, connect, attach, fasten

list NOUN • *a list of names*
▶ register, catalogue, index, file, roll

428

DICTIONARY

list *VERB* to make a list of

list² *VERB* (of a ship) to lean over to one side ▶ **list** *NOUN*

listen *VERB* to try to hear
▶ **listener** *NOUN*

listless *ADJECTIVE* too tired to do much

lit *past tense of* **light**¹

litany *NOUN* **litanies** a formal prayer with fixed responses

literacy *NOUN* the ability to read and write

literal *ADJECTIVE* **1** meaning exactly what is said **2** word for word

literally *ADVERB* really; exactly as stated

literary (lit-er-er-i) *ADJECTIVE* to do with literature

literate *ADJECTIVE* able to read and write

literature *NOUN* **1** novels, plays, and other written works **2** the books and writings on a subject

lithe *ADJECTIVE* flexible and supple

litmus *NOUN* a blue substance that is turned red by acids and can be turned back to blue by alkalis

litre *NOUN* a measure of liquid, about 1.75 pints

litter *NOUN* **1** rubbish or untidy things lying about **2** young animals born to a mother at one time **3** a tray of absorbent material used as a cat's toilet

litter *VERB* to leave litter about in a place

little *ADJECTIVE* **less**, **least** small in amount or size

little *NOUN* a small amount

liturgy *NOUN* **liturgies** a form of public worship used in churches
▶ **liturgical** *ADJECTIVE*

live¹ (rhymes with *give*) *VERB* **1** to have life; to be alive **2** to have a home *lives in Glasgow* **3** to pass your life in a certain way *lived as a hermit*

live² (rhymes with *hive*) *ADJECTIVE* **1** alive **2** connected to an electric

THESAURUS

list *VERB* • *to list the names*
▶ record, write down, register, itemize

listen *VERB* • *They weren't listening.*
▶ pay attention, take notice
listen to • *Listen to what I say.*
▶ pay attention to, take notice of, hear, heed

litter *NOUN* • *to clear up the litter*
▶ rubbish, refuse, junk, waste, debris, trash • *a litter of puppies*
▶ brood

little *ADJECTIVE* • *a little book*
▶ small, tiny, minute, miniature,

mini • *a little person* ▶ small, slight, short, diminutive • *in a little while* ▶ short, brief • *a little problem* ▶ minor, trivial, unimportant, insignificant

live *VERB* • *We live in Glasgow.*
▶ reside, have a home, dwell, lodge • *enough to live on* ▶ exist, subsist, survive • *The plants will not live much longer.* ▶ last, survive, stay alive • *to live a happy life* ▶ spend, pass

live *ADJECTIVE* • *live animals* ▶ living, alive, breathing • *a live show*

DICTIONARY

current 3 (of a broadcast) transmitted while it is actually happening **4** burning *live coals*

livelihood NOUN a way of earning money to support yourself

lively ADJECTIVE **livelier, liveliest** full of life or action ▸ **liveliness** NOUN

liven VERB to make or become lively

liver NOUN an organ of the body that purifies the blood

livery NOUN **liveries** a uniform worn by male servants

livestock NOUN farm animals

livid ADJECTIVE **1** bluish-grey **2** furious

living NOUN **1** the state of being alive **2** the way a person lives **3** a way of earning money

lizard NOUN a reptile with a rough skin and a long tail

llama (lah-ma) NOUN a South American animal like a camel but with no hump

load NOUN **1** something carried; a burden **2** the total amount of an electric current **3** (*informal*) a large amount *a load of nonsense*

load VERB **1** to put a bullet or shell into a gun or film into a camera **2** to enter programs or data into a computer **3** to put a load in or on **4** to fill heavily **5** to add a weight to

loaf[1] NOUN **loaves** a shaped mass of bread

loaf[2] VERB to spend time idly ▸ **loafer** NOUN

loam NOUN rich soil ▸ **loamy** ADJECTIVE

loan NOUN something lent, especially money **on loan** being lent

loan VERB to lend

loath (rhymes with *both*) ADJECTIVE unwilling

loathe (rhymes with *clothe*) VERB to hate very much ▸ **loathing** NOUN

loathsome ADJECTIVE causing disgust; revolting

lob VERB **lobbing, lobbed** to throw, hit, or kick a ball high into the air

lobby NOUN **lobbies 1** an entrance hall **2** a group who try to influence MPs or officials

THESAURUS

▸ real-time, actual, unrecorded • *a live rail* ▸ electrified, connected • *a live issue* ▸ topical, current, relevant, contemporary

lively ADJECTIVE • *a lively town* ▸ busy, bustling, crowded • *a lively person* ▸ vivacious, exuberant, energetic, active • *a lively colour scheme* ▸ bright, vivid, colourful, bold

livid ADJECTIVE • *livid with them* ▸ furious, fuming, seething, infuriated

load NOUN • *a load of goods* ▸ cargo, consignment, vanload, lorryload, shipment • *a load of books* ▸ lot, large number of, large amount of

load VERB • *to load the luggage* ▸ pack, stow, store, stack

a b c d e f g h i j k l m n o p q r s t u v w x y z

lobby VERB **lobbies, lobbied** to try to persuade an MP or other person to support your cause

lobe NOUN **1** a rounded part of an organ of the body **2** the soft part at the bottom of the ear

lobster NOUN a large shellfish with eight legs and two long claws

local ADJECTIVE belonging to a particular place or a small area
▸ **locally** ADVERB

local NOUN (informal) **1** someone who lives in a particular district **2** a pub near a person's home

locality NOUN **localities** a district or location

locate VERB to discover where something is *have located the fault* **be located** to be situated in a particular place

location NOUN the place where something is

loch NOUN a lake in Scotland

lock¹ NOUN **1** a fastening that is opened with a key or other device **2** a section of a canal in which boats can be raised or lowered to a different level **3** the distance that a vehicle's front wheels can turn **lock, stock, and barrel** completely

lock VERB **1** to fasten or secure with a lock **2** to store away securely **3** to

become fixed in one place **lock up** to shut in or imprison

lock² NOUN a clump of hair

locker NOUN a small cupboard with a lock, for leaving your belongings

locket NOUN a small ornamental case for a portrait or lock of hair, worn round the neck

locks PLURAL NOUN the hair of the head

locksmith NOUN a person who makes and mends locks

locomotive NOUN a railway engine

locomotive ADJECTIVE to do with movement *locomotive power*
▸ **locomotion** NOUN

locum NOUN a doctor who takes the place of another for a time

locus NOUN (Maths) the path traced by a moving point, or made by points placed in a certain way

locust NOUN a kind of grasshopper that moves in large swarms destroying plants

lodge NOUN **1** a small house at the gates of a park **2** a porter's room at the entrance to a building

lodge VERB **1** to live in rented rooms **2** to make a formal complaint **3** to become stuck

lodger NOUN a person who pays to live in rented rooms

local ADJECTIVE • *the local library*
▸ nearby, neighbourhood, regional

locate VERB • *He located the letter at last.* ▸ find, discover, track

down, detect • *The boiler room is located in the basement.*
▸ situate, site, position, place

lock VERB • *to lock the door*
▸ fasten, secure, shut, bolt, close

a
b
c
d
e
f
g
h
i
j
k
l
m
n
o
p
q
r
s
t
u
v
w
x
y
z

a
b
c
d
e
f
g
h
i
j
k
l
m
n
o
p
q
r
s
t
u
v
w
x
y
z

lodgings *PLURAL NOUN* rooms rented for living in

loft *NOUN* a room or space under a roof

lofty *ADJECTIVE* **loftier**, **loftiest** **1** tall **2** proud or noble ▶ **loftily** *ADVERB*

log *NOUN* **1** a large piece cut from a fallen tree **2** a record of a voyage or flight

log *VERB* **logging**, **logged** to enter facts in a log **log on** or **off** to start or finish using a computer

loganberry *NOUN* **loganberries** a dark red fruit like a blackberry

logarithm *NOUN* one of a series of numbers set out in tables which make it possible to do sums by adding and subtracting instead of multiplying and dividing

logbook *NOUN* **1** a book in which a log of a voyage is kept **2** the registration document of a motor vehicle

log cabin *NOUN* a hut built of logs

loggerheads *PLURAL NOUN* **at loggerheads** disagreeing or quarrelling

logic *NOUN* **1** the process of reasoning **2** a system or method of reasoning

logical *ADJECTIVE* using logic; reasoning or reasoned correctly ▶ **logically** *ADVERB*

logo *NOUN* **logos** a printed symbol used by a business company etc. as its emblem

loin *NOUN* the side and back of the body between the ribs and the hip bone

loiter *VERB* to linger or stand about idly

loll *VERB* **1** to lean lazily against something **2** to hang loosely

lollipop *NOUN* a large round hard sweet on a stick

lolly *NOUN* **lollies** (*informal*) **1** a lollipop **2** (*informal*) money

lone *ADJECTIVE* solitary

lonely *ADJECTIVE* **lonelier**, **loneliest** **1** sad when you are on your own **2** solitary **3** not often visited or used ▶ **loneliness** *NOUN*

lonesome *ADJECTIVE* feeling lonely

long[1] *ADJECTIVE* **1** measuring a lot from one end to the other **2** taking a lot of time **3** having a certain length *10 metres long*

long *ADVERB* **1** for a long time *Have you been waiting long?* **2** at a long time before or after *long ago* **3** throughout a time *all night long*

long[2] *VERB* to feel a strong desire

logical *ADJECTIVE* • *logical arguments* ▶ clear, sound, sensible, rational, reasonable

lonely *ADJECTIVE* • *to feel lonely* ▶ alone, solitary, friendless, abandoned • *a lonely road* ▶ deserted, remote, secluded

long *ADJECTIVE* • *long hair* ▶ lengthy • *a long wait* ▶ lengthy, prolonged, extended

long *VERB* **long for** • *We longed for the holidays.* ▶ yearn for, dream of

DICTIONARY

longhand NOUN ordinary writing, not shorthand

longing NOUN a strong desire

longitude NOUN the distance east or west of the Greenwich meridian, measured in degrees

long jump NOUN an athletic contest of juming as far as possible along the ground in one leap

long-range ADJECTIVE covering a long distance or period of time

longship NOUN a long narrow warship used by the Vikings

long-sighted ADJECTIVE able to see distant things clearly but not things that are close

long wave NOUN a radio wave of a wavelength above one kilometre and a frequency less than 300 kilohertz

long-winded ADJECTIVE talking or writing at great length

loo NOUN **loos** (informal) a toilet

loofah NOUN a rough sponge made from a dried gourd

look VERB **1** to turn the eyes to see **2** to face in a particular direction **3** to have a certain appearance to look sad **look after 1** to protect or take care of **2** to be in charge of **look for** to try to find **look forward to** to be waiting eagerly for **look into** to investigate **look out** to be careful

look NOUN **1** the act of looking; a gaze or glance **2** general appearance

lookout NOUN **1** the act of watching for something keep a lookout **2** a place for keeping watch **3** a person who keeps watch **4** (informal) a person's own fault or concern That's his lookout.

loom¹ NOUN a machine for weaving cloth

loom² VERB to appear suddenly and threateningly

THESAURUS

longing NOUN • a longing for home ► yearning, craving, desire, need

look VERB • everywhere you look ► see, stare, gaze, regard, survey, glance, peer • Things look difficult. ► seem, appear • to look after an invalid ► take care of, care for, attend to, mind, watch over **look at** • I looked at her. ► glance at, watch, observe **look for 1** I was looking for my wallet. ► search for, hunt for, try to find **2** looking for trouble ► ask for, provoke, invite, attract, encourage **3** to

look up the answer ► find, search for, research

look NOUN • have a look ► glance, glimpse, peek, peep, sight (of) • the look on his face ► expression • a house with a Tudor look ► appearance, air • this year's new look ► fashion, vogue, style

lookout NOUN • a lookout on the bridge ► sentry, guard, watchman • That's their lookout. ► concern, responsibility, problem

loom VERB • The cathedral loomed above them. ► tower, soar, rise • Shapes loomed out of the mist. ► appear, emerge, come into view

a
b
c
d
e
f
g
h
i
j
k
l
m
n
o
p
q
r
s
t
u
v
w
x
y
z

DICTIONARY

a b c d e f g h i j k **l** m n o p q r s t u v w x y z

loop NOUN **1** the shape made by a curve crossing itself **2** a piece of string etc. made into this shape

loop VERB **1** to make into a loop **2** to enclose in a loop

loophole NOUN a way of avoiding a rule or promise without breaking it

loose ADJECTIVE **1** not tight or firmly fixed **2** not tied up or shut in **3** not packed in a box or packet **4** not exact *a loose translation*
► **loosely** ADVERB

loose VERB **1** to loosen **2** to untie or release

⚠ **USAGE**

Do not confuse this word with *lose*.

loose-leaf ADJECTIVE (of a folder) having each sheet of paper separate and able to be removed

loosen VERB to make or become loose or looser

loot NOUN stolen things; goods taken from an enemy

loot VERB to take loot from
► **looter** NOUN

lop VERB **lopping, lopped** to cut away branches or twigs

lope VERB to run with a long jumping stride

lopsided ADJECTIVE with one side lower or smaller than the other

lord NOUN **1** a nobleman **2** a master or ruler

lordly ADJECTIVE **lordlier, lordliest 1** to do with a lord **2** proud or haughty

lordship NOUN a title used in speaking to or about a lord

lore NOUN a set of traditional facts or beliefs

lorry NOUN **lorries** a large motor vehicle for carrying heavy loads

lose VERB **lost 1** to be without something you once had **2** to fail to keep or obtain **3** to be defeated in a contest or argument **4** to cause the loss of **5** (of a clock

THESAURUS

loop NOUN • *a loop of wire* ► coil, ring, twist, curl, hoop, circle

loop VERB • *Loop a rope round the animal's neck.* ► coil, wind, twist, bend, curl

loose ADJECTIVE • *a loose screw* ► wobbly, insecure, unfastened, unfixed • *a wild animal loose in the grounds* ► free, at large, at liberty • *loose trousers* ► baggy, loose-fitting

loosen VERB • *to loosen the knots* ► ease, free, slacken, untie

• *to loosen your grip* ► weaken, relax

loot NOUN • *a sack full of loot* ► booty, spoils, plunder

loot VERB • *to loot a place* ► raid, plunder, pillage, ransack

lopsided ADJECTIVE • *a lopsided load* ► uneven, unbalanced, asymmetrical

lose VERB • *I've lost my passport.* ► mislay, misplace, forget • *to lose time* ► waste, squander • *The home side lost 3–0.* ► be beaten, be defeated

DICTIONARY

or watch) to become behind the correct time ► **loser** NOUN

⚠ **USAGE**
Do not confuse this word with **loose**.

loss NOUN **1** the act of losing something **2** something lost **at a loss** unsure

lost past tense and past participle of **lose**

lost ADJECTIVE **1** not knowing where you are or which way to go **2** missing or strayed

lot NOUN **1** a large number or amount *a lot of friends* *lots of time* **2** a person's fate or situation in life **3** something for sale at an auction **4** a piece of land **a lot** very much *a lot better* **the lot** or **the whole lot** everything

loth ADJECTIVE another spelling of **loath**

lotion NOUN a liquid for putting on the skin

lottery NOUN **lotteries** a way of raising money by selling numbered tickets and giving prizes to winners

lotus NOUN a kind of tropical water lily

loud ADJECTIVE **1** producing a lot of noise **2** unpleasantly bright *loud colours*

loudspeaker NOUN a device that changes electrical signals into sound

lounge NOUN a comfortable room

lounge VERB to sit in a lazy and relaxed way

louse NOUN **lice** a small insect that lives as a parasite on animals, people, or plants

lousy ADJECTIVE **lousier, lousiest** (*informal*) very bad or unpleasant

lout NOUN a bad-mannered man

lovable ADJECTIVE easy to love

love NOUN **1** great liking or affection **2** sexual affection **3** a loved person **4** no score in tennis **in love** feeling strong love

love VERB to feel love for

lovely ADJECTIVE **lovelier, loveliest 1** beautiful **2** very pleasant or enjoyable ► **loveliness** NOUN

THESAURUS

lot NOUN **a lot of** or **lots of** • *a lot of friends* ► many, plenty of, a large amount or number • *A new lot of tourists arrived.* ► set, group, batch

loud ADJECTIVE • *loud music* ► noisy, blaring, deafening, booming • *loud colours* ► gaudy, garish, bold, lurid

lovable ADJECTIVE • *a lovable kitten* ► adorable, dear, sweet, cute

love NOUN • *to show your love* ► fondness, affection, adoration,

devotion, friendship • *his true love* ► beloved, darling, dear

love VERB • *She told him she loved him.* ► care for, feel deeply for, adore, treasure • *We all love the holidays.* ► like, enjoy, take pleasure in, appreciate

lovely ADJECTIVE • *to look lovely* ► beautiful, attractive, good-looking, pretty, charming, delightful • *a lovely morning* ► pleasant, fine, glorious, wonderful

a
b
c
d
e
f
g
h
i
j
k
l
m
n
o
p
q
r
s
t
u
v
w
x
y
z

a
b
c
d
e
f
g
h
i
j
k
l
m
n
o
p
q
r
s
t
u
v
w
x
y
z

lover NOUN **1** someone who loves something *a music lover* **2** an unmarried person having a sexual relationship

lovesick ADJECTIVE longing for someone you love

low[1] ADJECTIVE **1** only reaching a short way up **2** below average in importance, quality, amount, etc. **3** unhappy **4** not high-pitched *low notes*

low[2] VERB to moo like a cow

lower ADJECTIVE, ADVERB less high

lower VERB to make or become lower

lowlands PLURAL NOUN flat low-lying country ▶ **lowland** ADJECTIVE

lowly ADJECTIVE **lowlier, lowliest** humble ▶ **lowliness** NOUN

loyal ADJECTIVE firmly supporting your friends or country etc. ▶ **loyally** ADVERB, **loyalty** NOUN

loyalist NOUN a person who is loyal to the government in a revolt

lozenge NOUN **1** a small flavoured tablet containing medicine **2** a diamond shape

lubricant NOUN a lubricating substance

lubricate VERB to oil or grease something so that it moves smoothly ▶ **lubrication** NOUN

lucid ADJECTIVE **1** clear and easy to understand **2** thinking clearly ▶ **lucidly** ADVERB

luck NOUN **1** the way things happen **2** good fortune

luckless ADJECTIVE unlucky or unfortunate

lucky ADJECTIVE **luckier, luckiest** bringing or resulting from good luck ▶ **luckily** ADVERB

lucrative (loo-kruh-tiv) ADJECTIVE profitable

ludicrous ADJECTIVE ridiculous or laughable ▶ **ludicrously** ADVERB

ludo NOUN a game played with counters on a board

THESAURUS

low ADJECTIVE • *a low wall* ▶ short, small, shallow • *low prices* ▶ reasonable, cheap, inexpensive • *Supplies were getting low.* ▶ sparse, scarce, inadequate • *to feel low* ▶ depressed, unhappy • *a low rumbling sound* ▶ soft, deep

lower VERB • *to lower the flag* ▶ bring down, drop, take down • *to lower interest rates* ▶ reduce, decrease

loyal ADJECTIVE • *a loyal friend* ▶ faithful, true, devoted, dependable, reliable

luck NOUN • *They could not believe their luck.* ▶ good fortune, good luck, success • *Our luck will change.* ▶ fate, fortune, destiny • *Luck had brought them there.* ▶ chance

lucky ADJECTIVE • *a lucky guess* ▶ fortunate, timely • *lucky to have such good friends* ▶ fortunate, blessed, favoured

ludicrous ADJECTIVE • *a ludicrous suggestion* ▶ absurd, ridiculous, idiotic

DICTIONARY

lug VERB **lugging, lugged** to drag or carry something heavy

lug NOUN **1** an ear-like part on an object, for carrying or fixing it **2** (informal) an ear

luggage NOUN suitcases and bags taken on a journey

lugubrious (lug-oo-bree-us) ADJECTIVE gloomy or mournful

lukewarm ADJECTIVE **1** slightly warm **2** not enthusiastic *lukewarm applause*

lull VERB **1** to soothe or calm **2** to give a false feeling of being safe

lull NOUN a short period of quiet

lullaby NOUN **lullabies** a song to send a baby to sleep

lumbago NOUN pain in the lower back

lumber NOUN unwanted furniture or junk

lumber VERB **1** to leave someone with an unpleasant task **2** to move in a clumsy way

lumberjack NOUN a person who fells trees and cuts timber

luminous ADJECTIVE glowing in the dark ► **luminosity** NOUN

lump NOUN **1** a solid piece of something **2** a swelling

lump VERB to put or treat things together in a group **lump it** (informal) to put up with something unwelcome

lumpy ADJECTIVE **lumpier, lumpiest** containing or covered in lumps

lunacy NOUN **lunacies** insanity or foolishness

lunar ADJECTIVE to do with the moon

lunatic NOUN an insane person ► **lunatic** ADJECTIVE

lunch NOUN a meal eaten in the middle of the day

lunch VERB to eat lunch

luncheon NOUN (formal) lunch

lung NOUN either of the two parts of the body, in the chest, used in breathing

lunge VERB to thrust the body forward suddenly ► **lunge** NOUN

lupin NOUN a garden plant with tall spikes of flowers

lurch[1] VERB to stagger or lean over suddenly ► **lurch** NOUN

lurch[2] NOUN **leave somebody in the lurch** to leave them in difficulties

lure VERB to tempt into a trap ► **lure** NOUN

THESAURUS

luggage NOUN • *a rack for luggage* ► bags, cases, baggage, belongings

lull VERB • *The singing lulled her to sleep.* ► soothe, calm, pacify, quieten

lull NOUN • *a lull in the fighting* ► pause, respite, break, gap

lump NOUN • *a lump of bread* ► chunk, hunk, block, wedge, piece, portion, slab, wad • *a lump on the head* ► swelling, bump, growth

lure VERB • *to lure people into debt* ► tempt, entice, coax, persuade

a
b
c
d
e
f
g
h
i
j
k
l
m
n
o
p
q
r
s
t
u
v
w
x
y
z

lurid (lewr-id) ADJECTIVE **1** very bright or gaudy **2** sensational and shocking

lurk VERB to wait where you cannot be seen

luscious (lush-us) ADJECTIVE delicious

lush ADJECTIVE **1** growing thickly and strongly **2** luxurious

lust NOUN powerful sexual desire ► **lustful** ADJECTIVE

lust VERB to have a powerful desire

lustre NOUN brightness or brilliance

lustrous ADJECTIVE bright and shining

lusty ADJECTIVE **lustier, lustiest** strong and vigorous ► **lustily** ADVERB

lute NOUN a stringed musical instrument with a pear-shaped body

luxuriant ADJECTIVE growing abundantly

⚠ USAGE

Do not confuse this word with *luxurious*.

luxuriate VERB to enjoy something as a luxury

luxurious ADJECTIVE expensive and comfortable ► **luxuriously** ADVERB

⚠ USAGE

Do not confuse this word with *luxuriant*.

luxury NOUN **luxuries** **1** something expensive but inessential **2** expensive and comfortable surroundings

Lycra NOUN (trademark) a thin stretchy material

lying present participle of **lie**[1] and **lie**[2]

lymph (limf) NOUN a colourless fluid from the flesh or organs of the body

lynch VERB to join together to execute someone without a proper trial

lynx NOUN a wild animal like a large cat with sharp sight

lyre NOUN an ancient musical instrument like a small harp

lyric (li-rik) NOUN **1** a short poem that expresses the poet's feelings **2** the words of a song

lyrical ADJECTIVE **1** like a song **2** expressing poetic feelings ► **lyrically** ADVERB

THESAURUS

lurk VERB • to lurk in doorways ► skulk, loiter, lie in wait, hide

lush ADJECTIVE • lush vegetation ► rich, luxuriant, abundant, profuse, prolific, flourishing

luxurious ADJECTIVE • luxurious surroundings ► comfortable, sumptuous, grand, opulent, plush

luxury NOUN • a life of luxury ► wealth, comfort, ease, opulence, splendour

Mm

mac NOUN (informal) a mackintosh

macabre (mak-ahbr) ADJECTIVE strange and horrible

macaroni NOUN pasta in the form of short tubes

macaroon NOUN a small sweet cake or biscuit made with ground almonds

macaw (ma-kaw) NOUN a brightly coloured parrot with a long tail

mace NOUN an ornamental rod or staff carried by a mayor or other official

machete (mash-et-ee) NOUN a broad heavy knife used as a tool or weapon

machine NOUN a piece of equipment with parts that together perform a task

machine VERB to make with a machine

machine gun NOUN a gun that fires a rapid succession of bullets

machinery NOUN **1** machines **2** the moving parts of a machine **3** an organized system

macho (mach-oh) ADJECTIVE masculine in an aggressive way

mackerel NOUN a sea fish used as food

mackintosh NOUN a raincoat

mad ADJECTIVE **madder, maddest 1** ill in the mind; insane **2** extremely foolish **3** very keen or excited *mad about football* **4** (informal) angry ▸ **madness** NOUN

madam NOUN a polite way of addressing a woman

madden VERB to make mad or angry

madly ADVERB very much *madly in love*

madrigal NOUN a song for several voices singing different parts together

maelstrom (mayl-strom) NOUN **1** a great whirlpool **2** a state of great confusion

maestro (my-stroh) NOUN **maestros** a famous musician

magazine NOUN **1** a regular publication with articles, stories, and features **2** the part of a gun that holds the cartridges **3** a store for weapons and ammunition

maggot NOUN the larva of some kinds of fly

magic NOUN **1** the art of making things happen by a mysterious power **2** mysterious tricks performed for entertainment **3** an

THESAURUS

machine NOUN • *The machine made a noise.* ▸ apparatus, appliance, device, contraption, mechanism

mad ADJECTIVE • *He thought he was going mad.* ▸ insane, deranged, demented, crazy • *a mad idea* ▸ foolish, stupic, crazy, insane

• *still mad with us* ▸ angry, cross, furious, infuriated, irate, enraged, incensed

magic NOUN • *seemed like magic* ▸ sorcery, wizardry, witchcraft, the supernatural • *a party with magic* ▸ conjuring, conjuring tricks, illusion • *The place had lost*

enchanting quality ► **magic**
ADJECTIVE

magical **1** using magic
2 wonderful or marvellous
► **magically** ADVERB

magician NOUN **1** a person who
does magic tricks **2** a wizard

magistrate NOUN an official who
hears and judges minor legal cases

magma NOUN a molten substance
beneath the earth's crust

magnanimous (mag-nan-im-us)
ADJECTIVE generous and forgiving

magnate NOUN a wealthy
influential person, especially in
business

magnesia NOUN a white powder
that is a compound of magnesium,
used in medicine

magnesium NOUN a
silvery-white metal that burns
with a very bright flame

magnet NOUN a piece of iron or
steel that can attract metal

magnetic ADJECTIVE **1** having or
using the powers of a magnet
2 having the power to attract
people *a magnetic personality*

magnetism NOUN **1** the
properties and effects of magnetic
substances **2** great magnetic
charm and attraction

magnetize VERB to make into a
magnet

⚠️ **SPELLING**

This word can also be spelled
magnetise.

magnificent ADJECTIVE **1** grand or
splendid in appearance **2** excellent
► **magnificence** NOUN

magnify VERB **magnifies**,
magnified **1** to make something
look bigger than it really is **2** to
exaggerate ► **magnification**
NOUN

magnitude NOUN **1** size or extent
2 importance

magnolia NOUN a tree with large
white or pale-pink flowers

magpie NOUN a large black and
white bird related to the crow

mahogany NOUN a hard brown
wood

maid NOUN a female servant

maiden NOUN (old use) an
unmarried girl

maiden ADJECTIVE **1** not married *a
maiden aunt* **2** first *a maiden
voyage*

mail¹ NOUN letters and parcels sent
by post

mail VERB to send by post

mail² NOUN armour made of metal
rings joined together

THESAURUS

none of its magic. ► charm,
appeal, glamour
magical ADJECTIVE • *a magical day*
► wonderful, marvellous,
extraordinary
magnificent ADJECTIVE • *a
magnificent view* ► spectacular,

glorious, wonderful, gorgeous,
splendid, superb, breathtaking
• *a magnificent achievement*
► brilliant, superb, marvellous

magnify VERB • *to magnify an
image* ► enlarge, maximize,
amplify, expand

maim VERB to injure or disable

main ADJECTIVE largest or most important

main NOUN the main pipe or cable in a public system carrying water, gas, or electricity

mainland NOUN the main part of a country or continent

mainly ADVERB 1 chiefly 2 almost completely 3 usually

mainstay NOUN the chief support or main part

maintain VERB 1 to cause to continue or exist 2 to keep in good condition 3 to provide money for 4 to state that something is true

maintenance NOUN 1 the process of keeping something in good condition 2 money for food and clothing

maize NOUN a tall kind of corn with large seeds on cobs

majestic ADJECTIVE 1 stately and dignified 2 imposing
▶ **majestically** ADVERB

majesty NOUN **majesties** 1 the title of a king or queen 2 the state of being majestic

major ADJECTIVE 1 very important 2 of the musical scale with a semitone after the 3rd and 7th notes

major NOUN an army officer ranking next above a captain

majority NOUN **majorities** 1 the greatest part of a group of people or things 2 the amount by which the winner in an election beats the loser 3 the age at which a person legally becomes an adult

make VERB **made** 1 to bring into existence by putting things together 2 to cause or compel 3 to gain or earn 4 to achieve or reach 5 to reckon *What do you make the time?* 6 to result in or add up to *4 and 6 make 10.* 7 to perform an action etc. *to make an effort* 8 to arrange a bed for use **make out** to manage to see, hear, or

THESAURUS

maim VERB • *people maimed in the attack* ▶ injure, disable, mutilate, wound

main ADJECTIVE • *the main issues* ▶ chief, principal, most important, foremost, fundamental, crucial

mainly ADVERB • *The staff are mainly trainees.* ▶ chiefly, mostly, primarily, principally, especially

maintain VERB • *to maintain the private road* ▶ keep up, service, look after, take care of • *to maintain our links* ▶ continue, keep up, sustain, retain, preserve • *They maintain that they were*

never there. ▶ claim, assert, affirm, insist

majestic ADJECTIVE • *a majestic range of mountains* ▶ magnificent, grand, spectacular, splendid, impressive

major ADJECTIVE • *a major achievement* ▶ important, considerable, significant

make VERB • *to make furniture* ▶ build, construct, assemble, put together, manufacture, produce • *She made me tell her.* ▶ force, coerce, oblige, compel • *to make a noise* ▶ cause, create, generate • *The town made him their mayor.*

a
b
c
d
e
f
g
h
i
j
k
m
n
o
p
q
r
s
t
u
v
w
x
y
z

understand something **make up 1** to invent a story or excuse **2** to be friendly again ► **maker** NOUN

make NOUN a brand of goods

make-believe NOUN pretending or in fantasy

makeshift ADJECTIVE used when there is nothing better

make-up NOUN **1** cosmetics **2** the way something is made up

malady NOUN maladies an illness or disease

malaria NOUN a feverish disease spread by mosquitoes ► **malarial** ADJECTIVE

male ADJECTIVE belonging to the sex that reproduces by fertilizing egg cells produced by the female

male NOUN a male person, animal, or plant

malevolent (ma-lev-ol-ent) ADJECTIVE wishing to harm people ► **malevolence** NOUN

malfunction NOUN a fault or failure in a machine

malfunction VERB to fail to work properly

malice NOUN a desire to harm other people

malicious ADJECTIVE wishing to do harm

malign (mal-yn) ADJECTIVE **1** harmful **2** showing malice

malign VERB to say unpleasant and untrue things about someone ► **malinger** NOUN

malignant ADJECTIVE **1** (of a tumour) growing uncontrollably **2** full of malice

malinger VERB to pretend to be ill in order to avoid work ► **malingerer** NOUN

mall (mal or mawl) NOUN a shopping area

mallard NOUN a wild duck

malleable ADJECTIVE **1** able to be pressed or hammered into shape **2** easy to influence ► **malleability** NOUN

mallet NOUN a heavy wooden hammer

malnutrition NOUN bad health from lack of good food

malpractice NOUN wrongdoing by a professional person

malt NOUN dried barley used in brewing, making vinegar, etc.

maltreat VERB to treat badly ► **maltreatment** NOUN

mammal NOUN an animal of which the female gives birth to live young

► name, appoint, nominate, elect • to make mistakes ► commit, be responsible for • to make money ► earn, bring in • to make the lunch ► prepare, get ready, cook • to make a decision ► reach, come to, arrive at **make up** • to make up a story ► invent, fabricate, concoct, think up

make-believe NOUN • The garden was only make-believe. ► fantasy, pretence, fiction

malevolent ADJECTIVE • the malevolent gaze of his eyes ► malicious, hostile, spiteful

malice NOUN • actions prompted by malice ► spite, malevolence

a
b
c
d
e
f
g
h
i
j
k
l
m
n
o
p
q
r
s
t
u
v
w
x
y
z

mammoth NOUN an extinct elephant with curved tusks

mammoth ADJECTIVE huge

man NOUN **men** 1 a grown-up male human being 2 an individual person 3 human beings in general 4 a piece used in board games

man VERB **manning, manned** to supply with people to work something

manacle NOUN a fetter or handcuff

manacle VERB to fasten with manacles

manage VERB 1 to be in charge of a business or a group of people 2 to cope with something difficult
► **manageable** ADJECTIVE

management NOUN 1 the process of managing 2 people in charge

manager NOUN a person who manages something
► **managerial** (man-a-jeer-ee-al) ADJECTIVE

mandarin NOUN 1 an important official 2 a kind of small orange

mandate NOUN authority given to someone to carry out a certain task or policy

mandatory ADJECTIVE obligatory or compulsory

mandible NOUN the lower jaw

mandolin NOUN a musical instrument like a lute with a rounded back

mane NOUN the long hair on a horse's or lion's neck

manganese NOUN a hard brittle metal

mange NOUN a skin disease of dogs, cats, etc.

manger NOUN a trough in a stable for animals to feed from

mangle VERB to damage by crushing or cutting roughly

mango NOUN **mangoes** a tropical fruit with yellow pulp

mangy ADJECTIVE **mangier, mangiest** 1 scruffy or dirty 2 suffering from mange

manhandle VERB to treat or push roughly

manhole NOUN an opening large enough to let a person through

manhood NOUN the condition of being a man

mania NOUN 1 violent madness 2 great enthusiasm *a mania for sport*

maniac NOUN a person with mania

manic ADJECTIVE suffering from mania

manicure NOUN care and treatment of the hands and nails
► **manicurist** NOUN

a
b
c
d
e
f
g
h
i
j
k
l
m
n
o
p
q
r
s
t
u
v
w
x
y
z

THESAURUS

manage VERB • *to manage a team*
► be in charge of, run, organize, lead, supervise, control • *I don't know how we'll manage.* ► cope, survive, get along, make do • *a horse that's difficult to manage*
► control, handle, master, deal with

manager NOUN • *the manager of the department* ► director, head, executive, supervisor, boss

manifest ADJECTIVE clear and obvious ▶ **manifestly** ADVERB

manifest VERB to show a thing clearly ▶ **manifestation** NOUN

manifesto NOUN **manifestos** a public statement of policies

manifold ADJECTIVE of many kinds

manipulate VERB **1** to handle or arrange skilfully **2** to get someone to do what you want ▶ **manipulation** NOUN

mankind NOUN human beings in general

manly ADJECTIVE **manlier, manliest 1** suitable for a man **2** brave and strong ▶ **manliness** NOUN

manner NOUN **1** the way something happens or is done **2** a person's way of behaving **3** sort *all manner of things*

mannerism NOUN a person's particular gesture or way of speaking

manners PLURAL NOUN how a person behaves with other people

mannish ADJECTIVE (of a woman) like a man

manoeuvre (man-oo-ver) NOUN a difficult or skilful or cunning action

manoeuvre VERB to move carefully and skilfully ▶ **manoeuvrable** ADJECTIVE

manor NOUN a large country house and its land

manpower NOUN the number of people available for work

manse NOUN a church minister's house, especially in Scotland

mansion NOUN a large stately house

manslaughter NOUN the unlawful but unintentional killing of a person

mantle NOUN **1** a cloak **2** a covering *a mantle of snow*

mantra NOUN a word or phrase that is constantly repeated in meditation

manual ADJECTIVE worked by or done with the hands ▶ **manually** ADVERB

mankind NOUN • *to save nature from mankind* ▶ humankind, the human race, humanity, man

manly ADJECTIVE • *a manly physique* ▶ masculine, virile, muscular, well-built • *manly deeds* ▶ brave, courageous, heroic

manner NOUN • *a very efficient manner* ▶ way, fashion, style, method • *his unfriendly manner* ▶ attitude, demeanour, air, behaviour • *all manner of things* ▶ kind, sort, type **manners**

• *needs to learn some manners* ▶ politeness, civility, courtesy, etiquette, good behaviour

manoeuvre NOUN • *a skilful manoeuvre* ▶ movement, move, action, operation • *a diplomatic manoeuvre* ▶ stratagem, strategy, tactic • *military manoeuvres* ▶ exercise, operation

manoeuvre VERB • *He manoeuvred the trunk down the stairs.* ▶ move, guide, steer

a b c d e f g h i j k l m n o p q r s t u v w x y z

manual NOUN a handbook giving instructions

manufacture VERB to make things in large numbers
▶ **manufacture** NOUN, **manufacturer** NOUN

manure NOUN fertilizer made from animal dung

manuscript NOUN a written or typed document

many ADJECTIVE **more**, **most** great in number

many NOUN a large number of people or things *Many were found.*

map NOUN a diagram of part or all of the earth's surface or of the sky

map VERB **mapping**, **mapped** 1 to make a map of an area 2 to plan

maple NOUN a tree with broad leaves

mar VERB **marring**, **marred** to spoil

marathon NOUN a long-distance running race, especially one covering 26 miles 385 yards (42.195 km)

marauding ADJECTIVE going in search of plunder ▶ **marauder** NOUN

marble NOUN 1 a small glass ball used in games 2 limestone

polished and used in sculpture or building

March NOUN the third month of the year

march VERB to walk with regular steps ▶ **marcher** NOUN

march NOUN 1 a spell of marching 2 music suitable for marching to

mare NOUN a female horse or donkey

margarine NOUN a substance like butter, made from animal or vegetable fats

margin NOUN 1 an edge or border 2 the blank space at the edge of a page 3 the difference between two scores etc.

marginal ADJECTIVE very slight ▶ **marginally** ADVERB

marigold NOUN a yellow or orange garden flower

marijuana (ma-ri-hwah-na) NOUN a drug made from the hemp plant

marine (ma-reen) ADJECTIVE to do with the sea

marine NOUN a member of troops trained to serve at sea and on land

mariner (ma-rin-er) NOUN a sailor

marionette NOUN a puppet worked by strings

marital ADJECTIVE to do with marriage

THESAURUS

many ADJECTIVE • *many reasons* ▶ a lot of, plenty of, numerous, countless, various

march VERB • *Soldiers marched past.* ▶ file, troop, parade, stride

march NOUN • *a three-day march across the mountains*

▶ trek, hike, tramp, slog • *a protest march* ▶ rally, demonstration

margin NOUN • *the margin of the lake* ▶ edge, border, boundary • *by a narrow margin* ▶ difference, gap

maritime ADJECTIVE to do with the sea or ships

mark NOUN 1 a spot or stain etc. on something 2 a number or letter put as a grade on a piece of work 3 a distinguishing feature 4 a sign or symbol *a mark of respect* 5 a target

mark VERB 1 to make a mark on something 2 to give a mark to a piece of work 3 to pay attention to 4 to keep close to an opposing player in football etc. ▶ **marker** NOUN

marked ADJECTIVE distinct; noticeable *a marked improvement* ▶ **markedly** ADVERB

market NOUN 1 a place where items are bought and sold from stalls 2 a demand for a product

market VERB to offer for sale

marksman NOUN **marksmen** an expert in shooting at a target

marmalade NOUN jam made from oranges, lemons, etc.

marmoset NOUN a kind of small monkey

maroon[1] VERB to abandon or isolate in a deserted place

maroon[2] NOUN a dark red colour

marquee (mar-kee) NOUN a large tent used for a party, etc.

marquis NOUN a nobleman ranking above an earl

marriage NOUN 1 the state of being married 2 a wedding

marrow NOUN 1 a long vegetable with a thick green skin 2 the soft substance inside bones

marry VERB **marries, married** 1 to become a person's husband or wife 2 to join two people as husband and wife

marsh NOUN a low-lying area of wet ground ▶ **marshy** ADJECTIVE

marshal NOUN 1 an official who supervises a contest or ceremony etc. 2 an officer of very high rank *a Field Marshal*

marshal VERB **marshalling, marshalled** 1 to arrange neatly 2 to usher or escort

marshmallow NOUN a soft spongy sweet, usually pink or white

mark NOUN • *a dirty mark* ▶ spot, stain, blot, blotch, smudge • *a mark of respect* ▶ sign, token, symbol • *over the million mark* ▶ stage, point, level • *a higher mark* ▶ grade, score

mark VERB • *careful not to mark her white dress* ▶ stain, dirty, blot • *to mark your possessions* ▶ label, tag • *marked a new stage in the war* ▶ represent, signify • *to mark*

the Jubilee ▶ celebrate, commemorate • *Mark my words.* ▶ heed, note, take notice of • *exam papers to mark* ▶ correct, assess, grade

marked ADJECTIVE • *a marked improvement* ▶ distinct, noticeable, clear

maroon VERB • *a group of boys marooned on an island* ▶ strand, cast away, abandon

DICTIONARY

marsupial (mar-**soo**-pee-al) NOUN an animal that carries its young in a pouch on its stomach, e.g. a kangaroo

martial ADJECTIVE to do with war

martin NOUN a bird similar to a swallow

martinet NOUN a very strict person

martyr NOUN a person who is killed or made to suffer because of their beliefs ► **martyrdom** NOUN

martyr VERB to kill or torment someone as a martyr

marvel NOUN a wonderful thing

marvel VERB **marvelling, marvelled** to be filled with wonder

marvellous ADJECTIVE wonderful

marzipan NOUN a soft sweet food made with ground almonds

mascara NOUN a cosmetic for darkening the eyelashes

mascot NOUN a person, animal, or thing that is believed to bring good luck

masculine ADJECTIVE **1** to do with men **2** typical of or suitable for men **3** (in some languages) belonging to the class of words

which includes words referring to men ► **masculinity** NOUN

mash VERB to crush into a soft mass

mash NOUN (informal) mashed potato

mask NOUN a covering disguising or protecting the face

mask VERB **1** to cover with a mask **2** to disguise or conceal

masochist (**mas**-ok-ist) NOUN a person who gets pleasure from pain or humiliation ► **masochism** NOUN

mason NOUN a person who builds or works with stone

masonry NOUN **1** the stone parts of a building; stonework **2** a mason's work

masquerade NOUN a pretence

masquerade VERB to pretend to be something *masqueraded as a police officer*

Mass NOUN the Communion service in the Roman Catholic Church

mass NOUN **1** a large amount **2** a heap or other collection of matter **3** (Science) the quantity of physical matter that a thing contains

THESAURUS

marvel VERB **marvel at**
• *marvelled at their courage*
► admire, be amazed by, wonder at, be astonished by, be awed by, be surprised by

marvellous ADJECTIVE
• *a marvellous achievement*
► remarkable, amazing, extraordinary, wonderful

• *a marvellous time* ► excellent, wonderful, fantastic, lovely

mash VERB • *to mash potatoes*
► crush, pulp, cream, purée, smash, squash, grind

mask VERB • *Trees masked the view.* ► conceal, cover, obscure, hide

a
b
c
d
e
f
g
h
i
j
k
l
m
n
o
p
q
r
s
t
u
v
w
x
y
z

DICTIONARY

mass ADJECTIVE involving a large number of people *mass murder*

mass VERB to collect into a mass

massacre NOUN the killing of a large number of people

massacre VERB to kill a large number of people

massage (mas-ahzh) VERB to rub and press the body to make it less stiff or less painful ► **massage** NOUN

massive ADJECTIVE large and heavy

mast NOUN a tall pole holding up a ship's sails or a flag or aerial

master NOUN 1 a man in charge of something 2 a great artist, composer, etc.

master VERB 1 to learn a subject or a skill thoroughly 2 to bring under control

masterful ADJECTIVE
1 domineering 2 very skilful

masterly ADJECTIVE very skilful

mastermind NOUN 1 a very clever person 2 the person who plans and organizes a scheme or crime

mastermind VERB to plan and organize a scheme or crime

masterpiece NOUN a very fine piece of work

mastery NOUN full control or knowledge

mastiff NOUN a large kind of dog

masturbate VERB to get sexual pleasure by rubbing the genitals ► **masturbation** NOUN

mat NOUN 1 a small carpet 2 a small piece of material put on a table to protect the surface

matador NOUN a bullfighter who fights on foot

match¹ NOUN a small thin stick with a head that gives a flame when rubbed

match² NOUN 1 a game or contest between two teams or players 2 one person or thing that matches another 3 a marriage

match VERB 1 to be equal or similar to 2 to put teams or players to compete against each other 3 to find something similar or corresponding

THESAURUS

mass NOUN • *a mass of wet leaves* ► pile, heap, collection

mass ADJECTIVE • *a mass protest* ► large-scale, universal, widespread, popular

massive ADJECTIVE • *a massive building* ► huge, enormous, gigantic, immense, vast

master NOUN • *master of the country* ► ruler, chief, head, lord, governor • *a dog's master* ► owner, keeper • *a master of*

disguises ► expert (at), genius, virtuoso

master VERB • *to master his feelings* ► control, restrain, conquer • *to master a language* ► learn, grasp

match NOUN • *a cricket match* ► game, contest, competition, fixture, tournament

match VERB • *The hat matches her dress.* ► go with, suit, blend with, complement

a b c d e f g h i j k l m n o p q r s t u v w x y z

matchbox NOUN a box containing matches

matchstick NOUN the stem of a match

mate NOUN **1** (informal) a companion or friend **2** each of a mated pair of birds or animals **3** an officer on a merchant ship

mate VERB **1** to come or bring two together to breed **2** to put things together as a pair

material NOUN **1** anything used for making something else **2** cloth or fabric

material ADJECTIVE **1** to do with possessions, money, etc. **2** important *a material difference*

materialism NOUN the belief that possessions are important ► **materialistic** ADJECTIVE

materialize VERB **1** to appear or become visible **2** to happen

⚠ **SPELLING**

This word can also be spelled *materialise*.

maternal ADJECTIVE **1** to do with a mother **2** motherly ► **maternally** ADVERB

maternity NOUN motherhood

matey ADJECTIVE (informal) friendly and sociable

mathematician NOUN an expert in mathematics

mathematics NOUN the study of numbers, measurements, and shapes ► **mathematical** ADJECTIVE

maths NOUN mathematics

matinée NOUN an afternoon performance at a theatre or cinema

matins NOUN a morning church service

matriarch (may-tree-ark) NOUN a woman who is head of a family or tribe ► **matriarchal** ADJECTIVE, **matriarchy** NOUN

matrimony NOUN marriage ► **matrimonial** ADJECTIVE

matrix (may-triks) NOUN **matrices** **1** (Maths) a set of quantities arranged in rows and columns **2** a mould or framework

matron NOUN **1** a mature married woman **2** a woman in charge of nursing in a school, hospital, etc. ► **matronly** ADJECTIVE

matt ADJECTIVE having a dull surface

matted ADJECTIVE tangled into a mass

matter NOUN **1** something you can touch or see **2** a substance **3** things of a certain kind *printed matter* **4** something to be thought about or done *a serious matter* **5** a quantity *in a matter of minutes*

matter VERB to be important

THESAURUS

material NOUN • *material for making curtains* ► fabric, cloth, textile • *organic material* ► matter, substance, stuff • *collecting material for an article* ► data, information, facts, statistics, evidence

matter NOUN • *vegetable matter* ► material, substance, stuff • *a serious matter* ► affair, business, subject, issue

matter VERB • *It doesn't matter.* ► make a difference, be important, count

a
b
c
d
e
f
g
h
i
j
k
l
m
n
o
p
q
r
s
t
u
v
w
x
y
z

a
b
c
d
e
f
g
h
i
j
k
l
m
n
o
p
q
r
s
t
u
v
w
x
y
z

matter-of-fact ADJECTIVE keeping to facts; not imaginative or emotional

matting NOUN rough material for covering floors

mattress NOUN a thick layer of soft material in a covering, used on a bed

mature ADJECTIVE **1** fully grown or developed **2** grown-up
▶ **maturity** NOUN

mature VERB to make or become mature

maudlin ADJECTIVE feebly sentimental

maul VERB to injure by handling or clawing

mausoleum (maw-sol-ee-um) NOUN a magnificent tomb

mauve (mohv) ADJECTIVE a pale purple colour

maverick NOUN an independent or eccentric person

maxim NOUN a short saying giving a general truth

maximize VERB to make as great or large as possible

⚠ **SPELLING**

This word can also be spelled *maximise*.

maximum NOUN **maxima** or **maximums** the greatest possible number or amount

maximum ADJECTIVE greatest or most

May NOUN the fifth month of the year

may AUXILIARY VERB **may**, **might** **1** used to express permission *You may go now.* **2** used to express possibility *It may be true.* **3** used to express wish *Long may it last.* **4** used to express uncertainty *whoever it may be.*

maybe ADVERB perhaps; possibly

mayday NOUN an international radio signal calling for help

mayfly NOUN **mayflies** an insect that lives for a short time in spring

mayhem NOUN violent confusion or damage

mayonnaise NOUN a savoury sauce used with salads

mayor NOUN the person in charge of the council in a town or city

mayoress NOUN the wife of a mayor

maypole NOUN a decorated pole round which people dance on 1 May

maze NOUN a complicated network of paths designed as a puzzle

Mb ABBREVIATION megabyte(s)

me PRONOUN the form of **I** used as the object of a verb or after a preposition

mead NOUN an alcoholic drink made from honey and water

THESAURUS

mature ADJECTIVE • *a mature woman* ▶ adult, grown-up, fully-grown • *The children were mature for their age.*
▶ responsible, sensible, reliable, dependable

maximum NOUN • *Production reached its maximum.* ▶ limit, peak, ceiling, highest point

maximum ADJECTIVE • *a maximum speed of 80 kph* ▶ greatest, highest, top, most

meadow NOUN a field of grass

meagre ADJECTIVE barely enough *a meagre diet*

meal¹ NOUN food served and eaten at one sitting

meal² NOUN coarsely-ground grain ▸ **mealy** ADJECTIVE

mean¹ VERB **meant** (ment) **1** to have as an equivalent or explanation **2** to intend **3** to indicate or have as a result

mean² ADJECTIVE **meaner, meanest 1** not generous; miserly **2** unkind or spiteful **3** poor in quality or appearance ▸ **meanness** NOUN

mean³ NOUN a point or number midway between two extremes

mean ADJECTIVE midway between two points

meander (mee-an-der) VERB to take a winding course

meaning NOUN what something means ▸ **meaningful** ADJECTIVE, **meaningless** ADJECTIVE

means NOUN a way of achieving something **by all means** certainly

means PLURAL NOUN money or other wealth

meantime NOUN **in the meantime** meanwhile

meanwhile ADVERB in the time between two events

measles NOUN an infectious disease with red spots

measly ADJECTIVE (*informal*) not adequate or generous

measure VERB **1** to find the size, amount, or extent of **2** to be a certain size ▸ **measurable** ADJECTIVE

measure NOUN **1** a unit used for measuring **2** a device used in measuring **3** the size or quantity of something **4** something done for a particular purpose *measures to stop vandalism*

THESAURUS

meagre ADJECTIVE • *meagre earnings* ▸ inadequate, paltry, scanty

mean ADJECTIVE • *too mean to leave a tip* ▸ stingy, miserly, parsimonious • *mean of them to leave* ▸ unkind, nasty, cruel, spiteful

mean VERB • *The sign means stop.* ▸ indicate, signify, show • *What do you think they mean?* ▸ suggest, intend, imply • *I mean to find him.* ▸ intend, plan, aim

meaning NOUN • *the meaning of the word* ▸ sense, definition, explanation, significance • *Life has*

little meaning for them. ▸ value, worth, significance

means NOUN • *modern means of communication* ▸ method, mode, way • *the means for such a lifestyle* ▸ resources, funds, money, finance • *a person of means* ▸ wealth, riches, substance, property

measure VERB • *to measure the effects of the disaster* ▸ evaluate, assess, gauge, determine

measure NOUN • *special measures to monitor noise* ▸ step, action, procedure, operation • *a measure of success* ▸ gauge, standard, touchstone

a
b
c
d
e
f
g
h
i
j
k
l
m
n
o
p
q
r
s
t
u
v
w
x
y
z

measurement NOUN **1** the process of measuring something **2** a size or amount found by measuring

meat NOUN animal flesh used as food ▸ **meaty** ADJECTIVE

mechanic NOUN a person who maintains or repairs machinery

mechanical ADJECTIVE **1** to do with machines **2** done or doing things without thought
▸ **mechanically** ADVERB

mechanics NOUN **1** the study of movement and force **2** the study or use of machines

mechanism NOUN **1** the moving parts of a machine **2** a process

mechanized ADJECTIVE equipped with machines ▸ **mechanization** NOUN

⚠ **SPELLING**

This word can also be spelled *mechanised*.

medal NOUN a metal disc, star, or cross given for bravery or an achievement

medallion NOUN a large medal worn as an ornament

medallist NOUN a winner of a medal

meddle VERB to interfere or tinker ▸ **meddler** NOUN

meddlesome ADJECTIVE liking to meddle

media *plural of* **medium** NOUN
the media newspapers, radio, and television

medial ADJECTIVE **1** in the middle **2** average

median ADJECTIVE in the middle

median NOUN **1** a median point or line **2** (*Maths*) the middle number in a set of numbers **3** a straight line passing from a point of a triangle to the centre of the opposite side

mediate VERB to negotiate between sides in a dispute
▸ **mediation** NOUN, **mediator** NOUN

medical ADJECTIVE to do with the treatment of disease ▸ **medically** ADVERB

medicated ADJECTIVE containing a medicine

medication NOUN **1** a medicine **2** treatment using medicine

medicine NOUN **1** a substance taken to cure a disease **2** the study and treatment of diseases
▸ **medicinal** (med-iss-in-al) ADJECTIVE

medieval ADJECTIVE of Europe from about 1000 to 1453

mediocre ADJECTIVE not very good; ordinary ▸ **mediocrity** NOUN

medal NOUN • *to win a medal*
▸ honour, decoration, award, trophy

meddle VERB • *meddling in our affairs* ▸ interfere, pry, snoop

medicine NOUN • *modern medicine* ▸ medical science,

healing, surgery • *a dose of medicine* ▸ medication, remedy, drug, prescription

mediocre ADJECTIVE • *a mediocre result* ▸ ordinary, indifferent, average, unexceptional

DICTIONARY

meditate VERB to think deeply and quietly ► **meditation** NOUN

medium ADJECTIVE neither large nor small; moderate

medium NOUN **mediums** or **media** **1** a thing in which something exists or moves **2** a person who claims to communicate with the dead

medium wave NOUN a radio wave of a frequency between 300 kilohertz and 3 megahertz

medley NOUN **medleys 1** an assortment **2** a collection of tunes

meek ADJECTIVE **meeker**, **meekest** quiet and obedient ► **meekly** ADVERB

meet VERB **met 1** to come together or into contact **2** to go to receive an arrival **3** to pay a bill or

cost **4** to satisfy or fulfil *to meet your needs*

meet NOUN a gathering of riders and hounds for a hunt

meeting NOUN **1** the act of coming together **2** a number of people who have come together

megabyte NOUN (ICT) a unit of information roughly equal to one million bytes

megaphone NOUN a funnel-shaped device for amplifying the voice

melancholy ADJECTIVE sad; gloomy

melancholy NOUN sadness or depression

melee (mel-ay) NOUN **1** a confused fight **2** a muddle

THESAURUS

medium ADJECTIVE • *of medium height* ► average, middling, normal, standard

medium NOUN • *a powerful medium of communication* ► method, means, way, vehicle • *a happy medium* ► average, midpoint, middle way, compromise

meek ADJECTIVE • *a meek response* ► gentle, mild, docile, unassuming

meet VERB • *She met an old friend.* ► encounter, come across, bump into, chance on • *I'll meet you at the airport.* ► collect • *to meet a challenge* ► face, encounter, experience • *to meet requirements* ► satisfy, fulfil • *to meet once a month* ► gather, assemble, come

together, convene • *where the two roads meet* ► join, converge, merge, intersect

meeting NOUN • *in time for the meeting* ► gathering, assembly, conference • *their very first meeting* ► encounter, contact, get-together • *the meeting of three rivers* ► convergence, junction, confluence

melancholy ADJECTIVE • *melancholy music* ► sad, sorrowful, mournful • *a melancholy mood* ► sad, unhappy, despondent, gloomy, depressed

melancholy NOUN • *a feeling of melancholy* ► sadness, sorrow, dejection, depression

a
b
c
d
e
f
g
h
i
j
k
l
m
n
o
p
q
r
s
t
u
v
w
x
y
z

453

a
b
c
d
e
f
g
h
i
j
k
l
m
n
o
p
q
r
s
t
u
v
w
x
y
z

mellow ADJECTIVE **mellower, mellowest 1** soft and rich in flavour, colour, or sound **2** more kindly with age

mellow VERB to make or become mellow

melodic ADJECTIVE to do with melody

melodious ADJECTIVE pleasant to listen to

melodrama NOUN a play full of excitement and exaggerated emotion ▶ **melodramatic** ADJECTIVE

melody NOUN **melodies** a pleasing tune

melon NOUN a large sweet fruit with a yellow or green skin

melt VERB **1** to make or become liquid by heating **2** to disappear slowly

member NOUN a person belonging to a particular society or group ▶ **membership** NOUN

membrane NOUN a thin skin or similar covering

memento NOUN **mementoes** a souvenir

memo (mem-oh) NOUN **memos** a note from one person to another in an office

memoir (mem-wahr) NOUN a biography written by someone who knew the person

memoirs (mem-wahrz) PLURAL NOUN an account of a person's life written by that person

memorable ADJECTIVE **1** worth remembering **2** easy to remember ▶ **memorably** ADVERB

memorandum NOUN **memoranda** or **memorandums** a note to remind yourself of something

memorial NOUN something to remind people of a person or event ▶ **memorial** ADJECTIVE

memorize VERB to get into your memory

⚠ **SPELLING**

This word can also be spelled *memorise*.

memory NOUN **memories 1** the ability to remember **2** something you remember **3** (ICT) the part of a computer where information is stored

menace NOUN **1** a threat or danger **2** a troublesome person or thing

menace VERB to threaten with harm or danger

menagerie NOUN a small zoo

THESAURUS

mellow ADJECTIVE • *a mellow voice*
▶ smooth, melodious, sweet • *a mellow temperament*
▶ easy-going, tolerant, good-natured, affable

melt VERB • *The ice was melting.*
▶ thaw, unfreeze, defrost

memorial NOUN • *a memorial to victims of the war* ▶ monument, remembrance, shrine, plaque

menace NOUN • *a menace to society* ▶ danger, threat, risk
• *That child is a menace.*
▶ nuisance, pest

mend VERB **1** to repair **2** to make or become better ► **mender** NOUN

menial (meen-ee-al) ADJECTIVE needing little or no skill or thought ► **menially** ADVERB

menial NOUN a person who does menial work

meningitis NOUN a disease causing inflammation of the membranes (*meninges*) round the brain and spinal cord

menopause NOUN the time of life when a woman stops menstruating

menstruate VERB to bleed from the womb about once a month ► **menstruation** NOUN, **menstrual** ADJECTIVE

mental ADJECTIVE to do with the mind ► **mentally** ADVERB

mentality NOUN **mentalities** a person's mental ability or attitude

menthol NOUN a solid white peppermint-flavoured substance

mention VERB to speak or write about briefly ► **mention** NOUN

mentor NOUN an experienced and trusted adviser

menu NOUN **menus 1** a list of food available **2** (*ICT*) a list of options shown on a computer screen

mercantile ADJECTIVE to do with trade or trading

mercenary ADJECTIVE working only for money or some other reward

mercenary NOUN **mercenaries** a soldier hired to serve in a foreign army

merchandise NOUN goods for sale

merchant NOUN a person involved in trade

merchant navy NOUN the ships and sailors that carry goods for trade

merciful ADJECTIVE showing mercy ► **mercifully** ADVERB

merciless ADJECTIVE showing no mercy; cruel ► **mercilessly** ADVERB

mercury NOUN a heavy silvery liquid metal used in thermometers

mercy NOUN **mercies 1** kindness or pity shown to a wrongdoer or enemy etc. **2** something to be thankful for

mere ADJECTIVE not more than *a mere child*

THESAURUS

mend VERB • *to mend faulty wiring* ► repair, fix, renovate • *socks to mend* ► patch, repair, darn • *a quarrel that a few kind words can mend* ► put right, resolve

mention VERB • *mentioned that he would be here* ► state, say, remark, observe • *Better not to*

mention the score. ► refer to, allude to, touch on, talk about

merciful ADJECTIVE • *a merciful God* ► compassionate, forgiving

merciless ADJECTIVE • *a merciless leader* ► cruel, pitiless, ruthless

mercy NOUN • *to beg for mercy* ► clemency, compassion, leniency, forgiveness

DICTIONARY

merely ADVERB only; simply

merge VERB to combine or blend

merger NOUN the combining of two business companies

meridian NOUN a line on a map or globe from the North Pole to the South Pole

meringue (mer-ang) NOUN a crisp cake made from egg white and sugar

merit NOUN 1 a quality that deserves praise 2 excellence

merit VERB to deserve

meritorious ADJECTIVE deserving praise

mermaid NOUN a mythical sea creature with a woman's body and a fish's tail

merriment NOUN cheerful behaviour

merry ADJECTIVE **merrier**, **merriest** cheerful and lively
▶ **merrily** ADVERB

merry-go-round NOUN a roundabout at a fair

mesh NOUN 1 the open spaces in a net or sieve 2 material made like a net

mesh VERB (of gears) to engage

mesmerize VERB to fascinate or hold a person's attention completely

⚠ **SPELLING**

This word can also be spelled *mesmerise*.

mess NOUN 1 a dirty or untidy state 2 a difficult or confused situation 3 (in the armed forces) a dining room

mess VERB **mess about** to behave stupidly or idly **mess up** to do something badly

message NOUN 1 a piece of information sent from one person to another 2 the main theme of a book, film, etc.

THESAURUS

merge VERB • *to merge the two organizations* ▶ combine, amalgamate, integrate, unite • *The two parties will merge.* ▶ unite, join together, come together, combine • *The motorways merge ahead.* ▶ join, meet, converge

merit NOUN • *writers of merit* ▶ excellence, value, worth, importance

merit VERB • *to merit consideration* ▶ deserve, warrant, be worthy of

merry ADJECTIVE • *a merry ringing of bells* ▶ jolly, cheerful, light-hearted, joyful

mess NOUN • *a mess in the kitchen* ▶ muddle, untidiness, chaos, clutter, confusion, shambles • *to get into a mess* ▶ predicament, quandary, trouble

mess VERB **mess about** or **around** *to stop messing around* ▶ fool about or around, play about or around **mess up** *Try not to mess this up.* ▶ ruin, spoil, botch, bungle

message NOUN • *to send a message* ▶ communication, note, letter, memo

a
b
c
d
e
f
g
h
i
j
k
l
m
n
o
p
q
r
s
t
u
v
w
x
y
z

messenger NOUN a person who carries a message

Messiah (mis-I-a) NOUN **1** a promised saviour **2** Christ

messy ADJECTIVE **messier, messiest** dirty and untidy

metabolism (mit-ab-ol-izm) NOUN the process by which food is built up into living material in a plant or animal ► **metabolic** ADJECTIVE

metal NOUN a chemical substance that conducts heat and electricity and melts when it is heated ► **metallic** ADJECTIVE

metallurgy (mit-al-er-jee) NOUN the study of metals ► **metallurgist** NOUN

metamorphosis (met-a-mor-fo-sis) NOUN **metamorphoses** a complete change by a living thing

metaphor NOUN the use of a word or phrase in a way that is not literal, e.g. *to break your heart* ► **metaphorical** ADJECTIVE

mete VERB **mete out** to deal out something unpleasant

meteor NOUN a piece of rock or metal in space that burns up when it enters the earth's atmosphere

meteoric ADJECTIVE rapid and brilliant *a meteoric career*

meteorite NOUN the remains of a meteor that has landed on the earth

meteorology NOUN the study of the conditions of the climate and weather ► **meteorological** ADJECTIVE, **meteorologist** NOUN

meter NOUN a device for measuring how much of something has been used

meter VERB to measure with a meter

⚠ **USAGE**

Do not confuse this word with **metre**.

methane (mee-thayn) NOUN an inflammable gas produced by decaying matter

method NOUN **1** a way of doing something **2** methodical behaviour

methodical ADJECTIVE doing things in a systematic way ► **methodically** ADVERB

meths NOUN (informal) methylated spirits, a liquid fuel made from alcohol

meticulous ADJECTIVE careful and precise

metre NOUN **1** a unit of length in the metric system, about 39 ½ inches **2** rhythm in poetry

⚠ **USAGE**

Do not confuse this word with **meter**.

metric ADJECTIVE to do with a measuring system based on

THESAURUS

messy ADJECTIVE • *messy work* ► dirty, filthy, grubby, grimy • *a messy room* ► untidy, disorganized, chaotic

method NOUN • *a new method of gathering data* ► way,

manner, technique (for), process, style

methodical ADJECTIVE • *a methodical approach to working* ► organized, systematic, painstaking, logical

decimal units (metre, litre, and gram)

metrical ADJECTIVE in rhythmic metre, not prose

metronome NOUN a device that marks the beat in music

metropolis NOUN the chief city of a country or region
▸ **metropolitan** ADJECTIVE

mettle NOUN courage or strength of character

mew VERB to make a cat's cry
▸ **mew** NOUN

mews NOUN a row of houses in a small street or square, originally stables

miasma (mee-az-ma) NOUN unpleasant or unhealthy air

mica NOUN a mineral used to make electrical insulators

mice plural of **mouse**

microbe NOUN a micro-organism

microchip NOUN a tiny piece of silicon designed to work like an electric circuit

microcosm NOUN a world in miniature; something regarded as resembling something else on a very small scale

microfiche NOUN a piece of film on which pages of information are photographed in reduced size

microfilm NOUN a length of film on which written or printed

material is photographed in reduced size

microorganism NOUN a microscopic creature, e.g. a bacterium or virus

microphone NOUN an electrical device that picks up sound waves for recording, amplifying, or broadcasting

microprocessor NOUN the central processing unit of a computer, consisting of one or more microchips

microscope NOUN an instrument with lenses that magnify tiny objects or details

microscopic ADJECTIVE extremely small

microwave NOUN 1 a very short electromagnetic wave 2 an oven that uses microwaves to heat or cook food

microwave VERB to cook in a microwave oven

mid ADJECTIVE 1 in the middle of mid-July 2 middle in his mid thirties

midday NOUN the middle of the day; noon

middle NOUN the point that is at the same distance from all sides or edges or ends

middle ADJECTIVE 1 placed or happening in the middle 2 moderate in size or rank etc.

middle NOUN • the middle of the room ▸ centre, midpoint • the middle of the earth ▸ centre, core, heart, kernel

middle ADJECTIVE • Remove the middle pin. ▸ central, midway, mean, medial, median, half-way, inner, inside

DICTIONARY

middle-aged ADJECTIVE aged between about 40 and 60 ▶ **middle age** NOUN

middle class or **classes** NOUN the class of people including business and professional people ▶ **middle-class** ADJECTIVE

middling ADJECTIVE of medium size or quality

midge NOUN a small insect like a gnat

midget NOUN an extremely small person or thing ▶ **midget** ADJECTIVE

midland ADJECTIVE **1** to do with the middle part of a country **2** to do with the Midlands

midnight NOUN twelve o'clock at night

midriff NOUN the front part of the body above the waist

midst NOUN the middle

midway ADVERB halfway

midwife NOUN **midwives** a person trained to look after a woman during childbirth

might[1] NOUN great strength or power

might[2] AUXILIARY VERB (the past tense of **may**) used to express possibility *It might be true.*

mighty ADJECTIVE strong or powerful ▶ **mightily** ADVERB

migraine NOUN a severe kind of headache

migrant NOUN a person or animal that migrates or has migrated

migrate VERB to leave one country or place and settle in another ▶ **migration** NOUN

mike NOUN (*informal*) a microphone

mild ADJECTIVE **milder, mildest 1** gentle **2** not strongly flavoured **3** warm and pleasant ▶ **mildly** ADVERB

mildew NOUN a white coating of fungus on damp surfaces ▶ **mildewed** ADJECTIVE

mile NOUN a measure of distance equal to 1,760 yards (about 1.6 kilometres)

mileage NOUN **1** the number of miles travelled **2** benefit or advantage

milestone NOUN an important event

milieu (meel-yer) NOUN **milieus** or **milieux** surroundings

militant ADJECTIVE **1** eager to fight **2** forceful or aggressive ▶ **militancy** NOUN

military ADJECTIVE to do with soldiers or the armed forces

militate VERB to be a strong influence against something

⚠ **USAGE**

Do not confuse this word with *mitigate*.

THESAURUS

might NOUN • *I pulled with all my might.* ▶ strength, force, power, energy

mighty ADJECTIVE • *a mighty blow* ▶ powerful, forceful, violent, hefty

mild ADJECTIVE • *a mild voice* ▶ gentle, soft, calm • *The weather turned mild.* ▶ warm, calm

militant ADJECTIVE • *militant opponents of the regime* ▶ aggressive, assertive, hostile

militia (mil-ish-a) NOUN **militias** a military force of civilians

milk NOUN a white liquid produced by female mammals to feed their young ▶ **milky** ADJECTIVE

milk VERB to take the milk from a cow or other animal

milkshake NOUN a drink made from milk whisked with sweet fruit flavouring

milk tooth NOUN **milk teeth** one of the first set of teeth of a child or animal

mill NOUN **1** a place or machine for grinding corn **2** a grinding machine *a pepper mill* **3** a factory *a paper mill*

mill VERB **1** to grind or crush in a mill **2** to move in a confused crowd ▶ **miller** NOUN

millennium NOUN **millenia** or **millenniums** a period of 1,000 years

millet NOUN a kind of cereal with tiny seeds

milligram NOUN one thousandth of a gram

millilitre NOUN one thousandth of a litre

millimetre NOUN one thousandth of a metre

milliner NOUN a person who makes and sells women's hats ▶ **millinery** NOUN

million NOUN **millions** or **million** one thousand thousand (1,000,000) ▶ **millionth** ADJECTIVE, NOUN

millionaire NOUN a person who has a million pounds or dollars

millipede NOUN an insect with many legs

millstone NOUN a heavy responsibility

mime NOUN acting without words

mime VERB to perform a mime

mimic VERB **mimicking, mimicked** to imitate someone in an imitating or mocking way ▶ **mimicry** NOUN

mimic NOUN a person who mimics others

mimosa NOUN a tree with small yellow flowers

minaret NOUN the tall tower of a mosque

mince VERB to chop into small pieces ▶ **mincer** NOUN

mince NOUN minced meat

mincemeat NOUN a sweet mixture of currants, raisins, apple, etc. used in pies

mince pie NOUN a pie filled with mincemeat

mind NOUN **1** the ability to think, feel, and remember **2** a person's opinion or intention *changed my mind*

THESAURUS

mimic VERB • *She could mimic anyone.* ▶ imitate, impersonate, copy

mimic NOUN • *a clever mimic* ▶ impersonator, imitator

mind NOUN • *They were all people with brilliant minds.* ▶ brain, intellect, intelligence, sense, wits, understanding, head, mentality

DICTIONARY

mind VERB **1** to look after **2** to be careful about **3** to object to
► **minder** NOUN

mindful ADJECTIVE taking thought or care

mindless ADJECTIVE done without thinking

mine ¹ POSSESSIVE PRONOUN belonging to me

mine ² NOUN **1** a place where minerals are dug from the ground **2** an explosive device in the ground or sea

mine VERB **1** to dig from a mine **2** to lay explosive mines in

minefield NOUN **1** an area of explosive mines **2** something with hidden dangers or problems

miner NOUN a person who works in a mine

mineral NOUN **1** a hard inorganic substance found in the ground **2** a cold non-alcoholic drink

mineralogy (min-er-al-o-jee) NOUN the study of minerals
► **mineralogist** NOUN

mineral water NOUN water containing mineral salts or gases

minestrone (mini-stroh-nee) NOUN a soup containing vegetables and pasta

mingle VERB to mix or blend

miniature ADJECTIVE **1** very small **2** on a small scale

minim NOUN a note in music, lasting twice as long as a crotchet (♩)

minimal ADJECTIVE very little; as little as possible

minimize VERB to make as small as possible

> ⚠ **SPELLING**
>
> This word can also be spelled *minimise*.

minimum NOUN **minima** or **minimums** the lowest possible number or amount

minimum ADJECTIVE least or smallest

minion NOUN a humble assistant

THESAURUS

mind VERB • *I'll mind your bags.* ► look after, watch, guard, attend to • *Mind the step.* ► be careful of, pay attention to, watch out for • *Do you mind if I eat my lunch?* ► care, object, be upset, complain

mingle VERB • *to mingle with other people* ► socialize, mix, circulate • *Country smells mingled with the aroma of barbecues.* ► combine, merge, join

miniature ADJECTIVE • *a miniature village* ► tiny, small-scale, diminutive

minimize VERB • *to minimize the risk of fire* ► reduce, keep down, lessen • *should not minimize their importance* ► underestimate, play down

minimum NOUN • *Costs are kept to a minimum.* ► lower limit, base, lowest point

minimum ADJECTIVE • *the minimum wage* ► lowest, least, smallest, bottom

minister NOUN **1** a person in charge of a government department **2** a member of the clergy ▶ **ministerial** ADJECTIVE

minister VERB to attend to people's needs

ministry NOUN **ministries 1** a government department **2** the work of the clergy

mink NOUN **1** an animal like a stoat **2** its brown fur

minnow NOUN a tiny freshwater fish

minor ADJECTIVE **1** of less importance **2** of the musical scale with a semitone after the second note

minor NOUN a person under the age of legal responsibility

minority NOUN **minorities 1** the smallest part of a group **2** a small group that is different

minstrel NOUN a travelling musician in medieval times

mint[1] NOUN **1** a plant with fragrant leaves used as flavouring **2** peppermint or a sweet flavoured with this

mint[2] NOUN the place where coins are made **in mint condition** like new

mint VERB to make coins

minuet NOUN a slow stately dance

minus PREPOSITION with the next number or thing subtracted

minus ADJECTIVE less than zero *minus ten degrees* (-10°)

minuscule ADJECTIVE extremely small

minute[1] (min-it) NOUN **1** one sixtieth of an hour **2** a very short time **3** one sixtieth of a degree (used in measuring angles)

minute[2] (my-newt) ADJECTIVE very small or detailed

minutes PLURAL NOUN a summary of things said at a meeting

minx NOUN a cheeky or mischievous girl

miracle NOUN something wonderful, believed to have a supernatural cause ▶ **miraculous** ADJECTIVE

mirage (mi-rahzh) NOUN something that seems to be there but is not

mire NOUN **1** a swamp **2** deep mud

mirror NOUN a surface of reflecting material

mirror VERB to reflect in or like a mirror

mirth NOUN merriment or laughter ▶ **mirthful** ADJECTIVE

misadventure NOUN a piece of bad luck

minor ADJECTIVE • *minor alterations* ▶ small, trivial, unimportant

minute NOUN • *I'll only be a minute.* ▶ moment, short while, second

minute ADJECTIVE • *a minute insect* ▶ tiny, minuscule, diminutive

miracle NOUN • *a miracle of modern technology* ▶ marvel, wonder, phenomenon

miraculous ADJECTIVE • *a miraculous escape* ▶ amazing, astounding, astonishing, extraordinary, incredible

a b c d e f g h i j k l m n o p q r s t u v w x y z

misappropriate VERB to take dishonestly ► **misappropriation** NOUN

misbehave VERB to behave badly ► **misbehaviour** NOUN

miscalculate VERB to calculate incorrectly ► **miscalculation** NOUN

miscarriage NOUN **1** the birth of a baby before it has developed **2** a failure of justice

miscellaneous (mis-el-ay-nee-us) ADJECTIVE of various kinds; mixed

miscellany (mis-el-an-ee) NOUN **miscellanies** a collection or mixture of different things

mischance NOUN misfortune

mischief NOUN **1** naughty or troublesome behaviour **2** trouble caused by this

mischievous ADJECTIVE naughty or troublesome

misconception NOUN a mistaken idea

misconduct NOUN bad behaviour by someone in authority

misdemeanour NOUN a minor offence or crime

miser NOUN a person who hoards money and spends little ► **miserly** ADJECTIVE

miserable ADJECTIVE **1** very unhappy or uncomfortable **2** unpleasant *miserable weather*

misery NOUN **miseries** great unhappiness

misfire VERB to fail to fire or have the right effect

misfit NOUN a person who does not fit in well with other people

misfortune NOUN **1** bad luck **2** an unlucky event or accident

misgiving NOUN a feeling of doubt or slight mistrust

misguided ADJECTIVE guided by mistaken ideas or beliefs

mishap (mis-hap) NOUN an unlucky accident

misjudge VERB to judge wrongly ► **misjudgement** NOUN

mislay VERB **mislaid** to lose for a short time

THESAURUS

misbehave VERB • *They were misbehaving again.* ► behave badly, be naughty, be disobedient

miscellaneous ADJECTIVE • *miscellaneous jobs* ► various, varied, assorted

mischief NOUN • *plotting mischief* ► misbehaviour, naughtiness, disobedience, pranks

mischievous ADJECTIVE • *mischievous children* ► naughty,

badly behaved, disobedient • *a mischievous grin* ► playful, impish

miserable ADJECTIVE • *felt too miserable to eat* ► unhappy, sad, dejected, despondent, depressed • *miserable surroundings* ► dreary, dismal, gloomy

misery NOUN • *her silent misery* ► unhappiness, distress, depression, despair, grief, suffering

a
b
c
d
e
f
g
h
i
j
k
l
m
n
o
p
q
r
s
t
u
v
w
x
y
z

mislead VERB **misled** to give somebody a wrong idea deliberately

misnomer NOUN an unsuitable name for something

misprint NOUN a mistake in printing

misrule NOUN bad government

Miss NOUN a title put before a girl's or unmarried woman's name

miss VERB **1** to fail to hit, reach, catch, see, hear, or find something **2** to feel the loss or absence of **3** to notice that something has gone

miss NOUN a failure to hit something

misshapen ADJECTIVE badly shaped

missile NOUN a weapon or other object fired or thrown at a target

missing ADJECTIVE lost or absent

mission NOUN **1** an important task to be done **2** a military or scientific expedition

missionary NOUN **missionaries** a person sent to another country to spread a religion

misspell VERB **misspelt** or **misspelled** to spell wrongly

mist NOUN **1** damp cloudy air **2** condensed water vapour
► **misty** ADJECTIVE

mist VERB to become covered in mist

mistake NOUN something wrong

mistake VERB **mistook, mistaken 1** to misunderstand **2** to choose or identify wrongly

mistaken ADJECTIVE wrong or incorrect

mister NOUN (informal) a form of address to a man

mistletoe NOUN a plant with white berries

mistreat VERB to treat badly

mistress NOUN **1** a woman in charge of something **2** a man's lover who is not his wife

mistrust VERB to have no trust in
► **mistrust** NOUN

THESAURUS

mishap NOUN • an unfortunate mishap ► accident, misfortune

mislead VERB • Colin had misled her. ► deceive, fool, misinform

miss VERB • to miss a catch ► drop, fumble, let slip • to miss the train ► be too late for, fail to catch • to miss your friends ► pine for, long for • to miss a chance ► let slip, let go, forfeit

missing ADJECTIVE • the missing books ► lost, mislaid, disappeared

mist NOUN • the early morning mist ► fog, haze • the mist on the windows ► condensation, steam

mistake NOUN • to make mistakes ► error, slip, blunder, misjudgement, oversight

mistake VERB • I mistook their meaning. ► misunderstand, misinterpret, confuse, get wrong, misjudge

misty ADJECTIVE • misty weather ► foggy, hazy, cloudy • a misty window ► misted, clouded

misunderstand VERB
misunderstood to get a wrong idea or impression of
▶ **misunderstanding** NOUN

misuse (mis-yooz) VERB **1** to use incorrectly **2** to treat badly
▶ **misuse** (mis-yooss) NOUN

mite NOUN **1** a tiny creature **2** a small child

mitigate VERB to make less severe
▶ **mitigation** NOUN

⚠️ USAGE
Do not confuse this word with *militate*.

mitre NOUN **1** a tall pointed bishop's hat **2** a joint in wood

mitten NOUN a glove with a combined part for the fingers

mix VERB **1** to blend or unite things into one **2** to socialize **mix up** to confuse

mix NOUN a mixture

mixed ADJECTIVE containing two or more kinds

mixture NOUN something made of different things mixed together

mix-up NOUN a state of confusion

mnemonic (nim-on-ik) NOUN words that help you to remember something

moan VERB **1** to make a long low sound of pain **2** to grumble
▶ **moan** NOUN

moat NOUN a deep wide ditch round a castle, filled with water

mob NOUN a large noisy crowd

mob VERB **mobbing, mobbed** to crowd round

mobile ADJECTIVE able to be moved or carried easily ▶ **mobility** NOUN

mobile NOUN **1** a hanging decoration that moves in air currents **2** a mobile phone

mix VERB • *to mix ingredients*
▶ blend, combine, merge, amalgamate • *to mix with people*
▶ associate, socialize, mingle **mix up** • *I've mixed up the two dates.*
▶ confuse, muddle up

mixed ADJECTIVE • *a mixed collection*
▶ assorted, varied, diverse, miscellaneous • *mixed ingredients*
▶ combined, amalgamated • *Their reactions were mixed.*
▶ ambivalent, equivocal, uncertain

mixture NOUN • *a strange mixture of people* ▶ assortment, variety, combination, blend, hotchpotch

moan VERB • *to moan with pain*
▶ groan, cry, howl • *Everyone*

moaned about the food.
▶ complain, grumble

moan NOUN • *moans of pain*
▶ groan, cry, howl • *moans about the awful food* ▶ complain, grumble

mob NOUN • *an angry mob*
▶ crowd, horde, rabble, riot

mob VERB • *Fans mobbed her.*
▶ crowd round, swarm round

mobile ADJECTIVE • *mobile again after his operation* ▶ moving, walking, able to move • *a mobile library* ▶ travelling, itinerant, peripatetic • *mobile in your career*
▶ adaptable, flexible, versatile

mobilize VERB to bring together for war or other activity
► **mobilization** NOUN

⚠️ **SPELLING**

This word can also be spelled *mobilise*.

moccasin NOUN a soft leather shoe

mock VERB to make fun of

mock ADJECTIVE imitation; not real

mockery NOUN **mockeries** ridicule or contempt

mode NOUN **1** the way a thing is done **2** what is fashionable

model NOUN **1** a small-scale copy **2** a particular design **3** a person who poses for an artist or displays clothes **4** a person or thing worth copying

model VERB **modelling**, **modelled** **1** to make a model of **2** to design or plan using another thing as an example **3** to work as a model

modem (moh-dem) NOUN a device linking a computer to a telephone line

moderate (mod-er-at) ADJECTIVE **1** not extremely small or great or hot etc. **2** not extreme *moderate opinions* ► **moderately** ADVERB

moderate (mod-er-ayt) VERB to make or become moderate
► **moderation** NOUN

modern ADJECTIVE **1** belonging to recent times **2** fashionable
► **modernity** NOUN

modernize VERB to make more modern

⚠️ **SPELLING**

This word can also be spelled *modernise*.

modest ADJECTIVE **1** not vain or boastful **2** moderate in size or appearance ► **modesty** NOUN

modicum NOUN a small amount

mock VERB • *He mocked her behind her back.* ► ridicule, jeer at, make fun of, laugh at, tease

mock ADJECTIVE • *mock disbelief* ► pretend, imitation, false, fake

model ADJECTIVE • *a model railway* ► miniature, toy, replica • *a model pupil* ► ideal, perfect, exemplary

model NOUN • *a working model* ► replica, copy, representation • *a model of good behaviour* ► ideal, paragon

moderate ADJECTIVE • *a moderate success* ► average, modest, mediocre, reasonable

modern ADJECTIVE • *modern art* ► contemporary, present-day, current • *modern clothes* ► fashionable, stylish

modernize VERB • *to modernize production methods* ► update, renovate, refurbish, rebuild

modest ADJECTIVE • *a modest increase in income* ► slight, small, moderate, limited • *modest about their achievements* ► unassuming, humble, bashful, coy

a
b
c
d
e
f
g
h
i
j
k
l
m
n
o
p
q
r
s
t
u
v
w
x
y
z

modify VERB **modifies, modified** to change something slightly
▶ **modification** NOUN

module NOUN **1** a self-contained component **2** a unit of study
▶ **modular** ADJECTIVE

mogul (moh-gul) NOUN an influential person

mohair NOUN fine silky wool from an angora goat

moist ADJECTIVE slightly wet

moisten VERB to make slightly wet

moisture NOUN water in tiny drops

molar NOUN a wide tooth at the back of the jaw

molasses NOUN dark syrup from raw sugar

mole¹ NOUN a small furry animal that burrows

mole² NOUN a small dark spot on skin

molecule NOUN the smallest part into which a substance can be divided without changing its chemical nature ▶ **molecular** ADJECTIVE

molest VERB to annoy or pester
▶ **molestation** NOUN

mollify VERB **mollifies, mollified** to make less angry

mollusc NOUN an animal with a soft body, e.g. a snail

molten ADJECTIVE (of metal) made liquid by great heat

moment NOUN **1** a very short time **2** a particular time

momentary ADJECTIVE lasting only a moment ▶ **momentarily** ADVERB

momentous ADJECTIVE very important

momentum NOUN the ability to keep moving or developing

monarch NOUN a king, queen, emperor, or empress

monarchy NOUN **monarchies** a place or government with a monarch

monastery NOUN **monasteries** a place where monks live
▶ **monastic** ADJECTIVE

Monday NOUN the day of the week following Sunday

money NOUN coins and banknotes
▶ **monetary** ADJECTIVE

mongoose NOUN **mongooses** a small tropical animal

mongrel (mung-rel) NOUN a dog of mixed breeds

monitor NOUN **1** a device for watching or testing **2** a screen that displays computer data **3** a school pupil with special responsibility

THESAURUS

modify VERB • *to modify your views*
▶ change, alter, amend, adapt

moist ADJECTIVE • *the moist earth*
▶ damp, soggy, wet

moment NOUN • *She waited for a moment.* ▶ minute, second, little

while, short time • *the moment the rain stops* ▶ instant, minute

momentous ADJECTIVE • *a momentous decision*
▶ important, significant, historic, crucial

a
b
c
d
e
f
g
h
i
j
k
l
m
n
o
p
q
r
s
t
u
v
w
x
y
z

monitor VERB to watch or test work being done or the person doing it

monk NOUN one of a community of religious men living according to rules

monkey NOUN **monkeys 1** an animal with long arms, hands with thumbs, and often a tail **2** a mischievous child

monochrome ADJECTIVE in one colour

monocle NOUN a lens for one eye

monogamy NOUN marriage to only one person at a time

monogram NOUN a design made of letters

monolithic ADJECTIVE (of an organization) huge and difficult to change

monologue NOUN a speech by one person

monopolize VERB to take or dominate the whole of

⚠ **SPELLING**

This word can also be spelled *monopolise*.

monopoly NOUN **monopolies 1** the exclusive right to sell something **2** complete possession or use of something by one group

monotonous ADJECTIVE dull because it does not change

monotony NOUN lack of change or variety

monsoon NOUN a strong wind with rain in the Indian Ocean

monster NOUN **1** a large frightening creature **2** a cruel person

monster ADJECTIVE (informal) huge

monstrosity NOUN **monstrosities** a monstrous thing

monstrous ADJECTIVE **1** like a monster; huge and ugly **2** shocking or outrageous

month NOUN each of the twelve parts into which a year is divided

📖 **WORD HISTORY**

from an Old English word meaning 'moon' (because time was measured by the phases of the moon)

monthly ADJECTIVE, ADVERB happening or done once a month

monument NOUN a statue or building put up as a memorial
▶ **monumental** ADJECTIVE

moo VERB **moos, mooing, mooed** to make the low deep sound of a cow ▶ **moo** NOUN

THESAURUS

monotonous ADJECTIVE • *a monotonous job* ▶ boring, tedious, dull, dreary

monster NOUN • *a monster of a man* ▶ giant, colossus • *behaving like a monster* ▶ beast, brute, savage

monstrous ADJECTIVE • *a monstrous wave* ▶ huge, enormous, massive, colossal, gigantic • *a monstrous winged creature* ▶ grotesque, hideous, horrible, repulsive • *a monstrous injustice* ▶ appalling, dreadful, shocking, abominable

DICTIONARY

mood NOUN the way someone feels

moody ADJECTIVE **moodier, moodiest** gloomy or sullen
▶ **moodily** ADVERB

moon NOUN **1** the natural satellite of the earth seen at night **2** a satellite of any planet

moon VERB to go about in a dreamy way

moonlight NOUN light from the moon ▶ **moonlit** ADJECTIVE

moor¹ NOUN an area of rough land

moor² VERB to fasten a boat

moorhen NOUN a small waterbird

mooring NOUN a place where a boat can be moored

moose NOUN a North American elk

moot ADJECTIVE open to debate

mop NOUN **1** a soft pad on a stick, used for cleaning floors etc. **2** a thick mass of hair

mop VERB **mopping, mopped** to clean or wipe with a mop etc.

mope VERB to be sad and gloomy

moped (moh-ped) NOUN a small motorcycle with pedals

moral ADJECTIVE **1** to do with right and wrong **2** virtuous

moral NOUN a lesson in right behaviour taught by a story or event

morale (mor-ahl) NOUN the level of confidence of people

morality NOUN standards of behaviour

moralize VERB to speak about right and wrong behaviour

⚠ **SPELLING**

This word can also be spelled *moralise*.

morals PLURAL NOUN standards of behaviour

morass (mo-rass) NOUN **1** a marsh or bog **2** a confused mass

moratorium NOUN **moratoriums** a temporary ban

morbid ADJECTIVE thinking about gloomy things

more ADJECTIVE (comparative of **much** and **many**) greater in amount or degree

more NOUN a greater amount

more ADVERB **1** to a greater extent *more beautiful* **2** again *once more*

THESAURUS

mood NOUN • *in a bad mood*
▶ temper, humour, disposition, frame of mind • *to be in the right mood* ▶ atmosphere, feeling, tone, ambience

moody ADJECTIVE • *quiet and moody*
▶ sulky, sullen, gloomy, changeable, temperamental

mope VERB • *It was no use moping.*
▶ brood, fret, sulk

moral I ADJECTIVE • *moral issues*
▶ ethical, social • *a very moral*

person ▶ good, honest, virtuous, honourable, decent

moral NOUN • *a moral to the story*
▶ lesson, message, meaning, point

morbid ADJECTIVE • *a morbid story*
▶ macabre, gruesome, grisly • *a morbid outlook* ▶ gloomy, depressed, melancholy

more ADJECTIVE • *more money*
▶ additional, extra, added, increased, supplementary

a
b
c
d
e
f
g
h
i
j
k
l
m
n
o
p
q
r
s
t
u
v
w
x
y
z

a
b
c
d
e
f
g
h
i
j
k
l
m
n
o
p
q
r
s
t
u
v
w
x
y
z

moreover ADVERB besides; in addition

morning NOUN the early part of the day before noon

moron NOUN (informal) a stupid person ▶ **moronic** ADJECTIVE

morose ADJECTIVE bad-tempered

morphine NOUN a drug made from opium, used to lessen pain

Morse code NOUN a signalling code using short and long sounds or flashes of light (dots and dashes) to represent letters

morsel NOUN a small piece of food

mortal ADJECTIVE 1 not living for ever 2 causing death ▶ **mortally** ADVERB

mortal NOUN a human being

mortality NOUN 1 the state of being mortal 2 the number of people who die over a period

mortar NOUN 1 a mixture of sand, cement, and water used in fixing bricks etc. 2 a hard bowl for pounding substances with a pestle 3 a short cannon for firing shells at a high angle

mortarboard NOUN an academic cap with a stiff square top

mortgage (mor-gij) NOUN a loan to buy a house, with the house as security

mortgage VERB to offer as security

mortify VERB **mortifies**, **mortified** to humiliate

mortuary NOUN **mortuaries** a place where dead bodies are kept before being buried or cremated

mosaic (mo-zay-ik) NOUN a picture or design made from small coloured pieces of stone or glass

mosque (mosk) NOUN a Muslim place of worship

mosquito NOUN **mosquitoes** a kind of gnat that sucks blood

moss NOUN a plant growing in clumps in damp places ▶ **mossy** ADJECTIVE

most ADJECTIVE (superlative of **much** and **many**) greatest in amount or degree

most NOUN the greatest amount

most ADVERB 1 to the greatest extent 2 very or extremely

mostly ADVERB mainly

motel NOUN a roadside hotel for motorists

moth NOUN an insect like a butterfly, which flies at night

mother NOUN a female parent ▶ **motherhood** NOUN, **motherly** ADJECTIVE

mother VERB to look after in a caring way

mother-in-law NOUN **mothers-in-law** the mother of a person's husband or wife

morose ADJECTIVE • looking very morose ▶ bad-tempered, sullen, gloomy, surly, moody

morsel NOUN • a few morsels of food ▶ bite, mouthful, nibble

mostly ADVERB • reading books, mostly novels ▶ mainly, chiefly, predominantly, primarily, principally, normally, typically, usually, generally, largely

DICTIONARY

mother-of-pearl NOUN a pearly substance lining the shells of mussels etc.

motif (moh-teef) NOUN a repeated design or theme

motion NOUN 1 a way of moving 2 a proposal at a meeting

motion VERB to signal by a gesture

motivate VERB to give a motive or reason to ► **motivation** NOUN

motive NOUN what makes a person do something

motive ADJECTIVE producing movement

motley ADJECTIVE having many colours or kinds

motor NOUN a machine providing power to drive machinery etc.

motor VERB to travel in a car

motorbike NOUN a motorcycle

motorcade NOUN a procession of cars

motorcycle NOUN a two-wheeled road vehicle with an engine ► **motorcyclist** NOUN

motorist NOUN a person who drives a car

motorway NOUN a major road with several lanes for fast traffic

mottled ADJECTIVE marked with spots or patches of colour

motto NOUN **mottoes** a short saying

mould¹ NOUN a hollow container for setting liquid in a special shape

mould VERB to give a particular shape or character to

mould² NOUN a furry growth of tiny fungi

moulder VERB to decay into dust

mouldy ADJECTIVE **mouldier**, **mouldiest** covered with mould

moult VERB (of an animal) to shed feathers, hair, or skin

mound NOUN 1 a pile of earth or stones etc. 2 a small hill

mount VERB 1 to climb or go up 2 to get on a horse or bicycle etc. 3 to increase in amount 4 to place or fix in position 5 to organize

mount NOUN 1 a mountain 2 something on which an object is mounted 3 a horse for riding

mountain NOUN 1 a very high hill 2 a large heap or amount

THESAURUS

motive NOUN • to establish a motive for the attacks ► reason, grounds, intention, purpose

mould NOUN • cheese with mould on it ► mildew, fungus • molten metal poured into a mould ► cast, die

mould VERB • figures moulded in bronze ► shape, form, fashion,

sculpt • to mould your character ► form, shape, influence

mouldy ADJECTIVE • mouldy bread ► mildewed, mouldering, stale

mount VERB • to mount an exhibition ► put on, organize, present, show • to mount a horse ► climb on to, get on, get astride • Our savings were mounting. ► grow, increase

a
b
c
d
e
f
g
h
i
j
k
l
m
n
o
p
q
r
s
t
u
v
w
x
y
z

mountaineer NOUN a person who climbs mountains
► **mountaineering** NOUN

mountainous ADJECTIVE **1** having many mountains **2** huge

mourn VERB to be sad when someone has died ► **mourner** NOUN, **mournful** ADJECTIVE

mouse NOUN **mice 1** a small furry animal with a long thin tail **2** (ICT) a device moved around by hand to control the movements of a cursor on a computer screen

mousse (mooss) NOUN a creamy flavoured pudding

moustache (mus-tahsh) NOUN hair growing on a man's upper lip

mousy ADJECTIVE **mousier, mousiest 1** a light brown colour **2** dull and timid

mouth NOUN **1** the opening through which food is taken into the body **2** the place where a river enters the sea **3** an opening or outlet

mouth VERB to form words without saying them

mouthful NOUN **mouthfuls** an amount of food that can be put in the mouth

mouthpiece NOUN the part of a musical instrument etc. put to the mouth

move VERB **1** to take or go from one place to another **2** to affect a person's feelings **3** to put forward a formal statement for discussion
► **movable** ADJECTIVE, **mover** NOUN

move NOUN **1** a movement or action **2** a player's turn in a game

movement NOUN **1** the act of moving or being moved **2** a group of people working together for a cause **3** (Music) a main division of a work

movie NOUN (American) (informal) a cinema film

moving ADJECTIVE causing strong emotion

mourn VERB • mourning his dead wife ► grieve for, weep for, pine for

mouth NOUN • He opened his mouth. ► jaws, lips • the mouth of the cave ► entrance, opening • the mouth of a river ► outlet, estuary

move VERB • He moved to the bench under the tree. ► go, walk, proceed, advance • The traffic moved slowly forward. ► edge, creep, crawl, slide • I'll move the chair closer to the table. ► carry, take, transport • We'll need to move quickly. ► act, take action,

take steps, make a move • Things are starting to move. ► progress, make progress, develop • She moved from London to the country. ► relocate, move house, migrate • The voices moved them deeply. ► touch, affect, impress

move NOUN • to talk over the next move ► step, action, initiative, tactic, ploy • It's your move. ► turn, go

moving ADJECTIVE • a moving train ► travelling, on the move • a moving story ► touching, poignant, emotional, heart-warming, inspiring

DICTIONARY

mow VERB **mowed, mown** to cut grass etc. with a machine or scythe **mow down** to knock down and kill ▸ **mower** NOUN

MP ABBREVIATION **MPs** Member of Parliament

m.p.h. ABBREVIATION miles per hour

MP3 NOUN (ICT) a system of compressing audio files so that they can be downloaded from the Internet

Mr (mist-er) NOUN a title put before a man's name

Mrs (mis-iz) NOUN a title put before a married woman's name

Ms (miz) NOUN a title put before a married or unmarried woman's name

much ADJECTIVE **more, most** existing in a large amount

much NOUN a large amount

much ADVERB **1** greatly or considerably *much to my surprise* **2** approximately *much the same*

muck NOUN **1** farmyard manure **2** dirt or filth ▸ **mucky** ADJECTIVE

mucous (mew-kus) ADJECTIVE like or covered with mucus

mucus (mew-kus) NOUN the moist sticky substance in the throat etc.

mud NOUN wet soft earth

muddle VERB **1** to jumble or mix things up **2** to confuse

muddle NOUN a muddled state

muddy ADJECTIVE **muddier, muddiest 1** covered in mud **2** vague and unclear

muesli (mooz-lee) NOUN a breakfast food made of mixed cereals, dried fruit, and nuts

muff NOUN a tube-shaped piece of warm material for keeping the hands warm

muffin NOUN **1** a flat toasted bun **2** a small sponge cake

muffle VERB **1** to cover or wrap for protection or warmth **2** to deaden the sound of

muffler NOUN a scarf

THESAURUS

muck NOUN • *cleaning the muck off the windows* ▸ dirt, grime, filth, mud

mucky ADJECTIVE • *mucky shoes* ▸ dirty, messy, muddy, filthy, grubby

muddle NOUN • *a muddle over the time of the train* ▸ confusion, misunderstanding, mix-up • *the muddle in the kitchen* ▸ mess, disorder, chaos, shambles

muddle VERB • *Her explanation muddled him.* ▸ confuse, bewilder, puzzle • *Don't muddle the papers.* ▸ disorganize, mix up, jumble up

muddy ADJECTIVE • *muddy boots* ▸ dirty, mucky, filthy, grubby • *muddy ground* ▸ waterlogged, boggy, marshy, soft

muffled ADJECTIVE • *a muffled cry* ▸ faint, indistinct, muted

473

DICTIONARY

mug NOUN **1** a large straight-sided cup **2** (*informal*) a person who is easily deceived **3** (*informal*) the face

mug VERB **mugging, mugged** to attack and rob in the street ▸ **mugger** NOUN

muggy ADJECTIVE **muggier, muggiest** unpleasantly warm and damp

mulberry NOUN **mulberries** a purple or white fruit like a blackberry

mule NOUN an animal that is the offspring of a donkey and a mare

mull VERB **mull over** to think about carefully

mullet NOUN a kind of fish used as food

multiple ADJECTIVE having many parts or elements

multiple NOUN a number that contains another number an exact number of times

multiply VERB **multiplies, multiplied 1** to take a number a given quantity of times **2** to make or become many ▸ **multiplication** NOUN

multitude NOUN a great number of people or things

mum[1] NOUN (*informal*) mother

mum[2] ADJECTIVE (*informal*) silent *keep mum*

mumble VERB to speak indistinctly ▸ **mumble** NOUN

mummy[1] NOUN **mummies** (*informal*) mother

mummy[2] NOUN **mummies** an embalmed dead body in ancient Egypt

mumps NOUN an infectious disease that makes the neck swell painfully

munch VERB to chew steadily and noisily

mundane ADJECTIVE ordinary; not exciting

municipal ADJECTIVE to do with a town or city

municipality NOUN **municipalities** a town or city with local government

mural NOUN a picture painted on a wall

murder VERB to kill a person unlawfully and deliberately

murder NOUN the act of murdering a person ▸ **murderous** ADJECTIVE

murderer NOUN a person who commits murder

THESAURUS

mug VERB • *were mugged on their way home* ▸ attack, assault, rob

muggy ADJECTIVE • *muggy weather* ▸ humid, close, clammy, sultry, sticky

mull VERB **mull over** • *a few suggestions to mull over*

▸ consider, ponder, think about, contemplate

multiply VERB • *The problems began to multiply.* ▸ increase, proliferate, mount up • *The hedgehogs multiplied rapidly.* ▸ breed, reproduce

a b c d e f g h i j k l m n o p q r s t u v w x y z

murky ADJECTIVE **murkier, murkiest** dark and gloomy

murmur VERB **1** to make a low continuous sound **2** to speak in a soft voice ▶ **murmur** NOUN

muscle NOUN **1** body tissue which contracts and relaxes to produce movement **2** physical strength ▶ **muscular** ADJECTIVE

muse VERB to think deeply

museum NOUN a place where historical or scientific objects are displayed

mush NOUN soft pulp

mushroom NOUN an edible fungus with a dome-shaped top

mushroom VERB to appear suddenly in large numbers

mushy ADJECTIVE **mushier, mushiest 1** soft and wet **2** sentimental

music NOUN pleasant or interesting sounds made by instruments or by the voice

musical ADJECTIVE **1** to do with music **2** talented in music

musical NOUN a play or film with songs

musician NOUN someone who plays a musical instrument

musk NOUN a strong-smelling substance used in perfumes ▶ **musky** ADJECTIVE

musket NOUN a gun with a long barrel, formerly used by soldiers

musketeer NOUN a soldier armed with a musket

Muslim NOUN someone who follows the religion of Islam

muslin NOUN thin soft cotton cloth

mussel NOUN a black shellfish

must AUXILIARY VERB **1** used to express necessity *We must go.* **2** used to express certainty *You must be joking!*

mustang NOUN a wild horse of North America

mustard NOUN a hot yellow paste used to flavour food

muster VERB to assemble or gather together

mustn't must not

musty ADJECTIVE **mustier, mustiest** smelling or tasting mouldy

mutate VERB to undergo a change in form ▶ **mutation** NOUN

mute ADJECTIVE **1** not able to speak **2** (of a letter) not pronounced

muted ADJECTIVE made quiet or less intense

mutilate VERB to damage by breaking or cutting off a part ▶ **mutilation** NOUN

mutiny NOUN **mutinies** a rebellion by members of the armed forces ▶ **mutinous** ADJECTIVE

mutiny VERB **mutinies, mutinied** to take part in a mutiny

THESAURUS

murky ADJECTIVE • *a murky sky* ▶ gloomy, grey, dark, overcast, foggy, sombre

musical ADJECTIVE • *musical sounds* ▶ tuneful, melodic, harmonious, sweet-sounding

DICTIONARY

mutter VERB **1** to speak in a low voice **2** to grumble ▶ **mutter** NOUN

mutton NOUN meat from a sheep

mutual ADJECTIVE **1** given or done to each other *mutual respect* **2** shared *a mutual friend* ▶ **mutually** ADVERB

muzzle NOUN **1** an animal's nose and mouth **2** a cover put over an animal's nose and mouth to prevent it biting **3** the open end of a gun

muzzle VERB to put a muzzle on

my ADJECTIVE belonging to me

myriad (mirri-ad) ADJECTIVE very many ▶ **myriad** NOUN

myrrh (mer) NOUN a substance used in perfumes and medicine

myself PRONOUN I or me and nobody else *I cut myself. I myself have said it.* **by myself** alone; on my own

mysterious ADJECTIVE full of mystery

mystery NOUN **mysteries** something that cannot be explained

mystic ADJECTIVE **1** having a spiritual meaning **2** filling people with wonder

mystical ADJECTIVE having a special spiritual meaning ▶ **mysticism** NOUN

mystify VERB **mystifies, mystified** to puzzle or bewilder ▶ **mystification** NOUN

mystique (mis-teek) NOUN an air of mystery or secret power

myth NOUN **1** an ancient story about gods and heroes **2** an untrue story or belief

mythical ADJECTIVE **1** imaginary; found only in myths **2** to do with myths

mythology NOUN **mythologies** a collection of myths ▶ **mythological** ADJECTIVE

myxomatosis (miks-om-at-oh-sis) NOUN a disease that kills rabbits

THESAURUS

mutual ADJECTIVE • *mutual respect* ▶ joint, shared, reciprocal

mysterious ADJECTIVE • *disappeared in mysterious circumstances* ▶ strange, puzzling, odd, peculiar, curious, weird

mystery NOUN • *Their disappearance remains a mystery.* ▶ puzzle, enigma, riddle,

conundrum • *events surrounded in mystery* ▶ secrecy, uncertainty

mystify VERB • *a problem that mystified us* ▶ puzzle, perplex, baffle, confuse

mythical ADJECTIVE • *a story based on mythical events* ▶ legendary, mythological, imaginary, fabled, fictional

Nn

nab VERB **nabbing, nabbed**
(*informal*) **1** to catch or arrest **2** to
seize or grab

nag [1] VERB **nagging, nagged 1** to
pester or criticize about minor
things **2** (of a pain) to hurt
constantly

nag [2] NOUN (*informal*) a horse

nail NOUN **1** the hard covering over
the end of a finger or toe **2** a thin
pointed piece of metal for
fastening wood etc.

nail VERB **1** to fasten with nails **2** to
catch or arrest

naive (nah-eev) ADJECTIVE innocent
and trusting ► **naivety** NOUN

naked ADJECTIVE **1** without any
clothes or covering **2** obvious *the
naked truth*

name NOUN **1** the word or words
by which a person, place, or thing
is known **2** a person's reputation

name VERB **1** to give a name to **2** to
state the name of **3** to specify

nameless ADJECTIVE not having a
name

namely ADVERB that is to say

namesake NOUN a person or
thing with the same name as
another

nanny NOUN **nannies** a woman
who looks after young children

> **WORD HISTORY**
> from the name *Ann*

nanny goat NOUN a female goat

nap [1] NOUN a short sleep

nap [2] NOUN short raised fibres on
cloth

nape NOUN the back of the neck

napkin NOUN a piece of cloth or
paper used for wiping the lips or
fingers

nappy NOUN **nappies** a piece of
cloth or padding put round a
baby's bottom to absorb the urine
and faeces

narcissus NOUN **narcissi** or
narcissuses a garden flower like a
daffodil

narcotic NOUN a drug that makes
a person sleepy or unconscious
► **narcotic** ADJECTIVE

narrate VERB to tell a story
► **narration** NOUN, **narrator** NOUN

narrative NOUN a spoken or
written account of something

narrow ADJECTIVE **1** not wide or
broad **2** uncomfortably close
► **narrowly** ADVERB

THESAURUS

nag VERB • *has been nagging me for
days* ► pester, harass, badger

naive ADJECTIVE • *I was naive in those
days.* ► innocent, ingenuous,
inexperienced

naked ADJECTIVE • *a naked statue*
► nude, bare, unclothed,
undressed

name VERB • *to name her Clio*
► call, dub, baptize • *to name the
victims* ► identify, specify • *to
name a successor* ► choose,
nominate, appoint

narrow ADJECTIVE • *a narrow space*
► tight, close, confined, cramped

a
b
c
d
e
f
g
h
i
j
k
l
m
n
o
p
q
r
s
t
u
v
w
x
y
z

narrow VERB to make or become narrower

narrow-minded ADJECTIVE not tolerant of other beliefs and ways

nasal ADJECTIVE **1** to do with the nose **2** sounding through the nose

nasturtium (na-ster-shum) NOUN a garden plant with round leaves and bright flowers

nasty ADJECTIVE **nastier, nastiest** unpleasant or unkind

nation NOUN a community of people living under one government ► **national** ADJECTIVE

nationalism NOUN the desire for a country to be independent ► **nationalist** NOUN, **nationalistic** ADJECTIVE

nationality NOUN **nationalities** the condition of belonging to a nation

nationalize VERB to put an industry or business under state ownership ► **nationalization** NOUN

⚠ SPELLING

This word can also be spelled *nationalise*.

nationwide ADJECTIVE, ADVERB over the whole of a country

native NOUN a person born in a particular place

native ADJECTIVE originating in or belonging to a particular place

nativity NOUN **nativities** a person's birth

natty ADJECTIVE **nattier, nattiest** (informal) neat and smart ► **nattily** ADVERB

natural ADJECTIVE **1** produced by nature **2** normal **3** having an ability from birth **4** (of a note in music) neither sharp nor flat ► **naturally** ADVERB

natural NOUN a natural note in music; a sign (♮) that shows this

natural history NOUN the study of plants and animals

naturalist NOUN an expert in natural history

naturalize VERB to give a person full rights as a citizen ► **naturalization** NOUN

⚠ SPELLING

This word can also be spelled *naturalise*.

THESAURUS

• *a narrow majority* ► small, slim, slender

nasty ADJECTIVE • *a nasty taste* ► unpleasant, disagreeable, disgusting, horrible • *a nasty person* ► unkind, unfriendly, unpleasant, mean, spiteful • *nasty weather* ► unpleasant, rough

nation NOUN • *to broadcast to the nation* ► country, people,

population • *the nations of the world* ► country, land, state

natural ADJECTIVE • *a natural tendency* ► innate, inborn, instinctive • *a natural manner* ► genuine, sincere, unaffected • *a natural leader* ► born, untaught • *natural for them to want more information* ► understandable, reasonable, logical

DICTIONARY

nature NOUN **1** everything in the world that was not made by people **2** the qualities and characteristics of a person or thing *a loving nature* **3** a kind or sort *things of that nature*

naturist NOUN a person who practises nudism ► **naturism** NOUN

naught NOUN *(old use)* nothing

naughty ADJECTIVE **naughtier, naughtiest 1** badly behaved or disobedient **2** slightly indecent ► **naughtiness** NOUN

nausea (naw-zee-a) NOUN a feeling of sickness or disgust ► **nauseating** ADJECTIVE

> **WORD HISTORY**
> from Greek *nausia* 'seasickness', from *naus* 'ship'

nauseous ADJECTIVE sickening; disgusting

nautical ADJECTIVE to do with ships or sailors

naval ADJECTIVE to do with a navy

nave NOUN the main central part of a church

navel NOUN the hollow in the abdomen where the umbilical cord was attached

navigable ADJECTIVE suitable for ships to sail in ► **navigability** NOUN

navigate VERB **1** to sail on a river or sea **2** to calculate the route of a ship, aircraft, or vehicle ► **navigation** NOUN, **navigator** NOUN

navvy NOUN **navvies** a labourer working on a road, railway, canal, etc.

navy NOUN **navies** a country's warships and crews

navy blue NOUN a dark blue colour, the colour of naval uniform

nay ADVERB *(old use)* no

Nazi (nah-tsee) NOUN **Nazis** a member of the National Socialist Party in Germany in 1933–45 ► **Nazism** NOUN

NB ABBREVIATION note well

near ADVERB, ADJECTIVE not far away

near PREPOSITION not far away from

near VERB to come near to

nearby ADJECTIVE near

nearly ADVERB almost

THESAURUS

nature NOUN • *the beauties of nature* ► the natural world, the living world, the environment, the countryside • *not in his nature to complain* ► character, personality, temperament • *coins, medals, and things of that nature* ► kind, type, sort

naughty ADJECTIVE • *a naughty child* ► badly behaved, mischievous, disobedient

near ADJECTIVE • *a near neighbour* ► nearby, close, adjacent, next-door, bordering • *A decision is near.* ► close, approaching, imminent, impending • *near relatives* ► close, dear, closely related

nearly ADVERB • *nearly finished* ► almost, practically, virtually, more or less

a
b
c
d
e
f
g
h
i
j
k
l
m
n
o
p
q
r
s
t
u
v
w
x
y
z

neat ADJECTIVE **neater, neatest**
1 simple and tidy **2** not diluted

neaten VERB to make something
neat

nebula NOUN **nebulae** or **nebulas**
a bright or dark patch in the sky

nebulous ADJECTIVE indistinct or
vague

necessary ADJECTIVE needed;
essential ► **necessarily** ADVERB

necessitate VERB to make
necessary

necessity NOUN **necessities**
1 need **2** something needed

neck NOUN **1** the part of the body
that joins the head to the
shoulders **2** a narrow part of
something

necklace NOUN an ornament worn
round the neck

nectar NOUN **1** a sweet liquid
collected by bees from flowers **2** a
delicious drink

nectarine NOUN a kind of peach
with a thin smooth skin

need VERB **1** to be without
something you should have **2** to
have to do something *You need to
answer.*

need NOUN **1** something needed
2 a situation where something is
necessary *no need to cry* **3** great
poverty or hardship

needful ADJECTIVE necessary

needle NOUN **1** a thin pointed
piece of steel used in sewing
2 something thin and pointed **3** a
pointer

needle VERB to provoke

needless ADJECTIVE not necessary

needlework NOUN sewing or
embroidery

needy ADJECTIVE **needier, neediest**
very poor

nefarious (nif-air-ee-us) ADJECTIVE
wicked

THESAURUS

neat ADJECTIVE • *a neat bedroom*
► tidy, orderly, spick-and-span,
immaculate • *hair tied in a neat
bun* ► compact, elegant, trim
• *neat writing* ► regular, well
formed, elegant • *a neat solution*
► clever, ingenious, inventive
• *neat whisky* ► undiluted,
straight

necessary ADJECTIVE • *necessary
repairs* ► important, essential,
vital, unavoidable, needed,
obligatory, compulsory

need VERB • *to need more milk*
► require, want, be short of, be in

need of, lack • *to need someone*
► depend on, rely on

need NOUN • *no need to say
anything* ► necessity, obligation,
call, requirement • *basic human
needs* ► requirement, essential,
necessity

needless ADJECTIVE • *needless
expense* ► unnecessary,
unwanted, superfluous

needy ADJECTIVE • *day centres for the
needy* ► poor, deprived,
destitute, underprivileged

negate VERB **1** to make ineffective **2** to disprove or deny ► **negation** NOUN

negative ADJECTIVE **1** that says 'no' *a negative answer* **2** looking only at the bad aspects **3** (of a test) showing no sign of what is being tested **4** less than nought; minus **5** to do with the kind of electric charge carried by electrons ► **negatively** ADVERB

negative NOUN **1** a negative statement **2** a film with the dark and light parts reversed

neglect VERB to fail to do something or attend to something

neglect NOUN the state of being neglected

negligent ADJECTIVE showing a lack of care ► **negligence** NOUN

negligible ADJECTIVE not big or important enough to bother about

negotiable ADJECTIVE able to be changed after being discussed

negotiate VERB **1** to discuss with others to reach an agreement **2** to arrange after discussion **3** to get

over an obstacle ► **negotiation** NOUN, **negotiator** NOUN

Negro NOUN **Negroes** a member of a dark-skinned people originating in Africa

neigh VERB to make the cry of a horse ► **neigh** NOUN

neighbour NOUN a person who lives near another ► **neighbouring** ADJECTIVE

neighbourhood NOUN **1** the surrounding district or area **2** a district

neighbourly ADVERB helpful to local people

neither ADJECTIVE, PRONOUN not one or the other of two

neither ADVERB (used with **nor**) not either of two possibilities

neolithic ADJECTIVE of the later part of the Stone Age

neon NOUN a gas that glows when electricity passes through it

nephew NOUN the son of a person's brother or sister

neglect VERB • *to neglect your work* ► ignore, pay no attention to, let slide, forget, abandon

neglect NOUN • *years of neglect* ► negligence, carelessness, dereliction of duty, inattention

negligible ADJECTIVE • *a negligible difference* ► tiny, trifling, trivial, insignificant

negotiate VERB • *to negotiate a better deal* ► work out, hammer

out, agree on • *refused to negotiate* ► consult, confer, discuss terms, talk • *several sharp bends to negotiate* ► get round, deal with

neighbourhood NOUN • *a quiet neighbourhood* ► district, area, locality, vicinity

neighbourly ADJECTIVE • *a neighbourly offer of help* ► friendly, considerate, kind

a
b
c
d
e
f
g
h
i
j
k
l
m
n
o
p
q
r
s
t
u
v
w
x
y
z

nerve NOUN **1** any of the fibres in the body that carry messages to and from the brain **2** courage; calmness **3** impudence

nerve-racking ADJECTIVE causing anxiety or stress

nervous ADJECTIVE **1** easily upset or scared **2** to do with the nerves *a nervous illness*

nervy ADJECTIVE **nervier, nerviest** nervous

nest NOUN **1** a structure in which birds rear their young **2** a set of similar things

nestle VERB to curl up comfortably

nestling NOUN a bird that is too young to leave the nest

net[1] NOUN material made of pieces of thread, cord, or wire etc. joined together in a criss-cross pattern with holes between **the Net** the Internet

net VERB **netting, netted** to cover or catch with a net

net[2] ADJECTIVE remaining after items have been deducted *income net of tax*

netball NOUN a game in which two teams try to throw a ball into a high net hanging from a ring

nether ADJECTIVE lower

netting NOUN a piece of net

nettle NOUN a wild plant with leaves that sting when they are touched

nettle VERB to annoy or provoke

network NOUN **1** an organization with parts that work together

neuralgia NOUN pain along a nerve

neuron or **neurone** NOUN a cell that is part of the nervous system

neurotic ADJECTIVE nervously and obsessively anxious

neuter ADJECTIVE neither masculine nor feminine

neutral ADJECTIVE **1** not supporting either side in a war **2** not distinctive ▶ **neutrality** NOUN

neutral NOUN a gear that disconnects the engine

neutralize VERB to stop from having any effect
▶ **neutralization** NOUN

⚠ **SPELLING**

This word can also be spelled *neutralise*.

neutron NOUN a particle of matter with no electric charge

never ADVERB **1** at no time; not ever **2** not at all

nevertheless ADVERB in spite of this; although this is a fact

THESAURUS

nerve NOUN • *It takes some nerve.* ▶ courage, bravery, daring, determination • *the nerve to ask for more* ▶ cheek, audacity, effrontery

nervous ADJECTIVE • *a nervous person* ▶ highly-strung, nervy, anxious, excitable • *feeling a little*

nervous ▶ anxious, worried, apprehensive, concerned

neutral ADJECTIVE • *a neutral umpire* ▶ impartial, unbiased, objective, even-handed • *neutral colours* ▶ dull, indefinite, indeterminate

new ADJECTIVE **1** not existing before **2** just made, bought, etc.
► **newly** ADVERB

newcomer NOUN a person who has arrived recently

newfangled ADJECTIVE new and unfamiliar in method or style

new moon NOUN the moon at the beginning of its cycle, visible as a thin crescent

news NOUN information about recent events

newsagent NOUN a shopkeeper who sells newspapers

newspaper NOUN a daily or weekly publication containing news reports, articles, etc.

newt NOUN a small animal like a lizard, living near or in water

newton NOUN a unit for measuring force

next ADJECTIVE, ADVERB nearest; coming immediately after

next door ADVERB, ADJECTIVE in the next house or room

next of kin NOUN a person's closest relative

nib NOUN the pointed metal part of a pen

nibble VERB to take quick small bites

nice ADJECTIVE **nicer**, **nicest** **1** pleasant or kind **2** precise or careful ► **nicely** ADVERB

nicety (ny-sit-ee) NOUN **niceties** **1** precision **2** a small detail

niche (neesh) NOUN **1** a recess in a wall **2** a suitable place

nick NOUN a small cut or notch

nick VERB **1** to make a nick in **2** (informal) to steal **3** (informal) to arrest

nickel NOUN a silvery white metal

nickname NOUN a name used instead of a person's real name

nicotine NOUN an oily substance found in tobacco

niece NOUN the daughter of a person's brother or sister

niggardly ADJECTIVE mean or stingy

niggle VERB **1** to fuss over details **2** to be a small but constant worry

nigh ADVERB, PREPOSITION (old use) near

THESAURUS

new ADJECTIVE • *new ways of beating crime* ► modern, recent, up-to-date • *new ideas* ► fresh, original, innovative, creative, different • *new labs at the school* ► additional, extra, more, supplementary • *I felt like a new person.* ► changed, improved, restored, revived

news NOUN • *the news of his death* ► report, announcement, account, information (about)

next ADJECTIVE • *in the next street* ► adjacent, neighbouring, adjoining • *the next train* ► soonest, following, subsequent

nice ADJECTIVE • *a nice time* ► pleasant, agreeable, enjoyable, wonderful, delightful • *nice people* ► pleasant, kind, likeable, agreeable, friendly • *nice food* ► delicious, tasty, well-cooked • *nice weather* ► pleasant, warm, sunny

a
b
c
d
e
f
g
h
i
j
k
l
m
n
o
p
q
r
s
t
u
v
w
x
y
z

night NOUN **1** the dark hours between sunset and sunrise **2** a particular night or evening

nightfall NOUN the beginning of night

nightie NOUN (*informal*) a nightdress

nightingale NOUN a small brown bird that sings sweetly

> **WORD HISTORY**
>
> from an Old English word meaning 'night-singer' (because nightingales sing in the evening)

nightly ADJECTIVE, ADVERB happening every night

nightmare NOUN **1** a frightening dream **2** an unpleasant experience ▶ **nightmarish** ADJECTIVE

nil NOUN nothing or nought

nimble ADJECTIVE able to move quickly ▶ **nimbly** ADVERB

nine NOUN, ADJECTIVE the number 9 ▶ **ninth** ADJECTIVE, NOUN

nineteen NOUN, ADJECTIVE the number 19 ▶ **nineteenth** ADJECTIVE, NOUN

ninety NOUN, ADJECTIVE **nineties** the number 90 ▶ **ninetieth** ADJECTIVE, NOUN

nip VERB **nipping**, **nipped** **1** to pinch or bite quickly **2** (*informal*) to go quickly

nip NOUN **1** a quick pinch or bite **2** sharp coldness *a nip in the air* **3** a small amount *a nip of brandy*

nipper NOUN (*informal*) a young child

nipple NOUN the part of a mother's breast from which a baby sucks milk

nippy ADJECTIVE **nippier**, **nippiest** (*informal*) **1** quick or nimble **2** cold

nit NOUN a parasitic insect or its egg

nit-picking NOUN the pointing out of small faults

nitrate NOUN a substance got from nitric acid, used as a fertilizer

nitric acid (ny-trik) NOUN a strong acid containing nitrogen

nitrogen (ny-tro-jen) NOUN a gas that makes up about four-fifths of air

no ADJECTIVE not any *no money*

no ADVERB **1** used to deny or refuse something **2** not at all *no better*

No. or **no.** ABBREVIATION number

nobility NOUN **nobilities 1** a noble state **2** the aristocracy

noble ADJECTIVE **nobler**, **noblest 1** of high social rank **2** good or impressive ▶ **nobly** ADVERB

noble NOUN a person of high social rank ▶ **nobleman** NOUN, **noblewoman** NOUN

nobody PRONOUN no person; no one

nocturnal ADJECTIVE active at night

nod VERB **nodding**, **nodded** to move the head up and down ▶ **nod** NOUN

node NOUN a swelling like a small knob

nodule NOUN a small knob or lump

THESAURUS

noble ADJECTIVE • *a noble family* ▶ aristocratic, high-born • *a noble deed* ▶ honourable, virtuous, brave, gallant

noise NOUN a sound, especially a loud or unpleasant one ► **noisy** ADJECTIVE

nomad NOUN a member of a tribe that moves from place to place ► **nomadic** ADJECTIVE

no man's land NOUN an area that does not belong to anybody

nominal ADJECTIVE **1** in name only *the nominal ruler* **2** small *a nominal fee* ► **nominally** ADVERB

nominate VERB to propose as a candidate in an election ► **nomination** NOUN ► **nominee** NOUN

nonchalant (non-shal-ant) ADJECTIVE calm and casual ► **nonchalance** NOUN

nondescript ADJECTIVE having no special qualities

none PRONOUN **1** not any **2** no one

none ADVERB not at all *none too sure*

nonentity NOUN **nonentities** an unimportant person

non-existent ADJECTIVE not existing or unreal

non-fiction NOUN books and writing about real people and events

non-flammable ADJECTIVE not able to be set on fire

nonplussed ADJECTIVE puzzled or confused

nonsense NOUN **1** meaningless words **2** foolish ideas ► **nonsensical** (non-sens-ik-al) ADJECTIVE

non-stop ADJECTIVE, ADVERB without stopping

noodles PLURAL NOUN pasta in long narrow strips

nook NOUN a sheltered corner

noon NOUN twelve o'clock midday

no one NOUN no person; nobody

noose NOUN a loop in a rope that tightens when the rope is pulled

nor CONJUNCTION and not

norm NOUN **1** a standard or average type, amount, etc. **2** normal or expected behaviour

normal ADJECTIVE **1** usual or ordinary **2** natural and healthy ► **normality** NOUN, **normally** ADVERB

north NOUN **1** the direction to the left of a person who faces east

a
b
c
d
e
f
g
h
i
j
k
l
m
n
o
p
q
r
s
t
u
v
w
x
y
z

THESAURUS

noise NOUN • *the noise from the street* ► sound, din, clamour, racket, uproar, crash, clatter

noisy ADJECTIVE • *a noisy machine* ► loud, deafening, ear-splitting, thunderous • *a noisy argument* ► loud, vociferous, rowdy, shouting

nonsense NOUN • *talking nonsense* ► rubbish, balderdash, gibberish, drivel

non-stop ADJECTIVE • *non-stop fun and laughter* ► continuous, constant, uninterrupted, unending, never-ending

non-stop ADVERB • *to work non-stop* ► continuously, all the time, steadily, round the clock

normal ADJECTIVE • *a perfectly normal couple* ► ordinary, average, typical, conventional, everyday • *in the normal way*

2 the northern part of a country, city, etc.

north ADJECTIVE, ADVERB towards or in the north; coming from the north

north-east NOUN, ADJECTIVE, ADVERB midway between north and east ▸ **north-easterly** ADJECTIVE, **north-eastern** ADJECTIVE

northerly ADJECTIVE **1** coming from the north **2** facing the north

northern ADJECTIVE of or in the north

northerner NOUN a person from the north of a country

northward ADJECTIVE, ADVERB towards the north ▸ **northwards** ADVERB

north-west NOUN, ADJECTIVE, ADVERB midway between north and west ▸ **north-westerly** ADJECTIVE, **north-western** ADJECTIVE

nose NOUN **1** the part of the face that is used for breathing and smelling **2** the front end or part

nose VERB to go forward cautiously

nosedive NOUN a steep downward dive by an aircraft

nostalgia (nos-tal-ja) NOUN longing for the past ▸ **nostalgic** ADJECTIVE

nostril NOUN either of the two openings of the nose

nosy ADJECTIVE **nosier, nosiest** (informal) inquisitive or prying

not ADVERB used to express a negative

notable ADJECTIVE worth noticing ▸ **notably** ADVERB

notation NOUN a system of symbols representing numbers, quantities, etc.

notch NOUN a small V-shape cut into a surface

notch VERB to cut a notch in **notch up** to score or achieve

note NOUN **1** something written down as a reminder **2** a short letter **3** a banknote **4** a single sound in music **5** a sound or quality that indicates something *a note of warning* **6** notice or attention *take note*

note VERB **1** to write down **2** to pay attention to

THESAURUS

▸ usual, customary, standard, regular, routine

nosy ADJECTIVE • *too nosy for his own good* ▸ inquisitive, prying, curious

notable ADJECTIVE • *with some notable exceptions* ▸ significant, important, noteworthy, remarkable • *a notable statesman* ▸ prominent, famous, distinguished

note NOUN • *left her a note* ▸ message, communication, letter, memo • *to make a note of an address* ▸ record, reminder • *notes written in the margin* ▸ comment, annotation, remark

note VERB • *noted the new cafe* ▸ observe, notice, see, remark • *to note your suggestion* ▸ consider, bear in mind, take into account • *Note the dates in your*

DICTIONARY

noted ADJECTIVE famous for a particular reason *an area noted for its beaches*

notepaper NOUN paper for writing letters

noteworthy ADJECTIVE important or remarkable

nothing NOUN **1** no thing; not anything **2** no amount; nought

nothing ADVERB **1** not at all **2** in no way *nothing like as good*

notice NOUN **1** a printed announcement **2** attention *escaped my notice* **3** a formal announcement of leaving a job or dismissing an employee

notice VERB to see or become aware of

noticeable ADJECTIVE easily seen or noticed ► **noticeably** ADVERB

notify VERB **notifies**, **notified** to tell someone formally or officially ► **notifiable** ADJECTIVE, **notification** NOUN

notion NOUN a vague idea

notional ADJECTIVE guessed and not definite

notorious ADJECTIVE well-known for something bad ► **notoriety** (noh-ter-I-it-ee) NOUN

notwithstanding PREPOSITION in spite of

nougat (noo-gah) NOUN a chewy sweet made from nuts and sugar or honey

nought NOUN **1** the figure 0 **2** nothing

noun NOUN a word that stands for a person, place, or thing

nourish VERB to keep a person, animal, or plant alive with food

nourishment NOUN **1** the process of nourishing **2** food

nova (noh-va) NOUN **novae** a star that suddenly brightens for a time

novel NOUN a story that fills a whole book ► **novelist** NOUN

novel ADJECTIVE new and unusual

novelty NOUN **novelties** **1** newness and originality **2** something new and unusual **3** a cheap toy

November NOUN the eleventh month of the year

THESAURUS

diary. ► write down, jot down, enter, record

notice NOUN • *a notice pinned on the door* ► announcement, message, note, poster, sign • *to escape your notice* ► attention, observation

notice VERB • *I noticed the door was open.* ► observe, perceive, see, spot • *to notice a smell of gas* ► detect, perceive

notify VERB • *to be notified of any changes* ► inform, advise, tell

notion NOUN • *wild notions* ► idea, belief, concept, thought, opinion

nourish VERB • *to nourish their children* ► feed, provide for, support

novel ADJECTIVE • *a novel idea* ► new, original, innovative, unconventional, unusual

DICTIONARY

novice NOUN **1** a beginner **2** a person preparing to be a monk or nun

now ADVERB **1** at this time **2** by this time **3** immediately

now CONJUNCTION as a result of or at the same time as *Now that you have come, we'll start.*

nowadays ADVERB at the present time

nowhere ADVERB not anywhere

noxious ADJECTIVE unpleasant and harmful

nozzle NOUN the spout of a hose, pipe, or tube

nuance NOUN a slight difference

nub NOUN **1** a small knob or lump **2** the central point of a problem

nuclear ADJECTIVE **1** to do with a nucleus **2** using the energy created by the nuclei of atoms

nucleus NOUN **nuclei 1** a central part **2** the central part of an atom or of a seed

nude ADJECTIVE not wearing any clothes; naked ▸ **nudity** NOUN

nudge VERB **1** to poke a person gently **2** to push slightly ▸ **nudge** NOUN

nudism NOUN the belief that going naked is beneficial ▸ **nudist** NOUN

nugget NOUN **1** a rough lump of gold **2** a valuable fact

nuisance NOUN an annoying person or thing

null ADJECTIVE not legally valid

nullify VERB **nullifies**, **nullified** to make invalid

numb ADJECTIVE unable to feel or move

numb VERB to make numb

number NOUN **1** a symbol or word indicating how many or identifying something **2** a quantity of people or things **3** one issue of a magazine or newspaper **4** a song

number VERB **1** to mark with numbers **2** to count **3** to amount to

THESAURUS

nude ADJECTIVE • *nude bathing* ▸ naked, undressed, bare

nudge VERB • *She nudged him in his side.* ▸ poke, prod, shove, jog

nuisance NOUN • *what a nuisance for you* ▸ inconvenience, annoyance, bother, worry, pain

numb ADJECTIVE • *hands numb with cold* ▸ dead, frozen, insensitive, unfeeling

numb VERB • *to numb your senses* ▸ deaden, paralyse, desensitize, freeze, anaesthetize

number NOUN • *a line of numbers* ▸ figure, numeral, integer, digit • *a large number of children* ▸ quantity, amount, collection, crowd, multitude • *a musical number* ▸ item, piece, song

number VERB • *Visitors numbered over ten million.* ▸ total, add up to, amount to, come to

numeral NOUN a symbol that represents a certain number

numerate (new-mer-at) ADJECTIVE having a good understanding of numbers ► **numeracy** NOUN

numerator NOUN the number above the line in a fraction, e.g. 3 in $\frac{3}{4}$

numerical ADJECTIVE to do with or consisting of numbers ► **numerically** ADVERB

numerous ADJECTIVE many

nun NOUN one of a community of religious women living according to rules

nunnery NOUN **nunneries** a convent

nuptial ADJECTIVE to do with marriage

nurse NOUN a person trained to look after sick or injured people

nurse VERB 1 to look after someone who is ill or injured 2 to feed a baby at the breast 3 to hold carefully

nursery NOUN **nurseries** 1 a place where young children are looked

after 2 a place where plants are grown

nursery rhyme NOUN a simple rhyme or song of the kind that young children like

nurture VERB 1 to train and educate 2 to nourish

nut NOUN 1 a fruit with a hard shell containing a kernel 2 a small piece of metal with a hole in the middle, for screwing on a bolt ► **nutty** ADJECTIVE

nutmeg NOUN the hard seed of a tropical tree, grated and used in cooking

nutrient (new-tree-ent) NOUN a nourishing substance

nutrition NOUN 1 nourishment 2 the study of what nourishes people ► **nutritious** ADJECTIVE

nutshell NOUN **in a nutshell** stated very briefly

nuzzle VERB to rub gently with the nose

nylon NOUN a strong synthetic cloth or fibre

nymph NOUN a female spirit in myths

THESAURUS

numeral NOUN • written in numerals ► figure, digit, integer, number

numerous ADJECTIVE • numerous reasons ► many, several, a lot of, copious, abundant

nurse VERB • She nursed her old father. ► look after, take care of, tend, treat

nutritious ADJECTIVE • nutritious food ► healthy, nourishing, wholesome

Oo

O INTERJECTION oh

oaf NOUN a stupid or clumsy person

oak NOUN a large tree with seeds called acorns

OAP ABBREVIATION old-age pensioner

oar NOUN a pole with a flat blade at one end, used for rowing a boat

oasis (oh-ay-sis) NOUN a fertile place in a desert, with a spring or well of water

oath NOUN a solemn promise

oatmeal NOUN a food of ground oats

oats PLURAL NOUN a cereal used to make food

obedient ADJECTIVE doing what you are told; willing to obey ► **obedience** NOUN

obelisk NOUN a tall pillar as a monument

obese (o-beess) ADJECTIVE very fat ► **obesity** NOUN

obey VERB to do what you are told to do

obituary NOUN **obituaries** a newspaper announcement of a person's death

object (ob-jikt) NOUN **1** something that can be seen or touched **2** an aim or purpose **3** a person or thing to which an action or feeling is directed an object of pity **4** (*Grammar*) the word or words naming who or what is acted on by a verb or a preposition, e.g. *him* in *The dog bit him* and *against him*

object (ob-jekt) VERB to say that you do not approve of something or do not agree ► **objector** NOUN

objection NOUN a reason for not approving of something

objectionable ADJECTIVE unpleasant or nasty

objective NOUN an aim or intention

objective ADJECTIVE not influenced by personal opinions ► **objectivity** NOUN

THESAURUS

oath NOUN • *an oath of allegiance* ► vow, pledge, promise

obedient ADJECTIVE • *an obedient child* ► dutiful, compliant, respectful, well-behaved

obey VERB • *to obey without question* ► take orders (from), submit (to) • *to obey orders* ► follow, carry out, abide by

object NOUN • *an object found on the beach* ► article, item, thing • *the object of the exercise* ► aim, objective, purpose, point

object VERB • *if you don't object* ► mind, protest **object to** • *to object to a suggestion* ► oppose, protest against, be against, disapprove of

objection NOUN • *many objections to the idea* ► protest, challenge, complaint, disapproval, opposition

objectionable ADJECTIVE • *an objectionable person* ► unpleasant, offensive, disagreeable, nasty

DICTIONARY

obligation NOUN a promise or duty you have to fulfil

obligatory ADJECTIVE compulsory; not optional

oblige VERB **1** to force or compel **2** to help and please someone **be obliged to** to feel gratitude towards

obliging ADJECTIVE polite and helpful

oblique (ob-leek) ADJECTIVE **1** slanting **2** not saying something in a direct way

obliterate VERB to blot out or remove all traces of ► **obliteration** NOUN

oblivion NOUN **1** the state of being forgotten **2** the state of being unconscious

oblivious ADJECTIVE completely unaware of something

oblong ADJECTIVE rectangular in shape and longer than it is wide ► **oblong** NOUN

obnoxious ADJECTIVE very unpleasant; objectionable

oboe NOUN a high-pitched woodwind instrument ► **oboist** NOUN

obscene (ob-seen) ADJECTIVE indecent in an offensive way ► **obscenity** NOUN

obscure ADJECTIVE **1** difficult to see or understand **2** not well-known

obscure VERB to make obscure; to darken or conceal

obscurity NOUN the state of being obscure or unknown

obsequious (ob-seek-wee-us) ADJECTIVE too willing to obey or serve someone

observance NOUN the practice of obeying a law or custom

observant ADJECTIVE quick at observing or noticing things

observation NOUN **1** the act of observing or watching **2** a comment or remark

THESAURUS

obligation NOUN • *an obligation to help* ► responsibility, duty, requirement

obligatory ADJECTIVE • *Use of seat-belts is obligatory.* ► compulsory, mandatory, required

oblige VERB • *cannot oblige them to agree* ► force, compel, require, make

obscene ADJECTIVE • *obscene literature* ► indecent, pornographic, immoral

obscure ADJECTIVE • *an obscure disease* ► unknown, little-known, unheard-of

obscure VERB • *Clouds obscured the sun.* ► hide, conceal, cover

observant ADJECTIVE • *an observant eye* ► alert, attentive, watchful, perceptive, sharp-eyed

observation NOUN • *sent to hospital for observation* ► monitoring, examination, inspection, surveillance • *useful observations* ► remark, comment, opinion

observatory NOUN
  observatories a building with equipment for observing the stars or weather

observe VERB **1** to see and notice **2** to obey a law or rule **3** to keep a custom or religious festival **4** to make a remark ▶ **observer** NOUN

obsess VERB to occupy a person's thoughts constantly ▶ **obsessive** ADJECTIVE

obsession NOUN an idea or feeling that dominates a person's mind

obsolescent ADJECTIVE going out of use or fashion ▶ **obsolescence** NOUN

obsolete ADJECTIVE not used any more; out of date

obstacle NOUN something that stands in the way

obstetrics NOUN the branch of medicine and surgery that deals with childbirth

obstinate ADJECTIVE **1** keeping firmly to your own ideas or ways, even though they may be wrong **2** difficult to overcome or deal with ▶ **obstinacy** NOUN

obstreperous (ob-strep-er-us) ADJECTIVE noisy and unruly

obstruct VERB to stop a person or thing from getting past ▶ **obstruction** NOUN

obtain VERB to get or be given something

obtrusive ADJECTIVE unpleasantly noticeable

obtuse ADJECTIVE slow to understand

obtuse angle NOUN an angle of between 90° and 180°

obverse NOUN the side of a coin or medal showing the head or chief design

THESAURUS

observe VERB • *observed friends over by the bar* ▶ notice, see, perceive, spot • *observed that he looked unhappy* ▶ remark, comment, mention • *could observe what was going on* ▶ watch, view, monitor, witness • *to observe the rules* ▶ obey, follow, abide by

observer NOUN • *merely an observer* ▶ spectator, onlooker, viewer, watcher, witness

obsolete ADJECTIVE • *obsolete machinery* ▶ out of date, antiquated, old-fashioned, dated

obstacle NOUN • *a major obstacle in the negotiations* ▶ barrier,

hurdle, hindrance, obstruction, difficulty

obstinate ADJECTIVE • *too obstinate to see the advantages* ▶ stubborn, inflexible, intractable, headstrong

obstruct VERB • *a road obstructed by cars* ▶ block, jam, clog up • *obstructing the course of justice* ▶ impede, hinder, hamper

obstruction NOUN • *an obstruction to learning* ▶ barrier, hindrance, drawback, difficulty, impediment

obtain VERB • *to obtain permission* ▶ get, acquire, secure

obvious ADJECTIVE easy to see or understand ► **obviously** ADVERB

occasion NOUN **1** the time when something happens **2** a special event **3** a suitable time

occasion VERB (formal) to cause

occasional ADJECTIVE **1** happening from time to time but not frequently **2** for special occasions ► **occasionally** ADVERB

occult ADJECTIVE to do with supernatural or magic things

occupant NOUN someone who occupies a place ► **occupancy** NOUN

occupation NOUN **1** a person's job or profession **2** something done to pass the time **3** the act of capturing a country by force

occupational ADJECTIVE caused by an occupation *an occupational disease*

occupy VERB **occupies**, **occupied** **1** to live in a place **2** to fill a space or position **3** to capture a country and place troops in it **4** to keep someone busy ► **occupier** NOUN

occur VERB **occurring**, **occurred** **1** to happen or exist **2** to be found **3** to come into a person's mind

occurrence NOUN something that happens

ocean NOUN the water that surround the continents of the earth ► **oceanic** ADJECTIVE

ochre (oh-ker) NOUN **1** a mineral used as a pigment **2** a pale brownish yellow

THESAURUS

obvious ADJECTIVE • *obvious that she's unhappy* ► clear, plain, evident, apparent

occasion NOUN • *on several occasions* ► instance, time • *a special occasion* ► event, affair, celebration • *if the occasion arises* ► opportunity, chance

occasional ADJECTIVE • *occasional rain* ► intermittent, sporadic, infrequent, irregular, rare

occasionally ADVERB • *only spoke occasionally* ► sometimes, from time to time, now and then, intermittently, infrequently

occupation NOUN • *your name and occupation* ► job, profession, work, employment • *a favourite leisure occupation* ► pastime,

hobby, interest, activity • *the occupation of the country* ► invasion, annexation, seizure, takeover

occupy VERB • *occupies the top floor* ► live in, inhabit, reside in • *problems that occupied her mind* ► absorb, engage, preoccupy • *to occupy a country* ► capture, seize, invade, take over

occur VERB • *everything that occurred that morning* ► happen, take place, come about • *a disease that occurs in tropical climates* ► be found, exist, be prevalent, appear

occurrence NOUN • *a common occurrence* ► event, happening, incident

a
b
c
d
e
f
g
h
i
j
k
l
m
n
o
p
q
r
s
t
u
v
w
x
y
z

o'clock ADVERB used after a number to give the time *one o'clock*

octagon NOUN a flat shape with eight sides and eight angles
▶ **octagonal** ADJECTIVE

octave NOUN the interval of eight steps between one musical note and the next note of the same name

octet NOUN **1** a group of eight musicians **2** a piece of music for eight musicians

October NOUN the tenth month of the year

octopus NOUN **octopuses** a sea creature with eight long tentacles

odd ADJECTIVE **1** strange or unusual **2** (of a number) not able to be divided exactly by 2, e.g. 3, 5, 7, etc. **3** left over from a pair or set *an odd sock* **4** of various kinds *odd jobs* ▶ **oddly** ADVERB

oddity NOUN **oddities** a strange person or thing

oddments PLURAL NOUN scraps or pieces left over

odds PLURAL NOUN the chances that a certain thing will happen **at odds with** in conflict with **odds and ends** small things of various kinds

ode NOUN a poem addressed to a person or thing

odious (oh-dee-us) ADJECTIVE extremely unpleasant; hateful

odium (oh-dee-um) NOUN general hatred or disgust

odour NOUN an unpleasant smell
▶ **odorous** ADJECTIVE

odyssey (od-iss-ee) NOUN **odysseys** a long adventurous journey

oesophagus (ee-sof-a-gus) NOUN **oesophagi** the gullet

oestrogen (ees-tro-jen) NOUN a hormone which develops female physical characteristics

of PREPOSITION **1** belonging to **2** concerning; about **3** made from **4** in relation to

off PREPOSITION **1** away or down from **2** not taking or wanting *off your food* **3** deducted from

off ADVERB **1** away or down **2** not working or happening **3** completely *Finish it off.* **4** (of food) beginning to go bad

offal NOUN the organs of an animal (e.g. liver and kidneys) used as food

off-colour ADJECTIVE slightly unwell

offence NOUN **1** an illegal action **2** a feeling of resentment

odd ADJECTIVE • *an odd thing to do*
▶ strange, peculiar, weird, curious, unusual, bizarre • *an odd person* ▶ eccentric, strange, peculiar, weird • *odd socks*
▶ unmatched, different

offence NOUN • *guilty of an offence*
▶ crime, misdemeanour, wrongdoing, misdeed, transgression • *to cause offence*
▶ annoyance, anger, upset, displeasure, indignation

DICTIONARY

offend VERB **1** to cause offence to **2** to do wrong

offensive ADJECTIVE **1** causing offence **2** disgusting **3** *offensive weapons*

offensive NOUN an attack

offer VERB **1** to present something for someone to accept **2** to say you are willing to do or pay something

offer NOUN **1** the act of offering **2** an amount offered **3** a reduced price

offering NOUN something offered

offhand ADJECTIVE **1** said or done without preparation **2** casual and rude

office NOUN **1** a room or building used for business work **2** a government department **3** an important job or position

officer NOUN **1** a person in charge of others, especially in the armed forces **2** an official **3** a member of the police force

official ADJECTIVE **1** done or said by someone with authority **2** done as part of a job or position *official duties* ▸ **officially** ADVERB

⚠ **USAGE**

Do not confuse this word with *officious*.

official NOUN a person who holds a position of authority

officiate VERB to be in charge of a meeting, event, etc.

officious ADJECTIVE too ready to give orders; bossy ▸ **officiously** ADVERB

⚠ **USAGE**

Do not confuse this word with *official*.

offing NOUN **in the offing** about to arrive or happen

▶ **WORD HISTORY**

The *offing* was the horizon of the sea seen from the land, so that a ship *in the offing* would soon arrive.

off-licence NOUN a shop selling alcoholic drinks to be drunk away from the shop

THESAURUS

offend VERB • *I didn't mean to offend you.* ▸ upset, hurt, annoy, insult • *prisoners who offend again* ▸ break the law, commit a crime, do wrong

offensive ADJECTIVE • *offensive remarks* ▸ insulting, derogatory, disrespectful, abusive, rude

offer VERB • *to offer advice* ▸ provide, give, extend, make available, suggest • *offered to help in the search* ▸ volunteer, come forward, present yourself • *a job offering good prospects* ▸ provide, afford

offer NOUN • *a business offer* ▸ bid, proposal, proposition

official ADJECTIVE • *an official inquiry* ▸ authorized, approved, proper, authentic • *an official function* ▸ formal, ceremonial

official NOUN • *An official escorted us.* ▸ officer, functionary, representative, executive

officious ADJECTIVE • *an officious person* ▸ self-important, bumptious, bossy

a
b
c
d
e
f
g
h
i
j
k
l
m
n
o
p
q
r
s
t
u
v
w
x
y
z

495

off-putting ADJECTIVE making you less keen on something

offset VERB **offsetting, offset** to cancel out or make up for something

offshoot NOUN something developed from something else

offshore ADJECTIVE **1** from the land towards the sea **2** in the sea some distance from the shore

offside ADJECTIVE, ADVERB (of a player in football etc.) in a position not allowed by the rules of the game

offspring NOUN **offspring 1** a person's child or children **2** the young of an animal

often ADVERB many times; in many cases

ogle VERB to stare at someone attractive

ogre NOUN **1** a cruel giant in fairy tales **2** a terrifying person

oh EXCLAMATION an exclamation of pain, surprise, delight, etc.

ohm NOUN (Science) a unit of electrical resistance

oil NOUN **1** a thick slippery liquid that will not dissolve in water **2** a kind of petroleum used as fuel **3** oil paint ► **oily** ADJECTIVE

oil VERB to put oil on machinery to make it work smoothly

oil rig NOUN a structure with equipment for drilling for oil

oilskin NOUN cloth made waterproof by treatment with oil

ointment NOUN a cream or slippery paste for putting on sore skin and cuts

OK or **okay** ADVERB, ADJECTIVE (informal) all right

old ADJECTIVE **1** not new; born or made or existing from a long time ago **2** of a particular age *ten years old* **3** former or original *our old house* of old long ago; in the distant past

old age NOUN the time when a person is old

olden ADJECTIVE of former times

old-fashioned ADJECTIVE old in style; no longer fashionable

olive NOUN **1** a small green or black bitter fruit **2** the tree from which this comes

olive branch NOUN an offer of peace or friendship after a quarrel

Olympic Games or **Olympics** PLURAL NOUN a series of international sports contests held every four years in a different part of the world ► **Olympic** ADJECTIVE

THESAURUS

off-putting ADJECTIVE • *off-putting remarks* ► discouraging, intimidating, unsettling

often ADVERB • *She often asks about you.* ► frequently, regularly, repeatedly, many times

OK or **okay** ADJECTIVE • *Is everything OK now?* ► all right, satisfactory, fine, in order, acceptable

old ADJECTIVE • *an old man* ► elderly, aged, advanced in years • *old buildings* ► historic, dilapidated, ramshackle, ruined • *old clothes* ► worn, shabby, threadbare • *the old days* ► past, former, bygone

old-fashioned ADJECTIVE • *a big old-fashioned bathroom* ► out of date, outmoded, antiquated

ombudsman NOUN
ombudsmen an official who investigates complaints against government organizations

omega (oh-meg-a) NOUN the last letter of the Greek alphabet, equivalent to a long Roman o

omelette NOUN eggs beaten and cooked in a pan

omen NOUN a sign of what is going to happen

ominous ADJECTIVE suggesting trouble soon or in the future

omission NOUN something that has been omitted or not done

omit VERB **omitting, omitted 1** to miss something out **2** to fail to do something

omnibus NOUN a book or radio or television programme containing several stories or episodes that were previously published or broadcast separately

omnipotent ADJECTIVE having unlimited power

omniscient (om-niss-ee-ent) ADJECTIVE knowing everything
► **omniscience** NOUN

omnivorous (om-niv-er-us) ADJECTIVE eating all kinds of food
► **omnivore** NOUN

on PREPOSITION **1** supported by; covering; added or attached to

the sign on the door **2** close to; towards **3** during; at the time of *on my birthday* **4** concerning *a book on butterflies*

on ADVERB **1** so as to be on something *Put it on.* **2** further forward *Move on!* **3** working; in action

once ADVERB **1** for one time or on one occasion **2** formerly

once NOUN one time *just this once*

once CONJUNCTION as soon as

oncoming ADJECTIVE approaching; coming towards you

one ADJECTIVE **1** single **2** individual or united

one NOUN **1** the smallest whole number, 1 **2** a person or thing alone

one PRONOUN **1** a person or thing previously mentioned **2** a person; any person *One likes to help.*
► **oneself** PRONOUN

onerous (ohn-er-us or on-er-us) ADJECTIVE difficult to bear or do

one-sided ADJECTIVE **1** with one side much stronger or active than the other **2** unfair *a one-sided account*

ongoing ADJECTIVE continuing to exist or be in progress

onion NOUN a round vegetable with a strong flavour

omit VERB • *to omit a name from the list* ► leave out, miss out, exclude, ignore, cut, drop, eliminate • *I omitted to tell you about the party.* ► forget, neglect, fail

ongoing ADJECTIVE • *an ongoing problem* ► continuing, persistent, constant • *A road improvement programme is ongoing.* ► under way, in progress, progressing, evolving, continuing

a
b
c
d
e
f
g
h
i
j
k
l
m
n
o
p
q
r
s
t
u
v
w
x
y
z

a
b
c
d
e
f
g
h
i
j
k
l
m
n
o
p
q
r
s
t
u
v
w
x
y
z

online ADJECTIVE, ADVERB connected to a computer, the Internet, etc.

onlooker NOUN a spectator

only ADJECTIVE being the one person or thing of a kind *my only wish*

only ADVERB no more than; and that is all *only three left*

onset NOUN 1 a beginning *the onset of winter* 2 an attack

onslaught NOUN a fierce attack

onto PREPOSITION to a position on

onus (oh-nus) NOUN the duty or responsibility

onward ADVERB, ADJECTIVE going forward; further on ▶ **onwards** ADVERB

onyx NOUN a stone like marble, with different colours in layers

ooze VERB 1 to flow out or trickle slowly 2 to allow to flow out slowly

opal NOUN a kind of stone with a rainbow sheen

opaque (o-payk) ADJECTIVE not able to be seen through

open ADJECTIVE 1 not closed or fastened 2 not covered or blocked up 3 spread out; unfolded 4 not restricted *open access* 5 letting in visitors or customers 6 with wide empty spaces *open country* 7 honest and frank 8 not decided *an open mind* 9 willing or likely to receive *open to suggestions*

open VERB 1 to make or become open 2 to begin ▶ **opener** NOUN

open-air ADJECTIVE happening out of doors

opening NOUN 1 a space or gap; a place where something opens 2 a beginning 3 an opportunity

openly ADVERB without secrecy

opera NOUN a stage drama in which all or most of the words are sung ▶ **operatic** ADJECTIVE

operate VERB 1 to make a machine work 2 to be in action 3 to perform a surgical operation

operation NOUN 1 a piece of work or method of working 2 surgery on the body to take away or repair

THESAURUS

ooze VERB • *Blood oozed from a wound.* ▶ seep, leak, flow, dribble

open ADJECTIVE • *open access* ▶ free, unrestricted, clear, unobstructed, available • *open country* ▶ sweeping, rolling • *open about his feelings* ▶ frank, honest, candid, truthful

opening NOUN • *an opening in the wall* ▶ doorway, gateway, entry, hole, chink, crack • *openings in accountancy* ▶ opportunity, chance

operate VERB • *The alarms were not operating.* ▶ work, function, run • *a machine that's difficult to operate* ▶ work, use, utilize, handle, drive • *The doctors will need to operate.* ▶ perform surgery, carry out an operation

operation NOUN • *a business operation* ▶ enterprise, undertaking, procedure, transaction • *military operations* ▶ campaign, exercise, action, manoeuvre • *the smooth operation of the system*

a part of it **3** a planned military activity ► **operational** ADJECTIVE

operative ADJECTIVE working or functioning

operator NOUN a person who works something, especially a telephone switchboard

operetta NOUN a short light opera

opinion NOUN what you think of something; a belief or judgement

opinionated ADJECTIVE having and expressing strong opinions regardless of others

opium NOUN a drug made from the juice of certain poppies

opponent NOUN a person or group opposing another in a contest or war

opportune ADJECTIVE **1** (of a time) suitable for a purpose **2** happening at a suitable time ► **opportunely** ADVERB

opportunist NOUN a person who is quick to seize opportunities ► **opportunism** NOUN

opportunity NOUN **opportunities** a good chance to do a particular thing

oppose VERB **1** to argue or fight against **2** to contrast **be opposed to** to be strongly against

opposite ADJECTIVE **1** placed on the other or further side **2** moving away from or towards each other **3** completely different

opposite NOUN an opposite person or thing

opposite PREPOSITION opposite to; facing

opposition NOUN **1** the act of opposing; resistance **2** the people who oppose something **the Opposition** the chief political party opposing the one that is in power

THESAURUS

► running, functioning, working, management • *a surgical operation* ► biopsy, surgery, transplant

opinion NOUN • *to have an opinion* ► belief, view, point of view, thought, idea, attitude

opponent NOUN • *to face an opponent* ► adversary, opposition, rival, competitor, enemy • *an opponent of reform* ► objector (to), opposer

opportunity NOUN • *a good opportunity* ► chance, possibility

oppose VERB • *opposed plans for a new runway* ► object to, be against, protest against,

disapprove of • *I shan't oppose you.* ► resist, withstand, defy

opposite ADJECTIVE • *a house opposite the church* ► facing, across from • *the opposite wall* ► opposing, facing • *fought on opposite sides* ► rival, opposing, enemy

opposite NOUN • *to do the opposite* ► contrary, reverse, antithesis

opposition NOUN • *to meet with opposition* ► resistance, hostility, disapproval, unfriendliness, competition • *won over the opposition* ► opponents, opposing side

DICTIONARY

oppress VERB 1 to govern or treat people cruelly or unjustly 2 to worry someone or make them very sad ▶ **oppression** NOUN, **oppressor** NOUN

oppressive ADJECTIVE 1 cruel or harsh 2 worrying and difficult to bear 3 (of the weather) humid

opt VERB to choose **opt out** to decide not to take part

optic ADJECTIVE to do with the eye or sight

optical ADJECTIVE to do with sight

optician NOUN a person who tests the eyesight and provides glasses and contact lenses

optics NOUN the study of sight and of light

optimist NOUN a person who expects that things will turn out well ▶ **optimism** NOUN, **optimistic** ADJECTIVE

optimum ADJECTIVE best; most favourable ▶ **optimal** ADJECTIVE

option NOUN 1 the right or power to choose 2 something that may be chosen

optional ADJECTIVE that you can choose to do

opulent ADJECTIVE wealthy or luxurious ▶ **opulence** NOUN

or CONJUNCTION used to show a choice

oracle NOUN (in the ancient world) a shrine of a god where people sought advice about the future

oral ADJECTIVE 1 spoken, not written 2 to do with or using the mouth ▶ **orally** ADVERB

oral NOUN a spoken exam or test

orange NOUN 1 a citrus fruit with reddish-yellow peel 2 a reddish-yellow colour

orangeade NOUN an orange-flavoured drink

orang-utan NOUN a large reddish-brown ape with long arms

oration NOUN a long formal speech

orator NOUN a public speaker ▶ **oratorical** ADJECTIVE

oratorio NOUN **oratorios** a long piece of choral music on a religious theme

oratory NOUN the art or practice of making speeches

orb NOUN a sphere or globe

THESAURUS

oppress VERB • *gloomy feelings that oppressed him* ▶ depress, weigh down, burden, hang over • *had been oppressed by successive invaders* ▶ persecute, repress, suppress, keep down

oppressive ADJECTIVE • *an oppressive dictatorship* ▶ dictatorial, autocratic, authoritarian, brutal, harsh • *oppressive weather* ▶ humid, muggy, sultry, hot, stifling

option NOUN • *little option but to agree* ▶ choice, alternative, possibility

oral ADJECTIVE • *oral evidence* ▶ spoken, verbal

orbit NOUN 1 the curved path of an object moving round a planet 2 a range of control ► **orbital** ADJECTIVE

orbit VERB to move in an orbit

orchard NOUN a piece of ground with fruit trees

orchestra NOUN a group of musicians playing together under a conductor ► **orchestral** ADJECTIVE

orchestrate VERB 1 to arrange music for an orchestra 2 to coordinate carefully ► **orchestration** NOUN

orchid NOUN a plant with brightly coloured flowers in unusual shapes

ordain VERB 1 to make a person a member of the Christian clergy 2 to declare or order by law

ordeal NOUN a difficult or unpleasant experience

order NOUN 1 a command 2 a request for goods to be supplied 3 the way things are arranged *alphabetical order* 4 a satisfactory condition *working order* 5 obedience to laws 6 a kind or sort *bravery of the highest order* 7 a group of monks or nuns who live by religious rules **in order that** or **in order to** for the purpose of

order VERB 1 to command 2 to ask for goods to be supplied 3 to put into order

orderly ADJECTIVE 1 arranged neatly or well 2 well-behaved and obedient

orderly NOUN **orderlies** 1 a soldier who assists an officer 2 an assistant in a hospital

ordinal number NOUN a number that shows a thing's position in a series, e.g. first, second, third, etc.

ordinance NOUN a command or decree

ordinary ADJECTIVE normal or usual; not special **out of the ordinary** unusual ► **ordinarily** ADVERB

THESAURUS

orbit NOUN • *the earth's orbit round the sun* ► course, path, circuit

ordeal NOUN • *a four-year ordeal as a captive* ► trial, suffering, test, nightmare

order NOUN • *the order to charge* ► command, instruction, direction, decree • *to restore order* ► peace, control, calm, quiet • *do things in a set order* ► sequence, arrangement • *an order for a hundred storage boxes* ► request, booking, demand, application • *skills of a very high order* ► type, kind, sort

order VERB • *ordered them to leave* ► instruct, command, direct • *to order tickets* ► book, reserve, apply for • *to order your thoughts* ► arrange, organize, sort out, set in order

orderly ADJECTIVE • *an orderly withdrawal* ► methodical, systematic, well organized • *to form an orderly queue* ► neat, tidy, well behaved

ordinary ADJECTIVE • *an ordinary day's work* ► usual, normal, typical, habitual, customary • *ordinary people* ► average,

a b c d e f g h i j k l m n o p q r s t u v w x y z

ordination NOUN the act of ordaining someone as a member of the clergy

ordnance NOUN weapons and other military equipment

ore NOUN rock with a valuable mineral in it

oregano (o-ri-gah-noh) NOUN a wild herb used in cooking

organ NOUN 1 a keyboard instrument with sound produced by air forced through pipes 2 a part of the body with a particular function

organic ADJECTIVE 1 to do with the organs of the body 2 to do with living things 3 grown without the use of chemical fertilizers and pesticides

organism NOUN a living thing

organist NOUN a person who plays the organ

organization NOUN 1 a group of people working together in business, government, etc. 2 the process of organizing

⚠ **SPELLING**

This word can also be spelled *organisation*.

organize VERB 1 to plan and prepare 2 to form people into a group to work together 3 to put in order

⚠ **SPELLING**

This word can also be spelled *organise*.

orgasm NOUN the climax of sexual excitement

Orient NOUN the East

oriental ADJECTIVE to do with eastern countries

orientate VERB 1 to face or place something in a certain direction 2 to get your bearings
▶ **orientation** NOUN

orienteering NOUN the sport of finding your way across rough country

orifice NOUN an opening in the body

origami (o-rig-ah-mee) NOUN the art of folding paper into special shapes

origin NOUN 1 the point or cause from which something began 2 a person's family background

THESAURUS

normal, typical • *Life seemed so ordinary.* ▶ routine, humdrum, dull, unremarkable, unexciting

organization NOUN • *the organization of trips and visits* ▶ planning, coordination, arrangement, running • *an international organization* ▶ institution, enterprise, operation, company

organize VERB • *to organize a demonstration* ▶ coordinate, plan, bring together, run • *to organize your ideas* ▶ order, structure, develop, put in order

origin NOUN • *the origin of the universe* ▶ beginning, start, birth, emergence • *of Irish origin* ▶ descent, ancestry, parentage, family

DICTIONARY

original ADJECTIVE **1** existing from the start **2** new in its design etc. **3** producing new ideas ▸ **originality** NOUN, **originally** ADVERB

originate VERB **1** to cause to begin; to create **2** to have as an origin

ornament NOUN an object displayed or worn as a decoration

ornamental ADJECTIVE decorative rather than useful

ornamentation NOUN artistic decoration

ornate ADJECTIVE elaborately decorated

ornithology NOUN the study of birds ▸ **ornithologist** NOUN

orphan NOUN a child whose parents have died

orphanage NOUN a home for orphans

orthodox ADJECTIVE **1** holding accepted beliefs **2** conventional or normal ▸ **orthodoxy** NOUN

orthopaedic (orth-o-pee-diks) ADJECTIVE to do with diseases and injuries of the bones and muscles

oscillate VERB **1** to move to and fro **2** to waver or vary ▸ **oscillation** NOUN

osmosis NOUN the passing of fluid into a porous partition into another more concentrated fluid

ostensible ADJECTIVE apparent, but not necessarily true or genuine *ostensible reasons* ▸ **ostensibly** ADVERB

ostentatious ADJECTIVE making a showy display ▸ **ostentation** NOUN

osteopath NOUN a person who treats disease by manipulating the bones and muscles ▸ **osteopathy** NOUN

ostracize VERB to exclude a person from a group ▸ **ostracism** NOUN

⚠ **SPELLING**

This word can also be spelled *ostracise*.

ostrich NOUN a large long-legged bird that cannot fly

other ADJECTIVE **1** different **2** additional or remaining **3** just recent or past *the other day*

other NOUN, PRONOUN the other person or thing

THESAURUS

original ADJECTIVE • *the original inhabitants* ▸ earliest, first, initial, indigenous • *an original idea for a story* ▸ new, creative, fresh, unusual, imaginative • *an original painting* ▸ authentic, genuine, real

originate VERB • *Where did the rumour originate?* ▸ arise, start, begin, emerge, crop up • *not clear who originated the idea* ▸

conceive, invent, create, introduce

ornament NOUN • *a plain style without ornament* ▸ decoration, embellishment, trimming • *a shelf covered with ornaments* ▸ trinket, knick-knack

orthodox ADJECTIVE • *orthodox views* ▸ conventional, mainstream, established, conservative, traditional

a
b
c
d
e
f
g
h
i
j
k
l
m
n
o
p
q
r
s
t
u
v
w
x
y
z

otherwise ADVERB **1** if things happen differently **2** in other ways **3** differently *cannot do otherwise*

otter NOUN a fish-eating river animal with webbed feet and a flat tail

ought AUXILIARY VERB **1** expressing duty or need *We ought to stay.* **2** expressing probability *They ought to be home soon.*

oughtn't ought not

ounce NOUN a unit of weight equal to $\frac{1}{16}$ of a pound (about 28 grams)

our ADJECTIVE belonging to us

ours POSSESSIVE PRONOUN belonging to us *These seats are ours.*

⚠ **USAGE**

It is incorrect to write *our's.*

ourselves PRONOUN we and nobody else *We hurt ourselves. We ourselves have said it.* **by ourselves** alone; on our own

oust VERB to drive a person out from a position or office

out ADVERB **1** away from a particular place or position **2** into the open or into existence **3** no longer burning or shining **4** in error *out by 10%* **5** to or at an end; completely *sold out* **6** strongly or openly *to speak out* **7** (in cricket)

no longer batting **out of doors** in the open air

out-and-out ADJECTIVE thorough or complete

outback NOUN the remote inland districts of Australia

outbreak NOUN the beginning of something unpleasant or violent, e.g. disease or war

outburst NOUN a sudden bursting out of anger or laughter etc.

outcast NOUN a person who has been rejected by family or society

outcome NOUN a result of events

outcry NOUN **outcries** a strong protest

outdated ADJECTIVE out of date

outdo VERB **outdoes**, **outdid**, **outdone** to do better than

outdoor ADJECTIVE done or used in the open air

outdoors ADVERB in the open air

outer ADJECTIVE nearer to the outside ► **outermost** ADJECTIVE

outfit NOUN **1** a set of clothes or equipment **2** (*informal*) a team or organization

outgoings PLURAL NOUN expenditure

outgrow VERB **outgrew**, **outgrown 1** to become too old or

outbreak NOUN • *an outbreak of disease* ► epidemic, plague, rash, spate • *the outbreak of war* ► start, beginning, onset

outcome NOUN • *the outcome of the election* ► result, consequence, conclusion, upshot

outcry NOUN • *an outcry about the state of the railways* ► protest, complaint, furore

outdo VERB • *to outdo everyone else* ► surpass, outshine, exceed, be better than, beat

a
b
c
d
e
f
g
h
i
j
k
l
m
n
o
p
q
r
s
t
u
v
w
x
y
z

DICTIONARY

big for **2** to grow faster or larger than

outhouse NOUN a small building separate from the main one

outing NOUN a journey for pleasure

outlandish ADJECTIVE looking or sounding strange

outlast VERB to last longer than

outlaw NOUN a person who is excluded from legal rights and protection

outlaw VERB **1** to make a person an outlaw **2** to forbid or ban

outlay NOUN an amount of money spent

outlet NOUN **1** a way for something to get out **2** a way of expressing feelings **3** a place from which goods are sold

outline NOUN **1** a line showing a boundary or shape **2** a summary

outline VERB **1** to make an outline of **2** to summarize

outlive VERB to live or last longer than

outlook NOUN **1** a view from a window **2** a mental attitude **3** future prospects

outlying ADJECTIVE remote

outmoded ADJECTIVE no longer useful or fashionable

outnumber VERB to be more in number than

out of date ADJECTIVE no longer valid or fashionable

outpatient NOUN a person who visits a hospital for treatment but does not stay there

outpost NOUN a distant settlement

output NOUN **1** the amount of goods etc. produced **2** the information or results from a computer

outrage NOUN something wicked or cruel that shocks people

THESAURUS

outing NOUN • *outings to the coast* ► trip, excursion, jaunt, expedition

outlaw NOUN • *notorious outlaws* ► bandit, brigand, fugitive, desperado, criminal

outlet NOUN • *an outlet for fumes* ► vent, duct, channel, opening • *high street outlets* ► shop, store, retailer

outline NOUN • *the outline of a building* ► profile, silhouette, shape, form

outlook NOUN • *a glorious outlook over the valley* ► view, prospect, panorama • *different in character*

and outlook ► attitude, way of thinking, viewpoint, frame of mind • *the economic outlook* ► prospects, forecast, prognosis, prediction

out of date ADJECTIVE • *an out-of-date passport* ► expired, lapsed, invalid • *a machine that was out of date* ► old-fashioned, outdated, obsolete

outrage NOUN • *the sense of outrage* ► anger, indignation, fury, disgust • *Their suffering is an outrage.* ► scandal, disgrace, atrocity

a
b
c
d
e
f
g
h
i
j
k
l
m
n
o
p
q
r
s
t
u
v
w
x
y
z

outrage VERB to shock and anger people

outrageous ADJECTIVE **1** very wicked **2** very extravagant

outright ADVERB **1** completely **2** frankly *Tell him outright.*

outright ADJECTIVE thorough or complete *an outright lie*

outrun VERB **outrunning, outran, outrun** to run faster or further than

outset NOUN the beginning of something

outside NOUN the outer side, surface, or part

outside ADJECTIVE **1** on or coming from the outside **2** remote or slight

outside ADVERB on or to the outside; outdoors

outside PREPOSITION on or to the outside of *outside the door*

outsider NOUN **1** a person who does not belong **2** a contestant with little chance of winning

outsize ADJECTIVE much larger than average

outskirts PLURAL NOUN the outer districts of a town

outspoken ADJECTIVE speaking or spoken frankly

outstanding ADJECTIVE **1** extremely good or distinguished **2** not yet paid or dealt with

outstrip VERB **outstripping, outstripped 1** to run faster or further than **2** to be or do better than

outward ADJECTIVE **1** on the outside **2** going or facing outwards

outward ADVERB outwards

outwardly ADVERB on the outside; as it appears

outwards ADVERB towards the outside

outweigh VERB be more important than

outwit VERB **outwitting, outwitted** to deceive with cunning

outrageous ADJECTIVE • *an outrageous slur* ► disgraceful, shocking, scandalous, appalling • *outrageous stories* ► far-fetched, extravagant, unbelievable • *an outrageous price* ► excessive, exorbitant, extortionate

outside NOUN • *the outside of the building* ► exterior, facade, surface, skin

outside ADJECTIVE • *an outside light* ► exterior, external, outdoor

• *outside interference* ► external, foreign, alien • *an outside chance of rain* ► slight, remote, faint

outspoken ADJECTIVE • *outspoken remarks* ► frank, forthright, candid, blunt

outstanding ADJECTIVE • *an outstanding musician* ► excellent, exceptional, superb • *outstanding questions* ► unresolved, unsettled, remaining

outwit VERB • *to outwit the enemy* ► outsmart, dupe, fool, trick

ova plural of **ovum**

oval ADJECTIVE shaped like an egg
► **oval** NOUN

ovary NOUN **ovaries** either of the two female organs in which egg cells are produced

ovation NOUN a round of applause

oven NOUN a closed space for cooking or heating food or for baking clay

over PREPOSITION **1** above **2** more than **3** concerning *quarrelled over money* **4** across the top of; on or to the other side of **5** in superiority or preference to *a victory over their enemy*

over ADVERB **1** from an upright position *fall over* **2** so that a different side shows *Turn it over.* **3** at or to a place *Walk over to our house.* **4** remaining *nothing left over* **5** all through *Think it over.* **6** at an end *The lesson is over.*

over NOUN a series of six balls bowled in cricket

overall ADJECTIVE including everything *the overall cost*

overall ADVERB in general *has improved overall*

overall NOUN a light coat worn to protect other clothes when working

overalls PLURAL NOUN a combined bib and trousers worn over other clothes to protect them

overarm ADJECTIVE, ADVERB with the arm lifted above shoulder level

and coming down in front of the body

overawe VERB to overcome a person with awe

overbearing ADJECTIVE domineering

overboard ADVERB into the water from a ship

overcast ADJECTIVE covered with cloud

overcoat NOUN a warm outdoor coat

overcome VERB **overcame**, **overcome 1** to win a victory over **2** to have a strong physical or emotional effect on **3** to find a way of dealing with

overcrowded ADJECTIVE having too many people

overdo VERB **overdid**, **overdone 1** to do something too much **2** to cook food for too long

overdose NOUN too large a dose of a drug

overdraft NOUN the amount by which a bank account is overdrawn

overdraw VERB **overdrew**, **overdrawn** to draw more money from a bank account than you have in it

overdue ADJECTIVE not paid or arrived etc. by the proper time

overestimate VERB to estimate too highly

THESAURUS

overcome VERB **1** *strong enough to overcome the enemy* ► defeat, beat, conquer, overpower,

vanquish **2** *to overcome your fear* ► control, master, conquer, get the better of

overflow VERB to flow over the edge ► **overflow** NOUN

overgrown ADJECTIVE covered with weeds or unwanted plants

overhang VERB **overhung** to jut out over something

overhaul VERB to examine and repair ► **overhaul** NOUN

overhead ADJECTIVE, ADVERB **1** directly above **2** in the sky

overheads PLURAL NOUN the expenses of running a business

overhear VERB **overheard** to hear something you were not meant to hear

overjoyed ADJECTIVE filled with great joy

overland ADJECTIVE, ADVERB travelling over the land

overlap VERB **overlapping, overlapped 1** to lie across part of **2** to happen partly at the same time ► **overlap** NOUN

overleaf ADVERB on the other side of the page

overload VERB to put too great a load on

overlook VERB **1** not to notice or consider something **2** to ignore a wrong deliberately **3** to have a view of something

overlord NOUN a supreme lord

overnight ADJECTIVE, ADVERB **1** of or during a night *an overnight stop; can stay overnight* **2** very quick or quickly

overpower VERB to defeat by greater strength

overpowering ADJECTIVE very strong

overrate VERB to have too high an opinion of ► **overrated** ADJECTIVE

override VERB **overrode, overridden 1** to overrule **2** to be more important than ► **overriding** ADJECTIVE

overrule VERB to reject a suggestion etc. by using your authority

overrun VERB **overrunning, overran, overrun 1** to grow or spread over

overseas ADVERB across or beyond the sea; abroad

oversee VERB **oversaw, overseen** to watch over or supervise ► **overseer** NOUN

overshadow VERB **1** to cast a shadow over **2** to make a person or thing seem unimportant

oversight NOUN a mistake made by not noticing something

overt ADJECTIVE done or shown openly

overflow VERB • *The water tank overflowed.* ► spill over, flow over, brim over, flood

overjoyed ADJECTIVE • *overjoyed at the birth of a daughter* ► thrilled, delighted, ecstatic

overlook VERB • *willing to overlook the mistake* ► ignore, disregard, take no notice of, excuse • *The house overlooks a car park.* ► look out on, have a view of, face

DICTIONARY

overtake VERB **overtook, overtaken** to catch up with or pass someone ahead

overthrow VERB **overthrew, overthrown** to remove from power by force ▶ **overthrow** NOUN

overtime NOUN **1** time spent working outside the normal hours **2** payment for this

overtone NOUN a feeling or quality suggested but not expressed

overture NOUN **1** an orchestral introduction **2** an attempt to start a discussion

overturn VERB **1** to turn over or upside down **2** to reverse a legal decision

overweight ADJECTIVE too heavy

overwhelm VERB **1** to bury or drown beneath a huge mass **2** to overcome completely
▶ **overwhelming** ADJECTIVE

overwrought ADJECTIVE upset and anxious

ovulate VERB to produce an egg cell from an ovary

ovum (oh-vum) NOUN **ova** a female cell that can develop into a new individual when it is fertilized

owe VERB **1** to have a duty to pay or give something to someone **2** to have something thanks to another person or thing *owed their lives to the pilot's skill* **owing to** because of; caused by

owl NOUN a bird of prey with large eyes, flying at night

own ADJECTIVE belonging to yourself or itself **on your own** alone

own VERB **1** to have as your property **2** to acknowledge or admit **own up** to confess

owner NOUN the person who owns something ▶ **ownership** NOUN

ox NOUN **oxen** a large animal kept for its meat and for pulling carts

oxide NOUN a compound of oxygen and one other element

oxygen NOUN a gas that exists in the air and is essential to life

oyster NOUN a kind of shellfish with a shell that can contain a pearl

ozone NOUN a form of oxygen with a sharp smell

THESAURUS

overthrow VERB • *The emperor was finally overthrown.* ▶ depose, oust, remove, drive out, defeat

overturn VERB • *The boat overturned in a squall.* ▶ capsize, turn over, keel over • *The decision was overturned.* ▶ overrule, override, revoke, reverse

owing ADJECTIVE **owing to** • *would not use the lifts, owing to claustrophobia* ▶ because of, as a result of, on account of, thanks to

own VERB • *to own a house* ▶ possess, be the owner of, have **own up to** • *to own up to the mistake* ▶ confess, admit, acknowledge

a
b
c
d
e
f
g
h
i
j
k
l
m
n
o
p
q
r
s
t
u
v
w
x
y
z

Pp

p. ABBREVIATION page

pace NOUN **1** one step in walking or running **2** speed of walking or running *a slow pace*

pace VERB to walk with slow or regular steps

pacemaker NOUN **1** a person who sets the pace for another in a race **2** an electronic device put into the body by surgery to keep the heart beating

pacifist (pas-if-ist) NOUN a person who refuses to support violent means ► **pacifism** NOUN

pacify VERB **pacifies**, **pacified 1** to calm a person **2** to bring peace to a country

pack NOUN **1** a collection of things wrapped or tied together **2** a set of playing cards **3** a bag carried on your back **4** a large amount *a pack*

of lies **5** a group of hounds or wolves etc.

pack VERB **1** to put things into a suitcase, bag, box etc. **2** to crowd together

package NOUN **1** a parcel or packet **2** a number of things offered together ► **packaging** NOUN

packet NOUN a small parcel

pact NOUN an agreement or treaty

pad¹ NOUN **1** a soft thick mass of material **2** a piece of soft material worn for protection **3** a set of sheets of paper fastened together **4** the soft fleshy part under an animal's foot or the end of a finger or toe **5** a platform for launching a rocket

pad VERB **padding**, **padded** to put a pad on or in **pad out** to make something last longer

pad² VERB **padding**, **padded** to walk softly

THESAURUS

pace NOUN • *moved back a few paces* ► step, stride, stride • *traffic moving at a slow pace* ► speed, rate • *quickened their pace* ► stride, walk, speed

pace VERB • *to pace up and down* ► walk, stride, march

pacify VERB • *difficult to pacify him now* ► appease, placate, calm, soothe

pack NOUN • *a pack of cigarettes* ► package, packet, container, carton, box • *walkers with packs on their backs* ► backpack,

rucksack • *a pack of animals* ► group, herd, troop

pack VERB • *to pack a case* ► fill, load, stuff • *decided to pack her belongings* ► bundle, parcel, wrap, store • *Visitors pack the local museums.* ► throng, crowd into, fill

pact NOUN • *a non-aggression pact* ► treaty, alliance, agreement

pad NOUN • *a pad of cotton wool* ► wad, cushion, pillow • *made notes on a pad* ► notebook, notepad, jotter

padding NOUN material used to pad things

paddle VERB 1 to move a boat along with a paddle 2 to walk about with bare feet in shallow water

paddle NOUN 1 a short oar with a broad blade 2 a spell of paddling

paddock NOUN a small field for keeping horses

paddy field NOUN a field where rice is grown

padlock NOUN a detachable lock with a hinged metal loop that passes through a ring or chain

padlock VERB to lock with a padlock

paediatrics (peed-ee-at-riks) NOUN the study of children's diseases
► **paediatric** ADJECTIVE, **paediatrician** NOUN

> **WORD HISTORY**
> from Greek *paidos* 'of a child' and *iatros* 'doctor'

pagan (pay-gan) NOUN a person who does not believe in one of the chief religions ► **pagan** ADJECTIVE, **paganism** NOUN

page[1] NOUN a piece of paper that is part of a book or newspaper etc.; one side of this

page[2] NOUN 1 a boy or man employed as an attendant 2 a young boy attending a bride at a wedding

pageant NOUN 1 a play or entertainment on a historical subject 2 a procession of people in costume as an entertainment
► **pageantry** NOUN

pager NOUN a small radio device that can receive messages

pagoda (pag-oh-da) NOUN a tower or temple in Asia, shaped like a tall pyramid

paid past tense of **pay**
put paid to (*informal*) to put an end to

pail NOUN a bucket

pain NOUN 1 an unpleasant feeling caused by injury or disease 2 suffering in the mind

pain VERB to cause suffering or distress to

painful ADJECTIVE causing pain or distress ► **painfully** ADVERB

painless ADJECTIVE not causing any pain or distress

painstaking ADJECTIVE very careful and thorough

paint NOUN a liquid substance put on a surface to colour it

paint VERB 1 to put paint on a surface 2 to make a picture with paints

paintbrush NOUN a brush for putting paint on a surface

painter NOUN a person who paints

pain NOUN • *a pain in his tooth* ► ache, soreness, tenderness, discomfort • *the pain of losing a child* ► grief, sorrow, distress

painful ADJECTIVE • *a painful wound* ► sore, hurting, tender, agonizing, excruciating • *a painful experience* ► unpleasant, traumatic

a
b
c
d
e
f
g
h
i
j
k
l
m
n
o
p
q
r
s
t
u
v
w
x
y
z

painting NOUN **1** a painted picture **2** the use of paints to make a picture

pair NOUN **1** a set of two things or people **2** something made of two joined parts *a pair of scissors*

pair VERB to put two things together as a pair **pair off** to form a couple

pal NOUN (informal) a friend

palace NOUN a large house where a king, queen, or other important person lives

palatable ADJECTIVE pleasant to eat

palate NOUN **1** the roof of the mouth **2** a person's sense of taste

⚠ **USAGE**

Do not confuse this word with *palette* and *pallet*.

palatial (pa-lay-shal) ADJECTIVE like a palace; large and splendid

pale[1] ADJECTIVE almost white *a pale face* **2** not bright in colour or light *pale green*

pale[2] NOUN a boundary **beyond the pale** beyond what is acceptable

palette NOUN a board on which an artist mixes paints

⚠ **USAGE**

Do not confuse this word with *palate* and *pallet*.

palindrome NOUN a word or phrase that reads the same backwards as forwards, e.g. *radar* or *Madam, I'm Adam*

paling NOUN a fence made of wooden posts or railings

palisade NOUN a fence of pointed sticks or boards

pall[1] (pawl) NOUN **1** a cloth spread over a coffin **2** a dark covering *a pall of smoke*

pall[2] (pawl) VERB to seem dull or uninteresting after a while

pallet NOUN **1** a mattress stuffed with straw **2** a hard narrow bed **3** a large platform for stacking and transporting goods

⚠ **USAGE**

Do not confuse this word with *palate* and *palette*.

palliative NOUN something that lessens pain or suffering

pallid ADJECTIVE pale from illness

pallor NOUN paleness of a person's face

palm NOUN **1** the flat inner part of the hand **2** a tropical tree with large leaves and no branches

palm VERB **palm off** to fool a person into accepting something

palpable ADJECTIVE **1** able to be touched or felt **2** obvious *a palpable lie* ▶ **palpably** ADVERB

palpitate VERB (of the heart) to beat hard and quickly
▶ **palpitation** NOUN

palsy (pawl-zee) NOUN (old use) paralysis

paltry (pol-tree) ADJECTIVE small and almost worthless *a paltry amount*

pampas NOUN wide grassy plains in South America

THESAURUS

pale ADJECTIVE • *a pale face* ▶ white, pallid, wan, ashen • *a pale shade of* pink ▶ light, soft, muted, pastel • *a pale light* ▶ dim, weak, watery

pampas grass NOUN a tall grass with long feathery flowers

pamper VERB to treat or look after someone very kindly and indulgently

pamphlet NOUN a leaflet or booklet giving information on a subject

pan NOUN **1** a wide container with a flat base, used in cooking **2** something shaped like this **3** the bowl of a lavatory

panacea (pan-a-see-a) NOUN a cure for all kinds of diseases or troubles

panache (pan-ash) NOUN a confident stylish manner

pancake NOUN a thin round cake of batter fried on both sides

pancreas (pan-kree-as) NOUN a gland near the stomach, producing insulin and digestive juices

panda NOUN a large bear-like black-and-white animal found in China

pandemonium NOUN uproar and confusion

pander VERB **pander to** to give someone whatever they want

pane NOUN a sheet of glass in a window

panel NOUN **1** a long flat piece of wood, metal, etc. that is part of a door, wall, piece of furniture, etc.

2 a flat board with controls or instruments on it **3** a group of people chosen to discuss or decide something ► **panelled** ADJECTIVE, **panelling** NOUN

pang NOUN a sudden sharp pain

panic NOUN sudden uncontrollable fear ► **panicky** ADJECTIVE

panic VERB **panicking, panicked** to fill or be filled with panic

pannier NOUN a bag or basket hung on one side of a bicycle, motorcycle, or horse

panorama NOUN a view or picture of a wide area ► **panoramic** ADJECTIVE

pansy NOUN **pansies** a small brightly coloured garden flower

pant VERB to take short quick breaths after running or working hard

panther NOUN a large black leopard

panties PLURAL NOUN (informal) short knickers

pantile NOUN a curved tile for a roof

pantomime NOUN **1** a Christmas entertainment, usually based on a fairy tale **2** mime

pantry NOUN **pantries** a small room for storing food; a larder

pants PLURAL NOUN (informal) **1** underpants or knickers **2** (American) trousers

THESAURUS

pamper VERB • to pamper a child ► spoil, indulge

panel NOUN • a control panel ► console, board • a panel of judges ► group, team, board

panic NOUN • rushed out in panic ► alarm, fright, fear, terror

panic VERB • no need to panic yet ► be alarmed, take fright, lose your head, overreact

pap NOUN **1** soft food suitable for babies **2** trivial entertainment; nonsense

papacy (pay-pa-see) NOUN the position of Pope

papal (pay-pal) ADJECTIVE to do with the Pope

paper NOUN **1** a substance made in thin sheets from wood, rags, etc., used for writing or printing or drawing on or for wrapping **2** a newspaper **3** wallpaper **4** a document **5** a set of examination questions

paper VERB to cover a wall or room with wallpaper

paperback NOUN a book with a thin flexible cover

papier mâché (pap-yay mash-ay) NOUN paper made into pulp and moulded to make models, ornaments, etc.

paprika (pap-rik-a) NOUN a powdered spice made from red pepper

papyrus (pap-y-rus) NOUN paper made from the stems of a plant like a reed, used in ancient Egypt

par NOUN **1** an average or normal amount or condition **2** (in golf) the number of strokes that a good player should normally take for a hole or course

parable NOUN a story told to teach people a moral

parabola (pa-rab-ol-a) NOUN a curve like the path of an object thrown into the air and falling down again ▶ **parabolic** ADJECTIVE

parachute NOUN an umbrella-like device on which people or things can float to the ground from an aircraft

parade NOUN **1** a procession of people or things **2** an assembly of troops for inspection or drill **3** a public square or promenade

parade VERB **1** to move in a parade **2** to assemble for a parade **3** to display in an obvious way

paradise NOUN **1** heaven **2** a place of great happiness

paradox NOUN a statement that seems to contradict itself but which contains a truth, e.g. 'More haste, less speed' ▶ **paradoxical** ADJECTIVE

paraffin NOUN a kind of oil used as fuel

paragon NOUN a person or thing that seems perfect

paragraph NOUN one or more sentences on a single subject, forming a section of a piece of writing and beginning on a new line

parakeet NOUN a kind of small parrot

parallel ADJECTIVE (of lines etc.) side by side and the same distance

THESAURUS

parade NOUN • *a military parade* ▶ procession, march, cavalcade, display, pageant, review, show

parade VERB • *to parade through the city* ▶ process, troop, march past • *paraded up and down the corridor* ▶ walk, stride, strut

apart from each other for their whole length

parallel NOUN **1** something similar or corresponding **2** a comparison **3** a line that is parallel to another **4** a line of latitude

parallel VERB **paralleling, paralleled** to be similar to or correspond to

parallelogram NOUN a four-sided figure with opposite sides equal and parallel

paralyse VERB **paralysing, paralysed 1** to cause paralysis in **2** to make unable to move *be paralysed with fear*

paralysis NOUN a state of being unable to move a muscle or muscles, especially because of disease or injury

paramedic NOUN a member of an ambulance crew or other person trained to assist medical staff

parameter NOUN a quantity or factor that is variable and affects other things by its changes

paramilitary ADJECTIVE organized like a military force but not part of the armed services

paramount ADJECTIVE more important than anything else

paranoia NOUN **1** a mental illness in which a person wrongly believes that other people want to hurt them **2** an unjustified suspicion and mistrust of others
▶ **paranoid** ADJECTIVE

paranormal ADJECTIVE beyond what is normal and can be rationally explained

parapet NOUN a low wall along the edge of a balcony, bridge, roof, etc.

paraphernalia NOUN numerous pieces of equipment, belongings, etc.

paraphrase VERB to express the meaning of something in different words ▶ **paraphrase** NOUN

paraplegia NOUN paralysis of the lower half of the body
▶ **paraplegic** NOUN

parasite NOUN an animal or plant that lives in or on another, from which it gets its food ▶ **parasitic** ADJECTIVE

parasol NOUN a light umbrella used to give shade from the sun

paratroops PLURAL NOUN troops trained to be dropped from aircraft by parachute
▶ **paratrooper** NOUN

parcel NOUN an item wrapped up for sending by post

parcel VERB **parcelling, parcelled 1** to wrap something up as a parcel **2** to divide into shares

parched ADJECTIVE **1** very dry **2** very thirsty

parchment NOUN a kind of heavy paper, originally made from animal skins

pardon NOUN **1** forgiveness **2** the cancelling of a punishment

THESAURUS

parcel NOUN • *a parcel of food*
▶ package, packet, pack, bundle

pardon VERB • *The king would pardon them.* ▶ forgive, excuse, reprieve

pardon VERB **1** to forgive or excuse someone **2** to cancel a person's punishment

pare (say as pair) VERB **1** to trim by cutting away the edges **2** to reduce gradually

parent NOUN **1** a mother or father; a living thing that has produced young **2** a source from which others are derived *the parent company* ► **parental** (pa-rent-al) ADJECTIVE

parentage NOUN the identity of a person's parents

parenthesis (pa-ren-thi-sis) NOUN **parentheses 1** extra words put into a sentence, usually between brackets or dashes **2** either of a pair of brackets in writing

pariah (pa-ry-a) NOUN an outcast

parish NOUN a district with its own church

parishioner NOUN someone who lives in a particular parish

parity NOUN equality

park NOUN a large public area with grass and trees

park VERB to leave a vehicle in a place for a time

parka NOUN a warm jacket with a hood attached

Parkinson's disease NOUN a disease that causes trembling of the arms and legs and stiff muscles

parley VERB to hold a discussion with someone ► **parley** NOUN

parliament NOUN the assembly that makes a country's laws ► **parliamentary** ADJECTIVE

parlour NOUN (old use) a sitting room

parochial ADJECTIVE **1** to do with a church parish **2** interested only in your own area

parody NOUN **parodies** an amusing imitation of the style of a writer, composer, literary work, etc.

parody VERB **parodies, parodied** to make or be a parody of

parole NOUN the release of a prisoner before the end of a sentence on condition of good behaviour *on parole*

parole VERB to release on parole

paroxysm (pa-roks-izm) NOUN an outburst of rage, jealousy, laughter, etc.

parrot NOUN a brightly coloured tropical bird that can imitate human speech

parry VERB **parries, parried 1** to turn aside an opponent's weapon or blow **2** to avoid an awkward question

parsimonious ADJECTIVE sparing in the use of something ► **parsimony** NOUN

parsley NOUN a plant with crinkled green leaves used to flavour and decorate food

THESAURUS

park NOUN • *The children went off to play in the park.* ► recreation ground, playground

park VERB • *She parked her car outside the house.* ► leave, station

a b c d e f g h i j k l m n o p q r s t u v w x y z

parsnip NOUN a plant with a yellow root used as a vegetable

parson NOUN a member of the clergy, especially a rector or vicar

parsonage NOUN a parson's house

part NOUN **1** some but not all of a thing or number of things **2** character played by an actor **3** the words spoken by a character in a play **4** a contribution to an activity *played an important part in the project* **5** one side in an agreement or dispute **take part** to join in an activity

part VERB to separate or divide **part with** to give away or get rid of

partake VERB **partook, partaken partake of 1** to eat or drink **2** to take part in

partial ADJECTIVE **1** not complete or total *a partial eclipse* **2** favouring one side **be partial to** to be fond of ▶ **partially** ADVERB

partiality NOUN **1** a preference for one side over another **2** a liking

participant NOUN someone who takes part in something

participate VERB to take part in something ▶ **participation** NOUN, **participator** NOUN

participle NOUN a word formed from a verb and used to form certain tenses (e.g. *It has gone, It is going*) or the passive (e.g. *We were guided to our seats*), or as an adjective (e.g. *a guided missile, a guiding light*)

particle NOUN a very small piece or amount

particular ADJECTIVE **1** of this one and no other *This particular stamp is very rare.* **2** special **take particular care 3** fussy; choosing carefully *very particular about his clothes* **in particular** especially ▶ **particularly** ADVERB

particulars PLURAL NOUN details or facts

part NOUN • *only one part of the story* ▶ bit, piece, portion, segment, section, episode, chapter • *The machine needs a new part.* ▶ component, element, unit • *the lead part in the play* ▶ role, character • *another part of town* ▶ region, district, neighbourhood, quarter • *their part in the affair* ▶ involvement, role

part VERB • *to part on good terms* ▶ separate, leave, say goodbye **part with** *to part with your money* ▶ give up, relinquish, hand over

partial ADJECTIVE • *a partial recovery* ▶ limited, incomplete

particle NOUN • *not a single particle of food left* ▶ bit, piece, scrap, crumb, drop, fragment

particular ADJECTIVE • *This particular stamp is very rare.* ▶ specific, certain, distinct • *take particular care* ▶ special, exceptional, unusual • *very particular about his clothes* ▶ fussy, finicky, fastidious

particulars PLURAL NOUN • *to take your particulars* ▶ details, facts, information

a
b
c
d
e
f
g
h
i
j
k
l
m
n
o
p
q
r
s
t
u
v
w
x
y
z

parting NOUN 1 leaving or separation 2 a line where hair is combed in different directions

partisan NOUN 1 a strong supporter of a party or group etc. 2 a member of an organization resisting the authorities in a conquered country

partisan ADJECTIVE strongly supporting a particular cause

partition NOUN 1 a thin wall dividing a room or space 2 the act of dividing a country into separate parts

partition VERB 1 to divide something into separate parts 2 to divide a room or space with a partition

partly ADVERB to some extent but not completely

partner NOUN 1 one of a pair of people who do something together 2 a person who jointly owns a business with others 3 a husband, wife, or lover
▶ **partnership** NOUN

partner VERB to be a person's partner

part of speech NOUN any of the groups into which words are

divided in grammar (noun, pronoun, adjective, verb, adverb, preposition, conjunction, exclamation)

partook past tense of **partake**

partridge NOUN a game bird with brown feathers

part-time ADJECTIVE, ADVERB working for only some of the normal hours

party NOUN **parties** 1 a gathering of people for enjoyment 2 a group working or travelling together 3 an organized group of people with similar political beliefs 4 a person who is involved in an action or lawsuit etc. *the guilty party*

pass VERB 1 to go past; to go or move in a certain direction 2 to move something in a certain direction 3 to give or transfer something to another person 4 (in ball games) to kick or throw the ball to another player 5 to be successful in a test or exam 6 to approve or accept 7 to occupy time 8 to happen 9 to come to an end 10 to utter a remark 11 (in a game, quiz, etc.) to choose not to

partner NOUN • *a business partner*
▶ colleague, associate, ally, comrade, companion • *asked to bring their partners to the party*
▶ girlfriend or boyfriend, husband or wife

party NOUN • *a birthday party*
▶ celebration, gathering, festivity, function, get-together • *a political party* ▶ group, faction, alliance

• *a search party* ▶ team, crew, squad, group

pass VERB • *heavy traffic passing through the village* ▶ drive, go, move, stream, progress • *passed him the sugar* ▶ hand, give • *The storm passed.* ▶ blow over, fade, come to an end • *as time passed* ▶ elapse, go by, tick by

answer or make a move **pass out**
to faint

pass NOUN **1** the act of passing
something **2** success in an
examination **3** (in ball games) a
kick or throw of the ball to another
player **4** a permit to go in or out of
a place **5** a route through a gap in a
range of mountains **6** a critical
state of affairs *come to a pretty*
pass

passable ADJECTIVE **1** able to be
passed **2** acceptable but not very
good ▸ **passably** ADVERB

passage NOUN **1** a way through
something **2** a journey by sea or air
3 a section of a piece of writing or
music **4** passing *the passage of*
time

passageway NOUN a passage or
way through

passenger NOUN a person who is
driven or carried in a car, train,
ship, or aircraft etc.

passion NOUN **1** strong emotion
2 great enthusiasm

passionate ADJECTIVE full of
passion

passive ADJECTIVE **1** not resisting or
fighting **2** acted upon and not
active **3** (of a verb) in the form
used when the subject of the
sentence receives the action, e.g.
is sold in Milk *is sold in the shop.*

Passover NOUN a Jewish religious
festival commemorating the
freeing of the Jews from slavery in
Egypt

passport NOUN an official
document entitling the holder to
travel abroad

password NOUN **1** a secret word
or phrase used to distinguish
friends from enemies **2** a word
keyed in to gain access to certain
computer files

past ADJECTIVE of the time gone by
the past week

past NOUN the time gone by

past PREPOSITION **1** beyond *past the*
school **2** after *past midnight*

pasta NOUN an Italian food
consisting of a dried paste made
from flour and shaped into
macaroni, spaghetti, etc.

paste NOUN **1** a soft, moist, and
sticky substance **2** a thick glue for

THESAURUS

pass NOUN • *a pass through the*
mountains ▸ route, way, gap • *a*
bus pass ▸ permit, ticket

passage NOUN • *The passage of*
time ▸ passing, advance, march,
progress • *a sea passage*
▸ crossing, journey, voyage,
cruise • *a narrow passage*
▸ corridor, walkway, hallway • *a*
passage between the houses
▸ alley, path, lane, track • *a*

passage from a book ▸ excerpt,
extract, section, episode

passion NOUN • *a passion for sport*
▸ enthusiasm, interest (in),
fanaticism • *spoke with a fierce*
passion ▸ emotion, feeling,
vehemence

passionate ADJECTIVE • *a*
passionate appeal for help
▸ emotional, heartfelt

sticking paper **3** a soft edible mixture

paste VERB **1** to stick something on a surface with paste **2** to coat with paste **3** (ICT) to insert text cut or copied from another place

pastel NOUN **1** a crayon that is like chalk **2** a light delicate colour

pasteurize VERB to purify milk by heating and then cooling it

⚠️ **SPELLING**

This word can also be spelled *pasteurise*.

pastille NOUN a small flavoured sweet for sucking

pastime NOUN a hobby or interest that a person follows in their spare time

pastor NOUN a member of the clergy in charge of a church

pastoral ADJECTIVE **1** to do with country life **2** to do with a pastor or a pastor's duties

pastry NOUN pastries **1** dough made with flour, fat, and water, rolled flat and baked **2** a small cake with pastry

pasture NOUN land covered with grass etc. for cattle to graze on

pasty¹ (pas-tee) NOUN **pasties** pastry with a filling of meat and vegetables

pasty² (pay-stee) ADJECTIVE **pastier**, **pastiest** looking pale and unhealthy

pat VERB **patting**, **patted** to tap gently with the open hand

pat NOUN **1** a patting movement or sound **2** a small piece of butter or other soft substance

patch NOUN **1** a piece of material or metal etc. put over a hole or damaged place **2** an area that is different from its surroundings **3** a piece of ground **4** a small area or piece of something *patches of fog*

patch VERB to put a patch on

patchwork NOUN needlework in which small pieces of different cloth are sewn edge to edge

patchy ADJECTIVE **patchier**, **patchiest** occurring in patches; uneven ▸ **patchily** ADVERB

pâté (pat-ay) NOUN paste made of meat, fish, or vegetables

patent NOUN an official statement giving an inventor the sole right to make or sell an invention

patent ADJECTIVE **1** protected by a patent *patent medicines* **2** obvious

pastime NOUN • *an enjoyable pastime* ▸ hobby, activity, recreation, diversion, amusement, entertainment, occupation, game, sport, relaxation

pat VERB • *patted her hand* ▸ tap, touch, stroke, rub

patch NOUN • *jeans covered in patches* ▸ mend, repair • *going through a difficult patch* ▸ period, time, spell • *a vegetable patch* ▸ plot, strip, row, area

patch VERB • *to patch his jacket at the elbow* ▸ mend, repair, cover, darn, fix

a
b
c
d
e
f
g
h
i
j
k
l
m
n
o
p
q
r
s
t
u
v
w
x
y
z

patent VERB to be given a patent for something

patent leather NOUN glossy leather

patently ADVERB clearly or obviously *is patently untrue*

paternal ADJECTIVE **1** to do with a father **2** fatherly

paternity NOUN **1** fatherhood **2** the state of being the father of a particular baby

path NOUN **1** a narrow way for walking along **2** a line along which a person or thing moves **3** a course of action

pathetic ADJECTIVE **1** making you feel pity or sympathy **2** completely inadequate or useless ▸ **pathetically** ADVERB

pathological ADJECTIVE **1** to do with pathology or disease **2** (*informal*) compulsive *a pathological liar*

pathology NOUN the study of diseases of the body ▸ **pathologist** NOUN

pathos (pay-thoss) NOUN a quality of making people feel pity or sympathy

patience NOUN **1** the state of being patient **2** a card game for one person

patient ADJECTIVE able to wait for a long time or put up with trouble or inconvenience without getting anxious or angry ▸ **patiently** ADVERB

patient NOUN a person receiving treatment from a doctor or dentist

patio NOUN **patios** a paved area beside a house

patriarch NOUN **1** the male head of a family or tribe **2** a bishop of high rank in the Orthodox Christian Church ▸ **patriarchal** ADJECTIVE

patrician NOUN an ancient Roman noble

patrician ADJECTIVE aristocratic

patriot NOUN someone who loves their country and supports it loyally

patriotic ADJECTIVE loyal to your country ▸ **patriotism** NOUN

patrol VERB **patrolling, patrolled** to walk or travel regularly over an area to guard it

THESAURUS

path NOUN • *a path by the railway* ▸ footpath, track, alley, lane • *The path was blocked.* ▸ way, route

pathetic ADJECTIVE • *a pathetic wave of the hand* ▸ pitiful, plaintive, sad, touching • *a pathetic attempt* ▸ inadequate, feeble

patience NOUN • *waited with great patience* ▸ calmness,

toleration, perseverance, endurance, self-control

patient ADJECTIVE • *tried to stay patient* ▸ calm, self-controlled, composed, tolerant, understanding

patrol VERB • *Guards patrol the estate.* ▸ police, tour, inspect, keep watch on

a
b
c
d
e
f
g
h
i
j
k
l
m
n
p
q
r
s
t
u
v
w
x
y
z

patrol NOUN **1** a patrolling group of people, ships, aircraft, etc. **2** a group of Scouts or Guides

patron NOUN **1** someone who supports a person or cause **2** a regular customer

patronage NOUN support given by a patron

patronize VERB **1** to be a regular customer of a particular shop, restaurant, etc. **2** to talk to someone in a way that shows you think them inferior

> ⚠ **SPELLING**
>
> This word can also be spelled *patronise*.

patron saint NOUN a saint who is thought to protect a particular place or activity

patter[1] NOUN a series of light tapping sounds

patter VERB to make light tapping sounds

patter[2] NOUN the quick talk of a comedian, salesperson, etc.

pattern NOUN **1** a repeated arrangement of lines, shapes, or colours etc. **2** a thing to be copied to make something **3** the regular way in which something happens **4** an excellent example or model

patty NOUN **patties** a small pie or pasty

paucity NOUN (*formal*) smallness of number or quantity

paunch NOUN a large belly

pauper NOUN a person who is very poor

pause NOUN a temporary stop in speaking or doing something

pause VERB to stop something for a short time

pave VERB to lay a hard surface on a road or path etc.

pavement NOUN a paved path along the side of a street

pavilion NOUN **1** a building for use by players and spectators at a sports ground **2** a large ornamental building

paw NOUN the foot of an animal that has claws

paw VERB to touch or scrape something with a hand or foot

pawn[1] NOUN **1** the least valuable piece in chess **2** a person whose actions are controlled by somebody else

pawn[2] VERB to leave something with a pawnbroker as security for a loan

THESAURUS

patrol NOUN • *on patrol all night* ▶ watch, guard, duty, surveillance • *a four-man patrol* ▶ guard, lookout, party, task force

pattern NOUN • *patterns drawn in the sand* ▶ design, shape, arrangement, decoration, ornamentation • *actions that*

might set a pattern ▶ example, model, standard, guide, norm

pause NOUN • *a short pause in the music* ▶ break, interruption, interval, rest, wait

pause VERB • *paused for a moment* ▶ wait, hesitate, stop, delay, rest

pawnbroker NOUN a shopkeeper who lends money to people in return for objects that they leave as security

pawpaw NOUN an orange-coloured tropical fruit used as food

pay VERB paid 1 to give money in return for goods or services 2 to give what is owed *pay your debts* 3 to be profitable or worthwhile *It pays to advertise.* 4 to give or express *to pay a compliment* 5 to suffer a penalty

pay NOUN salary or wages

payable ADJECTIVE that must be paid

payee NOUN a person to whom money is paid or is to be paid

payment NOUN 1 the act of paying 2 money paid

payphone NOUN a public telephone operated by coins or a card

payroll NOUN a list of employees entitled to be paid

PC ABBREVIATION 1 personal computer 2 police constable

PE ABBREVIATION physical education

pea NOUN 1 the small round green seed of a climbing plant, growing inside a pod and used as a vegetable 2 the plant bearing these pods

peace NOUN 1 a time when there is no war or disorder 2 quietness and calm

peaceable ADJECTIVE fond of peace; not quarrelsome or warlike
▶ **peaceably** ADVERB

peaceful ADJECTIVE quiet and calm
▶ **peacefully** ADVERB

peach NOUN a round soft juicy fruit with a pinkish or yellowish skin and a large stone

peacock NOUN a large bird with a long brightly coloured tail that it can spread out like a fan

peahen NOUN a female peacock

peak NOUN 1 a pointed top, especially of a mountain 2 the highest or most intense part of something 3 the part of a cap that

THESAURUS

pay VERB • *Why pay more?*
▶ spend, part with • *He'd pay me for the broken window.*
▶ reimburse, refund, repay • *to pay your debts* ▶ settle, discharge, clear • *make them pay for this* ▶ suffer, make amends, atone

pay NOUN • *an increase in pay*
▶ income, earnings, salary, wages

peace NOUN • *not easy to get any peace* ▶ calm, quiet, silence,

relaxation • *to long for peace*
▶ order, harmony, non-violence

peaceful ADJECTIVE • *a peaceful part of the country* ▶ quiet, restful, tranquil, secluded, calm, relaxing • *use peaceful methods*
▶ non-violent

peak NOUN • *mountain peaks*
▶ summit, tip, top, crest, crown
• *the peak of a career* ▶ height, highest point, zenith, climax

sticks out in front ▶ **peaked**
ADJECTIVE

peak VERB to reach a highest point
or value

peaky ADJECTIVE **peakier, peakiest**
pale and unwell

peal NOUN **1** the loud ringing of a
bell or bells **2** a loud burst of
thunder or laughter

peal VERB (of bells) to ring loudly

peanut NOUN a small round nut
that grows in a pod in the ground

peanut butter NOUN roasted
peanuts crushed into a paste

pear NOUN a juicy fruit that narrows
near the stalk

pearl NOUN a small shiny white ball
found in the shells of some oysters
and used as a jewel ▶ **pearly**
ADJECTIVE

peasant NOUN a person who
belongs to a farming community,
especially in poor areas
▶ **peasantry** NOUN

peat NOUN rotted plant material
dug out of the ground and used as
fuel

pebble NOUN a small round stone
▶ **pebbly** ADJECTIVE

peck VERB **1** to bite at something
quickly with the beak **2** to kiss
someone lightly

peck NOUN **1** a quick bite by a bird
2 a light kiss

peckish ADJECTIVE (informal) slightly
hungry

peculiar ADJECTIVE **1** strange or
unusual **2** belonging to a
particular person, place, or thing

peculiarity NOUN **peculiarities** a
distinctive feature

pedal NOUN a lever pressed by the
foot to operate a bicycle, car,
machine, etc.

pedal VERB **pedalling, pedalled** to
move or work something,
especially a bicycle, by means of
pedals

pedant NOUN a pedantic person

pedantic ADJECTIVE too concerned
with minor details or formalities
▶ **pedantically** ADVERB

peddle VERB **1** to go from house to
house selling small goods **2** to sell
illegal drugs

pedestal NOUN the base for a
statue or pillar etc.

pedestrian NOUN a person who is
walking

pedestrian ADJECTIVE ordinary and
dull

pedestrian crossing NOUN a
place where traffic has to stop to
allow pedestrians to cross the road

peculiar ADJECTIVE • *Something
peculiar was happening.*
▶ strange, odd, unusual, weird,
curious, funny, extraordinary • *to
feel peculiar* ▶ unwell, ill, sick,
poorly

peculiarity NOUN • *a peculiarity
of the local weather* ▶ oddity,
idiosyncrasy, quirk • *the
peculiarity of the arrangement*
▶ strangeness, oddness,
bizarreness

pedigree NOUN a list of a person's or animal's ancestors

pediment NOUN a wide triangular part decorating the top of a building

pedlar NOUN a person who goes from house to house selling small things

peek VERB to have a quick look at something ▶ **peek** NOUN

peel NOUN the skin of certain fruits and vegetables

peel VERB 1 to remove the peel or covering from 2 to come off in strips 3 to lose a covering or layer of skin

peelings PLURAL NOUN strips of skin peeled from potatoes etc.

peep VERB 1 to look quickly or secretly 2 to look through a narrow opening 3 to come briefly into view ▶ **peep** NOUN

peer¹ VERB to look at something closely or with difficulty

peer² NOUN 1 a member of the nobility 2 someone who is equal to another in rank, merit, or age etc.

peerage NOUN 1 peers collectively 2 the rank of a peer

peer group NOUN a group of people of roughly the same age or status

peerless ADJECTIVE without an equal; better than the others

peeved ADJECTIVE (informal) annoyed

peevish ADJECTIVE irritable

peewit NOUN a lapwing

peg NOUN a piece of wood, plastic, etc. for fastening things together or hanging things on

peg VERB pegging, pegged 1 to fix with pegs 2 to keep wages or prices at a fixed level

pejorative (pij-orra-tiv) ADJECTIVE showing disapproval; derogatory

Pekinese NOUN a small dog with short legs, a flat face, and long silky hair

pelican NOUN a large bird with a pouch in its long beak for storing fish

pelican crossing NOUN a pedestrian crossing controlled by lights

pellet NOUN a tiny ball of metal, food, paper, etc.

pell-mell ADVERB, ADJECTIVE in a hasty untidy way

pelmet NOUN an ornamental strip of wood etc. above a window, used to conceal a curtain rail

pelt¹ VERB 1 to throw a lot of things at 2 to run fast 3 to rain very hard

pelt² NOUN an animal skin

THESAURUS

peep VERB • *to peep through the keyhole* ▶ peek, peer, look

peep NOUN • *have a peep at the baby* ▶ peek, glance, glimpse, look

pelt VERB • *pelting each other with snowballs* ▶ bombard, shower, attack • *It was pelting down outside.* ▶ pour, teem • *The boys pelted home.* ▶ rush, dash, run, sprint

pelvis NOUN the round framework of bones at the lower end of the spine ▶ **pelvic** ADJECTIVE

pen[1] NOUN an instrument with a point for writing with ink

pen[2] NOUN an enclosure for cattle, sheep, etc.

pen VERB **penning, penned** to shut animals etc. into a pen

penal (peen-al) ADJECTIVE to do with the punishment of criminals

penalize VERB to punish

⚠️ SPELLING

This word can also be spelled *penalise*.

penalty NOUN **penalties 1** a punishment **2** a point or advantage given to one side in a game when the other side has broken a rule

penance NOUN a punishment willingly suffered to show regret for a wrong

pence PLURAL NOUN SEE **penny**

penchant NOUN a liking or inclination

pencil NOUN an instrument for drawing or writing, made of a stick of graphite in a cylinder of wood or metal

pencil VERB **pencilling, pencilled** to write or mark with a pencil

pendant NOUN an ornament worn on a chain round the neck

pending ADJECTIVE **1** waiting to be decided or settled **2** about to happen

pending PREPOSITION while waiting for; until *pending approval*

pendulum NOUN a weight hung to swing to and fro, especially in the works of a clock

penetrable ADJECTIVE able to be penetrated

penetrate VERB to make or find a way through or into something ▶ **penetration** NOUN

penetrating ADJECTIVE **1** showing great insight **2** clearly heard

penfriend NOUN a friend with whom you exchange letters without meeting

penguin NOUN an Antarctic seabird that cannot fly

penicillin NOUN an antibiotic obtained from mould

peninsula NOUN a piece of land almost surrounded by water ▶ **peninsular** ADJECTIVE

penis (peen-iss) NOUN the part of the body with which a male urinates and has sexual intercourse

penitence NOUN regret for having done wrong ▶ **penitent** ADJECTIVE

penknife NOUN **penknives** a small folding knife

pen-name NOUN a name used by an author instead of their real name

pennant NOUN a long pointed flag

THESAURUS

penetrate VERB • *to penetrate the surface* ▶ pierce, puncture, perforate • *to penetrate defences* ▶ infiltrate, get through

penniless ADJECTIVE having no money

penny NOUN **pennies** or **pence** 1 a British coin worth $\frac{1}{100}$ of a pound 2 a former coin worth $\frac{1}{12}$ of a shilling

pension NOUN an income of regular payments made to someone who is retired, widowed, or disabled

pension VERB **pension off** to make someone retire early

pensioner NOUN a person who receives a pension

pensive ADJECTIVE deep in thought

pentagon NOUN a flat shape with five sides ► **pentagonal** ADJECTIVE

pentathlon NOUN an athletic contest consisting of five events

Pentecost NOUN 1 the Jewish harvest festival, fifty days after Passover 2 Whit Sunday

penthouse NOUN a flat at the top of a tall building

pent-up ADJECTIVE shut in *pent-up feelings*

penultimate ADJECTIVE last but one

penumbra NOUN an area that is partly shaded, e.g. during an eclipse

penury NOUN (formal) great poverty

peony NOUN **peonies** a plant with large round red, pink, or white flowers

people PLURAL NOUN 1 human beings 2 men, women, and children belonging to a particular country, area, etc.

people NOUN a community or nation *a warlike people the English-speaking peoples*

people VERB to fill a place with people

pep NOUN (informal) vigour or energy

pepper NOUN 1 a hot-tasting powder used to flavour food 2 a bright green, red, or yellow vegetable ► **peppery** ADJECTIVE

pepper VERB 1 to sprinkle with pepper 2 to pelt with small objects

peppercorn NOUN the dried black berry from which pepper is made

peppermint NOUN 1 a kind of mint used for flavouring 2 a sweet flavoured with this mint

pepperoni NOUN beef and pork sausage seasoned with pepper

pep talk NOUN (informal) a talk given to encourage people

per PREPOSITION for each *£5 per person*

per annum ADVERB for each year; yearly

penniless ADJECTIVE • *a penniless student* ► poor, impoverished, destitute, poverty-stricken

people NOUN • *Many people were hungry.* ► folk, men, women and children, individuals, human beings • *to appeal to the people* ► nation, electorate, voters • *a proud and brave people* ► nation, race

a
b
c
d
e
f
g
h
i
j
k
l
m
n
o
p
q
r
s
t
u
v
w
x
y
z

perceive VERB to see, hear, or understand clearly

per cent ADVERB for or in every hundred *three per cent* (3%)

percentage NOUN an amount or rate expressed as a proportion of 100

perceptible ADJECTIVE able to be seen or heard or noticed
► **perceptibly** ADVERB

perception NOUN **1** the ability to see or hear or understand something **2** the receiving of information through the senses

perceptive ADJECTIVE quick to see or understand things

perch¹ NOUN **1** a place where a bird sits or rests **2** a seat high up

perch VERB to rest or place on a perch

perch² NOUN perch an edible freshwater fish

percolate VERB to flow or force through small holes or spaces
► **percolation** NOUN

percolator NOUN a pot for making coffee

percussion NOUN musical instruments (e.g. drums and cymbals) played by being struck or shaken

peregrine NOUN a kind of falcon

perennial ADJECTIVE lasting for many years ► **perennially** ADVERB

perennial NOUN a plant that lives for many years

perfect (per-fikt) ADJECTIVE **1** so good that it cannot be made any better **2** complete *perfect strangers* **3** (of a verb) showing a completed action, e.g. *He has arrived.* ► **perfectly** ADVERB

perfect (per-fekt) VERB to make perfect

perfection NOUN a perfect state

perfectionist NOUN a person who is only satisfied if something is done perfectly

perforate VERB **1** to make tiny holes in something **2** to pierce
► **perforated** ADJECTIVE,
perforation NOUN

perceive VERB • *to perceive someone in the distance* ► see, discern, notice, recognize, spot • *to perceive a meaning* ► understand, comprehend, grasp • *to perceive the world in different ways* ► consider, view

perceptive ADJECTIVE • *perceptive questions* ► discerning, astute, shrewd, intelligent

perfect ADJECTIVE • *the start to a perfect day* ► superb, excellent,

wonderful, marvellous, idyllic, blissful • *in perfect condition* ► impeccable, immaculate, spotless, pristine • *a perfect copy* ► exact, precise, faithful, accurate • *the perfect birthday present* ► ideal, suitable, appropriate, • *perfect strangers* ► complete, absolute, utter, total

perfect VERB • *to perfect a technique* ► improve, refine

DICTIONARY

perform VERB **1** to do something in front of an audience **2** to do or carry out a process ► **performer** NOUN

performance NOUN **1** the act of performing **2** an entertainment in a theatre, on television, etc.

perfume NOUN **1** a pleasant smell **2** a liquid with a pleasant smell

perfume VERB to give a pleasant smell to

perfunctory ADJECTIVE done without much care or interest ► **perfunctorily** ADVERB

perhaps ADVERB it may be; possibly

peril NOUN an immediate danger

perilous ADJECTIVE immediately dangerous ► **perilously** ADVERB

perimeter NOUN **1** an outer edge or boundary **2** the distance round the edge

⚠ **USAGE**

Do not confuse this word with *parameter*.

period NOUN **1** a length of time **2** the time allowed for a lesson in school **3** the time when a woman menstruates **4** (in punctuation) a full stop

periodic ADJECTIVE occurring at regular intervals ► **periodically** ADVERB

periodical NOUN a magazine published at regular intervals

periodic table NOUN (Science) a table in which the chemical elements are arranged in order of increasing atomic number

peripatetic ADJECTIVE going from place to place

peripheral ADJECTIVE **1** of minor importance **2** at the edge or boundary

periphery NOUN **peripheries** the part at the edge or boundary

periscope NOUN a tube and mirrors allowing a viewer to see things that are otherwise out of sight

THESAURUS

perform VERB • *to perform a function* ► fulfil, carry out, accomplish, achieve • *to perform a play* ► present, stage, put on, produce • *performs best at a low temperature* ► work, function, operate

performer NOUN • *sung by the original performers* ► singer, entertainer, artist, musician, actor, actress

perfume NOUN • *an exotic perfume* ► scent, toilet water, eau de cologne • *the sweet perfume of*

roses ► smell, scent, fragrance, aroma

perhaps ADVERB • *Perhaps they have left.* ► maybe, possibly, conceivably

peril NOUN • *the perils of the sea* ► danger, hazard, risk **in peril** • *in great peril* ► in danger, at risk, in jeopardy

period NOUN • *long periods of separation* ► spell, span, stretch, time • *an early period of history* ► age, era, epoch, time • *a double period of science* ► lesson, class

a
b
c
d
e
f
g
h
i
j
k
l
m
n
o
p
q
r
s
t
u
v
w
x
y
z

a
b
c
d
e
f
g
h
i
j
k
l
m
n
o
p
q
r
s
t
u
v
w
x
y
z

perish VERB **1** to die or be destroyed **2** to rot ► **perishable** ADJECTIVE

perished ADJECTIVE (informal) feeling very cold

perishing ADJECTIVE (informal) freezing cold *It's perishing outside!*

periwinkle NOUN **1** a trailing plant with blue or white flowers **2** a winkle

perjure VERB **perjure yourself** to lie under oath

perjury NOUN the crime of telling a lie when under oath in a lawcourt

perk[1] VERB **perk up** to become more cheerful

perk[2] NOUN (informal) something extra given to a worker

perky ADJECTIVE **perkier, perkiest** lively and cheerful

perm NOUN treatment of hair to give it long-lasting waves or curls

perm VERB to give a perm to hair

permafrost NOUN a permanently frozen layer of soil in polar regions

permanent ADJECTIVE lasting for always or for a very long time ► **permanence** NOUN, **permanently** ADVERB

permeable ADJECTIVE able to be permeated by fluids etc. ► **permeability** NOUN

permeate VERB to spread into every part of

permissible ADJECTIVE permitted

permission NOUN the right to do something given by someone in authority

permissive ADJECTIVE letting people do what they wish; too tolerant or liberal

permit (per-mit) VERB **permitting, permitted** to give permission or a chance to do something

permit (per-mit) NOUN written or printed permission to do something *a fishing permit*

permutation NOUN **1** the changing of the order of a set of things **2** a changed order *3, 1, 2 is a permutation of 1, 2, 3.*

pernicious ADJECTIVE very harmful

peroxide NOUN a chemical used for bleaching hair

perpendicular ADJECTIVE upright; at a right angle to a line or surface

perish VERB • to perish in the floods ► die, lose your life • rubber starting to perish ► decay, decompose, disintegrate, rot

permanent ADJECTIVE • a permanent solution ► lasting, durable, long-term, irreversible,

everlasting • his first permanent job ► stable, fixed, secure

permission NOUN • permission to leave early ► authorization, consent, approval, agreement

permit VERB • would not permit release of the documents ► allow, authorize, agree to, consent to

DICTIONARY

perpetrate VERB to commit a crime, error, etc. ► **perpetrator** NOUN

perpetual ADJECTIVE **1** lasting for ever or for a long time **2** constant; continual ► **perpetually** ADVERB

perpetuate VERB to cause to continue or be remembered for a long time *a statue to perpetuate his memory*

perplex VERB to bewilder or puzzle ► **perplexity** NOUN

persecute VERB to be continually cruel to somebody ► **persecution** NOUN

persevere VERB to go on doing something even though it is difficult ► **perseverance** NOUN

persist VERB **1** to continue firmly or obstinately **2** to continue to happen or exist

persistent ADJECTIVE continuing; persisting ► **persistence** NOUN, **persistently** ADVERB

person NOUN **1** a human being; a man, woman, or child **2** (*Grammar*) any of the three groups of personal pronouns and forms taken by verbs, referring to the person speaking (e.g. *I*, *we*), the person addressed (e.g. *you*), or a person spoken about (e.g. *he* or *she* or *they*)

personable ADJECTIVE pleasing in appearance and behaviour

personage NOUN an important or well-known person

personal ADJECTIVE **1** belonging to or concerning a particular person *personal belongings* **2** private *personal business* **3** criticizing a person's appearance or character *personal remarks*

personal computer NOUN a small computer designed for a single user

THESAURUS

perpetual ADJECTIVE • *perpetual daylight* ► continuous, constant, uninterrupted, ceaseless, non-stop

perplex VERB • *questions that perplex you* ► baffle, bewilder, puzzle, confuse

persevere VERB • *to persevere in spite of difficulties* ► continue, persist, keep going, carry on

persist VERB • *to persist with questions* ► continue, persevere, keep going, carry on • *if the pain persists* ► continue, carry on, last, linger, remain

persistent ADJECTIVE • *their more persistent critics* ► determined, tenacious, single-minded • *a persistent knocking on the door* ► continuing, constant, incessant, endless, non-stop

person NOUN • *the person responsible* ► individual, man or woman, human being

personal ADJECTIVE • *the author's personal experiences* ► own, individual, particular • *a personal letter* ► private, confidential, secret

a
b
c
d
e
f
g
h
i
j
k
l
m
n
o
p
q
r
s
t
u
v
w
x
y
z

a
b
c
d
e
f
g
h
i
j
k
l
m
n
o
p
q
r
s
t
u
v
w
x
y
z

personality NOUN **personalities**
1 a person's character 2 a famous
person

personally ADVERB 1 in person
2 as far as I am concerned

personify VERB **personifies,
personified** to represent a quality
or idea as a person
▸ **personification** NOUN

personnel NOUN the people
employed by a large organization

perspective NOUN 1 the
impression of depth and space in a
picture or scene 2 a person's point
of view

Perspex NOUN (trademark) a tough
transparent plastic

perspicacious ADJECTIVE quick to
notice or understand things
▸ **perspicacity** NOUN

perspire VERB to sweat
▸ **perspiration** NOUN

persuade VERB to make someone
believe or agree to do something

persuasion NOUN 1 the act of
persuading 2 a firm belief

persuasive ADJECTIVE likely to
persuade someone; convincing

pert ADJECTIVE cheeky ▸ **pertly**
ADVERB

pertain VERB be relevant to
something *evidence pertaining to
the crime*

pertinent ADJECTIVE relevant to a
subject being discussed

perturb VERB to worry someone a
lot ▸ **perturbation** NOUN

peruse VERB to read something
carefully ▸ **perusal** NOUN

pervade VERB to spread all
through

perverse ADJECTIVE obstinately
doing something unreasonable or
unwanted ▸ **perversely** ADVERB,
perversity NOUN

pervert (per-vert) VERB 1 to turn
something from the right course
of action 2 to make a person
behave wickedly or abnormally
▸ **perversion** NOUN

THESAURUS

personality NOUN • *a warm
personality* ▸ character, nature,
disposition, temperament • *a
television personality* ▸ celebrity,
star, superstar

perspective NOUN • *to see the
events from a different perspective*
▸ outlook, viewpoint, point of
view, slant, angle **in perspective**
• *to put the matter in perspective*
▸ in context, in proportion

persuade VERB • *not able to
persuade them to agree*
▸ convince, tempt, coax, talk into,
pressurize, urge

persuasive ADJECTIVE • *persuasive
talk* ▸ convincing, compelling,
plausible, strong, influential

perverse ADJECTIVE • *a perverse
attitude* ▸ contrary, awkward,
unreasonable, obstinate,
rebellious

a
b
c
d
e
f
g
h
i
j
k
l
m
n
o
p
q
r
s
t
u
v
w
x
y
z

pessimist NOUN a person who expects that things will turn out badly ► **pessimism** NOUN, **pessimistic** ADJECTIVE, **pessimistically** ADVERB

pest NOUN **1** a destructive insect or animal, such as a locust or mouse **2** a nuisance

pester VERB to keep annoying someone with questions or requests

pesticide NOUN a substance for killing harmful insects and other pests

pestilence NOUN a deadly epidemic

pestle NOUN a tool with a heavy rounded end for pounding substances in a mortar

pet NOUN **1** a tame animal kept in the home **2** a favourite person

pet ADJECTIVE favourite or particular

pet VERB **petting, petted** to stroke or pat someone affectionately

petal NOUN each of the separate coloured parts of a flower

peter VERB **peter out** to become gradually less and cease to exist

petition NOUN a formal written request signed by many people

petition VERB to submit a petition to ► **petitioner** NOUN

petrel NOUN a kind of seabird

petrify VERB **petrifies, petrified 1** to terrify someone so much they cannot move **2** to turn to stone

petrochemical NOUN a chemical substance obtained from petroleum or natural gas

petrol NOUN a liquid made from petroleum, used as fuel for engines

petroleum NOUN an oil found underground and refined to make fuel

petticoat NOUN a dress-length item of underwear worn by a woman or girl under a skirt or dress

petting NOUN affectionate touching or fondling

pettish ADJECTIVE irritable or bad-tempered; peevish

petty ADJECTIVE **pettier, pettiest 1** unimportant or trivial **2** mean and small-minded ► **pettily** ADVERB, **pettiness** NOUN

---

pessimistic ADJECTIVE • *pessimistic about the economic future* ► negative, fatalistic, gloomy, defeatist, resigned

pest NOUN • *becoming a pest* ► nuisance, bother, annoyance, irritation • *crop pests* ► insect, bug, parasite

pester VERB • *don't pester him with silly questions* ► annoy, bother, irritate, harass, nag

pet ADJECTIVE • *a pet rabbit* ► tame, domestic • *her own pet scheme* ► favourite, precious, special, personal

pet VERB • *petting the kitten* ► pat, stroke, cuddle

petty ADJECTIVE • *petty reasons* ► trivial, minor, unimportant, insignificant

a
b
c
d
e
f
g
h
i
j
k
l
m
n
o
p
q
r
s
t
u
v
w
x
y
z

petty cash NOUN cash kept in an office for small payments

petty officer NOUN a non-commissioned officer in the navy

petulant ADJECTIVE irritable or bad-tempered ► **petulance** NOUN

petunia NOUN a garden plant with funnel-shaped flowers

pew NOUN a long wooden seat in a church

pewter NOUN a grey alloy of tin and lead

pH NOUN a measure of the acid or alkaline content of a solution

> **WORD HISTORY**
>
> from the first letter of German *Potenz* 'power' and H, the symbol for hydrogen

phantom NOUN **1** a ghost **2** something that does not really exist

Pharaoh (fair-oh) NOUN the title of a king in ancient Egypt

pharmaceutical ADJECTIVE to do with medicines and drugs

pharmacist NOUN a person who prepares and sells medicines

pharmacy NOUN **pharmacies 1** a shop selling medicines **2** the process of preparing medicines

phase NOUN a stage in the progress or development of something

phase VERB to do something in planned stages

pheasant NOUN a game bird with a long tail

phenomenal ADJECTIVE amazing or remarkable ► **phenomenally** ADVERB

phenomenon NOUN **phenomena** a remarkable event or fact

phial NOUN a small glass bottle

philander VERB (of a man) to have casual affairs with women ► **philanderer** NOUN

philanthropy NOUN concern for and generosity to fellow human beings ► **philanthropic** ADJECTIVE, **philanthropist** NOUN

philately (fil-at-il-ee) NOUN stamp-collecting ► **philatelist** NOUN

philistine NOUN a person who dislikes the arts and creative works

philology NOUN the study of words and their history ► **philological** ADJECTIVE, **philologist** NOUN

philosopher NOUN an expert in philosophy

philosophical ADJECTIVE **1** to do with philosophy **2** calm after a misfortune or disappointment ► **philosophically** ADVERB

THESAURUS

phantom NOUN • *a phantom appearing at night* ► ghost, spectre, spirit, apparition

phase NOUN • *the final phase of the war* ► stage, part, period, chapter

phenomenal ADJECTIVE • *a phenomenal memory* ► remarkable, extraordinary, amazing, astonishing, sensational

philosophical ADJECTIVE • *philosophical ideas*

philosophy NOUN **philosophies**
1 the study of truths about life,
morals, etc. **2** a set of ideas or
principles or beliefs

philtre (fil-ter) NOUN a love potion

phlegm (flem) NOUN thick mucus
that forms in the throat and lungs
during a cold

phlegmatic (fleg-mat-ik) ADJECTIVE
not easily excited or worried
▶ **phlegmatically** ADVERB

phobia (foh-bee-a) NOUN great or
abnormal fear of something

phoenix (feen-iks) NOUN a
mythical bird that was believed to
burn itself to death and be born
again from the ashes

phone NOUN a telephone

phone VERB to telephone

phonecard NOUN a plastic card
used to work some public
telephones

phonetic (fon-et-ik) ADJECTIVE **1** to
do with speech sounds
2 representing speech sounds
▶ **phonetically** ADVERB

phoney ADJECTIVE **phonier**,
phoniest (informal) sham; not
genuine

phosphorus NOUN a chemical
substance that glows in the dark

photo NOUN (informal) a
photograph

photocopy NOUN **photocopies** a
copy of a document or page etc.
made by photographing it on
special paper

photocopy VERB **photocopies**,
photocopied to make a
photocopy of ▶ **photocopier**
NOUN

photoelectric ADJECTIVE using the
electrical effects of light

photogenic ADJECTIVE looking
attractive in photographs

photograph NOUN a picture
made by the effect of light on film,
using a camera

photograph VERB to take a
photograph of ▶ **photographer**
NOUN

photography NOUN the process
of taking photographs
▶ **photographic** ADJECTIVE

photosynthesis NOUN the
process by which plants convert
sunlight into complex substances
that give off oxygen

phrase NOUN **1** a group of words
that form a unit in a sentence or
clause **2** a short section of a tune

phrase VERB to express in words

THESAURUS

▶ theoretical, analytical, abstract,
academic, intellectual
• *philosophical about life's
problems* ▶ calm, composed,
resigned, stoical

phoney ADJECTIVE • *a phoney name*
▶ false, bogus, sham, fake

phrase NOUN • *searched for the
right phrase* ▶ expression,
wording, form of words, idiom

phrase VERB • *how to phrase the
question* ▶ express, word,
formulate, present

a
b
c
d
e
f
g
h
i
j
k
l
m
n
o
p
q
r
s
t
u
v
w
x
y
z

a b c d e f g h i j k l m n o p q r s t u v w x y z

phraseology NOUN the way something is worded

physical ADJECTIVE **1** to do with the body rather than the mind **2** to do with things that can be touched or seen ► **physically** ADVERB

physician NOUN a doctor, especially one who is not a surgeon

physicist (fiz-i-sist) NOUN an expert in physics

physics (fiz-iks) NOUN the study of the properties of matter and energy (e.g. heat, light, sound, and movement)

physiognomy (fiz-ee-on-o-mee) NOUN the features of a person's face

physiology NOUN the study of the body and its parts and how they function ► **physiological** ADJECTIVE, **physiologist** NOUN

physiotherapy NOUN the treatment of a disease or injury by massage, exercises, etc. ► **physiotherapist** NOUN

physique NOUN a person's build

pi NOUN the symbol (π) of the ratio of the circumference of a circle to its diameter, approximately 3.142

pianist NOUN a person who plays the piano

piano NOUN **pianos** a large musical instrument with a keyboard

piccolo NOUN **piccolos** a small high-pitched flute

pick[1] VERB **1** to separate a flower or fruit from its plant **2** to choose carefully **3** to pull bits off or out of **4** to open a lock with an instrument other than a key **5** to provoke a fight or quarrel **6** to steal from someone's pocket **pick on** to single out for criticism **pick up 1** to collect **3** to learn or acquire something **4** to get better or recover

pick NOUN **1** a choice **2** the best of a group

pick[2] NOUN a pickaxe

pickaxe NOUN a heavy pointed tool with a long handle, used for breaking up hard ground etc.

picket NOUN **1** a striker or group of strikers who try to persuade other people not to go into a place of work during a strike **2** a pointed post as part of a fence

picket VERB to put a picket at a place of work

pickle NOUN **1** a strong-tasting food made of preserved vegetables **2** (informal) a mess

THESAURUS

physical ADJECTIVE • *physical appearance* ► bodily, corporal • *our physical existence* ► earthly, material, mortal, terrestrial

pick VERB • *to pick fruit* ► gather, collect, pluck, harvest • *to pick a card* ► choose, select, take

pick on • *always picking on them* ► victimize, bully, persecute, tease

pick NOUN • *Take your pick.* ► choice, preference, selection, option • *the pick of the bunch* ► best, finest, top, cream

pickle VERB to preserve food in vinegar or salt water

pickpocket NOUN a thief who steals from pockets and bags

picnic NOUN a meal eaten in the open air, e.g. on an outing

picnic VERB picnicking, picnicked to have a picnic ▶ **picnicker** NOUN

pictorial ADJECTIVE with or using pictures ▶ **pictorially** ADVERB

picture NOUN 1 a painting, drawing, or photograph of a person or thing 2 a film at the cinema 3 how something seems; an impression

picture VERB 1 to show in a picture 2 to imagine

picturesque ADJECTIVE forming an attractive scene

pidgin NOUN a simplified form of a language used by people who do not speak the same language

pie NOUN a baked dish of meat, fish, or fruit covered with pastry

piebald ADJECTIVE having patches of black and white

piece NOUN 1 a part or portion of something 2 a separate thing or example 3 a work of writing, music, etc. 4 one of the objects used to play a game on a board 5 a coin *a 50p piece*

piece VERB to put pieces together to make something

piecemeal ADJECTIVE, ADVERB done or made one piece at a time

pie chart NOUN a circle divided into sectors to show the way in which something is divided up

pier NOUN 1 a long platform built out into the sea for walking on 2 a pillar supporting a bridge or arch

pierce VERB to make a hole through

piercing ADJECTIVE 1 very loud and high-pitched 2 penetrating; very strong *a piercing wind*

piety NOUN a religious and devout state or attitude

THESAURUS

picture NOUN • *a picture of Napoleon* • painting, portrait, likeness, depiction, image • *wanted to take a picture of them* ▶ photograph, snap, shot

picture VERB • *The man is pictured on the right.* • show, depict, illustrate, represent • *can picture them clearly* ▶ visualize, imagine, envisage

picturesque ADJECTIVE
• *picturesque views* ▶ attractive, pretty, beautiful, charming, pleasant

piece NOUN • *a piece of cheese* ▶ bit, chunk, lump, hunk, portion, fragment, morsel • *a piece of furniture* ▶ item • *wrote a piece for the newspaper* ▶ article, story, feature, account

pierce VERB • *could pierce armour* ▶ penetrate, puncture, perforate, make a hole in

piercing ADJECTIVE • *a piercing screech* ▶ shrill, sharp, high-pitched, ear-splitting • *a piercing pain* ▶ stabbing, intense, excruciating

a
b
c
d
e
f
g
h
i
j
k
l
m
n
o
p
q
r
s
t
u
v
w
x
y
z

piffle NOUN (informal) nonsense

pig NOUN **1** a fat animal with short legs and a blunt snout, kept for its meat **2** (informal) a greedy or dirty person

pigeon NOUN a bird with a fat body and small head

pigeonhole NOUN a small compartment for holding letters, messages, or papers, for collection

piggyback NOUN a ride on a person's back or shoulders

piggy bank NOUN a money box in the shape of a pig with a slot on top

pig-headed ADJECTIVE stubborn

piglet NOUN a young pig

pigment NOUN **1** a substance that colours animal and plant tissue **2** a substance that gives colour to paint, inks, dyes, etc.
▶ **pigmentation** NOUN

pigsty NOUN **pigsties 1** a partly-covered pen for pigs **2** a filthy room or house

pigtail NOUN a plait of hair at the back of the head

pike NOUN **1** a heavy spear **2** a large freshwater fish

pilchard NOUN a small sea fish

pile NOUN **1** a number of things on top of one another **2** (informal) a large amount **3** a large impressive

building **4** a raised surface on fabric, carpet, etc.

pile VERB to put things in a pile

pile-up NOUN a road accident involving several vehicles

pilfer VERB to steal things of little value

pilgrim NOUN a person who travels to a holy place

pilgrimage NOUN a journey to a holy place

pill NOUN a small solid piece of medicine for swallowing

pillage VERB to carry off goods using force; to plunder ▶ **pillage** NOUN

pillar NOUN a tall stone or wooden post

pillar box NOUN a postbox standing in a street

pillion NOUN a seat behind the driver on a motorcycle

pillory NOUN **pillories** a wooden framework with holes for a person's head and hands, in which offenders were formerly made to stand as a punishment

pillory VERB **pillories, pilloried** to expose a person to public ridicule or anger

pillow NOUN a cushion for a person's head to rest on, especially in bed

THESAURUS

pile NOUN • a pile of stones ▶ heap, stack, mass, mound, mountain, collection, hoard • There was a pile of work still left to do. ▶ plenty, lots, a lot, a great deal, masses, heaps

pile VERB • piled everything into a corner ▶ heap, stack, pack, jam, load, store

pillar NOUN • pillars supporting the roof ▶ column, pier, support, buttress

DICTIONARY

pillowcase or **pillowslip** *NOUN* a cloth cover for a pillow

pilot *NOUN* **1** a person who flies an aircraft **2** a person who steers a ship in and out of a port **3** a guide

pilot *VERB* **1** to be the pilot of an aircraft or ship **2** to guide or steer

pilot *ADJECTIVE* testing something on a small scale *a pilot scheme*

pilot light *NOUN* **1** a small flame that lights a larger burner on a gas cooker etc. **2** an electric indicator light

pimp *NOUN* a man who obtains clients for prostitutes

pimple *NOUN* a small round raised spot on the skin ▶ **pimply** *ADJECTIVE*

PIN *ABBREVIATION* personal identification number; a number used as a password at a cash machine, computer, etc.

pin *NOUN* **1** a short thin piece of metal with a sharp point and a rounded head, used to fasten pieces of cloth or paper etc. **2** a pointed device for fixing or marking something **pins and needles** a tingling feeling

pin *VERB* **pinning, pinned 1** to fasten with a pin or pins **2** to hold someone firmly so they cannot move **3** to fix the blame or responsibility on someone

pinafore *NOUN* an apron with a bib top

pinball *NOUN* a game in which metal balls are shot across a table and score points when they strike targets

pincer *NOUN* the claw of a shellfish such as a lobster

pincers *PLURAL NOUN* a tool with two parts that are pressed together for gripping

pinch *VERB* **1** to squeeze something tightly between two things, especially between the finger and thumb **2** (*informal*) to steal

pinch *NOUN* **1** a pinching movement **2** a small amount *a pinch of salt*

pine[1] *NOUN* an evergreen tree with needle-shaped leaves

pine[2] *VERB* **1** to feel an intense longing **2** to become weak through longing

pineapple *NOUN* a large tropical fruit with a tough prickly skin and yellow flesh

ping *VERB* to make a short sharp ringing sound ▶ **ping** *NOUN*

ping-pong *NOUN* table tennis

pink *ADJECTIVE* pale red

pink *NOUN* **1** a pale red colour **2** a garden plant with fragrant flowers

pinnacle *NOUN* **1** a pointed ornament on a roof **2** a high pointed piece of rock **3** the highest point of something

THESAURUS

pin *VERB* • *pinned a badge on him*
▶ fasten, attach, fix, stick

pinch *VERB* • *She pinched his arm.*
▶ nip, squeeze, crush, tweak

• *Someone pinched my pen while I wasn't looking.* ▶ steal, take, pilfer, snatch, nick, swipe, filch

pinpoint ADJECTIVE exact or precise *with pinpoint accuracy*

pinpoint VERB to find or identify precisely

pinprick NOUN a small annoyance

pinstripe NOUN one of the very narrow stripes that form a pattern in cloth ▸ **pinstriped** ADJECTIVE

pint NOUN a measure for liquids, equal to one-eighth of a gallon

pin-up NOUN (informal) a picture of an attractive or famous person for pinning on a wall

pioneer NOUN one of the first people to go to a place or to develop an idea

pioneer VERB to be the first to develop something

pious ADJECTIVE very religious; devout

pip NOUN 1 a small hard seed of an apple, pear, orange, etc. 2 one of the stars on the shoulder of an army officer's uniform 3 a short high-pitched sound

pip VERB pipping, pipped (informal) to defeat by a small amount

pipe NOUN 1 a tube through which water or gas etc. can flow 2 a narrow tube with a bowl at one end for smoking tobacco 3 a tube forming a musical instrument or part of one

pipe VERB 1 to send something along pipes 2 to transmit music by wire or cable 3 to play music on a pipe or the bagpipes

pipe dream NOUN an impossible wish

pipeline NOUN a pipe for carrying oil or water etc. a long distance

piper NOUN a person who plays a pipe or bagpipes

pipette NOUN a small glass tube used in a laboratory

piping NOUN 1 pipes; a length of pipe 2 a decorative line of icing etc. on a cake 3 a long narrow piece of separate fabric on the edge of clothing, upholstery, etc.

piping ADJECTIVE shrill *a piping voice* **piping hot** very hot

pippin NOUN a kind of apple

piquant (pee-kant) ADJECTIVE 1 pleasantly sharp and appetizing *a piquant smell* 2 pleasantly stimulating ▸ **piquancy** NOUN

pique (peek) NOUN a feeling of hurt pride

pique VERB to hurt the pride of

piracy NOUN the activity of pirates

piranha NOUN a South American freshwater fish that has sharp teeth and eats flesh

THESAURUS

pioneer VERB • *to pioneer new methods* ▸ develop, introduce, create, discover, invent

pious ADJECTIVE • *a remarkably pious woman* ▸ religious, devout, devoted, spiritual, dutiful

pirate NOUN a person who attacks and robs ships at sea ▶ **piratical** ADJECTIVE

pirouette NOUN a spinning movement of the body while balanced on the point of the toe or on one foot

pirouette VERB to perform a pirouette

pistachio NOUN **pistachios** a nut with a green kernel

pistil NOUN the part of a flower that produces the seed

pistol NOUN a small gun held in the hand

piston NOUN a disc or cylinder that fits inside a tube in which it moves up and down as part of an engine or pump etc.

pit NOUN **1** a deep hole **2** a hollow **3** a coal mine **4** the part of a race circuit where cars are refuelled and repaired during a race

pit VERB **pitting, pitted 1** to make holes or hollows in **2** to put somebody in a competition with somebody else ▶ **pitted** ADJECTIVE

pitch¹ NOUN **1** a piece of ground marked out for cricket, football, etc. **2** the highness or lowness of a voice or a musical note **3** intensity

or strength *at fever pitch* **4** the steepness of a roof or other slope

pitch VERB **1** to throw or fling **2** to set up a tent or camp **3** to fall heavily **4** to move up and down on a rough sea **5** to set something at a particular level **6** (of a bowled ball in cricket) to strike the ground

pitch² NOUN a black sticky substance like tar

pitch-black or **pitch-dark** NOUN completely black or dark

pitched battle NOUN a battle between armies in prepared positions

pitcher NOUN a large jug

pitchfork NOUN a large fork with two prongs, used for lifting hay

piteous ADJECTIVE arousing pity ▶ **piteously** ADVERB

pitfall NOUN an unsuspected danger or difficulty

pith NOUN the spongy substance in the stems of certain plants or lining the rind of oranges etc.

pithy ADJECTIVE **pithier, pithiest 1** like pith; containing pith **2** short and full of meaning *pithy comments*

pitiable ADJECTIVE arousing pity; pitiful

pirate NOUN • *Pirates attacked the ship.* ▶ marauder, privateer, buccaneer

pit NOUN • *a deep pit in the ground* ▶ hole, ditch, trench, shaft, hollow, depression, trough

pitch NOUN • *voices rising in pitch* ▶ tone, timbre, key • *reached such*

a pitch ▶ level, point, degree • *the pitch of the roof* ▶ steepness, angle, gradient, slope • *no players left on the pitch* ▶ playing field, field, ground

pitch VERB • *to pitch a tent* ▶ put up, raise, erect • *pitched the ball into the next-door garden*

a b c d e f g h i j k l m n o p q r s t u v w x y z

a
b
c
d
e
f
g
h
i
j
k
l
m
n
o
p
q
r
s
t
u
v
w
x
y
z

pitiful ADJECTIVE arousing pity; pathetic ▶ **pitifully** ADVERB

pitiless ADJECTIVE showing no pity ▶ **pitilessly** ADVERB

pittance NOUN a small allowance of money

pity NOUN **1** the feeling of being sorry for someone else's pain or trouble **2** a cause for regret *It's a pity you can't come.*

pity VERB **pities**, **pitied** to feel pity for

pivot NOUN a point or part on which something turns or balances

pivot VERB to turn on a pivot

pivotal ADJECTIVE **1** fixed on a pivot **2** of crucial importance

pixel (piks-el) NOUN each of the tiny dots on a computer display screen from which the image is formed

pixie NOUN a small fairy or elf

pizza (peets-a) NOUN an Italian dish of a savoury mixture baked on a flat piece of dough

pizzicato ADJECTIVE, ADVERB (Music) played by plucking the strings instead of using the bow

placard NOUN a displayed poster or notice

placate VERB to make someone feel calmer and less angry

place NOUN **1** an area or position **2** a seat **3** a job **4** a person's home *at my place* **5** a duty or function *not my place to interfere* **6** a point in a series of things *in the first place* **in place of** instead of **take place** to happen

place VERB to put in a particular place

placebo (plas-ee-boh) NOUN **placebos** a substance with no physical effect, given as if it were a medicine

placenta NOUN a piece of body tissue that provides a fetus with nourishment in the womb

placid ADJECTIVE calm and peaceful; not easily made anxious or upset ▶ **placidly** ADVERB, **placidity** NOUN

▶ throw, fling, toss, hurl, lob, sling, bowl • *a boat pitching in the storm* ▶ lurch, toss, roll

pitiful ADJECTIVE • *a pitiful sight* ▶ sad, pathetic, touching, distressing, heartbreaking

pity NOUN • *felt pity for us* ▶ compassion, sympathy, understanding, mercy, forgiveness **a pity** • *a pity it was so cold* ▶ shame, unfortunate

pity VERB • *pitied people who had to ask for money* ▶ feel sorry for, feel for, sympathize with

place NOUN • *a foreign place* ▶ region, locality, resort, city, town, village • *the ideal place to work in* ▶ spot, location, venue • *a place of their own* ▶ home, house, flat, accommodation, residence, property • *a place on the committee* ▶ position, place

place VERB • *placed the shopping on the table* ▶ put, set, lay, deposit, leave • *was placed second overall* ▶ rank, grade

DICTIONARY

plagiarize VERB to use someone else's writings or ideas as if they were your own
► **plagiarism** NOUN, **plagiarist** NOUN

> ⚠ **SPELLING**
>
> This word can also be spelled *plagiarise*.

plague NOUN **1** a dangerous illness that spreads quickly **2** a large number of pests

plague VERB to pester or annoy

plaice NOUN **plaice** a flat edible sea fish

plaid (plad) NOUN cloth with a tartan or similar pattern

plain ADJECTIVE **1** simple; not decorated or elaborate **2** not beautiful or ugly **3** easy to see or hear or understand **4** frank and straightforward ► **plainly** ADVERB, **plainness** NOUN

plain NOUN a large area of flat country

> ⚠ **USAGE**
>
> Do not confuse this word with *plane*.

plain clothes NOUN civilian clothes worn instead of a uniform, e.g. by the police

plaintiff NOUN someone who brings a complaint against another person to a lawcourt

plaintive ADJECTIVE sounding sad *a plaintive cry*

plait (plat) VERB to weave several strands of hair or rope into one length

plait NOUN a length of hair or rope that has been plaited

plan NOUN **1** a way of doing something thought out in advance **2** a drawing showing the parts of something **3** a map of a town or district

plan VERB **planning, planned** to make a plan for something ► **planner** NOUN

THESAURUS

plague NOUN • *the effects of the plague* ► pestilence, blight, epidemic • *a plague of flies* ► infestation, invasion, swarm

plague VERB • *fears which returned to plague her* ► afflict, torment • *was being plagued with questions* ► pester, badger, harass, annoy

plain ADJECTIVE • *decorated in a plain style* ► simple, basic, unadorned, unelaborate • *a plain appearance* ► ordinary, unattractive, ugly • *forms written in plain English* ► clear, simple, straightforward, understandable • *was plain that*

someone had been there ► obvious, clear, evident, apparent

plan NOUN • *a clever plan* ► scheme, idea, proposal, strategy, suggestion • *a plan of the building* ► chart, diagram, map, layout

plan VERB • *to plan a journey* ► organize, arrange, work out • *to plan a new garden* ► design, devise, sketch out • *We plan to go abroad.* ► intend, propose, aim, mean

plane¹ NOUN **1** an aeroplane **2** a tool for making wood smooth by scraping its surface **3** a flat or level surface

plane VERB to smooth wood with a plane

plane ADJECTIVE flat or level *a plane surface*

⚠ **USAGE**

Do not confuse this word with *plain*.

plane² NOUN a tall tree with broad leaves

planet NOUN any of the large round masses that move in an orbit round the sun ▶ **planetary** ADJECTIVE

📜 **WORD HISTORY**

from Greek *planetes* 'wanderer' (because *planets* seem to move among the stars)

plank NOUN a long flat piece of wood

plankton NOUN microscopic plants and animals floating in the sea, lakes, etc.

plant NOUN **1** a living thing that cannot move, makes its food from chemical substances, and usually has a stem, leaves, and roots **2** a factory or its equipment

plant VERB **1** to put something in soil for growing **2** to fix something firmly in place ▶ **planter** NOUN

plantation NOUN **1** a large area of land where cotton, tobacco, or tea etc. is planted **2** an area of planted trees

plaque (plak) NOUN **1** a flat piece of metal or porcelain fixed on a wall as an ornament or memorial **2** a film that forms on teeth and gums, containing bacteria

plasma NOUN the colourless liquid part of blood, carrying the corpuscles

plaster NOUN **1** a covering put over the skin to protect a cut **2** a mixture of lime, sand, and water etc. for covering walls and ceilings **3** plaster of Paris, or a cast made of this

plaster VERB **1** to cover a surface with plaster **2** to cover something thickly

plaster of Paris NOUN a white paste used for making moulds or for casts round a broken leg or arm

plastic NOUN a light synthetic substance that can be moulded into a special shape

plastic ADJECTIVE **1** made of plastic **2** soft and easy to mould ▶ **plasticity** NOUN

plastic surgery NOUN surgery to repair injured parts of the body

plate NOUN **1** an almost flat circular object for eating or serving food **2** a thin flat sheet of metal, glass, etc. **3** an illustration in a book

THESAURUS

plant NOUN • *industrial plant*
▶ machinery, machines, equipment, apparatus **plants**
▶ greenery, growth, flora, vegetation

plant VERB • *to plant seeds* ▶ sow, bury • *to plant an idea in the mind* ▶ put, establish, introduce

plate NOUN • *a plate of food*
▶ dish, platter, plateful, portion

DICTIONARY

plate VERB **1** to coat metal with a thin layer of gold, silver, tin, etc. **2** to cover with sheets of metal

plateau (plat-oh) NOUN **plateaux** or **plateaus** a flat area of high land

plateful NOUN **platefuls** an amount that will fill a plate

platform NOUN **1** a flat raised area for passengers to stand on at a railway station **2** a raised surface for someone speaking to an audience

platinum NOUN a valuable silver-coloured metal that does not tarnish

platitude NOUN a remark that has been used so often that it is no longer interesting ► **platitudinous** ADJECTIVE

platoon NOUN a small group of soldiers

platter NOUN a flat dish or plate

platypus NOUN an Australian animal with a beak like a duck, which lays eggs but is a mammal

plaudits PLURAL NOUN expressions of approval

plausible ADJECTIVE seeming to be genuine but perhaps deceptive *a plausible excuse* ► **plausibility** NOUN, **plausibly** ADVERB

play VERB **1** to take part in a game, sport, or amusement **2** to make music or sound with a musical instrument etc. **3** to perform a part in a play or film **play up** (*informal*) to tease or annoy someone

play NOUN **1** the activity of playing **2** a story acted on a stage or on radio or television

player NOUN **1** an actor **2** a member of a sports team **3** someone who plays a musical instrument

playful ADJECTIVE **1** wanting to play; full of fun **2** done in fun; not serious ► **playfully** ADVERB

playground NOUN a piece of ground for children to play on

THESAURUS

• *a brass plate on the door* ► plaque, nameplate, sign

plausible ADJECTIVE • *a plausible explanation* ► credible, believable, convincing

play VERB • *children playing in the garden* ► enjoy yourself, amuse yourself, have fun • *to play indoor sports* ► take part in, participate in, join in, compete in • *The two sides play each other.* ► compete against, take on, challenge • *someone to play Hamlet* ► act, perform, portray, take the role of • *to play a musical instrument* ► perform on, make music on

play NOUN • *a balance between work and play* ► amusement, entertainment, relaxation, enjoyment, leisure, fun • *a play by Shakespeare* ► drama, theatrical work, tragedy, comedy, show

player NOUN • *players on stage* ► actor or actress, performer, artist • *new players in the team* ► team member, sportsman or sportswoman, competitor, contestant • *players in an orchestra* ► musician, performer

playful ADJECTIVE • *in a playful mood* ► lively, frisky, jolly

a b c d e f g h i j k l m n o p q r s t u v w x y

DICTIONARY

playgroup NOUN a supervised group of young children who play together

playing card NOUN each of a set of cards used for playing games

playing field NOUN a field used for outdoor games

playmate NOUN a person a child plays games with

play-off NOUN an extra match to decide a draw or tie

plaything NOUN a toy

playschool NOUN a nursery school or playgroup

playwright NOUN a person who writes plays

plea NOUN 1 a request or appeal 2 an excuse 3 a formal statement of guilt or not guilt made in a lawcourt by an accused person

plead VERB 1 to beg someone to do something 2 to state formally in a lawcourt that you are guilty or not guilty 3 to give something as an excuse

pleasant ADJECTIVE pleasing; giving pleasure ► **pleasantly** ADVERB, **pleasantness** NOUN

pleasantry NOUN **pleasantries** a friendly or good-humoured remark

please VERB 1 to make a person feel satisfied or glad 2 used in polite requests *Please ring the bell.* 3 to think suitable *Do as you please.*

pleased ADJECTIVE happy or glad

pleasurable ADJECTIVE causing pleasure

pleasure NOUN 1 a feeling of satisfaction or gladness 2 something that pleases

pleat NOUN a flat fold made by doubling cloth on itself ► **pleated** ADJECTIVE

plectrum NOUN **plectrums** or **plectra** a small piece of metal or bone etc. for plucking the strings of a musical instrument

THESAURUS

• *playful remarks* ► light-hearted, joking, teasing

plea NOUN • *a plea for mercy* ► appeal, request • *his plea that he had been ill* ► excuse, defence

plead VERB • *to pleaded for mercy* ► beg, implore, request, appeal

...sant ADJECTIVE • *a pleasant ...oon* ► enjoyable, pleasing, ...le, delightful, lovely ...people* ► friendly, ...likeable, affable, ...ured

please VERB • *did her best to please them* ► make happy, satisfy, amuse, delight, entertain • *Do what you please.* ► want, like, wish

pleased ADJECTIVE • *pleased to see you* ► happy, glad, delighted, thrilled

pleasure NOUN • *found pleasure in smart clothes* ► enjoyment, happiness, satisfaction, contentment, delight, joy • *the pleasures that children bring* ► joy, delight, enjoyment

549

DICTIONARY

pledge NOUN **1** a solemn promise **2** something given as security for a loan

pledge VERB **1** to promise solemnly to do or give something **2** to give as security

plentiful ADJECTIVE existing in large numbers; abundant
▶ **plentifully** ADVERB

plenty NOUN as much as is needed or wanted

plethora NOUN too large a quantity of something

pleurisy (ploor-i-see) NOUN inflammation of the membrane round the lungs

pliable ADJECTIVE **1** easy to bend; flexible **2** easy to influence or control ▶ **pliability** NOUN

pliant ADJECTIVE pliable

pliers PLURAL NOUN a tool with jaws for gripping things

plight NOUN a difficult situation

plimsoll NOUN a canvas sports shoe with a rubber sole

Plimsoll line NOUN a mark on a ship's side showing how deep it may legally go down in the water when loaded

plinth NOUN a block or slab forming the base of a column

plod VERB **plodding, plodded 1** to walk slowly and heavily **2** to work steadily ▶ **plodder** NOUN

plonk NOUN (informal) cheap wine

plonk VERB (informal) to put something down clumsily or heavily

plop VERB **plopping, plopped** to make the sound of something dropping into water ▶ **plop** NOUN

plot NOUN **1** a secret plan **2** the story in a play, novel, or film **3** a small piece of land

plot VERB **plotting, plotted 1** to make a secret plan **2** to make a chart or graph of something

plough NOUN a farming implement for turning the soil over

THESAURUS

plentiful ADJECTIVE • *a plentiful supply* ▶ abundant, copious, ample, inexhaustible

plenty NOUN • *a time of plenty* ▶ prosperity, wealth, affluence, luxury **plenty of** • *plenty of time* ▶ a lot of, a great deal of, much, enough

plight NOUN • *the plight of the homeless* ▶ difficulty, predicament

plod VERB • *plodded down the road* ▶ trudge, tramp, stomp • *to plod*

through the whole book ▶ plough, wade, trawl

plot NOUN • *a plot against the government* ▶ conspiracy, intrigue, plan, scheme • *a complicated plot* ▶ storyline, story, narrative • *vegetables in a plot* ▶ piece of ground, patch

plot VERB • *was plotting their downfall* ▶ plan, scheme, devise • *plotting against the government* ▶ conspire, scheme, intrigue

plough VERB **1** to turn over soil with a plough **2** to go through something with great effort or difficulty

ploughshare NOUN the cutting blade of a plough

plover (pluv-er) NOUN a kind of wading bird

ploy NOUN a clever manoeuvre to gain an advantage

pluck VERB **1** to pick a flower or fruit **2** to pull the feathers off a bird **3** to pull something up or out **4** to pull a string (e.g. on a guitar) and let it go again

pluck NOUN courage or spirit

plucky ADJECTIVE **pluckier, pluckiest** brave or spirited
▸ **pluckily** ADVERB

plug NOUN **1** something used to stop a hole **2** a device that fits into a socket to connect wires to an electricity supply **3** (informal) a piece of publicity

plug VERB **plugging, plugged 1** to stop up a hole **2** (informal) to publicize something

plum NOUN **1** a soft juicy fruit with a pointed stone **2** a reddish-purple colour

plumage (ploom-ij) NOUN a bird's feathers

plumb VERB **1** to measure the depth of water **2** to fit a room or building with plumbing **3** to solve a mystery

plumb ADJECTIVE exactly upright; vertical

plumb ADVERB (informal) exactly *plumb in the middle*

plumber NOUN a person who fits and mends plumbing

plumbing NOUN **1** the water pipes, water tanks, and drainage pipes in a building **2** the work of a plumber

plumb line NOUN a cord with a weight on the end, used to measure depth or to see whether a surface is vertical

plume NOUN **1** a large feather **2** something shaped like a feather *a plume of smoke* ▸ **plumed** ADJECTIVE

plummet NOUN a plumb line or the weight on its end

plummet VERB **1** to drop downwards rapidly **2** to decrease rapidly in value

plump¹ ADJECTIVE slightly fat; rounded ▸ **plumpness** NOUN

plump VERB to make rounded *plump up a cushion*

plump² VERB **plump for** (informal) to choose

THESAURUS

pluck NOUN • *needed a lot of pluck*
▸ courage, daring, nerve

plug NOUN • *a plug in a bottle*
▸ stopper, cork, bung

plug VERB • *to plug a leak* ▸ seal, stop up, block up, close

plump ADJECTIVE • *a plump child*
▸ chubby, podgy, tubby, fat

plunder VERB to rob a person or place using force, especially during a war or riot ▶ **plunderer** NOUN

plunder NOUN 1 the act of plundering 2 goods that have been plundered

plunge VERB 1 to go or push forcefully into something 2 to fall or go downwards suddenly 3 to go or force into action etc. ▶ **plunge** NOUN

plural NOUN the form of a noun or verb when it stands for more than one person or thing *The plural of 'child' is 'children'.* ▶ **plural** ADJECTIVE

plus PREPOSITION used to show addition *2 plus 2 equals four* (2 + 2 = 4).

plus ADJECTIVE 1 (of a grade) slightly higher *B plus* 2 more than zero *a temperature between minus ten and plus ten degrees*

plush NOUN a thick velvety cloth used in furnishings ▶ **plushy** ADJECTIVE

plutonium NOUN a radioactive substance used in nuclear weapons and reactors

ply¹ NOUN **plies** 1 a thickness or layer of wood or cloth etc. 2 a strand in yarn *4-ply wool*

ply² VERB **plies, plied** 1 to use or wield a tool or weapon 2 to work at a trade or business 3 to keep supplying someone with something

plywood NOUN strong thin board made of layers of wood glued together

p.m. ABBREVIATION after noon

pneumatic (new-mat-ik) ADJECTIVE filled with or worked by compressed air *a pneumatic drill* ▶ **pneumatically** ADVERB

pneumonia (new-moh-nee-a) NOUN a serious illness caused by inflammation of one or both lungs

PO ABBREVIATION 1 Post Office 2 postal order

poach VERB 1 to cook slowly in liquid 2 to steal game or fish from someone else's land or water ▶ **poacher** NOUN

pocket NOUN 1 a small bag-shaped part, especially in a piece of clothing 2 an isolated part or area *pockets of rain*

pocket VERB 1 to put into a pocket 2 to steal

pocket money NOUN money given to a child to spend by its parents

THESAURUS

plunder VERB • *Pirates plundered towns and villages.* ▶ loot, pillage, raid, ransack, steal from

plunge VERB • *plunge into the lake* ▶ dive, leap, jump, throw yourself

• *plunge the knife into the cheese* ▶ thrust, force, stab, shove, stick
• *plunge a hand in the water* ▶ dip, immerse, sink • *to plunge to the ground* ▶ dive, plummet, fall, drop, crash, swoop

a
b
c
d
e
f
g
h
i
j
k
l
m
n
o
p
q
r
s
t
u
v
w
x
y
z

pockmark NOUN a scar or mark left on the skin by a disease
► **pockmarked** ADJECTIVE

pod NOUN a long seed-container of a pea or bean plant

podcast NOUN a radio broadcast that can be downloaded from the Internet and played on a computer or MP3 player

podgy ADJECTIVE **podgier**, **podgiest** short and fat

podium (poh-dee-um) NOUN **podiums** or **podia** a small platform on which a music conductor or someone making a speech stands

poem NOUN a piece of poetry

poet NOUN a person who writes poetry

poetic ADJECTIVE of or like poetry
► **poetically** ADVERB

poetry NOUN writing arranged in short lines, usually with a particular rhythm and sometimes with rhymes

pogrom NOUN an organized massacre of people

poignant (poin-yuhnt) ADJECTIVE very moving or distressing
poignant memories ► **poignancy** NOUN

point NOUN **1** the narrow or sharp end of something **2** a dot *a decimal point* **3** a particular place or time **4** a detail or characteristic *has some good points* **5** the important or essential idea *keep to the point* **6** purpose or value *no point in hurrying* **7** an electrical socket **8** a device for changing a train from one track to another

point VERB **1** to show where something is, especially by holding out a finger etc. towards it **2** to aim or direct *to point a gun* **3** to fill in the parts between bricks with mortar or cement **point out** to draw attention to

point-blank ADJECTIVE **1** (of a shot) fired from close to the target **2** direct and straightforward *a point-blank refusal*

point-blank ADVERB in a direct manner *refused point-blank*

pointed ADJECTIVE **1** with a point at the end **2** (of a remark) clearly

poetic ADJECTIVE • *poetic language*
► expressive, lyrical, emotional, imaginative

point NOUN • *the point of a needle*
► tip, end, spike • *points of light*
► spot, speck, dot • *At this point, the door opened.* ► moment, instant, time • *to get to the point*
► meaning, essence, crux • *an interesting point* ► detail, fact, idea, thought • *some good points*
► characteristic, feature, attribute

• *not much point in staying*
► purpose, reason, aim, benefit
• *a point further down the road*
► place, position, location, spot

point VERB • *to point a gun* ► aim, direct, train **point out** • *pointed out a picture* ► show, signal, indicate

pointed ADJECTIVE • *the pointed end of the stick* ► sharp, tapered, spiky

directed at a person ► **pointedly**
ADVERB

pointer NOUN **1** a rod used to point at something **2** a dog that points with its muzzle towards birds that it scents **3** a hint

pointless ADJECTIVE having no purpose ► **pointlessly** ADVERB

point of view NOUN **points of view** a way of looking at or thinking about something

poise NOUN **1** a dignified self-confident manner **2** a state of balance

poise VERB to balance

poised ADJECTIVE **1** dignified and self-confident **2** prepared or ready

poison NOUN a substance that can harm or kill a living thing if swallowed or absorbed into the body ► **poisonous** ADJECTIVE

poison VERB **1** to give poison to; to kill with poison **2** to put poison in something **3** to corrupt or spoil something *He poisoned their minds.* ► **poisoner** NOUN

poisonous ADJECTIVE containing poison and causing death or harm

poke VERB **1** to prod or jab **2** to push out or forward

poke NOUN a prod or poking movement

poker[1] NOUN a metal rod for poking a fire

poker[2] NOUN a card game in which players bet on who has the best cards

poky ADJECTIVE **pokier, pokiest** small and cramped

polar ADJECTIVE **1** to do with or near the North Pole or South Pole **2** to do with either pole of a magnet ► **polarity** NOUN

polar bear NOUN a white bear living in Arctic regions

polarize VERB **1** (*Science*) to keep vibrations of light waves etc. to a single direction **2** to divide into two opposing groups ► **polarization** NOUN

⚠ **SPELLING**

This word can also be spelled *polarise*.

Polaroid NOUN (*trademark*) a type of plastic which reduces the brightness of light passing through it

Polaroid camera NOUN (*trademark*) a camera that produces a finished photograph a few seconds after taking it

pole[1] NOUN a long slender rounded piece of wood or metal

pole[2] NOUN **1** a point on the earth's surface that is as far north (**North**

THESAURUS

pointless ADJECTIVE • *a pointless exercise* ► useless, futile, vain, meaningless

poisonous ADJECTIVE • *poisonous gases* ► toxic, lethal, noxious • *a poisonous insect* ► venomous, deadly

poke VERB • *poked her with his elbow.* ► prod, dig, jab, nudge

poky ADJECTIVE • *a poky room* ► tiny, small, cramped

pole NOUN • *a fence held with poles* ► post, pillar, stake, stick, support, shaft

Pole) or as far south (**South Pole**) as possible **2** each end of a magnet or electric cell

polecat NOUN an animal of the weasel family

polemical ADJECTIVE attacking a person's opinion or actions

pole star NOUN the star above the North Pole

pole vault NOUN an athletic contest in which competitors jump over a high bar with the help of a long flexible pole

police NOUN officials who enforce laws and catch criminals

police VERB to keep order in a place by means of police

policeman NOUN **policemen** a male police officer

police officer NOUN a member of the police

policewoman NOUN **policewomen** a female police officer

policy NOUN **policies 1** the aims or plans of a person or group **2** an insurance agreement

polio NOUN poliomyelitis

poliomyelitis NOUN a disease that can cause paralysis

polish VERB **1** to make smooth and shiny by rubbing **2** to make a thing better with small corrections
polish off to finish off

polish NOUN **1** a substance used in polishing **2** a shine

polite ADJECTIVE having good manners ▶ **politely** ADVERB, **politeness** NOUN

politic ADJECTIVE prudent or wise

political ADJECTIVE connected with the governing of a country or region ▶ **politically** ADVERB

politician NOUN a person involved in politics

politics NOUN the business of governing a country or region

polka NOUN a lively dance for couples

poll (say as pole) NOUN **1** the process of voting at an election **2** the number of votes cast **3** an opinion poll

poll VERB to receive a certain number of votes in an election

pollen NOUN powder produced by the anthers of flowers, containing male cells for fertilizing other flowers

THESAURUS

police VERB • to police an area
▶ control, supervise, watch over, patrol

policy NOUN • the school's policy on truancy ▶ strategy, code of practice, approach (to) • always a good policy to read the instructions ▶ practice, habit, rule

polish VERB • to polish shoes
▶ shine, clean, brush up, wax

polish NOUN • a bright polish
▶ shine, sheen, gloss, lustre

polite ADJECTIVE • too polite to complain ▶ well-mannered, courteous, respectful, civil, well behaved

poll NOUN • a poll on banning smoking ▶ vote, survey, ballot, referendum

pollinate VERB to fertilize a plant with pollen ▶ **pollination** NOUN

pollutant NOUN something that pollutes

pollute VERB to make the air, water, etc. dirty or impure ▶ **pollution** NOUN

polo NOUN a game like hockey, with players on horseback

polo neck NOUN a high round turned-over collar ▶ **polo-necked** ADJECTIVE

poltergeist NOUN a ghost or spirit that throws things about noisily

polyester NOUN a synthetic material used to make clothing

polygamy NOUN the practice of having more than one wife at a time ▶ **polygamous** ADJECTIVE

polyglot ADJECTIVE knowing or using several languages

polygon NOUN a flat shape with many sides ▶ **polygonal** ADJECTIVE

polyhedron NOUN a solid shape with many sides

polymer NOUN a substance whose molecule is formed from a large number of simple molecules combined

polystyrene NOUN a kind of plastic used for insulating or packing

polythene NOUN a lightweight plastic used to make bags, wrappings, etc.

polyunsaturated ADJECTIVE (of fats) not forming cholesterol in the blood

pomegranate NOUN a tropical fruit with many seeds

pomp NOUN solemn splendour on public occasions

pompom NOUN a ball of coloured threads used as a decoration

pompous ADJECTIVE full of excessive dignity and self-importance ▶ **pomposity** NOUN

pond NOUN a small lake

ponder VERB to think deeply and seriously

ponderous ADJECTIVE **1** heavy and awkward **2** laborious and dull

pong NOUN (informal) an unpleasant smell

pontiff NOUN the Pope

pontificate VERB to give your opinions in a pompous way

pontoon¹ NOUN a boat or float supporting a bridge over a river

pontoon² NOUN a card game in which players try to get cards whose value totals 21

pony NOUN **ponies** a small horse

ponytail NOUN a bunch of long hair tied at the back of the head

pony-trekking NOUN travelling across country on a pony for pleasure ▶ **pony-trekker** NOUN

poodle NOUN a dog with thick curly hair

a
b
c
d
e
f
g
h
i
j
k
l
m
n
o
p
q
r
s
t
u
v
w
x
y
z

THESAURUS

pompous ADJECTIVE • *a pompous bore* ▶ self-important, haughty, arrogant, conceited, puffed-up, pretentious

DICTIONARY

pool NOUN **1** an area or patch of still water **2** the fund of money staked in a gambling game **3** a group of things shared by several people **4** a game resembling billiards

pool VERB to put money or things together for sharing

poor ADJECTIVE **1** having little money or other resources **2** not good; inadequate *poor work* **3** deserving pity

poorly ADVERB **1** in a poor way; badly **2** unwell; slightly ill

pop¹ NOUN **1** a small explosive sound **2** a fizzy drink

pop VERB **popping, popped 1** to make a pop **2** (*informal*) to go or put something somewhere quickly

pop² NOUN modern popular music

popcorn NOUN maize heated so that it bursts and forms fluffy balls

Pope NOUN the head of the Roman Catholic Church

poplar NOUN a tall slender tree

poplin NOUN a plain woven cotton material

poppy NOUN **poppies** a plant with large red flowers

populace NOUN the general public

popular ADJECTIVE **1** liked or enjoyed by many people **2** held or believed by many people *popular beliefs* **3** intended for the general public ▶ **popularity** NOUN, **popularly** ADVERB

popularize VERB to make generally liked or known ▶ **popularization** NOUN

⚠ **SPELLING**

This word can also be spelled *popularise*.

populate VERB to supply with a population; to inhabit

population NOUN the people who live in a district or country

porcelain NOUN fine china

porch NOUN a shelter outside the entrance to a building

porcupine NOUN an animal covered with long prickles

pore¹ NOUN a tiny opening in the skin, allowing moisture to pass through

THESAURUS

pool NOUN • *a pool of water* ▶ pond, puddle, lake • *a pool of cars* ▶ supply, fleet, stock, reserve

poor ADJECTIVE • *a scheme to rehouse poor families* ▶ badly off, hard-up, impoverished, destitute • *poor work* ▶ inferior, substandard, unsatisfactory, mediocre, shoddy • *The poor man was left waiting.* ▶ unfortunate, unlucky

poorly ADJECTIVE • *began to feel poorly* ▶ ill, unwell, sick, off colour, queasy

pop VERB • *Corks were popping everywhere.* ▶ crack, go bang, explode, burst

popular ADJECTIVE • *a popular student* ▶ well-liked, favourite, admired, accepted • *a popular product* ▶ fashionable, modish, well-known

a
b
c
d
e
f
g
h
i
j
k
l
m
n
o
p
q
r
s
t
u
v
w
x
y
z

pore[2] VERB **pore over** to study closely

⚠ **USAGE**

Do not confuse this word with *pour*.

pork NOUN meat from a pig

pornography NOUN obscene pictures or writings
▶ **pornographic** ADJECTIVE

porous ADJECTIVE allowing liquid or air to pass through

porpoise (por-pus) NOUN a sea animal like a small whale

porridge NOUN a food made by boiling oatmeal to a thick paste

port[1] NOUN **1** a harbour **2** a town with a harbour **3** the left-hand side of a ship or aircraft facing forward

port[2] NOUN a strong red Portuguese wine

portable ADJECTIVE able to be carried

portal NOUN a doorway or gateway

portcullis NOUN a heavy grating that can be lowered in grooves to block the gateway to a castle

portend VERB to be a warning of something unwelcome

portent NOUN an omen; a sign that something will happen
▶ **portentous** ADJECTIVE

portentous ADJECTIVE **1** serving as a sign **2** solemn

porter NOUN **1** a person who carries luggage or other goods **2** an official at the entrance to a large building

portfolio NOUN **portfolios 1** a case for holding documents or drawings **2** a government minister's special responsibility

porthole NOUN a window in the side of a ship or aircraft

portico NOUN **porticoes** or **porticos** a roof supported on columns, forming a porch of a building

portion NOUN a part or share given to someone

portion VERB to divide something into portions

portly ADJECTIVE **portlier, portliest** slightly fat
▶ **portliness** NOUN

portrait NOUN **1** a picture of a person or animal **2** a description in words

portray VERB **1** to make a picture of a person or scene etc. **2** to describe or show ▶ **portrayal** NOUN

port NOUN • *A liner had entered the port.* ▶ harbour, seaport, marina, dock

portable ADJECTIVE • *a portable computer* ▶ mobile, movable, lightweight, easy to carry

portion NOUN • *a large portion of rice* ▶ helping, serving, plateful, bowlful, share, ration • *the rear portion of the train* ▶ section, part

• *their portion of the inheritance* ▶ share, allocation

portrait NOUN • *a portrait of the King* ▶ painting, picture , drawing, depiction, likeness

portray VERB • *The artist portrayed her in profile.* ▶ paint, draw, sketch, depict • *The novel portrays London life.* ▶ describe, depict, illustrate, evoke

a
b
c
d
e
f
g
h
i
j
k
l
m
n
o
p
q
r
s
t
u
v
w
x
y
z

pose NOUN **1** a position or posture of the body **2** a way of behaving to make a particular impression

pose VERB **1** to take up a pose **2** to pretend **3** to present *poses a problem for us*

poser NOUN **1** a puzzling question or problem **2** a person who tries to impress people

posh ADJECTIVE (informal) **1** very smart; high-class *a posh restaurant* **2** upper-class *a posh accent*

position NOUN **1** the place where something is or should be **2** the way a person or thing is placed or arranged *a standing position* **3** a situation or condition *in an awkward position* **4** a job
▶ **positional** ADJECTIVE

position VERB to put in a certain position

positive ADJECTIVE **1** definite or certain **2** agreeing or consenting

a positive answer **3** confident and hopeful **4** (of a test) showing signs of what is being tested **5** greater than nought **6** to do with the kind of electric charge that lacks electrons **7** (of a photograph) with the light and dark parts as normal
▶ **positively** ADVERB

posse (poss-ee) NOUN a group of people helping a sheriff

possess VERB **1** to have or own **2** to control someone's thoughts or behaviour ▶ **possessor** NOUN

possessed ADJECTIVE seeming to be controlled by strong emotion or an evil spirit

possession NOUN **1** something someone owns **2** the state of owning something

possessive ADJECTIVE **1** wanting to possess and keep things for yourself **2** (Grammar) (of an adjective or pronoun) showing

THESAURUS

pose NOUN • *a gracious pose*
▶ attitude, stance, position, posture • *only a pose* ▶ pretence, act, show

pose VERB • *to pose a threat*
▶ present, constitute • *to pose a number of questions* ▶ raise, ask, put forward, suggest • *posed for a local artist* ▶ sit, model

posh ADJECTIVE • *a posh hotel*
▶ smart, stylish, high-class, luxury

position NOUN • *the position of the house* ▶ location, situation, setting, site • *a standing position* ▶ posture, pose, stance • *in an*

awkward position ▶ situation, circumstances, predicament • *a position in banking* ▶ job, post

positive ADJECTIVE • *was positive they would come* ▶ certain, sure, convinced, confident • *positive proof* ▶ definite, conclusive, clear • *positive criticism* ▶ helpful, constructive, useful • *a positive attitude* ▶ optimistic, confident, hopeful • *was a positive nightmare* ▶ absolute, utter, complete

possess VERB • *to possess a house* ▶ own, have • *A strange feeling possessed him.* ▶ preoccupy, obsess, dominate

that someone owns something (e.g. *mine*, *their*)

possibility NOUN **possibilities**
1 the fact of being possible
2 something that may exist or happen etc.

possible ADJECTIVE able to exist, happen, be done, or be used

possibly ADVERB 1 in any way *can't possibly do it* 2 perhaps

possum NOUN an opossum

post NOUN 1 an upright piece of wood, concrete, etc. fixed in the ground 2 the collecting and delivering of letters, parcels, etc. 3 letters and parcels 4 a job 5 the place where someone is on duty

post VERB 1 to send a letter or parcel etc. by post 2 to put up a notice or poster etc. 3 to place information on an Internet site 4 to place someone on duty

postage NOUN the charge for sending something by post

postal ADJECTIVE of the post; by post

postal order NOUN a document bought from a post office for sending money by post

postbox NOUN a box for posting letters

postcard NOUN a card for sending messages by post

postcode NOUN a group of letters and numbers included in an address to help in sorting the post

poster NOUN a large sheet of paper with an announcement or advertisement

posterior ADJECTIVE 1 situated at the back 2 coming after

posterior NOUN the buttocks

posterity NOUN future generations of people

postgraduate NOUN a person who does university study after a first degree

post-haste ADVERB with great speed

posthumous (poss-tew-mus) ADJECTIVE coming or happening after a person's death
▶ **posthumously** ADVERB

postman NOUN **postmen** someone who delivers letters

postmark NOUN an official mark put on a postal item to show the place and date of posting

post-mortem NOUN an examination of a dead body to discover the cause of death

post office NOUN 1 an office for sending letters and parcels 2 the national organization for postal services

THESAURUS

possible ADJECTIVE • *a possible improvement* ▶ feasible, achievable, attainable, viable • *a possible explanation* ▶ plausible, believable, conceivable, likely

post NOUN • *a wooden post* ▶ pole, pillar, stake, stick • *The post hasn't come yet.* ▶ mail, letters • *The post will be advertised.* ▶ job, position, vacancy

a
b
c
d
e
f
g
h
i
j
k
l
m
n
p
q
r
s
t
u
v
w
x
y
z

postpone VERB to fix a later time for ► **postponement** NOUN

postscript NOUN an addition at the end of a letter or book

postulate VERB to propose that something is true as part of an argument ► **postulation** NOUN

posture NOUN a particular position of the body

post-war ADJECTIVE of the time after a war

posy NOUN **posies** a small bunch of flowers

pot NOUN **1** a deep usually round container **2** (informal) a lot of something **pots of money pot luck** (informal) whatever is available

pot VERB **potting, potted** to put into a pot

potash NOUN potassium carbonate

potassium NOUN a soft silvery-white metal substance that is essential for living things

potato NOUN **potatoes** a starchy white tuber growing underground, used as a vegetable

potent ADJECTIVE powerful; strong ► **potency** NOUN

potentate NOUN a powerful monarch or ruler

potential (po-ten-shal) ADJECTIVE capable of happening or developing *a potential winner* ► **potentially** ADVERB

potential NOUN the ability of a person or thing to develop in the future

pothole NOUN **1** a deep natural hole in the ground **2** a hole in a road

potion NOUN a liquid for drinking as a medicine etc.

potpourri (poh-poor-ee) NOUN a scented mixture of dried petals and spices

pot shot NOUN a casual shot

potted ADJECTIVE **1** shortened or abridged *a potted account* **2** preserved in a pot *potted shrimps*

potter [1] NOUN a person who makes pottery

potter [2] VERB to work or move about in a leisurely way

pottery NOUN **potteries 1** items made of baked clay **2** the craft of making these things **3** a place where pottery is made

potty [1] ADJECTIVE **pottier, pottiest** (informal) eccentric or foolish

potty [2] NOUN **potties** (informal) a small bowl used by a young child instead of a toilet

pouch NOUN **1** a small bag or pocket **2** a fold of skin in which a kangaroo etc. keeps its young

pouffe (poof) NOUN a low padded stool

poultice NOUN a soft hot dressing put on a sore or inflamed place

poultry NOUN birds (e.g. chickens and geese) kept for their eggs and meat

THESAURUS

postpone VERB • *They had to postpone the game because of the* *bad weather.* ► put off, defer, delay, hold over, suspend

DICTIONARY

pounce VERB to jump or swoop down quickly on something
► **pounce** NOUN

pound[1] NOUN 1 a unit of money (in Britain = 100 pence) 2 a unit of weight equal to 16 ounces or about 454 grams

pound[2] NOUN an enclosure for animals or vehicles

pound[3] VERB 1 to hit something hard and often 2 to run or go heavily 3 (of the heart) to beat fast

pour VERB 1 to flow or make something flow 2 to rain heavily 3 to arrive in large numbers

⚠ **USAGE**

Do not confuse this word with *pore*.

pout VERB to push the lips out when annoyed or sulking ► **pout** NOUN

poverty NOUN 1 the state of being poor 2 a lack or scarcity *a poverty of ideas*

powder NOUN 1 a mass of fine dry particles 2 a medicine or cosmetic etc. made as a powder 3 gunpowder

powder VERB 1 to put powder on 2 to make into powder

powdery ADJECTIVE 1 covered in powder 2 like powder

power NOUN 1 strength or energy 2 an ability *the power of speech* 3 political authority or control 4 a powerful country or organization 5 mechanical or electrical energy 6 (*Science*) the rate of doing work, measured in watts or horsepower 7 (*Maths*) the product of a number multiplied by itself *The third power of 2 = 2 x 2 x 2 = 8.*

powerboat NOUN a powerful motor boat

powerful ADJECTIVE having great power or influence ► **powerfully** ADVERB

powerless ADJECTIVE having no power or influence

power station NOUN a building where electricity is produced

THESAURUS

pounce VERB **pounce on** • *The animal pounced on its prey.*
► jump on, spring on, leap on, swoop on, attack

pound VERB • *pounded his fists on the desk* ► beat, strike, thump, batter, bang

pour VERB • *Blood poured from the wound.* ► spill, stream, flow, gush

poverty NOUN • *years of poverty*
► want, hardship, shortage, need

power NOUN • *the power of speech*
► faculty, capability, capacity, ability • *where the real power lies*
► control, authority, influence

• *the power to impose a curfew*
► right, authority • *a speech of great power* ► force, strength, intensity, energy

powerful ADJECTIVE • *a powerful blow* ► violent, hard, strong, forceful • *a powerful ruler*
► strong, dominant, commanding • *a powerful physique* ► strong, muscular, sturdy, mighty • *a powerful argument* ► strong, convincing, compelling

powerless ADJECTIVE • *felt powerless*
► helpless, impotent, ineffective, defenceless, weak

a
b
c
d
e
f
g
h
i
j
k
l
m
n
o
p
q
r
s
t
u
v
w
x
y
z

559

pp. ABBREVIATION pages

practicable ADJECTIVE able to be done

⚠ **USAGE**

Do not confuse this word with *practical*.

practical ADJECTIVE **1** able to do or make useful things **2** likely to be useful **3** involving activity rather than just theory

⚠ **USAGE**

Do not confuse this word with *practicable*.

practical NOUN a lesson or examination in which something has to be made or done

practical joke NOUN a trick played on someone

practically ADVERB **1** in a practical way **2** almost *I've practically finished.*

practice NOUN **1** the process of doing something repeatedly to become better at it **2** action and not theory *works well in practice* **3** the professional business of a

doctor, lawyer, etc. **4** a habit or custom

⚠ **USAGE**

See the note at **practise**.

practise VERB **1** to do something repeatedly to become better at it **2** to do something habitually *Practise what you preach.* **3** to work as a doctor, lawyer, etc.

⚠ **USAGE**

Note the spelling: *practice* for the noun, *practise* for the verb.

practised ADJECTIVE experienced or expert

practitioner NOUN a professional worker, especially a doctor

pragmatic ADJECTIVE treating things in a practical way *a pragmatic approach to the problem* ▸ **pragmatically** ADVERB, **pragmatism** NOUN

prairie NOUN a large area of flat grass-covered land in North America

praise VERB **1** to say good things about a person or thing **2** to honour God in words

praise NOUN words that praise

THESAURUS

practical ADJECTIVE • *practical experience* ▸ real, actual, hands-on • *practical solutions* ▸ sensible, realistic, workable • *a practical gadget* ▸ handy, useful

practically ADVERB • *I've practically finished.* ▸ almost, nearly, virtually

practice NOUN • *a common practice* ▸ custom, habit, routine, tradition • *needs practice* ▸ training, rehearsal, preparation

practise VERB • *to practise for a music exam* ▸ do exercises, prepare, rehearse, train • *customs that are still practised* ▸ follow, carry out, observe

praise VERB • *praised them for their bravery* ▸ commend, applaud, compliment, congratulate, admire

praise NOUN • *deserve our praise* ▸ approval, acclaim, admiration, commendation, applause

a b c d e f g h i j k l m n o **p** q r s t u v w x y z

praiseworthy ADJECTIVE deserving praise

pram NOUN a four-wheeled carriage for a baby, pushed by a person walking

prance VERB to move about in a lively or happy way

prank NOUN a practical joke or mischievous action

prawn NOUN an edible shellfish like a large shrimp

pray VERB **1** to talk to God **2** to ask earnestly for something

prayer NOUN words used in praying

preach VERB to give a religious or moral talk ▸ **preacher** NOUN

preamble NOUN the introduction to a speech or book or document etc.

pre-arranged ADJECTIVE arranged beforehand

precarious ADJECTIVE not safe or secure ▸ **precariously** ADVERB

precaution NOUN something done to prevent future trouble or danger

precede VERB to come or go before something else

⚠ **USAGE**

Do not confuse this word with *proceed*.

precedence (press-i-dens) NOUN the right to be first or go first

precedent (press-i-dent) NOUN a previous case used as an example to be followed

precept NOUN a rule for action or conduct

precinct NOUN **1** a part of a town where traffic is not allowed **2** the area round a cathedral or other large building

precious ADJECTIVE **1** very valuable **2** greatly loved

precious ADVERB (informal) very *precious little*

precipice NOUN a steep cliff

precipitate VERB **1** to make something happen **2** to throw or send down

precipitate ADJECTIVE hurried or hasty *a precipitate departure*

precipitation NOUN rain, snow, or hail falling

precipitous ADJECTIVE very steep ▸ **precipitously** ADVERB

precis (pray-see) NOUN **precis** a summary

precise ADJECTIVE exact; clearly stated ▸ **precisely** ADVERB

precision NOUN accuracy

preclude VERB to prevent from happening

THESAURUS

prank NOUN • *a prank that went wrong* ▸ trick, practical joke, hoax, stunt

precaution NOUN • *an extra precaution* ▸ safeguard, safety measure, defence

precious ADJECTIVE • *a precious collection* ▸ valuable, priceless, rare • *her most precious possession* ▸ treasured, cherished, valued, prized, favourite

precise ADJECTIVE • *the precise measurements* ▸ exact, accurate, correct • *at the precise moment* ▸ exact, particular • *precise work* ▸ careful, meticulous, detailed

precocious ADJECTIVE (of a child) unusually advanced or developed
► **precociously** ADVERB

preconceived ADJECTIVE (of an idea) formed before full information is available
► **preconception** NOUN

precursor NOUN an earlier form of a person or thing

predator (pred-a-ter) NOUN an animal that hunts or preys on others ► **predatory** ADJECTIVE

predecessor NOUN an earlier holder of a job or position

predestine VERB to determine beforehand ► **predestination** NOUN

predicament (prid-ik-a-ment) NOUN a difficult or unpleasant situation

predicate NOUN (Grammar) the part of a sentence that says something about the subject, e.g. 'is short' in Life is short.

predict VERB to say what will happen in the future
► **predictable** ADJECTIVE

prediction NOUN something predicted

predispose VERB to influence in advance ► **predisposition** NOUN

predominant ADJECTIVE most important or noticeable
► **predominance** NOUN, **predominantly** ADVERB

predominate VERB to be the largest or most important or most powerful

pre-empt VERB to take action to prevent or block something
► **pre-emptive** ADJECTIVE

preen VERB (of a bird) to smooth its feathers with its beak

prefabricated ADJECTIVE made in sections ready to be assembled
► **prefabrication** NOUN

preface (pref-as) NOUN an introduction at the beginning of a book or speech

preface VERB to add introductory words to

prefect NOUN **1** a senior pupil in a school, given authority to help to keep order **2** a regional official in some countries

prefer VERB **preferring**, **preferred 1** to like one person or thing more than another **2** (formal) to put forward a request

preferable (pref-er-a-bul) ADJECTIVE liked better; more desirable
► **preferably** ADVERB

preference (pref-er-ens) NOUN a greater liking

preferential (pref-er-en-shal) ADJECTIVE favoured above others preferential treatment

prefix NOUN (Grammar) a word or syllable joined to the front of a word to change or add to its

predict VERB • to predict a victory
► forecast, foretell, foresee, prophesy

prefer VERB • to prefer tea ► like better, choose, favour, opt for

meaning, as in *disorder*, *outstretched*, *unhappy*

pregnant ADJECTIVE having a fetus in the womb ► **pregnancy** NOUN

prehistoric ADJECTIVE belonging to ancient times before written records ► **prehistory** NOUN

prejudice NOUN an unfair opinion or dislike ► **prejudiced** ADJECTIVE

preliminary ADJECTIVE coming before an important action or event

prelude NOUN **1** a thing that comes before **2** a short piece of music

premature ADJECTIVE coming before the usual or proper time ► **prematurely** ADVERB

premeditated ADJECTIVE planned beforehand

premier (prem-ee-er) ADJECTIVE first in importance, order, or time

premier NOUN a prime minister or other head of government

premiere (prem-yair) NOUN the first public performance of a play or film

premises PLURAL NOUN a building and its grounds

premiss (prem-iss) NOUN a statement used as the basis for reasoning

premium NOUN **1** an amount or instalment paid to an insurance company **2** an extra charge or payment

premonition NOUN a feeling that something is about to happen

preoccupied ADJECTIVE thinking mainly about one thing ► **preoccupation** NOUN

preparation NOUN **1** the process of getting something ready **2** something done to get ready for an event or activity **3** something prepared, e.g. a medicine

preparatory ADJECTIVE preparing for something

prepare VERB to get ready; to make something ready

preponderate VERB to be greater or more important than others ► **preponderance** NOUN

preposition NOUN a word used with a noun or pronoun to show place, position, time, or means, e.g. *at* home, *in* the hall, *on* Sunday, *by* train

prepossessing ADJECTIVE pleasant or attractive

THESAURUS

prejudice NOUN • *widespread prejudice* ► discrimination, bias, favouritism, intolerance, racism, sexism

prejudice VERB • *might prejudice the jury* ► influence, bias

preoccupied ADJECTIVE • *anxious and preoccupied* ► pensive, thoughtful, lost in thought

preoccupied with • *preoccupied with work* ► engrossed in, absorbed in, involved with, wrapped up in

prepare VERB • *to prepare a presentation* ► write, put together, get ready • *to prepare for the future* ► plan, make arrangements, get ready

a
b
c
d
e
f
g
h
i
j
k
l
m
n
o
p
q
r
s
t
u
v
w
x
y
z

a
b
c
d
e
f
g
h
i
j
k
l
m
n
o
p
q
r
s
t
u
v
w
x
y
z

preposterous ADJECTIVE completely absurd or foolish

prerequisite NOUN something necessary before something else can be done

prerogative NOUN a right or privilege belonging to one person or group

prescribe VERB 1 to advise a person to use a particular medicine or treatment 2 to say what should be done

⚠ **USAGE**

Do not confuse this word with *proscribe*.

prescription NOUN 1 a doctor's written order for a medicine 2 the medicine prescribed

prescriptive ADJECTIVE laying down rules

presence NOUN 1 the state of being present 2 a person's impressive appearance or manner

present[1] (prez-ent) ADJECTIVE 1 being in a particular place 2 to do with now; existing now

present (prez-ent) NOUN present times or events; the time now

present[2] (prez-ent) NOUN something given or received as a gift

present (priz-ent) VERB 1 to give something formally 2 to introduce someone to another person 3 to put on a play or other entertainment 4 to show 5 to cause or provide something *This presents a problem.*
▶ **presentation** NOUN, **presenter** NOUN

presentable ADJECTIVE fit to be presented to other people; looking good

presentation NOUN 1 the act of presenting something 2 something presented 3 a talk or demonstration 4 the way in which something is shown

presentiment NOUN a feeling that something bad is about to happen

presently ADVERB 1 soon; shortly 2 now

preservative NOUN a substance added to food to preserve it

preserve VERB to keep something safe or in good condition
▶ **preserver** NOUN, **preservation** NOUN

preserve NOUN 1 jam made with fruit boiled with sugar 2 a place or activity associated with a particular person or group

THESAURUS

present ADJECTIVE (with the stress on *pres-*) • *a doctor was present.*
▶ in attendance, at hand, nearby, available • *their present value*
▶ current, present-day, existing

present VERB • *to present prizes*
▶ hand out, give out, award, grant
• *to present their work* ▶ show, display, exhibit, submit

presently ADVERB • *will be there presently* ▶ shortly, soon, directly
• *is presently abroad* ▶ currently, at present, now

preserve VERB • *action to preserve wildlife* ▶ protect, safeguard, conserve • *to preserve them from harm* ▶ protect, guard, shield

preside VERB to be in charge of a meeting etc.

president NOUN **1** the person in charge of a club, society, or council etc. **2** the head of state in a republic ▶ **presidency** NOUN, **presidential** ADJECTIVE

press VERB **1** to put weight or force on something **2** to make something by pressing **3** to make clothes smooth by ironing them **4** to urge

press NOUN **1** a device for pressing things **2** a machine for printing things **3** a firm that prints or publishes books etc. **4** newspapers and journalists

press conference NOUN an interview with a group of journalists

pressing ADJECTIVE needing immediate action; urgent

press-up NOUN an exercise performed by lying face down and pressing down with the hands to lift the body

pressure NOUN **1** continuous pressing **2** the force with which something presses **3** the force of the atmosphere on the earth's surface **4** strong influence or persuasion

pressurize VERB **1** to maintain a compartment at a constant air pressure **2** to influence or persuade someone ▶ **pressurization** NOUN

⚠️ **SPELLING**

This word can also be spelled *pressurise*.

prestige (pres-teej) NOUN good reputation ▶ **prestigious** ADJECTIVE

✏️ **WORD HISTORY**

from Latin *praestigiae* 'conjuring tricks': *prestige* originally meant 'trickery'

presumably ADVERB according to what you may presume

presume VERB **1** to suppose or assume to be true **2** to be bold enough *I won't presume to advise you.* ▶ **presumption** NOUN

presumptive ADJECTIVE presuming something

presumptuous ADJECTIVE too bold or confident ▶ **presumptuously** ADVERB

press VERB • *She pressed his hand.* ▶ squeeze, grip, clutch • *to press clothes* ▶ iron, smooth, flatten • *Press them to answer.* ▶ urge, beg, persuade

pressure NOUN • *pressure on the foundations* ▶ force, load, weight, strain, stress • *under pressure to accept the offer* ▶ coercion, duress, intimidation

presume VERB • *We presume there will be a charge.* ▶ assume, expect, suppose, guess, believe • *won't presume to advise you* ▶ dare, have the nerve, have the audacity, be so bold as

presumptuous ADJECTIVE • *a presumptuous attitude* ▶ arrogant, bold, impudent, insolent, cheeky

DICTIONARY

presuppose VERB to suppose or assume beforehand
► **presupposition** NOUN

pretence NOUN an attempt to pretend that something is true

pretend VERB 1 to behave as if something is true or real when you know it is not 2 to put forward a claim

pretender NOUN a person who claims a throne or title

pretension NOUN 1 a doubtful claim 2 showy behaviour

pretentious ADJECTIVE 1 trying to impress 2 showy or ostentatious
► **pretentiously** ADVERB

pretext NOUN a reason put forward to conceal the true reason

pretty ADJECTIVE **prettier, prettiest** attractive in a delicate way ► **prettiness** NOUN

pretty ADVERB quite *pretty silly*

prevail VERB 1 to be the most frequent or general 2 to be victorious

prevalent (prev-a-lent) ADJECTIVE most frequent or common
► **prevalence** NOUN

prevaricate VERB to be evasive or misleading ► **prevarication** NOUN

prevent VERB 1 to stop something from happening 2 to stop a person from doing something
► **prevention** NOUN

preventive or **preventative** ADJECTIVE helping to prevent something

preview NOUN a showing of a film or play etc. before its general release

previous ADJECTIVE existing or happening before; preceding
► **previously** ADVERB

prey (say as pray) NOUN an animal that is hunted or killed by another for food

prey VERB **prey on 1** to hunt or take as prey 2 to worry or obsess

price NOUN 1 the amount of money to be paid for something

THESAURUS

pretend VERB • *pretended to understand* ► claim, allege, affect • *Let's pretend we're ghosts.* ► imagine, make believe

pretentious ADJECTIVE • *smaller, less pretentious restaurants* ► ostentatious, showy, flashy

pretty ADJECTIVE • *a pretty little garden* ► attractive, lovely, beautiful, charming, appealing

prevail VERB • *attitudes that prevailed then* ► exist, hold, be prevalent • *Common sense prevailed.* ► win, triumph

prevent VERB • *too late to prevent it* ► stop, avert, avoid, head off • *try to prevent crime* ► stop, thwart, deter, discourage

previous ADJECTIVE • *the previous three years* ► preceding, last

price NOUN • *the price of the holiday* ► cost, terms, amount, charge (for) • *Isolation was one price of their peaceful existence.* ► consequence, result, downside, sacrifice

DICTIONARY

2 something that must be given or done to achieve something

price VERB to decide the price of

priceless ADJECTIVE **1** very valuable **2** (informal) very amusing

prick VERB **1** to make a tiny hole in **2** to hurt somebody with a pin or needle etc. **prick up your ears** to start listening closely

prick NOUN **1** the act of pricking **2** a feeling of pricking

prickle NOUN **1** a small thorn **2** a sharp spine on a hedgehog or cactus etc. **3** a feeling of pricking

prickle VERB to feel or cause a pricking feeling

prickly ADJECTIVE **pricklier**, **prickliest** **1** full of prickles **2** stinging or pricking **3** touchy; irritable

pride NOUN **1** a feeling of pleasure or satisfaction with what you have achieved **2** something that makes you feel proud **3** dignity or self-respect **4** too high an opinion of yourself **5** a group of lions

pride VERB **pride yourself on** to be proud of

priest NOUN **1** a member of the clergy in certain Christian Churches **2** a person who conducts religious ceremonies in a non-Christian religion
▶ **priesthood** NOUN

priestess NOUN a female priest in a non-Christian religion

prig NOUN a self-righteous person
▶ **priggish** ADJECTIVE

prim ADJECTIVE **primmer**, **primmest** formal and correct in manner

prima donna (preem-uh) NOUN **1** the chief female singer in an opera **2** a woman who is temperamental

primary ADJECTIVE first or most important ▶ **primarily** ADVERB

primary colour NOUN one of the colours (red, yellow, and blue) from which all others can be made by mixing

primary school NOUN a school for the first stage of education

primate NOUN **1** an animal of the group that includes human beings, apes, and monkeys **2** an archbishop

THESAURUS

priceless ADJECTIVE • *a priceless collection* ▶ precious, valuable, irreplaceable

prick VERB • *prick the lid first* ▶ pierce, puncture, perforate, stab

prickly ADJECTIVE • *a prickly bush* ▶ spiky, spiny, thorny, bristly, scratchy

pride NOUN • *Pride prevented him from accepting.* ▶ conceit, vanity,

arrogance • *took great pride in the work* ▶ satisfaction, pleasure, sense of achievement • *a source of great pride* ▶ self-esteem, self-respect

prim ADJECTIVE • *looking prim* ▶ demure, proper, formal, strait-laced

primary ADJECTIVE • *the primary aim* ▶ main, chief, principal, key

prime ADJECTIVE **1** chief; most important **2** excellent; first-rate

prime NOUN the best time or stage of something *in the prime of life*

prime VERB **1** to prepare something for use or action **2** to put a coat of liquid on a surface to prepare it for painting **3** to equip a person with information

prime minister NOUN the head of a government

prime number NOUN a number (e.g. 2, 3, 5, 7, 11) that can be divided exactly only by itself and one

primer NOUN **1** a liquid for priming a surface **2** an elementary textbook

primeval ADJECTIVE belonging to the earliest times of the world

primitive ADJECTIVE at an early stage of civilization or development

primrose NOUN a pale yellow flower that blooms in spring

prince NOUN **1** the son of a king or queen **2** a man or boy in a royal family ▸ **princely** ADJECTIVE

princess NOUN **1** the daughter of a king or queen **2** a woman or girl in a royal family **3** the wife of a prince

principal ADJECTIVE chief or most important ▸ **principally** ADVERB

principal NOUN the head of a college or school

⚠ **USAGE**

Do not confuse this word with *principle*.

principality NOUN **principalities** a country ruled by a prince

principle NOUN **1** a general truth, belief, or rule **2** a rule of conduct

⚠ **USAGE**

Do not confuse this word with *principal*.

print VERB **1** to put words or pictures on paper by using a machine or computer **2** to write with letters not joined together **3** to press a mark or design etc. on a surface **4** to make a photograph from a negative

print NOUN **1** printed lettering or words **2** a mark made by

THESAURUS

prime ADJECTIVE • *the prime reason* ▸ main, chief, principal, key • *prime farming land* ▸ best, choice, superior, first-class, top-quality

primitive ADJECTIVE • *primitive peoples* ▸ ancient, early, prehistoric • *primitive tools* ▸ crude, basic, rudimentary, simple, rough

principal ADJECTIVE • *the principal objection* ▸ main, chief, prime, most important, foremost

principle NOUN • *a person of principle* ▸ honour, integrity, morality • *a basic principle of physics* ▸ rule, law, formula

principles PLURAL NOUN • *stick to your principles* ▸ morals, values, standards, code of behaviour

print NOUN • *print that is difficult to read* ▸ type, typeface, lettering • *prints of feet in the sand* ▸ mark, impression, indentation, stamp • *a print of the painting* ▸ copy, reproduction, photograph

a b c d e f g h i j k l m n o p q r s t u v w x y z

something pressing on a surface **3** a printed picture, photograph, or design

printed circuit NOUN an electric circuit made by pressing thin metal strips on a board

printer NOUN **1** someone who prints books or newspapers **2** a machine that prints on paper from computer data

printout NOUN printed information produced by a computer

prior ADJECTIVE earlier or more important than something else *a prior engagement*

prior NOUN the chief monk of a religious order

prioritize VERB to put tasks etc. in order of importance

⚠ **SPELLING**

This word can also be spelled *prioritise*.

priority NOUN **priorities 1** the state of being earlier or more important than something else **2** something considered more important than other things

priory NOUN **priories** a religious house of certain monks or nuns

prise VERB to lever something out or open

prism (prizm) NOUN **1** a solid piece of glass with triangular ends,

which breaks up light into the colours of the rainbow **2** (*Maths*) a solid shape with ends that are triangles or polygons which are equal and parallel

prison NOUN a place where criminals are kept as a punishment

prisoner NOUN **1** a person kept in a prison **2** a captive

pristine ADJECTIVE in its original condition; unspoilt

privacy NOUN a state of being private

private ADJECTIVE **1** belonging to a particular person or group **2** confidential *private talks* **3** quiet and secluded **4** not holding public office *a private citizen* **5** not run by the state *private medicine*

private NOUN a soldier of the lowest rank

privation NOUN loss or lack of something needed

privatize VERB to transfer from the state to private owners ▶ **privatization** NOUN

⚠ **SPELLING**

This word can also be spelled *privatise*.

privet NOUN an evergreen shrub used to make hedges

privilege NOUN a special right or advantage given to one person or group ▶ **privileged** ADJECTIVE

THESAURUS

private ADJECTIVE • *a private beach*
▶ personal, exclusive, individual
• *private talks* ▶ secret, confidential • *her private thoughts*
▶ personal, secret, hidden

• *somewhere private to talk*
▶ quiet, secluded, isolated

privilege NOUN • *special privileges*
▶ benefit, entitlement, advantage, prerogative

a
b
c
d
e
f
g
h
i
j
k
l
m
n
o
p
q
r
s
t
u
v
w
x
y
z

privy ADJECTIVE **privy to** sharing in a secret

prize NOUN **1** an award given to the winner of a game or competition etc. **2** something taken from an enemy

prize VERB to value very much

pro[1] NOUN **pros** (*informal*) a professional

pro[2] NOUN **pros and cons** reasons for and against something

probability NOUN **probabilities 1** likelihood **2** something that is probable

probable ADJECTIVE likely to happen or be true

probably ADVERB very likely

probation NOUN **1** a period of testing a person's suitability at the start of a job **2** the release of a prisoner on good behaviour and under supervision

probation officer NOUN an official who supervises a person on probation

probe NOUN **1** a long thin instrument used to inspect a wound **2** an unmanned spacecraft used for exploring **3** an investigation

probe VERB **1** to explore or look at with a probe **2** to investigate

problem NOUN **1** something difficult to deal with or understand **2** something that has to be done or answered

problematic or **problematical** ADJECTIVE difficult or uncertain

procedure NOUN an orderly way of doing something

proceed VERB **1** to go forward or onward **2** to go on to do something *proceeded to explain the idea*

⚠ **USAGE**

Do not confuse this word with *precede*.

proceedings PLURAL NOUN **1** things that happen; activities **2** a lawsuit

prize NOUN • *to win a prize*
► award, reward, trophy

prize VERB • *to prize your freedom*
► value, appreciate, cherish

probable ADJECTIVE • *the most probable cause of the crash*
► likely, plausible, believable, expected

probe NOUN • *a space probe*
► exploration, expedition • *a police probe*
► inquiry, investigation

probe VERB • *underwater vehicles probing the depths* ► explore, penetrate • *to probe the evidence*
► investigate, examine, look into, scrutinize

problem NOUN • *a page of problems to solve* ► puzzle, question, riddle, mystery • *a big problem for them* ► difficulty, complication, worry, dilemma, snag

procedure NOUN • *a special procedure* ► process, course of action, routine, system

proceeds PLURAL NOUN the money made from a sale or event

process NOUN **processes** a series of actions for making or doing something

process VERB to put something through a process

procession NOUN a number of people or vehicles etc. moving steadily forward in line

processor NOUN **1** a machine that processes things **2** the part of a computer that controls all its operations

proclaim VERB to announce officially or publicly

proclamation NOUN an official announcement

procrastinate VERB to put off doing something
▶ **procrastination** NOUN

procreate VERB to produce offspring by the natural process of reproduction ▶ **procreation** NOUN

procure VERB to obtain or acquire
▶ **procurement** NOUN

prod VERB **prodding, prodded 1** to poke **2** to stimulate someone into action ▶ **prod** NOUN

prodigal ADJECTIVE wasteful or extravagant ▶ **prodigally** ADVERB, **prodigality** NOUN

prodigious ADJECTIVE wonderful or enormous ▶ **prodigiously** ADVERB

prodigy NOUN **prodigies 1** a young person with exceptional abilities **2** a wonderful thing

produce (prod-yooss) VERB **1** to make or create; to bring something into existence **2** to bring something out so that it can be seen **3** to organize the performance of a play, making of a film, etc. **4** to extend a line further ▶ **producer** NOUN

produce (prod-yooss) NOUN things produced, especially by farmers

producer NOUN a person who produces a play, film, etc.

product NOUN **1** something produced **2** the result of multiplying two numbers

THESAURUS

process NOUN • *a simple process*
▶ operation, procedure, method, system

process VERB • *to process claims quickly* ▶ deal with, handle, see to • *to process crude oil* ▶ refine, treat

procession NOUN • *A procession passed through the town.*
▶ parade, march

proclaim VERB • *to proclaim peace*
▶ declare, announce

prod VERB • *prodded the potatoes*
▶ jab, poke, stab, dig, nudge • *someone to prod him into action*
▶ goad, spur, stir, prompt

produce VERB • *produced laughter*
▶ cause, give rise to, provoke, bring about, result in • *produced his passport* ▶ show, display, present, bring out • *to produce a play* ▶ stage, mount, present, put on

production NOUN **1** the process of making or creating something **2** the amount produced **3** a version of a play, opera, etc.

productive ADJECTIVE **1** producing a lot of things **2** producing good results ► **productivity** NOUN

profane ADJECTIVE showing disrespect for holy things

profanity NOUN **profanities** a word or words that show disrespect for holy things

profess VERB **1** to declare or express **2** to claim *professed to be an authority*

profession NOUN **1** an occupation that needs special training, such as medicine or law **2** a declaration *professions of loyalty*

professional ADJECTIVE **1** to do with a profession **2** doing work as a full-time job for payment **3** done with a high standard of skill ► **professional** NOUN

professor NOUN a university teacher of the highest rank ► **professorship** NOUN

proffer VERB to offer

proficient ADJECTIVE trained to do something with skill ► **proficiency** NOUN

profile NOUN **1** a side view of a person's face **2** a short description of a person's character or career

profit NOUN **1** the extra money obtained by selling something for more than it cost to buy or make **2** an advantage gained

profit VERB to gain an advantage or benefit

profitable ADJECTIVE providing a profit or benefit ► **profitably** ADVERB

profligate ADJECTIVE wasteful and extravagant ► **profligacy** NOUN

profound ADJECTIVE **1** very deep or intense *a profound interest* **2** showing great knowledge or understanding *a profound remark* ► **profoundly** ADVERB, **profundity** NOUN

profuse ADJECTIVE lavish or plentiful ► **profusion** NOUN

progeny (proj-in-ee) NOUN offspring or descendants

prognosis NOUN **prognoses** a prediction about how a disease will develop

THESAURUS

professional ADJECTIVE
• *professional life* ► working, business • *professional judgement* ► expert, qualified, skilled, trained • *professional actors* ► paid, salaried, full-time • *a thoroughly professional journalist* ► conscientious, businesslike

profit NOUN • *a modest profit* ► return, surplus, yield

profits • *an increase in profits* ► income, revenue, takings, earnings

profound ADJECTIVE • *a profound interest* ► sincere, deep • *a profound disagreement* ► complete, total • *a very profound remark* ► learned, wise, intelligent

program NOUN a series of coded instructions for a computer

program VERB **programming, programmed** to put instructions into a computer by means of a program ▸ **programmer** NOUN

programme NOUN **1** a list of planned events **2** a pamphlet giving details of a play, concert, football match, etc. **3** a show, play, or talk etc. on radio or television

progress (proh-gress) NOUN **1** forward movement; an advance **2** a development or improvement

progress (pro-gress) VERB **1** to move forward **2** to develop or improve

progression NOUN **1** the process of moving forward or developing **2** (*Maths*) a sequence of numbers each having the same relation to the one before

progressive ADJECTIVE **1** moving forward or developing **2** in favour of political or social reform **3** (of a disease) becoming more severe

prohibit VERB to forbid or ban ▸ **prohibition** NOUN

prohibitive ADJECTIVE (of prices) too high for most people to afford

project (proj-ekt) NOUN **1** a plan or scheme **2** a piece of research into a subject

project (pro-jekt) VERB **1** to stick out **2** to show a picture on a screen **3** to give people a particular impression ▸ **projection** NOUN

projectile NOUN a missile

projector NOUN a machine for showing films or photographs on a screen

proletariat (proh-lit-air-ee-at) NOUN the ordinary working people

proliferate VERB to increase in numbers ▸ **proliferation** NOUN

prolific ADJECTIVE producing a lot *a prolific author*

prologue (proh-log) NOUN an introduction to a poem or play etc.

prolong VERB to make a thing longer or make it last for a long time

prom NOUN (*informal*) **1** a promenade **2** a promenade concert **3** (*American*) a formal school dance

progress NOUN • *major progress in medical research* ▸ advance, development, improvement, breakthrough • *The weather made further progress difficult.* ▸ advance, movement, headway

progress VERB • *Plans are progressing slowly.* ▸ advance, develop, move forward, proceed

prohibit VERB • *a law prohibiting advertising* ▸ forbid, ban, disallow, make illegal

project NOUN • *a conservation project* ▸ scheme, plan, proposal, enterprise, idea • *a history project* ▸ assignment, piece of research, piece of work, task

prolong VERB • *to prolong the discussion* ▸ lengthen, extend, continue, stretch out

a
b
c
d
e
f
g
h
i
j
k
l
m
n
o
p
q
r
s
t
u
v
w
x
y
z

a
b
c
d
e
f
g
h
i
j
k
l
m
n
o
p
q
r
s
t
u
v
w
x
y
z

promenade (prom-in-**ahd**) NOUN a place suitable for walking, especially beside the seashore

promenade concert a concert at which part of the audience stands

prominence NOUN 1 conspicuousness 2 fame

prominent ADJECTIVE 1 easily seen; conspicuous *in a prominent position* 2 sticking out 3 important ► **prominently** ADVERB

promiscuous ADJECTIVE 1 having casual sexual relationships 2 indiscriminate ► **promiscuity** NOUN

promise NOUN 1 a statement that you will do or not do something 2 an indication of future success

promise VERB to make a promise

promising ADJECTIVE likely to be good or successful

promontory NOUN **promontories** a piece of high land jutting into a sea or lake

promote VERB 1 to move a person to a higher rank or position 2 to help the progress of 3 to publicize or advertise ► **promotion** NOUN

prompt ADJECTIVE immediate; not involving delay *a prompt reply* ► **promptly** ADVERB

prompt ADVERB exactly *at 7.20 a.m. prompt*

prompt VERB 1 to cause or encourage a person to do something 2 to remind an actor or speaker of the words to speak next ► **prompter** NOUN

promulgate VERB to make known to the public; to proclaim ► **promulgation** NOUN

prone ADJECTIVE lying face downwards **prone to** likely to do or suffer from something *is prone to exaggerate*

THESAURUS

prominent ADJECTIVE • *a prominent politician* ► important, well-known, leading, distinguished

promise NOUN • *You have my promise.* ► word, assurance, pledge, commitment, guarantee, vow • *shows great promise* ► potential, ability, aptitude, talent

promise VERB • *promised to pay for the damage* ► agree, undertake, guarantee • *promised they'd be there* ► give your word, vow, swear

promote VERB • *was promoted to manager* ► upgrade, move up • *will promote the new place* ► advertise, publicize, push • *promoting equal opportunities* ► champion, advance, encourage

prompt ADJECTIVE • *a prompt reply* ► quick, swift, rapid, speedy

prompt VERB • *not sure what prompted the outburst* ► cause, give rise to, bring about, lead to

prone ADJECTIVE • *a man lying prone on the floor* ► face down, on your front, prostrate • *is prone to exaggerate* ► apt, inclined, liable

prong NOUN each of the spikes on a fork ► **pronged** ADJECTIVE

pronoun NOUN a word used instead of a noun (e.g. *I, we, who, this*)

pronounce VERB **1** to say a sound or word in a particular way **2** to declare formally

pronounced ADJECTIVE noticeable *a pronounced limp*

pronouncement NOUN a declaration

pronunciation NOUN the way a word is pronounced

⚠ **SPELLING**

Note the spelling -nunc- and not -nounc-.

proof NOUN **1** evidence that shows something to be true **2** a copy of printed matter made for checking before other copies are printed

proof ADJECTIVE able to resist something *bullet-proof*

prop[1] NOUN a support made of a long piece of wood or metal

prop VERB **propping, propped** to support something by leaning it against a surface

prop[2] NOUN an object or piece of furniture used in a play or film

propaganda NOUN biased or misleading publicity intended to make people believe something

propagate VERB **1** to breed or reproduce **2** to spread an idea or belief

propel VERB **propelling, propelled** to push something forward

propeller NOUN a device with blades that spin round to drive an aircraft or ship

propensity NOUN **propensities** a natural tendency

proper ADJECTIVE **1** suitable or right **2** respectable **3** (*informal*) complete or thorough *a proper nuisance* ► **properly** ADVERB

proper noun NOUN the name of an individual person or thing, e.g. *Mary, London, Spain*, usually written with a capital first letter

property NOUN **properties 1** a thing or things that belong to somebody **2** a building or land

THESAURUS

pronounce VERB • *difficult to pronounce* ► say, enunciate, articulate • *pronounced them cured* ► declare, proclaim, announce

proof NOUN • *need proof of purchase* ► evidence, confirmation, verification

prop NOUN • *supported by steel props* ► post, strut, support

prop VERB • *propped the bike against a wall* ► lean, rest, stand

prop up • *The old tree was propped up with posts.* ► support, hold up

proper ADJECTIVE • *a proper job* ► real, genuine • *not considered proper* ► respectable, correct, decent • *apply through the proper channels* ► correct, right, appropriate, official

property NOUN • *left all his property to a nephew* ► possessions, belongings, assets, valuables • *property to buy abroad*

a
b
c
d
e
f
g
h
i
j
k
l
m
n
o
p
q
r
s
t
u
v
w
x
y
z

owned by someone **3** a quality or characteristic

prophecy NOUN **prophecies 1** a statement that predicts what will happen **2** the action of prophesying

prophesy VERB **prophesies, prophesied** to say what will happen in the future

prophet NOUN **1** a person who makes prophecies **2** a religious teacher believed to be inspired by God

prophetic ADJECTIVE saying or showing what will happen in the future

propitious ADJECTIVE favourable

proponent NOUN a person who favours something

proportion NOUN **1** a part or share of a whole thing **2** a ratio **3** the correct relation of size, amount, or importance

proportional or **proportionate** ADJECTIVE in proportion; according to a ratio

proportional representation NOUN a system in which each political party has a number of Members of Parliament in proportion to the number of votes for all its candidates

proposal NOUN **1** the act of proposing **2** something proposed **3** an offer of marriage

propose VERB **1** to suggest an idea or plan etc. **2** to plan or intend to do something **3** to ask someone to marry you

proposition NOUN **1** a suggestion or offer **2** a statement **3** (*informal*) an undertaking or problem *a difficult proposition*

propound VERB to put forward an idea for consideration

proprietor NOUN the owner of a shop or business

propriety NOUN **proprieties 1** the state of being proper **2** correct behaviour

propulsion NOUN forward movement

prosaic ADJECTIVE dull and ordinary

proscribe VERB to forbid by law

⚠ **USAGE**

Do not confuse this word with *prescribe*.

prose NOUN ordinary writing or speech as distinct from verse

prosecute VERB **1** to bring a criminal charge against someone **2** to continue with something
▸ **prosecutor** NOUN

▸ buildings, houses • *the medicinal properties of garlic*
▸ quality, attribute, characteristic

proposal NOUN • *a proposal to build a new road* ▸ plan, scheme, suggestion, recommendation

propose VERB • *proposed Greece for their next holiday*
▸ suggest, put forward, recommend • *How do you propose to find the money?* ▸ plan, intend mean, aim

DICTIONARY

prosecution NOUN **1** the process of prosecuting **2** the lawyers prosecuting someone in a lawcourt

prospect (pros-pekt) NOUN **1** a possibility or expectation *little prospect of success* **2** a wide view

prospect (pro-spekt) VERB to explore in search of gold or some other mineral ► **prospector** NOUN

prospective ADJECTIVE expected to be or to happen *prospective customers*

prospectus NOUN a booklet describing a school, business, company, etc.

prosper VERB to be successful

prosperous ADJECTIVE successful or rich

prosperity NOUN success and wealth

prostitute NOUN a person who offers sexual intercourse for payment ► **prostitution** NOUN

prostrate ADJECTIVE lying face downwards

prostrate VERB **prostrate yourself** to lie flat on the ground in submission ► **prostration** NOUN

protagonist NOUN the main character in a play

protect VERB to keep safe from harm or injury ► **protection** NOUN

protective ADJECTIVE giving protection

protector NOUN a defender or guardian

protectorate NOUN a country that is under the protection of a stronger country

protégé (prot-ezh-ay) NOUN a person who is guided and supported by a more experienced person

protein NOUN a substance found in living things and an essential part of the human and animal diet

protest (proh-test) NOUN a statement or action showing disapproval

protest (pro-test) VERB **1** to make a protest **2** to declare firmly *protested their innocence* ► **protester** NOUN

THESAURUS

prospect NOUN • *little prospect of success* ► chance, expectation, likelihood, possibility

prosper VERB • *The country continues to prosper.* ► thrive, do well, flourish

prosperous ADJECTIVE • *a prosperous part of the country* ► rich, affluent, wealthy

protect VERB • *anxious to protect their families* ► defend, guard, safeguard, keep safe, save

protest NOUN • *a wave of protests* ► complaint, objection • *a large protest in the town* ► demonstration, rally, march

protest VERB • *protesting against the export of animals* ► demonstrate, object • *protested that the music was too loud* ► complain, object, grumble • *protested their innocence* ► maintain, insist on

a
b
c
d
e
f
g
h
i
j
k
l
m
n
o
p
q
r
s
t
u
v
w
x
y
z

577

Protestant NOUN a member of any of the western Christian Churches separated from the Roman Catholic Church

protocol NOUN correct or official procedure

proton NOUN a particle of matter with a positive electric charge

prototype NOUN the first model of something, from which others are copied

protract VERB to make something last longer than usual
▶ **protracted** ADJECTIVE

protractor NOUN an instrument for measuring angles

protrude VERB to stick out from a surface ▶ **protrusion** NOUN

proud ADJECTIVE **1** pleased with yourself or someone else who has done well **2** causing pride *a proud moment* **3** full of self-respect *too proud to ask for help* **4** having too high an opinion of yourself
▶ **proudly** ADVERB

prove VERB **1** to show that something is true **2** to turn out *a forecast that proved to be true*
▶ **provable** ADJECTIVE

proven (proh-ven) ADJECTIVE proved of proven ability

proverb NOUN a well-known saying that states a truth, e.g. *Many hands make light work.*

proverbial ADJECTIVE **1** referred to in a proverb **2** well-known

provide VERB **1** to supply or make available **2** to prepare for something *to provide for emergencies* **provided** or **providing that** on condition that

providence NOUN wise preparation for the future

provident ADJECTIVE wisely providing for the future; thrifty

providential ADJECTIVE happening very luckily
▶ **providentially** ADVERB

province NOUN **1** a major division of a country **2** a person's area of special knowledge or responsibility

provincial (pro-vin-shul) ADJECTIVE **1** to do with the provinces **2** culturally limited or narrow-minded

provision NOUN **1** the providing of something **2** a statement in a legal document

provisional ADJECTIVE arranged or agreed on for the time being
▶ **provisionally** ADVERB

THESAURUS

proud ADJECTIVE • *too proud to admit a mistake* ▶ conceited, arrogant, vain, big-headed • *a proud people* ▶ noble, dignified, self-respecting **proud of** • *so proud of her garden* ▶ pleased with, delighted with, thrilled with, satisfied with

prove VERB • *evidence that proves their innocence* ▶ confirm, corroborate, demonstrate, establish • *a story that proved to be true* ▶ turn out, be found

provide VERB • *willing to provide food* ▶ supply, furnish, contribute, donate, lay on

DICTIONARY

provisions PLURAL NOUN supplies of food and drink

proviso (prov-y-zoh) NOUN **provisos** a condition insisted on in advance

provocative ADJECTIVE likely to make someone angry

provoke VERB **1** to make a person angry **2** to cause or give rise to ► **provocation** NOUN

prow NOUN the front end of a ship

prowess NOUN great ability or daring

prowl VERB to move about quietly or cautiously ► **prowler** NOUN

proximity NOUN nearness

proxy NOUN **proxies** a person authorized to act for another person

prude NOUN a person who is easily shocked by things to do with sex ► **prudish** ADJECTIVE

prudent ADJECTIVE careful and cautious ► **prudence** NOUN, **prudently** ADVERB

prune¹ NOUN a dried plum

prune² VERB to cut off unwanted parts of a tree or bush etc.

pry VERB **pries**, **pried** to look into or ask about someone else's private business

PS ABBREVIATION postscript

psalm (sahm) NOUN a religious song

pseudonym NOUN a false name used by an author

psychedelic (sy-ker-**del**-ik) ADJECTIVE having vivid colours and patterns

psychiatrist (sy-ky-a-trist) NOUN a doctor who treats mental illnesses ► **psychiatric** ADJECTIVE, **psychiatry** NOUN

psychic (sy-kik) ADJECTIVE **1** supernatural **2** having the power to predict the future **3** to do with the mind or soul

psychoanalysis NOUN investigation of a person's mental processes by psychotherapy ► **psychoanalyst** NOUN

psychology NOUN the study of the mind ► **psychological** ADJECTIVE, **psychologist** NOUN

psychotherapy NOUN treatment of mental illness by psychological methods ► **psychotherapist** NOUN

ptarmigan (tar-mig-an) NOUN a bird of the grouse family

pterodactyl (te-ro-dak-til) NOUN an extinct flying reptile

PTO ABBREVIATION please turn over

pub NOUN a building licensed to serve alcoholic drinks; a public house

THESAURUS

provisions PLURAL NOUN • were running out of provisions ► supplies, food and drink, stores

provoke VERB • better not to provoke him ► annoy, irritate,

anger, offend • to provoke interest ► arouse, prompt, cause

pry VERB • didn't mean to pry ► interfere, meddle, snoop

a
b
c
d
e
f
g
h
i
j
k
l
m
n
o
p
q
r
s
t
u
v
w
x
y
z

puberty NOUN the time when a young person is developing physically into an adult

pubic ADJECTIVE to do with the lower front part of the abdomen

public ADJECTIVE belonging to or known by people in general ► **publicly** ADVERB

public NOUN people in general

publican NOUN the person in charge of a pub

publication NOUN 1 the process of publishing 2 a published book or newspaper etc.

public house NOUN a building licensed to serve alcoholic drinks; a pub

publicity NOUN advertising and other methods of bringing things to people's attention

publicize VERB to bring something to people's attention; advertise

⚠️ **SPELLING**

This word can also be spelled *publicise*.

public school NOUN a private school that charges fees

publish VERB 1 to have something printed and sold to the public 2 to

announce in public ► **publisher** NOUN

puce ADJECTIVE of a brownish-purple colour

puck NOUN a hard rubber disc used in ice hockey

pucker VERB to wrinkle

pudding NOUN 1 the sweet course of a meal 2 a food made from suet and flour

puddle NOUN a shallow patch of liquid on the ground

puerile ADJECTIVE silly and childish

puff NOUN 1 a short blowing of breath, wind, or smoke etc. 2 a soft pad for putting powder on the skin 3 a cake of light pastry filled with cream

puff VERB 1 to blow out puffs of smoke etc. 2 to breathe with difficulty 3 to inflate or swell something

puffin NOUN a seabird with a large striped beak

puffy ADJECTIVE **puffier**, **puffiest** puffed out; swollen

pug NOUN a small dog with a flat face like a bulldog

pugnacious ADJECTIVE wanting to fight; aggressive

puke VERB (informal) to vomit

THESAURUS

public ADJECTIVE • *public gardens* ► communal, open, community • *is public knowledge by now* ► general, common, widely known

publish VERB • *a new book which was published last year* ► issue,

bring out, produce, print • *private letters that should not be published* ► make public, make known, announce, publicize

puff NOUN • *a puff of wind* ► gust, blast, breath, draught • *a puff of grey smoke* ► cloud, curl, whiff

580

pull VERB **1** to make a thing come towards you or after you **2** to move by a driving force *The car pulled into the road.* **pull in** to move to the side of the road **pull off** to achieve ▶ **pull** NOUN

pullet NOUN a young hen

pulley NOUN **pulleys** a wheel with a rope, chain, or belt over it, used for lifting or moving loads

pullover NOUN a knitted piece of clothing for the top half of the body

pulp NOUN **1** the soft moist part of fruit **2** any soft moist mass ▶ **pulpy** ADJECTIVE

pulpit NOUN a small enclosed platform for the preacher in a church

pulsate VERB to expand and contract rhythmically ▶ **pulsation** NOUN

pulse¹ NOUN **1** the rhythmical movement of the arteries as blood is pumped through them by the beating of the heart **2** a throb

pulse VERB to throb or pulsate

pulse² NOUN the edible seed of peas, beans, lentils, etc.

pulverize VERB to crush into powder

⚠️ **SPELLING**

This word can also be spelled *pulverise*.

puma NOUN a large American brown cat

pumice NOUN a kind of porous stone used as an abrasive especially for removing hard skin

pummel VERB **pummelling**, **pummelled** to hit repeatedly with the fists

pump¹ NOUN a machine that pushes air or liquid into or out of something, or along pipes

pump VERB **1** to move air or liquid with a pump **2** (*informal*) to question someone **pump up** to inflate

pump² NOUN a canvas sports shoe with a rubber sole

pumpkin NOUN a large round fruit with a hard orange skin

pun NOUN a joking use of a word sounding the same as another, e.g. 'When is coffee like earth? When it is ground.'

punch¹ VERB **1** to hit someone with your fist **2** to make a hole in something

punch¹ NOUN **1** a hit with a fist **2** a device for making holes in paper, metal, leather, etc. **3** force or vigour

punch² NOUN a drink made by mixing wine or spirits and fruit juice in a bowl

THESAURUS

pull VERB • *pulled a chair to the table* ▶ drag, draw, tug, heave • *cars pulling trailers* ▶ tow, haul • *to pull huge crowds* ▶ attract, draw, bring in **to pull a muscle** ▶ strain, sprain, wrench

pump VERB • *to pump water out* ▶ drain, draw off, empty

punch VERB • *punched him in the stomach* ▶ hit, strike, thump • *punched a hole in the wall* ▶ bore, pierce

a
b
c
d
e
f
g
h
i
j
k
l
m
n
o
p
q
r
s
t
u
v
w
x
y
z

punchline NOUN words that give the climax of a joke or story

punctilious ADJECTIVE careful about correct behaviour and detail

punctual ADJECTIVE doing things exactly at the time arranged
▶ **punctuality** NOUN, **punctually** ADVERB

punctuate VERB 1 to put punctuation marks into writing 2 to include or interrupt *a speech punctuated with cheers*

punctuation NOUN marks such as commas, full stops, and brackets put into a piece of writing to make it easier to read

puncture NOUN a small hole made by something sharp, especially in a tyre

puncture VERB to make a puncture in

pundit NOUN a person who is an authority on something

pungent (pun-jent) ADJECTIVE having a strong taste or smell
▶ **pungency** NOUN

punish VERB to make a person suffer for doing wrong

punishment NOUN 1 the act of punishing 2 something suffered for doing wrong

punitive (pew-nit-iv) ADJECTIVE inflicting or intended as a punishment

punk NOUN 1 a loud aggressive style of rock music 2 a person who listens to this music

punnet NOUN a small container for soft fruit

punt[1] NOUN a flat-bottomed boat, moved by pushing a pole against the bottom of a river

punt VERB to travel in a punt

punt[2] VERB to kick a football after dropping it from your hands and before it touches the ground

punter NOUN 1 a person who bets 2 (informal) a customer

puny ADJECTIVE **punier**, **puniest** small and weak

pup NOUN 1 a puppy 2 a young seal

pupa NOUN **pupae** a chrysalis

pupil NOUN 1 a person being taught, especially at school 2 the opening in the centre of the eyeball

puppet NOUN 1 a doll that can be made to move by fitting it over your hand or working it by strings or wires 2 a person whose actions are controlled by someone else

puppy NOUN **puppies** a young dog

purchase VERB to buy
▶ **purchaser** NOUN

purchase NOUN 1 something that is bought 2 the act of buying 3 a firm hold or grip

purdah NOUN the Muslim or Hindu custom of keeping women from the sight of men or strangers

THESAURUS

punish VERB • *to punish the culprits* ▶ discipline, penalize, make an example of, correct, scold, chastise

puny ADJECTIVE • *looked small and puny* ▶ weak, feeble

pupil NOUN • *an able pupil* ▶ student, scholar, learner

pure ADJECTIVE **1** not mixed with anything else *pure gold* **2** clean or clear *pure spring water* **3** free from evil or sin **4** mere; nothing but *pure nonsense* ▶ **purely** ADVERB

purgatory NOUN **1** (in Roman Catholic belief) a place in which souls are purified by punishment before they can enter heaven **2** a state of temporary suffering

purge VERB to get rid of unwanted people or things

purge NOUN an act of purging

purify VERB **purifies, purified** to make pure ▶ **purification** NOUN

purist NOUN a person who insists on correctness, especially in language

Puritan NOUN a Protestant in the 16th and 17th centuries who wanted simpler religious ceremonies and strictly moral behaviour

puritan NOUN a person with strict morals ▶ **puritanical** ADJECTIVE

purity NOUN a pure state

purl VERB to knit with a stitch that makes a ridge towards the person knitting ▶ **purl** NOUN

purloin VERB (formal) to steal

purple ADJECTIVE of a deep reddish-blue colour

purport (per-port) VERB to claim *a letter purporting to be from the council*

purpose NOUN **1** what you intend to do; a plan or aim **2** determination **on purpose** deliberately

purposeful ADJECTIVE determined ▶ **purposefully** ADVERB

purposely ADVERB on purpose

purr VERB to make the low murmuring sound that a cat makes when pleased ▶ **purr** NOUN

purse NOUN **1** a small pouch for carrying money **2** (American) a handbag

purse VERB to draw your lips tightly together in disapproval

purser NOUN a ship's officer in charge of accounts

pursue VERB **1** to chase someone in order to catch them **2** to continue with or work at *to pursue a career* ▶ **pursuer** NOUN

pursuit NOUN **1** the act of pursuing **2** a regular activity

THESAURUS

pure ADJECTIVE • *pure gold*
▶ genuine, real • *pure spring water*
▶ clean, fresh, clear, unpolluted

purpose NOUN • *made their purpose clear* ▶ intention, motive
• *can't see any purpose in doing it*
▶ point, advantage, benefit, gain
• *actions that show purpose*
▶ determination, resolve,

single-mindedness **on purpose**
• *did it on purpose* ▶ deliberately, intentionally, knowingly

pursue VERB • *pursued a fox*
▶ chase, go after, follow • *to pursue a career* ▶ follow, carry on, continue

pursuit NOUN • *gave up the pursuit*
▶ chase, hunt, search • *outdoor*

a
b
c
d
e
f
g
h
i
j
k
l
m
n
p
q
r
s
t
u
v
w
x
y
z

purvey VERB (formal) to supply food etc. as a trade ► **purveyor** NOUN

pus NOUN a thick yellowish substance produced in infected tissue, e.g. in an abscess or boil

push VERB **1** to push a thing away from you **2** to move yourself by using force *pushed in front of us* **3** to try to force someone to do or use something

push NOUN a pushing movement or effort

pushchair NOUN a folding chair on wheels, for a young child to be pushed in

pushy ADJECTIVE **pushier**, **pushiest** unpleasantly assertive and eager

puss or **pussy** NOUN **pusses** or **pussies** (informal) a cat

pussyfoot VERB to act too cautiously and timidly

put VERB **putting**, **put** This word has many uses, including **1** to move a person or thing to a place or position **2** to make a person or thing do or experience something or be in a certain condition *put the light on put me in a good mood* **3** to express in words *Try to put it tactfully.* **put off** to postpone **put up** to construct or build **put up with** to tolerate

putrid (pew-trid) ADJECTIVE rotting and stinking

putt VERB to hit a golf ball gently towards the hole ► **putt** NOUN

putty NOUN a soft paste that sets hard, used for fitting glass into windows

puzzle NOUN **1** a difficult question or problem **2** a game or toy that sets a problem to solve

THESAURUS

pursuits ► activity, pastime • *the pursuit of knowledge* ► search (for), quest (for)

push VERB • *pushed a chair against the door* ► shove, thrust, press, nudge • *pushed a few things into a bag* ► pack, cram, squash, squeeze, jam, ram • *tried to push his way through* ► force, shove, elbow, jostle • *better not to push them to come* ► pressurize, force

push NOUN • *felt a push in the back* ► shove, thrust, prod, nudge, jolt, poke

put VERB • *put the case on the table* ► place, leave, set, deposit,

position, stand, settle • *wasn't sure how to put it* ► express, word, phrase • *put a tax on it* ► impose, levy • *put the cost at over a million* ► estimate, reckon, calculate, assess • *some ideas to put to you* ► submit, present, propose, suggest **put off** • *to put off a decision* ► postpone, defer, delay **put up** • *put up a shed in the garden* ► erect, build, construct **put up with** • *will not put up with it* ► tolerate, stand for, accept

puzzle NOUN • *a hard puzzle to solve* ► problem, riddle, question

puzzle VERB **1** to make someone confused by something that is difficult to think patiently about how to solve something ▸ **puzzled** ADJECTIVE, **puzzlement** NOUN

PVC ABBREVIATION polyvinyl chloride, a plastic used to make clothing, pipes, flooring, etc.

pygmy (pig-mee) NOUN **pygmies** **1** a very small person or thing **2** a member of certain unusually short peoples of equatorial Africa

pyjamas PLURAL NOUN a loose jacket and trousers worn in bed

pylon NOUN a tall steel framework supporting electric cables

pyramid NOUN **1** a structure with a square base and with sloping sides that meet in a point at the top **2** an ancient Egyptian tomb shaped like this

pyre NOUN a pile of wood for burning a dead body as part of a funeral ceremony

python NOUN a large snake that kills its prey by crushing it

THESAURUS

puzzle VERB • *a response that puzzled me* ▸ confuse, perplex, baffle, mystify, bewilder

puzzled ADJECTIVE • *a puzzled look* ▸ confused, baffled, perplexed, mystified, bewildered

Qq

quack VERB to make the harsh cry of a duck ► **quack** NOUN

quad (kwod) NOUN **1** a quadrangle **2** a quadruplet

quadrangle NOUN a rectangular courtyard with buildings round it

quadrant NOUN a quarter of a circle

quadrilateral NOUN a flat geometric shape with four sides

quadruped NOUN an animal with four feet

quadruple ADJECTIVE **1** four times as much or as many **2** having four parts

quadruple VERB to make or become four times as much or as many

quadruplet NOUN each of four children born to the same mother at one time

quaff (kwof) VERB to drink eagerly

quagmire NOUN a bog or marsh

quail ¹ NOUN a bird related to the partridge

quail ² VERB to feel or show fear

quaint ADJECTIVE attractively odd or old-fashioned

quake VERB to tremble; to shake with fear

quake NOUN an earthquake

Quaker NOUN a member of a religious group called the Society of Friends, founded in the 17th century

qualification NOUN **1** a skill or ability that makes someone suitable for a job **2** a statement that qualifies

qualify VERB **qualifies, qualified 1** to make or become able to do something **2** to make a remark or statement less extreme **3** (of an adjective) to add meaning to a noun ► **qualified** ADJECTIVE

quality NOUN **qualities 1** the degree of goodness or worth **2** something special in a person or thing

qualm (kwahm) NOUN a doubt about whether something you have done is fair or right

quandary NOUN **quandaries** a difficult situation or decision

quantify VERB **quantifies, quantified** to describe or express as an amount or a number

quantity NOUN **quantities 1** the amount there is of something **2** a large amount

THESAURUS

quaint ADJECTIVE • *a quaint little teashop* ► charming, picturesque, sweet

qualified ADJECTIVE • *a qualified doctor* ► trained, professional, certified • *qualified approval* ► cautious, half-hearted, limited

quality NOUN • *work of a high quality* ► standard, class, grade • *many good qualities* ► characteristic, feature, attribute

quantity NOUN • *a large quantity* ► amount, number, total, volume

quantum NOUN a quantity or amount

quantum leap or **quantum jump** NOUN a sudden large increase or advance

quarantine NOUN the process of keeping a person or animal isolated in case they have a disease

quarrel NOUN an angry disagreement

quarrel VERB **quarrelling**, **quarrelled** to have a quarrel

quarrelsome ADJECTIVE fond of quarrelling

quarry [1] NOUN **quarries** an open place where stone for building is taken from the ground

quarry VERB **quarries**, **quarried** to dig from a quarry

quarry [2] NOUN **quarries** a hunted animal

quart NOUN two pints (1.13 litres)

quarter NOUN **1** each of four equal parts of a thing **2** three months, one-fourth of a year **3** a district or region **at close quarters** very close together

quarter VERB **1** to divide into quarters **2** to put soldiers etc. into lodgings

quarter-final NOUN each of the matches or rounds before a semi-final ▸ **quarter-finalist** NOUN

quarterly ADJECTIVE, ADVERB happening or produced once every three months

quarterly NOUN **quarterlies** a quarterly magazine

quarters PLURAL NOUN lodgings

quartet NOUN **1** a group of four musicians **2** a piece of music for four musicians

quartz NOUN a hard mineral, often in crystal form

quasar NOUN a huge remote star in the sky

quash VERB **1** to cancel or annul a previous decision **2** to crush a rebellion

quaver VERB to tremble or quiver

quaver NOUN **1** a quavering sound **2** a note in music (♪) lasting half as long as a crotchet

quay (kee) NOUN a landing place for loading and unloading ships

queasy ADJECTIVE **queasier**, **queasiest** feeling slightly sick ▸ **queasiness** NOUN

queen NOUN **1** a country's female ruler who reigns because of her birth **2** the wife of a king **3** a female bee or ant that produces eggs **4** the most powerful piece in

THESAURUS

quarrel NOUN • *a violent quarrel* ▸ argument, row, disagreement, dispute

quarrel VERB • *Try not to quarrel.* ▸ argue, disagree, squabble, bicker

quarter NOUN • *people from every quarter* ▸ district, neighbourhood, area

quaver VERB • *voice began to quaver* ▸ tremble, quiver, shake

DICTIONARY

chess **5** a playing card with a picture of a queen ▸ **queenship** NOUN

queen mother NOUN a king's widow who is the mother of the present king or queen

queer ADJECTIVE **1** strange or eccentric **2** slightly ill or faint ▸ **queerly** ADVERB, **queerness** NOUN

quell VERB **1** to crush a rebellion **2** to resist feeling fear, anger, etc.

quench VERB **1** to satisfy your thirst by drinking **2** to put out a fire or flame

query NOUN **queries 1** a question **2** a question mark

query VERB **queries, queried** to question whether something is true or correct

quest NOUN a long search for something

question NOUN **1** a sentence that asks something or needs an answer **2** a problem or matter to be discussed **3** a matter that may be doubted *no question of any refund* **out of the question** impossible

question VERB **1** to ask someone questions **2** to express doubt about something ▸ **questioner** NOUN

questionable ADJECTIVE causing doubt; not certainly true or honest or advisable

question mark NOUN the punctuation mark (?) placed after a question

questionnaire NOUN a written set of questions answered by a number of people to provide information for a survey

queue (kew) NOUN a line of waiting people or vehicles

queue VERB **queues, queueing, queued** to wait in a queue

quibble NOUN a trivial objection

quibble VERB to make trivial objections

quiche (keesh) NOUN an open tart with a savoury filling

quick ADJECTIVE **1** taking or needing only a short time **2** done in a short time **3** able to notice or learn or think quickly ▸ **quickly** ADVERB

THESAURUS

queer ADJECTIVE • *something queer going on* ▸ odd, strange, weird, peculiar, funny, bizarre • *feeling a bit queer* ▸ sick, unwell, poorly, queasy

question NOUN • *to answer the question* ▸ enquiry, query, demand • *the question of all their debts* ▸ issue, matter, subject, problem • *There is some question about who will be in charge.*

▸ uncertainty, doubt, dispute, controversy

question VERB • *being questioned by the police* ▸ interrogate, interview, cross-examine

questionable ADJECTIVE • *questionable arguments* ▸ debatable, doubtful, uncertain, unclear

quick ADJECTIVE • *a quick glance* ▸ brief, hasty, hurried, fleeting

quicken VERB to make or become quicker

quicksand NOUN an area of loose wet deep sand that sucks in anything resting or falling on top of it

quicksilver NOUN mercury

quid NOUN (informal) a pound in money

quiet ADJECTIVE **1** not making any sound or noise **2** calm and peaceful ▶ **quietly** ADVERB, **quietness** NOUN

quiet NOUN quietness

quieten VERB to make or become quiet

quiff NOUN an upright tuft of hair

quill NOUN **1** a pen made from a large feather **2** one of the spines of a hedgehog or porcupine

quilt NOUN a padded cover for a bed

quilted ADJECTIVE having a layer of padding fitted with lines of stitching

quin NOUN a quintuplet

quince NOUN a hard pear-shaped fruit used for making jam

quinine (kwin-een) NOUN a bitter-tasting medicine used to cure malaria

quintessential ADJECTIVE most essential or necessary

quintet NOUN **1** a group of five musicians **2** a piece of music for five musicians

quintuplet NOUN each of five children born to the same mother at one time

quip NOUN a witty remark

quirk NOUN **1** a peculiarity of a person's behaviour **2** an odd thing that happens by chance ▶ **quirky** ADJECTIVE

quit VERB **quitting**, **quitted** or **quit** **1** to leave or abandon **2** (informal) to stop doing something

THESAURUS

• *a quick worker* ▶ fast, swift, rapid, speedy, prompt • *no quick solution* ▶ instant, instantaneous, ready, sudden • *not as quick as the others in the class* ▶ bright, clever, intelligent

quickly ADVERB • *began to walk more quickly* ▶ fast, rapidly, speedily, swiftly • *quickly realized they had gone* ▶ soon, at once, straight away, immediately, suddenly

quiet ADJECTIVE • *a quiet village* ▶ peaceful, tranquil, calm, restful • *a quiet voice* ▶ soft, low, gentle, muffled • *a very quiet person* ▶ shy, reserved, calm, placid • *hard to keep rumours quiet* ▶ secret, silent, private, confidential

quit VERB • *to quit their house* ▶ leave, abandon, desert • *time to quit smoking* ▶ give up, stop, discontinue • *decided to quit her job* ▶ leave, resign from, retire from

DICTIONARY

quite ADVERB **1** completely or entirely **2** somewhat; to some extent

quits ADJECTIVE even or equal after paying someone back

quiver[1] VERB to tremble ▶ **quiver** NOUN

quiver[2] NOUN a container for arrows

quiz NOUN a competition in which people answer questions

quiz VERB **quizzes, quizzing, quizzed** to question someone closely

quizzical ADJECTIVE **1** in a questioning way **2** gently amused ▶ **quizzically** ADVERB

quota NOUN a fixed share that must be given or received by each in a group

quotation NOUN **1** the act of quoting **2** something quoted **3** a statement of a price

quotation marks PLURAL NOUN inverted commas (' ' or " "), used to mark a quotation

quote VERB **1** to repeat words first written or spoken by someone else **2** to state a price

quote NOUN a quotation

quotient (kwoh-shuhnt) NOUN the result of dividing one number by another

THESAURUS

quite ADVERB • *quite different* ▶ completely, totally, entirely, utterly, wholly • *was quite late by*

now ▶ rather, fairly, a bit, somewhat, comparatively, relatively

a
b
c
d
e
f
g
h
i
j
k
l
m
n
o
p
q
r
s
t
u
v
w
x
y
z

Rr

rabbi NOUN **rabbis** a Jewish religious leader

rabbit NOUN a furry burrowing animal with long ears

rabble NOUN a disorderly crowd or mob

rabid ADJECTIVE suffering from rabies

rabies NOUN a fatal disease that can be passed to humans by the bite of an infected dog or other animal

raccoon NOUN a furry North American animal with a bushy striped tail

race [1] NOUN a competition to be the first or fastest

race VERB **1** to compete in a race **2** to move fast ▶ **racer** NOUN

race [2] NOUN a large group of people having the same ancestors and physical characteristics

racecourse NOUN a place where horses are run

racehorse NOUN a horse bred or kept for racing

racetrack NOUN a track for horse or vehicle races

racial (ray-shul) ADJECTIVE to do with the races of the world ▶ **racially** ADVERB

racism or **racialism** NOUN **1** belief that a particular race is superior to others **2** discrimination against people because of their race ▶ **racist** or **racialist** NOUN

rack [1] NOUN **1** a framework used as a shelf or container **2** a former device for stretching people on

rack VERB to torment *was racked with guilt* **rack your brains** to think hard to solve a problem

rack [2] NOUN **go to rack and ruin** to become gradually worse from neglect

racket [1] NOUN a bat with strings stretched across a frame, used in tennis etc.

racket [2] NOUN **1** a loud noise or din **2** a dishonest or illegal business

racketeer NOUN a person involved in a dishonest or illegal business ▶ **racketeering** NOUN

racoon NOUN another spelling of **raccoon**

racquet NOUN another spelling of **racket** [1]

racy ADJECTIVE **racier, raciest** lively and slightly shocking in style

race NOUN • *won the race easily* ▶ contest, competition, chase, event • *people of different races* ▶ ethnic group, nation

race VERB • *children racing each other* ▶ run against, compete with, try to beat • *raced towards the house* ▶ dash, rush, sprint, dart, hurry, run, tear

racket NOUN • *machines making a frightful racket* ▶ noise, din, commotion

a b c d e f g h i j k l m n o p q r s t u v w x y z

a
b
c
d
e
f
g
h
i
j
k
l
m
n
o
p
q
r
s
t
u
v
w
x
y
z

radar NOUN a system that uses radio waves to show the position of objects that cannot be seen because of darkness, fog, distance, etc.

> **WORD HISTORY**
> from the first letters of *radio detection and ranging*

radial ADJECTIVE 1 to do with rays or radii 2 having spokes or lines that radiate from a central point
▶ **radially** ADVERB

radiant ADJECTIVE 1 radiating light or heat etc. 2 (of heat) radiated 3 looking bright and happy
▶ **radiance** NOUN, **radiantly** ADVERB

radiate VERB 1 to send out energy in rays 2 to give out a strong feeling or quality *radiate confidence* 3 to spread out from a central point

radiation NOUN 1 light, heat, or other energy radiated 2 the energy or particles sent out by a radioactive substance

radiator NOUN 1 a metal case that is heated electrically or by hot water 2 a device that cools the engine of a motor vehicle

radical ADJECTIVE 1 basic and thorough *radical changes* 2 wanting to make great reforms *a radical politician* ▶ **radically** ADVERB

radical NOUN a person who wants to make great reforms

radicle NOUN a root that forms in the seed of a plant

radio NOUN **radios** 1 the process of sending and receiving sound or pictures by means of electromagnetic waves 2 an apparatus for receiving or transmitting sound in this way 3 the activity of sound broadcasting

radio VERB **radios, radioing, radioed** to send a message to someone by radio

radioactive ADJECTIVE having atoms that send out radiation
▶ **radioactivity** NOUN

radiology NOUN the study of X-rays and similar radiation, especially in treating diseases
▶ **radiologist** NOUN

radiotherapy NOUN the use of radioactive substances in treating diseases

radish NOUN a small hard round red vegetable, eaten raw in salads

radium NOUN a radioactive substance used in radiotherapy

radius NOUN **radii** or **radiuses** 1 a straight line from the centre of a circle or sphere to the circumference 2 a range or distance from a central point

radon NOUN a radioactive gas used in radiotherapy

THESAURUS

radiant ADJECTIVE • *a radiant smile* ▶ beautiful, glowing, dazzling

radical ADJECTIVE • *radical changes* ▶ basic, fundamental, drastic, sweeping

DICTIONARY

raffia NOUN soft fibre from the leaves of a palm tree

raffle NOUN a kind of lottery, usually to raise money for a charity

raffle VERB to offer something as a prize in a raffle

raft NOUN a row of logs or planks tied together and used as a flat boat

rafter NOUN each of the sloping beams that help to hold up a roof

rag NOUN an old or torn piece of cloth **in rags** wearing old and torn clothes

rage NOUN great or violent anger **all the rage** fashionable for a short time

rage VERB 1 to be fiercely angry 2 to continue with great force *A storm was raging.*

ragged ADJECTIVE 1 torn or frayed 2 wearing torn clothes

ragtime NOUN a kind of jazz music

raid NOUN 1 a sudden attack 2 a surprise visit by police to discover criminal activity

raid VERB to make a raid on a place ▶ **raider** NOUN

rail[1] NOUN 1 a bar for hanging things on or forming part of a fence etc. 2 a long metal bar forming part of a railway track **by rail** on a train

rail[2] VERB to protest angrily or bitterly

railings PLURAL NOUN a fence made of metal bars

railroad NOUN (*American*) a railway

railway NOUN 1 a track of parallel metal bars for trains to travel on 2 a system of transport using rails

raiment NOUN (*old use*) clothing

rain NOUN drops of water that fall from the sky ▶ **rainy** ADJECTIVE

rain VERB 1 to fall as rain 2 to send down like rain *rained blows on them*

rainbow NOUN an arch of all the colours of the spectrum formed in the sky when the sun shines through rain

raincoat NOUN a waterproof coat

raindrop NOUN a single drop of rain

rainfall NOUN the amount of rain that falls in a particular place or time

rainforest NOUN a dense tropical forest in an area of heavy rainfall

THESAURUS

rage NOUN • *in a fit of rage* ▶ anger, fury, temper

ragged ADJECTIVE • *ragged clothes* ▶ tattered, torn, frayed, threadbare, shabby • *a ragged collection of men* ▶ disorganized, disorderly

raid NOUN • *an air raid* ▶ attack, assault, strike, onslaught, invasion • *a bank raid* ▶ robbery, burglary, hold-up

raid VERB • *raided towns on the border* ▶ attack, loot, plunder, ransack • *Burglars raided local jewellers.* ▶ rob, hold up, burgle

a b c d e f g h i j k l m n o p q r s t u v w x y z

raise VERB **1** to move something to a higher place or an upright position **2** to increase the amount or level of **3** to collect **4** to bring up young children or animals **5** to rouse or cause *raised a laugh with his joke* **6** to put forward *raised objections*

raisin NOUN a dried grape

rajah NOUN an Indian king or prince

rake NOUN a gardening tool with a row of short spikes fixed to a long handle, used for gathering leaves or smoothing earth

rake VERB **1** to gather or smooth with a rake **2** to search **rake up 1** collect **2** to remind people of unpleasant or embarrassing events in the past

rally NOUN **rallies 1** a large meeting to support a cause or share an interest **2** a competition in driving **3** a series of strokes in tennis before a point is scored **4** a recovery

rally VERB **rallies, rallied 1** to bring or come together for a united effort **2** to recover strength

RAM ABBREVIATION (ICT) random-access memory, with contents that a system can access directly without having to read through a sequence of items

ram NOUN **1** a male sheep **2** a device for ramming things

ram VERB **ramming, rammed** to push one thing hard against another

Ramadan NOUN the ninth month of the Muslim year, with strict fasting during the day

ramble NOUN a long walk in the country

ramble VERB **1** to go for a ramble **2** to speak or write aimlessly ► **rambler** NOUN

ramifications PLURAL NOUN the many effects of a plan or action

ramp NOUN a slope joining two different levels

rampage VERB to rush about or attack violently

rampage NOUN **on the rampage** behaving in a wild and violent way

THESAURUS

raise VERB • to raise a hand ► put up, lift • *A crane will raise the load.* ► lift, hoist • to raise prices ► increase, put up • *news that raised their hopes* ► encourage, improve • to raise children ► bring up, look after, educate • to raise questions ► bring up, introduce, mention, put forward • *need to raise £5,000* ► collect, get, make

rally VERB • to rally support ► muster, gather, round up, organize • *Our spirits rallied.* ► recover, improve, pick up

ram VERB • to ram another vehicle ► hit , strike, crash into, collide with

ramble VERB • to ramble in the countryside ► walk , roam, hike, stroll • *He was rambling about his schooldays.* ► chatter, prattle

rampant   rankle

rampant ADJECTIVE growing or spreading uncontrollably *rampant disease*

rampart NOUN a bank of earth or a wall built as a fortification

ramshackle ADJECTIVE badly made and rickety

ranch NOUN a large cattle farm in America

rancid ADJECTIVE smelling or tasting unpleasantly stale

rancour NOUN bitter resentment or hatred ▶ **rancorous** ADJECTIVE

random NOUN **at random** using no particular order or method

random ADJECTIVE done or taken at random *a random sample*
▶ **randomly** ADVERB

ranee (rah-nee) NOUN a rajah's wife or widow

range NOUN **1** a set of different things of the same type *a wide range of backgrounds* **2** the limits between which something varies *an age range of 15 to 18* **3** the distance that a gun can shoot, an aircraft can travel, a sound can be heard, etc. **4** a place with targets

for shooting practice **5** a line or series of mountains or hills **6** a large open area of grazing land or hunting ground **7** a kitchen fireplace with ovens

range VERB **1** to exist between two limits **2** to arrange **3** to move over a wide area

Ranger NOUN a senior Guide

ranger NOUN a keeper who patrols a park, forest, etc.

rank[1] NOUN **1** a line of people or things **2** a place where taxis wait **3** a position in a series of different levels *the rank of sergeant*

rank VERB **1** to put things in order according to their rank **2** to have a certain rank or place *ranks among the greatest writers*

rank[2] ADJECTIVE **1** growing too thickly and coarsely **2** smelling very unpleasant **3** unmistakably bad *rank injustice*

rank and file NOUN the ordinary people or soldiers, not the leaders

rankle VERB to cause lasting annoyance or resentment

ramshackle ADJECTIVE • *a ramshackle old house* ▶ dilapidated, tumbledown, derelict

random ADJECTIVE • *a random sample* ▶ arbitrary, chance, haphazard, casual, unplanned

range NOUN • *a range of mountains* ▶ chain, row, line • *a wide range of backgrounds* ▶ variety,

assortment, selection • *an age range of 15 to 18* ▶ span, scope

range VERB • *Prices range between £100 and £600* ▶ vary, extend, fluctuate • *Sheep ranged over the hills.* ▶ roam, wander

rank NOUN • *the rank of sergeant* ▶ level, grade, position, status, title • *a family of rank* ▶ distinction, importance, nobility

a
b
c
d
e
f
g
h
i
j
k
l
m
n
o
p
q
r
s
t
u
v
w
x
y
z

595

DICTIONARY

ransack VERB **1** to search thoroughly or roughly **2** to rob or pillage a place

ransom NOUN money that has to be paid for a prisoner to be set free

ransom VERB to free a prisoner by paying a ransom

rant VERB to speak loudly and violently

rap VERB **rapping, rapped** to knock loudly

rap NOUN **1** a rapping movement or sound **2** (informal) blame or punishment **3** rhymes spoken with a backing of rock music ▸ **rapper** NOUN

rape[1] NOUN the act of having sexual intercourse with someone by force

rape VERB to force someone to have sexual intercourse ▸ **rapist** NOUN

rape[2] NOUN a plant with bright yellow flowers, grown as food for sheep and for the oil obtained from its seed

rapid ADJECTIVE moving very quickly; swift ▸ **rapidly** ADVERB

rapidity NOUN great speed

rapids PLURAL NOUN part of a river where the water flows swiftly

rapier NOUN a thin lightweight sword

rapport (rap-or) NOUN a good relationship between people

rapt ADJECTIVE intent and absorbed; enraptured ▸ **raptly** ADVERB

rapture NOUN very great delight ▸ **rapturous** ADJECTIVE

rare ADJECTIVE **rarer, rarest 1** not often found or happening **2** (of air) thin and below normal pressure **3** (of meat) only lightly cooked ▸ **rarely** ADVERB, **rareness** NOUN

rarity NOUN **rarities 1** the state of being rare **2** something unusual or rare

rascal NOUN a dishonest or mischievous person ▸ **rascally** ADJECTIVE

rash[1] ADJECTIVE acting or done regardless of the possible risks or effects ▸ **rashly** ADVERB

rash[2] NOUN **1** an outbreak of spots or patches on the skin **2** a number of unwelcome events in a short time *a rash of accidents*

rasher NOUN a thin slice of bacon

rasp NOUN **1** a file with sharp points on its surface **2** a rough grating sound

rasp VERB **1** to scrape roughly **2** to make a rough grating sound or effect

raspberry NOUN **raspberries** a small soft red fruit

THESAURUS

rapid ADJECTIVE • *made rapid progress* ▸ fast, quick, swift, speedy, prompt

rare ADJECTIVE • *a rare moment of peace* ▸ uncommon, infrequent, scarce, occasional • *a person of*

rare abilities ▸ exceptional, remarkable, unusual, special

rash ADJECTIVE • *a rash promise* ▸ reckless, impulsive, impetuous, foolhardy

rat NOUN **1** an animal like a large mouse **2** an unpleasant or treacherous person

ratchet NOUN a row of notches on a bar or wheel in which a device catches to prevent it running backwards

rate NOUN **1** speed **2** a measure of cost, value, etc. *postage rates* **3** quality or standard *first-rate* **at any rate** anyway

rate VERB **1** to put a value on **2** to regard as *rated me among their friends*

rates PLURAL NOUN a local tax paid by owners of commercial land and buildings

rather ADVERB **1** slightly or somewhat **2** more willingly *would rather not go* **3** more exactly; instead of *is lazy rather than stupid*

ratify VERB ratifies, ratified to confirm or agree to something officially ▶ **ratification** NOUN

rating NOUN **1** the way something is rated **2** a sailor who is not an officer

ratio NOUN ratios the relationship between two numbers or amounts

ration NOUN an amount allowed to one person

ration VERB to share out in fixed amounts

rational ADJECTIVE **1** reasonable or sane **2** able to reason
▶ **rationally** ADVERB

rationale (rash-uhn-ahl) NOUN the reasons which explain a decision, belief, etc.

rationalize VERB **1** to make logical and consistent **2** to justify something by inventing a reasonable explanation **3** to reorganize and make more efficient ▶ **rationalization** NOUN

⚠ **SPELLING**

This word can also be spelled *rationalise*.

rations PLURAL NOUN a fixed daily amount of food issued to a soldier etc.

rat race NOUN a continuous struggle for success in a career, business, etc.

rattle VERB **1** to make a series of short sharp hard sounds **2** to make

rate NOUN • *moving along at a furious rate* ▶ speed, pace, tempo, velocity • *postage rates* ▶ charge, price, cost, fee, amount, figure

rather ADVERB • *It sounds rather difficult.* ▶ fairly, somewhat, quite, slightly • *would rather not go* ▶ sooner, preferably

ration NOUN • *a daily ration* ▶ allowance, allocation, quota, share, measure

ration VERB • *Fuel is rationed.* ▶ control, limit, restrict, allocate

rational ADJECTIVE • *a rational discussion* ▶ reasoned, logical, sensible, balanced, normal

rattle VERB • *Trucks rattled along the track.* ▶ clatter, jolt, shake

DICTIONARY

a person nervous or flustered
rattle off to say or recite rapidly

rattle NOUN 1 a rattling sound 2 a device or toy that rattles

rattlesnake NOUN a poisonous American snake with a tail that rattles

ratty ADJECTIVE **rattier, rattiest** (informal) irritable

raucous (raw-kus) ADJECTIVE loud and harsh

ravage VERB to do great damage to an area

ravages PLURAL NOUN damaging effects

rave VERB 1 to talk wildly or angrily 2 to talk enthusiastically

rave NOUN (informal) a large party or event with dancing to loud electronic music

raven NOUN a large black bird, related to the crow

ravenous ADJECTIVE very hungry
▶ **ravenously** ADVERB

ravine NOUN a deep narrow gorge or valley

raving ADJECTIVE mad; crazy

ravishing ADJECTIVE very beautiful

raw ADJECTIVE 1 not cooked 2 in the natural state; not yet processed 3 lacking experience *raw recruits*

4 with the skin removed *a raw wound* 5 cold and damp *a raw morning*

raw deal NOUN unfair treatment

raw material NOUN natural substances used in industry

ray[1] NOUN 1 a thin line of light, heat, or other radiation 2 each of a set of lines or parts extending from a centre 3 a trace of something *a ray of hope*

ray[2] NOUN a large sea fish with a flat body and a long tail

rayon NOUN a synthetic fibre or cloth made from cellulose

raze VERB to destroy a building or town completely

razor NOUN a device with a sharp blade used for shaving

reach VERB 1 to go as far as; to arrive at a place or thing 2 to stretch out your hand to get or touch something 3 to succeed in achieving something

reach NOUN 1 the distance a person or thing can reach 2 a distance you can easily travel *within reach of the sea*

react VERB 1 to respond to something; to have a reaction 2 to undergo a chemical change

THESAURUS

raw ADJECTIVE • *raw onion*
▶ uncooked, fresh • *raw materials*
▶ natural, untreated, unprocessed, basic • *a raw wound*
▶ sore, inflamed

ray NOUN • *a ray of light* ▶ beam, shaft, stream

reach VERB • *The walkers reached a village.* ▶ arrive at, get to, come to • *to reach a target* ▶ achieve, attain • *can't reach the switch* ▶ get hold of, grasp, touch

react VERB • *wondered how they would react* ▶ respond, reply, answer, behave

DICTIONARY

reaction NOUN **1** an effect or feeling produced in one person or thing by another **2** a chemical change **reactions** the ability to move in response to something *quick reactions*

reactionary ADJECTIVE opposed to progress or reform

reactor NOUN an apparatus for the controlled production of nuclear power

read VERB read (say as red) **1** to look at something written or printed and understand it or say it aloud **2** (of a computer) to copy, search, or extract data **3** to indicate or register *The thermometer reads 20°.* **4** to study a subject at university ▶ **readable** ADJECTIVE

reader NOUN **1** a person who reads **2** a book that helps you learn to read

readily (red-il-ee) ADVERB **1** willingly **2** easily; without any difficulty

reading NOUN **1** the activity of reading books **2** the figure shown on a meter or gauge etc.

ready ADJECTIVE **readier, readiest 1** fully prepared or willing **2** available to be used **3** quick or prompt **at the ready** ready for use or action ▶ **readiness** NOUN

reagent NOUN a substance used in a chemical reaction

real ADJECTIVE **1** existing or true **2** genuine *real pearls*

real estate NOUN (American) property consisting of land and buildings

realism NOUN the seeing or showing of things as they really are ▶ **realist** NOUN

realistic ADJECTIVE **1** true to life **2** seeing things as they really are ▶ **realistically** ADVERB

reality NOUN **realities 1** what is real *to face reality* **2** something real *the realities of the situation*

THESAURUS

reaction NOUN • *a strange reaction* ▶ response, reply, answer

read VERB • *to read a newspaper* ▶ peruse, study, glance at, pore over, dip into • *to read a story* ▶ read out, tell, recite • *The writing is not hard to read.* ▶ make out, decipher, understand

ready ADJECTIVE • *Is dinner ready?* ▶ available, done, prepared, set • *were ready to help us* ▶ willing, happy, pleased, glad • *a ready answer* ▶ prompt, quick, immediate

real ADJECTIVE • *real cream* ▶ genuine, natural • *real people* ▶ actual, existing • *not his real name* ▶ true, actual, proper • *to feel real remorse* ▶ sincere, genuine, honest, heartfelt

realistic ADJECTIVE • *a realistic portrayal of the events* ▶ authentic, truthful, true to life, lifelike, convincing • *a realistic plan* ▶ practical, sensible, reasonable

reality NOUN • *to distinguish reality from fantasy* ▶ truth, fact, the real world

DICTIONARY

realize VERB **1** to be fully aware of something **2** to make a hope or plan etc. happen *realized her ambition* ▸ **realization** NOUN

⚠ **SPELLING**

This word can also be spelled *realise*.

really ADVERB **1** truly or in fact **2** very *is really clever*

realm (relm) NOUN **1** a kingdom **2** an area of knowledge, interest, etc.

reams PLURAL NOUN a large quantity of writing

reap VERB **1** to cut down and gather corn when it is ripe **2** to obtain as the result of something done *reaped great benefit* ▸ **reaper** NOUN

reappear VERB to appear again

rear¹ NOUN the back part

rear ADJECTIVE placed at the rear

rear² VERB **1** to bring up children or animals **2** (of an animal) to rise on its hind legs

rearguard NOUN troops protecting the rear of an army

rearrange VERB to arrange in a different way or order ▸ **rearrangement** NOUN

reason NOUN **1** a cause or explanation **2** reasoning or common sense

reason VERB **1** to think and draw conclusions **2** to try to persuade by giving reasons

reasonable ADJECTIVE **1** sensible or logical **2** fair or moderate *reasonable prices* **3** fairly good *a reasonable standard of living* ▸ **reasonably** ADVERB

reassure VERB to restore someone's confidence by removing doubts and fears ▸ **reassurance** NOUN

THESAURUS

realize VERB • *I realized it was going to be difficult.* ▸ understand, grasp, comprehend, appreciate • *realized her ambition* ▸ achieve, accomplish, fulfil

realm NOUN • *the defence of the realm* ▸ kingdom, state

rear NOUN • *the rear of the house* ▸ back • *the rear of the queue* ▸ end, tail, back

rear ADJECTIVE • *one of its rear legs* ▸ back, hind

rear VERB • *to rear a child* ▸ bring up, raise, educate

reason NOUN • *the reason for leaving* ▸ cause, grounds, excuse, explanation, justification, incentive, motive • *arguments based on reason* ▸ reasoning, logic • *to lose your reason* ▸ sanity, mind, senses

reason VERB • *tried to reason with them* ▸ persuade, talk round, argue with, discuss with

reasonable ADJECTIVE • *a reasonable person* ▸ sensible, rational, logical, fair-minded • *a reasonable explanation* ▸ logical, convincing, plausible, believable • *reasonable prices* ▸ acceptable, fair, moderate

rebate NOUN a reduction in the amount to be paid; a partial refund

rebel (reb-el) VERB **rebelling, rebelled** to fight against the people in power

rebel (reb-el) NOUN 1 someone who rebels against the people in power 2 someone who rejects normal social conventions

rebellion NOUN 1 refusal to obey 2 an organized armed resistance to the people in power

rebellious ADJECTIVE refusing to obey authority

rebound VERB to bounce back after hitting something ► **rebound** NOUN

rebuff NOUN an unkind refusal or snub

rebuff VERB to snub

rebuild VERB **rebuilt** to build something again after it has been destroyed

rebuke VERB to speak severely to a person who has done wrong ► **rebuke** NOUN

rebut VERB **rebutting, rebutted** to reject an accusation or criticism ► **rebuttal** NOUN

recalcitrant ADJECTIVE disobedient or uncooperative ► **recalcitrance** NOUN

recall (ri-kawl) VERB 1 to bring back into the mind 2 to ask for something to be returned

recall (ree-kawl) NOUN 1 the ability to remember 2 an order to return something

recap VERB **recapping, recapped** (informal) to recapitulate ► **recap** NOUN

recapitulate VERB to state again the main points of what has been said ► **recapitulation** NOUN

recapture VERB 1 to capture again 2 to experience again a mood or feeling ► **recapture** NOUN

recede VERB 1 to go back from a certain point 2 (of a man's hair) to stop growing at the front of the head

receipt (ris-eet) NOUN 1 a written statement for money paid or something received 2 the act of receiving something

receive VERB 1 to take or get something that is given or sent to you 2 to experience something 3 to greet someone who comes

receiver NOUN 1 an apparatus for receiving radio and television broadcasts 2 the part of a telephone used for speaking and listening

THESAURUS

reassure VERB • tried hard to reassure us ► comfort, calm, encourage

rebel VERB • The people rebelled. ► revolt, mutiny, riot, rise up

rebel NOUN • The rebels took control. ► revolutionary, insurgent

rebellion NOUN • to crush the rebellion ► uprising, revolt, insurgency, mutiny, revolution

receive VERB • to receive an award i be given, earn, get, accept, gain • to receive injuries ► suffer, sustain, experience

DICTIONARY

recent ADJECTIVE happening or made or done a short time ago ► **recently** ADVERB

receptacle NOUN something for holding things; a container

reception NOUN 1 the way a person or thing is received 2 a formal party to receive guests 3 a place in a hotel or office where visitors are greeted 4 the quality of television or radio signals

receptionist NOUN a person who greets and deals with visitors, clients, etc.

receptive ADJECTIVE quick or willing to consider ideas etc.

recess NOUN 1 an alcove 2 a pause in work or business

recession NOUN 1 a reduction in a country's trade or prosperity 2 the act of moving back

recipe (ress-ip-ee) NOUN a set of instructions for preparing or cooking food

recipient NOUN a person who receives something

reciprocal (ris-ip-rok-al) ADJECTIVE given and received *reciprocal help reciprocal noun a reversed fraction is the reciprocal of ⅔.*

reciprocate VERB to do or feel the same thing in return

recital NOUN 1 the act of reciting 2 a musical entertainment by one performer or group

recite VERB to say aloud from memory ► **recitation** NOUN

reckless ADJECTIVE carelessly ignoring danger ► **recklessly** ADVERB

reckon VERB 1 to calculate or count up 2 to have as an opinion **reckon with** to take into account *didn't reckon with a rail strike*

reclaim VERB 1 to claim or get back 2 to make usable again *reclaimed land* ► **reclamation** NOUN

recline VERB to lean or lie back

recluse NOUN a person who lives alone and avoids company ► **reclusive** ADJECTIVE

recognition NOUN 1 the act of recognizing 2 acceptance as genuine or lawful

recognize VERB 1 to know a person or thing from before 2 to

THESAURUS

recent ADJECTIVE • *recent events* ► new, current, fresh, latest, present-day, up-to-date, contemporary, modern

reception NOUN • *a friendly reception* ► greeting, welcome • *a wedding reception* ► party, function, gathering, celebration, get-together

reckless ADJECTIVE • *a reckless driver* ► careless, dangerous, rash, heedless

reckon VERB • *reckoned the cost at about three thousand pounds* ► assess, estimate, calculate, work out • *I reckon she's keen on him.* ► think, believe, suspect

recognize VERB • *didn't recognize him in his smart suit* ► identify,

realize **3** to accept as genuine or lawful ► **recognizable** ADJECTIVE

⚠ **SPELLING**

This word can also be spelled recognise.

recoil VERB **1** to move back suddenly in shock or disgust **2** (of a gun) to jerk back when fired

recollect VERB to remember ► **recollection** NOUN

recommend VERB **1** to speak well of a person or thing **2** to advise a course of action
► **recommendation** NOUN

recompense VERB to repay or reward ► **recompense** NOUN

reconcile VERB **1** to make people friendly again after a quarrel **2** to make things agree **be reconciled to** to be willing to accept an unwelcome situation
► **reconciliation** NOUN

recondition VERB to overhaul and repair

reconnaissance (rik-on-i-sans) NOUN a survey of an area to gather information for military purposes

reconnoitre VERB to make a reconnaissance of an area

reconsider VERB to consider something again and perhaps change an earlier decision
► **reconsideration** NOUN

reconstitute VERB to form something again or differently

reconstruct VERB **1** to construct or build again **2** to create or act out past events again
► **reconstruction** NOUN

record (rek-ord) NOUN **1** a written or printed piece of information kept for the future **2** a disc on which sound has been recorded **3** the best performance in a sport etc. **4** facts known about a person's past life or career etc.

record (rik-ord) VERB **1** to put down in writing or other permanent form **2** to store sounds or pictures on a disc or magnetic tape etc. for replaying in the future

recorder NOUN **1** a kind of flute held downwards from the player's mouth **2** a person or thing that records something

recount[1] (ri-kownt) VERB to give an account of

recount[2] (ree-kownt) VERB to count again ► **recount** NOUN

know, remember, recall • *to recognize that he had been wrong*
► acknowledge, admit, accept

recommend VERB • *His doctor recommended surgery.* ► advise, counsel, propose, suggest • *The book is recommended by teachers.*
► approve of, commend, praise

record NOUN • *to keep a record*
► account, note, log • *break the world record* ► best **records**
• *historical records* ► documents, archives, evidence

record VERB • *recorded everything he heard* ► note, write down, transcribe, log • *to record a film*
► tape, video

recoup (ri-koop) VERB to recover the cost of an investment etc. or of a loss

recourse NOUN a source of help **have recourse to** to go to a person or thing for help

recover VERB 1 to get something back after losing it 2 to get well again after an illness or injury

recovery NOUN **recoveries** 1 the act of recovering something 2 a return to normal health or strength

recreation NOUN 1 enjoyable activity done in spare time 2 a game or hobby etc.
▶ **recreational** ADJECTIVE

recrimination NOUN an accusation made against a person who has accused you of something

recruit NOUN a new soldier or member

recruit VERB to enlist as a recruit
▶ **recruitment** NOUN

rectangle NOUN a shape with four sides and four right angles, usually longer than it is wide
▶ **rectangular** ADJECTIVE

rectify VERB **rectifies, rectified** to correct or put right
▶ **rectification** NOUN

rectitude NOUN moral goodness; honest or straightforward behaviour

rector NOUN a member of the Church of England clergy in charge of a parish

rectum NOUN the last part of the large intestine, ending at the anus

recuperate VERB to recover after an illness ▶ **recuperation** NOUN

recur VERB **recurring, recurred** to happen again ▶ **recurrence** NOUN

recurrent ADJECTIVE happening often or regularly

recurring decimal NOUN (Maths) a decimal fraction in which a digit or group of digits is repeated indefinitely, e.g. 0.666 …

recycle VERB to convert waste material into a form in which it can be used again

red ADJECTIVE **redder, reddest** of the colour of blood or a colour rather like this ▶ **redness** NOUN

red NOUN a red colour **in the red** in debt **see red** to become angry

THESAURUS

recover VERB • to recover stolen property ▶ find, get back, trace, track down, retrieve • to recover from an illness ▶ recuperate, convalesce, get better

recovery NOUN • a slow recovery from illness ▶ recuperation, convalescence, return to health • economic recovery

▶ improvement, revival, upturn
• recovery of the stolen property
▶ retrieval, recapture

red ADJECTIVE • a red dress ▶ scarlet, ruby, crimson, cherry, claret, maroon • red in the face
▶ flushed, blushing, ruddy, glowing, rosy • eyes were red
▶ bloodshot, inflamed, swollen

redden VERB to make or become red

reddish ADJECTIVE rather red

redeem VERB 1 to make up for faults 2 to buy something back or pay off a debt 3 to save a person from damnation ▸ **redeemer** NOUN, **redemption** NOUN

red-handed ADJECTIVE **catch red-handed** to catch someone in the act of committing a crime

redhead NOUN a person with reddish hair

red herring NOUN something that draws attention away from the main subject; a misleading clue

red-hot ADJECTIVE very hot; so hot that it has turned red

redolent (red-ol-ent) ADJECTIVE 1 having a strong smell *redolent of onions* 2 strongly reminding you of something *redolent of romance*

redoubtable ADJECTIVE brave; formidable

redress VERB to put right a situation that is wrong or unfair

redress NOUN 1 the act of setting right 2 compensation

red tape NOUN use of too many rules and forms in official business

reduce VERB 1 to make or become smaller or less 2 to force someone into a condition or situation *was reduced to borrowing*

reduction NOUN 1 the process of reducing 2 the amount by which something is reduced

redundant ADJECTIVE not needed, especially for a particular job ▸ **redundancy** NOUN

reed NOUN 1 a tall plant that grows in water or marshy ground 2 a thin strip that vibrates to make the sound in a clarinet or other wind instrument

reedy ADJECTIVE **reedier**, **reediest** 1 full of reeds 2 (of a voice) having a thin high tone

reef[1] NOUN a ridge of rock, coral, or sand near the surface of the sea

reef[2] VERB to shorten a sail by drawing in a strip (called a **reef**) at the top or bottom to reduce the area exposed to the wind

reef knot NOUN a symmetrical secure double knot

reek VERB to smell strongly or unpleasantly ▸ **reek** NOUN

reel NOUN 1 a round device on which cotton, thread, film, etc. is wound 2 a lively Scottish dance

reel VERB 1 to wind something on or off a reel 2 to stagger 3 to feel giddy or confused **reel off** to say something quickly

ref NOUN (*informal*) a referee

refer VERB **referring**, **referred** to pass a problem etc. to someone else **refer to 1** to mention or

THESAURUS

reduce VERB • *to reduce carbon emissions* ▸ lessen, lower, decrease, bring down

refer VERB • *His doctor referred him to a specialist.* ▸ pass, send,

transfer **refer to** • *to refer to notes* ▸ consult, look up • *Don't refer to this matter again.*
▸ mention, bring up, touch on, allude to

speak about **2** to look in a book etc. for information ▶ **referral** *NOUN*

referee *NOUN* **1** an official who ensures that players obey the rules of a game **2** someone willing to write in support of a candidate for a job

referee *VERB* to act as a referee

reference *NOUN* **1** the act of referring to something **2** a direction to information in a book **3** a supporting letter from a previous employer **in** *or* **with reference to** concerning or about

reference book *NOUN* a book (e.g. encyclopedia) that gives information

referendum *NOUN* **referendums** *or* **referenda** a vote on a particular question by all the people of a country

refill *VERB* to fill again

refill *NOUN* a container of a substance needed to refill something

refine *VERB* **1** to purify **2** to improve something with small changes

refined *ADJECTIVE* **1** purified **2** having good taste or manners

refinement *NOUN* **1** the action of refining **2** good taste or manners **3** an improvement

refinery *NOUN* **refineries** a factory for refining something *an oil refinery*

reflect *VERB* **1** to send back light, heat, or sound etc. from a surface **2** (of a mirror) to form an image of **3** to think something over **4** to be a sign of something

reflection *NOUN* **1** the process of reflecting **2** an image reflected, e.g. in a mirror

reflective *ADJECTIVE* thoughtful

reflector *NOUN* a device or surface that reflects light

reflex *NOUN* a movement or action done without any conscious thought

reflex angle *NOUN* an angle of more than 180°

reflexive pronoun *NOUN* (Grammar) any of the pronouns *myself, herself, himself,* etc., which refer back to the subject of a verb

refined *ADJECTIVE* • *refined sugar* ▶ purified, pure, processed • *a refined man* ▶ cultivated, sophisticated, well-mannered

reflect *VERB* • *The window reflected their faces.* ▶ mirror, send back, shine back • *Their looks reflected their feelings.* ▶ show, indicate, demonstrate, echo, match

reflection *NOUN* • *reflections in the water* ▶ image, likeness • *an accurate reflection of their ability* ▶ indication, demonstration, manifestation, expression, result • *needed some reflection before deciding* ▶ thought, deliberation, consideration, thinking

a
b
c
d
e
f
g
h
i
j
k
l
m
n
o
p
q
r
s
t
u
v
w
x
y
z

reform VERB **1** to make changes in something to improve it **2** to give up bad habits or practices
▶ **reformer** NOUN

reform NOUN **1** the process of reforming **2** a change or improvement

reformation NOUN the act of reforming **the Reformation** a 16th-century religious movement in Europe intended to reform the Roman Catholic Church, from which the Protestant Churches arose

refract VERB to bend a ray of light at the point where it enters water or glass etc. at an angle
▶ **refraction** NOUN

refrain¹ VERB to stop yourself from doing something

refrain² NOUN the chorus of a song

refresh VERB to make someone feel fresh and strong again
refresh someone's memory to remind someone of facts they may have forgotten

refreshing ADJECTIVE **1** producing new strength **2** pleasantly different or unusual

refreshment NOUN food and drink

refrigerate VERB to make and keep food cold to preserve it
▶ **refrigeration** NOUN

refrigerator NOUN a cabinet in which food is stored at a very low temperature

refuel VERB **refuelling, refuelled** to supply a ship or aircraft with more fuel

refuge NOUN a place where a person is safe from pursuit or danger

refugee NOUN someone who seeks refuge in another country

refund (ri-fund) VERB to pay money back

refund (ree-fund) NOUN money paid back

refurbish VERB to redecorate and brighten a place

refusal NOUN an act of refusing

refuse (ri-fewz) VERB to say that you will not do something when asked to

refuse (ref-yooss) NOUN waste material

refute VERB to show a person or statement to be wrong
▶ **refutation** NOUN

⚠️ **USAGE**
This word does not mean simply 'deny' or 'reject'.

reform VERB • will have to reform
▶ mend your ways, turn over a new leaf, do better • to reform the system ▶ change, reorganize, revolutionize

refresh VERB • A bit of air will refresh us. ▶ invigorate, freshen, revive • to refresh your memory
▶ prompt, jog

refuge NOUN • to seek refuge
▶ shelter, protection, safety, sanctuary • a refuge for the fugitives ▶ sanctuary, shelter, hideaway, hiding place

refuse VERB • to refuse an invitation
▶ turn down, decline, reject, say no to • to refuse permission
▶ deny, withhold

regain VERB **1** to get something back after losing it **2** to reach a place again

regal (ree-gal) ADJECTIVE **1** to do with a king or queen **2** dignified and splendid

regale VERB to entertain with conversation

regalia PLURAL NOUN the emblems of royalty or rank

regard VERB **1** to think of in a certain way *regarded the matter as serious* **2** to look or gaze at

regard NOUN **1** consideration or heed **2** respect **3** a gaze *with* or *in regard to* concerning; about

regarding PREPOSITION concerning; about

regardless ADVERB without considering something *regardless of the cost*

regards PLURAL NOUN kind wishes sent in a message

regatta NOUN a meeting for boat or yacht races

regency NOUN **regencies 1** being a regent **2** a period when a country is ruled by a regent

regenerate VERB to give new life or strength to something
► **regeneration** NOUN

regent NOUN a person appointed to rule in place of a king or queen

reggae (reg-ay) NOUN a West Indian style of music with a strong beat

regime (ray-zheem) NOUN a system of government or organization

regiment NOUN an army unit, usually divided into battalions or companies ► **regimental** ADJECTIVE

region NOUN a part of a country or of the world

regional ADJECTIVE to do with a region or regions ► **regionally** ADVERB

register NOUN **1** an official list **2** a book for recording information about school attendance **3** the range of a voice or musical instrument

register VERB **1** to list in a register **2** (of a gauge) to show a figure or amount **3** to make an impression on the mind ► **registration** NOUN

THESAURUS

regard VERB • *regard these as the best* ► consider, look on, view, judge • *regarded them closely* ► look at, observe, eye, watch

regard NOUN • *have due regard for cost* ► attention, care, consideration, notice, thought • *a high regard* ► respect, admiration, esteem

regardless ADJECTIVE • *carried on regardless* ► anyway, nonetheless, nevertheless

regardless of • *regardless of*

the cost ► irrespective of, disregarding

regime NOUN • *a military regime* ► government, administration

region NOUN • *the coastal region* ► district, area, territory, land

register VERB • *to register a protest* ► record, list, submit • *to register for a course* ► enrol, enlist, put your name down, apply • *to register relief* ► show, display, indicate

register office or **registry office** NOUN an office where marriages are performed and records of births, marriages, and deaths are kept

registrar NOUN an official whose job it is to keep written records or registers

registration number NOUN a series of letters and numbers identifying a motor vehicle

registry NOUN **registries** a place where registers are kept

regret NOUN a feeling of sorrow or disappointment

regret VERB **regretting, regretted** to feel regret about

regretful ADJECTIVE feeling regret ► **regretfully** ADVERB

regrettable ADJECTIVE to be regretted; unfortunate ► **regrettably** ADVERB

regular ADJECTIVE **1** happening or done always at certain times **2** even or symmetrical **3** normal or correct **4** belonging to a country's permanent armed forces ► **regularity** NOUN, **regularly** ADVERB

regulate VERB **1** to control by rules **2** to make a machine work at a certain speed ► **regulator** NOUN, **regulatory** ADJECTIVE

regulation NOUN **1** the process of regulating **2** a rule or law

regurgitate VERB to bring swallowed food up again into the mouth ► **regurgitation** NOUN

rehabilitate VERB to restore a person to a normal life after being in prison, ill, etc. ► **rehabilitation** NOUN

rehash VERB (informal) to reuse old ideas or material without much change or improvement

rehearse VERB to practise before performing to an audience ► **rehearsal** NOUN

reign VERB **1** to rule a country as king or queen **2** to prevail Silence reigned.

reign NOUN the time when a king or queen reigns

reimburse VERB to repay money spent ► **reimbursement** NOUN

rein NOUN each of a pair of straps used to guide a horse

regret VERB • to regret the decision ► be sorry about, repent • regretted her uncle's death ► mourn, lament, grieve over

regret NOUN • to express regret ► remorse, sorrow, shame, repentance, guilt • a feeling of regret ► sadness, sorrow

regrettable ADJECTIVE • a regrettable thing to say

► unfortunate, unwelcome, inappropriate

regular ADJECTIVE • a regular route to work ► routine, habitual, fixed, customary, typical, usual, normal • regular complaints ► frequent, constant, persistent • a regular rhythm ► even, steady

regulation NOUN • regulations about working hours ► rule, law, order

DICTIONARY

reincarnation NOUN the act of being born again into a new body

reindeer NOUN a kind of deer that lives in Arctic regions

reinforce VERB to strengthen by adding extra people or supports etc.

reinforcement NOUN 1 the process of reinforcing 2 something that reinforces

reinforcements PLURAL NOUN extra troops or ships etc. sent to strengthen a force

reinstate VERB to put a person or thing back into a former position ► **reinstatement** NOUN

reiterate VERB to say something again ► **reiteration** NOUN

reject (ri-jekt) VERB 1 to refuse to accept a person or thing 2 to throw away or discard ► **rejection** NOUN

reject (ree-jekt) NOUN a person or thing that is rejected

rejoice VERB to feel or show great joy

rejoin VERB to meet with again

rejoinder NOUN an answer or retort

rejuvenate VERB to make a person seem young again ► **rejuvenation** NOUN

relapse VERB to become worse again after improving ► **relapse** NOUN

relate VERB 1 to tell a story 2 to connect one thing with another 3 to understand and get on well with someone

related ADJECTIVE belonging to the same family

relation NOUN 1 a relative 2 the way one thing is related to another

relationship NOUN 1 the way in which people or things are related 2 the way in which people behave towards one another 3 an emotional or sexual association between two people

relative NOUN a person who is related to another

relative ADJECTIVE compared with the average *living in relative comfort* ► **relatively** ADVERB

relax VERB 1 to stop working; to rest 2 to become less anxious or worried 3 to make a rule etc. less strict or severe 4 to make a limb or muscle less stiff or tense ► **relaxed** ADJECTIVE, **relaxation** NOUN

THESAURUS

reject VERB • to reject an offer ► turn down, refuse, decline • to reject someone ► rebuff, spurn

rejection NOUN • rejection of the offer ► refusal, non-acceptance, dismissal • her rejection of him ► spurning, rebuff

rejoice VERB • to rejoice at the news ► celebrate, be happy, delight

relate VERB • many stories to relate ► tell, recount, narrate, describe • to relate the two incidents ► link, connect, associate

relax VERB • try to relax ► unwind, take it easy • to relax your grip ► loosen, slacken, weaken • helped to relax him ► calm, soothe, pacify

a b c d e f g h i j k l m n o p q **r** s t u v w x y z

DICTIONARY

relay VERB to pass on a message or broadcast

relay NOUN 1 a fresh group taking the place of another *working in relays* 2 a relay race 3 the process of relaying a broadcast

relay race NOUN a race between teams in which each person covers part of the distance

release VERB 1 to set free or unfasten 2 to let a thing fall or fly or go out 3 to make a film or record etc. available to the public

release NOUN 1 the act of releasing 2 a new film or record etc. 3 a device that unfastens something

relegate VERB 1 to put into a less important place 2 to place a sports team in a lower division of a league ▶ **relegation** NOUN

relent VERB to become less severe or strict

relentless ADJECTIVE not stopping or relenting ▶ **relentlessly** ADVERB

relevant ADJECTIVE connected with what is being discussed or dealt with ▶ **relevance** NOUN

reliable ADJECTIVE able to be relied on; trustworthy ▶ **reliability** NOUN, **reliably** ADVERB

reliance NOUN dependence or trust ▶ **reliant** ADJECTIVE

relic NOUN something that has survived from an earlier time

relief NOUN 1 the ending or lessening of pain, trouble, etc. 2 something that gives relief or help 3 help given to people in need 4 a person who takes over a turn of duty when another finishes 5 a method of making a map or design that stands out from a flat surface

relief map NOUN a map that shows hills and valleys by shading or moulding

relieve VERB to give relief to a person or thing **relieve of** to take something from a person

religion NOUN 1 belief in and worship of God or gods 2 a particular system of beliefs and worship

religious ADJECTIVE 1 to do with religion 2 believing firmly in a religion

THESAURUS

relevant ADJECTIVE • *relevant information* ▶ pertinent, applicable, significant, suitable

reliable ADJECTIVE • *reliable evidence* ▶ dependable, trustworthy, sound • *a reliable friend* ▶ faithful, trustworthy, dependable, true

relief NOUN • *It was a relief to be home.* ▶ consolation, comfort, solace • *relief from hard work* ▶ respite, release, ease, rest • *to*

bring relief to the flood victims ▶ help, aid, assistance

relieve VERB • *to relieve a pain* ▶ alleviate, ease, lessen • *to relieve the boredom* ▶ reduce, counteract • *It relieved us to see them.* ▶ reassure, comfort, console, soothe

religious ADJECTIVE • *religious music* ▶ spiritual, sacred, holy • *a religious person* ▶ devout, pious, holy, saintly

a
b
c
d
e
f
g
h
i
j
k
l
m
n
o
p
q
r
s
t
u
v
w
x
y
z

611

a
b
c
d
e
f
g
h
i
j
k
l
m
n
o
p
q
r
s
t
u
v
w
x
y
z

religiously ADVERB carefully and regularly

relinquish VERB to give something up

relish NOUN **1** great enjoyment **2** a flavouring for food

relish VERB to enjoy very much

relive VERB to remember something vividly, as though it was happening again

relocate VERB to move or be moved to a new place

reluctant ADJECTIVE not willing or eager ▶ **reluctance** NOUN, **reluctantly** ADVERB

rely VERB **relies, relied**
rely on 1 to trust a person or thing to help or support you **2** to be dependent on

remain VERB **1** to be left over **2** to stay or not leave

remainder NOUN **1** the remaining people or things **2** the number left after subtraction or division

remains PLURAL NOUN **1** all that is left over **2** ancient ruins or objects; relics **3** a dead body

remand VERB to send a prisoner back into custody while further evidence is being gathered **on remand** in prison while waiting for a trial

remark NOUN something said; a comment

remark VERB **1** to make a remark **2** to notice something

remarkable ADJECTIVE unusual or extraordinary ▶ **remarkably** ADVERB

remedial ADJECTIVE **1** helping to cure an illness **2** helping children who learn slowly

THESAURUS

reluctant ADJECTIVE • *was reluctant to admit it* ▶ unwilling, hesitant (about), unenthusiastic (about)

rely VERB **rely on** • *to rely on someone* ▶ depend on, count on, trust

remain VERB • *to remain in the same place* ▶ stay, continue, stop • *to remain in power* ▶ stay, continue, survive • *A few people remained.* ▶ be left, be present, survive

remains NOUN • *the remains of a sandwich* ▶ remainder, rest, remnant

remark NOUN • *remarks about the weather* ▶ comment, observation, statement, opinion

remark VERB • *He remarked that it was very quiet.* ▶ comment, observe, mention, note, state • *did not remark anything unusual* ▶ notice, observe, see, perceive

remarkable ADJECTIVE • *a remarkable journey* ▶ extraordinary, amazing, astonishing, wonderful, fantastic • *a remarkable achievement* ▶ outstanding, impressive, exceptional

remedy NOUN • *a remedy for flu* ▶ cure, treatment, medicine, antidote

remedy NOUN **remedies**
something that cures or relieves a
disease or problem

remedy VERB **remedies**,
remedied to be a remedy for

remember VERB **1** to keep
something in your mind **2** to bring
something back into your mind
▶ **remembrance** NOUN

remind VERB **1** to help a person
remember something **2** to make
you think of something because of
being similar

reminder NOUN something which
reminds you

reminisce (rem-in-iss) VERB to
think or talk about things from the
past

reminiscence NOUN something
remembered from the past

reminiscent ADJECTIVE reminding
you of something

remiss ADJECTIVE careless; not
doing your duty properly

remission NOUN **1** a period
during which an illness is less
serious **2** reduction of a prison
sentence

remit NOUN an officially given task
or area of activity

remittance NOUN **1** the sending
of money **2** the money sent

remnant NOUN a part or piece left
over

remonstrate VERB to make a
protest

remorse NOUN deep regret for
having done wrong

remorseful ADJECTIVE feeling
remorse ▶ **remorsefully** ADVERB

remorseless ADJECTIVE relentless;
cruel

remote ADJECTIVE **1** far away in
place or time **2** isolated **3** unlikely
or slight *a remote chance*
▶ **remotely** ADVERB

remote control NOUN **1** the
control of something from a
distance, usually by electricity or
radio **2** a device for doing this

removal NOUN the act of
removing or moving, especially to
a new home

remove VERB **1** to take something
away or off **2** to get rid of

remuneration NOUN pay or
reward for work done

remember VERB • *to remember a
poem* ▶ memorize, learn • *can't
remember where I put it* ▶ recall,
recollect, recognize • *Remember
she won't be there yet.* ▶ bear in
mind, keep in mind, not forget • *to
remember the past* ▶ reminisce
about, recall, look back on

remorse NOUN • *filled with
remorse* ▶ guilt, shame, sorrow,
repentance

remote ADJECTIVE • *a remote place*
▶ isolated, secluded,
out-of-the-way, faraway,
inaccessible • *a remote chance*
▶ slight, small, slim

remove VERB • *to remove a tooth*
▶ pull out, take out, extract
• *Please remove your rubbish.*
▶ take away, clear away • *decided
to remove the last sentence*
▶ delete, erase, strike out

a
b
c
d
e
f
g
h
i
j
k
l
m
n
o
p
q
r
s
t
u
v
w
x
y
z

Renaissance (ruh-nay-suhns) NOUN the revival of classical styles of art and literature in Europe in the 14th–16th centuries

renal (reen-uhl) ADJECTIVE to do with the kidneys

rename VERB to give a new name to

render VERB 1 to cause to become *rendered us speechless* 2 to give or perform something *quick to render help*

rendezvous (rond-ay-voo) NOUN an arranged meeting between two people, or the meeting place

rendition NOUN a performance of music, reading of a poem, etc.

renegade (ren-ig-ayd) NOUN a person who deserts a group or religion etc.

renew VERB 1 to restore something to its original condition or replace it with something new 2 to begin or make or give again ► **renewal** NOUN

renewable ADJECTIVE 1 able to be renewed 2 (of sources of energy, e.g. the sun or wind power) that cannot be used up

renounce VERB to give up or reject ► **renunciation** NOUN

renovate VERB to repair a thing and make it look new ► **renovation** NOUN

renowned ADJECTIVE famous ► **renown** NOUN

rent NOUN a regular payment for the use of a house, flat, etc.

rent VERB to have or allow the use of in return for payment

rental NOUN an amount paid as rent

renunciation NOUN the renouncing of something

reorganize VERB to change the way in which something is organized ► **reorganization** NOUN

⚠️ **SPELLING**

This word can also be spelled *reorganise.*

repair VERB to put something into good condition after it has been damaged or broken ► **repairable** ADJECTIVE

repair NOUN 1 the process of repairing 2 a mended place **in good repair** well maintained

reparation NOUN (formal) something done or paid to make up for damage or a loss

repartee NOUN witty replies and remarks

repatriate VERB to send someone back to their own country ► **repatriation** NOUN

repay VERB repaid 1 to pay back 2 to give in return ► **repayment** NOUN

• *penalties that had been removed* ► abolish, get rid of, do away with

repair VERB • *to repair the damage* ► mend, fix, put right, renovate

repair NOUN • *in need of repair* ► mending, fixing, renovation

repay VERB • *to repay a debt* ► pay back, settle, expunge • *to repay expenses* ► refund, reimburse, pay back, settle • *to repay their kindness* ► return, reciprocate

repeal VERB to cancel a law officially ► **repeal** NOUN

repeat VERB **1** to say or do the same thing again **2** to tell another person about something told to you

repeat NOUN **1** the act of repeating **2** a radio or television programme that is shown again

repeatedly ADVERB over and over again

repel VERB **repelling, repelled 1** to drive someone back **2** to push something away by means of a physical force **3** to disgust

repellent ADJECTIVE disgusting; revolting

repent VERB to be sorry for what you have done

repentance NOUN regret for what you have done ► **repentant** ADJECTIVE

repercussion NOUN an indirect result of something that has happened

repertoire (rep-er-twahr) NOUN a stock of songs or plays etc. that a person or company performs

repertory NOUN **repertories** a repertoire

repetition NOUN **1** the act of repeating **2** something repeated

repetitive ADJECTIVE full of repetitions

replace VERB **1** to put a thing back in its place **2** to take the place of **3** to put a new or different thing in place of ► **replacement** NOUN

replay NOUN **1** a sports match played again after a draw **2** the playing or showing again of a recording

replay VERB to play a game or recording again

replenish VERB **1** to fill again **2** to add a new supply of ► **replenishment** NOUN

replete ADJECTIVE full or well supplied

replica NOUN an exact copy

replicate VERB to make or become an exact copy of

repeat VERB • to repeat an experience ► have again, do again, redo, reproduce • to repeat a story ► say again, retell

repel VERB • to repel the invaders ► drive back, repulse • a device for repelling slugs ► deter, scare off • Such selfishness repelled me. ► disgust, revolt, sicken

repetition NOUN • a repetition of last week's incident ► repeat, recurrence, rerun

replace VERB • to replace a book on the shelf ► put back, return, reinstate • someone to replace him ► follow, take over from, succeed

replica NOUN • a replica of the ship ► copy, reproduction, model, reconstruction

a
b
c
d
e
f
g
h
i
j
k
l
m
n
o
p
q
r
s
t
u
v
w
x
y
z

reply NOUN **replies** something said or written to deal with a question, letter, etc.

reply VERB **replies**, **replied** to give a reply to

report VERB **1** to give an account of **2** to make a complaint or accusation against somebody **3** to tell someone in authority that you are present

report NOUN **1** a description or account **2** a statement of how someone has worked or behaved **3** an explosive sound

reporter NOUN a person who reports news for a newspaper, radio, or television

repose NOUN calm or rest

repository NOUN **repositories** a place for storing things

reprehensible ADJECTIVE deserving blame

represent VERB **1** to help someone by speaking or acting on their behalf **2** to symbolize or stand for **3** to be an example or equivalent of **4** to show a person

or thing in a picture or play etc. **5** to describe in a particular way
▶ **representation** NOUN

representative NOUN a person or thing that represents others

representative ADJECTIVE **1** representing others **2** typical of a group

repress VERB **1** to control by force **2** to restrain or suppress
▶ **repression** NOUN

repressive ADJECTIVE harsh or severe

reprieve NOUN cancellation of a punishment

reprieve VERB to give a reprieve to

reprimand NOUN an official rebuke

reprimand VERB to give someone a reprimand

reprisal NOUN an act of revenge

reproach VERB to tell someone you are upset and disappointed by something they have done
▶ **reproach** NOUN

reproachful ADJECTIVE upset and resentful ▶ **reproachfully** ADVERB

reply NOUN • to get a reply
▶ answer, response, acknowledgement, retort

reply VERB • She replied that they would just have to wait. ▶ answer, respond, retort **reply to** • He never replies to letters. ▶ answer, acknowledge, respond to

report VERB • to report an increase in exports ▶ announce, declare, communicate • to report him to the police ▶ inform on, make a

complaint against • to report for duty ▶ present yourself, arrive, turn up

report NOUN • a full report of the incident ▶ account, description, article, record

represent VERB • to represent a human quality ▶ stand for, symbolize, typify, personify • to represent their views ▶ speak for, express • The picture represents a winter scene. ▶ show, depict

616

DICTIONARY

reproduce VERB **1** to cause to exist or happen again **2** to make a copy of **3** to produce offspring

reproduction NOUN **1** a copy of a work of art **2** the process of producing offspring

reproductive ADJECTIVE to do with reproduction *the reproductive system*

reprove VERB to rebuke or criticize harshly ► **reproof** NOUN

reptile NOUN a cold-blooded creeping animal, e.g. a snake, lizard, or crocodile

republic NOUN a country that has an elected president ► **republican** ADJECTIVE

Republican NOUN a supporter of the Republican Party in the USA

repudiate VERB to reject or deny ► **repudiation** NOUN

repugnant ADJECTIVE unpleasant or disgusting ► **repugnance** NOUN

repulse VERB **1** to drive away or repel **2** to reject an offer etc.

repulsion NOUN **1** the act of repelling or repulsing **2** a feeling of disgust

repulsive ADJECTIVE disgusting

reputable (rep-yoo-ta-bul) ADJECTIVE having a good reputation ► **reputably** ADVERB

reputation NOUN the general opinion about a person or thing

repute NOUN reputation

reputed ADJECTIVE said or thought to be something *is reputed to be the best* ► **reputedly** ADVERB

request VERB **1** to ask for **2** to ask someone to do something

request NOUN **1** an act of asking **2** a thing asked for

requiem (rek-wee-em) NOUN **1** a special Mass for someone who has died **2** music for the words of this

require VERB **1** to need **2** to make someone do something

requirement NOUN what is required; a need

THESAURUS

reproduce VERB • *to reproduce drawings* ► copy, duplicate, print, repeat, photocopy • *animals that reproduce in large numbers* ► breed, multiply

repulsive ADJECTIVE • *a repulsive appearance* ► disgusting, revolting, repugnant, repellent

reputable ADJECTIVE • *a reputable builder* ► reliable, dependable, highly regarded, trustworthy

reputation NOUN • *to damage a reputation* ► good

name, standing, character, image

request VERB • *to request help* ► ask for, appeal for, call for, beg for • *They requested us to stop.* ► ask, call on, implore

request NOUN • *a request for assistance* ► appeal, plea, application, call

require VERB • *to require surgery* ► need • *a situation that required care* ► call for, need, necessitate • *required me to show my passport* ► order, instruct, oblige

requisite (rek-wiz-it) ADJECTIVE required or needed

requisite NOUN a thing needed

requisition VERB to take something over for official use

rescue VERB to save from danger, harm, etc. ▶ **rescuer** NOUN

rescue NOUN the action of rescuing

research NOUN special study or investigation

research VERB to do research into ▶ **researcher** NOUN

resemblance NOUN likeness or similarity

resemble VERB to be like another person or thing

resent VERB to feel indignant about or insulted by ▶ **resentment** NOUN

resentful ADJECTIVE bitter and indignant about something ▶ **resentfully** ADVERB

reservation NOUN 1 the act of reserving 2 something reserved *a hotel reservation* 3 an area of land kept for a special purpose 4 a doubt

reserve VERB 1 to keep or order something specially 2 to postpone or put aside

reserve NOUN 1 a person or thing kept ready for use 2 an extra player chosen for a team 3 an area of land kept for a special purpose *a nature reserve* 4 shyness

reserved ADJECTIVE 1 kept for special use 2 shy

reservoir (rez-er-vwar) NOUN a place where water is stored

reshuffle VERB to reorganize a group of people ▶ **reshuffle** NOUN

reside VERB to live in a particular place

residence NOUN 1 a place where a person lives 2 the state or time of living in a place

resident NOUN a person living in a particular place ▶ **resident** ADJECTIVE

residential ADJECTIVE 1 containing homes 2 providing accommodation *a residential course*

residue NOUN what is left over ▶ **residual** ADJECTIVE

resign VERB to give up your job or position **be resigned to** to accept something unwelcome

THESAURUS

rescue VERB • *Someone would rescue them.* ▶ set free, free, release, save • *I went back to rescue my belongings.* ▶ recover, retrieve, salvage

resemblance NOUN • *a close resemblance* ▶ similarity, likeness

resent VERB • *to resent interference* ▶ begrudge, object to, be annoyed about, dislike

resentful ADJECTIVE • *to feel resentful* ▶ aggrieved, indignant, angry, bitter, envious

reserve NOUN • *a reserve of money* ▶ supply, fund, store, hoard • *a wildlife reserve* ▶ reservation, sanctuary, park

resign VERB • *The manager resigned.* ▶ leave, stand down, step down, quit

DICTIONARY

resignation NOUN **1** acceptance of a difficulty without complaining **2** the act of resigning a job or position

resilient ADJECTIVE recovering quickly from illness or difficulty ▶ **resilience** NOUN

resin NOUN a sticky substance produced by plants or made artificially ▶ **resinous** ADJECTIVE

resist VERB to fight or act against

resistance NOUN **1** the act of resisting *armed resistance* **2** the ability of a substance to hinder the flow of electricity ▶ **resistant** ADJECTIVE

resistor NOUN a device that increases the resistance to an electric current

resit VERB **resitting, resat** to sit an examination again ▶ **resit** NOUN

resolute ADJECTIVE showing great determination ▶ **resolutely** ADVERB

resolution NOUN **1** a resolute manner **2** something you have

resolved to do **3** a formal decision **4** the solving of a problem etc.

resolve VERB **1** to decide firmly or formally **2** to solve a problem etc. **3** to overcome disagreements

resolve NOUN **1** something you have decided to do **2** great determination

resonant ADJECTIVE **1** resounding or echoing **2** suggesting a feeling, memory, etc. ▶ **resonance** NOUN

resonate VERB to resound or echo

resort VERB **resort to** to turn to or make use of

resort NOUN **1** a place where people go for relaxation or holidays **2** the act of resorting **the last resort** something tried when everything else has failed

resound VERB to fill a place with sound; to echo

resounding ADJECTIVE **1** loud and echoing **2** very great

resource NOUN **1** something that can be used **2** an ability

THESAURUS

resist VERB • *resisted all our attempts to persuade him* ▶ oppose, withstand, stand up to, defy, avoid • *unable to resist any longer* ▶ hold out, restrain yourself

resolute ADJECTIVE • *a resolute resistance* ▶ determined, firm, steadfast, tenacious

resolve VERB • *to resolve the matter* ▶ settle, sort out, solve • *to resolve to keep going* ▶ determine, decide, make up your mind

resort NOUN • *a seaside resort* ▶ holiday town, tourist spot • *the last resort* ▶ option, choice, alternative

resort VERB **resort to** • *to resort to threats* ▶ make use of, fall back on, turn to, use

resounding ADJECTIVE • *a resounding thump* ▶ loud, echoing, booming • *a resounding success* ▶ emphatic, decisive, great

DICTIONARY

a
b
c
d
e
f
g
h
i
j
k
l
m
n
o
p
q
r
s
t
u
v
w
x
y
z

620

resourceful ADJECTIVE good at finding ways of doing things

respect NOUN **1** admiration for the good qualities of someone or something **2** politeness or consideration **3** a detail or aspect *in every respect* **with respect to** concerning; to do with

respect VERB to have respect for

respectable ADJECTIVE **1** having good manners and character etc. **2** fairly good ► **respectability** NOUN, **respectably** ADVERB

respectful ADJECTIVE showing respect ► **respectfully** ADVERB

respecting PREPOSITION concerning; to do with

respective ADJECTIVE belonging to each one of several *went to their respective rooms*

respectively ADVERB in the same order as the people or things already mentioned *The American and British teams finished first and second respectively*

respiration NOUN the action of breathing ► **respiratory** ADJECTIVE

respirator NOUN a device that fits over a person's face to purify air before it is breathed

respite NOUN an interval of rest or relief

resplendent ADJECTIVE brilliant with colour or decoration

respond VERB **1** to reply **2** to act in answer to an event etc.

respondent NOUN the person answering

response NOUN **1** a reply **2** a reaction

responsibility NOUN **responsibilities 1** the state of being responsible **2** something for which a person is responsible

responsible ADJECTIVE **1** looking after a person or thing and having to take any blame **2** reliable and trustworthy **3** with important duties *a responsible job* **responsible for** causing or

THESAURUS

respect NOUN • *the respect due to a great writer* ► admiration, honour, esteem • *in every respect* ► aspect, characteristic, detail, way

respect VERB • *to respect them for their honesty* ► admire, esteem, think well of • *to respect their wishes* ► comply with, abide by, follow

respectable ADJECTIVE • *a respectable family* ► decent, reputable, honourable • *a respectable score* ► decent, adequate, reasonable

respective ADJECTIVE • *give the books back to their respective owners* ► separate, individual, own

respond VERB **respond to** • *to respond to an enquiry* ► answer, react to, reply to, acknowledge

response NOUN • *an angry response* ► answer, reply, retort, reaction

responsible ADJECTIVE • *a responsible tenant* ► trustworthy, reliable, dependable, sensible • *a responsible job* ► important, powerful, influential

DICTIONARY

bringing about ▸ **responsibly** *ADVERB*

responsive *ADJECTIVE* quick to respond

rest *NOUN* **1** a time of sleep or freedom from work **2** a support **3** an interval of silence between notes in music **the rest** the remaining part; the others

rest *VERB* **1** to have a rest **2** to be still **3** to allow to rest *sit and rest your feet* **4** to lean or place something so it is supported **5** to be left without further investigation etc. *let the matter rest*

restaurant *NOUN* a place where meals can be bought and eaten

restful *ADJECTIVE* giving a feeling of rest

restitution *NOUN* **1** the act of restoring something **2** compensation

restive *ADJECTIVE* restless or impatient

restless *ADJECTIVE* unable to rest or keep still

restore *VERB* **1** to put something back to its original place or condition **2** to clean and repair a work of art or building etc. ▸ **restoration** *NOUN*

restrain *VERB* to hold a person or thing back ▸ **restraint** *NOUN*

restrict *VERB* to keep within certain limits ▸ **restrictive** *ADJECTIVE*

restriction *NOUN* a rule or limit that restricts action

result *NOUN* **1** something produced by an action or condition etc. **2** the score or situation at the end of a game **3** the answer to a sum or calculation

THESAURUS

rest *NOUN* • *The rest of them went home.* ▸ remainder, others • *to need a rest* ▸ break, breathing space, time off, lie-down, nap • *alternating periods of rest and exercise* ▸ relaxation, leisure, inactivity

rest *VERB* • *She went to rest.* ▸ relax, lie down, have a nap • *He rested his bike against the wall.* ▸ prop, lean, stand

restful *ADJECTIVE* • *a restful night* ▸ relaxing, calm, peaceful, quiet

restore *VERB* • *to restore democracy* ▸ bring back,

reinstate • *to restore property to its rightful owners* ▸ return, give back • *to restore an old building* ▸ renovate, repair, rebuild, refurbish

restrict *VERB* • *to restrict your opportunities* ▸ limit, control, regulate, impede

result *NOUN* • *a result of the hot weather* ▸ consequence, effect, outcome, repercussion, upshot, product • *the result of a trial* ▸ verdict, decision, judgement • *the result of an exam* ▸ mark, grade, score • *the result of a calculation* ▸ answer, solution

DICTIONARY

result VERB **1** to happen as a result **2** to have a particular result *a game that resulted in a draw*

resultant ADJECTIVE happening as a result

resume VERB **1** to begin again after stopping **2** to take or occupy again *resumed our seats* ▶ **resumption** NOUN

résumé (rez-yoo-may) NOUN a summary

resurgence NOUN a rise or revival of something *a resurgence of interest*

resurrect VERB to bring back into use or existence

resurrection NOUN **1** the act of coming back to life after being dead **2** a revival **the Resurrection** in the Christian religion, the resurrection of Christ three days after his death

resuscitate VERB to revive an unconscious person ▶ **resuscitation** NOUN

retail VERB **1** to sell goods to the general public **2** to tell what happened ▶ **retailer** NOUN

retail NOUN the selling of goods to the general public

retain VERB **1** to continue to have **2** to hold in place

retake VERB **retook**, **retaken** to take a test or examination again

retaliate VERB **retaliates**, **retaliating**, **retaliated** to attack or insult someone in return ▶ **retaliation** NOUN

retarded ADJECTIVE not well developed, especially mentally

retch VERB to strain your throat as if vomiting

retention NOUN the act of retaining or keeping

retentive ADJECTIVE (of the memory) able to remember well

reticent ADJECTIVE reserved and discreet ▶ **reticence** NOUN

retina NOUN a layer of membrane at the back of the eyeball, sensitive to light

retinue NOUN a group of people accompanying an important person

retire VERB **1** to give up regular work at a certain age **2** to retreat or withdraw **3** to go to bed for the night ▶ **retirement** NOUN

retiring ADJECTIVE shy; avoiding company

THESAURUS

result VERB • *Several things resulted from this.* ▶ arise, come about, develop, emerge, happen

resume VERB • *to resume talks* ▶ restart, continue, start again, carry on

retain VERB • *to retain an interest* ▶ keep, hold on to, preserve • *to*

retain your composure ▶ keep control of, maintain • *to retain facts in the mind* ▶ remember, memorize, recall

retire VERB • *He retired two years ago.* ▶ stop working, give up work • *retired to her room* ▶ withdraw, retreat

a
b
c
d
e
f
g
h
i
j
k
l
m
n
o
p
q
r
s
t
u
v
w
x
y
z

etort NOUN a witty or angry reply

etort VERB to make a retort

etrace VERB to go back over *retraced our steps*

etract VERB 1 to pull back or in 2 to withdraw an offer or statement ▶ **retraction** NOUN

etreat VERB to draw back after being defeated or to avoid danger

etreat NOUN 1 an act of retreating 2 a quiet place

etribution NOUN a deserved punishment

etrieve VERB 1 to bring or get back 2 to rescue ▶ **retrieval** NOUN

etriever NOUN a breed of dog trained to retrieve game

etrograde ADJECTIVE 1 going backwards 2 becoming less good

etrospect NOUN in retrospect when looking back on the past

etrospective ADJECTIVE 1 looking back on the past 2 applying to the past as well as the future *a retrospective law*

return VERB 1 to come or go back 2 to give or send back 3 to elect to parliament

return NOUN 1 the act of returning 2 something returned 3 profit *a good return on savings* 4 a return ticket

return match NOUN a second match played between the same teams

return ticket NOUN a ticket for a journey to a place and back again

reunify VERB **reunifies, reunified** to make a divided country into one again ▶ **reunification** NOUN

reunion NOUN 1 the act of reuniting 2 a meeting of people after a long interval of time

reunite VERB to unite again after being separated

Rev. ABBREVIATION Reverend

rev VERB **revving, revved** (*informal*) to make an engine run quickly

rev NOUN (*informal*) a revolution of an engine

reveal VERB to let something be seen or known

THESAURUS

etreat VERB • *The army retreated in disarray.* ▶ withdraw, draw back, back away

etreat NOUN • *to make a hasty retreat* ▶ departure, escape, exit • *a holiday retreat* ▶ refuge, hideaway

etrieve VERB • *to retrieve the ball* ▶ get back, recover

eturn VERB • *I'll see you when I return.* ▶ come back, get back,

come home, reappear • *to return it to its owner* ▶ give back, send back, take back, restore • *to return to their normal state* ▶ go back, revert • *The pain returned.* ▶ happen again, recur, reappear • *to return a favour* ▶ reciprocate, repay

reveal VERB • *to reveal the truth* ▶ admit, confess, impart, divulge, tell, disclose, communicate,

a
b
c
d
e
f
g
h
i
j
k
l
m
n
o
p
q
r
s
t
u
v
w
x
y
z

DICTIONARY

reveille (riv-al-ee) NOUN a military waking signal on a bugle

revel VERB **revelling, revelled 1** to take great delight in something **2** to enjoy yourself in a lively and noisy way ▶ **reveller** NOUN

revelation NOUN **1** the act of revealing **2** something surprising that is revealed

revelry NOUN lively enjoyment

revels PLURAL NOUN lively and noisy festivities

revenge NOUN the act of harming somebody in return for harm they have done

revenge VERB to take revenge for harm done

revenue NOUN **1** a country's income from taxes etc. **2** a company's income

reverberate VERB to be repeated as an echo ▶ **reverberation** NOUN

revere (riv-eer) VERB to respect deeply

reverence NOUN a feeling of awe and deep or religious respect

Reverend NOUN the title of a member of the clergy

reverent ADJECTIVE feeling or showing reverence

reverie (rev-er-ee) NOUN a daydream

reversal NOUN **1** the act of reversing or being reversed **2** a piece of bad luck

reverse ADJECTIVE opposite in direction, order, or manner etc.

reverse NOUN **1** the reverse side, order, manner, etc. **2** a piece of misfortune **in reverse** the opposite way round

reverse VERB **1** to turn in the opposite direction or order etc. **2** to move backwards **3** to cancel a decision ▶ **reversible** ADJECTIVE

reverse gear NOUN a gear that allows a vehicle to move backwards

revert VERB to return to a former condition, subject, etc. ▶ **reversion** NOUN

review NOUN **1** an inspection or survey **2** a published opinion of a book, film, play, etc.

THESAURUS

expose • to reveal their secret ▶ disclose, divulge, broadcast, betray • The door opened to reveal a beautiful scene. ▶ show, expose, uncover, unveil

revenge NOUN • to seek revenge ▶ vengeance, retribution, retaliation

reverse NOUN • It was the reverse of the truth. ▶ opposite, contrary, antithesis, converse, inverse

reverse VERB • to reverse the order of events ▶ turn round, swap round, switch round • to reverse a vehicle ▶ back, drive backwards • to reverse a decision ▶ change, retract, revoke, overturn, repeal

review NOUN • a review of the year ▶ survey, report, analysis, look back (at) • book reviews ▶ criticism, write-up • a military review ▶ inspection, parade, display

review VERB **1** to write a review of a book, film, play, etc. **2** to reconsider **3** to inspect or survey ▶ **reviewer** NOUN

⚠️ **USAGE**

Do not confuse this word with *revue*.

revile VERB to criticize angrily ▶ **revilement** NOUN

revise VERB **1** to go over work in preparing for an examination **2** to alter or correct something ▶ **revision** NOUN

revitalize VERB to put new strength or vitality into something

⚠️ **SPELLING**

This word can also be spelled *revitalise*.

revive VERB to come or bring back to life, strength, use, etc. ▶ **revival** NOUN

revoke VERB to withdraw or cancel a decree or licence etc.

revolt VERB **1** to rebel **2** to disgust

revolt NOUN **1** a rebellion **2** a feeling of disgust

revolting ADJECTIVE disgusting

revolution NOUN **1** a rebellion that overthrows the government **2** a complete change **3** the process of revolving; one complete turn

revolutionary ADJECTIVE **1** involving a great change **2** to do with a political revolution

revolutionize VERB to make a great change in something

⚠️ **SPELLING**

This word can also be spelled *revolutionise*.

revolve VERB **1** to turn in a circle **2** to have as the most important element *a life that revolves around work*

revolver NOUN a pistol with a revolving mechanism

THESAURUS

review VERB • *to review the situation* ▶ consider, assess, evaluate, examine • *to review a book* ▶ criticize, evaluate

revise VERB • *to revise your opinion* ▶ reconsider, change, alter • *to revise for an exam* ▶ study, read up, cram

revive VERB • *The man was unconscious but soon revived.* ▶ regain consciousness, recover, come round • *Hot drinks will revive us.* ▶ refresh, invigorate, restore, freshen up

revolt VERB • *The people were about to revolt.* ▶ rebel, rise up, mutiny • *Their cruelty revolted us.* ▶ disgust, sicken, shock

revolt NOUN • *a revolt in the south of the country* ▶ rebellion, uprising, revolution, mutiny

revolting ADJECTIVE • *a revolting mess* ▶ disgusting, nauseating, offensive, sickening

revolution NOUN • *a popular revolution* ▶ rebellion, revolt, uprising, coup d'état • *a revolution of the earth* ▶ rotation, circuit, cycle, orbit • *a revolution in technology* ▶ transformation, dramatic change

revolve VERB • *The wheel began to revolve.* ▶ turn, go round, rotate, spin • *to revolve round the earth* ▶ circle, orbit

a
b
c
d
e
f
g
h
i
j
k
l
m
n
o
p
q
r
s
t
u
v
w
x
y
z

a
b
c
d
e
f
g
h
i
j
k
l
m
n
o
p
q
r
s
t
u
v
w
x
y
z

revue NOUN an entertainment of songs, sketches, etc.

⚠ **USAGE**
Do not confuse this word with *review*.

revulsion NOUN 1 strong disgust 2 a violent change of feeling

reward NOUN 1 something given in return for an achievement or service 2 a sum of money offered for help in catching a criminal or finding lost property

reward VERB to give a reward to

rewarding ADJECTIVE satisfying; worthwhile

rewind VERB to wind a cassette or videotape back to the beginning

rewrite VERB **rewrote, rewritten** to write something again or differently

rhapsody (rap-so-dee) NOUN **rhapsodies** 1 a statement of great delight about something 2 a romantic piece of music

rhetoric NOUN the effective use of words in public speaking
► **rhetorical** ADJECTIVE

rheumatism NOUN a disease that causes pain and stiffness in joints and muscles ► **rheumatic** ADJECTIVE

rhino NOUN **rhino** or **rhinos** (*informal*) a rhinoceros

rhinoceros NOUN a large animal with a horn or two horns on its nose

✏ **WORD HISTORY**
from Greek *rhinos* 'of the nose' and *keras* 'horn'

rhododendron NOUN an evergreen shrub with large trumpet-shaped flowers

rhombus NOUN a shape with four equal sides but no right angles

rhubarb NOUN a plant with thick reddish stalks used as fruit

rhyme NOUN 1 a similar sound in the endings of words 2 a poem with rhymes 3 a word that rhymes with another

rhyme VERB 1 to form a rhyme 2 to have rhymes

rhythm NOUN a regular pattern of beats, sounds, or movements

rhythmic or **rhythmical** ADJECTIVE having a rhythm
► **rhythmically** ADVERB

rib NOUN 1 each of the curved bones round the chest 2 a curved part or support ► **ribbed** ADJECTIVE

THESAURUS

reward NOUN • *a reward for loyal service* ► honour, award, prize • *to offer a reward* ► payment, compensation, present

reward VERB • *to be rewarded for bravery* ► decorate, honour, recognize • *to be rewarded for your work* ► pay, recompense, remunerate, compensate

rewarding ADJECTIVE • *a rewarding experience* ► satisfying, worthwhile, pleasing, fulfilling

rhyme NOUN • *the words of the rhyme* ► poem, verse, song

rhythm NOUN • *the rhythm of the poem* ► metre, flow • *the rhythm of the music* ► beat, throb, pulse

DICTIONARY

ribald (rib-ald) ADJECTIVE funny in a coarse way ► **ribaldry** NOUN

riband NOUN a ribbon

ribbon NOUN a narrow strip of material used for decoration or for tying

rice NOUN the seeds of a cereal plant grown in flooded fields in hot countries

rich ADJECTIVE **1** having a lot of money or property **2** having a large supply of something **3** (of colour, sound, or smell) pleasantly deep or strong **4** (of food) containing a lot of fat, butter, eggs, etc. **5** expensive or luxurious ► **richness** NOUN

riches PLURAL NOUN wealth

richly ADVERB **1** in a rich or luxurious way **2** fully or thoroughly *an award that is richly deserved*

Richter scale NOUN a scale (from 0–10) used to show the force of an earthquake

rick[1] NOUN a large neat stack of hay or straw

rick[2] VERB to sprain or wrench

rickets NOUN a disease caused by lack of vitamin D, causing deformed bones

rickety ADJECTIVE likely to break or fall down

rickshaw NOUN a two-wheeled carriage pulled by a person, used in the Far East

ricochet (rik-osh-ay) VERB **ricocheting, ricocheted** to bounce off something ► **ricochet** NOUN

rid VERB **ridding, rid** to make a person or place free from something unwanted **get rid of** to remove or throw away

riddle NOUN a puzzling question to be solved

riddled ADJECTIVE pierced with many holes *riddled with holes*

ride NOUN a journey on a horse, bicycle, etc. or in a vehicle

ride VERB **rode, ridden 1** to sit on a horse, bicycle, etc. and be carried along on it **2** to travel in a car, bus, train, etc. **3** to float or be carried

THESAURUS

rich ADJECTIVE • *rich people*
► wealthy, affluent, well-off, prosperous • *rich furnishings*
► luxurious, sumptuous, opulent, lavish • *rich agricultural land*
► fertile, productive • *rich colours*
► deep, full, strong, vibrant, vivid

riches NOUN • *the riches of royalty*
► wealth, money, affluence, fortune

rickety ADJECTIVE • *a rickety shed*
► shaky, unsteady, flimsy, ramshackle

rid VERB • *to rid the house of dangerous substances* ► clear, free **get rid of** • *to get rid of rubbish* ► dispose of, remove, throw out

riddle NOUN • *the riddle of the man's identity* ► puzzle, enigma, mystery

ride NOUN • *a short ride into town* ► journey, trip, drive, outing

627

DICTIONARY

supported on something *to ride the waves*

rider NOUN 1 someone who rides 2 an extra comment or statement

ridge NOUN 1 a long narrow higher part 2 a long narrow range of hills or mountains ▸ **ridged** ADJECTIVE

ridicule VERB to make fun of ▸ **ridicule** NOUN

ridiculous ADJECTIVE silly enough to laugh at ▸ **ridiculously** ADVERB

rife ADJECTIVE happening frequently

riff-raff NOUN disreputable people

rifle NOUN a gun with a long barrel, held against the shoulder

rifle VERB to search through something in order to steal or steal something

rift NOUN 1 a crack or split 2 a disagreement between friends

rig[1] VERB **rigging**, **rigged** to provide a ship with ropes, spars, sails, etc. **rig out** to provide with clothes or equipment **rig up** to set up in a makeshift way

rig NOUN 1 a framework supporting the machinery for drilling an oil well 2 the arrangement of a ship's masts and sails etc.

rig[2] VERB **rigging**, **rigged** to arrange the result of an election dishonestly

rigging NOUN the ropes etc. that support a ship's mast and sails

right ADJECTIVE 1 on or towards the east if you are facing north 2 correct or true 3 fair or just 4 (of political groups) conservative ▸ **right-hand** ADJECTIVE

right ADVERB 1 on or towards the right *Turn right here.* 2 straight *Go right on.* 3 completely *Turn right round.* 4 exactly *right in the middle* 5 correctly or appropriately *Did I do that right?* **right away** immediately

right NOUN 1 the right-hand side or part etc. 2 what is morally good or fair or just 3 something that people are allowed to do or have *the right to vote in elections*

right VERB 1 to make a thing upright 2 to put right

right angle NOUN an angle of 90°

righteous ADJECTIVE doing what is right; virtuous ▸ **righteousness** NOUN

rightful ADJECTIVE deserved or proper *in her rightful place* ▸ **rightfully** ADVERB

right-handed ADJECTIVE using the right hand in preference to the left hand

THESAURUS

ridicule VERB • *too easy to ridicule them* ▸ mock, make fun of, laugh at, jeer at, humiliate

ridiculous ADJECTIVE • *a ridiculous thing to say* ▸ absurd, stupid, preposterous, ludicrous

right ADJECTIVE • *the right thing to do* ▸ appropriate, suitable, proper,

ideal • *the right answer* ▸ correct, accurate, exact, true, real • *not right to treat them in this way* ▸ fair, just, honest

right NOUN • *the right to speak* ▸ freedom, liberty, entitlement • *to have right on your side* ▸ justice, fairness, honesty

rightly ADVERB correctly or justifiably

rigid ADJECTIVE **1** stiff or firm *a rigid support* **2** strict ▸ **rigidity** NOUN

rigmarole NOUN a long rambling statement

rigorous ADJECTIVE **1** strict or severe **2** careful and thorough ▸ **rigorously** ADVERB

rigour NOUN strictness or severity

rile VERB (informal) to annoy

rim NOUN the outer edge of a cup, wheel, or other round object

rind NOUN the tough skin on bacon, cheese, or fruit

ring¹ NOUN **1** a circle **2** a thin circular piece of metal worn on a finger **3** the space where a circus performs **4** a square area for boxing or wrestling **5** a group of people

ring VERB **ringed** to put a ring round

ring² VERB **rang**, **rung** **1** to cause a bell to sound **2** to make a loud clear sound **3** to be filled with sound **4** to telephone

ring NOUN the act or sound of ringing

ringleader NOUN a person who leads others in rebellion, crime, etc.

ringlet NOUN a curl of hair

ringmaster NOUN the person in charge of a performance in a circus ring

ring road NOUN a road that goes round a town avoiding the centre

rink NOUN an enclosed area of ice for skating

rinse VERB to wash lightly in clear water

rinse NOUN **1** an act of rinsing **2** a liquid for colouring the hair

riot NOUN wild or violent behaviour by a crowd **run riot** to behave or spread in an uncontrolled way

riot VERB to take part in a riot

riotous ADJECTIVE **1** disorderly or unruly **2** boisterous *riotous laughter*

rip VERB **ripping**, **ripped** to tear roughly **rip off** (informal) to swindle or overcharge

rip NOUN a torn place

rigid ADJECTIVE • *a rigid container* ▸ stiff, hard, firm, inflexible • *rigid rules* ▸ strict, stern, harsh, uncompromising

ring NOUN • *a ring of fire* ▸ circle, loop, circuit • *a spy ring* ▸ network, organization, group

ring VERB • *to ring the area* ▸ surround, circle, encircle, enclose • *Bells were ringing.* ▸ peal, chime, toll, clang,

resound • *I'll ring you later.* ▸ phone, call, telephone

rinse VERB • *to rinse plates* ▸ wash, bathe, clean, sluice

riot NOUN • *to spark a riot* ▸ insurrection, uprising, tumult, commotion, disorder

riot VERB • *The crowd rioted.* ▸ rampage, run riot, revolt, rise up, rebel

rip VERB • *She ripped the note into tiny pieces.* ▸ tear, cut

a
b
c
d
e
f
g
h
i
j
k
l
m
n
o
p
q
r
s
t
u
v
w
x
y
z

ripe ADJECTIVE **riper, ripest 1** ready to be harvested or eaten **2** ready and suitable

ripen VERB to make or become ripe

rip-off NOUN (informal) a fraud or swindle

riposte (rip-ost) NOUN a quick clever reply

ripple NOUN a small wave or series of waves

ripple VERB to form ripples

rise VERB **rose, risen 1** go upwards **2** to increase *Prices will rise.* **3** to get up from lying, sitting, or kneeling **4** to get out of bed **5** to rebel *They rose in revolt against the tyrant.* **6** (of bread, cake, etc.) to swell by the action of yeast **7** (of a river) to begin its course

rise NOUN **1** the action of rising; an upward movement **2** an increase in wages, prices, etc. **3** an upward slope **give rise to** to cause

rising NOUN a rebellion

risk NOUN a chance of harm or loss

risk VERB **1** to take the chance of harming or losing *risked their lives* **2** to accept the risk of harm or loss *risks injury each time he climbs*

risky ADJECTIVE **riskier, riskiest** full of risk

rite NOUN a solemn or religious ceremony

ritual NOUN the series of actions used in a religious or other ceremony ▶ **ritual** ADJECTIVE, **ritually** ADVERB

rival NOUN a person or thing that competes with another ▶ **rivalry** NOUN

rival VERB **rivalling, rivalled** to be a rival of

> **WORD HISTORY**
> from Latin *rivalis* 'someone getting water from the same river (as someone else)', and therefore a *rival*

ripe ADJECTIVE • *a ripe melon*
▶ mature, tender, juicy

rise VERB • *to rise into the air*
▶ ascend, go up, fly up, climb
• *The walls rose above us.* ▶ tower, loom • *Prices have risen.*
▶ increase, grow, go up • *She rose from her chair.* ▶ stand up, get up, jump up

rise NOUN • *a rise in prices*
▶ increase, jump

risk NOUN • *to face the risk*
▶ chance, likelihood, possibility, danger • *a plan that involves risk*
▶ hazard, danger, uncertainty

risk VERB • *didn't want to risk being caught* ▶ chance • *to risk*

everything ▶ endanger, jeopardize, gamble, chance

risky ADJECTIVE • *a risky plan*
▶ dangerous, hazardous, unsafe, uncertain

rival NOUN • *the main rival for the job* ▶ competitor, adversary, challenger, opponent

rival VERB • *Few countries rival Greece for its beauty.* ▶ compete with, contend with, equal, match

rivalry NOUN • *a growing rivalry between the two teams*
▶ competitiveness, competition, opposition

river NOUN a large natural stream of water flowing through land

rivet NOUN a strong nail or bolt for holding pieces of metal together

rivet VERB **1** to fasten with rivets **2** to hold firmly *was riveted to the spot* **3** to fascinate *a riveting performance*

roach[1] NOUN a small freshwater fish

roach[2] NOUN (*informal*) (*American*) a cockroach

road NOUN **1** a level way with a hard surface for traffic to travel on **2** a way or course *the road to success*

road rage NOUN aggressive behaviour by motorists

roadway NOUN the part of the road used by traffic

roadworthy ADJECTIVE (of a vehicle) safe to be used on roads

roam VERB to wander ▶ **roam** NOUN

roan ADJECTIVE (of a horse) brown or black with many white hairs

roar NOUN a loud deep sound like that made by a lion

roar VERB **1** to make a roar **2** to laugh loudly

roast VERB to cook meat etc. in an oven or by exposing it to heat

roast ADJECTIVE roasted *roast beef*

roast NOUN **1** meat for roasting **2** roast meat

rob VERB **robbing**, **robbed** to take or steal from *robbed me of my watch*

robber NOUN a person who robs

robbery NOUN **robberies** an act of robbing

robe NOUN a long loose piece of clothing

robin NOUN a small brown bird with a red breast

robot NOUN **1** a machine that looks or acts like a person **2** a machine operated by remote control ▶ **robotic** ADJECTIVE

robust ADJECTIVE strong and vigorous ▶ **robustly** ADVERB

rock[1] NOUN **1** a large stone or boulder **2** the hard part of the

THESAURUS

roam VERB • *to roam over the hills*
▶ wander, rove, ramble, stray

roar VERB • *He roared at them to stop.* ▶ shout, bellow, yell, bawl
• *A motorbike roared past.*
▶ speed, zoom, whizz • *to roar with laughter* ▶ howl, hoot, guffaw

roar NOUN • *the roars of the crowd*
▶ shout, yell, bellow, howl

rob VERB • *to rob a bank* ▶ burgle, hold up, steal from, break into, raid, loot • *was attacked and*

robbed ▶ mug, hold up • *had been robbed of their victory*
▶ cheat, deprive

robber NOUN • *attacked by robbers*
▶ thief, brigand, bandit, criminal

robbery NOUN • *a wave of robberies* ▶ burglary, theft, housebreaking, shoplifting, hold-up, mugging

rock NOUN • *a castle on a rock*
▶ cliff, crag, outcrop • *rocks strewn across the road* ▶ boulder, stone

earth's crust **3** a hard stick-shaped sweet

rock² VERB to move gently backwards and forwards

rock NOUN **1** a rocking movement **2** rock music

rock and roll or **rock 'n' roll** NOUN a kind of popular dance music with a strong beat

rocker NOUN **1** a thing that rocks something or is rocked **2** a rocking chair

rockery NOUN **rockeries** a mound or bank in a garden, with plants growing among stones

rocket NOUN **1** a device propelled into the air by burning gases, used to send up a missile or a spacecraft **2** a firework that shoots into the air

rocket VERB **1** to move quickly upwards **2** to increase rapidly

rocking chair NOUN a chair that can be rocked by a person sitting in it

rocking horse NOUN a model of a horse that can be rocked by a child sitting on it

rock music NOUN popular music with a heavy beat

rocky¹ ADJECTIVE **rockier, rockiest** **1** like rock **2** full of rocks

rocky² ADJECTIVE **rockier, rockiest** unsteady

rod NOUN **1** a long thin stick or bar **2** a stick with a line attached for fishing

rodent NOUN an animal with large front teeth for gnawing, e.g. a rat or mouse

rodeo NOUN **rodeos** a show of riding skills by cowboys

roe¹ NOUN a mass of eggs or reproductive cells in a fish's body

roe² NOUN a kind of small deer

rogue NOUN a dishonest or mischievous person ► **roguery** NOUN

roguish ADJECTIVE playful and mischievous

role NOUN **1** a performer's part in a play or film etc. **2** a purpose or function

roll VERB **1** to move along by turning over and over **2** to form into the shape of a cylinder or ball **3** to flatten something by rolling a rounded object over it **4** to rock from side to side **5** to pass steadily

---

THESAURUS

rock VERB • *to rock gently* ► sway, swing • *The ship rocked in the storm* ► toss, lurch, pitch, roll

rocky ADJECTIVE • *a rocky hillside* ► stony, craggy, pebbly, rugged • *a rocky table* ► unsteady, shaky, wobbly

rod NOUN • *an iron rod* ► bar, pole, baton

rogue NOUN • *behaving like a rogue* ► villain, scoundrel, rascal, crook

role NOUN • *had a small role in the film* ► part, character • *the role of government adviser* ► function, position, post, job

roll VERB • *The wheel began to roll down the hill.* ► spin, rotate,

The years rolled on. **6** (of thunder) to make a rumbling sound

roll NOUN **1** something rolled into a cylinder **2** a small portion of baked bread **3** an official list of names **4** a long vibrating sound *a drum roll*

roll-call NOUN the calling of names from a list

roller NOUN **1** a cylinder used for flattening or spreading things, or on which something is wound **2** a long swelling sea wave

Rollerblade NOUN (*trademark*) a skating boot with a line of wheels for rolling over the ground

roller coaster NOUN a fairground ride with a series of alternate steep descents and ascents

roller skate NOUN a shoe with wheels for rolling over the ground

rollicking ADJECTIVE boisterous and full of fun

rolling pin NOUN a heavy cylinder for rolling out pastry

rolling stock NOUN railway engines and carriages etc.

Roman ADJECTIVE to do with ancient or modern Rome or its people
► **Roman** NOUN

Roman alphabet NOUN the alphabet in which most European languages are written

Roman Catholic ADJECTIVE belonging to or to do with the Christian Church that has the Pope as its leader ► **Roman Catholicism** NOUN

Roman Catholic NOUN a member of this Church

romance NOUN **1** tender feelings and experiences connected with love **2** a love affair or story **3** an imaginative story about heroes

Roman numerals PLURAL NOUN letters that represent numbers (I = 1, V = 5, X = 10, etc.), used by the ancient Romans

romantic ADJECTIVE **1** to do with love or romance **2** sentimental or unrealistic ► **romantically** ADVERB

Romany NOUN **Romanies 1** a Gypsy **2** the language of Gypsies

romp VERB to play in a lively way
► **romp** NOUN

rompers PLURAL NOUN a one-piece suit of clothing for a baby or young child

rondo NOUN **rondos** a piece of music with a recurring theme

revolve, turn, whirl, reel • *rolled the paper into a ball* ► wind, fold, coil, twist, curl, screw • *The ship began to roll.* ► lurch, pitch, toss, reel • *to roll out pastry* ► smooth, flatten, level • *Thunder rolled.* ► rumble, boom, resound, reverberate

roll NOUN • *a roll of paper* ► reel, spool, cylinder, drum

romantic ADJECTIVE • *handsome and romantic* ► loving, tender, affectionate • *romantic stories* ► sentimental, exotic, glamorous • *romantic ideas* ► idealistic, unrealistic

roof NOUN **1** the covering on top of a building, shelter, or vehicle **2** the top inside surface of the mouth

rook NOUN **1** a black crow that nests in groups **2** a chess piece shaped like a castle

rook VERB (informal) to swindle or overcharge

room NOUN **1** a part of a building with its own walls and ceiling **2** available space *plenty of room*

roomy ADJECTIVE **roomier, roomiest** having plenty of space

roost VERB (of birds) to perch or settle for sleep

roost NOUN a place where birds roost

rooster NOUN (American) a cockerel

root[1] NOUN **1** the part of a plant that grows under the ground and absorbs nourishment from the soil **2** a source or basis **3** a number in relation to the number it produces when multiplied by itself *9 is the square root of 81 (9 × 9 = 81).*

root VERB **1** to grow roots **2** to fix firmly **root out** to find and get rid of

root[2] VERB **1** (of an animal) to turn up ground in search of food **2** to find by rummaging

rope NOUN a strong thick cord made of twisted strands of fibre

rope VERB to fasten with a rope
rope in to persuade someone to take part

rosary NOUN **rosaries** a string of beads for keeping count of prayers said

rose[1] NOUN **1** a shrub that has showy flowers often with thorny stems **2** a deep pink colour

rose[2] past tense of **rise**

rosemary NOUN an evergreen shrub with fragrant leaves, used in cooking

rosette NOUN a large circular badge made of ribbon

Rosh Hashanah or **Rosh Hashana** NOUN the Jewish New Year

roster NOUN a list showing people's turns to be on duty etc.

rostrum NOUN a platform for one person

rosy ADJECTIVE **rosier, rosiest**
1 deep pink **2** hopeful or cheerful *a rosy future* ▶ **rosiness** NOUN

rot VERB **rotting, rotted** to decay or go soft

rot NOUN **1** the process of rotting **2** (informal) nonsense

roomy ADJECTIVE • *a roomy apartment* ▶ spacious, large, sizeable

root NOUN • *the root of a plant* ▶ tuber, rhizome • *the root of the problem* ▶ source, origin, cause

rope NOUN • *a rope attached to the boat* ▶ cable, cord, line

rot NOUN • *rot in the roof timbers* ▶ decay, mould, mildew, dry rot

rot VERB • *The wood had begun to rot.* ▶ decay, decompose, perish, crumble, disintegrate

DICTIONARY

rota (roh-ta) NOUN a list of duties and the people who must do them

rotary ADJECTIVE going round like a wheel

rotate VERB 1 to go round like a wheel 2 to arrange or happen in a series ► **rotation** NOUN

rote NOUN **by rote** from memory or by routine

rotor NOUN a rotating part of a machine or helicopter

rotten ADJECTIVE 1 rotted **rotten wood** 2 (informal) very bad or unpleasant

rotund ADJECTIVE rounded or plump ► **rotundity** NOUN

rouble (roo-bul) NOUN the unit of money in Russia

rouge (roozh) NOUN a reddish cosmetic for colouring the cheeks ► **rouge** VERB

rough ADJECTIVE 1 not smooth; uneven 2 not gentle or careful; violent **a rough push** 3 not exact

a rough guess 4 (of the weather or the sea) wild and stormy ► **roughly** ADVERB

rough VERB **rough it** to do without basic comforts **rough out** to draw or plan something roughly

roughage NOUN fibre in food, which helps digestion

roughen VERB to make or become rough

roughshod ADJECTIVE **ride roughshod over** to treat someone badly or unkindly

> **WORD HISTORY**
> a *roughshod* horse had shoes with the nail heads sticking out to prevent slipping

roulette (roo-let) NOUN a gambling game with bets placed on where the ball in a rotating disc will come to rest

round ADJECTIVE 1 shaped like a circle or ball 2 full or complete *a round dozen* 3 returning to the

THESAURUS

rotten ADJECTIVE • *rotten wood*
► decayed, decaying, crumbling, disintegrating • *rotten meat*
► bad, mouldy, mouldering, putrid

rough ADJECTIVE • *rough ground*
► bumpy, rugged, uneven, rocky, stony • *rough skin* ► dry, chapped, coarse, bristly, unshaven • *rough treatment* ► harsh, severe, hard, tough, stern • *rough weather* ► violent, stormy • *a rough sea* ► choppy, turbulent, wild • *a rough voice* ► harsh, grating, gruff, hoarse • *rough lads*
► rowdy, boisterous, disorderly

• *rough workmanship*
► amateurish, careless, clumsy, crude, unskilful • *a rough idea*
► vague, approximate, inexact • *a rough drawing* ► quick, sketchy, hasty, preliminary

roughly ADVERB • *roughly equal*
► about, around, approximately, more or less • *pulled his arm roughly away* ► violently, forcefully

round ADJECTIVE • *a round window*
► circular, spherical, curved • *a round figure* ► plump, chubby, rotund

start *a round trip* **in round figures** or **numbers** approximately, without giving exact units

round ADVERB **1** in a circle or curve *Go round to the back.* **2** to every person *Hand the cakes round.* **3** in a new direction *Turn your chair round.* **4** to someone's house or place of work *Come round after lunch.* **come round** to become conscious again **round about 1** near by **2** approximately

round PREPOSITION **1** on all sides of *a fence round the field* **2** in a curve or circle at an even distance from *The earth moves round the sun.* **3** to all parts of *Show them round the house.* **4** on the further side of *is round the corner*

round NOUN **1** the usual route of a postman etc. **2** one stage in a competition **3** a volley of shots from a gun **4** a whole slice of bread **5** a number of drinks bought together

round VERB **1** to make or become round **2** to travel round **round off**

to complete the last stages of **round up** to gather together

roundabout NOUN **1** a circular structure at a junction of roads, which traffic goes round **2** a circular revolving ride at a fair

roundabout ADJECTIVE indirect; not straight

rounders NOUN a game in which players try to hit a ball and run round a circuit

Roundhead NOUN an opponent of King Charles I in the English Civil War (1642–9)

roundly ADVERB severely *were roundly criticized*

round trip NOUN a trip to one or more places and back again

rouse VERB **1** to make or become awake **2** to cause to become active or excited

rousing ADJECTIVE loud or exciting *a rousing speech*

rout VERB to defeat completely
▶ **rout** NOUN

round NOUN • *the second round of the competition* ▶ stage, heat, game

round VERB • *to round the corner* ▶ travel round, turn **round off** • *to round off the evening* ▶ end, finish, complete **round up** • *to round up sheep* ▶ herd, drive together, assemble

roundabout ADJECTIVE • *a roundabout route* ▶ indirect, circuitous, long, meandering

rouse VERB • *was roused by the church bells* ▶ awaken, wake up • *to rouse feelings* ▶ provoke, stir up, spark off, kindle • *can be angry when he's roused* ▶ anger, annoy, provoke, incite

rousing ADJECTIVE • *a rousing speech* ▶ stirring, inspiring, moving

rout VERB • *to rout the enemy* ▶ crush, defeat

a b c d e f g h i j k l m n o p q r s t u v w x y z

route (*say as* root) NOUN the way taken to get to to a place

routine (roo-teen) NOUN a regular way of doing things ▸ **routinely** ADVERB

rove VERB to roam or wander ▸ **rover** NOUN

row¹ (rhymes with go) NOUN a line of people or things

row² (rhymes with go) VERB to make a boat move with oars ▸ **rower** NOUN

row³ (rhymes with cow) NOUN 1 a loud noise 2 a quarrel

rowan (roh-an) NOUN a tree that bears hanging bunches of red berries

rowdy ADJECTIVE **rowdier, rowdiest** noisy and disorderly ▸ **rowdiness** NOUN

rowing boat NOUN a boat that is rowed with oars

royal ADJECTIVE to do with a king or queen

royalty NOUN **royalties 1** being royal **2** a royal person or persons in the presence of royalty **3** a payment made to an author or composer etc. for each copy of a work sold or for each performance

rub VERB **rubbing, rubbed** to move something backwards and forwards while pressing it on something else **rub out** to remove by rubbing ▸ **rub** NOUN

rubber NOUN 1 a strong elastic substance used for making tyres, balls, hoses, etc. 2 a piece of rubber for erasing pencil marks ▸ **rubbery** ADJECTIVE

rubbish NOUN 1 things that are worthless or not wanted 2 nonsense

rubble NOUN broken pieces of brick or stone

THESAURUS

route NOUN • *the route home* ▸ way, road, direction, path, journey

routine NOUN • *their evening routine* ▸ procedure, pattern, method, system • *a dance routine* ▸ act, performance, number

row NOUN • *a row of plants* ▸ line, string, chain, series

row • *to have a row* ▸ argument, quarrel, squabble, fight • *making a dreadful row* ▸ noise, racket, rumpus, din

rowdy ADJECTIVE • *a rowdy mob* ▸ unruly, disorderly, noisy, badly behaved, wild

royal ADJECTIVE • *the royal family* ▸ regal, imperial, majestic

rub VERB • *to rub the skin* ▸ stroke, knead, massage • *to rub lotion* ▸ apply (to), smear, smooth, spread, put on **rub out** • *to rub out the name* ▸ remove, erase, delete

rubbish NOUN • *household rubbish* ▸ refuse, waste, garbage, junk, litter, trash • *to talk rubbish* ▸ nonsense, claptrap, drivel

rubble NOUN • *piles of rubble* ▸ debris, ruins, remains, wreckage

rubella NOUN an infectious disease which causes a red rash

ruby NOUN **rubies** a red jewel

ruck VERB to crease or wrinkle
▶ **ruck** NOUN

rucksack NOUN a bag carried on the back

ructions PLURAL NOUN protests and noisy argument

rudder NOUN a hinged upright piece at the back of a ship or aircraft, used for steering

ruddy ADJECTIVE **ruddier, ruddiest** red and healthy-looking

rude ADJECTIVE **ruder, rudest** 1 impolite 2 indecent or improper 3 roughly made; crude 4 vigorous and hearty *in rude health*
▶ **rudely** ADVERB, **rudeness** NOUN

rudimentary ADJECTIVE 1 basic or elementary 2 not fully developed *rudimentary wings*

rudiments PLURAL NOUN the basic principles of a subject

rueful ADJECTIVE regretful
▶ **ruefully** ADVERB

ruff NOUN 1 a starched pleated frill worn round the neck 2 a ring of feathers round a bird's neck

ruffian NOUN a violent lawless person

ruffle VERB 1 to disturb the smoothness of a thing 2 to upset or annoy someone

rug NOUN 1 a thick mat 2 a thick blanket

rugby or **rugby football** NOUN a kind of football game using an oval ball that players carry or kick

rugged ADJECTIVE 1 having an uneven surface or outline; craggy 2 strong or sturdy

ruin NOUN 1 severe damage or destruction 2 a building that has fallen down

ruin VERB to damage or spoil completely ▶ **ruination** NOUN

ruinous ADJECTIVE 1 causing ruin 2 in ruins; ruined

rule NOUN 1 something that people have to obey 2 ruling; governing *foreign rule* 3 a carpenter's ruler **as a rule** usually

rude NOUN • *a rude person*
▶ impolite, discourteous, disrespectful, ill-mannered, offensive • *a rude joke* ▶ coarse, vulgar

ruffle VERB • *to ruffle the leaves* ▶ stir, agitate, disturb • *to ruffle your hair* ▶ rumple, tousle, dishevel, mess up

rugged ADJECTIVE • *rugged country* ▶ rough, uneven, rocky, craggy

ruin NOUN • *to face ruin* ▶ bankruptcy, failure, collapse, downfall • *the ruin of all their hopes* ▶ destruction, disintegration, failure **ruins** • *the ruins of the house* ▶ remains, rubble, debris, wreckage

ruin VERB • *Rain had ruined the day.* ▶ spoil, wreck, destroy, blight

rule NOUN • *the rules about reporting a fire* ▶ regulation, law, principle • *foreign rule* ▶ control, administration, command, authority, government

DICTIONARY

rule VERB **1** to govern or reign **2** to make a decision **3** to draw a straight line with a ruler

ruler NOUN **1** a person who governs **2** a strip of wood, metal, or plastic with straight edges, used for measuring and drawing straight lines

ruling NOUN a decision or judgement

rum NOUN a strong alcoholic drink made from sugar

rumble VERB to make a deep heavy continuous sound
▸ **rumble** NOUN

ruminate VERB **1** (of an animal) to chew the cud **2** to think hard about something

rummage VERB to turn things over or move them about while looking for something
▸ **rummage** NOUN

rummy NOUN a card game in which players try to form sets of cards

rumour NOUN information that spreads to a lot of people but may not be true

rumour VERB **be rumoured** to be spread as a rumour

rump NOUN the hind part of an animal

rumple VERB **1** to crumple **2** to make untidy

rump steak NOUN a piece of meat from the rump of a cow

rumpus NOUN (informal) an uproar or angry protest

run VERB **running, ran, run 1** to move with quick steps and both feet off the ground at each stride **2** to flow **3** to produce a flow of liquid **4** to work or function **5** to manage or organize **6** to compete in a contest **7** to extend **8** to go or take in a vehicle **run away** to

THESAURUS

rule VERB • to rule an empire
▸ govern, run, control, command, lead, reign over • The king ruled for less than a year. ▸ reign, be ruler, be in power • The judge ruled about costs. ▸ decree, order, pronounce, decide **rule out** • cannot rule anything out
▸ exclude, discount, dismiss

ruler NOUN • a much-respected ruler
▸ leader, sovereign, governor, monarch, president (of a republic), head of state

ruling NOUN • a ruling from the president ▸ decision, judgement, pronouncement, decree, order

rumble VERB • Thunder rumbled in the distance. ▸ boom, echo, reverberate

run VERB • We ran across the field.
▸ sprint, race, jog, tear, dash, rush, speed, bolt • buses not running ▸ operate, go • The car has not been running well.
▸ function, perform, work • left the engine running ▸ operate, tick over, go • Water ran down the wall. ▸ stream, trickle, flow, pour, spill • was running a small business ▸ manage, be in charge of • to run a car ▸ maintain, keep, own • She ran me back to my

a b c d e f g h i j k l m n o p q **r** s t u v w x y z

leave a place secretly or quickly **run down 1** to run over **2** to stop gradually **3** (*informal*) to speak unkindly about **run into 1** to collide with **2** to happen to meet **run out** to have used up a supply **run over** to knock down with a moving vehicle

run NOUN **1** the action of running **2** a point scored in cricket or baseball **3** a continuous series of events etc. **4** an enclosure for animals **5** a series of damaged stitches **6** a track *a ski run* **on the run** escaping from the police

runaway NOUN someone who has run away

runaway ADJECTIVE **1** having run away or out of control **2** won easily *a runaway victory*

rundown ADJECTIVE **1** tired and in bad health **2** in bad condition

rung[1] NOUN each of the steps on a ladder

rung[2] *past participle of* **ring**[2]

runner NOUN **1** a person or animal that runs in a race **2** a groove, rod, or roller for a thing to move on

runner-up NOUN **runners-up** someone who comes second in a competition

running *present participle of* **run. in the running** having a chance of success

running ADJECTIVE continuous; without an interval *four days running*

runny ADJECTIVE **runnier, runniest 1** flowing like liquid *runny honey* **2** producing a flow of liquid *a runny nose*

run-of-the-mill ADJECTIVE ordinary, not special

runway NOUN a long hard surface for aircraft to take off and land

rupee NOUN the unit of money in India and Pakistan

rupture VERB to break or burst ▶ **rupture** NOUN

rural ADJECTIVE to do with the countryside

ruse NOUN a deception or trick

rush[1] VERB **1** to move or act quickly **2** to make someone hurry **3** to attack or capture by dashing forward

THESAURUS

house. ▶ drive, take, bring • *to run tests* ▶ carry out, complete, do • *The road runs north.* ▶ extend, stretch, go **run away** • *The prisoners ran away.* ▶ escape, flee, bolt **run out** • *My subscription has run out.* ▶ expire, end

run NOUN • *a run across the park* ▶ jog, dash, sprint, trot, gallop, race • *a run in the car* ▶ drive,

ride, trip, journey • *a run of bad luck* ▶ sequence, stretch, series • *a chicken run* ▶ enclosure, compound, coop, pen

runny ADJECTIVE • *a runny mixture* ▶ watery, thin, liquid

rural ADJECTIVE • *rural communities* ▶ country, agricultural

rush VERB • *to rush home* ▶ hurry, hasten, dash, run, race, tear

rush NOUN **1** a hurry **2** a sudden movement **3** a sudden great demand

rush[2] NOUN a plant with a thin stem that grows near water

rush hour NOUN the time when traffic is busiest

rusk NOUN a kind of hard dry biscuit for babies

russet NOUN a reddish-brown colour

rust NOUN **1** a red or brown coating that forms on iron or steel exposed to damp **2** a reddish-brown colour

rust VERB to make or become rusty

rustic ADJECTIVE **1** rural **2** made of rough timber or branches

rustle VERB **1** to make a sound like paper being crumpled **2** to steal horses or cattle **rustle up** (informal) to produce quickly *rustle up a meal* ► **rustle** NOUN

rustler NOUN someone who rustles horses or cattle

rusty ADJECTIVE **rustier, rustiest 1** coated with rust **2** less skilful from lack of practice

rut NOUN a deep track made by a wheel in soft ground **in a rut** following a dull routine

ruthless ADJECTIVE merciless or cruel ► **ruthlessly** ADVERB

rye NOUN a cereal used to make bread, biscuits, etc.

THESAURUS

rush NOUN • *a frantic rush* ► hurry, haste, dash, race • *a rush of water* ► flood, gush • *a sudden rush for the doors* ► charge, stampede

rustic ADJECTIVE • *rustic surroundings* ► rural, country, agricultural • *a rustic wooden seat* ► plain, simple, crude, rough

rusty ADJECTIVE • *a rusty spanner* ► corroded, discoloured, rotten

ruthless • *a ruthless dictator* ► brutal, cruel, merciless

a
b
c
d
e
f
g
h
i
j
k
l
m
n
o
p
q
r
s
t
u
v
w
x
y
z

Ss

S. *ABBREVIATION* **1** south **2** southern

sabbath *NOUN* a weekly day for rest and prayer, Saturday for Jews, Sunday for Christians

sabbatical (sa-bat-ikal) *NOUN* a period of paid leave granted to a university teacher for study or travel

sable *NOUN* **1** a kind of dark fur **2** (*poetical use*) black

sabotage *NOUN* deliberate damage or disruption to hinder an enemy, organization, etc.

sabotage *VERB* to damage or destroy by sabotage

saboteur *NOUN* a person who commits sabotage

sabre *NOUN* **1** a heavy sword with a curved blade **2** a light fencing sword

sac *NOUN* a bag-shaped part in an animal or plant

saccharin (sak-er-in) *NOUN* a sweet substance used as a substitute for sugar

sachet (sash-ay) *NOUN* a small sealed packet containing shampoo, sugar, etc.

sack¹ *NOUN* a large bag made of strong material **the sack** (*informal*) dismissal from a job

sack *VERB* (*informal*) to dismiss someone from a job

sack² *VERB* (*old use*) to plunder a captured town in a violent destructive way ► **sack** *NOUN*

sacrament *NOUN* a Christian religious ceremony such as baptism or Holy Communion

sacred *ADJECTIVE* holy; to do with God or a god

sacrifice *NOUN* **1** the offering of something to please a god, e.g. a killed animal **2** the act of giving up something valuable to benefit someone else **3** something sacrificed ► **sacrificial** *ADJECTIVE*

sacrifice *VERB* to offer something or give it up as a sacrifice

sacrilege (sak-ril-ij) *NOUN* disrespect for something sacred ► **sacrilegious** *ADJECTIVE*

sacrosanct *ADJECTIVE* sacred or respected and therefore not to be harmed

sad *ADJECTIVE* **sadder, saddest** unhappy; showing or causing sorrow ► **sadly** *ADVERB*, **sadness** *NOUN*

THESAURUS

sack *NOUN* • *a sack of flour* ► bag, pack

sack *VERB* • *to sack an employee* ► dismiss, give notice to, get rid of, lay someone off

sacred *ADJECTIVE* • *a sacred place* ► holy, blessed, consecrated • *sacred music* ► religious, spiritual

sacrifice *VERB* • *to sacrifice their lives* ► give up, forfeit • *to sacrifice an animal* ► offer up, kill, slaughter

sad *ADJECTIVE* • *sad to be leaving* ► unhappy, dejected, despondent, depressed, miserable • *a sad story* ► distressing, upsetting, depressing, tragic

sadden VERB to make a person sad

saddle NOUN 1 a seat put on the back of a horse or other animal 2 the seat of a bicycle 3 a ridge of high land between two peaks

saddle VERB 1 to put a saddle on a horse etc. 2 to burden someone with a task or problem

sadist (say-dist) NOUN a person who enjoys hurting or humiliating other people ► **sadism** NOUN, **sadistic** ADJECTIVE

safari NOUN an expedition to see or hunt wild animals

safari park NOUN a park where wild animals are kept in enclosures to be seen by visitors

safe ADJECTIVE 1 not in danger 2 not dangerous ► **safely** ADVERB

safe NOUN a strong cupboard or box for keeping valuables

safeguard NOUN a protection

safeguard VERB to protect

safety NOUN freedom from harm or danger

safety pin NOUN a U-shaped pin with a clip fastening over the point

saffron NOUN 1 a deep yellow colour 2 a kind of crocus with orange-coloured stigmas which are dried and used as flavouring for food

sag VERB **sagging, sagged** 1 to sink in the middle from pressure 2 to hang down loosely ► **sag** NOUN

saga (sah-ga) NOUN a long story with many episodes or adventures

sagacious (sa-gay-shus) ADJECTIVE shrewd and wise ► **sagacity** NOUN

sage¹ NOUN a kind of herb used in cooking

sage² ADJECTIVE wise

sage NOUN a wise person

sago NOUN a starchy white food used to make puddings

said past tense of **say**

sail NOUN 1 a large piece of strong cloth attached to a mast etc. to catch the wind and make a ship or boat move 2 a short voyage 3 an arm of a windmill **set sail** to begin a voyage by sea

sail VERB 1 to travel in a ship or boat 2 to start a voyage 3 to control a

safe ADJECTIVE • **safe from attack** ► secure, protected, guarded, invulnerable • **The children were all safe.** ► unharmed, unhurt, uninjured, out of danger • **a safe driver** ► reliable, sensible, trustworthy, responsible • **a safe medicine** ► harmless, innocuous

safeguard NOUN • **a safeguard against burglary** ► protection, defence, precaution, security

safety NOUN • **the safety of passengers** ► security,

protection, welfare • **a place of safety** ► refuge, shelter, sanctuary, protection

sag VERB • **to sag in the middle** ► hang down, sink, dip, droop

sail VERB • **to sail in the Mediterranean** ► cruise, voyage, boat • **The ferry sails at midday.** ► put to sea, set sail, leave harbour • **to sail a boat** ► steer, navigate, skipper, captain

ship or boat **4** to move quickly and smoothly

sailor NOUN **1** a person who sails **2** a member of a ship's crew or of a navy

saint NOUN a holy or very good person ▶ **saintly** ADJECTIVE

sake NOUN **for the sake of** in order to get or achieve something **for someone's sake** to help or please them

salad NOUN a mixture of vegetables eaten raw or cold

salamander NOUN a small lizard-like animal

salami NOUN a spiced sausage eaten cold

salary NOUN **salaries** a regular monthly wage

sale NOUN **1** the act of selling **2** a period of selling goods at reduced prices **for sale** or **on sale** available to be bought

salesperson NOUN a person employed to sell goods

salient (say-lee-ent) ADJECTIVE most noticeable or important *the salient features*

saline ADJECTIVE containing salt

saliva NOUN the natural liquid in a person's or animal's mouth

salivate (sal-iv-ayt) VERB to form a lot of saliva ▶ **salivation** NOUN

sallow ADJECTIVE (of the skin) slightly yellow

sally NOUN **sallies 1** a sudden rush forward **2** an excursion **3** a lively or witty remark

sally VERB **sallies, sallied** to make a sudden attack

salmon (sam-on) NOUN **salmon** a large edible fish with pink flesh

salmonella (sal-mon-el-a) NOUN a bacterium that can cause food poisoning

salon NOUN **1** a large elegant room **2** a room or shop where a hairdresser etc. receives customers

saloon NOUN **1** a car with a hard roof and a separate boot **2** a more comfortable bar in a pub

salsa NOUN **1** a hot spicy sauce **2** a modern Latin American dance

salt NOUN **1** sodium chloride, the white substance that gives sea water its taste and is used for flavouring food **2** a chemical compound of a metal and an acid ▶ **salty** ADJECTIVE

salt VERB to flavour or preserve food with salt

salubrious ADJECTIVE good for people's health

salutary ADJECTIVE having a good effect *salutary advice*

salutation NOUN a greeting

salute VERB **1** to raise the right hand to your head as a sign of respect **2** to greet **3** to admire something openly

THESAURUS

sake NOUN **for the sake of** • *for the sake of his family* ▶ for the good

of, in the interests of, for the benefit of

salute NOUN **1** the act of saluting **2** the firing of guns as a sign of greeting or respect

salvage VERB to save or rescue damaged goods or cargo
▶ **salvage** NOUN

salvation NOUN **1** the act of saving from loss or damage **2** (in Christianity) saving the soul from sin

salve NOUN **1** a soothing ointment **2** something that soothes a person's conscience or pride

salve VERB to soothe a person's conscience or pride

salvo NOUN **salvoes** or **salvos** a volley of shots

same ADJECTIVE **1** of one kind; exactly alike or equal **2** not changing; not different

sample NOUN a small amount that shows what something is like

sample VERB **1** to take a sample of **2** to try part of

sanatorium NOUN **sanatoriums** or **sanatoria** a hospital for people recovering from illnesses or with illnesses that cannot be cured

sanctify VERB **sanctifies**, **sanctified** to make holy or sacred

sanctimonious ADJECTIVE making a show of being virtuous or pious

sanction NOUN **1** action taken against a country **2** a penalty for disobeying a law **3** permission or authorization

sanction VERB to permit or authorize

sanctity NOUN a holy or sacred state

sanctuary NOUN **sanctuaries 1** a safe place or refuge **2** an area where wildlife is protected **3** the part of a church where the altar stands

sand NOUN the tiny particles that cover the ground in deserts, beaches, etc.

sand VERB to smooth or polish with sandpaper ▶ **sander** NOUN

sandal NOUN a lightweight shoe with straps over the foot

sandalwood NOUN a scented wood from a tropical tree

sandbag NOUN a bag filled with sand, used to build defences

sandpaper NOUN paper coated with sand for smoothing rough surfaces

sands PLURAL NOUN a beach or sandy area

THESAURUS

same ADJECTIVE • *the same person*
▶ identical, selfsame **the same**
• *houses that all looked the same*
▶ similar, identical, alike, comparable, matching • *to stay the same* ▶ unchanged, unvarying

sample NOUN • *samples of their work* ▶ specimen, example, demonstration, illustration • *a sample of a thousand voters*
▶ cross section

sample VERB • *to sample the food*
▶ try, test, inspect

sandstone NOUN rock made of compressed sand

sandwich NOUN slices of bread with a filling between them

sandwich VERB to put a thing between two others

sandy ADJECTIVE **sandier, sandiest 1** like sand **2** covered with sand **3** a yellowish-red colour

sane ADJECTIVE **1** having a healthy mind; not mad **2** sensible
► **sanity** NOUN

sanguine (sang-gwin) ADJECTIVE cheerful and optimistic

sanitary ADJECTIVE **1** free from germs and dirt; hygienic **2** to do with sanitation

sanitation NOUN arrangements for drainage and the disposal of sewage

sanitize VERB to clean and disinfect

⚠️ **SPELLING**

This word can also be spelled *sanitise*.

sanity NOUN a sane state

sap NOUN the juice inside a plant or tree

sap VERB **sapping, sapped** to take away strength gradually

sapling NOUN a young tree

sapphire NOUN a bright-blue jewel

sarcasm NOUN use of irony or humour to mock someone

📝 **WORD HISTORY**

from Greek *sarkazein* 'to tear the flesh'

sarcastic ADJECTIVE using sarcasm
► **sarcastically** ADVERB

sardine NOUN a small sea fish, sold packed tightly in oil

sardonic ADJECTIVE grimly amusing
► **sardonically** ADVERB

sari NOUN **saris** a length of cloth worn wrapped round the body by Indian women and girls

sarong NOUN a strip of cloth worn tucked round the waist or under the armpits by men and women in south-east Asia

sartorial ADJECTIVE to do with clothes

sash NOUN a strip of cloth worn round the waist or over one shoulder

sash window NOUN a window that slides up and down

SAT ABBREVIATION standard assessment task

satanic (suh-tan-ik) ADJECTIVE to do with or like Satan, the Devil in Jewish and Christian teaching

satchel NOUN a bag worn on the shoulder for carrying school books

satellite NOUN **1** a spacecraft put in orbit round a planet **2** a moon moving in an orbit round a planet

THESAURUS

sane ADJECTIVE • *helps to keep you sane* ► rational, normal, balanced, reasonable, sensible

sarcastic ADJECTIVE • *a sarcastic remark* ► mocking, contemptuous, ironic, scornful, sneering

DICTIONARY

3 a country controlled by a more powerful neighbour

satellite television NOUN television broadcasting in which the signals are transmitted by a satellite

satiated ADJECTIVE having as much as or more than you want

satin NOUN a silky material that is shiny on one side

satire NOUN **1** use of humour or exaggeration to ridicule people in power **2** a play or poem etc. that does this ► **satirical** ADJECTIVE

satisfaction NOUN **1** the act of satisfying **2** the state of being satisfied **3** something that satisfies a desire etc.

satisfactory ADJECTIVE good enough; adequate ► **satisfactorily** ADVERB

satisfy VERB **satisfies, satisfied 1** to give someone what they need or want **2** to convince **3** to fulfil needs etc.

satsuma NOUN a kind of mandarin orange originally grown in Japan

saturate VERB **1** to make very wet **2** to make something take in as much as possible of something ► **saturation** NOUN

Saturday NOUN the day of the week following Friday

sauce NOUN **1** a thick liquid served with food to add flavour **2** (informal) cheek or impudence

saucepan NOUN a metal cooking pan with a handle at the side

saucer NOUN a shallow dish on which a cup is placed

saucy ADJECTIVE **saucier, sauciest** cheeky or impudent ► **saucily** ADVERB

sauna NOUN a room or compartment filled with steam, used as a kind of bath

saunter VERB to walk slowly and casually ► **saunter** NOUN

sausage NOUN a tube-shaped skin filled with seasoned minced meat

savage ADJECTIVE wild and fierce; cruel ► **savagery** NOUN

savage NOUN a savage or primitive person

savage VERB to attack fiercely

savannah or **savanna** NOUN a grassy plain with no trees

save VERB **1** to keep safe or free from harm **2** to keep for later use **3** to avoid wasting something **4** (ICT) to store data in a file **5** (in sports) to prevent an opponent from scoring ► **save** NOUN

save PREPOSITION except

THESAURUS

satisfactory ADJECTIVE • *a satisfactory method* ► adequate, acceptable, suitable, sufficient, all right

satisfy VERB • *to satisfy demand* ► fulfil, meet, fill • *Nothing would satisfy him.* ► content, make happy

savage ADJECTIVE • *savage dogs* ► fierce, wild, ferocious, vicious, untamed • *a savage assault* ► fierce, ferocious, brutal, cruel, sadistic

save VERB • *to save someone from harm* ► protect, defend, guard • *to save all the passengers*

a
b
c
d
e
f
g
h
i
j
k
l
m
n
o
p
q
r
s
t
u
v
w
x
y
z

savings PLURAL NOUN money saved

saviour NOUN a person who saves someone

savour NOUN the taste or smell of something

savour VERB **1** to enjoy the taste or smell of **2** to have a certain taste or smell

savoury ADJECTIVE **1** tasty but not sweet **2** having an appetizing taste or smell

savoury NOUN **savouries** a savoury dish

saw[1] NOUN a tool with a jagged edge for cutting wood or metal etc.

saw VERB **sawed**, **sawn** to cut with a saw

saw[2] past tense of **see**[1]

sawdust NOUN powder made when wood is cut by a saw

saxophone NOUN a brass wind instrument with a curved flared opening ► **saxophonist** NOUN

say VERB **said 1** to speak or express in words **2** to give an opinion

say NOUN the power to decide something

saying NOUN a well-known phrase or proverb

scab NOUN a hard crust that forms over a wound ► **scabby** ADJECTIVE

scabbard NOUN the sheath of a sword or dagger

scabies (skay-beez) NOUN a contagious skin disease caused by a parasite

scaffold NOUN a platform on which criminals are executed

scaffolding NOUN a structure of poles and platforms for workers to stand on while building or repairing a house etc.

scald VERB to burn yourself with hot liquid or steam ► **scald** NOUN

scale[1] NOUN **1** a series of units or degrees for measuring **2** a series of musical notes in a fixed pattern **3** proportion or ratio **4** the relative size or importance of something

scale VERB to climb

scale[2] NOUN **1** each of the thin overlapping parts on the outside

THESAURUS

► rescue, free, release, liberate
• *to save money* ► put by, set aside, store up • *to save petrol* ► economize on, cut back on, use wisely

say VERB • *could not say his name* ► speak, utter, articulate • *'It's snowing,' he said.* ► observe, remark, declare, state, announce, answer, reply • *He says he didn't do it.* ► claim, maintain, assert, insist
• *to say a prayer* ► recite, utter

• *What are you trying to say?*
► express, put into words, communicate • *cannot say what might happen* ► guess, imagine, judge

saying NOUN • *the saying about too many cooks* ► proverb, adage, maxim

scale NOUN • *the scale of the tragedy* ► size, extent, scope, magnitude

scale VERB • *to scale a fence* ► climb, clamber up

DICTIONARY

of a fish, snake, etc. **2** a hard substance formed by hard water or on teeth

scalene (skay-leen) ADJECTIVE (of a triangle) having unequal sides

scales PLURAL NOUN a device for weighing

scallop NOUN a shellfish with two hinged fan-shaped shells ▶ **scalloped** ADJECTIVE

scalp NOUN the skin on the top of the head

scalp VERB to cut or tear the scalp from

scalpel NOUN a small knife with a thin sharp blade, used in surgery

scaly ADJECTIVE **scalier, scaliest** covered in scales or scale

scam NOUN (informal) a dishonest scheme or swindle

scamp NOUN a rascal

scamper VERB to run quickly or playfully ▶ **scamper** NOUN

scampi PLURAL NOUN large prawns

scan VERB **scanning, scanned 1** to look at every part of **2** to glance at **3** (of poetry) to be rhythmically correct **4** to sweep a radar or electronic beam over an area

scan NOUN **1** an act of scanning **2** an examination using a scanner

scandal NOUN **1** something shameful or disgraceful **2** gossip about people's faults and wrongdoings ▶ **scandalous** ADJECTIVE

scandalize VERB to shock by doing or saying something shameful or disgraceful

⚠ **SPELLING**

This word can also be spelled *scandalise*.

scanner NOUN **1** a machine that examines things by means of light or other rays **2** a machine that converts printed text, pictures, etc. into machine-readable form

scansion NOUN the scanning of verse

scant ADJECTIVE barely enough or adequate

scanty ADJECTIVE **scantier, scantiest** small in amount or extent ▶ **scantily** ADVERB

scapegoat NOUN a person who bears the blame or punishment for others

THESAURUS

scan VERB • *to scan the horizon* ▶ study, examine, view, survey • *to scan a newspaper* ▶ skim, glance through, flick through

scandal NOUN • *newspapers full of scandal* ▶ gossip, rumour, sensation • *a scandal that the hospital has to close* ▶ disgrace, outrage, injustice

scandalous ADJECTIVE • *a scandalous way to treat people* ▶ shameful, disgraceful, shocking, outrageous, appalling • *scandalous behaviour* ▶ improper, shameful, disreputable

scanty ADJECTIVE • *scanty evidence* ▶ meagre, sparse, minimal, negligible, insufficient

a b c d e f g h i j k l m n o p q r s t u v w x y z

scar NOUN **1** the mark left by a cut or burn etc. **2** psychological harm caused by an unpleasant experience

scar VERB **scarring, scarred** to make a scar or scars on

scarab NOUN an ornament or symbol carved in the shape of a beetle

scarce ADJECTIVE **scarcer, scarcest 1** not plentiful or enough **2** rare

scarcely ADVERB only just; only with difficulty

scarcity NOUN **scarcities** a shortage

scare VERB to frighten

scare NOUN **1** a fright **2** a sudden sense of alarm

scarecrow NOUN a figure dressed in old clothes, set up to frighten birds away

scarf NOUN **scarves** a strip of material worn round the neck or head

scarlet ADJECTIVE, NOUN a bright red colour

scarp NOUN a steep slope on a hill

scary ADJECTIVE **scarier, scariest** (informal) frightening

scathing ADJECTIVE severely critical

scatter VERB **1** to throw or send in all directions **2** to leave quickly in all directions

scatterbrain NOUN a careless forgetful person

scavenge VERB to search for useful things among rubbish
▶ **scavenger** NOUN

scenario NOUN **scenarios 1** a summary of the plot of a play etc. **2** an imagined series of events or set of circumstances

scene NOUN **1** the place where something has happened **2** a part of a play or film **3** a view as seen by a spectator **4** an angry or noisy outburst **5** an area of activity

scar NOUN • *a scar on his cheek*
▶ mark, blemish

scar VERB • *The wound scarred his face.* ▶ disfigure, mark

scarce ADJECTIVE • *Supplies became scarce.* ▶ sparse, meagre, in short supply, hard to find, insufficient

scarcely ADVERB • *could scarcely walk* ▶ barely, hardly, only just

scare VERB • *I didn't mean to scare you.* ▶ frighten, alarm, startle, shock, terrify

scare NOUN • *gave them a scare*
▶ fright, shock, start

scared ADJECTIVE • *too scared to go out alone* ▶ frightened, afraid, anxious, alarmed, terrified, panic-stricken

scary ADJECTIVE • *a scary old house*
▶ frightening, eerie, spooky, creepy, terrifying

scatter VERB • *The crowd quickly scattered.* ▶ disperse, break up, disband • *to scatter breadcrumbs*
▶ sprinkle, strew, spread

scene NOUN • *the scene of the accident* ▶ site, place, position, spot, location • *a beautiful scene*
▶ view, vista, outlook, panorama • *to cause a scene* ▶ fuss, commotion, disturbance, row

a
b
c
d
e
f
g
h
i
j
k
l
m
n
o
p
q
r
s
t
u
v
w
x
y
z

scenery NOUN **1** the natural features of a landscape **2** things put on a stage to make it look like a place

scenic ADJECTIVE having fine natural scenery

scent NOUN **1** a pleasant smell **2** a liquid perfume **3** an animal's smell that other animals can detect

scent VERB **1** to discover something by its scent **2** to put scent on or in

sceptic (skep-tik) NOUN a sceptical person

sceptical (skep-tik-al) ADJECTIVE inclined to question things
► **sceptically** ADVERB, **scepticism** NOUN

sceptre NOUN a rod carried by a king or queen as a symbol of power

schedule (shed-yool) NOUN a programme or timetable of planned events or work

schedule VERB **1** to put into a schedule **2** to arrange for a certain time

schematic (skee-mat-ik) ADJECTIVE in the form of a diagram or chart

scheme NOUN a plan of action

scheme VERB to make plans; to plot

schism (sizm) NOUN the splitting of a group into two opposing sections

schizophrenia (skid-zo-free-nee-a) NOUN a kind of mental illness in which people affected cannot relate their thoughts and feelings to reality
► **schizophrenic** ADJECTIVE & NOUN

scholar NOUN **1** a person who has studied a subject thoroughly **2** a person who has been awarded a scholarship ► **scholarly** ADJECTIVE

scholarship NOUN **1** a grant of money given to a student to pay for their education **2** the knowledge and methods of scholars

scholastic ADJECTIVE to do with schools or education

school[1] NOUN **1** a place where children are taught **2** the pupils in a school **3** a group of people who

scent NOUN • *the scent of roses*
► smell , perfume, fragrance, aroma • *a bottle of scent*
► perfume, toilet water, cologne • *to pick up the scent* ► trail, track

sceptical ADJECTIVE • *sceptical about all their excuses* ► dubious, doubtful, unsure, suspicious, uncertain

schedule NOUN • *a busy work schedule* ► timetable, agenda, programme, diary

scheme NOUN • *a national reading scheme* ► plan, project, proposal, programme, system

scheme VERB • *schemed to overthrow the emperor* ► plot, intrigue, plan

scholar NOUN • *a leading scholar* ► academic, authority, expert, intellectual

have the same beliefs or style of work etc.

school VERB to teach or train

school[2] NOUN a shoal of fish or whales etc.

schooling NOUN 1 education in a school 2 training

schoolteacher NOUN a person who teaches in a school

schooner (skoon-er) NOUN a sailing ship with two masts

science NOUN 1 the study of the physical world by means of observation and experiment 2 a branch of this, such as chemistry, physics, or biology

science fiction NOUN stories about imaginary scientific discoveries or space travel and life on other planets

scientific ADJECTIVE 1 to do with science or scientists 2 studying things systematically
▶ **scientifically** ADVERB

scientist NOUN an expert in science

scintillating ADJECTIVE lively and witty

scissors PLURAL NOUN a cutting instrument with two blades that close against each other

scoff[1] VERB to speak contemptuously

scoff[2] VERB (informal) to eat greedily

scold VERB to speak angrily to

scone NOUN a soft flat plain cake

scoop NOUN 1 a deep spoon for serving ice cream etc. 2 a news story published exclusively by one newspaper

scoop VERB to lift or hollow out with a scoop

scooter NOUN 1 a kind of motorcycle with small wheels 2 a board with wheels and a long handle, pushed along by foot

scope NOUN 1 opportunity or possibility 2 the range or extent of a subject

scorch VERB to burn slightly

scorching ADJECTIVE (informal) very hot

scientific ADJECTIVE • scientific research ▶ science-based, technical, technological • scientific methods ▶ systematic, methodical, analytical, rigorous

scoff VERB scoff at • inclined to scoff at such theories ▶ mock, ridicule, sneer at, make fun of

scold VERB • to scold children ▶ tell off, reprimand, rebuke

scoop VERB scoop out • to scoop out holes in the sand ▶ dig, excavate, hollow to scoop out the flesh of the fruit ▶ remove, scrape out, spoon out

scope NOUN • beyond the scope of the inquiry ▶ extent, limit, range, reach • plenty of scope for new ideas ▶ opportunity, chance, room

scorch VERB • was scorched by the fire ▶ burn, singe, char, blacken

score NOUN **1** the number of points or goals made in a game **2** (old use) a group of twenty **3** written or printed music

score VERB **1** to get a point or goal in a game **2** to keep a count of the score **3** to mark with lines or cuts **4** to write out a musical score ▶ **scorer** NOUN

scores PLURAL NOUN very many

scorn NOUN contempt

scorn VERB **1** to treat with contempt **2** to refuse indignantly

scornful ADJECTIVE contemptuous ▶ **scornfully** ADVERB

scorpion NOUN an animal with eight legs and a poisonous sting

scotch¹ NOUN whisky made in Scotland

scotch² VERB to put an end to an idea or rumour etc.

scot-free ADJECTIVE without harm or punishment

scoundrel NOUN a wicked or dishonest person

scour¹ VERB to rub something until it is clean and bright ▶ **scourer** NOUN

scour² VERB to search thoroughly

scourge (skerj) NOUN something that causes suffering

Scout NOUN a member of the Scout Association, an organization for boys

scout NOUN someone sent out to collect information

scout VERB **1** to act as a scout **2** to search an area thoroughly

scowl NOUN an angry frown

scowl VERB to frown angrily

scrabble VERB to grope or struggle to reach or get something

scraggy ADJECTIVE **scraggier**, **scraggiest** thin and bony

scram EXCLAMATION (informal) go away!

scramble VERB **1** to move quickly and awkwardly **2** to struggle to do or get something **3** to cook eggs by beating them and heating them in a pan **4** to mix things together **5** to alter a radio or telephone signal so that it has to be decoded

scramble NOUN **1** a climb or walk over rough ground **2** a struggle to

score NOUN • the final score of the game ▶ result, total, mark

score VERB • to score double points ▶ earn, win, gain, achieve • to score the surface ▶ cut, mark, scratch, scrape

scorn NOUN • treated the remark with scorn ▶ contempt, disdain, derision, ridicule

scorn VERB • to scorn such practices ▶ despise, scoff at, ridicule, mock

scour VERB • to scour the junk shops for bargains ▶ search, comb, hunt through

scowl VERB • to scowl angrily ▶ glower, frown, glare, grimace

scramble VERB • scrambled down the slope ▶ clamber, climb, crawl, scrabble • two men scrambling for the gun ▶ scuffle, jostle, tussle • quickly scrambled into the plane ▶ hurry, dash, rush

do or get something **3** a motorcycle race over rough country

scrap[1] NOUN **1** a small piece **2** rubbish or waste material

scrap VERB **scrapping**, **scrapped** to get rid of something useless or unwanted

scrap[2] NOUN (*informal*) a fight

scrap VERB **scrapping**, **scrapped** (*informal*) to fight

scrape VERB **1** to rub or damage something by passing something hard over it **2** to make a harsh sound by rubbing against a rough or hard surface **3** to remove by scraping **4** to get something by great effort or care **scrape through** to succeed by a small margin

scrape NOUN **1** a scraping movement or sound **2** a mark etc. made by scraping **3** (*informal*) an awkward situation

scrappy ADJECTIVE **scrappier**, **scrappiest** untidy or carelessly done

scratch VERB **1** to mark or cut the surface of a thing with something sharp **2** to rub the skin with fingernails or claws **3** to withdraw from a race or competition

scratch NOUN **1** a mark made by scratching **2** the action of scratching **from scratch** from the start **up to scratch** good enough ▶ **scratchy** ADJECTIVE

scrawl NOUN untidy handwriting

scrawl VERB to write in a scrawl

scrawny ADJECTIVE **scrawnier**, **scrawniest** thin and bony

scream NOUN **1** a loud cry of pain, fear, anger, or excitement **2** a loud piercing sound **3** (*informal*) an amusing person or thing

scream VERB to make a scream

scrap NOUN • *a few scraps of food*
▶ bit, piece, crumb, fragment
• *not a scrap of evidence* ▶ shred, speck, ounce • *a lorry loaded with scrap* ▶ junk, rubbish, waste

scrap VERB • *to scrap the plan*
▶ abandon, cancel, drop, ditch

scrape VERB • *scraped her skin on the wall* ▶ graze, scratch • *to scrape your boots* ▶ scrub, rub, clean

scrape NOUN • *to get into a scrape*
▶ difficulty, predicament, tight spot, trouble

scrappy ADJECTIVE • *a scrappy game*
▶ disjointed, disorganized

scratch VERB • *to scratch the table top* ▶ scrape, mark, score, gouge
• *Thorns scratched his legs.*
▶ graze, prick, cut

scratch NOUN • *scratches in the paint* ▶ gash, mark, line, scrape
• *to get a scratch* ▶ graze, cut, laceration

scream NOUN • *a scream of pain*
▶ yell, shriek, shout, screech, roar, howl

scream VERB • *She screamed at them to stop.* ▶ yell, shriek, shout, bawl, screech, roar, howl

screech VERB to make a harsh high-pitched sound ▶ **screech** NOUN

screen NOUN 1 a surface for showing films 2 a device for displaying television pictures or computer data 3 a vehicle's windscreen 4 a movable panel used to hide, protect, or divide something

screen VERB 1 to protect, hide, or divide with a screen 2 to show a film or television pictures on a screen 3 to check someone for the presence of a disease 4 to check whether a person is suitable for a job

screenplay NOUN the script of a film, with instructions to the actors

screw NOUN 1 a metal pin with a spiral thread round it, holding things together by being twisted in 2 something twisted 3 a propeller on a ship or motor boat

screw VERB 1 to fasten with a screw or screws 2 to fit or turn by twisting

screwdriver NOUN a tool for turning screws

scribble VERB 1 to write quickly or untidily 2 to make meaningless marks ▶ **scribble** NOUN

scribe NOUN 1 a person who made copies of manuscripts 2 (in biblical times) a professional religious scholar ▶ **scribal** ADJECTIVE

scrimp VERB to use money very carefully

script NOUN 1 handwriting 2 the text of a play, film, broadcast talk, etc.

scripture NOUN 1 sacred writings 2 (in Christianity) the Bible

scroll NOUN 1 a roll of paper or parchment used for writing 2 a spiral design

scroll VERB to move the display on a computer screen up or down

scrotum (skroh-tuhm) NOUN the pouch of skin containing the testicles

scrounge VERB to get something without paying for it ▶ **scrounger** NOUN

scrub[1] VERB scrubbing, scrubbed 1 to rub or clean with a hard brush 2 (informal) to cancel ▶ **scrub** NOUN

scrub[2] NOUN land covered with low trees and bushes

scruff NOUN the back of the neck

scruffy ADJECTIVE scruffier, scruffiest shabby and untidy ▶ **scruffily** ADVERB

screen NOUN • a computer with a 17-inch screen ▶ monitor • a screen dividing the room ▶ partition, divider, curtain

screen VERB • a hedge screening the dustbins ▶ hide, conceal • to screen applicants ▶ vet, scrutinize

scribble VERB • to scribble a note ▶ write, scrawl, dash off, jot down

scrub VERB • to scrub the floor ▶ wash, clean, brush

scruffy ADJECTIVE • scruffy jeans ▶ shabby, worn, ragged, dirty • to look scruffy ▶ unkempt, untidy, dishevelled, messy

scrum NOUN a group of forwards from each side in rugby football who push against each other to get possession of the ball

scrumptious ADJECTIVE (informal) delicious

scrunch VERB 1 to crunch 2 to crush or crumple

scruple NOUN a feeling of doubt about whether something is morally right

scrupulous ADJECTIVE 1 careful and conscientious 2 strictly honest or honourable

scrutinize VERB to look at carefully

⚠ SPELLING

This word can also be spelled scrutinise.

scrutiny NOUN scrutinies a careful examination of something

scuba diving NOUN swimming underwater using a tank of air strapped to your back

scuff VERB 1 to drag your feet while walking 2 to scrape with your foot

scuffle NOUN a confused fight or struggle

scuffle VERB to take part in a scuffle

scullery NOUN sculleries a small room next to a kitchen, used for washing and cleaning

sculpt VERB to make sculpture

sculptor NOUN a person who makes sculptures

sculpture NOUN 1 the art of making shapes by carving wood or stone or casting metal 2 a shape made in this way

scum NOUN froth or dirt on top of a liquid

scupper VERB to wreck plans or chances

scurf NOUN flakes of dry skin
► **scurfy** ADJECTIVE

scurrilous ADJECTIVE rude, insulting, and probably untrue

scurry VERB scurries, scurried to run with quick short steps

scurvy NOUN a disease caused by lack of vitamin C

scuttle¹ NOUN a container for coal in a house

scuttle² VERB 1 to hurry away 2 to sink a ship deliberately

scythe NOUN a tool with a long curved blade for cutting grass or corn

scythe VERB to cut with a scythe

sea NOUN 1 the salt water that covers most of the earth's surface 2 a large lake 3 a large area of something a sea of faces

seaboard NOUN a coastline or coastal region

seafaring ADJECTIVE, NOUN working or travelling on the sea
► **seafarer** NOUN

seafood NOUN fish or shellfish from the sea used as food

seagull NOUN a seabird with long wings

THESAURUS

scuff VERB • scuff the toes of your shoes ► scrape, scratch, graze

scuffle NOUN • sounds of a scuffle
► fight, brawl, tussle

sea horse NOUN a small fish that swims upright, with a head like a horse's head

seal[1] NOUN a sea mammal with thick fur or bristles

seal[2] NOUN **1** a piece of metal with an engraved design for pressing on a soft substance to leave an impression **2** this impression made on a piece of wax **3** something designed to close an opening **4** a small decorative sticker

seal VERB **1** to close something by sticking two parts together **2** to close securely **3** to press a seal on **4** to settle or decide **seal off** to prevent people getting to an area

sea level NOUN the level of the sea halfway between high and low tide

sealing wax NOUN a substance that is soft when heated but hardens when cooled, used for sealing documents

sea lion NOUN a kind of large seal

seam NOUN **1** the line where two edges of cloth or wood etc. join **2** a layer of coal in the ground

seaman NOUN a sailor

seamanship NOUN skill in seafaring

seamy ADJECTIVE **seamier**, **seamiest** sordid or unattractive

seance (say-ahns) NOUN a meeting at which people try to make contact with the dead

sear VERB to scorch or burn

search VERB to look carefully to find something ▶ **search** NOUN

search engine NOUN (ICT) a computer program that searches the Internet

searching ADJECTIVE examining closely and thoroughly

searchlight NOUN a light with a strong beam that can be turned in any direction

searing ADJECTIVE (of a pain) sharp and burning

seasick ADJECTIVE sick because of the movement of a ship

seaside NOUN a place by the sea where people go for holidays

season NOUN **1** each of the four main parts of the year (spring, summer, autumn, winter) **2** the time of year when an activity takes place

THESAURUS

seal NOUN • *the queen's seal* ▶ emblem, crest, stamp

seal VERB • *to seal an envelope* ▶ stick down, close, fasten • *to seal a jar* ▶ stop up, close, plug • *to seal the agreement* ▶ confirm, complete, clinch, settle

search VERB • *to search for clues* ▶ look, hunt, poke about, seek • *to search the woods* ▶ comb, explore • *to search the luggage* ▶ check, examine, inspect

search NOUN • *a search for somewhere to eat* ▶ look, check, hunt, exploration

a
b
c
d
e
f
g
h
i
j
k
l
m
n
o
p
q
r
s
t
u
v
w
x
y
z

season VERB **1** to give extra flavour to food **2** to dry and treat timber etc. for use

seasonal ADJECTIVE **1** for or to do with a season **2** happening in a particular season

seasoning NOUN a substance used to season food

season ticket NOUN a ticket that can be used repeatedly for a period of time

seat NOUN **1** a thing made or used for sitting on **2** a place on a council or committee, in parliament, etc. **3** the buttocks **4** the place where something is based or located

seat VERB **1** to place in or on a seat **2** to have enough seats for

seat belt NOUN a strap to hold a person securely in a seat

seating NOUN **1** the seats in a place **2** the arrangement of seats

seaweed NOUN a plant or plants that grow in the sea

seaworthy ADJECTIVE (of a ship) fit for a sea voyage ► **seaworthiness** NOUN

secateurs PLURAL NOUN clippers held in the hand for pruning plants

secede VERB to withdraw from being a member of an organization ► **secession** NOUN

secluded ADJECTIVE quiet and sheltered from view ► **seclusion** NOUN

second[1] ADJECTIVE **1** next after the first **2** another *a second chance* **3** less good *second quality* **second thoughts** doubts about a decision

second NOUN **1** a person or thing that is second **2** an attendant of a fighter in a boxing match, duel, etc. **3** one-sixtieth of a minute of time or of a degree used in measuring angles

second VERB **1** to assist someone **2** to support a proposal

second[2] (sik-ond) VERB to transfer a person temporarily to other work ► **secondment** NOUN

secondary ADJECTIVE **1** coming after or from something **2** less important

secondary colour NOUN a colour made by mixing two primary colours

secondary school NOUN a school for pupils of more than about 11 years old

second-hand ADJECTIVE bought from or used by a previous owner

secondly ADVERB in the second place; as the second one

seat NOUN • *not enough seats for everyone* ► chair, bench, sofa, stool

second ADJECTIVE • *a second chance* ► additional, extra, further, another

second NOUN • *Putting the things away will only take a second.* ► moment, instant, bit • *Chris was acting as his second.* ► assistant, attendant, right-hand man or woman

second nature NOUN behaviour that has become automatic or habitual

second-rate ADJECTIVE inferior; not very good

second sight NOUN the ability to foresee the future

secrecy NOUN the state of keeping things secret

secret ADJECTIVE 1 that must not be told or shown to other people 2 not known by everybody
► **secretly** ADVERB

secret NOUN something secret

secretary (sek-ret-ree) NOUN **secretaries** 1 a person who helps with letters, answers the telephone, etc. in an office 2 the chief assistant of a government minister or ambassador
► **secretarial** ADJECTIVE

secrete VERB 1 to hide something 2 to produce a substance in the body ► **secretion** NOUN

secretive (seek-rit-iv) ADJECTIVE liking or trying to keep things secret

sect NOUN a group of people whose beliefs differ from those of others in the same religion

sectarian (sekt-air-ee-an) ADJECTIVE belonging to or supporting a sect

section NOUN 1 a part of something 2 a cross-section

sector NOUN 1 one part of an area 2 a part of something *the private sector* 3 (Maths) a section of a circle between two lines drawn from its centre to its circumference

secular ADJECTIVE to do with worldly affairs, not with religion

secure ADJECTIVE 1 safe against attack 2 certain not to slip or fail 3 reliable ► **securely** ADVERB

secure VERB 1 to make secure 2 to fasten firmly 3 to obtain

security NOUN **securities** 1 a secure state; safety 2 precautions against theft or spying etc. 3 something given as a guarantee for a debt

sedate ADJECTIVE calm and dignified

THESAURUS

secret ADJECTIVE • *secret information* ► confidential, classified • *a secret location* ► private, secluded, hidden, remote

secretive ADJECTIVE • *very secretive about his plans*
► uncommunicative, unforthcoming, tight-lipped

section NOUN • *each section of the application form* ► part, portion
• *the reference section of your*

library ► department, part, division

secure ADJECTIVE • *secure windows*
► locked, sealed, impregnable
• *We felt secure indoors.* ► safe, protected • *The ladder needs to be made secure.* ► stable, steady, firm

secure VERB • *to secure the door*
► fasten, close, lock, shut, bolt
• *to secure a good job* ► obtain, acquire, get

sedate VERB to give a sedative to ► **sedation** NOUN

sedative NOUN a medicine that makes a person calm

sedge NOUN a grass-like plant growing in marshes or near water

sediment NOUN fine particles of solid matter at the bottom of liquid

sedimentary ADJECTIVE (of rock) formed from particles that have settled on a surface

sedition NOUN speeches or actions intended to make people rebel ► **seditious** ADJECTIVE

seduce VERB 1 to persuade a person to have sexual intercourse 2 to lead astray with temptations ► **seduction** NOUN

seductive ADJECTIVE 1 sexually attractive 2 tempting

see VERB **saw**, **seen** 1 to perceive with the eyes 2 to meet or visit 3 to understand 4 to imagine 5 to consider *shall see what we can do* 6 to make sure 7 to discover *see who it is* 8 to escort *see to* attend to

seed NOUN 1 a fertilized part of a plant, capable of growing into a new plant 2 a seeded player in a competition

seed VERB 1 to plant or sprinkle seeds in 2 to name the best players and arrange for them not to play against each other in the early rounds of a tournament

seedling NOUN a young plant growing from a seed

seedy ADJECTIVE **seedier**, **seediest** 1 full of seeds 2 shabby and disreputable

seeing CONJUNCTION considering

seek VERB **sought** 1 to search for 2 to try to do or obtain something

seem VERB to give the impression of being something

seemly ADJECTIVE (old use) (of behaviour etc.) proper or suitable

seep VERB to ooze slowly out or through something ► **seepage** NOUN

THESAURUS

see VERB • *Did you see that?*
► catch sight of, glimpse, discern, make out, recognize • *could see how difficult it was* ► understand, realize, grasp • *shall see what we can do* ► consider, think about, decide • *can see trouble ahead* ► foresee, envisage, imagine • *went to see the doctor* ► visit, consult, talk to • *I saw an old friend in town.* ► meet, encounter, run into • *offered to see her home* ► take, escort, accompany • *must see what the dog is up to* ► find

out, discover, ascertain **see to** • *to see to the repairs* ► attend to, deal with, sort out, organize

seek VERB • *to seek the enemy*
► look for, search for, pursue, hunt • *to seek advice* ► ask for, get • *seeking compensation* ► request, try to obtain • *We seek to please.* ► try, attempt

seem VERB • *seemed too afraid to speak* ► appear, look, sound

seep VERB • *Smoke seeped into the room.* ► leak, ooze, escape, trickle

a
b
c
d
e
f
g
h
i
j
k
l
m
n
o
p
q
r
s
t
u
v
w
x
y
z

DICTIONARY

seer NOUN a prophet

see-saw NOUN a plank balanced in the middle so that two people can sit, one on each end, and make it go up and down

seethe VERB 1 to be angry or excited 2 to bubble and surge like water boiling

segment NOUN a part that is separated from other parts

segregate VERB 1 to separate people of different religions, races, etc. 2 to isolate a person or thing ▶ **segregation** NOUN

seismic (sy-zmik) ADJECTIVE to do with earthquakes

seize VERB 1 to take hold of suddenly or forcibly 2 to take possession of by force or by legal authority 3 to take eagerly 4 to have a sudden effect on *Panic seized us.* **seize up** to become jammed

seizure NOUN 1 the act of seizing 2 a sudden fit, as in epilepsy or a heart attack

seldom ADVERB rarely; not often

select VERB to choose a person or thing

select ADJECTIVE 1 carefully chosen 2 (of a club etc.) choosing its members carefully

selection NOUN 1 the process of selecting 2 a person or thing selected 3 a group selected from a larger group 4 a range of goods from which to choose

selective ADJECTIVE choosing or chosen carefully ▶ **selectively** ADVERB

self NOUN **selves** 1 a person as an individual 2 a person's particular nature *is her old self again*

self-centred ADJECTIVE concerned only with yourself; selfish

self-confident ADJECTIVE confident of your own abilities

self-conscious ADJECTIVE embarrassed or awkward in the presence of other people

self-contained ADJECTIVE (of accommodation) complete in itself

self-control NOUN the ability to control your own behaviour ▶ **self-controlled** ADJECTIVE

self-defence NOUN 1 the process of defending yourself 2 techniques for doing this

THESAURUS

seize VERB • *seized her arm* ▶ grab, snatch • *to seize the enemy's camp* ▶ capture, take • *Officers seized the stolen goods.* ▶ confiscate, impound

seldom ADVERB • *was seldom away for long* ▶ rarely, not often

select VERB • *to select a book* ▶ choose, pick, appoint, vote

for, nominate, decide on, elect

selective ADJECTIVE • *very selective in their reading* ▶ discerning, discriminating, careful

self-conscious ADJECTIVE • *self-conscious about asking* ▶ embarrassed, bashful, awkward, uncomfortable

a
b
c
d
e
f
g
h
i
j
k
l
m
n
o
p
q
r
s
t
u
v
w
x
y
z

a
b
c
d
e
f
g
h
i
j
k
l
m
n
o
p
q
r
s
t
u
v
w
x
y
z

self-employed ADJECTIVE working independently, not for an employer

self-evident ADJECTIVE obvious and not needing proof

self-important ADJECTIVE having a high opinion of yourself; pompous

selfish ADJECTIVE doing what you want and not thinking of other people ▸ **selfishly** ADVERB

selfless ADJECTIVE thinking of other people; considerate

self-made ADJECTIVE rich or successful from your own efforts

self-raising ADJECTIVE (of flour) making cakes rise without needing to have baking powder etc. added

self-respect NOUN respect for yourself

self-righteous ADJECTIVE smugly sure that you are behaving virtuously

selfsame ADJECTIVE the very same

self-satisfied ADJECTIVE very pleased with yourself

self-service ADJECTIVE at which customers serve themselves

sell VERB **sold 1** to exchange something for money **2** to have something available for people to buy **3** to be on sale at a certain price *It sells for £5.99.* ▸ **seller** NOUN

sell-by date NOUN a date marked on a product, after which it should not be sold

sell-out NOUN an entertainment etc. for which all the tickets have been sold

selves plural of **self**

semantic (sim-an-tik) ADJECTIVE to do with the meanings of words ▸ **semantically** ADVERB

semaphore NOUN a system of signalling by holding flags out with the arms in positions indicating letters of the alphabet

semblance NOUN an outward appearance or apparent likeness

semen (seem-en) NOUN a white liquid produced by males and containing sperm

semibreve NOUN the longest musical note normally used (𝅝), lasting four times as long as a crotchet

semicircle NOUN half a circle ▸ **semicircular** ADJECTIVE

semicolon NOUN a punctuation mark (;) used to mark a break that is stronger than a comma

semiconductor NOUN a substance that can conduct electricity but not as well as most metals do

semi-detached ADJECTIVE (of a house) joined to another house on one side only

THESAURUS

selfish ADJECTIVE • *a selfish attitude* ▸ self-centred, inconsiderate, egocentric

sell VERB • *The shop sells basic provisions.* ▸ stock, trade in, deal in • *to sell a house* ▸ put on the market, dispose of

semifinal NOUN a match or round whose winner will take part in the final

seminar NOUN a meeting for advanced discussion and research on a subject

semiquaver NOUN a note in music (♬), equal in length to one quarter of a crotchet

semi-skimmed ADJECTIVE (of milk) having had some of the cream taken out

Semitic (sim-it-ik) ADJECTIVE to do with the Semites, the group of people that includes the Jews and Arabs

semitone NOUN half a tone in music

semolina NOUN hard round grains of wheat used to make milk puddings and pasta

senate NOUN 1 the governing council in ancient Rome 2 the upper house of the parliament of the United States, France, and other countries ► **senator** NOUN

send VERB sent 1 to make a person or thing go or be taken

somewhere 2 to cause to become *was sending me crazy* **send for** to order to come or be brought ► **sender** NOUN

senile ADJECTIVE weak and forgetful because of old age ► **senility** NOUN

senior ADJECTIVE 1 older than someone else 2 higher in rank 3 for older children *a senior school* ► **seniority** NOUN

senior NOUN 1 a person who is older or higher in rank 2 a member of a senior school

senior citizen NOUN an elderly person, especially a pensioner

senna NOUN the dried pods or leaves of a tropical tree, used as a laxative

sensation NOUN 1 a feeling 2 an excited condition or a cause of this

sensational ADJECTIVE causing great excitement or interest ► **sensationally** ADVERB

sense NOUN 1 the ability to see, hear, smell, touch, or taste 2 the ability to feel or appreciate something 3 the power to think or make decisions 4 meaning

THESAURUS

send VERB • *I'll send you a letter.*
► post, mail, dispatch, forward
• *to send a satellite into orbit*
► launch, propel, shoot • *was sending me crazy* ► make, drive
send for • *to send for the police*
► call, fetch, summon

sensation NOUN • *a sensation of floating* ► feeling, sense, impression • *to cause a sensation*

► commotion, excitement, stir, scandal

sensational ADJECTIVE • *a sensational murder trial*
► shocking, horrifying, scandalous • *Her singing was sensational.* ► amazing, extraordinary, remarkable, wonderful

sense NOUN • *a sense of guilt*
► feeling, awareness, sensation

a
b
c
d
e
f
g
h
i
j
k
l
m
n
o
p
q
r
s
t
u
v
w
x
y
z

663

a b c d e f g h i j k l m n o p q r **s** t u v w x y z

DICTIONARY

sense VERB **1** to feel; to get an impression **2** to detect

senseless ADJECTIVE **1** not showing good sense **2** unconscious

sensibility NOUN **sensibilities** sensitiveness or delicate feeling

sensible ADJECTIVE having or showing good sense ▶ **sensibly** ADVERB

sensitive ADJECTIVE **1** strongly affected by something *sensitive to light* **2** receiving impressions quickly and easily *sensitive fingers* **3** easily hurt or offended **4** considerate about other people's feelings **5** needing to be dealt with tactfully *a sensitive subject* ▶ **sensitively** ADVERB, **sensitivity** NOUN

sensitize VERB to make a thing sensitive to something

⚠️ **SPELLING**

This word can also be spelled *sensitise*.

sensor NOUN a device or instrument for detecting a physical property such as light, heat, or sound

sensory ADJECTIVE **1** to do with the senses **2** receiving sensations

sensual ADJECTIVE **1** to do with physical pleasure **2** liking or suggesting physical or sexual pleasures

sensuous ADJECTIVE giving pleasure to the senses, especially by being beautiful or delicate

sentence NOUN **1** a group of words that express a complete thought and form a statement, question, exclamation, or command **2** the punishment announced to a convicted person in a lawcourt

sentence VERB to give someone a sentence in a lawcourt

sentiment NOUN **1** an opinion **2** sentimentality

sentimental ADJECTIVE showing or arousing excessive feelings of

THESAURUS

• They had the sense to leave.
▶ wisdom, common sense, intelligence *• no sense in saying anything* ▶ point, purpose *• the sense of the message* ▶ meaning, significance

sense VERB *• We sensed that they didn't trust us.* ▶ feel, suspect, realize, get the impression

senseless ADJECTIVE *• a senseless crime* ▶ pointless, futile, needless, silly, foolish, stupid *• He was knocked senseless.*
▶ unconscious, comatose, out cold

sensible ADJECTIVE *• a sensible person* ▶ wise, prudent, careful, shrewd, intelligent *• sensible clothes* ▶ practical, functional, comfortable

sensitive ADJECTIVE *• sensitive to light* ▶ responsive, susceptible, affected (by) *• sensitive handling of the problem* ▶ tactful, thoughtful, considerate, sympathetic *• a sensitive person* ▶ emotional, easily upset

sentimental ADJECTIVE *• a sentimental attachment to their old home* ▶ emotional, nostalgic

sadness, pity, etc.
► **sentimentality** NOUN

sentinel NOUN a guard or sentry

sentry NOUN **sentries** a soldier on guard duty

sepal NOUN each of the leaves forming the calyx of a bud

separable ADJECTIVE able to be separated

separate (sep-er-at) ADJECTIVE **1** not joined to anything **2** not shared
► **separately** ADVERB

separate (sep-er-ayt) VERB **1** to make or keep separate **2** to become separate **3** to stop living together as a couple
► **separation** NOUN

September NOUN the ninth month of the year

septet NOUN **1** a group of seven musicians **2** a piece of music for seven musicians

septic ADJECTIVE infected with harmful bacteria that cause pus to form

sequel NOUN **1** a book or film etc. that continues the story of an earlier one **2** something that

follows or results from an earlier event

sequence NOUN **1** the order in which things happen **2** a series of things

sequin NOUN a tiny bright disc sewn on clothes etc. to decorate them

serenade NOUN a song or tune of a kind played by a man under his lover's window

serenade VERB to sing or play a serenade

serene ADJECTIVE calm and peaceful
► **serenity** (ser-en-iti) NOUN

serf NOUN a farm labourer who worked for a landowner in the Middle Ages, and who was not allowed to leave ► **serfdom** NOUN

sergeant (sar-jent) NOUN a soldier or policeman in charge of others

sergeant major NOUN a soldier who is one rank higher than a sergeant

serial NOUN a story or film etc. that is presented in separate parts

⚠ **USAGE**
Do not confuse this word with *cereal*.

THESAURUS

• *a sentimental story* ► maudlin, mawkish, soppy

separate ADJECTIVE • *tried to keep the two groups separate* ► apart, segregated, divided, isolated • *a separate kitchen* ► distinct, detached

separate VERB • *It was difficult to separate them.* ► divide, part, break up, split up • *We separated at the station and I went home.*

► part company, split up • *His parents separated.* ► split up, break up, divorce

sequel NOUN • *a sequel to the novel* ► continuation • *the immediate sequel* ► consequence, result, upshot

sequence NOUN • *the sequence of events* ► succession, order, progression, series

DICTIONARY

series NOUN series **1** a number of things following or connected with each other **2** a number of separate radio or television programmes with the same characters or on the same subject

serious ADJECTIVE **1** solemn and thoughtful **2** needing careful thought **3** sincere *a serious attempt* **4** causing anxiety *a serious accident* ▸ **seriously** ADVERB

sermon NOUN a talk given by a preacher as part of a religious service

serpent NOUN a snake

serrated ADJECTIVE having a notched edge

serum (seer-um) NOUN the thin pale yellow liquid that remains from blood when the rest has clotted and that contains antibodies

servant NOUN a person who works or serves in someone else's house

serve VERB **1** to work for a person or organization or country etc. **2** to sell things to people in a shop **3** to give out food at a meal **4** to spend time doing something **5** to be suitable for something *will serve our purpose* **6** to start play in tennis etc. by hitting the ball *it serves you right* you deserve it

serve NOUN a service in tennis etc.

server NOUN **1** a person or thing that serves **2** (ICT) a computer or program that controls or supplies information to several computers in a network

service NOUN **1** the activity of working for a person or organization or country etc. **2** something that supplies a need *a bus service* **3** the army, navy, or air force *the armed services* **4** a religious ceremony **5** provision of goods, food, etc. **6** a set of dishes and plates etc. for a meal **7** maintenance of a vehicle or machine etc. **8** the action of serving in tennis etc.

service VERB **1** to repair or keep a vehicle or machine etc. in working order **2** to supply with services

THESAURUS

series NOUN • *a series of kidnappings* ▸ succession, sequence, string, chain, spate

serious ADJECTIVE • *a serious expression* ▸ solemn, grave, earnest, thoughtful • *a serious disagreement* ▸ important, significant, urgent, crucial, grave • *serious injuries* ▸ severe, critical, bad, acute, terrible, grave • *serious about leaving* ▸ sincere, in earnest, genuine

servant NOUN • *a servant carrying a tray* ▸ attendant, valet, butler, maid

serve VERB • *to serve a master* ▸ attend, assist, look after • *will serve our purpose* ▸ fulfil, satisfy • *to serve food* ▸ give out, dish up, provide

service NOUN • *the terms of service* ▸ employment, work, duty • *a church service* ▸ ceremony

service VERB • *to service a car* ▸ maintain, repair, check

DICTIONARY

serviceable ADJECTIVE suitable for ordinary use or wear

service station NOUN a place beside a road, where petrol and various services are available

serviette NOUN a piece of cloth or paper used to keep your clothes or hands clean at a meal

servile ADJECTIVE too willing to serve or obey others ► **servility** NOUN

serving NOUN a helping of food

sesame NOUN an African plant with seeds that can be eaten or used to make an edible oil

session NOUN 1 a meeting or series of meetings 2 a time spent doing one thing *a recording session*

set VERB **set** 1 to put or fix 2 to make ready to work *to set the alarm* 3 to make or become firm or hard 4 to give someone a task 5 to put into a condition *set them free* 6 (of the sun) to go down below the horizon **set off** or **out** to begin a journey **set up** to arrange or organize

set NOUN 1 a group of people or things that belong together 2 a radio or television receiver 3 (*Maths*) a collection of things that have a common property 4 the scenery or stage for a play or film 5 a group of games in a tennis match 6 a badger's burrow

set ADJECTIVE 1 fixed or arranged in advance 2 ready or prepared to do something **set on** determined about

setback NOUN something that stops progress or slows it down

set square NOUN a device shaped like a right-angled triangle, used in drawing parallel lines etc.

settee NOUN a long soft seat with a back and arms

setter NOUN a dog of a long-haired breed that can be trained to stand rigid when it scents game

setting NOUN 1 the way or place in which something is set 2 music for the words of a song etc. 3 a set of cutlery or crockery for one person at a meal

settle VERB 1 to arrange or decide 2 to make or become calm or

THESAURUS

set VERB • *to set the bags on the table* ► put, place, deposit, position • *to set a date* ► fix, decide on, agree on • *The sun was setting.* ► go down, sink • *The jelly has set.* ► harden, solidify **set off** or **out** • *We set off for the airport.* ► start out, leave, depart

set NOUN • *a set of new proposals* ► collection, group, series, batch

• *a fashionable set of people*
► circle, clique, group, crowd

settle VERB • *to settle a dispute* ► resolve, clear up, put an end to, find a solution to • *to settle their affairs* ► sort out, put in order • *A bird settled on a branch.* ► land, alight • *to settle your nerves* ► calm, soothe

comfortable or orderly **3** to go and live somewhere **4** to come to rest on something **5** to pay a bill or debt

settlement NOUN **1** the act of settling something **2** the way something is settled **3** a small number of settlements or houses in a new area

settler NOUN one of the first people to settle in a new country

set-up NOUN (*informal*) the way something is organized or arranged

seven NOUN, ADJECTIVE the number 7 ► **seventh** ADJECTIVE & NOUN

seventeen NOUN, ADJECTIVE the number 17 ► **seventeenth** ADJECTIVE & NOUN

seventy NOUN, ADJECTIVE the **seventies** the number 70 ► **seventieth** ADJECTIVE & NOUN

sever VERB to cut or break off ► **severance** NOUN

several ADJECTIVE, NOUN more than two but not many

severally ADVERB separately

severe ADJECTIVE **1** strict; not gentle or kind **2** intense or forceful *severe*

weather **3** very plain ► **severely** ADVERB, **severity** NOUN

sew VERB sewn or sewed **1** to join things together by using a needle and thread **2** to work with a needle and thread or with a sewing machine

⚠ **USAGE**

Do not confuse this word with sow.

sewage (soo-ij) NOUN liquid waste matter carried away in drains

sewer (soo-er) NOUN a large underground drain for carrying away sewage

sex NOUN **1** each of the two groups (*male* and *female*) into which living things are placed according to their functions in the process of reproduction **2** sexual intercourse

sexism NOUN discrimination against people of a particular sex ► **sexist** ADJECTIVE & NOUN

sextant NOUN an instrument for measuring the angle of the sun and stars, used for finding a position when navigating

sextet NOUN **1** a group of six musicians **2** a piece of music for six musicians

THESAURUS

sever VERB • *to sever an arm* ► cut off, chop off, amputate, remove • *to sever relations* ► break off, end

several ADJECTIVE • *did it several times* ► many, some, a number of, a few, various

severe ADJECTIVE • *a severe threat of starvation* ► serious, acute, grave

• *severe weather* ► harsh, extreme, stormy • *a severe pain* ► acute, intense, painful, excruciating • *a severe test of their stamina* ► demanding, difficult • *severe criticism* ► fierce, harsh, scathing • *severe penalties* ► strict, harsh, draconian • *furnishings in a severe style* ► plain, simple, stark

DICTIONARY

sexual ADJECTIVE **1** to do with sex or the sexes **2** (of reproduction) happening by the fusion of male and female cells ▶ **sexuality** NOUN, **sexually** ADVERB

sexual intercourse NOUN the physical act in which a man puts his erect penis into a woman's vagina and sends semen into her womb

sexy ADJECTIVE **sexier, sexiest** (informal) sexually attractive or exciting

shabby ADJECTIVE **shabbier, shabbiest 1** in a poor or worn-out condition **2** poorly dressed **3** unfair or dishonourable *a shabby trick* ▶ **shabbily** ADVERB

shack NOUN a roughly-built hut

shackle NOUN an iron ring for fastening a prisoner's wrist or ankle

shackle VERB **1** to put shackles on a prisoner **2** to restrict or limit someone

shade NOUN **1** slight darkness when light is blocked **2** a device that reduces or shuts out bright light **3** a colour; the strength of a colour **4** a slight difference

shade VERB **1** to shelter something from bright light **2** to make part of a drawing darker **3** to move gradually from one state or quality to another *evening shading into night* ▶ **shading** NOUN

shadow NOUN **1** the dark shape that falls on a surface when something is between the surface and a light **2** an area of shade **3** a slight trace ▶ **shadowy** ADJECTIVE

shadow VERB **1** to cast a shadow on something **2** to follow a person secretly

shady ADJECTIVE **shadier, shadiest 1** giving shade *a shady tree* **2** in the shade *a shady place* **3** (informal) not completely honest *a shady deal*

shaft NOUN **1** a long slender rod or straight part **2** a ray of light **3** a deep narrow hole

THESAURUS

shabby ADJECTIVE • *shabby clothes* ▶ worn, scruffy, ragged • *a shabby coffee bar* ▶ run-down, scruffy, seedy

shade NOUN • *to lie in the shade* ▶ shadow, shelter • *the shade of evening* ▶ darkness, twilight, gloominess • *a shade over the window* ▶ blind, screen, curtain • *a shade of blue* ▶ hue, tinge, tone, colour

shadow NOUN • *He lingered in the shadow.* ▶ shade, darkness,

gloom • *a shadow on the wall* ▶ silhouette, outline, shape • *not a shadow of doubt* ▶ trace, scrap, shred

shady ADJECTIVE • *a shady footpath* ▶ shaded, shadowy, dark, sunless • *shady deals* ▶ dubious, suspicious, dishonest

shaft NOUN • *a wooden shaft* ▶ pole, rod, stick, post • *a shaft of light* ▶ ray, beam • *a shaft in a mine* ▶ passage, tunnel

shaggy ADJECTIVE **shaggier, shaggiest 1** having long rough hair or fibre **2** (of hair) thick and untidy

shah NOUN the title of the former ruler of Iran

shake VERB **shook, shaken 1** to move quickly up and down or from side to side **2** to shock or upset **3** (of the voice) to tremble

shake NOUN **1** a shaking movement **2** (informal) a milkshake

shaky ADJECTIVE **shakier, shakiest** unsteady or wobbly ▸ **shakily** ADVERB

shale NOUN a kind of stone that splits easily into layers

shall AUXILIARY VERB **1** used with I and we to refer to the future *I shall arrive tomorrow.* **2** used with I and we in questions or suggestions *Shall I shut the door?* **3** used for emphasis *You shall go.*

shallot NOUN a kind of small onion

shallow ADJECTIVE **shallower, shallowest 1** not deep *shallow water* **2** not capable of deep feelings *a shallow character*

shallows PLURAL NOUN a shallow part of a stretch of water

sham NOUN something that is not genuine; a pretence ▸ **sham** ADJECTIVE

sham VERB **shamming, shammed** to pretend

shamble VERB to walk or run in a lazy or awkward way

shambles NOUN a scene of great disorder or bloodshed

shambolic ADJECTIVE (informal) chaotic or disorganized

shame NOUN **1** a feeling of sorrow or guilt for an action **2** dishonour or disgrace **3** something you regret

shame VERB make a person feel ashamed

shamefaced ADJECTIVE looking ashamed

shameful ADJECTIVE disgraceful ▸ **shamefully** ADVERB

THESAURUS

shaggy ADJECTIVE • *a shaggy coat* ▸ thick, hairy, bushy, woolly, fleecy

shake VERB • *The building seemed to shake.* ▸ tremble, quiver, shudder, shiver, judder, wobble • *She shook her umbrella at them.* ▸ wave, waggle, brandish • *The news shook them.* ▸ shock, startle, upset, alarm

shaky ADJECTIVE • *a shaky table* ▸ unsteady, wobbly, rickety • *a shaky voice* ▸ quavering, unsteady

sham NOUN • *Their appearance was a sham.* ▸ pretence, act, fraud

shame NOUN • *the shame of being found out* ▸ humiliation, disgrace, remorse, embarrassment

shame VERB • *to be shamed in public* ▸ humiliate, mortify, embarrass • *to shame the family name* ▸ discredit, degrade, taint, tarnish

shameful ADJECTIVE • *a shameful waste* ▸ disgraceful, deplorable, scandalous

a
b
c
d
e
f
g
h
i
j
k
l
m
n
o
p
q
r
s
t
u
v
w
x
y
z

shameless ADJECTIVE not showing any shame ► **shamelessly** ADVERB

shampoo NOUN **shampoos** 1 a liquid for washing the hair 2 a substance for cleaning a carpet etc. 3 a wash with shampoo

shampoo VERB **shampoos**, **shampooed** to wash or clean with a shampoo

> **WORD HISTORY**
> originally 'to massage', from Hindi *champo* 'to press'

shamrock NOUN a plant like clover, the national emblem of Ireland

shank NOUN 1 the leg from the knee to the ankle 2 a long narrow part

shan't shall not

shanty NOUN **shanties** 1 a crude dwelling or shack 2 a sailors' song with a chorus

shanty town NOUN a settlement consisting of shanties

shape NOUN 1 a thing's outline; the appearance an outline produces 2 proper form or condition 3 the general form or condition of something

shape VERB 1 to make into a particular shape 2 to develop

shapeless ADJECTIVE having no definite shape

shapely ADJECTIVE **shapelier**, **shapeliest** having an attractive shape

share NOUN 1 a part given to one person or thing out of something that is divided 2 each of the equal parts forming a business company's capital

share VERB 1 to give portions of something to two or more people 2 to have or use or experience something jointly with others

shareholder NOUN a person who owns shares in a company

shark NOUN a large sea fish with sharp teeth 2 a person who exploits or cheats people

sharp ADJECTIVE 1 with an edge or point that can cut or make holes 2 quick at noticing or learning things 3 clear or distinct 4 steep or pointed *a sharp bend* 5 forceful or severe *a sharp pain* 6 loud and shrill *a sharp cry* 7 slightly sour 8 (*Music*) one semitone higher than the natural note *C sharp*

THESAURUS

shape NOUN • *the shape of the room* ► form, outline, profile, silhouette • *in good shape* ► condition, health, state

shape VERB • *to shape clay* ► form, fashion, mould

share NOUN • *a share of the profits* ► portion, part, division, allocation, allowance

share VERB • *to share the costs* ► divide, split, distribute, apportion, allocate

sharp ADJECTIVE • *a sharp pain* ► acute, intense, fierce, severe, stabbing • *a sharp wind* ► cold, bitter, biting • *sharp words* ► harsh, cutting, scathing • *a sharp image* ► distinct, clear, crisp • *a sharp mind* ► intelligent, perceptive

sharp ADVERB **1** sharply *Turn sharp right.* **2** punctually or precisely *at six o'clock sharp*

sharp NOUN (*Music*) a note one semitone higher than the natural note; the sign (#) that indicates this

sharpen VERB to make or become sharp ▶ **sharpener** NOUN

sharp practice NOUN dishonest or barely honest dealings

shatter VERB **1** to break violently into small pieces **2** to destroy hopes etc. **3** to upset greatly

shave VERB **1** to cut growing hair off the skin with a razor **2** to cut or scrape a thin slice off something ▶ **shaver** NOUN

shave NOUN the act of shaving the face **a close shave** (*informal*) a narrow escape

shaven ADJECTIVE shaved

shavings PLURAL NOUN thin strips shaved off a piece of wood or metal

shawl NOUN a piece of material worn round the shoulders or head or wrapped round a baby

she PRONOUN the female person or animal being talked about

sheaf NOUN **1** a bundle of cornstalks tied together **2** a

bundle of arrows, papers, etc. held together

shear VERB **sheared** or, *in sense 1,* **shorn 1** to cut or trim, especially wool from a sheep **2** to break because of a sideways force ▶ **shearer** NOUN

⚠ USAGE

Do not confuse this word with *sheer*.

shears PLURAL NOUN a large pair of scissors used for cutting grass etc.

sheath NOUN **1** a cover for the blade of a knife or sword etc. **2** a close-fitting cover **3** a condom

sheathe VERB to put into a sheath or cover

shed[1] NOUN a simple building used for storing things or as a workshop

shed[2] VERB **shedding, shed 1** to let something fall or flow **2** to get rid of

sheen NOUN a shine or gloss

sheep NOUN **sheep** an animal that eats grass and has a thick fleecy coat, kept in flocks for its wool and its meat

sheepdog NOUN a dog trained to guard and herd sheep

sheepish ADJECTIVE embarrassed or ashamed

sheer ADJECTIVE **1** complete or thorough *sheer stupidity*

shatter VERB • *The glass shattered.*
▶ break, smash, splinter, crack
• *Their hopes were shattered.*
▶ destroy, wreck, ruin, dash

shed NOUN • *a garden shed* ▶ hut, shack, shelter

shed VERB • *A lorry had shed its load.* ▶ spill, drop, scatter

sheer ADJECTIVE • *sheer stupidity*
▶ utter, complete, absolute, total • *a sheer drop* ▶ vertical, abrupt

DICTIONARY

2 vertical *a sheer drop* **3** (of material) thin and transparent

sheer VERB to swerve or move sharply away

⚠ **USAGE**

Do not confuse this word with **shear**.

sheet NOUN **1** a large piece of lightweight material used in pairs on a bed **2** a whole flat piece of paper, glass, or metal **3** a wide area of water, ice, flame, etc.

sheikh (shayk) NOUN an Arab chief

shelf NOUN **shelves** **1** a flat piece of hard material fixed to a wall or in a piece of furniture for placing things on **2** a flat level surface that sticks out

shell NOUN **1** the hard outer covering of an egg, nut, etc., or of an animal such as a snail, crab, or tortoise **2** the walls or framework of a building, ship, etc. **3** a metal case filled with explosive, fired from a large gun

shell VERB **1** to take something out of its shell **2** to fire explosive shells at

shellfish NOUN **shellfish** a sea animal that has a shell

shelter NOUN **1** a structure that protects people from rain, wind, danger, etc. **2** protection

shelter VERB **1** to provide with shelter **2** to protect **3** to find a shelter

shelve VERB **1** to put things on shelves **2** to postpone or reject a plan etc. **3** to slope

shepherd NOUN a person who looks after sheep

shepherd VERB to guide or direct people

shepherd's pie NOUN a dish of minced beef or lamb covered with mashed potato

sherbet NOUN a fizzy sweet powder or drink

sheriff NOUN the chief law officer of a county

sherry NOUN **sherries** a kind of strong wine

shield NOUN **1** a large piece of metal, wood, etc. carried to protect the body in fighting **2** a

THESAURUS

sheet NOUN • *a sheet of paper*
► piece, page • *a sheet of glass*
► pane, panel • *a sheet of ice*
► layer, film, covering, surface

shell NOUN • *a hard shell* ► case, casing, crust, husk • *the shell of a building* ► frame, framework, skeleton

shelter NOUN • *a shelter against the wind* ► shield, screen, barrier • *to provide shelter* ► protection, refuge, sanctuary, safety • *a*

shelter for the homeless
► sanctuary, refuge, haven

shelter VERB • *The hut sheltered us from the storm.* ► protect, keep safe, shield, cover, screen • *The walkers sheltered in doorways.*
► take shelter, seek protection, take cover • *to shelter someone on the run* ► hide, harbour

shield NOUN • *a shield against corrosion* ► protection, barrier, defence

DICTIONARY

model of a triangular shield used as a trophy **3** a protection

shield VERB to protect from harm or discovery

shift VERB **1** to move or cause to move **2** (of an opinion or situation) to change slightly

shift NOUN **1** a change of position or condition **2** a group of workers who start work as another group finishes **3** a straight dress with no waist

shifty ADJECTIVE evasive; untrustworthy ► **shiftily** ADVERB

shilling NOUN a former British coin, equal to 5p

shilly-shally VERB **shilly-shallies, shilly-shallied** to be indecisive

shimmer VERB to shine with a quivering light ► **shimmer** NOUN

shin NOUN the front of the leg between the knee and the ankle

shin VERB **shinning, shinned** to climb by using the arms and legs

shine VERB **shone** or, in sense 4, **shined 1** to give out or reflect light; be bright **2** to be excellent **3** to aim a light **4** to polish *Have you shined your shoes?*

shine NOUN **1** brightness **2** a polish

shingle NOUN pebbles on a beach

shingles NOUN an infectious disease producing a painful rash

shiny ADJECTIVE **shinier, shiniest** shining or glossy

ship NOUN a large boat for journeys sea

ship VERB **shipping, shipped** to transport goods etc., especially by ship

shipment NOUN **1** the process of shipping goods **2** an amount shipped

shipping NOUN **1** ships *a danger to shipping* **2** the transporting of goods by ship

shipshape ADJECTIVE in good order; tidy

shipwreck NOUN **1** the wrecking of a ship by storm or accident **2** a wrecked ship ► **shipwrecked** ADJECTIVE

shipyard NOUN a place where ships are built or repaired

shire NOUN a county

shirk VERB to avoid work or a duty ► **shirker** NOUN

THESAURUS

shield VERB • *to shield the eyes from the sun* ► protect, shade, screen, cover

shift VERB • *to shift furniture* ► move, rearrange, reposition • *Their opinions had shifted.* ► change, alter

shine VERB • *The sun shone.* ► beam, gleam, glow, glint,

sparkle, flash • *to shine shoes* ► polish, brush, buff • *one thing they all shone at* ► excel, stand out

shine NOUN • *a shine on the furniture* ► polish, sheen, lustre

shiny ADJECTIVE • *shiny black boots* ► bright, glossy, gleaming, shining, polished

DICTIONARY

shirt NOUN a piece of light clothing for the top half of the body, with a collar and sleeves

shirty ADJECTIVE **shirtier, shirtiest** (informal) annoyed; irritable

shiver VERB to tremble with cold or fear ► **shiver** NOUN, **shivery** ADJECTIVE

shoal NOUN a large number of fish swimming together

shock NOUN 1 a sudden unpleasant surprise 2 great weakness caused by pain or injury etc. 3 the effect of a violent shake or knock 4 an effect caused by electric current passing through the body 5 a bushy mass of hair

shock VERB 1 to give someone a shock 2 to seem improper or scandalous to

shock absorber NOUN a device for absorbing jolts and vibrations in a vehicle

shocking ADJECTIVE 1 causing indignation or disgust 2 (informal) very bad *shocking weather*

shock wave NOUN a sharp change in pressure in the air around an explosion or an object moving very quickly

shod past tense of **shoe**

shoddy ADJECTIVE **shoddier, shoddiest** badly made or done *shoddy work*

shoe NOUN 1 a stiff covering for the foot 2 a horseshoe 3 something shaped or used like a shoe

shoe VERB **shoes, shoeing, shod** to fit with a shoe or shoes

shoehorn NOUN a curved piece of stiff material for easing on a shoe

shoelace NOUN a cord for lacing up and fastening a shoe

shoo VERB **shoos, shooed** to frighten or drive away

shoot VERB **shot** 1 to fire a gun or missile etc. 2 to hurt or kill by shooting 3 to move or send very quickly 4 to kick or hit a ball at a goal 5 to film or photograph

shoot NOUN a new growth on a plant

shooting star NOUN a meteor

shop NOUN 1 a building where goods are sold 2 a workshop

THESAURUS

shiver VERB • *shivering in the cold*
► tremble, quiver, shake

shock NOUN • *the shock of an explosion* ► impact, blow, vibration • *The news came as a shock.* ► blow, upset, surprise, bombshell • *It gave him a shock.* ► surprise, fright, scare, jolt • *in a state of shock* ► trauma, distress

shock VERB • *a brutal attack that shocked the community* ► horrify, appal, stun, outrage, disgust

shocking ADJECTIVE • *the whole shocking story* ► horrifying, appalling, terrible, distressing, upsetting

shoddy ADJECTIVE • *shoddy work* ► careless, slapdash • *shoddy goods* ► poor-quality, cheap, trashy

shoot VERB • *shot him from a window* ► hit, kill, gun down, snipe at • *A motorcycle shot past.* ► race, dash, zoom, fly, rush

a
b
c
d
e
f
g
h
i
j
k
l
m
n
o
p
q
r
s
t
u
v
w
x
y
z

shop VERB **shopping**, **shopped** to buy things in shops ► **shopper** NOUN

shop floor NOUN the workers in a factory

shopkeeper NOUN a person who owns or manages a shop

shoplifter NOUN a person who steals from a shop ► **shoplifting** NOUN

shopping NOUN **1** the activity of buying goods in shops **2** goods bought

shop steward NOUN a trade-union official who represents fellow workers

shore¹ NOUN the land along the edge of a sea or of a lake

shore² VERB to prop up with beams etc.

shorn past participle of **shear**

short ADJECTIVE **1** not long in distance or time **2** not tall **3** not having enough of something **4** bad-tempered; curt **5** (of pastry) rich and crumbly because it contains a lot of fat

short ADVERB abruptly; suddenly *stopped short*

shortage NOUN a lack or scarcity

shortbread NOUN a rich sweet biscuit, made with butter

short circuit NOUN a fault in an electrical circuit in which current flows along a shorter route than the normal one

short-circuit VERB to cause a short circuit

shortcoming NOUN a fault or failure to reach a good standard

short cut NOUN a route or method that is quicker than the usual one

shorten VERB to make or become shorter

shortfall NOUN an amount less than needed or expected

shorthand NOUN a set of special signs for writing words down as quickly as people say them

shortlist NOUN a list of the most suitable people or things, from which a final choice will be made

shortlist VERB to put on a shortlist

shortly ADVERB **1** in a short time; soon **2** in a few words **3** curtly

shorts PLURAL NOUN trousers with legs that stop at or above the knee

short-sighted ADJECTIVE **1** unable to see things at a distance clearly **2** lacking imagination or foresight

short ADJECTIVE • *a short piece of string* ► small, little • *a short person* ► small, little, petite, diminutive • *a short account of the trip* ► brief, concise • *a short look* ► cursory, fleeting, momentary • *Supplies were short.* ► low, scant • *a short manner* ► curt, abrupt, sharp

shortage NOUN • *a shortage of water* ► scarcity, lack

shorten VERB • *to shorten an essay* ► cut down, reduce, cut, abridge

shortly ADVERB • *shortly afterwards* ► soon, presently, directly

676

DICTIONARY

short-tempered ADJECTIVE irritable

short-term ADJECTIVE to do with a short period of time

short wave NOUN a radio wave of a wavelength between 10 and 100 metres and a frequency of about 3 to 30 megahertz

shot[1] past tense of **shoot**

shot[2] NOUN **1** the firing of a gun or missile etc. **2** something fired from a gun **3** a person judged by skill in shooting *a good shot* **4** a heavy metal ball thrown as a sport **5** a stroke in tennis, cricket, billiards, etc. **6** a photograph or filmed scene **7** (*informal*) an attempt **8** an injection of a drug or vaccine

shotgun NOUN a gun for firing small shot at close range

should AUXILIARY VERB **1** used to say what someone ought to do *You should have told me* **2** used to say what someone expects *They should be here soon.* **3** used with *I* and *we* to make a polite statement *I should like to come* **4**

shoulder NOUN the part of the body between the neck and the arm

shoulder VERB **1** to take on your shoulder **2** to accept responsibility or blame

shoulder blade NOUN either of the two large flat bones at the top of your back

shouldn't should not

shout NOUN a loud cry or call

shout VERB to give a shout

shove VERB to push roughly
▶ **shove** NOUN

shovel NOUN a tool like a spade with the sides turned up, used for lifting

shovel VERB **shovelling, shovelled 1** to move or clear with a shovel **2** (*informal*) to scoop or push quickly and in large amounts *He shovelled the pasta into his mouth.*

show VERB **showed, shown 1** to allow or cause to be seen **2** to make a person understand *Show me how to use it.* **3** to guide *Show him in.* **4** to treat in a certain way *showed us kindness.* **5** to be visible

show off to try to impress people

show up to make or be clearly visible

THESAURUS

shot NOUN • *A shot rang out.*
▶ bang, blast, explosion • *a shot of us on the beach* ▶ photo, photograph, snap • *a winning shot* ▶ stroke, hit, strike

shout VERB • *'Come on,' she shouted.* ▶ cry, call, yell, exclaim, shriek, scream

shove VERB • *She shoved the bag in the back of the van.* ▶ push,

thrust, force • *Two men shoved past them.* ▶ push, barge

show VERB • *I can show you how to do it.* ▶ demonstrate, explain • *a hole in the sleeve that won't show* ▶ be visible, be seen, be obvious • *It just shows what you can do if you try.* ▶ demonstrate, illustrate, prove • *The gallery is showing her*

a
b
c
d
e
f
g
h
i
j
k
l
m
n
o
p
q
r
s
t
u
v
w
x
y
z

show NOUN **1** a display or exhibition **2** an entertainment

showdown NOUN a final test or confrontation

shower NOUN **1** a brief fall of rain or snow **2** a lot of small things coming or falling like rain **3** a device for spraying water to wash a person's body

shower VERB **1** to fall or send things in a shower **2** to wash under a shower

showjumping NOUN a competition in which riders ride horses over fences and other obstacles

showman NOUN **showmen 1** someone who is good at entertaining ▶ **showmanship** NOUN

show-off NOUN a person who tries to impress people boastfully

showroom NOUN a large room where goods are displayed

showy ADJECTIVE **showier, showiest** brightly or highly decorated

shrapnel NOUN pieces of metal scattered from an exploding shell

shred NOUN **1** a tiny piece torn or cut off something **2** a small amount *not a shred of evidence*

shred VERB **shredding, shredded** to cut into shreds ▶ **shredder** NOUN

shrew NOUN a small mouse-like animal

shrewd ADJECTIVE having good sense and judgement ▶ **shrewdly** ADVERB

shriek NOUN a shrill cry or scream

shriek VERB to give a shriek

shrift NOUN **short shrift** curt treatment

shrill ADJECTIVE sounding very high and piercing ▶ **shrilly** ADVERB

shrimp NOUN a small shellfish, pink when boiled

new work. ▶ exhibit, display • *to show impatience* ▶ reveal, communicate • *He showed them to their seats.* ▶ take, escort, accompany

show NOUN • *a show of strength* ▶ display, exhibition, impression, pretence • *to watch the show* ▶ entertainment, performance, production, spectacle

shower NOUN • *a shower of rain* ▶ fall, drizzle, downpour

showy ADJECTIVE • *showy fake jewellery* ▶ gaudy, flashy, ostentatious

shred NOUN • *not a shred of evidence* ▶ scrap, speck, ounce **shreds** • *torn to shreds* ▶ tatters, ribbons, rags

shrewd ADJECTIVE • *a shrewd politician* ▶ clever, astute, sharp, intelligent

shriek VERB • *to shriek with laughter* ▶ scream, screech, squeal, howl, yell

shrill ADJECTIVE • *a shrill voice* ▶ piercing, high-pitched

a b c d e f g h i j k l m n o p q r s t u v w x y z

shrine NOUN an altar, chapel, or other sacred place

shrink VERB **shrank, shrunk 1** to make or become smaller **2** to move back to avoid something **3** to avoid doing something from fear, embarrassment, etc.

shrinkage NOUN the amount by which something shrinks

shrivel VERB **shrivelling, shrivelled** to make or become dry and wrinkled

shroud NOUN **1** a cloth in which a dead body is wrapped **2** a covering

shroud VERB **1** to wrap in a shroud **2** to cover or conceal *was shrouded in mist*

Shrove Tuesday NOUN the day before Lent, when pancakes are eaten

shrub NOUN a woody plant smaller than a tree; a bush ▶ **shrubby** ADJECTIVE

shrubbery NOUN **shrubberies** an area planted with shrubs

shrug VERB **shrugging, shrugged** to raise your shoulders to show uncertainty or lack of interest ▶ **shrug** NOUN

shrunken ADJECTIVE having shrunk

shudder VERB **1** to shiver violently with horror, fear, or cold **2** to make a strong shaking movement ▶ **shudder** NOUN

shuffle VERB **1** to walk without lifting the feet **2** to rearrange playing cards by sliding them over each other to get them into random order **3** to shift or rearrange ▶ **shuffle** NOUN

shun VERB **shunning, shunned** to avoid; to keep away from something

shunt VERB to move things to a different position

shut VERB **shutting, shut 1** to move a door, lid, or cover etc. so that it blocks an opening **2** to bring or fold parts together **shut down 1** to stop something working **2** to stop business **shut up 1** to shut securely **2** (*informal*) to stop talking or making a noise

shutter NOUN **1** a panel that can be closed over a window **2** the device in a camera that opens and closes to let in light ▶ **shuttered** ADJECTIVE

shuttle NOUN **1** a holder carrying the weft thread across a loom in

shrink VERB • *to shrink in the wash* ▶ become smaller, contract, dwindle, shrivel • *to shrink in alarm* ▶ draw back, cower, cringe

shrivel VERB • *The plants were shrivelling in the heat.* ▶ wilt, wither, droop

shudder VERB • *shuddered at the thought of it* ▶ shake, quiver, shiver, tremble

shuffle VERB • *He shuffled over to the fireplace.* ▶ shamble, hobble, stumble • *She shuffled the cards.* ▶ mix, jumble

shut VERB • *I'll shut the window.* ▶ close, fasten, lock, bolt, secure **shut up** • *told them to shut up* ▶ be quiet, be silent, stop talking

weaving **2** a train, bus, or aircraft that makes short journeys between two points

shuttle VERB to move, travel, or send backwards and forwards

shuttlecock NOUN a small rounded piece of cork or plastic with a crown of feathers, used in badminton

shy ADJECTIVE **shyer**, **shyest** afraid to meet or talk to other people; timid ▸ **shyly** ADVERB

shy VERB **shies**, **shied** to jump or move suddenly in alarm

SI NOUN an internationally recognized system of metric units of measurement, including the metre and kilogram

Siamese cat NOUN a breed of cat with short pale fur and darker face, ears, tail, and feet

sibling NOUN a brother or sister

sick ADJECTIVE **1** physically or mentally unwell **2** vomiting or likely to vomit **3** distressed or disgusted **4** (of humour) dealing with serious subjects in an unpleasant or upsetting way **sick of** tired of

sicken VERB **1** to begin to be ill **2** to distress or disgust ▸ **sickening** ADJECTIVE

sickle NOUN a tool with a narrow curved blade, used for cutting corn etc.

sickly ADJECTIVE **1** often ill; unhealthy **2** making people feel sick *a sickly smell* **3** weak *a sickly smile*

sickness NOUN **1** illness **2** a disease **3** vomiting

side NOUN **1** a surface, especially one joining the top and bottom of something **2** a line that forms part of the boundary of a triangle, square, etc. **3** the part near the edge and away from the centre **4** the place next to a person or thing *stood at my side* **5** one aspect or view *all sides of the problem* **6** one of two groups or teams etc. who oppose each other **on the side** as a sideline

side ADJECTIVE at or on a side *the side door*

side VERB **side with** to support a person in an argument

THESAURUS

shy ADJECTIVE • *too shy to speak* ▸ reserved, timid, bashful, modest, self-conscious

sick ADJECTIVE • *had been sick all week* ▸ ill, unwell, poorly, queasy, nauseous *sick of having to wait* ▸ fed up with, tired of

sicken VERB • *All that waste sickened us.* ▸ disgust, revolt, appal

sickly ADJECTIVE • *a sickly child* ▸ unhealthy, poorly, weak, feeble

side NOUN • *an address label on one side* ▸ surface, face, flank • *by the side of the lake* ▸ edge, border, boundary, limit • *on the wrong side of the road* ▸ half, part, carriageway • *both sides in the argument* ▸ point of view, opinion, viewpoint, angle • *the*

sideboard NOUN a long piece of furniture with drawers and cupboards and a flat top

sideburns PLURAL NOUN strips of hair growing on each side of a man's face

side effect NOUN an extra (usually bad) effect that a medicine has on a person

sideline NOUN 1 something done in addition to your main job 2 each of the lines on the two long sides of a sports pitch

sidelong ADJECTIVE towards one side; sideways

sideshow NOUN a small entertainment forming part of a large one, e.g. at a fair

sidetrack VERB to take someone's attention away from the main subject

sidewalk NOUN (American) a pavement

sideways ADVERB, ADJECTIVE 1 to or from one side 2 with one side facing forwards

siding NOUN a short railway line by the side of a main line

sidle VERB to walk in a shy or nervous manner

siege NOUN the surrounding of a place in order to capture it or force someone to surrender

sierra NOUN a range of mountains with sharp peaks, in Spain or parts of America

siesta (see-est-a) NOUN an afternoon rest

sieve (siv) NOUN a device with a fine mesh, used to separate the smaller or soft parts of something from the larger or hard parts

sieve VERB to put through a sieve

sift VERB 1 to sieve 2 to analyse facts or information carefully

sigh NOUN a sound made by breathing out heavily from tiredness, sadness, relief, etc.

sigh VERB to make a sigh

sight NOUN 1 the ability to see 2 a view or glimpse *caught sight of them* 3 a thing that can be seen or is worth seeing *a lovely sight* 4 an unsightly thing *I must look a sight.* 5 a device for aiming a gun or telescope etc.

⚠ **USAGE**

Do not confuse this word with *site*.

sight VERB 1 to see or observe something 2 to aim a gun or telescope etc.

sighted ADJECTIVE able to see

sight-reading NOUN playing or singing music at sight, without preparation

winning side in the conflict
► faction, army • *the home side*
► team, squad

sight NOUN • *His sight was failing.*
► eyesight, vision • *almost in sight*
► range, view • *the first sight of*

land ► view, glimpse • *an impressive sight* ► spectacle, scene

sight VERB • *sighted survivors in the water* ► spot, make out, notice, see

a
b
c
d
e
f
g
h
i
j
k
l
m
n
o
p
q
r
s
t
u
v
w
x
y
z

sightseeing NOUN visiting interesting places in a town etc.
▶ **sightseer** NOUN

sign NOUN **1** something that shows that a thing exists *signs of decay* **2** a mark, notice, etc. having a special meaning **3** an action or movement giving an instruction **4** any of the twelve divisions of the zodiac, represented by a symbol

sign VERB **1** to make a sign or signal **2** to write your signature on a letter or document **3** to use signing

signal NOUN **1** a gesture, sound, etc. that gives information or an instruction **2** a message made up of such things **3** a sequence of electrical impulses or radio waves

signal VERB **signalling, signalled** to make a signal to

signal box NOUN a building from which railway signals, points, etc. are controlled

signalman NOUN a person who controls railway signals

signatory NOUN **signatories** a person who signs an agreement etc.

signature NOUN **1** a person's name written by himself or herself **2** (*Music*) a set of signs after the clef in a score, showing the key the music is written in

signature tune NOUN a special tune used to introduce a particular programme, performer, etc.

signet ring NOUN a ring with a person's initials or a design engraved on it

significance NOUN meaning or importance

significant ADJECTIVE **1** having a meaning; full of meaning **2** important ▶ **significantly** ADVERB

signify VERB **signifies, signified 1** to be a sign or symbol of **2** to indicate **3** to be important

signing or **sign language** NOUN a way of communicating by

sign NOUN • *signs of decay*
▶ indication, hint, clue, proof, warning • *gave the sign to begin*
▶ signal, cue, gesture, nod • *a sign of affection* ▶ token, marker, symptom • *to put up a sign*
▶ notice, poster, publicity, advertisement • *walls daubed with signs* ▶ symbol, mark

signal NOUN • *gave the signal to move forward* ▶ sign, gesture, wave, nod

signal VERB • *signalled to him to stop.* ▶ gesture, indicate, motion

significance NOUN • *the significance of her remarks*
▶ importance, meaning, relevance

significant ADJECTIVE • *produced some significant results*
▶ important, meaningful, informative • *a significant effect*
▶ considerable, important, sizeable

signify VERB • *Red signifies danger.*
▶ mean, denote, represent

using gestures etc. instead of sounds, used mainly by deaf people

signpost NOUN a sign at a road junction etc. showing the names and distances of places down each road

Sikh (seek) NOUN a member of a religion founded in northern India, believing in one God and accepting some Hindu and some Islamic beliefs ▸ **Sikhism** NOUN

silage NOUN fodder made from green crops stored in a silo

silence NOUN absence of sound or speaking

silence VERB to make a person or thing silent

silencer NOUN a device for reducing the sound made by a gun or a vehicle's exhaust system etc.

silent ADJECTIVE 1 without any sound 2 not speaking ▸ **silently** ADVERB

silhouette (sil-oo-et) NOUN 1 a dark shadow seen against a light background 2 a portrait of a person in profile, showing the outline only in solid black

silicon NOUN a substance found in many rocks, used in making transistors, chips for microprocessors, etc.

silk NOUN 1 a fine soft thread or cloth made from the fibre produced by silkworms 2 a length of silk thread used for embroidery ▸ **silken** ADJECTIVE, **silky** ADJECTIVE

silkworm NOUN the caterpillar of a kind of moth, which spins a cocoon

sill NOUN a strip of stone, wood, or metal below a window or door

silly ADJECTIVE **sillier, silliest** foolish or unwise ▸ **silliness** NOUN

silo (sy-loh) NOUN **silos** 1 a pit or tower for storing green crops or corn or cement etc. 2 an underground place for storing a missile

silt NOUN sediment laid down by a river or sea etc.

silt VERB **silt up** to become blocked with silt

silver NOUN 1 a shiny white precious metal 2 the colour of silver 3 coins or objects made of silver or silver-coloured metal ▸ **silvery** ADJECTIVE

silver ADJECTIVE 1 made of silver 2 coloured like silver

silver VERB to make or become silvery

silver medal NOUN a medal awarded for second place in a competition

silence NOUN • *a long period of silence* ▸ quiet, stillness, tranquillity, peace

silent ADJECTIVE • *to remain silent* ▸ quiet, speechless, unspeaking, voiceless, dumb, mute, taciturn, reticent

silly ADJECTIVE • *a silly thing to do* ▸ foolish, unwise, stupid, rash, reckless

silver wedding NOUN a 25th wedding anniversary

SIM card NOUN a card in a mobile phone, storing its number and other information

similar ADJECTIVE nearly the same; of the same kind ► **similarly** ADVERB

similarity NOUN **similarities** **1** a close resemblance **2** a similar feature

simile (sim-il-ee) NOUN a comparison of one thing with another, e.g. *as brave as a lion*

simmer VERB to boil very gently **simmer down** to calm down

simper VERB to smile in a silly affected way ► **simper** NOUN

simple ADJECTIVE **simpler**, **simplest** **1** easy; not complicated or elaborate **2** plain or ordinary *a simple cottage* **3** lacking sense or intelligence ► **simplicity** NOUN

simple-minded ADJECTIVE naive or foolish

simpleton NOUN a foolish person

simplify VERB **simplifies**, **simplified** to make simple or easy

to understand ► **simplification** NOUN

simply ADVERB **1** in a simple way *Explain it simply.* **2** without doubt; completely *was simply marvellous* **3** only or merely *is simply a question of time*

simulate VERB **1** to reproduce the appearance or conditions of **2** to pretend to have a feeling ► **simulation** NOUN

simulator NOUN a device for simulating actual conditions or events

simultaneous ADJECTIVE happening at the same time ► **simultaneously** ADVERB

sin NOUN **1** the breaking of a religious or moral law **2** a very bad action

sin VERB **sinning**, **sinned** to commit a sin ► **sinner** NOUN

since CONJUNCTION **1** from the time when **2** because

since PREPOSITION from a certain time *nothing since January*

since ADVERB between then and now *hasn't been seen since*

similar ADJECTIVE • *similar in appearance* ► alike, identical, the same • *hills and similar features* ► comparable to • *views similar to my own* ► like, comparable to

similarity NOUN • *a startling similarity between them* ► resemblance, likeness

simple ADJECTIVE • *a simple method* ► easy, straightforward,

uncomplicated • *written in simple language* ► clear, plain, simple, honest lives • ordinary, unpretentious, unsophisticated

simply ADVERB • *was simply marvellous* ► absolutely, completely, utterly • *She did it simply because we asked her to.* ► merely, purely, solely

sin NOUN • *to commit a sin* ► offence, wrong

sincere ADJECTIVE truly felt or meant *sincere thanks*
▶ **sincerely** ADVERB, **sincerity** NOUN

sine NOUN (in a right-angled triangle) the ratio of the length of a side opposite one of the acute angles to the length of the hypotenuse

sinew NOUN strong tissue that connects a muscle to a bone

sinewy ADJECTIVE slim, muscular, and strong

sinful ADJECTIVE **1** guilty of sin **2** wicked ▶ **sinfully** ADVERB

sing VERB sang, sung **1** to make musical sounds with the voice **2** to perform a song ▶ **singer** NOUN

singe (sinj) VERB singeing to burn slightly

single ADJECTIVE **1** one only; not double or multiple **2** suitable for one person *a single bed* **3** separate *every single thing* **4** not married

single VERB **single out** to pick out or distinguish

single file NOUN a line of people one behind the other

single-handed ADJECTIVE without help

single-minded ADJECTIVE having one purpose only

single ticket NOUN a ticket for a journey to a place but not back

singly ADVERB in ones; one by one

sing-song ADJECTIVE having a repeated rising and falling rhythm

sing-song NOUN informal singing by a gathering of people

singular NOUN the form of a noun or verb used when it stands for only one person or thing *The singular is 'child', the plural is 'children'*

singular ADJECTIVE uncommon or extraordinary *a person of singular courage* ▶ **singularly** ADVERB

sinister ADJECTIVE **1** looking evil or harmful **2** wicked *a sinister motive*

sink VERB sank, sunk **1** to go or cause to go under the surface or to the bottom of the sea etc. **2** to go or fall slowly downwards *sank to their knees* **3** to push something sharp deeply into something *sank its teeth into a bone* **4** to drill a well **5** to invest money **sink in** to be understood

sink NOUN a fixed basin with a drainpipe and taps

THESAURUS

sincere ADJECTIVE • *sincere thanks* ▶ heartfelt, honest, genuine, truthful

sinful ADJECTIVE • *sinful behaviour* ▶ wicked, wrong, evil

single ADJECTIVE • *only a single biscuit left* ▶ solitary, lone • *He had remained single all his life.* ▶ unattached, unmarried • *every*

single word ▶ individual, particular

sinister • *words with a sinister undertone* ▶ menacing, threatening

sink VERB • *The sun sank below the horizon.* ▶ descend, dip, fall, drop • *The ship sank.* ▶ founder, go down

a
b
c
d
e
f
g
h
i
j
k
l
m
n
o
p
q
r
s
t
u
v
w
x
y
z

a
b
c
d
e
f
g
h
i
j
k
l
m
n
o
p
q
r
s
t
u
v
w
x
y
z

sinuous ADJECTIVE bending or curving

sinus (sy-nus) NOUN a hollow part in the bones of the skull, connected with the nose

sip VERB **sipping, sipped** to drink in small mouthfuls ▸ **sip** NOUN

siphon NOUN **1** a pipe or tube in the form of an upside-down U, arranged so that liquid is forced up it and down to a lower level **2** a bottle containing soda water which is released through a tube

siphon VERB to flow or draw out through a siphon

sir NOUN **1** a word used when speaking politely to a man **2 Sir** the title given to a knight or baronet

sire NOUN the male parent of a horse or dog etc.

sire VERB to be the sire of

siren NOUN **1** a device that makes a loud wailing sound as a signal **2** a dangerously attractive woman

sirloin NOUN beef from the upper part of the loin

sissy NOUN **sissies** a timid or cowardly person

sister NOUN **1** a daughter of the same parents as another person **2** a woman who is a fellow member or worker **3** a nun **4** a senior hospital nurse ▸ **sisterly** ADJECTIVE

sisterhood NOUN **1** companionship between women **2** a society or association of women

sister-in-law NOUN **sisters-in-law 1** the sister of a person's husband or wife **2** the wife of a person's brother

sit VERB **sitting, sat 1** to rest with your body supported on the buttocks **2** to cause someone to sit **3** (of birds) to stay on the nest to hatch eggs **4** to be a candidate in an examination **5** to be situated; to stay **6** (of a lawcourt etc.) to be assembled for business

sitcom NOUN (informal) a television comedy with a continuing storyline

site NOUN the place where something happens or happened or is built etc. a camping site

⚠ USAGE
Do not confuse this word with sight.

site VERB to provide with a site; to locate

sit-in NOUN a protest in which demonstrators sit down in a public place

sitter NOUN **1** a person posing for a portrait **2** a person who babysits

sitting NOUN **1** the time when people are served a meal **2** the

sit VERB • A bird sat on a branch. ▸ settle, perch, ensconce yourself • The hall sits about a hundred people. ▸ seat, accommodate • Parliament sits again

today. ▸ meet, assemble, convene

site NOUN • the site for the new hospital ▸ location, situation, spot

time when a parliament etc. is conducting business

sitting room NOUN a room with comfortable chairs for sitting in

situated ADJECTIVE in a particular place or situation

situation NOUN 1 a position with its surroundings 2 a state of affairs at a certain time 3 a job

six NOUN, ADJECTIVE the number 6 **at sixes and sevens** in a muddle
► **sixth** ADJECTIVE, NOUN

sixth form NOUN a form for students aged 16–18 in a secondary school

sixth sense NOUN the ability to know something by instinct or intuition

sixteen NOUN, ADJECTIVE the number 16 ► **sixteenth** ADJECTIVE, NOUN

sixty NOUN, ADJECTIVE the number 60 **sixties** ► **sixtieth** ADJECTIVE, NOUN

size NOUN 1 the measurements or extent of something 2 any of the series of standard measurements in which certain things are made

size VERB to arrange according to size **size up 1** to form an opinion about

sizeable ADJECTIVE fairly large

sizzle VERB to make a crackling or hissing sound

skate[1] NOUN 1 a boot with a steel blade on the sole, used for sliding on ice 2 a roller skate

skate VERB to move on skates
► **skater** NOUN

skate[2] NOUN skate a large flat sea fish

skateboard NOUN a small board with wheels, used for riding on as a sport ► **skateboarding** NOUN

skeleton NOUN 1 the framework of bones of the body 2 the shell or other hard part of a crab etc. 3 a framework of a building etc.
► **skeletal** ADJECTIVE

sketch NOUN 1 a rough drawing or painting 2 a short account of something 3 a short amusing play

sketch VERB to make a sketch of

sketchy ADJECTIVE **sketchier, sketchiest** rough and not detailed or careful

THESAURUS

situation NOUN • new houses in a pleasant situation ► location, position, setting • The financial situation improved.
► circumstances, position, state of affairs, predicament

size NOUN • the vast size of the main bedroom ► dimensions, proportions, area • the size of the job ► scale, extent, scope, range

sizeable ADJECTIVE • a sizeable reward ► large, substantial, considerable

sketch NOUN • a sketch of the scene ► drawing, outline, picture, plan • a comic sketch ► scene, skit, turn

sketch VERB • to sketch a scene ► draw, depict

sketchy ADJECTIVE • sketchy information ► incomplete, imperfect, incomplete

skew ADJECTIVE askew or slanting

skew VERB **1** to make a thing askew **2** to make something biased or distorted

skewer NOUN a long pin pushed through meat to hold it together during cooking

skewer VERB to pierce with a skewer

ski (skee) NOUN **skis** each of a pair of long narrow strips fixed under the feet for moving quickly over snow

ski VERB **skies**, **skiing**, **skied** to travel on skis ▸ **skier** NOUN

skid VERB **skidding**, **skidded** to slide accidentally without control ▸ **skid** NOUN

skilful ADJECTIVE having or showing great skill ▸ **skilfully** ADVERB

skill NOUN the ability to do something well ▸ **skilled** ADJECTIVE

skilled ADJECTIVE **1** highly trained or experienced **2** (of work) needing skill

skim VERB **skimming**, **skimmed 1** to remove something from the surface of a liquid **2** to move quickly over a surface or through

the air **3** to read something quickly

skimp VERB to supply or use less than is needed

skimpy ADJECTIVE **skimpier**, **skimpiest** scanty or too small

skin NOUN **1** the outer covering of a person's or animal's body **2** the outer layer of a fruit **3** a film formed on the surface of a liquid

skin VERB **skinning**, **skinned** to take the skin off

skin diving NOUN swimming under water with breathing apparatus but without a diving suit ▸ **skin diver** NOUN

skinflint NOUN a miserly person

skinny ADJECTIVE **skinnier**, **skinniest** very thin

skip VERB **skipping**, **skipped 1** to move along lightly with a hop on each leg **2** to jump with a skipping rope **3** to go quickly from one subject to another **4** to miss out

skip NOUN **1** a skipping movement **2** a large container for builders' rubbish

skipper NOUN (informal) a captain

THESAURUS

skilful ADJECTIVE • a skilful negotiator ▸ expert, skilled, capable, talented, brilliant

skill NOUN • work that needs skill ▸ expertise, ability, aptitude, talent

skilled ADJECTIVE • a skilled engineer ▸ experienced, trained, qualified, expert

skim VERB • The boat skimmed on the water. ▸ glide, slide, float

skin NOUN • an animal's skin ▸ hide, pelt • the skin of an apple ▸ peel, rind

skinny ADJECTIVE • skinny people ▸ thin, lean, scrawny, lanky, emaciated

skip VERB • She skipped along the path. ▸ dance, prance, trip • We can skip the details. ▸ dispense with, forget

a b c d e f g h i j k l m n o p q r s t u v w x y z

skipping rope NOUN a rope that is swung over the head and under the feet while jumping

skirmish NOUN (informal) a minor fight or conflict

skirt NOUN **1** a piece of clothing for a woman or girl that hangs from the waist **2** the lower part of a dress

skirt VERB to go round the edge of

skirting NOUN a narrow board round the wall of a room, close to the floor

skit NOUN a satirical sketch or parody

skittish ADJECTIVE lively and excitable

skittle NOUN a bottle-shaped object that people try to knock down by bowling a ball in the game called skittles

skive VERB (informal) to dodge work
► **skiver** NOUN

skulk VERB to loiter stealthily

skull NOUN the framework of bones of the head

skunk NOUN a furry North American animal that sprays a bad-smelling fluid to defend itself

sky NOUN skies the space above the earth

skylark NOUN a lark that sings while it hovers high in the air

skylight NOUN a window in a roof

skyline NOUN the outline of land or buildings seen against the sky

skyscraper NOUN a very tall building

slab NOUN a thick flat piece

slack ADJECTIVE **1** not pulled tight **2** not busy or working hard

slack NOUN the slack part of a rope etc.

slack VERB to avoid work; to be lazy
► **slacker** NOUN

slacken VERB to make or become slack

slacks PLURAL NOUN loose casual trousers

slag NOUN waste material separated from metal in smelting

slain past participle of **slay**

slalom NOUN a ski race down a zigzag course

slam VERB slamming, slammed **1** to shut loudly **2** to hit violently
► **slam** NOUN

slander NOUN a spoken untrue statement that damages a person's reputation
► **slanderous** ADJECTIVE

slander VERB to make a slander against ► **slanderer** NOUN

slang NOUN very informal words used by a particular group of people ► **slangy** ADJECTIVE

slant VERB **1** to slope **2** to present news or information from a particular point of view

slab NOUN • slabs of rock ► piece, block, chunk, lump

slack ADJECTIVE • The rope went slack. ► limp, loose

slacken VERB • to slacken your grip ► loosen, relax, release

slant VERB • slant to the right ► tilt, lean, slope, incline

a
b
c
d
e
f
g
h
i
j
k
l
m
n
o
p
q
r
s
t
u
v
w
x
y
z

slant NOUN a slope

slap VERB **slapping, slapped 1** to hit with the palm of the hand or with something flat **2** to apply roughly *slapped paint on the walls*
▶ **slap** NOUN

slapdash ADJECTIVE hasty and careless

slapstick NOUN comedy with people hitting each other, falling over, etc.

slash VERB **1** to cut or strike with a long sweeping movement **2** to reduce prices greatly

slash NOUN **1** a slashing cut **2** a slanting line (/) used in writing and printing

slat NOUN a thin strip of wood etc. overlapping with others to form a screen

slate NOUN a piece of flat grey rock used in covering a roof or (formerly) for writing on

slate VERB **1** to cover a roof with slates **2** (*informal*) to criticize harshly

slaughter VERB **1** to kill an animal for food **2** to kill people or animals in large numbers

slaughter NOUN the killing of large numbers of people or animals

slaughterhouse NOUN a place where animals are killed for food

slave NOUN a person who is owned by another and has to work for the owner ▶ **slavery** NOUN

slave VERB to work very hard

slavery NOUN **1** the state of being a slave **2** the system of having slaves

slavish ADJECTIVE **1** like a slave **2** showing no independence or originality

slay VERB **slew, slain** (*literary*) to kill

sled NOUN a sledge

sledge NOUN a vehicle with runners for travelling over snow
▶ **sledging** NOUN

sledgehammer NOUN a large heavy hammer

sleek ADJECTIVE smooth and shiny

sleep NOUN the state in which the eyes are closed, the body relaxed, and the mind unconscious

slap VERB • *She wanted to slap him.* ▶ smack, strike, hit • *slapped paint on the walls* ▶ spread, daub, plaster

slash VERB • *Someone had slashed the tyres.* ▶ cut, slit, rip, tear • *Prices were slashed.* ▶ reduce, cut

slaughter VERB • *A whole legion was slaughtered.* ▶ massacre, butcher, kill, murder, slay

slave NOUN • *work done by slaves* ▶ serf, servant

slavery NOUN • *a life that amounted to slavery* ▶ bondage, captivity

sleek ADJECTIVE • *sleek dark hair* ▶ silky, glossy, shiny

sleep NOUN • *to have a sleep* ▶ snooze, nap, rest, doze

DICTIONARY

sleep VERB **slept** to have a sleep

sleeper NOUN **1** someone who is asleep **2** each of the wooden or concrete beams on which the railway lines rest **3** a railway carriage fitted for sleeping in

sleeping bag NOUN a padded bag to sleep in, especially when camping

sleepless ADJECTIVE unable to sleep

sleepwalker NOUN a person who walks while asleep
▶ **sleepwalking** NOUN

sleepy ADJECTIVE **sleepier, sleepiest 1** feeling a need to sleep **2** quiet and lacking activity
▶ **sleepily** ADVERB

sleet NOUN a mixture of rain and snow or hail

sleeve NOUN **1** the part of an item of clothing that covers the arm **2** a record cover

sleeveless ADJECTIVE without sleeves

sleigh (say as slay) NOUN a large sledge pulled by horses

sleight (say as slight) NOUN **sleight of hand** skill in using the hands to do conjuring tricks etc.

slender ADJECTIVE **1** slim and graceful **2** slight or small a slender chance

sleuth (slooth) NOUN a detective

slew past tense of **slay**

slice NOUN **1** a thin piece cut off something **2** a portion

slice VERB **1** to cut into slices **2** to cut from a larger piece **3** to cut cleanly

slick ADJECTIVE **1** done or doing things quickly and cleverly **2** slippery

slick NOUN **1** a large patch of oil floating on water **2** a slippery place

slide VERB **slid 1** to move or cause to move smoothly on a surface **2** to move quietly or secretly

slide NOUN **1** a sliding movement **2** a smooth surface on which people or things can slide **3** a photograph for projecting on a screen **4** a small glass plate on which objects are viewed under a

THESAURUS

sleep VERB • *He had slept for about an hour.* ▶ snooze, doze, rest, slumber

sleepy ADJECTIVE • *to feel sleepy*
▶ tired, drowsy, weary, heavy-eyed • *a sleepy little town*
▶ quiet, peaceful, tranquil, dull

slender ADJECTIVE • *a slender youth*
▶ slim, lean, thin, graceful

slice NOUN • *a slice of bread*
▶ piece, sliver (= thin slice), chunk (= thick slice)

slice VERB • *to slice a tomato* ▶ cut up, chop, carve

slick ADJECTIVE • *a slick marketing campaign* ▶ smooth, efficient, polished, professional

slide VERB • *The spoon slid across the table.* ▶ glide, slither, skim, skid, slip

DICTIONARY

microscope **5** a fastener to keep hair tidy

slight ADJECTIVE very small; not serious or important

slight VERB to insult by treating as unimportant ► **slight** NOUN

slightly ADVERB rather; a little

slim ADJECTIVE **slimmer, slimmest 1** thin and graceful **2** small; hardly enough *a slim chance*

slim VERB **slimming, slimmed** to become thinner by dieting ► **slimmer** NOUN

slime NOUN an unpleasant wet slippery substance

slimy ADJECTIVE **slimier, slimiest 1** covered in slime **2** wet and slippery

sling NOUN **1** a band placed round the neck and supporting an injured arm **2** a looped strap used to throw a stone etc.

sling VERB **slung 1** to hang loosely **2** (*informal*) to throw carelessly

slink VERB **slunk** to move in a stealthy or guilty way

slinky ADJECTIVE **slinkier, slinkiest** sleek and smooth in appearance or movement

slip VERB **slipping, slipped 1** to slide accidentally or lose balance **2** to move or put quickly and quietly **3** to escape from *It slipped my mind.* **slip up** to make a mistake

slip NOUN **1** an accidental slide or fall **2** a mistake **3** a small piece of paper **4** a petticoat **5** a pillowcase

slipper NOUN a soft comfortable shoe for wearing indoors

slippery ADJECTIVE smooth or wet and difficult to stand on or hold

slip road NOUN a road for entering or leaving a motorway

slipshod ADJECTIVE careless or untidy

slipstream NOUN a current of air driven backward as an aircraft or vehicle moves forward

THESAURUS

slight ADJECTIVE • *a slight problem* ► small, modest, insignificant, minor, trivial

slightly ADVERB • *slightly bigger* ► a little, a bit, rather, somewhat

slim ADJECTIVE • *a slim person* ► slender, lean, slight, thin • *a slim chance* ► faint, slender, remote

slimy ADJECTIVE • *a slimy mess* ► slithery, slippery, sticky, greasy

slink VERB • *They slunk round to the back of the house.* ► creep, sneak, slip

slip VERB • *slipping on the icy ground* ► slide, slither, fall, trip, stumble • *slipped quietly out of the door* ► creep, sneak, slink, steal

slip NOUN • *a slip of paper* ► piece, scrap • *to make a slip* ► mistake, error

slippery ADJECTIVE • *The floor was wet and slippery.* ► slithery, greasy, slippy

slit NOUN a narrow straight cut or opening

slit VERB **slitting, slit** to make a slit

slither VERB to slip or slide unsteadily

sliver NOUN a thin strip of wood or glass etc.

slob NOUN (informal) an untidy or lazy person

slobber VERB to dribble from the mouth

sloe NOUN a small dark plum-like fruit

slog VERB **slogging, slogged** (informal) **1** to hit hard **2** to work or walk hard and steadily ▶ **slog** NOUN

slogan NOUN a phrase used to advertise a product or idea

sloop NOUN a small sailing ship with one mast

slop VERB **slopping, slopped** to spill liquid over the edge of its container

slope VERB to lie or turn at an angle; to slant

slope NOUN **1** a sloping surface **2** the amount by which something slopes

sloppy ADJECTIVE **sloppier, sloppiest 1** liquid and splashing

easily **2** careless and untidy **3** weakly sentimental

slops PLURAL NOUN **1** slopped liquid **2** liquid waste matter

slosh VERB (informal) **1** to splash or slop **2** to pour liquid carelessly

slot NOUN a narrow opening to put flat things in ▶ **slotted** ADJECTIVE

slot VERB **slotting, slotted** to put something into a place where it fits

sloth (rhymes with both) NOUN **1** laziness **2** a slow-moving South American animal that lives in trees

slothful ADJECTIVE lazy

slot machine NOUN a machine worked by putting a coin in a slot

slouch VERB to stand or move in a lazy awkward way ▶ **slouch** NOUN

slovenly ADJECTIVE careless or untidy

slow ADJECTIVE **1** not quick; taking more time than is usual **2** showing a time earlier than the correct time *Your watch is slow.* **3** not able to understand quickly ▶ **slowly** ADVERB

slow VERB to go or cause to go more slowly

slit NOUN • *a slit in a fence*
▶ opening, chink, gap, crack
• *make a slit in the side of the box*
▶ cut, incision

slit VERB • *to slit open a letter* ▶ cut, tear, rip

slope VERB • *The garden slopes gently.* ▶ slant, fall or rise, incline

slope NOUN • *a steep slope*
▶ incline, gradient, slant

sloppy ADJECTIVE • *a sloppy mixture*
▶ liquid, runny, slushy, watery
• *sloppy work* ▶ careless, slapdash

slot NOUN • *put a coin in the slot*
▶ slit, chink, opening

slow ADJECTIVE • *at a slow pace*
▶ leisurely, unhurried, moderate, steady, plodding

slow VERB • *to slow to a halt*
▶ reduce speed, decelerate, brake

a
b
c
d
e
f
g
h
i
j
k
l
m
n
o
p
q
r
s
t
u
v
w
x
y
z

slow motion NOUN movement in a film or on television which has been slowed down

sludge NOUN thick mud

slug NOUN **1** a small slimy animal like a snail without a shell **2** a pellet for firing from a gun

sluggish ADJECTIVE slow-moving; not alert

sluice (slooss) NOUN **1** a sluice gate **2** a channel carrying off water

sluice VERB to wash with a flow of water

sluice gate NOUN a sliding barrier for controlling a flow of water

slum NOUN an area of dirty overcrowded houses

slumber VERB to sleep ► **slumber** NOUN

slump VERB to fall heavily or suddenly

slump NOUN a sudden fall in prices or trade

slur VERB **slurring, slurred 1** to pronounce words indistinctly **2** (Music) to mark with a slur in music

slur NOUN **1** a slurred sound **2** something that harms a person's reputation **3** (Music) a curved line placed over notes that are to be played smoothly without a break

slurp VERB to eat or drink with a loud sucking sound ► **slurp** NOUN

slurry NOUN **slurries** a semi-liquid mixture of water and cement, etc.

slush NOUN **1** partly melted snow **2** (informal) sentimental talk or writing ► **slushy** ADJECTIVE

sly ADJECTIVE **slyer, slyest 1** unpleasantly cunning or secret **2** mischievous and knowing ► **slyly** ADVERB

smack[1] NOUN **1** a slap **2** a loud sharp sound *hit the wall with a smack* **3** a loud kiss **4** a slight flavour or trace

smack VERB to slap or hit hard **smack of** to suggest *a decision that smacks of favouritism*

smack ADVERB (informal) forcefully or directly *went smack through the window*

smack[2] NOUN a small fishing boat

small ADJECTIVE **1** not large; less than the usual size **2** not important or significant

smallholding NOUN a small farm ► **smallholder** NOUN

small hours PLURAL NOUN the hours after midnight

small-minded ADJECTIVE selfish; petty

smallpox NOUN a serious contagious disease that causes a

THESAURUS

sly ADJECTIVE • *a sly individual* ► cunning, crafty, clever, wily

smack VERB • *lost control and smacked him* ► slap, strike, hit

small ADJECTIVE • *a small packet* ► little, tiny, minute, diminutive,

minuscule • *a small person* ► short, little, slight, petite • *made small changes* ► minor, trivial, insignificant, unimportant • *small portions* ► meagre, inadequate, insufficient

fever and produces spots that leave permanent scars on the skin

small print NOUN the details of a contract, especially if in very small letters or difficult to understand

small talk NOUN conversation about unimportant things

smarmy ADJECTIVE **smarmier, smarmiest** (*informal*) polite and flattering in an exaggerated way

smart ADJECTIVE **1** neat and elegant; dressed well **2** clever **3** forceful; brisk *a smart pace* ► **smartly** ADVERB

smart VERB to feel a stinging pain ► **smart** NOUN

smart card NOUN a plastic card which stores information in electronic form

smarten VERB to make or become smarter

smash VERB **1** to break noisily into pieces **2** to hit or move with great force **3** to destroy or defeat completely

smash NOUN **1** the action or sound of smashing **2** a collision between vehicles **3** (*informal*) a smash hit

smash hit NOUN (*informal*) a very successful song, show, etc.

smashing ADJECTIVE (*informal*) very good or attractive

smattering NOUN a slight knowledge of a subject

smear VERB **1** to rub something greasy or sticky on a surface **2** to try to damage someone's reputation ► **smeary** ADJECTIVE

smear NOUN **1** something smeared **2** a sample of tissue taken to check for faulty cells which may cause cancer **3** a malicious rumour

smell VERB **smelt** or or **smelled 1** to be aware of something from the sense organs of the nose **2** to give out a smell

smell NOUN **1** the act of smelling **2** the ability to smell things **3** something that can be smelt

smelly ADJECTIVE **smellier, smelliest** having a bad smell

smelt VERB to melt ore for its metal

---

smart ADJECTIVE • *a smart appearance* ► elegant, well dressed, stylish, chic • *a smart person* ► clever, bright, intelligent, sharp • *a smart hotel* ► fashionable, high-class, exclusive • *a smart pace* ► brisk, fast, quick

smash VERB • *to smash a window* ► break, shatter, crack **smash into** • *to smash into a lamppost* ► crash into, collide with, hit

smear VERB • *to smear grease* ► daub, spread, wipe, rub • *was smeared with paint* ► cover, coat, streak

smell NOUN • *a lovely smell* ► fragrance, scent, perfume • *a smell of cooking* ► aroma, odour • *a bad smell* ► odour, stench, stink, reek

DICTIONARY

smile NOUN an expression on the face that shows pleasure or amusement, with the lips stretched and turning upwards at the ends

smile VERB to give a smile

smirk NOUN a self-satisfied smile

smirk VERB to give a smirk

smith NOUN **1** a person who makes things out of metal **2** a blacksmith

smithy NOUN **smithies** a blacksmith's workshop

smitten ADJECTIVE **1** suddenly affected by a disease **2** having a sudden fondness or attraction

smock NOUN a long loose shirt worn over other clothes

smog NOUN thick smoky fog

smoke NOUN **1** the mixture of gas and solid particles given off by a burning substance **2** a period of smoking tobacco ► **smoky** ADJECTIVE

smoke VERB **1** to give out smoke **2** to inhale and exhale smoke from a cigarette, cigar, etc. **3** to preserve meat or fish by treating it with smoke ► **smoker** NOUN

smokeless ADJECTIVE without producing smoke

smokescreen NOUN something that conceals what is happening

smooth ADJECTIVE **1** having an even surface without lumps, etc. **2** moving without bumps or jolts **3** not harsh **4** without problems or difficulties ► **smoothly** ADVERB

smooth VERB to make smooth

smother VERB **1** to suffocate **2** to put out a fire by covering it **3** to cover thickly

smoulder VERB **1** to burn slowly without a flame **2** to feel a hidden emotion

smudge NOUN a dirty mark made by rubbing ► **smudgy** ADJECTIVE

smudge VERB to make a smudge on

smug ADJECTIVE self-satisfied ► **smugly** ADVERB

smuggle VERB to bring goods into a country etc. secretly or illegally ► **smuggler** NOUN

smut NOUN a small piece of soot or dirt ► **smutty** ADJECTIVE

THESAURUS

smile VERB • *He smiled at her.*
► beam, grin, smirk

smooth ADJECTIVE • *a smooth road*
► even, level, flat • *a smooth surface* ► shiny, polished, glossy • *a smooth sea* ► calm, still, tranquil • *a smooth talker* ► suave, articulate, slick • *the smooth running of the engine* ► regular, steady, rhythmic • *a smooth operation*

► straightforward, efficient, well-run

smother VERB • *She was smothered with a pillow.*
► suffocate, asphyxiate • *to smother the flames* ► put out, extinguish

smudge NOUN • *a smudge on the paper* ► smear, mark, stain, blot

smug ADJECTIVE • *a smug look*
► self-satisfied, conceited

DICTIONARY

snack NOUN **1** a small meal **2** food eaten between meals

snag NOUN **1** an unexpected difficulty **2** a tear in material

snail NOUN a small animal with a soft body and a shell

snake NOUN a reptile with a long narrow body and no legs

snap VERB **snapping, snapped 1** to break suddenly or with a sharp sound **2** to bite suddenly or quickly **3** to speak quickly and angrily **4** to take a quick photograph of **snap up** to grab something offered

snap NOUN **1** the action or sound of snapping **2** a photograph **3** a card game in which players shout 'Snap!' when they see two similar cards

snap ADJECTIVE sudden *a snap decision*

snappy ADJECTIVE **snappier, snappiest 1** quick and lively **2** irritable

snapshot NOUN a quickly taken photograph

snare NOUN **1** a trap for catching birds or animals **2** something attractive but dangerous

snare VERB to catch in a snare

snarl[1] VERB **1** to growl angrily **2** to speak in a bad-tempered way
► **snarl** NOUN

snarl[2] VERB to make or become tangled or jammed

snatch VERB to take quickly, eagerly, or by force

snatch NOUN **1** the act of snatching **2** a short part of a song, conversation, etc.

sneak VERB **1** to move quietly and secretly **2** to tell tales

sneak NOUN someone who tells tales

sneaky ADJECTIVE **sneakier, sneakiest** dishonest or deceitful
► **sneakily** ADVERB

sneer VERB to speak or behave in a scornful way ► **sneer** NOUN

sneeze VERB to send out air suddenly and uncontrollably through the nose and mouth to get rid of something irritating the nostrils ► **sneeze** NOUN

snide ADJECTIVE sneering in a sly way

sniff VERB **1** to draw in air through the nose **2** to smell something
► **sniff** NOUN

sniffle VERB to sniff slightly
► **sniffle** NOUN

snigger VERB to giggle in a sly way
► **snigger** NOUN

snip VERB **snipping, snipped** to cut in small quick cuts ► **snip** NOUN

snipe NOUN a marsh bird with a long beak

THESAURUS

snag NOUN • *a snag in the plan*
► problem, catch, hitch, setback

snap VERB • *The rope snapped.*
► break, split • *The dogs were snapping.* ► snarl, growl, bark

snap ADJECTIVE • *a snap decision*
► quick, instant, on-the-spot

snatch VERB • *Thieves snatched her handbag.* ► steal, seize, grab

sneak VERB • *to sneak in quietly*
► creep, steal, slip

snide ADJECTIVE • *snide remarks*
► disparaging, sarcastic, scornful, sneering

a
b
c
d
e
f
g
h
i
j
k
l
m
n
o
p
q
r
s
t
u
v
w
x
y
z

a b c d e f g h i j k l m n o p q r s t u v w x y z

snipe VERB **1** to shoot at people from a hiding place **2** to criticize in a sly way ► **sniper** NOUN

snippet NOUN a small piece of news, information, etc.

snivel VERB **snivelling, snivelled** to cry or complain in a whining way

snob NOUN a person who despises those who have not got wealth, power, or particular tastes ► **snobbery** NOUN, **snobbish** ADJECTIVE

snooker NOUN a game played with cues and 21 balls on a cloth-covered table

snoop VERB to ask or look around secretly ► **snooper** NOUN

snooty ADJECTIVE **snootier, snootiest** (informal) haughty and contemptuous

snooze VERB (informal) to have a short sleep ► **snooze** NOUN

snore VERB to breathe noisily while sleeping ► **snore** NOUN

snorkel NOUN a tube through which a swimmer under water can breathe under water ► **snorkelling** NOUN

snort VERB to make a rough sound through the nose ► **snort** NOUN

snout NOUN an animal's projecting nose and jaws

snow NOUN frozen drops of water that fall from the sky in small white flakes

snow VERB to come down as snow

snowball NOUN snow pressed into a ball for throwing

snowball VERB to grow quickly in size or intensity

snowdrift NOUN a bank of snow piled up by the wind

snowdrop NOUN a small white flower that blooms in early spring

snowflake NOUN a flake of snow

snowman NOUN **snowmen** a figure made of snow

snowplough NOUN a vehicle for clearing a road or railway of snow

snowshoe NOUN a frame like a tennis racket for walking on soft snow

snowy ADJECTIVE **snowier, snowiest 1** with snow falling **2** covered with snow **3** pure white

snub VERB **snubbing, snubbed** to treat in a scornful or unfriendly way

snub NOUN an act of snubbing

snub-nosed ADJECTIVE having a short turned-up nose

snuff[1] NOUN powdered tobacco for taking into the nose by sniffing

snuff[2] VERB to put out a candle

snuffle VERB to sniff in a noisy way ► **snuffle** NOUN

snug ADJECTIVE **snugger, snuggest 1** cosy **2** fitting closely ► **snugly** ADVERB

snuggle VERB to curl up comfortably

THESAURUS

snippet NOUN • snippets of information ► piece, scrap, shred

snivel VERB • Stop snivelling! ► cry, sniff, sob

snub VERB • snubbed them by early ► insult, offend, rebuff

snug ADJECTIVE • The cottage was warm and snug. ► cosy, comfortable, homely

so ADVERB **1** to such an extent *Why are you so cross?* **2** very *The film is so boring.* **3** also *I was wrong but so were you* **and so on** and other similar things

so CONJUNCTION for that reason

soak VERB to make very wet **soak up** to take in a liquid like a sponge ▶ **soak** NOUN

so-and-so NOUN **so-and-sos** a person or thing that need not be named

soap NOUN **1** a substance used with water for washing and cleaning things **2** a soap opera ▶ **soapy** ADJECTIVE

soap VERB to put soap on

soap opera NOUN a television serial about the everyday lives of a group of people

> ✏ **WORD HISTORY**
>
> called this because the first soap operas in America were sponsored by soap manufacturers

soar VERB **1** to rise high in the air **2** to increase rapidly

sob VERB **sobbing, sobbed** to make a gasping sound when crying ▶ **sob** NOUN

sober ADJECTIVE **1** not drunk **2** serious and calm **3** not bright or showy

sober VERB to make or become sober

so-called ADJECTIVE named in what may be the wrong way

soccer NOUN football

sociable ADJECTIVE liking to be with other people

social ADJECTIVE **1** living in a community, not alone **2** to do with life in a community **3** concerned with people's welfare *a social worker* **4** helping people to meet each other *a social club* **5** sociable ▶ **socially** ADVERB

socialism NOUN a political system in which wealth is shared equally between people, and the main industries and trade etc. are controlled by the state

socialist NOUN a person who believes in socialism

socialize VERB to meet other people socially

> ⚠ **SPELLING**
>
> This word can also be spelled *socialise.*

social security NOUN money and other assistance provided by the state to those in need

social services PLURAL NOUN welfare services provided by the state, including schools, hospitals, and pensions

THESAURUS

soak VERB • *soak the beans in liquid* ▶ immerse, steep, submerge. • *Rain had soaked the ground.* ▶ drench, saturate **soak up** • *A sponge soaks up water.* ▶ absorb, take up

soar VERB • *Birds soared overhead.* ▶ climb, glide, drift • *Prices continue to soar.* ▶ rise, escalate

sociable ADJECTIVE • *lively and sociable* ▶ friendly, outgoing, gregarious

a
b
c
d
e
f
g
h
i
j
k
l
m
n
o
p
q
r
s
t
u
v
w
x
y
z

699

society NOUN **societies 1** people living together in a group or nation **2** a group of people organized for a particular purpose **3** company or companionship

sociology NOUN the study of human society and social behaviour ▸ **sociologist** NOUN

sock[1] NOUN a piece of clothing covering the foot and the lower part of the leg

sock[2] VERB (informal) to hit hard ▸ **sock** NOUN

socket NOUN **1** a hollow into which something fits **2** a device into which an electric plug or bulb is put

sod NOUN a piece of turf

soda NOUN **1** a substance made from sodium, such as baking soda **2** soda water

soda water NOUN water made fizzy with carbon dioxide

sodden ADJECTIVE made very wet

sodium NOUN a soft white metallic element from which salt and other substances are formed

sofa NOUN a long soft seat with a back and arms

soft ADJECTIVE **1** not hard or firm; easily pressed **2** smooth, not rough or stiff **3** gentle; not loud **4** (of a drink) not alcoholic **5** (of a drug) not likely to be addictive **6** (of water) free of minerals that reduce lathering **7** lenient ▸ **softly** ADVERB

soften VERB to make or become soft or softer

soft-hearted ADJECTIVE sympathetic and easily moved

software NOUN computer programs and data, which are not part of the machinery of a computer

soggy ADJECTIVE **soggier**, **soggiest** wet and soft

soil NOUN **1** loose earth in which plants grow **2** territory

soil VERB to make dirty

solace NOUN a comfort for someone who is unhappy or disappointed

solar ADJECTIVE from or to do with the sun

society NOUN • *a modern society* ▸ civilization, nation, culture, community • *our position in society* ▸ the community, the population, the public • *a local history society* ▸ association, club, group, organization

soft ADJECTIVE • *a soft pillow* ▸ comfortable,springy, squashy • *soft ground* ▸ swampy, marshy, boggy • *soft music* ▸ gentle,

soothing, melodious • *a soft voice* ▸ quiet, low, faint • *soft colours* ▸ pale, pastel, muted • *a soft fabric* ▸ velvety, silky, smooth • *too soft with them* ▸ lenient, indulgent

soggy ADJECTIVE • *a pile of soggy clothes* ▸ wet, soaked, sodden

soil NOUN • *garden soil* ▸ earth, loam, ground • *on Scottish soil* ▸ territory, land

solar panel NOUN a panel designed to produce energy from the sun's rays

solar system NOUN the sun and the planets that revolve round it

solder NOUN a soft alloy that is melted to join metal

solder VERB to join with solder

soldier NOUN a member of an army

sole ¹ NOUN **soles** or, *in sense 2*, **sole** **1** the bottom surface of a foot or shoe **2** a flat edible sea fish

sole VERB put a sole on a shoe

sole ² ADJECTIVE single; only *the sole survivor* ▸ **solely** ADVERB

solemn ADJECTIVE **1** serious **2** dignified or formal

sol-fa NOUN a system of syllables (*doh, ray, me fah, so, la, te*) used to represent the notes of the musical scale

solicit VERB to ask for or try to obtain ▸ **solicitation** NOUN

solicitor NOUN a lawyer who advises clients

solid ADJECTIVE **1** not hollow; having no space inside **2** keeping its shape; not liquid or gas **3** continuous *for two solid hours* **4** firm or strongly made *a solid*

foundation **5** showing solidarity; unanimous ▸ **solidly** ADVERB

solid NOUN **1** a solid thing **2** a shape that has three dimensions

solidarity NOUN unity and support between people

solidify VERB **solidifies, solidified** to make or become solid

solidity NOUN the state of being solid

solids PLURAL NOUN food that is not liquid

soliloquy (sol-il-ok-wee) NOUN **soliloquies** a speech in a play in which a character expresses thoughts alone, without other characters hearing

solitaire NOUN a game of cards or marbles for one person

solitary ADJECTIVE **1** alone or lonely **2** single; by itself

solitude NOUN a solitary state

solo NOUN **solos** something sung, played, danced, or done by one person ▸ **solo** ADJECTIVE

soloist NOUN a musician or singer who performs a solo

solstice (sol-stiss) NOUN either of the two times in each year when the sun is at its furthest point

a
b
c
d
e
f
g
h
i
j
k
l
m
n
o
p
q
r
s
t
u
v
w
x
y
z

THESAURUS

sole ADJECTIVE • *the sole survivor* ▸ one, only, single

solemn ADJECTIVE • *a solemn look* ▸ serious, earnest, sombre • *a solemn occasion* ▸ dignified, formal, grand, stately, majestic, impressive

solid ADJECTIVE • *solid metal* ▸ hard, firm, dense, rigid • *solid evidence* ▸ firm, genuine, convincing

solitary ADJECTIVE • *a solitary existence* ▸ lonely, unsociable, friendless, isolated • *a solitary village* ▸ isolated, remote, secluded

north or south of the equator, 21 June and 22 December

soluble ADJECTIVE able to be dissolved

solution NOUN 1 a liquid in which something is dissolved 2 the answer to a problem or puzzle

solve VERB to find the answer to a problem or puzzle

solvent ADJECTIVE having enough money to pay debts ► **solvency** NOUN

solvent NOUN a liquid used for dissolving something

sombre ADJECTIVE dark and gloomy

some ADJECTIVE 1 a few; a little *some apples some sugar* 2 an unknown person or thing *some person* 3 about *some 30 minutes*

some PRONOUN a certain number or amount *Some of them were late.*

somebody or **someone** NOUN 1 some person 2 an important person

somehow ADVERB in some way

somersault NOUN a movement in which you turn head over heels before landing on your feet

somersault VERB to perform a somersault

something NOUN a thing which you cannot or do not want to name

sometime ADVERB at some time not specified

sometime ADJECTIVE former *her sometime friend*

sometimes ADVERB at some times but not always

somewhat ADVERB to some extent

somewhere ADVERB in or to some place

son NOUN a male child

sonar NOUN a device using reflected sound waves to locate objects under water

sonata NOUN a piece of music for one instrument or two, in several movements

song NOUN 1 a tune for singing 2 singing *burst into song*

songbird NOUN a bird that sings sweetly

sonic ADJECTIVE to do with sound waves

son-in-law NOUN **sons-in-law** a daughter's husband

sonnet NOUN a poem of 14 lines

soon ADVERB 1 in a short time from now 2 not long after something

THESAURUS

solution NOUN • *a solution of ammonia in water* ► mixture, blend • *no easy solution to the problem* ► answer, resolution

solve VERB • *to solve the problem* ► resolve, sort out, deal with

sombre ADJECTIVE • *sombre colours* ► dark, dull • *a sombre expression* ► serious, solemn

song NOUN • *She sang an old song.* ► tune, melody, air

soon ADVERB • *We'll be there soon.* ► shortly, presently, before long, in a while

DICTIONARY

sooner ADVERB rather; in preference *I'd sooner wait.*

soot NOUN black powder left by smoke ► **sooty** ADJECTIVE

soothe VERB 1 to calm or comfort 2 to ease pain or distress ► **soothing** ADJECTIVE

sop NOUN something unimportant given to pacify or persuade someone

sophisticated ADJECTIVE 1 having refined or cultured tastes or experience 2 complicated ► **sophistication** NOUN

soporific ADJECTIVE causing sleep or drowsiness

sopping ADJECTIVE very wet; drenched

soppy ADJECTIVE **soppier, soppiest** silly and sentimental

soprano NOUN **sopranos** a woman or boy with a high singing voice

sorcerer NOUN a magician ► **sorceress** NOUN

sorcery NOUN magic or witchcraft

sordid ADJECTIVE 1 dirty and nasty 2 dishonourable and selfish *sordid motives*

sore ADJECTIVE 1 painful or smarting 2 (*informal*) annoyed or offended 3 urgent *in sore need*

sore NOUN a sore place

sorely ADVERB seriously; very *was sorely tempted to leave*

sorrel[1] NOUN a herb with sharp-tasting leaves

sorrel[2] NOUN a reddish-brown horse

sorrow NOUN 1 unhappiness or regret caused by loss or disappointment 2 a cause of this

sorrow VERB to feel sorrow

sorrowful ADJECTIVE feeling sorrow ► **sorrowfully** ADVERB

sorry ADJECTIVE **sorrier, sorriest** 1 feeling regret 2 feeling pity or sympathy 3 wretched *in a sorry state*

sort NOUN a group of things or people that are similar

sort VERB to arrange things in groups according to their size,

THESAURUS

soothe VERB • *spoke gently to soothe him* ► calm, comfort, console, still

soothing ADJECTIVE • *a soothing ointment* ► healing • *soothing words* ► calming, relaxing, comforting

sore ADJECTIVE • *a sore arm* ► painful, aching, tender, injured

sorrow NOUN • *The loss caused him great sorrow.* ► sadness, unhappiness, regret, misery, grief

sorry ADJECTIVE • *sorry for what they had done* ► apologetic, ashamed (of), regretful, remorseful, repentant • *felt sorry for them* ► sympathetic, compassionate, full of pity • *in a sorry state* ► pitiful, wretched, pathetic

sort NOUN • *don't like that sort of film* ► type, kind, variety, genre, style

sort VERB • *Eggs are sorted by size.* ► class, grade, group, categorize

sort out • *to sort out the*

a
b
c
d
e
f
g
h
i
j
k
l
m
n
o
p
q
r
s
t
u
v
w
x
y
z

a
b
c
d
e
f
g
h
i
j
k
l
m
n
o
p
q
r
s
t
u
v
w
x
y
z

kind, etc. **sort out** to resolve a problem or difficulty

SOS NOUN an urgent appeal for help

sought past tense of **seek**

soul NOUN 1 the spiritual part of a person that is believed by some to be immortal 2 a person's mind and emotions etc. 3 a person *not a soul anywhere* 4 a perfect example of something *the soul of discretion*

soulful ADJECTIVE having or showing deep feeling ▶ **soulfully** ADVERB

sound¹ NOUN 1 vibrations that travel through the air and can be detected by the ear 2 sound reproduced in a film etc. 3 a mental impression *don't like the sound of it*

sound VERB 1 to produce or cause to produce a sound 2 to give an impression *They sound angry.* 3 to test by noting the sounds heard

sound² VERB to test the depth of water beneath a ship **sound out** to try to find out a person's opinion about something

sound³ ADJECTIVE 1 in good condition; not damaged 2 healthy;

not diseased 3 reasonable or correct *sound ideas* 4 reliable or secure *a sound investment* 5 thorough or deep *a sound sleep* ▶ **soundly** ADVERB

sound⁴ NOUN a narrow stretch of water

sound barrier NOUN the resistance of the air to objects moving at speeds near the speed of sound

sound bite NOUN a short memorable extract from a speech or statement by a politician etc.

sound effects PLURAL NOUN sounds produced artificially to make a play, film, etc. more realistic

soundtrack NOUN the sound that goes with a cinema film

soup NOUN liquid food made from stewed bones, meat, fish, vegetables, etc.

sour ADJECTIVE 1 tasting sharp like unripe fruit 2 stale and unpleasant *sour milk* 3 bad-tempered

sour VERB to make or become sour

source NOUN 1 the place from which something comes 2 the starting point of a river

THESAURUS

difficulties ▶ settle, resolve, deal with

sound VERB • *A signal sounded.* ▶ be heard, resound, resonate, make a noise • *to sound the alarm* ▶ set off, operate • *They sound angry.* ▶ seem, appear

sound ADJECTIVE • *sound advice* ▶ good, sensible, reasonable,

dependable • *sound foundations* ▶ firm, solid, well built, stable • *a sound investment* ▶ wise, well chosen • *a sound sleep* ▶ deep, prolonged

sour ADJECTIVE • *a sour taste* ▶ sharp, acid, bitter • *a sour look* ▶ embittered, resentful

source NOUN • *the source of the problem* ▶ cause, origin

south NOUN **1** the direction to the right of a person who faces east **2** the southern part of a country, city, etc.

south ADJECTIVE, ADVERB towards or in the south; coming from the south

south-east NOUN, ADJECTIVE,, ADVERB midway between south and east
▶ **south-easterly** ADJECTIVE, **south-eastern** ADJECTIVE

southerly ADJECTIVE **1** coming from the south **2** facing the south

southern ADJECTIVE of or in the south

southerner NOUN a person from the south of a country

southward ADJECTIVE, ADVERB towards the south
▶ **southwards** ADVERB

south-west NOUN, ADJECTIVE, ADVERB midway between south and west
▶ **south-westerly** ADJECTIVE, **south-western** ADJECTIVE

souvenir (soo-ven-eer) NOUN something given or kept as a reminder of a person, place, or event

sou'wester NOUN a waterproof hat with a wide flap at the back

sovereign NOUN **1** a king or queen who is the ruler of a country **2** an old British gold coin worth £1

sovereign ADJECTIVE **1** supreme *sovereign power* **2** having sovereignty *sovereign states*

sovereignty NOUN the power a country has to govern itself

sow[1] (rhymes with *go*) VERB **sown** or or **sowed** **1** to put seeds into the ground to grow **2** to cause feelings or ideas to develop
▶ **sower** NOUN

⚠ **USAGE**
Do not confuse this word with *sew*.

sow[2] (rhymes with *cow*) NOUN a female pig

soya bean NOUN a kind of bean from which edible oil and flour are made

soy sauce or **soya sauce** NOUN a Chinese or Japanese sauce made from fermented soya beans

spa NOUN a health resort where there is a spring of water containing mineral salts

space NOUN **1** the whole area outside the earth, where the stars and planets are **2** an area or volume **3** an empty area; a gap **4** an interval of time

space VERB to arrange things with spaces between them

spacecraft NOUN spacecraft a vehicle for travelling in space

• *the source of the river* ▶ start, beginning, spring, origin, head

sow VERB *Sow the seeds in rows.* ▶ plant, scatter, spread, distribute, put in the ground

space NOUN • *space for ten people* ▶ room, capacity, accommodation, seating • *few green spaces left* ▶ area, expanse • *spaces between the houses* ▶ gap, interval, opening

spaceman NOUN **spacemen** a traveller in space, especially in stories

spaceship NOUN a manned spacecraft

spacious ADJECTIVE providing a lot of space

spade[1] NOUN a tool with a long handle and a wide blade for digging

spade[2] NOUN a playing card with black heart-like shapes on it

spaghetti NOUN pasta made in long thin strands

span NOUN **1** the length from end to end or across something **2** the part between two uprights of an arch or bridge **3** the length of a period of time **4** the distance from the tip of the thumb to the tip of the little finger when the hand is spread out

span VERB **spanning, spanned** to reach from one side or end to the other

spangle NOUN a small piece of glittering material

spaniel NOUN a kind of dog with long ears and silky fur

spank VERB to smack a person on the bottom as a punishment

spanner NOUN a tool for gripping and turning the nut on a bolt etc.

spar[1] NOUN a strong pole used for a mast or boom etc. on a ship

spar[2] VERB **sparring, sparred 1** to practise boxing **2** to quarrel or argue

spare VERB **1** to afford to give or do without **2** to be merciful towards someone **3** to avoid making a person suffer something *Spare me the details.* **4** to use or treat economically *No expense will be spared.*

spare ADJECTIVE **1** not used but kept ready in case it is needed **2** thin or lean

spark NOUN **1** a tiny glowing particle **2** a flash produced electrically **3** a trace *a spark of hope*

spark VERB to give off a spark or sparks

sparkle VERB **1** to shine with tiny flashes of light **2** to be lively and witty ► **sparkle** NOUN

sparkler NOUN a hand-held firework that gives off sparks

spacious ADJECTIVE • *a spacious room* ► big, large, roomy, sizeable

span VERB • *A bridge spans the river.* ► cross, bridge, pass over, extend across

spare VERB • *can't spare the money* ► afford, do without • *would not spare the hostages* ► pardon, show mercy to

spare ADJECTIVE • *a spare set of keys* ► extra, additional, supplementary • *spare paper* ► leftover, surplus, unwanted

spark NOUN • *a spark of light* ► flash, gleam, glint, flicker

sparkle VERB • *Lights sparkled in the distance.* ► glitter, glint, glisten, glimmer, twinkle

sparrow NOUN a small brown bird

sparse ADJECTIVE thinly scattered
> **sparsely** ADVERB

spartan ADJECTIVE simple and without comfort

spasm NOUN **1** a sudden involuntary movement of a muscle **2** a sudden brief spell of activity

spasmodic ADJECTIVE **1** happening or done at irregular intervals **2** to do with or caused by a spasm
> **spasmodically** ADVERB

spastic NOUN a person suffering from spasms of the muscles and jerky movements, especially caused by cerebral palsy
> **spastic** ADJECTIVE

⚠️ **USAGE**

This word can be offensive to some people. Use *person with cerebral palsy* instead.

spat *past tense of* **spit**[1]

spate NOUN a sudden flood or rush

spathe (rhymes with *bathe*) NOUN a large petal-like part of a flower, round a central spike

spatial ADJECTIVE to do with space

spatter VERB **1** to scatter in small drops **2** to splash *spattered with mud*

spatula NOUN a tool with a broad flexible blade, used for spreading or mixing

spawn NOUN the eggs of fish, frogs, toads, or shellfish

spawn VERB **1** to produce spawn **2** to produce in great quantities

spay VERB sterilize a female animal by removing the ovaries

speak VERB **spoke**, **spoken 1** to say something; to talk **2** to be able to talk in a specified foreign language **3** to give a speech

speaker NOUN **1** a person who is speaking **2** someone who makes a speech **3** a loudspeaker **the Speaker** an official who controls the debates in Parliament

spear NOUN a long pointed weapon for throwing or stabbing

spear VERB to pierce with a spear or with something pointed

spearmint NOUN mint used in cookery and for flavouring chewing gum

special ADJECTIVE **1** not ordinary or usual *a special occasion* **2** meant for a particular person or purpose *a special tool*

specialist NOUN an expert in one subject or branch of a subject

speciality NOUN **specialities 1** a special interest or ability **2** a special product

THESAURUS

sparse ADJECTIVE • *sparse vegetation*
> meagre, scarce, scant, minimal

speak VERB • *refused to speak about it* ▶ talk, say something, communicate • *He spoke for an*

hour. ▶ lecture, give a speech, hold forth

special ADJECTIVE • *a special occasion* ▶ important, exceptional, extraordinary • *a special tool* ▶ distinct, distinctive, characteristic, unique

a
b
c
d
e
f
g
h
i
j
k
l
m
n
o
p
q
r
s
t
u
v
w
x
y
z

specialize VERB to give particular attention or study to one subject or thing ► **specialization** NOUN

⚠ **SPELLING**

This word can also be spelled *specialise*.

specially ADVERB 1 in a special way 2 for a special purpose

species (spee-shiz) NOUN **species** 1 a group of animals or plants that are similar 2 a kind or sort

specific ADJECTIVE definite or precise ► **specifically** ADVERB

specification NOUN a detailed description of something

specify VERB **specifies, specified** to name or list precisely

specimen NOUN 1 a sample used for study 2 an example *a fine specimen*

speck NOUN a small spot or particle

speckle NOUN a small spot or mark ► **speckled** ADJECTIVE

spectacle NOUN 1 an impressive sight or display 2 a ridiculous sight

spectacles PLURAL NOUN a pair of glasses ► **spectacled** ADJECTIVE

spectacular ADJECTIVE impressive or striking

spectator NOUN a person who watches a game, event, etc.

spectre NOUN a ghost ► **spectral** ADJECTIVE

spectrum NOUN **spectra** or **spectrums** 1 the bands of colours seen in a rainbow 2 a wide range of things, ideas, etc.

speculate VERB 1 to form opinions without any definite evidence 2 to invest in money markets in the hope of making a profit but with the risk of loss ► **speculation** NOUN, **speculator** NOUN

speculative ADJECTIVE involving speculation

sped past tense of **speed**

speech NOUN 1 the action or power of speaking 2 a talk to an audience 3 a group of lines spoken by a character in a play

speechless ADJECTIVE too surprised or emotional to say anything

THESAURUS

specific ADJECTIVE • *no specific evidence* ► detailed, definite, precise

specimen NOUN • *a specimen of the handwriting* ► example, sample, illustration

speck NOUN • *a speck of dust* ► particle, bit, fleck, spot

spectacular ADJECTIVE • *a spectacular display*

► magnificent, splendid, impressive, dazzling

spectator NOUN • *Spectators lined the streets.* ► onlooker, watcher, viewer

speech NOUN • *the power of speech* ► speaking, talking • *His speech was slurred.* ► pronunciation, diction, articulation • *an after-dinner speech* ► talk, lecture, oration

speed NOUN **1** a measure of the time in which something moves or happens **2** quickness or swiftness

speed VERB **sped** or, in senses 2 and 3, **speeded**) **1** to go quickly **2** to make or become quicker **3** to drive faster than the legal limit
▶ **speeding** NOUN

speedboat NOUN a fast motor boat

speedometer NOUN a device in a vehicle, showing its speed

speedway NOUN a track for motorcycle racing

speedy ADJECTIVE **speedier, speediest** quick or swift
▶ **speedily** ADVERB

spell NOUN **1** a set of words supposed to have magical power **2** a period of time **3** a period of a certain work or activity etc.

spell³ VERB **spelled** or **spelt** **1** to put letters in the right order to make a word or words **2** (of letters) to form a word **3** to have as a result *Wet weather spells ruin for crops.*

spellbound ADJECTIVE entranced as if by a magic spell

spelling NOUN the way a word is spelled

spend VERB **spent** **1** to use money for payment **2** to use up energy etc. **3** to pass time

spendthrift NOUN a person who spends money extravagantly

sperm NOUN the male cell that fertilizes an ovum

spew VERB **1** to vomit **2** to send out in a stream

sphere NOUN **1** a perfectly round solid shape **2** a field of action or interest etc. ▶ **spherical** ADJECTIVE

spheroid NOUN a solid like a sphere but not perfectly round

sphinx NOUN a stone statue with the body of a lion and a human head, especially a massive one from ancient Egypt

spice NOUN **1** a strong-tasting substance used to flavour food **2** something that adds interest or excitement

spice VERB to flavour with spices

spick and span ADJECTIVE neat and clean

speed NOUN • *Check your speed.*
▶ velocity, pace, rate, tempo
• *done with amazing speed*
▶ rapidity, swiftness, alacrity, promptness

speed VERB • *We sped back home.*
▶ hurry, hasten, rush, dash

speedy ADJECTIVE • *a speedy response* ▶ quick, rapid, swift, fast, prompt

spell NOUN • *a magic spell*
▶ charm, incantation, enchantment • *a spell of dry weather* ▶ period, interval, stretch

spend VERB • *spent £50 on it*
▶ pay, fritter, squander • *spent all their time arguing* ▶ pass, fill, occupy

sphere NOUN • *a glass sphere*
▶ ball, globe, orb

a b c d e f g h i j k l m n o p q r s t u v w x y z

spicy ADJECTIVE **spicier**, **spiciest**
having a strong flavour from
spices

spider NOUN a small insect-like
animal with eight legs that spins
webs to catch insects on which it
feeds

spidery ADJECTIVE (of handwriting)
having long thin lines and sharp
angles

spike NOUN **1** a pointed piece of
metal **2** a sharp point ▶ **spiky**
ADJECTIVE

spike VERB **1** to fit with spikes **2** to
pierce with a spike

spill VERB **spilt** or **spilled 1** to let
something fall out of a container
2 to become spilt ▶ **spillage** NOUN

spill NOUN **1** the act of spilling
2 something spilt **3** a fall from a
horse, bicycle, etc.

spin VERB **spinning**, **spun 1** to
turn round and round quickly **2** to
make raw wool or cotton into
threads by pulling and twisting its
fibres **3** (of a spider or silkworm) to
make a web or cocoon **spin out** to
make something last longer

spin NOUN **1** a spinning movement
2 a short outing in a car

spinach NOUN a vegetable with
dark green leaves

spinal ADJECTIVE to do with the
spine

spindle NOUN **1** a thin rod on which
thread is wound **2** a pin or
bar on which something turns

spindly ADJECTIVE thin and long or
tall

spin dryer NOUN a machine in
which wet clothes are spun round
to dry them

spine NOUN **1** the line of bones
down the middle of the back **2** a
thorn or prickle **3** the edge of a
book where the pages are joined

spine-chilling ADJECTIVE
frightening and exciting

spineless ADJECTIVE **1** without a
backbone **2** lacking courage; weak

spinet NOUN a small harpsichord

spinning wheel NOUN a
machine for spinning fibre into
thread

spin-off NOUN an extra benefit or
result

spinster NOUN a woman who has
not married

THESAURUS

spike NOUN • tore her dress on a
spike ▶ prong, point, barb

spill VERB • He spilled his drink.
▶ knock over, tip over, upset, slop,
overturn • Water was spilling over.
▶ overflow, brim, run, pour • A
lorry had spilled its load. ▶ shed,
tip, scatter, drop • People spilled
into the streets. ▶ stream, pour,
swarm

spin VERB • A wheel spins on an axle.
▶ turn, rotate, revolve, gyrate,
whirl • My head was spinning.
▶ reel, swim

spine NOUN • a posture that is good
for the spine ▶ backbone • the
spines of a hedgehog ▶ needle,
quill, bristle

DICTIONARY

spiny ADJECTIVE covered with spines; prickly

spiral ADJECTIVE going round a central point and becoming gradually closer to it or further from it ▶ **spirally** ADVERB

spiral NOUN a spiral line or course

spiral VERB **spiralling, spiralled 1** to move in a spiral **2** to increase or decrease rapidly

spire NOUN a tall pointed part on top of a church tower

spirit NOUN **1** the soul **2** a person's mood or mind and feelings *in good spirits* **3** a ghost or a supernatural being **4** courage or liveliness **5** a kind of quality in something **6** a strong distilled alcoholic drink

spirit VERB to carry off quickly and secretly

spirited ADJECTIVE self-confident and lively

spirit level NOUN a glass tube of liquid with an air bubble in it, used to find out whether something is completely level

spiritual ADJECTIVE **1** to do with the human soul; not physical **2** to do with religion ▶ **spirituality** NOUN, **spiritually** ADVERB

spiritual NOUN a religious folk song, originally sung by black Christians in America

spiritualism NOUN the belief that the spirits of dead people communicate with the living ▶ **spiritualist** NOUN

spit[1] VERB **spat 1** to send out drops of liquid etc. from the mouth **2** to rain lightly

spit NOUN saliva or spittle

spit[2] NOUN **1** a long thin metal spike put through meat for roasting **2** a narrow strip of land extending into the sea

spite NOUN a desire to hurt or annoy someone **in spite of** not being prevented by *went out in spite of the rain*

spite VERB to hurt or annoy someone from spite

spiteful ADJECTIVE wishing to hurt or annoy someone ▶ **spitefully** ADVERB

spitting image NOUN an exact likeness

spittle NOUN saliva, especially when it is spat out

splash VERB **1** to make liquid fly about in drops **2** (of liquid) to fly

THESAURUS

spirit NOUN • *the body and the spirit* ▶ soul, inner being • *had a lot of spirit* ▶ enthusiasm, vigour, energy • *spirits haunting the place* ▶ ghost, spectre, phantom • *in good spirits* ▶ mood, humour

spite NOUN • *criticized her out of spite* ▶ malice, maliciousness, vindictiveness

spiteful ADJECTIVE • *spiteful remarks* ▶ malicious, hurtful, cruel, vicious, cruel, nasty

splash VERB • *A van splashed mud over us.* ▶ splatter, spray, slosh, slop, squirt • *Children splashed about in the water.* ▶ paddle, wade, wallow, slosh

a
b
c
d
e
f
g
h
i
j
k
l
m
n
o
p
q
r
s
t
u
v
w
x
y
z

about in drops **3** to make wet by splashing

splash NOUN **1** the action or sound or mark of splashing **2** a bright patch of colour or light

splatter VERB to splash noisily

splay VERB to spread or slope apart

spleen NOUN an organ of the body, close to the stomach, that helps to clean the blood

splendid ADJECTIVE **1** magnificent; full of splendour **2** excellent
► **splendidly** ADVERB

splendour NOUN a brilliant display or appearance

splice VERB to join pieces of rope etc. by twisting the strands together

splint NOUN a straight piece of wood etc. tied to a broken arm or leg to hold it firm

splinter NOUN a thin sharp piece of wood, glass, stone, etc. broken off a larger piece

splinter VERB to break into splinters

split VERB **splitting, split 1** to break apart along the length of something **2** to divide into parts **3** to divide among several people **split up** to end a relationship

split NOUN a break or tear caused by splitting **the splits** an acrobatic position in which the legs are stretched widely in opposite directions

split second NOUN a very brief moment of time

splodge NOUN a dirty mark or stain

splutter VERB **1** to make a quick series of spitting sounds **2** to speak quickly but not clearly
► **splutter** NOUN

splash NOUN • *a splash of colour*
► spot, patch, splodge, burst, dash

splendid ADJECTIVE • *in a splendid setting* ► magnificent, impressive, imposing, spectacular • *a splendid day out* ► wonderful, marvellous, excellent

splendour NOUN • *the splendour of the palace* ► magnificence, grandeur, sumptuousness, majesty

splinter NOUN • *a splinter of wood* ► sliver, chip, flake, fragment

splinter VERB • *The glass splintered.* ► shatter, crack, chip, smash

split VERB • *to split the curtain* ► tear, rip, slash, slit • *split the log with an axe* ► chop, cut, break • *splitting the proceeds* ► divide, share, distribute • *where the paths split* ► fork, divide, branch **split up** • *Her parents had split up.* ► separate, break up, divorce

split NOUN • *a large split in the rock* ► crack, fissure, crevice, break • *a split in the side* ► tear, rip, cut, slash, slit

spoil VERB **spoilt** or or **spoiled** 1 to damage or make useless 2 to damage the character of someone by pampering them

spoils PLURAL NOUN things stolen or gained in war

spoilsport NOUN a person who spoils other people's enjoyment

spoke [1] NOUN each of the bars or rods between the centre of a wheel and the rim

spoke [2] past tense of **speak**

spokesperson NOUN a person who speaks on behalf of others ▶ **spokesman** NOUN, **spokeswoman** NOUN

sponge NOUN 1 a sea creature with a soft porous body 2 the skeleton of this creature, or a piece of a similar substance, used for washing 3 a soft lightweight cake or pudding ▶ **spongy** ADJECTIVE

sponge VERB 1 to wipe or wash with a sponge 2 (informal) to get money or food without giving anything in return ▶ **sponger** NOUN

sponsor NOUN 1 a person or organization that provides money for an activity 2 someone who gives money to a charity in return for something achieved by another person ▶ **sponsorship** NOUN

sponsor VERB to be a sponsor for a person or thing

spontaneous ADJECTIVE happening or done naturally ▶ **spontaneity** NOUN, **spontaneously** ADVERB

spoof NOUN 1 a hoax 2 a parody

spook NOUN (informal) a ghost

spooky ADJECTIVE **spookier**, **spookiest** eerie or frightening

spool NOUN a rod or cylinder on which something is wound

spoon NOUN a small tool with a rounded bowl on a handle, used for lifting things to the mouth or for stirring

spoon VERB to take or lift with a spoon

spoonful NOUN **spoonfuls** the amount a spoon will hold

sporadic ADJECTIVE happening or found at irregular intervals; scattered ▶ **sporadically** ADVERB

spore NOUN a tiny reproductive cell of a plant such as a fungus or fern

sporran NOUN a pouch worn in front of a kilt

sport NOUN 1 an athletic activity; a game or pastime 2 games of this kind *keen on sport* 3 (informal) an obliging good-natured person

sport VERB 1 to amuse yourself 2 to wear

THESAURUS

spoil VERB • *didn't want to spoil her shoes* ▶ damage, harm, hurt, ruin
• *This could spoil everything.*
▶ ruin, wreck, upset, mess up
• *decided to spoil herself*
▶ indulge, pamper

spooky ADJECTIVE • *a spooky place at night* ▶ eerie, frightening, creepy, ghostly, weird

sport NOUN • *to enjoy sport*
▶ games, exercise

sporting ADJECTIVE **1** to do with or interested in sport **2** fair and generous

sporting chance NOUN a reasonable chance of success

sports car NOUN an open low-built fast car

sports jacket NOUN a man's casual jacket

sportsman NOUN **sportsmen** a man who takes part in sport

sportsmanship NOUN fair and generous behaviour in sport

sportswoman NOUN **sportswomen** a woman who takes part in sport

spot NOUN **1** a small round mark **2** a pimple **3** a small amount **4** a place **5** a drop **on the spot** without delay or change of place

spot VERB **spotting, spotted 1** to mark with spots **2** to notice or recognize ▶ **spotter** NOUN

spot check NOUN a random check on one of a group of people or things

spotless ADJECTIVE perfectly clean

spotlight NOUN a strong light that can shine on one small area

spotty ADJECTIVE **spottier, spottiest** marked with spots

spouse NOUN a person's husband or wife

spout NOUN **1** a pipe or similar opening from which liquid can pour **2** a jet of liquid

spout VERB **1** to come or send out as a jet of liquid **2** (informal) to speak for a long time

sprain VERB to injure a joint by twisting it ▶ **sprain** NOUN

sprat NOUN a small edible fish

sprawl VERB **1** to sit or lie with the arms and legs spread out loosely **2** to spread out loosely or untidily ▶ **sprawl** NOUN

spray VERB to scatter tiny drops of liquid over

spray NOUN **1** tiny drops of liquid sent through the air **2** a device for spraying liquid **3** a liquid for spraying **4** a single shoot with its leaves and flowers

spread VERB **spread 1** to open or stretch out to its full size **2** to make

spot NOUN • *a dirty spot on the carpet* ▶ stain, mark, smudge, smear • *a small spot on the skin* ▶ pimple, freckle, mole • *a fabric with small spots* ▶ dot, fleck • *a quiet spot near the sea* ▶ place, position, location, site

spot VERB • *spotted with grease* ▶ stain, mark, smudge, spatter • *spotted him in the garden* ▶ notice, observe, glimpse, see

spray VERB • *spraying water over the grass* ▶ sprinkle, spread • *Water sprayed into the air.* ▶ spout, gush, spurt

spray NOUN • *a spray of water* ▶ shower, sprinkling, splash • *a spray of flowers* ▶ bouquet, bunch, posy

spread VERB • *He spread his arms.* ▶ extend, stretch • *Spread the*

DICTIONARY

something cover a surface **3** to become longer or wider **4** to make or become more widely known

spread NOUN **1** the action or result of spreading **2** a thing's breadth or extent **3** a paste for spreading on bread **4** (*informal*) a large or grand meal

spreadeagled ADJECTIVE with arms and legs stretched out

spreadsheet NOUN a computer program for organizing figures etc. in a table

spree NOUN a period of carefree enjoyment

sprig NOUN a small branch or shoot

sprightly ADJECTIVE **sprightlier**, **sprightliest** lively and full of energy

spring VERB **sprang**, **sprung** **1** to jump; to move quickly or suddenly *sprang to his feet* **2** to originate or arise **3** to present or produce suddenly *spring a surprise on us*

spring NOUN **1** a coil of metal that returns to its original size after being bent, squeezed, or stretched **2** a springing movement **3** a place where water comes up naturally from the ground **4** the season when most plants begin to grow

springboard NOUN a springy board from which people jump in diving and gymnastics

spring-clean VERB to clean a house thoroughly in springtime

springy ADJECTIVE **springier**, **springiest** able to spring back easily after being bent, squeezed, or stretched

sprinkle VERB to make tiny drops or pieces fall on something
▶ **sprinkler** NOUN

sprinkling NOUN a small amount

sprint VERB to run very fast for a short distance ▶ **sprint** NOUN, **sprinter** NOUN

sprite NOUN an elf, fairy, or goblin

sprocket NOUN each of the row of teeth round a wheel, fitting into links on a chain

sprout VERB to start to grow; to put out shoots

sprout NOUN **1** a shoot of a plant **2** a Brussels sprout

spruce¹ NOUN a kind of fir tree

spruce² ADJECTIVE neat and trim; smart

spruce VERB to smarten *Spruce yourself up.*

spry ADJECTIVE **spryer**, **spryest** active and lively

THESAURUS

map on the table. ▶ open out, display • *to spread seeds*
▶ scatter, strew • *to spread information* ▶ communicate, broadcast, advertise • *The feelings were beginning to spread.*
▶ grow, increase, develop, proliferate

spring VERB • *He sprang to his feet.*
▶ leap, jump, bound

sprinkle VERB • *to sprinkle sugar over the cake* ▶ scatter, strew, drip

sprout VERB • *The seeds began to sprout.* ▶ grow, germinate, shoot up, develop

spud NOUN (informal) a potato

spur NOUN **1** a sharp device worn on the heel of a rider's boot to urge on a horse **2** a stimulus or incentive **3** a ridge that sticks out from a mountain **on the spur of the moment** on an impulse

spur VERB **spurring, spurred** to urge on

spurious ADJECTIVE not genuine

spurn VERB to reject scornfully

spurt VERB **1** to gush out **2** to increase your speed suddenly

spurt NOUN **1** a sudden gush **2** a sudden increase in speed or effort

sputter VERB to splutter

spy NOUN **spies** someone who works secretly to gather information about another country, organization, etc.

spy VERB **spies, spied 1** to be a spy **2** to keep watch secretly **3** to see or notice

squabble VERB to quarrel or bicker ▶ **squabble** NOUN

squad NOUN a small group of people working or being trained together

squadron NOUN a part of an army, navy, or air force

squalid ADJECTIVE dirty and unpleasant ▶ **squalidly** ADVERB

squall NOUN a sudden storm or gust of wind ▶ **squally** ADVERB

squalor NOUN dirty and unpleasant conditions

squander VERB to spend money or time wastefully

square NOUN **1** a flat shape with four equal sides and four right angles **2** an area surrounded by buildings **3** the result of multiplying a number by itself *9 is the square of 3 (9 = 3 x 3)*

square ADJECTIVE **1** having the shape of a square **2** forming a right angle *square corners* **3** equal or even *still square at full time* **4** used to give the length of each side of a square shape or object *The carpet is four metres square.* **5** used to give a measurement of an area *an area of 25 square metres*

square VERB **1** to make a thing square **2** to multiply a number by itself *5 squared is 25* **3** to make or be consistent **4** to settle or pay a debt

spur VERB • *was spurred to action* ▶ stimulate, encourage, drive, prompt

spurt VERB • *Blood spurted from his finger.* ▶ squirt, gush, shoot, stream

spy VERB • *We spied an adder in the grass.* ▶ notice, glimpse, spot, see **spy on** • *She sent you to*

spy on me. ▶ snoop on, watch, shadow

squabble VERB • *squabbling over money* ▶ argue, quarrel, bicker, fight

squalid ADJECTIVE • *squalid surroundings* ▶ dirty, filthy, grimy, grubby

squander VERB • *to squander money* ▶ waste, fritter away

square deal NOUN a deal that is honest and fair

squarely ADVERB directly or exactly *The ball hit him squarely in the mouth.*

square meal NOUN a good satisfying meal

square root NOUN the number that gives a particular number if it is multiplied by itself *3 is the square root of 9 (3 x 3 = 9)*

squash¹ VERB 1 to press something so that it becomes flat or out of shape 2 to force into a small space 3 to suppress or put an end to

squash NOUN 1 a crowded condition 2 a fruit-flavoured soft drink 3 an indoor game played with rackets and a soft ball

squash² NOUN a kind of gourd used as a vegetable

squat VERB **squatting, squatted** 1 to sit on your heels 2 to live in an unoccupied building without permission ► **squat** NOUN

squat ADJECTIVE short and fat

squatter NOUN someone who is squatting in a building

squawk VERB to make a loud harsh cry ► **squawk** NOUN

squeak VERB to make a short high-pitched cry or sound
► **squeak** NOUN, **squeaky** ADJECTIVE

squeal VERB to make a long shrill cry or sound ► **squeal** NOUN

squeamish ADJECTIVE easily disgusted or shocked

squeeze VERB 1 to press something from opposite sides 2 to force into or through a place *squeezed through a gap*

squeeze NOUN 1 the action of squeezing 2 an amount of liquid squeezed out *a squeeze of lemon* 3 a time when money is difficult to get or borrow

squelch VERB to make a sound like treading in thick mud ► **squelch** NOUN

squid NOUN a sea animal with tentacles

squiggle NOUN a short curly line

squint VERB 1 to be cross-eyed 2 to look with half-shut eyes at something ► **squint** NOUN

squire NOUN 1 a country landowner 2 a young nobleman who served a knight

squirm VERB to wriggle about from embarrassment or awkwardness

THESAURUS

squash VERB • *Someone had squashed the flowers.* ► crush, flatten, press, mangle, trample on, compress • *squashed a few things into his case* ► stuff, force, cram, pack • *The uprising was ruthlessly squashed.* ► suppress, quash, quell, put down

squat VERB • *to squat on the floor* ► crouch, stoop, sit

squeeze VERB • *He squeezed her hand.* ► press, clasp, grip • *She put her arm round and squeezed him.* ► hug, embrace, cuddle • *squeezed the audience into a tiny room* ► cram, push, ram, shove, stuff

DICTIONARY

squirrel NOUN a small animal with a bushy tail and red or grey fur, living in trees

squirt VERB to send or come out in a jet of liquid ▶ **squirt** NOUN

St. or **St** ABBREVIATION 1 Saint 2 Street

stab VERB **stabbing, stabbed** to pierce or wound with something sharp

stab NOUN 1 the action of stabbing 2 a sudden sharp pain 3 (informal) an attempt

stability NOUN a stable or steady state

stabilize VERB to make or become stable ▶ **stabilization** NOUN

⚠ **SPELLING**

This word can also be spelled *stabilise*.

stabilizer NOUN a device for keeping a vehicle or ship steady

⚠ **SPELLING**

This word can also be spelled *stabiliser*.

stable ADJECTIVE 1 steady and firm 2 sensible and dependable

stable NOUN a building where horses are kept

staccato ADVERB, ADJECTIVE (Music) played with each note short and separate

stack NOUN 1 a neat pile 2 (informal) a large amount *a stack of work*

stack VERB to pile in a stack

stadium NOUN **stadiums** or **stadia** a sports ground surrounded by seats for spectators

staff NOUN 1 the people who work in an office, shop, etc. 2 the teachers in a school or college

staff VERB to provide with a staff

stag NOUN a male deer

stage NOUN 1 a platform for performances in a theatre or hall 2 a point or part of a process, journey, etc.

stage VERB 1 to present a performance on a stage 2 to organize *staged a protest*

THESAURUS

squirt VERB • Water squirted from the nozzle. ▶ spurt, shoot, gush, spray • *squirted me with water* ▶ splash, spray, shower, spatter

stab VERB • *stabbed him in the arm* ▶ knife, spear, pierce, jab

stab NOUN • *a stab of pain* ▶ twinge, pang, sting

stable ADJECTIVE • Make sure the equipment is stable. ▶ steady, firm, secure • *a stable regime* ▶ strong, well-established, secure, lasting

stack NOUN • *a stack of magazines* ▶ heap, pile, mound, mass

stack VERB • *Boxes were stacked on the floor.* ▶ pile, heap, load

staff NOUN • *extra staff needed* ▶ personnel, assistants, employees, workers

stage NOUN • *the last stage of the journey* ▶ part, section, phase, portion • *a new stage in relations* ▶ point, phase

stage VERB • *to stage a performance* ▶ mount, put on, present, perform

stagecoach NOUN a horse-drawn passenger coach

stagger VERB 1 to walk unsteadily 2 to shock deeply 3 to arrange working hours etc. to begin and end at different times ► **stagger** NOUN, **staggering** ADJECTIVE

stagnant ADJECTIVE (of water) stale from not flowing

stagnate VERB 1 to be stagnant 2 to be dull through lack of activity or variety ► **stagnation** NOUN

staid ADJECTIVE steady and serious in manner; sedate

stain NOUN 1 a dirty mark 2 a blemish on someone's character or past record 3 a liquid used for staining

stain VERB 1 to make a stain on 2 to colour with a liquid that sinks into the surface

stained glass NOUN pieces of coloured glass held together in a lead framework to make a picture or pattern

stainless ADJECTIVE without a stain

stainless steel NOUN steel that does not rust easily

stair NOUN each of a set of fixed steps that lead from one floor to another

staircase NOUN a set of stairs

stairway NOUN a staircase

stake NOUN 1 a thick pointed stick driven into the ground 2 a post at which people were executed by burning 3 an amount of money bet on something **at stake** being risked

stake VERB 1 to fix or mark out with stakes 2 to bet or risk money etc.

stalactite NOUN a stony spike hanging like an icicle from the roof of a cave

stalagmite NOUN a stony spike standing like a pillar on the floor of a cave

stale ADJECTIVE 1 not fresh 2 dull and lacking new ideas

stalemate NOUN 1 a drawn position in chess when a player cannot make a move without putting the king in check 2 a situation in which neither side in an argument can win

stalk¹ NOUN a stem of a plant etc.

stalk² VERB 1 to track or hunt stealthily 2 to walk in a stiff or dignified way

THESAURUS

stagger VERB • *staggered up the road* ► totter, stumble, lurch • *was staggered by the answer* ► shock, astonish, amaze, flabbergast

stain NOUN • *a stain on his shirt* ► mark, spot, smear, smudge

stain VERB • *to stain your clothes* ► mark, dirty, soil • *to stain wood* ► dye, colour

stale ADJECTIVE • *stale bread* ► dry, hard, old

stalk NOUN • *the stalk of a plant* ► stem, shoot, branch

stalk VERB • *stalked them through the long grass* ► track, trail, hunt, pursue • *stalked out of the door* ► stride, strut

a b c d e f g h i j k l m n o p q r s t u v w x y z

stall NOUN **1** a table or counter from which things are sold **2** a place for one animal in a stable or shed

stall VERB **1** to lose power suddenly and stop **2** to delay or avoid giving an answer

stallion NOUN a male horse

stalls PLURAL NOUN the seats in the lowest level of a theatre

stalwart ADJECTIVE strong and faithful

stamen NOUN the part of a flower bearing pollen

stamina NOUN strength and ability to endure hard effort

stammer VERB to keep repeating the same syllables when speaking
► **stammer** NOUN

stamp NOUN **1** a small piece of gummed paper stuck to a letter or parcel to show the postage has been paid **2** a small device for pressing words or marks on something **3** a distinctive characteristic *bears the stamp of truth*

stamp VERB **1** to bang the foot heavily on the ground **2** to walk with loud heavy steps **3** to stick a postage stamp on **4** to press a mark or design etc. on **stamp out 1** to put an end to

stampede NOUN a wild rush by animals or people

stampede VERB to rush wildly in a crowd

stance NOUN **1** the way a person or animal stands **2** an attitude or point of view

stand VERB **stood 1** to be on your feet without moving **2** to rise to your feet **3** to set or be upright **4** to stay the same **5** to be a candidate for election **6** to tolerate or endure **7** to provide and pay for **stand for** to represent

stand NOUN **1** something made for putting things on **2** a stall for selling or displaying things **3** a grandstand **4** a stationary position *took his stand near the door* **5** resistance to attack *to make a stand*

stall NOUN • *a stall at the fair*
► stand, booth, kiosk

stamp NOUN • *an official stamp*
► mark, seal

stamp VERB • *stamped his foot*
► strike, bring down, thump

stamp out • *trying to stamp out bullying* ► eliminate, eradicate, end

stand VERB • *The choir stood for the final chorus.* ► rise, get to your feet, get up • *A house once stood on this spot.* ► situated, be located, be sited • *stood the packet on the table* ► put, place, set, position • *The offer still stands.* ► remain in force, remain valid, be unchanged • *can't stand noise* ► bear, abide, endure, tolerate, put up with **stand for** • *what the initials stand for* ► mean, represent, denote

stand NOUN • *a large vase on a stand* ► base, pedestal, support

standard NOUN **1** a level of achievement or quality *a high standard* **2** a thing used to measure or judge something else **3** a special flag

standard ADJECTIVE **1** of the usual or average quality or kind **2** regarded as the best and widely used *the standard book on the subject*

standardize VERB to make things have a standard size, quality, etc.
▸ **standardization** NOUN

⚠ **SPELLING**

This word can also be spelled *standardise*.

standard lamp NOUN a tall upright lamp that stands on the floor

standard of living NOUN the level of comfort and wealth that a country or person has

standby NOUN something or someone kept to be used if needed

stand-in NOUN a deputy or substitute

standing NOUN **1** a person's status or reputation **2** the period for which something has existed

stand-offish ADJECTIVE cold and formal; not friendly

standpoint NOUN a point of view

standstill NOUN a complete stop

stanza NOUN a verse of poetry

staple¹ NOUN **1** a small piece of wire pushed through papers and clenched to fasten them **2** a U-shaped nail

staple VERB to fasten with a staple or staples

staple² ADJECTIVE (of food or diet) main or usual

stapler NOUN a device for stapling papers together

star NOUN **1** a large mass of burning gas seen as a bright light in the night sky **2** a shape with points or rays sticking out from it **3** a famous performer or celebrity

star VERB **starring**, **starred 1** to be one of the main performers in a film or show **2** to have as a main performer **3** to mark with a star symbol

starboard NOUN the right-hand side of a ship or aircraft facing forward

📖 **WORD HISTORY**

from Old English words meaning 'rudder side' (because early sailing ships were steered by paddle on the right-hand side)

starch NOUN **1** a white carbohydrate in bread, potatoes, etc. **2** a substance used to stiffen clothes ▸ **starchy** ADJECTIVE

starch VERB to stiffen with starch

THESAURUS

standard NOUN • *a high standard* ▸ quality, level • *a standard of behaviour* ▸ norm, principle, benchmark, example • *the regimental standard* ▸ flag, banner, colours

standard ADJECTIVE • *the standard procedure* ▸ normal, usual, typical

star NOUN • *an international star* ▸ celebrity, big name, idol

stardom NOUN the state of being a star performer

stare VERB to look at something intensely ▸ **stare** NOUN

starfish NOUN a sea animal shaped like a star with five points

stark ADJECTIVE 1 complete or unmistakable 2 desolate and bare *a stark landscape*

stark ADVERB completely *stark naked*

starlight NOUN light from the stars

starling NOUN a noisy black bird with speckled feathers

starry ADJECTIVE full of stars

starry-eyed ADJECTIVE made happy by foolish dreams or unrealistic hopes

start VERB 1 to begin or cause to begin 2 to make a machine begin running 3 to jump suddenly from pain or surprise

start NOUN 1 a beginning 2 the place where a race starts 3 an advantage that someone starts

with *ten minutes' start* 4 a sudden movement

starter NOUN the first course of a meal

startle VERB to surprise or alarm

starve VERB 1 to suffer or die from lack of food 2 to deprive someone of something they need
▸ **starvation** NOUN

starving ADJECTIVE (*informal*) very hungry

stash VERB (*informal*) to store safely in a secret place

state NOUN 1 the quality or condition of a person or thing 2 an organized community under one government or forming part of a republic 3 a country's government 4 a grand style *arrived in state* 5 (*informal*) an excited or upset condition *got into a state*

state VERB to express in spoken or written words

stately ADJECTIVE **statelier**, **stateliest** dignified or grand

THESAURUS

stare VERB • *sat staring* ▸ gaze, gape, glare

start VERB • *The film starts at 8.* ▸ begin, commence • *to start a reading group* ▸ set up, establish, found • *A crash made us start.* ▸ jump, recoil, flinch

start NOUN • *the start of a long process* ▸ beginning, outset, birth, commencement • *the start of all our problems* ▸ origin, cause, source • *A noise gave us a start.* ▸ shock, jump, surprise

startle VERB • *A noise startled them.* ▸ alarm, frighten, scare

state NOUN • *the state of the economy* ▸ condition, situation, predicament, health • *a sovereign state* ▸ country, nation, land • *in a state* • *to get in a state* ▸ agitated, flustered, panicky

state VERB • *stated the company's objectives* ▸ announce, declare, express, communicate

stately ADJECTIVE • *a stately procession* ▸ dignified, majestic, grand

a
b
c
d
e
f
g
h
i
j
k
l
m
n
o
p
q
r
s
t
u
v
w
x
y
z

statement NOUN **1** words stating something **2** a formal account of facts

statesman NOUN **statesmen** someone who is skilled in governing a country
▶ **statesmanship** NOUN

static ADJECTIVE not moving or changing

static NOUN crackling or hissing on a telephone line, radio, etc.

static electricity NOUN electricity that is present in something, not flowing as current

station NOUN **1** a stopping place for trains, buses, etc. with platforms and buildings for passengers and goods **2** a building equipped for certain activities *police station* **3** a broadcasting company with its own frequency **4** a place where a person or thing stands

station VERB to put someone in a certain place

stationary ADJECTIVE not moving

⚠ **USAGE**
Do not confuse this word with *stationery*.

stationer NOUN a shopkeeper who sells stationery

stationery NOUN paper, envelopes, and other articles used in writing or typing

⚠ **USAGE**
Do not confuse this word with *stationary*.

statistic NOUN a piece of information expressed as a number ▶ **statistical** ADJECTIVE

statistics NOUN the study of information based on numbers

statue NOUN a stone or metal object in the form of a person or animal

statuette NOUN a small statue

stature NOUN **1** the natural height of the body **2** greatness gained by ability or achievement

status (stay-tus) NOUN position or rank in relation to others

statute NOUN a law passed by a parliament ▶ **statutory** ADJECTIVE

staunch ADJECTIVE firm and loyal

stave NOUN a set of five lines on which music is written

stave VERB **staved** or or **stove** to dent or break a hole in **stave off** to keep something away

stay VERB **1** to continue to be in the same place or state **2** to spend time in a place as a visitor

statement NOUN • *issued a brief statement* ▶ announcement, declaration, report

station NOUN • *a railway station* ▶ stopping place, terminus, platform • *a police station* ▶ establishment, base, depot

station VERB • *was stationed abroad* ▶ post, base, deploy

stationary ADJECTIVE • *The vehicles were stationary.* ▶ still, at a standstill, motionless

statue NOUN • *a statue of the emperor* ▶ figure, sculpture, effigy, carving

stay VERB • *told him to stay where he was* ▶ wait, remain, continue • *to stay calm* ▶ remain, keep • *to*

stay NOUN a time spent in a place

stead NOUN **in a person's stead** instead of this person

steadfast ADJECTIVE firm and not changing

steady ADJECTIVE **steadier, steadiest 1** not shaking or moving **2** continuing the same *a steady pace* ▶ **steadily** ADVERB

steady VERB **steadies, steadied** to make or become steady

steak NOUN a thick slice of meat or fish

steal VERB **stole, stolen 1** to take and keep something dishonestly **2** to move quietly

stealth NOUN quiet or furtive action or movement

stealthy (stelth-ee) ADJECTIVE **stealthier, stealthiest** quiet or furtive ▶ **stealthily** ADVERB

steam NOUN **1** gas or vapour produced by boiling water **2** power produced by steam

steam VERB **1** to produce steam **2** to move by the power of steam **3** to cook or treat with steam

steam engine NOUN an engine driven by steam

steamer NOUN a ship driven by steam

steamroller NOUN a heavy vehicle with a large roller used to flatten road surfaces

steamship NOUN a ship driven by steam

steamy ADJECTIVE **steamier, steamiest 1** covered in or full of steam **2** passionate

steed NOUN (literary) a horse

steel NOUN a strong metal made from iron and carbon

steel VERB **steel yourself** to find courage

steep[1] ADJECTIVE **1** sloping sharply **2** (of a price) unreasonably high ▶ **steeply** ADVERB

steep[2] VERB to soak thoroughly

THESAURUS

stay in a hotel ▶ lodge, reside, board, be accommodated

stay NOUN • *a long stay* ▶ visit, stop, break, holiday

steady ADJECTIVE • *The ladder isn't steady.* ▶ secure, stable, fixed, firm, safe • *a steady pace* ▶ constant, regular, even • *a steady girlfriend* ▶ regular, established, serious

steady VERB • *He steadied himself.* ▶ stabilize, balance

steal VERB • *tried to steal her camera* ▶ take, pilfer,

appropriate, rob, run off with • *stole quietly out of the room* ▶ creep, slink, sneak, tiptoe

stealthy ADJECTIVE • *stealthy movement* ▶ furtive, secretive, surreptitious

steamy ADJECTIVE • *steamy windows* ▶ misty, cloudy • *the hot steamy jungle* ▶ humid, muggy, sticky

steep ADJECTIVE • *steep cliffs overlooking the sea* ▶ sheer, vertical

steepen VERB to make or become steeper

steeple NOUN a church tower with a spire at the top

steeplechase NOUN a race across country or over hedges or fences

steeplejack NOUN a person who climbs tall chimneys or steeples to make repairs

steer[1] VERB to make a vehicle go in a certain direction

steer[2] NOUN a young castrated bull kept for its beef

steering wheel NOUN a wheel for steering a car, boat, etc.

stellar ADJECTIVE to do with a star or stars

stem[1] NOUN 1 the main central part of a tree or plant 2 a thin part on which a leaf, flower, or fruit is supported 3 a thin upright part of something 4 (*Grammar*) the main part of a word, to which endings are attached

stem VERB **stemming, stemmed** to stop the flow of **stem from** to have as a source

stench NOUN a strong unpleasant smell

stencil NOUN a piece of card, metal, or plastic with pieces cut out of it, used to produce a picture, design, etc.

stencil VERB **stencilling, stencilled** to produce or decorate with a stencil

step NOUN 1 a movement made by lifting the foot and setting it down 2 the sound of a person walking or running 3 a level surface for placing the foot in climbing 4 each of a series of things in a process

step VERB **stepping, stepped** to tread or walk **step in** to intervene **step up** to increase

stepbrother NOUN the son of your stepmother or stepfather

stepchild NOUN **stepchildren** a child of your husband or wife from an earlier marriage
  ▶ **stepdaughter** NOUN, **stepson** NOUN

stepfather NOUN a man who is married to your mother but was not your natural father

stepladder NOUN a folding ladder with flat treads

stepmother NOUN a woman who is married to your father but was not your natural mother

steppe NOUN a grassy plain with few trees

stepping stone NOUN 1 a stone for crossing a shallow stream 2 a stage in achieving something

steps PLURAL NOUN a stepladder

stepsister NOUN the daughter of your stepmother or stepfather

THESAURUS

steer VERB • *steered the car into the garage* ▶ drive, direct, guide

step NOUN • *took a step backwards* ▶ pace, stride, footstep • *taking a major step* ▶ decision, move,

action • *a first step* ▶ phase, stage

step VERB • *had to step over mounds rubble* ▶ tread, walk, trample

stereo ADJECTIVE stereophonic
stereo NOUN **stereos**
1 stereophonic sound or recording
2 a stereophonic CD player, record player, etc.
stereophonic ADJECTIVE using sound that comes from two different directions to give a natural effect
stereotype NOUN a fixed widely held idea of a type of person or thing
sterile ADJECTIVE 1 not fertile; barren 2 free from germs
► **sterility** NOUN
sterilize VERB 1 to make free from germs 2 to make a person or animal unable to reproduce
► **sterilization** NOUN

⚠ SPELLING

This word can also be spelled *sterilise*.

sterling NOUN British money in international trading
stern[1] ADJECTIVE strict and severe
► **sternly** ADVERB
stern[2] NOUN the back part of a ship
steroid NOUN a substance of a kind that includes certain hormones
stethoscope NOUN a device used for listening to sounds in a person's body

stew VERB to cook slowly in liquid
stew NOUN a dish of stewed meat or other food
steward NOUN 1 an official who looks after the passengers on a ship or aircraft 2 an official who looks after arrangements at a large public event
stewardess NOUN a female official on an aircraft
stick[1] NOUN 1 a long thin piece of wood 2 an implement used to hit the ball in hockey, polo, etc. 3 a long thin piece of something
stick[2] VERB **stuck** 1 to push a thing into something 2 to fix or be fixed by glue etc. 3 to become fixed and unable to move 4 (*informal*) to endure or tolerate **stick to** 1 to refuse to change
sticker NOUN an adhesive label or sign
sticking plaster NOUN a strip of adhesive material for covering cuts
stick insect NOUN an insect with a long thin body and legs, resembling a twig
stickleback NOUN a small fish with sharp spines on its back
stickler NOUN a person who insists on something *a stickler for punctuality*

THESAURUS

sterile ADJECTIVE • *sterile soil*
► infertile, barren, unproductive
• *a sterile bandage* ► clean, hygienic, sterilized, antiseptic

stern ADJECTIVE • *to look stern*
► strict, severe, harsh, serious

stick VERB • *Ben stuck a fork in the earth.* ► poke, jab, stab, thrust
• *stuck a message on the board*
► attach, fasten, fix, glue, pin • *A memory stuck in his mind.*
► remain, linger, stay **stick to**
• *stuck to his story* ► adhere to, keep to

DICTIONARY

sticky ADJECTIVE **stickier, stickiest**
1 able or likely to stick to things
2 (of weather) hot and humid
3 (informal) difficult or awkward *a sticky situation*

stiff ADJECTIVE **1** not bending or moving easily **2** thick or dense **3** difficult *a stiff climb* **4** formal in manner **5** severe or strong *a stiff fine*

stiffen VERB to make or become stiff

stifle VERB **1** to suffocate **2** to suppress *stifled a yawn*

stigma NOUN **1** a mark of disgrace **2** the part of a pistil that receives the pollen

stigmatize VERB to regard something as bad

⚠ **SPELLING**

This word can also be spelled *stigmatise*.

stile NOUN an arrangement of steps or bars for climbing over a fence

stiletto NOUN **stilettos** a shoe with a high pointed heel

still ADJECTIVE **1** not moving **2** silent **3** (of water) not fizzy

still ADVERB **1** without moving *standing still* **2** up to this or that time *were still young* **3** in a greater amount or degree *can do still better* **4** even so

still VERB to make or become still

still NOUN a photograph from a cinema film

stillborn ADJECTIVE (of a baby) born dead

still life NOUN **still lifes** a painting of lifeless things such as ornaments and fruit

stilted ADJECTIVE stiffly formal

stilts PLURAL NOUN posts or poles for supporting a person or building above the ground

stimulant NOUN something that stimulates

stimulate VERB **1** to make someone excited or enthusiastic **2** to make more lively or active
► **stimulation** NOUN

THESAURUS

sticky ADJECTIVE • *sticky tape*
► adhesive, gummed • *a sticky situation* ► difficult, tricky • *a sticky afternoon* ► humid, muggy, sultry

stiff ADJECTIVE • *a sheet of stiff cardboard* ► rigid, firm, hard • *a stiff paste* ► thick, firm • *stiff muscles* ► tight, aching, painful • *a stiff climb* ► difficult, strenuous, tough • *a stiff manner* ► formal, reserved, unfriendly • *a stiff fine* ► harsh, severe

stifle VERB • *almost stifled by the fumes* ► suffocate, choke, smother • *to stifle a cough* ► suppress, check

still ADJECTIVE • *to stand still* ► motionless, immobile, stationary, unmoving • *The evening was warm and still.* ► quiet, calm, silent

stimulate VERB • *to stimulate their interest* ► trigger, activate, kindle, rouse

a
b
c
d
e
f
g
h
i
j
k
l
m
n
o
p
q
r
s
t
u
v
w
x
y
z

stimulus NOUN **stimuli** something that stimulates or produces a reaction

sting NOUN **1** a sharp-pointed part of an animal or plant that can inject poison **2** a painful feeling caused by this

sting VERB **stung 1** to wound or hurt with a sting **2** to feel a sharp pain **3** to make someone feel upset or hurt *I was stung by this criticism.*

stingy (stin-jee) ADJECTIVE **stingier, stingiest** mean; not generous

stink NOUN an unpleasant smell

stink VERB **stank** or **stunk** to have an unpleasant smell

stint NOUN an amount or period of work

stint VERB to restrict to a small amount

stipulate VERB to insist on as part of an agreement ► **stipulation** NOUN

stir VERB **stirring, stirred 1** to mix a liquid or soft mixture by moving

it round **2** to start to move **3** to excite or stimulate ► **stirring** ADJECTIVE

stir NOUN **1** the action of stirring **2** a fuss or disturbance

stirring ADJECTIVE exciting; rousing

stirrup NOUN a metal part hanging from each side of a horse's saddle, as a support for the rider's foot

stitch NOUN **1** a loop of thread made in sewing or knitting **2** a sudden sharp pain in the side of the body

stitch VERB to sew or fasten with stitches

stoat NOUN a kind of weasel, also called an ermine

stock NOUN **1** items kept ready to be sold or used **2** a line of ancestors **3** a number of shares in a company's capital **4** liquid for soup, made by stewing meat, fish, or vegetables **5** the main stem of a tree or plant **6** the base, holder, or handle of an implement, weapon,

THESAURUS

sting NOUN • *a wasp sting* ► bite, prick, wound

sting VERB • *an insect that stings* ► bite, nip, prick • *made my eyes sting* ► smart, tingle, hurt, burn

stingy ADJECTIVE • *a stingy person* ► mean, miserly, penny-pinching

stink NOUN • *a dreadful stink* ► stench, reek, odour

stink VERB • *The room stank of smoke.* ► reek, smell

stir VERB • *to stir the mixture* ► mix, blend, beat, whisk • *stirred

in her sleep ► move slightly, tremble, twitch • *to stir the imagination* ► kindle, rouse, stimulate

stir NOUN • *The news caused a stir.* ► commotion, fuss, excitement

stitch VERB • *stitched a patch on his jeans* ► sew, tack, darn, mend

stock NOUN • *a stock of fuel* ► supply, store, hoard, reserve • *a review of the stock* ► goods, merchandise, wares

etc. **7** a garden flower with a sweet smell

stock VERB **1** to keep goods in stock **2** to provide a place with a stock of

stockade NOUN a fence made of stakes

stockbroker NOUN a broker who deals in stocks and shares

stock car NOUN an ordinary car strengthened for use in races where bumping is allowed

stock exchange NOUN a country's central place for buying and selling stocks and shares

stocking NOUN a piece of clothing covering the foot and part or all of the leg

stock market NOUN **1** a stock exchange **2** the buying and selling of stocks and shares

stockpile NOUN a large stock of things kept in reserve

stocks PLURAL NOUN a wooden framework with holes for a person's head and hands, in which offenders were formerly made to stand as a punishment

stock-still ADJECTIVE completely still

stocky ADJECTIVE **stockier, stockiest** short and solidly built

stodgy ADJECTIVE **stodgier, stodgiest** (of food) heavy and filling

stoical (stoh-ik-al) ADJECTIVE accepting pain or difficulty without complaining ► **stoically** ADVERB, **stoicism** NOUN

stoke VERB to put fuel in a furnace or on a fire

stole¹ NOUN a wide piece of material worn round the shoulders

stole² past tense of **steal**

stomach NOUN **1** the part of the body where food starts to be digested **2** the abdomen

stomach VERB to endure or tolerate

stone NOUN **1** a piece of rock **2** stones or rock as material, e.g. for building **3** a jewel **4** the hard case round the kernel of fruit **5** a unit of weight equal to 14 pounds (6.35 kg)

stone VERB **1** to throw stones at **2** to remove the stones from fruit

Stone Age NOUN the earliest period of human history, when tools and weapons were made of stone

stone-cold ADJECTIVE extremely cold

stoned ADJECTIVE (informal) under the influence of drugs or alcohol

stone-deaf ADJECTIVE completely deaf

a
b
c
d
e
f
g
h
i
j
k
l
m
n
o
p
q
r
s
t
u
v
w
x
y
z

THESAURUS

stodgy ADJECTIVE • *a stodgy pudding* ► starchy, heavy, solid, filling

stomach NOUN • *My stomach started to rumble.* ► gut, belly

stone NOUN • *throwing stones* ► rock, pebble, boulder • *a ring with a bright red stone* ► gem, jewel

a
b
c
d
e
f
g
h
i
j
k
l
m
n
o
p
q
s
t
u
v
w
x
y
z

stony ADJECTIVE **stonier, stoniest**
1 full of stones **2** hard like stone
3 unfriendly *a stony silence*

stooge NOUN *(informal)* an assistant
who does the routine work

stool NOUN a movable seat without
arms or a back

stoop¹ VERB **1** to bend the body
forwards and down **2** to lower
your standards *would not stoop to
lying* ▶ **stoop** NOUN

stop VERB **1** to bring or come to an
end **2** to be no longer moving or
working **3** to prevent or obstruct
4 to stay for a time **5** to fill a hole

stop NOUN **1** the act of stopping **2** a
place where a bus or train etc.
stops **3** a full stop **4** a lever or knob
that allows organ pipes to sound

stopcock NOUN a valve controlling
the flow of liquid in a pipe

stopgap NOUN a temporary
substitute

stoppage NOUN **1** an interruption
in the work of a factory etc. **2** a
blockage

stopper NOUN a plug for closing a
bottle etc.

stopwatch NOUN a watch for
timing, which can be started and
stopped

storage NOUN the storing of
things

store NOUN **1** a supply of things
kept for future use **2** a place where
things are kept until needed **3** a
large shop **in store** soon to
happen

store VERB to keep things until
needed

storey NOUN **storeys** one whole
floor of a building

⚠ **USAGE**

Do not confuse this word with *story*.

stork NOUN a large bird with long
legs and a long beak

storm NOUN **1** a strong wind
usually with rain, snow, etc. **2** a
violent attack or outburst
▶ **stormy** ADJECTIVE

stony ADJECTIVE • *a stony path*
▶ rough, rocky, pebbly, shingly • *a
stony silence* ▶ cold, unfriendly

stoop VERB • *stooped to pick up the
dog* ▶ crouch, bend, kneel, squat,
duck

stop VERB • *measures to stop violent
crime* ▶ prevent, reduce, put an
end to • *wanted to stop smoking*
▶ give up, discontinue, quit • *The
bus stopped near the corner.*
▶ halt, come to a halt, pull up
• *tried to stop her leaving*
▶ prevent, hinder, obstruct • *to*

stop the escape of blood ▶ stem,
staunch, block

stop NOUN • *come to a stop* ▶ halt,
end, standstill, conclusion

store NOUN • *a store of food*
▶ supply, stock, hoard, reserve
• *the coal store* ▶ storeroom,
storehouse • *a DIY store* ▶ shop,
outlet, supermarket

store VERB • *to store food for the
winter* ▶ keep, save, stow, put
aside, hoard

storm NOUN • *A storm blew up.*
▶ gale, tempest, hurricane • *a*

DICTIONARY

storm VERB **1** to rush violently or angrily **2** to attack and capture a place

story NOUN **stories** an account of a real or imaginary event

⚠ **USAGE**

Do not confuse this word with **storey**.

stout ADJECTIVE **1** rather fat **2** thick and strong ► **stoutly** ADVERB

stout NOUN a kind of dark beer

stove¹ NOUN **1** a device containing an oven or ovens **2** a device for heating a room

stove² past tense of **stave**

stow VERB to pack or store something away

stowaway NOUN someone who hides on a ship or aircraft to avoid paying the fare

straddle VERB **1** to sit or stand astride something **2** to be built across something

straggle VERB **1** to grow or spread in an untidy way **2** to lag behind ► **straggler** NOUN

straight ADJECTIVE **1** going continuously in one direction **2** level, horizontal, or upright **3** tidy; in proper order **4** honest and frank *a straight answer*

straight ADVERB **1** in a straight line or manner **2** directly; without delay *Go straight home.*

⚠ **USAGE**

Do not confuse this word with **strait**.

straight away ADVERB immediately

straighten VERB to make or become straight

straightforward ADJECTIVE **1** easy, not complicated **2** honest and frank

strain¹ VERB **1** injure or weaken something by stretching or working it too hard **2** to stretch

THESAURUS

storm of protest ► outburst, outcry, uproar

storm VERB • *to storm the building* ► attack, rush, charge • *stormed out in a rage* ► march, stomp

stormy ADJECTIVE • *stormy weather* ► blustery, tempestuous, gusty, wild

story NOUN • *a dramatic story* ► tale, account, narrative, yarn • *newspaper stories* ► report, article, feature, piece

stout ADJECTIVE • *a stout man* ► fat, plump, stocky, portly • *a stout pair of boots* ► strong, sturdy, robust

straight ADJECTIVE • *a straight stretch of road* ► direct, undeviating • *make the room straight* ► tidy, neat, orderly, shipshape • *a straight answer* ► honest, direct, frank

straight ADVERB • *walking straight into a trap* ► directly **straight away** • *went to see her straight away* ► at once, immediately

straightforward ADJECTIVE • *a straightforward explanation* ► simple, easy, uncomplicated • *straightforward people* ► honest, genuine, sincere

strain VERB • *strained a muscle in the last race* ► pull, sprain, twist,

tightly **3** to make a great effort **4** to put through a sieve or filter

strain NOUN **1** the act or force of straining **2** an injury caused by straining **3** something that uses up strength, resources, etc. **4** exhaustion

strain² NOUN **1** a breed or variety of animals, plants, etc. **2** an inherited characteristic

strainer NOUN a device for straining liquids

strait NOUN a narrow stretch of water connecting two seas

⚠ **USAGE**

Do not confuse this word with *straight*.

straitjacket NOUN a jacket with the sleeves tied round the sides for restraining a violent person

strait-laced ADJECTIVE very prim and proper

straits PLURAL NOUN **1** a strait **2** a difficult condition *found ourselves in dire straits*

strand¹ NOUN each of the threads or wires etc. twisted together to form a rope or cable

strand² NOUN a shore

stranded ADJECTIVE **1** left on sand or rocks in shallow water **2** left in a difficult or helpless position

strange ADJECTIVE **1** unusual or surprising **2** not known or seen before ► **strangely** ADVERB

stranger NOUN a person you do not know, or in a place they do not know

strangle VERB to kill by squeezing the throat to prevent breathing

stranglehold NOUN complete control over a person or process

strap NOUN a flat strip of leather etc. for fastening or holding things

wrench, hurt • *The dog strained at its leash.* ► tug, pull, stretch, haul • *She strained to hear.* ► try, struggle, make an effort • *Try not to strain yourself.* ► weaken, wear out, exhaust • *to strain a liquid* ► sieve, sift, filter

strain NOUN • *suffering from the strain* ► stress, pressure, tension, worry

strand NOUN • *a strand of hair* ► fibre, filament, thread

stranded ADJECTIVE • *jellyfish stranded on the beach* ► aground, marooned, high and dry • *stranded passengers* ► helpless, abandoned, deserted

strange ADJECTIVE • *heard a strange noise* ► funny, odd, weird, peculiar, curious, extraordinary • *a strange person* ► weird, eccentric, bizarre, unconventional • *hard to sleep in a strange house* ► unfamiliar, unknown, new

stranger NOUN • *They were strangers in the town.* ► newcomer, outsider, visitor, foreigner

strangle VERB • *The victim had been strangled.* ► throttle, choke

strap NOUN • *tied with straps* ► tie, belt, cord

a
b
c
d
e
f
g
h
i
j
k
l
m
n
o
p
q
r
s
t
u
v
w
x
y
z

DICTIONARY

strap VERB **strapping, strapped** to fasten with a strap

strapping ADJECTIVE tall and healthy-looking

strata plural of **stratum**

stratagem NOUN a cunning plan or trick

strategic ADJECTIVE 1 to do with strategy 2 giving an advantage ▸ **strategically** ADVERB

strategy NOUN **strategies** 1 a plan or policy designed to achieve something 2 the planning of a war or campaign

stratosphere NOUN a layer of the atmosphere between about 10 and 60 kilometres above the earth's surface

stratum NOUN **strata** a layer or level

straw NOUN 1 dry cut stalks of corn 2 a narrow tube for drinking through

strawberry NOUN **strawberries** a small red juicy fruit, with its seeds on the outside

stray VERB to leave a group or proper place and wander

stray ADJECTIVE 1 lost *a stray cat* 2 separated *a stray sock*

stray NOUN a stray animal

streak NOUN 1 a long thin line or mark 2 a trace 3 a spell of success, luck, etc. ▸ **streaky** ADJECTIVE

streak VERB 1 to mark with streaks 2 to move very quickly

stream NOUN 1 a small river 2 a flow of water, light, etc. 3 a constant passing of people or vehicles etc.

stream VERB 1 to move in or like a stream 2 to produce a stream of liquid 3 to organize pupils according to ability

streamer NOUN a long narrow ribbon or strip of paper etc.

streamline VERB 1 to give something a smooth shape to help it to move easily through air or water 2 to organize a process to be more efficient ▸ **streamlined** ADJECTIVE

street NOUN a road with houses beside it in a city or village

strength NOUN 1 the state of being strong 2 how strong a

THESAURUS

strap VERB • *strapped the bag to his bicycle* ▸ fasten, secure, tie, lash

stray VERB • *strayed into enemy territory* ▸ wander, drift, roam

streak NOUN • *black with streaks of white* ▸ strip, stripe, band, line

streak VERB • *faces streaked with tears* ▸ stain, smear, smudge • *Huge lorries streaked past him.* ▸ rush, speed, hurtle, zoom

stream NOUN • *a mountain stream* ▸ brook, burn, river, rivulet • *a stream of water* ▸ jet, flow, gush, spurt

stream VERB • *Water streamed through the hole.* ▸ flow, pour, gush, flood

street NOUN • *a quiet street* ▸ road, avenue

strength NOUN • *physical strength* ▸ power, brawn, muscle,

a b c d e f g h i j k l m n o p q r s t u v w x y z

person or thing is **3** an ability or good quality

strengthen VERB to make or become stronger

strenuous ADJECTIVE needing or using great effort ► **strenuously** ADVERB

stress NOUN **1** a force that presses, pulls, or twists **2** the extra force with which each part of a word is pronounced **3** distress caused by the problems of life ► **stressful** ADJECTIVE

stress VERB **1** to pronounce part of a word with extra emphasis **2** to emphasize a point or idea **3** to cause stress to

stretch VERB **1** to pull something or be pulled so that it becomes longer or larger **2** to extend or be continuous **3** to push out your

arms and legs as far as you can **4** to make high demand on resources, ability, etc.

stretch NOUN **1** the action of stretching **2** a continuous period of time or area of land or water

stretcher NOUN a framework for carrying a sick or injured person

strew VERB **strewn** or or **strewed** to scatter things over a surface

stricken ADJECTIVE badly affected by injury, illness, grief, etc.

strict ADJECTIVE **1** demanding obedience and good behaviour **2** complete or exact ► **strictly** ADVERB

stride VERB **strode**, **stridden** to walk with long steps

stride NOUN **1** a long step when walking or running **2** progress

THESAURUS

toughness, might• *has many strengths* ► quality, ability, strong point, talent

strengthen VERB • *Stone columns strengthen the walls.* ► support, reinforce, bolster, prop up • *to strengthen defences* ► reinforce, consolidate, bolster

strenuous ADJECTIVE • *years of strenuous work* ► hard, tough, demanding, exhausting • *has made strenuous efforts* ► determined, vigorous

stress NOUN • *under a lot of stress* ► anxiety, pressure, strain, tension, worry

stress VERB • *I stressed the importance of a balanced*

diet. ► emphasize, insist on, underline

stretch VERB • *stretched the rubber until it snapped* ► pull, strain, tighten • *The road stretched into the distance.* ► extend, continue

stretch out • *She stretched out on a couch.* ► recline, lie down, sprawl

stretch NOUN • *a five-hour stretch on duty* ► spell, stint, period • *a fine stretch of moorland* ► expanse, sweep, area

strict ADJECTIVE • *strict parents* ► severe, stern, harsh • *strict controls on spending* ► tough, stringent, rigorous • *a strict interpretation of the rule* ► exact, precise, correct

strident ADJECTIVE loud and harsh

strife NOUN conflict; fighting or quarrelling

strike VERB **struck 1** to hit with force **2** to attack or afflict suddenly **3** to make an impression on the mind *They strike me as being useful.* **4** to light a match **5** to refuse to work as a protest **6** to produce by pressing or stamping **7** (of a clock) to sound **8** to find gold or oil etc. by digging or drilling **strike off** or **out** to cross out

strike NOUN **1** a hit **2** an attack *an air strike* **3** refusal to work as a protest **4** a sudden discovery of gold or oil etc.

striker NOUN **1** a worker who is on strike **2** a football player whose role is to score goals

striking ADJECTIVE **1** impressive or attractive **2** noticeable
▶ **strikingly** ADVERB

string NOUN **1** thin cord made of twisted threads, used to fasten or tie things **2** a piece of wire or cord

etc. stretched and vibrated to produce sounds in a musical instrument **3** a line or series of things

string VERB **strung 1** to fit or fasten with string **2** to thread on a string

stringed ADJECTIVE (of a musical instrument) having strings

stringent (strin-jent) ADJECTIVE (of rules) strictly enforced

strings PLURAL NOUN stringed instruments

stringy ADJECTIVE **stringier**, **stringiest 1** like string **2** containing tough fibres

strip VERB **stripping**, **stripped 1** to take a covering or layer off something **2** to undress **3** to deprive a person of something

strip NOUN **1** a long narrow piece or area **2** the distinctive outfit worn by a sports team

strip cartoon NOUN a series of drawings telling a story

strike VERB • *struck my head on the beam* ▶ hit, knock, bump, smack, thump • *to strike without warning* ▶ attack, pounce • *The workforce threatened to strike.* ▶ down tools, stop work, take industrial action

strike NOUN • *The dispute ended in a strike.* ▶ stoppage, industrial action, walkout

striking ADJECTIVE • *a striking resemblance* ▶ noticeable, conspicuous, distinctive, obvious

string NOUN • *a piece of string* ▶ twine, cord, line, rope

string VERB • *Lights were strung across the road.* ▶ hang, link, thread, connect

strip VERB • *stripped and climbed into the shower* ▶ undress, take off your clothes • *Thieves had stripped the house.* ▶ empty, clear out, loot

strip NOUN • *a narrow strip of land* ▶ band, ribbon, belt • *a new strip for the team* ▶ outfit, kit

a
b
c
d
e
f
g
h
i
j
k
l
m
n
o
p
q
r
s
t
u
v
w
x
y
z

stripe NOUN **1** a long narrow band of colour **2** a band of cloth on the sleeve of a uniform showing rank
▶ **striped** ADJECTIVE, **stripy** ADJECTIVE

strive VERB **strove**, **striven** to try hard

strobe NOUN a light that flashes on and off continuously

stroke¹ NOUN **1** a hit **2** a movement of the arms and legs in swimming **3** an action or effort *a stroke of genius* **4** the sound made by a clock striking **5** a sudden illness that often causes paralysis

stroke² VERB to move the hand gently along a surface ▶ **stroke** NOUN

stroll VERB to walk in a leisurely way ▶ **stroll** NOUN, **stroller** NOUN

strong ADJECTIVE **1** having great power or effect **2** not easy to break, damage, or defeat **3** great in intensity *strong feelings* **4** having a lot of flavour or smell

5 of a certain number *an army 5,000 strong*

stronghold NOUN a strong fortified place

strove past tense of **strive**

structure NOUN **1** something that has been built **2** the way something is built or organized
▶ **structural** ADJECTIVE

structure VERB to organize or arrange into a system or pattern

struggle VERB **1** to move about violently in trying to get free **2** to make strong efforts to do something **3** to try to overcome an opponent or difficulty

struggle NOUN **1** the action of struggling **2** a hard fight or great effort

strum VERB **strumming**, **strummed** to sound a guitar by running your fingers across the strings

strut VERB **strutting**, **strutted** to walk proudly or stiffly

stripe NOUN • *a stripe down the side*
▶ line, strip, band, bar

stroke NOUN • *a swift stroke of the axe* ▶ blow, swipe, hit

stroke VERB • *to stroke the dog*
▶ pat, caress, fondle, touch

stroll VERB • *strolled round the grounds* ▶ wander, saunter, amble, dawdle

strong ADJECTIVE • *a strong lad*
▶ tough, muscular, powerful, brawny, well built, strapping • *a strong lock* ▶ sturdy, firm, durable, secure • *a strong interest*

▶ keen, eager, deep • *a cup of strong coffee* ▶ highly flavoured, pungent • *a strong argument*
▶ convincing, forceful, persuasive

structure NOUN • *a tall structure*
▶ construction, edifice, building

struggle VERB • *We struggled to get free.* ▶ work hard, try, strive, strain, wrestle, wriggle

struggle NOUN • *a struggle to finish in time* ▶ effort, challenge, battle • *gave themselves up without a struggle* ▶ fight, scuffle, brawl

DICTIONARY

strut NOUN **1** a bar strengthening a framework **2** a strutting walk

stub NOUN **1** a short stump left after use **2** the part of a cheque, ticket, etc. for keeping

stub VERB **stubbing, stubbed** to bump a toe painfully

stubble NOUN **1** short stalks of corn left after harvesting **2** short hairs growing after shaving

stubborn ADJECTIVE **1** refusing to give way; obstinate **2** difficult to remove or deal with

stubby ADJECTIVE **stubbier, stubbiest** short and thick

stuck past tense and past participle of **stick**

stuck ADJECTIVE unable to move or make progress

stuck-up ADJECTIVE (informal) conceited or snobbish

stud[1] NOUN a small curved lump or knob

stud VERB **studding, studded** to set or decorate with studs etc.

stud[2] NOUN a stallion

student NOUN a person who studies a subject, especially at a college or university

studio NOUN **studios 1** the room where a painter or photographer etc. works **2** a place where cinema films are made **3** a room from which radio or television programmes are broadcast

studious ADJECTIVE studying hard

study VERB **studies, studied 1** to spend time learning about something **2** to look at carefully

study NOUN **studies 1** the process of studying **2** a subject studied **3** a room used for studying **4** a piece of music for playing as an exercise **5** a drawing done for practice

THESAURUS

stubborn ADJECTIVE • too stubborn to admit a mistake ► obstinate, strong-willed, headstrong, pig-headed

stuck ADJECTIVE • The door was stuck. ► jammed, fixed, immovable • was stuck and needed help ► confused, baffled, at a loss

stuck-up ADJECTIVE • a bunch of stuck-up businessmen ► arrogant, conceited, snobbish

student NOUN • a student at the university ► undergraduate, postgraduate, scholar • a student

at the local school ► pupil, schoolchild • a nursing student ► trainee

studious ADJECTIVE • a studious pupil ► serious-minded, hard-working, diligent

study VERB • studied the information ► examine, analyse, survey, investigate, inspect • to study languages ► learn, be taught

study NOUN • two years of study ► learning, education, schooling • a study dealing with all aspects of the subject ► essay, article, report

a
b
c
d
e
f
g
h
i
j
k
l
m
n
o
p
q
r
s
t
u
v
w
x
y
z

737

DICTIONARY

stuff NOUN **1** a substance or material **2** possessions

stuff VERB **1** to fill tightly **2** to fill with stuffing **3** to push a thing into something **4** (*informal*) to eat greedily

stuffing NOUN **1** material used to fill the inside of something **2** a savoury mixture put into meat or poultry etc. before cooking

stuffy ADJECTIVE **stuffier, stuffiest 1** lacking fresh air **2** with blocked breathing passages **3** formal and uninteresting ▶ **stuffily** ADVERB

stumble VERB **1** to trip and lose your balance **2** to speak hesitantly or uncertainly **stumble across** or **on** to find accidentally ▶ **stumble** NOUN

stump NOUN **1** the bottom of a tree trunk left in the ground **2** something left when the main part is cut off or worn down **3** each of the three upright sticks of a wicket in cricket

stump VERB **1** to put a batsman out by knocking the bails off the stumps **2** to be too difficult or puzzling for

stumpy ADJECTIVE **stumpier, stumpiest** short and thick

stun VERB **stunning, stunned 1** to knock unconscious **2** to daze or shock

stunt[1] VERB to prevent from growing or developing

stunt[2] NOUN **1** a daring action **2** something done to attract attention

stupefy VERB **stupefies, stupefied** to make a person dazed ▶ **stupefaction** NOUN

stupendous ADJECTIVE amazing or tremendous ▶ **stupendously** ADVERB

stupid ADJECTIVE **1** not clever or thoughtful **2** without reason or common sense ▶ **stupidity** NOUN

THESAURUS

stuff NOUN • *some wet stuff on the floor* ▶ matter, substance, material • *Leave your stuff here.* ▶ belongings, possessions, things

stuff VERB • *stuffed everything in a drawer* ▶ pack, push, cram, shove, squeeze • *foam to stuff the cushions* ▶ fill, pad, pack

stuffy ADJECTIVE • *a stuffy atmosphere* ▶ airless, close, stifling, unventilated • *a stuffy lecture on citizenship* ▶ dull, boring

stumble VERB • *stumbled on a loose paving stone* ▶ trip, tumble, lose your balance • *stumbled*

through the speech ▶ stammer, stutter

stump VERB • *a question that stumped us* ▶ baffle, puzzle, perplex, confuse

stun VERB • *a blow that stunned him* ▶ daze, knock out • *The results stunned everyone.* ▶ amaze, astonish, stagger, shock

stunt NOUN • *a circus stunt* ▶ trick, feat, performance

stupid ADJECTIVE • *not as stupid as they seem* ▶ foolish, silly, unintelligent, empty-headed, dim, thick • *a stupid thing to do*

DICTIONARY

stupor (stew-per) NOUN a dazed condition

sturdy ADJECTIVE **sturdier**, **sturdiest** strong and solid ► **sturdily** ADVERB

sturgeon NOUN a large edible fish

stutter VERB to stammer ► **stutter** NOUN

sty [1] NOUN **sties** a pigsty

sty [2] or **stye** NOUN **sties** or **styes** a sore swelling on an eyelid

style NOUN **1** the way something is done, said, or written **2** fashion or elegance ► **stylistic** ADJECTIVE

style VERB to design or arrange something ► **stylist** NOUN

stylish ADJECTIVE elegant or fashionable

suave (swahv) ADJECTIVE smoothly polite

sub NOUN (informal) **1** a submarine **2** a subscription **3** a substitute

subconscious ADJECTIVE to do with mental processes of which we are not fully aware ► **subconscious** NOUN

subcontinent NOUN a mass of land smaller than a continent

subdivide VERB to divide into smaller parts ► **subdivision** NOUN

subdue VERB **1** to overcome or bring under control **2** to make quieter or gentler ► **subdued** ADJECTIVE

subject (sub-jekt) NOUN **1** the person or thing being talked or written about or dealt with **2** something that is studied **3** (Grammar) the word or words naming who or what does the action of an active verb, e.g. The dog in The dog bit him **4** someone who is ruled by a monarch or government

subject (sub-jekt) ADJECTIVE ruled by a monarch or government; not independent **subject to 1** having to obey **2** liable to **3** depending on

subject (sub-jekt) VERB **1** to make a person or thing undergo something **2** to bring a country under your control ► **subjection** NOUN

THESAURUS

► foolish, silly, unwise, idiotic, ridiculous

sturdy ADJECTIVE • a sturdy fellow ► strong, strapping, big, brawny, well-built • a pair of sturdy shoes ► stout, strong, tough, robust

style NOUN • an old-fashioned style of writing ► manner, tone, way • the latest styles ► design, pattern, fashion, vogue • dresses with style ► elegance, refinement, taste

stylish ADJECTIVE • stylish clothes ► fashionable, elegant, chic, trendy, smart

subdued ADJECTIVE • in a subdued mood ► serious, sober, reflective, thoughtful

subject NOUN • a subject for discussion ► theme, topic, matter, question • a British subject ► citizen, passport-holder

a
b
c
d
e
f
g
h
i
j
k
l
m
n
o
p
q
r
s
t
u
v
w
x
y
z

DICTIONARY

subjective ADJECTIVE **1** existing in a person's mind **2** depending on a person's own taste or opinions etc.

subjunctive NOUN the form of a verb used to indicate what might happen, e.g. *were* in *if I were you*

sublime ADJECTIVE noble or impressive

submarine NOUN a ship that can travel under water

submarine ADJECTIVE under the sea

submerge VERB to go or put under water

submission NOUN **1** the act of submitting to someone **2** something offered for consideration

submissive ADJECTIVE willing to obey

submit VERB **submitting, submitted 1** to let someone have authority over you **2** to put forward for consideration

subordinate ADJECTIVE **1** less important **2** lower in rank

subordinate NOUN a person working under someone's authority or control

subordinate VERB to treat as being less important
▶ **subordination** NOUN

subordinate clause NOUN (*Grammar*) a clause which adds details to the main clause of the sentence, but cannot be used as a sentence by itself

subscribe VERB **1** to pay regularly for a service, membership, etc. **2** to contribute money **3** to say that you agree *We cannot subscribe to this theory.*
▶ **subscriber** NOUN

subscription NOUN money paid to subscribe to something

subsequent ADJECTIVE coming after in time or order
▶ **subsequently** ADVERB

subside VERB **1** to become less strong or intense **2** to sink

subsidence NOUN the gradual sinking of an area of land

subsidiary ADJECTIVE less important; secondary

THESAURUS

submissive ADJECTIVE • *Be polite, but not submissive.* ▶ meek, passive, servile, docile

submit VERB • *had only submitted under duress.* ▶ give in, yield, back down, surrender • *to submit your ideas* ▶ present, offer, tender, put forward

subordinate ADJECTIVE • *a subordinate role* ▶ inferior, lower,

lesser, secondary, subsidiary, minor, junior

subordinate NOUN • *the manager and three subordinates* ▶ assistant, junior, inferior, dependant, employee

subside VERB • *wait for the storm to subside* ▶ die down, abate, diminish • *The flood waters had begun to subside.* ▶ recede, fall back

subsidize VERB to pay a subsidy to

> ⚠ **SPELLING**
> This word can also be spelled *subsidise*.

subsidy NOUN **subsidies** money paid to help or support a person or group

subsist VERB to keep yourself alive ▶ **subsistence** NOUN

substance NOUN **1** matter of a particular kind **2** the essential part of something

substantial ADJECTIVE **1** of great size, value, or importance **2** solidly built

substantially ADVERB mostly; essentially

substantiate VERB to produce evidence to prove something ▶ **substantiation** NOUN

substitute NOUN a person or thing that replaces another

substitute VERB to put or use one person or thing instead of another ▶ **substitution** NOUN

subterfuge NOUN a trick or deception

subterranean ADJECTIVE underground

subtitle NOUN **1** words shown on the screen during a foreign-language film, translating the words spoken

subtle (sut-el) ADJECTIVE **1** slight and difficult to detect or describe **2** faint or delicate ▶ **subtlety** NOUN, **subtly** ADVERB

subtotal NOUN the total of part of a group of figures

subtract VERB to take away a part or number from a greater one ▶ **subtraction** NOUN

suburb NOUN a district outside the central part of a city ▶ **suburban** ADJECTIVE

subversive ADJECTIVE tending to weaken or overthrow authority

subvert VERB to weaken or overthrow ▶ **subversion** NOUN

subway NOUN **1** an underground passage for pedestrians **2** an underground railway

THESAURUS

substance NOUN • *a strange sticky substance* ▶ material, matter, stuff • *the substance of the story* ▶ essence, gist, theme, meaning

substantial ADJECTIVE • *a substantial building* ▶ strong, sturdy, solid • *substantial improvements* ▶ significant, sizeable, big

substitute NOUN • *no substitute for experience* ▶ replacement, alternative (to)

substitute VERB • *can substitute yoghurt for cream cheese* ▶ change, exchange, swop, replace

subtle ADJECTIVE • *a subtle change* ▶ mild, slight, faint, delicate • *subtle colours* ▶ delicate, pale, muted, subdued

subtract VERB • *must be subtracted from the total* ▶ deduct, take away

a
b
c
d
e
f
g
h
i
j
k
l
m
n
o
p
q
r
s
t
u
v
w
x
y
z

a
b
c
d
e
f
g
h
i
j
k
l
m
n
o
p
q
r
s
t
u
v
w
x
y
z

succeed VERB **1** to achieve what you wanted or intended **2** to come after another person or thing **3** to become the next king or queen

success NOUN **1** the achievement of something wanted **2** a person or thing that does well

successful ADJECTIVE having success; being a success
▶ **successfully** ADVERB

succession NOUN **1** a series of people or things **2** the process of following in order **3** the right of becoming the next king or queen **in succession** one after another

successive ADJECTIVE following one after another *on successive days* ▶ **successively** ADVERB

successor NOUN a person or thing that comes after another

succinct (suk-sinkt) ADJECTIVE expressed briefly

succour (suk-er) NOUN help given in time of need

succulent ADJECTIVE **1** juicy and tasty **2** (of plants) having thick juicy leaves or stems

succumb (suk-um) VERB to give way to something overpowering

such ADJECTIVE **1** of the same kind; similar **2** of the kind described *There's no such thing.* **3** so great or intense **such as** for example

suchlike ADJECTIVE of that kind

suck VERB **1** to take in liquid or air through almost-closed lips or to hold in the mouth an draw flavour from **3** to pull or draw in **suck up** to absorb ▶ **suck** NOUN

sucker NOUN an organ or device that can stick to a surface by suction **2** a shoot coming up from a root **3** (*informal*) someone easily deceived

suckle VERB to feed on milk from the mother's breast or teat

suction NOUN **1** the process of sucking **2** production of a vacuum so that things are sucked into the empty space

sudden ADJECTIVE happening or done quickly or without warning
▶ **suddenly** ADVERB, **suddenness** NOUN

THESAURUS

succeed VERB • *important to succeed* ▶ be successful, do well, thrive, flourish, triumph, be victorious • *succeeded him as President* ▶ replace, take over from

success NOUN • *ways of judging success* ▶ achievement, accomplishment, fame • *the success of the plan* ▶ effectiveness, completion • *an instant success* ▶ triumph, hit, sensation

successful ADJECTIVE • *a successful business* ▶ thriving, flourishing, prosperous, profitable

succession NOUN • *a succession of menial jobs* ▶ series, sequence, string, run

suck VERB **suck up** • *to suck up water* ▶ soak up, absorb

sudden ADJECTIVE • *a sudden explosion* ▶ unexpected, abrupt, sharp • *a sudden decision* ▶ quick, rash, impetuous

DICTIONARY

suds *PLURAL NOUN* froth on soapy water

sue *VERB* to start a lawsuit to claim money from

suede (swayd) *NOUN* leather with one side rubbed to make it velvety

suet *NOUN* hard fat from cattle and sheep, used in cooking

suffer *VERB* 1 to feel pain or sadness 2 to experience something bad 3 to become worse or be badly affected

suffering *NOUN* pain or hardship

suffice *VERB* to be enough

sufficient *ADJECTIVE* enough
▶ **sufficiency** *NOUN*, **sufficiently** *ADVERB*

suffix *NOUN* (*Grammar*) a word or syllable joined to the end of a word to change or add to its meaning, as in *sufficiently* and *suffocation*

suffocate *VERB* 1 to make prevent someone from breathing 2 to suffer or die because breathing is prevented ▶ **suffocation** *NOUN*

suffrage *NOUN* the right to vote in political elections

suffuse *VERB* to spread through or over something

sugar *NOUN* a sweet food obtained from the juices of various plants
▶ **sugary** *ADJECTIVE*

suggest *VERB* 1 to put forward an idea or plan for someone to consider 2 to cause an idea or possibility to come into the mind
▶ **suggestive** *ADJECTIVE*

suggestion *NOUN* 1 the act of suggesting 2 something suggested

suggestive *ADJECTIVE* suggesting something, especially something indecent

suicide *NOUN* 1 the act of killing yourself deliberately 2 a person who does this ▶ **suicidal** *ADJECTIVE*

suit *NOUN* 1 a matching set of clothes worn together 2 each of the four sets of cards (clubs, hearts, diamonds, spades) in a pack of playing cards 3 a lawsuit

⚠ USAGE
Do not confuse this word with *suite*.

THESAURUS

suffer *VERB* • *hated to see him suffer* ▶ feel pain, be in pain, be in distress • *suffered a defeat*
▶ experience, meet with, receive, sustain, encounter • *Their relationship will suffer.*
▶ deteriorate, decline, be damaged

suffering *NOUN* • *suffering inflicted on the population*
▶ hardship, distress, misery, pain, sorrow, grief

suggest *VERB* • *We suggested an outing.* ▶ propose, recommend, advise, put forward • *The evidence suggests we could be right.*
▶ imply, indicate, hint

suggestion *NOUN* • *a few suggestions* ▶ recommendation, proposal, idea, plan

suit *NOUN* • *wore a dark suit*
▶ outfit, set of clothes, ensemble

a
b
c
d
e
f
g
h
i
j
k
l
m
n
o
p
q
r
s
t
u
v
w
x
y
z

a b c d e f g h i j k l m n o p q r **s** t u v w x y z

DICTIONARY

suit VERB **1** to be suitable or convenient for a person or thing **2** to make a person look attractive

suitable ADJECTIVE satisfactory or right for a particular person, purpose, or occasion ► **suitability** NOUN, **suitably** ADVERB

suitcase NOUN a travelling case for carrying clothes

suite (say as sweet) NOUN **1** a set of furniture **2** a set of rooms **3** a set of short pieces of music

⚠ USAGE

Do not confuse this word with *suit*.

suitor NOUN a man who wants to marry a particular woman

sulk VERB to be silent and in a bad mood because you are cross about something

sulky ADJECTIVE **sulkier, sulkiest** silent and in a bad mood ► **sulkily** ADVERB

sullen ADJECTIVE sulking and gloomy

sulphur NOUN a yellow chemical used in industry and medicine ► **sulphurous** ADJECTIVE

sulphuric acid NOUN a strong colourless acid containing sulphur

sultan NOUN the ruler of certain Muslim countries

sultana NOUN a raisin without seeds

sultry ADJECTIVE **sultrier, sultriest 1** hot and humid **2** passionate

sum NOUN **1** an amount of money **2** a total **3** a problem in arithmetic

sum VERB **summing, summed sum up** to give a summary

summarize VERB to make or give a summary of

⚠ SPELLING

This word can also be spelled *summarise*.

summary NOUN **summaries** a statement of the main points of something

summary ADJECTIVE **1** brief **2** done or given hastily ► **summarily** ADVERB

summer NOUN the warm season between spring and autumn ► **summery** ADJECTIVE

THESAURUS

suit VERB • *terms to suit all pockets* ► satisfy, accommodate, be suitable for, please • *Black doesn't suit me.* ► look attractive on, look right on, flatter

suitable ADJECTIVE • *a suitable time* ► convenient, appropriate, acceptable • *a film suitable for all age groups* ► appropriate (to), suited (to)

sulk VERB • *was sulking in his room* ► mope, brood

sulky ADJECTIVE • *a row of sulky faces* ► moody, sullen, surly, glum

sum NOUN • *a large sum of money* ► amount, quantity • *a sum you can do in your head* ► calculation, problem

summary NOUN • *a summary of the main arguments* ► resumé, review, summing-up • *a summary of a story* ► synopsis, precis, abridgement

DICTIONARY

summit *NOUN* **1** the top of a mountain or hill **2** a meeting between world leaders

summon *VERB* **1** to order someone to come or appear **2** to call people together **summon up** to find strength or courage or energy

summons *NOUN* a command to appear in a lawcourt

sump *NOUN* a metal case holding oil at the bottom of an engine

sumptuous *ADJECTIVE* splendid and expensive-looking

sun *NOUN* **1** the star round which the earth travels **2** light and warmth from the sun

sunbathe *VERB* to expose your body to the sun

sunbeam *NOUN* a ray of sun

sunburn *NOUN* redness of the skin caused by the sun ▸ **sunburnt** *ADJECTIVE*

sundae (sun-day) *NOUN* a mixture of ice cream and fruit, nuts, cream, etc.

Sunday *NOUN* the first day of the week, for Christians a day of rest and worship

sundial *NOUN* a device that shows the time by a shadow on a dial

sundown *NOUN* sunset

sundries *PLURAL NOUN* various small things

sundry *ADJECTIVE* various or several

sunflower *NOUN* a tall flower with golden petals

sunglasses *PLURAL NOUN* dark glasses to protect the eyes from strong sunlight

sunken *ADJECTIVE* sunk deeply into a surface

sunlight *NOUN* light from the sun ▸ **sunlit** *ADJECTIVE*

sunny *ADJECTIVE* **sunnier**, **sunniest** **1** full of sunshine **2** cheerful

sunrise *NOUN* the rising of the sun in the morning

sunset *NOUN* the setting of the sun in the evening

sunshine *NOUN* sunlight with no cloud between the sun and the earth

sunstroke *NOUN* illness caused by too much exposure to the sun

suntan *NOUN* a brown colour of the skin caused by the sun ▸ **suntanned** *ADJECTIVE*

THESAURUS

summit *NOUN* • *the summit of the mountain* ▸ top, peak, crest, cap

summon *VERB* • *was summoned to Washington* ▸ send for, call, order, invite • *to summon a meeting* ▸ call, convene, assemble

sunny *ADJECTIVE* • *sunny spells and showers* ▸ bright, clear, fine,

cloudless • *a sunny smile* ▸ cheerful, happy, joyful

sunrise *NOUN* • *Their day begins at sunrise.* ▸ dawn, daybreak, daylight

sunset *NOUN* • *a beautiful sky at sunset* ▸ dusk, twilight, sundown

a
b
c
d
e
f
g
h
i
j
k
l
m
n
o
p
q
r
s
t
u
v
w
x
y
z

sup VERB **supping, supped** to drink liquid in sips or spoonfuls

super ADJECTIVE (*informal*) excellent or superb

superb ADJECTIVE magnificent or excellent

supercilious ADJECTIVE haughty and scornful

superficial ADJECTIVE **1** on the surface **2** not deep or thorough ► **superficially** ADVERB

superfluous ADJECTIVE more than is needed

superhuman ADJECTIVE **1** beyond human ability **2** divine

superimpose VERB to place one thing on top of another

superintend VERB to supervise

superintendent NOUN **1** a supervisor **2** a police officer above the rank of inspector

superior ADJECTIVE **1** higher in position or rank **2** better than another person or thing **3** showing conceit ► **superiority** NOUN

superior NOUN a person or thing that is superior to another

superlative ADJECTIVE of the highest degree or quality

superlative NOUN the form of an adjective or adverb that expresses 'most', e.g. *biggest*, *most quickly*

supermarket NOUN a large self-service shop that sells food etc.

supernatural ADJECTIVE not having a natural explanation

superpower NOUN one of the most powerful nations of the world

supersede VERB to take the place of something

supersonic ADJECTIVE faster than the speed of sound

superstition NOUN a belief or action that is not based on reason or evidence ► **superstitious** ADJECTIVE

superstore NOUN a large supermarket

THESAURUS

super ADJECTIVE • *a super place to live* ► excellent, superb, first-rate, marvellous, wonderful

superb ADJECTIVE • *a superb view of the mountains* ► excellent, marvellous, magnificent, wonderful

superficial ADJECTIVE • *superficial wounds* ► surface, slight, shallow • *similarities that are purely superficial* ► cosmetic, slight, on the surface • *a superficial study of the subject* ► casual, perfunctory

superfluous ADJECTIVE • *superfluous material* ► excess, spare, extra, unwanted, unnecessary

superior ADJECTIVE • *superior status* ► senior, higher-level, more important • *a superior technology* ► first-class, top-quality, choice, fine • *a superior attitude* ► arrogant, haughty, disdainful

DICTIONARY

supervise VERB to be in charge of a person or activity
► **supervision** NOUN

supervisor NOUN a person who supervises others

supper NOUN a meal eaten in the evening

supplant VERB to take the place of a person or thing

supple ADJECTIVE bending easily; flexible ► **supplely** ADVERB

supplement NOUN 1 something added 2 an extra section of a book or newspaper ► **supplementary** ADJECTIVE

supplement VERB to add to something

supply VERB **supplies**, **supplied** to provide what is needed
► **supplier** NOUN

supply NOUN **supplies** 1 an amount available for use 2 the action of supplying

support VERB 1 to keep something from falling or sinking 2 to give help or encouragement to 3 to provide with the necessities of life ► **supporter** NOUN, **supportive** ADJECTIVE

support NOUN 1 the action of supporting 2 a person or thing that supports

THESAURUS

supervise VERB • people to supervise the children ► be in charge of, be responsible for, watch over

supervisor NOUN • working for a new supervisor ► manager, director, overseer, boss

supplement VERB • to supplement the family income ► add to, top up, boost

supply NOUN • a supply of food ► quantity, amount, store, reserve **supplies** • a week's supplies ► provisions, stores, rations, necessities

supply VERB • to supply people's needs ► provide, fulfil, fill • unable to supply us with what we needed ► equip, provide

support VERB • walls too weak to support the roof ► carry, bear, hold up, prop up, underpin

• wanted to support her during her difficult time ► comfort, encourage, console, reassure • to support a family ► maintain, provide for, feed, keep • to support medical research ► contribute to, sponsor, subsidize, fund • evidence to support the idea ► prove, substantiate, confirm, agree with, argue for

support NOUN • financial support ► backing, funding, aid, subsidy • emotional support ► encouragement, comfort, relief, strength, friendship • a shelf resting on three supports ► prop, brace, pillar, foundation

supporter NOUN • football supporters ► enthusiast, follower, fan • a supporter of the project ► champion, advocate, backer

DICTIONARY

suppose VERB 1 to think that something is likely to happen or be true 2 to consider as a suggestion *Suppose you tell them.* **be supposed to** to be expected to ► **supposition** NOUN

supposedly ADVERB so people suppose or think

suppress VERB 1 to put an end to something by force 2 to keep something from being known ► **suppression** NOUN

supremacy NOUN highest authority or power

supreme ADJECTIVE 1 most important or highest in rank 2 greatest *supreme courage*

surcharge NOUN an extra charge

sure ADJECTIVE 1 completely confident of being right 2 certain to happen or do something 3 reliable; undoubtedly true

surely ADVERB 1 certainly or securely 2 it must be true *Surely you were there.*

surf NOUN the white foam of waves breaking on a rock or shore

surf VERB 1 to go surfing 2 to browse through the Internet

surface NOUN 1 the outside of something 2 any of the sides of an object 3 an outward appearance

surface VERB 1 to put a surface on a road, path, etc. 2 to come up to the surface from under water

surfboard NOUN a board used in for riding on the waves

surfeit (ser-fit) NOUN too much

surfing NOUN the sport of riding on a surfboard ► **surfer** NOUN

surge VERB 1 to move powerfully forward 2 to increase dramatically ► **surge** NOUN

surgeon NOUN a doctor who treats disease or injury usually by cutting open and repairing the affected parts of the body

surgery NOUN **surgeries** 1 the work of a surgeon 2 the place where a doctor or dentist treats patients

THESAURUS

suppose VERB • *I suppose you will be going.* ► assume, expect, guess, presume, imagine • *Suppose you tell them.* ► imagine, pretend

suppress VERB • *to suppress the rebellion* ► quash, quell, crush, put an end to • *to suppress feelings* ► hide, conceal, stifle, control

sure ADJECTIVE • *I'm sure they will be safe.* ► certain, convinced, confident, positive • *is sure to ask* ► bound, certain, likely • *a sure*

sign ► clear, undoubted, undeniable

surf VERB • *surfing the Internet* ► browse, explore, search

surface NOUN • *the surface of the ball* ► outside, exterior, veneer, covering • *a cube with six surfaces* ► face, side, plane

surface VERB • *A new idea has surfaced.* ► come up, rise, appear, emerge

surge VERB • *The crowd surged forward.* ► rush, sweep, push, stream

a b c d e f g h i j k l m n o p q r s t u v w x y z

DICTIONARY

surgical ADJECTIVE to do with surgery

surly ADJECTIVE **surlier, surliest** bad-tempered and unfriendly
▶ **surliness** NOUN

surmise VERB to guess or suspect

surmount VERB to overcome an obstacle or difficulty

surname NOUN the name held by members of a family

surpass VERB to do or be better than others

surplus NOUN an amount left over after spending or all that was needed ▶ **surplus** ADJECTIVE

surprise NOUN **1** something unexpected **2** the feeling caused by something unexpected

surprise VERB **1** to be a surprise to **2** to come upon or attack unexpectedly

surprising ADJECTIVE causing surprise; unexpected
▶ **surprisingly** ADVERB

surreal ADJECTIVE using images from dreams and the subconscious

surrealism NOUN a surreal style of painting etc. ▶ **surrealist** NOUN, **surrealistic** ADJECTIVE

surrender VERB **1** to stop fighting and give yourself up to an enemy **2** to hand something or someone over to another person
▶ **surrender** NOUN

surreptitious ADJECTIVE stealthy

surrogate (su-rog-at) NOUN a deputy or substitute ▶ **surrogate** ADJECTIVE

surround VERB to come or be all round a person or thing

surroundings PLURAL NOUN the conditions or area around a person or thing

surveillance (ser-vay-lans) NOUN a close watch kept on a person or thing

survey (ser-vay) NOUN **1** a general look at something **2** an inspection of an area, building, etc.

THESAURUS

surplus NOUN • *a fruit surplus*
▶ excess, surfeit, glut

surprise ▶ NOUN • *looked at him in surprise* ▶ amazement, astonishment, incredulity, wonder • *might be a surprise to you* ▶ shock, revelation, bolt from the blue

surprise VERB • *information that will surprise you* ▶ astonish, amaze, astound, shock, stagger, flabbergast • *surprised an intruder* ▶ discover, come upon

surrender VERB • *The rebels surrendered.* ▶ give up,

capitulate, yield • *to surrender personal freedoms* ▶ give up, relinquish

surround VERB • *The garden surrounds an old house.*
▶ encircle, enclose, skirt • *found herself surrounded by angry faces*
▶ besiege, engulf, hedge in

surroundings NOUN • *in beautiful surroundings*
▶ environment, location, setting, neighbourhood

survey NOUN • *a survey of public opinion* ▶ poll, census, count, study • *a survey of the house*

a
b
c
d
e
f
g
h
i
j
k
l
m
n
o
p
q
r
s
t
u
v
w
x
y
z

a b c d e f g h i j k l m n o p q r s t u v w x y z

DICTIONARY

survey (ser-vay) VERB to make a survey of; to inspect

surveyor NOUN someone qualified to make a survey of land, buildings, etc.

survival NOUN 1 the process or likelihood of surviving 2 something that has survived

survive VERB 1 to stay alive; to continue to exist 2 to remain alive after an accident or disaster 3 to live longer than ▸ **survivor** NOUN

susceptible (sus-ept-ib-ul) ADJECTIVE likely to be affected by something ▸ **susceptibility** NOUN

suspect (sus-pekt) VERB 1 to have reason to think a person guilty of something 2 to believe that something is possible

suspect (sus-pekt) NOUN a person who is suspected of a crime etc.

suspect (sus-pekt) ADJECTIVE thought to be dangerous or unreliable *a suspect package*

suspend VERB 1 to hang something up 2 to stop something for a time 3 to remove a person from a position for a time 4 to keep something from falling or sinking in air or liquid

suspender NOUN a fastener to hold up a sock or stocking by its top

suspense NOUN an anxious or uncertain feeling while waiting for something to happen

suspension NOUN 1 the act of suspending 2 the springs etc. in a vehicle that lessen the effect of rough road surfaces 3 a liquid containing pieces of solid material which do not dissolve

suspension bridge NOUN a bridge supported by cables

suspicion NOUN 1 a feeling of doubt; a lack of trust 2 a slight belief

THESAURUS

▸ inspection, assessment, examination, valuation

survey VERB • *to survey the scene* ▸ observe, view, look at • *stood back to survey his work* ▸ examine, inspect, study

survive VERB • *enough water to survive* ▸ remain alive, live, carry on, keep going • *Six people survived the crash.* ▸ live through, withstand

suspect ADJECTIVE • *suspect packages* ▸ suspicious, dubious

suspect VERB • *hope they don't suspect anything* ▸ doubt,

distrust, mistrust, have doubts about • *suspect another visit may not be possible.* ▸ think, expect, imagine, guess

suspend VERB • *Sacks were suspended from hooks.* ▸ hang, sling, swing, dangle • *to suspend trading* ▸ interrupt, discontinue • *have been suspended from school* ▸ exclude, dismiss, expel

suspense NOUN • *building up suspense* ▸ tension, uncertainty, expectation, excitement, drama

suspicion NOUN • *my suspicions about them* ▸ doubt, misgiving, reservation

DICTIONARY

suspicious ADJECTIVE feeling or causing suspicion ▸ **suspiciously** ADVERB

sustain VERB 1 to keep someone alive 2 to keep something happening 3 to undergo or suffer 4 to support or uphold ▸ **sustainable** ADJECTIVE

sustenance NOUN food and drink; nourishment

svelte ADJECTIVE slim and graceful

swab (swob) NOUN a mop or pad for cleaning or wiping

swab VERB **swabbing, swabbed** to clean or wipe with a swab

swagger VERB to walk or behave in a conceited way ▸ **swagger** NOUN

swallow[1] VERB 1 to make something go down your throat 2 to believe something improbable **swallow up** to absorb completely ▸ **swallow** NOUN

swallow[2] NOUN a small bird with a forked tail and pointed wings

swamp NOUN a marsh ▸ **swampy** ADJECTIVE

swamp VERB 1 to flood 2 to overwhelm

swan NOUN a large usually white waterbird with a long neck

swansong NOUN a person's last performance or work

swap VERB **swapping, swapped** to exchange one thing for another ▸ **swap** NOUN

swarm NOUN a large number of insects or birds etc. flying or moving together

swarm VERB 1 to gather or move in a swarm 2 be crowded with people

swarthy ADJECTIVE **swarthier, swarthiest** having a dark complexion

swashbuckling ADJECTIVE daring and fond of adventure

swastika NOUN an ancient symbol in the form of a cross with its ends bent at right angles

THESAURUS

suspicious ADJECTIVE • *was suspicious of his visitor* ▸ doubtful, distrustful, unsure, wary • *a suspicious character* ▸ dubious, disreputable, untrustworthy

sustain VERB • *to sustain a large population* ▸ maintain, keep, provide for • *bread and cheese to sustain them* ▸ nourish, feed

swamp NOUN • *rain turning the fields into a swamp* ▸ marsh, bog, quagmire

swamp VERB • *A tidal wave swamped the region.* ▸ flood, inundate, engulf, submerge

swap VERB • *Jane swapped her stamps for some coins.* ▸ exchange, barter, switch

swarm VERB • *Reporters swarmed everywhere.* ▸ crowd, throng, flock **be swarming with** • *The beaches were swarming with tourists.* ▸ be overrun with, be crawling with, be teeming with

DICTIONARY

a b c d e f g h i j k l m n o p q r **s** t u v w x y z

swat VERB **swatting, swatted** to hit or crush a fly etc.

swathe¹ NOUN **1** a broad strip or area **2** a line of cut corn or grass

swathe² VERB to wrap in layers of bandages etc.

sway VERB **1** to move gently from side to side **2** to influence ▶ **sway** NOUN

swear VERB **swore, sworn 1** to make a solemn promise **2** to make a person take an oath *swore them to secrecy* **3** to use words that are rude or shocking

swear word NOUN a word considered rude or shocking

sweat NOUN moisture given off by the body through the pores of the skin ▶ **sweaty** ADJECTIVE

sweat VERB to give off sweat

sweater NOUN a jersey or pullover

sweatshirt NOUN a thick casual jersey

swede NOUN a large kind of turnip with purple skin and yellow flesh

sweep VERB **swept 1** to clean or clear with a broom or brush etc. **2** to move or remove quickly **3** to go smoothly and quickly

swept out of the room ▶ **sweeper** NOUN

sweep NOUN **1** the process of sweeping *Give this room a good sweep.* **2** a sweeping movement **3** a chimney sweep **4** a sweepstake

sweeping ADJECTIVE general or wide-ranging *sweeping changes*

sweepstake NOUN a form of gambling on sporting events in which the money staked is divided among the winners

sweet ADJECTIVE **1** tasting as if it contains sugar; not bitter **2** very pleasant *a sweet smell* **3** charming or delightful ▶ **sweetly** ADVERB

sweet NOUN **1** a piece of sweet food made with sugar, chocolate, etc. **2** a pudding

sweetcorn NOUN the juicy yellow seeds of maize

sweeten VERB to make or become sweet

sweetener NOUN an artificial substance used instead of sugar

sweetheart NOUN a person's lover

sweet pea NOUN a climbing plant with fragrant flowers

THESAURUS

sway VERB • *corn swaying in the breeze* ▶ swing, bend, rock, wave

swear VERB • *swore he had told the truth* ▶ promise, give your word, vow • *heard him swear loudly* ▶ curse, blaspheme

sweep VERB • *time to sweep the floor* ▶ brush, clean, scrub, wipe

• *A bus swept past.* ▶ sail, glide, hurtle, whizz

sweet ADJECTIVE • *The tea was too sweet.* ▶ sugary • *a sweet smell* ▶ fragrant, aromatic, scented • *a sweet song* ▶ melodious • *a sweet little baby* ▶ cute, pretty, delightful

DICTIONARY

swell VERB **swollen** or or **swelled**
1 to make or become larger 2 to
increase in amount or force

swell NOUN 1 the process of
swelling 2 the rise and fall of the
sea's surface

swelling NOUN a swollen place

swelter VERB to feel
uncomfortably hot ► **sweltering**
ADJECTIVE

swerve VERB to turn suddenly to
one side ► **swerve** NOUN

swift ADJECTIVE quick or rapid
► **swiftly** ADVERB

swift NOUN a small bird like a
swallow

swig VERB **swigging**, **swigged**
(informal) to drink in large
mouthfuls ► **swig** NOUN

swill VERB to pour water over or
through something

swill NOUN a sloppy mixture of
waste food given to pigs

swim VERB **swimming**, **swam**,
swum 1 to move the body
through water 2 to cross by
swimming 3 to float 4 to be
covered with or full of liquid *eyes*

swimming in tears 5 to feel
dizzy
► **swimmer** NOUN

swim NOUN the action of
swimming *went for a swim*

swimming bath NOUN a public
swimming pool

swimsuit NOUN a one-piece
swimming costume

swindle VERB to cheat a person in
business etc. ► **swindle** NOUN,
swindler NOUN

swine NOUN **swine** 1 a pig
2 (informal) an unpleasant person

swing VERB **swung** 1 to move
back and forth or in a circle 2 to
change opinion or mood

swing NOUN 1 a swinging
movement 2 a swinging seat 3 the
amount by which votes or
opinions etc. change 4 a kind of
jazz music

swingeing (swin-jing) ADJECTIVE
severe or powerful

swipe VERB 1 to hit with a
swinging blow 2 (informal) to steal
3 pass a credit card through an
electronic reading device
► **swipe** NOUN

THESAURUS

swell VERB • *could feel his stomach
swelling* ► expand, distend,
enlarge, inflate, bulge • *The
population was swelling.*
► increase, expand, grow

swerve VERB • *The car swerved.*
► turn aside, change direction,
veer

swift ADJECTIVE • *a swift reply*
► quick, rapid, prompt,
immediate, punctual

swindle VERB • *had been swindled
out of a lot of money* ► cheat,
defraud, trick, fleece, dupe,
deceive, con

swindle NOUN • *an insurance
swindle* ► fraud, fiddle, racket,
deception, sham

swing VERB • *The inn sign swung in
the wind.* ► sway, flap, dangle,
rock

a
b
c
d
e
f
g
h
i
j
k
l
m
n
o
p
q
r
s
t
u
v
w
x
y
z

swirl VERB to move round rapidly in circles ► **swirl** NOUN

swish VERB to move with a hissing sound ► **swish** NOUN

swish ADJECTIVE (informal) smart and fashionable

switch NOUN **1** a device pressed or turned to start or stop something working **2** a change of opinion or methods **3** a mechanism for moving the points on a railway track **4** a flexible rod or whip

switch VERB **1** to turn on or off with a switch **2** to change something suddenly **3** to replace one thing with another

switchback NOUN a railway at a fair, with steep slopes

switchboard NOUN a panel with switches etc. for making telephone connections

swivel VERB **swivelling, swivelled** to turn on a pivot or central point

swollen past participle of **swell**

swoon VERB to faint ► **swoon** NOUN

swoop VERB **1** to come down with a rushing movement **2** to make a sudden attack ► **swoop** NOUN

swop VERB **swopping, swopped** another spelling of **swap**

sword (sord) NOUN a weapon with a long pointed blade fixed in a handle or hilt

swordfish NOUN **swordfish** a large sea fish with a long sword-like upper jaw

sworn ADJECTIVE **1** given under oath *sworn testimony* **2** determined to remain so *sworn enemies*

swot VERB **swotting, swotted** (informal) to study hard

swot NOUN a person who studies hard

sycamore NOUN a tall tree with winged seeds, often grown for its timber

sycophant NOUN a person who tries to win favour by flattering someone ► **sycophantic** ADJECTIVE

syllable NOUN a word or part of a word that has one vowel sound when you say it ► **syllabic** ADJECTIVE

syllabus NOUN a summary of the things to be studied in a course

symbol NOUN **1** a thing used as a sign **2** a mark or sign with a special meaning (e.g. +, -, and x, in mathematics)

⚠ USAGE

Do not confuse this word with *cymbal*.

THESAURUS

switch NOUN • *the switch on the dashboard* ► button, control, key, lever

switch VERB • *to switch places* ► change, swap, exchange, replace, substitute

swoop VERB • *Birds swooped across the path.* ► dive, plunge, drop, fly down

symbol NOUN • *the Red Cross symbol* ► logo, badge, crest • *a symbol of freedom* ► emblem, token, sign, representation

DICTIONARY

symbolic ADJECTIVE acting as a symbol of something
► **symbolically** ADVERB

symbolism NOUN the use of symbols to represent ideas

symbolize VERB to make or be a symbol of something

⚠️ **SPELLING**

This word can also be spelled *symbolise*.

symmetrical ADJECTIVE able to be divided into two halves which are exactly the same but the opposite way round ► **symmetrically** ADVERB

symmetry NOUN the quality of being symmetrical or well-proportioned

sympathetic ADJECTIVE showing or feeling sympathy for someone
► **sympathetically** ADVERB

sympathize VERB to show or feel sympathy

⚠️ **SPELLING**

This word can also be spelled *sympathise*.

sympathy NOUN **sympathies**
1 the sharing or understanding of other people's feelings 2 a feeling of pity or tenderness towards someone who is hurt or in trouble

symphony NOUN **symphonies** a long piece of music for an orchestra, in several movements
► **symphonic** ADJECTIVE

symptom NOUN a sign that a disease or condition exists
► **symptomatic** ADJECTIVE

synagogue (sin-a-gog) NOUN a place where Jews worship

synchronize VERB 1 to make things happen at the same time 2 to put watches or clocks to the same time ► **synchronization** NOUN

⚠️ **SPELLING**

This word can also be spelled *synchronise*.

syncopate VERB to change the strength of beats in a piece of music ► **syncopation** NOUN

syndicate NOUN a group of people or firms working or acting together

syndrome NOUN 1 a set of symptoms 2 a set of characteristic opinions, behaviour, etc.

synod (sin-od) NOUN a church council

THESAURUS

sympathetic ADJECTIVE • *a sympathetic smile* ► caring, comforting, understanding, compassionate

sympathize VERB **sympathize with** • *We sympathize with your opinions.* ► understand, agree

with, support • *sympathized with their plight* ► commiserate with, be sorry for, identify with, feel for

sympathy NOUN • *to express sympathy* ► commiseration, pity, compassion, understanding

a
b
c
d
e
f
g
h
i
j
k
l
m
n
o
p
q
r
s
t
u
v
w
x
y
z

synonym (sin-o-nim) NOUN a word that means the same or almost the same as another word
▶ **synonymous** (sin-on-im-us) ADJECTIVE

synopsis (sin-op-sis) NOUN **synopses** a summary

syntax (sin-taks) NOUN the way words are arranged to make phrases or sentences ▶ **syntactic** ADJECTIVE

synthesis (sin-thi-sis) NOUN **syntheses** the combining of different things to make a whole

synthesize (sin-thi-syz) VERB to make something by combining parts

⚠ **SPELLING**

This word can also be spelled *synthesise*.

synthetic ADJECTIVE artificially made; not natural
▶ **synthetically** ADVERB

syringe NOUN a device for sucking in a liquid and squirting it out

syrup NOUN a thick sweet liquid
▶ **syrupy** ADJECTIVE

system NOUN **1** a set of parts, things, or ideas organized to work together **2** a way of doing something

systematic ADJECTIVE methodical; carefully planned
▶ **systematically** ADVERB

synthesizer NOUN an electronic musical instrument that can make a wide range of sounds

⚠ **SPELLING**

This word can also be spelled *synthesiser*.

THESAURUS

synthetic ADJECTIVE • *a synthetic material* ▶ artificial, imitation, man-made

system NOUN • *a reform of the system* ▶ organization, structure, framework, network, institution

• *a system for recording accidents* ▶ procedure, process, scheme, arrangement, method

systematic ADJECTIVE • *systematic teaching* ▶ methodical, ordered, organized, structured

Tt

tab NOUN a small flap or strip that sticks out

tabby NOUN **tabbies** a grey or brown cat with dark stripes

tabernacle NOUN (in the Bible) the portable shrine used by the Israelites during their wanderings in the desert

table NOUN **1** a piece of furniture with a flat top on legs **2** a set of facts or figures displayed in columns

table VERB to put forward for discussion

tableau (tab-loh) NOUN **tableaux** a dramatic or attractive scene

tablecloth NOUN a cloth for covering a table

tablespoon NOUN a large spoon for serving food

tablet NOUN **1** a pill **2** a solid piece of soap **3** an inscribed piece of stone or wood etc.

table tennis NOUN a game played on a table divided by a net, with bats and a small light ball

tabloid NOUN a newspaper with small pages and many photographs

taboo ADJECTIVE not to be done or used or talked about

taboo NOUN **taboos** a subject or action that is disapproved of

tabular ADJECTIVE arranged in a table or in columns

tabulate VERB to arrange information in a table
► **tabulation** NOUN

tacit (tas-it) ADJECTIVE implied or understood without spoken

taciturn (tas-i-tern) ADJECTIVE saying very little

tack NOUN **1** a short nail with a flat top **2** a tacking stitch **3** a course of action or policy *to change tack*

tack VERB **1** nail something down with tacks **2** fasten material together with long stitches **3** sail a zigzag course to take advantage of what wind there is

tackle VERB **1** to try to deal with **2** to try to get the ball from an opponent in a game **3** to talk to someone about an awkward matter

tackle NOUN **1** equipment, especially for fishing **2** a set of

table NOUN • *a table showing monthly rainfall* ► chart, diagram, graph

tablet NOUN • *a tablet of soap* ► bar, piece, block • *a headache tablet* ► pill, capsule, caplet

tackle VERB • *to tackle the problem* ► deal with, attend to, sort out,

handle, set about • *An opposing player tackled him.* ► challenge, intercept, take on • *decided to tackle him about her pay* ► confront, approach, challenge

tackle NOUN • *fishing tackle* ► gear, equipment, kit • *penalized for a late tackle* ► challenge, interception

DICTIONARY

ropes and pulleys **3** the act of tackling in a game

tacky¹ ADJECTIVE **tackier, tackiest** sticky; not quite dry

tacky² ADJECTIVE **tackier, tackiest** (*informal*) showing poor taste or style

tact NOUN skill in not offending people

tactful ADJECTIVE showing tact
▶ **tactfully** ADVERB

tactical ADJECTIVE to do with tactics
▶ **tactically** ADVERB

tactics NOUN **1** the skilful arrangement of troops etc. **2** methods used to achieve something

tactile ADJECTIVE to do with the sense of touch

tactless ADJECTIVE showing a lack of tact

tadpole NOUN the larva of a young frog or toad

taffeta NOUN a stiff silky material

tag NOUN **1** a label fixed to something **2** a game in which one person chases the others

tag VERB **tagging, tagged 1** to label with a tag **2** to add as an extra **tag along** to go with other people

tail NOUN **1** the part at the end or rear of something **2** the side of a coin opposite the head

tail VERB **1** to remove stalks from fruit **2** to follow someone closely **tail off** to become fewer, smaller, etc.

tailback NOUN a line of traffic stretching back from an obstruction

tailless ADJECTIVE not having a tail

tailor NOUN a person who makes men's clothes

tailor VERB **1** to make or fit clothes **2** to adapt for a special purpose

taint VERB to spoil with a small amount of a bad quality

taint NOUN something that spoils

take VERB **took, taken 1** to get something into your hands or possession or control etc. **2** to carry or convey **3** to make use of *to take a taxi* **4** to undertake or enjoy *to take a holiday* **5** to study

THESAURUS

tact NOUN • *treated them with great tact* ▶ consideration, sensitivity, thoughtfulness, understanding

tactful ADJECTIVE • *a tactful reminder* ▶ considerate, discreet, polite, sensitive, thoughtful

tactless ADJECTIVE • *upset by his tactless remark* ▶ insensitive, thoughtless, indiscreet, clumsy

tag VERB • *Each bottle was tagged.* ▶ label, mark

tail NOUN • *the tail of the queue* ▶ back, end, rear

tail VERB • *Reporters had tailed him for months.* ▶ follow, shadow, stalk, pursue **tail off** • *number of visitors tailed off* ▶ decrease, lessen, fade, wane, drop away

take VERB • *Many prisoners were taken.* ▶ catch, seize, capture, arrest • *He took her hand gently.* ▶ clasp, clutch, grasp, grab, grip

DICTIONARY

or teach a subject **6** to make an effort *taking the trouble* **7** to experience a feeling *to take offence* **8** to tolerate **9** to need **10** to write down *to take notes* **11** to make a photograph **12** to subtract **13** to assume *I take it you agree.* **take after** to resemble **take in** to deceive **take off** (of an aircraft) to become airborne **take on** to accept a task or challenge **take to** to develop a liking or ability for **take up 1** to occupy space or time etc. **2** to accept an offer

takeaway NOUN **1** a place that sells cooked meals for customers to take away **2** a meal from this

take-off NOUN the process of an aircraft becoming airborne

takeover NOUN the act of one business company taking control of another

takings PLURAL NOUN money received by a business

talcum powder NOUN a scented powder put on the skin

tale NOUN a story

talent NOUN a special ability
▶ **talented** ADJECTIVE

talisman NOUN **talismans** an object supposed to bring good luck

talk VERB **1** to speak or have a conversation **2** to be able to speak

talk NOUN **1** a conversation or discussion **2** an informal lecture **3** gossip or rumour

talkative ADJECTIVE talking a lot

THESAURUS

• *Someone had taken his car.*
▶ steal, remove, make off with, pinch • *Take ten percent from the total.* ▶ subtract, deduct • *It takes a long time.* ▶ need, require, call for, necessitate • *more than he could take* ▶ tolerate, bear, put up with, endure • *I'll take you home.* ▶ accompany, drive, bring, guide, transport **take in** • *a confidence trick that fools everyone in* ▶ fool, deceive, dupe, trick **take on** d took on more responsibilities ▶ accept, assume **take up** • *a cupboard that takes up a lot of space* ▶ occupy, use up

tale NOUN • *a tale of dragons and heroes* ▶ story, narrative, account

talent NOUN • *a talent for music*
▶ gift, aptitude, ability, flair, skill

talented ADJECTIVE • *a talented young player* ▶ gifted, able, accomplished, skilful, brilliant

talk VERB • *was talking to a friend*
▶ speak, chat, converse (with), have a chat

talk NOUN • *a lot of talk*
▶ conversation, chatter, discussion, dialogue • *a talk in the village hall* ▶ lecture, speech, presentation

talkative ADJECTIVE • *a talkative taxi driver* ▶ chatty, communicative, loquacious

DICTIONARY

tall ADJECTIVE **1** higher than the average • *a tall tree* **2** measured from the bottom to the top • *10 metres tall*

tall story NOUN **tall stories** (*informal*) a story that is hard to believe

tally NOUN **tallies** the total amount of a debt or score

tally VERB **tallies, tallied** to correspond or agree with something else

Talmud NOUN writings containing Jewish religious law

talon NOUN a strong claw

tambourine NOUN a circular musical instrument with metal discs round it, tapped or shaken to make it jingle

tame ADJECTIVE **1** (of animals) gentle and not afraid of people **2** not exciting; dull

tame VERB to make an animal become tame

tamper VERB to meddle or interfere with something

tampon NOUN a plug of soft material that a woman puts into her vagina to absorb the blood during menstruation

tan NOUN **1** a light brown colour **2** brown colour in skin exposed to the sun

tan VERB **tanning, tanned 1** to make or become brown by exposing skin to the sun **2** to make an animal's skin into leather by treating it with chemicals

tandem NOUN a bicycle for two riders, one behind the other

tandoori NOUN a style of Indian cooking using a clay oven

tang NOUN a strong flavour or smell

tangent NOUN a straight line touching the outside of a curve or circle

tangerine NOUN a kind of small orange

tangible ADJECTIVE **1** able to be touched **2** real or definite ▸ **tangibly** ADVERB

tangle VERB to make or become twisted and confused ▸ **tangle** NOUN

tango NOUN **tangos** a ballroom dance with gliding steps

THESAURUS

tall ADJECTIVE • *a tall man* ▸ large, big • *a tall building* ▸ high, lofty, towering

tame ADJECTIVE • *a tame animal* ▸ domesticated, gentle, trained • *a tame evening out* ▸ dull, boring, unexciting

tame VERB • *Wild rabbits can be tamed.* ▸ domesticate, break in, train

tamper VERB **tamper with** • *to tamper with the controls* ▸ interfere with, meddle with, fiddle about with

tangle VERB • *had managed to tangle her hair* ▸ knot, twist, ravel • *A dolphin had become tangled in the net.* ▸ trap, ensnare, catch, enmesh

tangle NOUN • *a tangle of wires and cables* ▸ mass, muddle, jumble, confusion

tank

tank *NOUN* **1** a large container for a liquid or gas **2** a heavy armoured military vehicle

tankard *NOUN* a large drinking mug of silver or pewter

tanker *NOUN* **1** a large ship for carrying oil **2** a large lorry for carrying a liquid

tanner *NOUN* a person who tans leather

tannin *NOUN* a substance obtained from the bark or fruit of various trees (also found in tea), used in tanning and dyeing

tantalize *VERB* to torment by offering something that cannot be reached

⚠️ **SPELLING**

This word can also be spelled *tantalise*.

tantamount *ADJECTIVE* equivalent *a request tantamount to a command*

tantrum *NOUN* an outburst of bad temper

tap¹ *NOUN* a device for letting out liquid or gas in a controlled flow

tap *VERB* **tapping, tapped 1** to take liquid out of **2** to obtain supplies or information etc. from **3** to fix a device to a telephone line to overhear conversations

tap² *NOUN* **1** a quick light hit **2** tap-dancing

tap *VERB* **tapping, tapped** to hit a person or thing quickly and lightly

tap dance *NOUN* a dance performed wearing shoes that make elaborate tapping sounds on the floor ► **tap dancer** *NOUN*

tape *NOUN* **1** a narrow strip of cloth, paper, plastic, etc. **2** a narrow magnetic strip for making recordings **3** a tape recording **4** a tape measure

tape *VERB* **1** fix, cover, or surround something with tape **2** record something on magnetic tape

taper *VERB* to make or become thinner at one end

taper *NOUN* a long thin candle

tape recorder *NOUN* a machine for recording sound on magnetic tape

tapestry *NOUN* **tapestries** a cloth with pictures or patterns woven or embroidered on it

tapeworm *NOUN* a long flat worm lives as a parasite in the intestines

tapioca *NOUN* a starchy food in hard white grains obtained from cassava

tapir *NOUN* a pig-like animal with a long flexible snout

tar *NOUN* a thick black liquid made from coal or wood etc. and used in making roads

tar *VERB* **tarring, tarred** to coat with tar

tarantula *NOUN* a large poisonous spider

THESAURUS

tap *NOUN* • *I was startled by a tap at the window.* ► knock, rap, knocking, touch

tap *VERB* • *tapped on the door* ► knock, rap • *tapped her shoulder* ► pat, touch, poke, nudge, strike

tardy ADJECTIVE **tardier, tardiest**
slow or late ▶ **tardily** ADVERB

target NOUN **1** an object aimed at
in shooting **2** a person or thing
being criticized, ridiculed, etc. **3** a
sum of money or other objective
aimed at

target VERB to aim at or have as a
target

tariff NOUN a list of prices or
charges

tarmac NOUN an area surfaced
with tarmacadam, especially on an
airfield

tarmacadam NOUN a mixture of
tar and broken stone, used for
making a hard surface on roads,
etc.

tarnish VERB **1** to make or become
less shiny **2** to spoil or blemish

tarot (rhymes with *barrow*) PLURAL
NOUN a system of fortune-telling
using special cards

tarpaulin NOUN a large sheet of
waterproof cloth

tarragon NOUN a plant with leaves
used to flavour salads etc.

tarry VERB **tarries, tarried** to stay
for a while; to linger

tart[1] NOUN **1** a pie containing fruit
or a sweet filling **2** a piece of pastry
with jam etc. on top

tart[2] ADJECTIVE **1** sour **2** sharp in
manner

tartan NOUN a pattern with
coloured stripes crossing each
other, especially one used by a
Scottish clan

tartar NOUN a hard chalky deposit
that forms on teeth

task NOUN a piece of work to be
done

tassel NOUN a hanging bundle of
threads used as a decoration

taste VERB **1** to take a small
amount of food or drink to try its
flavour **2** to be able to perceive
flavours **3** to have a certain flavour

taste NOUN **1** the feeling caused
by something placed on it **2** the ability to taste
things **3** the ability to judge
beautiful or suitable things well
4 a liking **5** a small amount of food
or drink

tasteful ADJECTIVE showing good
taste ▶ **tastefully** ADVERB

target NOUN • *the target of attacks*
▶ victim, object • *a target of
£100,000* ▶ goal, objective, aim,
ambition

tart ADJECTIVE • *a tart taste* ▶ sharp,
sour, tangy

task NOUN • *a daunting task* ▶ job,
undertaking, chore, duty

taste VERB • *tasted her food*
▶ sample, test, try, sip

taste NOUN • *a strange taste*
▶ flavour, savour • *have a
taste of the pudding* ▶ mouthful,
bite, nibble, sip • *a person
of taste* ▶ judgement,
discrimination, style • *a taste
for travel* ▶ liking, fondness,
desire

tasteful ADJECTIVE • *a tasteful decor*
i smart, stylish, refined

DICTIONARY

tasteless ADJECTIVE **1** having no flavour **2** showing poor taste

tasty ADJECTIVE **tastier, tastiest** having a pleasant taste

tattered ADJECTIVE badly torn or ragged

tatters PLURAL NOUN badly torn pieces

tattoo VERB **tattoos, tattooing, tattooed** to mark a design on the skin using a needle and dyes

tattoo NOUN **tattoos 1** a tattooed picture or pattern **2** an entertainment of military music, marching, etc.

tatty ADJECTIVE **tattier, tattiest 1** shabby and untidy **2** cheap and gaudy

taunt VERB to jeer at or insult
▶ **taunt** NOUN

taut ADJECTIVE stretched tightly
▶ **tautly** ADVERB

tautology NOUN **tautologies** a form of saying the same thing twice in different words, e.g. *a free gift*

tavern NOUN (old use) an inn or public house

tawdry ADJECTIVE **tawdrier, tawdriest** cheap and gaudy

tawny ADJECTIVE a brownish-yellow colour

tax NOUN **1** money collected from the public by the government, used for public purposes **2** a strain or burden

tax VERB **1** to put a tax on **2** to charge someone a tax **3** to put a strain or burden on

taxation NOUN a system of collecting taxes

taxi NOUN **taxis** a car that can be hired for short journeys for payment

taxi VERB **taxis, taxiing, taxied** (of an aircraft) to move along the ground before or after flying

taxidermist NOUN a person who stuffs the skins of dead animals to make them lifelike ▶ **taxidermy** NOUN

taxpayer NOUN a person who pays tax

TB ABBREVIATION tuberculosis

tea NOUN **1** the dried leaves of an evergreen shrub **2** a drink made from these **3** a meal in the afternoon or early evening

teacake NOUN a kind of flat bun

teach VERB **taught** to give a person knowledge or skill

THESAURUS

tasteless ADJECTIVE • *tasteless vegetables* ▶ flavourless, bland, insipid, weak, watery • *a tasteless remark* ▶ crude, indelicate, uncouth, vulgar

tasty ADJECTIVE • *Tasty food was laid out on every table.* ▶ delicious, appetizing, luscious, mouth-watering

taunt VERB • *taunted him about his shabby clothes* ▶ tease, jeer at, mock, ridicule

taut ADJECTIVE • *a taut rope* ▶ tight, tense, firm, rigid

teach VERB • *taught me to swim*
▶ instruct, train, coach • *teaches children with special needs*
▶ educate, tutor

a
b
c
d
e
f
g
h
i
j
k
l
m
n
o
p
q
r
s
t
u
v
w
x
y
z

teacher NOUN a person who teaches at a school

teak NOUN a hard strong wood

teal NOUN a kind of duck

team NOUN **1** a set of players in certain games and sports **2** a group of people working together

team VERB to put or join together in a team

teapot NOUN a pot with a lid and a handle, for making and pouring tea

tear[1] (teer) NOUN a drop of the water that comes from the eyes when crying

tear[2] (tair) VERB **tore, torn 1** to pull apart or into pieces **2** to become torn **3** to run hurriedly

tear NOUN a split made by tearing

tearful ADJECTIVE crying easily
▶ **tearfully** ADVERB

tear gas NOUN a gas that makes the eyes water painfully

tease VERB to amuse yourself by . making fun of someone

tease NOUN a person who often teases others

teasel NOUN a plant with bristly heads

teaser NOUN a problem or puzzle

teaspoon NOUN a small spoon for stirring tea etc.

teat NOUN **1** a nipple through which a baby sucks milk **2** the cap of a baby's feeding bottle

technical ADJECTIVE **1** to do with technology **2** to do with a particular subject *technical terms*

technicality NOUN **technicalities** a technical word, phrase, or detail

technically ADVERB according to the strict facts, rules, etc.

technician NOUN a person who looks after scientific equipment in a laboratory

technique NOUN a method of doing something skilfully

technology NOUN the study of machinery, engineering, and how things work ▶ **technological** ADJECTIVE

teddy bear NOUN a soft furry toy bear

tedious ADJECTIVE annoyingly slow or long

tedium NOUN a dull or boring time or experience

tee NOUN **1** the flat area from which golfers strike the ball at the start of

THESAURUS

team NOUN • *the local cricket team*
▶ squad, side • *a production team*
▶ group, crew, gang

tear VERB • *Don't tear your clothes.*
▶ rip, slit, snag, split • *tore the packet open* ▶ rip, pull • *I tore round to the shop.* ▶ rush, hurry, race, speed

tear NOUN • *a tear in my jeans*
▶ rip, hole, split, slit

tease VERB • *Friends teased him about his hair.* ▶ make fun of, laugh at, mock, taunt

tedious ADJECTIVE • *tedious work*
▶ dull, boring, monotonous, dreary

play for each hole **2** a small peg for resting a golf ball to be struck

teem VERB **1** to be full of something **2** to rain very hard

teen ADJECTIVE, NOUN (informal) a teenager

teenage ADJECTIVE to do with teenagers ▸ **teenaged** ADJECTIVE

teenager NOUN a person in their teens

teens PLURAL NOUN the time of life between 13 and 19 years of age

tee-shirt NOUN another spelling of **T-shirt**

teeter VERB to stand or move unsteadily

teeth plural of **tooth**.

teethe VERB (of a baby) to have its first teeth beginning to grow

teetotal ADJECTIVE not drinking alcohol ▸ **teetotaller** NOUN

telecommunications PLURAL NOUN communications over a long distance, e.g. by telephone, telegraph, radio, or television

telegram NOUN a message sent by telegraph

telegraph NOUN a way of sending messages by using electric current along wires or by radio

telepathy (til-ep-ath-ee) NOUN communication of thoughts from

one person's mind to another without speaking, writing, or gestures ▸ **telepathic** ADJECTIVE

telephone NOUN a device or system using electric wires or radio etc. to enable one person to speak to another who is some distance away

telephone VERB to speak to a person on the telephone

telephonist NOUN a person who operates a telephone switchboard

telescope NOUN an instrument using lenses to magnify distant objects ▸ **telescopic** ADJECTIVE

telescope VERB **1** make or become shorter by sliding overlapping sections into each other **2** compress or condense something so that it takes less space or time

teletext NOUN a system for displaying news and information on a television screen

televise VERB to broadcast by television

television NOUN **1** a system using radio waves to reproduce a view of scenes, events, or plays etc. on a screen **2** an apparatus for receiving these pictures

tell VERB told **1** to use words to make a thing known to someone

THESAURUS

tell VERB • *Tell them what happened.*
▸ inform, advise, let know
• *They told us there would be another train.* ▸ assure, promise, inform • *I'll tell you a secret.*
▸ disclose, reveal, confess, admit
• *to tell your story* ▸ recount,

narrate, relate, describe • *told us to leave* ▸ order, instruct, direct
• *not easy to tell them apart*
▸ distinguish, differentiate

tell off • *told them off for being late* ▸ reprimand, scold, rebuke

2 to speak *telling the truth* 3 to order 4 to reveal a secret 5 to decide or distinguish 6 to have an effect *The strain was beginning to tell.* **tell off** (*informal*) to scold or reprimand

telling ADJECTIVE having a strong effect or meaning *a telling answer*

tell-tale NOUN a person who tells tales

tell-tale ADJECTIVE revealing or indicating something *a tell-tale spot of jam on his chin*

temerity NOUN rashness or boldness

temper NOUN 1 a person's mood 2 an angry mood **lose your temper** to become angry

temper VERB 1 to harden or strengthen metal etc. by heating and cooling it 2 to moderate or soften the effects of something *temper justice with mercy*

temperament NOUN a person's nature and typical behaviour *a nervous temperament*

temperamental ADJECTIVE 1 likely to become excitable or moody 2 to do with temperament ▶ **temperamentally** ADVERB

temperate ADJECTIVE (of a climate) neither extremely hot nor extremely cold

temperature NOUN 1 how hot or cold a person or thing is 2 an abnormally high body temperature

tempest NOUN a violent storm

tempestuous ADJECTIVE 1 stormy 2 violent or passionate

template NOUN a thin sheet used as a guide for cutting or shaping

temple[1] NOUN a building in which a god is worshipped

temple[2] NOUN the part of the head between the forehead and the ear

tempo NOUN *tempos* or *tempi* the speed or rhythm of music

temporary ADJECTIVE lasting for a limited time only ▶ **temporarily** ADVERB

tempt VERB to try to persuade or attract someone

temptation NOUN 1 the act of tempting 2 something that tempts

ten NOUN, ADJECTIVE the number 10

tenable ADJECTIVE able to be held or defended

temper NOUN • *a calm temper* ▶ temperament, nature, character, personality • *walked out in a temper* ▶ rage, fury, tantrum **lose your temper** • *was near losing my temper* ▶ become angry, fly into a rage

temporary ADJECTIVE • *a temporary solution* ▶ short-term, interim, short-lived, momentary

tempt ▶ • *tempted him to stay* ▶ entice, lure, persuade, coax

temptation NOUN • *the temptation to call him* ▶ urge, desire, impulse • *the temptations of city life* ▶ attraction, appeal, lure, pull, enticement

DICTIONARY

tenacious ADJECTIVE **1** holding or clinging firmly to something **2** firm and determined

tenacity NOUN firmness and determination

tenant NOUN a person who rents a house, building, or land etc. from a landlord ► **tenancy** NOUN

tend VERB **1** to be inclined or likely to do something **2** to look after

tendency NOUN **tendencies** the way a person or thing is likely to behave

tender[1] ADJECTIVE **1** easy to chew **2** easily hurt or damaged **3** (of a part of the body) painful when touched **4** gentle and loving ► **tenderly** ADVERB

tender[2] VERB to offer formally *He tendered his resignation.*

tender NOUN a formal offer to supply goods or carry out work at a stated price

tendon NOUN a strong strip of tissue joining muscle to bone

tendril NOUN **1** a thread-like part by which a climbing plant clings to a support **2** a thin curl of hair etc.

tenement NOUN a large house divided into flats

tenet NOUN a firm belief

tenner NOUN (*informal*) a ten-pound note

tennis NOUN a game played with rackets and a ball on a court with a net across the middle

> **WORD HISTORY**
>
> from French *tenez!* 'receive (the ball)!', which the player serving called out

tenon NOUN a piece of wood shaped to fit into a mortise

tenor NOUN **1** a male singer with a high voice **2** the general meaning or drift

tense[1] NOUN the form of a verb that shows when something happens: *past*, *present*, and *future*

tense[2] ADJECTIVE **1** tightly stretched **2** nervous or worried

tense VERB to make or become tense

tension NOUN **1** how tightly stretched a rope or wire is **2** a feeling of anxiety or nervousness

tent NOUN a movable shelter made of canvas or other material

tentacle NOUN a long flexible part of certain animals (e.g. snails, octopuses), used for feeling or grasping or for moving

THESAURUS

tend VERB ► *to tend the sick* ► look after, care for, treat, nurse **tend to** ► *tends to get lost* ► be inclined to, be liable to, have a tendency to

tender ADJECTIVE ► *tender food* ► soft, succulent, juicy ► *Her ankle felt tender.* ► sore, painful, sensitive ► *a tender person* ► kind, caring, gentle, compassionate

tense ADJECTIVE ► *tense muscles* ► taut, tight, strained ► *was feeling tense* ► anxious, nervous, edgy, stressed

tension NOUN ► *the tension of the ropes* ► tightness, tautness ► *The tension was unbearable.* ► stress, strain, anxiety, suspense, excitement

a
b
c
d
e
f
g
h
i
j
k
l
m
n
o
p
q
r
s
t
u
v
w
x
y
z

tentative ADJECTIVE cautious; trying something out *a tentative suggestion*

tenterhooks PLURAL NOUN **on tenterhooks** tense and anxious

tenth ADJECTIVE, NOUN next after the ninth

tenuous ADJECTIVE very slight or thin

tenure (ten-yoor) NOUN the holding of a position of employment, or of land, accommodation, etc.

tepee NOUN a traditional Native American tent made with animal skins

tepid ADJECTIVE slightly warm

term NOUN **1** the period when a school or college is open **2** a definite period **3** a word or expression

term VERB to call something by a certain term

terminal NOUN **1** the place where something ends **2** a building where air passengers arrive or depart **3** a connection in an electric circuit or battery etc. **4** a monitor and keyboard linked to a computer network

terminal ADJECTIVE (of a fatal disease) in the last stage
▶ **terminally** ADVERB

terminate VERB to stop finally
▶ **termination** NOUN

terminology NOUN
terminologies the technical terms of a subject

terminus NOUN **termini 1** the end of something **2** the last station on a railway or bus route

termite NOUN a small insect that eats wood

terms PLURAL NOUN **1** a relationship between people *We are all on friendly terms.* **2** conditions offered or accepted

tern NOUN a seabird with long wings

terrace NOUN **1** a level area on a slope or hillside **2** a paved area beside a house **3** a row of joined houses ▶ **terraced** ADJECTIVE

terracotta NOUN **1** a kind of pottery **2** a brownish-red colour

terrain NOUN an of land of a particular type *hilly terrain*

terrapin NOUN a small turtle

terrestrial ADJECTIVE to do with the earth or land

terrible ADJECTIVE very bad; awful
▶ **terribly** ADVERB

terrier NOUN a kind of small lively dog

terrific ADJECTIVE (*informal*) **1** very great **2** excellent ▶ **terrifically** ADVERB

term NOUN • *a term of office*
▶ period, spell, session • *a technical term* ▶ word, expression

terrible ADJECTIVE • *had a terrible time* ▶ dreadful, horrible, awful, ghastly • *a terrible smell*
▶ disgusting, nasty, unpleasant, horrible

terrific ADJECTIVE • *heard a terrific thud* ▶ huge, mighty, tremendous, colossal • *a terrific story* ▶ excellent, wonderful, marvellous, first-class

terrify VERB **terrifies, terrified** to make someone very afraid

territorial ADJECTIVE to do with a country's territory

territory NOUN **territories** an area of land belonging to a country or person

terror NOUN **1** very great fear **2** a terrifying person or thing

terrorist NOUN a person who uses violence for political purposes
▶ **terrorism** NOUN

terrorize VERB to frighten someone by threatening them
▶ **terrorization** NOUN

⚠ **SPELLING**

This word can also be spelled *terrorise*.

terse ADJECTIVE using few words; concise or curt

test NOUN **1** a brief examination **2** a way of discovering the abilities or presence of a person or thing

test VERB to carry out a test on

testament NOUN **1** a written statement **2** either of the two main parts of the Bible, the Old Testament and the New Testament

testicle NOUN either of the two glands in the scrotum where semen is produced

testify VERB **testifies, testified 1** to give evidence under oath **2** be evidence or proof of something

testimonial NOUN a letter describing someone's abilities, character, etc.

testimony NOUN **testimonies** evidence, especially given under oath

test match NOUN a cricket match between different countries

testosterone (test-ost-er-ohn) NOUN a male sex hormone

test tube NOUN a tube of thin glass with one end closed, used for experiments in chemistry etc.

testy ADJECTIVE **testier, testiest** easily annoyed; irritable

tetanus NOUN a disease that makes the muscles stiff, caused by bacteria

tetchy ADJECTIVE **tetchier, tetchiest** easily annoyed; irritable

tether VERB to tie an animal with a rope

tether NOUN a rope for tethering an animal **at the end of your tether** unable to bear any more

text NOUN **1** the words of something written or printed **2** a novel, play, etc., studied for a course **3** a text message

THESAURUS

terrify VERB • *The prospect terrified him.* ▶ frighten, scare, horrify, petrify

terror NOUN • *overwhelmed by terror* ▶ fear, alarm, fright, horror, panic

test NOUN • *will have to pass a test* ▶ exam, examination,

assessment • *a series of scientific tests* ▶ trial, experiment, study, investigation

test VERB • *experiments to test the idea* ▶ check, evaluate, examine, analyse • *a chance to test your DIY skills* ▶ try out, put to the test, trial

text VERB to send a text message by mobile phone

textbook NOUN a book for teaching and learning about a subject

textiles PLURAL NOUN kinds of cloth; fabrics

text message NOUN a written message sent on a mobile phone

texture NOUN the way that the surface of something feels

than CONJUNCTION, PREPOSITION compared with another person or thing *is taller than I am is taller than me*

thank VERB to tell someone that you are grateful to them

thankful ADJECTIVE grateful
► **thankfully** ADVERB

thankless ADJECTIVE not likely to win thanks from people

thanks PLURAL NOUN 1 statements of gratitude 2 (*informal*) thank you

thanksgiving NOUN an expression of gratitude, especially to God

that ADJECTIVE, PRONOUN the one there *That book is mine. Whose is that?*

that ADVERB to such an extent *not that good*

that RELATIVE PRONOUN which, who, or whom *the record that I wanted*

that CONJUNCTION used to introduce a wish, reason, result, etc. *so hard that no one could solve it I hope that you are well.*

thatch NOUN straw or reeds used to make a roof

thatch VERB to make a roof with thatch

thaw VERB to stop being frozen

thaw NOUN a period of warm weather that thaws ice and snow

the DETERMINER a particular one; that or those

theatre NOUN 1 a building in which plays etc. are performed to an audience 2 the acting and production of plays 3 a hospital room for performing surgical operations

theatrical ADJECTIVE 1 to do with plays or acting 2 exaggerated and showy ► **theatrically** ADVERB

thee PRONOUN (*old use*) you (referring to one person and used as the object of a verb or after a preposition)

theft NOUN stealing

their ADJECTIVE belonging to them *Their coats are here.*

⚠ **USAGE**
Do not confuse this word with **there**.

theirs POSSESSIVE PRONOUN belonging to them *The coats are theirs.*

⚠ **USAGE**
It is incorrect to write **their's**.

THESAURUS

thankful ADJECTIVE • *was thankful for the moonlight* ► grateful, pleased (about), happy (about)

thanks NOUN • *expressed his thanks* ► gratitude, appreciation, acknowledgement

thaw VERB • *The snow was beginning to thaw.* ► melt, unfreeze, soften, defrost

theft NOUN • *the theft of jewels* ► robbery, stealing, burglary

them PRONOUN the form of **they** used as the object of a verb or after a preposition *We saw them.*

theme NOUN **1** the subject of a piece of writing, conversation, etc. **2** a melody

theme park NOUN an amusement park with rides and attractions based on a particular subject

theme tune NOUN a special tune used to announce a particular programme, performer, etc.

themselves PRONOUN they or them and nobody else *They cut themselves. They themselves have said it.* **by themselves** alone; on their own

then ADVERB **1** at that time **2** after that; next **3** in that case

thence ADVERB from that place

theologian NOUN an expert in theology

theology NOUN the study of religion ▶ **theological** ADJECTIVE

theorem NOUN a mathematical statement reached by reasoning

theoretical ADJECTIVE based on theory and not on practice or experience ▶ **theoretically** ADVERB

theorize VERB to form a theory or theories

⚠ **SPELLING**

This word can also be spelled *theorise.*

theory NOUN **theories 1** an idea or set of ideas put forward to explain something **2** the principles of a subject

therapeutic ADJECTIVE treating or curing a disease etc.

therapy NOUN **therapies** treatment of a physical or mental illness without using surgery or artificial medicines ▶ **therapist** NOUN

there ADVERB **1** in or to that place etc. **2** used to call attention to something

⚠ **USAGE**

Do not confuse this word with *their.*

thereabouts ADVERB near there

thereafter ADVERB from then or there onwards

thereby ADVERB by that means; because of that

therefore ADVERB for that reason

therm NOUN a unit for measuring heat, especially from gas

thermal ADJECTIVE to do with heat; worked by heat

thermodynamics NOUN the science of the relation between heat and other forms of energy

thermometer NOUN a device for measuring temperature

Thermos NOUN (*trademark*) a kind of vacuum flask

theme NOUN • *the dominant theme of the book* ▶ topic, subject, question • *a musical theme* ▶ melody, tune

theory NOUN • *theories based on experiments* ▶ hypothesis, idea, argument, belief, thesis, assumption

a
b
c
d
e
f
g
h
i
j
k
l
m
n
o
p
q
r
s
t
u
v
w
x
y
z

771

a
b
c
d
e
f
g
h
i
j
k
l
m
n
o
p
q
r
s
t
u
v
w
x
y
z

thermostat NOUN a device that controls the temperature of a room or piece of equipment

thesaurus (thi-sor-us) NOUN **thesauruses** or **thesauri** a kind of dictionary listing words in sets according to their meaning

these plural of **this**.

thesis NOUN **theses 1** a theory put forward **2** a long essay written for a university degree

they PRONOUN **1** the people or things being talked about **2** people in general **3** he or she; a person *If anyone is late they will not be admitted.*

they're they are

⚠ **USAGE**

Do not confuse this word with *their* or *there*.

thick ADJECTIVE **1** measuring a lot between its opposite surfaces **2** measuring from one side to the other *ten centimetres thick* **3** (of a line) broad, not fine **4** crowded with things; dense **5** not flowing easily **6** (informal) stupid
► **thickness** NOUN

thicken VERB to make or become thicker

thicket NOUN a close group of shrubs and small trees

thickset ADJECTIVE **1** having a stocky or burly body **2** closely placed or crowded

thief NOUN **thieves** a person who steals

thieving NOUN stealing

thigh NOUN the part of the leg between the hip and the knee

thimble NOUN a small cap worn over the finger to push the needle in sewing

thin ADJECTIVE **thinner**, **thinnest 1** not thick; not fat **2** feeble *a thin excuse* **3** (of a liquid) watery

thin VERB **thinning**, **thinned** to make or become less thick **thin out** to make or become less dense or crowded

thine POSSESSIVE PRONOUN (old use) yours (referring to one person)

thing NOUN an object; something which can be seen, touched, thought about, etc.

THESAURUS

thick ADJECTIVE • *a thick wad of notes*
► fat, broad, wide, solid, substantial • *thick fog* ► dense, solid, impenetrable • *a thick smooth paste* ► stiff, concentrated, viscous

thicken VERB • *to thicken the sauce*
► stiffen, concentrate, reduce

thief NOUN • *A thief stole the jewels.*
► robber, burglar, housebreaker, shoplifter

thin ADJECTIVE • *was thin for his age*
► slim, slender, slight, skinny • *thin material* ► fine, delicate, light • *a thin liquid* ► light, runny, watery, dilute

thin VERB • *to thin the paint*
► dilute, water down, weaken **thin out** • *The crowds began to thin out.* ► decrease, dwindle

thing NOUN • *full of weird things*
► object, item, artefact, article,

DICTIONARY

things *PLURAL NOUN* **1** personal belongings **2** circumstances

think *VERB* **thought 1** to use the mind to form connected ideas **2** to have an idea or opinion **3** to intend or plan *thinking of buying a guitar* ▶ **think** *NOUN*

third *ADJECTIVE* next after the second ▶ **thirdly** *ADVERB*

third *NOUN* **1** a person or thing that is third **2** one of three equal parts of something

Third World *NOUN* the poorest countries of Asia, Africa, and South America

thirst *NOUN* **1** a feeling of dryness in the mouth and throat, causing a desire to drink **2** a strong desire

thirst *VERB* to have a strong desire for something

thirsty *ADJECTIVE* **thirstier, thirstiest 1** needing to drink **2** eager for something

thirteen *NOUN, ADJECTIVE* the number 13 ▶ **thirteenth** *ADJECTIVE, NOUN*

thirty *NOUN, ADJECTIVE* the number 30 **thirties** ▶ **thirtieth** *ADJECTIVE, NOUN*

this *ADJECTIVE, PRONOUN* the one here *This house is ours. Whose is this?*

this *ADVERB* to such an extent *not this big*

thistle *NOUN* a prickly wild plant with purple, white, or yellow flowers

thither *ADVERB* (old use) to that place

thong *NOUN* **1** a narrow strip of leather etc. used for tying and fastening **2** a style of knickers with just a narrow strip at the back

thorax *NOUN* the part of the body between the head or neck and the abdomen ▶ **thoracic** *ADJECTIVE*

thorn *NOUN* **1** a small pointed growth on the stem of a plant **2** a thorny tree or shrub

thorny *ADJECTIVE* **thornier, thorniest 1** having many thorns; prickly **2** difficult *a thorny problem*

THESAURUS

device • *A strange thing happened.* i event, occurrence, incident, deed **things** • *put the things in the car* ▶ belongings, possessions, equipment • *Things will improve.* ▶ circumstances, conditions

think *VERB* • *Do you think they will come?* ▶ believe, expect, imagine, consider, conclude • *thought hard for a few moments* ▶ concentrate, ponder, deliberate, reflect • *was thought worthy of high office* ▶ consider, deem, judge **think about**

• *thinking about the future.*
▶ consider, contemplate
think of • *thought of all the good times* ▶ recall, remember, recollect

thirst *NOUN* • *a thirst for knowledge*
▶ appetite, hunger, longing, craving, desire

thirsty *ADJECTIVE* • *were hot and thirsty* ▶ dehydrated, dry, parched • *thirsty for adventure*
▶ eager, hungry, yearning, longing

a
b
c
d
e
f
g
h
i
j
k
l
m
n
o
p
q
r
s
t
u
v
w
x
y
z

thorough ADJECTIVE **1** careful and detailed **2** complete in every way ► **thoroughly** ADVERB, **thoroughness** NOUN

thoroughbred ADJECTIVE bred of pure or pedigree stock ► **thoroughbred** NOUN

thoroughfare NOUN a public road open at both ends

those plural of **that**.

thou PRONOUN (old use) you (referring to one person)

though CONJUNCTION in spite of the fact that; even if *We can phone them, though they may have left.*

though ADVERB however *She's right, though.*

thought[1] NOUN **1** something you think; an idea or opinion **2** the process of thinking

thought[2] past tense of **think**.

thoughtful ADJECTIVE **1** thinking a lot **2** showing consideration for other people ► **thoughtfully** ADVERB

thoughtless ADJECTIVE **1** careless; not thinking of what may happen **2** inconsiderate

thousand NOUN, ADJECTIVE the number 1,000 ► **thousandth** ADJECTIVE & NOUN

thrash VERB **1** to beat with a stick or whip **2** (informal) to defeat thoroughly **3** to move violently

thread NOUN **1** a length of cotton, wool, etc. **2** the spiral ridge round a screw **3** a theme or idea running through a story, argument, etc.

thread VERB **1** to put a thread through the eye of a needle **2** to pass a strip of film etc. through or round something **3** to put beads on a thread **4** to make your way through a crowd etc.

threadbare ADJECTIVE (of cloth) having a worn surface

threat NOUN **1** a warning of harm or punishment **2** a sign of something undesirable **3** a person or thing causing danger

THESAURUS

thorough ADJECTIVE • *a thorough inquiry* ► rigorous, detailed, in-depth • *thorough in their work* ► careful, conscientious, methodical, meticulous • *a thorough nuisance* ► utter, complete, absolute

thought NOUN • *shared his thoughts with us* ► idea, belief, opinion • *deep in thought* ► thinking, contemplation

thoughtful ADJECTIVE • *thoughtful comments* ► intelligent, profound • *was thoughtful of you to visit*

► considerate, kind, caring, unselfish

thoughtless ADJECTIVE • *was thoughtless to rush off* ► inconsiderate, unkind, uncaring

thrash VERB • *was thrashed severely* ► beat, whip, flog • *thrashed her arms about* ► jerk, toss, flail

threat NOUN • *bomb threats* ► warning, ultimatum • *a threat to world peace* ► danger, risk, hazard

774

DICTIONARY

threaten VERB **1** to make threats against **2** to be a threat or danger to

three NOUN, ADJECTIVE the number 3

thresh VERB to beat corn to separate the grain from the husks

threshold NOUN **1** a slab of stone or board etc. under a doorway **2** a beginning of something great *on the threshold of a discovery*

threw past tense of **throw**

thrice ADVERB (old use) three times

thrift NOUN careful management of money or resources

thrifty ADJECTIVE **thriftier, thriftiest** careful about spending money ▸ **thriftily** ADVERB

thrill NOUN a feeling of excitement

thrill VERB to have or give a feeling of excitement

thriller NOUN an exciting story about crime or spying

thrilling ADJECTIVE very exciting

thrive VERB **throve, thrived** or or **thriven** to prosper or be successful

throat NOUN **1** the passage in the neck that takes food and drink down into the body **2** the front of the neck

throb VERB **throbbing, throbbed** to beat or vibrate with a strong rhythm ▸ **throb** NOUN

throes PLURAL NOUN severe pain

thrombosis NOUN the formation of a clot of blood in the body

throne NOUN **1** a ceremonial chair for a king, queen, or bishop **2** the position of king or queen *heir to the throne*

throng NOUN a crowd of people

throng VERB to crowd

throttle NOUN a device that controls the flow of fuel to an engine

throttle VERB to strangle

through PREPOSITION **1** from one end or side to the other end or side of *Light came through the window.*

THESAURUS

threaten VERB • *were threatening us with angry looks* ▸ intimidate, menace, bully, terrorize • *to threaten our safety* ▸ endanger, put at risk

thrill NOUN • *was a thrill to work with them* ▸ adventure, excitement, pleasure, sensation

thrill VERB • *The idea thrilled him.* ▸ excite, delight, exhilarate, rouse, stimulate

thrilling ADJECTIVE • *a thrilling adventure* ▸ exciting, gripping, exhilarating

thrive VERB • *The plants were thriving.* ▸ flourish, grow, prosper, do well

throb VERB • *The music throbbed.* ▸ pound, pulsate, beat

throb NOUN • *the dull throb of the car's stereo* ▸ beat, rhythm, pounding

throttle VERB • *to throttle someone* ▸ strangle, choke

DICTIONARY

2 by means of; because of *We lost it through carelessness.*

through ADVERB **1** from one end or side to the other *We squeezed through.* **2** with a telephone connection made *I'll put you through.* **3** finished *I'm through with the work.*

through ADJECTIVE **1** leading through *a through road* **2** not involving a change *a through train*

throughout PREPOSITION, ADVERB all the way through

throve past tense of **thrive**.

throw VERB **threw, thrown 1** to send through the air **2** to put in a place carelessly or hastily **3** to move part of your body quickly *threw his head back* **4** to put someone in a certain condition etc. *threw us into confusion* **5** to confuse or upset **6** to move a switch or lever **7** to hold a party
► **throw** NOUN

thrush NOUN a songbird with a speckled breast

thrust VERB **thrust** to push hard
► **thrust** NOUN

thud VERB **thudding, thudded** to make the dull sound of a heavy fall
► **thud** NOUN

thug NOUN a rough and violent person

> **WORD HISTORY**
> from Hindi *thag* 'thief, swindler'

thumb NOUN the short thick finger set apart from the other four

thumb VERB to turn the pages of a book etc. quickly with your thumb

thump VERB **1** to hit or knock heavily **2** to throb or beat strongly
► **thump** NOUN

thunder NOUN **1** the rumbling noise heard with lightning **2** a loud noise

thunder VERB **1** to sound with thunder **2** to speak with a loud deep voice

thunderbolt NOUN a flash of lightning with a simultaneous crash of thunder

thunderous ADJECTIVE extremely loud *thunderous applause*

thunderstorm NOUN a storm with thunder and lightning

THESAURUS

throw VERB • *throw the ball*
► toss, fling, hurl, pitch, lob, cast
• *The horse threw its rider.*
► unseat, dislodge **throw away**
• *lots of stuff to throw away*
► discard, dispose of, get rid of

thrust VERB • *thrust a book into my hands* ► push, shove, force, press, stick

thud VERB • *footsteps thudding across the garden* ► bang, thump, crash

thud NOUN • *heard a loud thud*
► bang, thump, clunk, crash

thump VERB • *thumped the table with his fist* ► bang, hit, strike, pound, beat, knock

thump NOUN • *sat down with a thump* ► bang, thud, clunk, crash • *the heavy thump of rock music* ► beat, rhythm, pounding

a b c d e f g h i j k l m n o p q r s t u v w x y z

Thursday NOUN the day of the week following Wednesday

thus ADVERB **1** in this way **2** therefore

thwart VERB to prevent from achieving something

thy ADJECTIVE (old use) your (referring to one person)

thyme (say as time) NOUN a herb with fragrant leaves

thyroid gland NOUN a large gland at the front of the neck

tiara NOUN a woman's jewelled ornament worn like a crown

tic NOUN an unintentional twitch of a face muscle

tick¹ NOUN **1** a mark (✓) put by something to show that it is correct or has been checked **2** a regular clicking sound made by a clock or watch **3** (informal) a moment

tick VERB **1** to mark with a tick **2** to make the sound of a tick **tick off** (informal) to scold or reprimand

tick² NOUN a tiny bloodsucking insect

ticket NOUN **1** a printed piece of paper or card allowing a person to

travel, enter a theatre, etc. **2** a notice of a traffic offence attached to a vehicle

tickle VERB **1** to touch a person's skin lightly to produce a slight tingling feeling **2** to amuse or please

ticklish ADJECTIVE **1** likely to react to tickling **2** awkward or difficult

tidal ADJECTIVE to do with tides

tidal wave NOUN a huge sea wave

tiddler NOUN (informal) a small fish

tiddlywink NOUN a small counter flicked into a cup by pressing with another counter

tide NOUN **1** the regular rise and fall in the level of the sea **2** (old use) a time or season *Christmastide*

tide VERB **tide someone over** to provide them with their needs for a time

tidings PLURAL NOUN (formal) news

tidy ADJECTIVE **tidier, tidiest 1** neat and orderly **2** (informal) fairly large
► **tidily** ADVERB, **tidiness** NOUN

tidy VERB **tidies, tidied** to make a place tidy

tie VERB **tying 1** to fasten with string, ribbon, etc. **2** to arrange

THESAURUS

thwart VERB • *The bad weather thwarted us.* ► frustrate, hinder, prevent

tick VERB • *could hear my watch ticking* ► click, beat • *tick the box* ► mark, indicate

ticket NOUN • *a ticket to the game* ► pass, permit, voucher, coupon • *a price ticket* ► label, tag, sticker

tickle VERB • *tickled her toes* ► touch, stroke

tidy ADJECTIVE • *a tidy desk* ► neat, orderly, uncluttered, shipshape

tidy VERB • *started to tidy the room* ► clean up, put in order, set straight, arrange

tie VERB • *tied the dog to a lamppost* ► fasten, secure, attach, tether, bind

into a knot or bow **3** to have the same score as another competitor

tie NOUN **1** a strip of material worn under the collar of a shirt and knotted in front **2** a result when two or more competitors have equal scores **3** one of the matches in a competition **4** a close connection or bond

tier (teer) NOUN each of a series of rows or levels ▸ **tiered** ADJECTIVE

tiff NOUN a slight quarrel

tiger NOUN a large wild animal of the cat family, with yellow and black stripes

tight ADJECTIVE **1** fitting very closely **2** firmly fastened **3** fully stretched; tense **4** in short supply **5** mean; stingy **6** severe or strict *tight security* **7** (informal) drunk ▸ **tightly** ADVERB

tighten VERB to make or become tighter

tightrope NOUN a rope or wire stretched tightly high above the ground, on which acrobats perform

tights PLURAL NOUN an item of clothing that fits tightly over the feet, legs, and lower part of the body

tigress NOUN a female tiger

tile NOUN a thin square piece of baked clay or other material, used in rows for covering roofs, walls, or floors ▸ **tiled** ADJECTIVE

till[1] PREPOSITION, CONJUNCTION until

till[2] NOUN a drawer or box for money in a shop; a cash register

till[3] VERB to plough land for cultivation

tiller NOUN a handle used to turn a boat's rudder

tilt VERB to move into a sloping position

tilt NOUN a sloping position **at full tilt** at full speed or force

timber NOUN **1** wood for building **2** a wooden beam

time NOUN **1** all the years of the past, present, and future **2** a particular period or portion of time **3** an occasion *saw it for the first time* **4** a period available for something *not enough time* **5** (Music) rhythm depending on the number and stress of beats in the bar **in time 1** not late **2** eventually **on time** punctual

tight ADJECTIVE • *The rope was pulled tight.* ▸ taut, stretched, rigid, stiff • *a tight grip* ▸ firm, fast, secure • *a tight lid* ▸ sealed, airtight • *a tight space* ▸ small, compact, constricted, snug, poky • *very tight with money* ▸ mean, stingy, miserly • *tight security* ▸ strict, stringent, rigorous, severe, tough

tilt VERB • *The cupboard tilted alarmingly.* ▸ lean, slant, slope, tip

time NOUN • *in the time of Queen Mary* ▸ age, era, period • *He lived here for a time.* ▸ while, period • *took a long time* ▸ while, interval, duration • *the best time to come* ▸ moment, point, stage, date

DICTIONARY

time VERB **1** to measure how long something takes **2** to arrange a time for

timeless ADJECTIVE not affected by the passing of time

timely ADJECTIVE happening at a suitable or useful time

timer NOUN a device for timing things

times PLURAL NOUN (Maths) multiplied by *Five times three is 15 (5 x 3 = 15)*

timetable NOUN a list showing the times when things will happen, e.g. when buses or trains will arrive and depart, or when classes will take place

timid ADJECTIVE easily frightened ▶ **timidity** NOUN

timing NOUN **1** the choice of time to do something **2** the time when something happens

timorous ADJECTIVE timid

timpani PLURAL NOUN kettledrums

tin NOUN **1** a silvery-white metal **2** a metal container for food

tin VERB **tinning, tinned** to seal food in a tin

tinder NOUN a dry substance that burns easily

tinge VERB **tingeing 1** to colour something slightly **2** to add a slight amount of another feeling *relief was tinged with sadness* ▶ **tinge** NOUN

tingle VERB to have a slight pricking feeling ▶ **tingle** NOUN

tinker NOUN (old use) a person travelling about to mend pots and pans etc.

tinker VERB to work at something casually, trying to improve or mend it

tinkle VERB to make a gentle ringing sound ▶ **tinkle** NOUN

tinny ADJECTIVE **tinnier, tinniest 1** like tin **2** (of a sound) unpleasantly thin and high-pitched

tinsel NOUN strips of glittering material used for decoration

tint NOUN a shade of colour, especially a pale one

tint VERB to colour something slightly

tiny ADJECTIVE **tinier, tiniest** very small

THESAURUS

timid ADJECTIVE • *a timid smile* ▶ shy, bashful, sheepish, coy

tingle VERB • *made his feet tingle* ▶ itch, prickle, sting

tingle NOUN • *a strange tingle in her fingers* ▶ itch, prickling, stinging, pins and needles

tinker VERB • *tinkering with his bike* ▶ fiddle, play, meddle, tamper

tint NOUN • *a yellowish tint* ▶ tinge, shade, hue, colour

tiny ADJECTIVE • *a tiny room* ▶ minute, miniature, diminutive, mini

DICTIONARY

tip¹ NOUN the part at the extreme top or end of something

tip VERB **tipping, tipped** to put a tip on something

tip² NOUN **1** a small gift of money given to a waiter etc. **2** a small piece of advice

tip VERB **tipping, tipped 1** to give a tip to **2** to name as a likely winner
tip off to give a hint or warning to

tip³ VERB **tipping, tipped 1** to tilt or topple **2** to dispose of rubbish

tip NOUN **1** the action of tipping something **2** a place where rubbish is tipped

tipple VERB to drink small amounts of alcohol ▶ **tipple** NOUN

tipsy ADJECTIVE **tipsier, tipsiest** slightly drunk

tiptoe VERB **tiptoes, tiptoeing, tiptoed** to walk quietly on your toes

tiptop ADJECTIVE (informal) very best **in tiptop condition**

tirade (ty-rayd) NOUN a long angry speech

tire VERB to make or become tired
▶ **tiring** ADJECTIVE

tired ADJECTIVE feeling that you need to sleep or rest **tired of** bored or impatient with

tireless ADJECTIVE having a lot of energy

tiresome ADJECTIVE annoying

tissue NOUN **1** tissue paper **2** a paper handkerchief **3** the substance forming part of the body of an animal or a plant

tissue paper NOUN thin soft paper used for wrapping and packing

tit¹ NOUN a kind of small bird

tit² NOUN **tit for tat** something equal given in return

titanic (ty-tan-ik) ADJECTIVE huge; gigantic

> **WORD HISTORY**
>
> from the *Titans*, gigantic ancient Greek gods and goddesses

THESAURUS

tip NOUN • *tip of the arrow* ▶ end, point, sharp end • *the tip of a mountain* ▶ summit, peak, pinnacle, top • *paid his bill and left a tip* ▶ gratuity, gift • *a tip for tourists this year* ▶ hint, suggestion, advice, warning • *a rubbish tip* ▶ dump, heap, pit

tip VERB • *was tipping to one side* ▶ lean, incline, slant, slope, tilt • *tipped the water into the sink* ▶ empty, dump, spill, unload • *capable of tipping a small boat*

▶ overturn, capsize, turn over, upset

tire VERB • *The long walk tired us.* ▶ exhaust, fatigue, wear out, drain

tired ADJECTIVE • *was tired after all the excitement* ▶ exhausted, sleepy, wearied, worn out **tired of** • *grew tired of waiting* ▶ bored with, fed up with, sick of

tiresome ADJECTIVE • *a tiresome person* ▶ annoying, irritating

tiring ADJECTIVE • *Shopping can be tiring.* ▶ exhausting, demanding, difficult

titbit NOUN a small amount of something

tithe NOUN a tax of one-tenth of a year's income formerly paid to support the church

titillate VERB to stimulate or excite pleasantly ▸ **titillation** NOUN

title NOUN 1 the name of a book, film, song, etc. 2 a word used to show a person's rank or position 3 a sports championship 4 a legal right

titled ADJECTIVE having a title as a member of the nobility

titter VERB to giggle ▸ **titter** NOUN

TNT ABBREVIATION trinitrotoluene, a powerful explosive

to PREPOSITION 1 used to show direction or arrival *went to Australia* 2 used to show a limit *worked to midnight* 3 used to show giving or receiving *lent it to them* 4 used to show a ratio *three to one* 5 used to show a connection *the key to the door* 6 used in comparisons *was nothing to what might happen* used before a verb, forming an infinitive *hope to see you*

to ADVERB 1 nearly closed *Push the door to.* **to and fro** backwards and forwards

toad NOUN a animal like a frog that lives mainly on land

toadstool NOUN a poisonous fungus with a round top

toast VERB 1 to heat bread etc. to make it brown and crisp 2 to drink in honour of someone

toast NOUN 1 toasted bread 2 a call to drink in honour of someone

toaster NOUN an electrical device for toasting bread

tobacco NOUN the dried leaves of certain plants used for smoking

tobacconist NOUN a shopkeeper who sells cigarettes, cigars, etc.

toboggan NOUN a small sledge used for sliding downhill ▸ **tobogganing** NOUN

today NOUN, ADVERB this present day

toddler NOUN a young child who has just started to walk

to-do NOUN **to-dos** a fuss or commotion

toe NOUN 1 each of the separate parts at the end of the foot 2 the front part of a shoe or sock **on your toes** alert

toffee NOUN a sticky sweet made from heated butter and sugar

toga (toh-ga) NOUN a long loose piece of clothing worn by men in ancient Rome

together ADVERB with another person or thing

toggle NOUN a short piece of wood etc. used like a button

toil VERB to work or move with great effort

toil NOUN hard work

together ADVERB • *all speaking together* ▸ simultaneously, at the same time, at once, collectively, concurrently, in chorus, in unison

toil VERB • *toiled all day* ▸ work, labour, slave, sweat

toil NOUN • *years of hardship and toil* ▸ work, labour, drudgery, effort

toilet NOUN **1** a bowl connected by pipes to a drain, used for disposing of urine and faeces **2** a room containing a toilet

toiletries PLURAL NOUN soap, cosmetics, etc.

token NOUN **1** a piece of metal etc. that can be used instead of money **2** a sign or signal of something

tolerable ADJECTIVE able to be tolerated ▸ **tolerably** ADVERB

tolerant ADJECTIVE willing to accept other people's behaviour and opinions ▸ **tolerance** NOUN

tolerate VERB **1** to allow something you do not approve of **2** to put up with something unpleasant ▸ **toleration** NOUN

toll[1] NOUN **1** a charge made for using a road, bridge, etc. **2** loss or damage caused

toll[2] VERB to ring a bell slowly

tom NOUN a male cat

tomahawk NOUN a small axe used by Native Americans

tomato NOUN tomatoes a soft round red or yellow fruit eaten as a vegetable

tomb NOUN a place where someone is buried

tombola NOUN a kind of lottery

tomboy NOUN a girl who enjoys rough noisy games etc.

tombstone NOUN a memorial stone set up over a grave

tome NOUN a large heavy book

tomorrow NOUN, ADVERB the day after today

tom-tom NOUN a drum beaten with the hands

ton NOUN **1** a unit of weight equal to 2,240 pounds or 1,016 kilograms **2** a large amount

tone NOUN **1** a sound in music or of the voice **2** each of the five larger intervals between notes in a musical scale **3** a shade of a colour **4** the quality or character of something ▸ **tonal** ADJECTIVE

token NOUN • a book token ▸ voucher, coupon • a token of good faith ▸ symbol, sign, mark, reminder

tolerable ADJECTIVE • barely tolerable ▸ bearable, acceptable, endurable • a tolerable time ▸ satisfactory, adequate, fair, mediocre

tolerant ADJECTIVE • a tolerant person ▸ understanding, open-minded, fair

tolerate VERB • attitudes that are difficult to tolerate ▸ accept,

forgive, condone • cannot tolerate pain ▸ put up with, bear, stand, endure

tomb NOUN • the tomb of the king ▸ burial place, sepulchre, grave, crypt

tone NOUN • an angry tone of voice ▸ quality, expression, sound, intonation • paint with a pink tone ▸ tint, tinge, hue, shade • the arrogant tone of the letter ▸ mood, manner, attitude

tone VERB be harmonious in colour

tone down to make quieter or less intense

tone-deaf ADJECTIVE unable to distinguish different musical notes

tongs PLURAL NOUN a tool with two arms joined at one end, used to pick up or hold things

tongue NOUN 1 the long soft muscular part that moves about inside the mouth 2 a language 3 the leather flap on a shoe or boot under the laces

tonic NOUN 1 a medicine etc. that restores strength 2 anything that makes a person more energetic or cheerful 3 (Music) the keynote of a scale ▶ **tonic** ADJECTIVE

tonic water NOUN a fizzy mineral water with a slightly bitter taste

tonight NOUN, ADVERB this evening or night

tonne NOUN a metric ton (1,000 kilograms)

tonsil NOUN either of two small masses of soft tissue at the sides of the throat

tonsillitis NOUN inflammation of the tonsils

too ADVERB 1 also *Take the others too.* 2 more than is wanted or allowed etc. *too much sugar*

tool NOUN a device or instrument for doing a particular job

toolbar NOUN (ICT) a row of icons on a computer screen, selected with the mouse or cursor

toot NOUN a short sound produced by a horn

tooth NOUN **teeth** 1 each of the hard white bony parts rooted in the gums, used for biting and chewing 2 each of the sharp parts on a saw, cog, etc.

toothache NOUN a pain in a tooth

toothbrush NOUN a brush for cleaning the teeth

toothpaste NOUN a paste for cleaning the teeth

toothy ADJECTIVE **toothier, toothiest** having large teeth

top[1] NOUN 1 the highest part of something 2 the upper surface 3 the covering or stopper of a bottle, jar, etc. 4 an item of clothing for the upper part of the body **on top of** in addition to

top ADJECTIVE highest or best

top VERB **topping, topped** 1 to put a top on 2 to be at the top of **top up** to fill something partly empty

top[2] NOUN a toy that can be made to spin on its point

topaz NOUN a kind of gem, often yellow

tool NOUN • *a set of garden tools* ▶ implement, utensil, device, gadget

top NOUN • *the top of the mountain* ▶ summit, peak, tip, cap • *the top of the jar* ▶ lid, cap, cover

top ADJECTIVE • *an office on the top floor* ▶ highest, topmost, uppermost, upper • *a top golf professional* ▶ leading, finest, best, foremost, principal, chief

top hat NOUN a man's tall stiff black or grey hat

top-heavy ADJECTIVE too heavy at the top and likely to overbalance

topic NOUN a subject to write, learn, or talk about

topical ADJECTIVE connected with things that are happening now *a topical film*

topless ADJECTIVE naked on the top half of the body

topmost ADJECTIVE highest

topping NOUN food that is put on the top of a cake, pudding, pizza, etc.

topple VERB 1 to totter and fall 2 to overthrow someone in authority

topsy-turvy ADVERB, ADJECTIVE upside down; muddled

Torah (tor-uh) NOUN in Judaism, the law of God as given to Moses

torch NOUN 1 a small electric lamp held in the hand 2 a stick with burning material on the end

torment VERB 1 to make someone suffer greatly 2 to keep annoying someone ▶ **tormentor** NOUN

torment NOUN great suffering

torn past participle of **tear**².

tornado (tor-nay-doh) NOUN **tornadoes** a violent whirlwind

torpedo NOUN **torpedoes** a long tube-shaped missile fired under water

torpedo VERB **torpedoes**, **torpedoing**, **torpedoed** to attack or destroy a ship with a torpedo

torrent NOUN 1 a rushing stream or flow 2 a heavy downpour of rain

torrential ADJECTIVE (of rain) pouring down violently

torrid ADJECTIVE 1 hot and dry 2 passionate

torso NOUN **torsos** the trunk of the human body

tortoise NOUN a slow-moving animal with a shell over its body

tortoiseshell NOUN a mottled brown and yellow shell or colour

tortuous ADJECTIVE 1 full of twists and turns 2 complicated *tortuous logic*

topic NOUN • *a topic of your choice* ▶ subject, theme, matter, question

topical ADJECTIVE • *a news item of topical interest* ▶ current, contemporary, recent, up-to-date

topple VERB • *The winds toppled several pylons.* ▶ knock down, overturn, upset • *to topple sideways* ▶ fall, overbalance,

tumble • *to topple the government* ▶ bring down, overthrow, depose

torment VERB • *was tormented by jealousy* ▶ afflict, plague, bother • *loved tormenting her brother* ▶ tease, bait, annoy, bully

torrent NOUN • *a torrent of rain* ▶ downpour, deluge, flood, shower • *a torrent of words* ▶ cascade, rush, outburst, stream

DICTIONARY

torture VERB to make a person feel great pain or worry ► **torture** NOUN

Tory NOUN a Conservative **Tories** ► **Tory** ADJECTIVE

toss VERB 1 to throw into the air 2 to spin a coin to decide something according to which side of it is upwards after it falls 3 to move restlessly or from side to side ► **toss** NOUN

toss-up NOUN 1 the tossing of a coin 2 an even chance

tot[1] NOUN 1 a small child 2 (*informal*) a small amount of spirits *a tot of rum*

tot[2] VERB **totting, totted tot up** (*informal*) to add up

total ADJECTIVE 1 including everything 2 complete ► **totally** ADVERB

total NOUN the amount reached by adding everything

total VERB **totalling, totalled** 1 to add up the total 2 to have as a total

totalitarian ADJECTIVE having a form of government that does not allow opposition

totality NOUN **totalities** the whole of something

totem pole a pole carved or painted by Native Americans with the symbols (*totems*) of their tribes or families

totter VERB to walk unsteadily

toucan (too-kan) NOUN a tropical American bird with a huge beak

touch VERB 1 to put the hand or fingers lightly on something 2 to be or come together with no space between 3 to move or meddle with something 4 to affect someone's feelings 5 to reach a certain level **touch and go** uncertain or risky **touch on** to discuss briefly **touch up** to improve something slightly

touch NOUN 1 the action of touching 2 the ability to feel by touching 3 a small thing done *finishing touches* 4 a special skill or style of workmanship *hasn't lost her touch* 5 communication with someone *have lost touch with him* 6 the part of a football field outside the playing area

THESAURUS

torture VERB • to torture their victims ► be cruel to, hurt, persecute

toss VERB • tossed a ball in the air ► throw, fling, hurl, cast, pitch • Boats were tossing about. ► lurch, pitch, rock, roll, bob

total ADJECTIVE • total volume of sales ► complete, entire, full, overall, whole • a scene of total carnage ► sheer, utter, absolute, perfect

total VERB • costs that totalled £5,000 ► amount to, come to, add up to

touch VERB • She touched his arm. ► pat, brush, feel, rub, stroke, tap • Their sorrow touched him. ► move, affect, disturb, upset • The speed touched 100 m.p.h. ► reach, rise to **touch on** • The programme touched on recent events. ► refer to, deal with, mention

DICTIONARY

touching ADJECTIVE causing pity or sympathy

touchline NOUN one of the lines that mark the side of a sports pitch

touchy ADJECTIVE **touchier, touchiest** sensitive; easily offended

tough ADJECTIVE **1** strong; difficult to break or damage **2** difficult to chew **3** able to tolerate hardship **4** firm or severe **5** difficult to do

toughen VERB to make or become tough

tour NOUN a journey visiting several places

tour VERB to make a tour

tourism NOUN the industry of providing services for tourists

tourist NOUN a person who visits places for pleasure

tournament NOUN a series of games or contests

tourniquet (toor-nik-ay) NOUN a strip of material pulled tightly round an arm or leg to stop bleeding from an artery

tousled ADJECTIVE untidy or ruffled

tout VERB to try to sell something or get business

tout NOUN a person who sells tickets for an event at more than the official price

tow [1] (rhymes with go) VERB to pull something along behind you

tow NOUN an act of towing

tow [2] (rhymes with go) NOUN short light-coloured fibres of flax or hemp

toward PREPOSITION towards

towards PREPOSITION **1** in the direction of **2** in relation to; regarding *behaved kindly towards us* **3** as a contribution to *some money towards a new bicycle*

towel NOUN a piece of cloth for drying the skin after washing

towelling NOUN thick material used for towels

THESAURUS

touching ADJECTIVE • *a touching letter of sympathy* ► moving, poignant, emotional

touchy ADJECTIVE • *was touchy and uncooperative* ► sensitive, prickly, irritable, grumpy

tough ADJECTIVE • *tough boots* ► strong, stout, hard-wearing, indestructible, well-made • *a tough physique* ► sturdy, muscular, strong, brawny, burly • *tough food* ► chewy, leathery, gristly, rubbery, hard • *a tough climb* ► difficult, arduous, strenuous, exhausting

tour NOUN • *a tour round the lakes* ► journey, expedition, trip, drive, excursion

tour VERB • *to tour the area* ► travel round, visit, explore

tourist NOUN • *a group of tourists* ► sightseer, holidaymaker, visitor, traveller

tournament NOUN • *a golf tournament* ► competition, contest, championship, match

tow VERB • *to tow the barge* ► pull, drag, tug, draw, haul

a
b
c
d
e
f
g
h
i
j
k
l
m
n
o
p
q
r
s
t
u
v
w
x
y
z

DICTIONARY

tower NOUN a tall narrow building

tower VERB to be very high

town NOUN a place with many houses, shops, offices, and other buildings

town hall NOUN a building with offices for the local council

towpath NOUN a path beside a canal or river, originally used by horses towing barges

toxic ADJECTIVE poisonous; caused by poison ▸ **toxicity** NOUN

toxin NOUN a natural poisonous substance in the body

toy NOUN a thing to play with

toy ADJECTIVE 1 made as a toy 2 (of a dog) of a very small breed

toy VERB **toy with** to handle or consider idly

trace NOUN 1 a mark left by a person or thing 2 a small amount

trace VERB 1 to copy a picture or map etc. by drawing over it on transparent paper 2 to find a person or thing by following evidence

traceable ADJECTIVE able to be traced

track NOUN 1 a mark or marks left by a moving person or thing 2 a rough path made by regular use 3 a road or area of ground specially prepared for racing 4 a set of rails for trains or trams etc. 5 each of the songs or pieces of music on a CD, tape, etc. 6 a continuous band round the wheels of a tank or tractor etc. **keep** or **lose track of** to stay or fail to stay informed about something

track VERB 1 to follow the tracks left by a person or animal 2 to follow or observe something as it moves

tracksuit NOUN a warm loose suit worn by athletes for training or jogging

tract NOUN 1 an area of land 2 a pamphlet containing a short religious essay

traction NOUN 1 the action of pulling 2 the ability of a vehicle to grip the ground 3 a medical treatment in which an injured arm, leg, etc. is pulled gently for a long time

THESAURUS

tower VERB • Buildings towered over them. ▸ loom, rear, rise

town NOUN • moved to an industrial town ▸ city, urban area

toxic ADJECTIVE • toxic fumes ▸ poisonous, noxious, dangerous, harmful

trace NOUN • The animal had left no trace. ▸ trail, track, mark, sign • could find no trace of blood ▸ sign, remnant, remains

trace VERB • can trace the map from an atlas ▸ copy, draw, outline, sketch, make a copy of • trying to trace the owner ▸ track down, find, discover, detect

track NOUN • an animal's tracks ▸ trail, mark, scent, footprint • a track across the fields ▸ path, way, footpath, lane, trail • a racing track ▸ course, circuit

track VERB • He tracked a bear all day. ▸ follow, trail, pursue, stalk

a
b
c
d
e
f
g
h
i
j
k
l
m
n
o
p
q
r
s
t
u
v
w
x
y
z

tractor NOUN a motor vehicle for pulling farm machinery and loads

trade NOUN 1 the buying and selling of goods 2 an occupation or craft

trade VERB to buy and sell things

trademark NOUN a firm's registered symbol or name used to distinguish its goods etc. from others

tradesman NOUN **tradesmen** a person who sells or delivers goods

trade union NOUN a group of workers organized to help and protect workers in their own trade or industry

trader NOUN a person who buys and sells

tradition NOUN 1 the passing down of beliefs or customs etc. from one generation to another 2 something passed on in this way

traditional ADJECTIVE 1 belonging to a tradition 2 established over a long period ▶ **traditionally** ADVERB

traffic NOUN 1 vehicles, ships, or aircraft moving along a route 2 illegal trading

traffic VERB **trafficking, trafficked** to trade in something illegally

traffic lights PLURAL NOUN coloured lights used as a signal to traffic at road junctions etc.

tragedy NOUN **tragedies** 1 a play with unhappy events or a sad ending 2 a sad or distressing event

tragic ADJECTIVE 1 sad or distressing 2 to do with tragedies *a tragic actor* ▶ **tragically** ADVERB

trail NOUN 1 a track, scent, or other sign left where something has passed 2 a path or track through the countryside

THESAURUS

trade NOUN • *international trade* ▶ commerce, buying and selling, dealing • *to practise a trade* ▶ craft, occupation, job

trade VERB • *trading in diamonds* ▶ deal, traffic, buy and sell, do business • *traded her old car for a new model* ▶ exchange, barter, swap

tradition NOUN • *an old tradition* ▶ custom, practice, habit

traditional ADJECTIVE • *a traditional ceremony* ▶ customary, established, time-honoured, typical

• *traditional beliefs* ▶ popular, folk

traffic NOUN • *road traffic* ▶ vehicles, cars

tragedy NOUN • *the tragedy of their son's death* ▶ disaster, catastrophe, calamity

tragic ADJECTIVE • *a tragic accident* ▶ sad, catastrophic, disastrous, dreadful, appalling

trail NOUN • *the trail of its prey* ▶ track, footprints, mark, scent • *a trail of clues* ▶ series, string, stream, chain • *a nature trail* ▶ path, route, track

a b c d e f g h i j k l m n o p q r s t u v w x y z

DICTIONARY

trail VERB **1** to follow the trail of **2** to drag or be dragged along behind **3** to follow someone more slowly or wearily **4** to hang down or float loosely **5** (of a voice) to become fainter

trailer NOUN **1** a truck or other container pulled along by a vehicle **2** a short extract advertising a film or television programme

train NOUN **1** a railway engine pulling a line of linked carriages or trucks **2** a number of people or animals moving in a line **3** a series of things **4** part of a long dress or robe that trails behind

train VERB **1** to give an instruction or practice **2** to practise for a sporting event **3** to make something grow in a particular direction **4** to aim a gun or camera etc.

trainee NOUN a person who is being trained

trainer NOUN **1** a person who trains people or animals **2** a soft rubber-soled shoe

traipse VERB to walk wearily; to trudge

trait (say as tray or trayt) NOUN one of a person's characteristics

traitor NOUN someone who betrays their country or friends

trajectory NOUN **trajectories** the path taken by a moving object such as a bullet or rocket

tram NOUN a public passenger vehicle running on rails in the road

tramp NOUN **1** a homeless person who walks from place to place **2** a long walk **3** the sound of heavy footsteps

tramp VERB **1** to walk with heavy footsteps **2** to walk for a long distance

trample VERB to tread heavily on something

trampoline NOUN a large piece of canvas joined to a frame by springs, used in gymnastics for bouncing on

THESAURUS

trail VERB • Someone was trailing her. ► follow, shadow, stalk, tail • The car was trailing a caravan. ► draw, pull, tow • The children were trailing behind. ► straggle, linger, lag, dawdle

train VERB • had three assistants to train ► teach, instruct, coach, educate • The team was training hard. ► practise, exercise, get fit • training their guns ► aim, point, direct

traitor NOUN • was denounced as a traitor ► betrayer, defector, deserter, collaborator

tramp NOUN • an old tramp ► beggar, vagrant, homeless person • a tramp across the fields ► trek, trudge, march

tramp VERB • tramped over the wet grass ► trudge, trek, hike, plod

trample VERB **trample on** • A dog had trampled on the tulips. ► tread on, stamp on, crush, flatten

a
b
c
d
e
f
g
h
i
j
k
l
m
n
o
p
q
r
s
t
u
v
w
x
y
z

a
b
c
d
e
f
g
h
i
j
k
l
m
n
o
p
q
r
s
t
u
v
w
x
y
z

trance NOUN a dreamy or unconscious state like sleep

tranquil ADJECTIVE calm and quiet

tranquillity NOUN a state of calm

tranquillizer NOUN a medicine used to make a person feel calm

⚠ **SPELLING**

This word can also be spelled *tranquilliser*.

transact VERB to conduct business

transaction NOUN an item of business

transatlantic ADJECTIVE across or on the other side of the Atlantic Ocean

transcend VERB to go beyond or do better than

transcribe VERB to copy or write out ► **transcription** NOUN

transcript NOUN a written copy

transfer VERB **transferring, transferred 1** to move a person or thing to another place **2** to hand over ► **transferable** ADJECTIVE, **transference** NOUN

transfer NOUN **1** the transferring of a person or thing **2** a picture or design transferred to another surface

transfix VERB to make unable to move because of fear or surprise etc.

transform VERB to change completely the form or appearance of ► **transformation** NOUN

transformer NOUN a device used to change the voltage of an electric current

transfusion NOUN the process of injecting blood taken from one person into another person

transgress VERB to break a rule or law etc. ► **transgression** NOUN

transient ADJECTIVE not lasting or staying for long

transistor NOUN a tiny semiconductor that controls a flow of electricity

transit NOUN the process of travelling from one place to another

transition NOUN the process of changing from one condition or form etc. to another ► **transitional** ADJECTIVE

transitive ADJECTIVE (of a verb) having a direct object, e.g. *hear* in *we can hear you*

transitory ADJECTIVE existing for a time but not lasting

translate VERB to put something into another language ► **translator** NOUN

translation NOUN **1** the process of translating **2** something translated

transliterate VERB to write a word in the letters of a different alphabet or language ► **transliteration** NOUN

THESAURUS

trance NOUN • *lost in a trance* ► daze, dream

tranquil ADJECTIVE • *a tranquil village* ► peaceful, quiet, calm

transfer VERB • *The books will be transferred to the central library.* ► move, shift, relocate, convey, transmit

DICTIONARY

translucent ADJECTIVE allowing light to shine through but not transparent

transmission NOUN **1** the process of transmitting **2** a broadcast **3** the gears by which power is transmitted from the engine to the wheels of a vehicle

transmit VERB **transmitting, transmitted 1** to send or pass on from one person or place to another **2** to send out a signal or broadcast etc. ▶ **transmitter** NOUN

transparency NOUN **transparencies 1** the state of being transparent **2** a transparent photograph viewed on a screen

transparent ADJECTIVE able to be seen through

transpire VERB **1** (of information) to become known **2** to happen

transplant VERB **1** to move a plant to another place to grow **2** to transfer a body part to another person or animal ▶ **transplantation** NOUN

transplant NOUN **1** the process of transplanting **2** something transplanted

transport VERB to take from one place to another ▶ **transportation** NOUN

transport NOUN the process or means of transporting people, animals, or things

transpose VERB **1** to change the position or order of **2** to put a piece of music into a different key ▶ **transposition** NOUN

transverse ADJECTIVE lying across

trap NOUN **1** a device for catching and holding animals **2** a plan or trick for detecting or cheating someone **3** a two-wheeled carriage pulled by a horse

trap VERB **trapping, trapped 1** to catch or hold in a trap **2** to prevent someone from escaping an unpleasant situation

trapdoor NOUN a door in a floor, ceiling, or roof

trapeze NOUN a bar hanging from two ropes as a swing for acrobats

trapezium NOUN a figure of four sides of which two are parallel

trapezoid NOUN a figure of four sides, none of them parallel

THESAURUS

transmit VERB • *to transmit a programme* ▶ broadcast, send out • *to transmit messages* ▶ send, communicate, pass on

transparent ADJECTIVE • *a transparent fabric* ▶ see-through, translucent, clear

transport VERB • *The goods will be transported by rail.* ▶ take, carry, convey, ship, bring, fetch, move

trap NOUN • *animal traps* ▶ snare, noose, net • *rode straight into a trap* ▶ ambush, ambuscade • *The last question was a trap.* ▶ trick, ploy

trap VERB • *a way of trapping the fox* ▶ capture, catch, snare • *a question designed to trap them* ▶ trick, deceive, fool

a
b
c
d
e
f
g
h
i
j
k
l
m
n
o
p
q
r
s
t
u
v
w
x
y
z

a
b
c
d
e
f
g
h
i
j
k
l
m
n
o
p
q
r
s
t
u
v
w
x
y
z

trapper NOUN someone who traps wild animals for their fur

trappings PLURAL NOUN clothes or possessions showing rank or position

trash NOUN rubbish or nonsense
▸ **trashy** ADJECTIVE

trauma NOUN a shock that produces a lasting effect on the mind

traumatic ADJECTIVE very unpleasant or upsetting

travel VERB **travelling**, **travelled**
1 to move from place to place **2** to go on a journey ▸ **travel** NOUN

traveller NOUN **1** a person who travels **2** a person who does not settle in one place

traverse VERB to go across something ▸ **traversal** NOUN

travesty NOUN travesties a bad or ridiculous form of something *a travesty of the truth*

trawl VERB to fish by dragging a large net along the bottom of the sea

trawler NOUN a boat used in trawling

tray NOUN a flat piece of wood, metal, etc. usually with raised edges, for carrying cups, plates, food, etc.

treacherous ADJECTIVE
1 betraying someone **2** dangerous

treachery NOUN betrayal

treacle NOUN a thick sticky liquid produced when sugar is purified
▸ **treacly** ADJECTIVE

tread VERB **trod**, **trodden** to walk or put your foot on something

tread NOUN **1** a step in walking **2** the top surface of a stair **3** the part of a tyre that touches the ground

treadle NOUN a lever pressed with the foot to work a machine

treadmill NOUN **1** a mill wheel turned by the weight of people or animals treading on steps fixed round its edge **2** monotonous work

treason NOUN the act of betraying your country ▸ **treasonable** ADJECTIVE

THESAURUS

trash NOUN • *to dispose of trash*
▸ rubbish, waste, garbage, litter
• *was writing trash* ▸ rubbish, nonsense, drivel

travel VERB • *travelled to Russia*
▸ journey, go, tour

travel NOUN • *more time for travel*
▸ touring, sightseeing, excursions, globetrotting

traveller NOUN • *weary travellers*
▸ tourist, voyager, passenger, holidaymaker, sightseer

treacherous ADJECTIVE • *a treacherous betrayal* ▸ traitorous, disloyal • *deep treacherous water*
▸ dangerous, hazardous, perilous

treachery NOUN • *an act of treachery* ▸ betrayal, disloyalty

tread VERB • *Walkers should tread carefully.* ▸ step, walk, proceed

treason NOUN • *was executed for treason* ▸ treachery, betrayal, rebellion

DICTIONARY

treasure NOUN **1** a store of precious metals or jewels **2** a precious thing or person

treasure VERB to value greatly

treasurer NOUN a person in charge of the money of a club, society, etc.

treasury NOUN **treasuries** a place where money and valuables are kept **the Treasury** the government department in charge of a country's income

treat VERB **1** to behave in a certain way towards **2** to deal with a subject **3** to give medical care to **4** to put through a chemical or other process **5** to pay for something pleasant for someone to have

treat NOUN **1** something special that gives pleasure **2** the process of treating someone

treatise NOUN a book or long essay on a subject

treatment NOUN **1** the process or manner of dealing with a person, animal, or thing **2** medical care

treaty NOUN **treaties** a formal agreement between two or more countries

treble ADJECTIVE three times as much or as many

treble NOUN **1** a treble amount **2** a person with a high-pitched or soprano voice

treble VERB to make or become three times as much or as many

tree NOUN a tall plant with a thick trunk and many branches

trefoil NOUN a plant with three small leaves (e.g. clover)

trek NOUN a long walk or journey

trek VERB **trekking, trekked** to go on a long walk or journey

trellis NOUN a wooden framework of crossing bars supporting climbing plants

tremble VERB to shake gently, especially with fear ▶ **tremble** NOUN

THESAURUS

treasure NOUN • *a chest of treasure* ▶ jewels, riches, gold, wealth

treasure VERB • *will treasure it for ever* ▶ prize, value, cherish

treat VERB • *treated her badly* ▶ behave towards, deal with, care for • *to treats all aspects of the subject* ▶ deal with, discuss, cover • *to treat an illness* ▶ cure, heal, tend • *to treat it as a joke* ▶ regard, consider, view

treat NOUN • *a special treat* ▶ indulgence, extravagance • *a*

birthday treat ▶ celebration, surprise, entertainment, outing

treatment NOUN • *his treatment of them* ▶ care, handling, management, behaviour (towards) • *responding to the treatment* ▶ therapy, medication

treaty NOUN • *signed a treaty* ▶ agreement, deal, settlement, pact, alliance

tremble VERB • *His hands were trembling.* ▶ shake, shiver, quake, quaver, quiver • *traffic making the house tremble* ▶ vibrate, shake, wobble, shudder

tremendous ADJECTIVE **1** very large; huge **2** excellent

tremor NOUN **1** a shaking or trembling movement **2** a slight earthquake

tremulous ADJECTIVE trembling from nervousness or weakness

trench NOUN a long narrow hole cut in the ground

trenchant ADJECTIVE strong and effective

trend NOUN the general direction in which something is going

trendy ADJECTIVE **trendier**, **trendiest** (informal) fashionable

trepidation NOUN fear and anxiety

trespass VERB to go on someone's land or property unlawfully
▶ **trespasser** NOUN

trespass NOUN (old use) wrongdoing; sin

tress NOUN a lock of hair

trestle NOUN each of a set of supports on which a board is rested to form a table ▶ **trestle table** NOUN

triad NOUN a group or set of three things

trial NOUN **1** a legal process of deciding whether a person is guilty of a crime **2** a test **3** an annoying person or thing

triangle NOUN **1** a flat shape with three sides and three angles **2** a percussion instrument made from a metal rod bent into a triangle

triangular ADJECTIVE having the shape of a triangle

triathlon NOUN an athletic contest consisting of three events

tribal ADJECTIVE to do with or belonging to a tribe

tribe NOUN **1** a group of families living in one area as a community **2** a set of people

tribesman or **tribeswoman** NOUN **tribesmen** or **tribeswomen** a member of a tribe

tribulation NOUN great trouble or hardship

tribunal (try-bew-nal) NOUN a committee appointed to hear evidence and give judgements when there is a dispute

tributary NOUN **tributaries** a river or stream that flows into a larger one

tribute NOUN **1** something said, done, or given to show respect or

THESAURUS

tremendous ADJECTIVE • a tremendous achievement ▶ great, wonderful, marvellous, extraordinary • a tremendous crash ▶ terrible, terrific, frightful, awful

trend NOUN • a downward trend ▶ tendency, movement, shift

• the latest trend ▶ fashion, vogue, craze, rage

trial NOUN • a criminal trial ▶ lawsuit, court case, hearing, tribunal • a new model undergoing trials ▶ test, testing, experiment

tribe NOUN • nomadic tribes ▶ people, race, nation, group

a b c d e f g h i j k l m n o p q r s t u v w x y z

admiration **2** payment formerly made by a country or ruler to a more powerful one

trice NOUN **in a trice** instantly

triceps (try-seps) NOUN the large muscle at the back of the upper arm

trick NOUN **1** a crafty or deceitful action **2** a skilful action done for entertainment **3** the cards picked up by the winner in a round of a card game

trick VERB to deceive or cheat by a trick

trickery NOUN the use of tricks; deception

trickle VERB to flow or move slowly ► **trickle** NOUN

trickster NOUN a person who tricks or cheats people

tricky ADJECTIVE **trickier, trickiest** difficult; needing skill or tact

tricolour (trik-ol-er) NOUN a flag with three coloured stripes

tricycle NOUN a vehicle like a bicycle but with three wheels

trident NOUN a three-pronged spear

trifle NOUN **1** a pudding of sponge cake with custard, fruit, cream, etc. **2** a small amount **3** something of little importance or value

trifle VERB **trifle with** to treat with little seriousness

trifling ADJECTIVE small in value or importance

trigger NOUN a lever that is pulled to fire a gun

trigger VERB **trigger off** to start something happening

trigonometry NOUN the calculation of distances and angles by using triangles

trill VERB to make a quivering musical sound ► **trill** NOUN

trillion NOUN **1** a million million **2** formerly, a million million million

trilogy NOUN **trilogies** a group of three stories, poems, or plays etc. on the same theme

trim ADJECTIVE neat and orderly

trim VERB **trimming, trimmed 1** to cut the edges or unwanted

tribute NOUN • *a tribute from friends* ► praise, accolade, appreciation, commendation • *a tribute to their courage* ► testimony, evidence (of), proof (of)

trick NOUN • *saw through every trick* ► ploy, ruse, scheme, deceit, fraud • *conjuring tricks* ► stunt, illusion, magic, feat

trick VERB • *annoyed at being tricked* ► fool, deceive, cheat, dupe, swindle

trickle VERB • *Sweat trickled down his sides.* ► drip, dribble, ooze, leak, run

tricky ADJECTIVE • *tricky negotiations* ► difficult, complicated, awkward, delicate

trim VERB • *had trimmed his beard* ► cut, crop, clip, tidy • *The curtains were trimmed with gold.* ► decorate, edge, embellish

trim ADJECTIVE • *trim gardens* ► neat, tidy, orderly, smart, well-kept

parts off **2** to decorate a piece of clothing

trim NOUN **1** the act of cutting or trimming **2** lace, ribbons, etc. used as decoration

trinket NOUN a small ornament or piece of jewellery

trio NOUN **trios 1** a group of three people or things **2** a group of three musicians **3** a piece of music for three musicians

trip VERB **tripping, tripped 1** to catch the foot on something and fall **2** to move with quick light steps **3** to operate a switch **trip up** to stumble

trip NOUN **1** a journey or outing **2** the action of tripping; a stumble **3** (informal) hallucinations caused by taking a drug

tripe NOUN **1** part of the stomach of a cow etc., used as food **2** (informal) nonsense

triple ADJECTIVE **1** consisting of three parts **2** three times as much or as many ▸ **triply** ADVERB

triple VERB to make or become three times as much or as many

triplet NOUN each of three children or animals born to the same mother at one time

triplicate NOUN **in triplicate** as three identical copies

tripod (try-pod) NOUN a stand with three legs, e.g. to support a camera

tripper NOUN a person who is making a pleasure trip

trite (rhymes with *kite*) ADJECTIVE not interesting as a reult of constant repetition; hackneyed *a few trite remarks*

triumph NOUN **1** a great success or victory **2** a celebration of a victory

triumph VERB **1** to be successful or victorious **2** to rejoice in success or victory

triumphal ADJECTIVE celebrating a success or victory

triumphant ADJECTIVE **1** victorious **2** rejoicing over a success or victory

trivia PLURAL NOUN unimportant details or pieces of information

trip VERB • *tripped over* ▸ stumble, totter, tumble, fall • *tripped along* ▸ run, skip

trip NOUN • *a trip to America* ▸ journey, visit, holiday, outing, voyage, expedition

triumph NOUN • *the party's election triumph* ▸ victory, win • *smiled in triumph* ▸ celebration, joy, jubilation • *The visit had been*

a triumph. ▸ success, achievement

triumph VERB **triumph over** • *had triumphed over his enemies* ▸ overcome, defeat, conquer

triumphant ADJECTIVE • *a triumphant conclusion* ▸ successful, victorious, winning • *a triumphant look* ▸ jubilant, boastful

trivial ADJECTIVE having little value or importance ▸ **trivially** ADVERB

troll NOUN (in myths and legends) a giant or a friendly but mischievous dwarf

trolley NOUN **trolleys 1** a small table on wheels or castors **2** a small cart or truck **3** a basket on wheels, used in supermarkets

trolleybus NOUN a bus powered by electricity from overhead wires

trombone NOUN a large brass musical instrument with a sliding tube

troop NOUN **1** an organized group of soldiers **2** a number of people moving along together

⚠ USAGE
Do not confuse this word with *troupe*.

troop VERB to move along as a group

trooper NOUN a soldier in the cavalry or in an armoured unit

troops PLURAL NOUN armed forces

trophy NOUN **trophies 1** a cup etc. given as a prize **2** something taken in war or hunting

tropic NOUN a line of latitude about 23° north of the equator (**tropic of Cancer**) or 23° south of the equator (**tropic of Capricorn**) **the tropics** the hot regions between these two latitudes

tropical ADJECTIVE to do with the tropics *tropical fish*

trot VERB **trotting, trotted 1** (of a horse) to run at a medium pace lifting the feet high **2** to run slowly with short steps

trot NOUN a trotting run

trotter NOUN a pig's foot used for food

troubadour (troo-bad-or) NOUN a travelling singer in medieval France

trouble NOUN **1** difficulty or distress **2** a cause of these **take trouble** to take great care

trouble VERB **1** to cause trouble to **2** to make the effort to do something *Nobody troubled to ask.*

trivial ADJECTIVE • *a trivial offence* ▸ unimportant, insignificant, minor

troop NOUN • *a troop of tourists* ▸ group, party, band, bunch

troop VERB • *saw the others troop in* ▸ march, file, flock

trophy NOUN • *a sports trophy* ▸ award, cup, medal, prize • *trophies of war* ▸ spoils, booty, loot

trot VERB • *He trotted into the house.* ▸ run, jog, scurry, scamper, scuttle

trouble NOUN • *the trouble they caused* ▸ difficulty, bother, problems, distress, anxiety

trouble VERB • *Something was troubling him.* ▸ bother, worry, distress, upset • *sorry to trouble you* ▸ disturb, interrupt, bother

troublesome ADJECTIVE causing trouble or annoyance

trough (trof) NOUN 1 a long narrow open container of water or food for animals 2 the low part between two waves or ridges 3 a long region of low air pressure

trounce VERB to defeat heavily

troupe (say as troop) NOUN a company of actors, dancers, etc.

⚠ **USAGE**

Do not confuse this word with troop.

trousers PLURAL NOUN a piece of clothing worn over the lower half of the body, with a separate part for each leg

trousseau (troo-soh) NOUN trousseaus or trousseaux a bride's collection of clothing etc. for married life

trout NOUN a freshwater fish used for food

trowel NOUN 1 a small garden tool with a curved blade for lifting or scooping 2 a small tool with a flat blade for spreading mortar

truant NOUN a pupil who stays away from school without permission **play truant** to be a truant ▶ **truancy** NOUN

truce NOUN an agreement to stop fighting for an agreed time

truck NOUN 1 a lorry 2 an open railway goods wagon

truculent ADJECTIVE defiant and aggressive ▶ **truculence** NOUN

trudge VERB to walk slowly and heavily

true ADJECTIVE **truer**, **truest** 1 representing what has really happened or exists 2 genuine or proper 3 accurate 4 loyal or faithful

truffle NOUN 1 an underground fungus with a rich flavour 2 a soft chocolate sweet

truism NOUN a statement so obviously true that it is not worth making it

truly ADVERB 1 truthfully 2 sincerely or genuinely 3 accurately 4 loyally or faithfully

troublesome ADJECTIVE • a troublesome knee injury ▶ annoying, irritating, tiresome

truancy NOUN • determined to crack down on truancy ▶ absenteeism, shirking, skiving

truant NOUN • a truant from school ▶ absentee, skiver **play truant** • admitted to playing truant ▶ be absent, skive

truce NOUN • The enemy broke the truce. ▶ ceasefire, armistice, pact, peace, treaty

true ADJECTIVE • a true story ▶ factual, accurate, correct, right • a true copy ▶ exact, faithful, genuine, real • a true friend ▶ loyal, faithful, devoted, dependable • the true owner ▶ legal, legitimate, rightful

truly ADVERB • Tell us truly what you think. ▶ truthfully, frankly, honestly • truly remarkable ▶ really, absolutely • am truly glad for you ▶ sincerely, genuinely

a b c d e f g h i j k l m n o p q r s t u v w x y z

DICTIONARY

trump NOUN a playing card of a suit that ranks above the others for one game

trump VERB to beat a card by playing a trump

trumpet NOUN a metal wind instrument with a narrow tube that widens near the end

trumpet VERB 1 to blow a trumpet 2 (of an elephant) to make a loud sound with its trunk
▶ **trumpeter** NOUN

truncated ADJECTIVE made shorter

truncheon NOUN a short thick stick carried as a weapon by police officers

trundle VERB to roll along heavily

trunk NOUN 1 the main stem of a tree 2 an elephant's long flexible nose 3 a large box for transporting or storing clothes etc. 4 the human body except for the head, arms, and legs 5 (American) the boot of a car

trunks PLURAL NOUN shorts worn by men and boys for swimming

truss NOUN 1 a bundle of hay etc. 2 a padded belt worn to support a hernia

truss VERB to tie up securely

trust VERB 1 to believe that a person or thing is good, truthful, or reliable 2 to let a person have or use something believing they will treat it well 3 to hope **trust to** to rely on *is trusting to luck*

trust NOUN 1 the belief that a person or thing can be trusted 2 responsibility 3 a legal arrangement in which money is entrusted to a person with instructions on how to use it

trustee NOUN a person who looks after money entrusted to them

trustful ADJECTIVE willing to trust
▶ **trustfully** ADVERB

trustworthy ADJECTIVE able to be trusted; reliable

trusty ADJECTIVE trustier, trustiest trustworthy or reliable

truth NOUN 1 something that is true 2 the quality of being true

THESAURUS

trunk NOUN • *the trunk of a tree*
▶ stem, stock • *a person's trunk*
▶ torso, frame, body • *locked the trunk* ▶ chest, case, box, crate

trust VERB • *doesn't trust me to do it*
▶ believe in, have confidence in, have faith in, rely on • *We trust they will be here soon.* ▶ hope, expect, presume

trust NOUN • *grateful for your trust*
▶ confidence, faith, belief,

reliance • *a position of trust*
▶ responsibility, obligation

trustworthy ADJECTIVE
• *trustworthy and hard-working*
▶ reliable, dependable, responsible, honest

truth NOUN • *doubted the truth of these statements* ▶ accuracy, truthfulness, veracity, honesty
• *an acknowledged truth* ▶ fact, certainty

a
b
c
d
e
f
g
h
i
j
k
l
m
n
o
p
q
r
s
t
u
v
w
x
y
z

truthful ADJECTIVE **1** telling the truth **2** true *a truthful account* ► **truthfully** ADVERB

try VERB **tries, tried 1** to make an effort to do something **2** to test something by using or doing it **3** to decide in a lawcourt whether a person is guilty of a crime **4** to be a strain on

try NOUN **tries 1** an attempt **2** (in rugby football) a score achieved by the putting the ball down behind the opposing goal line

trying ADJECTIVE tiresome or annoying

tsar (zar) NOUN the title of the former ruler of Russia

tsetse fly (tee-see) NOUN **tsetse flies** a tropical African fly that can cause sleeping sickness

T-shirt NOUN a short-sleeved shirt shaped like a T

tsunami NOUN **tsunamis** a huge sea wave caused by an underwater earthquake

tub NOUN a round open container

tuba (tew-ba) NOUN a large brass wind instrument with a deep tone

tubby ADJECTIVE **tubbier, tubbiest** short and fat

tube NOUN **1** a long hollow piece of metal, plastic, rubber, glass, etc.,

for liquids or gases to pass along **2** a flexible container with a screw cap

tuber NOUN a short thick rounded root or underground stem of a plant (e.g. a potato)

tuberculosis NOUN a disease of people and animals, effecting the lungs

tubing NOUN tubes; a length of tube

tubular ADJECTIVE shaped like a tube

tuck VERB **1** to push a loose edge into something **2** to put something away in a small space

tuck NOUN **1** a flat fold stitched in a piece of clothing **2** (*informal*) sweets and cakes etc.

Tuesday NOUN the day of the week following Monday

tuft NOUN a bunch of close threads, grass, hair, etc.

tug VERB **tugging, tugged 1** to pull something hard or suddenly **2** to tow a ship

tug NOUN **1** a hard or sudden pull **2** a small powerful boat used for towing larger ones

THESAURUS

truthful ADJECTIVE • is always truthful ► honest, sincere, frank

try VERB • *Try to respond positively.* ► aim, attempt, endeavour, make an effort • *Why not try another school?* ► evaluate, examine, check out

try NOUN • have another try ► attempt, endeavour, effort, test

tuck VERB • *tucked his shirt into his jeans* ► push, ease, slip, shove

tug VERB • *He tugged the rope.* ► pull, heave, drag, haul

DICTIONARY

tug of war NOUN **tugs of war** a contest between two teams pulling a rope from opposite ends

tuition NOUN teaching, especially of a small group

tulip NOUN a large cup-shaped flower on a tall stem growing from a bulb

tumble VERB **1** to fall or roll over suddenly or clumsily **2** to move or push quickly and carelessly ► **tumble** NOUN

tumbledown ADJECTIVE falling into ruins

tumbler NOUN a drinking glass with no stem or handle

tummy NOUN **tummies** (informal) the stomach

tumour (tew-mer) NOUN an abnormal lump on or in the body

tumult (tew-mult) NOUN an uproar; a state of noisy confusion

tumultuous ADJECTIVE noisy and excited

tun NOUN a large cask or barrel

tuna (tew-na) NOUN **tuna** a large edible sea fish with pink flesh

tundra NOUN a vast Arctic region with no trees

tune NOUN **1** a pleasant series of musical notes **2** the music of a song **in tune** at the correct musical pitch

tune VERB **1** put a musical instrument in tune **2** adjust a radio or television set to receive a certain channel **3** adjust an engine so that it runs smoothly ► **tuner** NOUN

tuneful ADJECTIVE having a pleasant tune

tungsten NOUN a grey metal used to make steel

tunic NOUN **1** a jacket worn as part of a uniform **2** a piece of clothing reaching from the shoulders to the hips or knees

tunnel NOUN an underground passage

tunnel VERB **tunnelling, tunnelled** to make a tunnel

turban NOUN a covering for the head made by wrapping a strip of cloth round a cap

turbine NOUN a machine or motor driven by a flow of water, steam, or gas

turbot NOUN **turbot** a large flat edible sea fish

turbulence NOUN violent and uneven movement of air or water

turbulent ADJECTIVE **1** moving violently and unevenly **2** involving much change and disagreement

tureen NOUN a deep dish with a lid, for serving soup

THESAURUS

tumble VERB • *He tumbled into the water.* ► topple, stumble, fall, collapse, pitch • *People tumbled out of the room.* ► hurry, rush, pile

tune NOUN • *singing a tune* ► melody, song, air, strain, theme

tunnel NOUN • *a tunnel under the river* ► underpass, passage, subway

a
b
c
d
e
f
g
h
i
j
k
l
m
n
o
p
q
r
s
t
u
v
w
x
y
z

DICTIONARY

turf NOUN short grass and the earth round its roots

turf VERB to cover the ground with turf

turgid ADJECTIVE 1 swollen and thick 2 pompous and tedious

turkey NOUN **turkeys** a large bird kept for its meat

turmoil NOUN wild confusion or agitation

turn VERB 1 to move round or to a new direction 2 to change in appearance etc. **turned pale** 3 to make something change 4 to move a switch or tap etc. to control something 5 to pass a certain time *It was turning midnight.* 6 to shape something on a lathe **turn down** 1 to reduce the flow or sound of something 2 to reject **turn out** 1 to happen in a certain way **turn up** 1 to appear or arrive 2 to increase the flow or sound of something

turn NOUN 1 a turning movement 2 a place where there is a change of direction 3 an opportunity or duty etc. that comes to each person in succession 4 a short performance in an entertainment

5 (*informal*) an attack of illness **in turn** in succession; one after another

turncoat NOUN someone who changes their principles or beliefs

turning NOUN a place where one road meets another

turnip NOUN a plant with a large white root used as a vegetable

turnout NOUN the number of people who attend a meeting, vote at an election, etc.

turnover NOUN 1 the amount of sales achieved by a business 2 the rate at which workers leave and are replaced

turnpike NOUN (*old use*) a road at which a toll is charged

turnstile NOUN a revolving gate that lets one person through at a time

turntable NOUN a circular revolving platform or support

turpentine NOUN a kind of oil used for thinning paint, cleaning paintbrushes, etc.

turps NOUN (*informal*) turpentine

THESAURUS

turmoil NOUN • *in a state of turmoil* ▶ confusion, chaos, disorder, mayhem

turn VERB • *The wheel started to turn.* ▶ go round, revolve, rotate, whirl, roll • *turned pale* ▶ become, go, grow • *The house will be turned into apartments.* ▶ convert, adapt, transform, change • *The path turned to the*

right. ▶ bend, curve, twist **turn down** • *turned down her application* ▶ reject, refuse

turn NOUN • *hot water at the turn of a tap* ▶ twist, spin, twirl, rotation, cycle • *a turn in the road* ▶ bend, corner, curve • *your turn to speak* ▶ chance, opportunity, time • *a comic turn* ▶ act, performance, show

turquoise NOUN **1** a sky-blue or greenish-blue colour **2** a blue jewel

turret NOUN **1** a small tower on a castle or other building **2** a revolving structure containing a gun

turtle NOUN a sea animal that looks like a tortoise

tusk NOUN a long pointed tooth sticking out from the mouth of an elephant, walrus, etc.

tussle NOUN a struggle or conflict

tussle VERB to struggle or fight

tutor NOUN **1** a private teacher, especially of one pupil **2** a teacher of students in a college or university

tutorial NOUN a meeting for students to discuss a subject with their tutor

tutu (too-too) NOUN **tutus** a ballet dancer's short stiff frilled skirt

TV ABBREVIATION television

twaddle NOUN (informal) nonsense

twain NOUN, ADJECTIVE (old use) two

twang NOUN **1** a sharp sound like that of a wire when plucked **2** a nasal tone in a person's voice

twang VERB to make a sharp sound like that of a wire when plucked

tweak VERB to pinch and twist or pull something sharply ▶ **tweak** NOUN

tweed NOUN thick woollen material of mixed colours

tweeds PLURAL NOUN clothes made of tweed

tweet VERB to make the chirping sound of a small bird ▶ **tweet** NOUN

tweezers PLURAL NOUN small pincers for picking up or pulling out small things

twelve NOUN, ADJECTIVE the number 12 ▶ **twelfth** ADJECTIVE, NOUN

twenty NOUN, ADJECTIVE the number 20 **twenties** ▶ **twentieth** ADJECTIVE, NOUN

twice ADVERB **1** two times; on two occasions **2** double the amount

twiddle VERB to turn something round or over and over in an idle way

twig[1] NOUN a small shoot on a branch or stem of a tree or shrub

twig[2] VERB **twigging, twigged** (informal) to realize what something means

twilight NOUN dim light from the sky after sunset or before sunrise

twill NOUN material woven with a diagonal pattern

twin NOUN either of two children or animals born to the same mother at one time

twine NOUN strong thin string

twine VERB to twist or wind together or round something

twinge NOUN a sudden sharp pain

twinkle VERB to shine with tiny flashes of light ▶ **twinkle** NOUN

twinkle VERB • *We could see the lights twinkling on the trees outside.* ▶ glitter, glint, shine, flash, sparkle

a
b
c
d
e
f
g
h
i
j
k
l
m
n
o
p
q
r
s
t
u
v
w
x
y
z

twinned ADJECTIVE forming a pair; matching

twirl VERB to twist quickly ▸ **twirl** NOUN

twist VERB **1** to turn the ends of something in opposite directions **2** to turn round or from side to side **3** to bend out of the proper shape **4** to pass threads or strands round something or each other **5** to distort the meaning of

twist NOUN **1** a twisting movement or action **2** an unexpected development in a story

twit NOUN (informal) a silly or foolish person

twitch VERB to move or pull with a slight jerk ▸ **twitch** NOUN

twitter VERB to make quick chirping sounds ▸ **twitter** NOUN

two NOUN, ADJECTIVE the number 2

two-faced ADJECTIVE insincere or deceitful

tycoon NOUN a rich and influential business person

tying present participle of **tie**

type NOUN **1** a kind or sort **2** letters or figures etc. designed for use in printing

type VERB to write something by using a typewriter or computer

typecast VERB **typecast** to keep giving an actor the same kind of role to play

typewriter NOUN a machine with keys that are pressed to print letters or figures etc. on paper ▸ **typewritten** ADJECTIVE

typhoid fever NOUN a serious infectious disease with fever, caused by bacteria

typhoon NOUN a violent hurricane in the western Pacific or East Asian seas

typhus NOUN an infectious disease causing fever, weakness, and a rash

THESAURUS

twirl VERB • twirled round the room ▸ spin, turn, twist, whirl, wheel, gyrate, pirouette

twist VERB • Girders were twisted in the explosion. ▸ crush, buckle, mangle • twisted a strand of hair ▸ coil, curl, wind • twisted an ankle ▸ sprain, wrench • was twisting his words ▸ distort, change, alter

twist NOUN • a firm twist ▸ turn, screw, spin • a twist in the rope ▸ coil, curl, loop, tangle, knot • an

unexpected twist to the story ▸ quirk, oddity

twitch VERB • The bushes twitched. ▸ tremble, jerk, jump

two-faced ADJECTIVE • a two-faced liar ▸ deceitful, insincere, dishonest, hypocritical

type NOUN • an unusual type of injury ▸ kind, sort, class, form • printed in small type ▸ print, characters, typeface, font

typical ADJECTIVE **1** having the usual characteristics or qualities **2** usual in a particular person or thing *It was typical of him to forget.*
▶ **typically** ADVERB

typify VERB **typifies**, **typified** to be a typical example of something

typist NOUN a person who works with a typewriter

tyrannical or **tyrannous** ADJECTIVE harsh and cruel

tyrannize VERB to rule harshly

⚠ **SPELLING**

This word can also be spelled *tyrannise*.

tyrannosaurus NOUN a huge flesh-eating dinosaur that walked upright on large hind legs

tyranny NOUN **tyrannies** rule by a tyrant

tyrant NOUN a person who rules cruelly and unjustly

tyre NOUN a rubber covering round a wheel of a road vehicle

typical ADJECTIVE • *a typical feature*
▶ characteristic, distinctive, particular, representative, special
• *a fairly typical week* ▶ average, ordinary, normal, conventional, standard

tyrant NOUN • *behaved like a tyrant*
▶ despot, dictator

a
b
c
d
e
f
g
h
i
j
k
l
m
n
o
p
q
r
s
t
u
v
w
x
y
z

Uu

a
b
c
d
e
f
g
h
i
j
k
l
m
n
o
p
q
r
s
u
v
w
x
y
z

ubiquitous (yoo-bik-wit-us) ADJECTIVE existing or found everywhere

udder NOUN the bag-like part of a cow, ewe, female goat, etc. from which milk is taken

UFO ABBREVIATION unidentified flying object

ugly ADJECTIVE **uglier, ugliest** **1** unpleasant to look at or hear **2** hostile and threatening *ugly scenes* ► **ugliness** NOUN

UK ABBREVIATION United Kingdom

ukulele (yoo-kul-ay-lee) NOUN a small guitar with four strings

ulcer NOUN a sore on the inside or outside of the body

ulterior ADJECTIVE beyond what is obvious or stated *an ulterior motive*

ultimate ADJECTIVE furthest in a series of things; final ► **ultimately** ADVERB

ultimatum NOUN a final demand or statement with a threat of action if it is not followed

ultramarine NOUN a deep bright blue

ultrasonic ADJECTIVE (of sound) beyond the range of human hearing

ultrasound NOUN sound with an ultrasonic frequency

ultraviolet ADJECTIVE (of light rays) beyond the violet end of the spectrum and not visible to the human eye

umber NOUN a kind of brown pigment

umbilical cord NOUN the long tube through which an unborn baby receives nourishment in the womb

umbrage NOUN **take umbrage** to be offended

umbrella NOUN a circular piece of material stretched over a folding frame with a central stick as a handle, used for protection from rain

> **WORD HISTORY**
>
> from Italian *ombrella* 'little shadow' (because the first umbrellas were used as protection from the heat of the sun)

umpire NOUN a referee in cricket, tennis, and some other games

umpire VERB to act as an umpire

umpteen ADJECTIVE (*informal*) many; a lot of

UN ABBREVIATION United Nations

unable ADJECTIVE not able to do something

unaccountable ADJECTIVE **1** unable to be explained **2** not accountable for what you do ► **unaccountably** ADVERB

unadulterated ADJECTIVE pure; not mixed with other things

unaided ADJECTIVE without help

THESAURUS

ugly ADJECTIVE • *an ugly building*
► unattractive, unsightly, plain,

hideous • *ugly scenes* ► angry, threatening, unpleasant

unanimity NOUN a state of complete agreement

unanimous ADJECTIVE with everyone agreeing *a unanimous decision* ▶ **unanimously** ADVERB

unassuming ADJECTIVE modest; not arrogant or pretentious

unavoidable ADJECTIVE not able to be avoided

unaware ADJECTIVE not aware

unawares ADVERB unexpectedly; without warning

unbalanced ADJECTIVE 1 not balanced 2 slightly mad or mentally ill

unbearable ADJECTIVE not able to be endured ▶ **unbearably** ADVERB

unbeatable ADJECTIVE unable to be defeated or surpassed

unbeaten ADJECTIVE not defeated or surpassed

unbecoming ADJECTIVE 1 not making a person look attractive 2 not suitable or fitting

unbeknown ADJECTIVE
unbeknown to without someone knowing

unbelievable ADJECTIVE not able to be believed; incredible
▶ **unbelievably** ADVERB

unborn ADJECTIVE not yet born

unbridled ADJECTIVE not controlled or restrained *unbridled rage*

unbroken ADJECTIVE not broken or interrupted

uncalled for ADJECTIVE not justified or necessary

uncanny ADJECTIVE **uncannier**, **uncanniest** strange or mysterious

unceremonious ADJECTIVE offhand or abrupt

uncertain ADJECTIVE 1 not known certainly 2 not sure 3 not reliable
▶ **uncertainty** NOUN

uncle NOUN 1 the brother of your father or mother 2 your aunt's husband

uncomfortable ADJECTIVE not comfortable ▶ **uncomfortably** ADVERB

uncommon ADJECTIVE not common; unusual

unavoidable ADJECTIVE
• *unavoidable job losses*
▶ inevitable, necessary

unaware ADJECTIVE • *unaware of what had happened* ▶ ignorant, oblivious

unbearable ADJECTIVE • *The pain was unbearable.* ▶ intolerable, unendurable

unbelievable ADJECTIVE • *an unbelievable story* ▶ incredible, implausible, far-fetched, unconvincing

uncalled for ADJECTIVE • *rudeness that is uncalled for*
▶ unnecessary, gratuitous, inappropriate

uncanny ADJECTIVE • *an uncanny silence* ▶ eerie, unnatural, weird, creepy

uncertain ADJECTIVE • *an uncertain outcome* ▶ unclear, unknown, unforeseeable • *was uncertain what to say* ▶ unsure, undecided

uncomfortable ADJECTIVE
• *uncomfortable plastic chairs*
▶ hard, cramped, stiff, tight,

uncompromising ADJECTIVE not allowing a compromise; inflexible

unconcerned ADJECTIVE not caring about something

unconditional ADJECTIVE without any conditions; absolute
▸ **unconditionally** ADVERB

unconscious ADJECTIVE **1** not conscious **2** not aware of things

uncontrollable ADJECTIVE unable to be controlled or stopped
▸ **uncontrollably** ADVERB

uncooperative ADJECTIVE not cooperative

uncouth ADJECTIVE rude and rough in manner

uncover VERB **1** to remove the covering from **2** to reveal

undecided ADJECTIVE **1** not yet settled or certain **2** not having decided

undeniable ADJECTIVE impossible to deny; clearly true
▸ **undeniably** ADVERB

under PREPOSITION **1** below or beneath **2** less than **3** governed or controlled by **4** in the process of *under repair* **5** according to the rules of *permitted under the agreement* **under way** in motion or in progress

under ADVERB in or to a lower place or level or condition *The diver went under.*

underarm ADJECTIVE, ADVERB moving the hand and arm forward and upwards

undercarriage NOUN an aircraft's landing wheels and their supports

underclothes PLURAL NOUN clothes worn next to the skin, under other clothing
▸ **underclothing** NOUN

undercover ADJECTIVE done or doing things secretly

undercurrent NOUN **1** a current below the surface **2** an underlying feeling or influence

undercut VERB **undercutting**, **undercut** to sell at a lower price than a competitor

underdeveloped ADJECTIVE **1** not fully developed or grown **2** (of a country) poor and lacking modern industrial development

underdog NOUN a person or team regarded as likely to lose

underdone ADJECTIVE not fully cooked

underestimate VERB to make too low an estimate of

underfoot ADVERB on the ground; under your feet

THESAURUS

lumpy • *an uncomfortable silence*
▸ awkward, uneasy, embarrassed

unconscious ADJECTIVE • *was unconscious in hospital*
▸ concussed, knocked out, comatose **unconscious of**

• *unconscious of the danger*
▸ unaware of, ignorant of

uncover VERB • *uncovered a secret door* ▸ reveal, find, expose • *to uncover the causes of the problem*
▸ detect, discover, expose

DICTIONARY

undergarment NOUN an item of underwear

undergo VERB **undergoes**, **undergoing**, **underwent**, **undergone** to experience or endure

undergraduate NOUN a university student studying for a first degree

underground ADJECTIVE, ADVERB **1** under the ground **2** done or working in secret

underground NOUN a railway that runs through tunnels under the ground

undergrowth NOUN bushes and other plants growing closely

underhand ADJECTIVE sly or secretive

underline VERB **1** to draw a line under **2** to emphasize

underling NOUN a subordinate

underlying ADJECTIVE **1** forming the basis of something *the underlying causes*

undermine VERB to weaken something gradually

underneath PREPOSITION, ADVERB below or beneath

underpants PLURAL NOUN an item of men's underwear covering the lower part of the body

underpass NOUN a road that passes under another

underpin VERB **underpinning**, **underpinned** to strengthen or support

underprivileged ADJECTIVE lacking the normal standard of living or rights in a community

underrate VERB to have too low an opinion of

undersized ADJECTIVE of less than the normal size

understand VERB **understood** **1** to know what something means **2** to know how someone feels or why they behave in a certain way **3** to have been told **4** to take for granted

understandable ADJECTIVE **1** able to be understood **2** reasonable or natural
▶ **understandably** ADVERB

understanding NOUN **1** the power to understand or think **2** sympathy or tolerance **3** agreement

understanding ADJECTIVE sympathetic and helpful

THESAURUS

undergo VERB • *to undergo surgery* ▶ experience, endure, go through, put up with, face

understand VERB • *could not understand it* ▶ comprehend, grasp, follow, take in • *I understood they would be there.* ▶ believe, think, suppose, conclude

understanding NOUN
• *our understanding of the past* ▶ knowledge, comprehension, grasp • *reacted with deep understanding*
▶ compassion, sympathy
• *to reach an understanding*
▶ agreement, arrangement, deal, pact

a
b
c
d
e
f
g
h
i
j
k
l
m
n
o
p
q
r
s
t
u
v
w
x
y
z

understatement NOUN an incomplete or restrained statement of facts or truth

understudy NOUN **understudies** an actor who learns a part to be able to play it if the usual performer is ill or absent

undertake VERB **undertook, undertaken 1** to agree or promise to do something **2** to take on a task or responsibility

undertaker NOUN a person who arranges funerals and burials or cremations

undertaking NOUN **1** a job or task being undertaken **2** a promise or guarantee

undertone NOUN **1** a low or quiet tone **2** an underlying quality or feeling

underwater ADJECTIVE, ADVERB beneath the surface of water

underwear NOUN clothes worn next to the skin, under other clothing

underweight ADJECTIVE not heavy enough

underwent past tense of **undergo**.

underworld NOUN **1** the world of crime (in myths and legends) **2** the place where the spirits of the dead exist

undesirable ADJECTIVE not wanted; objectionable

undo VERB **undoes, undoing, undid, undone 1** to unfasten or unwrap **2** to cancel the effect of

undoing NOUN **be someone's undoing** to be the cause of their ruin or failure

undoubted ADJECTIVE not doubted; accepted
▸ **undoubtedly** ADVERB

undress VERB to take your clothes off

undue ADJECTIVE excessive; too great

undulate VERB **1** to move like waves **2** to have a wavy appearance ▸ **undulation** NOUN

unduly ADVERB excessively; more than is reasonable

undying ADJECTIVE lasting forever

unearth VERB **1** to dig up **2** to find by searching

unearthly ADJECTIVE strange and frightening

uneasy ADJECTIVE **1** worried or anxious **2** uncomfortable
▸ **uneasily** ADVERB

uneatable ADJECTIVE not fit to be eaten

uneconomic ADJECTIVE not profitable

THESAURUS

undertake VERB • *undertook to visit them* ▸ agree, promise • *to undertake an assignment* ▸ begin, embark on, take on

undo VERB • *to undo the safety belt* ▸ unfasten, release, untie,

unbutton, unlock, unhitch, loosen

uneasy ADJECTIVE • *was uneasy about the decision* ▸ anxious, nervous, worried • *an uneasy atmosphere* ▸ uncomfortable, tense, awkward

DICTIONARY

unemployed ADJECTIVE not having a job ► **unemployment** NOUN

unending ADJECTIVE not coming to an end

unequal ADJECTIVE **1** not equal in amount, size, or value **2** not giving the same opportunities ► **unequalled** ADJECTIVE

unequivocal ADJECTIVE completely clear; not ambiguous

unerring ADJECTIVE making no mistake

uneven ADJECTIVE **1** not level or regular **2** not equally balanced ► **unevenly** ADVERB

unexceptionable ADJECTIVE not in any way objectionable

unexceptional ADJECTIVE not exceptional; quite ordinary

unexpected ADJECTIVE not expected ► **unexpectedly** ADVERB

unfair ADJECTIVE not fair; unjust ► **unfairly** ADVERB, **unfairness** NOUN

unfaithful ADJECTIVE not faithful or loyal

unfamiliar ADJECTIVE not familiar ► **unfamiliarity** NOUN

unfasten VERB to open the fastenings of

unfavourable ADJECTIVE not favourable ► **unfavourably** ADVERB

unfeeling ADJECTIVE not caring about other people's feelings

unfit ADJECTIVE **1** not suitable **2** not in perfect health from lack of exercise

unfold VERB **1** to open or spread out **2** to make or become known slowly *as the story unfolds*

unforeseen ADJECTIVE not foreseen; unexpected

unforgettable ADJECTIVE too good to forget

unforgivable ADJECTIVE not able to be forgiven

unfortunate ADJECTIVE **1** unlucky **2** unsuitable or regrettable ► **unfortunately** ADVERB

unfounded ADJECTIVE not based on facts

THESAURUS

unemployed ADJECTIVE • *am unemployed at the moment* ► out of work, jobless

uneven ADJECTIVE • *uneven ground* ► bumpy, rough, rutted • *an uneven contest* ► unequal, unfair, one-sided

unexpected ADJECTIVE • *an unexpected error* ► unforeseen, unpredictable, chance

unfair ADJECTIVE • *an unfair decision* ► unjust, unreasonable • *unfair advantages* ► undeserved, unreasonable, unjustified

unfaithful ADJECTIVE • *an unfaithful friend* ► disloyal, untrustworthy

unfamiliar ADJECTIVE • *an unfamiliar sight* ► strange, unusual, curious

unforgettable ADJECTIVE • *an unforgettable experience* ► memorable, striking, remarkable

unfortunate ADJECTIVE • *unfortunate people* ► unlucky, unsuccessful, poor, unhappy

a b c d e f g h i j k l m n o p q r s t u v w x y z

unfriendly ADJECTIVE not friendly

unfurl VERB to unroll or spread out

ungainly ADJECTIVE awkward or clumsy

ungracious ADJECTIVE not kindly or courteous

ungrateful ADJECTIVE not showing thanks

unguarded ADJECTIVE **1** not guarded **2** without thought; indiscreet

unhappy ADJECTIVE **1** not happy; sad **2** unfortunate or unsuitable *an unhappy coincidence*
▶ **unhappily** ADVERB

unhealthy ADJECTIVE **1** not healthy **2** likely to damage health *an unhealthy diet*

unheard of ADJECTIVE never known or done before

unhinged ADJECTIVE mentally ill or unbalanced

unicorn NOUN (in legends) an animal like a horse with a straight horn growing from its forehead

uniform NOUN special clothes worn by members of an organization, school, etc.

uniform ADJECTIVE always the same; not varying *of uniform size*
▶ **uniformity** NOUN

unify VERB **unifies, unified** to make into one thing
▶ **unification** NOUN

unilateral ADJECTIVE done by one person or group or country etc.

unimportant ADJECTIVE not important; trivial

uninhabited ADJECTIVE with nobody living there

uninhibited ADJECTIVE having no inhibitions

uninterested ADJECTIVE not interested; showing or feeling no concern

union NOUN **1** the joining of things together **2** a trade union

Union Jack NOUN the flag of the United Kingdom

unique ADJECTIVE being the only one of its kind ▶ **uniquely** ADVERB

unisex ADJECTIVE suitable for both sexes

unison NOUN **1** agreement **2** harmony of speaking or singing

unfriendly ADJECTIVE • *an unfriendly manner* ▶ hostile, aggressive, unpleasant

unhappy ADJECTIVE • *The news made him unhappy.* ▶ sad, melancholy, miserable, despondent, depressed

unhealthy ADJECTIVE • *was looking unhealthy* ▶ sickly, unwell, poorly, weak • *an unhealthy*

environment ▶ dirty, insanitary, unhygienic

unimportant ADJECTIVE • *Size is unimportant.* ▶ insignificant, irrelevant

unique ADJECTIVE • *a unique name* ▶ distinctive, special, individual • *a unique opportunity* ▶ remarkable, outstanding, extraordinary

DICTIONARY

unit NOUN **1** an amount used as a standard in measuring or counting **2** a single item of equipment used with others *a sink unit* **3** (Maths) any whole number less than 10

unite VERB **1** to join together **2** to make or become one thing

unity NOUN **unities 1** complete agreement **2** something whole that is made up of parts **3** (Maths) the number one

universal ADJECTIVE to do with everyone or everything
▶ **universally** ADVERB

universe NOUN everything that exists, including the earth and all the stars and planets

university NOUN **universities** a place where people study at an advanced level after leaving school

unjust ADJECTIVE not fair or just

unkempt ADJECTIVE looking untidy or neglected

unkind ADJECTIVE not kind
▶ **unkindly** ADVERB

unknown ADJECTIVE not known or named

unlawful ADJECTIVE not legal

unleaded ADJECTIVE (of petrol) without added lead

unleash VERB **1** to release a dog from a leash **2** to show an emotion

unleavened (un-lev-end) ADJECTIVE (of bread) made without yeast or other substances that would make it rise

unless CONJUNCTION except if; if ... not *We cannot go unless we are invited.*

unlike PREPOSITION not like; not typical of *It was unlike him to say that.*

unlike ADJECTIVE not alike; different

unlikely ADJECTIVE **unlikelier, unlikeliest** not likely to happen or be true

unlimited ADJECTIVE very great or very many

unload VERB to remove the cargo from a ship, vehicle, etc.

THESAURUS

unite VERB • *to unite the population*
▶ unify, bring together, join • *united to solve the problem* ▶ combine, join forces, cooperate

universal ADJECTIVE • *a universal fear* ▶ common, general, widespread, worldwide, global

unjust ADJECTIVE • *an unjust decision* ▶ unfair, unreasonable, biased, one-sided

unkind ADJECTIVE • *says unkind things* ▶ cruel, spiteful, thoughtless, unfeeling

unknown ADJECTIVE • *unknown destinations* ▶ unidentified, unnamed, mysterious, strange • *an unknown planet* ▶ undiscovered, unexplored

unlikely ADJECTIVE • *It is unlikely they will come.* ▶ doubtful, improbable • *an unlikely explanation* ▶ implausible, far-fetched, unconvincing

unlock VERB to open by undoing a lock

unlucky ADJECTIVE having or bringing bad luck ► **unluckily** ADVERB

unmarried ADJECTIVE not married

unmask VERB 1 to remove a person's mask 2 to reveal what a person or thing really is

unmentionable ADJECTIVE too bad or embarrassing to be spoken of

unmistakable ADJECTIVE not able to be mistaken for another person or thing ► **unmistakably** ADVERB

unmitigated ADJECTIVE total and absolute *an unmitigated disaster*

unnatural ADJECTIVE not natural or normal ► **unnaturally** ADVERB

unnecessary ADJECTIVE not necessary; more than is necessary

unnerve VERB to make someone lose courage or determination

unoccupied ADJECTIVE not occupied

unofficial ADJECTIVE not official ► **unofficially** ADVERB

unorthodox ADJECTIVE not generally accepted

unpack VERB to take things out of a suitcase, bag, box, etc.

unpaid ADJECTIVE 1 not yet paid 2 not receiving payment

unparalleled ADJECTIVE having no parallel or equal

unpick VERB to undo the stitching of

unpleasant ADJECTIVE not pleasant; nasty

unpopular ADJECTIVE not much liked

unprecedented ADJECTIVE never having happened before

unprepossessing ADJECTIVE not attractive

unprincipled ADJECTIVE lacking good moral principles

unprofitable ADJECTIVE not producing a profit or advantage ► **unprofitably** ADVERB

unqualified ADJECTIVE 1 not officially qualified 2 not limited *unqualified approval*

unlucky ADJECTIVE • *was unlucky not to get a medal* ► unfortunate • *an unlucky number* ► inauspicious, jinxed, ill-fated

unnatural ADJECTIVE • *an unnatural silence* ► abnormal, unusual, uncanny, strange, weird • *Her voice sounded unnatural.* ► affected, self-conscious

unnecessary ADJECTIVE • *unnecessary risks* ► needless,

uncalled for, unjustified, unneeded, unwanted, excessive

unpleasant ADJECTIVE • *an unpleasant experience* ► disagreeable, distressing, nasty, horrible

unpopular ADJECTIVE • *an unpopular tax* ► hated, disliked, unwanted, despised • *was unpopular at school* ► disliked, friendless

unravel VERB **unravelling,
unravelled 1** to disentangle **2** to
undo something knitted **3** to solve
a mystery

unreal ADJECTIVE not real;
imaginary

unreasonable ADJECTIVE **1** not
reasonable **2** excessive or unjust
▶ **unreasonably** ADVERB

unreliable ADJECTIVE not reliable
or trustworthy

unremitting ADJECTIVE never
stopping or relaxing; persistent

unrequited ADJECTIVE (of love) not
returned or rewarded

unrest NOUN trouble or rioting by
people who are dissatisfied

unripe ADJECTIVE not yet ripe

unrivalled ADJECTIVE having no
equal

unroll VERB to open something
that has been rolled up

unruly ADJECTIVE difficult to control;
disorderly ▶ **unruliness** NOUN

unsaturated ADJECTIVE (of fats)
forming cholesterol in the blood

unsavoury ADJECTIVE unpleasant
or disgusting

unscathed ADJECTIVE not harmed

unscrew VERB to undo something
that has been screwed up

unscrupulous ADJECTIVE having
no scruples about doing wrong

unseemly ADJECTIVE not proper or
suitable; indecent

unseen ADJECTIVE not seen; invisible

unselfish ADJECTIVE not selfish;
generous

unsettle VERB to make someone
feel uneasy or anxious
▶ **unsettling** ADJECTIVE

unsettled ADJECTIVE **1** not settled
or calm **2** (of weather) likely to
change

unshakeable ADJECTIVE strong
and firm *an unshakeable belief*

unsightly ADJECTIVE ugly

unskilled ADJECTIVE not having or
not needing special skill

unsolicited ADJECTIVE not asked
for *unsolicited advice*

unsound ADJECTIVE **1** not reliable
2 not firm or strong **3** not healthy
of unsound mind

unspeakable ADJECTIVE too bad to
be described

unsteady ADJECTIVE not steady or
secure

unstinting ADJECTIVE giving
generously

unstuck ADJECTIVE **come unstuck**
(*informal*) to fail or go wrong

THESAURUS

unreal ADJECTIVE • *an unreal state of
affairs* ▶ false, artificial, fake,
imaginary

unreasonable ADJECTIVE • *was
being unreasonable* ▶ unfair,
unjust, uncooperative • *making
unreasonable demands*
▶ excessive, exorbitant

unreliable ADJECTIVE • *The figures
are unreliable.* ▶ inaccurate,
misleading, deceptive • *friends
who prove unreliable*
▶ untrustworthy, irresponsible

unsteady ADJECTIVE • *an unsteady
table* ▶ shaky, rickety, unstable,
wobbly

unsuccessful ADJECTIVE not successful ► **unsuccessfully** ADVERB

unsuitable ADJECTIVE not suitable

unsure ADJECTIVE not confident or certain

unsuspecting ADJECTIVE unaware of a danger etc.

untenable ADJECTIVE not able to be justified or defended

unthinkable ADJECTIVE too bad or too unlikely to be worth considering

unthinking ADJECTIVE thoughtless

untidy ADJECTIVE **untidier, untidiest** not tidy; in a mess ► **untidily** ADVERB

untie VERB **unties, untied** to undo something that has been tied

until PREPOSITION, CONJUNCTION up to a particular time or event

untimely ADJECTIVE happening too soon or at an unsuitable time

unto PREPOSITION (old use) to

untold ADJECTIVE **1** not yet told **2** too great to be counted *untold wealth*

untoward ADJECTIVE inconvenient or unfortunate

untrue ADJECTIVE not true

untruth NOUN an untrue statement; a lie

untruthful ADJECTIVE not telling the truth ► **untruthfully** ADVERB

unused ADJECTIVE **1** (un-yoozd) not yet used *an unused stamp* **2** (un-yoost) not accustomed *unused to flying*

unusual ADJECTIVE not usual; strange ► **unusually** ADVERB

unveil VERB **1** to remove a veil or covering from something **2** to reveal

unwanted ADJECTIVE not wanted

unwarranted ADJECTIVE not justified; uncalled for

unwary ADJECTIVE careless about danger

unwell ADJECTIVE not in good health

unwieldy ADJECTIVE awkward to move or handle because of its size or shape

⚠ **USAGE**

Do not spell this word *unwieldly*.

unsuitable ADJECTIVE • *an unsuitable choice* ► inappropriate, unsatisfactory

unsure ADJECTIVE • *unsure about what to do* ► uncertain, doubtful, sceptical

untidy ADJECTIVE • *an untidy bedroom* ► messy, cluttered, disorganized, chaotic • *untidy hair* ► scruffy, dishevelled, bedraggled, unkempt

untie VERB • *began to untie the string* ► undo, loosen, unfasten

untrue ADJECTIVE • *The claims were untrue.* ► wrong, false, incorrect, mistaken

unusual ADJECTIVE • *an unusual story* ► strange, odd, curious, weird

unwell ADJECTIVE • *was feeling unwell* ► ill, sick, poorly

a b c d e f g h i j k l m n o p q r s t u v w x y z

unwilling ADJECTIVE not willing
  ► **unwillingly** ADVERB

unwind VERB unwound **1** to pull out from a reel etc. **2** (informal) to relax after work or stress

unwise ADJECTIVE not wise; foolish
  ► **unwisely** ADVERB

unwitting ADJECTIVE unintended
  ► **unwittingly** ADVERB

unworn ADJECTIVE not yet worn

unworthy ADJECTIVE not worthy or deserving

unwrap VERB unwrapping, unwrapped to open something that is wrapped

up ADVERB **1** to or in a higher place or position or level *Prices went up.* **2** so as to be upright *stand up* **3** out of bed *not up yet* **4** completely *eat it up* **5** finished *Time is up.* **6** (informal) happening *Something is up.* **up to 1** until **2** occupied with something **3** capable of **4** needed from *up to us to help*

up PREPOSITION upwards along *A lizard ran up the wall.*

up-and-coming ADJECTIVE (informal) likely to become successful

upbringing NOUN the way someone is educated as a child

update VERB to bring up to date
  ► **update** NOUN

upgrade VERB **1** to improve a machine by installing new parts **2** to promote to a higher rank
  ► **upgrade** NOUN

upheaval NOUN a sudden violent change or disturbance

uphill ADVERB up a slope

uphill ADJECTIVE **1** going up a slope **2** difficult *an uphill struggle*

uphold VERB upheld to support or maintain a decision or belief etc.

upholster VERB to put a soft padded covering on furniture

upholstery NOUN soft covering and padding on furniture

upkeep NOUN **1** the process of keeping something in good condition **2** the cost of this

uplands PLURAL NOUN the higher parts of a country or region
  ► **upland** ADJECTIVE

uplifting ADJECTIVE making you feel more cheerful

upload VERB (ICT) to move data from a personal computer to a computer network

upon PREPOSITION (formal) on

upper ADJECTIVE higher in place or rank etc.

upper-class ADJECTIVE belonging to the highest class in society, the aristocracy

uppermost ADJECTIVE highest

THESAURUS

unwilling ADJECTIVE • *unwilling helpers* ► reluctant, unenthusiastic, uncooperative

update VERB • *to update the information* ► review, amend,

upgrade, correct, revise, modernize

upheaval NOUN • *would be a major upheaval* ► disruption, commotion, disturbance

a
b
c
d
e
f
g
h
i
j
k
l
m
n
o
p
q
r
s
t
u
v
w
x
y
z

upright ADJECTIVE **1** vertical or erect **2** honest or honourable

upright NOUN an upright post or rod forming a support

uprising NOUN a rebellion or revolt

uproar NOUN an outburst of noise or excitement or anger

uproarious ADJECTIVE very noisy

uproot VERB **1** to remove a plant and its roots from the ground **2** to make someone leave their home

upset VERB **upsetting, upset 1** to overturn or knock over **2** to make a person unhappy or distressed **3** to disturb or disrupt plans etc.

upset ADJECTIVE **1** unhappy or distressed **2** slightly ill *an upset stomach*

upset NOUN **1** a slight illness **2** an unexpected result or setback

upshot NOUN the eventual outcome

upside down ADVERB, ADJECTIVE **1** with the upper part underneath **2** in a mess; very untidy

upstairs ADVERB, ADJECTIVE to or on a higher floor

upstart NOUN a person who has risen suddenly to a high position and behaves arrogantly

upstream ADJECTIVE, ADVERB in the direction from which a stream flows

uptake NOUN **quick on the uptake** quick to understand

uptight ADJECTIVE (*informal*) tense and nervous

up to date ADJECTIVE **1** modern or fashionable **2** having or providing the most recent information

⚠ **USAGE**

Use hyphens before a noun: *an up-to-date edition* but *an edition that is up to date.*

upward ADJECTIVE, ADVERB towards what is higher ► **upwards** ADVERB

uranium NOUN a radioactive grey metal used as a source of nuclear energy

urban ADJECTIVE to do with a town or city

THESAURUS

upright ADJECTIVE • *upright stones with carvings* ► perpendicular, vertical, erect • *upright citizens* ► honourable, honest, respectable

uproar NOUN • *There was an uproar at the decision.* ► outcry, clamour, protest • *They found the place in uproar.* ► turmoil, confusion, chaos

upset VERB • *upset a pot of paint* ► tip over, knock over, spill • *would never want to upset anyone*

► distress, trouble, hurt • *to upset the natural balance* ► disrupt, disturb

upset ADJECTIVE • *was upset about leaving* ► distressed, dismayed, troubled, unsettled • *an upset stomach* ► queasy

uptight ADJECTIVE • *trying not to get uptight about it* ► tense, anxious, stressed

up to date ADJECTIVE • *up-to-date computer programs* ► current, latest, new, modern

DICTIONARY

urbane *ADJECTIVE* having smoothly polite manners ► **urbanity** *NOUN*

urbanize *VERB* to change a place into a town-like area ► **urbanization** *NOUN*

⚠ **SPELLING**

This word can also be spelled *urbanise.*

urchin *NOUN* a poor child wearing dirty or ragged clothes

urge *VERB* 1 to try to persuade a person to do something 2 to drive people or animals onward 3 to recommend or advise

urge *NOUN* a strong desire or wish

urgent *ADJECTIVE* needing to be done or dealt with immediately ► **urgency** *NOUN*, **urgently** *ADVERB*

urinal *NOUN* a bowl or trough fixed to the wall in a public toilet, into which men may urinate

urinate *VERB* to pass urine out of your body ► **urination** *NOUN*

urine *NOUN* waste liquid that collects in the bladder and is passed out of the body ► **urinary** *ADJECTIVE*

urn *NOUN* 1 a large metal container for heating water 2 a vase holding the ashes of a cremated person

US or **USA** *ABBREVIATION* United States (of America)

us *PRONOUN* the form of **we** used when it is the object of a verb or after a preposition

usable *ADJECTIVE* able to be used

usage *NOUN* 1 the way something is used 2 the way words are used in a language

use (yooz) *VERB* to perform an action or job with something **used to** 1 was or were in the habit of doing *We used to go by train.* 2 accustomed to *I'm used to their rudeness.*

use (yooss) *NOUN* 1 the action of using something 2 a purpose *another use for the box* 3 the quality of being useful *It is no use at all.*

used (yoozd) *ADJECTIVE* not new; second-hand

useful *ADJECTIVE* able to be used effectively ► **usefully** *ADVERB*

THESAURUS

urge *VERB* • *We would urge people to take care.* ► encourage, advise, appeal to • *to urge caution* ► advise, recommend, suggest • *urged his crew on* ► drive, spur, push

urgent *ADJECTIVE* • *in urgent need of repair* ► immediate, pressing, grave, serious

use *VERB* • *They use the garden like an extra room.* ► make use of, utilize, employ • *to use a lawn mower* ► work, operate, handle

• *to use all your judgement* ► exercise, apply, make use of

use *NOUN* • *not much use for them now* ► need, call, demand, necessity • *the use of video equipment* ► utilization, employment, operation • *no use in arguing* ► point, purpose, advantage, value

useful *ADJECTIVE* • *can offer useful advice* ► helpful, beneficial, positive • *a useful tool* ► handy, practical, convenient, efficient

a
b
c
d
e
f
g
h
i
j
k
l
m
n
o
p
q
r
s
u
v
w
x
y
z

819

DICTIONARY

useless ADJECTIVE having no use or effect

user NOUN a person who uses something

user-friendly ADJECTIVE designed to be easy to use

usher NOUN a person who shows people to their seats in a theatre etc.

usher VERB to lead or escort someone

usual ADJECTIVE happening or done always or most of the time
▸ **usually** ADVERB

usurp VERB to take power or a right etc. illegally ▸ **usurpation** NOUN, **usurper** NOUN

utensil (yoo-ten-sil) NOUN a tool or device used in a house *cooking utensils*

uterus NOUN the womb

utility NOUN **utilities 1** usefulness **2** an organization that supplies water, gas, electricity, etc. to the public

utilize VERB to find a use for

⚠ **SPELLING**

This word can also be spelled *utilise*.

utmost ADJECTIVE extreme or greatest *with the utmost care* **do your utmost** to do all you can

Utopia NOUN an imaginary place where everything is perfect
▸ **Utopian** ADJECTIVE

utter[1] VERB to say or speak

utter[2] ADJECTIVE complete or absolute ▸ **utterly** ADVERB

utterance NOUN something said

uttermost ADJECTIVE, NOUN extreme; utmost

U-turn NOUN **1** a U-shaped turn made by a vehicle **2** a complete change of policy

THESAURUS

useless ADJECTIVE • *useless information* ▸ worthless, pointless, futile • *a useless suggestion* ▸ impractical, unusable, ineffective, hopeless • *is useless at spelling* ▸ bad, inept, incompetent

usual ADJECTIVE • *his usual choice* ▸ normal, customary, habitual, regular, routine

usually ADVERB • *He usually went home alone.* ▸ normally, generally, habitually, routinely, regularly

utter VERB • *too stunned to utter a word* ▸ say, speak, communicate, express

utter ADJECTIVE • *utter disbelief* ▸ absolute, complete, total

utterly ADVERB • *utterly pointless* ▸ absolutely, completely, totally

a b c d e f g h i j k l m n o p q r s t u v w x y z

DICTIONARY

Vv

vacancy NOUN **vacancies 1** a job that has not been filled **2** an available room in a hotel etc.

vacant ADJECTIVE **1** empty; not filled or occupied **2** (of a look) showing no interest or expression

vacate VERB to give up a place or position

vacation NOUN **1** a holiday time **2** the act of vacating a place etc.

vaccinate VERB to inoculate with a vaccine ▸ **vaccination** NOUN

vaccine (vak-seen) NOUN a substance used to provide immunity against a disease

> **WORD HISTORY**
>
> from Latin *vacca* 'cow' (because serum from cows was used to protect people from smallpox)

vacillate VERB to keep changing your mind

vacuous ADJECTIVE empty-headed; unintelligent

vacuum NOUN a space with no air in it

vacuum cleaner NOUN a machine for sucking up dust and dirt etc.

vacuum flask NOUN a container with double walls that have a vacuum between them, for keeping liquids hot or cold

vagabond NOUN a person with no settled home or regular work

vagaries PLURAL NOUN strange features or whims *the vagaries of fashion*

vagina NOUN the passage leading from a woman's vulva to the womb

vagrant (vay-grant) NOUN a person with no settled home or regular work ▸ **vagrancy** NOUN

vague ADJECTIVE **1** not definite or clear **2** not thinking clearly or precisely ▸ **vaguely** ADVERB

vain ADJECTIVE **1** useless *vain attempts* **2** conceited, especially about your appearance **in vain** with no result; uselessly ▸ **vainly** ADVERB

> ⚠ **USAGE**
>
> Do not confuse this word with *vane* or *vein*.

valance NOUN a short curtain round the frame of a bed or above a window

vale NOUN a valley

valentine NOUN **1** a card sent on St Valentine's day (14 February) to

THESAURUS

vacant ADJECTIVE • *a vacant site* ▸ unused, unoccupied, empty, available • *a vacant expression* ▸ blank, expressionless, absent-minded

vague ADJECTIVE • *vague promises* ▸ indefinite, imprecise, inexact, unspecific • *vague shapes* ▸ hazy,

unclear, indistinct, blurred • *vague plans* ▸ uncertain, inexact, indefinite

vain ADJECTIVE • *vain attempts to stop them* ▸ unsuccessful, ineffective, futile • *a vain person* ▸ conceited, arrogant, self-satisfied, boastful

a b c d e f g h i j k l m n o p q r s t u **v** w x y z

a loved person **2** a person who receives a valentine

valet (val-ay or val-it) NOUN a man's personal servant

valiant ADJECTIVE brave or courageous ▸ **valiantly** ADVERB

valid ADJECTIVE **1** legally able to be used *a valid passport* **2** (of reasoning) sound and logical ▸ **validity** NOUN

valley NOUN **valleys** a long low area between hills, often with a river flowing through it

valour NOUN bravery

valuable ADJECTIVE worth a lot of money; of great value ▸ **valuably** ADVERB

valuables PLURAL NOUN valuable items

value NOUN **1** the price or worth of something **2** how useful or important something is *the value of regular exercise* **3** (Maths) the number or quantity represented by a figure etc.

value VERB **1** to think something to be valuable or important **2** to estimate the value of ▸ **valuation** NOUN

valueless ADJECTIVE having no value

valve NOUN **1** a device for controlling the flow of gas or liquid **2** a flap in the heart or in a vein, controlling the flow of blood **3** a device controlling the flow of electricity in old televisions, radios, etc. **4** either of the two parts of the shell of oysters etc.

vampire NOUN a dead person who is supposed to rise at night and suck blood from living people

van[1] NOUN **1** a covered vehicle for carrying goods **2** a railway carriage for luggage or goods

van[2] NOUN the vanguard

vandal NOUN a person who deliberately damages public property ▸ **vandalism** NOUN

vandalize VERB to damage things as a vandal

⚠ **SPELLING**

This word can also be spelled *vandalise.*

vane NOUN **1** a weathervane **2** the blade of a propeller, sail of a windmill, etc.

⚠ **USAGE**

Do not confuse this word with *vain* or *vein.*

THESAURUS

valid ADJECTIVE • *a valid passport* ▸ current, up-to-date • *a valid conclusion* ▸ legitimate, reasonable

valuable ADJECTIVE • *valuable jewellery* ▸ expensive, precious, costly, priceless • *a valuable experience* ▸ helpful, useful, worthwhile, beneficial

value NOUN • *to double in value* ▸ price, cost, worth • *the value of regular exercise* ▸ importance, benefit, usefulness

value VERB • *is valued at £5,000* ▸ assess, evaluate, price • *to value good advice* ▸ appreciate, prize, rate highly

vanguard NOUN **1** the leading part of an army **2** the first people to adopt a practice or idea

vanilla NOUN a flavouring obtained from the pods of a tropical plant

vanish VERB to disappear completely

vanity NOUN conceit; a state of being vain

vanquish VERB to defeat completely

vantage point NOUN a place offering a good view of something

vapid ADJECTIVE dull and uninteresting

vaporize VERB to change or be changed into vapour

⚠️ SPELLING
This word can also be spelled *vaporise*.

vapour NOUN a visible gas to which some substances can be converted by heat

variable ADJECTIVE likely to vary; changeable

variable NOUN something that varies or can vary

variance NOUN a state of differing or disagreeing

variant NOUN a different form of something ► **variant** ADJECTIVE

variation NOUN **1** the amount by which something varies **2** a different form of something

varicose ADJECTIVE (of veins) permanently swollen

varied ADJECTIVE of different sorts

variegated (vair-ig-ay-tid) ADJECTIVE having patches of different colours

variety NOUN **varieties 1** a set of different things of the same type **2** the quality of not always being the same; variation **3** a particular kind **4** an entertainment with various short acts

various ADJECTIVE **1** of several kinds **2** several ► **variously** ADVERB

varnish NOUN a liquid that dries to form a hard shiny coating

varnish VERB to cover with varnish

vary VERB **varies, varied 1** to make or become different **2** to be different

THESAURUS

vanish VERB • *He vanished into the garden.* ► disappear, leave • *Their fears had vanished.* ► evaporate, melt away, end

variable ADJECTIVE • *of variable quality* ► changing, varying, irregular

varied ADJECTIVE • *a varied choice* ► mixed, diverse, assorted

variety NOUN • *Variety adds interest.* ► diversity, variation, change • *a variety of subjects*

► assortment, array, mixture, range • *sixteen varieties of chocolate* ► kind, sort, type, form

various ADJECTIVE • *can be done in various ways* ► different, diverse, varied, assorted • *various political groups* ► several, numerous, many

vary VERB • *Prices vary enormously.* ► differ, fluctuate, change • *You can vary the size of your pictures.* ► alter, adjust, modify

a
b
c
d
e
f
g
h
i
j
k
l
m
n
o
p
q
r
s
t
u
v
w
x
y
z

vascular ADJECTIVE consisting of tubes or similar vessels for circulating blood, sap, or water in animals or plants *the vascular system*

vase NOUN a tall open container for holding flowers

vast ADJECTIVE very great in area ▶ **vastly** ADVERB

VAT ABBREVIATION value added tax; a tax on goods and services

vat NOUN a large container for liquid

vaudeville (vawd-vil) NOUN a kind of variety entertainment

vault VERB to jump over something while supporting yourself with your hands or with a pole

vault NOUN 1 a vaulting jump 2 an arched roof 3 an underground room or burial chamber

vaulted ADJECTIVE having an arched roof

VDU ABBREVIATION visual display unit

veal NOUN calf's flesh used as food

vector NOUN (Maths) a quantity that has size and direction, such as velocity (which is speed in a certain direction) ▶ **vectorial** ADJECTIVE

Veda NOUN the most sacred literature of Hindus

veer VERB to change direction

vegan NOUN a person who does not eat or use any animal products

vegetable NOUN a plant that can be used as food

vegetarian NOUN a person who does not eat meat or fish ▶ **vegetarianism** NOUN

vegetate VERB to live a dull or inactive life

vegetation NOUN plants that are growing

vehement ADJECTIVE showing strong feeling ▶ **vehemence** NOUN, **vehemently** ADVERB

vehicle NOUN a machine with wheels used for transport on land

veil NOUN a piece of thin material worn to cover the face or head

veil VERB 1 to cover something with a veil 2 to hide something partly

vein NOUN 1 any of the tubes that carry blood to the heart 2 a line or streak on a leaf, insect's wing, etc. 3 a long deposit of mineral or ore in rock 4 a mood or manner *in a serious vein*

⚠ **USAGE**

Do not confuse this word with *vain* or *vane*.

vellum NOUN smooth parchment or writing paper

velocity NOUN speed in a given direction

velvet NOUN a woven material with soft furry fibres on one side ▶ **velvety** ADJECTIVE

vendetta NOUN a long-lasting bitter quarrel or feud

vending machine NOUN a slot machine for buying drinks, chocolate, etc.

THESAURUS

vast ADJECTIVE • *travelled vast distances* ▶ huge, great,   enormous, immense, colossal, tremendous

DICTIONARY

vendor NOUN a seller, especially of a house

veneer NOUN **1** a thin layer of fine wood covering the surface of a cheaper wood **2** an outward show *a veneer of politeness*

venerable ADJECTIVE worthy of respect or honour, especially because of great age

venerate VERB to honour with great respect ► **veneration** NOUN

venereal disease (vin-eer-ee-al) NOUN a disease passed on by sexual intercourse

venetian blind NOUN a window blind of adjustable horizontal strips

vengeance NOUN action taken in revenge

vengeful ADJECTIVE seeking revenge

venison NOUN deer's flesh as food

Venn diagram NOUN (*Maths*) a diagram of circles showing the relationships between sets

venom NOUN **1** poison produced by snakes, scorpions, etc. **2** hatred or spite ► **venomous** ADJECTIVE

vent NOUN an opening to let out smoke or gas etc. **give vent to** to express feelings openly

vent VERB to express feelings openly

ventilate VERB to let air move freely in and out of a room etc. ► **ventilation** NOUN

ventilator NOUN a device or opening for ventilating a room

ventriloquist NOUN an entertainer who makes their voice sound as if it comes from another source ► **ventriloquism** NOUN

venture NOUN a risky undertaking

venture VERB to dare or be bold enough to do or say something

venue NOUN the place where a meeting, sports match, etc. is held

veracity NOUN truthfulness

veranda NOUN a terrace with a roof, along the side of a house

verb NOUN a word that shows what a person or thing is doing, e.g. *bring, came, sing, were*

verbal ADJECTIVE **1** to do with or in words **2** spoken, not written *a verbal statement*. **3** to do with verbs ► **verbally** ADVERB

verbatim ADVERB, ADJECTIVE in exactly the same words

verbose ADJECTIVE using more words than are needed

verdant ADJECTIVE (of grass or fields) green

verdict NOUN a judgement or decision made after consideration, especially that made by a jury

THESAURUS

vengeance NOUN • *to swear vengeance* ► revenge, retribution, retaliation

venture NOUN • *a new venture* ► enterprise, undertaking,

project, scheme, endeavour, operation

verdict NOUN • *the jury's verdict* ► judgement, decision, ruling, conclusion

a
b
c
d
e
f
g
h
i
j
k
l
m
n
o
p
q
r
s
t
u
v
w
x
y
z

DICTIONARY

verge NOUN **1** a strip of grass along the edge of a road or path **2** the extreme edge or brink of something

verge VERB **verge on** to be close to

verger NOUN a church caretaker and attendant

verify VERB **verifies, verified** to check or show that something is true or correct ▶ **verifiable** ADJECTIVE, **verification** NOUN

veritable ADJECTIVE real; rightly named *a veritable villain* ▶ **veritably** ADVERB

vermicelli (ver-i-**chel**-ee) NOUN pasta made in long thin threads

vermilion NOUN, ADJECTIVE a bright red colour

vermin PLURAL NOUN animals or insects that cause damage or carry disease, such as rats and fleas ▶ **verminous** ADJECTIVE

vernacular NOUN the ordinary language of a country or district

verruca NOUN a wart on the sole of the foot

versatile ADJECTIVE able to do or be used for different things ▶ **versatility** NOUN

verse NOUN **1** writing arranged in short lines with a particular rhythm **2** a group of lines forming a unit in a poem or song **3** a numbered section of a chapter in the Bible

versed ADJECTIVE **versed in** knowledgeable about

version NOUN **1** a particular person's account of something **2** a special or different form of something

versus PREPOSITION against; competing with

vertebra NOUN **vertebrae** each of the bones forming the backbone

vertebrate NOUN an animal that has a backbone

vertex NOUN **vertices** the highest point of a cone or triangle, or of a hill etc.

vertical ADJECTIVE at right angles to the horizontal; upright ▶ **vertically** ADVERB

vertigo NOUN a feeling of dizziness and loss of balance

verve (verv) NOUN enthusiasm and liveliness

THESAURUS

verge NOUN • *the grass verge* ▶ edge, bank, kerb • *on the verge of collapse* ▶ brink, point, threshold

verge VERB **verge on** • *laughter verging on hysterics* ▶ border on, approach, come close to

versatile ADJECTIVE • *a versatile teacher* ▶ adaptable, flexible,

resourceful, all-purpose, all-round

version NOUN • *our version of the story* ▶ account, explanation, interpretation • *a new version of the software* ▶ form, type, model

vertical ADJECTIVE • *a vertical post* ▶ upright, perpendicular, standing • *a vertical drop* ▶ sheer, steep

DICTIONARY

very ADVERB **1** to a great amount; extremely **2** (used for emphasis) *the very next day*

very ADJECTIVE **1** exact or actual *her very words* **2** extreme *the very end*

vessel NOUN **1** a ship or boat **2** a container for liquid **3** a tube carrying fluid in the body of an animal or plant

vest NOUN a sleeveless item of underwear worn on the upper part of the body

vestibule NOUN an entrance hall or lobby

vestige NOUN a trace of something that once existed

vestment NOUN a ceremonial garment worn by the clergy or choir at a service

vestry NOUN **vestries** a room in a church where the vestments are kept

vet NOUN a veterinary surgeon

vet VERB **vetting, vetted** to make a careful check of a person or thing

vetch NOUN a plant of the pea family

veteran NOUN a person who has long experience, especially an ex-member of the armed forces

veterinary surgeon NOUN a person trained to give medical treatment to animals

veto (vee-toh) NOUN **vetoes 1** a refusal to let something happen **2** the right to prohibit something

veto VERB **vetoes, vetoing, vetoed** to refuse or prohibit something

vex VERB to annoy or cause worry to ▸ **vexation** NOUN

vexed question NOUN a problem that is difficult or much discussed

via PREPOSITION **1** through; by way of *London to Exeter via Bristol* **2** by means of

viable ADJECTIVE able to work or exist successfully ▸ **viability** NOUN

viaduct NOUN a long arched bridge carrying a road or railway over a valley

vibrant ADJECTIVE full of energy; lively

vibrate VERB **1** to shake rapidly to and fro **2** to make a throbbing sound ▸ **vibration** NOUN

vicar NOUN a member of the Church of England clergy in charge of a parish

THESAURUS

very ADVERB • *felt very ashamed*
▸ extremely, highly, deeply, exceedingly, truly

very ADJECTIVE • *her very words*
▸ actual, identical, exact, precise
• *the very end* ▸ extreme

veto VERB • *vetoed the proposal*
▸ reject, refuse, throw out, disallow

vibrant ADJECTIVE • *vibrant colour*
▸ bright, vivid, brilliant, intense
• *a vibrant personality*
▸ vivacious, dynamic, alert, energetic

vibrate VERB • *The machine began to vibrate.* ▸ tremble, shake, shudder, judder

DICTIONARY

vicarage NOUN the house of a vicar

vice¹ NOUN **1** evil or wickedness **2** a bad habit or fault

vice² NOUN a device for gripping something and holding it firmly while you work on it

vice versa ADVERB the other way round

vicinity NOUN **vicinities** the area near or round a place

vicious ADJECTIVE **1** cruel and aggressive **2** severe or violent
▸ **viciously** ADVERB

vicious circle NOUN a situation in which a problem produces an effect which in turn makes the problem worse

victim NOUN someone who is killed or harmed

victimize VERB to single out for cruel or unfair treatment
▸ **victimization** NOUN

⚠ **SPELLING**

This word can also be spelled *victimise.*

victor NOUN the winner

Victorian ADJECTIVE belong to the time of Queen Victoria (1837–1901) ▸ **Victorian** NOUN

victory NOUN **victories** success won against an opponent in a battle, contest, or game
▸ **victorious** ADJECTIVE

video NOUN **videos 1** a video recorder or cassette **2** a recording on videotape

video VERB **videos, videoing, videoed** to record on videotape

video recorder or **video cassette recorder** NOUN a device for recording and playing video cassettes

videotape NOUN magnetic tape suitable for recording television programmes

vie VERB **vies, vied** to compete

view NOUN **1** what can be seen from one place **2** range of vision **3** an opinion **in view of** because of

view VERB **1** to look at **2** to consider or regard

THESAURUS

vicious ADJECTIVE • *vicious street fighting* ▸ brutal, savage, fierce, ferocious • *a vicious streak* ▸ cruel, malicious, spiteful, vindictive

victim NOUN • *the victim of an attack* ▸ target, casualty, sufferer, fatality

victimize VERB • *had been victimizing workers* ▸ persecute, intimidate, mistreat, harass

victorious ADJECTIVE • *victorious in the second round* ▸ triumphant, successful, winning

victory NOUN • *a victory in the games* ▸ win, success, triumph

view NOUN • *a magnificent view* ▸ outlook, panorama, vista, scene • *caught a brief view of them* ▸ sight, look, glance, peek • *They came into view.* ▸ sight, range of vision • *an official view* ▸ opinion, viewpoint, belief, opinion

view VERB • *to view the scene* ▸ look at, inspect, survey, examine

viewer NOUN someone who watches a television programme

viewpoint NOUN **1** an opinion or point of view **2** a place giving a good view

vigil NOUN a period of staying awake to keep watch or to pray

vigilant ADJECTIVE watchful; alert ▶ **vigilance** NOUN

vigilante (vij-il-an-tee) NOUN a member of an unofficial group organized to try to prevent crime in a community

vigorous ADJECTIVE full of strength and energy ▶ **vigorously** ADVERB

vigour NOUN strength and energy

Viking NOUN a Scandinavian trader and pirate in the 8th–10th centuries

vile ADJECTIVE **1** extremely disgusting **2** very bad or wicked ▶ **vilely** ADVERB

vilify VERB **vilifies, vilified** to say unpleasant things about ▶ **vilification** NOUN

villa NOUN a house, especially a holiday home abroad

village NOUN a group of houses in a small country district ▶ **villager** NOUN

villain NOUN a wicked person or a criminal ▶ **villainous** ADJECTIVE, **villainy** NOUN

vindicate VERB **1** to clear of blame or suspicion **2** to prove to be true or worthwhile ▶ **vindication** NOUN

vindictive ADJECTIVE wanting revenge; spiteful ▶ **vindictively** ADVERB

vine NOUN a climbing or trailing plant producing grapes

vinegar NOUN a sour liquid used to flavour food or in pickling

vineyard (vin-yard) NOUN a plantation of vines for making wine

vintage NOUN **1** the harvest of a season's grapes **2** the wine made from this **3** the year or period from which something comes

vinyl NOUN a kind of plastic

viola[1] (vee-oh-la) NOUN a musical instrument like a large violin

viola[2] (vy-ol-a) NOUN a plant of the kind including violets and pansies

violate VERB **1** to break a law, agreement, etc. **2** to treat a person or place with disrespect or violence ▶ **violation** NOUN

vigilant ADJECTIVE • *important to remain vigilant* ▶ watchful, alert, observant

vigorous ADJECTIVE • *vigorous exercise* ▶ strenuous, energetic, brisk

vigour NOUN • *acted with vigour* ▶ energy, force, vitality, dynamism

vile ADJECTIVE • *a cup of vile coffee* ▶ nasty, horrible, foul, disgusting • *a vile conspiracy* ▶ wicked, evil, despicable

villain NOUN • *one of history's great villains* ▶ wrongdoer, rogue, scoundrel, criminal, reprobate

a
b
c
d
e
f
g
h
i
j
k
l
m
n
o
p
q
r
s
t
u
v
w
x
y
z

violence NOUN 1 physical force that causes harm or injury 2 strength or intensity

violent ADJECTIVE 1 using or involving violence 2 strong or intense *a violent dislike*
▶ **violently** ADVERB

violet NOUN 1 a small plant with purple flowers 2 purple

violin NOUN a musical instrument with four strings, played with a bow ▶ **violinist** NOUN

VIP ABBREVIATION very important person

viper NOUN a small poisonous snake

virgin NOUN a person who has never had sexual intercourse
▶ **virginity** NOUN

virgin ADJECTIVE not yet touched or used *virgin snow*

virile ADJECTIVE having masculine strength or vigour ▶ **virility** NOUN

virtual ADJECTIVE being something in effect though not strictly in fact

virtually ADVERB nearly or almost

virtual reality NOUN an image or environment produced by a computer that is so realistic that it seems to be part of the real world

virtue NOUN 1 moral goodness, or a particular form of this 2 a good quality or advantage **by virtue of** because of

virtuoso NOUN virtuosos a person with outstanding skill in singing or playing music
▶ **virtuosity** NOUN

virtuous ADJECTIVE morally good
▶ **virtuously** ADVERB

virulent ADJECTIVE 1 strongly poisonous or harmful 2 bitterly hostile ▶ **virulence** NOUN

virus NOUN 1 a tiny living thing smaller than a bacterium, which can cause disease 2 a hidden set of instructions in a computer program that is designed to destroy data

visa NOUN an official mark put on a passport to show that the holder has permission to enter a foreign country

viscount (vy-kownt) NOUN a nobleman ranking below an earl

viscous ADJECTIVE (of a liquid) thick and gluey ▶ **viscosity** NOUN

visibility NOUN the distance you can see clearly

visible ADJECTIVE able to be seen or noticed ▶ **visibly** ADVERB

violence NOUN • *reacted with violence* ▶ brutality, savagery, cruelty, barbarity • *the violence of the blow* ▶ force, strength, power, ferocity

violent ADJECTIVE • *violent clashes* ▶ brutal, vicious, aggressive

virtue NOUN • *the virtue of a simple life* ▶ goodness, righteousness

• *Punctuality is one of his virtues.*
▶ strength, quality, good point

virtuous ADJECTIVE • *led a virtuous life* ▶ moral, righteous, upright, honourable

visible ADJECTIVE • *a visible pattern* ▶ noticeable, obvious, conspicuous, recognizable

a b c d e f g h i j k l m n o p q r s t u v w x y z

DICTIONARY

vision NOUN **1** the ability to see **2** something seen in the imagination or in a dream **3** foresight and wisdom **4** a beautiful person or thing

visionary ADJECTIVE imaginative or fanciful

visionary NOUN **visionaries** a person with imaginative ideas and plans

visit VERB **1** to go to see a person or place **2** to stay somewhere for a while

visit NOUN **1** the act of going to see a person or place **2** a short stay

visitation NOUN an official visit

visitor NOUN someone who visits

visor (vy-zer) NOUN **1** a part of a helmet that can be pulled down to cover the face **2** a shield to protect the eyes from bright light

vista NOUN a long view

visual ADJECTIVE to do with or used in seeing; to do with sight
► **visually** ADVERB

visual display unit NOUN a device like a television screen that displays computer data

visualize VERB to form a mental picture of ► **visualization** NOUN

⚠️ **SPELLING**

This word can also be spelled *visualise*.

vital ADJECTIVE **1** necessary for life **2** essential; very important
► **vitally** ADVERB

vitality NOUN liveliness or energy

vitamin NOUN any of a number of chemical substances that are essential to keep people and animals healthy

vitriolic ADJECTIVE **1** fiercely critical

vivacious ADJECTIVE happy and lively ► **vivacity** NOUN

vivid ADJECTIVE **1** bright and strong or clear **2** clear and lively
► **vividly** ADVERB

THESAURUS

vision NOUN • blurred vision
► eyesight, sight • had seen a vision ► apparition, mirage, ghost, hallucination • a plan that had vision ► foresight, insight, imagination

visit VERB • wanted to visit the old woman ► call on, go to see, pay a call on, stay with, descend on • recently visited Moscow ► travel to, make a trip to, spend time in

visit NOUN • their first visit to Rome
► trip, outing, excursion, day out • paid a final visit ► call, stay

visitor NOUN • a welcome visitor
► guest, caller • The site attracts

many visitors. ► tourist, holidaymaker, sightseer

visualize VERB • can visualize the scene ► picture, imagine, envisage

vital ADJECTIVE • vital to keep going
► essential, crucial, important, necessary

vitality NOUN • full of vitality
► energy, vivacity, dynamism, exuberance

vivid ADJECTIVE • vivid blue flowers
► bright, brilliant, colourful, vibrant • a vivid account of the incident ► clear, graphic, dramatic, lively

a b c d e f g h i j k l m n o p q r s t u v w x y z

a
b
c
d
e
f
g
h
i
j
k
l
m
n
o
p
q
r
s
t
u
v
w
x
y
z

vivisection NOUN the practice of performing experiments on live animals

vixen NOUN a female fox

vocabulary NOUN **vocabularies** 1 all the words used in a particular subject or language 2 the words a person uses 3 a list of words with their meanings

vocal ADJECTIVE to do with or using the voice ► **vocally** ADVERB

vocalist NOUN a singer

vocation NOUN 1 a person's job or occupation 2 a strong desire to do a particular kind of work

vocational ADJECTIVE teaching the skills needed for particular work *vocational training*

vociferous ADJECTIVE expressing views noisily and forcefully

vodka NOUN a strong alcoholic drink made from potatoes or grain

vogue NOUN the current fashion

voice NOUN 1 sounds uttered by the mouth, especially in speaking, singing, etc. 2 the ability to speak or sing 3 the right to express an opinion

voice VERB to express something in words

void ADJECTIVE 1 empty 2 having no legal validity

void NOUN an empty space or hole

volatile ADJECTIVE 1 (of a liquid) evaporating quickly 2 changing quickly in mood or behaviour ► **volatility** NOUN

volcano NOUN **volcanoes** a mountain with an opening from which lava, ashes, and hot gases are thrown out when it erupts ► **volcanic** ADJECTIVE

vole NOUN a small animal like a rat

volition NOUN **of your own volition** choosing for yourself

volley NOUN **volleys** 1 a number of bullets or shells etc. fired at the same time 2 a return of the ball in tennis etc. before it touches the ground

volley VERB to send or hit something in a volley or volleys

volleyball NOUN a game in which two teams hit a large ball over a net with their hands

volt NOUN (Science) a unit for measuring electric force

voltage NOUN electric force measured in volts

voluble ADJECTIVE talking a lot ► **volubly** ADVERB

volume NOUN 1 the amount of space filled by something 2 an amount or quantity *the volume of work* 3 the strength of sound 4 a book, especially one of a set

voluminous ADJECTIVE large or bulky

voluntary ADJECTIVE 1 done or acting willingly 2 (of work) done without pay ► **voluntarily** ADVERB

volunteer VERB 1 to offer to do something without being asked 2 to provide willingly or freely

voice NOUN • *no emotion in his voice* ► tone, accent, speaking, speech

voluntary ADJECTIVE • *voluntary work* ► unpaid, optional

DICTIONARY

volunteer NOUN a person who volunteers

voluptuous ADJECTIVE **1** giving a luxurious feeling **2** (of a woman) having an attractively curved figure

vomit VERB to bring up food from the stomach through the mouth
▶ **vomit** NOUN

voodoo NOUN a form of witchcraft and magic especially in the West Indies

voracious (vor-**ay**-shus) ADJECTIVE **1** having a large appetite **2** very eager *a voracious reader*
▶ **voracity** NOUN

vortex NOUN **vortices** a whirlpool or whirlwind

vote VERB to show which person or thing you prefer by putting up your hand, marking a paper, etc.
▶ **voter** NOUN

vote NOUN **1** the action of voting **2** the right to vote

vouch VERB **vouch for** to support or guarantee

voucher NOUN a piece of paper that can be exchanged for goods or money

vow NOUN a solemn promise, especially to God

vow VERB to make a vow

vowel NOUN any of the letters *a*, *e*, *i*, *o*, *u*, and sometimes *y*

voyage NOUN a long journey on water or in space

voyage VERB to make a voyage
▶ **voyager** NOUN

vulgar ADJECTIVE **1** rude or indecent **2** lacking good manners
▶ **vulgarity** NOUN

vulgar fraction NOUN a fraction shown by numbers above and below a line (e.g. $\frac{2}{3}$)

vulnerable ADJECTIVE able to be hurt or harmed or attacked
▶ **vulnerability** NOUN

vulture NOUN a large bird that feeds on dead animals

vulva NOUN the outer parts of the female genitals

vying present participle of **vie**

THESAURUS

vomit VERB • *the urge to vomit*
▶ be sick, retch, heave

vote NOUN • *a secret vote* ▶ ballot, poll, election, referendum

vote VERB • *voted in the election*
▶ cast a vote, go to the polls, ballot • *I vote we leave.* ▶ suggest, propose

vow NOUN • *a vow of silence*
▶ pledge, oath, promise

vow VERB • *vowed to do better*
▶ promise, pledge, swear

voyage NOUN • *The voyage lasted two weeks.* ▶ journey, passage, crossing

vulgar ADJECTIVE • *a vulgar picture*
▶ rude, indecent • *vulgar decorations* ▶ tasteless, gaudy, tacky • *vulgar behaviour*
▶ ill-mannered, impolite, coarse

vulnerable ADJECTIVE • *vulnerable when we are asleep* ▶ defenceless, unprotected, at risk, in danger

a
b
c
d
e
f
g
h
i
j
k
l
m
n
o
p
q
r
s
t
u
v
w
x
y
z

833

Ww

wad NOUN a pad or bundle of soft material, banknotes, papers, etc.

wadding NOUN soft material used for padding

waddle VERB to walk with short swaying steps like a duck
▶ **waddle** NOUN

wade VERB 1 to walk through water or mud etc. 2 to read through something long or difficult

wafer NOUN a kind of thin biscuit

waffle¹ NOUN a small cake made of batter and eaten hot

waffle² VERB (informal) to speak or write in a meaningless way
▶ **waffle** NOUN

waft VERB to carry or float gently through the air or over water

wag¹ VERB wagging, wagged to move quickly from side to side
▶ **wag** NOUN

wag² NOUN a person who makes jokes

wage NOUN or **wages** PLURAL NOUN a regular payment in return for work

wage VERB to carry on a war or campaign

wager NOUN a bet

wager VERB to bet

waggle VERB to move quickly to and fro ▶ **waggle** NOUN

wagon NOUN 1 a cart with four wheels, for carrying loads 2 an open railway truck

waif NOUN a homeless or neglected child

wail VERB to make a long sad cry
▶ **wail** NOUN

wainscot or **wainscoting** NOUN wooden panelling on the wall of a room

waist NOUN the narrow part in the middle of your body

⚠ **USAGE**

Do not confuse this word with *waste*.

waistcoat NOUN a short close-fitting jacket without sleeves, worn under a jacket

wait VERB 1 to stay or delay action until something happens 2 to be left to be dealt with later 3 to be a waiter or attendant

wait NOUN an act or time of waiting *a long wait*

waiter NOUN a man who serves food and drink in a restaurant

---

wad NOUN • *a wad of notes*
▶ bundle, roll • *a wad of cotton wool* ▶ lump, chunk

wag VERB • *The dog's tail began to wag.* ▶ wave, waggle, swing, shake

wage VERB • *to wage war* ▶ carry on, conduct, fight

wail VERB • *a wailing child* ▶ cry, howl, bawl

wait VERB • *She waited outside.*
▶ remain, rest, linger, stay

wait NOUN • *were ready after a short wait* ▶ interval, pause, delay, hold-up

waitress NOUN a woman who serves food and drink in a restaurant

waive VERB to be willing to go without a benefit or privilege

wake [1] VERB **woke**, **woken** 1 to become conscious after sleeping 2 to revive from sleeping

wake NOUN a gathering by the coffin of a dead person

wake [2] NOUN 1 the track left by a moving ship 2 currents of air left by a moving aircraft **in the wake of** coming after

wakeful ADJECTIVE unable to sleep

waken VERB to wake

walk VERB to move along on the feet at an ordinary speed
► **walker** NOUN

walk NOUN 1 a journey on foot 2 the manner of walking 3 a path for walking

walkabout NOUN an informal stroll among a crowd by an important visitor

walkie-talkie NOUN a small portable radio transmitter and receiver

walkover NOUN an easy victory

wall NOUN 1 an upright structure, forming a side of a building or room or enclosing an area 2 the outside part of something *the stomach wall*

wall VERB to enclose or block with a wall

wallaby NOUN **wallabies** a kind of small kangaroo

wallet NOUN a small flat folding case for holding banknotes, credit cards, etc.

wallflower NOUN a garden plant with fragrant flowers, blooming in spring

wallop VERB (*informal*) to hit or beat ► **wallop** NOUN

wallow VERB to roll about in water, mud, etc.

wallpaper NOUN paper covering the inside walls of rooms

walnut NOUN 1 an edible nut with a wrinkled surface 2 the wood from the tree that bears this nut

walrus NOUN a large sea animal with two long tusks

waltz NOUN a dance with three beats to a bar

waltz VERB to dance a waltz

wan (wonn) ADJECTIVE pale from being ill or tired

wand NOUN a thin rod used by a magician or conjuror

THESAURUS

wake VERB • *careful not to wake the baby* ► waken, rouse, disturb
• *woke up in the back of a car*
► awake, awaken, stir, come round

walk VERB • *decided to walk to work* ► go on foot, travel on foot
• *walked along the beach* ► stroll,

saunter, stride, march, trudge, proceed

walk NOUN • *went for a short walk*
► stroll, saunter, march, hike, trek

wand NOUN • *a magic wand*
► baton, stick, rod, staff

wander VERB **1** to go about without reaching a particular place **2** to leave the right route **3** to be distracted or digress
▶ **wanderer** NOUN

wander NOUN a wandering journey

wane VERB **1** (of the moon) to appear gradually smaller after being full **2** to become less or weaker

wane NOUN **on the wane** becoming less or weaker

wangle VERB (informal) to arrange something by trickery or clever planning

want VERB **1** to wish to have something **2** to be without something

want NOUN **1** a wish to have something **2** a lack or need

wanted ADJECTIVE (of a suspected criminal) sought by the police

wanting ADJECTIVE lacking in what is needed or usual

wanton ADJECTIVE pointless; without a motive wanton damage

war NOUN **1** fighting between nations or groups **2** a struggle or effort against crime, disease, etc.

warble VERB to sing with a trilling sound ▶ **warble** NOUN

warbler NOUN a kind of small songbird

ward NOUN **1** a room with beds in a hospital **2** a child looked after by a guardian **3** an area electing a councillor

ward VERB **ward off** to keep something away

warden NOUN an official in charge of a hostel, college, etc.

warder NOUN a guard in a prison

wardrobe NOUN **1** a cupboard for hanging clothes **2** a stock of clothes or costumes

ware NOUN manufactured goods of a certain kind hardware wares goods offered for sale

warehouse NOUN a large building for storing goods

wander VERB • wandering about the town ▶ roam, ramble, rove, walk • had wandered away
▶ stray, drift, veer

want VERB • wants to leave now ▶ wish, desire, hope, long • exactly what he wanted ▶ wish for, desire, long for, crave, fancy

want NOUN • trying to satisfy their wants ▶ demand, need,

requirement, wish • decaying for want of repair ▶ lack, need

war NOUN • suffered during the war ▶ conflict, fighting, hostilities, military action • a war against drugs ▶ campaign, crusade, battle, fight

ward VERB • ward off • to ward off evil spirits ▶ fend off, drive away • tried to ward off the blow
▶ deflect, parry, block

a b c d e f g h i j k l m n o p q r s t u v w x y z

warfare NOUN the act of fighting a war

warhead NOUN the part of a missile etc. containing the explosive

warlike ADJECTIVE 1 fond of making war 2 threatening war

warm ADJECTIVE 1 fairly hot 2 keeping the body warm 3 friendly or enthusiastic 4 close to the right answer

warm VERB to make or become warm

warm-blooded ADJECTIVE (of animals) having blood that is constantly warm

warmth NOUN 1 gentle heat 2 friendliness

warn VERB 1 to advise someone about a possible danger or difficulty 2 to give cautionary advice *warned us not to be late* **warn off** to advise someone to keep away or to avoid something

warning NOUN advice about a possible danger or difficulty

warp VERB 1 to bend or twist out of shape 2 to distort a person's ideas, judgement, etc.

warp NOUN 1 a warped condition 2 the lengthwise threads in weaving

warpath NOUN **on the warpath** angry and ready for a fight or argument

warrant NOUN a document authorizing a person to act in some way *a search warrant*

warrant VERB 1 to justify 2 to guarantee

warranty NOUN **warranties** a guarantee

warren NOUN 1 a network of rabbits' burrows 2 a building or place with many winding passages

warring ADJECTIVE involved in war

warrior NOUN a person who fights in battle

warship NOUN a ship used in war

wart NOUN a small hard lump on the skin

wartime NOUN a time of war

wary ADJECTIVE **warier, wariest** cautious and aware of possible danger or difficulty ▶ **warily** ADVERB

THESAURUS

warlike ADJECTIVE • *a warlike ruler* ▶ aggressive, belligerent, combative

warm ADJECTIVE • *warm weather* ▶ hot, balmy, summery, sultry, sunny, tropical • *a warm welcome* ▶ friendly, amiable, affable

warn VERB • *to warn patients of possible side effects* ▶ advise, alert, notify, inform, caution, remind, forewarn

warning NOUN • *warning of an attack* ▶ notice, forewarning, threat, hint, sign, omen

wary ADJECTIVE • *wary of giving her name* ▶ cautious, careful, suspicious, apprehensive

DICTIONARY

wash VERB **1** to clean with water or other liquid **2** to flow against or over something **3** to carry along by a moving liquid *was washed overboard* **4** (*informal*) to be believed *an excuse that won't wash* **wash up** to wash the dishes after a meal

wash NOUN **1** the action of washing **2** clothes etc. being washed **3** the disturbed water behind a moving ship **4** a thin coating of colour

washbasin NOUN a small sink for washing the hands and face

washer NOUN a small ring of rubber or metal etc. placed between two surfaces to fit them tightly together

washing NOUN clothes etc. being washed

washing machine NOUN a machine for washing clothes etc.

washing-up NOUN dishes and cutlery to be washed after a meal

washout NOUN (*informal*) a complete failure

wasn't was not

wasp NOUN a stinging insect with black and yellow stripes

wastage NOUN loss of something by waste

waste VERB **1** to use something extravagantly or without effect **2** to fail to use an opportunity etc. **3** to become gradually weaker or thinner

waste ADJECTIVE **1** left over or thrown away **2** not used or usable *waste land*

waste NOUN **1** the wasting of a thing **2** things that are not wanted or not used **3** an area of waste land

⚠ **USAGE**
Do not confuse this word with *waist*.

wasteful ADJECTIVE using something extravagantly or to no effect ► **wastefully** NOUN

wasteland NOUN a barren or empty area of land

wastrel NOUN a person who does nothing useful

THESAURUS

wash VERB • *need to wash it*
► clean, rinse, scrub, shampoo, mop, wipe, sponge

wash NOUN • *needed to go for a wash* ► bath, shower • *gave it a wash* ► clean, shampoo, scrub, wipe, rinse, hosing-down

waste VERB • *to waste time and money* ► squander, fritter away, throw away **waste away**
• *wasting away from malnutrition*
► become thinner, lose weight, weaken, decline

waste ADJECTIVE • *waste materials*
► unwanted, discarded • *waste ground* ► bare, empty, derelict, undeveloped

waste NOUN • *a waste of time*
► misuse, squandering, frittering away • *industrial waste*
► rubbish, refuse, effluent, garbage

wasteful ADJECTIVE • *a wasteful use of resources* ► extravagant, profligate, reckless

a b c d e f g h i j k l m n o p q r s t u v w x y z

watch VERB **1** to look at closely **2** to be on guard or ready for something **3** to pay careful attention to something *Watch where you put your feet.* **4** to take care of

watch NOUN **1** a small clock worn on the wrist **2** the action of watching **3** a turn of being on duty on a ship

watchdog NOUN **1** a dog kept to guard property **2** an official person or committee that monitors the activities of business companies

watchful ADJECTIVE watching closely; alert ▶ **watchfully** ADVERB

watchman NOUN **watchmen** a person employed to patrol an empty building

watchword NOUN a motto or slogan

water NOUN **1** a colourless tasteless liquid that is a compound of hydrogen and oxygen **2** a lake or sea **pass water** to urinate

water VERB **1** to sprinkle or supply with water **2** (of the eyes or mouth) to produce tears or saliva **water down** to dilute

water closet NOUN a toilet with a pan flushed by water

watercolour NOUN **1** paint made with water and not oil **2** a painting done with this paint

watercress NOUN a kind of cress that grows in water

waterfall NOUN a place where a river or stream flows over the edge of a cliff or large rock

water lily NOUN **water lilies** a water plant with broad leaves and large flowers

waterlogged ADJECTIVE completely soaked or swamped in water

watermark NOUN a design that can be seen in some kinds of paper when they are held up to the light

watermelon NOUN a large melon with a smooth green skin, red flesh, and watery juice

watermill NOUN a mill worked by a waterwheel

water polo NOUN a game played by teams of swimmers with a ball like a football

waterproof ADJECTIVE keeping out water

watershed NOUN **1** a ridge from which streams flow down on each side **2** a major change in events

water-skiing NOUN the sport of riding on water on a pair of skis, towed by a boat

watertight ADJECTIVE **1** made or fastened so that water cannot get in or out **2** (of an excuse etc.) completely convincing

waterway NOUN a river or canal for ships

waterwheel NOUN a large wheel turned by a flow of water

THESAURUS

watch VERB • *watched him closely* ▶ look at, observe, keep your eyes on, eye, gaze at • *someone*

to watch the children ▶ look after, mind, supervise, keep an eye on

a
b
c
d
e
f
g
h
i
j
k
l
m
n
o
p
q
r
s
t
u
v
w
x
y
z

waterworks PLURAL NOUN a place with pumping machinery etc. for supplying water

watery ADJECTIVE **1** like water **2** full of water **3** containing too much water

watt NOUN (Science) a unit of electric power

wattle NOUN **1** sticks and twigs woven together to make fences **2** an Australian tree with golden flowers **3** a red fold of skin hanging from the throat of a turkey

wave NOUN **1** the action of waving **2** a ridge moving along the surface of the sea etc. **3** a curling piece of hair **4** (Science) the wave-like movement of heat, light, sound, etc. **5** a sudden build-up of emotion

wave VERB **1** to move the hand to and fro as a greeting etc. **2** to move loosely as a flag etc. **3** to curl

wavelength NOUN the distance between corresponding points on

a sound wave or electromagnetic wave

waver VERB **1** to be unsteady **2** to hesitate

wavy ADJECTIVE **wavier**, **waviest** having waves or curves

wax[1] NOUN **1** a soft substance that melts easily, used to make candles, crayons, and polish **2** beeswax **3** a sticky substance in the ear
▶ **waxy** ADJECTIVE

wax VERB to coat or polish with wax

wax[2] VERB (of the moon) to appear gradually larger

waxen ADJECTIVE **1** made of wax **2** like wax

waxwork NOUN a model of a person etc. made in wax

way NOUN **1** how something is done **2** a manner *spoke in a friendly way* **3** a path or road **4** a route or direction **5** a distance to be travelled **6** an aspect *a good idea in some ways* **7** a condition or

THESAURUS

watery ADJECTIVE • *a bowl of watery porridge* ▶ runny, sloppy, thin, weak, tasteless • *watery eyes* ▶ damp, moist, tearful

wave NOUN • *gave a wave of her hand* ▶ gesture, shake, flourish • *surfers riding the waves* ▶ breaker, roller, surf • *hair flowing in long waves* ▶ curl, twist • *a wave of panic* ▶ feeling, surge

wave VERB • *waved to us to go over* ▶ beckon, gesture, signal, indicate • *waved his umbrella at them* ▶ shake, brandish, waggle

• *flags waving in the breeze* ▶ flap, flutter, quiver, move to and fro

waver VERB • *His voice began to waver.* ▶ tremble, falter, quaver • *was beginning to waver* ▶ hesitate, dither

wavy ADJECTIVE • *wavy hair* ▶ curly, curling, rippling

way NOUN • *was the best way* ▶ method, means, manner, approach • *helps in several ways* ▶ respect, aspect, detail, feature • *on the way home* ▶ road, route, journey, direction • *a long way to*

DICTIONARY

state *in a bad way* **give way 1** to collapse **2** to yield **in the way** forming an obstacle

waylay VERB **waylaid** to wait for someone and stop them

wayside NOUN **fall by the wayside** to fail to keep going

wayward ADJECTIVE wilfully doing what you want

WC ABBREVIATION water closet

we PRONOUN a word used to refer to the person speaking or writing together with others

weak ADJECTIVE **1** having little power or effect **2** easy to damage or defeat **3** not great in strength or intensity

weaken VERB to make or become weaker

weakling NOUN a weak person or animal

weakness NOUN **1** a lack of strength **2** a liking for something

weal NOUN a ridge raised on the flesh by a cane or whip etc.

wealth NOUN **1** a lot of money or property **2** a large quantity

wealthy ADJECTIVE **wealthier**, **wealthiest** having wealth; rich

wean VERB to make a baby take food other than its mother's milk

weapon NOUN a device used to harm or kill people in a battle or fight ▶ **weaponry** NOUN

wear VERB **wore**, **worn 1** to have clothes, jewellery, etc. on your body **2** to have a certain expression **3** to damage or

THESAURUS

go ▶ distance, length • *had to change his ways* ▶ habit, practice, routine

weak ADJECTIVE • *was in a weak position* ▶ vulnerable, exposed, defenceless • *a weak bridge* ▶ unsafe, unsteady, rickety, shaky, flimsy • *too weak to get up* ▶ feeble, frail, poorly, ill • *a weak joke* ▶ feeble, lame • *weak tea* ▶ watery, insipid, tasteless • *a weak light* ▶ dim, pale, faint

weaken VERB • *to weaken their power* ▶ reduce, sap, lessen, undermine • *Our enthusiasm had weakened.* ▶ dwindle, fade, flag, wane

weakness NOUN • *a weakness in the argument* ▶ fault, flaw, defect, imperfection • *a physical*

weakness ▶ infirmity, frailty, illness, vulnerability • *a weakness for chocolate* ▶ liking, fondness, penchant

wealth NOUN • *a person of wealth* ▶ affluence, riches, fortune, money, possessions • *a wealth of information* ▶ abundance, profusion, plenty

wealthy ADJECTIVE • *a wealthy family* ▶ rich, affluent, prosperous, well-off

wear VERB • *had to wear special clothing* ▶ dress in, put on, have on, wrap up in • *The tyres have worn well.* ▶ last, survive **wear off** • *The effect was wearing off.* ▶ fade, subside, lessen

a b c d e f g h i j k l m n o p q r s t u v w x y z

become damaged by use **4** to last while in use **wear off** to become less intense **wear out 1** to use or be used until it is useless **2** to exhaust

wear NOUN **1** clothes of a certain kind *evening wear* **2** gradual damage caused by use

wearisome ADJECTIVE causing tiredness or boredom

weary ADJECTIVE **wearier**, **weariest 1** tired from exertion **2** tiring *weary work* ► **wearily** ADVERB

weary VERB **wearies**, **wearied 1** to make weary **2** to grow tired of something

weasel NOUN a small fierce animal with a slender body and reddish-brown fur

weather NOUN the rain, snow, wind, sunshine etc. at a particular time or place **under the weather** feeling unwell

weather VERB **1** to expose to the effects of the weather **2** to survive a danger *to weather a storm*

weather-beaten ADJECTIVE damaged or affected by the weather

weathercock or **weathervane** NOUN a pointer that turns in the wind and shows its direction

weave VERB **wove**, **woven 1** to make material or baskets etc. by crossing threads or strips under and over each other **2** to put a story together **3** (*past tense & past participle* **weaved**) to twist and turn *weaving through the traffic* ► **weaver** NOUN

web NOUN **1** a cobweb **2** something complicated *a web of lies* **the Web** the World Wide Web

webbed or **web-footed** ADJECTIVE having toes joined by pieces of skin

weblog NOUN a personal diary or journal put on the Internet

web page NOUN a document forming part of a website

website NOUN a place on the Internet giving information about a subject, company, etc.

wed VERB to marry

wedding NOUN the ceremony at which a man and a woman get married

wedge NOUN **1** a piece of wood or metal etc. that is thick at one end and thin at the other, used to force surfaces apart or keep something in place **2** a wedge-shaped thing

wedge VERB **1** to keep something in place with a wedge **2** to pack tightly together

wear NOUN • *in formal wear* ► dress, clothes, clothing, outfit • *showed signs of wear* ► damage, deterioration, wear and tear

weary ADJECTIVE • *feeling sad and weary* ► tired, exhausted, worn out

wedding NOUN • *The wedding will be in the spring.* ► marriage, marriage ceremony

wedge VERB • *wedged the book into the shelf* ► squeeze, jam, cram, push

a b c d e f g h i j k l m n o p q r s t u v w x y z

wedlock NOUN the state of being married

Wednesday NOUN the day of the week following Tuesday

wee ADJECTIVE (Scottish) small; little

weed NOUN a wild plant that grows where it is not wanted

weed VERB to remove weeds from the ground

weedy ADJECTIVE **weedier, weediest** 1 full of weeds 2 thin and weak

week NOUN a period of seven days, especially from Sunday to the following Saturday

weekday NOUN a day other than Saturday or Sunday

weekend NOUN Saturday and Sunday

weekly ADJECTIVE, ADVERB happening or done once a week

weeny ADJECTIVE **weenier, weeniest** (informal) tiny

weep VERB **wept** 1 to shed tears; to cry 2 to ooze moisture

weeping ADJECTIVE (of a tree) having drooping branches

weevil NOUN a kind of small beetle

weft NOUN the threads on a loom that are woven across the warp

weigh VERB 1 to measure how heavy something is 2 to have a certain weight **weighs six kilograms** 3 be important or have influence **weigh up** to estimate or assess

weight NOUN 1 the amount that something weighs 2 a piece of metal of a specific weight, used in weighing things 3 a heavy object 4 importance or influence

weight VERB to attach a weight to

weighty ADJECTIVE **weightier, weightiest** 1 heavy 2 important or serious

weir (weer) NOUN a dam across a river or canal

weird ADJECTIVE very strange; uncanny

welcome NOUN a greeting or reception, especially a friendly one

welcome ADJECTIVE 1 pleased to receive or see 2 freely allowed **You are welcome to come.**

welcome VERB 1 to show pleasure when a person or thing arrives 2 to accept gladly

THESAURUS

weep VERB • began to weep ► cry, sob, shed tears, wail

weigh VERB **weigh** or **weigh up** • weighed up my chances ► consider, assess, examine, study

weight NOUN • attached a lot of weight to the idea ► importance, significance, authority, emphasis

weird ADJECTIVE • I heard a weird noise coming from the cellar.

► strange, peculiar, bizarre, creepy, spooky

welcome ADJECTIVE • welcome news ► pleasant, pleasing, encouraging

welcome VERB • We welcomed her warmly. ► greet, receive, meet • His colleagues welcomed his cheerfulness. ► appreciate, approve of, like, want

DICTIONARY

weld VERB **1** to join pieces of metal or plastic by heating and pressing them **2** to join into a whole

welfare NOUN people's health and happiness

welfare state NOUN a system in which the government funds health care, social services, etc.

well[1] NOUN **1** a deep hole dug to bring up water or oil from underground **2** a deep space, e.g. containing a staircase

well VERB to rise or flow up

well[2] ADVERB **better**, **best 1** in a good or suitable way **2** thoroughly *Polish it well.* **3** probably or reasonably *may well be the last chance*

well ADJECTIVE **1** in good health **2** satisfactory

well-being NOUN good health and comfort

wellingtons PLURAL NOUN rubber or plastic waterproof boots

> **WORD HISTORY**
>
> named after the first Duke of Wellington, who wore long leather boots

well-known ADJECTIVE **1** known to many people **2** known thoroughly

well-meaning ADJECTIVE having good intentions

wellnigh ADVERB almost

well off ADJECTIVE fairly rich and comfortable

well-read ADJECTIVE having read many books

well-to-do ADJECTIVE fairly rich

welsh VERB to cheat someone by avoiding paying a debt

welt NOUN **1** a strip or border **2** a weal

welter NOUN a confused mixture

wench NOUN (old use) a girl or young woman

wend VERB **wend your way** to go slowly but steadily

weren't were not

werewolf NOUN **werewolves** (in stories) a person who can change into a wolf

west NOUN **1** the direction where the sun sets **2** the western part of a country, city, etc.

THESAURUS

welfare NOUN • *the welfare of people at work* ▸ well-being, good, comfort, happiness, health

well ADVERB • *They behaved well.* ▸ satisfactorily, correctly, nicely, properly • *She sings well.* ▸ ably, skilfully, expertly • *Mix the ingredients well.* ▸ thoroughly, completely • *have been working well* ▸ carefully, conscientiously

• *to live well* ▸ comfortably, in comfort

well ADJECTIVE • *He was looking well.* ▸ healthy, fit, strong

well-known ADJECTIVE • *well-known music* ▸ familiar, popular • *a well-known family* ▸ famous, notable, prominent

well off ADJECTIVE • *was very well off* ▸ rich, wealthy, affluent, prosperous

west ADJECTIVE, ADVERB towards or in the west; coming from the west

westerly ADJECTIVE **1** coming from the west **2** facing the west

western ADJECTIVE of or in the west

western NOUN a film or story about cowboys in western North America

westward ADJECTIVE, ADVERB towards the west ► **westwards** ADVERB

wet ADJECTIVE **wetter, wettest 1** soaked or covered in liquid **2** (of paint etc.) not yet dry **3** (of weather) raining a lot ► **wetness** NOUN

wet VERB **wetting, wet** or or **wetted** to make wet

wet suit NOUN a close-fitting rubber suit worn by divers etc. to keep the body warm and dry

whack VERB (informal) to hit hard ► **whack** NOUN

whale NOUN a large sea mammal

whaler NOUN a person or ship that hunts whales

whaling NOUN the hunting of whales

wharf (worf) NOUN **wharves** or **wharfs** a quay for loading and unloading ships

what ADJECTIVE **1** used to ask the amount or kind of something *What book is that?* **2** used to

express degree *What a time we had!*

what PRONOUN **1** what thing or things *What did they say?* **2** the thing that *This is what you must do.*

whatever PRONOUN **1** anything or everything *whatever you like* **2** no matter what *whatever happens*

whatever ADJECTIVE of any kind or amount *Take whatever books you need.*

whatsoever ADJECTIVE at all

wheat NOUN a cereal plant from which flour is made ► **wheaten** ADJECTIVE

wheedle VERB to persuade by coaxing or flattering

wheel NOUN **1** a disc-shaped device that turns on a shaft, fitted to something to make it move **2** a steering wheel **3** a revolving disc used in shaping pottery

wheel VERB **1** to push a bicycle or trolley etc. along **2** to move in a curve or circle

wheelbarrow NOUN a small hand-pushed cart with a wheel at the front

wheelchair NOUN a chair on wheels for a disabled person

wheeze VERB to make a hoarse sound in breathing ► **wheeze** NOUN, **wheezy** ADJECTIVE

a
b
c
d
e
f
g
h
i
j
k
l
m
n
o
p
q
r
s
t
u
v
w
x
y
z

THESAURUS

wet ADJECTIVE • *a wet towel*
► damp, moist, soaked, sopping, dripping • *The ground was too wet.* ► waterlogged, sodden, boggy • *The paint was still*

wet. ► runny, sticky, tacky
• *wet weather* ► rainy, drizzly, showery

wet VERB • *wet your hair first*
► dampen, moisten, drench, soak

whelk NOUN a shellfish that looks like a snail

when ADVERB at what time *When can you come?*

when CONJUNCTION 1 at the time that *The bird flew away when I moved.* 2 although; considering that *Why stay when there's nothing to do?*

whence ADVERB, CONJUNCTION from where; from which

whenever CONJUNCTION at whatever time; every time

where ADVERB, CONJUNCTION in or to what place or that place

whereabouts ADVERB in or near what place

whereabouts PLURAL NOUN the place where something is

whereas CONJUNCTION but in contrast *Some people like sport, whereas others do not.*

whereby ADVERB by which

whereupon CONJUNCTION after which; and then

wherever ADVERB in or to whatever place

whet VERB **whetting, whetted** to sharpen a knife *his* **whet your appetite** to make you hungry

whether CONJUNCTION as one possibility; if *I don't know whether to believe them or not.*

whey (say as way) NOUN the watery liquid left when milk forms curds

which ADJECTIVE what particular *Which way did he go?*

which PRONOUN 1 what person or thing *Which is your desk?* 2 the person or thing referred to *the film, which is a western*

whichever PRONOUN, ADJECTIVE no matter which; any which

whiff NOUN a puff or slight smell of smoke, gas, etc.

while CONJUNCTION 1 during the time that; as long as *while you work* 2 although; but *She is dark, while her sister is fair.*

while NOUN a period of time *a long while*

while VERB **while away** to pass time idly

whilst CONJUNCTION while

whim NOUN a sudden wish

whimper VERB to cry or whine softly ► **whimper** NOUN

whimsical ADJECTIVE quaint and playful

whine VERB 1 to make a long high miserable cry 2 to complain in a petty way ► **whine** NOUN

whinge VERB **whinging** or **whingeing** (informal) to grumble persistently ► **whinge** NOUN

whinny VERB **whinnies, whinnied** to neigh gently ► **whinny** NOUN

whip NOUN 1 a strip of leather fixed to a handle and used for hitting people or animals 2 an official of a political party in Parliament 3 a pudding of whipped cream and flavouring

THESAURUS

whine VERB • *Mosquitos whined in my ears.* ► drone, hum • *sick of him whining to me* ► grumble, complain, moan

whip VERB whipping, whipped
1 to hit with a whip **2** to beat cream until it is thick **3** to move or take suddenly *whipped out a knife* **4** (*informal*) to steal **whip up** to stir up people's feelings etc.

whippet NOUN a racing dog like a small greyhound

whirl VERB to turn or spin quickly
► **whirl** NOUN

whirlpool NOUN a whirling current of water

whirlwind NOUN a strong wind that whirls round a central point

whirr VERB to make a continuous buzzing sound ► **whirr** NOUN

whisk VERB **1** to move or take away quickly and lightly **2** to beat eggs etc.

whisk NOUN **1** a kitchen tool used for whisking **2** a whisking movement

whisker NOUN **1** a long bristle growing near the mouth of a cat etc. **2** each of the hairs growing on a man's face ► **whiskery** ADJECTIVE

whisky NOUN whiskies a strong alcoholic drink made from grain

whisper VERB **1** to speak very softly **2** to talk secretly
► **whisper** NOUN

whist NOUN a card game for four people

whistle VERB to make a shrill sound by blowing through the lips or an instrument

whistle NOUN **1** a whistling sound **2** a device that makes a whistling sound

white ADJECTIVE **1** of the lightest colour, like snow or salt **2** having light-coloured skin **3** very pale from the effects of illness or fear etc. **4** (of coffee or tea) with milk

white NOUN **1** the lightest colour **2** the transparent part round the yolk of an egg

white elephant NOUN a useless possession that causes the owner a lot of trouble

white-hot ADJECTIVE extremely hot; so hot that heated metal looks white

white lie NOUN a harmless or trivial lie

whiten VERB to make or become whiter

whitewash NOUN a white liquid containing lime or powdered chalk, used for painting walls etc.

whitewash VERB **1** to cover with whitewash **2** to conceal a mistake

whither ADVERB, CONJUNCTION (*old use*) to what place

THESAURUS

whirl VERB • *dancers whirling round* ► spin, circle, twirl, rotate, turn

whisk VERB • *was whisked off to a studio* ► rush, speed, hurry, sweep • *whisk the eggs* ► beat, mix, whip

whisper VERB • *whispered something in his ear* ► murmur, mutter, mumble

white ADJECTIVE • *a white dress* ► ivory, snowy, pale , cream • *a face white with fear* ► pale, pallid, ashen, colourless

a
b
c
d
e
f
g
h
i
j
k
l
m
n
o
p
q
r
s
t
u
v
w
x
y
z

whiting NOUN a small sea fish with white flesh

Whitsun NOUN Whit Sunday and the days close to it

Whit Sunday the seventh Sunday after Easter

whittle VERB 1 to shape wood by trimming 2 to reduce something gradually

whizz or **whiz** VERB 1 to sound like something rushing through the air 2 to move very quickly

who PRONOUN which person or people; the particular person or people *the person who gave the money*

whoever PRONOUN 1 any or every person who 2 no matter who

whole ADJECTIVE 1 complete 2 not injured or broken

whole NOUN 1 the full amount 2 a complete thing **on the whole** considering everything

wholefood NOUN naturally produced food

wholehearted ADJECTIVE without doubts or reservations

wholemeal ADJECTIVE made from the whole grain of wheat

whole number NOUN a number without fractions

wholesale NOUN the selling of goods in large quantities to shops for selling to the public
▶ **wholesaler** NOUN

wholesale ADJECTIVE, ADVERB 1 on a large scale *wholesale destruction* 2 in the wholesale trade

wholesome ADJECTIVE good for health; healthy

wholly ADVERB completely or entirely

whom PRONOUN the form of **who** used when it is the object of a verb or comes after a preposition

whoop NOUN a loud cry of excitement

whoop VERB to make a whoop

whooping cough (hoop-ing) NOUN an infectious disease that causes coughing spasms and gasping for breath

whopper NOUN (informal) something very large

whopping ADJECTIVE (informal) very large or remarkable

who's who is; who has *Who's there? I don't know who's done it.*

⚠ **USAGE**
Do not confuse this word with *whose*.

whose PRONOUN belonging to whom or which *Whose house is that? He's a man whose opinion I respect.*

⚠ **USAGE**
Do not confuse this word with *who's*.

why ADVERB for what reason or purpose *Why did you do it? This is why I came.*

whole ADJECTIVE • *have read the whole book* ▶ entire, complete, full, total • *an ancient vase* *that was whole* ▶ intact, unbroken, undamaged, unharmed, perfect

abcdefghijklmnopqrstuvwxyz

wick NOUN the thread in the middle of a candle or in a lamp etc. that carries the fuel to the flame

wicked ADJECTIVE **1** morally bad or cruel **2** mischievous *a wicked smile* **3** (*informal*) excellent ► **wickedness** NOUN

wicker NOUN thin canes or twigs woven together to make baskets or furniture etc. ► **wickerwork** NOUN

wicket NOUN **1** a set of three stumps and two bails used in cricket **2** the strip of ground between the wickets

wide ADJECTIVE **1** measuring a lot from side to side **2** measuring from side to side *one metre wide* **3** covering a great range **4** missing the target *wide of the mark*

wide ADVERB **1** to the full extent *wide open* **2** missing the target *a shot that went wide* **3** over a large area *far and wide*

widely ADVERB among many people

widen VERB to make or become wider

widespread ADJECTIVE existing in many places or over a wide area

widow NOUN a woman whose husband has died ► **widowed** ADJECTIVE

widower NOUN a man whose wife has died

width NOUN how wide something is

wield VERB **1** to hold and use a weapon or tool **2** to have and use power or influence

wife NOUN **wives** the woman to whom a man is married

Wi-Fi NOUN (*ICT*) a system of transferring data from one computer to another using radio waves instead of wires

wig NOUN a covering of artificial hair

wiggle VERB to move from side to side ► **wiggle** NOUN, **wiggly** ADJECTIVE

wigwam NOUN a traditional Native American tent made with animal skins

wild ADJECTIVE **1** living or growing in its natural state **2** not cultivated *a wild landscape* **3** not controlled; violent or excited **4** strange or

THESAURUS

wicked ADJECTIVE • *a wicked act* ► evil, bad, sinful, immoral, corrupt • *a wicked smile* ► mischievous, playful, impish, cheeky

wide ADJECTIVE • *over a wide area* ► broad, extensive, vast, large • *a wide choice* ► extensive, comprehensive, wide-ranging, spread out, outspread

widen VERB • *plans to widen the motorway* ► broaden, make wider, expand, enlarge

widespread ADJECTIVE • *widespread protest* ► general, extensive, global • *Disease was widespread.* ► common, rife, prevalent

wild ADJECTIVE • *a wild animal* ► fierce, ferocious, untamed

unreasonable *wild ideas*
▶ **wildly** ADVERB

wilderness NOUN a wild
uncultivated area

wildfire NOUN **spread like
wildfire** (of rumours etc.) to
spread quickly

wild goose chase NOUN a futile
search

wildlife NOUN wild animals in their
natural setting

wile NOUN a piece of trickery

wilful ADJECTIVE **1** obstinately
determined **2** deliberate *wilful
damage* ▶ **wilfully** ADVERB

will[1] AUXILIARY VERB used to express
the future tense, questions, or
promises *They will arrive soon.
Will you shut the door? I will get
my revenge.*

will[2] NOUN **1** the mental power to
decide what you do **2** a chosen
decision *against my will*
3 determination *set to work with a
will* **4** a written statement of what
is to happen to a person's property
after their death

will VERB to use your will power
was willing you to win

willing ADJECTIVE ready and happy
to do what is wanted ▶ **willingly**
ADVERB

will-o'-the-wisp NOUN a
flickering spot of light seen on
marshy ground

willow NOUN a tree with long
flexible branches

will power NOUN strength of
mind to control what you do

willy-nilly ADVERB whether you
want to or not

wilt VERB **1** to lose freshness **2** to
lose strength or energy

wily ADJECTIVE **wilier, wiliest**
cunning or crafty

wimp NOUN (*informal*) a weak or
timid person

win VERB **winning, won 1** to
defeat opponents in a battle,
game, or contest **2** to get or
achieve by a victory or by using
effort or skill **win over** to gain
someone's favour or support

win NOUN a victory

THESAURUS

• *wild flowers* ▶ natural,
uncultivated, indigenous • *wild
ideas* ▶ crazy, strange, ridiculous,
mad • *wild behaviour* ▶ unruly,
rowdy, violent • *were wild with joy*
▶ excited, ecstatic, frantic • *a wild
guess* ▶ random, haphazard,
arbitrary

will NOUN • *lost the will to continue*
▶ determination, resolve,
intention, desire, wish

willing ADJECTIVE • *was willing to
help* ▶ prepared, ready, eager,
pleased • *willing helpers*

▶ enthusiastic, helpful,
cooperative

wilt VERB • *The flowers had begun
to wilt.* ▶ droop, fade, shrivel,
wither

wily ADJECTIVE • *outwitted by wily
opponents* ▶ clever, crafty,
shrewd, cunning, sly

win VERB • *a good chance of
winning* ▶ succeed, triumph,
come first, be victorious
• *managed to win their support*
▶ gain, obtain, earn, get

wince VERB to make a slight movement from pain or embarrassment etc.

winch NOUN a device using a rope or cable for lifting or pulling things

winch VERB to lift or pull with a winch

wind[1] (rhymes with *tinned*) NOUN **1** a current of air **2** gas in the stomach or intestines **3** breath used for running or speaking **4** the wind instruments of an orchestra

wind VERB to make a person out of breath

wind[2] (rhymes with *find*) VERB **wound 1** to go or turn in twists, curves, or circles **2** to tighten the spring of a clock or watch **3** to wrap round **wind up** (*informal*) to end up in a place or condition

windfall NOUN **1** a piece of unexpected good luck, especially money **2** a fruit blown off a tree by the wind

wind instrument NOUN a musical instrument played by blowing into it

windmill NOUN a mill worked by the wind turning its sails

window NOUN **1** an opening with glass in a wall or roof etc. to let in light and air **2** (*ICT*) a framed area on a computer screen

windpipe NOUN the tube by which air passes from the throat to the lungs

windscreen NOUN the window at the front of a motor vehicle

windsurfing NOUN the sport of riding on water on a board with a sail ▸ **windsurfer** NOUN

windward ADJECTIVE, ADVERB facing the wind

windy ADJECTIVE **windier**, **windiest** with a lot of wind

wine NOUN **1** an alcoholic drink made from grapes or other plants **2** a dark red colour

wing NOUN **1** each of the limbs of a bird, bat, or insect used for flying **2** each of the long flat parts on either side of an aircraft that support it in the air **3** a part extending from the main part of a building **4** the part of a vehicle body above a wheel **5** a player positioned at the edge of the pitch in football or hockey etc. **6** a section of a political party **7** each side of a theatre stage out of sight of the audience

wing VERB **1** to travel by means of wings **2** to wound a bird in the wing

winged ADJECTIVE having wings

THESAURUS

wind NOUN • *shivered in the cold wind* ▸ breeze, draught, gust, blast, gale

wind VERB • *He wound the cord tightly.* ▸ coil, loop, twist, curl,

roll • *The river winds like a serpent.* ▸ twist, snake, bend, meander

windy ADJECTIVE • *cold and windy* ▸ breezy, blowy, blustery, gusty, stormy

wink VERB **1** to close and open the eye quickly **2** (of a light) to flicker or twinkle

wink NOUN the action of winking

winkle NOUN a kind of edible shellfish

winkle VERB **winkle out** to get hold of information etc. with difficulty

winner NOUN **1** a person or animal etc. that wins **2** something successful

winnings PLURAL NOUN money won in gambling

winter NOUN the coldest season of the year, between autumn and spring

wintry ADJECTIVE cold and wet

wipe VERB to dry or clean by rubbing **wipe out** to cancel or destroy ► **wipe** NOUN

wiper NOUN a device fitted to a vehicle's windscreen to wipe it

wire NOUN **1** a strand of metal **2** a length of this carrying an electric current

wire VERB **1** to fit with wires to carry electric current **2** to fasten or strengthen with wire

wireless NOUN (old use) a radio

wireless ADJECTIVE not using electrical wires

wiring NOUN the system of electrical wires

wiry ADJECTIVE **wirier**, **wiriest 1** like wire **2** lean and strong

wisdom NOUN **1** the quality of being wise **2** wise sayings or writings

wisdom tooth NOUN a molar tooth at the back of the jaw of an adult

wise ADJECTIVE **1** judging well; showing good sense **2** knowledgeable ► **wisely** ADVERB

wish VERB **1** to feel or say what you would like to do or happen **2** to hope for for someone *I wish you luck.*

wish NOUN **1** something wished; a desire **2** the action of wishing

THESAURUS

wink VERB • *A light winked.*
► flash, gleam, flicker, sparkle, twinkle

winner NOUN • *the overall winner*
► victor, champion

wipe VERB • *wiped the table with a cloth* ► clean, rub, mop, wash, brush **wipe out** • *a hurricane that wiped out the town* ► destroy, obliterate

wisdom NOUN • *a lot of wisdom in their advice* ► sense, cleverness, prudence, judgement

wise ADJECTIVE • *a wise man*
► clever, intelligent, knowledgeable, sensible • *wise advice* ► sensible, prudent, appropriate, right

wish VERB • *if you wish to see them*
► want, hope **wish for** • *wished for wealth and happiness* ► desire, want, long for, fancy

wish NOUN • *their dearest wish*
► desire, ambition, longing, aim
• *must respect their wishes*
► request, order

DICTIONARY

wishbone NOUN a forked bone between the neck and breast of a chicken

wishful ADJECTIVE wanting something

wishful thinking NOUN the act of believing something to be true just because you want it to be

wisp NOUN 1 a few strands of hair or bits of straw etc. 2 a small streak of smoke or cloud etc. ▸ **wispy** ADJECTIVE

wistful ADJECTIVE sadly longing for something ▸ **wistfully** ADVERB

wit NOUN 1 intelligence or cleverness 2 a clever kind of humour 3 a witty person

witch NOUN (in stories) a woman with magic powers

witchcraft NOUN the use of magic for bad purposes

witch doctor NOUN a person who is believed to use magic to heal people

with PREPOSITION 1 in the company of *Come with me.* 2 having *a man with a beard* 3 using *hitting it with a hammer* 4 because of *shaking with laughter* 5 towards *angry with him* 6 against *was arguing*

with me 7 separated from *had to part with it*

withdraw VERB **withdrew**, **withdrawn** 1 to take back or away 2 to go away

withdrawal NOUN 1 the act of withdrawing 2 a sum of money taken out of an account 3 the process of no longer taking addictive drugs, often with unpleasant reactions

withdrawn ADJECTIVE shy or reserved

wither VERB to shrivel or wilt

withering ADJECTIVE (of a remark or look) scornful or sarcastic

withhold VERB **withheld** to refuse to give or allow something

within PREPOSITION, ADVERB inside; not beyond

without PREPOSITION 1 not having *without food* 2 free from *without fear*

withstand VERB **withstood** to endure or resist

witness NOUN 1 a person who sees or hears something happen 2 a person who gives evidence in a lawcourt

THESAURUS

withdraw VERB • *The objections have been withdrawn.* ▸ retract, take back • *The army was forced to withdraw.* ▸ retreat, draw back • *decided to withdraw from the talks* ▸ pull out (of), back out (of)

wither VERB • *The flowers had withered.* ▸ wilt, shrivel, droop

withhold VERB • *had withheld information* ▸ suppress, hide, hold back, keep secret

withstand VERB • *strong enough to withstand the storms* ▸ resist, survive

witness NOUN • *a witness to the incident* ▸ observer, onlooker, spectator, eyewitness

a
b
c
d
e
f
g
h
i
j
k
l
m
n
o
p
q
r
s
t
u
v
w
x
y
z

DICTIONARY

witness VERB **1** to be a witness of **2** to sign a document to confirm that it is genuine

witticism NOUN a witty remark

witty ADJECTIVE **wittier, wittiest** clever and amusing ► **wittily** ADVERB

wizard NOUN **1** (in stories) a magician **2** a person with amazing abilities ► **wizardry** NOUN

wizened ADJECTIVE full of wrinkles

woad NOUN a kind of blue dye formerly made from a plant

wobble VERB to move unsteadily from side to side ► **wobble** NOUN, **wobbly** ADJECTIVE

woe NOUN **1** sorrow or misfortune **2** a cause of this

woebegone ADJECTIVE looking unhappy

woeful ADJECTIVE **1** sorrowful **2** deplorable ► **woefully** ADVERB

wok NOUN a Chinese cooking pan shaped like a large bowl

wolf NOUN **wolves** a wild animal of the dog family that hunts in packs

wolf VERB to eat greedily

woman NOUN **women** a grown-up female human being

womanly ADJECTIVE having qualities typical of women

womb NOUN the organ in a female's body in which young develop before they are born

wombat NOUN an Australian animal like a small bear

wonder NOUN **1** a feeling of surprise and admiration **2** something that causes this

wonder VERB **1** to feel that you want to know **2** to feel wonder

wonderful ADJECTIVE marvellous or excellent ► **wonderfully** ADVERB

wonderment NOUN a feeling of wonder

THESAURUS

witness VERB • *had witnessed the crime* ► see, observe, be present at

witty ADJECTIVE • *a witty entertainer* ► humorous, amusing, funny, comic

wizard NOUN • *still under the wizard's spell* ► magician, sorcerer, enchanter

wobble VERB • *wobbling on a bicycle* ► sway, totter, be unsteady • *The glass wobbled.* ► tremble, shake, rock, vibrate

wobbly ADJECTIVE • *a table with a wobbly leg* ► unsteady, loose,

rickety, shaky • *feeling a bit wobbly* ► giddy, dizzy, faint

wonder NOUN • *were speechless with wonder* ► awe, admiration, amazement • *a wonder of nature* ► marvel, miracle

wonder VERB • *was wondering if they would come* ► speculate, ponder, ask yourself **wonder at** • *We wondered at such bravery.* ► admire, marvel at, be amazed by

wonderful ADJECTIVE • *had a wonderful time* ► excellent, marvellous, fantastic, amazing, terrific

wondrous ADJECTIVE (old use) wonderful

wont (wohnt) ADJECTIVE (old use) accustomed *was wont to dress in rags*

won't will not

woo VERB **woos, wooing, wooed** (old use) **1** to court a woman **2** to seek favour or support

wood NOUN **1** the substance of which trees are made **2** a large group of trees

wooded ADJECTIVE covered with growing trees

wooden ADJECTIVE **1** made of wood **2** showing no expression or life

woodland NOUN wooded country

woodlouse NOUN a small crawling creature able to roll into a ball

woodpecker NOUN a bird that taps tree trunks with its beak to find insects

woodwind NOUN wind instruments that are usually made of wood, e.g. the clarinet and oboe

woodwork NOUN **1** the making of wooden objects **2** things made out of wood

woodworm NOUN the larva of a beetle that bores into wood and damages it

woody ADJECTIVE **woodier, woodiest 1** like or made of wood **2** having many trees

woof NOUN the gruff bark of a dog

wool NOUN **1** the thick soft hair of sheep and goats etc. **2** thread or cloth made from this

woollen ADJECTIVE made of wool

woolly ADJECTIVE **1** covered with wool or hair **2** like wool; woollen **3** vague or confused
▸ **woolliness** NOUN

word NOUN **1** a set of sounds or letters with a meaning **2** a brief conversation **3** a promise **4** a command or spoken signal **5** a message *to send word*

word VERB to express in words

wording NOUN the way something is worded

word processor NOUN a type of computer or program used for editing and printing documents

wordy ADJECTIVE **wordier, wordiest** using many words; not concise

wore past tense of **wear**

THESAURUS

wood NOUN • *a nature trail through the wood* ▸ forest, woodland, trees, thicket • *a little cabin made from wood* ▸ timber, planks

woolly ADJECTIVE • *a sheep's woolly coat* ▸ fleecy, furry, downy, shaggy, soft

word NOUN • *another word for 'chuckle'* ▸ expression, term • *I give you my word.* ▸ promise, guarantee, assurance • *no word yet from the hospital* ▸ news, information, report, comment

word VERB • *how to word your CV* ▸ phrase, express, say

a
b
c
d
e
f
g
h
i
j
k
l
m
n
o
p
q
r
s
t
u
v
w
x
y
z

work NOUN **1** something you have to do that needs effort or energy **2** a job; employment **3** (Science) the result of applying a force to move an object **4** a piece of writing, painting, music, etc. *the works of Shakespeare*

work VERB **1** to do work **2** to have a job **3** to act or operate correctly **4** to operate a machine etc. **5** to shape or press etc. **6** to move gradually into a particular position *The screw had worked loose.* **work out 1** to find an answer by thinking or calculating **2** to have a particular result

workable ADJECTIVE that can be used or done; practical

worker NOUN a person who works in a particular industry

workforce NOUN the number of people who work in a particular place

working class NOUN people who are employed in manual or industrial work

workmanship NOUN skill in working; the result of this

work of art NOUN a fine picture, building, etc.

workout NOUN a session of physical exercise

works PLURAL NOUN **1** the moving parts of a machine **2** a factory or industrial site

workshop NOUN a place where things are made or mended

world NOUN **1** the earth with all its countries and peoples **2** all the people on the earth **3** a planet **4** everything to do with a certain activity *the world of sport* **5** a large amount *will do them a world of good*

worldly ADJECTIVE **1** to do with material things on earth **2** interested only in money, pleasure, etc.

worldwide ADJECTIVE, ADVERB over the whole world

World Wide Web NOUN a vast information system that connects sites and documents on the Internet

worm NOUN **1** a creeping animal with a long soft rounded or flat body and no backbone or limbs **2** an unimportant or unpleasant person

THESAURUS

work NOUN • *several days' work* ► labour, effort, toil • *looking for work abroad* ► employment, a job, a career

work VERB • *were working hard* ► labour, toil, slave • *works in a bank* ► have a job, be employed, earn a living • *The dishwasher was working again.* ► function, run, in working order • *how to work the*

coffee machine ► operate, use • *The plan had worked.* ► succeed, be successful **work out 1** *didn't quite work out as expected* ► turn out, happen, develop **2** *to work out the answer* ► calculate, solve

world NOUN • *around the world* ► earth, globe, planet • *the world of sport* ► field, area, realm

DICTIONARY

worm VERB to move along by wriggling or crawling **worm out** to get information from someone by constant questioning

worn *past participle of* **wear**.

worn out ADJECTIVE **1** tired and exhausted **2** damaged by use

worried ADJECTIVE feeling or showing worry

worry VERB **worries, worried** **1** to be troublesome to someone **2** to feel anxious ► **worrier** NOUN

worry NOUN **worries 1** the condition of worrying; anxiety **2** something that makes a person worry

worse ADJECTIVE, ADVERB more bad or more badly **worse off** less fortunate or well off

worsen VERB to make or become worse

worship VERB **worshipping, worshipped 1** to give praise or respect to God or a god **2** to love or admire greatly ► **worshipper** NOUN

worship NOUN **1** the act of worshipping **2** a title of respect for a mayor or certain magistrates

worst ADJECTIVE, ADVERB most bad or most badly

worsted NOUN a kind of woollen material

worth ADJECTIVE **1** having a certain value *is worth £100* **2** good or important enough for something *a book worth reading*

worth NOUN **1** value or usefulness **2** the amount that a certain sum will buy *five pounds' worth*

worthless ADJECTIVE having no value; useless

THESAURUS

worn out ADJECTIVE • *were worn out from the long walk*
► exhausted, tired out, weary, shattered

worried ADJECTIVE • *seemed worried about something*
► anxious, troubled, uneasy, tense, nervous

worry VERB • *Something was worrying her.* ► trouble, bother, upset • *was trying not to worry* ► be anxious, fret, panic • *Don't worry her while she's busy.*
► bother, pester, disturb

worry NOUN • *affected by worry*
► anxiety, unease, distress, fear, tension • *another worry*
► problem, difficulty, trouble

worsen VERB • *will worsen traffic problems* ► increase, exacerbate, aggravate • *The situation was worsening.* ► deteriorate, decline, degenerate

worship VERB • *They worshipped the sun.* ► pray to, revere, glorify • *worships his father* ► idolize, adore, dote on, love

worth NOUN • *knows her own worth* ► value, usefulness, merit, quality, strengths • *a fraction of its true worth* ► value, cost, price

worthless ADJECTIVE • *The certificate was worthless.*
► valueless, of no value • *Their advice proved worthless.*
► useless, futile, pointless

worthwhile ADJECTIVE deserving the time or effort needed

worthy ADJECTIVE **worthier, worthiest** having great merit; deserving respect or support
worthy of deserving *a charity worthy of our support*
► **worthiness** NOUN

would AUXILIARY VERB **1** used as the past tense of **will** *We said we would do it.* **2** used in questions and requests *Would you like to come? Would you come in, please?* **3** used to express a condition *They would tell us if they knew.*

would-be ADJECTIVE wanting or pretending to be *a would-be artist*

wouldn't would not

wound [1] (woond) NOUN **1** an injury caused by a cut, stab, or hit **2** a hurt to a person's feelings

wound VERB **1** to cause a wound to a person or animal **2** to offend someone

wound [2] (wownd) *past tense of* **wind** [2]

wraith NOUN a ghost

wrangle VERB to have a noisy argument or quarrel ► **wrangle** NOUN

wrap VERB **wrapping, wrapped** to put paper or cloth etc. round something as a covering **wrap up** to put on warm clothes

wrap NOUN a shawl, cloak, etc. worn for warmth

wrapper NOUN a piece of paper etc. wrapped round something

wrapping NOUN material used to wrap something

wrath (rhymes with *cloth*) NOUN fierce anger

wrathful ADJECTIVE fiercely angry ► **wrathfully** ADVERB

wreak (say as reek) VERB to inflict or cause *wreaked havoc*

wreath (reeth) NOUN a circle of flowers or leaves etc.

wreathe (reeth) VERB **1** to surround or decorate with a wreath **2** to cover *faces wreathed in smiles*

wreck VERB to damage or ruin something completely

wreck NOUN **1** a wrecked ship or building or car etc. **2** a person who

worthwhile ADJECTIVE • *do something worthwhile* ► useful, valuable, meaningful, important

worthy ADJECTIVE • *a worthy cause* ► admirable, commendable, deserving

wound NOUN • *a deep wound* ► injury, gash, cut

wound VERB • *a friend who had been wounded* ► injure, hurt, harm

wrap VERB • *wrapped paper round it* ► fold, wind, pack, place
• *wrapped himself in a towel* ► cover, envelop

wreck VERB • *had been wrecked in a storm* ► shipwreck, sink, destroy • *had wrecked his car* ► crash, smash • *wrecked their plans* ► ruin, spoil, put an end to

wreck NOUN • *the wreck of an ancient ship* ► wreckage, shipwreck, remains

a
b
c
d
e
f
g
h
i
j
k
l
m
n
o
p
q
r
s
t
u
v
w
x
y
z

is left very weak *a nervous wreck* **3** the wrecking of something

wreckage NOUN the remnants of something wrecked

wren NOUN a very small brown bird

wrench VERB to twist or pull violently

wrench NOUN **1** a wrenching movement **2** pain caused by parting **3** an adjustable tool like a spanner

wrest VERB to take something away using force

wrestle VERB **1** to fight an opponent, trying to throw them to the ground **2** to struggle with a problem or difficulty ▶ **wrestle** NOUN, **wrestler** NOUN

wretch NOUN **1** a miserable or pitiful person **2** a person who is disliked

wretched ADJECTIVE **1** miserable or unhappy **2** of bad quality

wriggle VERB to move with short twisting movements **wriggle out**

of to avoid work or blame etc.
▶ **wriggle** NOUN

wring VERB **wrung 1** to twist and squeeze water out of **2** to clasp the hands firmly **3** to get something by a great effort **wringing wet** wet enough for water to be squeezed out

wringer NOUN a device with a pair of rollers for squeezing water out of washed clothes etc.

wrinkle NOUN **1** a small furrow or ridge in the skin **2** a small crease in something

wrinkle VERB to make wrinkles in; to form wrinkles

wrist NOUN the joint that connects the hand and arm

wristwatch NOUN a watch for wearing on the wrist

writ (rit) NOUN a formal written command issued by a lawcourt etc.

write VERB **wrote, written 1** to form letters or words etc. **2** to be the author or composer of **3** to

THESAURUS

wreckage NOUN • *wreckage from the aircraft* ▶ debris, fragments, remains

wretched ADJECTIVE • *feeling tired and wretched* ▶ miserable, unhappy, despondent, ill
• *wretched conditions*
▶ atrocious, appalling, dreadful

wriggle VERB • *wriggled under the fence* ▶ twist, writhe, squirm, worm

wrinkle NOUN • *full of wrinkles*
▶ crease, fold, pucker, crinkle, line

wrinkle VERB • *wrinkled her nose*
▶ crease, crinkle, rumple, fold

write VERB • *wrote the details in a notebook* ▶ jot down, record, make a note of, note down, scribble • *has stopped writing to him* ▶ communicate (with), send letters, keep in touch • *wanted to write music*
▶ compose, create, compile, draft

DICTIONARY

send a letter **4** to enter data into a computer **write off** to regard as lost or useless ► **writer** NOUN

writhe VERB **1** to twist the body in pain **2** to wriggle

writing NOUN something written; a way of writing

wrong ADJECTIVE **1** incorrect; not true **2** not fair or morally right **3** not working properly
► **wrongly** ADVERB

wrong ADVERB wrongly *You guessed wrong.*

wrong NOUN something morally wrong; an injustice

wrong VERB to do wrong to someone

wrongdoer NOUN a person who does wrong ► **wrongdoing** NOUN

wrongful ADJECTIVE unfair or unjust; illegal ► **wrongfully** ADVERB

wrought ADJECTIVE (of metal) worked by being beaten out or shaped by hammering or rolling etc.

wry ADJECTIVE **wryer, wryest**
1 slightly mocking or sarcastic
2 twisted or bent out of shape
► **wryly** ADVERB, **wryness** NOUN

WWW ABBREVIATION World Wide Web

THESAURUS

writhe VERB • *writhing on the floor*
► wriggle, squirm, thrash about, twist

writing NOUN • *neat writing*
► handwriting, calligraphy, scribble, scrawl • *took up writing in old age* ► composition, literature

wrong ADJECTIVE • *the wrong answer* ► incorrect, inaccurate, erroneous, mistaken • *was wrong to do that* ► bad, dishonest, wicked, reprehensible
• *something wrong with the equipment* ► faulty, defective, amiss, out of order

a b c d e f g h i j k l m n o p q r s t u v w x y z

Xx

xenophobia NOUN a strong dislike of foreigners

Xmas NOUN (informal) Christmas

X-ray NOUN a photograph or examination of the inside of the body, made by a kind of radiation that can penetrate solid objects

X-ray VERB to make an X-ray of

xylophone (zy-lo-fohn) NOUN a musical instrument with a row of wooden bars struck with small hammers

Yy

yacht (yot) NOUN 1 a sailing boat used for racing or cruising 2 a private ship ► **yachting** NOUN

yachtsman or **yachtswoman** NOUN **yachtsmen** or **yachtswomen** someone who sails yachts

yak NOUN an Asian ox with long hair

yam NOUN the starchy potato-like tuber of a tropical plant

Yank or **Yankee** NOUN (informal) an American

> **WORD HISTORY**
> from a Dutch name *Janke*, the same as 'Johnny'

yank VERB (informal) to pull strongly and suddenly ► **yank** NOUN

yap VERB **yapping, yapped** to bark shrilly ► **yap** NOUN

yard NOUN 1 a measure of length, 36 inches or·91 centimetres 2 a long pole stretched from a mast to support a sail 3 an enclosed area used for a special purpose *a timber yard*

yardstick NOUN a standard for measuring or judging

yarn NOUN 1 thread spun by twisting fibres together 2 a long tale or story

yashmak NOUN a veil worn by Muslim women in some countries

yawn VERB 1 to open the mouth wide and breathe in deeply when feeling sleepy or bored 2 to form a wide opening *a yawning gap* ► **yawn** NOUN

ye PRONOUN (old use) you (referring to two or more people)

yea (yay) ADVERB (old use) yes

year NOUN 1 the time the earth takes to go round the sun, 365.25 days 2 a period of 12 months, especially the time from 1 January to 31 December ► **yearly** ADJECTIVE, ADVERB

yearling NOUN a one-year-old animal

yearn VERB to long for something

yeast NOUN a substance used to ferment beer and wine and to make bread etc. rise

yell VERB to give a shout ► **yell** NOUN

THESAURUS

yap VERB • *A dog yapped frantically.*
► yelp, bark, woof

yell VERB • *yelled at them to stop*
► shout, cry out, shriek, scream

a
b
c
d
e
f
g
h
i
j
k
l
m
n
o
p
q
r
s
t
u
v
w
x
y
z

a
b
c
d
e
f
g
h
i
j
k
l
m
n
o
p
q
r
s
t
u
v
w
x
y
z

yellow ADJECTIVE **1** of the colour of buttercups and ripe lemons **2** (informal) cowardly

yellow NOUN **1** the colour of buttercups and ripe lemons

yelp VERB to give a shrill bark or cry ▶ **yelp** NOUN

yen[1] NOUN plural **yen** a unit of money in Japan

yen[2] NOUN a longing

yeoman (yoh-man) NOUN plural **yeomen** formerly, a man who owned a small farm ▶ **yeomanry** NOUN

yes ADVERB used to agree to or accept something

yesterday NOUN, ADVERB **1** the day before today **2** the past

yet ADVERB **1** up to this time; by this time **2** eventually **3** in addition; even *found yet more of them*

yet CONJUNCTION nevertheless *It is strange, yet it is true.*

yeti NOUN a large animal thought to live in the Himalayas

yew NOUN an evergreen tree with green leaves and red berries

yield VERB **1** to give in or surrender **2** to agree to do what is asked **3** to produce as a crop or profit

yield NOUN the amount yielded or produced

yob NOUN (informal) an aggressive lout

yodel VERB **yodelling**, **yodelled** to sing with the voice continually varying in pitch

yoga NOUN a Hindu system of meditation and self-control, with physical exercises

yogurt or **yoghurt** NOUN milk thickened by the action of bacteria, giving it a sharp taste

yoke NOUN a curved piece of wood across the necks of animals pulling a load

⚠ **USAGE**

Do not confuse this word with *yolk*.

yoke VERB to harness or join with a yoke

yokel (yoh-kel) NOUN a simple country person

yolk (rhymes with *poke*) NOUN the round yellow part inside an egg

⚠ **USAGE**

Do not confuse this word with *yoke*.

Yom Kippur (yom kip-oor) NOUN the Day of Atonement, a Jewish religious festival

yonder ADJECTIVE, ADVERB (old use) over there

yore NOUN **of yore** of long ago *days of yore*

you PRONOUN **1** the person or people being spoken to *Who are you?* **2** anyone or everyone; one *You can never tell.*

young ADJECTIVE having lived or existed for only a short time

THESAURUS

young ADJECTIVE • *young people*
▶ youthful, teenage, adolescent

• *seem young for their age*
▶ immature, childish, babyish

862

DICTIONARY

young PLURAL NOUN children or young animals or birds

youngster NOUN a young person; a child

your ADJECTIVE belonging to you

⚠ USAGE
Do not confuse this word with *you're*.

you're you are

⚠ USAGE
Do not confuse this word with *your*.

yours POSSESSIVE PRONOUN something belonging to you

⚠ USAGE
It is incorrect to write *your's*.

yourself PRONOUN **yourselves** you and nobody else *You've cut yourself. You yourselves said it.* **by yourself** or **yourselves** alone; on your own

youth NOUN **1** the time of being young **2** a young man **3** young people

youthful ADJECTIVE young or looking young

youth hostel NOUN a hostel for young people hiking or on holiday

yo-yo NOUN **yo-yos** a round wooden or plastic toy that moves up and down on a string

Yule or **Yuletide** NOUN (*old use*) the Christmas festival

THESAURUS

young NOUN • *an instinct to protect their young* ► offspring, family, progeny, brood, issue, litter

youth NOUN • *spent most of her youth abroad* ► early life, early years, teenage years, adolescence, boyhood or girlhood, childhood, infancy, (*informal*) teens
• *a group of youths* ► young person, teenager, youngster, adolescent

a
b
c
d
e
f
g
h
i
j
k
l
m
n
o
p
q
r
s
t
u
v
w
x
y
z

Zz

a
b
c
d
e
f
g
h
i
j
k
l
m
n
o
p
q
r
s
t
u
v
w
x
y
z

zany ADJECTIVE **zanier, zaniest** funny in a crazy way

zap VERB **zapping, zapped** (informal) **1** to attack or destroy forcefully **2** to change television channels rapidly with a remote control ► **zapper** NOUN

zeal NOUN enthusiasm or keenness

zealot (zel-ot) NOUN a zealous person

zealous (zel-us) ADJECTIVE keen; enthusiastic

zebra NOUN a striped African animal of the horse family

zebra crossing NOUN a street crossing for pedestrians, marked with black and white stripes

zenith NOUN **1** the part of the sky directly above **2** the highest point

zephyr (zef-er) NOUN a soft gentle wind

zero NOUN **zeros 1** nought; the figure 0 **2** the point marked 0 on a scale

zest NOUN **1** great enjoyment or interest **2** orange or lemon peel

zestful ADJECTIVE full of enjoyment ► **zestfully** ADVERB

zigzag NOUN a line or route turning sharply from side to side

zigzag ADJECTIVE turning sharply from side to side

zigzag VERB **zigzagging, zigzagged** to move in a zigzag

zinc NOUN a white metal

zip NOUN **1** a fastener consisting of two strips with rows of small teeth made to interlock with a sliding tab **2** a sharp sound like a bullet going through the air

zip VERB **zipping, zipped 1** to fasten with a zip **2** to move quickly with a sharp sound

zither NOUN a musical instrument with strings stretched over a shallow body

zodiac (zoh-dee-ak) NOUN a strip of sky in which the sun, moon, and main planets are found, divided into twelve equal parts (called *signs of the zodiac*), each named after a constellation

zombie NOUN **1** (informal) a person who acts without thinking, from tiredness **2** (in voodoo) a corpse revived by witchcraft

zone NOUN an area set aside for a particular purpose

THESAURUS

zany ADJECTIVE • *a zany story about wizards* ► crazy, weird, bizarre

zero NOUN • *hopes reduced to zero* ► nothing, nought, nil

zest NOUN • *had a renewed zest for life* ► eagerness, energy, enthusiasm, zeal

zigzag ADJECTIVE • *a zigzag course* ► winding, meandering, twisting

zigzag VERB • *The path zigzagged down the cliff.* ► wind, meander, snake, twist

zone NOUN • *decided to leave the war zone* ► area, sector, region, district

zoo NOUN **zoos** a place where wild animals are kept so that people can look at them or study them

zoology NOUN the scientific study of animals ▶ **zoological** ADJECTIVE, **zoologist** NOUN

zoom VERB **1** to move rapidly with a low buzzing sound **2** (in photography) use a zoom lens ▶ **zoom** NOUN

zoom lens NOUN a camera lens that can be adjusted continuously to focus on things that are close up or far away

THESAURUS

zoom VERB • *A van zoomed past.*
▶ rush, speed, hurry, hurtle

a
b
c
d
e
f
g
h
i
j
k
l
m
n
o
p
q
r
s
t
u
v
w
x
y
z

Become a Word Explorer!

You don't need a map and a compass to be a word explorer.
You can explore the world of words equipped with your
dictionary and thesaurus. For example, you can:

- explore how to find the **best word**
- explore ways to avoid **overused words** and **common errors**
- explore effects like **similes**, **idioms**, and **proverbs**
- explore ideas to improve your **writing**

Explore: Prefixes and suffixes

Some common prefixes

A prefix is a group of letters joined to the beginning of a word to change its meaning, for example *re-* in *recapture* (= to capture again) and *un-* in *unknown* (= not known). Some prefixes already form part of the word, for example *com-* in *communicate* (= make contact with).

Once you know how prefixes work you can use them to give existing words new meanings. Because there are so many possible combinations, not all words that begin with prefixes can be included in this dictionary.

Here are some examples of the more common English prefixes:

Prefix	Meaning	Example
an-	not, without	anarchy – *no rules*
anti-	against	anti-British
arch-	chief	archbishop
auto-	self	automatic
co-	together	coeducation
com-, con-	together, with	communicate
contra-	against	contradict
cyber-	to do with electronic communication	cyberspace, cybercafe
de-	undoing or taking away	derail
dis-	not	dishonest
dis-	taking away	disconnect
eco-	to do with the ecology and the environment	ecosystem
em-, en-	in, into	embark, entrust
ex-	that used to be, former	ex-president
extra-	beyond, outside	extraordinary, extraterrestrial

Prefix	Meaning	Example
fore-	before, in front of	forefinger, foregoing
giga-	times 10^9 or (in ICT) 2^{30}	gigabyte
in- (also il-, im-, ir-)	not	incorrect, illegal, impossible, irrelevant
inter-	between	international
mega-	times 10^6 or (in ICT) 2^{20}	megabyte
mis-	wrong	misbehave
mono-	one, single	monotone
multi-	many	multimedia
non-	not	non-existent
over-	too much	overdo
poly-	many	polygon (many sided)
post-	after	post-war
pre-	before	prehistoric
pro-	supporting	pro-British
re-	again	recapture
semi-	half	semicircle
sub-	below	submarine
super-	over, beyond	superstore
tele-	at a distance	telecommunications
trans-	across	transport, transatlantic
ultra-	beyond	ultrasonic
un-	not, the opposite of	unknown, undo
under-	not enough	underdone

Some common suffixes

A suffix is a group of letters joined to the end of a word to change its meaning. For example, *-able* in *eatable* (= able to be eaten), *-er* in *maker* (= a person or machine makes something), and *-ness* in *happiness* (= the state of being happy).

Suffixes often modify a word's grammatical function, for instance *work* (verb), *worker* (noun) and *workable* (adjective).

As with prefixes suffixes can be used to make many different combinations and not all of them are included in this dictionary. You can also make words with more than one suffix, e.g. *childishness* and *childishly*.

Here are some examples of the more common English suffixes:

Suffix	Meaning	Example
-able (*also* **-ible, -uble**)	able to be	eatable, possible, soluble
-ant, -ent	someone who does something	attendant, superintendent
-dom	used to make nouns to do with condition or rank	martyrdom
-ee	someone who is affected	employee, refugee
-er	a person or thing that does something	maker, opener
-er	more	faster
-esque	in the style of	picturesque
-ess	a female person or animal	lioness, actress
-est	most	fastest
-ful	full (of)	beautiful, cupful
-hood	used to make nouns to do with state or condition	childhood, motherhood

Suffix	Meaning	Example
-ic	belonging to, associated with	Islamic, terrific
-ish	rather like, somewhat	childish, greenish
-ism	used to make nouns to do with systems and beliefs	capitalism, Hinduism
-ist	someone who does something or believes something	dentist, sexist
-itis	used to make nouns for illnesses involving inflammation	appendicitis
-ize or -ise	used to make verbs	criticize, televise
-less	not having, without	senseless
-let	small	booklet
-like	like, resembling	childlike
-ling	a small person or thing	seedling
-ly	used to make adverbs and adjectives	bravely, leisurely
-ment	used to make nouns	amusement
-ness	used to make nouns	kindness, happiness
-oid	like or resembling	celluloid
-or	a person or thing that does something	sailor, escalator
-ous	used to make adjectives	dangerous
-ship	used to make nouns	friendship, citizenship
-some	full of	loathsome
-tion	used to make nouns	abbreviation, ignition, completion
-ty	used to make nouns	ability, anxiety
-ward (also -wards)	in a particular direction	backward, northwards

Some tips on how to avoid common errors

all right | alright
Are you all right? It's cold all right.

The correct spelling is as two words: *all right*. Do not use the spelling *alright*, which is not generally acceptable in Standard English.

behalf
on behalf of means 'for the benefit of' or 'as the representative of': *We are collecting money on behalf of cancer research. I'd like to thank you on behalf of everyone here.* It does not mean 'by' or 'on the part of', and it is wrong to say, for example, ⊠ *It was a good result on behalf of the visiting side.*

different from | to | than
There are three prepositions that can be used after *different* when it means 'not the same': *from*, *to*, and *than*. The best one to use is *from*, because everyone accepts it: *The new model is very different from the last one.* You can also use *to*, although it is not much used in American English. *Than* is used in American English, but many people dislike it in British English and so you should avoid it.

double negatives
You should never use two negative words together to make a negative statement: ⊠ *I don't want no more.* ⊠ *They never said nothing about it.* (The correct versions are: *I don't want any more.* and *They never said anything about it.*) But you can use a negative word with a word beginning with a negative prefix like *in-* or *un-*, where the two negatives cancel each other out and produce a positive meaning: *The town is not unattractive* (i.e. *it is fairly attractive*).

enormity | enormousness
Enormity means more than just 'huge size'. It means 'great wickedness': *the enormity of the crime.* If you mean 'huge size', use *enormousness*: *the enormousness of the task*, not ⊠ *the enormity of the task.* (You can also use alternatives such as *immensity* and *vastness*.)

flaunt / flout

To *flaunt* something is to display it in a showy way: *He bought the most expensive item on the list just to flaunt his wealth.*

To *flout* a rule or instruction is to disobey it openly: *They must avoid flouting the health and safety regulations.*

Take care not to confuse these two words, as they sound similar.

I / me

You use *I* when it is the subject of a verb: *I want to see you.* Strictly speaking you should use *I* also in sentences such as *It is I who saw you*, because what comes after the verb *be* should 'agree' with what comes before, and *it* is the subject of the verb *be* (here in the form *is*). But in informal conversation it is acceptable to say *It is me* (or *It was him*).

You use *me* when it is the object of a verb or comes after a preposition such as *to* or *with*: *Give it to me. He came with me.*

You may be unsure whether to use *you and I* or *you and me* when you have more than one pronoun together. The rule is exactly the same: use *you and I* when it is the subject of the sentence and *you and me* when it is the object of a verb or comes after a preposition:

You and I were both there. This is a picture of you and me (not ⊠ This is a picture of you and I). Between you and me (not ⊠ between you and I), I don't think we can win.

infer / imply

To *imply* something is to suggest it without actually saying it: *Are you implying that I am mad?*

To *infer* something is to draw a conclusion from what someone says or does: *I inferred from the sounds in the house that someone was in.*

Take care not to use *infer* when you mean *imply*: *Are you inferring that I am mad?* means 'have you concluded that I am mad?' and not 'are you suggesting that I am mad?'.

it's / its

It is very important to remember the difference the apostrophe makes. *It's* (with an apostrophe) is short for 'it is' or 'it has': *It's [= it is] very late now. I think it's [= it has] been raining.*

Its (without an apostrophe) is a word like *his* and *their* (called a possessive determiner) and means 'belonging to it': *The cat licked its paw. The class wrote its own dictionary.*

who / whom

You use *who* when it is the subject of the sentence or clause: *Who is there? Do you know who that was?*

You use *whom* when it is the object of a verb or comes after a preposition: *Whom do you mean? He invited his friends, most of whom did not know each other. He knew the works of Shakespeare, whom he greatly admired. She was a woman whom everyone liked. This is the person to whom I spoke.*

But *whom* can sound a little formal and stiff. In everyday English, it is acceptable to use *who* instead of *whom* in questions: *Who do you mean?* When *whom* comes at the beginning of a clause without a comma before it, you can leave it out: *She was a woman everyone liked.* With prepositions, you can leave out *whom* and put the preposition at the end of the sentence: *This is the person I spoke to.*

Explore: Commonly misspelled words

In shorter words spelling problems are often caused by vowel combinations and by silent letters. The letters that cause trouble in the list below are in **blue**.

i before e	e before i	words including 'u'	silent letters
ch**ie**f	**ei**ghth	ga**u**ge	**k**nife
n**ie**ce	h**ei**ght	g**u**ard	**p**sychic
p**ie**rce	s**ei**ze	j**u**ice	rece**i**pt
pr**ie**st	w**ei**rd		**w**rite
s**ie**ge			
y**ie**ld			

In longer words problems can be caused by double or single letters, vowel combinations, letters that are not sounded out and silent letters. You need to pay careful attention to the parts of the words in **blue**.

eed or ede	i before e	e before i	words including 'u'
prec**ede**	achi**e**vement	dec**ei**ve	g**u**arantee
proc**eed**	misch**ie**vous	for**ei**gn	n**u**is**a**nce
supers**ede**	unwi**e**ldy	rece**i**pt	Portug**u**ese
		rec**ei**ve	pron**u**nciation
			s**au**sage

double or single letters

accommodate	disappoint	millennium
accommodation	disappointment	millionaire
address	dissect	necessary
aggressive	embarrass	parallel
beginning	embarrassment	questionnaire
cassette	exaggerate	recommend
colossal	harass	skilful
committee	harassment	threshold
disappear	install	unnecessary
disappearance	instalment	withhold

other difficult spellings

answer	government	separate
conscientious	idiosyncrasy	sergeant
consensus	length	signature
cylinder	library	strength
desperate	responsible	twelfth
diphthong	resuscitate	unconscious
ecstasy	rhythm	vengeance
extraordinary	sandwich	Wednesday
extravagant	scavenge	
February	secretary	

Explore: Overused words

One of the commonest reasons for using a thesaurus is to find alternatives for words that, for various reasons, are overused. Using some of these words can make your writing seem unsophisticated, like that of a young writer, or lazy as if you haven't bothered to come up with something better.

We overuse words for different reasons and need to adopt different strategies for avoiding them.

Opinions

The words below all express opinions, but not very clearly. If someone is **bad** think about what makes them bad. Would *evil* or *cruel* be better descriptions? If you **like** something do you *appreciate* it or are you *keen*? In most cases with these words if you add the word 'how' to it you will see the need for a better word. For instance, *The party was good. How good? The party was brilliant.*

all right	good	like	OK
bad	great	lovely	
beautiful	happy	nice	

Adjectives

The adjectives in the list below are amongst the first you learn. As you grow older you may wish to consider using more sophisticated expressions. Another point to consider is that most of these adjectives are neutral in their meanings but with a different choice of word you can show opinions. For instance, *A fat man* is neutral, *A plump man* conveys a similar idea but does not disapprove, *An obese man* suggests disapproval.

big	hard	old	small
bit	little	sad	thin
fat	new	short	

Verbs

Verbs convey ideas about actions and some actions occur very frequently; but that does not mean that we have to use the same word every time. One of the commonest verbs in writing is 'say' as it is used to tell us that someone has spoken; but there are many different ways of speaking and the thesaurus can help you to find more accurate and interesting alternatives. For instance, a speaker can *observe, remark, declare, state, announce, answer, reply,* or *respond.*

cry	go	look	run
eat	hit	move	say
get	laugh	put	walk

Intensifiers

An intensifier is used to answer the question *how much*? In writing, *very* is one of the commonest intensifiers and in informal speech *so* occurs frequently in sentences like *I was so excited.* One way of avoiding overuse of intensifiers is by careful word choice. Instead of saying *I was really happy*, you could write *I was ecstatic.* There are plenty of alternatives for *very* such as *extremely, highly,* and *deeply.*

really	so	very

Explore: Similes

Similes are comparisons using 'as' or 'like'. They can liven up your writing and of course you can make up your own.

similes using 'as':	
as blind as a bat	as good as gold
as bright as day	as graceful as a swan
as clear as a bell	as hard as nails
as clear as mud	as light as a feather
as cunning as a fox	as nutty as a fruitcake
as deep as the ocean	as pretty as a picture
as dry as a bone	as quiet as a mouse
as fit as a fiddle	as strong as an ox

similes using 'like':	
built like a tank	memory like an elephant's
chatter like a monkey	move like a snail
eat like a pig	run like a deer
eyes like a hawk	sing like a bird
fits like a glove	stand out like a sore thumb
fight like cats and dogs	swim like a fish

Explore: Idioms

Idioms are groups of words that have a meaning that is often impossible to work out on your own. This is frequently because they refer to ideas or beliefs that are no longer current. In a dictionary an idiom will often be listed at the end of an entry of its main word. Below are some interesting examples.

an Achilles' heel

a weak or bad point in a person who is otherwise strong or good [from the story of the Greek hero Achilles: his mother Thetis had dipped him in the River Styx because the water would prevent him from harm, but the water did not cover the heel by which she held him. So when the Trojan prince Paris killed Achilles he did it by throwing a spear into his heel.]

an albatross round someone's neck

something that is a constant worry or cause of feeling guilty [An albatross was supposed to bring good luck to sailors at sea. In Coleridge's 1798 poem *The Rime of the Ancient Mariner*, the mariner (= sailor) shoots an albatross and this brings a curse on the ship. The crew force the mariner to wear the dead albatross round his neck as a punishment.]

in seventh heaven

blissfully happy [In some religions, the seventh heaven is the last in a series of heavens that people's souls pass through after death.]

get out of bed on the wrong side

to be irritable all day [The idea is that you are irritable from the moment you get up in the morning.]

a stiff upper lip

you are said to have a stiff upper lip when you are brave and self-controlled when life is difficult or dangerous [Because the upper lip trembles when you are nervous or frightened. The phrase sounds British but in fact it occurs earliest in American writing.]

eat humble pie

to have to apologize or admit you were wrong about something [A play on the words *humble* and *umbles*, which were the inner organs of deer or other animals used in pies.]

under the weather

feeling unwell or fed up [A ship at sea was *under the weather* when a storm was overhead, making it uncomfortable for the people on board.]

the spitting image
a person who looks exactly like someone else
[From a strange old idea that a person could spit out an identical person from their mouth.]

have a chip on your shoulder
to feel jealous and resentful about life and the way you are treated compared with other people
[From an old American custom in which a person would place a chip of wood on their shoulder as a challenge to another person, who would accept the challenge by knocking the chip off.]

not turn a hair
to show no feeling or reaction
[Originally used about horses, whose hair becomes ruffled when they sweat.]

once in a blue moon
very rarely; hardly ever
[A blue moon is a second full moon in a month, which occurs rarely.]

out of the blue
without any warning; as a complete surprise
[Like something coming suddenly out of the blue of the sky.]

back to square one
back to the starting point after a failure or mistake
[Probably from the idea of going back to the first square as a penalty on a board game. Some people think the phrase is connected with early football commentaries, but this is unlikely.]

go hell for leather
at full speed
[From horse-riding, because the reins were made of leather, and people thought that going to hell must be very fast and reckless.]

break the ice
to make the first move in a conversation or undertaking
[From the idea of ships in very cold regions having to break through the ice to pass through.]

let the cat out of the bag
to reveal a secret by mistake
[Because cats do not like being confined, and it would be be hard to keep one in a bag in this way.]

full of beans
lively and energetic
[Horses used to be fed on beans to make them healthy.]

by hook or by crook
somehow or other; by any means possible
[From a practice in medieval times of allowing tenants to take as much firewood as they could from the trees by using these two tools.]

like water off a duck's back
having no effect on a person; making no impression
[Because water runs off the feathers of a duck without soaking through.]

from the horse's mouth
you get information straight from the horse's mouth when it comes from the person or

people who originated it or who are most likely to know about it
[The idea is of someone wanting to make a bet asking the horses themselves which one is likely to win the race.]

a wild goose chase
a pointless and hopeless search for something
[Originally a kind of horse race in which a leading horse had to run an erratic course which the other horses had to follow: wild geese run about in all directions.]

the lion's share
the largest share or part of something
[Because lions being very strong and fierce get the largest share of a killed animal's carcass; originally this expression meant 'all of something' as lions were not thought to share.]

have your cake and eat it
you say someone wants to have their cake and eat it when they seem to want to have or do two things when only one of them is possible
[Because if you eat your cake you cannot still have it: *have* here means 'keep'.]

come up to scratch
to be good or strong enough for what is needed
[*Scratch* is the line marking the start of a race or other sports event.]

on the ball
alert and quick to act
[A player in a game is on the ball when they have possession of it and are playing it well.]

show somebody the ropes
to give someone basic instruction in a task or activity
[From the days of sailing ships, when ropes were used to control the ship's rigging.]

hit the nail on the head
to say something exactly right or suitable
[From the idea of hitting a nail squarely on the head with a hammer, so that it goes in well.]

pass the buck
to leave something you should take responsibility for someone else to deal with
[In the game of poker the buck was a small piece placed in front of the dealer.]

rain cats and dogs
to rain very hard
[We cannot be sure where this phrase comes from and it may just be fanciful; originally is was the other way round: *rain dogs and cats*. One of the earliest uses is by Jonathan Swift, the author of *Gulliver's Travels*, in the 18th century.]

at sixes and sevens
with everything very confused and muddled
[The phrase is very old and is probably connected with; it may have something to do with throwing dice, because there is no 'seven' on a dice and so sixes and sevens would be impossible.]

Explore: Proverbs

A proverb is a sentence that gives a piece of advice or says something wise or true.

all's well that ends well
If things succeed in the end then it doesn't matter so much about the troubles or difficulties experienced on the way.

an apple a day keeps the doctor away If you eat well you will stay healthy and you won't need to see the doctor.

better late than never
Something done at the last moment is better than not doing it at all.

better safe than sorry
If in doubt it is better to be cautious than to take an unnecessary risk.

a bird in the hand is worth two in the bush
Something you already have is more valuable than something you might get or have been promised.

every cloud has a silver lining
Bad situations can often have some benefits.

a stitch in time saves nine
If you act promptly you will save yourself trouble later.
[From the idea of mending clothes with stitches: *nine* is used because it makes a good rhyme with *time*.]

strike while the iron's hot to act at the right moment [From metalwork, in which iron is shaped when hot by hitting it with a hammer.]

don't count your chickens before they hatch
Do not assume that something will happen until you are sure about it.

one good turn deserves another
If you do someone a favour you can expect another in return.

once bitten, twice shy
Someone who has had a bad experience will avoid the same situation another time.
[Someone who has been bitten by an animal or insect will stay away from them in future; *shy* here means 'cautious'.]

every picture tells a story
You can often tell what has happened from things you can see.
[The idea is of a picture illustrating a story in a book.]

there's no time like the present
It is best to get on with a task straight away and not delay.

the proof of the pudding is in the eating
You can often only tell how good or useful something is by trying it.

a rolling stone gathers no moss
Someone who does not settle down in one place does not become important or wealthy. [Because moss does not start to grow on stones that are moving.]

there's no smoke without fire
Rumours and reports usually have some truth about them . [If you can see smoke it usually means there is a fire near.]

two heads are better than one
You can usually do things better if you listen to advice.

where there's a will there's a way
You often need to be determined to overcome difficulties.

Some proverbs seem to contradict one another:

many hands make light work
A job can be done more easily if more people help to do it.

too many cooks spoil the broth
An activity might be badly done if too many people are involved in it.

....

more haste, less speed
If you rush or hurry over a task you will find it more difficult to do well.

time waits for no man
Do not delay in doing things that are important.

....

great minds think alike
Clever people often get the same ideas at the same time (often used jokingly when two people have the same idea or say the same thing).

fools seldom differ
Foolish or silly people will usually act or speak in the same way.

....

absence makes the heart grow fonder
People miss each other when they are apart.

out of sight out of mind
People forget each other or their problems when they are not immediately in front of them.

....

the squeaking wheel gets the grease
You often need to make a lot of noise or fuss to get attention.

silence is golden
It is often best to say nothing and keep quiet.

....

birds of a feather flock together
People of the same kind tend to like each other's company ['Birds of a feather' are birds of the same species.]

opposites attract
People often like other people who are very different in character from themselves.

....

the pen is mightier than the sword
Writing about people or things you do not like is often more effective than attacking them.

actions speak louder than words
It is often better to do something positive rather than just talk or think about doing it.

....

Explore: Writing

The importance of drafting

When you are writing a story, you are doing several things at once:

- Describing what is going on.
- Thinking about what will happen next.
- Remembering spellings.
- Deciding how your characters will develop.
- Thinking about how your story will end.
- Choosing the best words for your purpose.

This is a very complicated process and it is not surprising that writers neglect some parts of it from time to time. This is why almost all writers check their work for spelling when they have finished a writing session. With the help of a thesaurus you can check your word choice as well.

Choose nouns and verbs carefully

A great deal of power in descriptive writing comes from a good choice of verbs and nouns. If you find yourself employing too many commonly used verbs and nouns use the thesaurus to find more accurate alternatives. For instance, *I leapt on the bus* sounds much better than *I got on the bus*, and *I arrived at his mansion* tells the reader much more than *I came to his house*.

Use similes

See the list on page 880 for some common similes like *as fit as a fiddle*. Once you have an idea of the pattern of similes it is much better if you make up your own, using the thesaurus for ideas. Similes make descriptions more vivid and memorable:

The creature was so old, its face folded up like a concertina.

His progress down the room was about as slow as a glacier's.

Use idioms

An idiom is a phrase that doesn't mean exactly the same as the words in it. There is a list of common ones on page 881. Idioms are particularly appropriate in informal writing when you want the reader to feel relaxed and at home. For instance, *Passengers may have to put up with long delays* sounds much friendlier than *Passengers may have to endure long delays*.

Use opposites

In a first draft you might say something negative like *He did not give them a very warm welcome*. If you think of the opposites of warm, you could change your statement to *He gave them a cool welcome*. Equally, you can find an interesting opposite and make your statement negative. For instance you might start with *The painting was a fake* and change to *The painting was not genuine*.

You can show different shades of meaning by skilful use of opposites. Compare the difference between *She likes music* and *She does not dislike music*.

Don't just overuse 'said'

When you are writing dialogue in a story, try not to use the verb *say* each time. You can replace *said* with other verbs to make your dialogue much more varied and interesting. For example, *'Stop that racket!' snapped Miss Grump* sounds much more interesting than simply *said Miss Grump*.

Create your own words

You can add to the words by creating your own. Perhaps you are describing an alien whose skin is just a bit blue, or slightly purple: the word you want is *bluish* or *purplish*. Try creating a new word by starting with a word you know, or a word you have found in the dictionary or thesaurus, and adding one of these endings to it:

-ish (*purplish, shortish, hairyish*)

-less or **-free** (*a flowerless garden, a chocolate-free chin*)

-like (*a ghost-like shadow, a swan-like neck*)

-proof, (a *sword-proof shield*, a *dragon-proof castle*)

You can make up your own names for fears and likes by adding these endings:

-phobia (fear of something)

-phobe (someone who fears or hates something)

-philia (love of something)

-phile (someone who loves something)

For example, someone who loves bananas would be a *bananaphile*, whereas someone who hates football would be a *footballphobe*.

General tips for story writing

- Plan your story or description. Think of story 'hooks' for the beginning – and perhaps a twist or surprise at the end.
- You may find it helpful to discuss your writing with a friend before you write.
- Keep to your plan when you write.
- Focus on the character of the people in your story. Showing is better than telling.
- Think about the setting, and try to create a sense of atmosphere.
- Think about the pace of the story. It is often best to use short sentences for dramatic moments and longer sentences for description.
- Check over your use of dialogue. Does it move the story forward well?
- Watch out for any overused words. Try to choose other words.
- Write in well punctuated sentences.

Non-fiction

A dictionary and a thesaurus can help you with non-fiction, too. You need to be careful about the language you use—in non-fiction it is often more appropriate to use formal words and phrases, rather than informal ones. For example, *I arranged a day off school to organize the event* is a formal sentence. An informal way of saying it might be *I wangled a day off school*.

Use a dictionary to check your spelling and a thesaurus to find the best words.